...IN FINANCE, INSURANCE AND REAL ESTATE

Stephen A. Ross
Franco Modigliani Professor of Finance and Economics
...an School of Management, Massachusetts Institute of Technology
Consulting Editor

...nagement

...n
...nance

...llen
... Finance,

...d Marcus
...orporate Finance

... 5.0

...n Finance: Managing for
...lue Creation

...dair, and Nofsinger
...Applications and Theory
...dition

..., Adair, and Nofsinger
...: M Book
...dition

...ello
...s in Finance
...ond Edition

...rinblatt (editor)
...tephen A. Ross, Mentor: Influence
...hrough Generations

Grinblatt and Titman
Financial Markets and Corporate Strategy
Second Edition

Higgins
Analysis for Financial Management
Tenth Edition

Kellison
Theory of Interest
Third Edition

Ross, Westerfield, and Jaffe
Corporate Finance
Ninth Edition

Ross, Westerfield, Jaffe, and Jordan
Corporate Finance: Core Principles and Applications
Third Edition

Ross, Westerfield, and Jordan
Essentials of Corporate Finance
Seventh Edition

Ross, Westerfield, and Jordan
Fundamentals of Corporate Finance
Ninth Edition

Shefrin
Behavioral Corporate Finance: Decisions that Create Value
First Edition

White
Financial Analysis with an Electronic Calculator
Sixth Edition

Investments

Bodie, Kane, and Marcus
Essentials of Investments
Eighth Edition

Bodie, Kane, and Marcus
Investments
Ninth Edition

Hirt and Block
Fundamentals of Investment Management
Tenth Edition

Hirschey and Nofsinger
Investments: Analysis and Behavior
Second Edition

Jordan, Miller, and Dolvin
Fundamentals of Investments: Valuation and Management
Sixth Edition

Stewart, Piros, and Heisler
Running Money: Professional Portfolio Management
First Edition

Sundaram and Das
Derivatives: Principles and Practice
First Edition

Financial Institutions and Markets

Rose and Hudgins
Bank Management and Financial Services
Eighth Edition

Rose and Marquis
Financial Institutions and Markets
Eleventh Edition

Saunders and Cornett
Financial Institutions Management: A Risk Management Approach
Seventh Edition

Saunders and Cornett
Financial Markets and Institutions
Fifth Edition

International Finance

Eun and Resnick
International Financial Management
Sixth Edition

Robin
International Corporate Finance
First Edition

Real Estate

Brueggeman and Fisher
Real Estate Finance and Investments
Fourteenth Edition

Ling and Archer
Real Estate Principles: A Value Approach
Third Edition

Financial Planning and Insurance

Allen, Melone, Rosenbloom, and Mahoney
Retirement Plans: 401(k)s, IRAs, and Other Deferred Compensation Approaches
Tenth Edition

Altfest
Personal Financial Planning
First Edition

Harrington and Niehaus
Risk Management and Insurance
Second Edition

Kapoor, Dlabay, and Hughes
Focus on Personal Finance: An Active Approach to Help You Develop Successful Financial Skills
Third Edition

Kapoor, Dlabay, and Hughes
Personal Finance
Tenth Edition

INSTRUCTORS: ARE YOU LOOKING ... GET YOUR STUDENTS ACTIVELY INVOLVED IN REAL-WORLD INVESTING?

Give your students a practical application that will last them a lifetime by subscribing to STOCK-TRAK Portfolio Simulations

WWW.STOCKTRAK.COM

STOCK-TRAK is the most comprehensive online trading simulation featuring stocks, bonds, mutual funds, options, futures, spots, future options, and international stocks, **created specifically for classroom use**. ***STOCK-TRAK*** is used by **over 800 professors and 40,000 students** worldwide each year.

Students receive $500,000 of hypothetical money in a ***STOCK-TRAK*** brokerage account, a toll-free number for web page support and customer service, and 24/7 access to their accounts. **No other simulation can offer all of these features!**

Instructors customize ***STOCK-TRAK*** to fit their class by choosing the starting and ending date of their trading period, initial cash balance, and diversification requirements. Instructors also have **24/7 access** to their students' ranking and account detail so they can see exactly what their students are doing, and they receive weekly reports of class performance.

STOCK-TRAK can be used as **homework, end-of-course project, class contest, extra credit, or just as a discussion starter in class.**

There is a separate cost for using ***STOCK-TRAK*** with this text. Students who sign up using the Hirt/Block text and entering Promotional code: **HB0611** will receive $5.00 off the fee. Check out the Website at **www.stocktrak.com** for current prices for subscribing to a semester of ***STOCK-TRAK***, a demo of the product, and more ideas on how to use this simulation in class.

APPLY HIRT/BLOCK'S INVESTMENTS CONCEPTS WITH STOCK-TRAK!

FUNDAMENT

investm
managem

THE McGRAW-HILL/I

Financial Management

Block, Hirt, and Danielsen
Foundations of Financial Ma
Fourteenth Edition

Brealey, Myers, and Alle
Principles of Corporate F
Tenth Edition

Brealey, Myers, and A
Principles of Corporat
Concise
Second Edition

Brealey, Myers, a
Fundamentals of C
Seventh Edition

Brooks
FinGame Onlin

Bruner
Case Studies
Corporate Va
Sixth Editio

Cornett, A
Finance:
Second E

Cornet
Financ
First E

DeM
Cas
Se

G

FUNDAMENTALS OF

investment management

10e

Geoffrey A. Hirt
Professor of Finance
DePaul University

Stanley B. Block, CFA, CMM
Professor of Finance and Holder of the
Stan Block Endowed Chair in Finance
Texas Christian University

FUNDAMENTALS OF INVESTMENT MANAGEMENT, TENTH EDITION

This book is printed on acid-free paper.

1 2 3 4 5 6 7 8 9 0 RJE/RJE 1 0 9 8 7 6 5 4 3 2 1

ISBN 978-0-07-803462-6
MHID 0-07-803462-0

Vice President & Editor-in-Chief: *Brent Gordon*
Vice President and Director Specialized Publishing: *Janice Roerig-Blong*
Publisher: *Douglas Reiner*
Sponsoring Editor: *Michele Janicek*
Marketing Manager: *Melissa Caughlin*
Editorial Coordinator: *Kaylee Putbrese*
Project Manager: *Melissa M. Leick*
Design Coordinator: *Margarite Reynolds*
Cover Designer: *Studio Montage, St. Louis, Missouri*
Cover Image: *Photodisc/Getty Images*
Buyer: *Susan K. Culbertson*
Media Project Manager: *Balaji Sundararaman*
Typeface: *10.5/12 Garamond*
Compositor: *Aptara®, Inc.*
Printer: *RR Donnelley/Jefferson City*

Library of Congress Cataloging-in-Publication Data

Hirt, Geoffrey A.
Fundamentals of investment management / Geoffrey A. Hirt, Stanley B. Block.—10th ed.
p. cm.—(The McGraw-Hill/Irwin series in finance, insurance and real estate)
ISBN 978-0-07-803462-6 (hardback)
1. Investments. 2. Investments—United States. 3. Investment analysis. I. Block, Stanley B. II. Title.
HG4521.H579 2011
332.6—dc22

2011009720

dedication

To Michele Janicek, our executive editor at McGraw-Hill, who has supported us throughout the years with good advice, a dedicated staff, and much patience.

—Geoffrey A. Hirt, Chicago
Stanley B. Block, Ft. Worth

about the authors

Geoffrey A. Hirt Dr. Hirt is currently Professor of Finance at DePaul University. He received his PhD in Finance from the University of Illinois at Champaign-Urbana, his MBA from Miami University of Ohio, and his BA from Ohio-Wesleyan University. Geoff directed the Chartered Financial Analysts Study program for the Investment Analysts Society of Chicago from 1987 to 2001.

From 1987 to 1997 he was Chairman of the Finance Department at DePaul University and teaches Investments and Managerial Finance at DePaul. Dr. Hirt is past president of the Midwest Finance Association and former editor of the *Journal of Financial Education.* He served on the Board of Directors of the Investment Analysts Society of Chicago from 2002 to 2005 and on the editorial board of the *Journal of Investment Consulting.*

From 1998 through July of 2001 Dr. Hirt was Senior Vice President for Strategy and Planning at Mesirow Financial and also the Director of Equity Research. During that time he represented Mesirow Financial at the Pacific Pension Institute (PPI) and he remains a member of that organization today. During the last five years, Dr. Hirt has moderated seminars on various investment topics at PPI Asian Roundtables in Seoul, Singapore, Tokyo, Bangkok and Hong Kong.

Dr. Hirt has been a strong supporter and director of real dollar student managed investment funds during his career. In 2010, he and his wife Linda established a real dollar investment fund at DePaul University with a focus on international investing.

Dr. Hirt was the recipient of the "Spirit of DePaul" award in 2006. During the winter of 2007 he was a visiting professor at the University of Urbino in Italy, where he continues to be involved during the summer months. He enjoys gardening, golf, swimming and all types of music.

Stanley B. Block Professor Block teaches financial management and investments at Texas Christian University, where he received the Burlington Northern Outstanding Teaching Award and the M. J. Neeley School of Business Distinguished Teaching Award. His research interests include financial markets, mergers, and high-yield bonds. He has served as President of the Southwestern Finance Association and is a Chartered Financial Analyst and a Certified Cash Manager. He enjoys sports and has run the NY Marathon. Professor Block holds a BA from the University of Texas at Austin, an MBA from Cornell University, and a PhD from LSU.

In 2001, his former students established the Dr. Stan Block $1.5 million Endowed Chair in Finance at Texas Christian University. He is the first chairholder of the named chair. In 2006 Professor Block was selected as the "University's Most Outstanding Professor."

preface

Many changes have taken place in the financial markets since the first edition of *Fundamentals of Investment Management* was published in the early 1980s. However, the one constant has been a sincere commitment within this text to capture the excitement and enthusiasm that we feel for the topic of investment management.

Throughout the book, we attempt to present applied theory alongside real-world examples that illustrate the theory. Our goal is that by the time conscientious students complete an investment class using this textbook, they will be able to manage investments in the real world. We approach financial analysis the way it is done by many Wall Street firms. Geoff Hirt directed the CFA program for the Investment Analysts Society of Chicago (now the CFA Institute of Chicago) for 15 years and sat on the board of directors from 2002 to 2005. Stan Block has been a practicing CFA for over 20 years. Both of us have taught and advised student-managed investment funds at our universities and we bring this wealth of learning experience to the students who study from this text.

Both of us manage diversified portfolios. We are close to the markets on a daily basis and keep abreast of major developments in the economy, market structure, and globalization of the markets. Above all else, we have written a text that is user-friendly, but make no concessions to the importance of covering the latest and most important material for the student of investments.

KEY UPDATES TO THE TENTH EDITION

Organization

Perhaps the most significant change is our reorganization of the book for the tenth edition. We have added material on behavioral finance, and created a much larger section devoted to portfolio management, including a new chapter titled Alternative Investments: Private Equity and Hedge Funds. The last section of the book now includes the chapter on introductory theory and portfolio management, followed by chapters on duration and bond portfolio management, international investing, real assets, alternative investments, and measuring investment performance. Further reorganization of the chapters is as follows:

Part 1: We eliminated Chapter 4, formerly titled Investment Information. Today's students are very adept at finding information on the Internet, and many university libraries have electronic data accessible to the students from their home computers. We also have many Web links throughout the text, and we believed the space could be better used for more important material. In this instance, we moved the mutual fund chapter up from Chapter 18 to Chapter 4. This fits with the investing goals and objectives covered in Chapter 1, and also meshes with the stock market index material in Chapter 2. We also added to this chapter more information about exchange-traded funds.

Part 2: Chapters 5 through 8 have been our mainstay for financial analysis: economics, industry analysis, company valuation, and financial statement analysis. All material in these chapters has been extensively updated with refreshed examples. Chapter 7 has been reorganized and expanded to make the content more understandable for the student.

Part 3: Chapters 9 and 10 have been swapped. The chapter that deals with anomalies is now Chapter 9, as we thought it made more sense to have that chapter follow the section on fundamental analysis that we cover in Part 2. The former Chapter 9, A Basic View of Technical Analysis, is now Chapter 10, Behavioral

Finance and Technical Analysis. We have added introductory material on behavioral finance to the beginning of this chapter and have tried to show where technical analysis may in fact be trying to interpret some of the behavior we observe in investors.

Parts 4 and 5: Part 4 includes three chapters on bonds. Former Chapter 13 has been moved to Part 6 and is now Chapter 18. Part 5 includes three chapters on derivative instruments. Except for the move of former Chapter 13, both parts retain most of the organization of the last edition.

Part 6: As described earlier, Part 6 now includes all discussion of portfolio management, including a new chapter on private equity and hedge funds. All in all, we feel that moving some of the formerly earlier chapters into the portfolio section here made more sense than having them stand alone. In a portfolio context, these chapters combine to create a view of a diversified portfolio, and in the reordering of the chapters we tried to include more data on how these assets impact risk and return on a pure stock and bond portfolio. In the end we have collected together the asset classes of stocks, bonds, international securities, real estate and real assets, hedge funds, and private equity. These are the asset classes that are most often used by institutional investors to achieve a better risk-return trade-off than just a stock and bond portfolio.

Chapter Changes

Common Changes to All Chapters A great deal of new material has been added throughout the book. Although the financial crisis is fresh in our minds, we had a tough balancing act to determine just how much time we wanted to spend on this topic. We included material where relevant, but not so much as to make the book seem like a history book to the students. Topics like the subprime mortgage market, credit default swaps, Federal Reserve policy, and other related topics found their way into many chapters. In addition, tables, charts, and data have been updated throughout the text. For a more in-depth look at the changes made to this edition, see below, where we have highlighted chapter-specific changes.

PART ONE

Chapter 1

- Added more risk categories such as tax risk, operating risk, financial risk, and manager risk.
- Contrasted defined benefit and defined contribution retirement plans.
- Expanded the discussion of geometric vs. arithmetic returns, including the mathematical equation for calculating the geometric mean.
- Added new return data from the *Ibbotson Classic 2010 Yearbook*.
- Significantly expanded coverage of the equity risk premium and its use in the CAPM.

Chapter 2

- Updated our example of an IPO with the offering by Financial Engines, a company that was started by Bill Sharpe.
- Updated discussion of security markets organization to include the changes in market structure and competition, including the BATS and ICE exchanges.
- Added new Real World of Investing box on dark pools.
- Expanded coverage of program trading, with more on circuit breakers, the use of high-frequency trading, and the "flash crash."

Chapter 3

- Added a more comprehensive view of the Dow Jones Industrial Average and discussed how this price-weighted average is calculated.

Chapter 4

- Replaced sources of information material with mutual funds and included expanded coverage of exchange-traded funds and closed-end funds.
- Moved discussion on unit investment trusts from the appendix to the body of the text.
- Added new Real World of Investing box that covers socially responsible investing, including mutual funds that invest with a religious set of values. Many religions are covered, including Catholic, Christian, Mennonite, Islamic, and Jewish funds.
- Added material on target retirement, or life-cycle funds.
- Expanded coverage of mutual fund fees by asset class.
- Expanded the section on measuring mutual fund performance to include the Standard & Poor's SPIVA scorecard, comparing actively managed funds to index funds.

PART TWO

Chapter 5

- Added information on the financial crisis and how it has affected monetary policy as well as the fiscal policy initiatives of TARP and TALF.
- Added a new Real World of Investing box with information from the Congressional Budget Office on the budgetary treatment of companies such as General Motors, AIG, and Citigroup, now owned by the government.
- Deleted the section on business cycles and industry relationships.

Chapter 6

- Expanded coverage of industry life cycles to include a discussion of product life cycles.
- Replaced the old Real World of Investing box on brand names with a new, updated box discussing what a brand name is worth.
- Continued to use the pharmaceutical industry as an example throughout the chapter, but updated all tables and charts and included a new section on Obamacare and its implications for this industry.
- Expanded the discussion of sector rotation with a theoretical model based on Sam Stovall's S&P Guide to Sector Rotation.
- Added an appendix from Standard & Poor's Industry Surveys regarding how to analyze a pharmaceutical company.

Chapter 7

- Expanded coverage of the Capital Asset Pricing Model to include the deficiencies of beta as well as the problems with the equity risk premium.
- Added discussion on how to use corporate bond yields to calculate a stock's required return.
- Continued to use Johnson & Johnson as the company example for the valuation models, keeping the material from the pharmaceutical industry in Chapter 6 tied into the company valuation chapter. All J&J data were updated.
- Moved the sustainable growth model from the appendix to the body of the chapter. Also expanded this material to include a more complete discussion of

the model to help students evaluate company growth when using the dividend discount models.
- Added a new section discussing growth rates across the variables of per share data. We start with sales, net income, earnings, dividends, book value, and cash flow to show how the growth of these variables are related to one another.

Chapter 8

- Continued to use Johnson & Johnson for the ratio chapter, while all charts and tables have been updated.
- Expanded coverage of the difference between forward price-earnings ratios and trailing price-earnings ratios.

PART THREE

Chapter 9

- Swapped Chapters 9 and 10 (Chapter 9 in this edition was previously Chapter 10).
- Updated the material on merger and acquisition premiums.
- Updated the example of a White Knight with J. P. Morgan, Bear Sterns, and other forced marriages motivated by the financial crisis.
- Added a new Real World of Investing box concerning IBM's common stock repurchase program of over $100 billion since 1995 and $73 billion since 2003.
- Updated the Value Line Performance data.

Chapter 10

- Gave Chapter 10 a new title (Behavioral Finance and Technical Analysis) to reflect added coverage of behavioral finance, as this chapter now covers concepts such as market bubbles, the heuristics of representativeness, availability, anchoring-and-adjustment, prospect theory, overreaction, certainty effect, mental accounting, and framing.
- Added a new Real World of Investing box that highlights the misconception that the outcome of the Super Bowl is a predictor of the stock market.
- Added the fear index (VIX) and a graph of the CBOE SPX market volatility index to the technical analysis section.

PART FOUR

Chapter 11

- Made general updates to data and added information regarding the financial crisis.

Chapter 12

- Expanded explanation of the approximate yield to maturity and its weighted denominator.

Chapter 13

- Moved former Chapter 13 on duration to Part 6 as Chapter 18. The current Chapter 13 formerly was Chapter 14.
- Updated the Amazon convertible bond example.
- Updated all tables for convertible bonds selling at a discount, premium, and par, as well as the discussion that analyzes the bond information.
- Updated tables for warrants and added the terms *in-the-money warrants* and *out-of-the-money warrants*.

PART FIVE

Chapter 14

- Made general updates to data and content.

Chapter 15

- Updated the discussion of major commodity exchanges to reflect the consolidation in the industry.
- Updated data for the size and margin requirements of the various commodities.
- Added a section on credit default swaps.

Chapter 16

- Updated all tables and application examples.

PART SIX

Chapter 17

- Made general updates to data and content.

Chapter 18

- Expanded the Real World of Investing box to update the discussion of interest.
- Moved modified duration and convexity from the appendix to the body of the text.
- Added a table on the duration of U.S. Treasury securities from the one-month bill to the 30-year bond.
- Added a new section on bond portfolio strategies with changing interest rates.
- Added the use of bond ladders as one example of managing a bond portfolio, and created an example of a bond ladder for three successive periods in an environment of rising interest rates.
- Added a new section on bond swaps, including tax swaps and pure pickup-yield swaps.

Chapter 19

- Updated tables with new data for emerging and developed markets as well as the correlations between markets.
- Added material on the 20 largest U.S. multinationals, to give a better comparison of market size between small and large markets.
- Increased coverage of China and its impact on the global markets.
- Updated all the correlations of the developed markets and discussed what happens to correlations in times of global financial crisis.
- Updated the data and discussion of BRICs–Brazil, Russia, India, and China.
- Added a section on corporate governance to the list of problems with international investing.
- Expanded the coverage of exchange-traded funds as investment vehicles for international investing and included a table of correlation coefficients between ETFs covering 15 countries.

Chapter 20

- Created a large section dealing with real estate as an asset class that can diversify a portfolio by lowering risk and increasing return. This section includes many charts and tables that compare the returns and correlations of REITs to other asset classes, such as corporate and U.S. government bonds, large and small stocks, and treasury bills and inflation.

- Updated discussion of gold and silver prices.

Chapter 21

- This is a completely new chapter (titled Alternative Investments: Private Equity and Hedge Funds), which is divided into two parts: private equity and hedge funds.
- Presented an overview of the core satellite portfolio model and an explanation of how institutional investors use this concept for asset allocation strategies.
- Defined hedge funds as unregulated partnerships and discussed the various types of strategies hedge funds use, such as traditional long-short, merger arbitrage, convertible bond arbitrage, short only, and more.
- In the private equity section, discussed venture capital and its various stages of seed capital, early-stage, middle-stage, and late-stage funding. Included histories of returns by stage and the size of the markets over time.
- Included a Real World of Investing box featuring Kleiner Perkins Caufield & Byers, several companies they funded that became successful (such as Google), and several companies they hold in their portfolios that are still private.

Chapter 22

- Updated charts and graphs from *Ibbotson's Classic 2010 Yearbook.*
- Added a section on how returns and standard deviations change as the asset allocation within a portfolio moves from 100 percent stock to 100 percent bonds.

application example

One of the most important considerations in purchasing a closed-end fund is whether it is trading at a discount or premium from net asset value. First, let's look at the formula for net asset value.

$$\text{Net asset value (NAV)} = \frac{\text{Total market value of securities} - \text{Liabilities}}{\text{Shares outstanding}} \quad \textbf{(4–1)}$$

The **net asset value (NAV)** is equal to the current value of the securities owned by the fund minus any liabilities divided by the number of shares outstanding. For example, assume a fund has securities worth $140 million, liabilities of $5 million, and 10 million shares outstanding. The NAV is $13.50:

$$\text{NAV} = \frac{\$140 \text{ million} - \$5 \text{ million}}{10 \text{ million shares}} = \frac{\$135 \text{ million}}{10 \text{ million}} = \$13.50$$

The NAV is computed at the end of each day for a fund.

Application Examples

This text includes called-out examples to highlight key ideas and show them in action. This feature gives students a place to pause to make sure they understand the material covered in the chapter and gives instructors a place to launch classroom discussion.

holders' equity base provided by the owners of the firm. Ratio 13, total debt to total assets, looks at the total assets and the use of all debt. Each firm must consider its optimum capital structure, and the analyst should be aware of industry fluctuations in assessing the firm's proper use of leverage. J&J seems safe, given that its business is not subject to large swings in sales.

The last two debt-utilization ratios indicate the firm's ability to meet its cash payments due on fixed obligations such as interest, leases, licensing fees, or sinking-fund charges. The higher these ratios, the more protected the creditor's position. Use of the fixed-charge coverage is more conservative than interest earned since it includes all fixed charges. Now that most leases are capitalized and show up on the balance sheet, it is easier to understand that lease payments are similar in importance to interest expense. Charges after taxes such as sinking-fund payments must be adjusted to before-tax income. For example, if a firm is in the 40 percent tax bracket and must make a $60,000 sinking-fund payment, the firm would have had to generate $100,000 in before-tax income to meet that obligation. The adjustment would be as follows:

$$\text{Before-tax income required} = \frac{\text{After-tax payment}}{1 - \text{Tax rate}}$$

$$= \frac{\$60{,}000}{1 - 0.40} = \$100{,}000$$

Johnson & Johnson's fixed-charge coverage is the same as its interest-earned ratio because it has no fixed charges other than interest expense. Both ratios are very strong.

E. Price Ratios The **price ratios** relate the internal performance of the firm to the external judgment of the marketplace in terms of value. What is the firm's end result

Excel Examples

This feature will help your students understand how to use Excel for key investment topics—whether for homework, for projects, or for basic understanding. The actual spreadsheets are located at **www.mhhe.com/hirtblock10e** for students to access. An Excel icon appears in the margin next to examples that are illustrated by these spreadsheets.

the real world of investing

ESTATE PLANNING: THE ONLY TWO SURE THINGS ARE DEATH AND TAXES!! MAYBE?

We know the first is not going to go away (not even Elvis got out alive), but what about the second (taxes)? In this case, we are especially talking about the estate tax, or the taxes paid on your assets at time of death.

Fewer than 100,000 people pay the estate tax. The primary reason is that, starting in 2002, you had to have an estate of at least $1 million to owe the tax (there is a $1 million exemption). Also, there are tax planning devices that help you avoid part of the tax (lifetime gifts, trusts, the marital deduction, etc.). Nevertheless, for those who pay the estate tax, it is indeed an onerous burden.

During his or her lifetime, a successful person tends to pay 50 percent of every dollar earned in federal and state income taxes, local property taxes, state sales taxes, and excise taxes on foreign imports, alcoholic beverages, etc.

Then when he or she dies, an estate tax of up to 50 percent may be extracted. This double taxation may mean this person and his or her heirs may only get to keep 25 cents of each dollar earned; 75 cents could go to the government. Most people do not like that ratio.

To rectify this situation, the Bush administration and Congress decided to eliminate the estate tax as one of the provisions of the newly enacted Economic Growth and Tax Reconciliation Act of 2001.

But wait a minute. Don't rush out to die just because of the legislation. First of all, the elimination is a slow process and is enacted by progressively larger estate tax exemptions. The tax table reads like this:

Years	Exemptions
2002–03	$1.0 million
2004–05	1.5 million
2006–08	2.0 million
2009	3.5 million
2010	Total exemption
2011–12	5.0 million

Thus, a person who died in 2006 got a $2.0 million exemption and a death in 2009 qualified for a $3.5 million exemption. Finally there was no estate tax for those who died in 2010.

After the 2010 elections, the estate tax laws were changed in January 2011. The Republicans agreed to extend stimulus programs sought by the Democrats in exchange for an estate tax exemption of $5.0 million. The Democrats wanted a $3.5 million limit but accepted the higher amount. We do not know what the politicians will do from one minute to the next, much less during the next three or four years.

"Real World of Investing" Boxes

Timely and relevant, these boxes highlight topics of interest concerning corporations and investors. Aimed at bringing real life to the classroom, these boxes provide a link from the material learned in the student's investment class to the real business world.

Global Coverage

A new global icon cues students to specific areas of the text that focus on world issues and explain why students need to understand those markets.

MUTUAL FUND INFORMATION AND EVALUATING FUND PERFORMANCE

There are many sources of information on mutual funds. Morningstar is perhaps the leader on individual fund information. However, many financial magazines, such as *Forbes, SmartMoney,* and *Money,* have articles on mutual funds in every edition. Barron's publishes a quarterly review of mutual fund performance. The Value Line Investment survey publishes data on mutual funds, as does Standard & Poor's Netadvantage, an online service available at many university libraries. The American Association of Individual Investors publishes an annual mutual fund survey. Of course, you can look up a mutual fund family online, or call the toll-free number directly to request a prospectus. Online brokers at TD Ameritrade and E-trade, for example, have mutual fund screeners as part of their investor services.

For now, let's look at a Morningstar example, as seen in Figure 4–6, of the T. Rowe Price European Stock Fund. Morningstar ranks each mutual fund on a five-star system, with five stars signifying the highest quality and performance compared to the fund's peer group. At the top of the page, you will see that the T. Rowe Price European Fund is ranked four stars. On the top line, you will also see its ticker symbol. The data in the table are self-explanatory, but notice that the table includes annual returns, portfolio analysis, risk analysis, major company holdings, and more. The fund is also compared against market indexes on the left-hand side, in the middle of the page, under "Performance 10/22/2010." Shown there are comparisons for YTD, 12 months, 3 years, 5 years, and 10 years against the MSCI EAFE[3] index. Because this is an international European fund, it makes sense to use these European indexes as a benchmark for comparison purposes,

Objectives and Outlines

Every chapter starts with a list of objectives, which helps students focus on what they should know after reading the chapter. An outline of the chapter's main section headings will help guide students to the content they need.

OBJECTIVES

1. Understand the functions of financial markets.
2. Explain the role that the investment banker plays in an initial public offering.
3. Discuss the differences between floor trading and electronic trading.
4. Explain the potential impact of algorithmic program trading.
5. Understand the important legislation that affects the operations of the capital markets.

OUTLINE

The Market Environment
Market Functions
- Market Efficiency and Liquidity
- Competition and Allocation of Capital
- Secondary Markets
- Primary Markets

Organization of the Primary Markets: The Investment Banker
- Underwriting Function
- Distribution
- Investment Banking Competition

Organization of the Secondary Markets
- Stock Exchanges
- Consolidated Tape
- Listing Requirement for Firms
- Listing Fees

The Organization of the NYSE
- Trading on the NYSE
- The American Stock Exchange

The NASDAQ Stock Market
Electronic Communication Networks (ECNs)
Other Exchanges
- BATS Exchange
- The Chicago Board Options Exchange
- Intercontinental Exchange (ICE)
- Futures Markets

Over-The-Counter Markets
- Debt Securities Traded Over-The-Counter

Institutional Trading
Regulation of the Securities Markets
- Circuit Breakers and Program Trading
- Securities Act of 1933

"Exploring the Web" Boxes

At the end of each chapter, this box serves as a quick reference of pertinent chapter-related Web sites and short comments on what can be found at each site.

exploring the web

Web Address	Comments
www.aaii.com	A nonprofit Web site educating do-it-yourself investors
www.nasdaq.com	Provides information about Nasdaq stocks and market
www.nyse.com	Provides information about New York Stock Exchange listings and regulations
www.reit.com	Provides information and data about real estate investment trusts
http://quicken.intuit.com	Provides understandable coverage of financial planning and investing
www.morningstar.com	Contains evaluations of and information about stocks and mutual funds
www.business.com	Provides a searchable database for links to sites by industry
www.iclub.com	Provides information and education for investment club members
www.investopedia.com	Provides general education about stocks and investing
http://web.utk.edu/~jwachowi/part2.html	Site created by finance professor with links to information resources
www.investorwords.com	Provides links to finance sites and glossary of finance terminology
www.reuters.com	Contains business and financial market news for the United States and other countries
www.nasdaqtrader.com www.bloombergtradebook.com	These two Web sites represent electronic communication networks (ECNs) and the different companies and markets competing with traditional floor-based markets such as the NYSE.

PRACTICE PROBLEMS AND SOLUTIONS

Load funds

1. A fund is set up to charge a load. Its net asset value is $16.50 and its offer price is $17.30.
   a. What is the dollar value of the load (commission)?
   b. What percentage of the offer price does the load represent?
   c. What percentage of the net asset value does the load represent?
   d. Assume the fund increased in value by 30 cents the first month after you purchased 100 shares. What is the total dollar gain or loss? (Compare the total current value with the total purchase amount.)
   e. By what percentage would the net asset value of the shares have to increase for you to break even?

Total returns to a fund

2. Lee Kramer buys shares in the no-load Global Universe Fund on January 1 at a net asset value of $32.60. At the end of the year the price is $36.90. Also, the investor receives 90 cents in dividends and 50 cents in capital gains distributions. What is the total percentage return on the beginning net asset value? (Round to two places to the right of the decimal point.)

Solutions

1. *a.*

Offer price	$17.30
NAV	16.50
Commission (load)	$ 0.80

b. $\frac{\text{Load}}{\text{Offer price}} = \frac{\$0.80}{\$17.30} = 4.62\%$

c. $\frac{\text{Load}}{\text{NAV}} = \frac{\$0.80}{\$16.50} = 4.85\%$

d.

New NAV	$16.50 + $.30 =	$16.80
Number of shares		× 100
Current value		$1,680.00
Offer price		$17.30
Number of shares		× 100
Purchase amount		$1,730.00
Loss		($50.00)

e. You must earn the load of $0.80 on the net asset value of $16.50. The answer is 4.85 percent. This is the same as the answer to part *c.*

$$\frac{\text{Load}}{\text{NAV}} = \frac{\$0.80}{\$16.50} = 4.85\%$$

2.

Ending NAV	$36.90
Beginning NAV	−32.60
Change in NAV (+)	$ 4.30
Dividends distributed	$ 0.90
Capital gains distribution	0.50
Total return	$ 5.70

$$\frac{\text{Total return}}{\text{Beginning NAV}} = \frac{\$5.70}{\$32.60} = 17.48\%$$

[illegible] and Solutions

The [illegible] tional chapter problems [illegible] worked them out within the [illegible] so that the students can see how they were solved. This user-friendly feature increases students' comprehension of the material and gives them confidence to solve the rest of the end-of-chapter problems independently.

CRITICAL THOUGHT CASE—FOCUS ON ETHICS

Barry Minkow founded ZZZZ Best Co., a carpet-cleaning firm, when he was 15 years old. He ran the business from his family's garage in Reseda, California. The company became one of the biggest carpet-cleaning firms in California, and Minkow was a millionaire by age 18. Minkow took his company public by selling its stock when he was 21, and his personal worth was estimated at close to $10 million. At that time ZZZZ Best ("Zee Best") had 1,300 employees and 1987 sales of $4.8 million. Minkow boldly predicted that 1988 revenues would exceed $50 million.

In July 1990, ZZZZ Best management filed for bankruptcy protection and sued Minkow for misappropriating $21 million in company funds. In addition, several customers accused ZZZZ Best of overcharging them in a credit card scam. Minkow publicly admitted the overcharges but blamed them on subcontractors and employees. He also said he had fired those responsible and had personally repaid the charges.

The Securities and Exchange Commission (SEC) and other law enforcement agencies began investigating Minkow and his company. It became apparent that ZZZZ Best was built on a foundation of lies, dishonesty, and inconsistent accounting practices. The company had submitted phony credit card charges and had issued press releases claiming millions of dollars in bogus contracts, sending the price of the company's stock even higher. The SEC investigated other charges, including possible phony receivables, bogus financial accounting statements, organized crime connections, and securities law violations by Minkow and other executives. The SEC placed an independent trustee in charge of the company until its accounting records could be examined.

The Los Angeles Police Department investigated charges that ZZZZ Best was a money-laundering operation for organized crime. The investigation linked Minkow and ZZZZ Best with drug dealings and organized crime members.

These allegations ultimately led Minkow to resign from ZZZZ Best for "health reasons." But his resignation was not the end of his troubles. ZZZZ Best's new management sued Minkow for embezzling $3 million of the company's funds for his personal use and misappropriating $18 million to perform fictitious insurance

Critical Thought Cases

Critical Thought Cases, which examine investor behaviors, appear at the end of most chapters. Cases that reveal ethical dilemmas have a "Focus on Ethics" label. Each case is concluded with questions that guide students to dig deeper into the issues.

Investment Advisor Problems

This new feature puts students in the role of advisors. The problems depict situational dilemmas that investors might face and challenge the student to come up with a solution.

INVESTMENT ADVISOR PROBLEM

Carol Travis had recently shorted 400 shares of Pfizer, Inc., at $25 because of new federal regulations on Medicare. She put up half the value of the purchase, or $5,000, as margin.

Pfizer stock price	$ 25
Shares purchased	400
Total purchase	$10,000
Margin percentage (50%)	5,000

When the stock initially fell to $23.50 on a Friday, she was really excited. Based on the 400 shares she sold short, she had a $600 profit. However, over the weekend she searched PFE (Pfizer) on Yahoo Finance, **http://yahoo.finance.com**, and was surprised to read a story about Pfizer's new drug for osteoarthritis receiving FDA approval.

Since she saw the news before the market opened on Monday morning, she called her investment advisor, Kyle Turner. She told Kyle she wanted to immediately close out her short sale position at the quoted price of $23.50 that she had seen when the the market closed on the previous Friday.

Her investment advisor told her that would not be possible. Because of the positive news over the weekend, the stock was likely to open at a higher value. Carol became greatly concerned and anxiously awaited seeing the Monday morning opening price for Pfizer. She went into a mild panic attack when she saw there was a delayed opening on the stock. Her investment advisor explained there was an overload of buy orders that could not be matched with sell orders by specialists in the stock.

The stock finally opened at 10:30 EST at $26.53.

a. Based on the new stock price, how much is Carol's current margin position?
b. What is her percentage loss on her initial margin of $5,000?

Web Exercises

Web Exercises at the end of each chapter highlight specific chapter topics by having the student search the Internet for data and then spend time analyzing that data to solve exercises. Exercises range in topics from the focus on specific companies, SEC, NYSE, and government agencies, to commercial Web sites.

WEB EXERCISE

This chapter on capital markets focuses on long-term financing and the various stock markets. Each stock market has its own listing requirements, and this exercise will look at the New York Stock Exchange and Nasdaq listing requirements for comparative purposes. First, go to the New York Stock Exchange Web site at **www.nyse.com**.

1. Click on "Regulation" on the left side.
2. Then, click on "NYSE."
3. Then, click on "Listed Companies." After that, click on "Listing Standards." Look at U.S. Standards and answer the following questions in writing.
   a. How many round-lot holders are required to be listed?
   b. What is the required public shares outstanding?
   c. Under Alternative #1, what are the earnings requirements to be listed?
   d. What is the average global market capitalization requirement to be listed? (Disregard the "or" provision.)
4. Now go to the Nasdaq Web site at **www.nasdaq.com**.
5. Under the "Home" pulldown tab at the top, click on "Listing Center."
6. Next, under the "Listing Information-US" dropdown at the top, click on "Listing Standards & Fees."

CFA Questions

Many chapters also include questions and solutions from CFA Level I study materials. The CFA problems are designed to show students the relevancy of what is learned in their investment course to what is expected of certified professional financial analysts.

CFA MATERIAL

The following material contains sample questions and solutions from a prior Level I CFA exam. While the terminology is slightly different from that in this text, you can still view the skills necessary for the CFA exam.

CFA Exam Question

1. As a firm operating in a mature industry, Arbot Industries is expected to maintain a constant dividend payout ratio and constant growth rate of earnings for the foreseeable future. Earnings were $4.50 per share in the recently completed fiscal year. The dividend payout ratio has been a constant 55 percent in recent years and is expected to remain so. Arbot's return on equity (ROE) is expected to remain at 10 percent in the future, and you require an 11 percent return on the stock.
   a. Using the constant growth dividend discount model, *calculate* the current value of Arbot common stock. *Show* your calculations.

   After an aggressive acquisition and marketing program, it now appears that Arbot's earnings per share and ROE will grow rapidly over the next

SUPPLEMENTARY MATERIAL

All supplemental materials for both students and instructors can be found on the McGraw-Hill Web site for the tenth edition of *Fundamentals of Investment Management* at **www.mhhe.com/hirtblock10e**. All instructor supplements are password-protected. Student supplements are freely available for student and instructor access. Instructors should contact their McGraw-Hill representative for information on how to access the password-protected supplements. Print versions are available by request only (also through your publisher's representative). The following supplements are available for the tenth edition.

For Students

- *Multiple-Choice Quizzes.* Multiple-Choice Quizzes for each chapter, created by Martin St. John, consist of 10 multiple-choice questions that reflect key concepts from the text. These quizzes have instant grading and are a good self-study tool for students.

For Instructors

- *Test Bank.* The Test Bank, created by Martin St. John, offers true/false, multiple-choice, and essay questions for each chapter. The Test Bank is available in Word document format and through the EZ Test software.
- *Instructor's Manual.* The Instructor's Manual, created by Greg Arburn, contains chapter outlines, teaching notes, and answers to the text's Discussion Questions, Problems, Critical Thought Cases, Investment Advisor Problems, and Web Exercises.
- *PowerPoint Presentations.* PowerPoint Presentations for each chapter, created by Greg Arburn, contain coverage of each chapter's most important points, along with key tables and graphs. These slide shows can be edited by instructors to customize presentations.
- *Video Questions.* Questions to accompany the videos available to students are available for instructors. These questions can be assigned to students in conjunction with the videos as a homework assignment or quiz. Included are questions to ask students before and after they watch the video.

ACKNOWLEDGMENTS

We are grateful to the following individuals for their thoughtful reviews and suggestions for the tenth edition:

Elvan Aktas, Greg Arburn, Peter M. Basciano, Dr. Diane L. Boone, Brian Boscaljon, Alexander Deshkovski, Dov Fobar, Karen Gray, Charles Hannema, Thomas W. Harvey, Robert Jozkowski, Robert Kiss, Vivian Nazar, Rick Proctor, Vijayan Ramachandran, Narendar V. Rao, Rathin S. Rathinasamy, Rob Rittenhouse, Sheldon M. Sanders, Henry I. Silverman, Glenna Sumner, Sally Wells, Geungu Yu.

For their prior reviews and helpful comments, we are grateful to Grace C. Allen, Kristine Beck, Omar Benkato, Carol J. Billingham, Laurence E. Blose, Gerald A. Blum, Keith E. Boles, Jerry D. Boswell, Paul Bolster, Lynn Brown, John A. Cole, Joe B. Copeland, Marcia M. Cornett, Don R. Cox, James P. D'Mello, Betty Driver, John Dunkelberg, Adrian C. Edwards, Jane H. Finley, Steven Freund, Adam Gehr, Paul Grier, Richard Gritta, Arthur C. Gudikunst, Mahmoud Haddad, David Haraway, Gay B. Hatfield, David Heskel, Marcus Ingram, Joel R. Jankowski, Amir Jassim, Domingo Joaquin, Peppi Kenny, James Khule, Sheri Kole, Thomas M. Krueger, David Lawrence, Joe B. Lipscomb, David Louton, Carl Luft, John D. Markese, Kyle

Mattson, Cheryl McGaughey, Mike Miller, Majed Muhtaseb, Majed R. Muhtaseb, Harold Mulherin, Jamal Munshie, Peter Naylor, Winford Naylor, Carl C. Nielsen, Mike Nugent, Raj A. Padmaraj, Roger R. Palmer, John W. Peavy III, Richard Ponarul, Dave Rand, Spuma Rao, Linda Ravelle, Arnold Redman, Linda L. Richardson, Mark Rosa, Philip Russell, Tom S. Sale, Art Schwartz, Maneesh Sharma, Joseph F. Singer, Ira Smolowitz, Don Taylor, Frank N. Tiernan, George Troughton, Allan J. Twark, Howard E. Van Auken, Bismarck Williams, Glen Wood, Sheng Yang, and Zhong-Guo Zhou.

We would especially like to thank Alyssa Otterness and Kaylee Putbrese, Editorial Coordinators, for their outstanding editorial work on this project; Michele Janicek, Executive Editor, for her continued editorial support of this product; Melissa Caughlin for her significant support in marketing; and the entire team at McGraw-Hill/Irwin for their help and guidance in developing the tenth edition.

We are grateful for the support and encouragement provided by DePaul University and Texas Christian University. We thank Greg Arburn for creating the PowerPoint slides and the Instructor's Manual and Martin St. John for creating the Test Bank and Quizzes. We also thank Randy Fisher for his significant role in developing supplements for this text and updating Appendix F, Using Calculators for Financial Analysis. Additionally we would like to thank Agnieszka Dybowska and Tian Ye, our very competent research assistants at DePaul University, who effectively found information and data for many of the chapters. We would also like to thank Alex Wan of Mesirow Financial for creating Table 21–11 for this book. Lastly, I would be remiss if I didn't thank my friends and members of the Pacific Pension Institute for the continual investment education I get from interacting with them.

Geoffrey A. Hirt

Stanley B. Block

[brief] contents

contents

appendices

list of selected real world examples

CHAPTER 6

CHAPTER 7

CHAPTER 8

CHAPTER 9

CHAPTER 10

CHAPTER 11

CHAPTER 12

CHAPTER 13

CHAPTER 14

CHAPTER 15

CHAPTER 16

CHAPTER 17

CHAPTER 18

CHAPTER 19

CHAPTER 20

CHAPTER 21

CHAPTER 22

list of selected international examples

CHAPTER 20

CHAPTER 22

PART 1 [one]

INTRODUCTION TO INVESTMENTS

chapter one

1 THE INVESTMENT SETTING

OBJECTIVES

1. Understand the difference between financial and real assets.
2. Discuss the key considerations in setting investment objectives.
3. Appreciate the potential change in investment strategy caused by the tax law revisions.
4. Describe the relationship of risk and return.
5. Explain the three factors that make up the required rate of return for an investor.
6. Understand the career opportunities that are open to students in the field of investments.

OUTLINE

There is nothing more exciting than waking up in the morning and racing for the newspaper or computer screen to get the latest stock quotes. Everything that happens during the day affects your portfolio, whether it's a snowstorm in the Midwest, congressional testimony by the Federal Reserve Board chairman, or a surprise earnings announcement by a Fortune 500 company. There is no "free space" when your money is in play. You are always on real time with events in the United States, Europe, and the rest of the world.

These factors make investing very challenging, where winners can become losers, and losers winners. Take the case of IBM. The stock price of this renowned computer manufacturer reached a high of 175⅞ per share in 1987. At the time, security analysts thought that "Big Blue" could go up forever with its dominance in the traditional mainframe computer market and its emergence as the leader in the rapidly growing personal computer market. Such was not to be. With the conversion

www.ibm.com

of most computer applications from mainframes to microcomputers and the cloning of IBM products by its competitors, IBM rapidly lost market share and began to actually lose money in the early 1990s. This was in stark contrast to the $6 billion per year annual profits it had averaged for the prior decade. By mid-1993, the stock had fallen to 40⅝. Many investors threw up their hands in disgust and bailed out. Over a decade later, by the winter of 2011, the firm was once again showing a profit after massive layoffs of employees and restructuring of operations, and the stock price was *up* to the equivalent of $326 (the actual stock price was $163, but there was a two-for-one stock split during this time period).

Common stocks are not the only volatile investment. In the past two decades, silver has gone from $5 an ounce to $50 and back again to $12. The same can be said of investments in oil, real estate, and a number of other items. Commercial real estate lost more than 30 percent of its value in the late 1980s and then fully recovered by 2006. Other examples are constantly occurring on both the upside and the downside as fortunes are made and lost.

How does one develop an investment strategy in such an environment? Suggestions come from all directions. The investor is told how to benefit from the coming monetary disaster as well as how to grow rich in a new era of prosperity. The intent of this text is to help the investor sort out the various investments that are available and to develop analytical skills that suggest what securities and assets might be most appropriate for a given **portfolio**.

We shall define an **investment** as the commitment of current funds in anticipation of receiving a larger future flow of funds. The investor hopes to be compensated for forgoing immediate consumption, for the effects of inflation, and for taking a risk. Investments may take the form of stocks, bonds, real estate, and even rare paintings or old baseball cards.

FORMS OF INVESTMENT

In the text, we break down investment alternatives between financial and real assets. A **financial asset** represents a financial claim on an asset that is usually documented by some form of legal representation. An example would be a share of stock or a bond. A **real asset** represents an actual tangible asset that may be seen, felt, held, or collected. An example would be real estate or gold. Table 1–1 on page 4 lists the various forms of financial and real assets.

As indicated in the left column of Table 1–1, financial assets may be broken down into five categories. **Direct equity claims** represent ownership interests and include common stock as well as other instruments that can be used to purchase common stock, such as warrants and options. Warrants and options allow the holder to buy a stipulated number of shares in the future at a given price. Warrants usually convert to one share and are long term, whereas options are generally based on 100 share units and are short term in nature.

Indirect equity can be acquired through placing funds in investment companies (such as a mutual fund). The investment company pools the resources of many investors and reinvests them in common stock (or other investments). The individual enjoys the advantages of diversification and professional management (though not necessarily higher returns).

Financial assets may also take the form of **creditor claims** as represented by debt instruments offered by financial institutions, industrial corporations, or the government. The rate of return is often initially fixed, though the actual return may vary with changing market conditions. Other forms of financial assets are **preferred stock**, which is a hybrid form of security combining some of the elements of equity ownership and creditor claims, and **commodity futures**, which represent a contract to buy or sell a commodity in the future at a given price. Commodities may include wheat, corn, copper, or even such financial instruments as Treasury bonds or foreign exchange.

TABLE 1-1 Overview of Investment Alternatives

Financial Assets	Real Assets
1. Equity claims—direct	1. Real estate
Common stock	Office buildings
Warrants	Apartments
Options	Shopping centers
2. Equity claims—indirect	Personal residences
Investment company shares (mutual funds)	2. Precious metals
Exchange-traded funds	Gold
Pension funds	Silver
Whole life insurance	3. Precious gems
Retirement accounts	Diamonds
3. Creditor claims	Rubies
Savings accounts	Sapphires
Money market funds	4. Collectibles
Commercial paper	Art
Treasury bills, notes, bonds	Antiques
Municipal notes, bonds	Stamps
Corporate bonds (straight and convertible to common stock)	Coins
	Rare books
4. Preferred stock (straight and convertible to common stock)	5. Other
5. Commodity futures	Cattle
	Oil
	Common metals

As shown in the right column of Table 1–1, there are also numerous categories of real assets. The most widely recognized investment in this category is *real estate,* either commercial property or one's own residence. For greater risk, *precious metals* or *precious gems* can be considered, and for those seeking psychic pleasure as well as monetary gain, *collectibles* are an investment outlet. Finally, the *other* (*all-inclusive*) category includes cattle, oil, and other items that stretch as far as the imagination will go.

Throughout the text, each form of financial and real asset is considered. What assets the investor ultimately selects will depend on investment objectives as well as the economic outlook. For example, the investor who believes inflation will be relatively strong may prefer real assets that have a replacement value reflecting increasing prices. In a more moderate inflationary environment, stocks and bonds are preferred. The latter has certainly been the case in the last 15 years.

THE SETTING OF INVESTMENT OBJECTIVES

The setting of investment objectives may be as important as the selection of the investment. In actuality, they tend to go together. A number of key areas should be considered.

Risk and Safety of Principal

The first factor investors must consider is the amount of risk they are prepared to assume. In a relatively efficient and informed capital market environment, risk tends to be closely correlated with return. Most of the literature of finance would suggest that those who consistently demonstrate high returns of perhaps 20 percent or more are greater-than-normal risk takers. While some clever investors are able to prosper on their wits alone, most high returns may be perceived as compensation for risk.

And there is not only the risk of losing invested capital directly (a dry hole perhaps) but also the danger of a loss in purchasing power. At 6 percent inflation (compounded annually), a stock that is held for four years without a gain in value would represent a 26 percent loss in purchasing power.

Investors who wish to assume low risks will probably confine a large portion of their portfolios to short-term debt instruments in which the party responsible for payment is the government or a major bank or corporation. Some conservative investors may choose to invest in money market funds in which the funds of numerous investors are pooled and reinvested in high-yielding, short-term instruments. More aggressive investors may look toward longer-term debt instruments and common stock. Real assets, such as gold, silver, or valued art, might also be included in an aggressive portfolio.

It is not only the inherent risk in an asset that must be considered but also the extent to which that risk is being diversified away in a portfolio. Although an investment in gold might be considered risky, such might not be fully the case if it is combined into a portfolio of common stocks. Gold thrives on bad news, while common stocks generally do well in a positive economic environment. An oil embargo or foreign war may drive down the value of stocks while gold is advancing, and vice versa.

The age and economic circumstances of an investor are important variables in determining an appropriate level of risk. Young, upwardly mobile people are generally in a better position to absorb risk than are elderly couples on a fixed income. Nevertheless, each of us, regardless of our plight in life, has different risk-taking desires. Because of an unwillingness to assume risk, a surgeon earning $300,000 a year may be more averse to accepting a $2,000 loss on a stock than an aging taxicab driver.

One cruel lesson of investing is that conservative investments do not always end up being what you thought they were when you bought them. This was true of IBM as described at the beginning of the chapter. This has also been true of many other firms. Classic examples can be found in the drug industry where leading firms such as Merck and Pfizer, who have reputations for developing outstanding products for the cure of cardiovascular and other diseases, saw their stock values fall by 30 percent when a strong movement for health care regulation and cost containment began in the mid-1990s. Much crueler lessons were provided to dot-com investors in the late 1990s as "can't miss" $100 stocks became $2 disasters. The same could be said for investors in the energy company Enron, which shrank from $90 to 50¢ in 2001 and eventual bankruptcy. Even risk-averse investors in short-term U.S. Treasury bills saw their income stream decline from 6 percent to 1 percent over a four-year period as interest rates plummeted. This declining cash flow can be a shock to your system if you are living on interest income. The financial crisis of 2007–2009 was another nightmare for income-oriented investors, as companies cut over $50 billion of dividends and stock prices plummeted more than 50 percent from their 2007 peak.

Current Income versus Capital Appreciation

A second consideration in setting investment objectives is a decision on the desire for current income versus capital appreciation. Although this decision is closely tied to an evaluation of risk, it is separate.

In purchasing stocks, the investor with a need for current income may opt for high-yielding, mature firms in such industries as public utilities, chemicals, or apparel. Those searching for price gains may look toward smaller, emerging firms in high technology, energy, or electronics. The latter firms may pay no cash dividend, but the investor hopes for an increase in value to provide the desired return.

The investor needs to understand there is generally a trade-off between growth and income. Finding both in one type of investment is unlikely. If you go for high-yielding utilities, you can expect slow growth in earnings and stock price. If you opt for high growth with a biotechnology firm, you can expect no cash flow from the dividend.

Liquidity Considerations

Liquidity is measured by the ability of the investor to convert an investment into cash within a relatively short time at its fair market value or with a minimum capital loss on the transaction.

Most financial assets provide a high degree of liquidity. Stocks and bonds can generally be sold within a matter of seconds at a price reasonably close to the last traded value. Such may not be the case for real estate. Almost everyone has seen a house or piece of commercial real estate sit on the market for weeks, months, or years.

Liquidity can also be measured indirectly by the transaction costs or commissions involved in the transfer of ownership. Financial assets generally trade on a relatively low commission basis (perhaps ¼ to 1 percent), whereas many real assets have transaction costs that run from 5 percent to 25 percent or more.

In many cases, the lack of immediate liquidity can be justified if there are unusual opportunities for gain. An investment in real estate or precious gems may provide sufficient return to more than compensate for the added transaction costs. Of course, a bad investment will be all the more difficult to unload.

Investors must carefully assess their own situation to determine the need for liquidity. If you are investing funds to be used for the next house payment or the coming semester's tuition, then immediate liquidity will be essential, and financial assets will be preferred. If funds can be tied up for long periods, bargain-buying opportunities of an unusual nature can also be evaluated.

Short-Term versus Long-Term Orientation

In setting investment objectives, you must decide whether you will assume a short-term or long-term orientation in managing the funds and evaluating performance. You do not always have a choice. People who manage funds for others may be put under tremendous pressure to show a given level of performance in the short run. Those applying pressure may be a concerned relative or a large pension fund that has placed funds with a bank trust department. Even though you are convinced your latest investment will double in the next three years, the fact that it is currently down 15 percent may provide discomfort to those around you.

Market strategies may also be short term or long term in scope. Those who attempt to engage in short-term market tactics are termed *traders*. They may buy a stock at 15 and hope to liquidate if it goes to 20. To help reach decisions, short-term traders often use technical analysis, which is based on evaluating market indicator series and charting. Those who take a longer-term perspective try to identify fundamentally sound companies for a buy-and-hold approach. A long-term investor does not necessarily anticipate being able to buy right at the bottom or sell at the exact peak. Buy-and-hold investors also minimize their capital gains taxes.

Research has shown it is difficult to beat the market on a risk-adjusted basis. Given that the short-term trader encounters more commissions than the long-term investor because of more active trading, short-term trading as a rule is not a strategy endorsed by the authors.

the real world of investing

INFLATION—WHY SHOULD I WORRY?

Inflation has been very tame from the mid-1980s through the 2000s, with prices growing at 1 to 3 percent per year. This is a far cry from the double-digit inflation of 11.4 percent in 1979 and 13.4 percent in 1980. Even these rates would have to be considered mild compared with the triple-digit (100+ percent) inflation witnessed during the 1980s in such developing countries as Brazil, Israel, and Mexico.

As you plan your future, you might ask, "What effect could inflation have on my well-being?" If inflation is at 3 to 4 percent, the impact is not great. But observe in the table the effect of 6 percent sustained inflation over a 20-year time period. These values indicate why the Federal Reserve remains ever vigilant in trying to hold down the rate of inflation.

Impact of 6 Percent Inflation over 20 Years

	2010 Price	20 Years Later
Average automobile	$ 19,500	$ 62,536
Mercedes	44,000	141,108
Typical three-bedroom house	160,000	513,120
BBA starting salary	45,000	144,315
MBA starting salary	90,000	288,630
Average private college annual tuition	24,000	76,968
Ivy League annual tuition	40,000	128,280
Poverty level (family of four)	34,000	109,043

Tax Factors

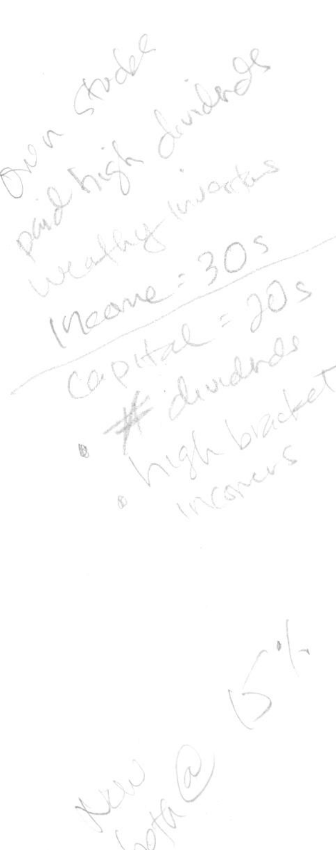

Investors in high tax brackets have different investment objectives than those in lower brackets or tax-exempt charities, foundations, or similar organizations. An investor in a high tax bracket may prefer municipal bonds where interest is not taxable, real estate with its depreciation and interest write-offs, or investments that provide tax credits or tax shelters.

The Tax Relief Act of 2003 changed tax considerations related to investments substantially, and you should be aware of these changes and their impact on portfolio strategy. Prior to the passage of the act, dividends were taxed as ordinary income (the same as salary, for example) and the maximum tax rate on dividends was 38.8 percent. However, long-term capital gains, that is, gains on securities held for over a year, were only taxed at a maximum rate of 20 percent.

For high-income, high-tax-bracket investors this made stocks with large capital gains potential much more desirable. They looked to companies such as Home Depot or eBay that paid little or no dividends, but used their funds instead to generate growth and hopefully capital gains for investors. Companies that paid high dividends such as Duke Energy or AT&T were often shunned by wealthy investors because of the tax consequences of owning these stocks.

However, the Tax Relief Act of 2003 put dividends and long-term capital gains on an equal footing. These tax rates were continued for two years at the beginning of 2011 in negotiations between the new Republican majority in the House of Representatives, the Democratic Senate, and President Obama. They both are now taxed at a maximum rate of 15 percent. This means that high-income investors may now seriously consider stocks with high dividends such as Verizon, Pfizer, or Southern Co. for their portfolios.

Ease of Management

Another consideration in establishing an investment program is ease of management. The investor must determine the amount of time and effort that can be devoted to an investment portfolio and act accordingly. In the stock market, this may determine whether you want to be a daily trader or assume a longer-term perspective. In real estate, it may mean the difference between personally owning and managing a handful of rental houses or going in with 10 other investors to form a limited partnership in which a general partner takes full management responsibility and the limited partners merely put up the capital.

Of course, a minimum amount of time must be committed to any investment program. Even when investment advisers or general partners are in charge, their activities must be monitored and evaluated.

In managing a personal portfolio, the investor should consider opportunity costs. If a lawyer can work for $200 per hour or manage his financial portfolio, a fair question would be, How much extra return can I get from managing my portfolio, or can I add more value to my portfolio by working and investing more money? Unless the lawyer is an excellent investor, it is probable that more money can be made by working.

Assume an investor can add a 2 percent extra return to his portfolio but it takes 5 hours per week (260 hours per year) to do so. If his opportunity cost is $40 per hour, he would have to add more than $10,400 ($40 × 260 hours) to his portfolio to make personal management attractive. If we assume a 2 percent excess return can be gained over the professional manager, the investor would need a portfolio of $520,000 before personal management would make sense under these assumptions. This example may explain why many high-income individuals choose to have professionals manage their assets.

Decisions such as these may also depend on your trade-off between work and leisure. An investor may truly find it satisfying and intellectually stimulating to manage a portfolio and may receive psychic income from mastering the nuances of investing. However, if you would rather ski, play tennis, or enjoy some other leisure activity, the choice of professional management may make more sense than a do-it-yourself approach.

Retirement and Estate Planning Considerations

Even the relatively young must begin to consider the effect of their investment decisions on their retirement and the estates they will someday pass along to their "potential families." Those who wish to remain single will still be called on to advise others as to the appropriateness of a given investment strategy for their family needs.

Most good retirement questions should not be asked at "retirement" but 40 or 45 years before because that's the period with the greatest impact. One of the first questions a person is often asked after taking a job on graduation is whether he or she wishes to set up an IRA. An IRA allows a qualifying taxpayer to deduct an allowable amount from taxable income and invest the funds at a brokerage house, mutual fund, bank, or other financial institution. The funds are normally placed in common stocks or other securities or in interest-bearing instruments, such as a certificate of deposit. The income earned on the funds is allowed to grow tax-free until withdrawn at retirement. As an example, if a person places $3,000 a year in an IRA for 45 consecutive years and the funds earn 10 percent over that time, $2,156,715 will have been accumulated.

Normally, private companies and governments have retirement plans. Most public employees, such as teachers, firefighters, and police, have a **defined benefit plan**. The defined benefit plan specifies the amount of the retirement benefit based on income and years of service. For example, a schoolteacher who teaches for 35 years and earned an average of $80,000 over the last four years of work may be entitled to 80 percent of his or her income ($64,000 per year) for the rest of his or her life. In some states and cities, this amount may be adjusted annually for inflation and not be included as taxable income for state income tax purposes. In the defined benefit plan, the public pension fund is responsible for managing the money and generating the benefits.

The second type of retirement plan is the **defined contribution plan**. This type of plan usually requires the employee to make contributions out of each paycheck into a retirement fund. Most plans match the employee contribution up to some limit. In the defined contribution plan, the employee is responsible for

the real world of investing

ESTATE PLANNING: THE ONLY TWO SURE THINGS ARE DEATH AND TAXES!! MAYBE?

We know the first is not going to go away (not even Elvis got out alive), but what about the second (taxes)? In this case, we are especially talking about the estate tax, or the taxes paid on your assets at time of death.

Fewer than 100,000 people pay the estate tax. The primary reason is that, starting in 2002, you had to have an estate of at least $1 million to owe the tax (there is a $1 million exemption). Also, there are tax planning devices that help you avoid part of the tax (lifetime gifts, trusts, the marital deduction, etc.). Nevertheless, for those who pay the estate tax, it is indeed an onerous burden.

During his or her lifetime, a successful person tends to pay 50 percent of every dollar earned in federal and state income taxes, local property taxes, state sales taxes, and excise taxes on foreign imports, alcoholic beverages, etc.

Then when he or she dies, an estate tax of up to 50 percent may be extracted. This double taxation may mean this person and his or her heirs may only get to keep 25 cents of each dollar earned; 75 cents could go to the government. Most people do not like that ratio.

To rectify this situation, the Bush administration and Congress decided to eliminate the estate tax as one of the provisions of the newly enacted Economic Growth and Tax Reconciliation Act of 2001.

But wait a minute. Don't rush out to die just because of the legislation. First of all, the elimination is a slow process and is enacted by progressively larger estate tax exemptions. The tax table reads like this:

Years	Exemptions
2002–03	$1.0 million
2004–05	1.5 million
2006–08	2.0 million
2009	3.5 million
2010	Total exemption
2011–12	5.0 million

Thus, a person who died in 2006 got a $2.0 million exemption and a death in 2009 qualified for a $3.5 million exemption. Finally there was no estate tax for those who died in 2010.

After the 2010 elections, the estate tax laws were changed in January 2011. The Republicans agreed to extend stimulus programs sought by the Democrats in exchange for an estate tax exemption of $5.0 million. The Democrats wanted a $3.5 million limit but accepted the higher amount. We do not know what the politicians will do from one minute to the next, much less during the next three or four years.

managing their own pension fund with mutual funds made available to them through their employer. Companies such as Vanguard and Fidelity and the College Teacher Retirement Fund offer retirement planning services and mutual funds to companies and universities. Defined contribution plans transfer the risk of money management from employers to employees and allow employees to choose a level of risk and return that meets their goals and objectives. An advantage to the employee is that the defined contribution is a more flexible retirement program, but a disadvantage is that employees don't know what their benefit will be when they retire. If you manage your money well, you can end up with a very healthy retirement benefit, but if you manage your money poorly, you can end up living well below what you expected.

Because many public and private pension funds are moving to defined contribution plans, it is important for everyone to know more about money management and the trade-offs between risk and return. As you will see, the type of investment can have a big impact on your rate of return and ending value of your portfolio.

MEASURES OF RISK AND RETURN

Now that you have some basic familiarity with the different forms of investments and the setting of investment goals, we are ready to look at concepts of measuring the return from an investment and the associated risk. The return you receive from any investment (stocks, bonds, real estate) has two primary components: capital gains or losses and current income.

application example

A one-period rate of return from an investment can be measured as:

$$\text{Rate of return} = \frac{(\text{Ending value} - \text{Beginning value}) + \text{Income}}{\text{Beginning value}} \quad \textbf{(1–1)}$$

Thus, if a share of stock goes from \$20 to \$22 in one year and also pays a dollar in dividends during the year, the total return is 15 percent. Using Formula 1–1:

$$\frac{(\$22 - \$20) + \$1}{\$20} = \frac{\$2 + \$1}{\$20} = \frac{\$3}{\$20} = 15\%$$

Where the formula is being specifically applied to stocks, it is written as:

$$\text{Rate of return 5} = \frac{P_1 - P_0 + D_1}{P_0} \quad \textbf{(1–2)}$$

where:

P_1 = Price at the end of the period.
P_0 = Price at the beginning of the period.
D_1 = Dividend income.

Assume that you have several one-year rates of return of 15, 20, −10, and 5 percent. How would you calculate the annualized rate of return? The geometric mean return makes the most financial sense, because financial returns often have negative returns, and an arithmetic average return creates an upward bias in the answer. The geometric return would take the 4th root of the product of four period returns minus one, where the percentages are expressed in decimals. For example:

$$\begin{aligned} R_G &= \sqrt[4]{(1 + .15)(1 + .20)(1 - .10)(1 + .05)} - 1 \\ &= \sqrt[4]{1.15 \times 1.20 \times .90 \times 1.05} - 1 \\ &= \sqrt[4]{1.3041} - 1 \\ &= 1.06863 - 1 \\ R_G &= .06863 \text{ or } 6.86\% \end{aligned}$$

The general equation for the geometric mean return would be

$$R_G = \sqrt[n]{(1 + r_1)(1 + r_2)(1 + r_3)\cdots(1 + r_n)} - 1$$

If we used an arithmetic average return, we would add all four returns (15% + 20% + −10% + 5%), which would give us a total of 30 percent, and divide by four periods. The average return would be 7.5 percent, which is quite a bit higher than the geometric mean return of 6.86 percent. This demonstrates how the arithmetic return is biased on the upside when a series of returns has negative numbers. This is a very important distinction, and Figure 1–4 on page 15 presents the contrast between the two types of returns for various investments.

Risk and Return Trade-Offs

The risk for an investment is related to the uncertainty associated with the outcomes from an investment. For example, an investment that has an absolutely certain return of 10 percent is said to be riskless. Another investment that has a likely or expected return of 12 percent, but also has the possibility of minus 10 percent in hard economic times and plus 30 percent under optimum circumstances, is said to be risky. An example of three investments with progressively greater risk is presented in Figure 1–1. Based on our definition of risk, investment

FIGURE 1-1 Examples of Risk

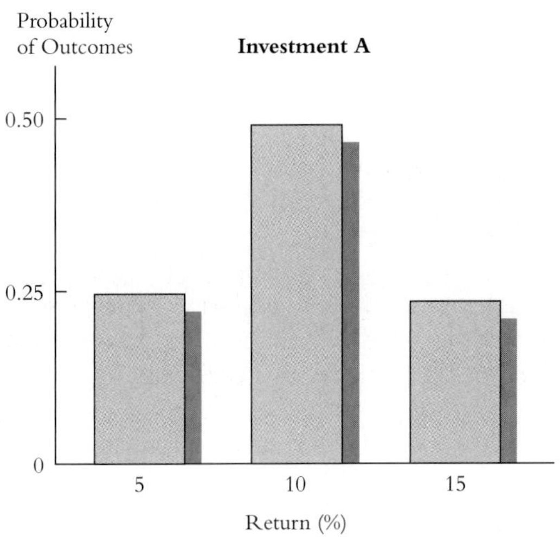

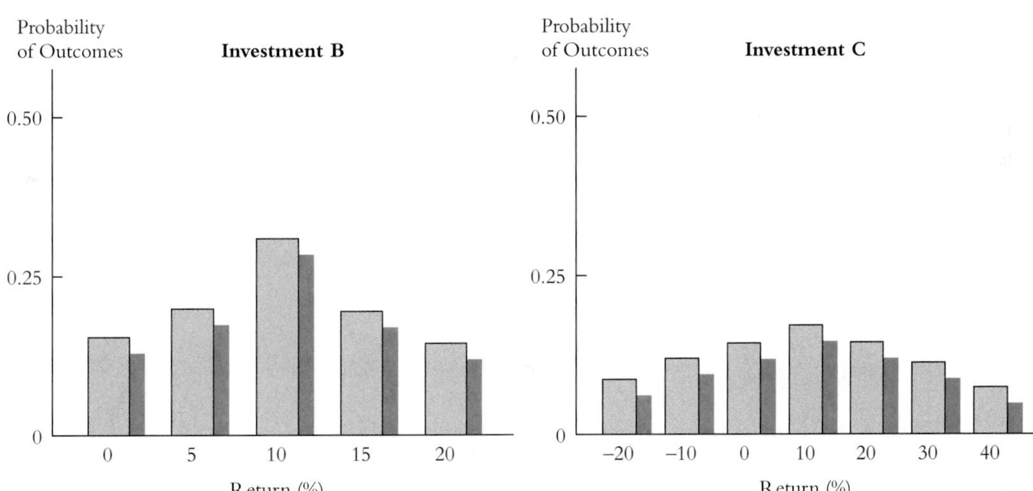

C is clearly the riskiest because of the large uncertainty (wide dispersion) of possible outcomes.

In the study of investments, you will soon observe that the desired or required rate of return for a given investment is generally related to the risk associated with that investment. Because most investors do not like risk, they will require a higher rate of return for a more risky investment. That is not to say the investors are unwilling to take risks—they simply wish to be compensated for taking the risk. For this reason, an investment in common stocks (which inevitably carries some amount of risk) may require an anticipated return 6 or 7 percent higher than a certificate of deposit in a commercial bank. This extra return of 6 or 7 percent represents a risk premium on top of the certificate of deposit return. You never know whether you will get the returns you anticipate, but at least your initial requirements will be higher to justify the risk you are taking.

Other Common Risks Investors are faced with lots of risks that may show up in quantitative measures but are sometimes hard to quantify easily. For example, if you put your money in an individual retirement account, you have a **tax risk**. IRA investors assume that their tax rate will be lower in retirement because they will have less income. But when you are 25 years old, how would you know what the tax rate will be 40 years later? Usually, the ability to compound your money tax-free should make up for any higher taxes in the future, but there is a risk present. Corporate finance textbooks often talk about **operating risk** and **financial risk**. Operating risk focuses on the volatility of operating earnings, and given the cyclical nature of the economy and the stability of the industry, this is a risk that can be measured. The greater the volatility of operating income, the greater the risk. Financial risk occurs when a firm uses too much financial leverage (high debt ratio) and risks bankruptcy. If a company has both high operating risk (airlines) and high financial risk (airlines), then there is a high probability that in an economic downturn, bankruptcy will occur (General Motors and Chrysler). If you are a mutual fund investor, you suffer from **manager risk**. There are good managers, bad managers, and lucky managers. One task of an investor is to measure the long-run performance of the manager. When a manager stays at a fund for a long time, his or her performance can be measured. But when there is a new manager or management by committee, it is hard to measure the manager's ability to perform with or above risk-adjusted market returns over time.

ACTUAL CONSIDERATION OF REQUIRED RETURNS

Let's consider how return requirements are determined in the financial markets. Although the following discussion starts out on a theoretical "what if" basis, you will eventually see empirical evidence that different types of investments do provide different types of returns.

Basically, three components make up the required return from an investment:

1. The real rate of return.
2. The anticipated inflation factor.
3. The risk premium.

Real Rate of Return

The **real rate of return** is the return investors require for allowing others to use their money for a given time period. This is the return investors demand for passing up immediate consumption and allowing others to use their savings until the funds are returned. Because the term *real* is employed, this means it is a value determined before inflation is included in the calculation. The real rate of return is also determined before considering any specific risk for the investment.

Historically, the real rate of return in the U.S. economy has been from 2 to 3 percent. During much of the 1980s and early 1990s, it was somewhat higher (4 to 6 percent), but in the 2000–2007 period the real rate of return came back to its normal level of 2 to 3 percent, which is probably a reasonable long-term expectation. With the financial crisis of 2007 lingering into 2011, the Federal Reserve Board kept U.S. interest rates at record lows to stimulate the economy. At the beginning of 2011, the real rate of return was actually negative. This means that investors in one-year treasury bills were actually losing purchasing power. In our examples, however, we will use the long-term average of 2 to 3 percent.

Because an investor is concerned with using a real rate of return as a component of a required rate of return, the past is not always a good predictor for any one year's real rate of return. The problem comes from being able to measure the real rate of return only after the fact by subtracting inflation from the nominal interest rate. Unfortunately, expectations and occurrence do not always match. The real rate of return is highly variable (for seven years in the 1970s and early 1980s, it was even negative). One of the problems investors face in determining required rates of return is the forecasting errors involving interest rates and inflation. These forecasting errors are more pronounced in short-run returns than in long-run returns. Let us continue with our example and bring inflation into the discussion.

Anticipated Inflation Factor

The anticipated inflation factor must be added to the real rate of return. For example, if there is a 2 percent real-rate-of-return requirement and the **anticipated rate of inflation** is 3 percent, we combine the two to arrive at an approximate 5 percent required return factor. Combining the real rate of return and inflationary considerations gives us the required return on an investment before explicitly considering risk. For this reason, it is called the risk-free required rate of return or, simply, **risk-free rate (R_F)**.

We can define the risk-free rate as:

$$\text{Risk-free rate} = (1 + \text{Real rate})(1 + \text{Expected rate of inflation}) - 1 \quad \textbf{(1–3)}$$

Plugging in numerical values, we would show:

$$\text{Risk-free rate} = (1.02)(1.03) - 1 = 1.0506 - 1 = 0.0506 \text{ or } 5.06\%$$

The answer is approximately 5 percent. You can simply add the real rate of return (2 percent) to the anticipated inflation rate (3 percent) to get a 5 percent answer or go through the more theoretically correct process of Formula 1–3 to arrive at 5.06 percent. Either approach is frequently used.

The risk-free rate (R_F) of approximately 5 percent applies to any investment as the minimum required rate of return to provide a 2 percent *real return* after inflation. Of course, if the investor actually receives a lower return, the real rate of return may be quite low or negative. For example, if the investor receives a 2 percent return in a 4 percent inflationary environment, there is a negative real return of 2 percent. The investor will have 2 percent less purchasing power than before he started. He would have been better off to spend the money *now* rather than save at a 2 percent rate in a 4 percent inflationary economy. In effect, he is *paying* the borrower to use his money. Of course, real rates of return and inflationary expectations change from time to time, so the risk-free required rate (R_F) also changes.

We have examined the two components that make up the minimum risk-free rate of return that apply to investments (stock, bonds, real estate, etc.). We now consider the third component, the risk premium. The relationship is depicted in Figure 1–2.

FIGURE 1-2 The Components of Required Rate of Return

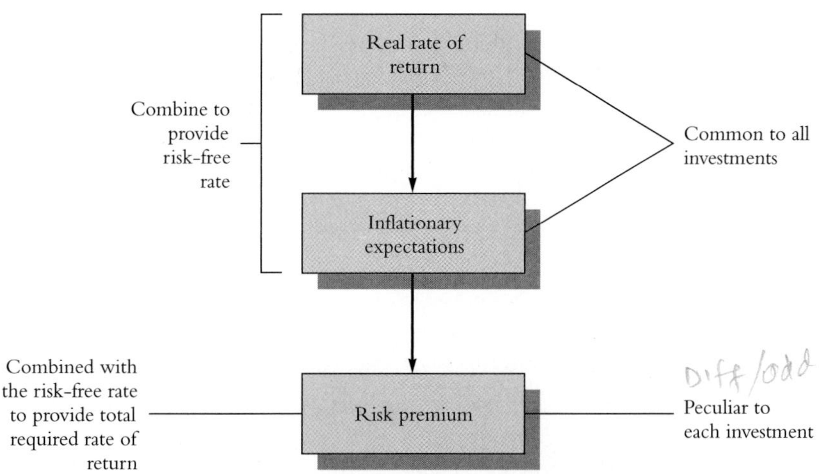

Risk Premium

The **risk premium** will be different for each investment. For example, for a federally insured certificate of deposit at a bank or for a U.S. Treasury bill, the risk premium approaches zero. All the return to the investor will be at the risk-free rate of return (the real rate of return plus inflationary expectations). For common stock, the investor's required return may carry a 6 or 7 percent risk premium in addition to the risk-free rate of return. If the risk-free rate were 5 percent, the investor might have an overall required return of 11 to 12 percent on common stock.

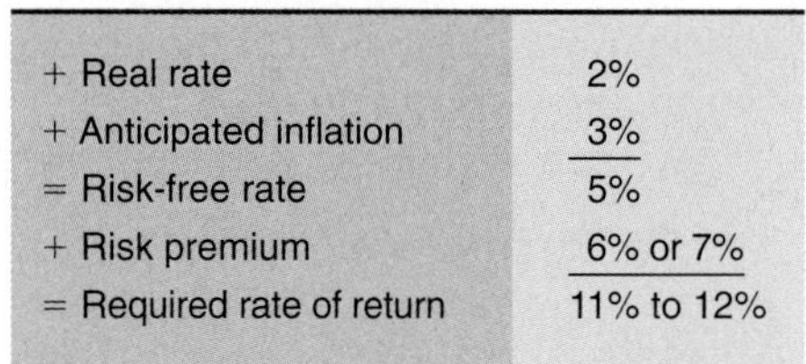

+ Real rate	2%
+ Anticipated inflation	3%
= Risk-free rate	5%
+ Risk premium	6% or 7%
= Required rate of return	11% to 12%

Corporate bonds fall somewhere between short-term government obligations (virtually no risk) and common stock in terms of risk. Thus, the risk premium may be 3 to 4 percent. Like the real rate of return and the inflation rate, the risk premium is not a constant but may change from time to time. If investors are very fearful about the economic outlook, the risk premium may be 8 to 10 percent as it was for junk bonds in 1990 and 1991.

The normal relationship between selected investments and their rates of return is depicted in Figure 1–3.

FIGURE 1-3 Risk-Return Characteristics

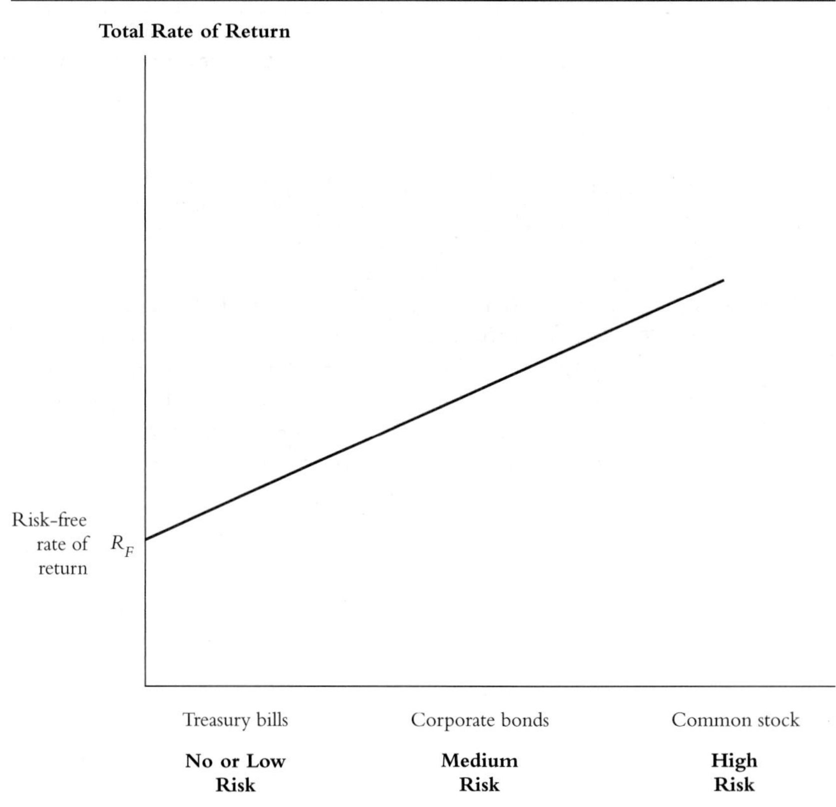

FIGURE 1-4 Basic Series: Summary Statistics of Annual Total Returns from 1926 to 2009

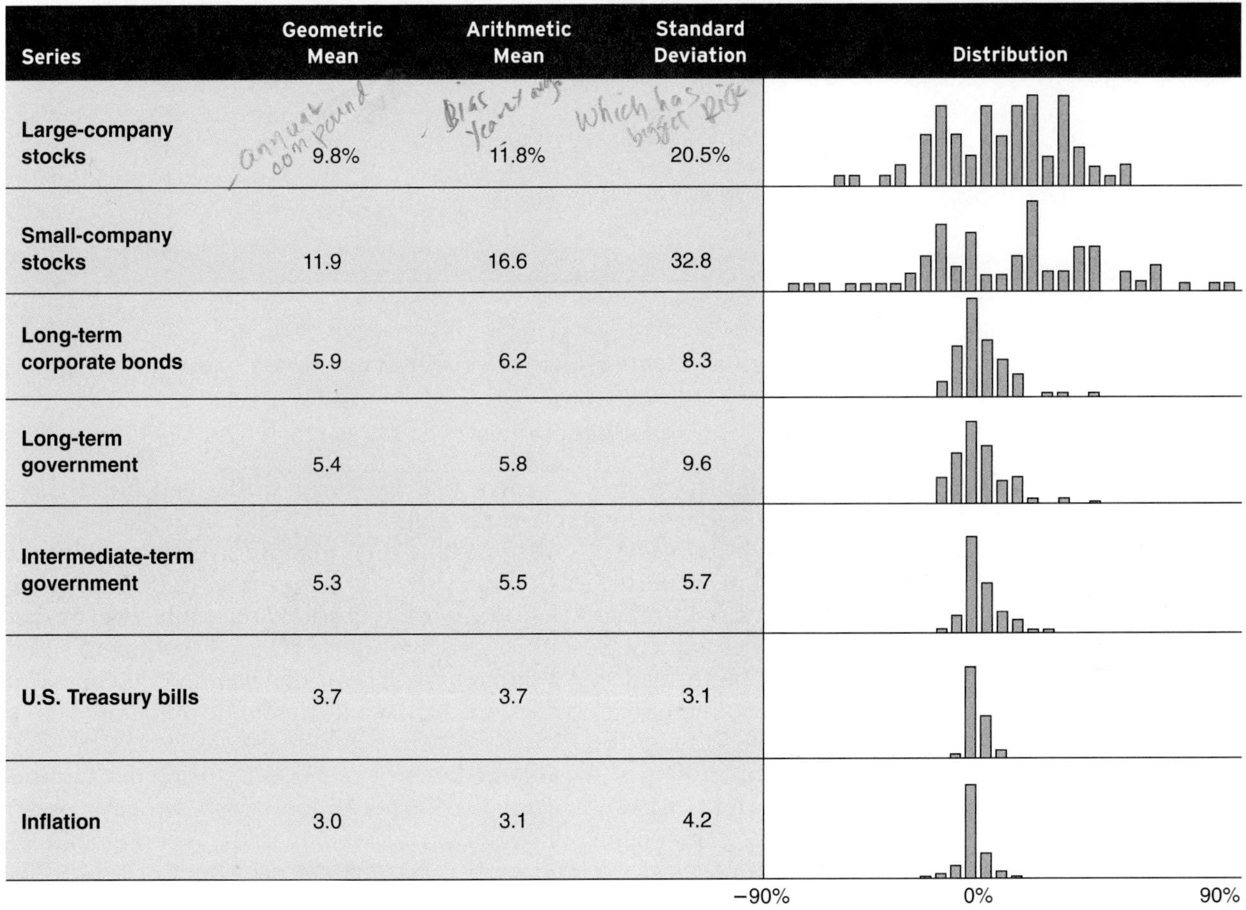

Series	Geometric Mean	Arithmetic Mean	Standard Deviation	Distribution
Large-company stocks	9.8%	11.8%	20.5%	
Small-company stocks	11.9	16.6	32.8	
Long-term corporate bonds	5.9	6.2	8.3	
Long-term government	5.4	5.8	9.6	
Intermediate-term government	5.3	5.5	5.7	
U.S. Treasury bills	3.7	3.7	3.1	
Inflation	3.0	3.1	4.2	

Source: *Stocks, Bonds, Bills and Inflation 2010 Yearbook.*

A number of empirical studies tend to support the risk-return relationships shown in Figure 1–3 over a long period. Perhaps the most widely cited are the Ibbotson and Associates data presented in Figure 1–4, which covers data for eight decades. Note that the high-to-low return scale is in line with expectations based on risk. Risk is measured by the standard deviation, which appears to the right of each security type. This distribution of returns indicates which security has the biggest risk. Figure 1–4 shows in practice what we discussed in theory earlier in the chapter; higher returns are normally associated with higher risk.

Of particular interest is the difference between the geometric mean return and the arithmetic mean return. The geometric mean is the compound annual rate of return while the arithmetic mean is a simple average of the yearly returns. The arithmetic mean is biased on the upside because it treats negative returns the same as positive returns. This is *not* true in reality. If you start with $1.00 and lose 50 percent, you now have 50 cents. To get back to your original investment, you need a 100 percent increase from 50 cents to $1.00.

Table 1–2, from the *Stocks, Bonds, Bills and Inflation 2010 Yearbook,* shows returns for nine different periods covering 84 years. An examination of the data indicates that returns are not consistent by decade. While large stocks have had somewhat inconsistent returns decade by decade, small stocks exhibited position returns every decade except for the 1920s. Even during the miserable most recent

TABLE 1-2 Compound Annual Rates of Return by Decade (in percent)

	1920s*	1930s	1940s	1950s	1960s	1970s	1980s	1990s	2000s†
Large company	19.2	−0.1	9.2	19.4	7.8	5.9	17.5	18.2	−0.9
Small company	−4.5	1.4	20.7	16.9	15.5	11.5	15.8	15.1	6.3
Long-term corporate	5.2	6.9	2.7	1.0	1.7	6.2	13.0	8.4	7.6
Long-term government	5.0	4.9	3.2	−0.1	1.4	5.5	12.6	8.8	7.7
Intermediate-term government	4.2	4.6	1.8	1.3	3.5	7.0	11.9	7.2	6.2
Treasury bills	3.7	0.6	0.4	1.9	3.9	6.3	8.9	4.9	2.8
Inflation	−1.1	−2.0	5.4	2.2	2.5	7.4	5.1	2.9	2.5

*Based on the period 1926–1929.

†Based on the period 2000–2009.

Source: *Stocks, Bonds, Bills and Inflation 2010 Yearbook.*

decade, when large stocks had negative returns, small stocks and bonds performed positively. Table 1–2 complements Figure 1–4 by showing that the average return for each category of investments is only that: an average, and not a return that should be expected each and every year. Over long periods of time, common stocks generally tend to perform at approximately the same level as real assets such as real estate, coins, stamps, and so forth, with each tending to show a different type of performance in a different economic environment.[1] Real assets tend to do best in inflationary environments, while moderate inflation favors financial assets.

Another way of looking at the required rate of return is by using the **Capital Asset Pricing Model (CAPM)**, which incorporates all the factors we have previously discussed but has a slightly different way of looking at the risk premium. In the CAPM, risk is divided into company risk and market risk. **Beta** measures the risk of a security relative to the market. Generally, the company's stock return is regressed against the return on the Standard and Poor's 500 Stock Index over a 60-month period. If there is a perfect correlation of returns, the beta of the company is calculated as 1.00, and the company's stock is considered to have risk equal to the market risk and expected returns equal to the market. If the beta is less than 1.00, the risk is less than the market and returns are expected to be less than market returns, and of course if the beta is greater than 1.00, the risk is greater than the market and returns are expected to be higher than market returns. Beta represents **systematic risk** that cannot be diversified away in a portfolio of stocks, and so it has special importance to the investor. The calculation of beta is covered in more detail in the section on portfolio management.

The second factor in calculating risk is the risk premium allocated to the stock market. We call this risk the **equity risk premium**. Again we use the Standard and Poor's 500 Index (large company returns found in Table 1–2) as our proxy for market returns. In many textbooks, the equity risk premium is given as $(K_M - R_F)$ and the terms are given. K_M refers to the expected return on the stock market and R_F refers to the expected risk free rate U.S. government securities. Unfortunately, in the real world K_M and R_F are not observable and must be

[1]Examples of other longer-term studies on comparative returns between real and financial assets are: Roger G. Ibbotson and Carol F. Fall, "The United States Wealth Portfolio," *The Journal of Portfolio Management*, Fall 1982, pp. 82–92; Roger G. Ibbotson and Lawrence B. Siegel, "The World Market Wealth Portfolio," *The Journal of Portfolio Management*, Winter 1983, pp. 5–17; and Alexander A. Robichek, Richard A. Cohn, and John J. Pringle, "Returns on Alternative Media and Implications for Portfolio Construction," *Journal of Business*, July 1972, pp. 427–43. (While Ibbotson and Siegel showed superior returns for metals between 1960 and 1980, metals have greatly underperformed other assets in the 1980s and 1990s.)

estimated, and so it is better to think of the equity risk premium as one term, ERP. The equity risk premium represents the extra return or premium the stock market must provide compared with the rate of return an investor can earn on U.S. Government Treasury Securities (a risk-free rate). Looking at Figure 1–4 again, we see that between 1926 and 2009 the mean return of large company stocks was 9.8 percent and of long-term government bonds was 5.4 percent. It is clear that stocks outperformed long-term government bonds by 4.4 percent. If we use U.S. Treasury bills as our risk-free rate, we have an equity risk premium of 6.1 percent (9.8 percent − 3.7 percent). An equity risk premium could be calculated in similar fashion for intermediate government bonds or long-term corporate bonds. The key to using the equity risk premium is to match the risk-free rate in the first term of the CAPM with the appropriate equity risk premium. For example, if you use the current long-term government rate in the CAPM you would use the 4.4 percent ERP, but if you used the Treasury bill rate you would use an ERP of 6.1 percent. If you were analyzing the stock of a small company, you could create equity risk premiums the same way, using the small stock returns from Figure 1–4. Table 1–3 shows the different equity risk premiums for large and small stocks that could be calculated from the data in Figure 1–4.

Recognize that we are assuming that historical equity risk premiums can be used as an estimate of the current equity risk premium in today's market environment. This is not always true. When investors are very optimistic, as they were with the Internet bubble in 1999–2001 and again with the housing bubble in 2006–2007, risk premiums can be very low, as investors don't perceive much risk in the markets. But the tide can turn fast. For example, when the financial crisis became the focal point of the U.S. economy in 2008 and 2009, risk premiums shot up quickly and stock price plummeted. The same panic occurred in 2010 with the Greek sovereign problem. So, although the historical average may be a good starting point, the equity risk premium can be adjusted up or down by the analyst based on his or her interpretation of the current risk situation.

You have to think not only about adjusting the equity risk premium, but also whether to use the long-term bond or the short-term Treasury bill for the risk-free rate. In times of a normal yield curve, where rates are not artificially depressed by the Federal Reserve, it probably doesn't make much of a difference which government security you use. But when the Federal Reserve Board has reduced short-term rates to extremely low levels to stimulate economic activity, you are probably better off using the long-term government bond yield. For example, in 2010, when one-year U.S. Treasury bills were yielding less than 1 percent, it would make no sense to use the short-term bills, because you would get an artificially low required rate of return that would cause you to overvalue stocks. Because common stocks have no maturity, it seems more realistic to use the long-term government bond for the risk-free rate. Additionally, the Federal Reserve generally doesn't manipulate long-term rates to stimulate the economy. How would we apply this CAPM to determine a required rate of return for an individual company's common stock?

TABLE 1-3 Historical Equity Risk Premiums, 1926-2009

Large stock return 9.8% − 5.4% long-term government bond = ERP of 4.4%
Large stock return 9.8% − 3.7% U.S. Treasury bill = ERP of 6.1%
Large stock return 9.8% − 5.3% intermediate government bond = ERP of 4.5%
Small stock return 11.9% − 5.4% long-term government bond = ERP of 6.5%
Small stock return 11.9% − 3.7% U.S. Treasury bill = ERP of 8.2%
Small stock return 11.9% − 5.3% intermediate government bond = ERP of 6.6%

application example

$$K_e = R_F = \beta(\text{ERP})$$

K_e = Required rate of return
R_F = Risk-free rate
β = Beta coefficient
K_M = Expected return on the market
$(K_M - R_F)$ = Equity risk premium (ERP)

Having discussed the beta and the equity risk premium, what is the appropriate value for the first-term, risk-free rate (R_F)?

$$K_e = \underset{\substack{\downarrow \\ \text{Risk-free rate}}}{R_F} + \underset{\substack{\downarrow \\ \text{Beta}}}{\beta}\underset{\substack{\searrow \\ \text{Equity risk premium}}}{(\text{ERP})}$$

By using the long-term government bond rate for our equity risk premium calculation, we have matched the long-term nature of common stock with the long-term returns generated by 20-year government bonds. For example, if the current long-term government bond has a yield of 4.6 percent, our ERP is 4.4 percent, and the beta for the market by definition is 1.00, then our required return for the stock market would be as follows:

$$K_e = R_F + \beta(\text{ERP})$$
$$= 4.6\% + 1.00(4.4\%)$$
$$K_e = 9.0\%$$

Now K_e, the required rate of return, can be used as a discount rate for future cash flows from an investment. If the company we are valuing has a beta different from 1.00, then the required return will reflect either higher or lower return for a company with higher or lower risk than the market. This methodology will be helpful as you work through the dividend valuation models presented in Chapter 7.

We have attempted to demonstrate the importance of risk in determining the required rate of return for an investment. We have tied the risk and return trade-off to historical data and given you several ways to calculate and think about the risk and return trade-off. This material will be used in later chapters, and so you may be referred back to Chapter 1 for a review of these concepts.

WHAT YOU WILL LEARN

The first part of the book covers the general framework for investing. You will look at an overview of the security markets (New York Stock Exchange, Chicago Board Options Exchange, and so on). Then you will examine the basics for participating in the market, such as opening an account, executing an order, investing individually or through a mutual fund, and so forth. Also in the first section of the book, you will become familiar with sources of important investment information so you can begin to make your university or public library, as well as your computer, valuable assets.

You will then go through the classic process of analyzing and valuing a security. You will start with examining the economy, then move to the industry level, and finally move to the actual company. The authors go through the process of putting a value on a stock. There is also heavy emphasis on financial analysis. Section Two provides an in-depth analysis of the Johnson & Johnson Company to demonstrate procedures for identifying the strengths and weaknesses of a company. For enthusiasts of charting and other forms of technical analysis, we examine the advantages and disadvantages of such approaches.

You will then move from stocks to bonds. Your level of interest should not diminish because bonds also offer an opportunity for income and, surprisingly, for large gains or losses. Because an emphasis of the book is to present the student with a wide investment horizon from which to choose, we then consider a variety of other investment alternatives. These include convertible securities and warrants, put and call options, commodities and financial futures, stock index futures and options, and real assets such as real estate and precious metals. We realize some of these terms may have little meaning to you now, but they soon will.

In the last section of the book, we consider the concepts of portfolio theory and how to put together the most desirable package of investments in terms of risk and return. The portfolio section includes chapters on bond management, international securities, real assets, private equity and hedge funds, and a final chapter on measuring portfolio risk adjusted returns. We also consider the consequences of investing in a reasonably efficient stock market environment, one in which information is acted on very quickly. Can superior return be achieved in such a setting?

Many students taking an investments course are not sure of their ultimate career goals. We hope this course can be equally valuable to a future banker, CPA, insurance executive, marketing manager, or anyone else. However, for those specifically considering a career in investments, the authors present a brief summary of career opportunities in Appendix 1A at the back of this chapter.

exploring the web

Web Address	Comments
www.aaii.com	**A nonprofit Web site educating do-it-yourself investors**
www.nasdaq.com	**Provides information about Nasdaq stocks and market**
www.nyse.com	**Provides information about New York Stock Exchange listings and regulations**
www.reit.com	**Provides information and data about real estate investment trusts**
http://quicken.intuit.com	**Provides understandable coverage of financial planning and investing**
www.morningstar.com	**Contains evaluations of and information about stocks and mutual funds**
www.business.com	**Provides a searchable database for links to sites by industry**
www.iclub.com	**Provides information and education for investment club members**
www.investopedia.com	**Provides general education about stocks and investing**
http://web.utk.edu/~jwachowi/part2.html	**Site created by finance professor with links to information resources**
www.investorwords.com	**Provides links to finance sites and glossary of finance terminology**
www.reuters.com	**Contains business and financial market news for the United States and other countries**
www.nasdaqtrader.com **www.bloombergtradebook.com**	**These two Web sites represent electronic communication networks (ECNs) and the different companies and markets competing with traditional floor-based markets such as the NYSE.**

KEY WORDS AND CONCEPTS

DISCUSSION QUESTIONS

1. How is an investment defined?
2. What are the differences between financial and real assets?
3. List some key areas relating to investment objectives.
4. Explain the concepts of direct equity and indirect equity.
5. How are equity and creditor claims different?
6. Do those wishing to assume low risks tend to invest long term or short term? Why?
7. How is liquidity measured?
8. Explain why conservative investors who tend to buy short-term assets differ from short-term traders.
9. How does the Tax Relief Act of 2003 affect the relative attractiveness of long-term capital gains versus dividend income? (A general statement will suffice.)
10. Why is there a minimum amount of time that must be committed to any investment program?
11. In a highly inflationary environment, would an investor tend to favor real or financial assets? Why?
12. What two primary components are used to measure the rate of return achieved from an investment?
13. Many people think of risk as the danger of losing money. Is this the same way that risk is defined in finance?
14. What are the three elements that determine the return an investor should require from an investment?
15. Explain how an investor receiving a 2 or 3 percent quoted return in an inflationary environment may actually experience a negative real rate of return.
16. In Figure 1–4 on page 15, what has been the highest return investment category over the 79-year period? What has been the lowest? Assuming risk is measured by the standard deviation, what can you say about the relationship of risk to return in Figure 1–4?

PROBLEMS

Rate of return

1. The price of the stock of Clarkson Corporation went from $50 to $56 last year. The firm also paid $2 in dividends. Compute the rate of return.

Rate of return

2. In the following year, the dividend was raised to $2.25. However, a bear market developed toward the end of the year, and the stock price declined from

$56 at the beginning of the year to $48 at the end of the year. Compute the rate of return or (loss) to stockholders.

Risk-free rate

3. Assume the real rate of return in the economy is 2.5 percent, the expected rate of inflation is 5 percent, and the risk premium is 5.8 percent. Compute the risk-free rate (Formula 1–3 on page 13) and required rate of return.

Required return

4. Assume the real return in the economy is 4 percent. It is anticipated that the consumer price index will go from 200 to 210. Shares in common stock are assumed to have a required return one-third higher than the risk-free rate. Compute the required return on common stock.

Geometric return

5. Sally is reviewing the performance of several portfolios in the family trusts. Trust A is managed by Wall Street Investment Advisors and Trust B is managed by LaSalle Street Investment Advisors. Both trusts are invested in a combination of stocks and bonds and have the following returns:

	Trust A	Trust B
Year 1	15%	12%
Year 2	10	15
Year 3	−4	−2
Year 4	25	20
Year 5	−8	−5

a. Calculate the annualized geometric and arithmetic returns over this 5-year period.

b. Which manager performed the best, and is there a significant enough difference for Sally to move her money to the winning manager?

c. Explain the difference between the geometric and arithmetic returns.

Capital Asset Pricing Model

6. Calculate the required rate of return for Campbell Corp. common stock. The stock has a beta of 1.3, and Campbell is considered a large capitalization stock. Current long-term government bonds are yielding 5.0% and the equity risk premium is 5.8%.

a. How would your required rate of return change if you used U.S. Treasury bills for your risk-free rate? Assume the current yield on T-bills is 1.25 percent. This is an artificially low rate because the Federal Reserve is trying to stimulate the economy out of a recession.

b. How would this difference in required returns affect the value of any cash flow you would evaluate?

Capital Asset Pricing Model

7. Fastchip is a small technology company with a beta of 1.5 and a market capitalization of $200 million. Currently, long-term government securities are yielding 5.0 percent, the equity risk premium is 5.8%, intermediate governments are yielding 4.0 percent, and T-bills are yielding 3.3 percent. Calculate the required rate of return using all three risk-free rates. Choose which one would be the most aggressive and which would be the most conservative to use in valuing cash flows. Which K_e would you prefer to use, and why?

WEB EXERCISE

Assume you want to see how the market is doing on a given day as well as get additional perspective on a given stock. There are literally hundreds of options. We will merely suggest one for now.

Go to **http://finance.yahoo.com**

1. Note the changes in the Dow Jones (DJIA), Nasdaq, and S&P 500 Index. Write a brief comment on whether they all moved in the same direction or not.

2. On the upper left-hand portion of the home page, you will see a search bar. Put in the symbol for any stock and click on "Get Quotes." If you do not have a preference, use IBM.
3. Write down the last trade value, the change, the previous close, the 52-week range, the P/E ratio, and the dividend yield. All these terms will take on greater meaning as you progress through the text.
4. On the left column you will see "Basic Chart." Click on this item. Describe when the stock hit its approximate high point (month and value) and its approximate low point (month and value). Based on the overall appearance of the chart, does the stock appear to have upward or downward momentum?
5. Click on "Competitors" along the left margin. Indicate how the company compares to other companies in the industry in terms of market capitalization (total market value). Write down the total values.

Note: From time to time, companies redesign their Web sites and occasionally a topic we have listed may have been deleted, updated, or moved into a different location.

APPENDIX 1A

CAREER OPPORTUNITIES IN INVESTMENTS

Career opportunities in the investment field include positions as stockbroker, security analyst, portfolio manager, investment banker, or financial planner.

Stockbroker

A stockbroker (an account executive) generally works with the public in advising and executing orders for individual or institutional accounts. Although the broker may have a salary base to cushion against bad times, most of the compensation is in the form of commissions. Successful brokers do quite well financially.

Most brokerage houses look for people who have effective selling skills as well as an interest in finance. In hiring, some brokerage houses require prior business experience and a mature appearance. Table 1A–1 lists both retail and

TABLE 1A-1 Major Retail Brokerage

Houses	Discount Brokers
CIBC World Markets	Bank of America
Cowen & Company	Charles Schwab
Deutsche Bank	E-Trade
Edward Jones	Fidelity
Goldman, Sachs & Co.	First Trade
Jefferies	Muriel Siebert
JPMorgan Securities	OptionsXpress
Merrill Lynch Credit Suisse	ShareBuilder
Morgan Stanley Smith Barney	TD Ameritrade
Raymond James	TradeKing
RBC Capital Markets	USAA
RBS Securities	WallStreet-E
UBS	Wells Trade
Wells Fargo Advisors	Zecco

discount brokerage houses in alphabetical order. There have been a lot of consolidations and bankruptcies in the last several years, and many well-known names, such as Lehman Brothers and Bear Stearns, are gone. TD Waterhouse merged into Ameritrade to become TD Ameritrade, and Quick & Reilly and Wachovia were gobbled up by Wells Fargo and became part of Wells Fargo Advisors.

Security Analyst or Portfolio Manager

Security analysts study various industries and companies and provide research reports to their clientele. Security analysts might work for a brokerage house, a bank trust department, or other type of institutional investor and often specialize in certain industries. They are expected to have an in-depth knowledge of overall financial analysis as well as the variables that influence their industry.

The role of the financial analyst has been upgraded over the years through a certifying program in which you can become a chartered financial analyst (CFA). There are approximately 50,000 CFAs in the United States and Canada. Achieving this designation calls for a three-year minimum appropriate-experience requirement and extensive testing over a three-year period. Each of the annual exams is six hours long (the fee changes from year to year). You can actually begin taking the exams while still in school (you can complete your experience requirement later).

Topics covered in the three years of exams are shown in Table 1A–2. An undergraduate or graduate degree in business with a major in finance or accounting or an economics degree is quite beneficial to the exam process (although other degrees are also acceptable). Of course, educational background must be supplemented with additional study prescribed by the Chartered Financial

TABLE 1A-2 Topics Covered in CFA Exams

Ethical and Professional Standards	
Applicable laws and regulations	Ethical conduct and professional obligations
Professional standards of practice	International ethical and professional considerations
Tools and Inputs for Investment Valuation and Management	
Quantitative methods and statistics	Microeconomics
Macroeconomics	Financial standards and accounting
Investment (Asset) Valuation	
Overview of the valuation process	Equity securities
Applying economic analysis in investment valuation	Fixed-income securities
Applying industry analysis in investment valuation	Other investments
Applying company analysis in investment valuation	Derivative securities
Portfolio Management	
Capital market theory	Equity portfolio management
Portfolio policies	Real estate portfolio management
Expectational factors	Specialized asset portfolio management
Asset allocation	Implementing the investment process
Fixed-income portfolio management	Performance management

Analysts Institute. The address for more information is: CFA Institute, P.O. Box 3668, Charlottesville, Virginia 22903 (phone 434-951-5499). The Web site location is www.cfainstitute.org.

While many security analysts are not CFAs, those who carry this designation tend to enjoy higher salaries and prestige. Top analysts are in strong demand, and six-figure to seven-figure salaries for top analysts are common. The magazine *Institutional Investor* picks an all-American team of security analysts—the best in energy, banking, and so on.

Portfolio managers are responsible for managing large pools of funds, and they are generally employed by insurance companies, mutual funds, bank trust departments, pension funds, and other institutional investors. They often rely on the help of security analysts and brokers in designing their portfolios. They not only must decide which stocks to buy or sell, but they also must determine the risk level with the optimum trade-off between the common stock and fixed-income components of a portfolio. Portfolio managers often rise through the ranks of stockbrokers and security analysts.

Investment Banker

Investment bankers primarily distribute securities from the issuing corporation to the public. Investment bankers also advise corporate clients on their financial strategy and may help to arrange mergers and acquisitions.

The investment banker is one of the most prestigious participants in the securities industry. Although the hiring of investment bankers was once closely confined to Ivy League graduates with the right family ties, such is no longer the case. Nevertheless, top academic credentials are still necessary.

Financial Planner

The field of financial planning is emerging to help solve the investment and tax problems of the individual investor. Financial planners may include specially trained representatives of the insurance industry, accountants, and certified financial planners (an individual may fall into more than one of these categories).

Certified financial planners (CFPs) are so designated by the College of Financial Planning, a division of the National Endowment for Financial Education. To qualify as a CFP, an applicant must demonstrate proficiency in the five following areas through extensive testing and training.

- Financial planning process and insurance.
- Investment planning.
- Income tax planning.
- Retirement planning and employee benefits.
- Estate planning.

Information on the CFP program can be obtained from the CFP Board, 4695 South Monaco Street, Denver, CO 80237-3403 (phone 303-220-4800) or from colleges or universities that sponsor CFP classes or programs. The Web site location is www.cfp.net.

chapter two

SECURITY MARKETS

OBJECTIVES

1. Understand the functions of financial markets.
2. Explain the role that the investment banker plays in an initial public offering.
3. Discuss the differences between floor trading and electronic trading.
4. Explain the potential impact of algorithmic program trading.
5. Understand the important legislation that affects the operations of the capital markets.

OUTLINE

THE MARKET ENVIRONMENT

The financial markets continue to change at a rapid pace. The last 10 years have been ones of deregulation, new laws, mergers, global consolidation, online (Internet) brokerage, electronic communication networks (ECNs), and the transformation of most securities markets from not-for-profit organizations to for-profit corporations with common stock available for purchase by the public. The first exchange to become a publicly traded company was the Chicago Mercantile Exchange (CME) at the end of 2001. The shares were offered at $34 per share and six years later they traded at over $500 per share. The Nasdaq Stock Market followed with a public offering, then the New York Stock Exchange, then the Chicago Board of Trade. No wonder these other markets were eager to "go public" after the CME's track record.

Once these securities markets became publicly traded companies, they had common stock to use for the acquisition of other markets. The New York Stock Exchange merged with Archipelago, one of the largest ECNs, and then in 2007 merged with Euronext, an electronic exchange in Europe trading derivative securities as well as common stock. The Nasdaq Stock Market acquired INET from Reuters, the largest ECN. Nasdaq also made a merger proposal to the London Stock Exchange but was rebuffed. Instead, they bought the OMX, a Nordic stock exchange. In addition, the two largest futures markets, the Chicago Mercantile Exchange (CME) and the Chicago Board of Trade (CBOT), merged and created the most dominant futures market in the world.

Significant changes in the banking laws preceded these structural changes in the securities markets. In 1999 Congress passed the Gramm-Leach-Bliley Act, which allowed financial institutions to offer the full financial services of commercial banking, investment banking, insurance, and brokerage firms. The combination of these services had been prohibited by the Glass Steagall Act, which was passed after the great crash of 1929, and essentially the Gramm-Leach-Bliley Act repealed these prohibitions.

Perhaps the most significant law was the Sarbanes-Oxley Act of 2002, which was enacted after the accounting frauds and scandals that took place during the stock market boom of the late 1990s. Members of management of companies such as Enron, WorldCom, Tyco, and others "cooked the books," and by 2007, many of the perpetrators were in jail. Unfortunately, the costs of compliance with Sarbanes-Oxley and the heavy penalties for those found guilty have had a significant negative effect on the willingness of foreign companies to list their shares on U.S. stock exchanges. As one example, during 2005, 24 of the 25 largest initial public offerings were listed on European stock exchanges. The Sarbanes-Oxley Act is a prime motivator for the U.S. exchanges to merge with foreign exchanges. Companies will be able to list on an exchange of their choice, and those companies choosing to be listed in Europe or Asia will not have to comply with Sarbanes-Oxley or with the rules and regulations of the U.S. Securities and Exchange Commission.

Subsequent to the Sarbanes-Oxley Act, the cost of compliance for small publicly listed companies has taken a very high percentage of their profits, and hundreds of small companies have returned to private ownership by buying back their shares from the public and delisting their stock from the public markets.

With all of the structural and legal changes that have taken place over the last several years, you may wonder how the markets actually function. What are these markets supposed to do?

MARKET FUNCTIONS

Many times people will call their stockbroker and ask, "How's the market?" What they are referring to is usually the market for common stocks as measured by the Dow Jones Industrial Average, the Standard & Poor's 500 Index, or some other measure of common stock performance. The stock market is not the only market. There are markets for each different kind of investment that can be made.

A **market** is simply a way of exchanging assets, usually cash, for something of value. It could be a used car, a government bond, gold, or diamonds. There doesn't have to be a central place where this transaction is consummated. As long as there can be communication between buyers and sellers, the exchange can occur. The offering party does not have to own what he sells but can be an agent acting for the owner in the transaction. For example, in the sale of real estate, the owner usually employs a real estate broker/agent who advertises and sells the property for a percentage commission. Not all markets have the same procedures, but certain trading characteristics are desirable for most markets.

Market Efficiency and Liquidity

In general, an **efficient market** occurs when prices respond quickly to new information, when each successive trade is made at a price close to the preceding price, and when the market can absorb large amounts of securities or assets without changing the price significantly. The more efficient the market, the faster prices react to new information; the closer in price is each successive trade; and the greater the amount of securities that can be sold without changing the price.

For markets to be efficient in this context, they must be liquid. **Liquidity** is a measure of the speed with which an asset can be converted into cash at its fair market value. Liquid markets exist when continuous trading occurs, and as the number of participants in the market becomes larger, price continuity increases along with liquidity. Transaction costs also affect liquidity. The lower the cost of buying and selling, the more likely it is that people will be able to enter the market.

Competition and Allocation of Capital

An investor must realize that all markets compete for funds: stocks against bonds, mutual funds against real estate, government securities against corporate securities, and so on. The competitive comparisons are almost endless. Because markets set prices on assets, investors are able to compare the prices against their perceived risk and expected return and thereby choose assets that enable them to achieve their desired risk-return trade-offs. If the markets are efficient, prices adjust rapidly to new information, and this adjustment changes the expected rate of return and allows the investor to alter investment strategy. Without efficient and liquid markets, the investor would be unable to do this. This allocation of capital occurs on both secondary and primary markets.

Secondary Markets

Secondary markets, such as the New York Stock Exchange and the NASDAQ stock market, are markets for existing assets that are currently traded between investors. These markets create prices and allow for liquidity. If secondary markets did not exist, investors would have no place to sell their assets. Without liquidity, many people would not invest at all. Would you like to own $10,000 of Microsoft common stock but be unable to convert it into cash if needed? If there were no secondary markets, investors would expect a higher return to compensate for the increased risk of illiquidity and the inability to adjust their portfolios to new information.

Primary Markets

Primary markets are distinguished by the flow of funds between the market participants. Instead of trading between investors as in the secondary markets, participants in the primary market buy their assets directly from the source of the asset. A common example would be a new issue of corporate bonds sold by AT&T. You would buy the bonds through a brokerage firm acting as an agent for AT&T's investment bankers. Your dollars would flow to AT&T rather than to another investor. The same would be true of buying a piece of art directly from the artist rather than from an art gallery.

Primary markets allow corporations, government units, and others to raise needed funds for expansion of their capital base. Once the assets or securities are sold in the primary market, they begin trading in the secondary market. Price competition in the secondary markets between different risk-return classes enables the primary markets to price new issues at fair prices to reflect existing risk-return relationships. So far, our discussion of markets has been quite general but applicable to most free markets. In the following sections, we will deal with the organization and structure of specific markets.

ORGANIZATION OF THE PRIMARY MARKETS: THE INVESTMENT BANKER

The most active participant in the primary market is the investment banker. Since corporations, states, and local governments do not sell new securities daily, monthly, or even annually, they usually rely on the expertise of the investment banker when selling securities.

Underwriting Function

The **investment banker** acts as a middleman in the process of raising funds and, in most cases, takes a risk by underwriting an issue of securities. **Underwriting** refers to the guarantee the investment banking firm gives the selling firm to purchase its securities at a fixed price, thereby eliminating the risk of not selling the whole issue of securities and having less cash than desired. The investment banker may also sell the issue on a **best-efforts** basis where the issuing firm assumes the risk and simply takes back any securities not sold after a fixed period. A very limited number of securities are **sold directly** by the corporation to the public. Of the three methods of distribution, underwriting is far and away the most widely used.

With underwriting, once the security is sold, the investment banker will usually make a market in the security, which means active buying and selling to ensure a continuously liquid market and wider distribution. In the case of best efforts and for direct offerings by the issuer, which are even smaller than best efforts, the firm assumes the risk of not raising enough capital and has no guarantees that a continuous market will be made in the company's securities.

Corporations may also choose to raise capital through private placements rather than through a public offering. With a private placement, the company may sell its own securities to a financial institution such as an insurance company, a pension fund, or a mutual fund, or it can engage an investment banker to find an institution willing to buy a large block of stock or bonds. Most private placements involve bonds (debt issues) instead of common stock. During the last decade, publicly offered bonds approximated 80 percent of the funds raised, with private placements accounting for about 20 percent. Publicly offered bonds issued through underwriters as opposed to privately placed issues are by far the most popular method of raising debt capital.

Distribution

In a public offering, the distribution process is extremely important, and on some large issues, an investment banker does not undertake this alone. Investment banking firms will share the risk and the burden of distribution by forming a group called a **syndicate**. The larger the offering in dollar terms, the more participants there generally are in the

FIGURE 2-1 Prospectus

10,600,000 Shares

Filed Pursuant to Rule 424(b)(4)
Registration No. 333–163581

retirement help for life®

Common Stock

This is an initial public offering of shares of common stock of Financial Engines, Inc.

Financial Engines is offering 5,868,100 of the shares to be sold in the offering. The selling stockholders identified in this prospectus are offering an additional 4,731,900 shares. Financial Engines will not receive any of the proceeds from the sale of the shares being sold by the selling stockholders.

Prior to this offering, there has been no public market for the common stock. Our common stock has been approved for listing on The Nasdaq Global Market under the symbol "FNGN."

See "Risk Factors" on page 15 to read about factors you should consider before buying shares of the common stock.

Neither the Securities and Exchange Commission nor any state securities commission has approved or disapproved of these securities or determined if this prospectus is truthful or complete. Any representation to the contrary is a criminal offense.

	Per Share	Total
Initial public offering price	$12.00	$127,200,000
Underwriting discounts and commissions	$ 0.84	$ 8,904,000
Proceeds, before expenses, to Financial Engines	$11.16	$ 65,487,996
Proceeds, before expenses, to the selling stockholders	$11.16	$ 52,808,004

To the extent that the underwriters sell more than 10,600,000 shares of common stock, the underwriters have the option to purchase up to an additional 1,590,000 shares from Financial Engines at the initial public offering price less the underwriting discounts and commissions.

The underwriters expect to deliver the shares against payment in New York, New York on March 19, 2010.

Goldman, Sachs & Co.

UBS Investment Bank

Piper Jaffray **Cowen and Company**

Prospectus dated March 15, 2010

syndicate. For example, the front page of the prospectus in Figure 2–1 for Financial Engines illustrates the participation of four investment banks in the syndicate. Financial Engines is located in Palo Alto, California, and was founded in 1996 by William Sharpe, 1990 Nobel laureate and professor emeritus at Stanford University, Joseph A. Grundfest, professor of law, and the late Craig Johnson, chairman of the Venture Law Group. The prospectus for Financial Engines describes the company as follows:

> We are a leading provider of independent, technology-enabled portfolio management services, investment advice, and retirement help to participants in employer-sponsored defined contribution plans, such as 401(k) plans. We help investors plan for retirement by offering personalized plans for saving and investing, as well as by providing assessments of retirement income needs and readiness, regardless of personal wealth or investment account size. We use our proprietary advice technology platform to provide our services to millions of retirement plan participants on a cost-efficient basis. We believe that our services have significantly lowered the cost and increased the accessibility to plan participants of independent, personalized portfolio management services, investment advice, and retirement help.

Of the 10.6 million shares offered for sale, Goldman Sachs underwrote 6.36 million shares, UBS Investment Bank 2.65 million shares, Piper Jaffray & Co. 848,000 shares, and Cowen and Company, LLC 742,000 shares. The underwriters had the option of purchasing an additional 1.59 million shares. This option is generally exercised if the offering is well accepted by the market and the stock price moves up from the original offer price ($12 per share in this case). Notice that Goldman Sachs, the lead underwriter, gets top billing, while the smaller participants show up at the bottom of the page.

Of the total $127.2 million raised, the company sold $63.2 million, and the existing stockholders sold $64.0 million. Management stated that the funds would be used for general corporate purposes and working capital. This is a classic case of founders, investors, and venture capitalists selling shares to gain liquidity and diversify their portfolio. Or you could say they were harvesting the fruits of their labors, and the market rewarded them with a 44 percent increase on the first day of the offering. The stock closed at $17.25.

It should be noted that the investment bankers make a commitment to purchase at a discount from the public price (in this case at only $11.16) and sell their allotted shares at the $12 offering price. If the Financial Engines stock price falls below the intended offering price of $12 per share while the shares are still being sold to the public, the investment bankers in the syndicate will not make their original estimated profit on the issue. If the stock price falls below $11.16 per share during the offering, the investment bankers could lose money.

For most initial public offerings (IPOs), the investment banker is extremely important as a link between the original issuer and the security markets. By taking much of the risk, the investment banker enables corporations and others to find needed capital and also allows other investors an opportunity for ownership of securities through purchase in the secondary (resale) market. One noticeable change in the investment banking industry is the globalization and increased size of the investment banks. Because the Financial Engines offering was small, only four investment banks shared $127.2 million dollars of the initial public offering. In some cases, a syndicate as small as 10 bankers can handle a $5 billion dollar (or larger) offering.

Another change that has affected the distribution and underwriting process is the increased use of shelf registration under SEC Rule 415. A shelf registration allows issuing firms to register their securities with the SEC and then sell them at will as funds are needed in the future. Over time, this allows bankers to buy portions of the shelf issue and immediately resell the securities to institutional clients without forming the normal syndicate or tying up capital for several weeks. Shelf registration is more popular with bond offerings than common stock offerings, where the traditional syndicated offering tends to dominate.

Investment Banking Competition

Table 2–1 shows the top 10 underwriters of global debt and equity offerings for the years 2008 and 2009. The list of bankers remains relatively the same from year to year, with some bankers moving up or down the list due to mergers and the fund-raising activities of their clients. In previous years the listing would have emphasized *U.S.* offerings of debt and equity but as more international and multinational companies raise capital around the world, the investment banking game has become *global*.

The total market share of the top 10 bankers has dropped from the late 1990s and early 2000s. This has allowed the smaller investment banks, specializing in medium-sized companies, to take some market share from the big players who are more dependent on large companies. In 2001 the top 10 investment bankers accounted for over 83 percent of the market share, while in 2009 they only accounted for 55.9 percent.

Bringing private companies public for the first time is called an **initial public offering (IPO)**, and distribution costs to the selling company are much higher than

TABLE 2-1 Top 10 Underwriters of Global Stocks and Bonds

Global Stocks and Bonds
U.S. Public, Rule 144a, Domestic and International Equity and Euro-Market Issues, Ranked by 2009 Proceeds

	2009			2008	
Manager	Proceeds (billions)	No. of Issues	Market Share	Proceeds (billions)	Rank
J.P. Morgan	**$ 618.9**	2,018	8.8%	**$ 426.2**	2
Citi	**449.0**	1,597	6.4	**275.1**	5
Barclays Capital	**448.8**	1,682	6.4	**395.6**	3
BofA-Merrill Lynch	**442.3**	1,804	6.3	**489.4**	1
Deutsche Bank	**381.9**	1,461	5.5	**278.9**	4
Goldman Sachs	**372.6**	1,075	5.3	**248.2**	6
Morgan Stanley	**321.4**	1,196	4.6	**216.5**	9
RBS	**296.6**	1,134	4.2	**228.3**	8
Credit Suisse	**295.8**	1,119	4.2	**212.8**	10
HSBC	**287.8**	1,200	4.1	**173.2**	11
Top 10 Totals	**$3,915.0**	14,286	55.9%	**$2,944.3**	
Industry Total	**$7,003.9**	25,318	100.0%	**$5,072.3**	

Source: *The Wall Street Journal,* January 4, 2010. Reprinted with permission of *The Wall Street Journal,* Copyright

offerings of additional stock by companies that are already public. Average fees from IPOs are usually between 1.5 and 2.0 percent higher than the fees for secondary offerings of publicly traded stock. The ranking for firms with proceeds from IPOs is shown in Table 2–2, with J.P. Morgan leading the field in global debt and equity.

Underwriting competition is like a decathlon; there are many events for each contestant. Table 2–3 provides a list of the categories in which investment bankers

TABLE 2-2 Initial Public Offerings (IPOs)

Global Equity and Equity-Related (U.S. Public, Rule 144a, Domestic and International Equity and Equity-Related Markets) | **(Continued) Global Debt (U.S. Public, Rule 144a and Euro-Market Issues)**

		Market Share				Market Share	
Manager	Amount (billions)	2009	2008	Manager	Amount (billions)	2009	2008
J.P. Morgan	**$105.5**	11.7%	11.6%	J.P. Morgan	**$ 514.8**	8.4%	8.0%
Goldman Sachs	**85.9**	9.5	9.6	Barclays Capital	**435.5**	7.1	8.4
Morgan Stanley	**72.5**	8.0	7.4	Citi	**391.8**	6.4	5.1
BofA-Merrill Lynch	**71.0**	7.9	12.7	BofA-Merrill Lynch	**371.6**	6.1	9.2
UBS	**60.8**	6.7	6.1	Deutsche Bank	**343.3**	5.6	5.7
Citi	**58.3**	6.5	7.6	Goldman Sachs	**286.7**	4.7	4.2
Credit Suisse	**51.0**	5.7	5.1	RBS	**281.4**	4.6	4.8
Deutsche Bank	**39.3**	4.4	4.1	HSBC	**270.1**	4.4	3.8
Nomura	**32.1**	3.6	1.7	Morgan Stanley	**250.0**	4.1	3.8
HSBC	**17.8**	2.0	0.9	Credit Suisse	**244.9**	4.0	4.1
Top 10 Totals	**$594.1**	65.8%	66.8%	**Top 10 Totals**	**$3,390.0**	55.5%	57.0%
Industry Total	**$903.0**	100.0%	100.0%	**Industry Total**	**$6,112.3**	100.0%	100.0%

Source: *The Wall Street Journal,* January 4, 2010. Reprinted with permission of *The Wall Street Journal,*

TABLE 2-3 **Who's Number 1?**

Leading Stock and Bond Underwriters, by 2009 Proceeds

Market Sector	No. 1 Ranked Manager	2009 Mkt. Share	Change from 2008 (pct. pts.)
Global Debt, Stock & Stock-Related	J.P. Morgan	8.8%	0.44
U.S. Debt, Equity & Equity-Related	J.P. Morgan	14.7	0.34
Stocks			
Global Common Stock	J.P. Morgan	11.7	0.48
Global Convertibles	J.P. Morgan	11.5	−1.92
Global Common Stock—U.S. Issuers	BofA-Merrill Lynch	18.0	−2.95
Global Convertibles—U.S. Issuers	Citi	20.6	4.57
Bonds			
U.S. Asset-backed Securities	Citi	21.5	8.71
U.S. Investment Grade Corporate Debt	Citi	15.3	1.68
U.S. High-Yield Corporate Debt	J.P. Morgan	16.1	−4.38
U.S. Mortgage-backed Securities	BofA-Merrill Lynch	18.3	−7.72
Syndicated Loans			
U.S. Syndicated Loans	J.P. Morgan	21.5	−0.36

Source: *The Wall Street Journal*, January 4, 2010. Reprinted with permission of *The Wall Street Journal*,

compete and the number one ranked investment bank in each category. While Merrill Lynch used to be the dominant player in many categories, it shows up in first place in only two of the categories. J.P. Morgan dominates the overall global markets and has a total of six first-place listings. Citi is strong in the corporate debt market and asset-backed securities. Each firm competes based on its expertise.

ORGANIZATION OF THE SECONDARY MARKETS

Once a new issue of securities has been sold by the investment banker or the U.S. Treasury, it begins trading in secondary markets that provide liquidity, efficiency, continuity, and competition. Secondary markets exist for corporate stocks and bonds; commodities such as gold, copper, wheat, sugar, and oil; foreign currencies; and U.S. treasury bills, notes, and bonds. Virtually any financial instrument or commodity can be traded in a secondary market. Without a secondary market, prices of assets would be hard to determine, and the ability to raise capital or liquidate assets would be very difficult and would be transacted in private markets where the liquidity and price efficiency would be less competitive and less transparent.

Stock Exchanges

Most of our discussion will be focused on stock markets. Stock exchanges such as the **New York Stock Exchange (NYSE)** and the American Stock Exchange began with a central location where trading between buyers and sellers occurred at trading posts located on the floor of the exchange. Modern exchanges like BATS and ICE are totally electronic and have no trading floor, while the New York Stock Exchange has moved to a hybrid system of floor trading coupled with electronic trading. The NASDAQ Stock Exchange has always been electronic without a central location. While a central location used to distinguish **organized exchanges** from the **over-the-counter markets**, this is not the case anymore. In addition, the last decade has seen the development of a new type of market called an **ECN**, or **electronic communication network**. In the next section we will present an overview of each market.

There are also regional exchanges such as the Chicago, Philadelphia, Cincinnati, and Boston Exchanges, but with the advent of electronic trading they have lost their reason to exist. Only the Chicago Stock Exchange is currently viable, with Philadelphia and Boston being bought by NASDAQ. Although these exchanges still exist, they mostly trade stocks in nationally listed companies, called dual trading. These small regional exchanges provide investors an alternative market to place trades. Very few trades are made in local companies, which is the historical reason for the existence of these exchanges.

Consolidated Tape

Although dual listing and trading have existed for decades, it was not until June 16, 1975, that a consolidated ticker tape was instituted. This allows brokers on the floor of one exchange to see prices of transactions on other exchanges in the dually listed stocks. There are two consolidated tapes, one that tracks New York Stock Exchange listings and one that tracks NASDAQ securities. All exchanges, ECNs, and third-market broker-dealers participate in the consolidated tape system.

Listing Requirements for Firms

One of the major factors identifying an exchange is its listing requirements. The only way a firm's securities can be traded on an exchange is if the company meets the listing requirements and has been approved by the board of governors of that exchange. All exchanges have minimum requirements that must be met before trading can occur in a company's common stock. Since the NYSE is the biggest exchange and generates the most dollar volume in large, well-known companies, its listing requirements are the most restrictive. However, while the Nasdaq Stock Market has less restrictive listing requirements than the NYSE, it lists many large technology companies such as Microsoft, Oracle, Apple, and Cisco Systems that would easily meet NYSE listing standards.

Initial Listing Although each case is decided on its own merits, there are minimum requirements that are specified by the exchanges. These requirements set minimums for the net income of the firm, the market value of publicly held shares, the number of shares publicly held, and the number of stockholders owning at least a round lot of 100 shares. Other exchanges have similar requirements, but the amounts are smaller. We have a Web exercise at the back of the chapter that takes you to the New York Stock Exchange Web site where you can look up the latest minimum standards for companies wanting to be listed on the NYSE. This is also true for the Nasdaq Web site.

www.nyse.com

Corporations desiring to be listed on the NYSE, Nasdaq, or elsewhere have decided that public availability of the stock on an exchange will benefit their shareholders by providing liquidity to owners or by allowing the company a more viable means for raising external capital for growth and expansion. The company must pay annual listing fees to the exchange and additional fees based on the number of shares traded each year.

Delisting The New York Stock Exchange also has the authority to remove (delist) a security from trading when the security fails to meet certain criteria. There is much latitude in these decisions, but generally, a company's security may be considered for delisting if there are fewer than 1,200 round-lot (100 shares) owners, 600,000 shares or fewer in public hands, and the total market value of the security

the real world of investing

1/1000 OF A SECOND DOES MATTER—HIGH FREQUENCY TRADING

As the stock exchanges and financial markets become ever more dominated by electronic trading systems, speed of order executions becomes extremely important for traders, brokers, and exchanges. Much like in the 100-yard dash, the fastest wins the prize. Only in the case of markets, 10 seconds isn't fast enough. The New York Stock Exchange reports that it takes approximately 7 seconds to fully execute a typical market order in the auction market on the floor of the exchange. Even online brokers like E*Trade guarantee trade execution in 2 seconds for a large number of stocks and often clear a trade in less than half a second. The NYSE also states that if you use their automated trading system, an order can be executed in 300 to 400 milliseconds or three- or four-tenths of a second.

However for traders we are not talking about seconds or even one-tenth of a second in financial markets. We are talking about milliseconds or 1/1000 of a second. Electronic exchanges such as NYSE-ARCA and the Nasdaq Stock Market account for approximately 50 percent of the trading volume in big name stocks with large volume. Globex, the electronic trading platform of the Chicago Mercantile Exchange, also accounts for about 80 percent of the volume in financial futures. The percentage of trades made electronically will continue to increase so that some day soon almost all of the volume on actively traded securities will be electronic.

Time is so important to algorithmic traders and hedge funds that even increasing trading speed by 1/1000 of a second makes a great difference in strategy implementation. Firms that employ extreme time-sensitive strategies are most often using their computers to search for bid/ask spread imbalances across markets. When they find a small price differential (even fractions of a penny) they use their computer programs to buy and sell almost instantaneously and pocket a small profit. By doing this often enough every day, those fractional pennies on millions of shares can add up. This arbitrage activity helps make the market very price efficient.

In fact, Tradebot System Inc. moved its trading computers from North Kansas City to New York and New Jersey in order to be located in the same buildings as the computers of the two largest electronic markets. Dave Cummings, the owner of Tradebot, estimated that the move allowed him to process trades in one millisecond rather than the twenty milliseconds by his computers when they were in Kansas City. The time savings were so important that Mr. Cummings estimates that he would be out of business if he hadn't made the move. It is estimated that over 40 other firms have their trading computers in the same two buildings. Renting space next to exchange computers has become a profit making center for the exchanges.

is less than $5 million. A company that easily exceeded these standards on first being listed may fall below them during hard times.

Listing Fees

www.nasdaq.com

One benefit for an exchange is the ability to charge listing fees to corporations trading on your exchange. The Nasdaq Web site has a calculator to demonstrate the difference between the fees on Nasdaq and the NYSE. According to the Nasdaq, a company having 100,000,000 shares outstanding would pay an annual listing fee of $61,750 to Nasdaq or $93,000 to the NYSE. There is also an initial listing fee for a company that just completed an initial public offering and is being listed for the first time. In this case Nasdaq would charge a one-time fee of $150,000 while the NYSE would charge $250,000. These fees change over time as exchanges adjust their fees for competitive reasons.

THE ORGANIZATION OF THE NYSE

The New York Stock Exchange has undergone a transformation from a not-for-profit corporation to a for-profit corporation and in the process has become a hybrid market consisting of traditional floor trading and electronic trading through its acquired subsidiary ArcaEx (formerly known as Archipelago). The NYSE also consummated a merger with Euronext in the first quarter of 2007. Euronext is the leading electronic European exchange having a presence in Amsterdam, Brussels, London, Lisbon, and Paris. It is also one of the leading derivative (futures, options) markets in the world. After the merger between the NYSE Group and Euronext, the combined exchange is now called NYSE Euronext and is the world's largest exchange. Its ticker symbol is NYX. In 2010, it had a combined market capitalization (number of shares outstanding of NYSE Euronext times its share price) of $7.5 billion, down from $27 billion in 2007.

In February of 2011 Deutsche Börse AG, located in Frankfurt, Germany, was in merger talks with the NYSE. At the time of this writing it was not clear what kind of regulatory hurdles this combination would generate in the U.S. and Europe. Deutsche Börse AG would end up as the majority shareholder of the combined entity. The offer caused other exchanges to consider bids for the NYSE but the merger agreement between the NYSE and the Deutsche Borse included a $339 breakup fee to be paid to the Deutsche Borse. This fee would increase the cost of a merger if the NYSE combined with another exchange. This potential merger highlights the global nature of the security markets and the transition to electronic trading.

Trading on the NYSE

Traditionally, the New York Stock Exchange had a fixed number of memberships that allowed members to trade on the floor. At its height in 2005, one membership traded for $3.5 million. These memberships were traded in for shares of stock in the NYSE Group (now NYSE Euronext), and members were given a trading license with an annual fee attached. There has been a slight redefinition of types of members, and currently there are two types: **floor brokers** and **specialists**.

Floor Brokers

Floor brokers act as agents for clients and execute buy and sell orders on the floor of the exchange. Floor brokers are further divided into **house brokers** and **independent brokers**. House brokers represent NYSE member firms such as Merrill Lynch or Morgan Stanley Smith Barney, which used to be known as investment houses. House brokers trade either for clients of the investment house or for the firm's direct account.

Independent brokers are individuals or are employees of very small "boutique" firms. These independent brokers can provide trade execution services to member firms or nonmember firms as well as to house brokers who need extra help. These brokers used to be referred to as $2 brokers or commission brokers because they were paid $2 for executing a trade for large brokerage houses. The New York Stock Exchange states that "Today, independent brokers are the NYSE's 'agent entrepreneurs.' They help a house broker manage order flow on a busy day, conduct business directly for the public, or execute special orders for customers. Their income is derived purely from commissions."

Specialists

Specialists consist of a limited number of firms that have been assigned specific stocks by the NYSE. These firms must have enough financial resources to make a market in the stocks they are assigned. By making a market, we mean they must stand ready to buy or sell 100 shares of each assigned stock at the current bid and ask prices. Specialists have five essential functions for the stocks to which they have been assigned:

1. Manage the auction process.
2. Execute special orders for floor brokers.
3. Serve as catalysts.
4. Provide capital.
5. Stabilize prices.

The five essential functions can be boiled down to two basic duties with regard to the stocks specialists supervise. First, they must handle any special orders that floor brokers might give. For example, a special order could limit the price someone is willing to pay for Time Warner (TWX) stock to $22 per share for 100 shares. If the broker reaches the TWX trading post and TWX is selling at $23 per share, the broker will leave the order with the specialist to execute if and when the stock of TWX falls to $22 or less. The specialist puts these special limit orders in his "book" with the date and time entered so he can execute orders at the same price by the earliest time of receipt. A portion of the broker's commission is then paid to the specialist.

The second major task of specialists is to maintain continuous, liquid, and orderly markets in their assigned stocks. This is not a difficult function in actively traded securities, such as Ford, Du Pont, and AT&T, but it becomes more difficult in those stocks where there are no large, active markets. For example, suppose you placed an order to buy 100 shares of Brush Engineering at the market price. If the broker reaches the trading post for Brush Engineering materials and no seller is present, the broker can't wait for one to appear since he has other orders to execute. Fortunately, the broker can buy the shares from the specialist who acts as a dealer—in this case buying for and selling from his own inventory. To ensure ability to maintain continuous markets, the exchange requires a specialist to have $500,000 or enough capital to own 5,000 shares of the assigned stock, whichever is greater. At times, specialists are under tremendous pressure to make a market for securities. A classic case occurred when President Reagan was shot in the 1980s, and specialists stabilized the market by absorbing wave after wave of sell orders.

Many market watchers believe competing dealers on the Nasdaq market provide more price stability and fluid markets than the NYSE specialist system.

Somewhat in response to these criticisms, the New York Stock Exchange created computer systems that help the specialists manage order inflows more efficiently. **Super Dot** (designated order transfer system) allows NYSE member firms to electronically transmit all market and limit orders directly to the specialist at the trading post or the member trading booth. This order-routing system takes orders and communicates executions of the orders directly back to the member firm on the same electronic circuit.

As a part of Super Dot, specialists are informed through OARS (Opening Automated Report Service) of market orders received before the opening bell. Another feature of Super Dot that greatly aids the specialist is the **Electronic Book**. This database covers stocks listed on the NYSE and keeps track of limit orders and market orders for the specialist. You can imagine the great improvement in recording, reporting, and error elimination over the old manual entry in the "specialist's book."

The American Stock Exchange

The American Stock Exchange (AMEX) became part of the NYSE Euronext group of exchanges in 2008. Traditionally the AMEX traded small companies with listing standards much less rigorous than those of the NYSE or NASDAQ and has primarily been a market for individual investors. Over time the American Stock Exchange moved to differentiate its activities from the major exchanges and became one of the biggest exchanges for put and call options. Later it focused on **exchange-traded funds**, closed-end funds, and structured products such as the Standard & Poor's 500 index (SPDRS) and the Dow Jones Industrial Average (DIAMONDS). Close to 100 exchange-traded funds are listed on the AMEX. More detail about these products will be covered in later chapters.

THE NASDAQ STOCK MARKET

The **Nasdaq Stock Market** used to be considered an over-the-counter market even though it had listing requirements for the companies that traded on its market. However, as of August 1, 2006, the Nasdaq became officially recognized as a national securities exchange by the Securities and Exchange Commission. This designation really doesn't change the way securities trade on the Nasdaq Stock Market but it does allow the exchange to charge some fees for data feeds and market information. As has historically been the case, all trades on the Nasdaq are done electronically, and there is no physical location, even though it is now called an exchange. Nasdaq is the second-largest exchange in the United States by dollar trading volume, but it often trades more shares on a daily basis than the NYSE.

Like the NYSE, the Nasdaq Stock Market has gone through a transformation from a not-for-profit company to a for-profit company. It did not have the same membership problems that the NYSE had, but it did have to separate itself from the regulatory body of the National Association of Securities Dealers (NASD). Its common stock trades on the Nasdaq Stock Market under the ticker symbol NDAQ. Nasdaq has always been an electronic stock exchange known for its trading technology and its listing of many of the world's largest technology companies such as Oracle, Cisco, Microsoft, Apple, Intel, and many others.

Nasdaq created SuperMontage, an electronic trading system that integrates the trading process with limit orders, time stamps for receipt of orders, multiple quotes, and more. It added to its technology and depth by acquiring the largest electronic communication network (ECN) called INET (the merged ECNs of Island and Instinet) and later BRUT, another ECN. Nasdaq integrated these ECNs' trading platforms into its own system and created more speed and price efficiency in order executions. Their trading system provides quotes on more than 6,000 stocks.

Listed stocks are divided between national market issues and small cap issues. As the name implies, the national market issues represent larger Nasdaq companies that must meet higher listing standards than the small cap market. The standards are not as high as those on the NYSE but cover most of the same areas: net tangible assets, net income, pretax income, public float (shares outstanding in the hands of the public), operating history, market value of the float, a minimum share price, the number of shareholders, and the number of market makers. Because the listing requirements are lower than those on the NYSE, many small public companies choose to begin trading on the Nasdaq Stock Market, and as they get larger, they often decide to stay there long after they have exceeded the listing requirements of the NYSE

Nasdaq prides itself on its corporate governance, efficiency, and surveillance systems that avoid conflicts of interest and market manipulation. With the passage of the Sarbanes-Oxley Act of 2002, corporate governance issues became more important to all publicly traded companies, and Nasdaq is no exception with its move to public ownership. It is incumbent on Nasdaq to be a corporate governance role model for its listed firms, and it has set a high standard in that area.

ELECTRONIC COMMUNICATION NETWORKS (ECNs)

ECNs are electronic trading systems that automatically match buy and sell orders at specified prices. ECNs are also known as alternative trading systems (ATSs) and have been given SEC approval to be more fully integrated into the national market system by choosing to act either as a broker–dealer or as an exchange. An ECN's subscribers can include retail and institutional investors, market makers, and broker–dealers. If a subscriber wants to buy a stock through an ECN, but there are no sell orders to match the buy order, the order cannot be executed. The ECN can wait for a matching sell order to arrive, or if the order is received during normal trading hours, the order can be routed to another market for execution. Some ECNs will let their subscribers see their entire order books, and some will even make their order books available on the Web. ECNs' bid and asked prices are included in Nasdaq's quotation montage, with the best bid and asked price being shown.

This helps create more efficient and transparent market prices and demonstrates how Nasdaq's open architecture allows firms with different computer technologies to compete in the same market.

Once upon a time ECNs were a competitive threat for the floor-based NYSE. They are no longer a threat because of the adage, "If you can't beat them, buy them." Both the New York Stock Exchange and Nasdaq have acquired the leading ECNs. New York acquired Archipelago (now NYSE ARCA) after the firm received exchange status from the SEC. Nasdaq acquired the INET and BRUT. There are still some ECNs in the market but they are not the dominant players because the exchanges now have their own ECNs.

OTHER EXCHANGES

BATS Exchange

The **BATS Exchange** was formed in 2005 as an electronic communications network and was granted exchange status by the SEC. It is a large electronic market and claims to be the third-largest exchange in the world based on the notional value of its trades. The NYSE and NASDAQ are larger. BATS trades securities listed on all exchanges and classifies them as NYSE (Tape A), regional exchanges (Tape B), and NASDAQ (Tape C). In 2009, BATS averaged one billion shares of matched trades per day. As an example of competitive volume, on July 30, 2010, BATS accounted for trades totaling 10.19 percent of the NYSE volume, 19.71 percent of the regional markets, and 13.10 percent of the NASDAQ volume. This is rather astonishing for an exchange that is a little more than five years old. The trick to BATS's success is of course software technology that reduces costs for the market participants.

BATS Europe is also growing fast; in its best month of 2010 it accounted for almost 8 percent of the volume for the 100 stocks in the (FTSE) index, traded on the London Stock Exchange. FTSE is an index managed by the *Financial Times,* similar to the Dow Jones Industrial Average being managed by the *Wall Street Journal.* BATS will continue to enter new markets and has plans for trading options and most likely other derivative products in the future. In an age of electronic markets, buyers and sellers gravitate to the most efficient trading systems. This allows successful electronic exchanges to compete anywhere in the world.

The Chicago Board Options Exchange

Trading in call options started on the Chicago Board Options Exchange (CBOE) in April 1973 and proved very successful. The number of call options listed grew from 16 in 1973 to more than 500 in 2006. A **call option** gives the owner the right to buy 100 shares of the underlying common stock at a set price for a certain period. The CBOE standardized call options into three-month, six-month, and nine-month expiration periods on a rotating monthly series. Other sequences have since been developed. The CBOE and the AMEX currently have many options that are dually listed, and the competition between them is fierce. The two exchanges also trade put options (options to sell). A number of smaller regional exchanges also provide for option trading.

A new wrinkle in the options game has been options on stock market indexes or industry groupings (called subindexes). The CBOE offers puts and calls on the Standard & Poor's 500 Index and the Dow Jones Industrial Average; the AMEX has options on the AMEX Market Value Index, and so on. More about options markets will be presented in Chapters 14 and 16.

Intercontinental Exchange (ICE)

The **Intercontinental Exchange (ICE)** was founded in 2000 to create a 24-hour electronic market for energy contracts. The goal was to consolidate a fragmented market, to create more liquidity and efficiency, and to lower the costs through the use of an electronic market. ICE touts its state-of-the-art electronic trading system, as do all electronic markets.

ICE was extremely successful in trading energy contracts and expanded its market reach through acquisitions. In 2001 it moved into the European energy futures market, and by 2005 ICE Futures Europe became the first fully electronic energy exchange. In the same year, it launched an initial public offering on the New York Stock Exchange and now trades under the ticker symbol ICE. In 2007 it acquired the New York Board of Trade. It is now called ICE Futures U.S., and it trades commodities such as sugar and coffee. In 2009 the Board of Governors of the Federal Reserve approved ICE as a bank holding company. In response to the outcry arising from the financial crisis of 2007–2009, it was approved to clear credit default swaps and today is the global leader for clearing credit default swaps.

Futures Markets

Futures markets have traditionally been associated with commodities and, more recently, also with financial instruments. Purchasers of commodity futures own the right to buy a certain amount of the commodity at a set price for a specified period. As the time runs out (expires), the futures contract is normally reversed (closed out) before expiration. Chicago is the center of the major futures market, and the CME Group is the largest in the world. In recent years it bought NYMEX holdings and merged with the Chicago Board of Trade (**www.cmegroup.com**).

There are significant changes in the structure of these markets. Futures exchanges are now publicly traded companies. The Chicago Mercantile Exchange listed shares on the New York Stock Exchange in December 2002. Exchanges are also consolidating and becoming electronic. Euronext (**www.euronext.com**), a leading electronic exchange, bought the London International Financial Futures Exchange (LIFFE) in 2002 and moved into the Chicago market to compete with the Chicago Mercantile Exchange. Eurex (**www.eurexchange.com**), another European electronic exchange, was approved by U.S. regulators to begin trading in Chicago and thus can offer its global customers competitive products listed on the CME. These markets are truly becoming global and low cost in nature. Chapters 15 and 16 cover the products that are traded on these exchanges.

OVER-THE-COUNTER MARKETS

Now that Nasdaq has exchange status, the remaining over-the-counter markets are the **over-the-counter bulletin board market (OTC.BB)** and the **pink sheets**. There is no listing requirement for the OTC.BB, but the companies trading in this market do file regulatory reports with the SEC. These are usually small companies, start-up companies, or companies controlled by a very few shareholders without a lot of trading activity or market following. Those companies listed on the "pink sheet" may be in the same category as those listed on the over-the-counter bulletin board market but they choose not to file reports to the SEC. Obviously companies trading on the pink sheets have very little public information available on which investors can base their investment decisions. This is the market where penny stocks trade. Stocks trading at less than a dollar per share are called penny stocks.

Being traded over-the-counter implies the trade takes place by telephone or electronic device, and dealers stand ready to buy or sell specific securities for their own accounts. These dealers will buy at a bid price (such as $19) and sell at an asked price (such as $19.13) that reflects the competitive market conditions.

OTC markets exist for stocks, corporate bonds, mutual funds, federal government securities, state and local bonds, commercial paper, negotiable certificates of deposits, and various other securities.

Debt Securities Traded Over-the-Counter

Debt securities trade over-the-counter. Actually, government securities of the U.S. Treasury provide the largest dollar volume of transactions on the OTC and account for billions of dollars in trades each week. These securities are traded by government securities dealers who are often associated with a division of a large financial institution, such as a New York or West Coast money market bank or a large brokerage house. These dealers make markets in government securities, such as Treasury bills and Treasury bonds, or federal agency securities such as Federal National Mortgage Association issues.

Municipal bonds of state and local governments are traded by specialized municipal bond dealers who, in most cases, work for large commercial banks. Commercial paper, representing unsecured, short-term corporate debt, is traded directly by *finance* companies, but a large portion of commercial paper sold by *industrial* companies is handled by OTC dealers specializing in this market. Every security has its own set of dealers and its own distribution system. On markets where large dollar trades occur, the spread between the bid and asked price could be as little as 1/16 or 1/32 of $1 per $1,000 of securities.

INSTITUTIONAL TRADING

Financial institutions, such as banks, pension funds, insurance companies, and investment companies (mutual funds), have always invested and traded in securities. Their importance can be seen in the fact that block trades of 10,000 shares or more carried out by financial institutions have averaged close to 50 percent of trades since 1984. As a contrast, block trades only accounted for 3.1 percent of total trades in 1965. Institutional investors are moving much of their trades to dark pools, and there is concern that their activities will have negative effects on the market. (See the box on dark pools for more details.)

Individual investors put their money into the market through intermediaries such as mutual funds, pension funds, profit-sharing plans, and individual retirement accounts (IRAs). Individuals who directly invest in the stock market have gone up and down with consumer sentiment and market returns. In 1987 the market crash scared many individual investors out of the market, but they came back during the bull market of the 1990s. This increased participation by the individual investor was made easier by the rise of electronic trading on the Internet with prices as low as $5 per trade. Brokerage firms such as Charles Schwab, Fidelity Investments, E*Trade, TD Ameritrade, and others offered small investors low-cost trades. This was a great benefit. As is always the case, bear markets and recessions cause individuals to move to the sidelines, and the market collapse of 2000–2002 and the financial crisis of 2007–2009 were no different. However, with the demographics of the baby boom generation reaching the high-income-savings years, it is expected that the individual investor will continue to have a significant place in our stock markets.

www.schwab.com

www.fidelity.com

www.etrade.com

www.tdameritrade.com

the real world of investing

DARK POOLS

Dark pools are electronic networks used by institutional investors to cross trades anonymously. They are called dark pools because no one can see into them. There are over 40 dark pools in existence. What has given rise to these trading platforms is the use of algorithmic trading models created by institutional investors. **Algorithmic trading** is the use of mathematical models that automatically execute trades when certain conditions exist. Every firm that has a proprietary model protects it as if it were Fort Knox. Algorithmic trading is widely used by hedge funds, high-frequency traders, mutual funds, large pension funds, and market makers. Some models may be simple; some may be mathematically complex. The models can determine the size and price of the trade as well as the timing of the trade. Sometimes it is called black-box trading because the trades occur with no human interaction.

There are independent dark pools and consortium-owned dark pools, as well as broker-dealer dark pools operated by firms or divisions of firms such as Credit Suisse, Fidelity Capital Market Services, Goldman Sachs, Merrill Lynch, and Morgan Stanley. Even the public exchanges are getting into the act. The NYSE Euronext has created SmartPool, a dark pool in Europe operated out of London. SmartPool is in partnership with HSBC (London), J. P. Morgan (U.S.), and BNP Paribas (France). NASDAQ also has a dark pool, and it was estimated that in 2009, 15–20 percent of the trades going to the NASDAQ stock market were routed to dark pools. Some experts estimate that over the next several years, 50 percent of all U.S. trading volume might be in dark pools; that is, if the Securities and Exchange Commission doesn't step in and make these systems more transparent.

Mary Shapiro, chairman of the SEC, was quoted as saying, "Participants in these private pools have access to information about a trade which other investors are denied." The reason for these dark pools, of course, is that when Goldman Sachs or Merrill Lynch trade for an institutional client, that client doesn't want the trade to be tracked and noticed by competitors. This would be especially true of hedge funds, mutual funds, and others who think that if competitors had access to their strategies it might negate what they were trying to do. In the old days these institutions would spread their trades around so that no one knew the whole scope of their activities.

There is concern in the SEC and Congress that dark pools create a two-tier market. The SEC wants to shine some light into these pools and make them more transparent by forcing dark pools to display bid and ask quotes if more than one-quarter of 1 percent of the stock outstanding is traded. This might accomplish more transparency, but some have argued that, given the number of dark pools, institutions will split their trades into several pools, allowing them to stay under the limit. Another concern besides less transparency is that there may be less liquidity and efficiency in public markets. This might negatively affect small to mid-sized companies, because dark pools trade only large global companies with billions of shares outstanding.

REGULATION OF THE SECURITIES MARKETS

Organized securities markets are regulated by the **Securities and Exchange Commission (SEC)** and by the self-regulation of the exchanges. The OTC market is regulated by the National Association of Securities Dealers. Three major laws govern the sale and subsequent trading of securities. The **Securities Act of 1933** pertains to new issues of securities, while the **Securities Exchange Act of 1934** deals with trading in the securities markets. The primary purpose of these laws was to protect unwary investors from fraud and manipulation and to make the markets more competitive and efficient. The **Securities Acts Amendments of 1975** main emphasis was on a national securities market.

Circuit Breakers and Program Trading

Occasionally markets fall out of bed and suffer huge declines in a short period of time. Sometimes the cause of these market drops can be identified, and other times they cannot. For example, on October 19, 1987, the Dow Jones Industrial Average (DJIA) dropped 508 points during the day, about a 22 percent decrease. This was the biggest one-day drop ever recorded, and many identified program trading as

TABLE 2-4 Program Trading

NEW YORK—Program trading in the week ended June 4 amounted to 28.0% of New York Stock Exchange average daily volume of 2.89 billion shares, or 810.7 million program shares traded per day.

Program trading encompasses a range of portfolio-trading strategies involving the purchase or sale of a basket of at least 15 stocks.

NYSE PROGRAM TRADING
Volume in millions of shares for the week ending June 4, 2010

Top 20 Firms	Index Arbitrage	Other Strategies	Total*
Goldman Sachs	0.1	409.3	442.4
Morgan Stanley	4.2	400.8	546.3
Wedbush Securities	—	291.7	291.7
SG Americas	17.5	212.7	230.2
Barclays Capital	—	209.1	291.4
Deutsche Bank	1.4	157.2	158.6
Credit Suisse	6.3	145.1	151.4
Penson Financial	—	135.0	135.0
RBC Capital	21.0	114.0	134.9
Schon-EX	—	130.6	130.6
J.P. Morgan	—	124.9	124.9
Merrill Lynch	—	99.4	102.7
BNP Paribas	—	79.2	79.2
UBS Securities	—	60.5	60.5
Millenco	—	48.0	48.0
Nomura Securities	—	34.6	34.6
Citigroup Global	—	27.1	41.7
Jefferies Execution	—	24.7	24.7
Credit Agricole	—	24.0	24.0
Fortis Clearing	—	21.5	21.5
Overall Total	**81.8**	**2,884.5**	**3,242.7**

*Total includes crossing session 2.

Source: The *Wall Street Journal,* June 11, 2010, p. c6. Reprinted with permission of *The Wall Street Journal,* Copyright

the culprit. **Program trading** simply means that computer trigger points are established in which large-volume trades can be initiated by institutional investors. For example, technical trading systems might automatically put in a sell order if the DJIA hits a certain price point. When many program traders act simultaneously, this process can have a major cumulative effect on the market. Understand that program trading was in its infancy then, and so it was an easy villain.

Table 2-4 is an example of the program-trading statistics that appear in the *Wall Street Journal* every day. In order to qualify as a program trade, a trade must include at least 15 stocks in the basket of securities bought or sold. As the table demonstrates, on June 4, 2010, program trades accounted for 28 percent of the NYSE daily volume. Program trades listed in the table would not include all algorithmic trading, as much of that is done with high-frequency trading programs where less than 15 different stocks would be traded. Both program trading and **high-frequency trading** rely on mathematical algorithms to trigger the trades without any human interaction.

Because of the 1987 collapse, the Securities and Exchange Commission put **circuit breakers** into effect in 1989. These circuit breakers would shut down the market for a period of time if a dramatic drop in stock prices occurred. Circuit breakers

FIGURE 2-2 **Circuit-Breaker Levels for First Quarter of 2010**

Source: © 2010 NYSE Euronext. All Rights Reserved. All rights in The Limit Order Book for Intel on the Archipelago Market are owned exclusively by NYSE Group, Inc., © 2007 NYSE Group, Inc., All Rights Reserved. This publication may not contain the most up-to-date information. Please see www.euronext.com.

for the market as of the first quarter of 2010 are shown in Figure 2–2. Notice that they are a function of time of day and percentage decrease.

As algorithmic trading and high-frequency trading on ECNs increases as a percentage of daily volume, the reality of more market jolts occurring is a concern. Regulators are concerned that high-frequency computer trades as well as other program trades could all react to negative information simultaneously and drive the market down dramatically.

On May 6, 2010, the market fell 1,000 points in a matter of minutes. This event became referred to as the **flash crash**. There has been no clear answer to what caused this crash, but those agencies investigating the decline have said that traders simply withdrew from the market on both the buy and sell sides as market anxiety rose over the European debt crisis. Investigating agencies did not rule out trading errors or computer cyber attacks, but found no evidence of these events. They also did not place the blame on algorithmic trading systems.

In response to this flash crash, the SEC instituted circuit breakers on individual stocks for all markets. Up until this time, only the New York Stock Exchange had circuit breakers on individual stocks. With all the different trading platforms and markets, there was no consistent system for dealing with this type of event. The new rule for individual stock circuit breakers is a trial program lasting only six months, but it has already paid off. Any company in the Standard and Poor's 500 Index that moves up or down by 10 percent or more during a five-minute period must be halted for five minutes while the markets digest the information or the error is corrected. Shortly after the rule was put into effect, the stock price movement of the *Washington Post* triggered the circuit breaker, and weeks later Citigroup stock suffered the same fate. Perhaps the most dramatic event was halting trade in Anadarko Petroleum on July 6, 2010, after its price was quoted at $99,999.99. The trade was canceled and the stock began trading again after a five-minute pause.

Securities Act of 1933

The Securities Act of 1933 was enacted after congressional investigations of the abuses present in the securities markets during the 1929 crash and again in 1931. The act's primary purpose was to provide full disclosure of all pertinent investment information whenever a corporation sold a new issue of securities. It is sometimes referred to as the "truth in securities" act. The Securities Act has several important features:

1. All offerings except government bonds and bank stocks that are to be sold in more than one state must be registered with the SEC.[1]
2. The registration statement must be filed 20 days in advance of the date of sale and include detailed corporate information. If the SEC finds the information misleading, incomplete, or inaccurate, it will delay the offering until the registration statement is corrected. The SEC in no way certifies that the security is fairly priced but only that the information seems to be factual and accurate. Under certain circumstances, the previously mentioned shelf registration is being used to modify the 20-day waiting period concept.
3. All new issues of securities must be accompanied by a *prospectus,* a detailed summary of the registration statement. Included in the prospectus is usually a list of directors and officers; their salaries, stock options, and shareholdings; financial reports certified by a certified public accountant (CPA); a list of the underwriters; the purpose and use for the funds to be provided from the sale of securities; and any other reasonable information that investors may need to know before they can wisely invest their money. A preliminary prospectus may be distributed to potential buyers before the offering date, but it will not contain the offering price or underwriting fees. It is called a red herring because stamped on the front in red letters are the words "Preliminary Prospectus."
4. Officers of the company and other experts preparing the prospectus or registration statement can be sued for penalties and recovery of realized losses if any information presented was fraudulent or factually wrong or if relevant information was omitted.

Securities Exchange Act of 1934

This act created the Securities and Exchange Commission to enforce the securities laws. It was empowered to regulate the securities markets and those companies listed on the exchanges. Specifically, the major points of the 1934 act are as follows:

1. Guidelines for insider trading were established. Insiders must hold securities for at least six months before they can sell them. This is to prevent them from taking quick advantage of information that could result in a short-term profit. All short-term profits were payable to the corporation. Insiders were generally thought to be officers, directors, major stockholders, employees, or relatives of key employees. In the last two decades, the SEC widened its interpretation to include anyone having information that was not public knowledge. This could include security analysts, loan officers, large institutional holders, and many others who had business dealings with the firm.

[1] Actually, the SEC did not come into existence until 1934. The Federal Trade Commission had many of these responsibilities before the formation of the SEC.

2. The Federal Reserve Board of Governors became responsible for setting margin requirements to determine how much credit one had available to buy securities.
3. Manipulation of securities by conspiracies between investors was prohibited.
4. The SEC was given control over the proxy procedures of corporations (a proxy is an absent stockholder vote).
5. In the act's regulation of companies traded on the markets, it required certain reports to be filed periodically. Corporations must file quarterly financial statements with the SEC, send annual reports to the stockholders, and file 10–K reports with the SEC annually. The 10–K report has more financial data than the annual report and can be very useful to an investor or loan officer. Most companies will now send 10–K reports to stockholders on request. The SEC also has company filings available on the Internet under its retrieval system called EDGAR.
6. The act required all securities exchanges to register with the SEC. In this capacity, the SEC supervises and regulates many pertinent organizational aspects of exchanges such as listing and trading mechanics.

The Securities Acts Amendments of 1975

The major focus of the Securities Acts Amendments of 1975 was to direct the SEC to supervise the development of a national securities market. No exact structure was put forth, but the law did assume that any national market would make extensive use of computers and electronic communication devices. Additionally, the law prohibited fixed commissions on public transactions and also prohibited banks, insurance companies, and other financial institutions from buying stock exchange memberships to save commission costs for their own institutional transactions. This was a worthwhile addition to the securities laws since it fosters greater competition and more efficient prices. Since this act was adopted, markets have not only become national but global.

Other Legislation

In addition to these three major pieces of legislation, a number of other acts deal directly with investor protection. For example, the **Investment Advisor Act of 1940** is set up to protect the public from unethical investment advisers. Any adviser with more than 15 public clients (excluding tax accountants and lawyers) must register with the SEC and file semiannual reports. The Investment Company Act of 1940 provides similar oversight for mutual funds and investment companies dealing with small investors. The act was amended in 1970 and currently gives the NASD authority to supervise and limit commissions and investment advisory fees on certain types of mutual funds.

Another piece of legislation dealing directly with investor protection is the Securities Investor Protection Act of 1970. The **Securities Investor Protection Corporation (SIPC)** was established to oversee liquidation of brokerage firms and to insure investors' accounts to a maximum value of $500,000 in case of bankruptcy of a brokerage firm. It functions much the same as the Federal Deposit Insurance Corporation. SIPC resulted from the problems encountered on Wall Street from 1967 to 1970 when share volume surged to then all-time highs, and many firms were unable to process orders fast enough. A back-office paper crunch caused Wall Street to shorten the hours the exchanges were formally open for new business, but even this didn't help. Investors lost large sums, and for many months, they were unable to use or get possession of securities held in their names. Even though SIPC insures these accounts, it still does not cover market value losses suffered while waiting to get securities from a bankrupt brokerage firm.

Insider Trading

The Securities Exchange Act of 1934 established the initial restrictions on insider trading. However, over the years, these restrictions have often proved to be inadequate. As previously indicated, the definition of *insider* may go beyond officers, directors, and major stockholders to include anyone with special insider knowledge. Both the Congress and the SEC are attempting to grapple with the issue of making punitive measures severe enough to discourage the illegal use of nonpublic information for profits.[2] Current and future legislation is likely to include tougher civil penalties and stiffer criminal prosecution. Also, the penalties for improper action will expand beyond simple recovery of profits to a penalty three or more times the profits involved.

The 1980s saw a rash of insider trading scandals involving major investment banking houses, traders, analysts, and investors. Ivan Boesky and Dennis Levine were the first of the well-known investors to end up in jail, and Michael Milken was not far behind. These insider trading scandals have plagued Wall Street and tarnished its image as a place where investors can get a fair deal.

On balance, all the legislation we have discussed has tended to increase the confidence of the investing public. In an industry where public trust is so critical, some form of supervision, whether public or private, is necessary and generally accepted.

[2] Insiders, of course, may make proper long-term investments in a corporation.

exploring the web

Web Address	Comments
www.nyse.com	**Provides information on regulations and market operations**
www.nasdaq.com	**Provides information about the Nasdaq market**
www.cboe.com	**Provides information about options traded on the Chicago Board Options Exchange**
www.marketwatch.com/tools/ipo	**Contains information about initial public offerings**

SUMMARY

A smoothly functioning market is one that is efficient and provides liquidity to the investor. The success of a primary market, in which new issues are generally underwritten by investment bankers, is highly dependent on the presence of an active resale (secondary) market.

Secondary markets may be established in the form of an organized exchange or as an over-the-counter market. The predominant organized market is the New York Stock Exchange (now called NYSE Euronext), but increasing attention is being directed to various other markets. The Nasdaq is the fastest-growing market and provides significant competition.

The dominant role of the institutional investor has had an enormous impact on the markets, with higher stock turnover and increasing market volatility. A major consolidation of market participants has also occurred on Wall Street. Institutions have had a large impact on market structure and liquidity through the use of program trading, dark pools and high frequency trading.

The term *market* is broadening with different types of new investment outlets as witnessed by the expansion of options, futures contracts on stock indexes, options

www.mhhe.com/hirtblock10e

on futures, and many other commodity trading mechanisms. Of equal importance, the term *market* must be viewed from a global viewpoint with securities trading throughout the world on a 24-hour basis.

Finally, problems or imperfections in the marketplace during critical time periods have led to a wide array of securities legislation. The legislation in the 1930s regulated the securities markets and created the SEC. Subsequent laws have dealt with restructuring the market and investor protection.

KEY WORDS AND CONCEPTS

algorithmic trading 41
BATS Exchange 38
best efforts 28
call options 38
circuit breakers 42
dark pools 41
efficient market 27
Electronic Book 36
electronic communication networks (ECNs) 33
exchange-traded funds (ETFs) 36
flash crash 43
floor brokers 35
high-frequency trading 42
house brokers 35
independent brokers 35
initial public offering (IPO) 30
Intercontinental Exchange (ICE) 39
Investment Advisor Act of 1940 45
investment banker 28
liquidity 27
market 27
Nasdaq Stock Market 36
New York Stock Exchange (NYSE) 32
organized exchange 32
over-the-counter bulletin board market (OTC.BB) 39
over-the-counter markets 32
pink sheets 39
primary markets 27
program trading 42
secondary markets 27
Securities Act of 1933 41
Securities Acts Amendments of 1975 41
Securities and Exchange Commission (SEC) 41
Securities Exchange Act of 1934 41
Securities Investor Protection Corporation (SIPC) 45
sold directly 28
specialists 35
Super Dot 36
syndicate 28
underwriting 28

DISCUSSION QUESTIONS

1. What is a market?
2. What is an efficient market?
3. What is the difference between primary and secondary markets?
4. What is the difference between an investment banker providing an underwriting function and a "best-efforts" offering?
5. What is a private placement?
6. What generally determines how firms are listed in a prospectus?
7. What are house brokers on the New York Stock Exchange?
8. How do critics think the specialist system on the NYSE might be improved?
9. Briefly describe the Nasdaq Stock Market.
10. What are electronic communication networks (ECNs)?
11. Define a block trade. What does the increase in the number of block trades since 1965 tend to indicate about the nature of investors in the market?
12. Indicate the primary purpose of the Securities Act of 1933. Why was it enacted? Does the SEC certify that a security is fairly priced?
13. How has the definition of an insider (inside trader) expanded over the past two decades?
14. Explain the purpose of the Securities Investor Protection Corporation (SIPC).
15. What impact have electronic markets had on markets overall?

WEB EXERCISE

This chapter on capital markets focuses on long-term financing and the various stock markets. Each stock market has its own listing requirements, and this exercise will look at the New York Stock Exchange and Nasdaq listing requirements for comparative purposes. First, go to the New York Stock Exchange Web site at **www.nyse.com**.

1. Click on "Regulation" on the left side.
2. Then, click on "NYSE."
3. Then, click on "Listed Companies." After that, click on "Listing Standards." Look at U.S. Standards and answer the following questions in writing.
   a. How many round-lot holders are required to be listed?
   b. What is the required public shares outstanding?
   c. Under Alternative #1, what are the earnings requirements to be listed?
   d. What is the average global market capitalization requirement to be listed? (Disregard the "or" provision.)
4. Now go to the Nasdaq Web site at **www.nasdaq.com**.
5. Under the "Home" pulldown tab at the top, click on "Listing Center."
6. Next, under the "Listing Information-US" dropdown at the top, click on "Listing Standards & Fees."
7. Under Initial Listing, Standard 1:
   a. What pretax earnings are required?
   b. What minimum bid price is required?
   c. How many market makers are required?
8. Scroll down further to "Liquidity Requirements." Using the first column, indicate:
   a. How many publicly held shares are required?
   b. What "Market Value" of the publicly held shares is required?

Note: From time to time, companies redesign their Web sites, and occasionally a topic we have listed may have been deleted, updated, or moved into a different location.

chapter three

PARTICIPATING IN THE MARKET

OBJECTIVES

1. Describe how an investor goes through the process of buying and selling securities.
2. Explain the difference between cash and margin accounts.
3. Describe the types of trading orders that can be executed.
4. Explain the tax implications of various investing strategies.
5. Understand how to measure the performance of securities in various markets through the use of market indexes.

OUTLINE

Either now or at some point in the future, you are likely to become an investor in the financial markets. You will need to know the mechanics of opening and trading in an account, the cost of trading, and basic tax considerations for an investor. This chapter walks you through the many steps that are involved. You will also need to know about various market indexes against which you will track the market and your own performance.

BUYING AND SELLING IN THE MARKET

When you decide to invest directly in common stocks or other assets, you will set up an account with a retail brokerage house or set up an online account. Some of the largest and better-known retail brokers are Merrill Lynch, Morgan Stanley, Smith Barney, and UBS, but there are many other good houses, both regional and national. When you set up your account, the account executive (often called stockbroker or financial consultant) will ask you to fill out a card listing your investment objectives, such as conservative, preservation of capital, income oriented, growth plus income, or growth. The account executive will also ask for your Social Security number for tax reporting, the level of your income, net worth, employer, and other information. Basically, the account executive needs to know your desire and ability to take risk in order to give good advice and proper management of your assets. Later in this section, we will also talk about discount brokers and online brokers, that is, brokers who charge very low commissions but give stripped-down service. These brokers are also very important, and a comparative analysis will be provided at that point in the chapter.

Cash or Margin Account

Your broker will need to know if you want a cash account or margin account. Either account allows you three business days to pay for any purchase. A cash account requires full payment, while a **margin account** allows the investor to borrow a percentage of the purchase price from the brokerage firm. The percentage of the total cost the investor must pay initially is called the margin and is set by the Federal Reserve Board. During the great crash in the 1920s, margin on stock was only 10 percent, but it was as high as 80 percent in 1968. It has been at 50 percent since January 1974. The margin percentage is used to control speculation. Historically, when the Board of Governors of the Federal Reserve System thinks markets are being pushed too high by speculative fervor, it raises the margin requirement, which means more cash must be put up. The Fed has been hesitant to take action in this area in recent times.

application example

Margin accounts are used mostly by traders and speculators or by investors who think their long-run return will be greater than the cost of borrowing. Most brokerage houses require a $2,000 minimum in an account before lending money, although many brokerage houses have higher limits. Here is how a margin account works. Assume you purchased 100 shares of Procter & Gamble (P&G) at $60 per share on margin and that margin is 50 percent:

Purchase: 100 shares at $60 per share	$6,000
Borrow: Cost × (1 − margin percentage)	−3,000
Margin: Equity contributed (cash or securities)	$3,000

You can borrow $3,000 or the total cost times (1 − margin percentage). The cost of borrowing is generally 1 to 2 percent above the prime rate, depending on the size of the account. Rather than putting up $3,000 in cash, a customer could put $3,000 of other approved financial assets into the account to satisfy the margin. Not all stocks may be used for margin purchases. The Securities and Exchange Commission publishes a list of approved securities that may be borrowed against.

One reason people buy on margin is to leverage their returns. Assume that P&G stock rises to $80 per share. The account would now have $8,000 in stock and an increase in equity from $3,000 to $5,000:

100 shares at $80	$8,000
Loan	−3,000
Equity (margin)	$5,000

This $2,000 increase in equity creates a 67 percent return on the initial $3,000 of equity. The 67 percent return was accomplished on the basis of only a 33 percent increase in the price of stock ($60 to $80). With the increased equity in the account, the customer could now purchase additional securities on margin.

Margin is a two-edged sword, however, and what works to your advantage in up markets works to your disadvantage in down markets. If P&G stock had gone down to $40, your equity would decrease to $1,000:

100 shares at $40	$4,000
Borrowed	−3,000
Equity (margin)	$ 1,000

Minimum requirements for equity in a margin account are called *minimum maintenance standards* (usually 25 percent). Your equity would now be at minimum maintenance standards where the equity of $1,000 equals 25 percent of the current market value of $4,000. A fall below $1,000 would bring a margin call for more cash or equity. Many brokerage firms have maintenance requirements above 25 percent, and when margin calls are made, the equity often needs to be increased to 35 percent or more of the portfolio value. Normally, you must maintain a $2,000 minimum in your account, so you would have been called for more equity when the stock was at $50 even though the minimum maintenance requirement had not yet been reached.

One feature of a margin account is that margined securities may not be delivered to the customer. In this case, the P&G stock would be kept registered in the street name of your retail brokerage house (e.g., Merrill Lynch), and your account would show a claim on 100 shares held as collateral for the loan. It is much like an automobile loan; you don't hold title to the car until you have made the last payment. In the use of margin, however, there is no due date on the loan. The use of margin increases risk and is not recommended for anyone who cannot afford large losses or who has no substantial experience in the market.

Long or Short? That Is the Question

Once you have opened the account of your choice, you are ready to buy or sell. When investors establish a position in a security, they are said to have a **long position** if they purchase the security for their account. It is assumed the reason they purchased the security was to profit on an increase in price over time and/or to receive dividend income.

Sometimes investors anticipate that the price of a security may drop in value. If they are long in the stock, some may sell out their position. Those who have no position at all may wish to take a **short position** to profit from the expected decline. When you short a security, you are borrowing the security from the broker and selling it with the obligation to replace the security in the future. How you can sell something you don't own is an obvious question. Your broker will simply lend you the security from the brokerage house inventory. If your brokerage house doesn't have an inventory of the particular stock you want to short, the firm will borrow the stock from another broker.

Once you go short, you begin hoping and praying that the price of the security will go down so that you can buy it back and replace the security at a lower price. In a perverse way, bad news starts to become good news. When you read the morning paper, you look for signs of unemployment, high inflation, and rising interest rates in hopes of a stock market decline.

A short sale can only be made on a trade where the price of the stock advances (an uptick), or if there is no change in price, the prior trade must have been positive. These rules are intended to stop a snowballing decline in stock values caused by short sellers.

application example

A margin requirement is associated with short selling, and it is currently equal to 50 percent of the securities sold short. Thus, if you were to sell 100 shares of Quaster short at $70 per share, you would be required to put up $3,500 in margin (50 percent of $7,000). In a short sale, the margin is considered to be good-faith money and obviously is not a down payment toward the purchase. The margin protects the brokerage house in case you start losing money on your account.

You would lose money on a short sales position if the stock you sold short starts going up. Assume Quaster goes from $70 to $80. Since you initially sold 100 shares short at $70 per share, you have suffered a $1,000 paper loss. Your initial margin or equity position has been reduced from $3,500 to $2,500:

Initial margin (equity)	$3,500
Loss	−1,000
Current margin (equity)	$2,500

We previously specified that there is a minimum 25 percent margin maintenance requirement in buying stock. A similar requirement exists in selling short. The equity position must equal at least 30 percent of the *current* value of the stock that has been sold short. In the present example, the equity position is equal to $2,500, and the current market value of Quaster is $8,000 ($80 × 100). Your margin percentage is 31.25 percent ($2,500 ÷ $8,000) or slightly above the minimum requirement. However, if the stock goes up another point or two and your losses increase, you will be asked to put up more margin to increase your equity position.

Of course, if the value of Quaster stock goes down from its initial base of $70, you would be making profits off the bad news. A 20-point drop in Quaster would mean a $2,000 profit on your 100 shares. Most market observers agree that it requires a "special breed of cat" to be an effective short seller. You often need nerves of steel and a contrarian outlook that cannot be easily shaken by good news.

One final point on selling short. In the last 10 or 15 years, some investors have chosen to use other ways to take a negative position in a security. These normally involve put and call options, which are discussed in Chapter 14. Both selling short and option transactions can be effectively utilized for strategic purposes.

TYPES OF ORDERS

When an investor places an order to establish a position, he or she has many different kinds of orders from which to choose. When the order is placed with the broker on a NYSE-listed stock, it is sent electronically to the exchange where it is executed by the company's floor broker in an auction market. Each stock is traded at a specific trading post on the floor of the exchange, so the floor broker knows exactly where to go to find other brokers buying and selling the same company's shares.

Most orders placed will be straightforward market orders to buy or sell. The market order will be carried by the floor broker to the correct trading post and will usually trade within a penny or a nickel of the last price. For example, if you want to sell 100 shares of AT&T at market, you would probably have no trouble finding a ready buyer since AT&T may be trading a few million shares per day. But if you wanted to sell 100 shares of Bemis, as few as 1,000 shares might be traded in a day, and no other broker would be waiting at the Bemis post to make a transaction with the floor broker. If the broker finds no one else wishing to buy the shares, he will transact the sale with the specialist who is always at the post ready to buy and sell 100-share round lots. If the broker wants to sell, the specialist will either buy the shares for her own account at 0.03 or 0.05 less than the last trade or will buy out of her book in which special orders of others are kept.

Two basic special orders are the limit order and the stop order. A **limit order** limits the price at which you are willing to buy or sell and ensures you will pay no more than the limit price on a buy or receive no less than the limit price on a sell. Assume you are trying to buy a thinly traded stock that fluctuates in value and you are afraid that with a market order you might risk paying more than you want. So you would place a limit order to buy 100 shares of MedQuist Inc., as an example, at $16.50 or a better price. The order will go to the floor broker who goes to the post to check the price. The broker finds MedQuist trading at its high for the day of $16.80, and so he leaves the limit order with the specialist who records it in his book. The entry will record the price, date, time, and brokerage firm. There may be other orders in front of yours at $16.50, but once these are cleared, and assuming the stock stays in this range, your order will be executed at $16.50 or less. Limit orders are used by investors to buy or sell thinly traded stocks or to buy securities at prices thought to be at the low end of a price range and to sell securities at the high end of the price range. Investors who calculate fundamental values have a basic idea of what they think a stock is worth and will often set a limit to take advantage of what they view to be discrepancies in values.

Many traders are certain they want their order to be executed if a certain price is reached. A limit order does not guarantee execution if orders are time stamped ahead of you on the specialist's book. In cases where you want a guaranteed "fill" of the order, a stop order is placed. A **stop order** is a two-part mechanism. It is placed at a specific price like a limit order, but when the price is reached, the stop turns into a market order that will be executed at close to the stop price but not necessarily at the exact price specified. Often, many short-term traders will view a common stock price with optimism for a certain trading strategy. When the stock hits the price, it may pop up on an abundance of buy orders or decline sharply on a large volume of sell orders, and your "fill" could be several dollars away from the top price. Assume Disney Corporation stock has been trading between $25 and $40 per share over the last six months, reaching both these prices three times. A trader may follow several strategies. One strategy would be to buy at $25 and sell at $40 using a stop buy and a stop sell order. Some traders may put in a stop buy at $41 thinking that if the stock breaks through its peak trading range it will go on to new highs, and finally some may put in a stop sell at $24 to either eliminate a long position or establish a short position with the assumption the stock has broken its support and will trend lower. When used to eliminate a long position, a stop order is often called a *stop-loss order*.

Limit orders and stop orders can be "day orders" that expire at the end of the day if not executed, or they can be GTC (good till canceled) orders. GTC orders will remain on the specialist's books until taken off by the brokerage house or executed. If the order remains unfilled for several months, most brokerage houses will send reminders that the order is still pending so that the client does not get caught buying stock for which he or she is unable to pay.

COST OF TRADING

Nowhere has the field of investments changed more than in the means and cost of trading. A decade ago, the basic choice was between full-service brokerage firms such as Merrill Lynch, Morgan Stanley Smith Barney, and discount brokers such as Charles Schwab and Fidelity. The discount brokers provided bare bones service

www.morganstanleysmithbarney.com

and generally charged 25 to 75 percent of the commissions charged by full-service brokers, who willingly provided research and stock analysis to clients, tax information, and help in establishing goals and objectives.

The nature of the landscape changed radically with the emergence of the Internet. Now, an investor can merely access an **online broker's** Web site to open an account, review the operating procedures and commission schedule, and initiate a trade. Confirmation of an electronic trade can take as little as 2 seconds, and almost all trades are completed within a minute.

application example

Online brokers such as TD Ameritrade and E*TRADE have become household names—and why not? A recent study by the American Association of Individual Investors indicated that for a 100-share trade, the average online broker charged $7. In comparison, the average discount broker charged $42, while a full-service broker charged $100.

To examine the effect of the pricing differential, assume 100 shares are traded at $40 per share for a total value of $4,000. Note the difference in percentage costs between the three types of brokers.

Online broker	$7/$4,000 = 0.17%
Discount broker	$42/$4,000 = 1.05%
Full-service broker	$100/$4,000 = 2.50%

www.TDameritrade.com
www.etrade.com

Because of the intense competition provided by online brokers, in the late 1990s many full-service and deep discount brokers began offering their clients the alternative of online trading. Merrill Lynch was the first major full-service broker to go this route, and Charles Schwab led the way among discount brokers. Others in the industry have followed the same path, so the landscape is blurred between full-service and deep discount brokers that offer an online alternative and pure online brokers. Even banks and mutual funds offer online trading through brokerage subsidiaries.

www.ml.com
www.schwab.com

While online trading is a very attractive trading alternative because of the low commission rate, it is not for everyone. For the less sophisticated investor or computer novice, full service (or even the discount broker) may be the way to go. The importance of explanations about long-term capital gains taxes, potential merger tender offers, retirement and estate planning, and so on, may outweigh savings in commissions. That is why most major traditional houses offer alternative ways to go. Nevertheless, for the sophisticated investor who knows his or her own mind, it is impractical to pay for additional unused and unnecessary services. While 25 to 30 percent of all trades are currently online, the number will undoubtedly double or triple in the next few years.

The Internet has not only influenced the way trades are executed but has given the individual investor access to instant information that was once in the private domain of large institutional investors such as mutual funds or bank trust departments. Individual investors can download balance sheets, income statements, up-to-the-minute press releases, and so on. They can also participate with other investors in chat rooms and e-mail the company for immediate answers to questions.

All of these options certainly represent progress, with one caveat. The intoxication of it all has led to a new class of "day traders," who attempt to beat the market on an hourly or by-the-minute basis. While some with exceptional skill have profited by this activity, all too many others get badly hurt when the market makes unexpected moves.

TAXES AND THE 2003 TAX ACT

In making many types of investments, an important consideration will be the tax consequences of your investment (taxes may be more significant than the brokerage commissions just discussed).

This section is intended only as a brief overview of tax consequences. For more information, consult a tax guide. Consultation with a CPA, CFP (certified financial planner), or similar sources may also be advisable.

Before we specifically talk about the tax consequences of investment *gains and losses,* let's briefly look at the tax rates for 2011. The rates are presented in Table 3–1. The values in the table will change very slightly each year for the rest of the decade. Be aware that the 2003 Tax Act, often referred to as the Bush Tax Act, expired at the end of 2010 and the U.S. Congress amended and extended most of the tax cuts. Capital gains taxes stayed the same and the tax brackets for 2011 were expanded.

TABLE 3-1 Tax Rates 2011

Taxable Income	Rate (%)
Single	
$0–8,500	10%
$8,501–34,500	15
$34,501–83,600	25
$83,601–174,400	28
$174,401–379,150	33
Over $379,150	35
Married (joint return)	
$0–17,000	10%
$17,001–69,000	15
$69,001–139,350	25
$139,351–212,300	28
$212,301–379,150	33
Over $379,150	35

application example

Refer to Table 3–1 and assume you have appropriately computed your taxable income after all deductions as $40,000. Further assume you are single so that you fall into a bracket in the upper portion of the table. How much is your tax obligation? The answer is shown below:

	Amount	Rate	Tax
First	$ 8,500	10%	$ 850
Next	26,000*	15	3,900
Next	5,500†	25	1,730
	$40,000		$6,480

*34,500-8,500
†40,000-34,500

The total tax is $6,480. The rates of 10, 15, and 25 percent are referred to as marginal tax rates. The average tax is a slightly different concept. It is simply the amount of taxes paid divided by taxable income, or 16.2 percent in this case:

$$\frac{\text{Taxes paid}}{\text{Taxable income}} = \frac{\$6,480}{\$40,000} = 16.2\%$$

Capital Gains and Dividends

A **capital gain or loss** occurs when an asset held for investment purposes is sold. A long-term capital gain takes place when an asset is held for more than a year, and the maximum tax rate is 15 percent. The Tax Relief Act of 2003 made a radical shift in tax policy by lowering the maximum tax rate on dividends to 15 percent. Previously, dividends had been taxed the same as other forms of income at a maximum rate in the mid-to-high 30 percent range.[1] Thus, the tax rate on long-term capital gains and dividends is the same, and high-income investors have little tax preference between high dividend stocks and low dividend stocks that attempt to provide capital gains.[2] This is a major shift in strategic considerations since the Tax Relief Act of 2003. This policy was extended for two years through 2012.

However, if an asset is not held for more than 12 months, its sale represents a short-term capital gain or loss, and the tax treatment is exactly the same as ordinary income. This means it is taxed at the rates shown in Table 3–1. For example, if a person is in the 35 percent tax bracket and sells a stock owned for only six months, the tax on the gain would be 35 percent. If he or she had held the asset for 12 months, the long-term capital gains tax rate on the gain would have been only 15 percent.

application example

As you can see, there are some strong inducements to go for the longer-term capital gains treatment over short-term capital gains rate. Assume an investor is in a 35 percent tax bracket and sells a stock at a $10,000 profit. Note the different amounts of taxes owed based on the holding period:

Holding Period	Profit	Tax Rate	Taxes
6 months	$10,000	35%	$3,500
Over 12 months	10,000	15	1,500

For investors putting their money into tax-deferred investments (such as an IRA or 401k), these tax considerations during the holding period are not relevant. Furthermore, taxes are only one of the many variables that should influence an investment decision.

[1] The maximum tax rate of 15 percent does not apply to Real Estate Investment Trusts and personal trusts.

[2] The one remaining advantage to long-term capital gains treatment is that the tax is deferred until the stock is sold, whereas the tax on dividends must be paid annually.

the real world of investing

WHO CHEATS ON THEIR INCOME TAXES?

Each year the government loses 17 cents out of every dollar due on income taxes because of cheating by taxpayers. The cheating may take the form of not reporting income or taking nonexistent or unjustified deductions. The total loss to the government is more than $100 billion a year. This represents the unpaid taxes of otherwise honest Americans, not the additional tens of billions hidden by drug czars and other hardened criminals. If all taxes were properly collected, a portion of our federal deficit could be wiped out.

The most frequent offenders are the self-employed. A General Accounting Office (GAO) study revealed that auto dealers, restaurateurs, and clothing store operators underreport their taxable income by nearly 40 percent. Doctors, lawyers, barbers, and *accountants* underpay (cheat?) on 20 percent of their revenues. The most proficient of the nonreporters are in the food-service industry. Collectively, waiters and waitresses fail to report 84 percent of their tips, according to the GAO.

Claiming deductions for dependent children that do not exist is another favorite approach. In 1987, the IRS began requiring taxpayers to report and verify the Social Security numbers of all dependents over five years of age. The following year 7 million fewer dependents were claimed as deductions. It seems that many people had been listing the same child two or three times and even claiming dogs, cats, and birds as tax-deductible dependents.

Of course, not all feel guilty about not paying their full share of taxes. A shipyard manager who did not report income from yacht repairs on the weekend told *Money* magazine, "The government squanders the money I already pay. Why give more?"

It should also be pointed out that when you have net investment losses in any one year, you can write off up to $3,000 of these losses against other taxable income (salary, interest income, etc.). Any unused balance can be carried forward into the future to be written off against future capital gains from investments or other forms of income.[3]

MEASURES OF PRICE PERFORMANCE: MARKET INDEXES

We now look at tracking market performance for stocks and bonds. Each market has several market indexes published by Dow Jones, Standard & Poor's, Value Line, and other financial services. These indexes allow investors to measure the performance of their portfolios against an index that approximates their portfolio composition; thus, different investors prefer different indexes. While a professional pension fund manager might use the Standard & Poor's 500 Stock Index, a mutual fund specializing in small stocks might prefer the Russell 2000 Index, and a small investor might use the Value Line Average or Russell 3000 as the best approximation of a portfolio's performance.

INDEXES AND AVERAGES

Dow Jones Averages

www.dj.com

Since there are many stock market indexes and averages, we will cover the most widely used ones. Dow Jones, publisher of *The Wall Street Journal* and *Barron's,* publishes several market averages of which the **Dow Jones Industrial Average (DJIA)** is the most popular. This average consists of 30 large industrial companies and is considered a "blue-chip" index (stocks of very high quality). Many people criticize the DJIA for being too selective and representing too few stocks. Nevertheless,

[3] At this point the discussion can become progressively more complicated in terms of balancing short- and long-term gains and losses against each other. The authors have decided these topics are better left for a tax course.

FIGURE 3-1 Dow Jones Industrial Average, June 11, 2010

Dow Jones Industrial Average

10172.53 ▲273.28, or 2.76%
High, low, open and close for each trading day of the past three months.

	Last	Year ago
Trailing P/E ratio	14.79	12.78
P/E estimate *	12.36	25.00
Dividend yield	2.72	3.31
Current divisor	0.132319125	

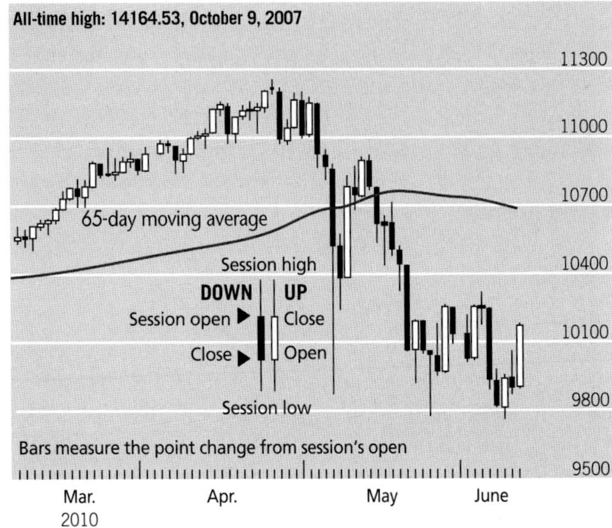

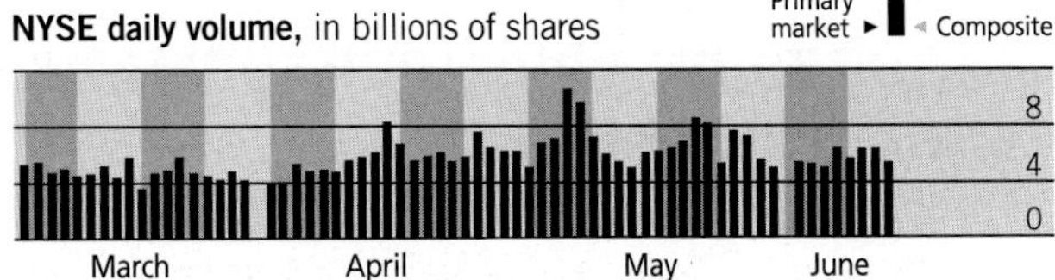

*P/E data based on as-reported earnings from Birinyi Associates Inc.

*Source: *The Wall Street Journal,* June 11, 2010, p. C4. Reprinted with permission of *The Wall Street Journal,* Copyright © 2010 by Dow Jones & Company., Inc. All Rights Reserved Worldwide.

the Dow Industrials do follow the general trend of the market, and these 30 common stocks comprise more than 25 percent of the market value of the 3,000 firms listed on the New York Stock Exchange. Figure 3–1 shows the price movements of the Dow Jones Industrial Average over a four-month period as well as daily volume in billions of shares.

Dow Jones also publishes an index of 20 transportation stocks and 15 utility stocks. At the top of Table 3–2, from *Barron's,* you see a listing of the daily changes for the three Dow Jones Averages on June 7, 2010. It also shows a Dow Jones 65-stock composite average that summarizes the performance of the Dow Jones industrial, transportation, and utility issues. Many other market averages are presented in the table, which we will discuss later.

For now, let's return to the Dow Jones Industrial Average of 30 stocks. The Dow Jones Industrial Average used to be a simple average of 30 stocks, but when a company splits its stock price, the average has to be adjusted. For the Dow Jones Industrials, the divisor in the formula has been adjusted downward from the original 30 to below 1. You can see the divisor in the upper right-hand corner

TABLE 3-2 Indexes and Averages Found in *Barron's*

THE WEEK IN STOCKS FOR THE MAJOR INDEXES

12-Month High	12-Month Low		Weekly High	Weekly Low	Friday Close	Friday Chg.	Weekly % Chg.	12-Month Chg.	12-Month % Chg.	Change From 12/31	Change From % Chg.
Dow Jones Averages											
11205.03	8146.52	**30 Indus**	10255.28	9931.97	9931.97	−204.66	−2.02	1168.84	13.34	−496.08	−4.76
4806.01	3062.96	**20 Transp**	4380.81	4157.17	4157.17	−178.89	−4.13	807.19	24.10	57.54	1.40
406.72	340.82	**15 Utilities**	364.31	353.02	354.27	−6.92	−1.92	9.67	2.81	−43.74	−10.99
3861.78	2812.05	**65 Comp**	3547.12	3416.79	3416.79	−92.61	−2.64	427.46	14.30	−149.89	−4.20
Dow Jones Indexes											
12745.82	8995.81	**US TSM**	11538.76	11121.91	11121.91	−281.07	−2.46	1467.14	15.20	−375.50	−3.27
304.59	216.19	**US Market**	275.60	265.81	265.81	−6.52	−2.39	33.92	14.63	−10.76	−3.89
123.48	76.67	**Internet**	114.75	109.01	111.00	−0.90	−0.80	26.19	30.88	1.38	1.26
New York Stock Exchange											
7728.96	5624.57	**Comp-z**	6860.39	6600.27	6600.27	−191.30	−2.82	517.63	8.51	−584.69	−8.14
5354.68	3661.97	**Financial-z**	4551.00	4341.28	4341.28	−170.86	−3.79	365.35	9.19	−379.74	−8.04
6732.71	5099.67	**Health Care-z**	5866.16	5687.02	5687.02	−63.57	−1.11	520.27	10.07	−740.25	−11.52
12007.48	9037.88	**Energy-z**	10157.38	9628.37	9760.61	−286.89	−2.86	−726.58	−6.93	−1654.42	−14.49
American Stock Exchange											
1987.68	1507.43	**Amex Comp**	1831.52	1789.51	1789.51	9.32	0.52	179.79	11.17	−35.44	−1.94
1237.73	907.94	**Major Mkt**	1132.68	1097.69	1097.69	−21.28	−1.90	124.17	12.75	−53.63	−4.66
Standard & Poor's Indexes											
553.87	412.29	**100 Index**	499.16	483.42	483.42	−9.64	−1.96	46.25	10.58	−30.67	−5.97
1217.28	879.13	**500 Index**	1102.83	1064.88	1064.88	−24.53	−2.25	124.79	13.27	−50.22	−4.50
1564.29	1141.95	**Indus**	1424.22	1376.93	1376.93	−27.12	−1.93	158.20	12.98	−71.86	−4.96
849.82	546.53	**MidCap**	767.72	736.27	736.27	−26.49	−3.47	140.17	23.51	9.60	1.32
394.65	255.51	**SmallCap**	356.68	339.53	339.53	−13.78	−3.90	59.44	21.22	6.90	2.07
Nasdaq Stock Market											
2530.15	1746.17	**Comp**	2303.03	2219.17	2219.17	−37.87	−1.68	369.75	19.99	−49.98	−2.20
2055.33	1404.78	**100 Index**	1895.66	1832.04	1832.04	−20.35	−1.10	338.83	22.69	−28.27	−1.52
2012.19	1286.14	**Indus**	1821.84	1750.18	1750.18	−46.66	−2.60	337.80	23.92	2.66	0.15
3902.14	2953.58	**Insur**	3636.12	3498.45	3498.45	−131.98	−3.64	353.29	11.23	−121.89	−3.37
2061.81	1497.78	**Banks**	1810.58	1730.52	1730.52	−77.58	−4.29	111.98	6.92	79.42	4.81
1281.81	847.33	**Computer**	1171.18	1130.71	1130.71	−9.68	−0.85	252.78	28.79	−37.55	−3.21
235.20	180.03	**Telecom**	206.70	199.41	199.84	−3.03	−1.49	2.84	1.44	−17.02	−7.85
Russell Indexes											
672.14	479.79	**1000**	609.06	587.76	587.76	−14.03	−2.33	74.00	14.40	−24.25	−3.96
741.92	479.27	**2000**	667.37	633.97	633.97	−27.64	−4.18	103.61	19.54	8.58	1.37
721.81	511.18	**3000**	653.66	629.97	629.97	−16.07	−2.49	81.24	14.81	−23.16	−3.55
632.77	439.11	**Value-v**	568.26	547.30	547.30	−16.74	−2.97	70.47	14.78	−18.97	−3.35
540.02	394.77	**Growth-v**	493.77	477.43	477.43	−8.22	−1.69	58.73	14.03	−22.79	−4.56
943.27	608.00	**MidCap**	855.59	820.42	820.42	−26.35	−3.11	158.42	23.93	4.70	0.58
Others											
2685.27	1612.75	**Value Line-a**	2420.28	2314.61	2314.61	−85.87	−3.58	538.16	30.29	55.16	2.44
361.46	229.77	**Value Line-g**	323.38	309.18	309.18	−11.80	−3.68	53.50	20.92	0.21	0.07
4816.72	2969.60	**DJ US Small TSM**	4320.81	4112.02	4112.02	−176.43	−4.11	816.78	24.79	91.32	2.27

High/Lows are based upon the daily closing index, a-Arithmetic Index. G-Geometric Index. V-Value 1000 and Growth 1000 y-Dec. 31, 1965=50 z-Dec. 31, 2002=5000

Source: *Barron's*, June 7, 2010, p. M44. Reprinted with permission of *Barron's*,

of Figure 3–1 is 0.132319125. Each time a company splits its shares of stock (or provides a stock dividend), the divisor is reduced to maintain the average at the same level as before the stock split. If this were not done, the lower-priced stock after the split would reduce the average, giving the appearance that investors were worse off.

The Dow Jones Industrial Average is a **price-weighted average,** which means each stock in the average is weighted by its price. To simplify the meaning of price weighted: if you had three stocks in a price-weighted average that had values of 10, 40, and 100, you would add the prices and divide by three. In this case, you would get an average of 50 (150 divided by 3). A price-weighted average is similar to what you normally use in computing averages. Price-weighted averages tend to give a higher weighting bias to high-price stocks than to low-price stocks.

Table 3–3 lists the 30 stocks in the Dow Jones Industrial Average as of August 6, 2010; their closing prices; the dollar change in price; the percentage change in price; and finally the impact of each stock's price change on the DJIA for the day. The divisor is given at the top of the table as 0.1321, and so each price change is divided by the divisor to determine the weighted change. For a good example, let's look at the entries for Caterpillar and Travelers. Both companies had a price decline of $0.40 for the day. In the case of Caterpillar the price change was −0.6 percent, and in the case of Travelers (the lower-priced stock) the price change was −0.8 percent. Yet both of these companies had a −3.03 weighted price change.

TABLE 3-3 Dow Jones Industrial Average, August 6, 2010

	DOW JONES INDUSTRIAL AVERAGE, AUGUST 6, 2010 EXAMPLE OF A PRICE-WEIGHTED INDEX DIVISOR = 0.1321				
	Ticker	Last Price	$ Price Change	% Price Change	Weighted Change
ALCOA	AA	$11.59	0.01	0.1%	0.08
AMERICAN EXPRESS	AXP	43.50	0.28	0.6	2.12
BOEING COMPANY	BA	68.70	(0.01)	0.0	−0.08
BANK OF AMERICA CORP	BAC	13.96	(0.06)	−0.4	−0.45
CATERPILLAR	CAT	71.56	(0.40)	−0.6	−3.03
CISCO SYSTEMS INC	CSCO	24.07	(0.10)	−0.4	−0.76
CHEVRON CORP	CVX	78.73	(0.34)	−0.4	−2.57
DUPONT E I DE NEMOURS & CO	DD	42.13	(0.35)	−0.8	−2.65
WALT DISNEY CO (THE)	DIS	35.00	0.02	0.1	0.15
GENERAL ELECTRIC CO	GE	16.45	(0.07)	−0.4	−0.53
HOME DEPOT INC.	HD	28.68	(0.03)	−0.1	−0.23
HEWLETT PACKARD CO	HPQ	46.30	(0.05)	−0.1	−0.38
INTL BUSINESS MACHINES	IBM	130.14	(1.04)	−0.8	−7.87
INTEL CORP	INTC	20.65	(0.02)	−0.1	−0.15
JOHNSON & JOHNSON	JNJ	59.96	0.20	0.3	1.51
JPMORGAN CHASE & CO	JPM	40.44	(0.83)	−2.1	−6.28
KRAFT FOODS INC	KFT	30.36	0.70	2.3	5.30
COCA COLA CO	KO	56.75	0.38	0.7	2.88
MCDONALDS CORP	MCD	71.74	1.29	1.8	9.77
3M COMPANY	MMM	87.29	(0.43)	−0.5	−3.26
MERCK & CO INC	MRK	34.98	(0.09)	−0.3	−0.68
MICROSOFT CORP	MSFT	25.55	0.18	0.7	1.36
PFIZER INC	PFE	16.24	0.05	0.3	0.38
PROCTER & GAMBLE CO	PG	60.02	0.16	0.3	1.21
AT&T INC	T	26.54	(0.20)	−0.8	−1.51
TRAVELERS COS INC (THE)	TRV	50.27	(0.40)	−0.8	−3.03
UNITED TECHNOLOGIES CORP	UTX	72.73	(0.47)	−0.6	−3.56
VERIZON COMMUNICATIONS	VZ	29.55	0.00	0.0	0.00
WALMART STORES INC	WMT	51.79	0.17	0.3	1.29
EXXON MOBIL CORP	XOM	61.97	(0.74)	−1.2	−5.60
					−16.58
Dow Jones Industrial Average	**.DJIA**	**10653.56**	**−21.42**	**−0.2%**	**−21.42**

Source: Reprinted with permission of *The Wall Street Journal,* Copyright © 2010 Dow Jones & Company, Inc. All Rights Reserved Worldwide.

Another good example is Chevron and DuPont. These two companies had price changes within a penny of each other, yet their impact is almost the same even though DuPont had a percentage move that was twice Chevron's. The highest-priced stock in the average is IBM, while the lowest-priced stock is Alcoa. If both stocks moved 10 percent, Alcoa (+1.16) would move the DJIA 8.77 points, while IBM (+13.01) would move the DJIA 98.52 points. Thus, we see a bias toward high-priced stock in the DJIA. This is why professional investors prefer the market-valued, weighted Standard & Poor's 500 Index as the best broad index of large-cap companies.

Standard & Poor's Indexes

www.standardandpoors.com

Standard & Poor's Corporation publishes a number of indexes. The best known is the **Standard & Poor's 500 Stock Index**. This index is widely followed by professional money managers and security market researchers as a measure of broad stock market activity. The S&P 500 Index and other Standard & Poor's Indexes can be seen toward the bottom of Table 3–2. The stocks in the S&P 500 Stock Index are equivalent to approximately 75 percent of the total value of the U.S. equities market.

In the summer of 1991, Standard & Poor introduced its MidCap Index. The **Standard & Poor's 400 MidCap Index** is composed of 400 middle-sized firms that have total market values between $200 million and $6.7 billion. The index was intended to answer the complaint that the S&P 500 Stock Index shows only the performance of larger firms. For example, Exxon Mobil, which is part of the S&P 500 Index, had a total market value of more than $316 billion in August 2010. By creating an index of middle-sized firms, portfolio managers with comparable-sized holdings could more accurately track their performance against an appropriate measure. The same is true for the **Standard & Poor's 600 SmallCap Index**, which provides an opportunity for comparison of stocks that are smaller than the MidCap. The **Standard & Poor's 1500 Stock Index**, also shown in Table 3–2, combines the S&P 500, the S&P 400 MidCap, and the S&P SmallCap 600. Figure 3–2 shows the S&P 500 fact sheet from the S&P Web site (**www.standardandpoors.com**) on June 30, 2010. It provides an overview of the index and the 10 sectors that are included in the index, as well as their weights in the S&P 500 Index and their individual sectors.

Standard & Poor's also has other special purpose indexes, some of which are not shown in Table 3–2. For example, the **Standard & Poor's 100 Index** is composed of 100 blue-chip stocks on which the Chicago Board Options Exchange has individual option contracts. (This terminology will become clearer when we study index options later in the text.) The S&P 100 Index closely mirrors the performance of the S&P 500 Stock Index.

All the S&P measures are true indexes in that they are linked to a base value. For the S&P 500 Stock Index, the base period is 1941–43. The base period price in 1941–43 was 10, so the SP 500 Stock Index price of 1,064.88 on June 7, 2010, as previously shown in Table 3–2, represents an increase of 1,064.88 percent over this 69-year-plus period. For the newer indexes, the base period does not go back as far.

Regardless of the base period, the important consideration is how much the index changed over a given time period (such as a day, month, or year) rather than the absolute value. For example, looking back at Table 3–2, you can see that the Dow Jones Industrial Average on June 7, 2010 is down 4.76 percent from December 31 (look at the last column to see the percentage change from the prior year) and that the Standard & Poor's 500 Stock Index is down 4.50 percent over a comparable time period. One might observe that this was a poor period for market performance in contrast to the 12-month percent change column, which shows the S&P 500 up 13.27 percent.

FIGURE 3-2 S&P 500 Fact Sheet

S&P 500

June 30, 2010

The large cap segment of the U.S. equities market, covering approximately 75% of the U.S. equities market.

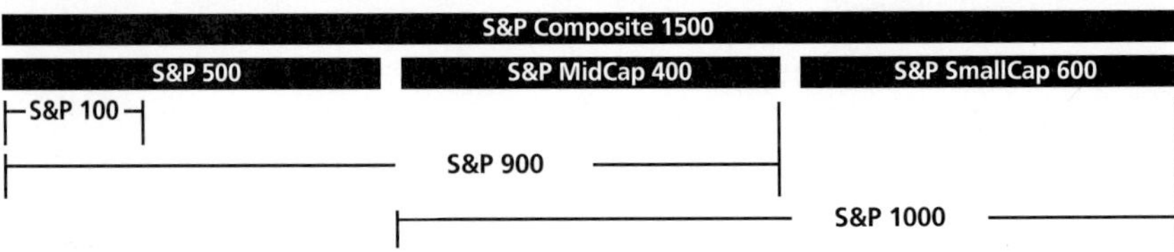

Index Performance

Returns	1 Month	−5.23%
	3 Month	−11.43%
	YTD	−6.65%
Annualized	1 Year	14.43%
Returns	3 Years	−9.81%
	5 Years	−0.79%
	7 Years	2.84%
Annualized	3 Years Std Dev	20.73%
Risk	5 Years Std Dev	16.83%
Sharpe Ratio	3 Years	−0.4515
	5 Years	−0.1146

5 Year Historical Performance

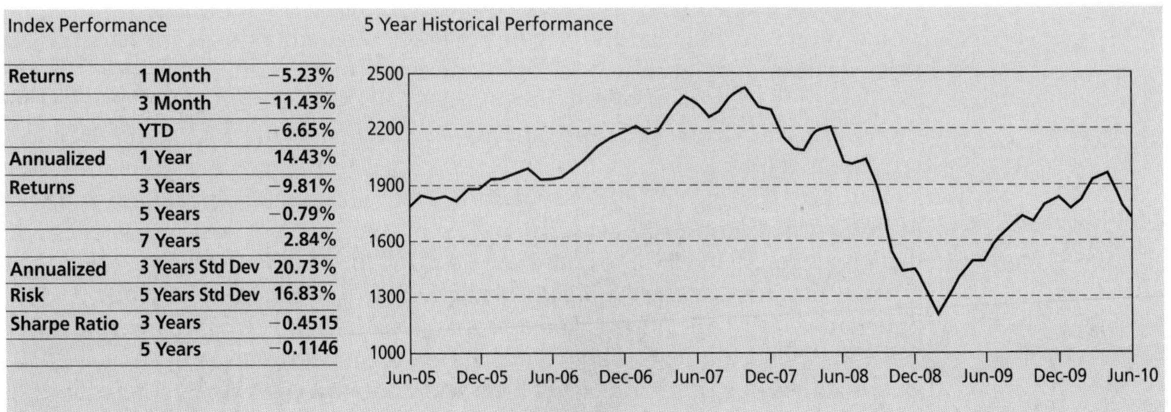

Top 10 Companies By Weight

Country	Company	Float Adjusted Market Cap ($ Million)	Index Weight	Sector Weight	Investable Weight Factor	GICS®Sector
United States	Exxon Mobil Corp	291,748.2	3.13%	25.39%	1.00	Energy
United States	Apple Inc.	228,876.7	2.46%	11.49%	1.00	Information Technology
United States	Microsoft Corp	175,440.7	1.88%	8.80%	0.87	Information Technology
United States	Procter & Gamble	172,736.6	1.85%	14.53%	1.00	Consumer Staples
United States	Johnson & Johnson	162,891.6	1.75%	12.69%	1.00	Health Care
United States	Intl Business Machines Corp	158,344.3	1.70%	7.95%	1.00	Information Technology
United States	General Electric Co	153,955.4	1.65%	13.88%	1.00	Industrials
United States	JP Morgan Chase & Co	145,660.0	1.56%	8.35%	1.00	Financials
United States	Bank of America Corp	144,173.4	1.55%	8.27%	1.00	Financials
United States	AT&T Inc	142,938.7	1.53%	48.21%	1.00	Telecommunication Services

Tickers

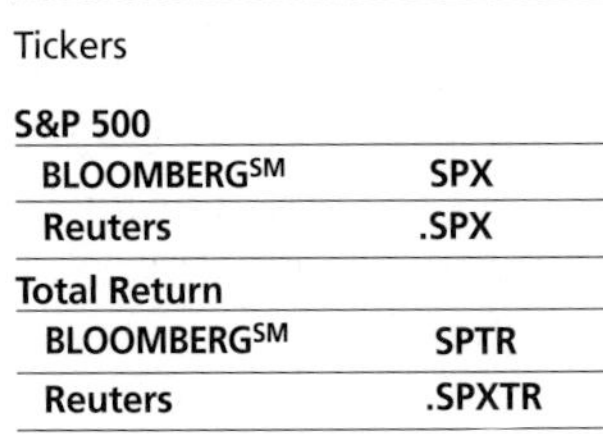

S&P 500	
BLOOMBERG℠	SPX
Reuters	.SPX
Total Return	
BLOOMBERG℠	SPTR
Reuters	.SPXTR

Sector Breakdown

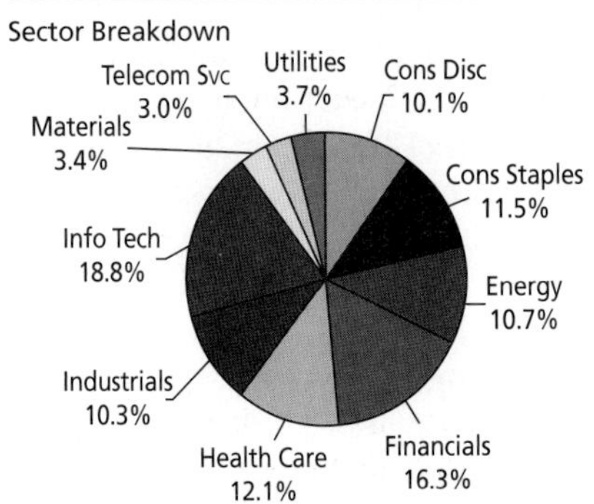

Index Portfolio Characteristics

Number of Companies	500
Adjusted Market Cap ($ Billion)	9,320.01
Company Size By Market Cap (Adjusted $ Billion):	
Average	18.64
Largest	291.75
Smallest	1.01
Median	8.29
% Weight Largest Company	3.13%
Top 10 Holdings (% Market Cap Share)	19.06%

Source: www.standardandpoors.com. *S&P 500 Fact Sheet*, June 30, 2010.

application example

The Standard & Poor's Indexes are **value-weighted indexes**, which means each company is weighted in the index by its own total market value as a percentage of the total market value for all firms. For example, in a value-weighted index comprising the following three firms, the weighting would be:

Stock	Shares	Price	Total Market Value	Weighting
A	150	$10	$ 1,500	12.0%
B	200	20	4,000	32.0
C	500	14	7,000	56.0
			$12,500	100.0%

In each case, the weighting is determined by dividing the total market value of the stock by the total market value for all firms. In the case of stock A, that would be $1,500 divided by $12,500, or 12 percent. The same procedure is followed for stocks B and C.

www.ge.com
www.exxon.com
www.att.com

Even though stock C has only the second-highest price, it makes up 56 percent of the average because of its high total market value based on 500 shares outstanding. This same basic effect carries through in the Standard & Poor's 500 Index, with large companies such as GE, Exxon, and AT&T having a greater impact on the index than smaller companies. Value-weighted indexes do not require special adjustments for stock splits because the increase in the number of shares automatically compensates for the decline in the stock value caused by the split.

Standard & Poor's, as well as others, also divides their indexes into growth and value indexes, usually based on prices to book value ratios. So the S&P 500 would have 250 stocks in a growth index and 250 stocks in a value index.

Value Line Average

www.valueline.com

The **Value Line Average** represents 1,700 companies from the New York and American stock exchanges and the Nasdaq market. Some individual investors use the Value Line Average because it more closely corresponds to the variety of stocks small investors may have in their portfolios.

Unlike the previously discussed price-weighted average (the Dow Jones Industrial Average) and value-weighted indexes (S&P 500), the Value Line Average is an **equal-weighted index**. This means each of the 1,700 stocks, regardless of market price or total market value, is weighted equally. It is as if there were $100 to be invested in each and every stock. In this case, IBM or ExxonMobil is weighted no more heavily than Wendy's International or Mattel Inc. This equal-weighting characteristic also more closely conforms to the portfolio of individual investors.

www.ibm.com
www.exxon.com
www.wendys.com
www.mattel.com

Other Market Indexes

www.nasdaq.com

Exchange Indexes Indexes are also computed and published by the New York Stock Exchange, American Stock Exchange, and Nasdaq. Each index is intended to represent the performance of stocks traded in a particular exchange or market. As is seen in Table 3–2 on page 59, the NYSE publishes a composite index as well as other indexes. Each index represents the stocks of a broad group or type of company.

the real world of investing

BABE RUTH CALLED SHOT HOME RUN IN THE 1932 WORLD SERIES WAS THE EQUIVALENT OF IBBOTSON AND SINQUEFIELD MARKET INDEX PREDICTION IN 1974

After taunting by the Chicago Cubs bench in the 1932 World Series, Babe Ruth bravely pointed his right finger to the grandstand and predicted he would hit a home run off Chicago Cubs Pitcher Charley Root. The legendary "Bambino" made good on his promise by taking two called strikes before sending a satellite shot into the bleachers at Wrigley Field in Chicago.

In 1974, when the Dow Jones Industrial Average was mired in a 10-year slump at a level of 800, financial researchers Ibbotson and Sinquefield stepped up to the plate and predicted that the Dow Jones Industrial Average would hit the seemingly astronomical level of 10,000 by November 1999. The mad "financial scientists" were only eight months off in their 25-year projection as the Dow Jones Industrial Average crashed through 10,000 on March 29, 1999. They used highly sophisticated statistical techniques and Monte Carlo analysis to make their prediction.

After such an incredible feat, one might assume the researchers would pack away their sophisticated crystal ball for posterity. After all, Babe Ruth never attempted another called shot home run.

But Roger Ibbotson of Ibbotson Associates stepped up to the plate again in 1998, and predicted the Dow Jones will hit a level of 100,000 by year-end 2025. Please stay tuned.

The Nasdaq also publishes a number of indexes, including the Nasdaq Composite, the Nasdaq 100, and other indexes that represent various sectors of the economy. The Nasdaq 100 is made up of the 100 largest firms in its market and is heavily populated by high-tech firms such as Microsoft, Intel, Oracle, and Cisco.

The Nasdaq Composite Index is often featured along with the Dow Jones Industrial Average and the Standard & Poor's 500 Index on the nightly news.

The American Exchange (AMEX) Composite Index is composed of all stocks trading on the American Stock Exchange. This index is also shown in Table 3–2 in the fourth section.

The indexes of the New York Stock Exchange, Nasdaq, and American Stock Exchange are all value-weighted indexes.

most compl[illegible]

Wilshire 5000 Another important index is the **Wilshire 5000 Equity Index** (**www.wilshire.com/indexes**). It is the most comprehensive index and represents the *total dollar volume* of all U.S. equity issues with readily available price data from the NYSE, AMEX, and Nasdaq stock markets. Originally the index included close to 5,000 stocks, but as the equity markets have grown it now includes more than 5,000 stocks. By the very fact of including total dollar volume, it is a value-weighted index. On August 6, 2010, the Wilshire Index had a value of $11,754.68 billion ($11.75 trillion). The index tells you the total value of virtually all important equities daily. Its all-time high was $15.8 trillion on October 9, 2007, and its 52-week low was on August 17, 2009. This demonstrates the volatility of the market during the financial crisis.

Russell Indexes The Russell indexes have also become popular in recent times. There are three separate but overlapping value-weighted indexes provided by Frank Russell Company, a money management consulting firm in Tacoma, Washington.[4] While only one is shown in Table 3–2, we shall discuss all three. The **Russell 3000 Index** comprises 3,000 U.S. stocks as measured by market capitalization (market value times shares outstanding). The other two

[4] Frank Russell Company has other indexes as well.

indexes allow you to see whether larger or smaller stocks are performing better. For example, the **Russell 1000 Index** includes only the largest 1,000 firms out of the Russell 3000, while the **Russell 2000** specifically includes the smallest 2,000 out of the Russell 3000. If the Russell 2000 is outperforming the Russell 1000, you can generally assume that smaller stocks are outperforming larger firms. The reverse would obviously be true if there is a superior performance by the Russell 1000.

International Stock Averages As the internationalization of investments has become progressively more important, so have international market indexes. *The Wall Street Journal* covers indexes throughout the world as shown in Table 3–4.

TABLE 3-4 International Stock Indexes

Region/Country	Index	Close	LATEST Net chg	LATEST % chg	YTD % chg
World	**The Global Dow**	**1757.30**	39.97	**2.33**	-11.4
	DJ Global Index	**210.12**	4.63	**2.25**	-7.4
	DJ Global ex U.S.	**178.66**	2.95	**1.68**	-11.2
World	**MSCI EAFE***	**1354.77**	23.10	**1.73**	-14.3
Americas	**DJ Americas**	**289.98**	8.27	**2.94**	-2.2
Brazil	**Sao Paulo Bovespa**	**63048.80**	1570.19	**2.55**	-8.1
Canada	**S&P/TSX Comp**	**11635.85**	185.21	**1.62**	-0.9
Mexico	**IPC All-Share**	**31910.22**	700.89	**2.25**	-0.7
Venezuela	**Caracas General**	**64625.51**	-78.04	**-0.12**	17.3
Europe	**Stoxx Europe 600**	**248.46**	3.86	**1.58**	-1.9
Euro zone	**Euro Stoxx**	**250.94**	5.07	**2.06**	-8.7
Belgium	**Bel-20**	**2463.32**	37.64	**1.55**	-1.9
France	**CAC 40**	**3516.64**	69.87	**2.03**	-10.7
Germany	**DAX**	**6056.59**	71.84	**1.20**	1.7
Israel	**Tel Aviv**	**1090.80**	0.87	**0.08**	-4.7
Italy	**FTSE MIB**	**19391.09**	478.18	**2.53**	-16.6
Netherlands	**AEX**	**325.42**	4.79	**1.49**	-3.0
Spain	**IBEX 35**	**9198.2**	329.50	**3.72**	-23.0
Sweden	**SX All Share**	**318.30**	6.46	**2.07**	6.3
Switzerland	**Swiss Market**	**6376.66**	57.48	**0.91**	-2.6
U.K.	**FTSE 100**	**5132.50**	46.64	**0.92**	-5.2
Asia-Pacific	**DJ Asia-Pacific**	**114.46**	1.29	**1.14**	-7.0
Australia	**S&P/ASX 200**	**4435.31**	49.99	**1.14**	-8.9
China	**Shanghai Composite**	**2562.58**	-21.29	**-0.82**	-21.8
Hong Kong	**Hang Seng**	**19632.70**	11.46	**0.06**	-10.2
India	**Bombay Sensex**	**16922.08**	264.19	**1.59**	-3.1
Japan	**Nikkei Stock Avg**	**9542.65**	103.52	**1.10**	-9.5
Singapore	**Straits Times**	**2779.58**	33.78	**1.23**	-4.1
South Korea	**Kospi**	**1651.70**	4.48	**0.27**	-1.8
Taiwan	**Weighted**	**7181.77**	110.10	**1.56**	-12.3

*Europe, Australia, FarEast, U.S.-dollar terms

Source: *The Wall Street Journal,* June 11, 2010. Reprinted with permission of *The Wall Street Journal,*

Of particular interest in the table is the first item, **the Global Dow**. This index covers the performance of all the world's markets combined and is down 11.4 percent year-to-date as of June 11, 2010, as shown in the last column. During this time period, China (Shanghai Composite) was down 21.8 percent. Particularly closely watched is Japan's **Tokyo Nikkei Stock Average**. Although this fact is not shown in the table, the Nikkei is down over 50 percent from its glory days of 25 years ago.

Bond Market Indicators Reports on performance in the many different types of bond markets are not easily found in *The Wall Street Journal* or other financial publications. Bonds are traded over the counter and are mostly traded by financial institutions. Bonds are most affected by interest rate movements; rising rates mean falling bond prices, and falling rates cause bond prices to rise. Investors usually judge bond market performance by yield-curve changes, risk characteristics, and interest rate spreads between various risk classes.

Table 3–5, from *Wall Street Journal's* Markets Data Center at **www.wsj.com**, provides a robust list of bond indexes. Merrill Lynch, Barclays Capital, and JPMorgan primarily provide these indexes. Barclays bought a large piece of Lehman Brothers and acquired the Lehman Brothers bond indexes in the process. The bonds are listed by category, including but not limited to: broad market, hourly treasury indexes, U.S. corporate indexes, high-yield bonds, U.S. agency indexes, and mortgage-backed, tax-exempt, and global government bonds.

The table contains the year-to-date (YTD) total return, which includes price change as well as interest payments (except for three indexes in the hourly treasury indexes.) The 52-week percentage change in the bond index is given, and you might notice that in this period of falling interest rates, most bond indexes had positive returns. A look at both the Barclays and the Merrill Lynch corporate indexes shows that this category has had a very good 52-week performance, with the Merrill Lynch high-yield debt index up 23 percent. As bond prices move up, the yield will go down, and vice versa. The 52-week yield range is given with the latest or current yield, as well as the high and low yield over this period. You can compare the latest yields and, except for the Merrill Lynch high-yield bonds (8.07 percent), there is no bond yielding over 6 percent. Most are yielding less than 4 percent. Bonds will be discussed fully in Part 4 of the text.

www.lipperweb.com

Mutual Fund Averages Lipper Analytical Services publishes the Lipper Mutual and Investment Performance Averages shown in Table 3–6 on page 68. It is interesting to observe the various categories that the funds are broken into to compute measures of performance. Also, observe in the next few columns of Table 3–6 that the starting point of the measurement period is very important in relation to relative performance.

Mutual funds and their performance have become progressively more important to investors in the United States and worldwide. Many of the 90 million investors in this country look to mutual funds to carry out their day-to-day investment activities. Mutual funds are covered in the next chapter to demonstrate the various alternatives investors have to match their goals and objectives with their investment strategies.

Direction of Indexes The directions of the indexes are closely related, but they do not necessarily move together. If a pension fund manager is trying to "outperform the market," then the choice of index may be crucial to whether the fund manager maintains his or her accounts. The important thing for you, as well as for a professional, when measuring success or failure of performance is to use an index that represents the risk characteristics of the portfolio being compared with the index.

TABLE 3-5 Tracking Bond Benchmarks, August 4, 2010

Closing Index values, return on investment, and yields paid to investors compared with 52-week highs and lows for different types of bonds. Preliminary data and data shown as "n.a." will update around 12 p.m. the following business day.

Index	Close	% Chg	YTD Total Return	52-wk % Chg	YIELD (%), 52-WEEK RANGE Latest	Low	High
Broad Market Barclays Capital							
U.S. Government/Credit	1753.53	−0.19	6.53	9.49	2.420	2.380	3.680
Barclays Aggregate	1538.53	−0.14	6.37	9.33	2.620	2.570	4.170
Hourly Treasury Indexes Barclays Capital							
Composite (Price Return)	1422.71	−0.18	4.11	3.81	1.770	1.720	2.670
Composite (Total Return)	11795.78	−0.18	6.03	7.15	1.770	1.720	2.670
Intermediate (Price Return)	1280.95	−0.17	3.39	3.11	1.470	1.430	2.320
Intermediate (Total Return)	10089.35	−0.16	5.13	6.13	1.470	1.430	2.320
Long-Term (Price Return)	1908.83	−0.30	8.96	8.09	3.700	3.610	4.600
Long-Term (Total Return)	18535.25	−0.28	12.10	13.42	3.700	3.610	4.600
U.S. Corporate Indexes Barclays Capital							
U.S. Corporate	1934.99	−0.20	7.73	13.86	3.950	3.910	5.560
Intermediate	1952.68	−0.19	7.04	13.02	3.340	3.300	5.220
Long-term	2265.04	−0.24	9.78	16.39	5.730	5.680	6.600
Double-A-rated(AA)	414.46	−0.19	6.34	10.35	3.090	3.050	4.380
Triple-B-rated(Baa)	453.87	−0.21	8.24	15.98	4.510	4.480	6.400
U.S. Agency Indexes Barclays Capital							
U.S. Agency	1419.90	−0.13	4.33	5.97	1.470	1.430	2.520
10–20 years	1308.08	−0.13	3.89	5.49	1.290	1.250	2.330
20-plus years	2192.70	−0.21	11.27	13.35	4.070	3.980	5.340
Mortgage-Backed Barclays Capital							
Mortgage-Backed	1632.04	−0.05	5.53	8.12	2.800	2.750	4.620
Ginnie Mae (GNMA)	1606.90	−0.06	6.53	8.79	2.780	2.710	4.610
Freddie Mae (FHLMC)	1469.01	−0.05	5.34	8.02	2.910	2.860	4.640
Fannie Mae (FNMA)	948.02	−0.04	5.31	7.93	2.740	2.690	4.600
Mortgage-Backed Merrill Lynch							
Ginnie Mae (GNMA)	602.17	−0.08	8.01	10.29	3.200	2.903	4.661
Fannie Mae (FNMA)	576.14	−0.11	8.02	9.31	3.380	3.251	4.671
Freddie Mae (FHLMC)	355.30	−0.14	8.06	9.31	3.470	3.335	4.710
U.S. Corporate Debt Merrill Lynch							
1–10 Year Maturities	1439.00	−0.16	7.40	13.58	3.480	3.426	5.326
10+ Year Maturities	1742.72	−0.13	10.52	18.57	5.750	5.677	6.695
Corporate Master	2038.66	−0.16	8.15	14.77	4.030	3.990	5.653
High Yield	1065.12	0.10	8.88	23.07	8.070	7.854	11.491
Yankee Bonds	1499.83	−0.09	7.03	12.44	3.400	3.375	4.911
Tax-Exempt Merrill Lynch							
Muni Master	n.a.	n.a.	n.a.	n.a.	n.a.	2.755	3.366
7–12 years	275.89	0.10	6.60	9.03	2.810	2.797	3.556
12–22 years	287.65	0.14	5.82	9.46	3.990	3.878	4.602
22-plus years	264.64	0.07	5.51	14.62	4.930	4.722	5.732
Bond Buyer 6% Muni	116.66	0.05	4.01	9.34	5.080	4.930	5.580
Yankee Barclays	1884.87	−0.10	6.90	11.13	3.080	3.060	4.400
Government Bonds J.P. Morgan†							
Global Government	434.35	0.05	5.09	6.75	2.310	2.310	2.940
Canada	604.92	−0.44	4.65	6.00	3.140	3.060	3.630
EMU§	274.48	0.13	4.04	5.29	3.380	3.330	3.770
France	535.14	0.19	6.95	8.45	2.760	2.710	3.560
Germany	399.76	0.16	6.98	8.30	2.510	2.390	3.430
Japan	247.99	0.25	3.08	4.61	1.080	1.080	1.470
Netherlands	430.47	0.21	6.95	8.74	2.580	2.470	3.510
U.K.	614.45	0.01	6.17	8.38	3.630	3.540	4.220
Emerging Markets**	517.14	0.155	10.84	18.46	5.859	5.859	7.335

Barclays data are preliminary. Barclays corporate indexes may be unavailable until midday the following business day.
*Constrained indexes limit individual issuer concentrations to 2%; the High Yield 100 are the 100 largest bonds.
†In local currency §Euro-zone bonds. **EMBI Global Index
Data from Dow Jones Indexes; Merrill Lynch; Barclays Capital; J.P. Morgan.
Source: http://online.wsj.com/mdc/public/page/2_3022-bondbnchmrk.html. Accessed August 5, 2010. Reprinted with permission of *The Wall Street Journal,*

TABLE 3-6 Lipper Mutual Fund Performance Indexes

Weekly Summary Report: 7/29/2010

Cumulative Performances with Dividends Reinvested

Current Value	No. Funds		12/31/09–07/29/2010	07/22/10–07/29/2010	07/01/10–07/29/2010	04/29/10–07/29/2010	07/30/09–07/29/2010
General Equity Indexes							
2,925.66	30	Capital Apprec Index	−0.65	+0.57	+6.12	−8.44	+13.43
7,770.39	30	Growth Fund Index	−0.79	+0.42	+6.59	−9.02	+14.35
1,112.36	30	Mid Cap Fund Indx	+2.47	+0.74	+6.85	−9.38	+18.63
275.56	30	Micro Cap Fund IX	+4.91	+2.12	+6.17	−10.64	+18.89
1,115.23	30	Small Cap Fund Index	+3.95	+1.45	+7.21	−10.03	+20.08
8,614.31	30	Growth & Income Index	−0.26	+0.77	+7.14	−7.93	+13.57
475.04	10	S&P 500 Fund Indx	−0.27	+0.73	+7.31	−8.33	+13.66
4,737.28	30	Equity Income Index	+0.17	+0.86	+7.46	−7.06	+13.93
Specialized Equity Indexes							
423.35	10	Hlth/Biotch Fd IX	−5.18	+0.45	+1.50	−11.43	+5.39
754.96	10	Sci & Tech Index	−1.57	−0.53	+6.96	−8.97	+15.14
551.57	30	Utility Fund Index	+0.63	+0.65	+8.15	−0.63	+11.56
443.42	10	Fincl Svs Fd Indx	+4.35	+2.20	+6.45	−11.50	+17.31
371.18	10	Real Estate Fd IX	+12.69	+2.38	+8.94	−5.81	+45.89
446.95	10	Gold Fund Index	+6.93	−1.59	−1.36	−3.88	+36.08
949.21	30	Global Fund Index	−1.46	+1.18	+7.95	−6.09	+11.74
1,114.24	30	International Index	−2.43	+1.88	+9.08	−3.94	+10.71
479.71	10	European Fd Index	−3.48	+1.83	+12.32	−3.21	+12.15
245.39	10	Pac Ex-Jpn Fd IX	+4.04	+1.50	+7.44	−0.69	+20.12
250.42	10	Pacific Reg Fd IX	+2.47	+1.81	+7.15	−3.90	+14.21
248.49	30	Emerg Mkt Fd Index	+2.62	+1.49	+9.00	−1.74	+22.62
Other Equity Indexes							
515.05	30	Flex Port Fd Indx	+1.35	+0.99	+5.52	−4.84	+13.03
359.34	10	Glbl Flx Fund IX	+1.77	+0.76	+4.70	−3.81	+14.28
6,208.81	30	Balanced Fund Index	+1.91	+0.55	+4.80	−3.89	+12.46
630.37	10	Conv Secur Index	+3.90	+0.57	+5.39	−4.45	+19.78
496.55	10	Income Fund Index	+3.34	+0.64	+3.30	−1.11	+12.93
Fixed-Income Indexes							
276.98	10	Intl Inc Fd IX	+3.93	+0.91	+2.59	+2.61	+10.16
387.10	30	Global Inc Fd IX	+4.07	+0.44	+1.66	+1.40	+12.39
159.27	10	Ultra Short Fd IX	+0.99	−0.18	+0.14	−0.18	+2.31
941.72	30	Gen Muni Dbt Indx	+4.50	+0.20	+1.08	+1.68	+11.29
537.89	30	Gen US Govt Fd IX	+6.38	−0.26	+0.02	+4.00	+8.77
613.00	10	GNMA Fund Index	+6.01	+0.22	+0.77	+3.40	+9.07
314.18	10	US Mortgage Fd IX	+5.94	+0.33	+0.74	+3.19	+9.78
1,447.10	30	A Rated Bnd Fd IX	+6.46	+0.12	+0.79	+2.83	+12.43
682.17	30	BBB Rated Fd IX	+7.66	+0.23	+1.47	+2.76	+14.56
1,294.34	30	HI Yid Bond Fd IX	+7.46	+0.94	+3.48	+0.52	+22.67
428.23	10	Ins Muni Fd Index	+3.86	+0.10	+0.91	+1.79	+8.81
400.97	10	HY Muni Dbt Fd IX	+6.54	+0.33	+1.24	+1.77	+20.27
169.46	10	Sh Muni Dbt Fd IX	+1.26	+0.08	+0.38	+0.69	+2.65
191.46	10	Sh-In Muni Dbt IX	+3.20	+0.21	+0.91	+1.75	+5.98
387.94	30	Intmdt Muni Fd IX	+3.99	+0.13	+1.16	+2.03	+7.91
311.71	30	Sht Inv Grd Fd IX	+3.49	+0.16	+0.64	+1.12	+7.06
299.91	30	Sh-In Inv Grd IX	+4.93	+0.18	+0.85	+2.13	+9.09
411.59	30	Intmdt Inv Grd IX	+7.17	+0.19	+1.06	+3.06	+13.13
274.08	10	Sh US Govt Fd IX	+2.34	+0.07	+0.28	+1.16	+3.75
339.55	30	Sh-In US Govt IX	+3.57	+0.08	+0.40	+1.96	+5.34
352.36	30	Intmdt US Govt IX	+6.36	−0.03	+0.44	+3.50	+8.67
205.17	10	CA Intmdt Muni IX	+4.47	+0.13	+1.23	+2.01	+8.46
523.58	30	CA Muni Dbt Fd IX	+5.13	+0.19	+1.19	+1.73	+12.53
233.67	10	MD Muni Dbt Fd IX	+4.24	+0.15	+1.08	+1.98	+9.40
382.56	10	MA Muni Dbt Fd IX	+4.29	+0.14	+1.01	+1.95	+9.59
281.33	10	MI Muni Dbt Fd IX	+4.10	+0.14	+0.89	+1.58	+10.11
370.92	10	MN Muni Dbt Fd IX	+4.17	+0.11	+0.97	+2.03	+9.15
288.77	10	NJ Muni Dbt Fd IX	+4.52	+0.21	+1.17	+1.53	+10.99
522.09	30	NY Muni Dbt Fd IX	+4.59	+0.16	+0.99	+1.63	+11.17
379.55	10	OH Muni Dbt Fd IX	+3.29	+0.08	+0.91	+1.52	+7.76
382.02	10	PA Muni Dbt Fd IX	+4.38	+0.11	+1.00	+1.71	+10.87
256.87	10	Muni Dbt VA Fd IX	+3.55	+0.17	+1.03	+1.32	+8.55

For a number of the Indexes no long-term historical data exist.

Source: Barron's online, http://online.barrons.com, August 1, 2010.

exploring the web

Web Address	Comments
www.mscibarra.com	**Provides information on bond and stock indexes and various modified indexes**
www.sec.gov	**Provides access to SEC filings**
http://finance.yahoo.com	**Profile pages on stock quotes provide access to company SEC filings**
www.standardandpoors.com	**Contains information about S&P indexes and the markets**
www.dowjones.com	**Provides information about the Dow Jones indexes**

SUMMARY

The potential investor must open an account. The investor may establish either a cash or a margin account and use the account to buy securities or to sell short (in which case a margin account is necessary). The investor can also execute a number of different types of orders such as a market order, a limit order, and a stop order. The latter two specify prices where the investor wishes to initiate transactions.

The investor must also consider the tax consequences of his or her actions. The Tax Relief Act of 2003 has caused many investors to rethink their investment strategy.

In gauging the movements in the market, the investor may view the Dow Jones Industrial Average, the Standard & Poor's 500 Stock Index, the Standard & Poor's MidCap Index, the Value Line Average of 1,700 companies, or the Nasdaq Averages (to name a few). To evaluate mutual funds, the investor may turn to the Lipper Mutual Fund Investment Performance Averages. Bond markets can be examined by indexes created by Barclays, Merrill Lynch, JPMorgan, and others. There also are a number of bond indexes and averages for foreign trading. The investor will try to evaluate performance in light of an index that closely parallels the makeup of the investor's portfolio.

KEY WORDS AND CONCEPTS

capital gain or loss 56
Dow Jones Industrial Average (DJIA) 57
equal-weighted index 63
limit order 53
long position 51
margin account 50
online broker 54
price-weighted average 59
Russell 1000 Index 65
Russell 2000 Index 65
Russell 3000 Index 64
short position 51
Standard & Poor's 100 Index 61
Standard & Poor's 400 MidCap Index 61
Standard & Poor's 500 Stock Index 61
Standard & Poor's 600 SmallCap Index 61
Standard & Poor's 1500 Stock Index 61
stop order 53
The Global Dow 66
Tokyo Nikkei Average 66
Value Line Average 63
value-weighted index 63
Wilshire 5000 Equity Index 64

DISCUSSION QUESTIONS

1. Explain the difference between a cash account and a margin account.
2. What is meant by the concept of minimum maintenance standards (or requirements) for margin?
3. Why is bad news "good news" to the short seller?
4. Explain what is meant by a limit order. How does a stop order differ from a limit order?
5. What is the difference between day orders and GTC orders?
6. On a 100-share trade, what would be the expected dollar commission with a full-service broker, a discount broker, and an online broker?
7. What is the difference between the meaning of the marginal tax rate and the average tax rate for a taxpayer?
8. Why is the Dow Jones Industrial Average considered a "blue-chip" measure of value?
9. How is the Dow Jones Industrial Average adjusted for stock splits?
10. What are the criticisms and a defense of the Dow Jones Industrial Average?
11. Explain the price-weighted average concept as applied to the Dow Jones Industrial Average.
12. What categories of stocks make up the Standard & Poor's 500 Stock Index?
13. Why was the Standard & Poor's MidCap Index created?
14. What is a value-weighted index? Explain the impact that large firms have on value-weighted indexes such as the S&P 500.
15. What is an equal-weighted average? Which average has this characteristic?
16. Fill in the table for the type of weighting system for the various indexes. Put an (x) under the appropriate weighting system.

	Price Weighted	Value Weighted	Equal Weighted
NYSE Composite Index	______	______	______
Value Line Average	______	______	______
S&P 500 Index	______	______	______
Dow Jones Industrial Average	______	______	______

17. If you did not wish a high-priced or heavily capitalized firm (one with high total market value) to overly influence your index, which of the weighting systems described in this chapter would you be likely to use?
18. Why might one say that the Wilshire 5000 Equity Index is the most comprehensive market measure?
19. If the Russell 2000 Index is outperforming the Russell 1000 Index, what can you generally assume about the relative performance of smaller versus larger stocks?

PRACTICE PROBLEMS AND SOLUTIONS

www.mhhe.com

Margin purchases

1. *a.* Assume you buy 100 shares of stock at $30 per share on margin (50 percent). If the price of the shares rises to $39, what is your percentage gain on the initial equity?
   b. What would be the percentage loss on the initial equity if the price decreased to $24?

Changing index values in a value-weighted index

2. Assume the following stocks make up a value-weighted index:

Corporation	Shares Outstanding	Market Price
Alpha	50,000	$30
Beta	5,000	10
Gamma	18,000	15
Delta	10,000	40

a. Compute the total market value and the weights assigned to each stock. Round up to two places to the right of the decimal point. (The weights may add up to slightly more or less than 100 percent due to rounding.)

b. Assume the shares of Alpha Corporation go up by 20 percent while the shares of Gamma Corporation go down by 40 percent. The other two stocks remain constant. What will be the newly established value for the index?

Solutions

1. *a.*

100 × $30	= $3,000	Price increase 100 × $39	= $3,900
Loan	= −1,500	Loan	= −1,500
Initial Equity	= $1,500	Equity (Ending)	= $2,400

$2,400 − $1,500 = $900 Gain

$$\frac{\$900 \text{ Gain}}{\$1{,}500 \text{ Initial margin (equity)}} = 60\% \text{ Gain}$$

b.

100 × $30	= $3,000	Price decrease 100 × $24	= $2,400
Loan	= −1,500	Loan	= −1,500
Initial Equity	= $1,500	Equity (Ending)	= $ 900

$900 − $1,500 = −$600 (Loss)

$$\frac{\$600 \text{ Loss}}{\$1{,}500 \text{ Initial margin (equity)}} = 40\% \text{ Loss}$$

2. *a.*

Corporation	Shares Outstanding	Market Price	Total Value	Weight
Alpha	50,000	$30	$1,500,000	67.57%
Beta	5,000	10	50,000	2.25
Gamma	18,000	15	270,000	12.16
Delta	10,000	40	400,000	18.02
			$2,220,000	100.00%

b.

Corporation	Shares Outstanding	Market Price	Total Value
Alpha	50,000	$36*	$1,800,000
Beta	5,000	10	50,000
Gamma	18,000	9†	162,000
Delta	10,000	40	400,000
			$2,412,000

* $30 × (1 + .20) = $30 × 120% = $36

† $15 × (1 − .40) = $15 × 60% = $9

$$\text{Index} = \frac{\$2{,}412{,}000}{2{,}220{,}000} = 108.65$$

PROBLEMS

Margin purchase

1. Assume you buy 100 shares of stock at $40 per share on margin (40 percent). If the price rises to $55 per share, what is your percentage gain on the initial equity?

Margin purchase

2. In problem 1, what would the percentage loss on the initial equity be if the price had decreased to $28?

Minimum margin

3. Assume you have a 25 percent minimum margin standard in problems 1 and 2. With a price decline to $28, will you be called upon to put up more margin to meet the 25 percent rule? Disregard the $2,000 minimum margin balance requirement.

Minimum margin

4. Recompute the answer to problem 3 based on a stock decline to $23.75.

Selling short

5. You sell 100 shares of Norton Corporation short. The price of the stock is $60 per share. The margin requirement is 50 percent.
   a. How much is your initial margin?
   b. If stock goes down to $42, what is your percentage gain or loss on the initial margin (equity)?
   c. If stock goes up to $67.50, what is your percentage gain or loss on the initial margin (equity)?
   d. In part *c*, if the minimum margin standard is 30 percent, will you be required to put up more margin? (Do the additional necessary calculations to answer this question.)

Margin purchase and selling short

6. You are very optimistic about the personal computer industry, so you buy 200 shares of Microtech Inc. at $45 per share. You are very pessimistic about the machine tool industry, so you sell short 300 shares of King Tools Corporation at $55. Each transaction requires a 40 percent margin balance.
   a. What is the initial equity in your account?
   b. Assume the price of each stock is as follows for the next three months (month-end). Compute the equity balance in your account for each month:

Month	Microtech Inc.	King Tools Corp.
October	$51	$48
November	39	62
December	37	40

Commission percentage

7. Lisa Loeb is considering buying 100 shares of CMA Record Company. The price of the shares is $52. She has checked around with different types of brokers and has been given the following commission quotes for the trade: online broker, $7; discount broker, $45; full-service broker, $98.
   a. Compute the percentage commission for all three categories.
   b. How many times larger is the percentage commission of the full-service broker compared with the online broker? Round to two places to the right of the decimal point for this answer.

Computing tax obligations

8. Compute the tax obligation for the following using Table 3–1 on page 55.
   a. An individual with taxable income of $59,000.
   b. A married couple with taxable income of $130,000.
   c. What is the average tax rate in part *b*?

Capital gains tax

9. Gill Thomas is in the 35 percent tax bracket. Her long-term capital gains tax rate is 15 percent. She makes $16,200 on a stock trade. Compute her tax obligation based on the following holding periods:
   a. 6 months.
   b. 14 months.

Selling short and capital gains

10. Al Rodriguez sells 500 shares of Gold Mine Corp. short at $80 per share. The margin requirement is 50 percent. The stock falls to $62 over a three-month time period, and he closes out his position.

a. How much is his initial margin?

b. What is his percentage gain or loss on his initial margin?

c. If he is in a 35 percent tax bracket for short-term capital gains and a 15 percent bracket for long-term capital gains, what is his tax obligation?

d. If the stock went up to $94 instead of down to $62, what would be his dollar loss?

e. Assuming this is his only transaction for the year, how large a tax deduction could he take against other income?

Price-weighted average

11. There are three stocks in a price-weighted index:

A	$100
B	20
C	60

a. What is the average value for the index?

b. Assume stock A goes down by 25 percent and stock B goes up by 25 percent, and stock C remains the same. What is the new average value for the index?

c. Explain why in part *b* the average changed with two stocks moving up and down by the same percentage amount.

Computing an index

12. Assume the following five companies are used in computing an index:

Company	Shares Outstanding	Base Period January 1, 1984 Market Price	Current Period December 31, 2007 Market Price
A	6,000	$ 6	$12
B	2,000	5	18
C	10,000	8	40
D	1,000	20	10
E	4,000	15	32

a. If the index is price weighted, what will be the value of the index on December 31, 2007? (Take the average price on December 31, 2007, and divide by the average price on January 1, 1984, and multiply by 100.)

b. If the index is value weighted, what will be the value of the index on December 31, 2007? (Take the total market value on December 31, 2007, and divide by the total market value on January 1, 1984, and multiply by 100.)

c. Explain why the answer in part *b* is different from the answer in part *a.*

Changing index values in a value-weighted index

13. Assume the following stocks make up a *value-weighted* index:

Corporation	Shares Outstanding	Market Price
Reese	4,000	$35
Robinson	16,000	4
Snider	6,000	10
Hodges	40,000	20

www.mhhe.com/hirtblock10e

a. Compute the total market value and the weights assigned to each stock. Round to two places to the right of the decimal point. (The weights may add up to slightly more than 100 percent due to rounding.)

b. Assume the price of the shares of the Snider Corporation goes up by 50 percent, while that of the Hodges Corporation goes down by a mere 10 percent. The other two stocks remain constant. What will be the newly established value for the index?

c. Explain why the index followed the pattern it did in part *b.*

Changing index values in a value-weighted index

14. In problem 13, if the initial price of the shares of the Snider Corporation doubles while that of the Hodges Corporation goes down by 7.5 percent, would the value of the index change? The other two stocks remain constant. Do the necessary computations.

CRITICAL THOUGHT CASE–FOCUS ON ETHICS

Elaine and Izzy Polanski have been happily married for the last 10 years. Elaine is a systems engineer for a major West Coast aerospace company, and Izzy is a pilot for a commuter airline flying out of Los Angeles International Airport. Together they anticipate a taxable income of $116,000.

Both Elaine and Izzy are concerned about their potential large tax obligation of $25,500. As the end of the year approached, they began to think of ways to reduce their anticipated taxable income. Izzy suggested they evaluate their stock portfolio to see if they might sell off a stock or two to create a deduction against taxable income. They have six stocks in their portfolio, and only one was trading at a loss from its original purchase price. They hold 500 shares of Atlantic Cellular Company, and the stock has fallen from $58 to $38 a share due to poor third-quarter earnings.

Before they make a decision to sell, Izzy and Elaine complete an intensive investigation of the company and find that the company still fundamentally sound. It is their view that investors overreacted to the poor third-quarter earnings announcement and that prospects for the fourth quarter look considerably better. Furthermore, they think that Atlantic Cellular Company has an excellent chance of winning a major contract with the U.S. Treasury Department on the installation and use of sophisticated telephone communication equipment. The other bidder on the contract is Atlas Corp., a firm in which Izzy and Elaine currently hold 1,000 shares. Since they purchased the stock of Atlas Corp. it has gone from $10 to $25.

To get a better feel for how the competition on the contract might turn out, Izzy tells Elaine he might give Gordon Lewis a call. Lewis is currently the vice president of Corporate Development at Atlantic Cellular Company and was Izzy's roommate in college. Elaine isn't sure this is such a good idea. Izzy counters with the argument that it is always best to be as fully informed as possible before making a decision and that Elaine, as a systems engineer, should know this better than anyone.

Questions

1. Do you think Izzy Polanski should call Gordon Lewis, his old college roommate, to get information on the contract bid?
2. Regardless of your answer to question 1, do you think the Polanskis should sell their stock in Atlantic Cellular Company? If they do sell the stock, what's the maximum deduction they can take from their taxable income this year?
3. What strategy do you recommend with their holdings in Atlas Corp.?

INVESTMENT ADVISOR PROBLEM

Carol Travis had recently shorted 400 shares of Pfizer, Inc., at $25 because of new federal regulations on Medicare. She put up half the value of the purchase, or $5,000, as margin.

Pfizer stock price	$ 25
Shares purchased	400
Total purchase	$10,000
Margin percentage (50%)	5,000

When the stock initially fell to $23.50 on a Friday, she was really excited. Based on the 400 shares she sold short, she had a $600 profit. However, over the weekend she searched PFE (Pfizer) on Yahoo Finance, **http://yahoo.finance.com**, and was surprised to read a story about Pfizer's new drug for osteoarthritis receiving FDA approval.

Since she saw the news before the market opened on Monday morning, she called her investment advisor, Kyle Turner. She told Kyle she wanted to immediately close out her short sale position at the quoted price of $23.50 that she had seen when the the market closed on the previous Friday.

Her investment advisor told her that would not be possible. Because of the positive news over the weekend, the stock was likely to open at a higher value. Carol became greatly concerned and anxiously awaited seeing the Monday morning opening price for Pfizer. She went into a mild panic attack when she saw there was a delayed opening on the stock. Her investment advisor explained there was an overload of buy orders that could not be matched with sell orders by specialists in the stock.

The stock finally opened at 10:30 EST at $26.53.

a. Based on the new stock price, how much is Carol's current margin position?

b. What is her percentage loss on her initial margin of $5,000?

c. If her investment advisor told her there was a 60 percent chance Pfizer, Inc., would go from its current price to $28 and a 40 percent chance it would ultimately fall to $21, should Carol maintain or close out her short sale position?

WEB EXERCISE

In this exercise, we get a better feel for the major market indexes. Go to **www.bloomberg.com**.

1. Click on "Market Data" across the top.
2. Click on "Stocks" along the right margin.
3. Then click on "Movers by Index" along the right margin. Scroll down and record the current price for 3M, Hewlett- Packard, and Procter and Gamble.
4. Which of the 30 Dow stocks had the largest percentage upside movement? Which had the largest percentage downside movement?
5. If you were using a price-weighted index, which stock would have the greatest impact on the DJIA?
6. Remaining in the "Movers by Index" page, click on Nikkei above the Dow Jones Indus. Avg. Snapshot and indicate which stocks had the highest volume and biggest price change in Nikkei 225 index.

Note: From time to time, companies redesign their Web sites, and occasionally a topic we have listed may have been deleted, updated, or moved into a different location.

www.mhhe.com/hirtblock10e

chapter four

INVESTMENT COMPANIES: MUTUAL FUNDS, EXCHANGE-TRADED FUNDS, CLOSED-END FUNDS, AND UNIT INVESTMENT TRUSTS

OBJECTIVES

1. Understand the concept of a mutual fund versus an exchange-traded fund.
2. Distinguish between closed-end and open-end funds.
3. Explain the difference between load and no-load funds.
4. Compute the net asset value of a fund.
5. Identify the key information sources for mutual funds.
6. Explain how to evaluate the performance of a mutual fund.

OUTLINE

The Securities and Exchange Commission regulates investment companies under the Investment Company Act of 1940, mentioned in Chapter 2. Investment companies include mutual funds, exchange-traded funds, closed-end funds, and unit investment trusts. Mutual funds are by far the largest of the four and have become a very important part of investing. Exchange-traded funds are growing rapidly and are challenging mutual funds as an alternative to investing in a diversified portfolio. Owning investment companies is an excellent way of getting a broad-based

FIGURE 4-1 U.S. Households Owning Mutual Funds, 1980–2009

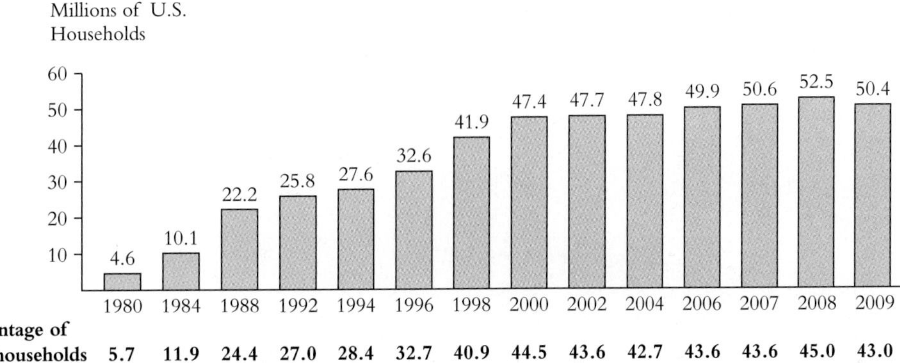

Percentage of U.S. households	5.7	11.9	24.4	27.0	28.4	32.7	40.9	44.5	43.6	42.7	43.6	43.6	45.0	43.0

Sources: *Investment Company Institute and U.S. Census Bureau.* See ICI Fundamentals, *"Ownership of Mutual Funds, Shareholder Sentiment, and Use of the Internet, 2009."*

portfolio of assets that would be virtually impossible for most individual investors. Additionally, as many companies move to defined-contribution retirement plans offering mutual funds for retirement portfolios, more and more workers have to understand how and where to invest their retirement funds.

According to the Investment Company Institute (www.ici.org), at the end of 2009 mutual funds were owned by 87 million people representing 50.4 million U.S. households, or 43 percent of all households. Assets held by investment companies totaled \$12.2 trillion at the end of 2009, broken down as follows: mutual funds (\$11.121 trillion), exchange-traded funds (\$777 billion), closed-end funds (\$228 billion), and unit investment trusts (\$38 billion). Worldwide, investment companies account for \$23 trillion of assets.

Figure 4–1 shows both the number and the percentage of U.S. households owning mutual funds from 1980 to 2009. Because most mutual fund investors are saving for retirement or education, they are long-term investors and are not likely to abandon mutual funds in down markets. Figure 4–1 shows that between 1998 and 2009 the percentage of households owning mutual funds has remained quite stable, fluctuating between 40.9 and 45 percent.

The concept of a mutual fund is best understood by an example. Suppose you and your friends are too busy to develop the expertise needed to manage your own assets. One of your neighbors, however, has had years of hands-on experience as a trustee of his company's pension fund. You and your friends decide to pool your money and have this experienced investor act as your investment advisor. He will be compensated by receiving a small percentage of the average amount of assets under his management during the forthcoming year.

By common agreement, the pooled money is to be invested in the common stock of large, stable companies with the objective of capital appreciation and moderate dividend income; funds not so invested are to be placed in short-term T-bills to earn interest. Group members collectively contribute \$100,000 and decide to issue shares in the fund at a rate of one share for each \$10 contributed—a total of 10,000 shares. Since you put in \$10,000, you receive 1,000 shares of the fund—or 10 percent of the fund's shares. Over the next few weeks, your investment advisor uses \$90,000 to purchase common stock in a number of companies representing several different industries and puts \$10,000 in T-bills. The portfolio is shown in Table 4–1.

Because you own 10 percent of this portfolio, you are entitled to 10 percent of all income paid out to shareholders and 10 percent of all realized capital gains or losses.

TABLE 4-1 **Companies Grouped by Different Industries to Get Some Diversification:**

Industries	Companies
Automobiles	Ford
Banking	Citigroup
Chemicals	Du Pont
Computers	Hewlett Packard
Financial services	Morgan Stanley Smith Barney
Oil	ExxonMobil
Pharmaceuticals	Eli Lilly
Semiconductors	Texas Instruments
Telecommunications	AT&T
Treasury bills: $10,000	

The initial value of the portfolio is $100,000, or $10 per share. Assume your investment manager picked some winning stocks, and the portfolio rises to $115,000. Now each share is worth $11.50.

Your group of investors has many characteristics of a mutual fund: ownership interest represented by shares, professional management, stated investment objectives, and a diversified portfolio of assets. A multibillion dollar mutual fund would operate with many of the same concepts and principles—only the magnitude of the operation would be thousands of times larger.

ADVANTAGES AND DISADVANTAGES OF MUTUAL FUNDS

Diversification The traditional way to think about diversification is to make sure you have securities from different industries in your portfolio. You want to invest in a variety of industries so that the economy does not affect all the companies equally. To help you achieve this diversification we have structured a portfolio as indicated in Table 4–1. Another way of diversifying a portfolio is to include different kinds of assets such as bonds, preferred stock, convertible securities, international securities, and real estate. Generally these asset classes are not highly correlated. The highest correlation would be +1.00, which would mean that the returns of two assets would go up and down together +100 percent of the time. If the correlation is −1.00, the returns on two assets would do the opposite; if one went up 10 percent the other would go down 10 percent.

It is extremely difficult to find assets that are negatively correlated, but it is easy to find assets that have a correlation of less than +1.00. When we combine assets together with correlations of less than +1.00, we help diversify a portfolio and reduce our risk. Mutual funds offer an efficient way to diversify your investments. For many small investors, diversification may be difficult to achieve. To have a properly diversified portfolio, it is suggested that the portfolio contain at least 20 stocks, and that also assumes the investor employs some risk-reduction optimization techniques. With the normal trading unit for listed stocks being 100 shares (called a round lot), accumulating a portfolio of 20 stocks could take $40,000 if we assume the average price per share was $20.

Investors can buy different types of mutual funds to achieve diversification. For example, they can buy a corporate or U.S. government bond fund, a domestic equity fund, an international equity fund, a real estate investment trust, a municipal bond fund, or a short-term money market fund, all of which have a correlation of less than +1.00 with each other. As we move into the next chapter, you will realize that international investing is a good way to diversify a portion of your portfolio.

Professional Management With a mutual fund you are also buying the expertise of the fund manager. In many cases, fund managers have a long history of investment experience and may be specialists in certain areas such as international securities, gold stocks, or municipal bonds. By entrusting your funds to a professional investor, you should get a diversified portfolio that meets your investment objectives. However, a careful investor should not assume that all professional investment managers generate above-average returns. You should select a manager with great care and study. Look at long-term returns of the fund for 3- to 5- and 10-year time periods. Don't be swayed by last year's results. Look at the longevity of the manager so that you know whether the performance numbers were generated by this investment manager or someone else. Research your choice thoroughly before choosing a manager. Our advice would be to use no-load (no commission) funds, with an eye on the aforementioned caveats, plus an eye for low expenses.

Time Savings For many people, managing money is a chore and can be very time consuming. By letting a professional manage their money they free time for leisure or more work. For example, if a lawyer or doctor was capable of making $200 or $300 per hour, why would she spend four hours per week managing a portfolio when she could make an extra $800 or $1,200 per week working. Over the course of a year she could work an additional 200 hours making an extra $40,000 to $60,000. However, you have to consider whether this doctor or lawyer could actually outperform a professional manager. On a million dollar portfolio, she would have to outperform the market by 4 to 6 percent just to recover the lost revenue she could have generated by working instead of managing her money. In most cases, the law of competitive advantage is true. Make your money doing what you do best. For many, golf, travel, fishing, sporting events, and myriad other leisure activities beat managing their money. However, it should be pointed out that for some professionals, managing their own money may be a form of leisurely escape.

Performance Having stated some of the advantages of mutual funds, let's look at the drawbacks. First, mutual funds, on average, do not outperform the market. That is to say that over long periods they do no better than the Standard & Poor's 500 Stock Index, the Dow Jones Industrial Average, and other benchmark indexes to which they are compared. Nevertheless, mutual funds do provide an efficient means for diversifying a portfolio. Also, only a minority of funds have had exceptional returns over time. This is why we suggest careful research before committing your money to a fund manager.

In regard to performance results, a mutual fund investor must also be sensitive to the excessive claims sometimes made by mutual fund salespeople. Often potential returns to the investor are emphasized without detailing the offsetting risk. The fact that a fund made 20 to 25 percent last year in no way ensures such a return in the future. In addition, returns have to be compared against proper benchmarks. You can't fairly compare the return on a large capitalization mutual fund against a small capitalization mutual fund because their risk is not the same.

Expenses Mutual funds have several types of expenses. You can incur sales commissions, management fees, and other costs. These fees will be discussed in more depth later in the chapter, but suffice it to say that the investor should be aware of all fees involved in the purchase and management of any mutual fund.

Selection Problems A final potential drawback to mutual funds is actually a reverse view of an advantage. With more than 8,100 mutual funds from which to choose, an investor has as much of a problem in selecting a mutual fund as a stock. For example, there are approximately 3,000 stocks on the New York Stock Exchange, considerably less than the number of mutual funds in existence. Nevertheless, if you sharpen your goals and objectives, you will be able to focus on a handful of funds that truly meet your needs.

Having discussed the general nature of mutual funds and some of their potential advantages and disadvantages, we now examine their actual mechanics. In the remainder of this chapter, we shall discuss closed-end versus open-end funds, load versus no-load funds, fund objectives, considerations in selecting a fund, and measuring the return on a fund. There is also a brief description of unit investment trusts (UITs).

CLOSED-END VERSUS OPEN-END FUNDS

There are basically two types of investment funds, the closed-end fund and the open-end fund. We shall briefly discuss the closed-end fund and then move on to the much more important type of arrangement, the open-end fund.

Actually, these terms refer to the manner in which shares are distributed and redeemed. A **closed-end fund** has a fixed number of shares, and purchasers and sellers of shares must trade with each other. You cannot buy the shares directly from the fund (except at the inception of the fund) because of the limitation on shares outstanding. Furthermore, the fund does not stand ready to buy the shares back from you.

As we shall eventually see, an open-end fund represents exactly the opposite concept. The **open-end fund** stands ready at all times to sell you new shares or buy back your old shares. Having made this distinction, let's stay with the closed-end fund for now. The shares of closed-end funds trade on security exchanges or over-the-counter just as any other stock might; but when you look for their prices in *Barron's,* you will find closed-end funds listed under a separate heading as illustrated in Table 4–2. This makes them more easily identifiable, but you still buy and sell them through a broker and pay a commission.

application example

One of the most important considerations in purchasing a closed-end fund is whether it is trading at a discount or premium from net asset value. First, let's look at the formula for net asset value.

$$\text{Net asset value (NAV)} = \frac{\text{Total market value of securities} - \text{Liabilities}}{\text{Shares outstanding}} \quad \textbf{(4–1)}$$

The **net asset value (NAV)** is equal to the current value of the securities owned by the fund minus any liabilities divided by the number of shares outstanding. For example, assume a fund has securities worth $140 million, liabilities of $5 million, and 10 million shares outstanding. The NAV is $13.50:

$$\text{NAV} = \frac{\$140\text{ million} - \$5\text{ million}}{10\text{ million shares}} = \frac{\$135\text{ million}}{10\text{ million}} = \$13.50$$

The NAV is computed at the end of each day for a fund.

TABLE 4-2 Closed-End Funds

Fund Name (Symbol)	Stock Exch	NAV	Market Price	Prem /Disc	52 Week Market Return
Friday, June 4, 2010					
General Equity Funds					
Adams Express (ADX)	♣N	11.17	9.44	– 15.5	14.4
AdvntClymrEnhG&I (LCM)	♣N	11.25	10.62	– 5.6	29.2
BlackRock Div Achvrs (BDV)	♣N	9.15	8.54	– 6.7	22.5
BlckRk Str Div Achvr (BDT)	♣N	10.35	9.03	– 12.8	26.6
Blue Chip Value Fd (BLU)	N	3.44	2.93	– 14.8	14.9
Boulder Growth & Income (BIF)	N	6.57	5.39	– 18.0	15.4
Boulder Tot Rtn (BTF)	N	15.55	12.86	– 17.3	31.7
Central Secs (CET)	A	22.93	18.90	– 17.6	24.9
DrmnClayDivInco (DCS)	♣N	14.76	12.47	– 15.5	23.9
CohenStrsCEOppFd (FOF)	N	12.57	11.58	– 7.9	24.0
CohenStrsDivMaj (DVM)	N	12.18	10.23	– 16.0	20.6
CornerstoneProgreRet (CFP)	A	5.33	6.50	+ 22.0	– 16.2
Cornerstone Str Val (CLM)	A	7.20	10.43	+ 44.9	31.4
Cornerstone Total Return (CRF)	♣A	6.31	9.58	+ 51.8	28.5
DenaliFund (DNY)	N	16.06	13.45	– 16.3	30.8
DWSDremanValueIncomeEdge (DHG)	♣N	14.03	12.19	– 13.1	51.2
Eagle Capital Growth (GRF)-c	A	7.27	6.09	– 16.2	25.3
EVTxAdvDivIncm (EVT)	♣N	15.18	14.03	– 7.6	24.0
Engex (EGX)	A	3.26	5.50	+ 68.7	203.8
Equus II (EQS)	♣N		2.68	NA	– 2.1
Foxby Corp (FXBY)	O	1.52	1.05	– 30.9	19.3
GabelliDiv&IncTr (GDV)	N	14.24	12.32	– 13.5	22.7
Gabelli Equity Tr (GAB)	N	4.78	4.62	– 3.3	5.3
General American (GAM)	N	25.70	22.30	– 13.2	17.2
JHancockTaxAdvDiv (HTD)	♣N	13.95	12.30	– 11.8	40.8
Librty AllStr Eq (USA)	N	4.82	4.15	– 13.9	23.6
Librty AllStr Gr (ASG)	N	3.86	3.51	– 9.1	35.3
NuvTaxAdvTRStrat (JTA)	N	10.79	10.14	– 6.0	33.8
OldMut/ClayLS (OLA)	♣N	8.82	8.24	– 6.6	16.7
RENN Glbl Entrepreneurs (RCG)	A	3.22	2.53	– 21.4	– 1.9
Royce Focus Trust (FUND)-a	♣O	6.80	5.99	– 11.9	13.3
Royce Micro-Cap Tr (RMT)-a	♣N	9.00	7.59	– 15.7	27.2
Royce Value Trust (RVT)-a	♣N	12.93	10.86	– 16.0	28.1
Source Capital (SOR)	N	48.21	43.20	– 10.4	29.7
SunAmericaFocAlphaGr (FGF)	N	14.82	13.88	– 6.3	36.0
SunAmericaFocAlphaLC (FGI)	N	13.71	13.03	– 5.0	26.3
Tri-Continental (TY)	♣N	13.42	11.34	– 15.5	21.6
Zweig (ZF)	♣N	3.36	3.05	– 9.2	17.3

Source: *Barron's,* Market Week, June 7, 2010, p. MW40. Reprinted with permission of *Barron's,*

Intuitively, one would expect a closed-end fund to sell at its net asset value, but that is not the case. Many funds trade at a discount from NAV because they have a poor record of prior performance, are heavily invested in an unpopular industry, or are thinly traded (illiquid). A few trade at a premium because of the known quality of their management, the nature of their investments, or the fact they have holdings in nonpublicly traded securities that are believed to be undervalued on their books. Note in Table 4–2 (second column from the right), the predominance of common stock funds trading at discounts from NAV in June 2010. The graph presented in Figure 4–2 on the bottom of page 82, tracks closed-end funds and indicates that, on average, closed-end funds sell at a discount of 8 to 11 percent. This has normally been the case over the last decade. Some researchers even use the fact that closed-end funds do not sell for what they are worth (in terms of their holdings) as evidence that the market is something less than truly efficient in valuing securities.

EXCHANGE-TRADED FUNDS

Exchange-traded funds (ETFs) began trading in 1993 and in recent years have increased their penetration into the investment company arena. Technically, an ETF is either a mutual fund or a unit investment trust. Most ETFs are designed to imitate the performance of a specific index, such as the Standard & Poor's 500 Index. Originally the Securities and Exchange Commission only allowed ETFs to track index funds, but in 2008 they allowed actively managed exchange-traded

the real world of investing

SOCIALLY RESPONSIBLE INVESTING AND RELIGION

Mutual funds have been known for their ability to create funds to match any index and investor objective. To this end fund managers have created sector funds, index funds, and a slew of other funds, including social investing funds. Socially responsible funds might avoid investing in companies that sell alcohol, tobacco, or gambling, or companies that are thought to be socially irresponsible. In today's environment, British Petroleum might fit into that category. But funds that combine religion and investing have added a new wrinkle to the fund category of socially responsible investing. There are over 90 funds available that cover a spectrum of religions and many different denominations. For example, Catholic funds tend to avoid companies that support abortion or contraception. One fund blocks investments in companies that are known to support gay rights. Some funds will not invest in entertainment companies that are not thought to be family oriented, and others will not invest in companies that advertise on TV programs that are violent or considered anti-family.

According to Daren Fonda, religious funds controlled $27 billion in assets at the end of 2009, almost three times more than in 1990.* Some suggest that religious individuals want professional advice from someone they trust to be socially responsible in making investment decisions. From the experience of one author, his church endowment board invested a portion of their endowment funds in socially responsible mutual funds to satisfy a segment of the congregation. In general, social investing funds are small funds and have higher expenses than large families of funds like Vanguard or Fidelity, and some are load funds. They generally don't outperform the S&P 500 Index, but they satisfy the needs of their investors, who are not necessarily looking for the highest return but perhaps a clean conscience. The seven funds listed below were highlighted in the January 2010 *SmartMoney* article by Daren Fonda. The list shows the religious group the fund focuses on as well as the ticker symbol (for publicly traded funds). Faith Shares has five exchange-traded funds one for Baptists (FZB), Catholics (FCV), Christians (FOC), Lutherans (FKL), and Methodists (FMV):

Mennonite Mutual Aid—Mennonites
GuideStone Funds—Southern Baptists and Evangelicals
Timothy Plan Large/Mid Cap Value (TLVCX)—Evangelicals
Foxhall Fund (DOIGX)—Christian
Amana Income Fund (AMANX)—Islamic Principles
LKCM Aquinas Growth (AQEGX)—Catholics
AMIDEX35 Israel Mutual Fund (AMDEX)—Jews

* Fonda, Daren, *SmartMoney*, January 2010, pp. 62–67.

FIGURE 4-2 Tracking Closed-End Funds

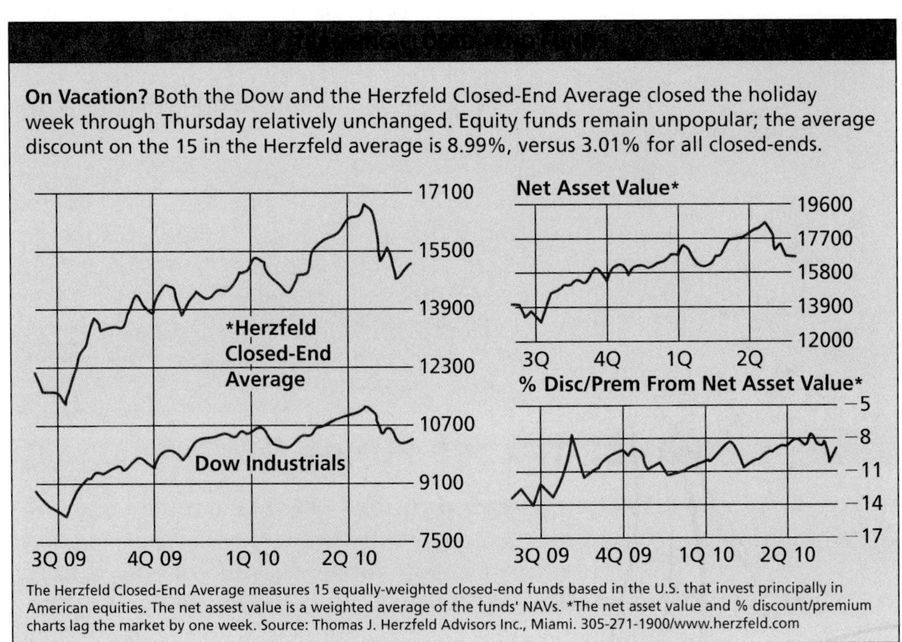

FIGURE 4-3 **Total Net Assets and Number of ETFs***
(billions of dollars, year-end, 1998–2009)

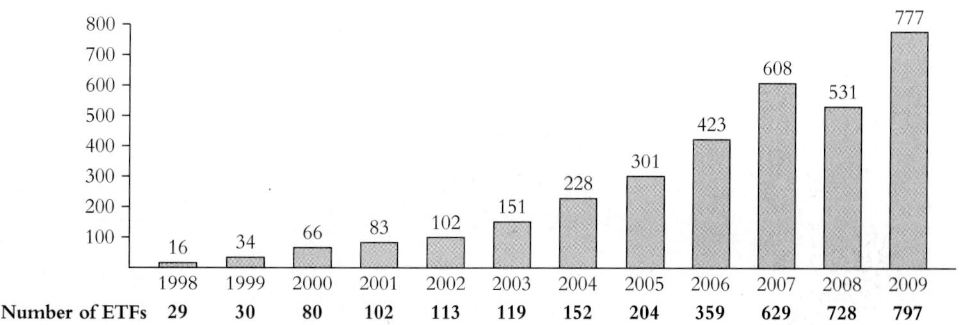

*ETF data prior to 2001 were provided by Strategic Insight Simfund; ETF data include ETFs not registered under the Investment Company Act of 1940; ETF data exclude ETFs that invest primarily in other ETFs.

Sources: Investment Company Institute and Strategic Insight Simfund. 2010 Investment Company Fact Book, p. 41. Copyright © 2010, Investment Company Institute, Washington D.C. Used with permission.

funds to operate as long as they made their portfolio transparent and available on their publicly accessible Web site.

Most funds are registered with the SEC under the Investment Company Act of 1940. The Commodity Futures Trading Commission regulates funds that invest in commodity futures contracts, whereas the SEC under the Act of 1933 regulates funds that invest in physical commodities. ETFs in the commodities category started in 2004 and already accounted for $74 billion in invested funds by year-end 2009. Figure 4–3 shows the growth in exchange-traded funds since 1998. Assets managed by ETFs grew from $16 billion in 1998 to $777 billion in 2009, and the number of funds mushroomed from 29 to 797 in this 12-year period. Of the $777 billion, $304 billion are invested in sector funds. ETF bond funds are very popular because investors have a hard time buying individual bonds. Bond exchange-traded funds have been a real growth area, having grown from $4 billion in 2002 to $107 billion at the end of 2009. Ninety percent of the assets in ETFs are index funds.

In Chapter 3 we discussed indexes such as the Dow Jones Industrial Average; the Standard & Poor's 400, 500, and 600; the Russell 3000, 2000, and 1000; and others. Some of the leading companies that manage exchange-traded funds are BlackRock (iShares), Inveseco (PowerShares), Proshares, State Street Global Advisors (SPDRs), and Vanguard. Actually, Barclays created the iShares, but BlackRock bought them. If you glance at Table 4–3, you will notice that in the left-hand column and top of the right-hand column, iShares has a long list of index funds, including the Russell funds, global market funds, and S&P funds. After some of the Russell and S&P funds you will see a V or a G for value or growth, as the index is divided into two categories. ProShares are noted for their short funds and leveraged funds. The "Ultra" in front of the fund means that the fund has leveraged the returns by two times the index. Direxion funds are not listed, but they also are leveraged, and some provide three times the return on the index. Both ProShares and Direxion have bull and bear funds for many different indexes. Vanguard, with a reputation as the leading low-cost mutual fund company, has also moved into the exchange-traded funds business. Table 4–3 includes the year-to-date return for each fund; this can be compared to the Lipper Indexes listed in the lower left-hand corner of the table.

One advantage of ETFs is that the assets in the portfolios are marked to market continuously, and you can trade them all day long at a price that is

TABLE 4-3 Exchange-Traded Funds

EXCHANGE-TRADED PORTFOLIOS

Largest 100 exchange-traded funds, latest session

Monday, June 14, 2010

ETF	SYMBOL	CLOSING PRICE	CHG (%)	YTD (%)
RegBkHldrs	RKH	77.09	**-1.55**	0.7
RetailHldrs	RTH	95.16	**0.44**	1.4
OilSvcHldrs	OIH	97.35	**-1.31**	-18.1
PharmaHldrs	PPH	60.31	**-0.08**	-8.6
BiotchHldrs	BBH	88.57	**0.34**	-9.2
SemiConHldrs	SMH	27.20	**0.44**	-2.6
iPathUBS Commd	DJP	38.17	**1.22**	-9.7
iShrBrclAggBd	AGG	105.81	**0.14**	2.5
iShrBrclIntCrBd	CIU	103.82	**0.06**	1.1
iShrBrclMBS BF	MBB	108.89	**0.06**	2.7
iShrBrcl1-3CrBd	CSJ	103.47	**-0.04**	-0.5
iShrBrclShrtTreas	SHV	110.22	**-0.01**	0.0
iShrTIPSBdFd	TIP	105.73	...	1.8
iShrComexGld	IAU	119.70	**-0.35**	11.5
iShrDJSelDiv	DVY	44.60	**0.22**	1.6
iShrDJUSRE	IYR	51.17	**1.19**	11.4
iShriBoxxFd	LQD	105.83	**-0.19**	1.6
iShr iBxxHYCorp	HYG	84.37	**0.13**	-4.0
iShrMSAusy	EWA	20.78	**0.73**	-9.0
iShrMSCI Bra	EWZ	64.97	**-1.04**	-12.9
iShrMSCI Can	EWC	26.66	**0.26**	1.3
iShrMSEAFE	EFA	49.22	**0.63**	-11.0
iShrMSCIEmrgMkt	EEM	38.77	**0.03**	-6.6
iShrMSCI HK	EWH	15.10	**0.07**	-3.6
iShrMSCI Jpn	EWJ	9.48	**0.64**	-2.7
iShrMSCI Pac	EPP	38.24	**0.26**	-7.6
iShrMSCI SK	EWY	45.93	**1.82**	-3.6
iShrMSCI Taiwn	EWT	11.39	**0.18**	-12.2
iShrRu1000G	IWF	48.71	**0.02**	-2.3
iShrRu1000	IWB	60.62	**-0.03**	-1.1
iShrRu1000V	IWD	57.39	**-0.30**	-0.0
iShrRu2000G	IWO	70.80	**0.48**	4.0
iShrRu2000	IWM	65.35	**0.63**	4.7
iShrRu2000V	IWN	61.27	**0.61**	5.6
iShrRu3000	IWV	64.78	...	-0.8
iShrRuMid	IWR	86.29	**0.38**	4.6
iShrRuMidVlu	IWS	39.07	**0.44**	5.7
iShrSP100	OEF	49.46	**-0.30**	-3.9
iShrSP400G	IJK	82.38	**0.46**	6.0
iShrSP500G	IVW	56.18	**-0.11**	-3.1
iShrSP500	IVV	109.88	**-0.10**	-1.7
iShrSP500V	IVE	52.80	**-0.13**	-0.4
iShrSP600	IJR	57.68	**0.54**	5.4
iShrsSP GSCI Cmdty	GSG	28.18	**1.18**	-11.4
iShrSP400	IJH	76.22	**0.43**	5.3
iShrTr40	ILF	44.18	**-0.83**	-7.6
iShrSP400V	IJJ	68.86	**0.46**	4.4
iShrSPUSPref	PFF	36.98	**0.08**	0.8
iShrSP NANatRes	IGE	33.31	**-0.51**	-2.9
iShsSPNtlAMTMunFd	MUB	103.80	**-0.15**	1.0
iShrSilverTr	SLV	17.86	**0.06**	8.0
iShrBrcl1-3	SHY	83.85	**0.02**	1.1
iShrBrcl7-10	IEF	93.32	**-0.09**	5.3
iShrBrcl20+	TLT	96.91	**-0.51**	7.8
iShrCohenSter	ICF	59.98	**1.10**	14.2
iShrChina25	FXI	40.11	**-0.40**	-5.1
iShrRuMidGrth	IWP	46.88	**0.28**	3.4
MktVecAgBusETF	MOO	38.23	**-0.65**	-12.7
MktVecGold	GDX	49.90	**-1.75**	8.0
MktVecRussia	RSX	29.33	...	-6.0
PwrShrDB CmFd	DBC	22.01	**0.27**	-10.6
PwrShrDB Agrcltr	DBA	23.79	**1.02**	-10.0
PwrShr DBGoldDblLng	DGP	32.58	**-0.64**	23.2
PwrShr DBGoldDblShrt	DZZ	11.08	**0.73**	-21.0
PwrShrDB DlrBull	UUP	25.23	**-0.90**	9.3
PwrShrs QQQ	QQQQ	45.49	**-0.02**	-0.6
♣ProShrShrtS&P	SH	52.11	**0.15**	-0.9
♣ProShrUltraFnl	UYG	55.40	**-0.68**	-1.6
♣ProShrUltra20	TBT	39.26	**0.85**	-21.3
♣ProShrsUShrt S&P	SDS	33.95	**0.29**	-3.1
RydexSPEqulWt	RSP	40.53	**0.01**	2.5
ConStplSel SPDR	XLP	26.62	**0.57**	0.6
HlthcarSel SPDR	XLV	29.21	**0.17**	-6.0
InduSelSctr SPDR	XLI	29.14	**-0.10**	4.9
MatrlsSel SPDR	XLB	30.37	**-0.98**	-7.9
TechSelSctr SPDR	XLK	21.70	**-0.18**	-5.4
UtilsSelSctr SPDR	XLU	29.39	**0.58**	-5.3
SPDR BarcHyld	JNK	37.65	**0.72**	-3.0
SPDR DJIA Tr	DIA	102.14	**-0.17**	-1.9
SPDR EngySelSct	XLE	54.04	**-0.52**	-5.2
SPDR FnclSelSct	XLF	14.45	**-0.41**	0.3
SPDR GldTr	GLD	119.60	**-0.34**	11.5
SPDR S&PMdCpTr	MDY	138.58	**0.60**	5.2
SPDR S&P 500	SPY	109.51	**-0.16**	-1.7
US NatGas	UNG	8.55	**4.65**	-15.2
US OilFd	USO	34.33	**0.29**	-12.6
VangdDivApp	VIG	46.40	**0.15**	-1.0
VangdEmrgMkt	VWO	38.84	**-0.08**	-5.3
VangdEurPacfc	VEA	30.36	**0.56**	-11.2
VangdEuro	VGK	42.04	**1.01**	-13.3
VangdAllWldxUS	VEU	39.70	**0.43**	-9.0
VangdGrowth	VUG	51.89	...	-2.2
VangdLgCap	VV	49.91	**-0.11**	-1.5
VangdMdCap	VO	62.86	**0.27**	4.9
VangdReit	VNQ	50.62	**1.24**	13.1
VangdShrtTrm	BSV	80.46	**0.01**	1.2
VangdSmCap	VB	60.62	**0.61**	5.7
VangdTtlBndMkt	BND	80.38	**0.02**	2.3
VangdTtlStock	VTI	56.00	**0.02**	-0.7
VangdValue	VTV	47.42	**-0.13**	-0.7

Lipper Indexes

Stock-Fund Indexes	PRELIM CLOSE	PERCENT CHANGE FROM PREV CLOSE	WK AGO	DEC. 31
Large-Cap Growth	3259.36	-0.17	+3.52	-3.10
Large-Cap Core	2375.58	-0.09	+3.79	-2.46
Large-Cap Value	10468.66	-0.19	+4.01	-1.87
Multi-Cap Growth	3053.76	+0.03	+4.16	-0.15
Multi-Cap Core	8113.39	+0.37	+4.38	-0.45
Multi-Cap Value	4465.00	+0.07	+4.40	-0.41
Mid-Cap Growth	862.21	+0.38	+5.62	+3.30
Mid-Cap Core	841.16	+0.26	+5.33	+3.37
Mid-Cap Value	1264.76	+0.15	+5.11	+3.50
Small-Cap Growth	600.37	+0.44	+5.15	+2.95
Small-Cap Core	499.35	+1.07	+5.77	+4.65
Small-Cap Value	812.50	+0.24	+4.82	+5.19
Equity Income Fd	4656.46	-0.17	+3.85	-1.54
Science and Tech Fd	749.83	-0.05	+3.37	-2.24
International Fund	1053.77	+1.19	+5.57	-7.72
Balanced Fund	6090.99		+2.38	-0.03
Bond-Fund Indexes				
Short Inv Grade	308.20	+0.09	-0.06	+2.32
Intmdt Inv Grade	401.44	-0.09	-0.38	+4.52
US Government	528.51	-0.49	-0.70	+4.53
GNMA	604.73	-0.08	-0.05	+4.58
Corp A-Rated Debt	1413.36	-0.12	-0.35	+3.98

Indexes are based on the largest funds within the same investment objective and do not include multiple share classes of similar funds.

Source: Lipper Inc.

Source: *The Wall Street Journal,* June 15, 2010, p. C9. Reprinted with permission of *The Wall Street Journal,*

almost exactly the net asset value of the stocks in the index. Mutual funds trade at ending day prices. For example, if you put in an order to buy open-end mutual fund shares at 1 p.m., your order will be filled at the closing NAV at 4 p.m. Eastern Standard Time. If you put in an order after the market closes, it will be filled after the next day's close. Because exchange-traded funds imitate an index, there are no real research costs, and therefore the expense ratios are usually lower than for mutual funds. One reason many investment companies have created so many indexes is that they can become profitable. One extra expense that exchange-traded funds have is a fee paid to the creator of the fund they imitate. For example, every ETF that uses a Standard & Poor's index pays S&P a fee for managing the construction of the index. All the ETF needs is to have a computer program that replicates the index, but Standard & Poor's continuously remodels the index for mergers, acquisitions, and market capitalization. Companies can move into and out of an index.

INVESTING IN OPEN-END FUNDS

As previously indicated, an open-end fund stands ready at all times to sell new shares or buy back old shares from investors at net asset value. More than 95 percent of the investment funds in the United States are open-ended. Actually, the term *mutual fund* applies specifically to *open-end* investment companies, although closed-end funds are sometimes loosely labeled as mutual funds as well. We shall be careful to make the distinction where appropriate.

Transactions with open-end funds are made at the net asset value as previously described in Formula 4–1 on page 80 (though there may be an added commission). If the fund has 100 million shares outstanding at an NAV of $10 per share ($1 billion) and sells 20 million more shares at $10 per share, the new funds ($200 million) are redeployed in investments worth $200 million, and the NAV remains unchanged. The only factor that changes the NAV is the up and down movement of the securities in the fund's portfolio. The primary distinctions between closed-end and open-end funds are presented in Table 4–4. All of our subsequent discussion will be about open-end (mutual) funds. These include such established names as Fidelity, Dreyfus, Vanguard, T. Rowe Price, and Templeton.

Load versus No-Load Funds

Some funds have established selling agreements with stockbrokers, financial planners, insurance agents, and others licensed to sell securities. These selling agents receive a commission for selling the funds. The funds are termed **load funds** because there is a commission associated with the purchase of the fund shares. The commission may run to 5.5 percent or higher.

Several stock funds are referred to as **low-load funds** because their sales charges are 2 to 3 percent instead of 5.5 percent. A number of funds also have a back-end load provision. While there may or may not be a front-end load in buying such a fund, there is an exit fee in selling a fund with a **back-end load** provision. The fee may be 2 to 3 percent of the selling price but typically declines with the passage of time.

TABLE 4-4 Distinction between Closed-End and Open-End Funds

	Method of Purchase	Number of Shares Outstanding	Shares Traded at Net Asset Value
Closed-End fund	Stock exchange or over-the-counter	Fixed	No—there may be a discount or premium from NAV; there will be a commission.
Open-End Fund			
Load fund	Usually through a full-line retail brokerage firm	Fluctuates	Yes—but there may be a high commission to buy the shares.
No-load fund	Direct from fund or through a discount or online broker	Fluctuates	Yes—no commission if bought direct from fund.

No-Load Funds

No-load funds do not charge commissions and are sold directly by the investment company through advertisements, prospectuses, and 800-number telephone orders.[1] Some wonder how no-load funds justify their existence since they charge no front-end commission to purchase their shares. The answer is because of the fee they charge to manage the assets in the fund. This management fee plus expenses normally average 0.75 to 1.50 percent. On a billion dollar fund, this represents approximately $10 million a year and can be more than adequate to compensate the fund managers. It should also be pointed out that load funds also have similar management fees.

The question then becomes, why pay the load (commission)? Studies indicate there is no significant statistical difference in the investment performance of load and no-load funds. Consequently, most astute investors shop around for a no-load fund to fit their needs rather than pay a commission. This statement is not intended to dismiss the possibility that apprehensive or uncomfortable investors may benefit from the consultation and advice of a competent mutual fund salesman or financial advisor, and thus receive a commensurate service from paying the commission. Also, some specialized funds may exist only in the form of load funds. However, whenever possible, investors are better off using the commission toward the purchase of new shares rather than the payment of a sales fee.

application example

If you invest $1,000 in a load mutual fund and pay a 5.00 percent commission, only 95 percent will go toward purchasing your shares. A $1,000 investment will immediately translate into a holding of $950.00. This means the fund must go up by $50.00 or 5.26 percent, just for you to break even:

$$\frac{\$50.00}{\$950.00} = 5.26\%$$

It used to be simple to figure out which funds charged a load and which ones were no-load funds. You could look in *The Wall Street Journal* or *Barron's* to find both the price and the NAV. If the price and the NAV were equal, there was no load (commission) and if the price was higher than the NAV, there was a load and the percentage could be calculated.

Let's assume that the net asset value of the Hirt Block Fund is $13.32 and the offer price is $13.98. This means the fund has a net asset value of $13.32 per share but is offered to the public for $13.98. The difference between $13.32 and $13.98 of $0.66 represents the commission:

$13.98	Offer price
13.32	NAV (net asset value)
$ 0.66	Commission

In this case, the commission represents 4.72 percent of the offer price ($0.66/$13.98 = 4.72%). You will buy a fund valued at $13.32 for $13.98 because of the sales charge.

The Wall Street Journal, Business Investors Daily, and many major city newspapers include mutual fund tables in their financial sections. However, with the ease of quotes on the Internet, the print media have cut back the depth of data provided. *Barron's,* a weekly publication of Dow Jones, has the most complete mutual fund section. Table 4–5 shows the NAV (net asset value), the weekly change in price, the YTD (year-to-date return) and the 3-year return. However, there is no indication as to whether the fund is a load or no-load fund.

[1] Some of these funds may have a small back-end load that declines to zero with the passage of time.

TABLE 4-5 Mutual Funds

	NAV	Net Chg	YTD % Ret	3-Yr % Ret
A				
AMF Funds:				
UltShrtMtg	7.36	0.00	2.3	-13.0
AcadnEm	15.54	-0.18	-6.5	-15.8
AdvOneAmerigoN n	11.07	-0.27	-4.3	-21.4
Alger Funds A:				
CapApr	12.10	-0.21	-5.5	-11.4
SpectraN	10.02	-0.18	-4.0	-4.2
Alger Funds I:				
SmCpGr I-2	26.01	-0.79	1.7	-18.7
Alger Funds Inst:				
CapApprI	17.29	-0.30	-5.3	-11.0
MidCpGrI	11.57	-0.41	-3.0	-30.8
SmCapGrI	22.53	-0.69	1.7	-19.0
AllianceBernstein:				
IntDurInstl	15.51	0.06	4.8	21.9
AllianceBernstein A:				
BalanA p	13.20	-0.15	-1.8	-19.0
BalWlthStrA p	10.47	-0.18	-3.3	-16.4
EmgMktDebtA p	8.42	-0.01	3.5	26.4
GlbThemGrA p	59.22	-1.50	-9.2	-13.9
GlobalBondA p	8.19	0.01	4.8	22.1
GrIncA p	2.79	-0.06	-5.1	-33.9
GrowthA p	30.60	-0.48	-3.9	-23.6
IntlGroA p	12.29	-0.28	-12.7	-35.5
IntlValA p	11.29	-0.35	-17.3	-51.2
LgCpGrA p	20.68	-0.43	-8.7	-7.0
MuCA A p	10.73	-0.02	4.1	12.0
MuNY A p	9.89	-0.01	3.4	13.8
NtlMuA p	9.83	-0.01	3.8	11.2
QualBndA p	10.58	0.04	5.1	19.3
SmMidCpValA p	14.52	-0.66	3.9	-15.7
WlthApprStrA t	9.97	-0.29	-7.4	-33.6
AllianceBernstein Adv:				
IntValAdv	11.52	-0.35	-17.2	-50.8
TxMgdWlthAppAdv	10.30	-0.28	-8.7	-33.7
WlthApprStr	9.99	-0.29	-7.2	-33.0
AllianceBernstein B:				
BalWlthStrB t	10.40	-0.18	-3.8	-18.3
AllianceBernstein C:				
BalWlthStrC t	10.42	-0.18	-3.7	-18.2
GlobalBondC t	8.22	0.01	4.5	19.5
AllianceBernstein I:				
GlbREInvII	7.30	-0.29	-6.8	-39.5
IntlVal I	11.36	-0.35	-17.2	-50.6
Allianz Fds Admin:				
NFJSmCpV	23.74	-0.73	2.5	-13.0
Allianz Fds Instl:				
NFJDivVal	9.72	-0.22	-6.0	-35.7
RCMTechI	37.57	-0.48	-1.5	-2.7
SmCpVl	24.88	-0.77	2.6	-12.4
Allianz Funds A:				
GrowthA	24.25	-0.37	-3.9	-15.6
NFJDivVal t	9.64	-0.22	-6.3	-36.4
NFJIntVal	17.01	-0.27	-10.6	-25.3
RenaisA	13.57	-0.32	-2.0	-26.3
SmCpV A	23.76	-0.74	2.5	-13.4
Allianz Funds C:				
NFJDivVal t	9.66	-0.22	-6.6	-37.8
SmCpVC p	22.75	-0.70	2.2	-15.3
Allianz Funds D:				
NFJDivVal tn	9.67	-0.21	-6.2	-36.4
Alpine Funds:				
DynamicDiv nr	4.04	-0.10	-13.3	-46.8
Intl RE n	19.07	-0.68	-16.0	-55.3
TxOptInc n	10.05	0.00	0.5	10.1
AmanaGrowth n	20.87	-0.33	-2.2	-8.1
AmanaIncome n	26.74	-0.54	-6.2	-10.6
Amer Beacon AMR:				
BalAmr n	11.39	-0.16	-0.3	-13.2
IntlAmr n	13.62	-0.38	-14.3	-34.2
LgCapAmr n	16.47	-0.45	-3.3	-29.7
SmCapAmr n	16.18	-0.73	2.8	-20.9
Amer Beacon Instl:				
IntlInst	13.54	-0.38	-14.4	-34.7
LgCapInst	16.66	-0.45	-3.4	-30.2
SmCpInst	16.27	-0.74	2.7	-21.5
Amer Beacon Inv:				
IntlEqInv n	13.36	-0.37	-14.6	-35.2
LgCapInv n	15.83	-0.43	-3.6	-30.9
SmCapInv n	15.90	-0.71	2.6	-22.1
American Century A:				
DivBndA t	10.80	0.04	3.7	25.0
EqIncA p	6.35	-0.11	-2.8	-17.5
HeritageA p	15.67	-0.53	0.5	-13.8
InfAdjBd pn	11.82	0.07	3.1	22.4
SmCpVal pn	7.46	-0.37	2.2	-9.7
StrModA p	5.71	-0.09	-2.4	-10.4
American Century Inv:				
Balanced n	14.01	-0.16	-0.2	-8.3
CaHYMu n	9.43	-0.02	5.1	8.1
CaLgTF n	10.90	-0.02	3.4	11.8
CaTxFBnd n	11.23	-0.01	2.8	14.7
DivBnd n	10.80	0.05	3.9	25.9
EmgMkt nr	6.83	-0.16	-10.4	-25.7
EqGro n	17.85	-0.41	-2.7	-28.0
EqInc n	6.35	-0.11	-2.8	-17.0
Gift n	22.22	-0.52	-3.2	-17.8
GinnieMae n	10.95	0.05	4.4	24.6
GlGold nr	21.79	-0.38	7.6	30.0
GovtBd n	11.26	0.06	4.1	25.5
Grwth n	21.35	-0.36	-3.1	-12.0
Heritage n	16.08	-0.54	0.7	-13.2
IncGro n	20.63	-0.51	-3.1	-32.8
InfAdjBd n	11.87	0.08	3.2	23.5
IntDisc nr	7.96	-0.14	-10.4	-39.0
IntlBnd n	13.08	-0.28	-9.4	9.0
Intl Gr n	8.56	-0.20	-12.5	-32.1
LgComVal n	4.76	-0.13	-5.5	-34.8
LivS2025 n	10.37	-0.15	-1.6	-9.3
American Century Inv:				
MdCapVal n	10.73	-0.27	0.2	-14.2
OneChAgg n	10.25	-0.19	-3.1	-16.0
OneChMod n	10.20	-0.15	-2.2	-9.8
Real n	15.08	-0.96	4.9	-39.2
Select n	31.17	-0.64	-5.8	-16.8
SGov n	9.78	0.01	1.4	14.1
SmCpVal n	7.49	-0.37	2.5	-9.0
StrAgg n	6.43	-0.12	-3.2	-15.5
StrMod n	5.72	-0.09	-2.3	-9.7
TxFr Bond:Inv n	11.08	-0.01	2.8	16.6
Ultra n	18.62	-0.27	-4.4	-15.6
Value n	4.95	-0.12	-3.7	-26.4
Vista n	13.06	-0.45	-3.2	-30.7
American Century Ist:				
DivBnd	10.80	0.05	3.9	26.6
EqInc	6.36	-0.11	-2.6	-16.3
Growth	21.53	-0.37	-3.1	-11.5
InfAdjBd	11.87	0.07	3.2	24.2
NTDvBnd	10.67	0.04	3.9	25.7
SmCapVal	7.52	-0.37	2.5	-8.5
American Funds Cl A:				
2015TarRetA p	8.39	-0.09	-2.9	-13.4
2020TarRetA p	8.14	-0.11	-3.8	-16.9
2025TarRetA p	7.97	-0.13	-4.9	-19.0
AmcpA p	16.03	-0.36	-3.4	-17.6
AMutlA p	22.14	-0.39	-3.8	-21.0
BalA p	15.85	-0.21	-1.7	-11.8
BondA p	12.09	0.04	4.2	6.8
CapIBA p	44.21	-0.62	-6.9	-20.3
CapWA p	19.56	-0.14	-1.6	14.4
CapWGrA	29.68	-0.70	-12.5	-25.2
EupacA p	33.54	-0.71	-12.5	-22.8
FdInvA p	30.65	-0.71	-6.0	-24.0
GovtA p	14.39	0.07	4.2	21.1
GwthA p	25.84	-0.49	-5.5	-22.3
HI TrA p	10.64	-0.04	3.2	7.5
HlnMuniA	13.89	-0.01	4.4	2.9
ICAA p	24.12	-0.50	-6.6	-24.7
IncoA p	14.77	-0.23	-3.6	-18.1
IntBdA p	13.39	0.04	3.0	11.8
IntlGrIncA p	25.98	-0.60	-12.4	NS
LtdTEBdA	15.60	-0.01	2.8	14.0
N PerA p	23.37	-0.40	-8.9	-18.5
NEcoA p	21.00	-0.35	-6.6	-20.1
NwWrldA	44.34	-0.60	-6.1	-11.1
SmCpA p	31.02	-0.66	-1.6	-23.3
STBFA p	10.09	0.02	1.4	9.6
STTxExBdA	10.12	0.00	1.2	NS
TECAA p	16.10	-0.03	4.3	10.0
TxExA p	12.20	-0.01	3.0	11.6
WshA p	23.20	-0.56	-5.3	-28.7
American Funds Cl B:				
AmcpB t	15.32	-0.35	-3.8	-19.5
AMutlB t	21.95	-0.39	-4.1	-22.8
BalB p	15.77	-0.21	-2.1	-13.8
BondB t	12.09	0.04	3.8	4.4
CapIBB t	44.17	-0.62	-7.2	-22.1
CapWGrB t	29.49	-0.69	-12.8	-26.9
EupacB t	33.14	-0.71	-12.8	-24.5
FdInvB t	30.53	-0.70	-6.3	-25.7
GwthB t	24.99	-0.47	-5.7	-24.0
HI TrB t	10.64	-0.04	2.9	5.0
ICAB t	23.99	-0.50	-6.9	-26.4
IncoB t	14.65	-0.23	-3.9	-20.0
N PerB t	22.96	-0.40	-9.2	-20.3
NwWrldB t	43.54	-0.60	-6.4	-13.1
SmCpB t	29.41	-0.63	-1.9	-25.1
WshB t	23.02	-0.56	-5.6	-30.3
Aquila Funds:				
HI TF A	11.41	0.00	1.8	13.5
ArbitrageI n	12.66	-0.01	-1.6	11.3
ArbitrageR pn	12.47	-0.02	-1.7	10.7
Ariel Investments:				
Apprec pn	34.42	-1.54	-2.9	-17.7
Ariel pn	38.56	-1.77	0.0	-27.2
Artio Global Funds:				
GlbHiIncA tn	10.36	-0.03	1.4	17.5
GblHiIncI r	9.97	-0.03	1.5	18.4
IntlEqA n	24.34	-0.42	-11.7	-36.7
IntlEqI r	24.95	-0.43	-11.7	-36.3
IntlEqII A tn	10.23	-0.18	-12.6	-33.2
IntlEqII I r	10.30	-0.18	-12.6	-32.7
TotRetI r	13.66	0.07	3.7	22.8
Artisan Funds:				
Intl n	17.32	-0.41	-16.2	-32.8
IntlSmCp nr	15.16	-0.29	-12.9	-25.8
IntlVal nr	21.51	-0.30	-6.9	-19.8
MidCap n	25.66	-0.51	0.4	-11.8
MidCapVal n	17.54	-0.42	-2.4	-13.0
SCapVal n	14.20	-0.53	-0.9	-10.4
SmCap n	13.18	-0.31	-3.4	-25.9
AssetMark Funds:				
CorPlsFxdInc p	9.29	0.05	5.0	17.0
Aston Funds:				
M&C Gro N n	20.94	-0.36	-6.7	-9.0
MidCapN pn	25.54	-1.01	-2.1	-7.4
B				
BBH Funds:				
BdMktN n	10.29	0.00	1.7	14.0
IntlEq	10.91	-0.21	-12.3	-27.5
BNY Mellon Funds:				
BondFd	13.11	0.06	3.4	23.4
EmgMkts	9.20	-0.13	-9.7	-6.9
IntlFd	8.90	-0.27	-14.7	-37.4
IntmBdFd	12.92	0.04	2.7	21.7
LgCpStk	7.25	-0.17	-2.6	-25.1
MA IntmMuni	13.05	-0.01	2.2	16.8
MidCpStk	9.54	-0.36	0.0	-23.0
NtlIntmMuni	13.42	-0.01	2.5	17.3
NtlShTMuni	12.92	-0.01	0.8	11.3
PA IntmMuni	12.67	-0.01	2.7	14.5
SmCpStk	9.36	-0.40	0.1	-30.0
Baird Funds:				
AggBdInst	10.54	0.06	5.0	18.4
IntBdInst	10.87	0.04	4.2	20.6
IntMunBdInst	11.45	0.00	2.0	20.3
ShtTBdInst	9.65	0.01	2.1	13.1
Baron Instl Shares:				
Growth	42.32	-0.73	2.3	NS
Baron Funds:				
Asset n	46.54	-1.18	0.7	-22.5
Growth n	42.22	-0.72	2.2	-18.5
Partners pn	16.49	-0.27	5.4	-27.5
SmallCap n	19.54	-0.51	1.5	-17.6
Bernstein Fds:				
Ca Mu n	14.57	-0.01	2.8	15.2
DivMu n	14.54	0.00	2.3	16.1
EmMkts n	25.91	-0.47	-10.9	-16.9
IntDur n	13.63	0.05	4.7	22.1
IntlPort n	12.75	-0.36	-15.7	-47.1
NYMu n	14.31	-0.01	2.3	15.9
ShDivMu n	12.70	0.00	0.6	10.3
ShtDur n	11.83	0.01	2.0	6.8
TxMgdIntl n	12.84	-0.37	-16.0	-47.5
BerwynInc n	12.90	-0.11	2.0	22.4
BlackRock Funds II:				
LP2020 I	14.20	-0.20	-2.6	-13.4
LP2030 I	12.69	-0.25	-4.4	-20.9
LP2040 I	15.07	-0.35	-5.9	-26.8
LPRet I	10.73	-0.08	-0.3	0.6
BlackRock Funds A:				
AssetAllocA	13.27	-0.15	-2.0	-9.3
BalCapFd p	19.73	-0.34	0.5	-16.2
BasicVal	21.73	-0.58	-5.6	-28.3
Eng&ResA p	28.56	-0.49	-10.3	-18.7
EqtyDivd p	14.78	-0.35	-6.2	-22.2
FdmtlGrth	18.55	-0.27	-3.7	-11.7
GlblAlloc p	17.11	-0.18	-4.4	-0.4
GlDnymcEq r	10.39	-0.20	-7.0	-18.5
GvtIncInvA	10.74	0.08	5.9	16.5
HighInc p	4.44	-0.02	5.4	8.1
HiYInvA	7.15	-0.03	5.5	12.2
HlthScOp p	26.78	-0.31	-3.3	7.6
InflProtBdA	10.98	0.06	3.5	25.7
IntlOppA p	26.43	-0.57	-12.8	-31.8
LatinAmr p	56.22	-1.04	-12.4	-0.1
LgCapCore p	9.61	-0.30	-2.4	-30.7
LgCapVal p	12.70	-0.40	-4.7	-34.7
MdCpValA p	9.65	-0.33	1.0	-24.6
NatlMuni p	10.23	0.00	4.1	12.2
S&P500Idx pn	13.07	-0.30	-4.0	-27.2
TotRet	10.90	0.04	5.1	NS
USOppA p	31.65	-1.06	-1.1	-9.7
ValueOp	15.28	-0.76	2.6	-31.7
BlackRock Funds B:				
GlblAlloc t	16.67	-0.18	-4.7	-2.9
BlackRock Funds Blrk:				
HiYBlk	7.15	-0.03	5.7	13.6
TotRet II	9.31	0.04	5.3	16.9
BlackRock Funds C:				
BasicVal t	20.37	-0.54	-5.9	-30.0
EqtyDivd t	14.48	-0.35	-6.5	-24.0
FdmtlGrth t	16.56	-0.25	-4.1	-14.0
GlblAlloc t	15.95	-0.17	-4.7	-2.7
InflProtBdC p	10.98	0.06	3.3	22.8
LgCapCore p	8.90	-0.29	-2.8	-32.6
BlackRock Funds Inst:				
ACpEngRes	12.47	-0.24	-7.1	-14.8
BalCapFd	19.81	-0.34	0.6	-15.4
BasicVal	21.88	-0.59	-5.5	-27.6
Bd II	9.39	0.03	3.6	19.2
EqtyDivd	14.81	-0.35	-6.1	-21.5
FdmtlGrth	19.15	-0.29	-3.7	-10.9
GlblAlloc	17.19	-0.18	-4.3	0.3
GNMA Ist	10.43	0.05	5.0	28.6
HiYldBd	7.15	-0.03	5.6	13.4
InflProtBdInst	11.07	0.06	3.7	26.7
IntlOppI	27.62	-0.59	-12.7	-31.2
IntVal	17.32	-0.43	-15.7	-38.3
LgCapCore p	9.83	-0.31	-2.4	-30.2
LgCapValue	12.91	-0.40	-4.7	-34.1
MuniIns	7.56	0.00	3.4	12.9
NatlMuni	10.23	0.00	4.2	13.1
PAMuni	10.92	-0.01	3.6	12.8
S&P500Idx	13.11	-0.30	-3.8	-26.6
ShTrmMuni	10.18	0.00	0.5	11.2
SmCpGrI	19.35	-0.53	-0.8	-17.3
TotRet	10.90	0.04	5.2	NS
TotRet II	9.29	0.04	5.3	16.5
US Opps	33.33	-1.11	-0.9	-8.3
BlackRock Funds R:				
GlblAlloc	16.56	-0.18	-4.6	-1.5
BlackRock Funds Svc:				
LowDurS	9.57	0.01	2.8	9.7
BrandesInstlE I	12.98	-0.26	-12.5	-35.7
Brandywine Funds:				
BlueFd n	20.99	-0.46	-2.8	-34.3
Brandywine n	21.21	-0.61	-3.3	-37.2
Bridgeway Funds:				
USCMkt n	12.21	-0.51	2.2	-30.2
BrownSmCoInst	33.92	-0.72	-5.4	5.8
Buffalo Funds:				
MidCap n	14.02	-0.33	3.1	-9.9
SmCap n	23.28	-0.82	3.6	-10.5
C				
C&OMktOpp n	19.23	0.21	-2.7	14.9
CG Cap Mkt Fnds:				
CoreFxdcm n	8.55	0.04	5.3	27.7
EmgMkt n	13.69	-0.23	-6.7	-13.2
IntlEq n	8.41	-0.19	-11.8	-34.2
LgGrw n	11.95	-0.24	-5.5	-19.0
LgVal n	7.48	-0.17	-5.6	-34.7
SmCpVal n	9.86	-0.32	3.2	-13.0
SmGrw n	15.56	-0.39	4.1	-17.5
CGM Funds:				
Focus n	26.65	-0.75	-10.4	-23.0
Mutl n	23.85	-0.56	-6.7	-3.6
Realty n	21.11	-1.25	1.3	-17.3
CRAQualInvFd	10.89	0.04	3.9	19.1
CRM Funds:				
MdCpVl I	23.15	-0.74	-4.6	-23.3
SmCpVl I	18.57	-0.64	-3.1	-23.5
Calamos Funds:				
ConvA p	18.44	-0.15	-1.1	2.3
ConvC t	18.35	-0.15	-1.5	0.0
ConvI	17.38	-0.14	-1.0	3.1
GlbGr&IncI	9.61	0.03	-0.7	-8.4
Gr&IncA p	27.17	-0.31	-4.9	-7.7
Gr&IncC t	27.28	-0.31	-5.2	-9.8
Gr&IncI	26.58	-0.30	-4.8	-7.0
GrowthA p	42.98	-0.76	-3.3	-19.8
GrowthB t	42.91	-0.77	-3.6	-21.5
GrowthC t	39.27	-0.70	-3.6	-21.5
GrowthI	46.74	-0.83	-3.2	-19.1
MktNeutA p	11.31	-0.07	-2.2	-1.2
MktNeutI	11.20	-0.08	-2.2	-0.6
Calvert Group:				
Inco p	15.71	0.03	3.1	9.5
ShtDurIncA t	16.40	0.02	1.5	16.7
Social p	24.72	-0.25	-0.2	-13.7
SocBd p	15.61	0.05	4.1	15.6
SocEq p	29.79	-0.64	-2.4	-13.5
Cambiar Funds:				
OpptyInv	14.54	-0.39	-6.7	-27.9
CausewayInst	9.96	-0.20	-11.9	-34.5
CausewayInv n	9.90	-0.19	-12.0	-34.9
ChamplainSmCo pn	11.65	-0.25	-0.7	-7.1
Clipper n	53.26	-1.43	-2.4	-35.5
Cohen & Steers:				
InstlRlty	31.58	-2.03	4.1	-28.7
IntlRltyA p	9.16	-0.19	-12.6	-46.2
IntlRltyI r	9.20	-0.19	-12.5	-45.7
RltyShs n	48.65	-3.16	4.0	-29.2
Colo Bonds	9.12	0.00	2.2	11.5
Columbia Class A:				
21CentryA t	11.37	-0.36	-2.2	-25.6
AcornA t	24.01	-0.78	0.1	-19.4
AcornIntA t	31.92	-0.50	-6.5	-22.2
AcornSelA t	22.25	-1.02	-2.5	-24.8
DivIncA t	11.30	-0.25	-4.1	-20.6
FedSecA	10.92	0.05	3.2	18.6
FocEqA t	18.29	-0.53	-4.6	-18.5
IntValA	12.17	-0.28	-13.4	-34.4
LgCpValA p	9.70	-0.34	-4.8	-32.0
MarsGrthA t	16.42	-0.46	-3.6	-23.3
MidCpValA	10.96	-0.43	-1.0	-29.2
SelLgCpGr t	9.79	-0.18	-3.1	NS
SmCapValA	36.77	-1.80	1.9	-18.7
SmCpVal II A p	10.99	-0.56	0.5	-23.5

Source: *Barron's* June 7, 2010, p. M36. Reprinted with permission of *Barron's*, Copyright © 2010 Dow Jones & Company, Inc. All Rights Reserved Worldwide.

www.morningstar.com

Now perhaps the best way to determine whether a mutual fund is load or no-load is to consult the *Morningstar Mutual Fund Survey* if you are only interested in no-load or low-load funds, or to consult the annual publication of the American Association of Individual Investors, *Individual Investor's Guide to the Top Mutual Funds.*

Over the last 20 years no-load funds have made steady inroads into what was once the market of the load fund. In 1984 load funds counted for about 70 percent of all equity mutual funds, and no-load funds accounted for the remaining 30 percent. By 2009 no-load funds had a slight edge over load funds, and net annual fund flows were skewed toward no-load funds. Table 4–6 shows a seven-year history with no-load funds accounting for approximately 89 percent of the new money flowing into mutual funds in 2009, as well as 65 percent of the assets.

Figure 4–4 shows the weekly cash flows into four categories of mutual funds. Investors pay attention to cash flows as a measure of risk. We can see that during

TABLE 4-6 Net New Cash Flow Was Greatest in No-Load Share Classes (*billions of dollars, 2003-2009*)

	2003	2004	2005	2006	2007	2008	2009
All long-term funds	**$216**	**$210**	**$192**	**$227**	**$223**	**−$226**	**$388**
Load	**48**	**44**	**30**	**33**	**14**	**−146**	**39**
Front-end load[1]	33	49	47	48	20	−99	19
Back-end load[2]	−19	−38	−48	−48	−44	−39	−24
Level load[3]	27	21	19	21	25	−12	37
Other load[4]	8	13	11	12	13	5	8
No-load[5]	**126**	**130**	**145**	**170**	**185**	**−54**	**323**
Retail	83	94	79	77	59	−104	138
Institutional	43	35	66	93	126	50	185
Variable annuities	**42**	**36**	**18**	**24**	**25**	**−27**	**26**

[1]Front-end load > 1 percent. Primarily includes A shares; includes sales where front-end loads are waived.

[2]Front-end load = 0 percent and CDSL > 2 percent. Primarily includes B shares.

[3]Front-end load ≤ 1 percent, CDSL ≤ 2 percent, and 12b-1 fee > 0.25 percent. Primarily includes C shares; excludes institutional share classes.

[4]All other load share classes not classified as front-end load, back-end load, or level load. Primarily includes retirement share classes known as R shares.

[5]Front-end load = 0 percent, CDSL = 0 percent, and 12b-1 fee ≤ 0.25 percent.

Note: Components may not add to the total because of rounding.

Sources: Investment Company Institute and Lipper

FIGURE 4-4 Mutual Funds

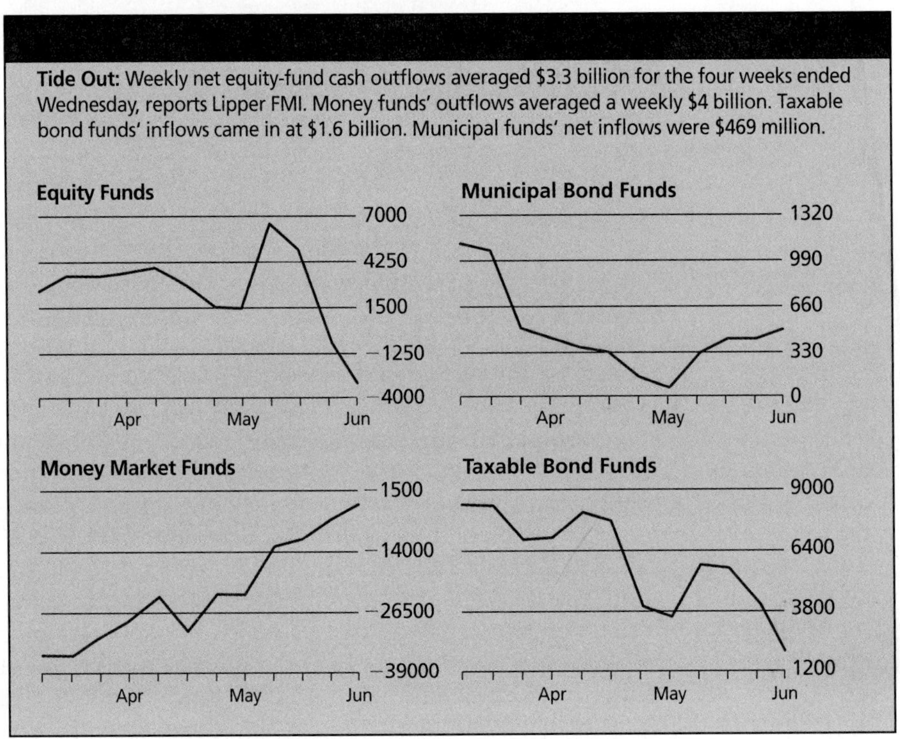

The charts above show four-week moving averages of net cash flow in millions of dollars.

Source: BARRON'S•Upper FMI

this time period cash flows to equities and bond funds were shrinking as investors sought the safety of money market funds.

Since load funds are sold by retail brokers, these changes indicate that investors are buying their mutual funds differently than in the past. There are several reasons for this change. First, many employers are using mutual fund supermarkets to provide pension plans for their employees. Plan participants buy directly from the fund through paycheck withdrawals and don't pay brokerage fees. Second, more investors are using discount brokers such as Charles Schwab, E-Trade, TD Ameritrade, and other online brokers. These brokers generally sell no-load funds to their clients for a small brokerage fee of $7 to $25 per trade.

DIFFERING OBJECTIVES AND THE DIVERSITY OF MUTUAL FUNDS

Recognizing that different investors have different objectives and sensitivities to risk, the mutual fund industry offers a large group of funds from which to choose. In 2007, there were more than 8,500 mutual funds, each unique in terms of stated objectives, investment policies, and current portfolio. To make some sense out of this much variety, funds can be classified in terms of their stated objectives, which are described in the following material.

Mutual Fund Categories

Money Market Funds **Money market funds** invest in short-term securities, such as U.S. Treasury bills and Eurodollar deposits, commercial paper, jumbo bank certificates of deposit (CDs), and repurchase agreements.

Money market funds are no-load, and most require minimum deposits of $500 to $1,000. Most have check-writing privileges, but usually the checks must be written for at least $250 to $500.

Because the maturities of assets held in money market portfolios generally range from 20 to 50 days, the yields of these funds closely track short-term market interest rates. Money market funds give small investors an opportunity to invest in securities that were once out of reach.

Growth Funds The pursuit of capital appreciation is the emphasis with **growth funds**. This class of funds includes those called aggressive growth funds and those concentrating on more stable and predictable growth. Both types invest primarily in common stocks. Aggressive funds concentrate on speculative issues, emerging small companies, and "hot" sectors of the economy and frequently use financial leverage to magnify returns. Regular growth funds generally invest in common stocks of more stable firms. They are less inclined to stay fully invested in stocks during periods of market decline, seldom use aggressive techniques such as leverage, and tend to be long term in orientation.

The best way to determine the type of growth fund is to carefully examine the fund's prospectus and current portfolio.

Growth with Income **Growth with income funds** pay steady dividends. Their stocks are attractive to investors interested in capital growth potential with a base of dividend or interest income. Funds that invest in such stocks are less volatile and risky than growth funds investing in small companies paying low or no dividends.

Balanced Funds **Balanced funds** combine investments in common stock and bonds and often preferred stock. They try to provide income plus some capital appreciation. Funds that invest in convertible securities are also considered balanced since the convertible security is a hybrid fixed-income security with the opportunity for appreciation if the underlying common stock rises.

FIGURE 4-5 **Index Funds as a Percentage of Total Mutual Fund Assets**

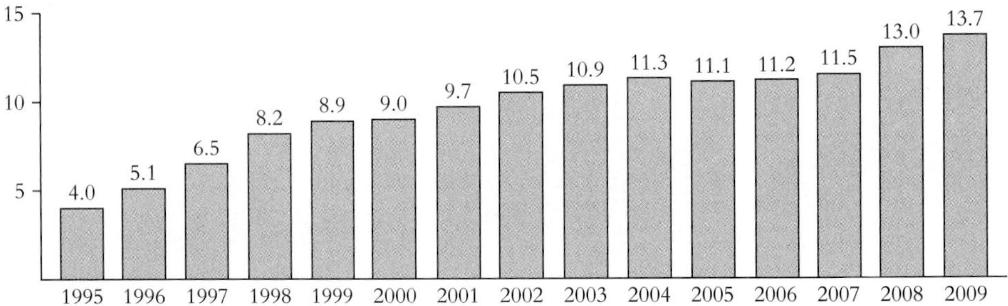

Source: Investment Company Fact Book, 2010, p. 33.

Index Funds **Index funds** are mutual funds that replicate a market index as closely as possible. It was pointed out earlier that exchange traded closed-end funds were index funds that traded on exchanges just like common stock. Conversely, index funds are open-end and may be purchased directly from the fund sponsor. As you may remember from Chapter 3, there are many indexes, including stock market indexes and bond market indexes as well as foreign and global indexes. If an investor truly believes that the market is efficient and that it is hard to outperform the market, he or she will try to reduce transaction costs and attempt to imitate the market. Index funds arose because of the efficient market hypothesis (presented in Chapter 9). A sizeable body of academic research indicates that it is difficult to outperform a market index unless you have superior information. Most investors do not have superior information and so index funds make sense.

Evidently, investors understand that if they can't beat the market, they should buy the market. According to the *Investment Company Fact Book*, 39 percent of all indexed mutual fund assets were invested in S&P 500 index funds.[2] Figure 4–5 shows that equity index funds are an ever-increasing percentage of total mutual fund assets, growing from 4.0 percent in 1995 to 13.7 percent at the end of 2009.

Bond Funds Income-oriented investors have always been attracted to bonds. Because bonds represent a contractual obligation on the part of the issuer to the bondholder, they normally offer a certain return. But as pointed out in Chapter 12, rising interest rates can undercut the market value of all classes of fixed-income securities. During the early 1980s and early 1990s, times of intense interest rate fluctuations, many bondholders watched the principal value of even their "safe" government bonds drop to 75 percent of face value. Bonds held in **bond mutual funds** were affected by the same market forces. Returns from bonds are historically lower than those from stocks, and bond funds are no exception.

Bond mutual funds can be roughly subdivided into corporate, government, and municipal funds.

Some corporate bond funds are particularly targeted to low-rated, high-yielding bonds. These funds are termed *junk bond funds* or *high yield bond funds.* They may have a yield of 3 or 4 percent over the typical corporate bond fund but also possess greater risk in terms of potential default by the securities in the bond portfolio. Just how much greater that risk is was discovered in the fall of 1989 when a number of low-rated bonds in these funds defaulted on their interest payments and prices for all junk bonds fell.

Because municipal bond funds buy only tax-exempt securities, interest income to shareholders is free of federal tax. Special tax-exempt funds also have been established for the benefit of investors in states with high state and local income taxes. For

[2] *Investment Company Fact Book*, 2010, p. 33.

example, fund managers of New York municipal bond funds establish portfolios of tax-exempt securities issued within the boundaries of that state. Under current tax law, interest income from these funds is exempt from federal, state, and local taxes for New York residents—a very appealing feature to high-bracket taxpayers.

Sector Funds Special funds have been created to invest in specific sectors of the economy. **Sector funds** exist for such areas as energy, medical technology, computer technology, leisure, and defense.

Because stock performance of companies within a particular industry, or sector, tends to be positively correlated, these funds offer investors less diversification potential. If an investor really likes a particular sector, such as biotech, but doesn't want to risk buying one stock, a sector fund provides diversification across the sector but not across the market.

Investors should be cautious with regard to the initial offering of new sector funds. An initial offering usually occurs after the sector has already been the subject of intense interest based on recent spectacular performance. As a result, stocks in that sector are often fully priced or overpriced.

Foreign Funds As will be noted in Chapter 19, investors seeking participation in foreign markets and foreign securities confront a number of obstacles, but the rewards can be remarkable. The mutual fund industry has made overseas investing convenient by establishing **foreign funds** whose policies mandate investing on an international basis (Templeton World Fund), within the markets of a particular locale (Canadian Fund, Inc.), or within a region (Merrill Lynch Pacific). Some funds even specialize in Third World countries.

A listing of various types of international funds is presented in Table 4–7. The mutual fund industry distinguishes between global and international funds. Global funds have foreign stocks plus U.S. stocks, while international funds have only foreign stocks.

www.sbs.gov.uk/phoenix

www.calvertgroup.com

www.usfunds.com

Specialty Funds Some mutual funds have specialized approaches that do not fit neatly into any of the preceding categories and so are called **specialty funds.** Their names are often indicative of their investment objectives or policies: the Phoenix Fund (rising from the ashes?), the Calvert Social Investment Fund, and United Services Gold Shares, to name just a few.

There is even a "fund of funds" (FundTrust) that manages a portfolio of different mutual fund shares.

TABLE 4-7 Internationally Oriented Funds

Name of Fund	Open- or Closed-End	Load or No-Load	Where Invested	Ticker
Templeton Emerging MKTS	Closed	—	Emerging MKTS	EMF
Central Europe and Russia	Closed	—	Europe	CEE
New Germany	Closed	None	Germany	GF
India Fund	Closed	—	India	IFN
Mexico Equity and Income	Closed	—	Mexico	MXE
Latin American Discovery	Closed	—	Latin America	LDF
Korea	Closed	—	Chile	KF
China	Closed	—	China	CHN
Scudder International Fund	Open	None	Mexico and Central America	SCINX
T. Rowe Price Latin American Fund A	Open	—	Latin America	PRLAX
Fidelity Europe Capital Appreciation	Open	3.00%	Europe	FECAX
Vanguard Europe Admiral	Open	—	Europe	VEUSX

Target Retirement Funds or Life-Cycle Funds Mutual funds that automatically adjust the risk profile of the fund as the investor gets older are referred to as **target funds,** or life-cycle funds. The basic premise of these funds is that an investor can take more risk when she is young and less risk as she gets older. So, as the investor ages, the portfolio mix shifts from a heavy emphasis on common stock to a heavy emphasis on fixed-income securities. As the investor gets closer to retirement, steady income generation becomes more important and there is less ability to withstand down markets and watch capital erode. As an example, let's look at the Vanguard Target Retirement Funds:

VANGUARD TARGET RETIREMENT 2020 (VTWNX)	Target Date 2016–2020	\$7.5 B	4 yrs
VANGUARD TARGET RETIREMENT 2025 (VTTVX)	Target Date 2021–2025	\$11.6 B	7 yrs
VANGUARD TARGET RETIREMENT 2030 (VTHRX)	Target Date 2026–2030	\$5.3 B	4 yrs
VANGUARD TARGET RETIREMENT 2035 (VTTHX)	Target Date 2031–2035	\$7.8 B	7 yrs
VANGUARD TARGET RETIREMENT 2040 (VFORX)	Target Date 2036–2040	\$3.2 B	4 yrs
VANGUARD TARGET RETIREMENT 2045 (VTIVX)	Target Date 2041–2045	\$4.2 B	7 yrs
VANGUARD TARGET RETIREMENT 2050 (VFIFX)	Target Date 2050+	\$1.3 B	4 yrs

Not all investors fit the average profile that a targeted or life-cycle fund follows. Some investors have a higher tolerance for risk, and others have a lower tolerance. The ability and willingness to take risk also depends on the investor's accumulated wealth. The more money you have available to you at retirement, the more risk you might be able to assume. Suppose that you can live on a \$2 million retirement nest egg, but you have managed to accumulate \$4 million. Your risk profile will be quite different from the profile for the investor who needs \$2 million and has only accumulated \$1.25 million. In other words, match your goals, objectives, and risk to the right fund, and don't assume that because you will retire in 2050 you need a 2050 target fund.

Matching Investment Objectives with Fund Types

Investors must consider how much volatility of return they can tolerate. Investors who require safety of principal with very little deviation of returns should choose money market funds first and intermediate-term bond funds second. They should also expect to receive lower returns based on historical evidence. While aggressive growth stock funds provide the highest return, they also have the biggest risk.

Liquidity objectives are met by all mutual funds since redemption can occur any time. If investors need income, bond funds provide the highest annual current yield, while aggressive growth funds provide the least. Growth-income and balanced funds are most appropriate for investors who want growth of principal with moderate current income.

Many investors diversify by fund type. For example, at one stage in the business cycle, an investor may want to have 50 percent of assets in U.S. common stocks, 35 percent in bonds, 10 percent in money market funds, and 5 percent in an international stock fund. These percentages could change as market conditions change. If interest rates are expected to decline, it would be better to have a higher percentage of bonds and fewer money market securities since bond prices will rise as rates decline. Investing with a "family of funds" allows the investor a choice of many different types of funds and the privilege of switching between funds at no or low cost. Some of the larger families of funds are managed by American Capital, Federated Funds, Fidelity Investments, T. Rowe Price Funds, and the Vanguard Group. In addition, most major retail brokerage firms, such as Merrill Lynch and Morgan Stanley Smith Barney, have families of mutual funds.

Each mutual fund has a unique history and management team. There is no guarantee that past performance will be repeated. Investors should check on a fund's longevity of management, historical returns, trading history, and management expenses. A very key instrument in providing information in this regard is the fund prospectus.

THE PROSPECTUS

The Investment Companies Act of 1940, which established the standard of practice for all investment companies, requires that the purchaser of fund shares be provided with a current prospectus. The **prospectus** contains information deemed essential by the SEC in providing "full disclosure" to potential investors regarding the fund's investment objectives and policies, risks, management, and expenses. The prospectus also provides information on how shares can be purchased and redeemed, sales and redemption charges (if any), and shareholders' services. Other fund documents are available to the public on request, including the Statement of Additional Information and the fund's annual and quarterly reports.

While it is beyond the scope of this chapter to provide a complete discourse on interpreting a prospectus, investors need to understand the following essentials.

Investment Objectives and Policies

This section is always found in the beginning of the prospectus. It usually describes the fund's basic objectives:

> The Fund will invest only in securities backed by the full faith and credit of the U.S. Government. At least 70 percent of the Fund's assets will be invested in certificates issued by the Government National Mortgage Association (GNMA). It may also purchase other securities issued by the U.S. Government, its agencies, or instrumentalities as long as these securities are backed by the full faith and credit of the U.S. Government.

The prospectus normally goes on to detail investment management policies under which it intends to operate—typically with regard to the use of borrowed money, lending of securities, or something like the following:

> The Fund may, under certain circumstances, sell covered call options against securities it is holding for the purpose of generating additional income.

Portfolio (or "Investment Holdings")

This section of the prospectus lists the securities held by the fund as of the date indicated. Since investment companies are only required to publish their prospectuses every 14 months, the information is probably dated. Still, the portfolio should be compared with the stated objectives of the fund to see if they are consistent.

Management Fees and Expenses

Besides sales and redemption charges, the prospectus also provides information and figures on fund managers' reimbursement and the fund's housekeeping expenses. Annual fees for the investment advisor are expressed as a percentage of the average daily net assets during the year (usually 0.50 percent). Other expenses include legal and auditing fees, the cost of preparing and distributing annual reports and proxy statements, directors' fees, and transaction expenses. When lumped together with investment advisory fees, a fund's total yearly expenses typically range from 0.50 percent for money market

TABLE 4-8 Expense Ratios for Selected Investment Objectives* (*percent, 2009*)

Investment Objective	10th Percentile	Median	90th Percentile	Average *Asset-Weighted*	Average *Simple*
Equity funds	**0.82**	**1.44**	**2.28**	**0.87**	**1.52**
Aggressive growth	0.91	1.49	2.33	1.03	1.58
Growth	0.78	1.33	2.16	0.91	1.43
Sector funds	0.92	1.62	2.50	0.98	1.70
Growth and income	0.52	1.21	2.00	0.56	1.25
Income equity	0.75	1.24	1.98	0.85	1.32
International equity	0.99	1.60	2.45	1.02	1.67
Hybrid funds	**0.63**	**1.20**	**2.00**	**0.84**	**1.28**
Bond funds	**0.52**	**0.96**	**1.73**	**0.65**	**1.08**
Taxable bond	0.50	0.99	1.80	0.65	1.09
Municipal bond	0.55	0.92	1.62	0.64	1.07
Money market funds	**0.22**	**0.50**	**0.91**	**0.34**	**0.54**

*Figures exclude mutual funds available as investment choices in variable annuities and mutual funds that invest primarily in other mutual funds.

Sources: Investment Company Institute and Lipper. Investment Company Factbook, 2010. Copyright © 2010, Investment Company Institute, Washington D.C. Used with permission.

funds to 2.5 percent for sector funds. Table 4–8 shows the range of fees for different investment objectives. Investors are quite sensitive to fees and have been attracted in recent years to low-cost mutual funds. Generally, there is no reason to pay more than the median expense or the asset-weighted average. Funds with large assets generally have lower expense fees. It is required that all expenses appear on one page in a table format.

A controversial SEC ruling—Rule 12b-1—allows mutual funds to use fund assets for marketing expenses, which are included in the expense ratio. Since marketing expenses have nothing to do with advancing shareholders' interests and everything to do with increasing the managers' fees, investors should be alert to this in the prospectus.

Turnover Rate A number of mutual funds trade aggressively in pursuit of profits; others do just the opposite. In one year, the Fidelity Contrafund had a 243 percent turnover rate; the rate for the Oppenheimer Special Fund was 9 percent.

In reality, transaction costs amount to more than just commissions, and they are not accounted for in the expense ratio. When fund assets are traded over-the-counter, the dealer's spread between the bid and asked price is not considered. Nor is the fact that large block trades—the kind mutual funds usually deal in—are made at less favorable prices than are smaller-volume transactions.

The prospectus also contains audited data on the turnover rate, the expense ratio, and other important data in the section on per share income and capital changes. In 1998 the SEC ordered mutual funds to provide shortened forms of the prospectus to investors who do not want to be overwhelmed with data.

DISTRIBUTION AND TAXATION

The selling of securities by a mutual fund manager results in capital losses or gains for the fund. After netting losses against gains, mutual funds distribute net capital gains to shareholders annually.

Funds with securities that pay dividends or interest also have a source of investment income. The fund, in turn, distributes such income to shareholders either quarterly or annually.

A fund that distributes at least 90 percent of its net investment income and capital gains is not subject, as an entity, to federal income tax. It is simply acting as a "conduit" in channeling taxable sources of income from securities held in the portfolio to the fund's shareholders. Most funds operate this way. But while the mutual fund may not be subject to taxation, its shareholders are.

At the end of every calendar year, each fund shareholder receives a Form 1099-DIV. This document notifies the shareholder of the amount and tax status of his or her distributions.

When the investor actually sells (redeems) shares in a mutual fund, another form of taxable event occurs. It is precisely the same as if stocks, bonds, or other securities were sold. The investor must consider the cost basis, the selling price, and any gain or loss and appropriately report the tax consequences on his or her tax form.

Tax Differences between Mutual Funds and Individual Stock Portfolios

When you manage your own portfolio of common stocks, you can choose when to sell a specific stock, and by having that choice, you control when you pay capital gains taxes. When you own a mutual fund, the manager decides when to buy and sell, so you end up with a capital gain or loss at the manager's discretion. This difference might not seem significant, but if you receive a bonus this year, you might want to take losses this year to offset some of the bonus income and wait until next year to take your gains. You might also want to wait until the gain is long term and taxed at a lower rate.

The initial purchase of a common stock sets the cost basis; if the stock goes up you have a gain, and if it goes down you have a loss. At least if the stock stays the same you have no gain or loss. This is not so with a mutual fund. When you buy fund shares, a portfolio of stocks already exists, and these stocks are held at either a gain or a loss. In rapidly rising bull markets, you may be buying into mutual funds that have large accumulated gains; if the manager decides to take those gains, you will have to pay the capital gains tax—even though the net asset value of your shares did not change. This would leave you with a negative return even though the price did not fall. This particular tax issue is what keeps more sophisticated investors from buying mutual funds during the last several months of the year.

SHAREHOLDER SERVICES

Most mutual funds offer a number of services to their shareholders. Some can be used in the investor's strategy. Common services include the following:

Automatic reinvestment. The fund reinvests all distributions (usually without sales charge). Shares and fractional shares are purchased at the net asset value. Purchases are noted on annual and periodic account statements.

Safekeeping. While shareholders are entitled to receive certificates for all whole shares, it is often convenient to let the fund's transfer agent hold the shares.

Exchange privilege. Many large management companies sponsor a family of funds. They may have five or more funds, each dedicated to a different investment objective. Within certain limits, shareholders are free to move their money between the different funds in the family on a net asset value basis. Transfers can often be done by telephone; a minimal charge is common to cover paperwork. These exchanges are taxable events.

Preauthorized check plan. Many people lack the discipline to save or invest regularly. Those who recognize this trait in themselves can authorize a management company to charge their bank account for predetermined amounts on a regular basis. The amounts withdrawn are used to purchase new shares.

Systematic withdrawal plan. Every shareholder plans to convert shares into cash at some time. The investor who wants to receive a regular amount of cash each month or quarter can do so by arranging for such a plan. The fund sells enough shares on a periodic basis to meet the shareholder's cash requirement.

Checking privileges. Most money market mutual funds furnish shareholders with checks that can be drawn against the account, provided that the account balance is above a minimum amount (usually $1,000). A per-check minimum of $250 to $500 is common.

INVESTMENT FUNDS, LONG-TERM PLANNING, AND DOLLAR-COST AVERAGING

Perhaps more than anything else, the liquidity and conveniences inherent in mutual funds lend themselves best to financial planning activities. The most important of these is the gradual accumulation of capital assets.

Using the preauthorized check plan, investors can have fixed amounts regularly withdrawn from their checking accounts to purchase fund shares. Just as savers can have their banks channel a specific amount from their paychecks into savings accounts, so too can investors make regular, lump-sum fund share purchases on an "out of sight, out of mind" basis. Reinvestment of distributions enhances this strategy.

What distinguishes the mutual fund from the bank savings strategy is the fact that fund shares are purchased at different prices. The investor can even use a passive strategy known as dollar-cost averaging. Under **dollar-cost averaging**, the investor buys a fixed dollar's worth of a given security at regular intervals regardless of the security's price or the current market outlook. By using such a strategy, investors concede they cannot outsmart the market. The intent of dollar-cost averaging is to avoid the common practice of buying high and selling low. In fact, investors are forced to do the opposite. Why? They commit a fixed-dollar amount each month (or year) and buy shares at the current market price. When the price is high, they are buying relatively fewer shares; when the price is low, they are accumulating more shares. An example is presented in Table 4–9. Suppose we use the preauthorized check plan to channel $200 per month into a mutual fund. The price ranges from a low of $12 to a high of $19.

Note that when the share price is relatively low, such as in January, we purchased a larger number of shares than when the share prices were high, as in

TABLE 4-9 Dollar-Cost Averaging

(1) Month	(2) Investment	(3) Share Price	(4) Shares Purchased
January	$ 200	$12	16.66
February	200	14	14.28
March	200	16	12.50
April	200	19	10.52
May	200	15	13.33
June	200	12	16.66
Totals	$1,200	$88	83.95 total shares
		Average price $14.67	Average cost $14.29

April. In this case, the share price ended in June at the same price it was in January ($12).

What would happen if the price merely ended up at the average price over the six-month period? The values in Column (3) total $88, so the average price over six months is $14.67 ($88/6). Actually, we would still make money under this assumption because the average *cost* is less than this amount. Consider that we invested $1,200 and purchased 83.95 shares. This translates to an average cost of only $14.29:

$$\frac{\text{Investment}}{\text{Shares purchased}} = \frac{\$1{,}200}{83.95} = \$14.29$$

The average cost ($14.29) is less than the average price ($14.67) because we bought relatively more shares at the lower price levels, and they weighed more heavily in our calculations. Thus, under dollar-cost averaging, investors can come out ahead over a period of investing fixed amounts, even if the share price ends up less than the average price paid on each transaction.

The only time investors lose money is if the eventual price falls below the average cost ($14.29) and they sell at that point. While dollar-cost averaging has its advantages, it is not without criticism. Clearly, if the share price continues to go down over a long period, it is hard to make a case for continued purchases. However, the long-term performance of most diversified mutual funds has been positive, and long-term investors may find this strategy useful in accumulating capital assets for retirement, children's education funds, or other purposes.

MUTUAL FUND INFORMATION AND EVALUATING FUND PERFORMANCE

There are many sources of information on mutual funds. Morningstar is perhaps the leader on individual fund information. However, many financial magazines, such as *Forbes, SmartMoney,* and *Money,* have articles on mutual funds in every edition. Barron's publishes a quarterly review of mutual fund performance. The Value Line Investment survey publishes data on mutual funds, as does Standard & Poor's Netadvantage, an online service available at many university libraries. The American Association of Individual Investors publishes an annual mutual fund survey. Of course, you can look up a mutual fund family online, or call the toll-free number directly to request a prospectus. Online brokers at TD Ameritrade and E-trade, for example, have mutual fund screeners as part of their investor services.

For now, let's look at a Morningstar example, as seen in Figure 4–6, of the T. Rowe Price European Stock Fund. Morningstar ranks each mutual fund on a five-star system, with five stars signifying the highest quality and performance compared to the fund's peer group. At the top of the page, you will see that the T. Rowe Price European Fund is ranked four stars. On the top line, you will also see its ticker symbol. The data in the table are self-explanatory, but notice that the table includes annual returns, portfolio analysis, risk analysis, major company holdings, and more. The fund is also compared against market indexes on the left-hand side, in the middle of the page, under "Performance 10/22/2010." Shown there are comparisons for YTD, 12 months, 3 years, 5 years, and 10 years against the MSCI EAFE[3] index. Because this is an international European fund, it makes sense to use these European indexes as a benchmark for comparison purposes,

[3] MSCI represents Morgan Stanley Capital International, headquartered in Geneva, Switzerland. EAFE stands for Europe, Australasia, and the Far East.

FIGURE 4-6 T. Rowe Price European Stock

Release date 10/22/2010 | FINRA Members: For internal use or client reporting purposes only Page 2 of 9

T. Rowe Price European Stock PRESX

Snapshot

Morningstar Rating™	Morningstar Category™	Net Assets (Mil)
★★★★	US OE Europe Stock	686.63(USD)

Portfolio Analysis 9/30/2010

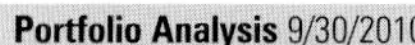

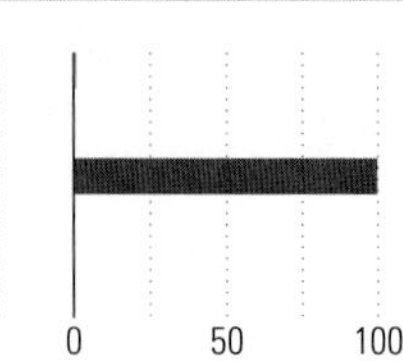

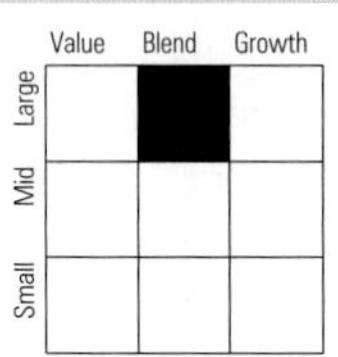

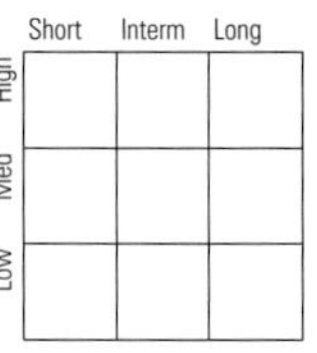

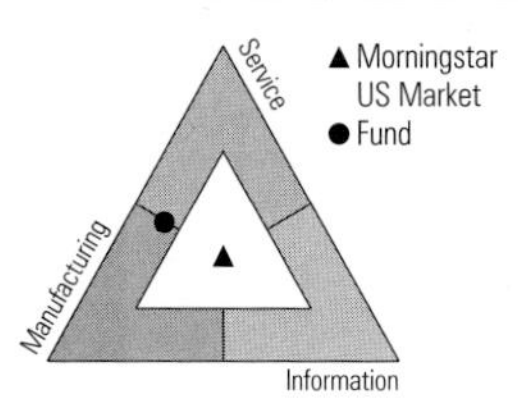

Asset Allocation	Long %	Short %	Net %
● Cash	0.54	0.00	0.54
● US Stock	0.00	0.00	0.00
● Non US Stock	99.46	0.00	99.46
● Bond	0.00	0.00	0.00
● Other	0.00	0.00	0.00

Fixed-income investment style data is as of —

Equity Investment Style	
Market Cap ($Mil)	16,525

Fixed-Income Investment Style	
Avg Effective Duration (Yrs)	—
Avg Effective Maturity (Yrs)	—
Avg Credit Quality	—

Stock Sectors	% Stocks
Information Economy	7.77
Service Economy	46.20
Manufacturing Economy	46.03

Sector data is calculated only using the long position holdings of the portfolio.

Performance 10/22/2010

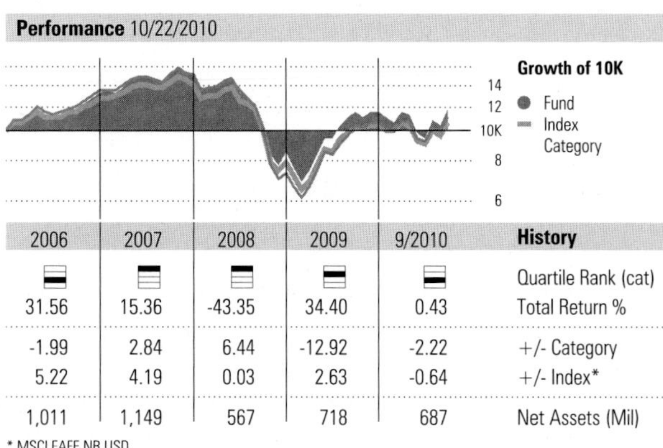

2006	2007	2008	2009	9/2010	History
					Quartile Rank (cat)
31.56	15.36	-43.35	34.40	0.43	Total Return %
-1.99	2.84	6.44	-12.92	-2.22	+/- Category
5.22	4.19	0.03	2.63	-0.64	+/- Index*
1,011	1,149	567	718	687	Net Assets (Mil)

* MSCI EAFE NR USD

Trailing Total Returns	Trailing Ret %	+/- Index‡	+/- Cat	% Rnk Cat	*Std Ret %
YTD	5.69	-0.34	-1.62	51	0.43
12 Mo	2.26	-3.25	-3.06	70	1.28
3 Yr Annualized	-6.93	1.35	1.77	20	-8.23
5 Yr Annualized	5.79	2.07	0.80	35	3.47
10 Yr Annualized	3.87	0.38	-2.51	68	2.82
Inception	7.53	2.79	-0.51	—	7.29

*Quarter-end data through 9/30/2010
‡MSCI EAFE NR USD

Ratings and Risk 9/30/2010

	Overall	3 Yr	5 Yr	10 Yr
Morningstar Rating™	★★★★	★★★★	★★★★	★★★
Number of Funds Rated	104	104	94	68
Morningstar Risk™	Average	Average	Average	Average
Morningstar Return™	Average	Above Avg	Average	Below Avg
Standard Deviation		29.10	23.69	20.84
Mean		-8.23	3.47	2.82

Top 10 Holdings 9/30/2010

YTD Return as of 10/22/2010	Sector	YTD Return %	% Assets
Royal Dutch Shell PLC B	Energy	—	3.59
Wirecard AG	Business Services	—	2.91
Telefonica, S.A. ADR	Telecommunications	—	2.79
Nestle SA	Consumer Goods	—	2.40
GEA Group Aktiengesellschaft	Industrial Materials	—	2.18
Experian PLC	Business Services	—	2.17
CIE Financiere Richemont SA	Consumer Services	—	2.11
Restaurant Group (The) PLC	Consumer Services	—	1.97
Credit Suisse Group	Financial Services	—	1.97
Roche Holding AG	Health Care	-10.60	1.86

% Assets in Top 10 Holdings	23.97
Total Number of Stock Holdings	73
Total Number of Bond Holdings	0
Turnover %	88
12-Month Yield %	3.40
30-Day SEC Yield %	0.00

Stewardship Grade

Overall Grade	Regulatory Issues	Board Quality	Manager Incentives
B	A	B	C
Grade Range: A B C D F	Fees	Corporate Culture	
	A	A	

Operations

Management	
Family	T. Rowe Price
Phone	800-638-5660
Inception	2/28/1990
Manager	Multiple
Tenure	5.00

Purchase Information	
Minimum Initial Purchase	2,500
Minimum IRA Purchase	1,000
Minimum Auto Investment Plan	0

Fees	
Front-End Load	—%
Deferred Load	—%
12b-1 Fee	None
Prospectus Net Expense Ratio	1.08%

and we find that on a 1-year basis, the T. Rowe Price European Stock fund underperformed both indexes. Other time periods tended to show mixed results.

Performance should always be measured against an appropriate benchmark. One common benchmark is the average performance of all competing mutual funds in the same fund category. Another and more rigorous performance comparison is against an index that measures the performance of a stock portfolio that matches the fund's investment objectives. That is why we compared the T. Rowe Price European Stock fund against the European indexes.

One warning: Past performance in no way guarantees future performance. A fund that did well in the past may do poorly in the future and vice versa.[4] Nevertheless, all things being equal, investors generally prefer funds that have a prior record of good performance. Investors do not know whether the funds can reproduce the performance, but at least the funds have indicated the capacity for good returns in the past. The same cannot be said for underperformers.

MEASURING MUTUAL FUND PERFORMANCE AVERAGES

Lipper Mutual Fund Performance Indexes

Lipper Mutual Fund Performance Indexes are perhaps the most widely known measure of mutual fund performance. Data are published weekly, monthly, quarterly, and annually in various forms, covering the many different categories of mutual funds. The benchmarks appear in print and online. An example of the Lipper weekly data appears in Table 3-6 on page 68 in Chapter 3, and so we will not repeat it.

American Association of Individual Investors

The AAII publishes an annual mutual fund survey called *The Individual Investor's Guide to the Top Mutual Funds*. This is an excellent source of information about mutual funds in general. The survey provides a long-term view of mutual fund performance by category for the last 5 years and returns for 3-, 5-, and 10-year periods. The returns are given in bull markets and bear markets. This provides information about which sectors may be defensive in down markets and which sectors might boom in up markets. Of course, to take advantage of this information the investor has to be able to forecast market trends. The performance data also provide the average expense ratio for each category, the yield, and the total risk index. The AAII performance data take a longer-term look at mutual fund performance than the Lipper Indexes. The 2010 data for the AAII performance benchmarks are shown in Table 4–10.

Standard & Poor's SPIVA Scorecard

The S&P SPIVA Scorecard is perhaps the best measure of average mutual fund performance and is available for free online at the S&P Web site (**www.standardandpoors.com**). The information provided in this report is comprehensive and more sophisticated than just simple return data. The scorecard compares fund performance to the S&P benchmark indexes and provides information about how many funds outperformed their benchmark index for each category. If the percentage is above 50, then on average the funds in the category did not

[4] The factor is covered more fully in Chapter 22.

TABLE 4-10 Performance of Category Averages and Index Benchmarks

Category		Annual Total Return (%)					Total Return (%)		Annual Total Return (%)			Yield (%)	Total Risk Index	Exp Ratio (%)
		2010	2009	2008	2007	2006	Bull	Bear	3-Yr	5-Yr	10-Yr			
Stk-LC	Large-Cap Stock	15.2	32.0	(38.6)	8.6	13.0	81.5	(50.7)	(2.7)	2.4	2.0	0.8	1.12	1.02
Stk-MC	Mid-Cap Stock	23.3	36.1	(39.7)	9.3	13.9	98.6	(51.3)	0.0	4.3	5.7	0.3	1.23	1.14
Stk-SC	Small-Cap Stock	26.6	36.5	(38.5)	2.4	14.5	112.0	(53.0)	1.5	4.3	7.3	0.2	1.33	1.29
LS	Long-Short	0.9	3.5	(12.4)	9.1	9.6	8.6	(14.7)	(3.1)	1.5	3.1	0.0	0.50	1.86
Contra	Contra Market	(26.1)	(34.7)	30.7	(5.6)	(8.1)	(57.1)	72.1	(17.1)	(12.2)	(8.4)	0.0	1.49	1.70
Sec-E	Energy/Resources Sector	21.2	52.8	(53.5)	42.9	13.7	111.4	(57.9)	(6.1)	7.2	10.9	0.9	1.80	1.24
Sec-F	Financial/Banking Sector	12.9	22.7	(45.9)	(10.1)	15.1	89.5	(62.9)	(9.8)	(6.6)	0.3	1.0	1.48	1.20
Sec-G	Gold Sector	41.5	59.0	(37.4)	23.7	33.1	129.2	(43.6)	11.1	17.5	24.8	2.9	2.19	1.33
Sec-H	Health Sector	11.2	28.5	(26.0)	11.3	3.5	60.5	(35.6)	1.5	3.8	3.7	0.3	1.00	1.03
Sec-R	Real Estate Sector	24.8	35.9	(44.2)	(13.5)	32.3	146.5	(66.4)	(2.5)	1.0	10.0	2.4	1.81	1.10
Sec-T	Technology Sector	19.9	62.5	(46.2)	16.0	9.8	111.7	(54.3)	1.4	5.7	(0.9)	0.0	1.35	1.41
Sec-TC	Telecommunications Sector	19.4	44.5	(44.2)	13.4	23.0	92.2	(53.7)	(1.8)	5.4	1.5	1.6	1.31	1.25
Sec-U	Utilities Sector	11.2	15.2	(32.9)	15.6	25.9	49.7	(43.2)	(5.0)	4.4	1.8	4.3	0.92	1.10
Sec-M	Miscellaneous Sector	27.5	40.7	(37.5)	8.6	15.4	125.8	(52.2)	2.6	6.0	6.9	1.2	1.41	1.16
IntS-Glb	Global Stock	14.4	33.7	(40.1)	13.5	20.2	78.7	(51.3)	(3.1)	4.1	4.8	0.9	1.10	1.42
IntS-F	Foreign Stock	13.8	38.5	(45.8)	12.9	25.9	91.4	(58.4)	(5.4)	3.7	5.0	1.4	1.34	1.20
IntS-R/C	Regional/Country Stock	16.1	57.5	(50.0)	26.8	26.7	122.3	(61.5)	(5.2)	6.0	8.4	1.1	1.57	1.41
IntS-E	Emerging Stock	19.8	80.0	(59.5)	40.3	33.8	155.0	(67.5)	(5.5)	9.2	15.1	0.7	1.76	1.63
Bal	Balanced: Domestic	11.6	21.9	(23.2)	6.9	11.1	50.8	(31.9)	1.2	4.2	4.8	1.8	0.69	0.94
Bal-Glb	Balanced: Global	13.0	24.9	(27.7)	9.6	11.6	59.8	(37.3)	0.4	4.3	4.3	3.5	0.78	1.01
TD2000	Target Date: 2000-2014	9.6	17.5	(17.6)	6.6	9.3	39.3	(24.9)	2.2	4.3	3.6	2.3	0.50	0.57
TD2015	Target Date: 2015-2029	12.6	24.9	(27.9)	7.0	12.5	59.0	(38.3)	0.4	3.8	2.2	1.9	0.78	0.70
TD2030	Target Date: 2030+	15.2	31.2	(35.8)	7.6	14.8	76.9	(48.0)	(0.9)	3.7	2.5	1.5	1.01	0.70
B-CHY	Corp High-Yield Bond	12.9	39.6	(20.8)	2.5	9.6	55.2	(20.5)	7.4	6.7	7.0	6.9	0.64	0.97
B-Cnvt	Convertible Bond	16.5	38.0	(29.3)	8.9	13.2	70.4	(34.1)	3.6	6.5	5.4	3.3	0.84	0.99
B-MB	Mortgage-Backed Bond	5.7	6.7	1.2	5.9	4.2	12.5	3.4	4.4	4.6	4.6	3.7	0.16	0.70
B-GvST	Gov't: Short-Term Bond	2.0	1.7	4.7	6.1	3.9	3.9	6.3	2.8	3.7	3.4	1.2	0.08	0.57
B-GvIT	Gov't: Interm-Term Bond	6.0	1.6	9.1	7.6	3.5	9.5	10.0	5.5	5.5	5.2	2.7	0.23	0.62
B-GvLT	Gov't: Long-Term Bond	11.5	(17.9)	30.7	10.4	(0.3)	4.4	20.0	5.9	5.5	6.4	3.1	0.85	0.86
B-IP	Inflation-Protected Bond	6.0	11.2	(2.5)	10.7	0.0	19.0	0.0	4.7	5.0	6.8	1.9	0.42	0.52
B-GenST	General Bond: Short-Term	4.8	9.8	(6.9)	3.9	4.6	15.5	(6.2)	2.1	2.8	3.6	2.5	0.21	0.67
B-GenIT	General Bond: Interm-Term	7.5	13.3	(2.2)	5.1	4.6	22.8	(1.7)	5.9	5.4	5.6	3.7	0.26	0.65
B-GenLT	General Bond: Long-Term	8.7	15.5	(2.8)	4.6	4.1	29.2	(4.7)	6.6	5.7	6.8	4.5	0.42	0.84
B-MNST	Muni Nat'l: Short-Term	1.3	4.5	1.3	3.6	3.3	4.4	3.6	2.4	2.7	3.2	1.7	0.10	0.55
B-MNIT	Muni Nati'l: Interm-Term	2.3	10.7	(1.2)	3.3	3.7	9.6	2.9	3.8	3.7	4.0	3.3	0.25	0.61
B-MNLT	Muni Nat'l: Long-Term	1.8	14.9	(5.4)	2.3	4.7	11.8	(0.5)	3.4	3.4	4.3	4.1	0.33	0.59
B-MHY	Muni Nat'l: High-Yield	3.5	27.4	(20.5)	(1.0)	6.9	22.9	(16.0)	1.5	2.1	4.1	5.1	0.51	0.64
IntB-Gen	Int'l Bond: General	5.6	12.3	(0.4)	7.3	5.5	24.4	(3.9)	5.5	5.9	6.2	3.3	0.43	0.90
IntB-E	Int'l Bond: Emerging	11.5	32.1	(16.7)	6.0	11.4	50.1	(19.1)	7.0	7.6	11.6	4.7	0.70	1.05
IntB-C	Int'l Bond: Currency	0.0	0.1	(2.3)	5.9	4.8	2.5	(2.2)	(1.5)	1.1	—	2.1	0.65	1.50
Index Benchmarks														
	S&P 500 Equal Weighted	21.9	46.3	(39.7)	1.5	15.8	118.2	(53.7)	2.4	4.8	6.3	—	1.29	—
	S&P 500	15.1	26.5	(37.0)	5.5	15.8	77.8	(50.9)	(2.9)	2.3	1.4	—	1.06	—
	S&P MidCap 400	26.6	37.4	(36.2)	8.0	10.3	106.5	(49.5)	3.5	5.7	7.2	—	1.25	—
	S&P SmallCap 600	26.3	25.6	(31.1)	(0.3)	15.1	106.3	(51.3)	3.0	4.6	7.7	—	1.33	—
	MSCI EAFE	8.2	32.5	(43.1)	11.6	26.9	77.0	(56.3)	(6.6)	2.9	3.9	—	1.28	—
	MSCI Europe	4.5	36.8	(46.1)	14.4	34.4	78.7	(58.9)	(8.3)	3.5	3.8	—	1.39	—
	MSCI Far East	16.6	12.8	(32.3)	0.3	8.9	58.8	(47.0)	(3.8)	(0.6)	2.1	—	1.02	—
	MSCI Pacific	16.1	24.3	(36.2)	5.6	12.5	74.1	(50.6)	(2.7)	1.8	4.3	—	1.11	—
	BarCap US Agg Bond	6.5	5.9	5.2	7.0	4.3	14.2	6.0	5.9	5.8	5.8	—	0.20	—
	BofA ML US Corp Bond	9.5	19.8	(6.8)	4.6	4.4	32.7	(7.2)	6.9	6.0	6.6	—	0.43	—
	BofA ML High Yield Bond	15.2	56.3	(26.2)	2.2	11.6	77.0	(26.2)	9.9	8.7	8.7	—	0.82	—
	BarCap GNMA Bond	6.7	5.4	7.9	7.0	4.6	11.8	10.7	6.6	6.3	5.9	—	0.16	—
	BarCap US Gov't 1-3 Yr	2.4	1.4	6.7	7.1	4.1	4.0	8.4	3.5	4.3	4.1	—	0.08	—
	BarCap US Gov't Interm	5.0	(0.3)	10.4	8.5	3.8	6.1	11.8	4.9	5.4	5.1	—	0.18	—
	BarCap US Gov't Long	9.4	(12.2)	22.7	9.7	2.1	5.8	16.0	5.6	5.7	6.6	—	0.65	—
	BarCap Municipal Bond	2.4	12.9	(2.5)	3.4	4.8	10.9	2.5	4.1	4.1	4.8	—	0.30	—
	Treasury Bills	0.2	0.2	1.4	4.4	4.9	0.2	1.9	0.6	2.2	2.2	—	0.01	—

Source: From AAII Journal, *The Individual Investor's Guide to the top Mutual Funds,* Feb. 2011, p. 6. Copyright © 2010. Used with permission.

TABLE 4-11 SPIVA: Percentage of U.S. Equity Funds Outperformed by Benchmarks

Fund Category	Comparison Index	One Year	Three Year	Five Year
All Domestic Equity Funds	S&P Composite 1500	41.67	54.06	60.61
All Large Cap Funds	S&P 500	50.75	49.41	60.80
All Mid Cap Funds	S&P MidCap 400	57.60	73.68	77.17
All Small Cap Funds	S&P SmallCap 600	32.22	63.21	66.60
All Multi Cap Funds	S&P Composite 1500	40.06	55.89	61.86
Large Cap Growth Funds	S&P 500 Growth	39.15	69.05	76.89
Large Cap Core Funds	S&P 500	52.06	49.59	65.12
Large Cap Value Funds	S&P 500 Value	46.24	26.36	38.76
Mid Cap Growth Funds	S&P MidCap 400 Growth	59.60	81.48	80.11
Mid Cap Core Funds	S&P MidCap 400	68.60	76.19	75.73
Mid Cap Value Funds	S&P MidCap 400 Value	47.83	74.42	70.24
Small Cap Growth Funds	S&P SmallCap 600 Growth	33.49	75.38	77.78
Small Cap Core Funds	S&P SmallCap 600	34.45	65.30	65.50
Small Cap Value Funds	S&P SmallCap 600 Value	26.27	48.39	48.81
MultiCap Growth Funds	S&P Composite 1500 Growth	44.68	72.94	67.88
MultiCap Core Funds	S&P Composite 1500	41.14	49.42	56.40
MultiCap Value Funds	S&P Composite 1500 Value	31.25	45.27	61.59
Real Estate Funds	S&P BMI United States REIT	35.00	52.33	57.33

Sources: SPIVA Scorecard, Year-End 2009, March 2010. S&P Indices, CRSP. For periods ending December 31, 2009. Outperformance is based upon equal weighted fund counts.

outperform their benchmark. The data show that for the one-year period of 2009 more than half of the funds outperformed their benchmark, but for a five-year period only 2 of the 17 categories outperformed the market. In other words, it is easier to have one good year than five good years in a row. These data are shown in Table 4–11.

The report also includes an analysis of style consistency, which shows whether the mutual fund is actually invested according to the style advertised in the prospectus. Because some funds might merge or liquidate during the period being analyzed, SPIVA adjusts for survivorship bias. Most funds that merge or liquidate have exhibited poor performance, so if the data only included funds that survived, the data would be biased upward. Therefore SPIVA adjusts for the survivorship bias.

Standard & Poor's SPIVA report for the 10-year period 2000 to 2009 shows a lack of consistent returns from year to year. Investors are often attracted to the fund that was a top performer in the previous year, but that fund might not duplicate its previous year's performance in the next year. The average of all domestic funds over this 10-year period shows that 52 percent of the funds did not outperform their benchmark. The data differ by category. Sixty-seven percent of small-cap growth funds and 65 percent of mid-cap value funds did not outperform. The 10-year average shows that no category consistently outperformed the benchmark.

The returns are net of management fees, but not net of load fees. Perhaps the reason so many professionally managed funds have difficulty outperforming their benchmark is that they cannot outperform the benchmark by a percentage that is greater than their fees. If a fund has fees of 1.5 percent, then they would have to outperform the market by 1.5 percent to equal the benchmark return. We can conclude from the data that on average it is hard to beat the market, and this may account for the increased use of index funds by individual investors and why they are attracted to no-load, low-expense funds.

TABLE 4-12 Annual Match Ups—No Clear Trends

	PERCENTAGE OF U.S. DOMESTIC EQUITY FUNDS OUTPERFORMED BY BENCHMARKS											
Fund Category	**Benchmark Index**	**2000**	**2001**	**2002**	**2003**	**2004**	**2005**	**2006**	**2007**	**2008**	**2009**	**Average**
All Domestic Funds	S&P Composite 1500	40.5	54.5	59.0	47.7	51.4	44.0	67.8	48.8	64.23	41.67	52.0
All Large-Cap Funds	S&P 500	36.9	57.6	61.0	64.6	61.6	44.5	69.1	44.8	54.34	50.75	54.5
All Mid-Cap Funds	S&P MidCap 400	78.9	67.3	70.3	56.4	61.8	76.0	46.7	46.4	74.74	57.60	63.6
All Small-Cap Funds	S&P SmallCap 600	70.7	66.4	73.6	38.8	85.0	60.5	63.6	45.0	83.77	32.22	62.0
Large-Cap Growth Funds	S&P 500 Growth	16.0	87.5	71.8	44.7	39.5	31.6	76.1	31.6	89.95	39.15	52.8
Large-Cap Core Funds	S&P 500	35.6	58.1	63.0	66.0	66.9	44.6	71.3	44.0	52.03	52.06	55.4
Large-Cap Value Funds	S&P 500 Value	54.5	20.6	39.4	78.5	83.2	58.8	87.7	46.3	22.17	46.24	53.7
Mid-Cap Growth Funds	S&P MidCap 400 Growth	78.4	79.0	86.9	31.7	59.6	78.5	34.8	39.3	88.95	59.60	63.7
Mid-Cap Core Funds	S&P MidCap 400	72.8	70.5	64.6	50.0	51.8	72.4	35.9	64.6	62.28	68.60	61.4
Mid-Cap Value Funds	S&P MidCap 400 Value	94.8	55.8	74.3	81.9	63.6	71.8	38.4	56.1	67.06	47.83	65.2
Small-Cap Growth Funds	S&P SmallCap 600 Growth	73.0	81.3	94.2	35.3	93.6	72.2	52.1	39.4	95.50	33.49	67.0
Small-Cap Core Funds	S&P SmallCap 600	66.8	65.6	75.2	33.3	82.9	61.4	62.8	51.9	82.46	34.45	61.7
Small-Cap Value Funds	S&P SmallCap 600 Value	74.4	48.7	37.5	49.3	77.5	46.0	76.7	39.8	72.55	26.27	54.9

Sources: SPIVA Scorecard, Year-End 2009, March 2010. Standard & Poor's 2000–2006, Standard & Poor's, CRSP 2007–2009.

The problem is that most people don't want to accept an average return. Our egos motivate us to try to outperform, and we think it should be possible. Now, on average, if 67 percent of the small-cap mutual funds did not outperform the market, that means that 33 percent did outperform. The question is: Can you find those funds in the 33 percent, and will they continue to outperform in the future? Picking the right mutual fund may be just as difficult as picking an individual stock. Table 4–12 shows the 10-year data for the SPIVA Scorecard at year-end 2009.

Computing Total Return on Your Investment

application example

Assume you own a fund for a year and want to determine the total return on your investment. There are three potential sources of return:

Change in net asset value (NAV)
Dividends distributed
Capital gains distributed[5]

Assume the following:

	\$14.05	Beginning NAV
	15.10	Ending NAV
	1.05	Change in NAV (+)
0.72	0.40	Dividends distributed
	0.32	Capital gains distributed
	\$ 1.77	Total return

[5] This represents net capital gains that the fund actually had as a result of selling securities. They are distributed to shareholders.

In this instance, there is a total return of $1.77. Based on a beginning NAV of $14.05, the return is 12.60 percent:

$$\frac{\text{Total return}}{\text{Beginning NAV}} = \frac{\$1.77}{\$14.05} = 12.60\%$$

As a further consideration, assume that instead of taking dividends and capital gains income in cash, you decide to automatically reinvest the proceeds to purchase new mutual fund shares. To compute the percentage return in this instance, you must compare the total value of your ending shares to the total value of your beginning shares. Assume you owned 100 shares to start, and you received $0.72 in dividends plus capital gains per share (see prior example). This would allow you to reinvest $72 (100 shares × $0.72 per share). Further assume you bought new shares at an average price of $14.40 per share. This would provide you with five new shares.[6]

$$\frac{\text{Dividends and capital gains allocated to the account}}{\text{Average purchase price of new shares}} = \frac{\$72}{\$14.40} = 5 \text{ new shares}$$

In comparing the ending and beginning value of the investment based on the example in this section, we show the following:

$$\text{Total return} = \frac{\begin{pmatrix}\text{Number of}\\ \text{ending shares}\\ \times \text{ Ending price}\end{pmatrix} - \begin{pmatrix}\text{Number of}\\ \text{beginning shares}\\ \times \text{ Beginning price}\end{pmatrix}}{\text{Number of beginning shares} \times \text{Beginning price}} \tag{4–2}$$

$$= \frac{(105 \times \$15.10) - (100 \times \$14.05)}{(100 \times \$14.05)}$$

$$= \frac{\$1{,}585.50 - \$1{,}405}{\$1{,}405}$$

$$= \frac{\$180.50}{\$1{,}405} = 12.85\%$$

In determining whether the returns computed in this section are adequate, you must compare your returns with the popular market averages and with the returns on other mutual funds. While the returns might be considered quite good for a conservative fund, such might not be the case for an aggressive, growth-oriented fund. You must also consider the amount of risk you are taking in the form of volatility of returns. These factors of risk and return are more fully developed in chapter 17 on portfolio management.

UNIT INVESTMENT TRUSTS (UITS)

Unit investment trusts (UITs) are investment companies organized for the purpose of purchasing a pool of securities—usually tax-exempt municipal bonds. UITs issue units to investors, representing a proportionate interest in the assets of the trust. Investors also receive a proportionate share in the interest or dividends received by the trust. UITs are the last type of investment company and the smallest by asset size.

According to the Investment Company Institute, by the end of 2009 there were a total of 6,000 unit trusts with a market value of $38 billion. While this is not a lot of money compared with mutual funds, unit trusts do meet a market niche for

[6] In this case, the number of new shares came out to be a whole number. It is also possible to buy fractional shares in a mutual fund.

specialized investors. Of these 6,000 trusts, more than 3,400 were tax-free bond trusts. While equity trusts only accounted for slightly more than 2,100 trusts, they made up the lion's share of the value with $24 billion.

Unit investment trusts have been in decline for some time. At their peak they had over $100 billion in assets and 13,700 trusts. These trusts have an expiration date, and if new ones are not started, their numbers will automatically decline. It could be that target-date funds and exchange-traded funds have taken a bite out of unit trusts.

Unit investment trusts are passive investments. They normally purchase assets and hold them for the benefit of owners for a specified period.

To understand UITs better, consider the following hypothetical example. Nuveen, Inc.—a prominent firm in this field—announces the formation of the next in its series of tax-exempt unit trusts: Nuveen Series 2050. Through advertising and selling agents, Nuveen will raise $4 million; investors will pay approximately $1,000 per unit. After deducting 2 to 3 percent for sales commissions, Nuveen will use the remaining cash to purchase large blocks of municipal securities from 10 to 20 different issuers. Once this diversified pool of bonds is acquired, Nuveen will play a passive role. It will collect and pass on to unit holders all interest payments received and all principal repayments resulting from maturing or recalled bonds. While UITs usually hold bonds until maturity, the trust custodian may sell off bonds whose future ability to pay interest and principal is altered by events.

Often, trusts are formed to purchase tax-exempt securities from issuers in specific, high-tax states, such as New York, Massachusetts, and Minnesota. Unit holders residing in these states expect to receive a stream of income exempt from federal, state, and local taxation.

Even unit investment trusts dedicated to tax-exempt bonds have different investment objectives. Some deal strictly in long-term, high-rated issues. Others seek higher yields by purchasing issues with low ratings.

Units of a trust are redeemable under terms set forth in the prospectus. In most cases, this means a unit holder can sell units back to the trust at their net asset value, which is the current market value of each trust unit.

A secondary market for unit trusts is evolving among broker-dealers. Investors seeking to acquire or sell units can sometimes find a better deal in this market. However, most investors in UITs do not intend to redeem early.

Investors in UITs benefit by professional selection of securities, by diversification, and by avoiding the housekeeping chores of collecting coupon payments. As a large buyer, a UIT can usually purchase securities at a better price than the individual who buys in small lots.

Essential Difference between a Unit Investment Trust and a Mutual Fund

There is an important difference between UITs and mutual funds. UITs are formed with the intention of keeping all the initially purchased assets until maturity. The investment strategy, as already described, is strictly passive. A UIT of $4 million with a 10-year life will draw interest over that time period, while only cashing in bonds as they mature and returning the funds to the investors. The UIT will cease to exist after 10 years. Because of the features just described, there is very little interest rate risk associated with UITs. Since all bonds are intended to be held until maturity, the investor can be reasonably well assured of recovering his initial investment (plus interest). The fact that interest rates and bond prices are changing at any point in time during the life of the UIT makes little difference.[7]

[7] Of course, if the investor needs to redeem shares before the end of the life of the trust, there will be fluctuations in value.

A bond-oriented mutual fund has no such assurance of recovering the initial investment. First, mutual funds have no stipulated life. Second, the bonds in the portfolio are actively managed and frequently sold off before their maturity dates at large profits or losses. Thus, the purchaser of a bond-oriented mutual fund may experience large capital gains or losses as well as receiving interest income.

The message is that if preservation of capital is of paramount importance to the investor, the UIT may be a better investment than a mutual fund. Of course, if one thinks interest rates are going down and bond prices up, the bond-oriented mutual fund would be a better investment.

exploring the web

Web Address	Comments
www.morningstar.com	**Basic site containing detailed information about mutual funds, portfolio tracking, and analysis**
www.my.yahoo.com	**Permits tracking of mutual funds in portfolios**
moneycentral.msn.com	**Provides information about mutual funds**

SUMMARY

Investment funds allow investors to pool their resources under the guidance of professional managers. Some funds are closed-end, which means there is a *fixed* number of shares, and purchasers and sellers of shares must deal with each other (via brokers). They normally cannot buy new shares from the fund. Much more important is the open-end fund, which stands ready at all times to sell new shares or buy back old shares. Actually, it is the open-end investment fund that technically represents the term *mutual fund.*

An important consideration with an open-end fund is whether it is a load fund or a no-load fund. The former requires a commission that may run as high as 7.25 percent, while the latter has no such charge. Because there is no proof that load funds deliver better performance than no-load funds, the investor should think long and hard before paying a commission.

Mutual funds may take many different forms such as those emphasizing money market management, growth in common stocks, bond portfolio management, special sectors of the economy (such as energy or computers), or foreign investments. The funds with an international orientation have enjoyed strong popularity with the increased awareness of globalization and the rise of emerging markets such as China, Brazil, Russia, and India.

Through examining a fund's prospectus, the investor can become familiar with the fund's investment objectives and policies, its portfolio holdings, its turnover rate, and the fund's management fees. The investor can also become aware of whether the fund offers such special services as automatic reinvestment of

www.mhhe.com/hirtblock10e

distributions (when desired), exchange privileges among different funds, systematic withdrawal plans, and check-writing privileges.

Return to fund holders may come in the form of capital appreciation or yield. Over the long term, mutual funds have not outperformed the popular market averages. However, they do offer an opportunity for low-cost, efficient diversification, and they normally have experienced management. Also, a minority of funds have turned in above-average performances.

KEY WORDS AND CONCEPTS

back-end load 85
balanced funds 89
bond mutual funds 90
closed-end fund 80
dollar-cost averaging 96
exchange-traded funds (ETFs) 81
foreign funds 91
growth funds 89
growth with income funds 89
index funds 90
load funds 85
low-load funds 85
money market funds 89
net asset value (NAV) 80
no-load funds 86
open-end fund 80
prospectus 93
sector funds 91
specialty funds 91
target funds 92
unit investment trusts (UITs) 103

DISCUSSION QUESTIONS

1. Do mutual funds, on average, outperform the market?
2. Do mutual funds generally provide efficient diversification?
3. Explain why the vast array of mutual funds available to the investor may be a partial drawback and not always an advantage.
4. What is the basic difference between a closed-end fund and an open-end fund?
5. Define net asset value. Do closed-end funds normally trade at their net asset value? What about open-end funds?
6. Is it mandatory that you pay a load fee when purchasing an open-end mutual fund? What is a low-load fund?
7. Should you get better performance from a load fund in comparison to a no-load fund?
8. If there is a difference between the net asset value (NAV) and the offer price for a mutual fund, what does that tell us about the fund?
9. How can you distinguish between regular growth funds and aggressive growth funds?
10. What type of fund is likely to invest in convertible securities?
11. Why might there be some potential danger in investing in sector funds?
12. What does Rule 12b-1 enable mutual funds to do? Is this normally beneficial to current mutual fund shareholders?
13. Are earnings of mutual funds normally taxed at the fund level or the shareholder level?
14. What is the advantage of investing in a mutual fund that offers an exchange privilege?
15. What is dollar-cost averaging? If you were a particularly astute investor at timing moves in the market, would you want to use dollar-cost averaging?

16. From the viewpoint of an individual investor, what is the potential tax disadvantage of investing in a mutual fund?
17. What is the difference between a unit trust and a mutual fund?

PRACTICE PROBLEMS AND SOLUTIONS

Load funds

1. A fund is set up to charge a load. Its net asset value is $16.50 and its offer price is $17.30.
   a. What is the dollar value of the load (commission)?
   b. What percentage of the offer price does the load represent?
   c. What percentage of the net asset value does the load represent?
   d. Assume the fund increased in value by 30 cents the first month after you purchased 100 shares. What is the total dollar gain or loss? (Compare the total current value with the total purchase amount.)
   e. By what percentage would the net asset value of the shares have to increase for you to break even?

Total returns to a fund

2. Lee Kramer buys shares in the no-load Global Universe Fund on January 1 at a net asset value of $32.60. At the end of the year the price is $36.90. Also, the investor receives 90 cents in dividends and 50 cents in capital gains distributions. What is the total percentage return on the beginning net asset value? (Round to two places to the right of the decimal point.)

Solutions

1. *a.*

Offer price	$17.30
NAV	16.50
Commission (load)	$ 0.80

b. $\frac{\text{Load}}{\text{Offer price}} = \frac{\$0.80}{\$17.30} = 4.62\%$

c. $\frac{\text{Load}}{\text{NAV}} = \frac{\$0.80}{\$16.50} = 4.85\%$

d.

New NAV	$16.50 + $.30 =	$16.80
Number of shares		× 100
Current value		$1,680.00
Offer price		$17.30
Number of shares		× 100
Purchase amount		$1,730.00
Loss		($50.00)

e. You must earn the load of $0.80 on the net asset value of $16.50. The answer is 4.85 percent. This is the same as the answer to part *c*.

$$\frac{\text{Load}}{\text{NAV}} = \frac{\$0.80}{\$16.50} = 4.85\%$$

2.

Ending NAV	$36.90
Beginning NAV	−32.60
Change in NAV (+)	$ 4.30
Dividends distributed	$ 0.90
Capital gains distribution	0.50
Total return	$ 5.70

$$\frac{\text{Total return}}{\text{Beginning NAV}} = \frac{\$5.70}{\$32.60} = 17.48\%$$

PROBLEMS

Net asset value

1. The Twenty-First Century closed-end fund has $350 million in securities, $8 million in liabilities, and 20 million shares outstanding. It trades at a 10 percent discount from net asset value (NAV).
   a. What is the net asset value of the fund?
   b. What is the current price of the fund?
   c. Suggest two reasons why the fund may be trading at a discount from net asset value.

Net asset value

2. The New Pioneer closed-end fund has $520 million in securities, $5 million in liabilities, and 10 million shares outstanding. It trades at a 5 percent premium above its net asset value (NAV).
   a. What is the net asset value of the fund?
   b. What is the current price of the fund?
   c. Why might a fund trade at a premium above its net asset value?

Load funds

3. In problem 2, if New Pioneer converted to an open-end fund trading at its net asset value with a 6 percent load (commission), what would its purchase price be?

Load vs. no-load

4. In problem 2, if New Pioneer converted to an open-end fund and traded at $51.50, would it be a load or no-load fund?

Load funds

5. An open-end fund is set up to charge a load. Its net asset value is $8.72, and its offer price is $9.25.
   a. What is the dollar value of the load (commission)?
   b. What percentage of the offer price does the load represent?
   c. What percentage of the net asset value does the load represent?
   d. Do load funds necessarily outperform no-load funds?
   e. How do no-load funds earn a return if they do not charge a commission?

Load funds

6. In problem 5, assume the fund increased in value by $0.30 the first month after you purchased 300 shares.
   a. What is your total dollar gain or loss? (Compare the total current value with the total purchase amount.)
   b. By what percentage would the net asset value of the shares have to increase for you to break even?

Comparative fund performance and loads

7. *a.* If you purchased a low-load fund at $10.30 and it had a net asset value of $10.00, what is the percent load?
   b. If the fund's net asset value went up by 33.72 percent, what would its new net asset value be?
   c. What is your dollar profit or loss per share based on your purchase price?
   d. What is your percentage return on your purchase price?

Total returns on a fund

8. An investor buys Go-Go Mutual Fund on January 1 at a net asset value of $21.20. At the end of the year, the price is $25.40. Also, the investor receives $0.50 in dividends and $0.35 in capital gains distributions. What is the total percent return on the beginning net asset value? (Round to two places to the right of the decimal point.)

Total returns on a fund

9. Dan Herman purchases the Ivy Tower New Horizon Fund at a net asset value of $11.25. During the year, he receives $0.50 in dividends and $0.14 in capital gains distributions. At the end of the year, the fund's price is $10.90. What is the total percentage return or loss on the beginning net asset value? (Round to two places to the right of the decimal point.)

Total returns with reinvestment

10. Alice Olivia had 200 shares of the Quest Fund on January 1. The shares had a value of $17.60. During the year she received $90 in dividends and $270 in capital gains distributions. She used the funds to purchase shares at an average

price of $18 per share. By the end of the year, the shares were up to $18.50. What is her percentage total return? Use Formula 4–2 on page 103 and round to two places to the right of the decimal point. Recall you first must determine the number of new shares.

Total returns with reinvestment

11. Tom Aaron had 300 shares of the New Decade Fund on January 1. The shares had a value of $23. During the year he received $150 in dividends and $450 in capital gains distributions. He used the funds to purchase shares at an average price of $25 per share. By the end of the year, the shares were all up to $27. What is the percentage of his total return? Use Formula 4–2 on page 103 and round to two places to the right of the decimal point. Recall that you first must determine the number of new shares.

Dollar-cost averaging

12. Under dollar-cost averaging, an investor will purchase $6,000 worth of stock each year for three years. The stock price is $40 in year 1, $30 in year 2, and $48 in year 3.

a. Compute the average price per share.
b. Compute the average cost per share.
c. Explain why the average cost is less than the average price.

INVESTMENT ADVISOR PROBLEM

Lou Samuels was really excited. After watching a commercial about the New Century Fund on NBC and talking to a representative of the mutual fund at an 800 number, he was ready to commit. And why not? The fund had an annualized compound rate of return of 16.6 percent over the last 10 years. Furthermore, he was impressed with the fact that it was a low-load fund with an initial commission of 3 percent and an exit (sales) commission of 0.75 percent. The mutual fund shares for this aggressive growth fund were currently selling at $36.

He planned to make the purchase the next morning. Although the fund kept its phone lines open during the evening, he had previously scheduled a tennis match with his investment advisor, Tony Roseman, and decided to tell him about the proposed investment first.

As they were warming up for the match, Lou told Tony about the exciting mutual fund he was about to invest in. Tony, a CFP, had been in the investment business long enough to know that investors are sometimes swept away by their enthusiasm and make hasty, not well-thought-out decisions.

a. What matters should the investment advisor point out to Lou?
b. By what percentage would the New Century Fund need to go up just for Lou to break even?

WEB EXERCISE

Many mutual fund sponsors have a large family of funds under management. One example of this is the Fidelity fund group. Go to **www.fidelity.com**.

1. Click on "Research" then click on "Mutual Funds."
2. Click on "Browse Fidelity Funds" on the right column.
3. Click on M in the directory and then find the Fidelity Magellan Fund.

www.mhhe.com/hirtblock10e

4. Click on the Fidelity Magellan Fund and record the following:
   a. 1-, 3-, 5-, 10-year returns
   b. Record the same for the "S&P Composite."
   c. How has Magellan done against the S&P Composite?
   d. Should investors be disappointed or pleased?
5. Scroll down and record the first five of the "Top 10 Holdings."
6. What percentage of the fund is invested in the United States? What is the "Percent Foreign Holdings"?

Note: From time to time, companies redesign their Web sites, and occasionally a topic we have listed may have been deleted, updated, or moved into a different location.

ANALYSIS AND VALUATION OF EQUITY SECURITIES

PART [two] 2

5

chapter five

ECONOMIC ACTIVITY

OBJECTIVES

1. Explain the concept of a top-down valuation process.
2. Discuss the role of the federal government in influencing economic policy.
3. Distinguish between the effects of fiscal policy and monetary policy.
4. Explain how inflation and trade policy influence the economy.
5. Describe the business cycle and how it relates to cyclical indicators.
6. Explain the relationship of the business cycle to various industries.

OUTLINE

To determine the value of the firm, fundamental analysis relies on long-run forecasts of the economy, the industry, and the company's financial prospects. Short-run changes in business conditions are also important in that they influence investors' required rates of return and expectations of corporate earnings and dividends. This chapter presents the basic information for analysis of the economy, while other chapters in this section focus on industry analysis and the individual firm.

Figure 5–1 presents an overview of the top-down valuation process as an inverted triangle. The process starts with a macroanalysis of the economy and then moves into industry variables. Next, common stocks are individually screened according to expected risk-return characteristics, and finally the surviving stocks are combined into portfolios of assets. This figure is not inclusive of all variables considered by an analyst but is intended to indicate representative areas applicable to most industries and companies.

FIGURE 5-1 Top-Down Overview of the Valuation Process

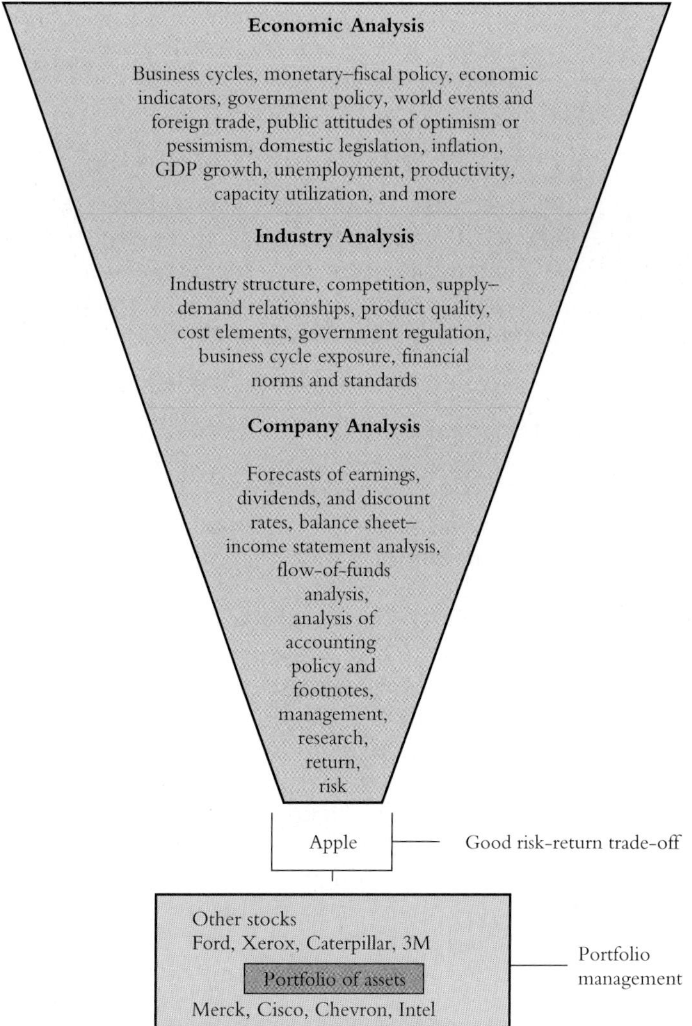

ECONOMIC ACTIVITY AND THE BUSINESS CYCLE

An investor begins the valuation process with an economic analysis. The hope is that an accurate forecast and examination of economic activity will provide the basis for accurate stock market predictions and indicate which industries may prosper. The analyst needs information on present and expected interest rates, monetary and fiscal policy, government and consumer spending patterns, and other economic data. To be successful, investors must understand business cycles and be able to forecast accurately. Unfortunately, these are not easy tasks, but the rewards can be significant if the timing is right.

Whether analysts use statistical methods, such as regression analysis and probability theory, or simply seat-of-the-pants judgment, they are still basing their forecast on expectations related to past data and experiences. Past information usually is not extrapolated into the future without being adjusted to conform with the subjective beliefs of the decision maker. Even when highly sophisticated statistical methods are used, subjectivity enters into the decision in some fashion.

Most likely, past knowledge will be helpful, but modifications for the present effects of worldwide currency fluctuations, international debt obligations, and other factors, which were not so important previously, need to be included in any forecast now. Since most companies are influenced to some degree by the general level of economic activity, a forecast will usually start with an analysis of the government's economic program.

Federal Government Economic Policy (A Short History)

Government economic policy is guided by the **Employment Act of 1946** and subsequent position statements by the Federal Reserve Board, the President's Council of Economic Advisors, and other acts of Congress. The goals established by the Employment Act still hold and cover four broad areas. These goals, the focus of monetary and fiscal policy, are as follows, with a second interpretation in parentheses:

1. Stable prices (a low inflation rate).
2. Business stability at high levels of production (low levels of unemployment).
3. Sustained real growth in gross domestic product (actual economic growth after deducting inflation).
4. A balance in international payments (primarily a balance of exports and imports but also including cash flows in and out of the United States).

1950–1970 These goals are often conflicting in that they do not all respond favorably to the same economic stimulus. Therefore, goal priorities and economic policies change to reflect current economic conditions. In the 1950s and early 1960s, the United States did not have an international trade or inflation problem, so economic policy focused on employment and economic growth. The economy grew rapidly between 1961 and 1969, and, because of the Vietnam War, unemployment reached very low levels. The demand for goods and competition for funds were very high during the war, and eventually war expenditures, large budget deficits, full employment, and large increases in the money supply caused many problems. Inflation accelerated to high levels, interest rates reached record heights, and an imbalance of international payments finally resulted in two devaluations of the U.S. dollar in the early 1970s.

1970–1990 By the time Jimmy Carter took office in January 1977, the primary goals were once again to reduce unemployment, control inflation, and create a moderate level of economic growth that could be sustained without causing more inflation (a very difficult task!). The achievement of these goals was thrown into the hands of the Federal Reserve Board. The Fed's tight money policy caused a rapid increase in interest rates to control inflation, and these high rates depressed common stock prices as the required rate of return by investors reached record levels.

Ronald Reagan inherited most of the problems Carter faced but tried new ways of reaching the goals. As the 1980s began, Reagan instituted a three-year tax cut to increase disposable income and stimulate consumption and thus economic growth, and, at the same time, he negotiated reductions in government spending. These policies were successful in sharply reducing inflation and creating strong growth in the gross domestic product (GDP), but they were accomplished with record government deficits. George H. Bush followed most of Reagan's domestic policies but focused more on international issues. In the middle of President Bush's term, the 90-month peacetime expansion came to an end with the start of a recession in July 1990. In looking back, the expansion that began in November 1982 created record employment, reduced unemployment percentages, and lowered interest rates and inflation from the high levels of 1980 and 1981. The stock market began a major bull market in 1982 in response to these improved conditions but also sustained the biggest one-day crash ever on October 19, 1987.

www.ibm.com
www.att.com

1990–2010 Unfortunately, the recession that began in July 1990 was extremely painful. Major companies such as IBM, AT&T, General Motors, and hundreds of others announced employee reductions totaling more than one-half million employees. In November 1992, President Clinton was elected to office on the promise of more jobs and universal health coverage. The economy was already benefiting from the recovery started in March 1991, and Clinton persuaded Congress to pass an increase in personal and corporate income taxes. Many economists thought the tax increase would create a "fiscal drag" on the economy by reducing spending. By the third quarter of 1992, the economy had slowed down considerably and stagnated at minimal real GDP growth. However, by year-end 1993, real GDP growth in the fourth quarter was more than 7 percent, and by the end of 1994 had stabilized at between 3.0 and 3.5 percent real growth. A Republican Congress was elected in 1994 and came into office in January 1995. President Clinton was elected for a second term in 1996, and he and Congress went to work on a balanced budget proposal. Spending was held in check, and tax revenues rose to record levels as a result of the long-term healthy growth of the economy.

The combination of these factors created large surpluses and projections of even larger surpluses in the coming years. Between 1997 and 2001 the U.S. Treasury was able to retire several hundred billion dollars of government debt. One of the results of deficit reduction is the loss of a fiscal stimulus created by government spending, and this can cause a drag on the economy if consumers don't pick up the slack. Consumers were more than happy to spend, and the economy rolled along until about 2000 when it slowed a little. The stock market started to decline in April 2000, and when George W. Bush took office in January 2001, he inherited a crumbling economy that had run out of steam after years of exceptional growth. By summer 2001, the economy managed to squeeze out a 0.2 percent growth in second quarter GDP, and the surplus was shrinking fast due to declining tax revenues and the tax cuts passed in the early days of the Bush administration. The third quarter of 2001, punctuated by the September 11th terrorist attack, generated a negative growth rate and the National Bureau of Economic Research declared a recession with a starting date of March 2001 and the end in November 2001. The economy picked up steam and managed reasonable growth in 2002 and 2003. However, President Bush's tax cuts coupled with large expenditures on the Iraqi war and homeland security, put the United States on course to have a $382 billion deficit for the fiscal year 2004 and a $309 billion deficit for fiscal year 2005. A strong economy in 2006 increased tax revenues and the U.S. deficit was reduced to $151 billion.

The economy grew throughout 2007, but in the first quarter of 2008 it recorded a negative real GDP growth rate of −0.7. The economy turned up briefly in the second quarter of 2008 and then recorded four quarters of negative real GDP growth that ended after the second quarter of 2009. Five out of six quarters of negative GDP growth signaled a severe recession that saw unemployment rise from 4.6 percent in 2006 to 10.1 percent by October 2009.

The cause of the problem was a housing bubble that gathered steam throughout 2005–2006 and finally burst in 2007, causing a financial crisis that was the most significant since the Great Depression of the 1930s. In 1999 the Clinton administration attempted to make mortgage financing more available for low-income, high-risk buyers. They enlisted the 20 largest banks and Fannie Mae and Freddie Mac (both quasi-governmental companies) to lower their credit standards. The Bush administration continued this policy, and over seven years, many new mortgages were made to "subprime" borrowers, or high-risk borrowers. Some of these mortgages required only a 5 or 10 percent down payment, or in some cases even nothing down. People were so sure that housing prices would never come down, they didn't worry about being overleveraged with too much debt. You can imagine how 5 percent equity in a house can be totally wiped out with a 5 percent decline in house prices. The conventional loan of 20 percent down would be more difficult to wipe out in a market downturn.

Many homeowners also took advantage of tax laws that allowed interest deductions on second mortgages (home equity loans), and as the value of their house went up, they borrowed against the increased equity to buy cars, boats, furniture, and many other things. Instead of paying down their mortgage in the traditional way, they kept increasing their borrowings. This new lending created increased demand, which caused housing prices in many areas of the United States to go up. Investors started speculating in hot spots like Florida, California, Arizona, and Nevada, and pushed up prices even more.

To exacerbate the problem, the banks and mortgage companies were bundling their mortgages into marketable securities and selling them off as asset-backed securities. Wall Street firms were creating billion-dollar mortgage portfolios with 10 tranches (pools) of mortgages, with triple A in the top pool and subprime high risk in the bottom pool. In many cases only the top 3 or 4 tranches were investment grade, but the rating agencies gave these mortgage-backed securities the highest AAA ratings. Many of these securities that were sold by banks and mortgage lenders eventually ended back in the banks' investment portfolios.

As housing prices peaked and started turning downward, homeowners began to default on their loans. Investors started to question the safety of their asset-backed securities. Bear Stearns, which had many collateralized mortgages in mortgage guarantees on its books, was forced into a fire sale to J.P. Morgan in 2008. It was either a fire sale or bankruptcy for Bear Stearns. Lehman Brothers was not so fortunate, and was forced into bankruptcy. Bank of America bought Merrill Lynch, and Morgan Stanley and Goldman Sachs, the last two major investment banks, became bank holding companies to benefit from the loans and guarantees by the Federal Reserve.

Congress allocated a loan fund of more than $800 billion to rescue financial institutions and another $800 billion stimulus bill to pour money into the economy. By the end of the first quarter of 2010, the U.S. federal deficit stood at $1.311 trillion, and accounted for over 11 percent of nominal GDP. Figure 5–2 shows that this is extremely high by historical standards and a great worry for future generations.

The recession that started in December 2008 increasingly worsened, as more and more people defaulted on their loans. Quite a few homeowners owned houses that were "under water"—the value of the house was less than the mortgage—and many simply walked away from their mortgages and sent the keys back to the lender. It will take many years for the housing market and the financial system to recover from this financial crisis. Congress passed a major financial reform bill in 2010, and the markets will eventually determine whether Congress got it right or

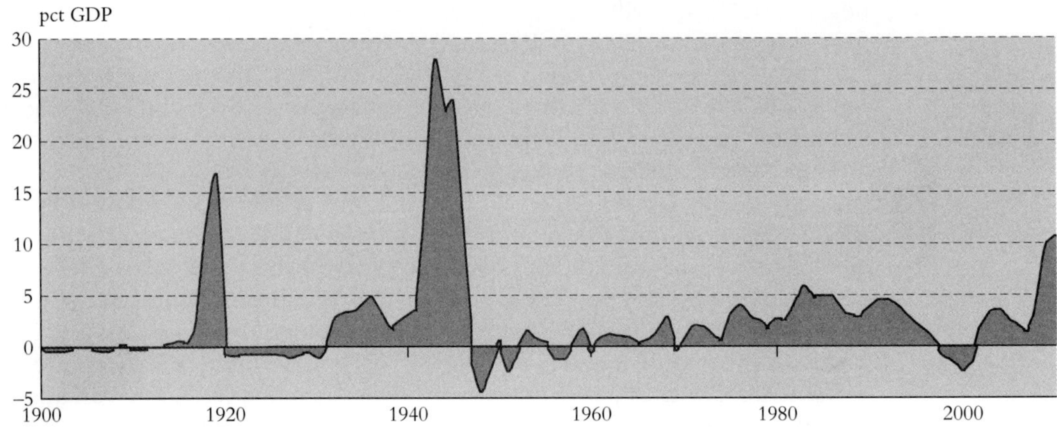

Source: www.usgovernmentspending.com. Copyright © 2010.

TABLE 5-1 Real Gross Domestic Product Percent Change from Year Ago

	2000	2001	2002	2003	2004	2005	2006	2007	2008	2009
Australia	3.3	2.5	3.9	3.2	3.6	3.2	2.6	4.7	2.4	1.3
Canada	5.2	1.8	2.9	1.9	3.1	3.0	2.9	2.5	0.4	−2.6
Chile	4.5	3.5	2.2	4.0	6.0	5.6	4.6	4.6	3.7	−1.5
China	8.4	8.3	9.1	10.0	10.1	10.4	11.6	13.0	9.6	8.7
Euro Area	4.0	1.9	0.9	0.8	2.0	1.8	3.1	2.7	0.5	−4.0
Japan	2.8	0.2	0.3	1.5	2.7	1.9	2.0	2.3	−1.2	−5.2
Mexico*	6.0	−0.9	0.1	1.4	4.0	3.2	4.9	3.3	1.5	−6.6
Singapore	10.1	−2.4	4.2	3.8	9.2	7.6	8.7	8.2	1.4	−2.0
United Kingdom	3.9	2.5	2.1	2.8	3.0	2.2	2.9	2.6	0.5	−4.9
United States	4.1	1.1	1.8	2.5	3.6	3.1	2.7	2.1	0.4	−2.4

Source: Federal Reserve Bank of St. Louis, August 2010, http://research.stlouisfed.org. From OECD Economic Outlook, 2010.

whether they overreacted and stifled lending. We will discuss some of the Federal Reserve Board's actions in response to this crisis later in the chapter.

International Trends The international landscape is also changing rapidly, and this includes changes in North America, South America, Europe, and Asia. In 2010, China overtook Japan as the second largest economy in the world, and Brazil has become a dominant economy in South America. The European Union suffered throughout the financial crisis, and in 2010 many countries, including Portugal, Ireland, Italy, Greece, and Spain ("PIIGS"), were in serious economic difficulties. The European Central Bank and the member countries had to guarantee loans to Greece and several large banks. They also set up a loan facility that could be used by countries in need. As we move into the realm of global investing, we can't ignore companies operating around the world, and we need to understand the trading relationships that exist between countries and how these may affect a country's GDP and companies within a region. Table 5–1 illustrates GDP growth rates of the United States's significant trading partners. China stands out from the crowd with the highest growth rates and a decade without any contractions. The world's developed economies, such as Canada, the Euro area, the United States, the United Kingdom, and Japan, have aging populations and slow growth relative to the Asian economies of China and Singapore, as well as Australia, which benefits from its relationship with Asia. Chile as a representative of South America was maintaining consistent and positive growth until 2009, when it suffered along with North America.

Fiscal Policy

Fiscal policy can be described as the government's taxing and spending policies. These policies can have a great impact on the direction of economic activity. One must realize at the outset that fiscal policy is cumbersome. It has a long implementation lag and is often motivated by political rather than economic considerations since Congress must approve budgets and develop tax laws. Figure 5–3 presents a historical picture of government expenditures and receipts. When the government spends more than it receives, it runs a **deficit** that must be financed by the Treasury. As the figure shows, the financial crisis and recession created the largest deficit on record.

A forecaster must pay attention to the size of the deficit and how it is financed to measure its expected impact on the economy. If the deficit is financed by the Treasury selling securities to the Federal Reserve, it is very expansive. The money

FIGURE 5-3 Federal Government Expenditures and Receipts

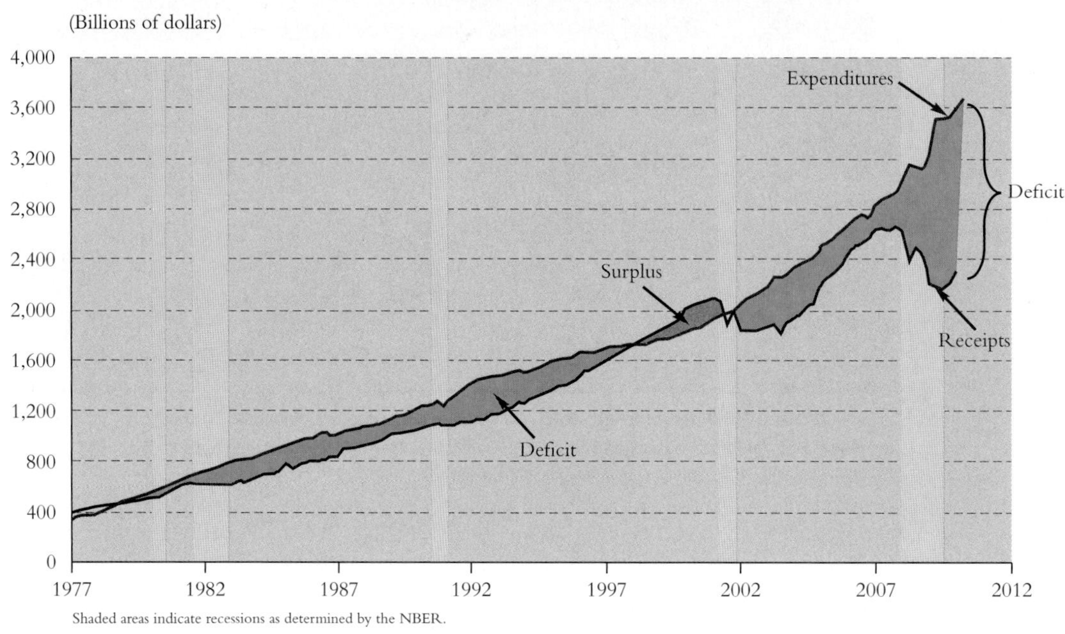

Source: 2010 Federal Reserve Bank of St. Louis: http://research.stlouisfed.org.

supply will increase without having any significant short-run effects on interest rates. If the deficit is financed by selling securities to banks and individuals, there is not the same expansion in the money supply, and short-term interest rates will rise unless the Federal Reserve intervenes with open-market trading.

A look at Figure 5–3 shows that **surpluses**, in which revenues exceed expenditures, have been virtually nonexistent from 1977 to 2010, and the annual deficit increased dramatically during 2008–2010. Surpluses tend to reduce economic growth as the government slows its demand for goods and services relative to its income. In an analysis of fiscal policy, the important consideration for the investor is the determination of the flow of funds. In a deficit economy, the government usually stimulates GDP by spending on socially productive programs or by increasing spending on defense, education, highways, or other government programs.

One other area of fiscal policy deals with the government's ability to levy import taxes or tariffs on foreign goods. As a free market economy, we have fought for years with our trading partners to open their countries' markets to U.S. goods. Figure 5–4 depicts the annual trade deficits that started piling up beginning in 1982. This deficit occurred because U.S. consumers purchased more foreign goods (imports) than U.S. companies sold to foreigners (exports). This occurred for several reasons; one was a lack of free markets with some of our trading partners, specifically Japan, and the robust health of the U.S. economy. The United States has been trying to open markets for U.S. goods with Japan, China, and other countries for the last several decades. The World Trade Organization (WTO) and its round of tariff negotiations have been instrumental in breaking down trade barriers during the last half of the 1990s, and in 2004 China was approved for membership in the WTO, which has had a positive effect on world trade.

Countries can create trade barriers either by setting up import tariffs or by taxes that raise the price of foreign goods and make them less competitive with domestic goods. This is a common way to protect domestic industries. The WTO deals with these issues through negotiations and if necessary through a world court to arbitrate complaints from one country against another.

FIGURE 5-4 Exports vs. Imports (balance of trade on current account)

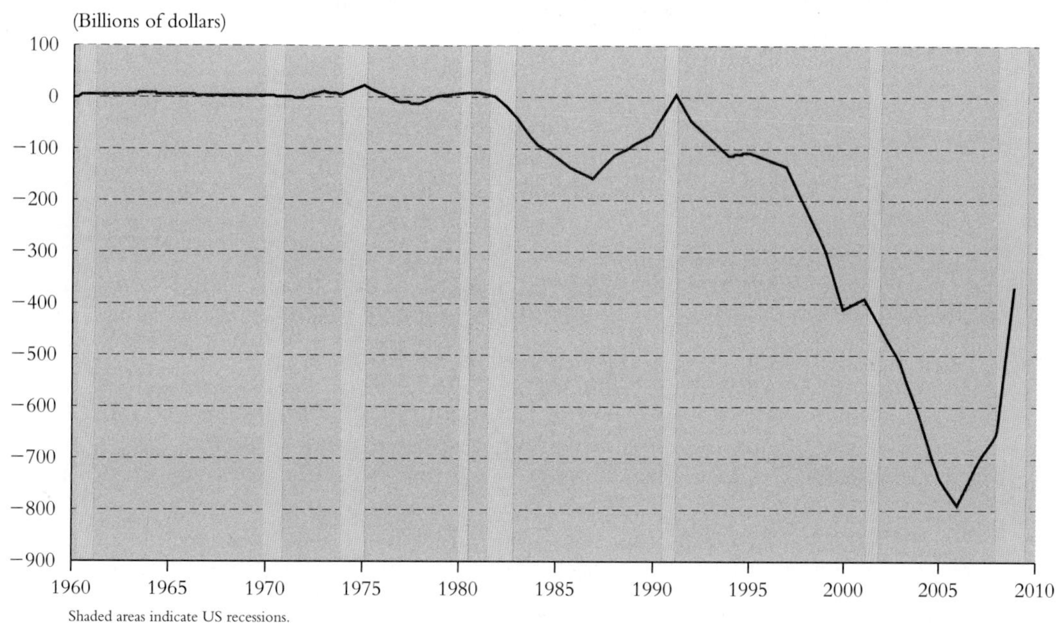

Source: Data from Federal Reserve Bank of St. Louis, FRED.

As Figure 5–4 shows, the U.S. trade deficit increased quite rapidly from 1996 to 2006, going from a negative \$89.4 billion in 1997 to a negative \$800 billion in 2006. As the U.S. dollar fell against other currencies, U.S. goods became relatively less expensive for foreigners, and the trade deficit has been improving since the 2006 bottom. For the year 2009, the United States's largest share of imports came from China (18.8 percent), Canada (14.4 percent), Mexico (11.2 percent), and Japan (6 percent).

The rising trade deficit during most of this time period was a function of the healthy U.S. economy and a strong dollar. When a country's economy is healthy with high employment and income, its citizens spend more in general and import more goods (especially high-priced luxury goods) from other countries. When there is a recession, people spend less, look for less expensive items, and import fewer goods. The second factor is the exchange rate between two currencies. For example, if the U.S. dollar rises against the British pound, U.S. goods become more expensive for British citizens, and British goods become less expensive for U.S. citizens. If the dollar exchange rate stays high or continues to rise, eventually British citizens change their buying habits and buy fewer U.S. goods, and U.S. citizens buy more British goods. This effect can also be seen in the U.S.–Japanese automobile market. As the Japanese yen rose against the dollar, in the early 1990s, Americans bought fewer Japanese cars and more U.S. domestic cars. The Japanese consumer did the opposite.

Since late 2002 the U.S. administration has been following a weak dollar policy as a way of curbing U.S. imports and raising U.S. exports. The euro has risen against the U.S. dollar by over 50 percent from its low to its peak, but unfortunately the United States's biggest trading deficit is with China, and the Chinese renmimbi has remained rather inflexible because the Chinese government has pegged the renmimbi to a basket of currencies including the U.S. dollar. In June 2010 they indicated that they will allow the yuan to be more flexible and rise against the U.S. dollar.

Short-term swings in exchange rates have little effect on imports and exports, but changes in long-term currency relationships eventually change import-export balances between countries. It usually takes more than a year before the effects of exchange rates on prices show up at the retail level and influence the buying patterns of consumers. As world trade increases, exchange rates and economic trends around the world become more important. While exchange rates and economic activity are influenced by fiscal policy, they are also affected by monetary policy, as discussed in the next section.

Monetary Policy

Monetary policy determines the "appropriate" levels for the money supply and interest rates that accomplish the economic goals of the Employment Act of 1946. Monetary policy is determined by the Federal Open Market Committee (FOMC), which includes the Federal Reserve Board of Governors and the 12 Federal Reserve bank presidents. Monetary policy can be implemented very quickly to reinforce fiscal policy or, when necessary, to offset the effects of fiscal policy.

The Federal Reserve has several ways to influence economic activity. First, it can raise or lower the reserve requirements on commercial bank time deposits or demand deposits. **Reserve requirements** represent the percent of total deposits that a bank must hold as cash in its vault or as deposits in Federal Reserve banks. An increase in reserve requirements contracts the money supply. The banking system has to hold larger reserves for each dollar deposited and is not able to lend as much money on the same deposit base. A reduction in reserve requirements has the opposite effect. The Fed also changes the discount rate periodically to reflect its attitude toward the economy. This **discount rate** is the interest rate the Federal Reserve charges commercial banks on very short-term loans. The Fed does not make a practice of lending funds to a single commercial bank for more than two or three weeks, and so this charge can influence an individual bank's willingness to borrow money for expansionary loans to industry. The Fed can also influence bank behavior by issuing policy statements, or jawboning.

Beyond these monetary measures, the tool most widely used is **open-market operations** in which the Fed buys and sells U.S. government securities for its own portfolio. When the Fed sells securities in the open market, purchasers write checks to pay for their securities, and demand deposits fall, causing a contraction in the money supply. At the same time, the increase in the supply of Treasury bills sold by the Fed forces prices down and interest rates up to entice buyers to part with their money. The Fed usually accomplishes its adjustments by selling securities to commercial banks, government securities dealers, or individuals.

If the Fed buys securities, the opposite occurs; the money supply increases, and interest rates go down. This tends to encourage economic expansion. As you will see in Chapter 7, the interest rate is extremely important in determining the required rate of return, or discount rate for a stock.

Figure 5–5 summarizes the four policy goals set by the Employment Act of 1946 and the monetary tools that help achieve these goals. The problem with monetary policy is that the four goals are not complementary, and so the Federal Reserve has to choose which goals it will focus upon given the state of the economy. If the economy is sluggish or contracting it will lower rates to stimulate the economy and employment. However, lowering rates will increase the outflow of foreign funds from the United States, and as the economy expands, inflation may increase. The early years of the millennium (2000–2004) demonstrate this goal conflict. The Federal Reserve was able to keep rates low to stimulate the economy, and excess capacity in the manufacturing sector allowed the economy to expand without creating too much inflation. Once the economy expands enough to reach capacity constraints, prices will start rising, and the Federal Reserve will have to raise rates, which will slow the economy. Rates did rise from 2004 to 2007, but then plummeted to extremely low levels as the Fed tried to stimulate the recession economy of 2008–2009. As of the fall of 2010, rates were still so low that one-year Treasury bills had a negative real rate of return.

application example

FIGURE 5-5 Economic Policy Goals and Monetary Policy

Goals	Raise Rates	Lower Rates
1. Sustainable Growth in Real GDP	Reduces economic growth	Stimulates economic growth
2. High Rates of Employment (low unemployment)	Reduces employment	Stimulates employment
3. Balance of International Payments	Strengthens domestic currency	Decreases domestic currency
a) Balance of Trade	Over time high rates will cause imports to go up, and exports down if the currency stays strong	Over time low rates will cause imports to go down and exports to go up if the currency stays weak
b) Cash Flows between Countries	Increases foreign investment inflows	Increases foreign investment outflows
4. Maintain Stable Prices (low inflation rate)	Reduces inflationary impact	Increases inflationary impact

Monetary Tools	To Raise Rates	To Lower Rates
Bank Reserve Requirements	Raise reserve requirements—Takes money out of banking system—Creates less loanable funds	Lower reserve requirements—Puts money into banking system—Creates more loanable funds
Discount Rate	An increase in the discount rate reduces banks' willingness to borrow from the Federal Reserve and contracts the economy	A decrease in the discount rate increases banks' willingness to borrow from the Federal Reserve and expands the economy
Federal Open-Market Committee Activity	Sells Treasury securities—Lowers prices and raises rates—Takes money out of economy	Buys Treasury securities—Raises prices and lowers rates—Puts money into economy
Jawboning (The art of the chairman of the Federal Reserve or governors of the Fed talking rates up or down in markets)	Say good things about GDP	Say bad things about GDP

In a sense, the Federal Reserve is always prioritizing the four goals, and by watching the Federal Reserve's monetary policy actions, an investor may be able to anticipate potential profitable investments. Analysts are continually playing chess with the Federal Reserve, trying to guess the next move, but the Federal Reserve is adept at not disclosing what the next move will be. In a perfect world, monetary and fiscal policy would create a balanced economy achieving all four goals. Unfortunately the economy has a tendency to move in cycles with changing demand and consumer behavior, international trade, and the hundreds of other factors making a perfect balance impossible.

The Fed's and the U.S. Treasury's Response to the Financial Crisis Sometimes the normal monetary and fiscal tools are not absolutely effective in very tough times. The Federal Reserve Bank and the U.S. Treasury, as well as Congress, were worried about the domino effect if the "too big to fail" banks started to declare bankruptcy. If a bank like Wachovia or CitiGroup were allowed to fail, this might bring down the whole financial system. During the fall of 2007, the markets for commercial paper, auction-rate preferred stock, and mortgage-backed securities were illiquid as participants withdrew from the markets. The Fed and the Treasury took some unorthodox approaches to the financial crisis.

The Fed acted as a market maker in the commercial paper market, buying and selling securities for their own account. They forced weak and potentially failing banks to merge with stronger banks. For example, Wells Fargo bought Wachovia Bank, J.P. Morgan bought Bear Stearns and Washington Mutual, PNC of Pittsburg bought National City Bank of Cleveland, and Bank of America bought Merrill Lynch and Countrywide Credit, the largest mortgage banker. The theory was that it would be better to force a merger than to endure a bankruptcy and subsequent financial chaos. There was also the possibility that the Federal Deposit Insurance Corporation didn't have enough resources to withstand the loan losses, and so it was better to work out a merger with the strong banks.

The U.S. Treasury convinced the U.S. Congress to provide $700 billion to support banks and financial institutions in financial trouble. The bill to allocate the money was named the **Troubled Asset Relief Program (TARP)**. Many banks were below their required capital adequacy standards and needed equity capital. They needed Tier 1 risk capital (common equity) and Tier 2 capital (preferred stock), and the Treasury now had the available capital to help out. TARP allowed the U.S. Treasury to purchase or insure up to $700 billion of troubled assets that were primarily subprime mortgages or securities collateralized by mortgages. The secretary of the Treasury was to work with the chairman of the Federal Reserve Board of Governors in allocating capital to the banking system. Additionally, the U.S. Treasury had to notify the appropriate committees of Congress of its actions.

First the Treasury bought preferred stock from banks to shore up their capital, and the five largest banks each sold the Treasury $25 billion in preferred stock. The preferred stock had warrants attached to buy common stock. This action was a first for the U.S. Treasury. Some banks, including J.P. Morgan, protested that they didn't need the money, but the Fed and Treasury insisted that all five banks take an equal amount in order to avoid signaling that some were weaker than others. PNC borrowed $6 billion to buy National City Bank. In the case of Citigroup, the preferred stock was later converted to common stock and the U.S. government ended up owning almost 40 percent of CitiGroup, which they began to sell in the open market during 2010. Originally TARP was expected to cost U.S. taxpayers about $350 billion, but it appears that the government loss may be less than $50 billion.

One of the more controversial uses of the TARP money was the purchase of General Motors after it was forced into a government-brokered bankruptcy. In 2010, GM returned to profitability and announced an initial public offering in August 2010. Another controversial loan was made to AIG Insurance, a company that had guaranteed many of the asset-backed securities that were in the securitized subprime mortgage pools. The day after the government let Lehman Brothers go bankrupt, they saved AIG with an $85 billion loan. At one time AIG owed the government $182 billion, a large percentage of the TARP bailout money.

Another program was called the **Term Asset-Backed Securities Loan Facility (TALF)**. This facility allowed the Federal Reserve to buy asset-backed securities backed by student loans, auto loans, loans to small business guaranteed by the Small Business Administration, and credit card loans. Originally the amount allocated was $200 billion, but this was later moved up to $1 trillion. The funds are not

the real world of investing

THE BUDGETARY TREATMENT OF COMPANIES OWNED BY THE GOVERNMENT

Investment made through the Troubled Asset Relief Program in General Motors (GM) and American International Group (AIG) have given the government a substantial ownership stake in those companies. The government currently owns nearly 80 percent of AIG and is likely to own about 60 percent of the reconstituted GM after it emerges from bankruptcy. In addition, if the planned conversion of preferred to common stock takes place, the government could own more than 30 percent of Citigroup. Such ownership by the government gives rise to questions about whether the companies' activities should be included in the federal budget.

Ownership is not the only relevant criterion for determining budgetary treatment, especially if the stake is meant to be temporary. In 1967, the President's Commission on Budget Concepts provided guidance for determining which activities should be included in the federal budget. Its report stated that the budget should include transactions that are within the federal sector and not subject to the economic disciplines of the marketplace."[1] The commission indicated the various aspects of ownership and control should be considered in judging whether to include an activity in the budget. But, the commission acknowledged, "the boundaries of the federal establishment are sometimes difficult to draw," no single answer to the question is conclusive, and decisions about including an activity must account for many relevant considerations.

The conservatorship Fannie Mae and Freddie Mac, government-sponsored enterprises that guarantee mortgages and mortgage-backed securities, is somewhat analogous although not completely parallel. Even though both institutions were created by the federal government and had long-standing links with the government, before conservatorship, each was considered a private company owned by shareholders; now the government owns warrants for nearly 80 percent of the value of each institution. Moreover, both are currently subjected to a degree of control that sometimes places the government's policy objectives ahead of corporate financial goals. The Congressional Budget Office (CBO) has therefore concluded that their operations should be considered federal.

As a substantial shareholder, the government could exert significant control over the operations of GM, AIG, and Citigroup, but it is not clear that it will. For example, although the government owns most of AIG's stock, it does not directly control any seats on the company's board of directors and it is not actively determining company policy. GM's situation could evolve somewhat differently; news reports suggest that the federal government will appoint some members of the board and could take a more active part in setting company policy. However, the administration has indicated that it does not plan to be an active participant in managing the carmaker's operations.

CBO does not currently believe that the full activities of GM, AIG, and Citigroup should be recorded as part of the federal budget. However, changes in the nature of the government's ownership or degree of control over those companies could provide sufficient basis for revisiting this issue and concluding that the financial transactions of one or more of those companies should be reflected in the budget.

By 2011, the government had sold off most of their stock in CitiGroup and GM did an initial public offering to pay off some of their loan to the government.

[1]See *Report of the President's Commission on Budget Concepts* (October 1967), p. 24.

Source: The Troubled Asset Relief Program: Report on Transactions through June 17, 2009. CBO, Congressional Budget office Report.

managed by the U.S. Treasury and therefore are solely under the jurisdiction of the Federal Reserve.

By 2010 the Federal Reserve's portfolio of assets had grown to over $2 trillion, which was more than twice its normal size. Instead of holding mostly securities of the U.S. Treasury, it now held commercial paper, mortgages, subprime loans, and asset-backed securities. The Associated Press reported that in 2009 the Federal Reserve paid the U.S. Treasury $46.1 billion out of the $52.1 billion they earned on their portfolio during the year. This was the largest profit and payment since the Fed began operating in 1914.

Many of these programs may still be winding down by the time you read this book, and you can check out the progress at the Web site of the Congressional Budget Office (**www.cbo.gov**). Books have also been published about the financial crisis and the government's programs; our attempt here is to make you familiar with the vast powers the Federal Reserve and the U.S. Treasury can possess in times of financial turmoil.

FIGURE 5-6 Real Growth and Inflation (quarterly % changes at annual rates)

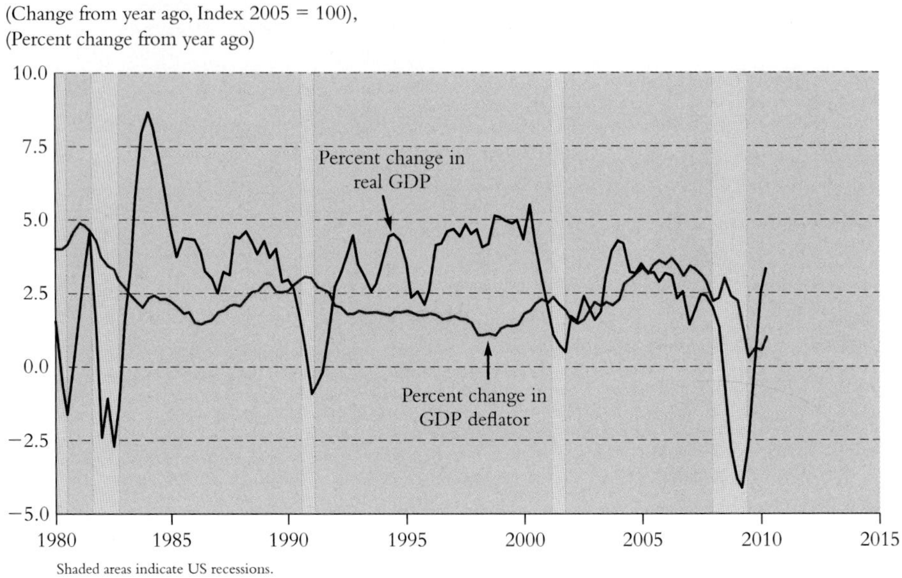

(Change from year ago, Index 2005 = 100),
(Percent change from year ago)

10.0
7.5
5.0
2.5
0.0
−2.5
−5.0

Percent change in real GDP

Percent change in GDP deflator

1980 1985 1990 1995 2000 2005 2010 2015

Shaded areas indicate US recessions.

Source: Federal Reserve Bank of St. Louis Economic Data (FRED).

Government Policy, Real Growth, and Inflation

In November 1991, the U.S. Commerce Department's Economic Bureau of Analysis shifted from gross national product to gross domestic product as the measure of economic activity for the U.S. economy. The **gross domestic product (GDP)** measurement makes us more compatible with the rest of the world and measures only output from U.S. factories and consumption within the United States. Gross domestic product does not include products made by U.S. companies in foreign countries, but gross national product did. Other U.S. economic measures such as employment, production, and capacity are also measured within the boundaries of the United States, and, with the switch to GDP, we now measure economic output consistently with these other variables.

Thirty years (120 quarters) of real GDP and inflation are shown in Figure 5–6. Real GDP reflects gross domestic product in constant dollars, which eliminates the effects of inflation from GDP. Real GDP measures output in physical terms rather than in dollars that are inflated by price increases. One common measure of inflation that most Americans are familiar with is the consumer price index, which is a basket of goods consumed by the average person. The GDP price deflator is a broader measure of inflation and is used in Figure 5–6.

Notice the relationship between real GDP and inflation. The healthy economy in the mid-1980s caused inflation to move upward from 1985 to 1990. However, by 1989, the real GDP growth declined, and a recession occurred in 1990 and early 1991. Inflation came down (with a lagged effect) and stayed relatively tame throughout most of the 1990s, but again in 2001 the economy went into a recession. The United States had three quarters of negative real GDP in 2000 and 2001 before the economy recovered in the third quarter of 2003 with a 7.8 percent growth in real GDP. Because real GDP is the measure of economic output in real physical terms, it does no good to stimulate the economy only to have all the gains eroded by inflation.

The recession of 2007–2009 was so severe that companies had no pricing power and inflation bottomed out at zero. Although the GDP price deflator turned up in early 2010, some measures of consumer price inflation were negative for several months in 2010, causing many economists to predict a deflationary price

FIGURE 5-7 Gross Domestic Product and Its Components for 2009

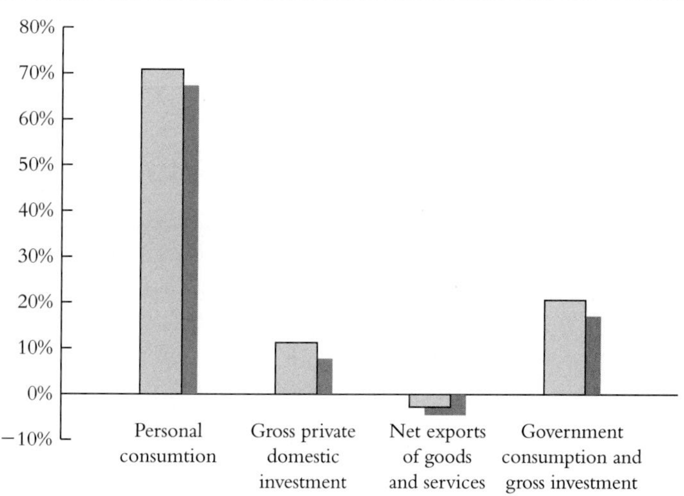

spiral. Deflation would benefit lenders, as they would get paid back in dollars with a larger purchasing power, but would hurt borrowers and those who hold assets.

To understand the major sectors of the economy and the relative influence of each sector, we divide gross domestic product into its four basic areas: personal consumption expenditures, government purchases, gross private investment, and net exports. Figure 5–7 shows the contribution of each one to the total GDP during 2009. It becomes clear from Figure 5–7 that personal consumption is the driving force behind economic growth. In fact consumer spending accounts for 70 percent of GDP. For this reason economic forecasters pay close attention to the mood of the consumer.

The University of Michigan surveys consumer expectations on a monthly basis and reports whether consumers are becoming more or less optimistic. Consumer expectations are a leading indicator of economic activity—when consumer confidence increases, this bodes well for spending; when consumer confidence decreases, this indicates a possible contraction in spending. Figure 5–8 presents a historical view of

FIGURE 5-8 Consumer Expectations, University of Michigan Surveys

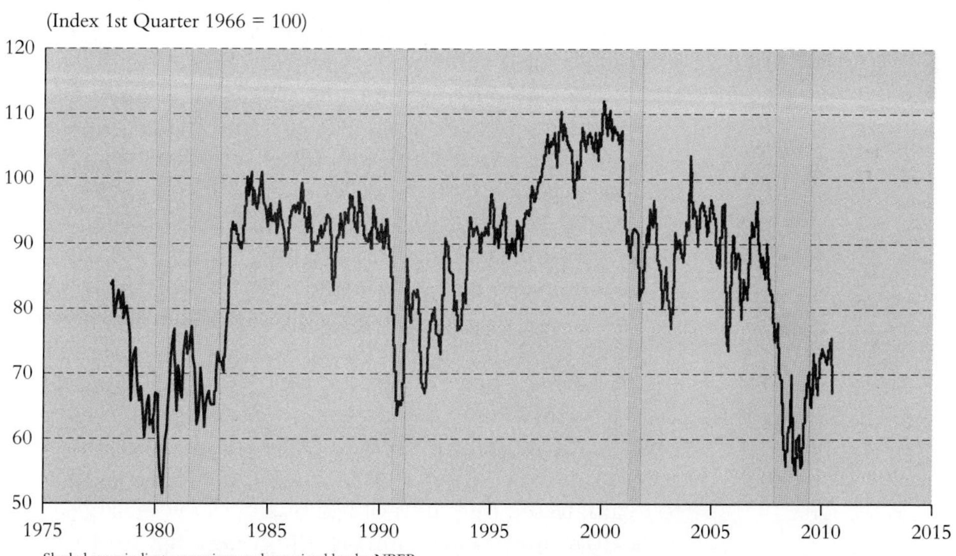

Sources: 2010 Federal Reserve Bank of St. Louis, http://research.stlouisfed.org; Survey Research Center, University of Michigan. © University of Michigan. Used with permission.

the index of consumer expectations. The shaded vertical lines represent recessions. In all cases consumer expectations turned down before a recession began and bottomed out before a recession was over. The negative views in 2009 were not quite as bad as in 1980. Looking at the period 1990–2001, we can see the large rise in confidence with many short-term reversals on the downside. In the next section we look at the cyclical nature of gross domestic product.

BUSINESS CYCLES AND CYCLICAL INDICATORS

The economy expands and contracts through a **business cycle** process. By measuring GDP and other economic data, we can develop a statistical picture of the economic growth pattern. Traditionally, the definition of a recession is two or more consecutive quarters of negative real GDP growth. However, the National Bureau of Economic Research (NBER) is the final authority in documenting cyclical turning points, and they have amended their definition of a recession as follows:

> The NBER does not define a recession in terms of two consecutive quarters of decline in real GDP. Rather, a recession is a significant decline in economic activity spread across the economy, lasting more than a few months, normally visible in real GDP, real income, employment, industrial production, and wholesale-retail sales.

Table 5–2 presents a historical picture of business cycle expansions and contractions in the United States. While the modern-day data may be more relevant, it is interesting to see that economic cycles have existed and been defined for 150 years.

Table 5–2 measures each contraction and expansion and then presents summary data at the bottom of the table for all business cycles and for cycles in peacetime only. A **trough** represents the end of a recession and the beginning of an expansion, and a **peak** represents the end of an expansion and the beginning of a recession. In general, we see on the last line of Table 5–2 that during nine peacetime cycles between 1945 and 2009, contractions (recessions) lasted an average of 11 months, while expansions averaged 55 months. Thus, one *complete* business cycle during modern *peacetimes* averages 65 to 66 months, or five and one-half years. The NBER declared that March 2001 was the beginning of a recession and the end of a 10-year expansion. This unusual dating of the recession occurred without two continuous quarters of negative real GDP growth, but in the face of months of declining manufacturing output, declining employment, and sagging consumer confidence. The NBER dated the end of the recession as November 2001. The next expansion lasted for 73 months until December 2007, and NBER dated the end of this recession as June 2009.

Predicting business cycles is easier said than done. It is important to realize that each business cycle is unique; no two cycles are alike. Some cycles are related to monetary policy; some are demand related; some are inventory induced. The length and depth of each are also different—some are shallow, and others deep; some are short, while others are long.

Additionally, not all industries or segments of the economy are equally affected by business cycles. However, if investors can make some forecast concerning the beginning and ending of the business cycle, they will be better able to choose which types of investments to hold over the various phases of the cycle.

So far, we have discussed the government's impact on the economy. Fiscal policy and monetary policy both provide important clues to the direction and magnitude of economic expansions and contractions. Other measures are used to evaluate the direction of the business cycle. These measures, called economic indicators, are divided into leading, lagging, and roughly coincident indicators. The NBER classifies indicators relative to their performance at economic peaks

TABLE 5-2 Business Cycle Expansions and Contractions in the United States

Contractions (Recessions) Start at the Peak of a Business Cycle and End at the Trough.

BUSINESS CYCLE REFERENCE DATES		DURATION IN MONTHS			
Peak	Trough	Contraction	Expansion	Cycle	
(Quarterly dates are in parentheses)		Peak to Trough	Previous Trough to This Peak	Trough from Previous Trough	Peak from Previous Peak
	December 1854 (IV)	—	—	—	—
June 1857 (II)	December 1858 (IV)	18	30	48	—
October 1860 (III)	June 1861 (III)	8	22	30	40
April 1865 (I)	December 1867 (I)	**32**	**46**	**78**	**54**
June 1869 (II)	December 1870 (IV)	18	18	36	50
October 1873 (III)	March 1879 (I)	65	34	99	52
March 1882 (I)	May 1885 (II)	38	36	74	101
March 1887 (II)	April 1888 (I)	13	22	35	60
June 1890 (III)	May 1891 (II)	10	27	37	40
January 1893 (I)	June 1894 (II)	17	20	37	30
December 1895 (IV)	June 1897 (II)	18	18	36	35
June 1899 (III)	December 1900 (IV)	18	24	42	42
September 1902 (IV)	August 1904 (III)	23	21	44	39
May 1907 (II)	June 1908 (II)	13	33	46	56
January 1910 (I)	January 1912 (IV)	24	19	43	32
January 1913 (I)	December 1914 (IV)	23	12	35	36
August 1918 (III)	March 1919 (I)	**7**	**44**	**51**	**67**
January 1920 (I)	July 1921 (III)	18	10	28	17
May 1923 (II)	July 1924 (III)	14	22	36	40
October 1926 (III)	November 1927 (IV)	13	27	40	41
August 1929 (III)	March 1933 (I)	43	21	64	34
May 1937 (II)	June 1938 (II)	13	50	63	93
February 1945 (I)	October 1945 (IV)	**8**	**80**	**88**	**93**
November 1948 (IV)	October 1949 (IV)	11	37	48	45
July 1953 (II)	May 1954 (II)	**10**	**45**	**55**	**56**
August 1957 (III)	April 1958 (II)	8	39	47	49
April 1960 (II)	February 1961 (I)	10	24	34	32
December 1969 (IV)	November 1970 (IV)	**11**	**106**	**117**	**116**
November 1973 (IV)	March 1975 (I)	16	36	52	47
January 1980 (I)	July 1980 (III)	6	58	64	74
July 1981 (III)	November 1982 (IV)	16	12	28	18
July 1990 (III)	March 1991 (I)	8	92	100	108
March 2001 (I)	November 2001 (IV)	8	120	128	128
December 2007 (IV)	June 2009 (II)	18	73	91	81
Average, All Cycles:					
1854–2009 (34 cycles)		16	38	55	55[a]
1854–1919 (16 cycles)		22	27	48	49[b]
1919–1945 (6 cycles)		18	35	53	53
1945–2009 (12 cycles)		11	60	71	71
Average, Peacetime Cycles:					
1854–2009 (29 cycles)		18	33	51	49[c]
1854–1919 (14 cycles)		22	24	46	47[d]
1919–1945 (5 cycles)		20	26	46	45
1945–2009 (9 cycles)[e]		11	55	66	65

[a] 31 cycles [b] 15 cycles [c] 26 cycles [d] 13 cycles [e] The current business cycle began in 2001 and still continues on, so it is not represented in the table as the book goes to press.

Note: Figures printed in **bold** are the wartime expansions (Civil War, World Wars I and II, Korean War, and Vietnam War); the wartime contractions; and the full cycles that include the wartime expansions.

Sources: NBER; the U.S. Department of Commerce, *Survey of Current Business,* October 1994, Table C-51. From Public Information Office, National Bureau of Economic Research, Inc., 1050 Massachusetts Avenue, Cambridge, MA 02138, 617-868-3900. http://www.nber.com/cycles/cyclesmain.html.

and troughs. **Leading indicators** change direction in advance of general business conditions and are of prime importance to the investor who wants to anticipate rising corporate profits and possible price increases in the stock market. **Coincident indicators** move approximately with the general economy, and **lagging indicators** usually change directions after business conditions have turned around.

The leading, lagging, and coincident indicators of economic activity are published by the Conference Board in its publication called *Business Cycle Indicators*. This publication includes moving averages, turning dates for recessions and expansions, cyclical indicators, composite indexes and their components, diffusion indexes,[1] and information on rates of change. Many of the series are seasonally adjusted and are maintained on a monthly or quarterly basis. This information is also available on its Web site **www.conference-board.org** for a fee.

Table 5–3 presents a summary of cyclical indicators by cyclical timing, with Part A of the table presenting timing at business cycle peaks and Part B showing timing at business cycle troughs. Thus, in the first part, we see the leading, coincident, and lagging indicators for business cycle peaks, and in the second part, similar indicators for the bottoming out of business cycles (troughs). While we would not expect you to study or learn all the leading or lagging indicators for a cyclical peak or trough, it is important that you know they are relied on by economists and financial analysts. Let's look more specifically at how they are used.

Economic Indicators

Of the 108 leading indicators shown in Parts A and B of Table 5–3, 61 lead at peaks and 47 lead at troughs. Of these, 10 basic indicators have been reasonably consistent in their relationship to the business cycle and are considered most important. These 10 leading indicators have been standardized and used to compute a composite index that is widely followed. It is a much smoother curve than each individual component since erratic changes in one indicator are offset by movements in other indicators. The same can be said for a similar index of four coincident indicators and six lagging indicators.

Figure 5–9 shows the performance of the composite index of leading, lagging, and coincident indicators over several past business cycles. The shaded areas are recessions as defined by the NBER. The numbers at the top of the graph give the year and month for the beginning and end of the recession (the shaded area). Look at the numbers above and below the lines. For example, the leading indicators have minus signs representing the number of months the Leading Indicator Index moved before a peak or a trough. The lagging indicators have plus signs representing the number of months the Lagging Index moved after the peak or trough.

While the composite index of leading indicators (top of Figure 5–9) has been a better predictor than any single indicator, it has varied widely over time. Table 5–4 presents the components for the 10 leading, 4 roughly coincident, and 7 lagging indicators.

Studies have found that the 10 leading indicators do not exhibit the same notice at peaks as they do at troughs. The notice before peaks is quite long, but the warning before troughs is very short, which means it is very easy to miss a turnaround to the upside, but on the downside you can be more patient waiting for confirmation from other indicators. Indicators occasionally give false signals.

[1] A diffusion index shows the pervasiveness of a given movement in a series. If 100 units are reported in a series, the diffusion index indicates what percentage followed a given pattern.

A. Timing at Business Cycle Peaks

Economic Process / Cyclical Timing	I. Employment and Unemployment (15 series)	II. Production and Income (10 series)	III. Consumption, Trade Orders, and Deliveries (13 series)	IV. Fixed Capital Investment (19 series)	V. Inventories and Inventory Investment (9 series)	VI. Price, Costs, and Profits (18 series)	VII. Money and Credit (28 series)
Leading (L) Indicators (61 series)	Marginal employment adjustments (3 series) Job vacancies (2 series) Comprehensive employment (1 series) Comprehensive unemployment (3 series)	Capacity utilization (2 series)	Orders and deliveries (6 series) Consumption and trade (2 series)	Formation of business enterprises (2 series) Business investment commitments (5 series) Residential construction (3 series)	Inventory investment (4 series) Inventories on hand and on order (1 series)	Stock prices (1 series) Sensitive commodity prices (2 series) Prices and profit margins (7 series) Cash flows (2 series)	Money (5 series) Credit flows (5 series) Credit difficulties (2 series) Bank reserves (2 series) Interest rates (1 series)
Roughly Coincident (C) indicators (24) series	Comprehensive employment (1 series)	Comprehensive output and income (4 series) Industrial production (4 series)		Consumption and trade commitments (1 series) Business investment expenditures (6 series)	Business investment (4 series)		Velocity of money (2 series) Interest rate (2 series)
Lagging (Lg) Indicators (19 series)	Comprehensive unemployment (2 series)			Business investment expenditures (1 series)	Inventories on hand and an order (4 series)	Unit labor costs and labor share (4 series)	Interest rate (4 series) Outstanding debt (4 series)
Timing Unclassified (U) (8 series)	Comprehensive unemployment (3 series)		Consumption and trade (1 series)	Business investment commitments (1 series)		Sensitive commodity prices (1 series) Profit and profit margins (1 series)	Interest rates (1 series)
B. Timing at Business Cycle Troughs							
Leading (L) Indicators (47 series)	Marginal employment adjustments (1 series)	Industrial production (1 series)	Orders and deliveries (5 series) Consumption and trade (4 series)	Formation of business enterprises (2 series) Business investment commitments (4 series) Residential construction (3 series)	Inventory investment (4 series)	Stock prices (1 series) Sensitive commodity prices (3 series) Profit and profit margins (6 series) Cash flows (2 series)	Money (4 series) Credit flows (5 series) Credit difficulties (2 series)
Roughly Coincident (C) indicators (23 series)	Marginal employment adjustments (2 series) Comprehensive employment (4 series)	Comprehensive output and income (4 series) Industrial production (3 series) Capacity utilization (2 series)	Consumption and trade (3 series)	Business investment commitments (1 series)		Profits and profit margins (2 series)	Money (1 series) Velocity of money (1 series)
Lagging (Lg) Indicators (41 series)	Job vacancies (2 series) Comprehensive employment (1 series) Comprehensive unemployment (5 series)		Orders and deliveries (1 series)	Business investment commitments (2 series) Business investment expenditures (7 series)	Inventories on hand and on order (5 series)	Unit labor costs and labor share (4 series)	Velocity of money (1 series) Bank reserves) (1 series) Interest rates (8 series) Outstanding debt (4 series)
Timing Unclassified (U) (1 series)							Bank reserves (1 series)

Source: *Business Conditions Digest* (U.S. Department of Commerce Bureau of Economic Analysis, July 1988).

FIGURE 5-9 U.S. Composite Indexes (2004=100)

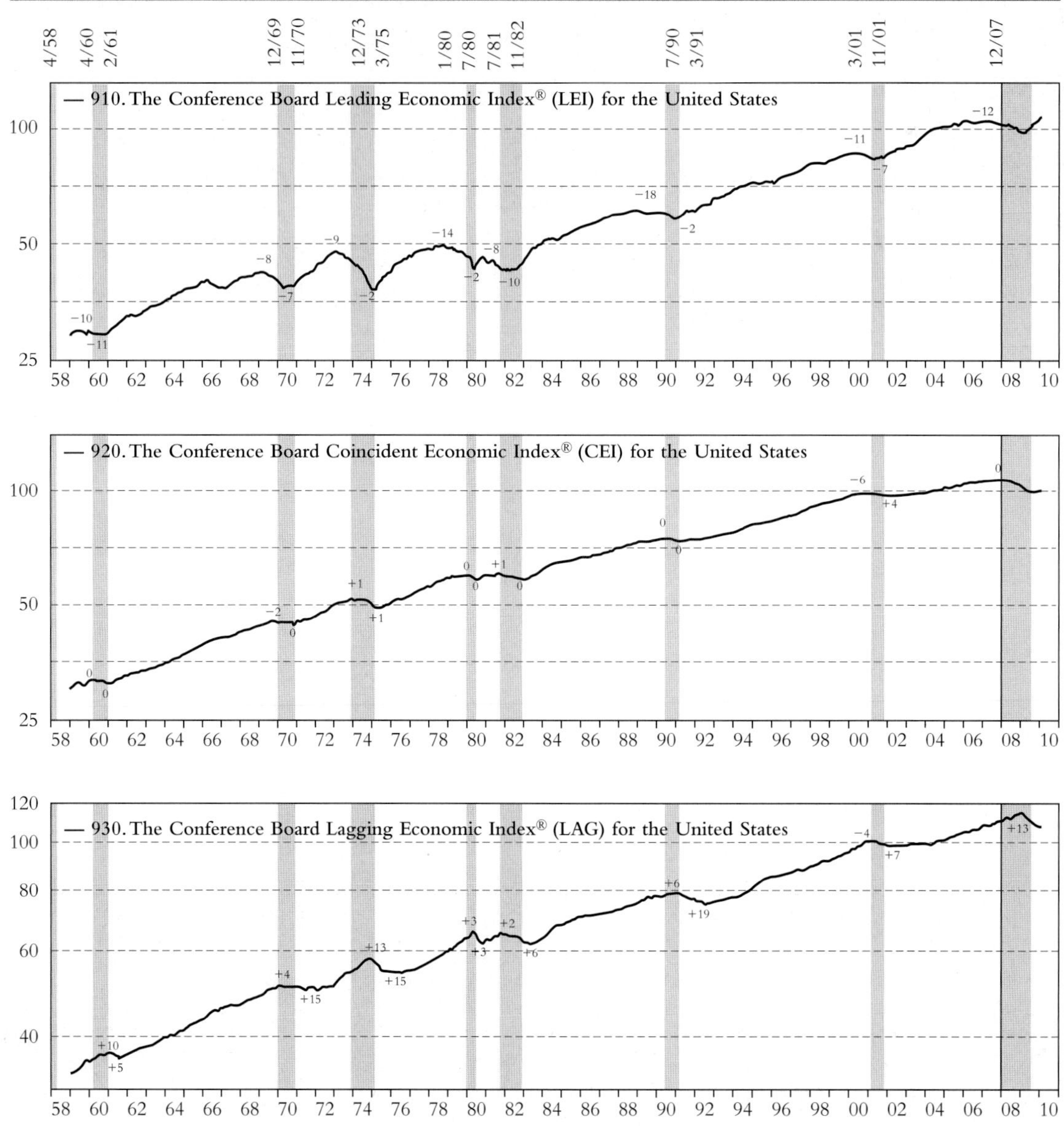

Shaded areas represent recessions.

Note: These data are for news analysis purposes only. Not for redistribution or public posting without express permission.

Source: The Conference Board. © 2010 The Conference Board. Used with permission.

Sometimes the indicators give no clear signal, and with the large variability of leads and lags versus the average lead time, an investor is lucky to get close to predicting economic activity within three or four months of peaks and troughs. Despite economic indicators and forecasting methods, investors cannot escape uncertainty in an attempt to manage their portfolios.

One very important fact is that the stock market is the most reliable and accurate of the 10 leading indicators. This presents a very real problem for us because our initial objective is to forecast (as well as we are able) changes in common stock prices. To do this, we are constrained by the fact that the stock market is anticipatory and, in fact, has worked on a lead time of nine months at peaks and five months at troughs.

application example

TABLE 5-4 Components of the Leading, Coincident, and Lagging Indicators

Leading Index:

1. Average weekly hours, manufacturing
2. Initial claims for unemployment insurance
3. Manufacturers' new orders, consumer goods and materials
4. Index of supplier deliveries, vendor performance
5. Manufacturers' new orders, nondefense capital goods
6. Building permits, new private housing units
7. Stock prices, 500 common stocks
8. Money supply, M2
9. Interest rate spread, 10-year Treasury bonds less federal funds
10. Index of consumer expectations

Coincident Index:

1. Employees on nonagricultural payrolls
2. Personal income less transfer payments
3. Industrial production
4. Manufacturing and trade sales

Lagging Index:

1. Average duration of unemployment, weeks
2. Ratio, manufacturing and trade inventories to sales
3. Labor cost per unit of output, manufacturing
4. Average prime rate
5. Commercial and industrial loans outstanding
6. Ratio, consumer installment credit outstanding to personal income
7. Consumer price index for services

Source: The Conference Board, February 2010. © 2010 The Conference Board. Used with permission.

STOCK PRICES AND ECONOMIC VARIABLES

Money Supply

One variable that has been historically popular as an indicator of the stock market is the money supply. The money supply is supposed to influence stock prices in several ways. Studies of economic growth and the money supply by Milton Friedman and Anna Schwartz found a long-term relationship between these two variables.[2]

Why does money matter? If you are a **monetarist**, money explains much of economic behavior. The quantity theory of money holds that as the supply of money increases relative to the demand for money, people will make adjustments in their portfolios of assets. If they have too much money, they will first buy bonds (a modification of the theory would now include Treasury bills or other short-term monetary assets), stocks, and finally, real assets. This is the direct effect of money on stock prices sometimes referred to as the *liquidity effect.*

The indirect effect of money on stock prices would be its impact on gross domestic product and corporate profits. As an increase or decrease in the money supply influences economic activity, it will eventually impact corporate earnings, dividends, and returns to investors.

[2] Milton J. Friedman and Anna J. Schwartz, "Money and Business Cycles," *Review of Economics and Statistics,* Supplement, February 1963.

FIGURE 5-10 The S&P 500, GDP, and Corporate Profits

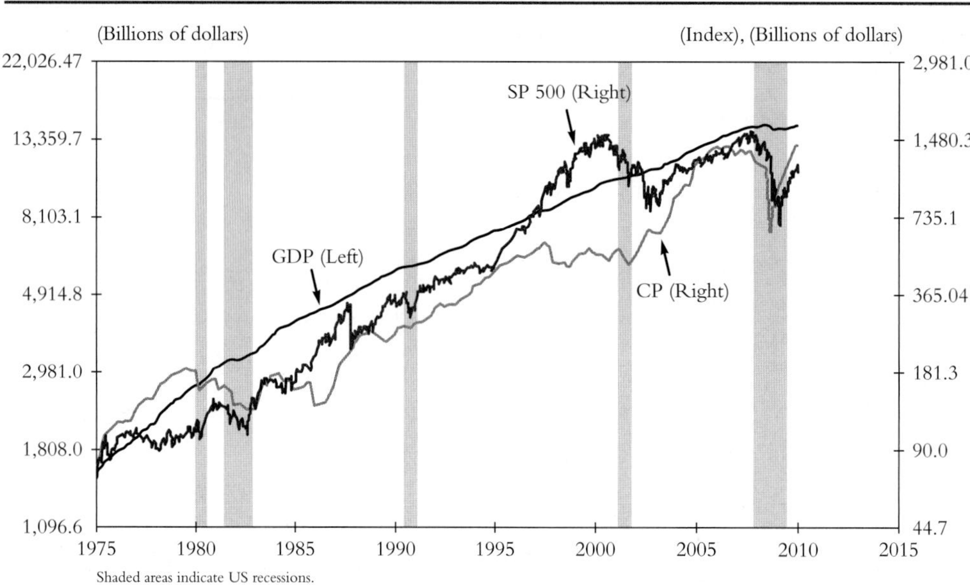

Source: Federal Reserve of St. Louis, http://research.stlouisfed.org. © Economagic, 2007.

Gross Domestic Product

There is a strong relationship between the long-run movement of the stock market and overall economic activity as measured by gross domestic product (GDP). Corporate profits are another measure of economic activity and are greatly influenced by growth in GDP. The relationship between these three variables appears in Figure 5–10, which plots the S&P Index and corporate profits on the right axis and GDP on the left axis. The data are plotted using log scale to get a better view of the relationship between variables that greatly differ in size. The first thing to observe is that, in general, the three variables follow the same trend line. There are a few periods where the trends diverge. For example, up to about 1996 there is a consistent relationship between the variables, but then the Internet/tech bubble of the late 1990s shows up dramatically. Stock prices rise while corporate earnings fall, and the S&P 500 moves above GDP for the first time in the series. The bubble breaks, and stock prices and earnings converge until the financial crisis of 2007–2009. While GDP declines, stock prices and corporate profits plunge in the middle of the recession and then turn up long before the recession is over.

Another point worth reiterating is that the stock market usually turns down before recessions and up before the recession is over (the recessions are depicted by the shaded areas). This has been true except for the 2001 recession, when the S&P 500 didn't turn up until April 2003. This was most likely because corporate earnings didn't turn up during the third quarter of 2003. In the 2007–2009 recession, corporate earnings surprised on the upside in both 2009 and 2010, even while the economy languished.

Industrial Production and Manufacturing

Even though manufacturing in the United States accounts for only about 20 percent of the U.S. GDP, it is still a very important sector and employs a large number of people. There are several very important relationships shown in Figure 5–11. First this figure with its series of three graphs shows the percentage change beginning in 1985. This is different than Figure 5–10, which showed total values over time.

Notice in the first graph of the percentage changes for the Standard & Poor's 500 Index that the stock market provides positive returns much more often than negative returns. Between 1985 and 2000 there were only a few periods with negative returns. However, the three-year period during 2000 to 2003 was one of the three or four

FIGURE 5-11 Stock Prices and Manufacturing Activity

Standard & Poor's 500 Index with Reinvested Dividends

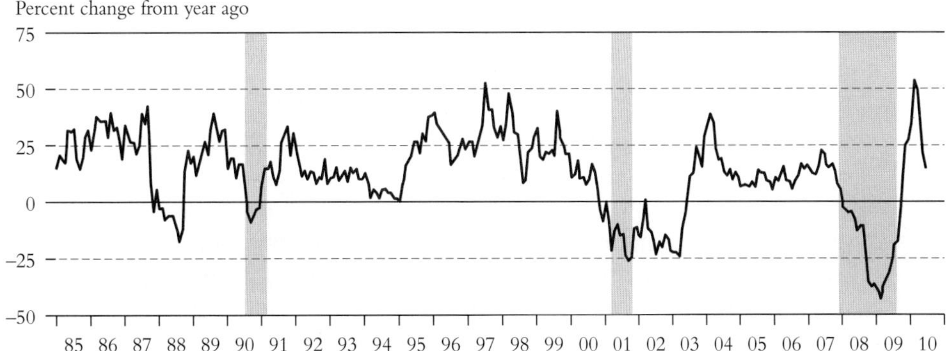

Industrial Production and Institute for Supply Management (ISM) Indexes

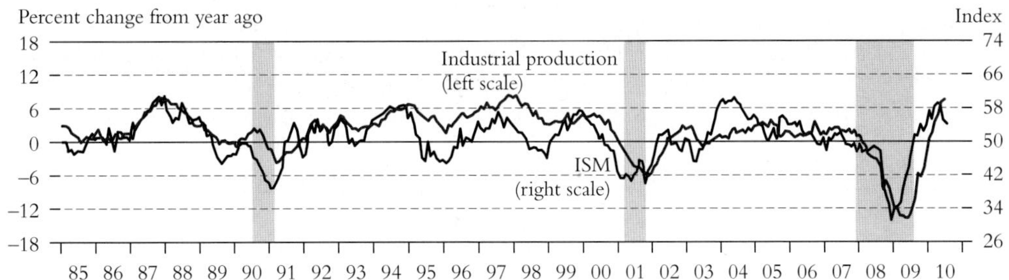

Output per Hour and Capacity Utilization, Manufacturing

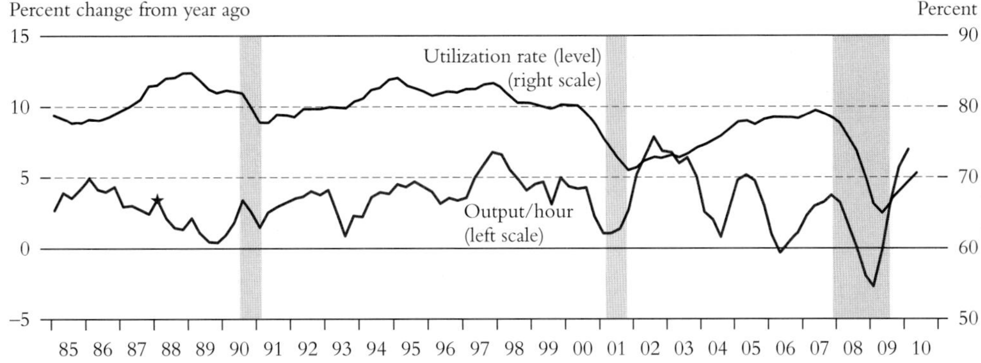

*Data from 1987 to the present are on a NAICS basis; data prior to 1987 are on an SIC basis and are not strictly comparable (see End Note).

Source: Research Division, *National Economic Trends,* Material reprinted from the Federal Reserve Bank of St. Louis, August 2010.

worst three-year periods since the Great Depression of the 1930s. The annual percentage change is given on the left axis, and there were many periods when returns were above 25 percent and in a few cases above 50 percent. In fact when the market recovered in 2003, the return reached 25 percent for the year and was positive until the recession of 2007–2009. Although the market fell more than 50 percent, it also recovered half of its loss within a year.

In the second panel we have industrial production as a percentage change from the period of the past year and the Institute for Supply Management Index (ISM) which is listed on the right scale. When the ISM is above 50, manufacturing is expanding, and when it is below 50, manufacturing is contracting. The last reading in the second panel for ISM is 58 which is a positive sign.

The last panel shows output per hour and capacity utilization and is important in helping an analyst forecast inflation and interest rates. One very important change in the economy is that worker productivity (measured on the left axis and shown as the bottom line) has been rising since the mid-1990s, which reversed the downward trend of the late 1980s. Productivity peaked in 2002 and has been quite volatile since then. Corporate America's investment in technology has started to pay off for the economy. Since bottoming out during the last recession, productivity has hit a new peak and continues to remain positive. Increases in productivity reduce the costs of production and keep a lid on the prices of manufactured products. The ability of management to continuously modernize their company's plants and equipment is central in a firm's maintaining a competitive position in the worldwide market.

Capacity utilization (right axis in the third panel of Figure 5–11) measures current manufacturing output against potential output. When the capacity utilization rate is low, companies use their most productive and efficient plant and equipment, but as demand for goods increases, less efficient plants and equipment are brought online. The less efficient equipment is more costly, and as profit margins are reduced, companies raise prices. This inflationary effect is generally thought to begin occurring when capacity utilization moves past 80 percent.

By the fall of 2006, capacity utilization was about 81 percent. As capacity utilization rises, companies use older less productive facilities and costs rise, but increased worker productivity can offset some cost pressures. Inflation was not on the horizon in the early part of 2004, but as capacity utilization increased, inflation picked up and the Federal Reserve raised the federal funds rate 18 times to slow down the economy and put a lid on inflation. The strategy seemed to be working and by the spring of 2007, GDP had slowed and inflation pressures were reduced. However, the housing bubble burst, and GDP declined, sending capacity utilization below 70 percent by 2009. During the recession many companies closed outdated plants. This is especially true of the automobile industry. You can further judge the wisdom of the Fed policy as you read the text.

exploring the web

Web Address	Comments
www.economy.com	**Provides access to economic data—some sources are fee based**
finance.yahoo.com	**Provides information about companies, markets, and the economy**
www.dismal.com	**Contains articles on economies and tracks information from U.S. and global sources**
www.fedstats.gov	**Has links to economic data**
www.freelunch.com	**Has links to other economic sites, has listings of economic reports and news events, and provides access to economic data**
www.smartmoney.com	**Has information and news about U.S. economy**
www.bea.gov	**Provides links to sources of U.S. government economic data**
www.ny.frb.org	**Contains links to New York Federal Reserve Bank analyses and data**
www.stls.frb.org/fred	**Contains historical interest rate, bond, and economic data—site is free**
www.mworld.com	**Provides industry and economic data as well as data on money flows into stock funds**
www.stat-usa.gov	**Provides general information about the U.S. economy**
www.bos.frb.org	**Home page of the Federal Reserve of Boston providing economic information**
http://trade.gov	**Provides access to U.S. government reports on international trade with reports being fee-based**

SUMMARY

The primary purpose of this chapter is to provide you with a process of valuation and an appreciation of some of the variables that should be considered. The valuation process is based on fundamental analysis of the economy, industry, and company. This method assumes decisions are made based on economic concepts of value over the long-term trend of the stock market. The purpose of the process is to eliminate losers from consideration in your portfolio and to thereby provide you with a good opportunity to build a sound portfolio.

The first step in the valuation process is an analysis of the economy and long-term economic trends. The difficulties of attaining government policy goals are discussed as trade-offs between conflicting objectives (high growth versus low inflation). Fiscal and monetary policy are discussed as the primary tools used to stimulate economic activity. Interest rates are influenced by inflation, with the end result being a higher required rate of return for the investor.

Business cycles are short-term swings in economic activity; they affect stock prices because they change investor expectations of risk and return. To forecast economic activity, cyclical indicators are presented as leading, lagging, and coincident indexes. The one index potentially most valuable to an investor is the composite index of 10 leading indicators.

KEY WORDS AND CONCEPTS

DISCUSSION QUESTIONS

1. As depicted in Figure 5–1 on page 113, what are the three elements in the valuation process?
2. As shown in Figure 5–5 on page 121, what are the four goals under the Employment Act of 1946?
3. What is fiscal policy? A one-sentence definition will suffice.
4. What is monetary policy?
5. How, specifically, can the Fed influence economic activity? Name three ways.
6. In regard to Federal Reserve open-market activity, if the Fed buys securities, what is the likely impact on the money supply? Is this likely to encourage expansion or contraction of economic activity?
7. What is the historical relationship between real GDP and inflation? What lesson might be learned from observing this relationship?
8. In terms of the business cycle, distinguish between a trough and a peak.
9. What are the four basic areas that make up gross domestic product? Over the past three decades, what area has been growing most rapidly?
10. What is the advantage of using a composite of indicators (such as the 10 leading indicators) over simply using an individual indicator?

11. Do leading indicators tend to give longer warnings before peaks or before troughs? What is the implication for the investor?

12. Comment on whether each of the following three industries is sensitive to the business cycle. If it is sensitive, does it do better in a boom period or a recession?

a. Automobiles

b. Pharmaceuticals

c. Housing

13. Observe the performance of the 10 leading indicators for the next month. Compare this with changes in stock prices and interest rates.

WEB EXERCISE

The Federal Reserve Board plays an important role in analyzing and regulating the economy. In this exercise, we will look at a couple of important reports that it provides. Go to **www.federalreserve.gov**.

1. Enter Beige Book in the search space and click on search.
2. Now click on "Beige Book." This book represents an important report that the Fed puts out describing economic conditions in various parts of the country. It is taken very seriously by stock and bond market investors.
3. Find the latest report on the calendar (the years are located at the bottom of the page) and click the HTML link on that date.
4. Next, on the left-hand side of the screen, click on the area of the country (Federal Reserve district) that covers your hometown.
5. Write a three-paragraph report on your area of the country.

Note: From time to time, companies redesign their Web sites, and occasionally a topic we have listed may have been deleted, updated, or moved into a different location.

www.mhhe.com/hirtblock10e

chapter
six

INDUSTRY ANALYSIS

OBJECTIVES

1. Explain the phases of the industry life cycle.
2. Relate dividend policy to the life cycle.
3. Describe the various economic structures of industries.
4. Explain the effect that government regulation can have on an industry.
5. Describe how to compare the performance of many companies within the same industry.
6. Explain the concept of rotational investing in which the investor shifts emphasis among industries during various phases of the business cycle.

OUTLINE

We saw in Chapter 5 that *economic analysis* is the first step in the valuation process. Figure 5–1 (back on page 113) is funnel shaped and leads from the economy to industry analysis and then to company analysis. This method of choosing common stocks is called the **top-down approach** because it goes from the macroeconomic viewpoint to the individual company. The opposite approach is the **bottom-up approach**, which starts with picking individual companies and then looks at the industry and economy to see if there is any reason an investment in the company should not be made. People who follow the bottom-up approach are sometimes referred to as **stock pickers**, as opposed to industry analysts.

Industry analysis is the second step in the top-down approach used in this text, and it focuses on industry life cycles and industry structure. Industries can be affected by government regulation, foreign and domestic competition, and the economic business cycle. As we shall also see, industry competition is affected by product quality, the cost structures within the industry, and the competitive strategies among companies in the industry. A starting point for industry analysis is determining where an industry's current position is in its industry life cycle.

INDUSTRY LIFE CYCLES

Industry life cycles are created because of economic growth, competition, availability of resources, and the resultant market saturation by the particular goods and services offered. Life-cycle growth influences many variables considered in the valuation process. The particular phase in the life cycle of an industry or company determines the growth of earnings, dividends, capital expenditures, and market demand for products.

An analysis of industry financial data helps place an industry on the life-cycle curve and, in turn, guides the analyst toward decisions on industry growth, the duration of growth, profitability, and potential rates of return. The analyst can determine whether all companies in the industry are in the same stage of the life cycle and translate company differences into various assumptions that will affect their individual valuations.

Industry Life Cycles vs. Product Life Cycles

Many individuals are familiar with the marketing product life cycle and impose that model on the industry life cycle found in finance. The product life cycle has four phases: development, growth, maturity, and decline. There is a big difference between an individual product and a company with hundreds or thousands of products. Companies and industries can try to reinvent themselves with new products (Apple), while an individual product (straight razor, electric knife, hairpins, etc.) saturates a market, reaches maturity, and maybe declines. The industry life cycle discussed in finance is more focused on growth and has one more phase to it than a product life cycle. The industry or company life cycle divides the growth phase into two parts: growth (accelerating growth) and expansion (decelerating growth). We do this because the price an investor is willing to pay for a company or companies within an industry is greatly influenced by its growth rate. The faster a company grows, the more valuable it can be, and investors want to know when that growth path will slow down, become stable, or even stop.

Dividend Policy and the Life-Cycle Curve

The dividend payout ratio has an important effect on company growth. As previously pointed out, the more funds a firm retains—and, thus, the lower the dividend payout—the greater the opportunity for growth. The dividend policy followed by management often provides the analyst with management's view of the company's ability to grow and some indication of where the company is on the life-cycle curve. For example, a firm paying out 50 percent of earnings in dividends is probably not in Phase I, II, or III of the life-cycle curve.

Figure 6–1 shows a five-stage industry life cycle (although it could very well be a company life cycle) and the corresponding dividend policy most likely to be found at each stage. The vertical scale on this graph is logarithmic, which means that a straight line on this scale represents a constant growth rate. The steeper the line, the faster the growth rate, and the flatter the line, the smaller the growth rate. The slope of the line in the life-cycle curve and how it changes over time is very important in the analysis of growth and its duration. We will examine each stage separately and learn why the dividend policy is important in placing an industry or company in a particular stage.

FIGURE 6-1 Industry Life Cycle

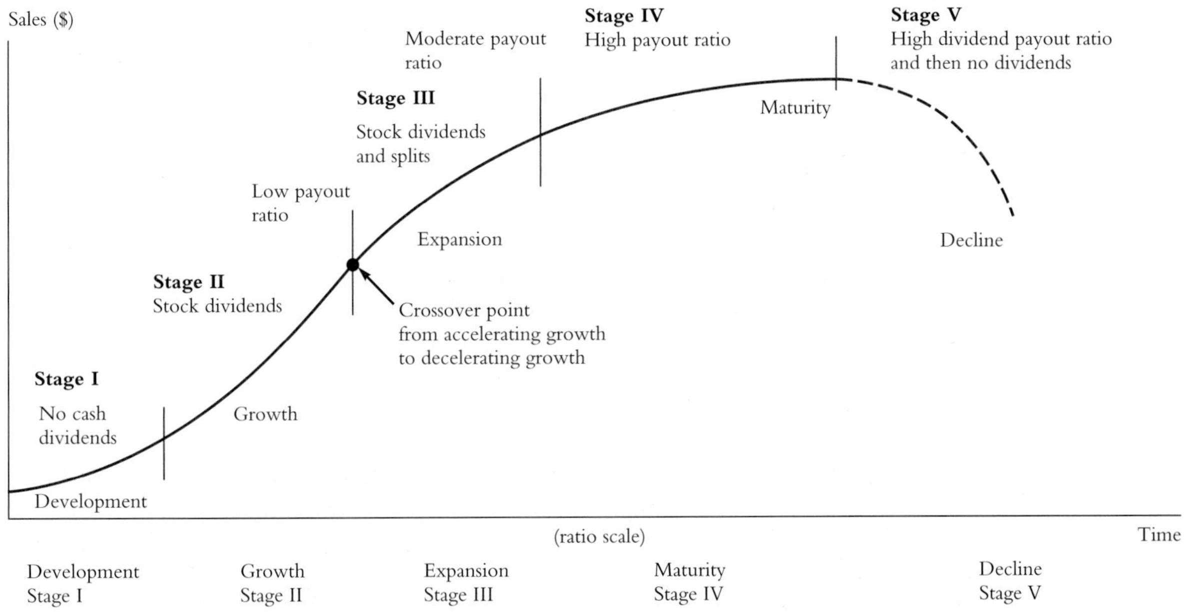

Development—Stage I

The development stage includes companies that are getting started in business with a new idea, product, or production technique that makes them unique. Firms in this stage are usually privately owned and are financed with the owner's money as well as with capital from friends, family, and a bank. If the company has some success, there is a probability that outside money from a venture capital group may increase the financing available to the company. In this stage, the company is also the industry or a subset of an existing industry. For example, when Steve Jobs started Apple Computer in the early 1970s, it was a development start-up company that created an entirely new industry. In the beginning, Apple was certainly not taken seriously by IBM, but now the personal computer (PC) industry and its related software products represent a sizable multibillion dollar industry much bigger than the old mainframe business of IBM and others.

The pharmaceutical industry has been around for a long time, but in the 1970s and 1980s many small biotechnology firms were founded that created drugs using different production and research techniques. Hundreds of small biotech firms using genetic techniques were created by entrepreneurs in medical research. This focus on medical research created a subset of the pharmaceutical industry, and, eventually, large companies such as Merck and Eli Lilly created joint partnerships with these companies. Some biotech firms such as Amgen and Genentech eventually produced successful drugs and became large companies themselves.

One thing all these firms have in common is their need for capital. A small firm in the initial stages of development (Stage I) pays no dividends because it needs all of its profits (if there are any) for reinvestment in new productive assets. If the firm is successful in the marketplace, the demand for its products will create growth in sales, earnings, and assets, and the industry or company will move into Stage II.

Growth—Stage II

Stage II growth represents an industry or company that has achieved a degree of market acceptance for its products. At this stage, earnings will be retained for reinvestment, and sales and returns on assets will be growing at an increasing rate. The increasing growth can be seen from the increasing slope of the line in Figure 6–1.

www.applecomputer.com

www.ibm.com

By 1978 Apple Computer's PC was so successful that Apple needed more capital for expansion than could be generated internally, so it made an initial public offering of common stock to finance a major expansion. The success of the personal computer enticed IBM to enter this segment of the market, and, eventually, the IBM PC—with its open architecture—was copied and cloned by companies such as Compaq (acquired by Hewlett-Packard), Gateway, and Dell.

Companies such as IBM entered the developing PC industry with a small amount of their total assets targeted at this market and were able to fund the move into this market with internal sources of capital. However, the other companies entering this market were "pure plays"; in other words, all they did was make personal computers. These companies were in the early part of Stage II, and they still needed to reinvest their cash flow back into research and development and into new plant and equipment.

In general, companies in Stage II become profitable, and, in their early stage of growth, they want to acknowledge to their shareholders that they have achieved profitability. Because they still need their internal capital, they often pay stock dividends (distributions of additional shares). A stock dividend preserves capital but often signals to the market that the firm made a profit. In the latter part of Stage II, low cash dividends may be paid out when the need for new capital declines as new sources of capital appear. A cash dividend policy is sometimes necessary to attract institutional investors to the company stock since some institutions cannot own companies that pay no dividends.

Obviously, industries in Stage I or early Stage II are very risky, and the investor does not really know if growth objectives will be met or if dividends will ever be paid. But if you want to have a chance to make an investment (after careful research) in a high-growth industry with large potential returns, then Stage I or II industries will provide you with opportunities for large gains. Since actual dividends are irrelevant in these stages, an investor will be purchasing shares for capital gains based on expected growth rather than on current income.

Expansion—Stage III

In Stage III, sales expansion and earnings continue but at a decreasing rate. As the industry crosses from the growth stage (accelerating growth) to the expansion stage (decelerating growth), the slope of the line in Figure 6–1 becomes less steep, signaling slower growth. It is this **crossover point** that is important to the analyst who will also be evaluating declining returns on investment as more competition enters the market and attempts to take away market share from existing firms. The industry has grown to the point where asset expansion slows in line with production needs, and the firms in the industry are more capable of paying cash dividends. Stock dividends and stock splits are still common in Stage III, and the dividend payout ratio usually increases from a low level of 5 to 15 percent of earnings to a moderate level of 25 to 30 percent of earnings by this stage.

Because industries and companies do not grow in a nice smooth line, it is often difficult to tell when the industry or company has crossed from Stage II growth to Stage III expansion. Determining the crossover point is extremely important to investors who choose to invest in growth companies. Once investors recognize that the past growth rate will not be extrapolated and, instead, is in decline, stock prices can take a sizable tumble as price-earnings ratios collapse because of slower growth expectations. Figure 6–2 demonstrates this relationship.

FIGURE 6-2 The Crossover Point

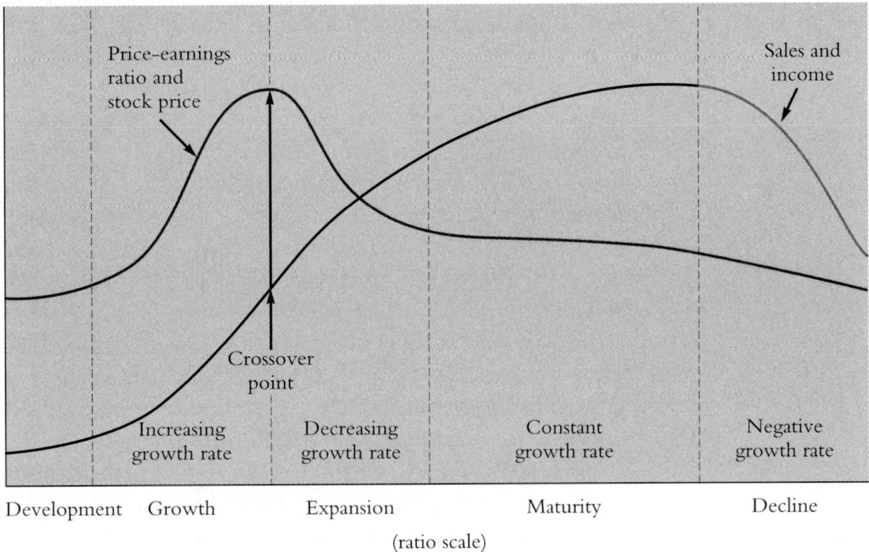

Maturity—Stage IV

Maturity occurs when industry sales grow at a rate equal to the economy as measured by the long-term trend in gross domestic product (GDP). Some analysts like to use the growth rate of the Standard & Poor's 500 Index for comparison because the growth rate of these 500 large companies sets the norm for mature companies.

Figure 6–3 graphs the Standard & Poor's 500 Index versus nominal gross domestic product rather than real GDP because corporate earnings are not adjusted for inflation. The graph uses a logarithmic scale on the *x*-axis (sometimes called ratio scale), which allows a comparison of growth rates or percentage returns between trend lines. As previously mentioned, a straight line on a vertical logarithmic scale

FIGURE 6-3 S&P 500 vs. Nominal GDP

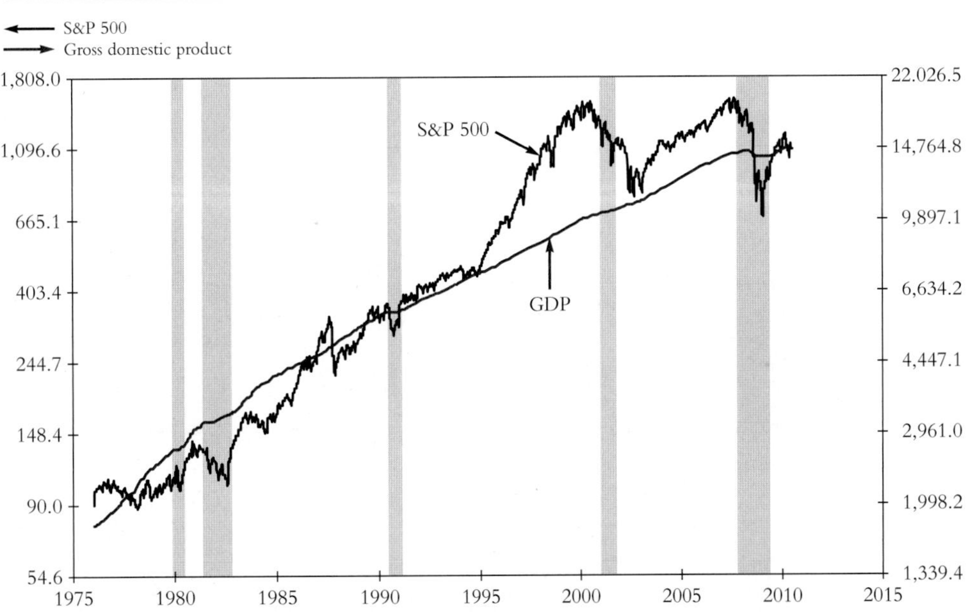

Source: St. Louis Federal Reserve Bank, FRED data. http://research.stlouis.org. Material reprinted from the Federal Reserve Bank of St. Louis.

represents a constant growth rate. The steeper the slope of the line, the higher the growth rate or percentage change. Notice that on the graph, the S&P 500 Index and gross domestic product track each other very well until about 1995. This was the beginning of the "tech or Internet bubble" in the stock market. The market soared to unreasonable heights during the 1996–1999 period because of the euphoria caused by the rise of Internet companies. As you can see, the market plummeted back to its long-term relationship with the GDP during 2000–2002. But the housing bubble burst and financial crisis again disrupted the relationship. The shaded areas denote recessions; notice the relationship between the S&P and GDP to recessions.

Grocery stores such as Albertsons, Kroger, Jewel, Piggly-Wiggly, Dominick's, A&P, and Safeway are good examples of a mature industry. This industry shows a fairly constant relationship between sales of grocery stores versus real gross domestic product. Since food consumption is a necessity, one would expect sales in this industry to follow population trends, inflation, and economic growth. However, even within a mature industry there may be changing trends such as organic foods that cause one grocery store chain to grow faster than the others. For example, Whole Foods, which specializes in organic foods, is a relatively new chain compared to Kroger or Safeway, and the company is adding stores and expanding its geographic territory, causing it to grow at a higher rate than the average for the industry.

In general, mature industries are related to growth in the overall economy. Firms in a mature industry have plant and equipment in place, financing alternatives are available domestically and internationally, and the cash flow from operations is usually enough to meet the growth requirements of the firm. Under these conditions, dividends will usually range from 40 to 50 percent of earnings. These percentages will be different from industry to industry, depending on individual characteristics. For example, dividend payouts in the electric utility industry can be much higher than 50 percent.

Figure 6–4 illustrates the mature industry of gas and electric utilities. Since the early 1970s the production of energy has pretty much followed the path of GDP, which is what you would expect from a mature industry. However, the graph shows a widening divergence from the historical relationship starting in about

FIGURE 6-4 Gas and Electric Utilities vs. GDP

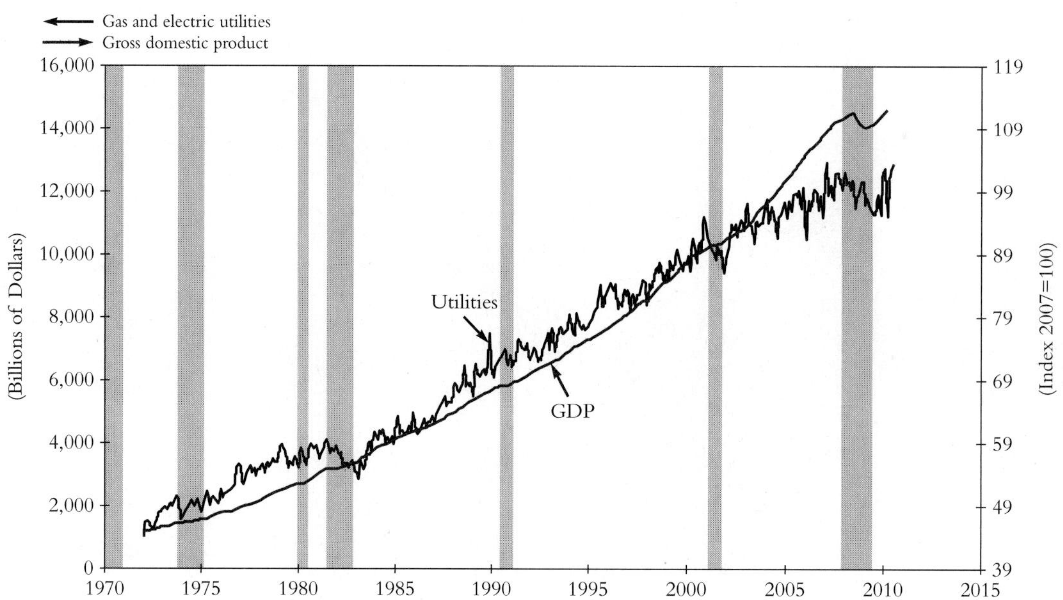

Source: St. Louis Federal Reserve Bank, FRED data. http://research.stlouis.org. Material reprinted from the Federal Reserve Bank of St. Louis.

2005. There could be several reasons for this. Consumers may have become more energy conscious as gas and electric prices rose and reduced their consumption of energy. We could hope that they used more energy-efficient lightbulbs, but that wouldn't account for such a large difference. Perhaps the widening gap is mostly due to the collapse of the housing market. With more home foreclosures and fewer people living in houses, energy consumption is bound to fall, and the graph shows the impact the recession has had. If you have less money, you will probably live hotter in the summer and colder in the winter (using less air conditioning and heating). New home construction is at an all-time low, and the housing stock is shrinking. As the economy recovers, the two trend lines may converge again.

Decline—Stage V

In unfortunate cases, industries suffer declines in sales if product innovation has not increased the product base over the years. Declining industries may be specific to a country; passenger trains are such an example. In Europe, passenger trains are common forms of transportation, while in the United States, passenger trains have been in decline for many decades because competition from automobiles, buses, and airplanes has cut into the market. Besides the famous buggy whip example, black-and-white televisions, vacuum tubes, and transistor radios are examples of products within an industry that have been in decline. In some cases, the companies producing these products repositioned their resources into growth-oriented products, and, in other cases, the companies went out of business.

Often it is not a whole industry that goes into decline but the weakest company in the industry that cannot compete. For example, the U.S. airline industry has been having problems for years, and the events of September 11, 2001, and a poor economy caused United Airlines, Delta Airlines, and Northwest Airlines to declare bankruptcy. United Airlines came out of bankruptcy in 2005 and Delta and Northwest emerged from bankruptcy in 2007. Delta and Northwest eventually merged and now fly as Delta. Bankruptcy allowed these companies to reduce costs by restructuring their labor contracts, their leases, and their debt repayment. Another example of potentially troubled companies in an otherwise mature industry can be found in the U.S. automobile industry. Saddled with high pension and retiree health care costs, and old plants and equipment, General Motors and Chrysler declared bankruptcy and both have restructured under U.S. government supervision. Ford managed to avoid bankruptcy and emerged from the recession with new products and a larger market share. To add to its success, Ford cars made the top ten list in J.D. Powers's quality rankings.

Dividend payout ratios of firms in decline sometimes rise to 100 percent or more of earnings. Often, the firm does not want to signal stockholders that it is in trouble, so it maintains its dividends in the face of falling earnings. This causes the payout ratio to soar until management realizes that the firm is bleeding to death and needs to conserve cash. Then, either drastic dividend cuts follow or there is an elimination of dividends entirely. Ford and GM fit this profile, but both are making progress with positive net income in 2010 and 2011. GM became a publicly traded company in late 2010 with a public offering of shares. The U.S. government was the beneficiary of the sale as GM was able to partially repay its government loans.

Growth in Nongrowth Industries

It is also important to realize that growth companies can exist in a mature industry and that not all companies within an industry experience the same growth path in sales, earnings, and dividends. Some companies are simply better managed, have better people, have more efficient assets, and have put more money into productive research and development that has created new or improved products.

www.nike.com
www.mcdonalds.com

Many U.S. companies, such as Nike and McDonald's, have found growth by expansion abroad. While their domestic markets are saturated and growing at the rate of GDP or less, the international demand for their products in Asia, Europe, eastern Europe, Russia, and China has allowed these two companies to maintain double-digit growth rates. This may also be true of other marketing-oriented companies with global trademarks such as Sony, PepsiCo, and Heineken.

Electric utilities are generally considered mature, but utilities in states such as Florida, Arizona, and the Carolinas, which have undergone rapid population explosions over the last decade, would still have higher growth rates than the industry in general.

Computer companies such as IBM were fast approaching maturity until technical innovations created new markets. Unfortunately for IBM, demand for its mainframe computers declined worldwide as personal computers and local area networks increased in flexibility and power. To combat this decline in its major product line, IBM restructured in an effort to revive growth from its personal computer, software, and service divisions.

The warning to the investor is not to become enamored with a company just because it is in a "growth industry." Its time of glory may have passed. Other investors improperly ignore companies that are in the process of revitalization. More will be said about growth stocks in Chapter 7.

INDUSTRY STRUCTURE

The structure of the industry is another area of importance for the analyst. Industry structure determines whether the companies in the industry are profitable, whether there are special considerations such as government regulations that positively or negatively affect the industry, and whether cost advantages and product quality create a dominant company within the industry.

A financial analyst may want to evaluate other significant factors for a given industry. For example, is the industry structure monopolistic like a regulated utility, oligopolistic like the automobile industry, partially competitive like the pharmaceutical industry, or very competitive like the industry for farm commodities? Questions of industry structure are very important in analyzing pricing structures and price elasticities that exist because of competition or the lack of it.

Economic Structure

We often look at the economic structure of an industry to determine how companies compete within the industry. **Monopolies** are generally not common in the United States because of our antitrust laws, but they have existed by government permission in the area of public utilities. In return for the monopoly, the government has the right to regulate rates of return on equity and assets and to approve customer fees. This sets the limits of growth and profitability and creates minimums and maximums for the analyst. Monopolies are almost always in mature industries, although the government may occasionally grant a monopoly on emerging technologies and even offer subsidies for the development of new technologies, especially in the defense industry.

Oligopolies have few competitors and are quite common in large mature U.S. industries such as automobiles, steel, oil, airlines, and aluminum to name a few. The competition between companies in an oligopoly can be intense, and profitability can suffer as a result of price wars and battles over market share. Increasingly, oligopolistic industries are facing international competition, which has altered their competitive strategies. Note that many of the industries previously mentioned have competition from other industrial countries such as Japan, Germany, the Netherlands, Britain, and France.

Pure competition in manufacturing is not widely found in the United States. The food processing industry may be the closest example of this economic form. Generally, companies in pure competition do not have a differentiated product such as corn, soybeans, and other commodities. Firms will often compete by trying to create perceived differences in product quality or service.

Other Economic Factors to Consider Questions of supply and demand relationships are very important because they affect the price structure of the industry and its ability to produce quality products at a reasonable cost. The cost variable can be affected by many factors. For example, high relative hourly wages in basic industries such as steel, autos, and rubber are somewhat responsible for the inability of the United States to compete in the world markets for these products. Availability of raw material is also an important cost factor. Industries such as aluminum and glass need to have an abundance of low-cost bauxite and silicon to produce their products. Unfortunately, the aluminum industry uses very large amounts of electricity in the production process, so the low cost of bauxite may be offset by the high cost of energy. Energy costs are of concern to all industries, but the availability of reasonably priced energy sources is particularly important to the airline and trucking industries. The list could go on and on, but as analysts become familiar with a specific industry, they learn the crucial variables.

Government Regulation Most industries are also affected by government regulation. This applies to the automobile industry, where safety and exhaust emissions are regulated, and to all industries where air, water, and noise pollution are of concern. Many industries engaged in interstate commerce—such as utilities, railroads, and telephone companies—have been strongly regulated by the government, but even these have begun to feel the effects of deregulation and competition. The telephone companies have begun a global expansion with international partners that is changing the face of competition for long-distance calling worldwide. Industries such as airlines, trucking, and natural gas production have been deregulated and are still undergoing structural changes within the industry as new competitive forces emerge. Most industries are affected by government expenditures; this is especially true for industries involved in defense, education, health care, and transportation.

These are but a few examples to alert you to the importance of having a thorough understanding of your industry. This is why in many large investment firms, trust departments, and insurance companies, analysts are assigned to only one industry or to several related industries so that they may concentrate their attention on a given set of significant factors. Perhaps one of the most important aspects of industry analysis is the competitive structure of the industry.

Competitive Structure

Industries consist of competing firms; some industries have many firms, others have few. Nevertheless, the existing firms compete with each other and employ different strategies for success. Increasingly, the competition is among large international companies where cultural values and production processes are different. It becomes important for the investment analyst to know the attractiveness of industries for long-term profitability and what factors determine an industry's long-term outlook.

As we discussed previously, just because an industry as a whole is in a certain life-cycle stage, all companies within that industry may not be in the same position. An individual company within the industry may have chosen a poor competitive position or an excellent competitive position. While the industry outlook is important, a company may be able to create a competitive position that shapes the industry environment. There are profitable firms in poor industries and unprofitable firms in good industries.

the real world of investing

IN ANALYZING AN INDUSTRY OR COMPANY, WHAT'S A BRAND NAME WORTH?

In our modern economy, a brand name is often worth as much as the brick or mortar. In recognizing this fact, Millward Brown Optimor, a global leader in marketing research and part of the British advertising group WPP, publishes the BRANDZ Top 100 Global Brands. Their 2010 analysis values the top 100 global brands at more than $2 trillion.

The first question is: How do you establish value? Millward Brown takes a three-step approach combining financial and marketing data from Bloomberg and DATAMONITOR.

The first step in their model takes corporate earnings adjusted for brand value to determine the intangible value created by the brand. The second step determines what percentage of the branded intangible earnings is attributed solely to the brand, as opposed to other factors such as price and location. The third step calculates future earnings based on the branded product. These future earnings are dependent on risk and growth and are adjusted for the brand category. If you multiply these three results, you end up with a brand value that is based on the power to increase sales and earnings and is quantified through taking the present value of the future impact of these variables:

Brand value = branded intangible earnings × % of brand contribution × future earnings.

Intangible assets such as brand names, patents, and trademarks are normally not quantified in the United States because of rulings by the Financial Standards Accounting Board (FSAB). However, financial analysts recognize their essential nature in valuing a firm. The lack of inclusion of intangible assets on the balance sheet (with the exception of postmerger goodwill) is one reason firms in the Standard & Poor's 500 Index trade on average at five times their accounting-determined book value. For companies in Great Britain and Australia, brand-name value must be included on the balance sheet, and this may be the reason a British marketing research firm is calculating these numbers.

Having said all this, which U.S. company had the most valuable brand name recognition? The answer is Google, with a value of $114 billion. Following are the top 10 U.S. companies in the BRANDZ list:

North America	(in billions)		(in billions)
Google	$114.2	McDonald's	$66.0
IBM	86.4	Marlboro	57.0
Apple	83.2	GE	45.1
Microsoft	76.3	HP	39.7
Coca-Cola	67.9	Walmart	39.4

Notice that the top four U.S. companies are in the technology/computer industry. Because this chapter covers industry analysis, we also show the top-ranked brand names in two industries where brand recognition is particularly important: automotive and fast food.

Automotive	(in billions)	Fast Food	(in billions)
BMW	$21.8	McDonald's	$66.0
Toyota	21.8	Subway	12.0
Honda	14.3	Starbucks	7.5
Mercedes	13.7	KCF[1]	7.1
Porsche	12.0	Pizza Hut[1]	3.4
Nissan	8.6	Tim Hortons's	3.3
Ford	7.0	Wendy's	2.5

[1] Both KCF and Pizza Hut are owned by Yum Brands.

Source: Millward Brown Optimor, BRANDZ Top 100 2010 Report, www.millwardbrown.com/brandz. "The Best Global Brands," *Business Week,* August 6, 2001.

Perhaps one of the most efficient ways to indicate competitive issues is to consider Michael Porter's elements of industry structure, often referred to as **Porter's Five Competitive Forces**.[1]

Porter divides the competitive structure of an industry into five basic competitive forces: (1) threat of entry by new competitors, (2) threat of substitute goods, (3) bargaining power of buyers, (4) bargaining power of suppliers, and (5) rivalry among existing competitors. All affect price and profitability. The first is the threat of entry by new competitors. If competitors can easily enter the market, firms may have to construct barriers to entry that raise the cost to the firm. This threat places a limit on prices that can be charged and affects profitability. A second force, as we know from economics, is the threat of substitute goods. If we can easily substitute one good for another, this will again affect the price that can be charged and profit

[1] Professor Porter is a leading business strategist at Harvard University.

margins. An example of this would be in the beverage industry. We can drink water (tap or bottled), beer, soft drinks, fruit juice, and so on. If not for the tremendous advertising expenditures from companies trying to get us to drink their beverages, the cost would be considerably lower.

www.walmart.com

Two other competitive forces are the bargaining power of buyers and the bargaining power of suppliers. A large buyer of goods (Wal-Mart) can influence the price suppliers can charge for their goods. Firms such as McDonald's have stringent requirements for their suppliers, and, because it is a powerful buyer, McDonald's expects and gets cost-efficient service and quality control from its suppliers. This behavior restricts the prices that suppliers can charge. On the other hand, there are many powerful suppliers, such as the Middle East oil cartel or DeBeers, the company that controls more than 70 percent of the worldwide diamond market. These suppliers control the cost of raw materials to their customers, and their behavior determines a major part of their customers' profitability.

The last competitive force is the rivalry among existing competitors. The extent of the rivalry affects the costs of competition—from the investment in plant and equipment to advertising and product development. The automobile industry is a reasonable example of intense rivalry that eventually caused Japanese auto manufacturers, for political reasons, to limit their exports to the United States and instead start producing automobiles in the United States. Because the threat of entry was thought to be small, U.S. automobile companies were complacent for years and did not modernize their production processes with new technology or work flow techniques. Once the Japanese took a large market share, the rivalry intensified and caused a restructuring of the whole U.S. automobile industry. The impact of intense rivalry, therefore, has the same effect as the threat of new entrants.

These five forces vary from industry to industry and directly affect the return on assets and return on equity. The importance of each factor is a function of industry structure or the economic and technical characteristics of an industry. These forces affect prices, costs, and investment in plants, equipment, advertising, and research and development. While each industry has a set of competitive forces that are most important to it in terms of long-run profitability, competitors will devise strategies that may change the industry structure. Strategies that change the environment may improve or destroy the industry structure and profitability. Sometimes it takes several years to see the impact of competitive strategies.

PHARMACEUTICAL INDUSTRY–AN EXAMPLE

Every industry has its own unique issues that arise from the economic and competitive structure of the industry. As we discussed on the previous pages, there is a lot to consider when analyzing an industry. For example the pharmaceutical industry is a global industry, and barriers to entry are high because it is not easy or cheap to develop new drugs. Additionally, drugs have predictable life cycles as they go through the development process, the approval process, and then the remainder of their life under patent protection, which may last no more that 10 years as a practical matter. Table 6–1 on the next page presents the leading pharmaceutical companies at the end of 2009 listed by U.S. sales.

Table 6–2, showing the top 15 pharmaceutical companies by global sales in 2009, demonstrates the global nature of this industry. Pfizer is the largest company on the list, and even though it is a U.S. company it has a worldwide presence, as do most companies in the industry. Seven different countries are represented in the list. Teva, an Israeli company, is the world's largest generic drug company, and Novartis, a Swiss company, produces both proprietary and generic drugs.

TABLE 6-1 Leading Pharmaceutical Companies—2009

Company	US PHARMA SALES (BIL. $)				
	2005	2006	2007	2008	2009
1. Pfizer	34.3	34.2	31.4	27.7	27.8
2. Merck	18.7	20.6	21.9	20.1	19.8
3. AstraZeneca	12.4	14.5	15.2	16.1	18.3
4. GlaxoSmithKline	17.0	18.7	18.3	16.5	15.0
5. Hoffman-La Roche	8.0	10.2	11.9	12.6	14.3
6. Novartis	12.6	13.6	13.5	12.2	13.4
7. Lilly	8.9	9.7	10.7	12.0	13.2
8. Johnson & Johnson	15.6	15.7	15.9	15.6	12.8
9. Amgen	11.6	14.2	13.6	12.8	12.5
10. Teva Pharmaceuticals	7.3	9.0	9.8	11.2	12.1
Total, Top 10	146.4	160.4	162.2	156.8	159.2
Total, US Market	247.3	270.3	280.5	285.7	300.3

* Pharmaceutical sales only.

Sources: IMS Health Inc. *Standard & Poor's Industry Surveys, Healthcare: Pharmaceuticals,* June 3, 2010, p. 9.

Life-Cycle Analysis

These large companies are for the most part somewhere in the expansion stage of their life cycle. While each new drug will go through a product life cycle, the portfolio of products for these companies is quite diversified, with each in a different phase of the cycle. Overall, the industry is growing faster than the economy and the Standard & Poor's 500 Index, but growth is decelerating rather than accelerating. Each company could be on a different part of the expansion curve. Table 6–3 depicts a comparative company analysis of pharmaceutical companies. Panel A

TABLE 6-2 Top 15 Pharmaceutical Companies by Global Sales—2009 (*Ranked by 2009 sales, in billions of US dollars*)

Company	2009 MARKET	
	Sales	Share (%)
1. Pfizer (U.S.)	57,024	7.9%
2. Merck (U.S.)	38,963	5.4
3. Novartis (Swiss)	38,460	5.3
4. Sanofi-Aventis (Franco German)	35,524	4.9
5. GlaxoSmithKline (British)	34,973	4.8
6. AstraZeneca (Swedish)	34,434	4.8
7. Roche (Swiss)	32,763	4.5
8. Johnson & Johnson (U.S.)	26,783	3.7
9. Lilly (U.S.)	20,310	2.8
10. Abbott (U.S.)	19,840	2.7
11. Teva (Israeli)	15,947	2.2
12. Bayer (German)	15,711	2.2
13. Boehringer Ingel (German)	15,275	2.1
14. Amgen (U.S.)	15,038	2.1
15. Takeda (Japanese)	14,352	2.0
Total, Top 15	415,397	57.3
Total, Global Market	724,465	100.0

Source: IMS Health. Standard and Poor's Industry Survey, *Pharmaceuticals: Europe,* June 2010, p. 16.

TABLE 6-3 Comparative Company Analysis–Health Care: Pharmaceuticals–Panel A

			Operating Revenues ($ millions)							CAGR (%)			Index Basis (1999 = 100)				
Ticker	Company	Yr. End	2009	2008	2007	2006	2005	2004	1999	10-Yr.	5-Yr.	1-Yr.	2009	2008	2007	2006	2005
Pharmaceuticals‡																	
ABT	*Abbott Laboratories	DEC	30,764.7	29,527.6 D	25,914.2	22,476.3	22,287.8 C	19,680.0 D	13,177.6	8.8	9.3	4.2	233	224	197	171	169
AGN	*Allergan Inc	DEC	4,503.6	4,403.4	3,938.9 A,C	3,063.3 A	2,319.2	2,045.6	1,452.4	12.0	17.1	2.3	310	303	271	211	160
BMY	*Bristol-Myers Squibb Co	DEC	18,808.0 D	20,597.0 D	19,348.0 D	17,914.0	19,207.0 D	19,380.0 A,C	20,222.0	(0.7)	(0.6)	(8.7)	93	102	96	89	95
ENDP	†Endo Pharmaceuticals Hldgs	DEC	1,460.8 A	1,260.5	1,085.6	909.7 A	820.2	615.1	138.5	26.6	18.9	15.9	1,054	910	784	657	592
FRX	*Forest Laboratories—CLA	#MAR	NA	3,845.1	3,718.3	3,360.3 A	2,912.1	3,113.8	881.8	NA	NA	NA	NA	436	422	381	330
JNJ	*Johnson & Johnson	DEC	61,897.0	63,747.0	61,035.0	53,194.0	50,434.0	47,348.0 A	27,471.0 A	8.5	5.5	(2.9)	225	232	222	194	184
KG	*King Pharmaceuticals Inc	DEC	1,776.5	1,565.1 A	2,136.9	1,988.5	1,772.9	1,304.4 D	348.3 A	17.7	6.4	13.5	510	449	614	571	509
LLY	*Lilly (Eli) & Co	DEC	21,836.0	20,378.0 A	18,633.5 A	15,691.0	14,645.3	13,857.9 A	9,912.9 D	8.2	9.5	7.2	220	206	188	158	148
MRX	†Medicis Pharmaceut CP—CLA	DEC	571.9	517.8 A	457.4	349.2	376.9	303.7	116.9 A	17.2	13.5	10.5	489	443	391	299	332
MRK	*Merck & Co	DEC	27,428.3 A	23,850.3	24,197.7	22,636.0	22,011.9	23,430.2	32,714.0	(1.7)	3.2	15.0	84	73	74	69	67
MYL	*Mylan Inc	DEC	5,090.5	5,137.6	2,178.8 H	1,611.8 A	1,257.2	1,253.4	790.1	20.5	32.4	(0.9)	644	650	276	204	159
PRX	§Par Pharmaceutical Cos Inc	DEC	1,193.2 A	578.1	769.7 D	725.2	432.3 D	690.0 A	80.3	31.0	11.6	106.4	1,486	720	958	903	538
PRGO	†Perrigo Co	JUN	2,006.9 D	1,817.2	1,447.4 A	1,366.8	1,024.1 A	898.2	877.6 F	8.6	17.4	10.4	229	207	165	156	117
PFE	*Pfizer Inc	DEC	49,934.0 A	48,341.0 A	48,209.0 A	48,201.0 A,C	51,298.0 A	52,516.0 A,C	16,204.0	11.9	(1.0)	3.3	308	298	298	297	317
SLXP	§Salix Pharmaceuticals Ltd	DEC	232.9	178.8	268.2	208.5	154.9 A	105.5	3.1	NM	17.2	30.3	7,530	5,780	8,672	6,742	5,008
VRX	†Valeant Pharmaceuticals Intl	DEC	830.5	657.0 A,C	872.2 D	907.2 C	823.9 A,C	682.5 D	747.4	1.1	4.0	26.4	111	88	117	121	110
VPHM	§Viropharma Inc	DEC	310.4	232.3 A	203.8	167.2	132.4	22.4	0.0	NM	69.2	33.6	**	**	**	**	NA
WPI	*Watson Pharmaceuticals Inc	DEC	2,793.0 A	2,535.5	2,496.7	1,979.2 A	1,646.2	1,640.6	689.2 A	15.0	11.2	10.2	405	368	362	287	239
Health Care Distributors‡																	
ABC	*Amerisourcebergen Corp	SEP	71,760.0	70,189.7 D	66,074.3	61,203.1	54,577.3 D	53,179.0	9,807.4 A	22.0	6.2	2.2	732	716	674	624	556
CAH	*Cardinal Health Inc	JUN	99,512.4 D	91,091.4	86,852.0 D	81,363.6 D	74,910.7	65,053.5	25,033.6 A,F	14.8	8.9	9.2	398	364	347	325	299
MCK	*Mckesson Corp	#MAR	108,702.0	106,632.0	101,703.0	92,977.0 D	88,050.0 D	80,514.6	36,712.5 A,C	11.5	6.2	1.9	296	290	277	253	240
MWIV	§MWI Veterinary Supply	SEP	941.3	831.4	710.1 A	606.2 A	496.7	394.3	NA	NA	19.0	13.2	**	**	**	**	NA
OMI	†Owens & Minor Inc	DEC	8,037.6	7,243.2 D	6,800.5	5,533.7 A	4,822.4	4,525.1	3,186.4 A	9.7	12.2	11.0	252	227	213	174	151
PDCO	*Patterson Companies Inc	#APR	NA	3,094.2	2,998.7	2,798.4	2,615.1	2,421.5	1,040.3	NA	NA	NA	NA	297	288	269	251
PMC	§Pharmerica Corp	DEC	1,841.2 A	1,947.3 A	1,217.8 A	NA	NA	NA	NA	NA	NA	(5.4)	**	**	**	**	NA
PSSI	§PSS World Medical Inc	#MAR	NA	1,952.7	1,855.8	1,741.6	1,619.4	1,473.8	1,793.5 A	NA	NA	NA	NA	109	103	97	90
HSIC	†Schein (Henry) Inc	DEC	6,538.3 D	6,394.9 D	5,920.2 D	5,153.1	4,635.9 A,C	4,060.3 A	2,285.7 A	11.1	10.0	2.2	286	280	259	225	203
Other Companies with Significant Pharmaceutical Operations																	
AZN	Astrazeneca PLC—ADR	DEC	33,187.0 F	32,215.0 F	30,270.0 A,F	26,999.0 A,F	24,143.0 F	21,741.0 F	17,950.0 A,C	6.3	8.8	3.0	185	179	169	150	135
BVF	Biovail Corp	DEC	821.5 A	758.3 A	843.9	1,068.8	935.5 D	886.5	151.8 A,F	18.4	(1.5)	8.3	541	500	556	704	616
ELN	Elan Corp PLC—ADR	DEC	820.9	761.8	516.4	497.3	426.7 D	464.0	1,007.8	(2.0)	12.1	7.8	81	76	51	49	42
GSK	GlaxoSmithKline PLC—ADR	DEC	47,092.9 A	36,391.1 A	46,017.9 A	46,089.8 A	37,854.9 A	39,191.8 A	13,711.3	13.1	3.7	29.4	343	265	336	336	276
NVS	Novartis AG—ADR	DEC	44,267.0 A	41,459.0 A	38,072.0 D	36,031.0 A,C	32,212.0 A	28,247.0 A	21,643.3 A	7.4	9.4	6.8	205	192	176	166	149
TEVA	Teva Pharmaceutical INDS—ADR	DEC	13,899.0	11,085.0 A	9,408.0	8,408.0 A	5,250.4	4,798.9 A	1,282.4 A	26.9	23.7	25.4	1,084	864	734	656	409

Note: Data as originally reported. CAGR-Compound annual growth rate.

‡S&P 1500 index group.

*Company included in the S&P 500.

†Company included in the S&P MidCap 400.

§Company included in the S&P SmallCap 600.

#Of the following calendar year.

**Not calculated; data for base year or end year not available. A-This year's data reflect an acquisition or merger. B-This year's data reflect a major merger resulting in the formation of a new company. C-This year's data reflect an accounting change. D-Data exclude discontinued operations. E-Includes excise taxes. F-Includes other (nonoperating) income. G-Includes sale of leased depts. H-Some or all data are not available, due to a fiscal year change.

Source: Standard & Poor's Industry Survey, *Healthcare: Pharmaceuticals,* June 3, 2010.

TABLE 6-3 Comparative Company Analysis—Health Care: Pharmaceuticals—Panel B

Ticker	Company	Yr. End	Net Income ($ millions) 2009	2008	2007	2006	2005	2004	1999	CAGR (%) 10-Yr.	5-Yr.	1-Yr.	Index Basis (1999 = 100) 2009	2008	2007	2006	2005
Pharmaceuticals‡																	
ABT	*Abbott Laboratories	DEC	5,745.8	4,734.2	3,606.3	1,716.8	3,372.1	3,175.8	2,445.8	8.9	12.6	21.4	235	194	147	70	138
AGN	*Allergan Inc	DEC	621.3	578.6	501.0	(127.4)	403.9	377.1	188.2	12.7	10.5	7.4	330	307	266	(68)	215
BMY	*Bristol-Myers Squibb Co	DEC	3,239.0	3,155.0	1,968.0	1,585.0	2,992.0	2,378.0	4,167.0	(2.5)	6.4	2.7	78	76	47	38	72
ENDP	†Endo Pharmaceuticals Hldgs	DEC	266.3	261.7	227.4	137.8	202.3	143.3	3.3	NM	13.2	1.8	NM	NM	NM	4,228	NM
FRX	*Forest Laboratories—CLA	#MAR	NA	767.7	967.9	454.1	708.5	838.8	112.7	NA	NA	NA	**	681	859	403	629
JNJ	*Johnson & Johnson	DEC	12,266.0	12,949.0	10,576.0	11,053.0	10,411.0	8,509.0	4,167.0	11.4	7.6	(5.3)	294	311	254	265	250
KG	*King Pharmaceuticals Inc	DEC	92.0	(333.1)	183.2	288.6	116.6	(50.6)	45.7	7.3	NM	NM	201	(730)	401	632	255
LLY	*Lilly (Eli) & Co	DEC	4,328.8	(2,071.9)	2,953.0	2,662.7	2,001.6	1,810.1	2,546.7	5.4	19.1	NM	170	(81)	116	105	79
MRX	†Medicis Pharmaceut CP—CLA	DEC	76.0	10.3	70.4	(75.8)	65.0	30.8	41.4	6.2	19.8	639.1	183	25	170	(183)	157
MRK	*Merck & Co	DEC	12,901.3	7,808.4	3,275.4	4,433.8	4,631.3	5,813.4	5,890.5	8.2	17.3	65.2	219	133	56	75	79
MYL	*Mylan Inc	DEC	232.6	(181.2)	(1,138.0)	217.3	184.5	203.6	154.2	4.2	2.7	NM	151	(117)	(738)	141	120
PRX	§Par Pharmaceutical Cos Inc	DEC	77.6	(45.9)	51.1	6.7	11.8	29.2	(1.8)	NM	21.6	NM	NM	NM	NM	NM	NM
PRGO	†Perrigo Co	JUN	141.1	135.8	73.8	71.4	(353.0)	80.6	1.5	NM	11.9	3.9	NM	NM	4,773	4,618	NM
PFE	*Pfizer Inc	DEC	8,621.0	8,026.0	8,213.0	11,024.0	8,094.0	11,332.0	3,199.0	10.4	(5.3)	7.4	269	251	257	345	253
SLXP	§Salix Pharmaceuticals Ltd	DEC	(43.6)	(47.0)	8.2	31.5	(60.6)	6.8	(4.6)	NM	NM	NM	NM	NM	NM	NM	NM
VRX	†Valeant Pharmaceuticals Intl	DEC	257.6	(190.3)	26.1	(64.1)	(185.8)	(136.3)	118.6	8.1	NM	NM	217	(160)	22	(54)	(157)
VPHM	§Viropharma Inc	DEC	(11.1)	67.6	95.4	66.7	113.7	(19.5)	(29.5)	NM	NM	NM	NM	NM	NM	NM	NM
WPI	*Watson Pharmaceuticals Inc	DEC	222.0	238.4	141.0	(445.0)	138.2	151.3	178.9	2.2	8.0	(6.9)	124	133	79	(249)	77
Health Care Distributors‡																	
ABC	*Amerisourcebergen Corp	SEP	511.9	469.1	493.8	468.0	291.9	468.4	70.9	21.9	1.8	9.1	722	661	696	660	412
CAH	*Cardinal Health Inc	JUN	1,142.8	1,315.9	839.7	1,244.7	1,046.7	1,524.7	456.3	9.6	(5.6)	(13.2)	250	288	184	273	229
MCK	*Mckesson Corp	#MAR	1,263.0	823.0	989.0	968.0	737.0	(156.7)	184.6	21.2	NM	53.5	684	446	536	524	399
MWIV	§MWI Veterinary Supply	SEP	24.9	19.9	16.9	13.8	4.6	2.5	NA	NA	58.1	25.0	**	**	**	**	NA
OMI	†Ownes & Minor Inc	DEC	116.9	101.3	72.7	48.8	64.4	60.5	28.0	15.4	14.1	15.4	418	362	260	174	230
PDCO	*Patterson Companies Inc	#APR	NA	199.6	224.9	208.3	198.4	183.7	64.5	NA	NA	NA	**	310	349	323	308
PMC	§Pharmerica Corp	DEC	42.2	5.0	(24.1)	NA	NA	NA	NA	NA	NA	744.0	**	**	**	**	NA
PSSI	§PSS World Medical Inc	#MAR	NA	58.0	56.8	50.5	44.3	39.4	22.2	NA	NA	NA	**	262	256	228	199
HSIC	†Schein (Henry) Inc	DEC	308.4	251.0	235.0	183.1	162.4	128.2	50.3	19.9	19.2	22.9	613	499	467	364	323
Other Companies with Significant Pharmaceutical Operations																	
AZN	Astrazeneca PLC—ADR	DEC	7,521.0	6,101.0	5,595.0	6,043.0	4,706.0	3,813.0	956.0	22.9	14.6	23.3	787	638	585	632	492
BVF	Biovail Corp	DEC	176.5	199.9	195.5	215.5	246.8	161.0	62.5	10.9	1.9	(11.7)	282	320	313	345	395
ELN	Elan Corp PLC—ADR	DEC	(162.3)	(35.2)	(665.9)	(408.7)	508.2	(368.3)	335.8	NM	NM	NM	(48)	(10)	(198)	(122)	151
GSK	GlaxoSmithKline PLC—ADR	DEC	8,942.0	6,727.7	10,346.1	10,554.9	8,059.5	8,246.5	2,924.8	11.8	1.6	32.9	306	230	354	361	276
NVS	Novartis AG—ADR	DEC	8,400.0	8,125.0	6,518.0	6,992.0	6,130.0	5,767.0	4,439.3	6.6	7.8	3.4	189	183	147	158	138
TEVA	Teva Pharmaceutical INDS—ADR	DEC	2,000.0	635.0	1,952.0	546.0	1,072.3	331.8	117.8	32.7	43.2	215.0	1,697	539	1,657	463	910

Note: Data as originally reported. CAGR-Compound annual growth rate.

‡S&P 1500 index group.

*Company included in the S&P 500.

†Company included in the S&P MidCap 400.

§Company included in the S&P SmallCap 600.

#Of the following calendar year.

**Not calculated; data for base year or end year not available.

shows the operating revenues of a selected group with their corresponding 1-year, 5-year and 10-year compound annual growth rates CAGR(%), while panel B displays the net income and growth rates for these companies.

As you analyze the growth rates in operating revenues for each company, you can see the variability from company to company. While many of the very large companies like Lilly (Eli) could be in the expansion stage of their life cycle, many of the smaller or medium-size firms such as ENDO Pharmaceuticals could be in the growth phase. Some companies such as Pfizer have not been successful in developing new products and demonstrated stagnant growth over the last five years. So while we can generalize about an industry, it is very difficult to assume all companies in the same industry are in the same phase of the life cycle. You might also notice that revenue growth does not always translate into growth in net income. A company's growth in net income may surpass its revenue growth because of the economies of scale achieved through merger activity and rising profit margins from the development of new drugs.

Government Regulation

These firms sell their drugs throughout the world and are regulated by many governments. It is quite possible for a drug to be approved in five European countries but not approved for sale in the United States. The U.S. Food and Drug Administration (FDA) is considered to be one of the most risk-averse and strict enforcement agencies in the world, and it is not unusual for drugs to be approved for use in other countries before receiving approval from the FDA. This is a controversial issue for people with a disease that needs to be treated with drugs not yet available in the United States. The FDA would respond that it is better to err on the side of peoples' health than to take the risk of fatal side effects with an unproven drug.

Figure 6–5 presents the annual number of drugs approved by the FDA between 1994 and 2009. The number of new drugs under development reached 2,900 in 2009, but of these only a few will make it through Phase I, II, and III trials and then be approved by the FDA. S&P states that for every 5,000 new compounds discovered, only one will make it to market.

Pharmaceuticals Gear Up for Obamacare The new health care reform passed by the U.S. Congress in 2010 will have a significant impact on the pharmaceutical industry, as it accounts for some of the negative views on the industry and

FIGURE 6-5 FDA Approvals*
(number of drugs)

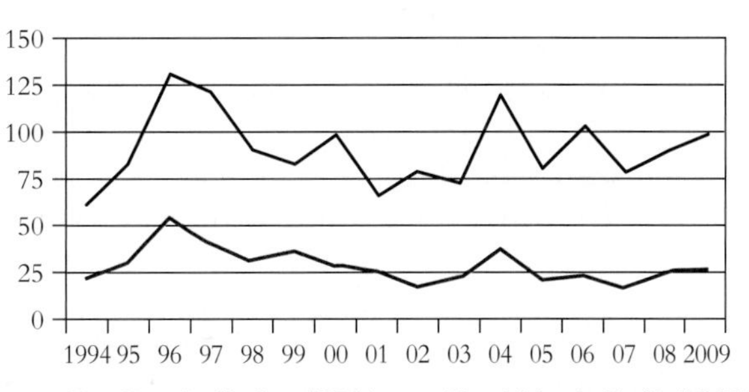

* Includes tentative NDA approvals under the President's Emergency Plan for AIDS Relief, starting in 2007.

Source: US Food & Drug Administration.

therefore the valuation of pharmaceutical companies. Quoting directly from the Standard & Poor's Industry Survey, we get their unedited view and the details of the bill.

> Representing the most sweeping and comprehensive federal healthcare legislation since the enactment of Medicare in 1965, the recently passed national healthcare legislation is expected to have a significant impact on nearly all segments of the U.S. healthcare industry for many years to come. Officially known as the Patient Protection and Affordable Care Act (PPACA), the new healthcare reform legislation was signed into law by President Obama on March 23, 2010.
>
> The law will require U.S. citizens and legal residents to have minimum essential health insurance coverage, require employers to provide coverage for their employees, and encourage the expansion of Medicaid eligibility in order to cover more persons under that program. Special exchanges are also expected to be set up whereby employers and individuals would be able to purchase health coverage at competitive rates.
>
> Funding for PPACA is expected to be derived through new taxes on individuals and healthcare companies, and reductions in spending for Medicare Advantage plans (the private managed care plans serving Medicare beneficiaries). Overall, PPACA is expected to cost about $938 billion over the 10 years from 2010 through 2019, with an indicated deficit reduction of $143 billion over that period, based on estimates made by the nonpartisan Congressional Budget Office (CBO), a research arm of Congress.[2]

The Cost of Healthcare Reform In June 2010, Standard & Poor's announced,

> We estimate the industry's contribution to healthcare reform over the next 10 years will exceed $100 billion, equal to roughly 3% of U.S. pharmaceutical expenditures on an annual basis. The major components of healthcare reform, from the pharmaceutical industry's perspective, are increased Medicaid rebates, Medicare Part D discounts, new fees in the form of excise taxes on pharmaceutical manufacturers, and expansion of the 340B price-discounting program.[3]

The impact of this law will be viewed and reevaluated by the market as time goes by. If the increased volume of drugs offsets the cost of compliance, then the industry's profitability may end up intact. Otherwise, the law will reduce profits.

Research and Development

One of the unique and extremely important areas for the pharmaceutical industry is the large amount of money invested in research and development. A very important ratio in this industry is the amount spent on research and development as a percentage of sales. Small companies are often at a disadvantage because they may only have enough money to work on a few drugs, while large companies like Pfizer can work on many chemical compounds and perhaps have a higher success rate. With only a 3.3 percent success rate in passing FDA approval, a great deal of research and development money is spent on failures.

In recent years, companies like Pfizer have merged with others to create very large companies that can pool their research resources to develop new drugs and achieve economies of scale. Mergers can also result from lack of research productivity. Large firms that have been unsuccessful at research may buy smaller companies with only one popular drug as a way of filling their product line. An analyst has to be careful in judging the research and development expense as a percentage of sales. Just because a company spends a large percentage of money on drug research doesn't mean they will be successful. What counts is how many successful drugs can be developed through the FDA

---

[2] Standard & Poor's Industry Survey, *Healthcare: Pharmaceuticals,* June 3, 2010, p. 1.

[3] Standard & Poor's Industry Survey, *Healthcare: Pharmaceuticals,* June 3, 2010, p. 2.

TABLE 6-4 Top Prescription Drugs of 2009 (*in billions of U.S. dollars*)

Product	Main Indication	Company	Country	SALES GROWTH			
				2009 Sales	2008-09 CER	2008-09 FER	Patent Expiration*
1. Lipitor	Hyperlipidemia	Pfizer	US	13.3	(0.3)	(2.6)	Jun-2011
2. Plavix	Thrombosis	Sanofi-Aventis/BMS	France/US	9.1	7.9	5.1	Nov-2011
3. Nexium	Ulcers/GERD	AstraZeneca	UK	8.2	7.1	5.2	May-2014
4. Seretide/Advair	Asthma/COPD	GlaxoSmithKline	UK	8.1	8.9	5.2	Sep-2011
5. Seroquel	Schizophrenia	AstraZeneca	UK	6.0	13.4	11.8	Sep-2011
6. Enbrel	Rheumatoid arthritis	Amgen/Wyeth	US	5.9	9.3	6.2	Oct-2012
7. Remicade	Rheumatoid arthritis	J&J/Schering-Plough	US	5.5	13.1	10.9	Dec-2018
8. Crestor	Dyslipidemia	AstraZeneca	UK	5.4	39.2	36.6	Jan-2016
9. Zyprexa	Schizophrenia	Eli Lilly	US	5.4	9.3	6.6	Oct-2011
10. Humira	Rheumatoid arthritis	Merck KGaA	Germany	5.0	31.8	27.7	Dec-2016
11. Avastin	Cancer (CRC, BC etc.)	Roche	Switzerland	5.0	27.2	25.1	Feb-2018
12. Singulair	Asthma/COPD	Merck & Co.	US	5.0	8.9	7.5	Aug-2012
13. Mabthera	NHL, RA, CLL	Roche	Switzerland	4.7	9.5	6.3	Dec-2014
14. Abilify	Schizophrenia, BD etc	Otsuka	Japan	4.7	31.7	30.7	Oct-2014
15. Lovenox	DVT, AF	Sanofi-Aventis	France	4.6	8.1	4.5	Feb-2012

CER-Constant exchange rate in US$. FER-Floating exchange rate. *Patent expiration dates are approximate for main indications in major markets (excluding line extentions) and subject to change, depending on the success of generic entries.

Sources: IMS Health; company reports; US Food & Drug Administration. *Standard & Poor's Industry Survey, Healthcare: Pharmaceuticals Europe*, June 2010, p. 15.

approval process, and the percentage of the drugs under development that actually improve the treatment of the targeted diseases.

A successful drug can reap large profits for a firm. Lipitor, the top-selling drug for 2009, is Pfizer's drug to reduce cholesterol, and it accounted for $13.3 billion of Pfizer's $57 billion sales in 2009. Table 6–4 presents the top prescription drugs in the global market for 2009, and if you count the winners you will see that Pfizer has two of the top 10 drugs.

The pharmaceutical industry lives and dies by its ability to create new chemical compounds that combat disease. The more effective the companies are in developing new drugs, the more profitable they will be and the more good they will do society. Advances in technology that allow researchers to analyze human genes have enabled scientists to better understand how genetic defects can cause many of our common diseases such as Alzheimer's disease, muscular dystrophy, and others. Many hope that new discoveries concerning genetics will allow researchers to move faster in solving some of the world's more puzzling medical problems. A new drug on average takes 10 years to develop and costs about $800 million (including the costs of unsuccessful compounds).

Product Diversity

The pharmaceutical industry is more complex than it might seem at first glance. Companies sell diagnostic and hospital supplies, nutritional supplements, human health products, animal health products, agricultural products, prescription pharmaceuticals, consumer products, and over-the-counter products such as aspirin and Tylenol. There are large and small companies, and even within the industry, companies concentrate their research efforts on targeted areas such as coronary, infectious, central nervous system, or pulmonary diseases. Within the industry there is not a lot of direct competition.

For example, it is unusual to find more than three drugs with high market shares treating the same problem. Usually one or two drugs dominate a market. Examining the product categories in Table 6–4, there are two cholesterol-reducing drugs in first and second place, two antiulcer drugs and two antianemia drugs in the top 10, with the other four leaders used for treating other ailments. Perhaps more important to the investor than a company's drugs currently in the market is the probability that its research laboratory is full of potential blockbuster drugs. Often stock prices are more influenced by a promising research pipeline than the current drugs that may come off patent in the next few years.

Patents and Generic Drugs

Drugs receive patent protection from the U.S. patent office and are protected from competition for a limited number of years. When a drug comes off patent protection, other companies are finally allowed to compete. Since the chemical makeup is available through the patent license, imitating some other company's chemical cocktail is not that difficult. Drugs imitated by other companies after a patent runs out are called generics, since they are copies. Once a generic duplicate hits the market, the profit on the original drug will shrink. Eli Lilly's Prozac is a case in point. This antidepressant generated close to $3 billion worth of sales for Lilly, but when it became available in generic form, Lilly lost approximately 80 percent of its Prozac sales. Of course, this is positive for consumers as they can buy the pills at a reduced price. Most pharmaceutical companies would like longer patent protection to insure that the profits from their discoveries can be reinvested in new research. (The normal protection period is now effectively 10 years.) In spite of complaints about inadequate patent protection, pharmaceutical companies generate high profit margins relative to many other industries.

Because this is a global industry, worldwide patent protection is a big issue. Many countries violate or don't enforce international patent protection. A company only needs to buy a pill and analyze it to determine its chemical formula and then manufacture the drug. This is usually easy for another pharmaceutical company to do. Patent violations and counterfeiting have been prevalent more in developing countries, especially Africa, where the AIDs epidemic is a serious problem. These violations have also occurred in India where many people can't afford the prices charged by the major global manufacturers. In recent years, companies have begun working with these governments to reduce the price of their drugs in exchange for more rigorous enforcement of the companies' patents. Table 6–4 also lists the patent expiration date of each top-selling drug. Some companies will have big holes to fill when generics are able to compete.

Demographics and Managed Care

Other issues that have a large effect on the pharmaceutical industry are demographics. As the world population ages, the demand for drugs will grow. Europe and Japan have relatively old populations, and the United States is rapidly aging. As the baby boomers age, their demand for drugs to treat all kinds of disease will increase. According to the *Standard & Poor's Industry Survey,* global demographics are bullish for the pharmaceutical industry. The drive to restrain rising drug prices through managed care and government programs will put downward pressure on company profit margins. The new Medicare coverage for drugs, while keeping a lid on prices, could create enough of an increased demand for drugs to overshadow any pricing constraints imposed on the pharmaceutical industry.

To keep yourself up to date on this industry or any other industry you are interested in analyzing, please refer to *Standard & Poor's Industry Surveys.* If your library subscribes to Standard & Poor's Net Advantage, you can access many industry reports online. Appendix 6A at the end of this chapter provides a guide on how to analyze the pharmaceutical industry.

INDUSTRY GROUPS AND ROTATIONAL INVESTING

One strategy of investment used by institutional investors and occasionally by individual investors is the concept of **rotational investing**. Rotational investing refers to the practice of moving in and out of various industries over the business cycle. As the business cycle moves from a trough to a peak, different industries benefit from the economic changes that accompany the cycle. Table 6–5 lists 10 Dow Jones Industry Groups; industries are classified into groups that are related in some form and that may exhibit similar behavior during different phases of the business cycle.

For example, as interest rates bottom out, houses become more easily financed and cost less per month to purchase. Because of this, housing stocks, home builders, lumber, and housing-related industries such as household durable goods benefit from the lower interest rates. Unfortunately, the collapse of the housing market in the most recent recession was not helped by low interest rates. But 2007–2010 was not a normal business cycle. Earnings of companies in these

TABLE 6-5 Dow Jones Industry Groups

Basic Materials
Chemicals
Chemicals, commodity
Chemicals, specialty
Forest products
Paper products
Aluminum
Mining, diversified
Other nonferrous (e.g., aluminum)
Precious metals
Steel

Consumer, Cyclical
Advertising
Broadcasting
Publishing
Auto manufacturers
Auto parts
Casinos
Entertainment
Recreation products and services
Restaurants
Toys
Home construction
Furnishings
Retailers
Retailers, apparel
Retailers, broadline
Retailers, drug-based
Retailers, specialty (e.g., drug and apparel)
Clothing and fabrics
Footwear
Airlines
Lodging

Consumer, Noncyclical
Consumer services
Cosmetics and personal care
Distillers and brewers
Food products
Soft drinks
Food retailers and wholesalers
Consumer products
Household products, durables
Household products, nondurables
Tobacco

Energy
Coal
Oil and gas
Oil, drilling
Oil, integrated majors
Oil, secondary
Oilfield equipment and services
Pipelines

Financial
Banks
Insurance, composite
Insurance, full line
Insurance, life
Insurance, property and casualty
Specialty finance
Real estate investment
Financial services, diversified
Savings and loans
Securities brokers

Health Care
Health care providers
Medical products
Advanced medical devices
Medical supplies
Pharmaceutical and biotech
Biotechnology
Pharmaceuticals

Industrial
Aerospace and defense
Building materials
Heavy construction
Containers and packaging
Industrial diversified
Industrial equipment
Advanced industrial equipment
Electrical components and equipment
Factory equipment
Heavy machinery
Industrial services
Pollution control and waste management
Industrial transportation
Air freight and couriers
Marine transportation
Railroads
Trucking
Transportation equipment

Technology
Hardware and equipment
Communications technology
Computers
Office equipment
Semiconductor and related
Software

Telecommunications
Fixed line communications
Wireless communications

Utilities
Electric
Gas
Water

fields are expected to rise, and investors start buying the common stocks of these companies before any profits are actually visible. The same could be said for the automobile industry because of the effect of low-cost financing.

Once an economic recovery is under way, the unemployment rate declines, personal income starts growing, and consumers start spending more. It may take six quarters or more of growth from the recessionary trough, but investors usually anticipate when the consumer will start spending again and bid prices of consumer cyclical stocks up before earnings increases appear. While automobile sales are affected by the lower interest rates, they also get a second boost from healthier and more affluent consumers.

When interest rates begin to rise, this is not good news for utility stocks. Utilities generate high dividend payouts and usually sell based on their dividend yield. As interest rates rise, utility stock prices fall along with prices of bonds. Another group that eventually loses favor after rates have risen somewhat from their bottom and are expected to continue rising is the banking sector. Rising rates eventually reduce bank lending and squeeze bank margins, which are small anyway.

Investors fearful of rising rates and a potential economic slowdown will often retreat into consumer noncyclical goods such as food, pharmaceuticals, beverages, and tobacco. A move into these industries is often considered defensive because the industries are not much influenced by economic downturns, so their earnings do not suffer nearly as much as cyclical industries.

Eventually, as the economy moves through its business cycle, inflation fears return as demand for products pushes up prices of goods. One possible move is into basic materials and energy. The pricing pressures in the economy spill over into rising prices for these commodities and rising profits for aluminum, oil, steel, and other companies in these industries. A move into these industry groups usually occurs later in the business cycle. Figure 6–6 from www.stockcharts.com presents one way to think about rotational investing.

While we do not necessarily endorse buying and selling common stocks in a rotational manner throughout the business cycle, many investors follow this approach, and you should be well aware of this strategy.

FIGURE 6-6 Sector Rotation Model

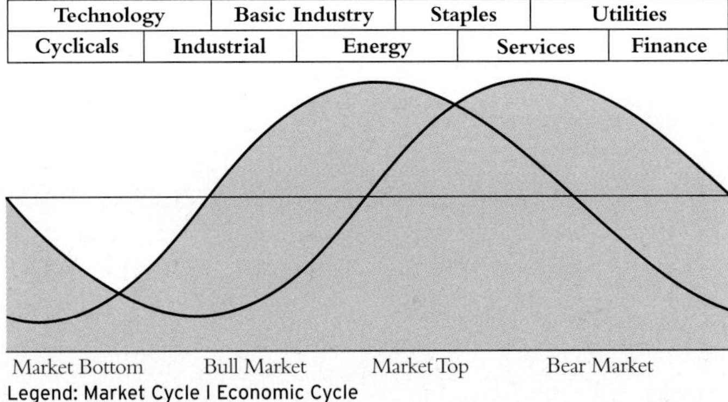

Legend: Market Cycle I Economic Cycle

This theoretical model is based on Sam Stovall's *S&P's Guide to Sector Rotation* and states that different sectors are stronger at different points in the economic cycle. The graph above shows these relationships and the order in which the various sectors should get a boost from the economy. The Market Cycle preceeds the Economic Cycle because investors try to anticipate economic effects. The PerfChart at the top of this page tries to help you see this effect.

Stage:	Full Recession	Early Recovery	Full Recovery	Early Recession
Consumer Expectations:	Reviving	Rising	Declining	Falling Sharply
Industrial Production:	Bottoming Out	Rising	Flat	Falling
Interest Rates:	Falling	Bottoming Out	Rising Rapidly (Fed)	Peaking
Yield Curve:	Normal	Normal (Steep)	Flattening Out	Flat/Inverted

Source: www.stockcharts.com.

exploring the web

Web Address	Comments
www.hoovers.com	Provides limited free information about sectors and industries
www.marketwatch.com/investing	Contains news and industry performance on daily basis
www.smartmoney.com	Provides sector and market performance—feature is map of market
www.wsj.com	Provides limited information about industry data; has searchable archive on articles about companies and industries—most content requires subscription to access
www.corporateinformation.com	Provides links to information on industries and by country—requires free registration
http://trade.gov/	Provides access to industry reports that are fee-based
www.investorguide.com	Has links to sites providing sector and industry information

SUMMARY

The preceding chapter presented a three-step model for stock valuation in Figure 5–1. Industry analysis as presented in this chapter is the second step in the top-down valuation process we use in the text. One of the most crucial issues in valuing a firm is its potential growth rates in sales, earnings, and cash flow. In order to have some idea of how fast a company can grow, we look at the underlying industry growth characteristics, especially its position on the life-cycle curve.

The industry life-cycle approach includes five stages: development, growth, expansion, maturity, and decline. The life-cycle process is depicted in Figures 6–1 and 6–2.

In addition to life-cycle analysis, the analyst must understand the importance of industry structure. Every industry has an economic structure, for example, monopoly, oligopoly, pure competition, or some other form of competition. The economic structure affects product pricing and returns. Government regulation is another issue that affects many industries. The government regulates profits (utilities), product quality (U.S. Food and Drug Administration), energy consumption (automobile efficiency), and many other areas of commerce such as transportation and education. Other areas that need to be examined are international competition, supply and demand relationships, availability of raw materials, energy costs, and so on. The pharmaceutical industry was given special attention in this chapter because of its significance to people of all ages and the many social issues associated with this industry.

KEY WORDS AND CONCEPTS

bottom-up approach 137
crossover point 140
industry life cycles 138
monopolies 144
oligopolies 144
Porter's Five Competitive Forces 146
pure competition 145
rotational investing 155
stock pickers 137
top-down approach 137

www.mhhe.com/hirtblock10e

DISCUSSION QUESTIONS

1. Distinguish between a "top-down approach" and a "bottom-up approach" to selecting stocks.
2. List the five stages of the industry life cycle. How does the pattern of cash dividend payments change over the cycle? (A general statement is all that is required.)
3. Why might a firm begin paying stock dividends in the growth stage?
4. If the investor does not correctly identify the crossover point between growth and expansion, what might happen to the price of the stock?
5. Suggest two companies that have continued to grow in nongrowth industries, and explain why.
6. Why are monopolies not common in the United States?
7. How would you describe the nature of competition in oligopolies, and what is the potential effect on profitability? How has international competition affected oligopolies?
8. What are the five competitive forces that affect prices and profitability in an industry?
9. As a follow-up to question 8, give two examples of powerful suppliers.
10. In the pharmaceutical industry, is government regulation tougher in the United States than in foreign countries?
11. Who has the greater advantage for research and development in the pharmaceutical industry, large drug companies or smaller ones?
12. What is meant by the concept of rotational investing?
13. Explain why low interest rates make housing stocks and other related stocks attractive.
14. If an investor fears higher inflation, what possible industries might he or she choose for investment?

WEB EXERCISE

Merck is one of the drug firms discussed in the chapter. We will now do further analysis. Go to **www.bloomberg.com**.

1. Enter MRK for Merck in the search box located across the top of the screen and press enter.
2. Scroll down the right-hand margin and record the value for the "Earnings Past 12 Months."
3. Record the "Last Dividend Reported" and divide by four.
4. Some have suggested Merck is not an expanding firm as depicted in Figure 6–1. The typical expanding firm does not pay out more than 25 to 30 percent of earnings in the form of dividends. How does Merck fare in this regard? Divide your answer to question 3 by your answer to question 2. Does Merck qualify as an expanding firm in terms of dividend policy? Write a one-sentence answer.

Note: From time to time, companies redesign their Web sites, and occasionally a topic we have listed may have been deleted, updated, or moved into a different location.

APPENDIX 6A

HOW TO ANALYZE A PHARMACEUTICAL COMPANY*

In evaluating a pharmaceutical company, there are important factors to consider. The most meaningful factors are its products, markets, and financial health.

*Source: *Standard & Poor's Industry Survey, Healthcare: Pharmaceuticals,* June 3, 2010, pp. 30–34.

Researching the Business

A thorough examination of the company's products and markets is the first step in the analysis. A pharmaceutical firm's drug portfolio is the main ingredient of its success.

Does the company sell primarily prescription or nonprescription products? Prices and profit margins of prescription drugs are significantly higher than those of nonprescription drugs, which are essentially mass-marketed consumer products. Patent protection is an important consideration for prescription drugs, whereas the success of nonprescription or over-the-counter (OTC) drugs is more closely linked to brandname recognition and promotional spending levels.

For both prescription and nonprescription drugmakers, company size and market share are important considerations. Pharmaceutical firms must have the critical mass to support heavy spending on research and development (R&D), as new product development is crucial to future success. In addition, these companies have to maintain a large sales force to market drugs in key domestic and foreign markets. Smaller drug companies, and even larger ones that depend heavily on one or two products, are more vulnerable to eventual patent expirations and competition from rival drugs.

With respect to market share, does the company dominate any key markets? Key markets are those with a large population whose chronic condition requires a daily regimen of maintenance therapy, thus offering the greatest sales opportunities. Medications for high blood pressure, elevated cholesterol levels, depression, ulcers, diabetes, and arthritis are examples. Oncology, once a niche therapeutic segment, is now exceedingly attractive because of its technological advances, growth rate, and profitability.

Prescription and nonprescription drug companies vary widely by the type of pharmaceuticals they offer and the markets that they serve. Does the company have a narrow or a broad product line? A broad product line is more desirable because greater diversification makes the company less dependent on a single product. It also makes the company more resilient to economic cycles and competition.

Prescription drugmakers, however, focus their product development and marketing efforts on select therapeutic areas. For many decades, Wyeth (formerly American Home Products) has dominated the female hormone replacement market with its Premarin family of products, while Pfizer Inc. has captured the lead in the growing cholesterol-reduction market with its popular drug Lipitor. Sometimes drugmakers create new markets with their discoveries, such as Pfizer's Viagra treatment for erectile dysfunction and Merck & Co. Inc.'s Proscar treatment for enlarged prostate glands. Launched in 2006, Merck's Gardasil vaccine for preventing infection with human papillomavirus (HPV)—believed to be the main cause of cervical cancer—has the potential to build a new market, in our opinion.

Nonprescription drugmakers do not have to fund major R&D projects, but they must maintain large advertising budgets to promote their products, which tend to face more competition than branded prescription drugs. As a result, most of the major firms have just a handful of truly successful product lines. Sales growth is slow for these businesses, with success highly dependent on the manufacturer's clout in the marketplace and overall market share.

If a prescription drugmaker has a diversification or acquisition program, has this been a plus or a minus? The program should be carefully analyzed to determine whether its initial objectives are being met or whether the program is hurting the company's performance. In general, large pharmaceutical companies regularly turn to smaller, more entrepreneurial companies as sources of innovation. Business development—the process of scouting for attractive deals and negotiating terms—is an integral part of a company's operating expertise and core strategy.

Prescription Drugmakers As noted earlier, most major prescription drugmakers tend to focus on a few specific therapeutic markets. Pfizer and Merck, for example, have carved out major stakes in the huge global antihypertensive and cholesterol-lowering drug markets by releasing a steady stream of new products in recent years. Eli Lilly

& Co. achieved phenomenal success in antidepressants with Prozac, which dominated the market for more than a decade until 2000, when it was overtaken by Pfizer's Zoloft. Eli Lilly's sales of Prozac eroded sharply following the loss of patent protection in August 2001. GlaxoSmithKline Plc has maintained dominance in respiratory drugs with its Advair and Flovent drugs.

In a healthcare market dominated by managed care, a company's relative size and the breadth of its product offerings have become increasingly important. Health maintenance organizations, preferred provider organizations, hospital chains, and other large-scale pharmaceutical purchasers prefer to deal with a limited number of large drug manufacturers that can offer them "one-stop shopping."

There are other factors when analyzing a prescription drugmaker. Questions to ask include the following:

- **When do the patents on the company's most important drugs expire?** If the expiration dates are within the next few years, is the company adequately preparing to make up for the revenues lost to generics competition? If a company loses its marketing exclusivity on key drugs without earning adequate profits from new products, it can find itself in difficult economic straits. Many of the leading US drugmakers, including Bristol-Myers Squibb Co., Merck, and Pfizer, are presently contending with fierce generics competition, with a wave of major drugs going off patent through 2011.
- **Have R&D efforts been productive?** In terms of R&D, the larger, well-funded firms typically have the advantage of being able to hire top scientists and to conduct more clinical trials, which are necessary to develop new drugs. Most leading drugmakers spend between 14% and 18% of their revenues on R&D. However, their success rates—in terms of lucrative new drugs—differ markedly. In addition, R&D productivity can be cyclical, with firms that generated a series of significant new products experiencing troughs before rebounding. In the 1990s, Merck and Pfizer had highly productive R&D programs, each spawning a number of blockbuster drugs.

  More recently, we think Merck has rejuvenated its pipeline with the launch of blockbusters such as Gardasil, and Januvia, a promising new treatment for type 2 diabetes. Pfizer also launched several promising drugs such as Lyrica for neuropathic pain and Chantix for smoking cessation. However, we think both Pfizer and Merck face steep patent challenges at the beginning of the next decade. Specifically, Merck's CozaarlHyzaar cardiovascular (sales of $3.6 billion in 2009), lost patent protection in 2010, and Pfizer's Lipitor cholesterol-lowering agent (sales of $11.4 billion in 2009) will lose patent protection in 2011.

  In the present managed care environment, companies with new drugs that are both therapeutic breakthroughs and cost effective hold the keys to success. New products that provide essentially identical results to existing therapies are less likely to reap big commercial rewards.
- **Has the company formed any promising alliances?** Large firms often benefit from alliances with smaller biotechnology and biopharmaceutical firms working on potentially lucrative new drugs. Conversely, a smaller company may find it necessary to team up with a larger partner to fund the clinical trials and commercialization of its discoveries.

  Business ventures with foreign companies can be a source of new products. For example, many drugs popular in the United States today were discovered by European and Japanese firms, but they are marketed by US drugmakers under royalty arrangements. Pfizer's Lipitor drug is sold under license from Sankyo Co. Ltd., of Japan.

  Many companies also maintain relationships with scientists at leading medical colleges or other organizations, such as the federal government's National Institutes of Health (NIH), which can funnel experimental products to drugmakers.

Bristol-Myers Squibb and GlaxoSmithKline, for example, have obtained major new drugs from these sources.

- **What is the company's international business profile?** The United States remains the most important market for US drugmakers, as well as for many foreign drug companies, because of its size and lack of government-imposed price constraints. Nonetheless, pharmaceutical markets elsewhere represent an attractive source of growth. Indeed, pharmaceutical sales in developing nations are expanding much faster than are those in the domestic market.

  Although the level of foreign business varies from company to company, the US pharmaceuticals industry currently derives about two-fifths of its revenues from sales outside the United States. Because many countries exercise strict price controls, foreign markets contribute a lower portion of profits than of sales.

  Which foreign markets has the company entered or does it plan to enter? Drugmakers should evaluate foreign markets carefully with respect to their individual risks and profit potential. In addition, it is important to assess the possible impact of changes in currency exchange rates.

  How diversified is the firm's foreign business? Foreign markets differ widely by level of pharmaceutical utilization, degree of government control over pricing, and the acceptance of clinical research from outside sources. Japan, for example, with the highest per capita consumption of prescription drugs in the world, is the largest single market outside the United States. However, the Japanese government generally requires across-the-board drug price cuts every few years.
- **How effective is the company in working with the FDA?** Because all drugs sold in the United States must first be cleared by the US Food and Drug Administration (FDA), a firm must be able to work with the agency and understand its criteria. Here again, size and experience can help. Most large, well-established drug companies are adept at working with the agency, while many smaller or newer firms are less proficient and often encounter major snags in obtaining approval for their products.

  Besides new drug applications, the FDA also inspects and monitors pharmaceutical plants for product integrity and quality control. (Several generic drugmakers ran into problems in this area a number of years ago.) In addition, the agency is expanding its role in postmarket surveillance of drug safety.
- **How effective is the company at working with third-party government and private payers?** Reimbursement is crucial for the commercial success of a product. Private and public payers alike are taking an increasingly hard line in evaluating the cost effectiveness of recently approved drugs. In Europe, several governments have established semi-independent organizations to make recommendations on whether a new drug should be reimbursed—and in some controversial cases, they have argued against coverage. The United States has not taken this approach, although it is considering the establishment of a reimbursement evaluation organization. US payers are increasingly differentiating drugs within the same class and placing them in separate tiers, with varying contributions from patients, aimed at giving patients incentives to use certain drugs. The ability to negotiate fair deals with Medicare over reimbursement for prescription drugs is also likely to be increasingly important to drug companies in the future.

Nonprescription Drugmakers While the prescription drug market depends on research-intensive innovation to differentiate among products and bolster sales, the nonprescription segment depends much more on consumer-directed marketing. The main factors that must be considered in evaluating a nonprescription drug company include the relative strength of its product offerings, its ability to develop new products, competitive pressures in each market segment, and the manufacturer's ability to support product sales through effective advertising and promotional campaigns.

www.mhhe.com/hirtblock10e

Companies with a strong presence in both prescription and nonprescription sectors typically generate the most successful OTC products, because most of the leading OTC medications on the market today started their lives as ethical, or prescription, drugs. Nonprescription drugmakers strive to cultivate broad consumer loyalty. For example, Johnson & johnson's Tylenol, launched as an OTC product in 1955, remains the best-selling nonprescription product in the US. This highly regarded analgesic has successfully fought off rival painkillers and cheaper private-label acetaminophen products, thanks to effective advertising that has built unmatched brand loyalty. The product has even survived recalls due to tampered packaging and reports of possible liver damage from overdosing or adverse reactions when combined with alcohol.

Strong recognition for an original brand also gives the manufacturer an ability to expand sales through line extensions. Leading OTC products, such as Tylenol, Advil, Bayer, and Motrin, have successfully broadened their consumer appeal through the addition of specialized formulations for children, combinations with other products, and extra-strength versions.

Analyzing Financial Statements

Once the analyst has reviewed a company's products and markets, a look at its financial statements is in order. The income statement contains some key figures and ratios (described below). Balance sheet and cash flow data provide further insight into a company's financial position and performance. Individual company statistics should be compared with those of rival companies and industry averages.

The Income Statement When looking at a pharmaceutical company's income statement, it is important to examine trends in sales growth; profit margins; R&D and selling, general, and administrative (SG&A) expenses; and return on equity.

- **What are the company's sales trends?** Examine the company's recent and historical sales performance. Has sales growth been consistent or volatile? How has growth been achieved: through volume, pricing, acquisitions, or through a combination of these?
- **How wide are operating margins?** Drug companies characteristically have high operating profit margins (operating earnings before depreciation and nonoperating items as a percentage of sales). Margins have contracted from their highs of about 40 percent in the early 1990s, due to reduced pricing flexibility. However, drug margins still exceed overall averages in other industries by a wide margin, averaging 32 percent in 2008, versus 17 percent for corporations in the S&P 500 Composite Stock index.

  The high margins reflect drugmakers' very low raw material costs and SG&A expenses per dollar of sales that are less than average. Although substantial costs are incurred during a drug's R&D phase, once those costs have been covered, most revenues flow to the bottom line. Companies that can consistently develop value-added, widely used drugs with long lives can command margins well above the industry average.

  It is important to note that companies can temporarily pump up margins by crimping R&D spending. While this tactic can provide short-term earnings improvement, it also undermines a drugmaker's ability to develop the new products needed to support future growth.

  Changes in a company's margins over a period of years can reveal management's effectiveness in improving the company's profitability. Restructuring and cost-streamlining efforts often can play a major role in boosting a company's profit margins.
- **What are the company's pretax and net returns?** Drug industry pretax and net income returns have historically been above the averages in other industries.

While the gap narrowed in recent years, as pharma margins contracted under more constrained managed care pricing and as patents expired, pharmaceutical margins still exceed the overall healthcare industry by a wide margin. Drugmakers' net earnings as a percentage of sales averaged about 16 percent between 2004 and 2008, versus an average of 6.4 percent for the S&P 500 over the same period.

The drug business is less capital intensive than most other industries, and it tends to have lower interest expense and depreciation as a percentage of sales. Drugmakers' profit margins also have been augmented by lower tax rates, R&D credits, and tax credits from manufacturing operations in Ireland and other areas. Lower-than-average drug industry tax rates also reflect the large portion of sales derived from countries with tax rates below those of the United States. Past tax credits from manufacturing operations in Puerto Rico now have been largely eliminated.

A company's geographic business mix should be examined to determine how its blended tax rate compares with others in the industry. But before comparing different companies' net returns, make sure that the reported results are truly comparable. Although current accounting standards require that discontinued operations be segmented out, nonrecurring items (such as restructuring charges, asset sales gains, foreign exchange gains and losses, and similar nonoperating items) are often buried in the category of "other income/expenses" and must be factored out when making comparisons. Accounting practices also vary for inventory and depreciation.

- **What is the return on stockholders' equity?** Return on equity (ROE), or net earnings as a percentage of average stockholders' equity, is viewed as a key measure of management's effectiveness in the pharmaceutical industry. The drug industry's average ROE of 19 percent between 2004 and 2008 ranked among the highest of all industries. The lofty ratio is essentially a function of the industry's relatively high profit margins. The comparable level for the S&P 500 was 12 percent.

Cash Flow Another way of looking at profits is cash flow—essentially, net earnings plus depreciation and other noncash charges. It provides a useful gauge of a company's capacity to finance capital projects. Cash flow as a percentage of sales for drugmakers is close to 23 percent, almost double the average percentage for US industrial companies.

The source and application of funds statement shows how a company allocates its cash flow, which is often a leading indicator of future growth. Firms investing heavily in acquisitions and capital projects are preparing to expand the business. Those paying out more in dividends are rewarding investors but retaining less cash for future growth.

Balance Sheet The balance sheet is a snapshot of a company's financial condition at a specific moment in time, so it should be examined to determine a company's financial health. For pharmaceutical companies, most balance sheet analysis focuses on liquidity. To assess a company's short-term liquidity, analysts look at its level of cash and marketable securities. Companies with large liquid assets also are better situated to make timely acquisitions.

A reliable check for liquidity is the current ratio, which measures the ratio of current assets to current liabilities. A healthy working capital ratio is essential to ensure that the company can adequately meet its current liabilities. This ratio always should be greater than 1.0. Any meaningful degradation in these items from previous reporting periods may signal a liquidity problem.

Debt leverage varies significantly among drugmakers. An appropriate debt load largely depends on a drug company's product line and the strength of its projected new product stream. The ratio of long-term debt to total capital from 2004 to 2008 was 21 percent, less than half the average for US industrial companies.

chapter seven

7 VALUATION OF THE INDIVIDUAL FIRM

OBJECTIVES

1. Understand the basic valuation process as it relates to earnings and dividends.
2. Explain the related concepts of risk and return.
3. Be able to use various present value–oriented valuation models.
4. Describe the role of the price-earnings ratio in determining value.
5. Explain how an individual stock's price-earnings ratio is related to the market.
6. Explain techniques for forecasting earnings per share.

OUTLINE

We have been building the foundation for the valuation of the individual firm, depicted in Figure 5–1 on page 113. **Valuation** is based on economic factors, industry variables, an analysis of the financial statements, and the outlook for the individual firm. Valuation determines the long-run fundamental economic value of a company's common stock. In the process, we try to determine whether a common stock is undervalued, overvalued, or fairly valued relative to its market price. The orientation in this chapter is mostly toward long-run concepts of valuation rather than toward determining short-term market pricing factors. The valuation concepts we develop in this chapter should be valuable to you in eventually developing your own portfolio.

BASIC VALUATION CONCEPTS

The valuation of common stock can be approached in several ways. Some models rely solely on dividends expected to be received during the future, and these are usually referred to as **dividend valuation models**. A variation on the dividend model is the **earnings valuation model**, which substitutes earnings as the main income stream for valuation. Earnings valuation models may also call for the determination of a price-earnings ratio, or multiplier of earnings, to determine value. Some models rely on long-run historical relationships between market price and sales per share, or market price and book value per share. Other methods may include the market value of assets, such as cash and liquid assets, replacement value of plant and equipment, and other hidden assets such as undervalued timber holdings. For the first part of our discussion, we develop the dividend valuation model and then go to earnings-related approaches.

REVIEW OF REQUIRED RETURN CONCEPTS: CAPITAL ASSET PRICING MODEL

As we move to the valuation models, it is helpful to review and consolidate the concepts of risk and required return presented in Chapter 1. Calculation of the required rate of return is extremely important because it is the rate at which future cash flows are discounted to reach a valuation. An investor needs to know the required rate of return on the various risk classes of assets to reach intelligent decisions to buy or sell.

Chapter 1 examined rates of returns for various assets and returns based on Ibbotson Associates data and explained how the risk-free rate is a function of both the real rate of return and an inflation premium. The required return was a function of the risk-free rate plus a risk premium for a specific investment.

In this section, we develop a simple methodology based on the capital asset pricing model for determining a required rate of return when valuing common stocks in a diversified portfolio. First, we determine the risk-free rate. The **risk-free rate** (R_F) is a function of the real rate of return and the expected rate of inflation. Some analysts express the risk-free rate as simply the addition of the real rate of return and the expected rate of inflation, while a more accurate answer is found as follows:

$$R_F \text{ (Risk-free rate)} = (1 + \text{Real rate})(1 + \text{Expected rate of inflation}) - 1 \qquad \textbf{(7–1)}$$

We now add a risk component to the risk-free rate to determine K_e, the total **required rate of return**. We show the following relationships.

$$K_e = R_F + b(K_M - R_F) \qquad \textbf{(7–2)}$$

where:

K_e = Required rate of return
R_F = Risk-free rate
b = Beta coefficient
K_M = Expected return for common stocks in the market
$(K_M - R_F)$ = Equity risk premium (ERP)

The risk-free rate, in practice, is normally assumed to be the return on U.S. Treasury securities. **Beta** measures individual company risk against the market risk (usually the S&P 500 Stock Index). Companies with betas greater than 1.00 have more risk than the market; companies with betas less than 1.00 have less risk than the market; and companies with betas equal to 1.00 have the same risk as the market. It stands to reason then that high beta stocks ($b > 1.00$) would have higher required returns than the market.

The last term ($K_M - R_F$) in Formula 7–2, the **equity risk premium** (ERP), is not observable from current market information because it is based on investor expectations. The equity risk premium represents the extra return or premium the stock market must provide compared with the rate of return an investor can earn on U.S.

Government Treasury securities. Between 1926 and 2009, the mean return of large company stocks was 9.8 percent and for government bonds 5.4 percent. It is clear that stocks outperformed long-term government bonds by 4.4 percent. If we use large-company stocks (the S&P 500) for our K_M and long-term government bonds for our R_F, then we have an equity risk premium of 4.4 percent.

In early finance courses K_M and R_F are usually given. In the real world they are thought of as one number and called the equity risk premium, or ERP. The equity risk premium represents the premium an investor would expect to receive for buying a more risky equity asset such as common stock, compared to the return an investor could expect to receive for a risk-free asset, namely a U.S. government security. In this case, history would create an expectation that the ERP would equal $(K_M - R_F)$ or (9.8–5.4) or 4.4 percent. An equity risk premium could be computed in a similar calculation for short-term Treasury bills, intermediate government securities, or long-term corporate bonds. We could also compute an equity risk premium for small stocks using the return on small stocks for our K_M. If an analyst were analyzing a small company, a small stock equity risk premium would be more appropriate than using a large stock equity risk premium. Please refer to Chapter 1 for the discussion of equity risk premiums.

application example

Having discussed the beta and the equity risk premium (the second term in Formula 7–2), what is the appropriate value for the first term, the risk-free rate (R_F)?

$$K_e = \underset{\substack{\uparrow \\ \text{Risk-free rate}}}{R_F} + \underset{\substack{\uparrow \\ \text{Beta}}}{b}\underset{\substack{\uparrow \\ \text{Equity risk premium}}}{(K_M - R_F)} \quad \textbf{(7–2)}$$

reproduced

By using the long-term government bond rate for our equity risk premium calculation we have matched the long-term nature of common stocks with the long-term returns generated by 20-year government bonds. For example, if the current long-term government bond has a yield of 4.6 percent return, and our ERP is 4.4 percent, and the beta for the market by definition is 1.00, then our required return for the stock market would be as follows:

$$\begin{aligned} K_e &= R_F + b(K_M - R_F) \\ &= 4.6\% + 1.00(4.4\%) \\ &= 9.0\% \end{aligned}$$

Now, K_e, the required rate of return, can be used as a discount rate for future cash flows from an investment. If the company we are valuing has a beta different from 1.00, then the required return will reflect either a higher or lower return for a company with higher or lower risk. This methodology will be helpful as you work through the dividend valuation models and other valuation models for common stock.

Deficiencies of Beta

Sometimes the Capital Asset Pricing Model gives us faulty information for one stock. Betas for individual stocks are not stable and have a tendency to revert to 1.0 over time. High beta stocks tend to move down, and low beta stocks tend to move up, and when put together in a large portfolio of stocks, the effects balance out. The other problem is that betas in up markets and down markets are different, and this makes them somewhat unreliable to use for one company. For example, when the S&P was falling from it peak in 1998 to 2001, stock prices for some companies, such as Budweiser (now owned by InBev, a Belgian-Brazilian beer giant), were fairly stable. As the market fell, Budweiser's stock price did not fall nearly as much as the

S&P 500, because it sells a product that has a fairly inelastic demand, which is why it is considered a defensive stock. This created a very low beta, because Bud's stock price was not highly correlated with the overall market. When you plugged a 0.5 beta into the CAPM, the result was a ridiculously low number—less than a U.S government bond. There are also many ways to calculate a beta and statistically adjust beta for its regression to the mean tendencies. Be careful: if you look in enough places for beta (Web sites, Merrill Lynch, Standard & Poor's, etc.), you may find two or three numbers that aren't at all the same. Then which one do you pick?

The Equity Risk Premium Problem

There is a problem with the equity risk premium, which is that it isn't stable. The equity risk premium jumps around with investors' risk aversion. When markets are booming and investors are greedy, investors may reduce the equity risk premium they desire because they are confident. On the other hand, when markets are in decline, as they were in 2008 and early 2010, investors are overcome with fear and need a very high equity risk premium to drag them into the stock market. Just because the long-term equity risk premium of stocks over long-term government bonds is 4.4 percent doesn't mean that it is a constant number that you can just plug into the formula. You need to determine your own required return parameters and risk aversion and decide whether the returns you expect to receive are high enough to compensate for the extra risk of owning the stock instead of the bond.

Using Bond Yields to Determine Required Returns

Finance students learn in their first class that stocks are riskier than bonds and therefore should have a higher return than a bond issued by the same company. To check up on the required rate of return generated by the CAPM, see if the company you are evaluating has a bond outstanding. You can usually find this information through Bloomberg or in the footnotes to the company's annual report. See how the bond yield compares to the required return on the stock. It should be lower. For example, assume that you compute K_e as 5.2 percent, and you find that the company has five bonds outstanding, with the highest yield to maturity at 6.5 percent. Does it make sense that your required rate of return on the stock is less than the yield to maturity on the bond? No, it doesn't, and besides that, the required rate of return on the stock should be the bond yield plus a risk premium. If we look back at Figure 1–4 in Chapter 1, we can see that corporate bonds had a long-term average return of 5.9 percent and stocks 9.8 percent, or a 3.9 percent equity risk premium for stocks over corporate bonds. It may be that the company you are analyzing could have a higher or lower risk premium than 3.9 percent, but that would be your judgment call.

$$\text{Alternative } K_e = \text{Company bond yield} + \text{Equity risk premium}$$

DIVIDEND VALUATION MODELS

The value of a share of stock may be interpreted by the shareholder as the present value of an expected stream of future dividends. Although in the short run, stockholders may be influenced by a change in earnings or other variables, the ultimate value of any holding rests with the distribution of earnings in the form of dividend payments. Although the stockholder may benefit from the retention and reinvestment of earnings by the corporation, at some point, the earnings must generally be translated into cash flow for the stockholder.[1] While dividend valuation models are theoretical in nature and subject to many limitations, they are the most frequently used models in the literature of finance. Perhaps this is because they demonstrate so well the relationship between the major variables affecting common stock prices.

[1] Some exceptions to this principle are noted later in the chapter.

General Dividend Model

A generalized stock valuation model based on future expected dividends can be stated as follows:

$$P_0 = \frac{D_1}{(1 + K_e)^1} + \frac{D_2}{(1 + K_e)^2} + \frac{D_3}{(1 + K_e)^3} + \cdots + \frac{D_\infty}{(1 + K_e)^\infty} \qquad \textbf{(7–3)}$$

where:

P_0 = Present value of the stock price
D_i = Dividend for each year, for example, 1, 2, 3 · · · ∞
K_e = Required rate of return (discount rate)

This model is very general and assumes the investor can determine the right dividend for each and every year as well as the annualized rate of return an investor requires.

Constant Growth Model

Rather than predict the actual dividend each year, a more widely used model includes an estimate of the growth rate in dividends. This model assumes a constant growth rate in dividends to infinity.

If a constant growth rate in dividends is assumed, Formula 7–3 can be rewritten as:

$$P_0 = \frac{D_0(1 + g)^1}{(1 + K_e)^1} + \frac{D_0(1 + g)^2}{(1 + K_e)^2} + \frac{D_0(1 + g)^3}{(1 + K_e)^3} + \cdots + \frac{D_0(1 + g)^\infty}{(1 + K_e)^\infty} \qquad \textbf{(7–4)}$$

where:

$D_0(1 + g)^1 = D_1$ = Dividends in the initial year
$D_0(1 + g)^2 = D_2$ = Dividends in year 2, and so on
g = Constant growth rate in the dividend

The current price of the stock should equal the present value of the expected stream of dividends. If we can correctly predict the growth of future dividends and determine the discount rate, we can estimate the true value of the stock.

For example, assume we wanted to determine the present value of ABC Corporation common stock based on this model. We shall assume ABC anticipates an 8 percent growth rate in dividends per share, and we will use a 12 percent discount rate as the required rate of return. The required rate of return is intended to provide the investor with a minimum rate of return based on the stock's beta. Twelve percent is sufficient to fulfill that function in this example.

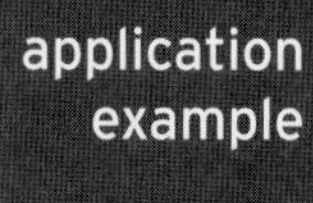

Rather than project the dividends for an extremely long period and then discount them back to the present, we can reduce previously presented Formula 7–4 to a more usable form:

$$P_0 = D_1/(K_e - g) \qquad \textbf{(7–5)}$$

This formula is appropriate as long as two conditions are met. The first is that the growth rate must be constant. For the ABC Corporation, we are assuming that to be the case. It is a constant 8 percent. Second, K_e (the required rate of return) must exceed g (the growth rate). Since K_e is 12 percent and g is 8 percent for the ABC Corporation, this condition is also met. Let's further assume D_1 (the expected dividend at the end of period 1) is \$3.38.

Using Formula 7–5, we determine a stock value of:

$$\begin{aligned} P_0 &= D_1/(K_e - g) \\ &= \$3.38/(0.12 - 0.08) \\ &= \$3.38/0.04 \\ &= \$84.50 \end{aligned}$$

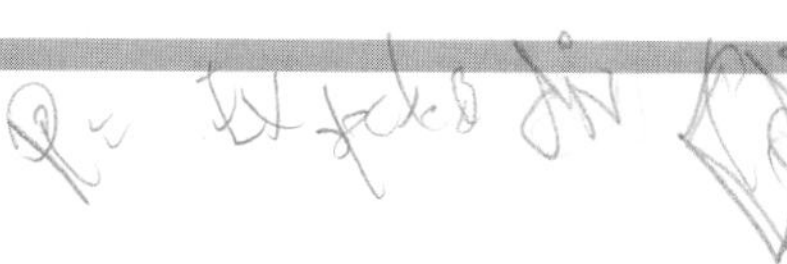

We must be aware that several things could be wrong with our analysis. First, our expectations of dividend growth may be too high for an infinite period. Perhaps 6 percent is a more realistic estimate of expected dividend growth. If we substitute our new estimate into Formula 7–5, we can measure the price effect as dividend growth changes from an 8 percent rate to a 6 percent rate:

$$
\begin{aligned}
P_0 &= \$3.38/(0.12 - 0.06) \\
&= \$3.38/0.06 \\
&= \$56.33
\end{aligned}
$$

A 6 percent growth rate (a 2 percent change) cuts the price down substantially from the prior value of \$84.50.

We could also misjudge our required rate of return, K_e, which could be higher or lower. A lower K_e would increase the present value of ABC Corporation, whereas a higher K_e would reduce its value. We have made these points to show how sensitive stock prices are to the basic assumptions of the model. Even though you may go through the calculations, the final value is only as accurate as your inputs. This is where a security analyst's judgment and expertise are important—in justifying the growth rate and required rate of return.

A Nonconstant Growth Model

Many analysts do not accept the premise of a constant growth rate in dividends or earnings. As we examined in Chapter 6, industries go through a life cycle in which growth is nonlinear. Growth is usually highest in the infancy and early phases of the life cycle, and as expansion is reached, the growth rate slows until the industry reaches maturity. At maturity, a constant, long-term growth rate that approximates the long-term growth of the macro economy may be appropriate for a particular industry.

Some companies in an industry may not behave like the industry in general. Companies constantly try to avoid maturity or decline, and so they strive to develop new products and markets to maintain growth.

In situations where the analyst wants to value a company without the constant-growth assumption, a variation of the constant-growth model is possible. Growth is simply divided into several periods with each period having a present value. The present value of each period is summed to attain the total value of the firm's share price. An example of a two-period model may illustrate the concept. Assume that JAYCAR Corporation is expected to have the growth pattern shown in Figure 7–1.

FIGURE 7-1 JAYCAR Growth Pattern

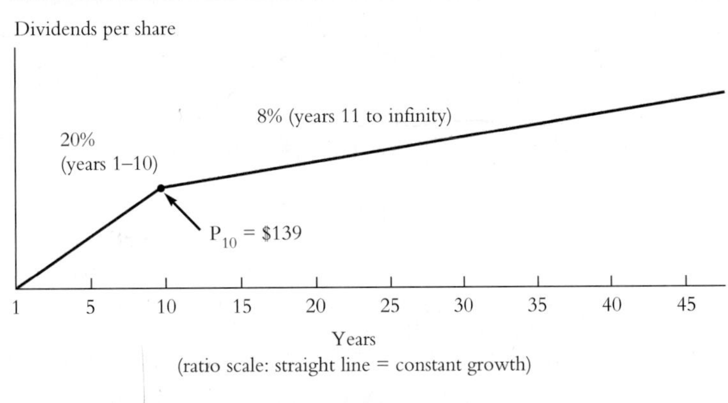

application example

It is assumed that JAYCAR will have a dividend growth rate of 20 percent for the next 10 years and an 8 percent perpetual growth rate after that. JAYCAR's dividend is expected to be $1 at the end of year one, and the appropriate required rate of return (discount rate) is 12 percent. Taking the present value for the first 10 years of dividends and then applying the constant dividend growth model for years 11 through infinity, we can arrive at an answer. First, we find the present value of the initial 10 years of dividends:

Year	Dividends (20% growth)	PV Factor (12%)[a]	Present Value of Dividends First 10 Years
1	$1.00	0.893	$ 0.89
2	1.20	0.797	0.96
3	1.44	0.712	1.03
4	1.73	0.636	1.10
5	2.07	0.567	1.17
6	2.48	0.507	1.26
7	2.98	0.452	1.35
8	3.58	0.404	1.45
9	4.29	0.361	1.55
10	5.15	0.322	1.66
			$12.42

[a] Present value factors are taken from Appendix C at the end of this book.

We then determine the present value of dividends after the 10th year. The dividend in year 11 is expected to be $5.56, or $5.15 (for year 10) compounded at the new, lower 8 percent growth rate ($5.15 × 1.08). Because the rest of the dividend stream will be infinite, Formula 7–5 can provide the value of JAYCAR at the end of year 10, based on a discount rate of 12 percent and an expected growth rate of 8 percent.

$$\begin{aligned} P_{10} &= D_{11}/(K_e - g) \\ &= \$5.56/(0.12 - 0.08) \\ &= \$5.56/0.04 \\ &= \$139 \end{aligned}$$

An investor would pay $139 at the end of the 10th year for the future stream of dividends from year 11 to infinity. To get the present value of the 10th year price, the $139 must be discounted back to the present by the 10-year PV factor for 12 percent from Appendix C (0.322). This part of the answer is $139.00 × 0.322, or $44.76. The two parts of this analysis can be combined to get the current valuation per share of $57.18.

Present value of the dividends from years 1 to 10	$12.42
Present value of 10th year price ($139.00 × 0.322)	44.76
Total present value of JAYCAR common stock	$57.18

Dividend valuation models are best suited for companies in the expansion or maturity life-cycle phase. Dividends of these companies are more predictable and usually make up a larger percentage of the total return than capital gains.

The Combined Dividend and Earnings Model

Another valuation model relies on earnings per share (EPS) and a price-earnings (P/E) ratio (earnings multiplier) combined with a finite dividend model. The value of the common stock can be viewed as a dividend stream plus a market price at the end of the dividend stream. We have selected Johnson & Johnson from the health care and pharmaceutical industry as our sample company for the valuation models that follow. We will use the Value Line Investment Survey for our Johnson & Johnson example, shown in Table 7–1. Assuming that we start

TABLE 7-1 Johnson & Johnson Value Line Investment Survey

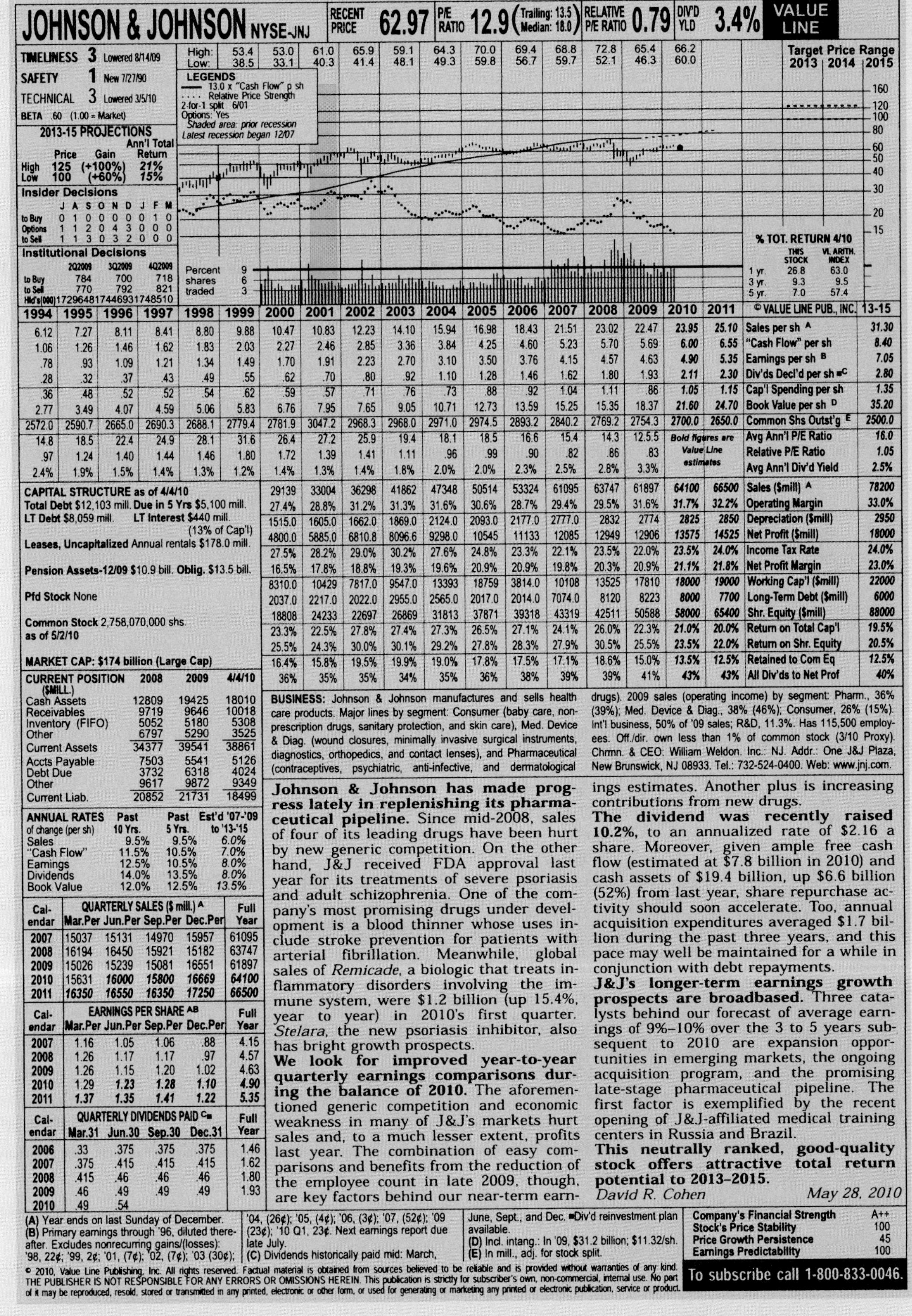

JOHNSON & JOHNSON NYSE-JNJ

RECENT PRICE 62.97 | P/E RATIO 12.9 (Trailing: 13.5 Median: 18.0) | RELATIVE P/E RATIO 0.79 | DIV'D YLD 3.4% | VALUE LINE

TIMELINESS 3 Lowered 8/14/09

SAFETY 1 New 7/27/90

TECHNICAL 3 Lowered 3/5/10

BETA .60 (1.00 = Market)

High:	53.4	53.0	61.0	65.9	59.1	64.3	70.0	69.4	68.8	72.8	65.4	66.2
Low:	38.5	33.1	40.3	41.4	48.1	49.3	59.8	56.7	59.7	52.1	46.3	60.0

Target Price Range 2013 | 2014 | 2015

LEGENDS
— 13.0 x "Cash Flow" p sh
.... Relative Price Strength
2-for-1 split 6/01
Options: Yes
Shaded area: prior recession
Latest recession began 12/07

2013-15 PROJECTIONS

	Price	Gain	Ann'l Total Return
High	125	(+100%)	21%
Low	100	(+60%)	15%

Insider Decisions

	J	A	S	O	N	D	J	F	M
to Buy	0	1	0	0	0	0	0	1	0
Options	1	1	2	0	4	3	0	0	0
to Sell	1	1	3	0	3	2	0	0	0

Institutional Decisions

	2Q2009	3Q2009	4Q2009
to Buy	784	700	718
to Sell	770	792	821
Hld's(000)	1729648	1744693	1748510

% TOT. RETURN 4/10

	THIS STOCK	VL ARITH. INDEX
1 yr.	26.8	63.0
3 yr.	9.3	9.5
5 yr.	7.0	57.4

1994	1995	1996	1997	1998	1999	2000	2001	2002	2003	2004	2005	2006	2007	2008	2009	2010	2011	© VALUE LINE PUB., INC.	13-15
6.12	7.27	8.11	8.41	8.80	9.88	10.47	10.83	12.23	14.10	15.94	16.98	18.43	21.51	23.02	22.47	**23.95**	**25.10**	Sales per sh A	**31.30**
1.06	1.26	1.46	1.62	1.83	2.03	2.27	2.46	2.85	3.36	3.84	4.25	4.60	5.23	5.70	5.69	**6.00**	**6.55**	"Cash Flow" per sh	**8.40**
.78	.93	1.09	1.21	1.34	1.49	1.70	1.91	2.23	2.70	3.10	3.50	3.76	4.15	4.57	4.63	**4.90**	**5.35**	Earnings per sh B	**7.05**
.28	.32	.37	.43	.49	.55	.62	.70	.80	.92	1.10	1.28	1.46	1.62	1.80	1.93	**2.11**	**2.30**	Div'ds Decl'd per sh ■C	**2.80**
.36	.48	.52	.52	.54	.62	.59	.57	.71	.76	.73	.88	.92	1.04	1.11	.86	**1.05**	**1.15**	Cap'l Spending per sh	**1.35**
2.77	3.49	4.07	4.59	5.06	5.83	6.76	7.95	7.65	9.05	10.71	12.73	13.59	15.25	15.35	18.37	**21.60**	**24.70**	Book Value per sh D	**35.20**
2572.0	2590.7	2665.0	2690.3	2688.1	2779.4	2781.9	3047.2	2968.3	2968.0	2971.0	2974.5	2893.2	2840.2	2769.2	2754.3	**2700.0**	**2650.0**	Common Shs Outst'g E	**2500.0**
14.8	18.5	22.4	24.9	28.1	31.6	26.4	27.2	25.9	19.4	18.1	18.5	16.6	15.4	14.3	12.5.5	*Bold figures are*	*Value Line estimates*	Avg Ann'l P/E Ratio	**16.0**
.97	1.24	1.40	1.44	1.46	1.80	1.72	1.39	1.41	1.11	.96	.99	.90	.82	.86	.83			Relative P/E Ratio	**1.05**
2.4%	1.9%	1.5%	1.4%	1.3%	1.2%	1.4%	1.3%	1.4%	1.8%	2.0%	2.0%	2.3%	2.5%	2.8%	3.3%			Avg Ann'l Div'd Yield	**2.5%**

2000	2001	2002	2003	2004	2005	2006	2007	2008	2009	2010	2011	© VALUE LINE PUB., INC.	13-15
29139	33004	36298	41862	47348	50514	53324	61095	63747	61897	**64100**	**66500**	Sales ($mill) A	**78200**
27.4%	28.8%	31.2%	31.3%	31.6%	30.6%	28.7%	29.4%	29.5%	31.6%	**31.7%**	**32.2%**	Operating Margin	**33.0%**
1515.0	1605.0	1662.0	1869.0	2124.0	2093.0	2177.0	2777.0	2832	2774	**2825**	**2850**	Depreciation ($mill)	**2950**
4800.0	5885.0	6810.8	8096.6	9298.0	10545	11133	12085	12949	12906	**13575**	**14525**	Net Profit ($mill)	**18000**
27.5%	28.2%	29.0%	30.2%	27.6%	24.8%	23.3%	22.1%	23.5%	22.0%	**23.5%**	**24.0%**	Income Tax Rate	**24.0%**
16.5%	17.8%	18.8%	19.3%	19.6%	20.9%	20.9%	19.8%	20.3%	20.9%	**21.1%**	**21.8%**	Net Profit Margin	**23.0%**
8310.0	10429	7817.0	9547.0	13393	18759	3814.0	10108	13525	17810	**18000**	**19000**	Working Cap'l ($mill)	**22000**
2037.0	2217.0	2022.0	2955.0	2565.0	2017.0	2014.0	7074.0	8120	8223	**8000**	**7700**	Long-Term Debt ($mill)	**6000**
18808	24233	22697	26869	31813	37871	39318	43319	42511	50588	**58000**	**65400**	Shr. Equity ($mill)	**88000**
23.3%	22.5%	27.8%	27.4%	27.3%	26.5%	27.1%	24.1%	26.0%	22.3%	**21.0%**	**20.0%**	Return on Total Cap'l	**19.5%**
25.5%	24.3%	30.0%	30.1%	29.2%	27.8%	28.3%	27.9%	30.5%	25.5%	**23.5%**	**22.0%**	Return on Shr. Equity	**20.5%**
16.4%	15.8%	19.5%	19.9%	19.0%	17.8%	17.5%	17.1%	18.6%	15.0%	**13.5%**	**12.5%**	Retained to Com Eq	**12.5%**
36%	35%	35%	34%	35%	36%	38%	39%	39%	41%	**43%**	**43%**	All Div'ds to Net Prof	**40%**

CAPITAL STRUCTURE as of 4/4/10
Total Debt $12,103 mill. **Due in 5 Yrs** $5,100 mill.
LT Debt $8,059 mill. **LT Interest** $440 mill.
(13% of Cap'l)
Leases, Uncapitalized Annual rentals $178.0 mill.

Pension Assets-12/09 $10.9 bill. **Oblig.** $13.5 bill.

Pfd Stock None

Common Stock 2,758,070,000 shs.
as of 5/2/10

MARKET CAP: $174 billion (Large Cap)

CURRENT POSITION ($MILL.)	2008	2009	4/4/10
Cash Assets	12809	19425	18010
Receivables	9719	9646	10018
Inventory (FIFO)	5052	5180	5308
Other	6797	5290	3525
Current Assets	34377	39541	38861
Accts Payable	7503	5541	5126
Debt Due	3732	6318	4024
Other	9617	9872	9349
Current Liab.	20852	21731	18499

ANNUAL RATES of change (per sh)	Past 10 Yrs.	Past 5 Yrs.	Est'd '07-'09 to '13-'15
Sales	9.5%	9.5%	6.0%
"Cash Flow"	11.5%	10.5%	7.0%
Earnings	12.5%	10.5%	8.0%
Dividends	14.0%	13.5%	8.0%
Book Value	12.0%	12.5%	13.5%

Cal-endar	QUARTERLY SALES ($ mill.) A Mar.Per	Jun.Per	Sep.Per	Dec.Per	Full Year
2007	15037	15131	14970	15957	61095
2008	16194	16450	15921	15182	63747
2009	15026	15239	15081	16551	61897
2010	15631	**16000**	**15800**	**16669**	**64100**
2011	**16350**	**16550**	**16350**	**17250**	**66500**

Cal-endar	EARNINGS PER SHARE AB Mar.Per	Jun.Per	Sep.Per	Dec.Per	Full Year
2007	1.16	1.05	1.06	.88	4.15
2008	1.26	1.17	1.17	.97	4.57
2009	1.26	1.15	1.20	1.02	4.63
2010	1.29	**1.23**	**1.28**	**1.10**	**4.90**
2011	**1.37**	**1.35**	**1.41**	**1.22**	**5.35**

Cal-endar	QUARTERLY DIVIDENDS PAID C■ Mar.31	Jun.30	Sep.30	Dec.31	Full Year
2006	.33	.375	.375	.375	1.46
2007	.375	.415	.415	.415	1.62
2008	.415	.46	.46	.46	1.80
2009	.46	.49	.49	.49	1.93
2010	.49	.54			

BUSINESS: Johnson & Johnson manufactures and sells health care products. Major lines by segment: Consumer (baby care, nonprescription drugs, sanitary protection, and skin care), Med. Device & Diag. (wound closures, minimally invasive surgical instruments, diagnostics, orthopedics, and contact lenses), and Pharmaceutical (contraceptives, psychiatric, anti-infective, and dermatological drugs). 2009 sales (operating income) by segment: Pharm., 36% (39%); Med. Device & Diag., 38% (46%); Consumer, 26% (15%). Int'l business, 50% of '09 sales; R&D, 11.3%. Has 115,500 employees. Off./dir. own less than 1% of common stock (3/10 Proxy). Chrmn. & CEO: William Weldon. Inc.: NJ. Addr.: One J&J Plaza, New Brunswick, NJ 08933. Tel.: 732-524-0400. Web: www.jnj.com.

Johnson & Johnson has made progress lately in replenishing its pharmaceutical pipeline. Since mid-2008, sales of four of its leading drugs have been hurt by new generic competition. On the other hand, J&J received FDA approval last year for its treatments of severe psoriasis and adult schizophrenia. One of the company's most promising drugs under development is a blood thinner whose uses include stroke prevention for patients with arterial fibrillation. Meanwhile, global sales of *Remicade*, a biologic that treats inflammatory disorders involving the immune system, were $1.2 billion (up 15.4%, year to year) in 2010's first quarter. *Stelara*, the new psoriasis inhibitor, also has bright growth prospects.

We look for improved year-to-year quarterly earnings comparisons during the balance of 2010. The aforementioned generic competition and economic weakness in many of J&J's markets hurt sales and, to a much lesser extent, profits last year. The combination of easy comparisons and benefits from the reduction of the employee count in late 2009, though, are key factors behind our near-term earnings estimates. Another plus is increasing contributions from new drugs.

The dividend was recently raised 10.2%, to an annualized rate of $2.16 a share. Moreover, given ample free cash flow (estimated at $7.8 billion in 2010) and cash assets of $19.4 billion, up $6.6 billion (52%) from last year, share repurchase activity should soon accelerate. Too, annual acquisition expenditures averaged $1.7 billion during the past three years, and this pace may well be maintained for a while in conjunction with debt repayments.

J&J's longer-term earnings growth prospects are broadbased. Three catalysts behind our forecast of average earnings of 9%–10% over the 3 to 5 years subsequent to 2010 are expansion opportunities in emerging markets, the ongoing acquisition program, and the promising late-stage pharmaceutical pipeline. The first factor is exemplified by the recent opening of J&J-affiliated medical training centers in Russia and Brazil.

This neutrally ranked, good-quality stock offers attractive total return potential to 2013–2015.

David R. Cohen *May 28, 2010*

(A) Year ends on last Sunday of December.
(B) Primary earnings through '96, diluted thereafter. Excludes nonrecurring gains/(losses): '98, 22¢; '99, 2¢; '01, (7¢); '02, (7¢); '03 (30¢); '04, (26¢); '05, (4¢); '06, (3¢); '07, (52¢); '09 (23¢); '10 Q1, 23¢. Next earnings report due late July.
(C) Dividends historically paid mid: March, June, Sept., and Dec. ■Div'd reinvestment plan available.
(D) Incl. intang.: In '09, $31.2 billion; $11.32/sh.
(E) In mill., adj. for stock split.

Company's Financial Strength	A++
Stock's Price Stability	100
Price Growth Persistence	45
Earnings Predictability	100

Source: "Johnson & Johnson," *The Value Line Investment Survey,* (New York: The Value Line Publishing, Inc., 2010).

application example

www.johnsonand johnson.com

TABLE 7-2 Johnson & Johnson Combined Dividend and Earnings Present Value Analysis

Part A: Present Value of Dividends for Five Years

Year	(1) Estimated Earnings per Share[a]	(2) Estimated Payout Ratio	(3) Estimated Dividends per Share	(4) Present Value Factor at K_e = 10.00%[b]	(5) Present Value of Cash Flows from Dividends
2011	$5.35	40%	$2.14	0.909	$1.95
2012	5.78	40	2.31	0.826	1.91
2013	6.24	40	2.50	0.751	1.88
2014	6.74	40	2.70	0.683	1.84
2015	7.28	40	2.91	0.621	1.81
	Present value of estimated dividends				$9.38

Part B: Present Value of Johnson & Johnson's 2011 Common Stock Price

Terminal Year	EPS	Estimated P/E Ratio	$Price_{2015}$	PV Factor	PV of 2011 Stock Price
2015	$7.28	15	$109.18	0.621	67.79
	Part A + Part B = the total PV at the beginning of 2011				$77.17

[a] The growth rate is assumed to be 8 percent from 2011 through 2015.

[b] The required return is assumed to be 10 percent which is more in line with its historical return.

The present value of the common stock for Johnson & Johnson at the beginning of 2011 is shown at the bottom of Table 7–2 to be $77.17. Note that Part A of Table 7–2 calculates the present value of the future dividends, while Part B is used to determine the present value of the future stock price at the end of 2015. These are assumed to be the two variables that determine that current stock price under this model.

In Part A, earnings per share is first projected for the next five years. The Johnson & Johnson payout ratio fluctuated between 34 and 43 percent from 2003 to 2010, and we estimate the payout ratio will average 40 percent over the next five years. The earnings are then multiplied by the company's estimated payout ratio of 40 percent to determine anticipated dividends per share for those five years (as indicated in column 3).

In Part B we use a price-earnings (P/E) ratio of 15 as a multiplier of earnings per share. A P/E ratio of 15 is lower than Johnson & Johnson's historical average, but given that the growth rate is slowing from the prior decade, a lower P/E ratio is a more conservative valuation metric. Using a P/E ratio of 15 and earnings per share of $7.28 calculated in part A, we expect a stock price of $109.18 at the end of 2015. When we discount this price back to the beginning of 2011, we get a present value of $67.79. The P/E ratio could be affected by a higher or lower expected growth rate in earnings per share, a change in risk, or another variable such as government regulations.

When the present value of the dividends of $9.38 from Part A is added to the $67.79 from Part B, the total present value of the stock is $77.17. Given that Johnson & Johnson was selling at $59 at the time of this analysis, this model would indicate that the stock is undervalued and a strong buy.

our valuation at the beginning of 2011, we develop a present value for the common stock listed on the New York Stock Exchange. The numbers are shown in Table 7–2.

AN ANALYSIS OF COMPANY GROWTH

Besides the required rate of return we covered earlier in the chapter, growth is probably an equally important variable. These two variables drive value. The faster a company grows, the more valuable it is and the higher its price will be relative to dividends, earnings, book value, cash flow, and sales. When the company starts to face diminishing growth, its price will fall relative to these variables. Notice how the value of a company changes when the growth rate is changed in the constant growth dividend model: price equals next year's dividend divided by the required return minus the growth rate, or

$$P_0 = D_1/(K_e\, g).$$

How can we estimate growth? One way is to run a regression of the variables to see how fast the company has been growing in the past. Unfortunately, too many investors assume that the past will repeat itself. Another way to approach growth is to use the Sustainable Growth Model based on the company's financial statements.

Sustainable Growth Model

The **sustainable growth model** looks at how much growth a firm can generate by maintaining the same financial relationships as the year before. The process of generating earnings using the sustainable growth model provides many insights into the financial interactions that produce earnings. This method requires an understanding of several ratios—we will examine the return on equity and the retention ratios.

The return on equity can take several forms. First, let's define equity to equal (1) assets − liabilities, (2) net worth, or (3) book value. These are all equal even though we call them by different names. We will use the term *book value* to equal the equity of the firm. The return on equity (ROE) is equal to:

$$\text{ROE} = \frac{\text{Net income or After-tax earnings}}{\text{Book value}} \qquad \textbf{(7–6)}$$

We can also express earnings and book value on a per share basis and the formula becomes:

$$\text{ROE} = \frac{\text{Earnings per share (EPS)}}{\text{Book value per share (BVPS)}} \qquad \textbf{(7–7)}$$

Because we are using the sustainable growth model, we want to know what the return on equity was, based on the book value at the beginning of the year. This makes sense because it is the book value at the beginning of the year that is in place to generate earnings. Assume the following:

$$\text{ROE} = \frac{\$1.20_{2011}\ \text{(full year)}}{\$6.44_{2010}\ \text{(year end)}^{2}} = 18.63\%$$

Because we want to forecast earnings per share, we will look at the process of growth on a per share basis. We can rearrange Formula 7–7 by multiplying both sides by the book value per share (BVPS) and we end up with:

$$\text{EPS} = \text{ROE} \times \text{BVPS} \qquad \textbf{(7–8)}$$

Using this information, we will examine how earnings per share can grow if the financial relationships stay the same from year to year. Let's say BVPS was $6.44

[2] We use year-end 2010 (beginning of 2011) BVPS to measure return on equity for 2011.

in 2010 (year-end) and return on equity was 18.63 percent, which we already computed. Substituting these numbers into Formula 7–8 gives us:

$$\text{EPS} = \text{ROE} \times \text{BVPS}$$
$$\$1.20 = 18.63\% \times \$6.44$$

This is the value of earnings per share for 2011. Future growth in earnings comes from the firm reinvesting in new plant and equipment and thus being able to generate more income for next year. In this case, the firm paid out a dividend of \$0.38 in 2011 and retained \$0.82 (\$1.20 − \$0.38). The \$0.82 gets added to the beginning book value per share to get ending book value of \$7.26 (\$6.44 + \$0.82) for 2011.

If the firm can continue to earn 18.63 percent on its equity, it will earn \$1.35 per share for 2012. This can be computed as follows:

$$\begin{aligned}\text{EPS}_{2012} &= \text{ROE} \times \text{BVPS}_{\text{year end 2011}}\\ &= 18.63\% \times \$7.26\\ &= \$1.353\end{aligned}$$

The growth rate in earnings per share using this model can be calculated by taking the increased earnings of \$0.153 and dividing by beginning earnings of \$1.20. This produces an earnings per share growth rate of 12.7 percent.

One of the conditions of growth is that the firm must retain some earnings. If the firm paid out all its earnings in dividends, it would start 2012 with the same book value and would experience no growth. The more earnings retained, the higher the growth rate would be. In this case, it retained \$0.82 out of \$1.20 in earnings. This is called the **retention ratio**, which is denoted by RR.

$$\begin{aligned}\text{Retention ratio (RR)} &= \frac{\text{Earnings per share} - \text{Dividends per share}}{\text{Earnings per share}}\\ &= (\$1.20 - \$.38)/\$1.20 \qquad \textbf{(7–9)}\\ &= 0.6833 \text{ or } 68.33\%\end{aligned}$$

The outcome of this analysis is that the growth in earnings per share is a function of the return on equity and the retention ratio. We can calculate growth in EPS as follows:

$$\begin{aligned}\text{Growth } (g) &= \text{Return on equity} \times \text{Retention ratio}\\ &= \text{ROE} \times \text{RR}\end{aligned} \qquad \textbf{(7–10)}$$

Using our example, we have:

$$\begin{aligned}g_{\text{eps}} &= 18.63\% \times 68.33\%\\ &= 12.7\%\end{aligned}$$

The sustainable growth model would predict a 12.7 percent growth rate for 2012 based on dividend policy and return on equity. This rate will continue into the future as long as the firm maintains its return on equity and its retention ratio.

Table 7–3 demonstrates how the growth rate is affected by the dividend payout ratio. In the first panel we start out with a 50 percent retention ratio and find that the company can grow at 10 percent. In the second panel the payout ratio is 25 percent and the company retains 75 percent. The extra money retained is reinvested, and the growth rate goes up to 15 percent. In the third panel, the opposite is true. The payout ratio is now 75 percent, the company retains only 25 percent, and the growth rate drops to 5 percent.

Like all models, this one can be misapplied if we again assume that the inputs will stay the same. The return on equity is affected by many variables, and so if the analyst takes a very careful view of the financial statements, he or she could adjust the ROE for changes they forecast in the profit margin, the asset turnover rate, or

TABLE 7-3 The Effects of a Changing Retention Ratio on Sustainable Growth

Book Value	ROE	EPS	Payout Ratio	Dividend Paid	Retention Ratio	Retained Earnings	Ending Book Value
$10.00	20.00%	$2.00	50.00%	$1.00	**50.00%**	$1.00	$11.00
11.00	20.00	2.20	50.00	1.10	**50.00**	1.10	12.10
12.10	20.00	2.42	50.00	1.21	**50.00**	1.21	13.31
13.31	20.00	2.66	50.00	1.33	**50.00**	1.33	14.64

Growth Rate = ROE × Retention Ratio = 10.0%

Book Value	ROE	EPS	Payout Ratio	Dividend Paid	Retention Ratio	Retained Earnings	Ending Book Value
$10.00	20.00%	$2.00	25.00%	$0.50	**75.00%**	$1.50	$11.50
11.50	20.00	2.30	25.00	0.58	**75.00**	1.73	13.23
13.23	20.00	2.65	25.00	0.66	**75.00**	1.98	15.21
15.21	20.00	3.04	25.00	0.76	**75.00**	2.28	17.49

Growth Rate = ROE × Retention Ratio = 15.0%

Book Value	ROE	EPS	Payout Ratio	Dividend Paid	Retention Ratio	Retained Earnings	Ending Book Value
$10.00	20.00%	$2.00	75.00%	$1.50	**25.00%**	$0.50	$10.50
10.50	20.00	2.10	75.00	1.58	**25.00**	0.53	11.03
11.03	20.00	2.21	75.00	1.65	**25.00**	0.55	11.58
11.58	20.00	2.32	75.00	1.74	**25.00**	0.58	12.16

Growth Rate = ROE × Retention Ratio = 5.0%

the financial leverage. If the analyst can make good forecasts, then this model can be more flexible in providing an estimated growth rate for the next year. One of its best uses is showing how the dividend policy affects the growth rate. This was first discussed in the industry life-cycle curves presented in Chapter 6. Another warning is that companies can't maintain super growth forever, and so what was once a growth company may now be only a growth stock or a mature company.

GROWTH STOCKS AND GROWTH COMPANIES

In assessing the worth of an investment, stockholders, analysts, and investors often make reference to such terms as growth stock and growth companies. As part of the process of improving your overall valuation skills, you should have some familiarity with these terms.

A **growth stock** may be defined as the common stock of a company generally growing faster than the economy or market norm. These companies are usually predictable in their earnings growth. Many of the more popular growth stocks, such as Disney, Coca-Cola, and McDonald's, are really in the middle-to-late stages of the expansion phase. They tend to be fully valued and recognized in the marketplace.

Growth companies, on the other hand, are those companies that exhibit rising returns on assets each year and sales that are growing at an increasing rate (growth phase of the life-cycle curve). Growth companies are found in stage 1 and 2 of the life-cycle curve discussed in Chapter 6. Growth companies may not be as well-known or recognized as growth stocks. Companies that may be considered to be growth companies might be in such industries as computer networking, cable television, cellular telephones, biotechnology, medical electronics, and so on. These companies are growing very rapidly, and extrapolations of growth trends can be very dangerous if you guess incorrectly. Growth companies have many things in common. Usually, they have developed a proprietary product that is patented and protected from competition like the original Xerox process. This market protection allows a high rate of return and generates cash for new-product development.

There are also other indicators of growth potential. Companies should have sales growth greater than the economy by a reasonable margin. Increasing sales should be translated into similar earnings growth, which means consistently stable and high profit margins. Additionally, the earnings growth should show up in earnings per share growth (no dilution of earnings through unproductive stock offers). The firm should have a low labor cost as a percentage of total cost since wages are prone to be inflexible on the downside but difficult to control on the upside.

The biggest error made in searching for growth-oriented companies is that the price may already be too high. By the time you identify the company, so has everyone else, and the price is probably inflated. If the company has one quarter where earnings do not keep up with expectations, the stock price could tumble. The trick is to find growth companies before they are generally recognized in the market, and this requires taking more risk in small companies trading over-the-counter.

Differing Growth Rates across Variables

Another challenge for the analyst is deciding which growth rate to focus on. Should earnings per share growth be more important than dividend per share growth or cash flow per share? If companies grew all their variables at a constant and equal rate, life would be simple to forecast. Look back at Table 7–1 for Johnson & Johnson. About two-thirds of the way down on the left-hand side, find the box titled Annual Rates of Change (per share). In this box we are presented with 10-year growth rates, 5-year growth rates, and a forecast for the average of the next three years. Johnson & Johnson is a fairly stable company compared to many others, but it still does not have equal growth rates across all variables. To take one variable as an example, let's look at five-year dividend growth compared to all other variables. It is growing faster than all the other variables, and so there is one conclusion you can draw quite simply, and that is that the payout ratio is rising. You can see in the large table that the payout ratio has gone from 34 percent in 2003 to 41 percent in 2010. Now the question is, how long can this last before the payout ratio reaches some upper limit?

Figure 7–2 shows the relationships between these variables as if a company were operating in the economists' fictitious world of perfect equilibrium. If all the lines are parallel, then the variables are all growing at the same rate. There are ratios between each of the variables that have to remain constant for this equal growth to occur. If sales and income grow at the same rate, then the profit margin has to be constant. If net income and earnings per share grow at the same rate, then the number of shares remains constant. Many companies buy back shares, and this allows earnings per share to grow faster than sales. If earnings per share and dividends per share grow at equal rates, then the payout ratio has to stay the same. By default the retention ratio would stay the same and book value per share would grow at an equal rate. Cash flow per share depends on noncash charges that are mostly depreciation expense, and so a company would have to maintain a consistent capital budgeting growth and depreciation expense to have cash flow grow at the same rate as earnings.

The message here is that by looking at the differences in growth rates, an analyst can make some assumptions about what is going on within the company without having to look at the ratios. Professors argue about which growth rates to use in dividend models, but in reality all these growth rates are connected, and it starts with sales growth. There are limits to growth and the ratios all have limits, so it is a good idea to know what the limits are and what is driving the growth. As we

FIGURE 7-2 Growth in Equilibrium

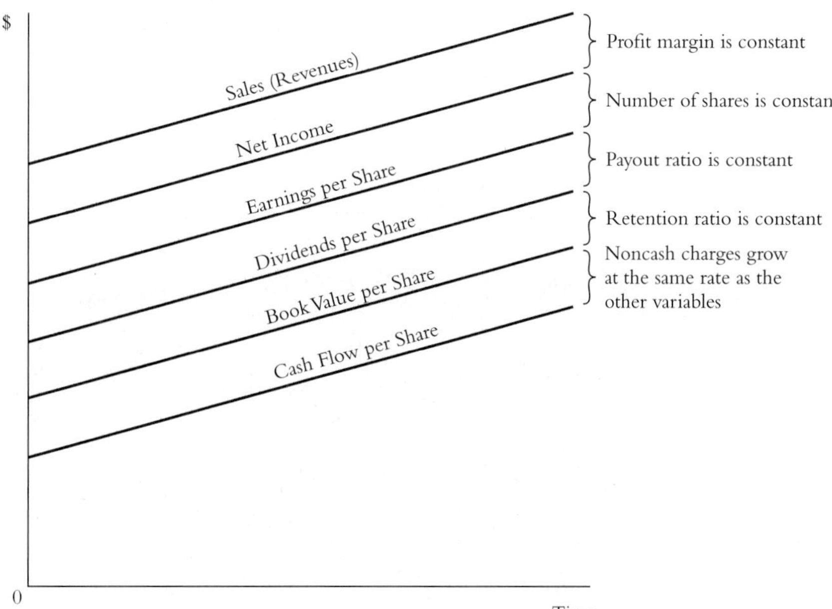

Ratio scale (semilogarithmic scale) where a straight line equals constant growth and parallel lines means they are all growing at the same rate.

move through the rest of the models, remember that growth is the main driving force behind company valuations, and the better you can forecast growth, the better investor you will be.

EARNINGS VALUATION MODEL AND THE PRICE-EARNINGS RATIO

The Price-Earnings Ratio

Mathematically, the **price-earnings ratio** (P/E) is simply the price per share divided by earnings per share, and it is ultimately set by investors in the market as they bid the price of a stock up or down in relation to its earnings. Price-earnings ratios are often expressed in the financial press as historical numbers using today's price divided by the latest 12-month earnings.

For companies with cyclical earnings, a P/E using the latest 12-month earnings might be misleading because these earnings could be high. If investors expect earnings to fall back to a normal level, they will not bid the price up in relation to this short-term cyclical swing in earnings per share, and the P/E ratio will appear to be low. But if earnings are severely depressed, investors will expect a return to normal higher earnings, and the price will not fall an equal percentage with earnings, and the P/E will appear to be high.

In the Johnson & Johnson example in Table 7–2 on page 172, we used a P/E of 15 in 2015. The P/E ratio is determined by historical analysis and by other factors such as expected growth in earnings per share. The P/E of a company is also affected by overall conditions in the stock market.

Even though the current P/E ratio for a stock is known, investors may not agree it is appropriate. Stock analysts and investors probably spend more time examining P/E ratios and assessing their appropriate level than any other variable. Although the use of P/E ratios in valuation approaches lacks the theoretical underpinning of the present value-based valuation models previously discussed in the chapter, P/E ratios are equally important. The well-informed student of investments

FIGURE 7-3 **Inflation and Price-Earnings Ratios**

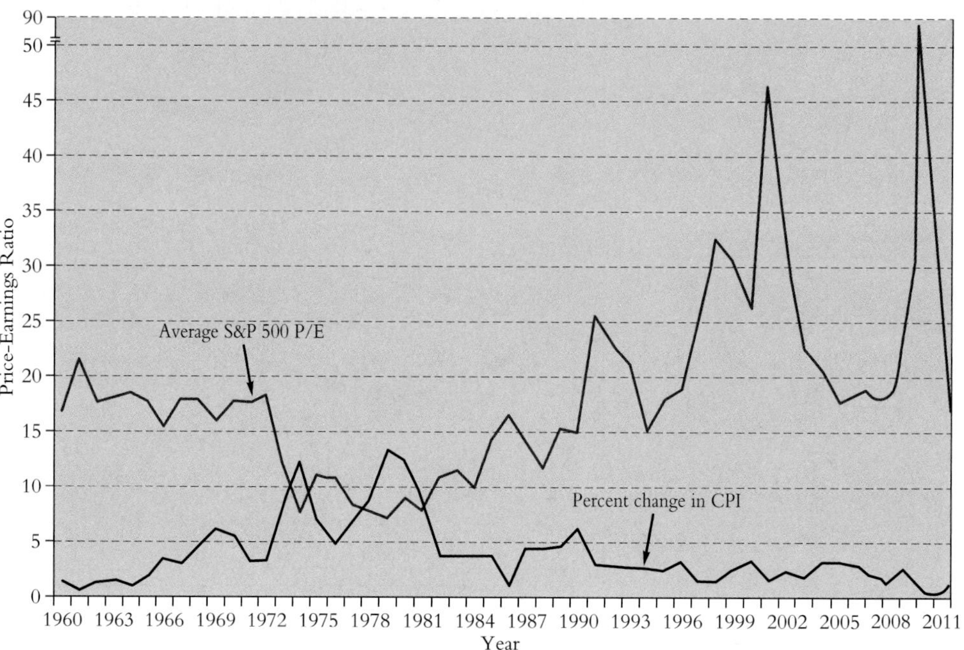

should have a basic understanding of both the theoretically based present value approach and the more pragmatic, frequently used P/E ratio approach.

What determines whether a stock should have a high or low P/E ratio? Let's first talk about the market for stocks in general, and then we will look at individual securities.

Stocks generally trade at a relatively high P/E ratio (perhaps 20 or greater) when there are strong growth prospects in the economy. However, inflation also plays a key role in determining P/E ratios for the overall market.

To illustrate the latter point, Figure 7–3 presents the relationship between the year-end Standard & Poor's 500 composite P/E ratio and the annual rate of inflation measured by the change in the consumer price index (CPI). The graphical relationship between these two variables shows they are inversely related. The price-earnings ratio goes down when the change in the CPI goes up, and the reverse is also true.

The dramatic drop in the P/E ratio in 1973–74 can be attributed in large measure to the rate of inflation increasing from 3.4 percent in 1972 to 12.2 percent in 1974, or a change of more than three times its former level. For a brief period in 1976, inflation decreased to an annual rate of less than 5 percent, only to soar to 13.3 percent by 1979. The average rate of inflation for 1982 was reduced to 3.8 percent, and the market responded by paying higher share prices for one dollar of earnings (that is, higher P/E ratios).

From 1983 through 1985, the consumer price index hovered around 3 to 4 percent, but in 1986, inflation subsided to 1.1 percent, and the S&P price-earnings ratio soared. In 1987, the S&P 500 P/E ratio remained high until the crash of October 1987 brought stock prices down to lower levels. During the sobering and risk-averse period after the crash, market prices were fairly stable.

As fears of higher inflation rose during 1989, the S&P 500 P/E ratio came back to the low-midrange of its 40-year history shown in Figure 7–3. The higher price-earnings ratios in 1991–93 reflect both the impact of falling inflationary expectations and depressed earnings suffered by corporations during the recessionary period of 1990–91 and the slow recovery in 1992 and 1993. As earnings grew quickly in 1994, 1995, and 1996, the Standard & Poor's 500 P/E ratio fell below 20 again. The economy in 1997 saw low inflation, strong economic growth, low unemployment, and reduced government deficits. This economy was described as a dream economy,

FIGURE 7-4 The S&P 500 Index with Earnings per Share and Derived Price-Earnings Ratio

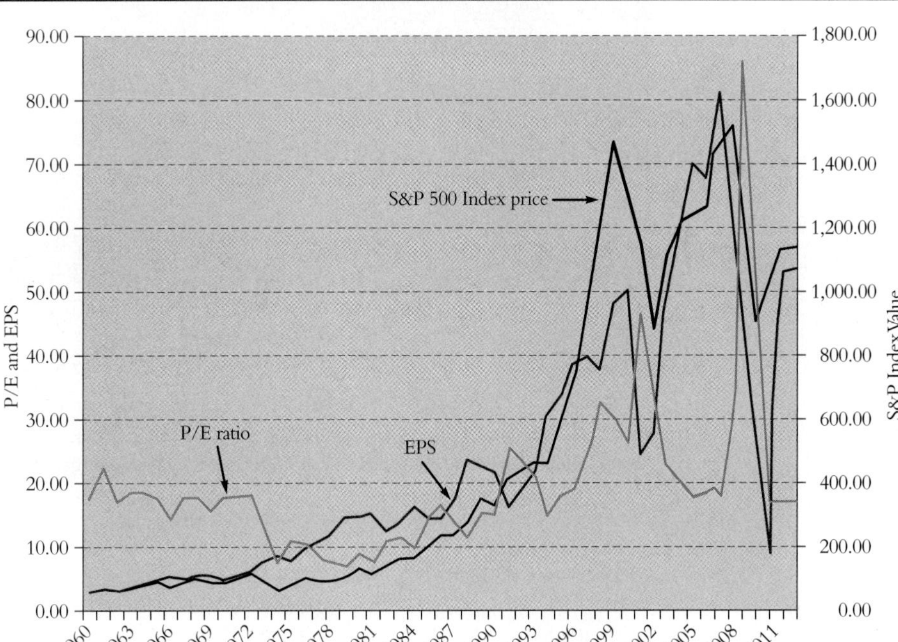

one that was perfectly balanced with GDP growth of 3.8 percent and inflation of 1.8 percent. In response, P/E ratios again soared above 21 times earnings, and the raging bull market, lasting through 1999, pushed P/E ratios over 30.

Collapsing earnings from 2000 to 2002 caused the S&P price-earnings ratio to soar to over 47, but with an earnings rebound in 2003 through 2006, the S&P P/E returned to a more reasonable level. By Thanksgiving in 2006, the S&P 500 Index had a P/E of 19.5. Figure 7–4 shows the S&P 500 Index with its corresponding earnings per share and resultant price-earnings ratio. When the economy suffers from a recession and major companies have collapsing earnings, the markets don't bid down prices of the securities to bargain basement prices because they understand that the earnings collapse is temporary. The result is a soaring price-earnings ratio. This can best be seen in 2002 to 2003 and also in 2009. The consumer price index was fairly steady from 2005 to 2008, ranging from 2.9 percent to 3.8 percent, but in 2009 the wheels came off the cart when the recession hit, and consumer prices fell 0.3 percent. Also, S&P 500 earnings per share fell from a high of $81.51 in 2006 to a low of $14.88 in 2008. The collapse in earnings per share caused the P/E ratio to soar in 2009, as it took several quarters for earnings to recover and the average P/E ratio of the four quarters hit 86.22. During the second quarter of 2009, the P/E ratio for the S&P 500 stocks stood at 122.41. By 2009, earnings per share had recovered, but the market was shaken, and these were not markets as usual. By 2010 earnings continued to recover and the price-earnings ratio for the S&P 500 stood at 17.1X in March of 2011.

In general, the price-earnings ratio indicates the market's response to many variables besides earnings. P/E ratios are affected by expected inflation, economic growth, government monetary and fiscal policies, leading indicators, international factors, the mood and confidence of the public, and much more. So while the price-earnings ratio seems to be a simple mathematical calculation, it reflects very complex interactions within a dynamic economy.

The P/E Ratio for Individual Stocks

Although the overall market P/E ratio is the collective average of individual P/Es, those factors that influence the market P/E do not necessarily affect P/E ratios of

TABLE 7-4 P/E and Expected Growth in EPS

Industry	Company	10-year Past Growth Rate in EPS[b]	Expected 5-yr. Growth Rate in EPS	P/E Fall 2006
Electric utility	FPL Group	3.50%	6.00%	15
Banking	Citigroup	13.00	8.00	12
Pharmaceuticals	Johnson & Johnson	15.50	8.50	17
Banking	Bank of America	11.50	9.00	12
Electric utility	Duke Energy	−6.50	9.50	17
Software	Microsoft	7.00	14.50	22
Retail, specialty lines	Best Buy	23.50	15.50	20
Software	Adobe Systems	18.00	16.50	34
Organic grocery[a]	Whole Foods Markets	22.00	17.00	42
Internet	eBay	97.50	19.00	42
Internet	Google	na	80.50[b]	50

[a] Some companies like Whole Foods sell at a premium P/E because organic food is in vogue and investors pay a social premium.

[b] All growth rates are from *Value Line Investment Surveys.*

individual companies consistently from one industry to another. An individual firm's P/E ratio is heavily influenced by its growth prospects and the risk associated with its future performance. Table 7–4 shows examples of growth rates and P/E ratios for different industries and firms.

Generally the higher the expected growth rate the higher the P/E ratio. Some companies like eBay have high P/E ratios even after their expected growth rates decline because they maintain an aura of quality and growth.

In addition to the future growth of the firm and the risk associated with that growth, investors and analysts also consider a number of other factors that influence a firm's P/E ratio. These cannot be easily quantified, but they affect a broad range of stocks. Included in this category are the debt-to-equity ratio and the dividend policy of the firm. All things being equal, the less debt a firm has, the more likely it is to be highly valued in the marketplace.

The dividend policy is more elusive. For firms that show superior internal reinvestment opportunities, low cash dividends may be desired. But maturing companies may be expected to pay a high cash dividend. For the latter group, a reduction in cash dividends may be associated with a lower P/E ratio if the dividend cut signals falling earnings per share.

Certain industries also traditionally command higher P/E ratios than others. Investors seem to prefer industries that have a high technology and research emphasis. Thus, firms in computers, medical research and health care, and sophisticated telecommunications often have higher P/E ratios than the market in general. This does not mean firms in these industries represent superior investments, but merely that investors value their earnings more highly.[3] Also, fads and other factors can cause a shift in industry popularity. For example, because Ronald Reagan emphasized military strength, defense-oriented stocks were popular during his administration. Jimmy Carter stressed the need for environmental control, and stocks dealing in air and water pollution control traded at high P/E ratios during his tenure. Bill Clinton's health care proposals lowered P/Es of pharmaceutical stocks dramatically until a Republican Congress killed his proposals. Tobacco and defense stocks rallied under George W. Bush.

The quality of management as perceived by those in the marketplace also influences a firm's P/E ratio. If management is viewed as being highly capable,

[3] William Kittrell, Geoffrey A. Hirt, and Roger Potter, "Price-Earnings Multiples, Investors' Expectations, and Rates of Return: Some Analytical and Empirical Findings" (paper presented at the 1984 Financial Management Association meeting).

clever, or innovative, the firm may carry a higher P/E ratio. Investors may look to magazines such as *Forbes* or *BusinessWeek,* which highlight management strategies by various companies.

Not only is the quality of management important to investors in determining the firm's P/E ratio, but the quality of earnings is also important. There are many interpretations of a dollar's worth of earnings. Some companies choose to use very conservative accounting practices so their reported earnings can be interpreted as being very solid by investors (they may even be understated). Other companies use more liberal accounting interpretations to report maximum earnings to their shareholders, and they, at times, overstate their true performance. It is easy to see that a dollar's worth of conservatively reported earnings (high quality earnings) may be valued at a P/E ratio of 20 to 25 times, whereas a dollar's worth of liberally reported earnings (low quality earnings) should be valued at a much lower multiple.

All of these factors affect a firm's P/E ratio. Thus, investors will consider growth in sales and earnings, future risk, the debt position, the dividend policy, the quality of management and earnings, and a multitude of other factors in arriving at the P/E ratio. The P/E ratio, like the price of the stock, is set by the interaction of the forces of demand and supply. Those firms that are expected to provide returns greater than the overall economy, with equal or less risk, generally have superior P/E ratios.

The Historical Short-Term Earnings Model

Often investors/speculators take a very short-term view of the market and ignore present value analysis with its associated long-term forecasts of dividends and earnings per share. Instead, they only use earnings per share and apply an appropriate multiplier to compute the estimated value.

application example

In Table 7–5, if we look at Johnson & Johnson's (J&J's) 10-year high and low P/E ratios we get a high average P/E of 20.27 and a low average P/E of 15.27, which gives us an average of 17.77. From Table 7–2 on page 172 we estimated Johnson & Johnson's 2011 earnings per share to be \$5.35. Using these data, we can come up with high, low, and average values for 2011.

$$\text{Price} = \text{EPS}_{2011} \times \text{P/E}_{\text{10-year high, average, low}}$$
$$\text{High price} = \$5.35 \times 20.27 = \$108.45$$
$$\text{Average price} = \$5.35 \times 17.77 = \$95.07$$
$$\text{Low price} = \$5.35 \times 15.27 = \$81.70$$

Given that Johnson & Johnson was selling at about \$59 per share at the time of this valuation, we could assume that it appears to be undervalued based on past history. Even at the low P/E, it is undervalued. Every valuation method has its limitations. Although this method is simplified by ignoring dividends and present value calculations, earnings need to be correctly estimated, and the appropriate price-earnings multiplier must be applied. Since the P/E is also a function of expected growth rates the analyst has to consider whether the future growth will be higher or lower than past growth and thereby adjust the P/E appropriately. Unfortunately, even if you have the correct forecast for EPS, there is no assurance that the market will agree with your forecast or your price-earnings ratio. You may have to wait for the price to adjust until the market comes to see things through your eyes. If we were to use four-year average P/E ratios, the average price would fall to \$71.83 with a high of \$80 and a low of \$63.

TABLE 7-5 Johnson & Johnson Relative P/E Model and Historical Ratio Models

Current Price = $59.00		August 2010				STOCK PRICE		J&J P/E RATIO		S&P 500 P/E RATIO		RELATIVE P/E RATIOS	
Year	SPS	DPS	EPS	CFPS	BVPS	High	Low	High	Low	High	Low	High	Low
2001	$10.83	$0.70	$1.91	$2.46	$ 7.95	$61.00	$40.30	31.94	21.10	47.39	24.59	0.67	0.86
2002	12.23	0.80	2.23	2.85	7.65	65.90	41.40	29.55	18.57	47.47	26.55	0.62	0.70
2003	14.10	0.92	2.70	3.36	9.05	59.10	48.10	21.89	17.81	30.73	20.90	0.71	0.85
2004	15.94	1.10	3.10	3.84	10.71	64.30	49.10	20.74	15.84	22.27	18.41	0.93	0.86
2005	16.98	1.28	3.50	4.25	12.73	70.00	59.80	20.00	17.09	20.32	16.83	0.98	1.02
2006	18.43	1.46	3.76	4.60	13.59	69.40	56.70	18.46	15.08	17.99	15.71	1.03	0.96
2007	21.51	1.62	4.15	5.23	15.25	68.80	59.70	16.58	14.39	23.65	16.53	0.70	0.87
2008	23.02	1.80	4.57	5.70	15.35	72.80	52.10	15.93	11.40	21.90	60.69	0.73	0.19
2009	22.47	1.93	4.63	5.69	18.37	65.40	46.30	14.13	10.00	136.13	70.07	0.10	0.14
2010	23.95	2.11	4.90	6.00	21.60	66.20	56.25	13.51	11.48	22.12	17.59	0.61	0.65
Average	**$17.95**	**$1.37**	**$3.55**	**$4.40**	**$13.23**	**$66.29**	**$50.98**	**20.27**	**15.27**	**39.00**	**28.79**	**0.71**	**0.71**
2011 estimates	SPS $26.20	DPS $ 2.39	EPS $5.35	CFPS $6.63	BVPS $24.22		Average Price $58.63 10-year average stock price for 2000–2010						

Relating an Individual Stock's P/E Ratio to the Market

Johnson & Johnson is the leading producer of health care products and pharmaceuticals. Everyone has probably used at least one of their products, such as Band-Aids, Q-tips, baby oil, or Tylenol, but you may not be familiar with the financial data presented in Table 7–5. This table provides a historical summary and an estimate of sales per share (SPS), dividends per share (DPS), earnings per share (EPS), cash flow per share (CFPS), and book value per share (BVPS). It also indicates Johnson & Johnson's high and low stock prices and the high and low P/E ratios for the company and the Standard & Poor's 500 Index and relative P/E ratios.

In the last three double columns, the high and low P/E ratios for Johnson & Johnson are compared with the high and low P/E ratios for the S&P 500. We calculate a relative price-earnings ratio as follows:

$$\text{Relative P/E} = \frac{\text{Company P/E}}{\text{S\&P 500 P/E}}$$

This market relative model compares the company P/E to the market P/E and tells us whether the company's stock has historically sold at a discount or premium to the market P/E.

For example, looking at Table 7–5, in the first row for 2001, Johnson & Johnson's high P/E ratio was 31.24 and the S&P 500 high P/E ratio was 47.39. When Johnson & Johnson's high P/E ratio is divided by the S&P 500 high P/E ratio, a relative P/E ratio of 0.67 is calculated. This indicates that Johnson & Johnson's high P/E ratio was 67 percent of the market or priced at a 33 percent discount to the market as represented by the S&P 500 Index. Over the 10 years we can see that Johnson & Johnson's relative P/E has fluctuated widely. Because the S&P P/E ratio was so unrealistic in 2009, Johnson & Johnson shows a relative low P/E ratio of 0.10 and a relative high P/E ratio of 0.14. Because Johnson & Johnson did not suffer an earnings collapse, as did the S&P 500, and their stock declined with the market, we get a relative P/E ratio that is probably meaningless.

In this case, if the analyst is going to use this model, she has to use data from the years that are more normal. There is nothing wrong with using selected years

TABLE 7-6 Projected Earnings and Relative P/E Valuation Model

	(1) Relative P/E[a]		(2) S&P 500 Current P/E[b]	(3) (1 × 2) Johnson & Johnson Calculated P/E		(4) Johnson & Johnson Estimated EPS^{2007}	(5) (3 × 4) Johnson & Johnson Value Based on Its P/E Relative to the S&P P/E
Average high P/E	0.71	×	17.46	12.40	×	$5.35	$66.32
Average low P/E	0.71	×	17.46	12.40	×	5.35	66.32
Average P/E	0.71	×	17.46	12.40	×	5.35	66.32

[a] Values taken from the last two columns of Table 7-5.

[b] The S&P 500 price-earnings ratio is taken from *Barron's,* August 23, 2010, p. M47.

that make sense. For example, knowing that Johnson & Johnson is a high-quality pharmaceutical company with stable earnings, the analyst might decide to use 2005, 2006, and 2007 as the baseline case. Clearly the data for 2001, 2002, 2008, and 2009 are corrupted by the abnormal market conditions that existed at that time. However, when you take a long-run 10-year view, some of the negative market bias may wash out. Because the bias should create a very conservative valuation for Johnson & Johnson, we will see what happens when we include all data for the last 10 years.

Looking at the 10-year average relative P/E ratio, we see that both the high and the low relative P/E ratios are at 0.71, or 71 percent of the S&P. Using these very conservative data to calculate a price in Table 7–6, we find that Johnson & Johnson is worth $66.32. If we believe that the inputs are realistic, then we would say that Johnson & Johnson's common stock is undervalued. Even though the relative P/E ratio is constant for the high, low, and average, we leave Table 7–6 with all three numbers to emphasize the point that it is very difficult to come up with a single point estimate for a stock.

OTHER HISTORICAL VALUATION MODELS AVERAGE PRICE RATIOS USING 4 AND 10-YEAR AVERAGES

application example

Notice that Table 7–5 also gives us estimates for earnings per share (EPS), sales per share (SPS), dividends per share (DPS), cash flow per share (CFPS), and book value per share (BVPS). Using the 10-year averages for price and per share data from Table 7–5 (bottom line), we can use the average price of $58.63 (right-hand bottom of Table 7–5) to determine the historical relationship. These models will simply determine whether the current stock price is selling above or below its historical valuation. It is up to the analyst to determine whether the past will be a good predictor of the future.

Using Table 7–5, we develop the five models in Table 7–7 below. In each case we calculate the historical price ratios and multiply the result times the value estimated for 2011. For example, in looking at the ratio of price to sales per share, the historical ratio is 3.266. If we multiply this historical ratio times the 2011 forecast for sales per share (SPS) of $26.20, we get an estimated target stock price of $85.57. The same procedure is followed for earnings per share, dividends per share, cash flow per share, and book value per share.

The analyst needs to look at the results of these models as information. In the case of Johnson & Johnson, all the models show that the current stock price of $59 is below fair value by as much as $43 per share. It is the analyst's job to make a judgment based on experience, expectations, and an in-depth knowledge of the company. These models do not provide foolproof values, only information that can be used to make a final judgment.

TABLE 7-7 Value Based on 2001–2010 Historical Price Ratios to Sales, Dividends, Cash Flow, and Book Value

		Historical Ratios	2011 Forecast	Estimated Target Price
Price to Earnings Per Share Value				
Average price/Average EPS	$58.63 / $ 3.55	16.51	$5.35	$ 88.32
Price to Sales Per Share Value				
Average price/Average SPS	$58.63 / $17.95	3.266	$26.20	$ 85.57
Price to Dividends Per Share Value				
Average price/Average DPS	$58.63 / $ 1.37	42.80	$ 2.39	$102.29
Price to Cash Flow Per Share Value				
Average price/Average CF	$58.63 / $ 4.40	13.32	$ 6.63	$ 88.34
Price to Dividends Per Share Value				
Average price/Average BVPS	$58.63 / $13.23	4.43	$13.23	$ 58.63

If you use the four-year average from 2007 to 2010 as the basis for your evaluation, the valuation models provide answers between $68.75 and $83.67. Using four years instead of 10 years eliminates the inflated P/E ratio caused by the "Internet Bubble." While the four-year model provides a lower valuation, it still indicates that Johnson & Johnson is undervalued. These calculations are shown in Table 7–8.

TABLE 7-8 Value Based on 2007–2010 Historical Price Ratios to Earnings, Sales, Dividends, Cash Flow, and Book Value

Average Price =	$60.94
Average Earnings Per Share	$4.56
Average Sales Per Share	$22.74
Average Dividends Per Share	$1.87
Average Cash Flow Per Share	$5.66
Average Book Value Per Share	$17.64

		Historical Ratios	2011 Forecast	Estimated Target Price
Price to Earnings Per Share Value				
Average price/Average EPS	58.633 / 4.5625	12.851	$ 5.35	**$68.75**
Price to Sales Per Share Value				
Average price/Average SPS	$60.94 / $22.74	2.680	$26.20	**$70.23**
Price to Dividends Per Share Value				
Average price/Average DPS	$60.94 / $ 1.87	32.678	$ 2.39	**$78.19**
Price to Cash Flow Per Share Value				
Average price/Average CF	$60.94 / $ 5.66	10.777	$ 6.63	**$71.47**
Price to Dividends Per Share Value				
Average price/Average BVPS	$60.94 / $17.64	3.454	$24.22	**$83.67**

the real world of investing

VALUING COMPANIES WITHOUT EARNINGS: EBITDA AND FREE CASH FLOW

In the high-tech, "new economy" era of the late 1990s and early 2000s, many popular companies did not achieve consistent earnings (or earnings at all). Examples include eBay, WorldCom, Oracle, and virtually every high-tech or telecommunications start-up firm.

For a firm with negative earnings per share, the concept of a price-earnings ratio is hardly applicable. For example, a company that has a loss of $0.75 a share and is assigned a P/E ratio of 20 by analysts would have a negative value of $15. No such concept exists in finance. For that reason, analysts looked for other values to track besides earnings. Some developed stock price to revenue, stock price to Web site hits, stock price to actual Web site sales (as opposed to just hits), and so on. All of these were done on a per share basis. While these new "metrics" were popular, sophisticated analysts looked for greater depth in their analysis.

The term EBITDA fits the bill. **EBITDA** stands for earnings before interest, taxes, depreciation, and amortization. Companies that have negative earnings may well have a positive EBITDA.

An example of computing EBITDA is shown here for a company with reported negative earnings of $5 million and 1 million shares outstanding:

Earnings	−$5,000,000
+ Amortization	1,000,000
+ Depreciation	6,000,000
+ Taxes	0
+ Interest	2,000,000
Earnings before interest, taxes, depreciation, and amortization (EBITDA)	$4,000,000
− Shares outstanding	1,000,000
EBITDA per share	$4.00

Amortization (line 2) usually represents the write-off of intangible assets (perhaps goodwill), while depreciation represents the write-off of physical assets (such as plant and equipment). The other terms are self-explanatory. EBITDA per share is very close to the concept of cash flow per share, but in addition to depreciation and amortization, taxes and interest are added back to earnings. What the analyst ends up with is operating income per share. In other words, this tells the analyst how much the company is making purely from its operations out in the plant before financing charges and taxes as well as non-cash charges. While the latter items are important in a traditional sense, the analyst needs to get a handle on something, and what better than how the company is doing on its actual day-to-day operations.

Once EBITDA is determined for a firm in a given industry, analysts look to other companies in the same industry to determine their stock price to EBITDA multiplier. Because this often is not commonly available data, the analyst may have to do the work on his or her own. Assume in this example that the industry average stock price/EBITDA ratio was 12×, then the firm with $4 in EBITDA per share might be valued at $48. If the firm has unusually bright prospects, it might be higher and the opposite would also be true.

Analysts may also use a slightly different concept of **free cash flow** per share by adding depreciation and amortization to earnings and subtracting out necessary capital expenditures and dividends (and dividing by the number of shares outstanding). Once again, an industry multiplier of stock price to free cashflow is developed and applied to free cash flow per share.

FORECASTING EARNINGS PER SHARE

The other side of choosing an appropriate P/E ratio is forecasting the earnings per share of a company with the proper growth rate. Investors can get earnings forecasts in several ways. They can rely on professional brokerage house research, investment advisory firms such as Value Line or Standard & Poor's, or financial magazines such as *Forbes, BusinessWeek, Worth,* or *Money,* or they can do it themselves.

Least Squares Trendline

One of the most common ways of forecasting earnings per share is to use regression or **least squares trend analysis**. The technique involves a statistical method whereby a trendline is fitted to a time series of historical earnings. This trendline, by definition, is a straight line that minimizes the distance of the individual observations from the line. Figure 7–5 depicts a scattergram for the earnings per share of XYZ Corporation. The earnings of this company have been fairly consistent, and

FIGURE 7-5 Least Squares Trendline for EPS of XYZ Corporation

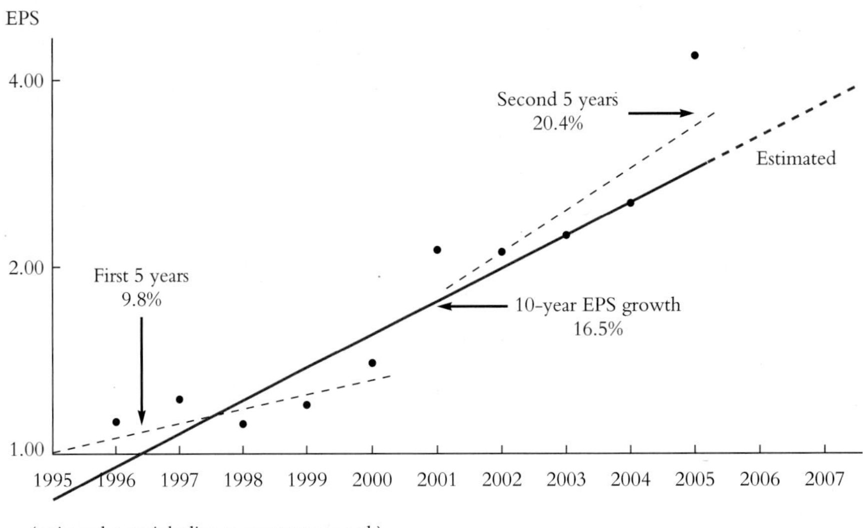

so we get a good trendline with a minimum of variation. The compounded growth rate for the whole 10-year period was 16.5 percent, with 9.8 percent for the first five years and 20.4 percent for the second five years. This shows up in Figure 7–5 as two distinct five-year trendlines. There are many statistical programs on PCs and mainframes that run regression analysis, and even handheld calculators have the ability to compute a growth rate from raw data.

Whenever a mechanical forecast is made, subjectivity still enters the decision in choosing the data that will be considered in the regression plot. If we compare two companies, one with consistent growth and one with cyclical growth, we find that the cyclical companies (e.g., autos, chemicals, airlines, forest products) are much more difficult to forecast than the consistent growth companies (e.g., pharmaceuticals, food, beverages). Cyclical companies are much more sensitive to swings in the economy and are likely to be in industries with high-priced durable goods where consumers can postpone purchases or where the economy has a direct effect on their products. Do not confuse cyclical with seasonal. Seasonal companies show earnings variability because their products have seasonal demand, such as fuel oil for winter heating and electricity for summer air conditioning or snowmobiles for winter. Cyclical companies have earnings related to the economy and exhibit variability over many years rather than three-month seasons.

Consistently growing companies often have higher P/E ratios on average than cyclical companies because investors are more confident in their future earnings. We compare two growth trends in Figure 7–6.

With cyclical companies you have to be careful not to start your forecast at a peak or trough period because you will get either biased-downward or -upward forecasts. Instead it is important to forecast cyclical companies throughout several business cycles with several peaks and troughs. Often the forecast for cyclical firms will cover 10 to 15 years of historical data, while the forecast for consistently growing firms might be based on five years of data.

The Income Statement Method

A more process-oriented method of forecasting earnings per share is to start with a sales forecast and create a standardized set of financial statements based on historical relationships. The sales forecast must be accurate if the earnings estimates are to have any significance. This method can be involved and provides a student with a very integrated understanding of the relationships that go into the creation of earnings.

FIGURE 7-6 Trendlines for Cyclical and Consistent Growth Companies

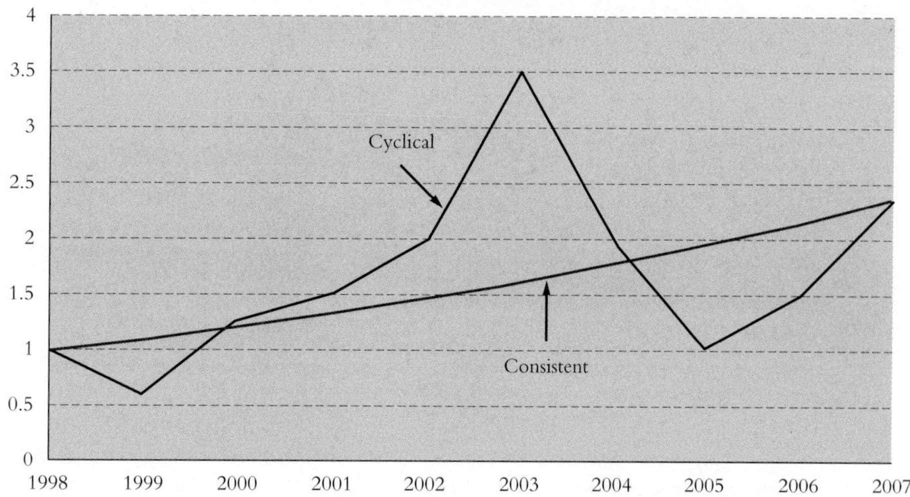

Several important factors are included in this method of forecasting. The analyst is forced to examine profitability and the resultant fluctuations in profit margins before and after taxes. The impact of short-term interest expense and any new bond financing can be factored into the analysis as well as any increase in shares of common stock from new equity financing.

application example

Some analysts use an abbreviated method of forecasting earnings per share. They use a sales forecast combined with after-tax profit margins. For example, let us assume the Hutchins Corporation has a sales and profit margin history as set forth in Table 7–9. The sales have been growing at a 10 percent growth rate, so the forecast is a simple extrapolation. However, the profit margin has fluctuated between 6.7 and 9.1 percent, with 8.2 percent being the average. Common stock outstanding has also grown by an average of 1.4 million shares per year. Given the cyclical nature of the profit margin, 8.2 percent was used for 2008, which is expected to be an average year. Nine percent was used for 2009, a year expected to be economically more robust for the firm. Multiplying the profit margin times the estimated sales produced an estimate of earnings that was divided by the number of shares outstanding to find the earnings per share. Once the EPS is found, it still must be plugged into an earnings valuation model to determine an appropriate value.

TABLE 7-9 Abbreviated Income Statement Method—Hutchins Corporation

Year	Sales ($000s)	×	After-Tax Profit Margin	=	Earnings ($000s)	–	Shares (000s)	=	Earnings per Share
2005	$1,250,000		7.9%		$ 98,750		30,000		$3.29
2006	1,375,000		9.1		125,125		31,500		3.97
2007	1,512,500		8.5		128,562		33,200		3.87
2008	1,663,750		6.7		111,471		35,000		3.18
2009	1,830,125		8.3		151,900		35,200		4.31
2010	2,013,137		8.5		171,117		37,000		4.62
2011e	2,214,452		8.2		181,585		38,400		4.73
2012e	2,435,896		9.0		219,230		39,800		5.50

e = Estimated.

the real world of investing

EVA: ECONOMIC VALUE ADDED: WHY IS IT IMPORTANT?

There is a valuation concept that has garnered attention at leading U.S. corporations such as Coca-Cola, AT&T, Eli Lilly, Merrill Lynch, and Monsanto. These firms are not nearly so interested at generating earnings per share as they are in maximizing economic value added (EVA).

Economic value added is based on the concept that decisions should be made or projects accepted only if net operating profit after taxes (NOPAT) exceeds the capital costs to finance the investment. If this rule is followed, then economic value will be added. To many readers, this may sound like the capital budgeting principle you learned in the first course in corporate finance, warmed over and served again as a hot new idea.

Not so, say the founders of the EVA concept at Stern Stewart & Co. (**www.sternstewart.com**) in New York.* EVA is an overriding concept that is intended to be applied to every decision the corporation makes, from investing overseas to adding three more widgets in the stockroom. The question repeatedly asked is, Is the firm earning an adequate return on the money investors entrusted to it? Even at the lowest levels of the organization, this question cannot be escaped.

Proponents of EVA say that all too often chief financial officers evaluate projects based on net present value, but they modify recommendations to meet earnings growth targets of the firm. Business unit evaluations may not be based on either parameter but rather on return on assets or some other unrelated profit goal set by top management. Bonuses for operating managers may be linked to demand–supply conditions within an industry. New-product introductions may be based on gross profit margin. Furthermore, the analysis for some decisions may be based on cash flow, while other decisions are linked to earnings per share. There is no coherent theme or goal, and stockholder wealth may be harmed in the process.

With EVA, the firm is assumed to always be working for the stockholder's benefit. Under the EVA concept, the firm will not accept a project or idea that does not earn back the cost of funds the stockholder provided. Economic value added is also intended to lead to market value added (MVA). MVA is another hot new topic and represents the total market value of the firm minus the total capital provided since day one (including the retained earnings). MVA requires a company's top managers to justify what they did with the money that was given to them. Did they increase the value and thereby produce a positive MVA as expected, or did they destroy contributed capital and generate a negative MVA?

MVA is thought to be linked to EVA because, according to Stern Stewart & Co., the way MVA increases is by consistently increasing EVA. In fact, MVA is intended to be the present value of all future EVAs.

Annual data on MVA and EVA for the 1,000 largest companies can be acquired directly from Stern Stewart & Co. of New York. *Fortune* magazine also publishes Stern Stewart & Co. data about the 200 top MVA creators toward the end of each year. (However, not all of these companies formally use EVA and MVA.)

Detractors of the EVA-MVA emphasis say it is not widely enough followed to truly affect value. They suggest that earnings per share is still the "king" on Wall Street. In spite of EVA, it is still quarterly earnings estimates that drive investors crazy. Only time will tell whether this hot new concept can permanently compete. Today, there are 300 to 350 firms that use EVA in their strategic development.

***EVA, The Real Key to Creating Wealth* (New York: Stern Stewart & Co., 1996–97).

ASSETS AS A SOURCE OF STOCK VALUE

Until now, our emphasis has been primarily on earnings and dividends as the sources of value. However, in certain industries, asset values may have considerable importance. These assets may take many forms—cash and marketable securities, buildings, land, timber, old movies, oil, and other natural resources. At times, any one of these assets may dominate a firm's value. Furthermore, companies with heavy cash positions are attractive merger and acquisition candidates because of the possibility that a firm with highly liquid assets could be taken over and its own cash used to pay back debt incurred in the takeover.

In the last two decades, natural resources also had an important influence on value. Let's briefly examine this topic.

Natural Resources

Natural resources such as timber, copper, gold, and oil often give a company value even if the assets are not producing an income stream. This is because of the present value of the future income stream that is expected as these resources are used up. Companies such as International Paper, Weyerhaeuser, and other forest product companies have timberlands with market values far in excess of their book values and, in some cases, in excess of their common stock prices.

Oil companies with large supplies of oil in the ground may have to wait 20 years before some of it is pumped, but there may be substantial value there. In the case of natural gas pipeline companies, increasing reserves have changed the way these companies are viewed by the market. They were previously considered similar to utilities because of their natural gas transmission systems, but now they are also being valued based on their hidden assets (energy reserves). The term **hidden assets** refers to assets that are not readily apparent to investors in a traditional sense but that add substantial value to the firm.

Investors should not overlook hidden assets because of naive extrapolation of past data or failure to understand an industry or company. Furthermore, assets do not always show up on the books of a company. They may be fully depreciated, like the movies *Raiders of the Lost Ark*, *101 Dalmatians*, or *Star Wars*, but still have substantial value in the television, VCR, or DVD market.

exploring the web

Web Address	Comments
my.yahoo.com	**Provides portfolio and stock tracking and screening—requires free registration**
www.marketwatch.com/investing	**Provides stock information, screening, and evaluation**
www.quicken.com	**Provides stock screening and analysis; has intrinsic value calculator**
www.valuepro.net	**Has free intrinsic value calculator—other services fee-based**
www.morningstar.com	**Provides stock screening and detailed evaluation with Quick Quotes**
www.fool.com	**Contains stock evaluation and information from Motley Fool**
www.wsj.com	**Provides company information along with news—most content requires subscription to access**
www.moneycentral.msn.com	**Has portfolio tracker, company information, investment information**
www.valuengine.com	**Provides stock analyses and forecasts, mainly fee-based—requires free registration**
www.pcquote.com	**Provides stock quotes, portfolio tracking, and news**
www.validea.com	**Provides fee-based valuation of stocks**
www.stockworm.com	**Provides stock analysis and screening**
www.zacks.com	**Provides consensus earnings forecasts**

SUMMARY

This chapter presents several common stock valuation models that rely on dividends and earnings per share. For the valuation to be accurate, the forecast of earnings and dividends needs to be correct.

Firms can be valued in many ways, and an analyst may use several methods to substantiate estimates. Valuation models based primarily on dividends look at future projections of dividends and the associated present values of the dividends. Assumptions must be made as to whether the dividend growth pattern is constant, accelerating, or decreasing.

Calculating the proper rate of return for the valuation of a company's stock is important. The Capital Asset Pricing Model is used as a method of calculating return. We also discuss the problems with beta and the equity risk premium. An alternate return method is presented where the company's corporate bond yield is used as a baseline for the required rate of return.

The analysis of a firm's growth rate is a very important part of the valuation process. We discuss the various ways of analyzing growth including the sustainable growth model and the relationship between the driving forces of growth. These driving forces of growth are a function of sales growth and the various relationships between profit margins, payout ratios, and number of shares outstanding.

Valuation using the earnings method requires that a price-earnings ratio be used as a multiplier of EPS. Price-earnings ratios are influenced by many variables such as growth, risk, capital structure, dividend policy, level of the market in general, industry factors, and more. A careful study of each situation must be concluded before choosing the appropriate P/E. The price-earnings ratio is a function of two fluctuating variables—earnings and price. The two variables combine to form a ratio that is primarily future oriented. High price-earnings ratios usually indicate positive expectations of the future, whereas low price-earnings ratios connote negative expectations.

To choose a P/E that is reasonable, the analyst must have some idea about the expected growth rate in earnings per share. Investors may find earnings estimates in investment advisory services, in statistical forecasts by brokerage houses, through their own time series statistical regression analysis, or by using the income statement method. Growth stocks were discussed more with the view of alerting the student to what to look for when trying to identify a growth stock or company than with the concept of valuation. The previously developed methods of valuation can be used on growth stocks as long as care is taken to evaluate the duration and level of growth.

We also presented some basic ideas about the value of companies based not on their earnings or dividend stream but on their assets such as cash or natural resources.

KEY WORDS AND CONCEPTS

DISCUSSION QUESTIONS

1. To determine the required rate of return, K_e, what factor is added to the risk-free rate? (Use Formula 7–2 on page 166.)
2. What does beta represent?
3. What does the equity risk premium (ERP) represent?
4. How is value interpreted under the dividend valuation model?

5. What two conditions are necessary to use Formula 7–5 on page 168?
6. How can companies with nonconstant growth be analyzed?
7. In considering P/E ratios for the overall market, what has been the relationship between price-earnings ratios and inflation?
8. What factors besides inflationary considerations and growth factors influence P/E ratios for the general market?
9. For cyclical companies, why might the current P/E ratio be misleading?
10. What two factors are probably most important in influencing the P/E ratio for an *individual stock?* Suggest a number of other factors as well.
11. What type of industries tend to carry the highest P/E ratios?
12. What is the essential characteristic of a least squares trendline?
13. What two elements go into an abbreviated income statement method of forecasting?
14. What is the difference between a growth company and a growth stock?
15. What are some industries in which there are growth companies?
16. How should a firm with natural resources be valued?
17. What is an example of a valuable asset that might not show any "value" on a balance sheet?
18. Do you think the sustainable growth model would be appropriate for a highly cyclical firm?
19. Based on the sustainable growth model, if a firm increases the dividend payout ratio (1 − the retention ratio), will this increase or decrease the growth in earnings per share in the future?

PRACTICE PROBLEMS AND SOLUTIONS

Constant growth dividend model

1. *a.* Assume D_1 = \$2.50, K_e = 11 percent, and g = 5 percent. Using Formula 7–5 on page 168, for the constant dividend growth model, compute P_0.
   b. If D_1 and K_e remain the same, but g goes up to 7 percent, what will the new stock price be?

Nonconstant growth dividend model

2. The Boswell Corporation anticipates a nonconstant growth pattern for dividends. Dividends at the end of year 1 are \$1.80 per share and are expected to grow by 12 percent per year until the end of year 3 (that's two years of growth). After year 3, dividends are expected to grow at 7 percent as far as the company can see into the future. All dividends are to be discounted back to present at a 10 percent rate (K_e = 10 percent).
   a. Project dividends for years 1 through 3 (the first year is already given). Round all values that you compute to two places to the right of the decimal point throughout this problem.
   b. Find the present value of the dividends in part *a.*
   c. Project the dividend for the fourth year (D_4).
   d. Use Formula 7–5 to find the present value of all future dividends, beginning with the fourth year's dividend. The present value you find will be at the end of the third year. Use Formula 7–5 as follows: $P_3 = D_4/(K_e - g)$.
   e. Discount back the value found in part *d* for three years at 10 percent.
   f. Add together the values from parts *b* and *e* to determine the present value of the stock.

Solutions

1. *a.*
$$\begin{aligned} P_0 &= D_1/(K_e - g) \\ &= \$2.50/(.11 - .05) \\ &= \$2.50/.06 \\ &= \$41.67 \end{aligned}$$

b. $P_0 = \$2.50/(.11 - .07)$
$P_0 = \$2.50/.04$
$P_0 = \$62.50$

2. *a.*

Year	Dividends (12% growth)
1	$1.80
2	2.02
3	2.26

b.

Year	Dividends	PV Factor 10%	PV of Dividends
1	$1.80	.909	$1.64
2	2.02	.826	1.67
3	2.26	.751	1.70
			$5.01

c. $D_4 = D_3(1 + g) = \$2.26\ (1.07) = \$2.42$

d. $P_3 = D_4(K_e - g)$
$= \$2.42/(.10 - .07)$
$= \$2.42/.03$
$= \$80.67$

e. PV of $80.67 for 3 years at 10%
$\$80.67 \times .751 = \$60.58$

f. Part *b* (first 3 years) $ 5.01
Part *e* (thereafter) 60.58
$65.59

PROBLEMS

1. Using Formula 7–1 on page 165, compute R_F (risk-free rate). The real rate of return is 3 percent and the expected rate of inflation is 5 percent.

Equity risk premium

2. If $R_F = 6$ percent, $b = 1.3$, and the ERP = 6.5 percent, compute K_e (the required rate of return).

Beta

3. If in problem 2 the beta (b) were 1.9 and the other values remained the same, what is the new value of K_e? What is the relationship between a higher beta and the required rate of return (K_e)?

Equity risk premium

4. Assume the same facts as in problem 2, but with an ERP of 9 percent. What is the new value for K_e? What does this tell you about investors' feelings toward risk based on the new ERP?

Constant growth dividend model

5. Assume $D_1 = \$1.60$, $K_e = 13$ percent, $g = 8$ percent. Using Formula 7–5 on page 168, for the constant growth dividend valuation model, compute P_0.

Constant growth dividend model

6. Using the data from problem 5:
   a. If D_1 and K_e remain the same, but g goes up to 9 percent, what will the new stock price be? Briefly explain the reason for the change.
   b. If D_1 and g retain their original value ($1.60 and 8 percent), but K_e goes up to 15 percent, what will the new stock price be? Briefly explain the reason for the change.

Proof of constant growth dividend model

7. Using the original data from problem 5, find P_0 by following the steps described.
   a. Project dividends for years 1 through 3 (the first year is already given). Round all values that you compute to two places to the right of the decimal point throughout this problem.
   b. Find the present value of the dividends in part *a* using a 13 percent discount rate.

c. Project the dividend for the fourth year (D_4).
d. Use Formula 7–5 on page 168 to find the value of all future dividends, beginning with the fourth year's dividend. The value you find will be at the end of the third year (the equivalent of the beginning of the fourth year).
e. Discount back the value found in part *d* for three years at 13 percent.
f. Observe that in part *b* you determined the percent value of dividends for the first three years and, in part *e*, the present value of an infinite stream after the first three years. Now add these together to get the total present value of the stock.
g. Compare your answers in part *f* to your answer to problem 5. There may be a slight 5 to 10 cent difference due to rounding. Comment on the relationship between following the procedures in problem 5 and problem 7.

Appropriate use of constant growth dividend model

8. If D_1 = \$3.00, K_e = 10 percent, and g = 8 percent, can Formula 7–5 be used to find P_0? Explain the reasoning behind your answer.

Appropriate use of constant growth dividend model

9. If D_1 = \$3.00, K_e = 10 percent, and g = 12 percent, can Formula 7–5 be used to find P_0? Explain the reasoning behind your answer.

Nonconstant growth dividend model

10. Leland Manufacturing Company anticipates a nonconstant growth pattern for dividends. Dividends at the end of year 1 are \$4.00 per share and are expected to grow by 20 percent per year until the end of year 4 (that's three years of growth). After year 4, dividends are expected to grow at 5 percent as far as the company can see into the future. All dividends are to be discounted back to present at a 13 percent rate (K_e = 13 percent).
a. Project dividends for years 1 through 4 (the first year is already given). Round all values that you compute to two places to the right of the decimal point throughout this problem.
b. Find the present value of the dividends in part *a*.
c. Project the dividend for the fifth year (D_5).
d. Use Formula 7–5 on page 168 to find the present value of all future dividends, beginning with the fifth year's dividend. The present value you find will be at the end of the fourth year. Use Formula 7–5 as follows: $P_4 = D_5/(K_e - g)$.
e. Discount back the value found in part *d* for four years at 13 percent.
f. Add together the values from parts *b* and *e* to determine the present value of the stock.

Nonconstant growth dividend model

11. The Fleming Corporation anticipates a nonconstant growth pattern for dividends. Dividends at the end of year 1 are \$2 per share and are expected to grow by 16 percent per year until the end of year 5 (that's four years of growth). After year 5, dividends are expected to grow at 6 percent as far as the company can see into the future. All dividends are to be discounted back to the present at a 10 percent rate (K_e = 10 percent).
a. Project dividends for years 1 through 5 (the first year is already given as \$2). Round all values that you compute to two places to the right of the decimal point throughout this problem.
b. Find the present value of the dividends in part *a*.
c. Project the dividend for the sixth year (D_6).
d. Use Formula 7–5 on page 168 to find the present value of all future dividends, beginning with the sixth year's dividend. The present value you find will be at the end of the fifth year. Use Formula 7–5 as follows: $P_5 = D_6/(K_e - g)$.
e. Discount back the value found in part *d* for five years at 10 percent.
f. Add together the values from parts *b* and *e* to determine the present value of the stock.
g. Explain how the two elements in part *f* go together to provide the present value of the stock.

Nonconstant growth dividend model

12. Rework problem 11 with a new assumption—that dividends at the end of the first year are $1.60 and that they will grow at 18 percent per year until the end of the fifth year, at which point they will grow at 6 percent per year for the foreseeable future. Use a discount rate of 12 percent throughout your analysis. Round all values that you compute to two places to the right of the decimal point.

Combined earnings and dividend model

13. J. Jones investment bankers will use a combined earnings and dividend model to determine the value of the Allen Corporation. The approach they take is basically the same as that in Table 7–2 on page 172 in the chapter. Estimated earnings per share for the next five years are:

2012	$3.20
2013	3.60
2014	4.10
2015	4.62
2016	5.20

a. If 40 percent of earnings are paid out in dividends and the discount rate is 11 percent, determine the present value of dividends. Round all values you compute to two places to the right of the decimal point throughout this problem.

b. If it is anticipated that the stock will trade at a P/E of 15 times 2012 earnings, determine the stock's price at that point in time and discount back the stock price for five years at 11 percent.

c. Add together parts *a* and *b* to determine the stock price under this combined earnings and dividend model.

P/E ratio analysis

14. Mr. Phillips of Southwest Investment Bankers is evaluating the P/E ratio of Madison Electronics Conveyors (MEC). The firm's P/E is currently 17. With earning per share of $2, the stock price is $34.

The average P/E ratio in the electronic conveyor industry is presently 16. However, MEC has an anticipated growth rate of 18 percent versus an industry average of 12 percent, so 2 will be added to the industry P/E by Mr. Phillips. Also, the operating risk associated with MEC is less than that for the industry because of its long-term contract with American Airlines. For this reason, Mr. Phillips will add a factor of 1.5 to the industry P/E ratio.

The debt-to-total-assets ratio is not as encouraging. It is 50 percent, while the industry ratio is 40 percent. In doing his evaluation, Mr. Phillips decides to subtract a factor of 0.5 from the industry P/E ratio. Other ratios, including dividend payout, appear to be in line with the industry, so Mr. Phillips will make no further adjustment along these lines.

However, he is somewhat distressed by the fact that the firm only spent 3 percent of sales on research and development last year, when the industry norm is 7 percent. For this reason he will subtract a factor of 1.5 from the industry P/E ratio.

Despite the relatively low research budget, Mr. Sanders observes that the firm has just hired two of the top executives from a competitor in the industry. He decides to add a factor of 1 to the industry P/E ratio because of this.

a. Determine the P/E ratio for MEC based on Mr. Phillips's analysis.

b. Multiply this times earnings per share, and comment on whether you think the stock might possibly be under- or overvalued in the marketplace at its current P/E and price.

P/E ratio analysis

15. Refer to Table 7–5 on page 182. Assume that because of unusually bright long-term prospects, analysts determine that Johnson & Johnson's P/E ratio in 2011 should be 10 percent above the average high J&J P/E ratio for the last 10 years. (Carry your calculation of the P/E ratio two places to the right of the decimal point in this problem.) What would the stock price be based on projected earnings per share of $5.35 (for 2011)?

P/E ratio analysis

16. Refer to problem 15, and assume new circumstances cause the analysts to reduce the anticipated P/E in 2011 to 20 percent below the average low J&J P/E for the last 10 years. Furthermore, projected earnings per share are reduced to $4.00. What would the stock price be?

Income statement method of forecasting

17. Security analysts following Health Sciences, Inc., use a simplified income statement method of forecasting. Assume that 2011 sales are $30 million and are expected to grow by 11 percent in 2012 and 2013. The after-tax profit margin is projected at 6.1 percent in 2012 and 5.9 percent in 2013. The number of shares outstanding is anticipated to be 700,000 in 2012 and 710,000 in 2013. Project earnings per share for 2012 and 2013. Round to two places to the right of the decimal point throughout the problem.

P/E ratio and price

18. The average P/E ratio for the industry that Health Science, Inc., is in is 24. If the company has a P/E ratio 20 percent higher than the industry ratio of 24 in 2012 and 25 percent higher than the industry ratio (also of 24) in 2013:

a. Indicate the appropriate P/E ratios for the firm in 2012 and 2013.

b. Combine this with the earnings per share data in problem 17 to determine the anticipated stock price for 2012 and 2013. Round to two places.

P/E ratio and price

19. Relating to problems 17 and 18, determine the price range in 2013 if the P/E ratio is between 27 and 33.

Sustainable growth model

20. The Bolten Corporation had earnings per share of $2.60 in 2012, and book value per share at the end of 2011 (beginning of 2012) was $13.

a. What was the firm's return on equity (book value) in 2012?

b. If the firm pays out $0.78 in dividends per share, what is the retention ratio? How much will book value per share be at the end of 2012? Add retained earnings per share for 2012 to book value per share at the beginning of 2012.

c. Assume the same rate of return on book value for 2013 as you computed in part *a* for 2012. What will earnings per share be for 2013? Multiply rate of return on book value (part *a*) by book value at the end of 2012 (second portion of part *b*).

d. What is the growth rate in earnings per share between 2012 and 2013?

e. If the firm continues to earn the same rate of return on book value and maintains the same earnings retention ratio, what will the sustainable growth rate be for the foreseeable future?

INVESTMENT ADVISOR PROBLEM

Hal Simmons put a lot of emphasis on the P/E ratio in analyzing stocks. He noted that Norton Software, Inc., had an average P/E of 29 over the last five years. The stock normally traded at a 10 percent premium above the S&P 500 Index P/E ratio.

Norton Software was a provider of protective, firewall software, and its products were in demand by many Fortune 500 companies. Its stock price, P/E ratio, and earnings per share over the last five years were as follows:

	NORTON SOFTWARE		
Year	Stock Price	P/E Ratio	EPS
2007	$42	20.3	$2.07
2008	51	22.2	2.30
2009	63	24.8	2.54
2010	79	28.1	2.81
2011	75	49.7	1.51

Hal currently had 500 shares of Norton Software, Inc., in his portfolio and was distressed by its poor stock performance in 2007. Its price was down $4 from 2010. However, Hal did note that the stock was trading at a five-year (and all-time) high P/E ratio of 49.7. Since he normally thought high P/E ratios were associated with strong future expectations, Hal took some comfort in the high P/E ratio. However, he had not read any positive news stories about Norton Software lately.

He decided to check out the situation with Jennifer Logan, his investment advisor. Jennifer was not only well versed in stock valuation but a Certified Financial Planner (CFP), indicating she was knowledgeable in matters such as insurance, tax issues, and estate planning.

Jennifer further analyzed Norton Software and could not find any evidence of strong positive events anticipated for the future either. She suggested the high P/E ratio of 49.7 might be related to a mathematical phenomenon associated with stocks that have irregular earnings. What might this mathematical property be?

WEB EXERCISE

Given that the valuation models in Chapter 7 focused on Johnson & Johnson, it seems only appropriate to continue the analysis using more current data from Johnson & Johnson's Web site. Go to **www.jnj.com**.

Click on the "Investors" tab on the front page and then scroll down the left column to "Stock Information." Then click on "Dividend History."

1. Look at the annual listing of dividends paid, and comment on the growth in dividends and the pattern of payment. What are your expectations for future growth of dividends?

2. Now, go back to the "Stock Information" tab and click on "Stock Quote & Chart." Under "Period" click on "History" and select the dates in the calendars for the past five years and click on "Refresh." By approximately what percentage has the price of Johnson & Johnson stock changed over the last five years? You can find the prices by moving the cursor along the graph or you can go to "Historic Stock Lookup" under "Stock Information" to get closing prices for individual dates.

3. Finally, under the "Stock Information" tab, click on "Trading Statistics." Examine the valuation ratios and compare to those found in Table 7-7 and Table 7-8 in the text. How do they compare? Is Johnson & Johnson valued above or below its historical averages?

Note: From time to time, companies redesign their Web sites and occasionally a topic we have listed may have been deleted, updated, or moved into a different location.

CFA MATERIAL

The following material contains sample questions and solutions from a prior Level I CFA exam. While the terminology is slightly different from that in this text, you can still view the skills necessary for the CFA exam.

CFA Exam Question

1. As a firm operating in a mature industry, Arbot Industries is expected to maintain a constant dividend payout ratio and constant growth rate of earnings for the foreseeable future. Earnings were $4.50 per share in the recently completed fiscal year. The dividend payout ratio has been a constant 55 percent in recent years and is expected to remain so. Arbot's return on equity (ROE) is expected to remain at 10 percent in the future, and you require an 11 percent return on the stock.

a. Using the constant growth dividend discount model, *calculate* the current value of Arbot common stock. *Show* your calculations.

After an aggressive acquisition and marketing program, it now appears that Arbot's earnings per share and ROE will grow rapidly over the next two years. You are aware that the dividend discount model can be useful in estimating the value of common stock even when the assumption of constant growth does not apply.

b. *Calculate* the current value of Arbot's common stock using the dividend discount model assuming Arbot's dividend will grow at a 15 percent rate for the next two years, returning in the third year to the historical growth rate and continuing to grow at the historical rate for the foreseeable future. *Show* your calculations.

Solution: Question 1—Morning Session (I–91) (15 points)

a. Constant growth (single-stage) dividend discount model:

$$\text{Value}_0 = \frac{D_1}{K - g}$$

where:

D_1 = Next year's dividend
K = Required rate of return
g = Constant growth rate
D_1 = $(\text{EPS}_0)(1 + g)(\text{P/O}) = (4.50)(1.045)(0.55) = \$2.59$
K = given at 11% or 0.11
g = $(\text{ROE})(1 - \text{P/O}) = (0.10)(1 - 0.55) = 0.045$

$$\text{Value}_0 = \frac{\$2.59}{11 - 0.045} = \frac{\$2.59}{0.065} = \$39.85$$

b. Multistage dividend discount model (where $g_1 = 0.15$ and g_2 is 0.045):

$$\text{Value}_0 = \frac{D_1}{1 + K} + \frac{D_2}{(1 + K)^2} + \frac{D_3/(K - g_2)}{(1 + K)^2}$$

D_1 = $(\text{EPS}_0)(1 + g_1)(\text{P/O}) = (4.50)(1.15)(0.55) = \$2.85$
D_2 = $(D_1)(1 + g_1) = (\$2.85)(1.15) = \$3.27$
K = given at 11% or 0.11
g_2 = 0.045
D_3 = $(D_2)(1 + g_2) = (\$3.27)(1.045) = \$3.42$

$$\begin{aligned}\text{Value}_0 &= \frac{\$2.85}{(1.11)} + \frac{\$3.27}{(1.11)^2} + \frac{\$3.42/(0.11 - 0.045)}{(1.11)^2}\\ &= \frac{\$2.85}{(1.11)} + \frac{\$3.27}{(1.11)^2} + \frac{\$52.62}{(1.11)^2}\\ &= \$2.56 + \$2.65 + \$42.71\\ &= \$47.92\end{aligned}$$

CFA Exam Question

2. The constant growth dividend discount model can be used both for the valuation of companies and for the estimation of the long-term total return of a stock.

Assume: $20 = Price of a stock today
8% = Expected growth rate of dividends
$0.60 = Annual dividend one year forward

a. Using *only* the above data, *compute* the expected long-term total return on the stock using the constant growth dividend discount model. *Show* calculations.

b. *Briefly discuss three* disadvantages of the constant growth dividend discount model in its application to investment analysis.

c. *Identify three* alternative methods to the dividend discount model for the valuation of companies.

Solution: Question 2—Morning Session (I–90)(10 points)
(Reading reference: Cohen, Zinbarg, & Ziekel, Chapter 10)

a. The dividend discount model is: $P = \dfrac{d}{k - g}$

where:

P = Value of the stock today
d = Annual dividend one year forward
k = Discount rate
g = Constant dividend growth rate

$$\text{Solving for } k\text{: } (k - g) = \frac{d}{p}\text{; then } k = \frac{d}{p} + g$$

So k becomes the estimate for the long-term return of the stock.

$$k = \frac{\$0.60}{\$20.00} + 8\% = 3\% + 8\% = 11\%$$

b. Many professional investors shy away from the dividend discount framework analysis due to its many inherent complexities.

(1) The model cannot be used where companies pay very small or no dividends and speculation on the level of future dividends could be futile. (Dividend policy may be arbitrary.)
(2) The model presumes one can accurately forecast long-term growth of earnings (dividends) of a company. Such forecasts become quite tenuous beyond two years out. (A short-term valuation may be more pertinent.)
(3) For the variable growth models, small differences in g for the first several years produce large differences in the valuations.
(4) The correct k or the discount rate is difficult to estimate for a specific company as an infinite number of factors affect it that are themselves difficult to forecast, e.g., inflation, riskless rate of return, risk premium on stocks, and other uncertainties.
(5) The model is not definable when $g > k$ as with growth companies, so it is not applicable to a large number of companies.
(6) Where a company has low or negative earnings per share or has a poor balance sheet, the ability to continue the dividend is questionable.
(7) The components of income can differ substantially, reducing comparability.

c. Three alternative methods of valuation would include: (1) price-earnings ratios; (2) price-asset value ratios (including market and book asset values); (3) price-sales ratios; (4) liquidation or breakup value; and (5) price–cash flow ratios.

chapter
eight

FINANCIAL STATEMENT ANALYSIS

OBJECTIVES

1. Understand the relationship between the income statement, balance sheet, and statement of cash flows.
2. Be able to break down and analyze ratios in six major categories.
3. Explain how the ratios can be applied to a specific company.
4. Be able to do long-term trend analysis based on the ratios.
5. Explain potential deficiencies that are often part of the published financial statements of companies.

OUTLINE

The Major Financial Statements
- Income Statement
- Balance Sheet
- Statement of Cash Flows

Key Financial Ratios for the Security Analyst
- Ratio Analysis
- Bankruptcy Studies
- Classification System

Uses of Ratios

Comparing Long-Term Trends

Deficiencies of Financial Statements
- Inflation Effects
- Inventory Valuation
- Extraordinary Gains and Losses
- Pension Fund Liabilities
- Foreign Exchange Transactions
- Other Distortions

Financial statements present a numerical picture of a company's financial and operating health. Since each company is different, an analyst needs to examine the financial statements for industry characteristics as well as for differences in accounting methods. The major financial statements are the balance sheet, the income statement, and the statement of cash flows. A very helpful long-term financial overview also is provided by a 5- or 10-year summary statement found in the corporate annual report. One must further remember that the footnotes to these statements are an integral part of the statements and provide a wealth of in-depth explanatory information. More depth can often be found in additional reports such as the 10–K filed with the Securities and Exchange Commission and obtainable from the company's Web site or the SEC's Edgar Web site.

www.freeedgar.com

Fundamental analysis depends on variables internal to the company, and the corporate financial statements are one way of measuring fundamental value and risk.

Financial statement analysis should be combined with economic and industry analysis before a final judgment is made to purchase or sell a specific security. Chapter 7 presented methods of valuation that used forecasts of dividends and earnings per share. Earnings per share (EPS) combined with an estimated price-earnings ratio was also used to get a future price. Careful study of financial statements provides the analyst with much of the necessary information to forecast earnings and dividends, to judge the quality of earnings, and to determine financial and operating risk.

THE MAJOR FINANCIAL STATEMENTS

In the first part of this chapter, we examine the three basic types of financial statements—the income statement, the balance sheet, and the statement of cash flows—with particular attention paid to the interrelationships among these three measurement devices. In the rest of the chapter, ratio analysis is presented in detail, and deficiencies of financial statements are discussed along with the role of the security analyst in interpreting financial statements.

Income Statement

The **income statement** is the major device for measuring the profitability of a firm over a period of time. An example of the income statement is presented in Table 8–1 for Johnson & Johnson, the company used in the previous chapter for valuation models. Johnson & Johnson calls their income statement the "Consolidated Statement of Earnings," which reflects that they have consolidated the activities of all their subsidiaries into this one statement. Note that an income statement is for a defined period, whether it is for one month, three months, or in this case one year. The statement is presented in a stair-step fashion so that we can examine the profit after each type of expense item is deducted.

TABLE 8-1 Consolidated Statements of Earnings

Johnson & Johnson and Subsidiaries
(dollars in millions except per share figures)

	2009	2008	2007
Sales to customers	**$61,897**	**63,747**	**61,095**
Cost of products sold	18,447	18,511	17,751
Gross profit	43,450	45,236	43,344
Selling, marketing and administrative expenses	19,801	21,490	20,451
Research expense	6,986	7,577	7,680
Purchased in-process research and development (Note 20)	—	181	807
Interest income	(90)	(361)	(452)
Interest expense, net of portion capitalized (Note 4)	451	435	296
Other (income) expense, net	(526)	(1,015)	534
Restructuring (Note 22)	1,073	—	745
Earnings before provision for taxes on income	15,755	16,929	13,283
Provision for taxes on income (Note 8)	3,489	3,980	2,707
Net earnings	**$12,266**	**12,949**	**10,576**
Basic net earnings per share (Notes 1 and 15)	**$ 4.45**	**4.62**	**3.67**
Diluted net earnings per share (Notes 1 and 15)	**$ 4.40**	**4.57**	**3.63**
Cash dividends per share	**$ 1.930**	**1.795**	**1.620**
Basic average shares outstanding (Notes 1 and 15)	**2,759.5**	**2,802.5**	**2,882.9**
Diluted average shares outstanding (Notes 1 and 15)	**2,789.1**	**2,835.6**	**2,910.7**

Source: *Johnson & Johnson Annual Report*, 2009, p. 37.

For 2009, Johnson & Johnson had sales of over $61 billion. After subtracting the cost of goods (products) sold, their gross profit was $43.45 billion. From gross profit they subtracted other expenses related to operations, such as selling, marketing, and administrative expenses; research expense; purchased in-process research and development; interest expense; and other expenses. Notice that there is also interest income of $90 million and interest expense of $451 million. The interest income is generated by their marketable securities found on the balance sheet. After subtracting expenses we arrive at earnings before taxes of $15.755 billion. After Johnson & Johnson pays taxes of $3.489 billion they have net earnings (earnings after taxes) of $12.266 billion.

When net earnings are divided by the number of shares outstanding we have basic net earnings per share of $4.45. Diluted earnings per share of $4.40 are five cents lower than basic net earnings per share because the number of shares used in the denominator includes new shares that might be created by the exercise of stock options or securities convertible into common stock. An examination of the two preceding years indicates that basic earnings are consistently diluted by four or five cents per share, indicating that dilution of earnings by the issuance of new shares is not a serious problem for Johnson & Johnson. Additionally, net earnings show an increase from $10.576 billion in 2007 to $12.266 billion in 2009. Is this a good or bad income statement? As we shall see later, the analyst's interpretation of the numbers will depend on historical figures, on industry data, and on the relationship of income to balance sheet items such as assets and net worth.

Balance Sheet

The **balance sheet** indicates what the firm owns and how these assets are financed in the form of liabilities or ownership interest. While the income statement purports to show the profitability of the firm, the balance sheet delineates the firm's holdings and obligations. Together, these statements are intended to answer two questions: How much did the firm make or lose? and What is a measure of its worth? A balance sheet for Johnson & Johnson is presented in Table 8–2.

Johnson & Johnson was chosen for analysis because of its international scope and its well-known products such as Band-Aids, Tylenol, Neutrogena skin care products, ORTHO contraceptives, baby products, and its many drugs that treat schizophrenia and bipolar mania, and anti-infective and immune disorders.

Note that the balance sheet is dated at the end of the year 2009. It does not represent the result of transactions for a specific month, quarter, or year but rather is a cumulative chronicle of all transactions that have affected the corporation since its inception. This is in contrast to the income statement, which measures results only over a short, quantifiable period. Generally, balance sheet items are stated on an original cost basis rather than at market value.

The balance sheet is divided into two basic parts: Assets and Liabilities, and Stockholders' Equity. Assets and Liabilities are separated into current and long-term categories with anything coming due in less than one year put into the current category and anything having a life of more than one year put into long term. There are several areas particular to Johnson & Johnson that are worth pointing out because they won't be found in many other companies.

Notice that at the end of 2009, Johnson & Johnson has $15.810 billion of cash and cash equivalents and $3.615 billion in marketable securities. This total of $19.425 billion is what accounted for the $90 million of interest income shown on the income statement. Secondly, in the long-term category of assets, you will find intangible assets of $16.323 billion. This represents the company's patents on its medical devices and pharmaceuticals, as well as its trademarks. This category represents more than 100 percent of the $14.759 billion in property, plant, and equipment found on the line right above it. Finally notice that the company has very little long-term debt.

TABLE 8-2 Consolidated Balance Sheets

Johnson & Johnson and Subsidiaries
At January 3, 2010, and December 28, 2009
(dollars in millions except share and per share data)

	2009	2008
Assets		
Current Assets		
Cash and cash equivalents (Notes 1 and 2)	$15,810	10,768
Marketable securities (Notes 1 and 2)	3,615	2,041
Accounts receivable trade, less allowances for doubtful accounts $333 (2008, $268)	9,646	9,719
Inventories (Notes 1 and 3)	5,180	5,052
Deferred taxes on income (Note 8)	2,793	3,430
Prepaid expenses and other receivables	2,497	3,367
Total Current Assets	**39,541**	**34,377**
Property, plant and equipment, net (Notes 1 and 4)	14,759	14,365
Intangible assets, net (Notes 1 and 5)	16,323	13,976
Goodwill (Notes 1 and 5)	14,862	13,719
Deferred taxes on income (Note 8)	5,507	5,841
Other assets	3,690	2,634
Total Assets	**$94,682**	**84,912**
Liabilities and Shareholders' Equity		
Current Liabilities		
Loans and notes payable (Note 7)	$ 6,318	3,732
Accounts payable	5,541	7,503
Accrued liabilities	5,796	5,531
Accrued rebates, returns and promotions	2,028	2,237
Accrued salaries, wages and commissions	1,606	1,432
Accrued taxes on income	442	417
Total Current Liabilities	**21,731**	**20,852**
Long-term debt (Note 7)	8,223	8,120
Deferred taxes on income (Note 8)	1,424	1,432
Employee related obligations (Notes 9 and 10)	6,769	7,791
Other liabilities	5,947	4,206
Total Liabilities	**44,094**	**42,401**
Shareholders' Equity		
Preferred stock—without par value (authorized and unissued 2,000,000 shares)	—	—
Common stock—par value $1.00 per share (Note 12) (authorized 4,320,000,000 shares; issued 3,119,843,000 shares)	3,120	3,120
Accumulated other comprehensive income (Note 13)	(3,058)	(4,955)
Retained earnings	70,306	63,379
	70,368	61,544
Less: common stock held in treasury, at cost (Note 12) (365,522,000 shares and 350,665,000 shares)	19,780	19,033
Total Shareholders' Equity	**50,588**	**42,511**
Total Liabilities and Shareholders' Equity	**$94,682**	**84,912**

Source: *Johnson & Johnson Annual Report,* 2009, p. 36.

Statement of Cash Flows

The third required financial statement, along with the balance sheet and income statement, is the **statement of cash flows**. Referred to as *Statement of Financial Accounting Standards (SFAS) No. 95,* it replaced the old statement of changes in financial position (and the sources and uses of funds statement).

The purpose of the statement of cash flows is to emphasize the critical nature of cash flow to the operations of the firm. Cash flow generally represents cash or cash-equivalent items that can easily be converted into cash within 90 days (such as a money market fund).

The income statement and balance sheet are normally based on the accrual method of accounting, in which revenues and expenses are recognized as they occur, rather than when cash actually changes hands. For example, a $100,000 credit sale may be made in December 2010 and shown as revenue for that year—despite the fact the cash payment would not be received until March 2011. When the actual payment is finally received under accrual accounting, no revenue is recognized (it has already been accounted for previously). The primary advantage of accrual accounting is that it allows us to match revenues and expenses in the period in which they occur to appropriately measure profit; but a disadvantage is that adequate attention is not directed to the actual cash flow position of the firm.

One can think of situations in which a firm made a $1 million profit on a transaction but will not receive the actual cash payment for two years. Or perhaps the $1 million profit is in cash, but the firm increased its asset purchases by $3 million (a new building). If you merely read the income statement, you might assume the firm is in a strong $1 million cash position; but if you go beyond the income statement to cash flow considerations, you would observe the firm is $2 million short of funds for the period.

As a last example, a firm might show a $100,000 loss on the income statement; but if it had a depreciation expense write-off of $150,000, the firm would actually have $50,000 in cash. Since depreciation is a noncash deduction, the $150,000 deduction in the income statement for depreciation can be added back to net income to determine cash flow.

The statement of cash flows addresses these issues by translating income statement and balance sheet data into cash flow information. A corporation that has $1 million in accrual-based accounting profits can determine whether it can actually afford to pay a cash dividend to stockholders, buy new equipment, or undertake new projects.

The three primary sections of the statement of cash flows are as follows:

1. Cash flows from operating activities.
2. Cash flows from investing activities.
3. Cash flows from financing activities.

After each of these sections is completed, the results are added to compute the net increase or decrease in cash flow for the corporation. An example of this process is shown in Figure 8–1. This statement informs us about how the cash was created (operations, investing, financing), where it was spent, and the net increase or decrease of cash for the entire year.

Let's look at Johnson & Johnson's statement of cash flows in Table 8–3 on page 205. Cash provided from operating activities (top one-third of the statement) was approximately $16.571 billion in 2009. The major items were net earnings and depreciation and amortization. Second, investing activities used $7.598 billion of cash with additions to property and the purchase and sale of investments being the major items.

In 2009, financing activities used $4.092 billion of cash. Johnson & Johnson issued new short-term debt to raise $9.484 billion and paid off $6.791 billion of short-term

FIGURE 8-1 Illustration of Concepts behind Statement of Cash Flows

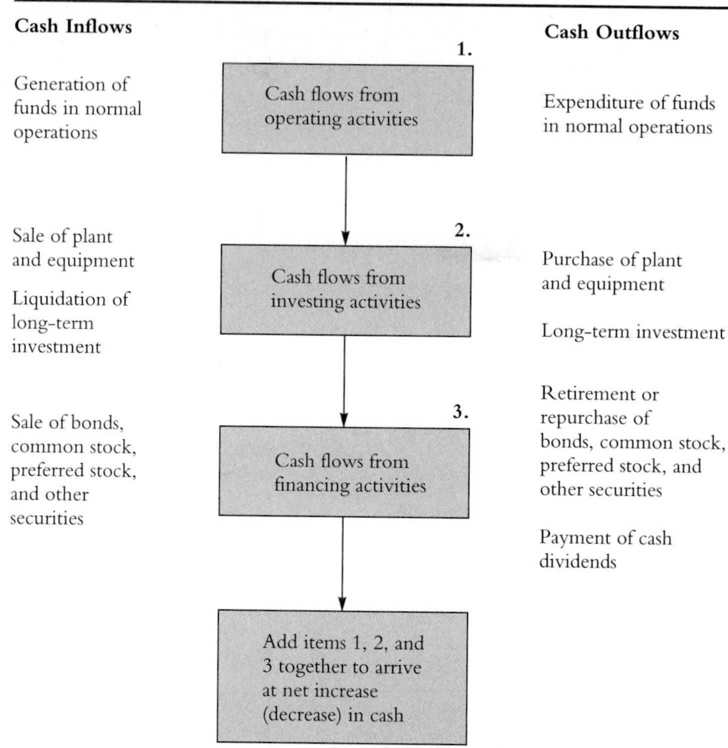

debt. Additionally, the company repurchased $2.130 billion of common stock and paid dividends of $5.327 billion. Because Johnson & Johnson is an international company, they also have to account for currency effects. The effect of exchange rate changes on cash and cash equivalents added $.161 billion from the cash flow statement; this is shown on the first line under "Net cash used by financing activities."

An analysis of this statement can pinpoint strengths or weaknesses in a company's cash flow. We can also see on the statement of cash flows that at the bottom of the cash flow statement, J&J gives us supplemental cash flow data that are not required to be reported in the three major categories but that are of interest to the shareholder. For example the supplemental section shows interest expenses, income taxes payments, treasury stock issued to employees for compensation, and details for the cash spent on acquisitions.

If we add cash flow from operating, investing, and financing activities we arrive at the following figures in billions of dollars for 2009:

Net cash provided by operating activities	$16.571 billion
Net cash provided by (used in) investing activities	(7.598)
Net cash used by financing activities	(4.092)
Effect of exchange rate adjustment	(.161)
Increase in cash after exchange rate adjustment	5.042
Cash and cash equivalents beg. of yr.	10.768
Cash and cash equivalents end of yr.	$15.810 billion

Notice that this ending cash balance is what appears on the balance sheet under cash. A careful analysis of the cash flow statements indicates how the company is generating cash. Johnson & Johnson is an example of a company with a good cash

TABLE 8-3 Consolidated Statements of Cash Flows

Johnson & Johnson and Subsidiaries
(dollars in millions)

	2009	2008	2007
Cash Flows from Operating Activities			
Net earnings	$ 12,266	12,949	10,576
Adjustments to reconcile net earnings to cash flows from operating activities:			
Depreciation and amortization of property and intangibles	2,774	2,832	2,777
Stock based compensation	628	627	698
Purchased in-process research and development	—	181	807
Intangible asset write-down (NATRECOR®)	—	—	678
Deferred tax provision	(436)	22	(1,762)
Accounts receivable allowances	58	86	22
Changes in assets and liabilities, net of effects from acquisitions:			
Decrease/(increase) in accounts receivable	453	(736)	(416)
Decrease/(increase) in inventories	95	(101)	14
(Decrease)/increase in accounts payable and accrued liabilities	(507)	(272)	2,642
Decrease/(increase) in other current and non-current assets	1,209	(1,600)	(1,578)
Increase in other current and non-current liabilities	31	984	564
Net Cash Flows from Operating Activities	**16,571**	**14,972**	**15,022**
Cash flows from investing activities			
Additions to property, plan and equipment	(2,365)	(3,066)	(2,942)
Proceeds from the disposal of assets	154	785	457
Acquisitions, net of cash acquired (Note 20)	(2,470)	(1,214)	(1,388)
Purchases of investments	(10,040)	(3,668)	(9,659)
Sales of investments	7,232	3,059	7,988
Other (primarily intangibles)	(109)	(83)	(368)
Net Cash Used by Investing Activities	**(7,598)**	**(4,187)**	**(5,912)**
Cash flows from financing activities			
Dividends to shareholders	(5,327)	(5,024)	(4,670)
Repurchase of common stock	(2,130)	(6,651)	(5,607)
Proceeds from short-term debt	9,484	8,430	19,626
Retirement of short-term debt	(6,791)	(7,319)	(21,691)
Proceeds from long-term debt	9	1,638	5,100
Retirement of long-term debt	(219)	(24)	(18)
Proceeds from the exercise of stock options/excess tax benefits	882	1,486	1,562
Net Cash Used by Financing Activities	**(4,092)**	**(7,464)**	**(5,698)**
Effect of exchange rate changes on cash and cash equivalents	161	(323)	275
Increase in cash and cash equivalents	**5,042**	**2,998**	**3,687**
Cash and cash equivalents, beginning of year (Note 1)	10,768	7,770	4,083
Cash and Cash Equivalents, End of Year (Note 1)	**$15,810**	**10,768**	**7,770**
Supplemental Cash Flow Data			
Cash paid during the year for:			
Interest	$ 533	525	314
Income taxes	2,363	4,068	4,099
Supplemental Schedule of Noncash Investing and Financing Activities			
Treasury stock issued for employee compensation and stock option plans, net of cash proceeds	$ 541	593	738
Conversion of debt	2	—	9
Acquisitions			
Fair value of assets acquired	$ 3,345	1,328	1,620
Fair value of liabilities assumed and non-controlling interests	(875)	(114)	(232)
Net Cash Paid for Acquisitions	**$ 2,470**	**1,214**	**1,388**

Source: *Johnson & Johnson Annual Report*, 2009, p. 39.

flow statement with cash generated by operations and is then spending cash on corporate growth through investment and financing. However, you might find some companies that are not so profitable and instead are liquidating inventory or reducing accounts receivable to generate cash. This would indicate either an unhealthy economic environment or a poor competitive position in the industry.

For example, during a recession a number of hard-pressed firms may have insufficient earnings to pay dividends or to maintain or expand long-term assets. In such cases, short-term debt may be used to meet long-term needs, and this can lead to a reduction of short-term working capital and a dangerous operating position. This statement of cash flows is a statement that is often overlooked as an analytical tool; however, it can tell you a lot about how the company operates.

KEY FINANCIAL RATIOS FOR THE SECURITY ANALYST

We just summarized the three major financial statements that will be the basis of your analysis in this section emphasizing financial ratios. Ratio analysis brings together balance sheet and income statement data to permit a better understanding of the firm's past and current health, which will aid you in forecasting the future outlook.

Ratio Analysis

Ratios are used in much of our daily life. We buy cars based on miles per gallon, we evaluate baseball players by their earned run averages and batting averages and basketball players by field goal and foul shooting percentages, and so on. These are all ratios constructed to judge comparative performances. Financial ratios serve a similar purpose, but you must know what is being measured to construct a ratio and to understand the significance of the resultant number.

Financial ratios are used to weigh and evaluate the operating performance and capital structure of the firm. While an absolute value such as earnings of $50,000 or accounts receivable of $100,000 may appear satisfactory, its acceptability can be measured only in relation to other values.

For example, are earnings of $50,000 actually good? If a company earned $50,000 on $500,000 of sales (10 percent profit-margin ratio), that might be quite satisfactory, whereas earnings of $50,000 on $5 million could be disappointing (a meager 1 percent return). After we have computed the appropriate ratio, we must compare our firm's results to the achievement of similar firms in the industry as well as to our own firm's past performance. Even then, this "number-crunching" process is not always adequate because we are forced to supplement our financial findings with an evaluation of company management, physical facilities, and numerous other factors.

Ratio analysis will not uncover "gold mines" for the analyst. It is more like a physical exam at the doctor's office. You hope you are all right, but if not, you may be content to know what is wrong and what to do about it. Just as with medical illness where some diseases are easier to cure than others, the same is true of financial illness. The analysts are the doctors. They determine the illness and keep track of management to see if they can administer the cure. Sometimes ailing companies can be very good values. Penn-Central went into bankruptcy, and its common stock could have been purchased at $2 per share for several years. In the 1990s, Penn-Central traded in the $17 to $27 range after a three-for-two stock split in 1982 and a two-for-one stock split in 1988. Chrysler and Lockheed (now Lockheed Martin) were both on the brink of bankruptcy in the 1970s until the government made guaranteed loans available. Both Chrysler and Lockheed could have been bought at less than $3 per share. After recovering and generating higher stock prices, they both split their common stock. These were all sick companies that returned to health, and any investor willing to take such great risk and buy their stocks would have been well rewarded.

www.daimlerchrysler.com

www.lockheedmartin.com

However, this is not always the case. The financial crisis of 2007–2009 brought down many companies such as Lehmann Brothers, General Motors, and Chrysler.

The U.S. government saved General Motors after it went through bankruptcy proceedings and owned over 60 percent of the common stock. Many referred to GM as "government motors." Chrysler went through bankruptcy proceedings and was bought by Fiat of Italy. In both cases the government intervened to save jobs. The U.S. Treasury recovered a portion of their investment through the sale of some of their common stock when GM went public in November of 2010.

Bankruptcy Studies

In a sense, ratio analysis protects an investor from picking continual losers more than it guarantees picking winners. Several studies have used ratios as predictors of financial failure. The most notable studies are by William Beaver and Edward Altman. Beaver found that ratios of failing firms signal failure as much as five years ahead of bankruptcy, and as bankruptcy approaches, the ratios deteriorate more rapidly, with the greatest deterioration in the last year. The Beaver studies also found (a) "Investors recognize and adjust to the new solvency positions of failing firms," and (b) "The price changes of the common stocks act as if investors rely upon ratios as a basis for their assessments, and impound the ratio information in the market prices."[1]

The first Altman research study indicated that five ratios combined were 95 percent accurate in predicting failure one year ahead of bankruptcy and were 72 percent accurate two years ahead of failure, with the average lead time for the ratio signal being 20 months.[2] Altman developed a Z score that was an index developed through multiple discriminate analysis that could predict failure. Altman modified and improved his model's accuracy even further by increasing the number of ratios to seven.[3] This service is currently sold to institutional investors by Zeta Services Inc. The Z (zeta) score relies on the following variables:

1. Retained earnings/total assets (cumulative profitability).
2. Standard deviation of operating income/total assets (measure of earnings stability during the last 10 years).
3. Earnings before interest and taxes/total assets (productivity of operating assets).
4. Earnings before interest and taxes/interest (leverage ratio, interest coverage).
5. Current assets/current liabilities (liquidity ratio).
6. Market value of common stock/book value of equity (a leverage ratio).
7. Total assets (proxy for size of the firm).

The greater the firm's bankruptcy potential, the lower its Z score. The ratios are not equally significant, but together they separate the companies into a correct bankruptcy group and nonbankruptcy group a high percentage of the time. Retained earnings/total assets has the heaviest weight in the analysis, and leverage is also very important. In the next section, we present six classifications of ratios that are helpful to the analyst. Many more could be used, but these represent the most widely used measures.

Classification System

We divide 20 significant ratios into six primary groupings:

A. Profitability ratios:
  1. Gross profit margin.
  2. After-tax profit margin.
  3. Return on assets.
  4. Return on equity.

[1] William H. Beaver, "Market Prices, Financial Ratios, and the Prediction of Failure," *Journal of Accounting Research,* Autumn 1968, p. 192.

[2] Edward I. Altman, "Financial Ratios, Discriminant Analysis, and the Prediction of Corporate Bankruptcy," *Journal of Finance,* September 1968, pp. 589–609.

[3] Edward I. Altman, *Corporate Financial Distress* (New York: John Wiley & Sons, 1983).

B. Asset-utilization ratios:
  5. Receivables turnover.
  6. Inventory turnover.
  7. Fixed-asset turnover.
  8. Total asset turnover.

C. Liquidity ratios:
  9. Current ratio.
  10. Quick ratio.
  11. Net working capital to total assets.

D. Debt-utilization ratios:
  12. Long-term debt to equity.
  13. Total debt to total assets.
  14. Times interest earned.
  15. Fixed charge coverage.

E. Price ratios:
  16. Price to earnings.
  17. Price to book value.
  18. Dividends to price (dividend yield).

F. Other ratios:
  19. Average tax rate.
  20. Dividend payout.

The users of financial statements will attach different degrees of importance to the six categories of ratios. To the potential investor, the critical consideration is profitability and debt utilization. For the banker or trade creditor, the emphasis shifts to the firm's current ability to meet debt obligations. The bondholder, in turn, may be primarily influenced by debt to total assets—while also eyeing the profitability of the firm in terms of its ability to cover interest payments in the short term and principal payments in the long term. Of course, the shrewd analyst looks at all the ratios, with different degrees of attention.

A. Profitability Ratios The **profitability ratios** allow the analyst to measure the ability of the firm to earn an adequate return on sales, total assets, and invested capital. The profit-margin ratios (1, 2) relate to income statement items, while the two return ratios (3, 4) relate the income statement (numerator) to the balance sheet (denominator). Many of the problems related to profitability can be explained, in whole or in part, by the firm's ability to effectively employ its resources. We shall apply these ratios to Johnson & Johnson's income statement and balance sheet for 2009, which were previously presented in Tables 8–1 and 8–2 on pages 200 and 202.

application example

Profitability Ratios (Johnson & Johnson, 2005—in millions)

1. Gross profit margin $= \dfrac{\text{Gross profit}}{\text{Sales (revenue)}} = \dfrac{\$43,450}{\$61,897} = 70.20\%$

2. After-tax profit margin $= \dfrac{\text{Net income}}{\text{Sales}} = \dfrac{\$12,266}{\$61,897} = 19.82\%$

3. Return on assets

   a. $\dfrac{\text{Net income}}{\text{Total assets}} = \dfrac{\$12,266}{\$94,682} = 12.95\%$

b. $\frac{\text{Net income}}{\text{Sales}} \times \frac{\text{Sales}}{\text{Total assets}}$

$\frac{\$12,266}{\$61,897} \times \frac{\$61,897}{\$94,682} = 12.95\%$

4. Return on equity

a. $\frac{\text{Net income}}{\text{Stockholder's equity}^4} = \frac{\$12,266}{\$50,588} = 24.25\%$

b. $\frac{\text{Return on assets}}{(1 - \text{Debt/Assets})^5} = \frac{12.95\%}{.5343} = 24.25\%$

The profitability ratios indicate that J&J is quite profitable, but the analysis of its return on equity using 4(b) indicates that its high return on stockholders' equity is partially a result of financing approximately 46.47 percent of assets with debt.

DuPont Analysis Notice that the return on assets and return on equity have parts (a) and (b), or two ways to determine the ratio. The methods employed in (b), which arise from the DuPont Company's financial system, help the analyst see the relationship between the income statement and the balance sheet. The return on assets is generated by multiplying the after-tax profit margin (income statement) by the asset-turnover ratio (combination income statement–balance sheet ratio).

www.dupont.com

The DuPont Company was a forerunner in stressing that satisfactory return on assets may be achieved through high profit margins or rapid turnover of assets, or a combination of both. The DuPont system causes the analyst to examine the sources of a company's profitability. Since the profit margin is an income statement ratio, a high profit margin indicates good cost control, whereas a high asset turnover ratio demonstrates efficient use of the assets on the balance sheet. Different industries have different operating and financial structures. For example, in the heavy capital goods industry (machinery and equipment), the emphasis is on a high profit margin with a low asset turnover, while in food processing, the profit margin is low, and the key to satisfactory returns on total assets is a rapid turnover of assets.

DuPont analysis further stresses that the return on equity stems from the return on assets adjusted for the amount of financial leverage by using the total debt-to-asset ratio. About 47 percent of the Johnson & Johnson's assets are financed by debt, and the return on equity reflects a fairly high level of debt financing because the return on equity of 24.25 percent is 87 percent higher than its return on assets of 12.95 percent. As a detective, the financial analyst can judge how much debt a company employs by comparing these two measures of return. Of course, you will want to check this clue with the debt-utilization ratios. The total relationship between return on assets and return on equity under the DuPont system is depicted in Figure 8–2.

Some analysts prefer a linear multiplicative approach to the DuPont analysis.

$$\underbrace{\frac{\text{Net income}}{\text{Sales}} \times \frac{\text{Sales}}{\text{Assets}}}_{\text{Return on assets}} \times \frac{\text{Assets}}{\text{Equity}} = \text{Return on equity}$$

Our major difference is that we divide the Return on assets by (1 − Debt/Assets) rather than multiply by Assets/Equity.

[4] A working definition of stockholders' equity is the preferred and common stock accounts plus retained earnings. Johnson & Johnson also has a few other adjustments. The total can be found on the second line from the bottom at the end of Table 8–2.

[5] Debt is equal to total liabilities on the balance sheet and can also be calculated by subtracting total equity from total assets.

FIGURE 8-2 DuPont Analysis

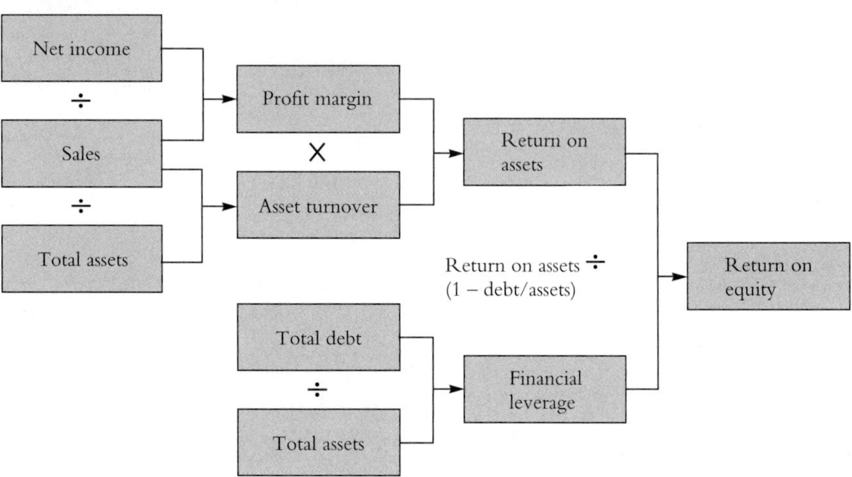

In computing return on assets and equity, the analyst must also be sensitive to the age of the assets. Plant and equipment purchased 15 years ago may be carried on the books far below its replacement value. A 20 percent return on assets that were purchased in the late 1990s and depreciated may be inferior to a 15 percent return on newly purchased assets.

B. Asset-Utilization Ratios With **asset-utilization ratios**, we measure the speed at which the firm is turning over accounts receivable, inventory, and longer-term assets. In other words, asset-utilization ratios measure how many times per year a company sells its inventory or collects its accounts receivable. For long-term assets, the utilization ratio tells us how productive the fixed assets are in terms of sales generation.

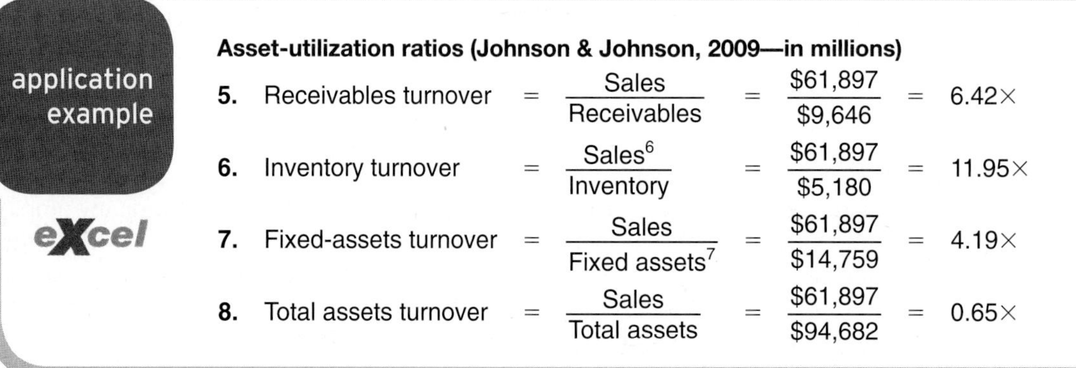

application example

eXcel

Asset-utilization ratios (Johnson & Johnson, 2009—in millions)

	Ratio		Formula		Calculation		Result
5.	Receivables turnover	=	Sales / Receivables	=	\$61,897 / \$9,646	=	6.42×
6.	Inventory turnover	=	Sales[6] / Inventory	=	\$61,897 / \$5,180	=	11.95×
7.	Fixed-assets turnover	=	Sales / Fixed assets[7]	=	\$61,897 / \$14,759	=	4.19×
8.	Total assets turnover	=	Sales / Total assets	=	\$61,897 / \$94,682	=	0.65×

The asset-utilization ratios relate sales on the income statement (numerator) to the various assets on the balance sheet. Given that Johnson & Johnson's products are a combination of household products and pharmaceuticals, the repeat nature of purchases creates a receivables turnover of 6.42×, which indicates that J&J gets paid close to every 56 days. The inventory turnover is very high at 11.95×, which shows that there is about a one-month inventory cycle, which certainly makes sense for the pharmaceutical side of the business.

[6] Some may prefer to use cost of goods sold in the numerator for theoretical reasons. We use sales to be consistent with Dun & Bradstreet, the well-known credit rating bureau.

[7] The fixed-asset value is equal to property, plant and equipment, net on the balance sheet.

The fixed-asset turnover ratio is relatively high at 4.19× because in the long-term asset area, J&J has a relatively small dollar amount invested in fixed assets (plant and equipment). The amount is only $14.759 billion. The nature of the business allows J&J to generate high margin products with a small investment in plant and equipment but requires a large investment in research and development.

The total asset turnover ratio of .65× is not so positive. There are many other assets causing this low turnover. Productive investment in research and development of expense of $6.986 billion ends up under the intangible category ($16.323 billion) in the long-term asset section. Patents on new drugs can have a life of up to 14 years. Also goodwill of $14.862 billion inflates assets as does the $19.4 billion in cash, cash equivalents, and marketable securities on their balance sheet. These three items of intangible assets, goodwill, and cash and marketable securities equal $50.6 billion and cause a low asset turnover ratio.

C. Liquidity Ratios The primary emphasis of the **liquidity ratios** is a determination of the firm's ability to pay off short-term obligations as they come due. These ratios can be related to receivables and inventory turnover in that a faster turnover creates a more rapid movement of cash through the company and improves liquidity. Again, remember that each industry will be different. A jewelry store chain will have much different ratios from a grocery store chain.

application example

excel

Liquidity ratios (Johnson & Johnson, 2009—in millions)

9. Current ratio =

$$\frac{\text{Current assets}}{\text{Current liabilities}} = \frac{\$39{,}541}{\$21{,}731} = 1.82\times$$

10. Quick ratio =

$$\frac{\text{Current assets} - \text{Inventory}}{\text{Current liabilities}} = \frac{\$34{,}361}{\$21{,}731} = 1.58\times$$

11. Net working capital to Total assets =

$$\frac{\text{Current assets} - \text{Current liabilities}}{\text{Total assets}} = \frac{\$17{,}810}{\$94{,}682} = 0.19\times$$

The first two ratios (current and quick) indicate whether the firm can pay off its short-term debt in an emergency by liquidating its current assets. The quick ratio looks only at the most liquid assets, which include cash, marketable securities, and receivables. Cash and securities are already liquid, but receivables usually will be turned into cash during the collection period. If there is concern about the firm's liquidity, the analyst will want to cross-check the liquidity ratios with receivables and inventory turnover to determine how fast the current assets are turned into cash during an ordinary cycle.

The last liquidity ratio is a measure of the percentage of current assets (after short-term debt has been paid) to total assets. This indicates the liquidity of the assets of the firm. The higher the ratio, the greater the short-term assets relative to fixed assets, and the safer a creditor is. In this example, the ratio of 0.19× is small, but indicates no problem given the solid current and quick ratios. Also consider that Johnson & Johnson has a cash and marketable securities balance of over $19 billion.

D. Debt-Utilization Ratios The **debt-utilization ratios** provide an indication of the way the firm is financed between debt (lenders) and equity (owners) and therefore helps the analyst determine the amount of financial risk present in the firm. Too much debt cannot only impair liquidity with heavy interest payments but can also damage profitability and the health of the firm during an economic recession or industry slowdown.

application example

eXcel

Debt-utilization ratios (Johnson & Johnson, 2009—in millions)

Ratio		Formula		Values		Result
12. Long-term debt to Equity	=	$\frac{\text{Long-term debt}}{\text{Stockholder's equity}}$	=	$\frac{\$\ 8{,}223}{\$50{,}588}$	=	0.16
13. Total debt to Total assets	=	$\frac{\text{Total debt}}{\text{Total assets}}$	=	$\frac{\$44{,}094}{\$94{,}682}$	=	0.47
14. Times interest earned	=	$\frac{\text{Income before interest and taxes}^{8}}{\text{Interest}}$	=	$\frac{\$16{,}206}{\$451}$	=	35.93
15. Fixed-charge coverage	=	$\frac{\text{Income before fixed charges and taxes}^{9}}{\text{Fixed charges}^{10}}$	=	$\frac{\$16{,}206}{\$451}$	=	35.93

We have already discussed the impact of financial leverage on return on equity, and the first two ratios in this category indicate to the analyst how much financial leverage is being used by the firm. The more debt, the greater the interest payments and the more volatile the impact on the firm's earnings. Companies with stable sales and earnings such as utilities can afford to employ more debt than those in cyclical industries such as automobiles or airlines. Ratio 12, long-term debt to equity, provides information concerning the long-term capital structure of the firm. In the case of J&J, long-term liabilities represent only 16 percent of the stockholders' equity base provided by the owners of the firm. Ratio 13, total debt to total assets, looks at the total assets and the use of all debt. Each firm must consider its optimum capital structure, and the analyst should be aware of industry fluctuations in assessing the firm's proper use of leverage. J&J seems safe, given that its business is not subject to large swings in sales.

The last two debt-utilization ratios indicate the firm's ability to meet its cash payments due on fixed obligations such as interest, leases, licensing fees, or sinking-fund charges. The higher these ratios, the more protected the creditor's position. Use of the fixed-charge coverage is more conservative than interest earned since it includes all fixed charges. Now that most leases are capitalized and show up on the balance sheet, it is easier to understand that lease payments are similar in importance to interest expense. Charges after taxes such as sinking-fund payments must be adjusted to before-tax income. For example, if a firm is in the 40 percent tax bracket and must make a $60,000 sinking-fund payment, the firm would have had to generate $100,000 in before-tax income to meet that obligation. The adjustment would be as follows:

$$\text{Before-tax income required} = \frac{\text{After-tax payment}}{1 - \text{Tax rate}}$$

$$= \frac{\$60{,}000}{1 - 0.40} = \$100{,}000$$

Johnson & Johnson's fixed-charge coverage is the same as its interest-earned ratio because it has no fixed charges other than interest expense. Both ratios are very strong.

E. Price Ratios The **price ratios** relate the internal performance of the firm to the external judgment of the marketplace in terms of value. What is the firm's end result

[8] Income before interest and taxes equals earnings before provision for taxes on income of $15,755 million plus the interest expense of $451 million as shown in Table 8–1.

[9] Because there are no other fixed charges besides interest, the numerators are the same in Formulas 14 and 15.

[10] The denominators are also the same in Formulas 14 and 15.

in market value? The price ratios indicate the expectations of the market relative to other companies. For example, a firm with a high price-to-earnings ratio has a higher market price relative to $1 of earnings than a company with a lower ratio.

eXcel

Debt-utilization ratios (Johnson & Johnson, 2009—in millions)

16. Price to Earnings[11] $= \frac{\text{Common stock price}}{\text{Earnings per share}} = \frac{59.00}{4.40} = 13.41$

17. Price to Book value $= \frac{\text{Common stock price}}{\text{Book value per share}^{12}} = \frac{59.00}{18.14} = 3.25$

18. Dividends to Price (dividend yield) $= \frac{\text{Dividends per share}}{\text{Common stock price}} = \frac{1.93}{59.00} = 3.27\%$

J&J's price-earnings ratio indicates that the firm's stock price represents $13.41 for every $1 of earnings. This number can be compared with that of other companies in the pharmaceutical industry and/or related industries. As indicated in Chapter 7, the price-earnings ratio (or P/E ratio) is influenced by the earnings and the sales growth of the firm and also by the risk (or volatility in performance), the debt-equity structure of the firm, the dividend-payment policy, the quality of management, and a number of other factors. The P/E ratio indicates expectations about the future of a company. Firms that are expected to provide greater returns than those for the market in general, with equal or less risk, often have P/E ratios higher than the overall market P/E ratio.

A better indicator of price-earnings ratios would be to use estimated earnings per share for 2010 of $4.75 for Johnson & Johnson. This would give a **forward P/E ratio** of 12.42 versus the **trailing P/E ratio** of 13.41 in ratio 16.

Expectations of returns and P/E ratios do change over time, as Table 8-4 illustrates. Price-earnings ratios for a selected list of U.S. firms in 1981, 1988, 1997, and 2010 show that during this 30-year period, price-earnings ratios generally rose between 1981 and 1997 and then fell back to more normal levels.

P/E ratios are more complicated than they may appear at first glance, and high P/E ratios can result from many sets of assumptions. They can be high because of expected rapid growth in earnings per share. They can fall, as they have in the

TABLE 8-4 Price-Earnings Ratios for Selected U.S. Corporations

		P/E Ratio[a]			
Corporation	Industry	12/31/81	10/24/88	8/13/97	6/4/10
ExxonMobil	International oil	5	12	19	14
Bank of America	Banking	7	9	17	dd[c]
Halliburton	Oil service	11	26	30	21
IBM	Computers	9	14	20	13
McDonald's	Restaurant franchise	10	15	22	16
Texas Instruments	Semiconductors	15	13	cc[b]	15
S&P 500	Market index	8	13	21	17

[a] P/E ratio is calculated by taking the market price and dividing by the previous 12 months' earnings per share.
[b] cc indicates that the P/E ratio is 100 or more.
[c] dd indicates that the company had a deficit.
Source: *Value Line Investment Survey* and *Barron's*.

[11] Stock price is July 2010 price, earnings per share is diluted earnings per share for 2009.

[12] Book value per share $= \frac{\text{Stockholder's equity}}{\text{Number of shares}} = \frac{\$50{,}588}{2{,}789} = \$18.14$

pharmaceutical industry, because of expected slower growth. Companies in cyclical industries are more of a problem; as earnings cycle from peak to trough, the P/E ratios may give conflicting signals. If the market knows that the earnings have peaked out and are expected to fall the P/E ratio will be low, but if earnings have bottomed out and are expected to move in an upward cycle the P/E ratio will be high. This phenomenon is the result of expectations and math. When the earnings peak, the market will not move the company's stock price up to really high levels and the P/E will shrink as EPS rise. When earnings trough, the market won't penalize the stock price as much as the decline in earnings, and the P/E ratio will rise.

The price-to-book-value ratio relates the market value of the company to the historical accounting value of the firm. In a company that has old assets, this ratio may be quite high, but in one with new, undepreciated fixed assets, the ratio might be lower. This information needs to be combined with a knowledge of the company's assets and of industry norms.

The **dividend yield** is part of the total return that an investor receives along with capital gains or losses. It is usually calculated by annualizing the current quarterly dividend since that is the cash value a current investor is likely to receive over the next year.

The price-to-earnings and price-to-book-value ratios are often used in computing stock values. The simple view of these ratios is that when they are relatively low compared with a market index or company history, the stock is a good buy. In the case of the dividend yield, the opposite is true. When dividend yields are relatively high compared with the company's historical data, the stock may be undervalued. Of course, the application of these simple models is much more complicated. The analyst has to determine if the company is performing the same as it was when the ratios were at what the analyst considers a normal level.

F. Other Ratios The other ratios are presented in category F to help the analyst spot special tax situations that affect the profitability of an industry or company and to determine what percentage of earnings are being paid to the stockholder and what is being reinvested for internal growth.

application example

excel

Other ratios (Johnson & Johnson, 2009—in millions)

19. Average tax rate $= \dfrac{\text{Income tax}}{\text{Taxable income}} = \dfrac{\$3{,}489}{\$15{,}755} = 22.15\%$

20. Dividend payout $= \dfrac{\text{Dividends per share}}{\text{Earnings per share}} = \dfrac{\$1.93}{\$4.40} = 43.86\%$

These other ratios are calculated to provide the analyst with information that may indicate unusual tax treatment or reinvestment policies. For example, the tax ratio for forest products companies will be low because of the special tax treatment given timber cuttings. A company's tax rate may also decline in a given year as a result of special tax credits. Thus, earnings per share may rise, but we need to know if it is from operations or favorable tax treatment. If it is from operations, we will be more sure of next year's forecast, but if it is from tax benefits, we cannot normally count on the benefits being continued into the future.

The **dividend-payout ratio** provides data concerning the firm's reinvestment strategies. It represents dividends per share divided by earnings per share. A high payout ratio tells the analyst that the stockholder is receiving a large part of the earnings and that the company is not retaining much income for investment in new plant and equipment. High payouts are usually found in industries that do not have great growth potential, while low payout ratios are associated with firms in growth industries.

Johnson & Johnson's tax rate is below the statutory rate of 35 percent, which can be attributed to its operations outside of the United States, which may have more favorable tax rates. The dividend payout ratio of 37 percent would indicate that J&J is somewhere between the expansion and maturity stages of its life cycle. Given Johnson & Johnson's record of increased earnings, it can be expected that the payout ratio will stay relatively constant and dividends will rise with earnings per share.

USES OF RATIOS

The previous section presented 20 ratios that may be helpful to the analyst when evaluating a firm. How can we further use the data gathered to check the health of companies we are interested in analyzing?

One way is to compare the company with the industry. This is becoming more difficult as companies diversify into several industries. Twenty years ago, many firms competed in only one industry, and ratio comparisons were more reliable. Now companies have a wide range of products and markets.

Let us see how Johnson & Johnson compares to its industry competitors based on selected ratios. The companies chosen for comparison include Abbott Laboratories, Sanolfi-Aventis, GlaxoSmithKline, and Novartis.

application example

The ratios presented in Table 8–5 can be found in the *Standard and Poor's Industry Surveys* available in most libraries either online or in print format.

TABLE 8-5 Comparative Data for Year Ending 2009

	Abbott Labs (United States)	Pfizer (United States)	GlaxoSmithKline (British)	J&J (United States)	Novartis AG (Swiss)
Operating revenues 2009 (in billions of dollars)	$30,764	$49,934	$47,092	$61,897	$44,267
5-yr. ann. growth of revenues	9.30%	−1.00%	3.70%	5.50%	9.40%
5-yr. ann. growth of net income	12.60%	−5.30%	1.60%	7.60%	7.80%
Profit margin	18.70%	17.30%	19.00%	19.80%	19.00%
Return on assets	12.10%	5.30%	14.10%	13.70%	9.70%
Return on equity	28.50%	11.70%	64.40%	26.40%	15.60%
Current ratio	1.8×	1.7×	1.4×	1.8×	17×
Debt to assets	56%	58%	77%	47%	40%
Dividend payout ratio	42%	65%	53%	43%	46%
Dividend yield (average)	3.25%	5.55%	5.55%	3.60%	4.05%
Price-earnings ratio (average)	13	12	10	12.5	12

Source: *S&P NetAdvantage,* Industry Surveys Health Care: Pharmaceuticals, June 3, 2010 and S&P Stock Reports, July 24, 2010.

The companies chosen are five of the biggest pharmaceutical companies in the world. In comparing growth rates for the five years of 2005–2009, we see that Novartis and Abbott Labs have the two highest revenue growth rates at 9.4 and 9.3 percent, respectively. Pfizer has a negative revenue growth rate, as several of their major drugs have come off patent protection and now compete with generic substitutes. This has also impacted their income growth rate in a negative fashion, as they have not been able to trim expenses fast enough to offset their revenue decline.

Abbott Labs and Johnson & Johnson (J&J) have been able to increase their income faster than their revenue due to rising profit margins. The rest of the competitors have faced declining profit margins, and their income growth rates have been smaller than their revenue growth rates.

An examination of profitability ratios shows that the profit margins (income/revenues) for these companies are all within a rather narrow range of 17 to 19 percent, but that the returns on assets and equity show quite a wide variation. The return on assets is probably a better view of total company profitability, because the return on equity is greatly influenced by the amount of total debt in the capital structure (as was demonstrated in the DuPont model earlier in the chapter). Another impact on the return on equity is the repurchase of common shares of stock. When a company repurchases shares and retires them, the equity base shrinks, causing an increase in the return on equity.

Comparing the return on assets to the return on equity gives the analyst (financial detective) clues as to how much leverage a company is using and whether they are possibly buying back shares of stock. In the case of GlaxoSmithKline, there is a very large difference between the return on assets (14.1%) and the return on equity (64.4%). It is not surprising then that GlaxoSmithKline has the highest debt to asset ratio of 77 percent and has reduced the number of shares outstanding from 5.873 billion in 2005 to 5.196 billion at the end of 2009. Novartis is on the other end of the spectrum with the lowest debt to asset ratio of 40 percent and very little financial leverage between the return on assets and return on equity. Novartis does have the second lowest return on assets, which is most likely caused by a lower asset turnover than its competitors. All five companies have reasonably safe current ratios and plenty of cash flow to cover short-term liabilities.

Johnson & Johnson has the second lowest debt to asset ratio at 47 percent and the second best return on assets. It has the second lowest dividend payout ratio and dividend yield and is plowing more money back into the company than Pfizer, Glaxo, and Novartis.

In summary, at the end of 2009 the market valued Abbott Labs highest with a price-earnings ratio of 13, Johnson & Johnson second with a price-earnings ratio of 12.5, and GlaxoSmithKline lowest with a price-earnings ratio of 10. During the last decade, common stocks of companies in the pharmaceutical industry have seen their P/E ratios fall from 20 times EPS to 10 to 13 times EPS. These P/E ratios declined over time because of slower growth, lower profitability, fewer new drug discoveries, and more government regulations. Most of the large companies in this industry have moved from being growth companies to mature companies.

It is important to understand that growth rates for these companies are quite dependent on the introduction of new drugs. Introducing a new drug is expensive because advertising costs are high, and the costs of research and development are being amortized. After several years, the new drug may become profitable as it gains market share. The point is, past growth rates are not a good predictor of future growth rates. Rather, the analyst looks at the "pipeline" of new drugs that are in clinical trials. Companies that are good at developing new drugs have higher growth rates and higher price-earnings ratios.

Johnson & Johnson's consistent growth is demonstrated in Figure 8–3 for the years 1999 through 2009. The graph shows both domestic and international sales. International sales account for approximately 50 percent of Johnson & Johnson's

FIGURE 8-3 U.S. and International Sales for 10 Years

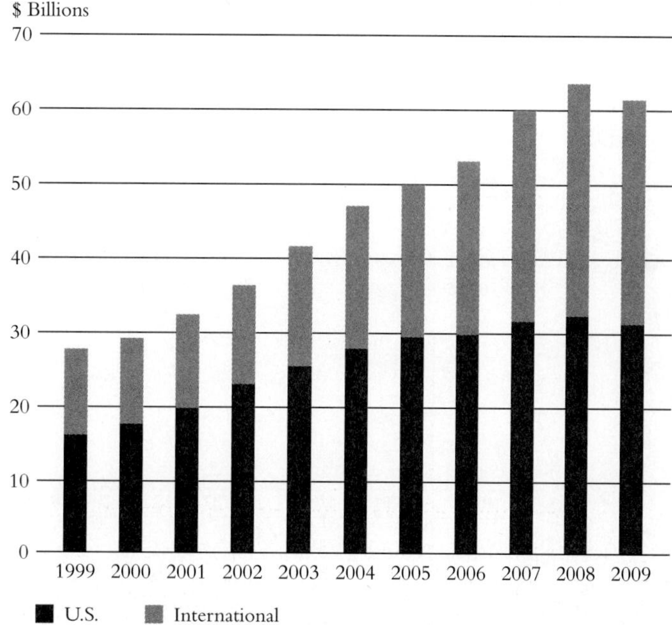

The five-year compound annual growth rates for worldwide, U.S., and international sales were 5.5%, 2.2%, and 9.6%, respectively. The 10-year compound annual growth rates for worldwide, U.S., and international sales were 8.5%, 7.1%, and 10.1%, respectively.

Source: *Johnson & Johnson's Annual Report, 2009*, p. 27.

revenues. The worldwide recession of 2008–2009 broke a nine-year string of improved sales both in the U.S. and abroad.

Because J&J is an international company, it may be affected by political and economic events abroad. Foreign price controls on pharmaceuticals are common. Earnings are affected by currency exchange rates and the fact that poor countries in the Third World are clamoring for drugs they can't afford. In 2004 Johnson & Johnson gave the rights to its very promising AIDS drug to a nonprofit medical foundation to develop, test, and if successful, distribute to countries in Africa. Johnson & Johnson retained the rights to sell the drug in the developed world.

For now we have just compared Johnson & Johnson to four competitors looking at ratios for a one-year period. Long-term trend analysis is also important because one year of data doesn't really tell an analyst much about the direction of the company's performance. Trend analysis can focus on increasing or decreasing performance as well as the volatility of the results.

COMPARING LONG-TERM TRENDS

Over the course of the business cycle, sales and profitability may expand and contract, and ratio analysis for any one year may not present an accurate picture of the firm. Therefore, we look at **trend analysis** of performance over a number of years to examine long-term performance. Depending on the type of business, an analyst might look at as many as ten years of data so that the analysis goes through at least one business cycle.

Table 8–6 presents the 10-year summary of selected financial data for Johnson & Johnson. Starting at the top, we can see that both domestic and international sales have been growing over the 10-year period, but that sales stagnated in 2008 and 2009 because of the worldwide recession. Research and development expense, which some feel is the lifeblood of the pharmaceutical industry, continued to grow until 2008 and 2009, when it appears that Johnson & Johnson cut back to help minimize expenses and keep earnings growing. Just eyeballing the research

TABLE 8-6 Summary of Operations and Statistical Data 1999-2009

Johnson & Johnson and Subsidiaries
(dollars in millions except per share figures)

	2009	2008	2007	2006	2005	2004	2003	2002	2001	2000	1999
Sales to customer—U.S.	$30,889	32,309	32,444	29,775	28,377	27,770	25,274	22,455	19,825	17,316	15,532
Sales to customer—International	31,008	31,438	28,651	23,549	22,137	19,578	16,588	13,843	12,492	11,856	11,825
Total Sales	**61,897**	**63,747**	**61,095**	**53,324**	**50,514**	**47,348**	**41,862**	**36,298**	**32,317**	**29,172**	**27,357**
Cost of products sold	18,447	18,511	17,751	15,057	14,010	13,474	12,231	10,498	9,622	8,987	8,559
Selling, marketing and administrative expenses	19,801	21,490	20,451	17,433	17,211	16,174	14,463	12,520	11,510	10,675	10,182
Research expense	6,986	7,577	7,680	7,125	6,462	5,344	4,834	4,094	3,704	3,186	2,821
Purchased in-process research and development	—	181	807	559	362	18	918	189	105	66	—
Interest income	(90)	(361)	(452)	(829)	(487)	(195)	(177)	(256)	(456)	(429)	(266)
Interest expense, net of portion capitalized	451	435	296	63	54	187	207	160	153	204	255
Other (income) expense, net	(526)	(1,015)	534	(671)	(214)	15	(385)	294	185	(94)	119
Restructuring	1,073	—	745	—	—	—	—	—	—	—	—
	46,142	46,818	47,812	38,737	37,398	35,017	32,091	27,499	24,823	22,595	21,670
Earnings before provision for taxes on income	15,755	16,929	13,283	14,587	13,116	12,331	9,771	8,799	7,494	6,577	5,687
Provision for taxes on income	3,489	3,980	2,707	3,534	3,056	4,151	2,923	2,522	2,089	1,813	1,554
Net Earnings	**12,266**	**12,949**	**10,576**	**11,053**	**10,060**	**8,180**	**6,848**	**6,277**	**5,405**	**4,764**	**4,133**
Percent of sales to customers	19.8	20.3	17.3	20.7	19.9	17.3	16.4	17.3	16.7	16.3	15.1
Diluted net earnings per share of common stock	$ 4.40	4.57	3.63	3.73	3.35	2.74	2.29	2.06	1.75	1.55	1.34
Percent return on average shareholder's equity	26.4	30.2	25.6	28.3	28.2	27.3	27.1	26.4	24.0	25.3	26.0
Percent Increase (Decrease) Over Previous Year:											
Sales to customers	(2.9)	4.3	14.6	5.6	6.7	13.1	15.3	12.3	10.8	6.6	14.9
Diluted net earnings per share	(3.7)	25.9	(2.7)	11.3	22.3	19.7	11.2	17.7	12.9	15.7	34.0
Supplementary Expense Data:											
Cost of materials and services[a]	$27,651	29,346	27,967	22,912	22,328	21,053	18,568	16,540	15,333	14,113	13,922
Total employment costs	14,587	14,523	14,571	13,444	12,364	11,581	10,542	8,942	8,153	7,376	6,727
Depreciation and amortization	2,774	2,832	2,777	2,177	2,093	2,124	1,869	1,662	1,605	1,592	1,510
Maintenance and repairs[b]	567	583	483	506	510	462	395	360	372	327	322
Total tax expense[c]	5,052	5,558	4,177	4,857	4,285	5,215	3,890	3,325	2,854	2,517	2,221
Supplementary Balance Sheet Data:											
Property, plant and equipment, net	14,759	14,365	14,185	13,044	10,830	10,436	9,846	8,710	7,719	7,409	7,155
Additions to property, plant and equipment	2,365	3,066	2,942	2,666	2,632	2,175	2,262	2,099	1,731	1,689	1,822
Total assets	94,682	84,912	80,954	70,556	58,864	54,039	48,858	40,984	38,771	34,435	31,163
Long-term debt	8,223	8,120	7,074	2,014	2,017	2,565	2,955	2,022	2,217	3,163	3,429
Operating cash flow	16,571	14,972	15,022	14,248	11,799	11,089	10,571	8,135	8,781	6,889	5,913
Common Stock Information											
Dividends paid per share	$ 1.930	1.795	1.620	1.455	1.275	1.095	0.925	0.795	0.700	0.620	0.550
Shareholders' equity per share	$ 18.37	15.35	15.25	13.59	13.01	10.95	9.25	7.79	8.05	6.82	5.73
Market price per share (year-end close)	$ 64.41	58.56	67.38	66.02	60.10	63.42	50.62	53.11	59.86	52.53	46.63
Average shares outstanding (millions)—basic	2,759.5	2,802.5	2,882.9	2,936.4	2,973.9	2,968.4	2,968.1	2,998.3	3,033.8	2,993.5	2,978.2
—diluted	2,789.1	2,835.6	2,910.7	2,961.0	3,002.8	2,992.7	2,995.1	3,049.1	3,089.3	3,075.2	3,090.4
Employees (Thousands)	**115.5**	**118.7**	**119.2**	**122.2**	**115.6**	**109.9**	**110.6**	**108.3**	**101.8**	**100.9**	**99.8**

[a] Net of Interest and other income.

[b] Also include in cost of materials and services category.

[c] Includes taxes on income, payroll, property, and other business taxes.

Source: *Johnson & Johnson Annual Report, 2009,* p. 66.

expenditures compared to total sales, it looks as if J&J spends between 11 and 12 percent of its sales on research and development. The real question for all firms in this industry is whether the expenditures result in new drugs that effectively treat disease and can pass the Federal Drug Administration's tough tests.

In the middle of the page we see a category called "Percent increase (decrease) over previous year." In this category we can look at diluted net earnings per share growth and see that between 2005 and 2009 growth was unpredictable, and through the whole 10-year period it was uneven, rising by as much as 34 percent in 1999 and falling by as much as 3.7 percent in 2009. This is why trend line growth analysis is important. Companies don't grow by equal percentages every year, and if they do, make sure that it is not because earnings are being "managed" to create a smooth path.

At the bottom of Table 8–6, Johnson & Johnson present common stock information. We can see that it has increased its dividend every year since 1999. This provides valuable information to the potential investor. The average stock price has tended to move in fits and starts, and even though earnings per share have increased, the price-earnings ratio has declined, leaving the stock price relatively flat between 2004 and 2009. We can also see that the number of shares outstanding has remained relatively stable, until 2006, when J&J began to buy back shares. When a company repurchases shares, it sends a signal to the market that they don't have a use for their excess cash that will generate a return equal to their return on equity. J&J built up a cash hoard and used it to buy back shares. This also helps increase the earnings per share, thus the EPS growth rate.

If we take a look at selected ratios and data over the last five years compared to competitors, how does Johnson & Johnson look? Figure 8–4 provides some

application example

FIGURE 8-4 Comparative Ratios for Johnson & Johnson and Competitors

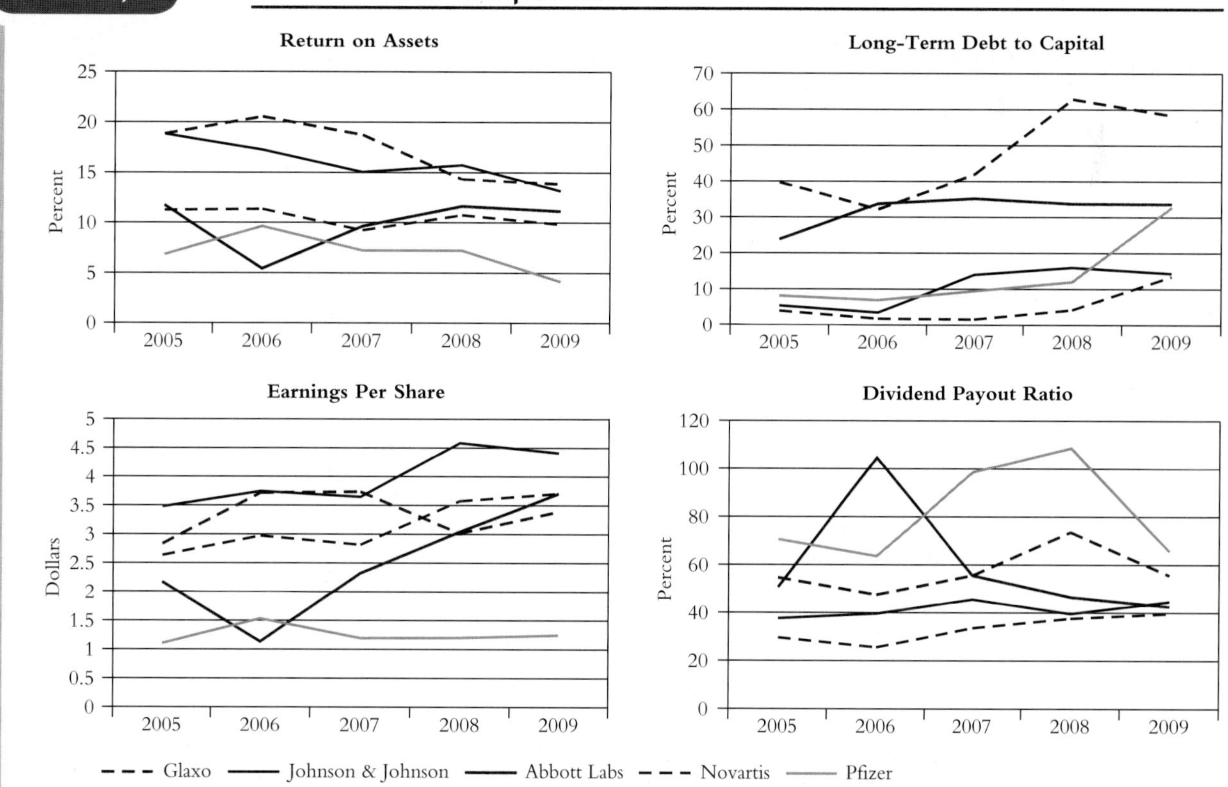

Source: 2009 company annual reports.

partial answers. On a comparative basis, we can see that all the companies had a lower return on assets in 2009 than they did in 2005. For Glaxo and J&J, there has been a steady decline, though they still maintained a slight edge over Abbott Labs and Novartis. Pfizer is struggling.

When we look at long-term debt to capital, we must remember that this ratio looks at long-term debt to long-term capital and ignores short-term debt and other liabilities. It is more of an examination of their capital structure, while total debt to total assets is more comprehensive. Long-term debt to capital does indicate that J&J and Novartis are the least leveraged and that Glaxo is the most leveraged. Abbott Labs has maintained the most stable debt ratio, while Pfizer's long-term debt to capital mushroomed with the purchase of Weyth in 2009.

As far as earnings per share goes, Abbott Labs had the best five-year trend, increasing from \$2.16 to \$3.69 (71%), while Novartis came in second at (41%) and J&J came in third at (27%). Glaxo and Pfizer are relatively flat. Looking at the dividend payout ratio tells a very interesting story about predictability and management's unwillingness to cut dividends when earnings fall. As Pfizer's earnings per share fell, it was reluctant to cut dividends, and it paid out 98 percent and 108 percent of its earnings in 2007 and 2008, respectively. In order to do this, Pfizer had to rely on its cash balances and increased debt to make the payments. This was clearly an unsustainable policy, and in 2009 it cut its dividend. On the other hand, the other four companies have relatively stable policies. Abbott Labs had a bad earnings year in 2006 and its payout ratio ballooned to 104 percent of earnings, but when its earnings popped back up to normal, so did its dividend payout ratio. Even this brief look provides a picture of three strong competitors: Johnson & Johnson, Abbott Labs, and Novartis, with Glaxo and Pfizer lagging behind.

DEFICIENCIES OF FINANCIAL STATEMENTS

Several differences occur between companies and industries, and, at times, inflation has additionally clouded the clarity of accounting statements. Some of the more important difficulties occur in the area of inflation-adjusted accounting statements, inventory valuation, depreciation methods, pension fund liabilities, research and development, deferred taxes, and foreign exchange accounting. We do not have space to cover all of them, but we will touch on the most important ones.

Inflation Effects

While inflation has been extremely mild in the last decade, the student who is preparing for a long-term career in finance should be aware of its potential effects for the future.

Inflation causes phantom sources of profit that may mislead even the most alert analyst. Revenue is almost always stated in current dollars, whereas plant and equipment or inventory may have been purchased at lower price levels. Thus, profit may be more a function of increasing prices than of satisfactory performance.

Distortion of inflation also shows up on the balance sheet since most of the values on the balance sheet are stated on a historical or original-cost basis. This may be particularly troublesome in the case of plant and equipment and inventory, which may now be worth two or three times the original cost or—from a negative viewpoint—may require many times the original cost for replacement.

TABLE 8-7 Comparison of Replacement-Cost Accounting to Historical-Cost Accounting

	10 CHEMICAL COMPANIES		8 DRUG COMPANIES	
	Replacement Cost	Historical Cost	Replacement Cost	Historical Cost
Increase in assets	28.4%	—	15.4%	—
Decrease in net income before taxes	(45.8)	—	(19.3)	—
Return on assets	2.8	6.2%	8.3	11.4%
Return on equity	4.9	13.5	12.8	19.6
Debt-to-assets ratio	34.3	43.8	30.3	35.2
Interest-coverage ratio (times interest earned)	7.1×	8.4×	15.4×	16.7×

Note: Replacement cost is but one form of current cost. Nevertheless, it is widely used as a measure of current cost.

Source: Jeff Garnett and Geoffrey A. Hirt, "Replacement Cost Data: A Study of the Chemical and Drug Industry for Years 1976 through 1978."

The accounting profession has been groping with this problem for decades, and the discussion becomes particularly intense each time inflation rears its ugly head. In October 1979, the Financial Accounting Standards Board (FASB) issued a ruling that required about 1,300 large companies to disclose **inflation-adjusted accounting** data in their annual reports. This information shows the effects of inflation on the financial statements of the firm. The ruling on inflation adjustment was extended for five more years in 1984 but was later made optional. As inflation temporarily slowed, many companies chose not to disclose inflation-adjusted statements in addition to the historical cost statements.

From a study of 10 chemical firms and 8 drug companies using current-cost (replacement-cost) data found in the financial 10–K statements these companies filed with the SEC, it was found that the changes shown in Table 8–7 occurred in their assets, income, and other selected ratios. The impact of these changes is important as an example of the changes that take place on ratio analysis during periods of high inflation.

The comparison of replacement-cost and historical-cost accounting methods in Table 8–7 shows that replacement cost increases assets but at the same time reduces income. This increase in assets lowers the debt-to-assets ratio since debt is a monetary asset that is not revalued because it is paid back in current dollars.

The decreased debt-to-assets ratio would indicate that the financial leverage of the firm decreased, but a look at the interest-coverage ratio tells a different story. Because the interest-coverage ratio measures the operating income available to cover interest expense, the declining income penalizes the ratio, and the firm shows a decreased ability to cover its interest cost.

As long as prices continue to rise in an inflationary environment, profits appear to feed on themselves. The main objection is that when prices do level off, management and unsuspecting stockholders have a rude awakening as expensive inventory is charged against softening retail prices. A 15 to 20 percent growth rate in earnings may be little more than an "inflationary illusion." Industries most sensitive to inflation-induced profits are those with cyclical products, such as lumber, copper, rubber, and food products, as well as those in which inventory is a significant percentage of sales and profits. Reported profits for the lumber industry have been influenced as much as 50 percent by inventory pricing, and profits of a number of other industries have been influenced by 15 to 20 percent.

Inventory Valuation

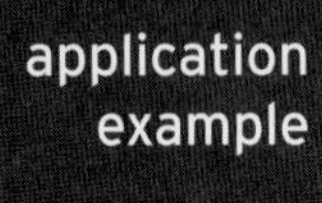

The income statement can show considerable differences in earnings, depending on the method of inventory valuation. The two basic methods are FIFO (first-in, first-out) and LIFO (last-in, first-out). In an inflationary economy, a firm could be reporting increased profits even though no actual increase in physical output occurred. The example of the Rhoades Company will illustrate this point. We first observe its income statement for 2010 in Table 8–8. It sold 1,000 units for $20,000 and shows earnings after taxes of $4,200 and an operating margin and after-tax margin of 35 percent and 21 percent, respectively.

Assume that in 2011 the number of units sold remains constant at 1,000 units. However, inflation causes a 10 percent increase in price, from $20 to $22 per unit as shown in Table 8–9. Total sales will go up to $22,000, but with no actual increase in physical

TABLE 8-8 Rhoades Corporation Income Statement

RHOADES CORPORATION
First-Year Income Statement
Net Income for 2010

Sales	$20,000	(1,000 units at $20)
Cost of goods sold	10,000	(1,000 units at $10)
Gross profit	10,000	
Selling and administrative expense	2,000	
Depreciation	1,000	
Operating profit	7,000	
Taxes (40 percent)	2,800	
Earnings after taxes	$ 4,200	
Operating margin	$7,000/$20,000 = 35%	
After-tax margin	$4,200/$20,000 = 21%	

TABLE 8-9 Rhoades Corporation Income Statement

RHOADES CORPORATION
Second-Year Income Statement Using FIFO and LIFO
Net Income for 2011

	FIFO		LIFO	
Sales	$22,000	(1,000 at $22)	$22,000	(1,000 at $22)
Cost of goods sold	10,000	(1,000 at $10)	11,000	(1,000 at $11)
Gross profit	12,000	11,000		
Selling and administrative expense	2,200	(10% of sales)	2,200	(10% of sales)
Depreciation	1,000		1,000	
Operating profit	8,800		7,800	
Taxes (40 percent)	3,520		3,120	
Earnings after taxes	$ 5,280		$ 4,680	
Operating margin	$8,800/$22,000 = 40%		$7,800/$22,000 = 35.4%	
After-tax margin	$5,280/$22,000 = 24%		$4,680/$22,000 = 21.2%	

volume. Further assume the firm uses FIFO inventory pricing so that inventory first purchased will be written off against current sales. We will assume that 1,000 units of 2010 inventory at a cost of $10 per unit are written off against 2011 sales revenue. If Rhoades used LIFO inventory and if the cost of goods sold went up 10 percent also, to $11 per unit, income will be less than under FIFO. Table 8–9 shows the 2005 income statement of Rhoades under both inventory methods.

The table demonstrates the difference between FIFO and LIFO. Under FIFO, Rhoades Corporation shows higher profit margins and more income even though no physical increase in sales occurs. This is because FIFO costing lags behind current prices, and the company generates "phantom profits" due to gains on inventory. Unfortunately, this inventory will need to be replaced next period at higher costs. When and if prices turn lower in a recessionary environment, FIFO will have the opposite effect and drag down earnings. LIFO inventory costing, on the other hand, relates current costs to current prices, and although profits rise in dollar terms from 2007, the margins stay basically the same. The only problem with LIFO inventory accounting is that low-cost layers of inventory build up on the balance sheet of the company and understate inventory. This will cause inventory turnover to appear higher than under FIFO.

While many companies shifted to LIFO accounting in the past, FIFO inventory valuation still exists in some industries, and the analyst must be alert to the consequences of both methods.

Extraordinary Gains and Losses

Extraordinary gains and losses may occur from the sale of corporate fixed assets, lawsuits, or similar events that would not be expected to occur often, if ever, again. Some analysts argue that such extraordinary events should be included in computing the current income of the firm, while others would leave them off when assessing operating performance. The choice can have a big impact on ratios that rely on earnings or earnings per share. Extraordinary gains can inflate returns and lower payout ratios if they are included in earnings. The analyst concerned about forecasting should include only those earnings from continuing operations; otherwise, the forecast will be seriously off its mark. Unfortunately, there is some inconsistency in the manner in which nonrecurring losses are treated despite determined attempts by the accounting profession to ensure uniformity.

Pension Fund Liabilities

One area of increasing concern among financial analysts is the unfunded liabilities of corporate pension funds. These funds eventually will have to pay workers their retirement income from the pension fund earnings and assets. If the money is not available from the pension fund, the company is liable to make the payments. These unfunded pensions may have to come out of earnings in future years, which would penalize shareholders and limit the corporation's ability to reinvest in new assets.

Foreign Exchange Transactions

Foreign currency fluctuations have a major impact on the earnings of those companies heavily involved in international trade. The drug industry is significantly affected, as well as firms like Coca-Cola, with more than 70 percent of operating income coming from foreign operations. Coca-Cola is a prime example of a company

the real world of investing

"WHEN DOES AGGRESSIVE ACCOUNTING CROSS THE LINE?"

Aggressive accounting and financial manipulation are still too often present even after recent accounting reforms.

In a survey of chief financial officers by *CFO Magazine* in 2004, the respondents indicated the factors that influenced them the most to engage in questionable activities were:*

Personal greed	79%
Weak boards of directors	58
Overbearing CEOs	45
Unrealistic shareholder expectations	34
Poor internal controls	33
Unrealistic budget targets	29

One of the most frowned-upon practices is the backdating of stock options. Normally options that are granted to high-ranking executives are at the price of the stock on the date the option is granted. Thus an option to purchase 50,000 shares may be granted to a CEO at $20 per share if that is the stock price on the day the option grant is approved by the board. But in some cases the option price mysteriously turns out to be backdated to an earlier date when the stock price was lower. Even though the stock may have been $20 on the date of the option grant (let's say October 1, 2006), the option is backdated to August 10 of the same year when the stock price was $15. Thus, this is actually a $5 gift to the CEO or $250,000 in immediate extra compensation (50,000 shares included in the option times $5).

Although backdating is not illegal as such, it takes on an extremely negative connotation when not properly reported as executive compensation and may call for SEC sanctions for improper accounting practices.

One firm that was called out on such charges in 2006 was UnitedHealth Group (UNH). Before this activity was exposed, UNH was ranked by *Forbes* magazine as one of America's "Most Admired Companies." The medical insurer had over 70 million customers and over $70 billion in revenue for 2006. Not only are the numbers impressive, but *Fortune* magazine further ranked UnitedHealth Group as the third most innovative company in any industry, trailing only Apple Computer and Google.

In October 2006, the board of directors of UnitedHealth Group and federal regulators were reviewing the past activity of option backdating that extended back to 1994. The company needed to restate prior income by taking a $286 million hit. Among the largest beneficiaries of backdated options was the CEO, Dr. William W. McGuire, who was forced to resign.

* Data from "It's Better (and worse) than you think," by Don Durfee, *CFO Magazine*, May 3, 2004.

affected by swings in the currency markets. For example, when the dollar declines relative to foreign currencies as it did between 2001 and 2004, earnings from foreign subsidiaries get translated into more U.S. dollars and help the earnings of U.S. companies such as Coca-Cola. The opposite is true when the dollar increases in value. Coca-Cola's foreign exchange currency transactions had a negative effect of $148 million in 2005. Because Coca-Cola is available in almost 200 countries, the firm has a diversification effect with some currencies rising and others falling. However, a major change in a given part of the world could cause this diversification effect to lose its impact.

Other Distortions

Other problems exist in accounting statements and methods of reporting earnings. A mention of some of them might provide you with areas that require further investigation. Additional areas for detective work are in accounting methods for the following: off balance sheet financing (e.g., Enron), research and development expenditures, deferred taxes, tax credits, merger accounting, intangible drilling and development costs, and percentage depletion allowances. As you can see, many issues cause analysts to dig further and to be cautious about accepting bottom-line earnings per share.

exploring the web

Web Address	Comments
www.zacks.com	**Provides detailed company financial information and ratios—mostly free**
www.investor.reuters.com	**Provides detailed financial information, including ratios and statements**
www.morningstar.com	**Provides financial information and ratios for free, some information fee-based**
www.investors.com	**From *Investor's Business Daily,* provides investment related charts and tools**
www.valueline.com	**A Web version of a print information source**
www.investopedia.com	**Provides tutorials on financial ratios**
www.ventureline.com	**Allows access to financial ratios and other analytics, requires registration for access, and is fee-based**

SUMMARY

Chapter 8 presents the basics of accounting statements and ratio analysis. After going through an income statement, a balance sheet, and the statement of cash flows, ratios are presented that help tie together these statements.

Ratio analysis is used to evaluate the operating performance and capital structure of a firm. Ratios will not help to find a gold mine, but they can help to avoid buying sick companies. Using ratio analysis, a brief description of two bankruptcy studies was given that emphasized the ability of ratios to spot troubled firms with a potential for failure.

Twenty ratios were classified into six categories that measured profitability, asset utilization, liquidity, debt utilization, relative prices, and taxes and dividend policy. Johnson & Johnson was used as an example as we computed each ratio. The DuPont method was presented to demonstrate the relationship between assets, sales, income, and debt for creating returns on assets and equity.

Ratios are best used when compared with industry norms, company trends, and economic and industry cycles. It is becoming more difficult to use ratio analysis on an industry basis as firms become more integrated and diversified into several industries.

Finally, the deficiencies of financial statements were discussed. The effect on ratios was examined for replacement cost versus historical cost data. Other distortions were discussed such as extraordinary gains and losses and pension fund liabilities.

Financial analysis is a science as well as an art, and experience certainly sharpens the skills. It would be unrealistic for someone to pick up all the complex relationships involved in ratio analysis immediately. This is why analysts are assigned industries they learn inside and out. After much practice, the analytical work is easier, and the true picture of financial performance becomes focused.

KEY WORDS AND CONCEPTS

asset-utilization ratios 210
balance sheet 201
debt-utilization ratios 211
dividend-payout ratio 214
dividend yield 214
extraordinary gains and losses 223
forward price-earnings ratio 213
income statement 200
inflation-adjusted accounting 221
liquidity ratios 211
price ratios 212
profitability ratios 208
statement of cash flows 203
trailing price-earnings ratio 213
trend analysis 217

DISCUSSION QUESTIONS

1. Does a balance sheet that is dated year-end 2007 reflect only transactions for that year?
2. Explain why the statement of cash flows is particularly relevant in light of the fact that the accrual method of accounting is used in the income statement and balance sheet.
3. Can we automatically assume that a firm that has an operating loss on the income statement has reduced the cash flows for the firm during the period?
4. What ratios are likely to be of greatest interest to the banker or trade creditor? To the bondholder?
5. If a firm's operating margin and after-tax margin are almost the same (an unusual case), what can we say about the firm?
6. Comment on the heavy capital goods industry and the food-processing industry in terms of performance under the DuPont system of analysis.
7. In computing return on assets, how does the age of the assets influence the interpretation of the values?
8. If a firm's return on equity is substantially higher than the firm's return on assets, what can the analyst infer about the firm?
9. How do the asset-utilization ratios relate to the liquidity ratios?
10. Can public utility firms better justify the use of high debt than firms in the automobile or airline industry? Comment.
11. Why will the fixed-charge-coverage ratio always be equal to or *less* than times interest earned?
12. What might a high dividend-payout ratio suggest to an analyst about a company's growth prospects?
13. Explain the probable impact of replacement-cost accounting on the ratios of return on assets, debt to total assets, and times interest earned for a firm that has substantial old fixed assets.

PRACTICE PROBLEMS AND SOLUTIONS

DuPont analysis

1. Given the following financial data: Net income/Sales = 4 percent; Sales/Total assets = 2.8 times; Debt/Total assets = 40 percent; compute:
   a. Return on assets.
   b. Return on equity.
   c. If the Debt/Total assets ratio were 70 percent, what would Return on equity be?

2. Assume the following financial data:

Short-term assets	$200,000
Long-term assets	300,000
Total assets	$500,000
Short-term debt	$100,000
Long-term debt	208,000
Total liabilities	308,000
Common stock	80,000
Retained earnings	112,000
Total stockholders' equity	$192,000
Total liabilities and stockholders' equity	$500,000
Total earnings (after tax)	$ 36,000
Dividends per share	$ 1.00
Stock price	$ 48.00
Shares outstanding	15,000

a. Compute the P/E ratio (stock price to earnings per share).
b. Compute the dividend yield.
c. Compute the payout ratio.
d. Compute the book value per share (note that book value equals stockholders' equity).
e. Compute the ratio of stock price to book value per share.

Solutions

1. *a.* $$\text{Return on assets} = \frac{\text{Net income}}{\text{Sales}} \times \frac{\text{Sales}}{\text{Total assets}}$$

$$11.2\% = 4\% \times 2.8$$

b. $$\text{Return on equity} = \frac{\text{Return on Assets}}{(1 - \text{Debt/Total assets})}$$

$$18.67\% = \frac{11.2\%}{(1 - .40)}$$

c. $$37.33\% = \frac{11.2\%}{(1 - .70)}$$

2. *a.* $$\text{P/E ratio} = \frac{\text{Price}}{\text{EPS}}$$

$$\text{EPS} = \frac{\text{Earnings}}{\text{Shares}} = \frac{\$36{,}000}{15{,}000} = \$2.40$$

$$\text{P/E} = \frac{\$48}{\$2.40} = 20\times$$

b. $$\text{Dividend yield} = \frac{\text{Dividends per share}}{\text{Common stock price}}$$

$$= \frac{\$1.00}{\$48} = 2.08\%$$

c. $$\text{Payout ratio} = \frac{\text{Dividends per share}}{\text{Earnings per share}}$$

$$= \frac{\$1.00}{\$2.40} = 41.67\%$$

d. Book value per share $= \dfrac{\text{Stockholders' equity}}{\text{Shares}}$

$$= \frac{\$192{,}000}{15{,}000}$$

$$= \$12.80$$

e. Stock price to book value $= \dfrac{\$48}{\$12.80} = 3.75\times$

PROBLEMS

Income statement

1. Singular Corp. has the following income statement data:

	2010	2011
Sales	\$500,000	\$700,000
Gross profit	161,300	205,000
Selling and administrative expense	45,200	74,300
Interest expense	15,200	29,100
Net income (after these and other expenses)	44,100	45,600

a. Compute the ratio of each of the last four items to sales for 2010 and 2011.
b. Based on your calculations, is the company improving or declining in its performance?

Balance sheet

2. A company has \$200,000 in inventory, which represents 20 percent of current assets. Current assets represent 50 percent of total assets. Total debt represents 30 percent of total assets. What is the stockholders' equity?

DuPont analysis

3. Given the following financial data: Net income/Sales = 4 percent; Sales/Total assets = 3.5 times; Debt/Total assets = 60 percent; compute:
a. Return on assets.
b. Return on equity.

DuPont analysis

4. Explain why in problem 3 return on equity was so much higher than return on assets.

DuPont analysis

5. A firm has assets of \$1,800,000 and turns over its assets 2.5 times per year. Return on assets is 20 percent. What is its profit margin (return on sales)?

DuPont analysis

6. A firm has assets of \$1,800,000 and turns over its assets 1.5 times per year. Return on assets is 25 percent. What is its profit margin (return on sales)?

DuPont analysis

7. A firm has a return on assets of 12 percent and a return on equity of 18 percent. What is the debt-to-total assets ratio?

DuPont analysis

8. In the year 2010, the average firm in the S&P 500 Index had a total market value of fives times stockholders' equity (book value). Assume a firm had total assets of \$10 million, total debt of \$6 million, and net income of \$600,000.
a. What is the percent return on equity?
b. What is the percent return on total market value? Does this appear to be an adequate return on the actual market value of the firm?

General ratio analysis

9. A firm has the following financial data:

Current assets	\$600,000
Fixed assets	400,000
Current liabilities	300,000
Inventory	200,000

If inventory increases by $100,000, what will be the impact on the current ratio, the quick ratio, and the net-working-capital-to-total-assets ratio? Show the ratios before and after the changes.

General ratio analysis

10. Given the following financial data, compute:
a. Return on equity.
b. Quick ratio.
c. Long-term debt to equity.
d. Fixed-charge coverage.

Assets:	
Cash	$ 2,500
Accounts receivable	3,000
Inventory	6,500
Fixed assets	8,000
Total assets	$20,000
Liabilities and stockholders' equity:	
Short-term debt	$ 3,000
Long-term debt	2,000
Stockholders' equity	15,000
Total liabilities and stockholders' equity	$20,000
Income before fixed charges and taxes	$ 4,400
Interest payments	800
Lease payment	400
Taxes (35 percent tax rate)	1,120
Net income (after taxes)	$ 2,080

Coverage of sinking fund

11. Assume in part *d* of problem 10 that the firm had a sinking fund payment obligation of $200. How much before-tax income is required to cover the sinking-fund obligation? Would lower tax rates increase or decrease the before-tax income required to cover the sinking fund?

Return on equity

12. In problem 10, if total debt were increased to 50 percent of assets and interest payments went up by $300, what would be the new value for return on equity?

Stock price ratios

13. Assume the following financial data:

Short-term assets	$300,000
Long-term assets	500,000
Total assets	$800,000
Short-term debt	$200,000
Long-term debt	168,000
Total liabilities	368,000
Common stock	200,000
Retained earnings	232,000
Total stockholders' equity	432,000
Total liabilities and stockholders' equity	$800,000
Total earnings (after-tax)	$ 72,000
Dividends per share	$ 1.44
Stock price	$ 45
Shares outstanding	24,000

a. Compute the P/E ratio (stock price to earnings per share).
b. Compute the book value per share (note that book value equals stockholders' equity).
c. Compute the ratio of stock price to book value per share.
d. Compute the dividend yield.
e. Compute the payout ratio.

Tax considerations and financial analysis

14. Referring to problem 13:
a. Compute after-tax return on equity.
b. If the tax rate were 40 percent, what could you infer the value of before-tax income was?
c. Now assume the same before-tax income computed in part *b*, but a tax rate of 25 percent; recompute after-tax return on equity (using the simplifying assumption that equity remains constant).
d. Assume the taxes in part *c* were reduced largely as a result of one-time nonrecurring tax credits. Would you expect the stock value to go up substantially as a result of the higher return on equity?

Divisional analysis

15. The Multi-Corporation has three different operating divisions. Financial information for each is as follows:

	Clothing	Appliances	Sporting Goods
Sales.	$3,000,000	$15,000,000	$25,000,000
Operating income	330,000	1,250,000	3,200,000
Net income (A/T)	135,000	870,000	1,400,000
Assets.	1,200,000	10,000,000	8,000,000

a. Which division provides the highest operating margin?
b. Which division provides the lowest after-tax profit margin?
c. Which division has the lowest after-tax return on assets?
d. Compute net income (after-tax) to sales for the entire corporation.
e. Compute net income (after-tax) to assets for the entire corporation.
f. The vice president of finance suggests the assets in the Appliances division be sold off for $10 million and redeployed in Sporting Goods. The new $10 million in Sporting Goods will produce the same after-tax return on assets as the current $8 million in that division. Recompute net income to total assets for the entire corporation assuming the above suggested change.
g. Explain why Sporting Goods, which has a lower return on sales than Appliances, has such a positive effect on return on assets.

Approaches to security evaluation

16. Security Analyst A thinks the Collins Corporation is worth 14 times current earnings. Security Analyst B has a different approach. He assumes that 45 percent of earnings (per share) will be paid out in dividends and the stock should provide a 4 percent current dividend yield. Assume total earnings are $12 million and that 5 million shares are outstanding.
a. Compute the value of the stock based on Security Analyst A's approach.
b. Compute the value of the stock based on Security Analyst B's approach.
c. Security Analyst C uses the constant dividend valuation model approach presented in Chapter 7 as Formula 7–5 on page 168. She uses Security Analyst B's assumption about dividends (per share) and assigns a growth rate, *g*, of 9 percent and a required rate of return (K_e) of 12 percent. Is her value higher or lower than that of the other security analysts?

Combining DuPont analysis with P/E ratios

17. Sarah Bailey is analyzing two stocks in the semiconductor industry. It is her intention to assign a P/E of 16 to the average firm in the industry. However, she will assign a 20 percent premium to the P/E of a company that uses conservative financing in its capital structure. This is because of the highly cyclical nature of the industry.

Two firms in the industry have the following financial data:

	Palo Alto Semiconductors	Burr Ridge Semiconductors
Net income/Sales	5.0%	4.2%
Sales/Total assets	2.1×	3.5×
Debt/Total assets	60%	30%
Earnings	$40 million	$15 million
Shares	$16 million	$6.25 million

a. Compute return on stockholders' equity for each firm. Use the DuPont method of analysis. Which is higher?
b. Compute earnings per share for each company. Which is higher?
c. Applying the 20 percent premium to the P/E ratio of the firm with the more conservative financial structure and the industry P/E ratio to the other firm, which firm has the higher stock price valuation?

CRITICAL THOUGHT CASE–FOCUS ON ETHICS

Barry Minkow founded ZZZZ Best Co., a carpet-cleaning firm, when he was 15 years old. He ran the business from his family's garage in Reseda, California. The company became one of the biggest carpet-cleaning firms in California, and Minkow was a millionaire by age 18. Minkow took his company public by selling its stock when he was 21, and his personal worth was estimated at close to $10 million. At that time ZZZZ Best ("Zee Best") had 1,300 employees and 1987 sales of $4.8 million. Minkow boldly predicted that 1988 revenues would exceed $50 million.

In July 1990, ZZZZ Best management filed for bankruptcy protection and sued Minkow for misappropriating $21 million in company funds. In addition, several customers accused ZZZZ Best of overcharging them in a credit card scam. Minkow publicly admitted the overcharges but blamed them on subcontractors and employees. He also said he had fired those responsible and had personally repaid the charges.

The Securities and Exchange Commission (SEC) and other law enforcement agencies began investigating Minkow and his company. It became apparent that ZZZZ Best was built on a foundation of lies, dishonesty, and inconsistent accounting practices. The company had submitted phony credit card charges and had issued press releases claiming millions of dollars in bogus contracts, sending the price of the company's stock even higher. The SEC investigated other charges, including possible phony receivables, bogus financial accounting statements, organized crime connections, and securities law violations by Minkow and other executives. The SEC placed an independent trustee in charge of the company until its accounting records could be examined.

The Los Angeles Police Department investigated charges that ZZZZ Best was a money-laundering operation for organized crime. The investigation linked Minkow and ZZZZ Best with drug dealings and organized crime members.

These allegations ultimately led Minkow to resign from ZZZZ Best for "health reasons." But his resignation was not the end of his troubles. ZZZZ Best's new management sued Minkow for embezzling $3 million of the company's funds for his personal use and misappropriating $18 million to perform fictitious insurance restoration work. The suit charged that Minkow actually diverted this money to an associate's refurbishing business, which was part of an elaborate scheme designed to allow Minkow to take corporate funds for his own and others' personal use. According to the suit, these discrepancies in the company's accounting practices were the reasons behind the bankruptcy filing. As a result ZZZZ Best's accounting firm quit.

Questions

1. Given the extent of fraud in this case, should ZZZZ Best's accounting firm be held responsible for not discovering the fraudulent activities?
2. What are the responsibilities of the broker and financial analyst in recommending the company to investors? To what extent are they responsible for their investment recommendations?

WEB EXERCISE

We will look at Eli Lilly's financial ratios. Go to **www.lilly.com**.

1. Click on "Investors" along the upper-right part of the screen.
2. Then click on "Financial Information."
3. Next select "Key Ratios."
4. Assume Lilly had the following targets for each of the financial ratios listed below. Write a one-sentence description (for each) of how the firm did against the target and the implications.
   a. Yield 3%
   Does the comparison enhance or restrict Lilly's growth potential?
   b. Total debt/equity 40%
   Does the comparison enhance or restrict Lilly's return on equity?
   c. Price/book 7×
   Does the comparison indicate that Lilly is likely to be overpriced or underpriced?
   d. Gross margin 81%
   Profit margin 22.5%
   How is Lilly doing in terms of its profitability ratios?
   e. Quick ratio .70
   Current ratio 1.75
   In comparing these two ratios to the targets, what might you infer about the level of inventory Lilly carries?

Note: From time to time, companies redesign their Web sites, and occasionally a topic we have listed may have been deleted, updated, or moved into a different location.

CFA MATERIAL

The following material contains sample questions and solutions from a prior Level I CFA exam. While the terminology is slightly different from that in this text, you can still view the skills necessary for the CFA exam.

CFA Exam Question

Question 1 is composed of two parts, for a total of 15 minutes.

1. As shown in Table I, Tennant's operating results have been less favorable during the 1980s than the 1970s based on three representative years, 1975, 1981, and 1987. To develop an explanation, you decide to examine Tennant's

operating history employing the industrial life-cycle model, which recognizes four stages as follows:

I. Early development. II. Rapid expansion. III. Mature growth.

TABLE I Tennant Company

Selected Historic Operating and Balance Sheet Data
As of December 31, 1975, 1981, and 1987
(in thousands)

	1975	1981	1987
Net sales	$47,909	$109,333	$166,924
Cost of goods sold	27,395	62,373	95,015
Gross profits	20,514	46,960	71,909
Selling, general, and administrative expenses	11,895	29,649	54,151
Earnings before interest and taxes	8,619	17,311	17,758
Interest on long-term debt	0	53	248
Pretax income	8,619	17,258	17,510
Income taxes	4,190	7,655	7,692
After-tax income	$ 4,429	$ 9,603	$ 9,818
Total assets	$33,848	$ 63,555	$106,098
Total common stockholders' equity	25,722	46,593	69,516
Long-term debt	6	532	2,480
Total common shares outstanding	5,654	5,402	5,320
Earnings per share	$ 0.78	$ 1.78	$ 1.85
Dividends per share	0.28	0.72	0.96
Book value per share	4.55	8.63	13.07

IV. Stabilization or decline.

a. Describe the behavior of revenues, profit margins, and total profits as a company passes through *each* of the *four* stages of the industrial life cycle.

b. Using 1975, 1981, and 1987 results as representative, discuss Tennant's operating record from 1975 through 1987 in terms of the industrial life-cycle record. (*15 minutes*)

Solution: Question 1—Morning Section (I–88) (15 points)

a. During the early development stage, revenue growth is rapid. However, profit margins are negative until revenues reach a critical mass. From that point forward, rapidly improving margins combine with continued strong revenue growth to create extremely rapid earnings progress.

Profit margins continue to expand during the rapid expansion phase but level out during the mature growth phase. Despite gradual tapering of profit margins, earnings continue to rise during the mature growth phase due to continuing revenue growth. However, earnings progress is significantly slower than during the rapid expansion phase.

The final stage of earnings stabilization or decline is characterized by a continuing moderation in the rate of sales growth and deteriorating profit margins. In the extreme, declining revenues in combination with decreasing profit margins lead to significant earnings declines.

b. Tennant appeared to be in the rapid expansion to the mature growth stage between 1975 and 1981. Although pretax margins weakened, the company was able to double pretax earnings, while sales revenues increased even more rapidly. However, a sharp change occurred after 1981. Sales growth moderated, and profit margins declined sharply. On this basis, Tennant clearly entered the mature growth stage between 1981 and 1987. Based on profit trends, it could be argued that the company had progressed to Stage IV, stabilization and decline. However, a continuation of reasonably strong revenue growth suggests this is not the case.

(Good answers to this question will recognize that the life cycle of a corporation is identified primarily by trends in revenue growth and profit margins. An ideal answer might include simple calculations along the line shown below.)

	1975	1981	1987
Sales	$47,909	$109,333	$166,924
Percent change during prior 6 years	N.A.	128.2%	52.7%
Pretax earnings	$ 8,619	$ 17,311	$ 17,758
Percent change during prior 6 years	N.A.	100.8%	2.6%
Pretax margins	18.0%	15.8%	10.6%

Question 2 is composed of two parts, for a total of 25 minutes.

2. The director of research suggests that you use the DuPont model to analyze the components of Tennant's return on equity during 1981 and 1987 to explain the change that has occurred in the company's return on equity. She asks you to work with the five factors listed below.

I. EBIT margin.
II. Asset turnover.
III. Interest burden.
IV. Financial leverage.
V. Tax retention rate.

a. Compute 1981 and 1987 values of *each* of these *five* factors. (*15 minutes*)

b. Identify the individual component that had the greatest influence on the change in return on equity from 1981 and 1987, and briefly explain the possible reasons for the changes in the value of this component between the two years. (*10 minutes*)

Solution: Question 2—Morning Section (I–88) (25 points)

a.

Tennant Equity Return Components	Value 1981	1987
I. EBIT margins	15.8%	10.6%
II. Asset turnover	1.72×	1.57×
III. Interest burden	0.1%	0.2%
IV. Financial leverage	1.36×	1.53×
V. Tax retention rate	55.6%	56.1%

b. Increases in financial leverage and the tax retention rate acted to increase return on equity between 1981 and 1987. Declining EBIT margins, a decline in asset turnover, and an increase in interest burden tended to reduce profitability.

The dominant factor was the 33 percent decline in EBIT margins. This is due to the increase in SG&A and Tennant's entering mature growth. Interest burden was a relatively trivial factor, and the tax-retention rate changed only nominally. The decrease in asset turnover and increase in financial leverage were more meaningful but tended to cancel each other.

ISSUES IN EFFICIENT MARKETS

PART 3 [three]

chapter nine

EFFICIENT MARKETS AND ANOMALIES

OBJECTIVES

1. Explain the efficient market hypothesis and the various forms it can take.
2. Relate the efficient market hypothesis to fundamental and technical analyses.
3. Understand the potential for abnormal returns in special investment situations. These are considered to be market anomalies.
4. Explain how abnormal returns might occur in mergers, new public issues, exchange listings, stock repurchases, and other investment opportunities.
5. Be familiar with the latest theories about the relationship of book value to market value, low P/E ratios, and small size to superior market returns.
6. Discuss the problem of distinguishing between superior returns and incorrect measurement of returns.

OUTLINE

EFFICIENT MARKET HYPOTHESIS

In this chapter, we shift our attention from fundamental analysis (discussed in Chapters 5–8) to that of examining market efficiency. We now view any contradictions between the assumptions of fundamental or technical analysis and the findings of the **efficient market hypothesis (EMH)**.

Earlier in the text, we said that an efficient market is one in which new information is very rapidly processed so that securities are properly priced at any given time.[1] An important premise of an efficient market is that a large number of profit-maximizing participants are concerned with the analysis and valuation of securities. This would seem to describe the security market environment in the United States. Any news on IBM, AT&T, an oil embargo, or tax legislation is likely to be absorbed and acted on very rapidly by profit-maximizing individuals. For this reason, the efficient market hypothesis assumes that no stock price can be in disequilibrium or improperly priced for long. There is almost instantaneous adjustment to new information. The EMH applies most directly to large firms trading on the major security exchanges.

The efficient market hypothesis further assumes that information travels in a random, independent fashion and that prices are an unbiased reflection of all currently available information.

More generally, the efficient market hypothesis is stated and tested in three different forms: the weak form, the semistrong form, and the strong form. We shall examine each of these and the related implications for technical and fundamental analysis.

WEAK FORM OF THE EFFICIENT MARKET HYPOTHESIS

The **weak form of the efficient market hypothesis** suggests there is no relationship between past and future prices of securities. They are presumed to be independent over time. Because the efficient market hypothesis maintains that current prices reflect all available information and information travels in a random fashion, it is assumed that there is little or nothing to be gained from studying past stock prices. If the weak form is true, then technical analysis doesn't work. (Technical analysis is presented in Chapter 10.)

The weak form of the efficient market hypothesis has been tested in two different ways—tests of independence and trading rule tests.

Tests of Independence

Tests of independence have examined the degree of correlation between stock prices over time and have found the correlation to be consistently small (between +0.10 and −0.10) and not statistically significant. This indicates that stock price changes are independent.[2] A further test is based on the frequency and extent of runs in stock price data. A run occurs when there is no difference in direction between two or more price changes. An example of a series of data and some runs is presented below:

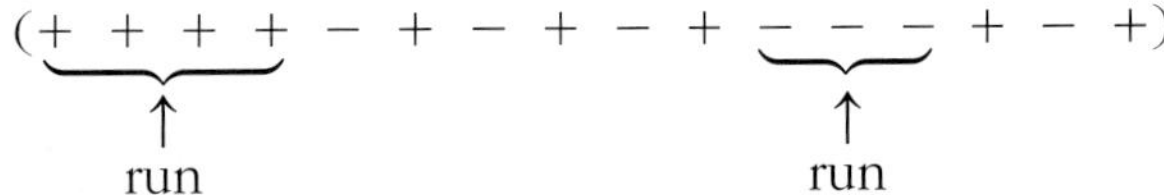

Runs can be expected in any series of data through chance factors, but an independent data series should not produce an unusual amount of runs. Statistical tests have indicated that security prices generally do not produce any more runs than would be expected through the process of random number generation.[3]

[1] A slightly more precise definition is that securities are priced in an unbiased fashion at any given time. Because information is assumed to travel in a random, independent fashion, there is no consistent upside or downside pricing bias mechanism. Although the price adjustment is not always perfect, it is unbiased and cannot be anticipated in advance.

[2] Sidney S. Alexander, "Price Movements in Speculative Markets: Trends or Random Walks," *Industrial Management Review,* May 1961, pp. 26; and Eugene F. Fama, "The Behavior of Stock Market Prices," *Journal of Business,* January 1965, pp. 34–105.

[3] Ibid.

This also tends to indicate that stock price movements are independent over time.[4]

Trading Rule Tests

A second method of testing the weak form of the efficient market hypothesis (that past trends in stock prices are not helpful in predicting the future) is through trading rule tests. Because practicing market technicians maintain that tests of independence (correlation studies and runs) are too rigid to test the assumptions of the weak form of the efficient market hypothesis, additional tests by academic researchers have been developed. These are known as trading rule or filter tests. These tests determine whether a given trading rule based on past price data, volume figures, and so forth can be used to beat a naive buy-and-hold approach. The intent is to simulate the conditions under which a given trading rule is used and then determine whether superior returns were produced after considering transaction costs and the risks involved.

As an example of a trading rule, if a stock moves up 5 percent or more, the rule might be to purchase it. The assumption is that this represents a breakout and should be considered bullish. Similarly, a 5 percent downward movement would be considered bearish and call for a sell strategy (rather than a buy-low/sell-high strategy, this is a follow-the-market-trend strategy). Other trading rule tests might be based on advance-decline patterns, short sales figures, and similar technical patterns. Research results have indicated that in a limited number of cases, trading rules may produce slightly positive returns, but after commission costs are considered, the results are neutral and sometimes negative in comparison to a naive buy-and-hold approach.[5]

Implications for Technical Analysis

The results of the *tests of independence* and *trading rules* would seem to uphold the weak form of the efficient market hypothesis. Security prices do appear to be independent over time or, more specifically, move in the pattern of a random walk.

Some challenge the research on the basis that academic research in this area does not capture the personal judgment an experienced technician brings forward in reading charts. There is also the fact that there are an infinite number of trading rules, and not all of them can or have been tested. Nevertheless, research on the weak form of the EMH still seems to suggest that prices move independently over time, that past trends cannot be used to easily predict the future, and that charting and technical analysis may have limited value.

SEMISTRONG FORM OF THE EFFICIENT MARKET HYPOTHESIS

The **semistrong form of the efficient market hypothesis** maintains that all public information is already impounded into the value of a security, and therefore, one cannot use fundamental analysis to determine whether a stock is undervalued or overvalued. If the semistrong form is true, then fundamental analysis doesn't work.

---

[4] A possible exception to this rule was found in small stocks. A sample study is Jennifer Conrad and Gantam Kaul, "Time Variation and Expected Returns," *Journal of Business,* October 1988, pp. 409–25.

[5] Eugene F. Fama and Marshall Blume, "Filter Rules and Stock Market Trading Profits," *Journal of Business,* supplement, January 1966, pp. 226–41; and George Pinches, "The Random Walk Hypothesis and Technical Analysis," *Financial Analysts Journal,* March–April 1970, pp. 104–10.

Basically, the semistrong form of the efficient market hypothesis supports the notion that there is no learning lag in the distribution of public information. When a company makes an announcement, investors across the country assess the information with equal speed. Also, a major firm listed on the New York Stock Exchange could hardly hope to utilize some questionable accounting practice that deceptively leads to higher reported profits and not expect sophisticated analysts to pick it up. (This may not be equally true for a lesser known firm that trades over-the-counter and enjoys little investor attention.)

Researchers have tested the semistrong form of the EMH by determining whether investors who acted on the basis of newly released public information have been able to enjoy superior returns. If the market is efficient in a semistrong sense, this information is almost immediately impounded in the value of the security, and little or no trading profits would be available. The implications are that one could not garner superior returns by trading on public information about stock splits, earnings reports, or other similar items.

Tests on the semistrong form of the efficient market hypothesis have generally been on the basis of risk-adjusted returns. Thus, the return from a given investment strategy must be compared with the performance of popular market indicators with appropriate risk adjustments. As will be described in Chapter 17, the risk measurement variable is usually the beta. After such adjustments are made, the question becomes: Are there abnormal returns that go beyond explanations associated with risk? If the answer is yes and can be shown to be statistically significant, then the investment strategy may be thought to refute the semistrong form of the efficient market hypothesis. The investor must also cover transaction costs in determining that a given strategy is superior.

For example, assume a stock goes up 15 percent. The security is 20 percent riskier than the market. Further assume the overall market goes up by 10 percent. On a risk-adjusted basis, the security would need to go up in excess of 12 percent (the 10 percent market return $\times$ 1.2 risk factor) to beat the market. In the above case, the stock with the 15 percent gain beat the market on a risk-adjusted basis.

Tests examining the impact of such events as stock splits and stock dividends, corporate announcements, and changes in accounting policy indicate that the market is generally efficient in a semistrong sense. For example, a study by Fama, Fisher, Jensen, and Roll indicated that almost all of the market impact of a stock split occurs before a public announcement.[6] There is little to be gained from acting on the announcement.

According to the semistrong form of the efficient market hypothesis, investors not only digest information very quickly, but they also are able to see through mere changes in accounting information that do not have economic consequences. For example, the switching from accelerated depreciation to straight-line depreciation for financial reporting purposes (but not tax purposes) tends to make earnings per share look higher but provides no economic benefit for the firm. Research studies indicate this has no positive impact on valuation.[7]

Similarly, investors are not deceived by mere accounting changes related to inventory policy, reserve accounts, exchange translations, or other items that appear to have no economic benefits. The corporate treasurer who switches from LIFO to FIFO accounting to make earnings look better in an inflationary economy will probably not see the firm's stock price rise because investors look at the economic consequences of higher taxes associated with the action and disregard the

[6] Eugene F. Fama, Lawrence Fisher, Michael G. Jensen, and Richard Roll, "The Adjustment of Stock Prices to New Information," *International Economic Review,* February 1969, pp. 2–21.

[7] T. Ross Archibald, "Stock Market Reaction to Depreciation Switch-Back," *Accounting Review,* January 1972, pp. 22–30; and Robert S. Kaplan and Richard Roll, "Investor Evaluation of Accounting Information: Some Empirical Evidence," *Journal of Business,* April 1972, pp. 225–57.

mere financial accounting consequences of higher reported profits.[8] Under this circumstance, the effect on stocks may be neutral or negative.

Implications for Fundamental Analysis

www.gm.com

If stock values are already based on the analysis of all available public information, it may be assumed that little is to be gained from additional fundamental analysis. Under the semistrong form of the efficient market hypothesis, if Apple is trading at $350, the assumption is that every shred of public information about Apple has been collected and evaluated by thousands of investors, and they have determined an equilibrium price of $350. The assumption is that anything you read in *The Wall Street Journal* or Standard & Poor's publications has already been considered many times over by others and is currently impounded in the value of the stock. If you were to say you think Apple is really worth $400 because of some great new product, proponents of the semistrong form of the efficient market hypothesis would suggest that your judgment cannot be better than the collective wisdom of the marketplace in which everyone is trying desperately to come out ahead.

Ironically, although many suggest that fundamental analysis may not lead to superior profits in an efficient market environment, it is fundamental analysis itself that makes the market efficient. Because everyone is doing fundamental analysis, there is little in the way of unabsorbed or undigested information. Therefore, one extra person doing fundamental analysis is unlikely to achieve superior insight.

Although the semistrong form of the efficient market hypothesis has research support, there are exceptions. For example, Basu and other more recent studies have found that a portfolio of stocks with low P/E ratios consistently provides better returns than a portfolio of stocks with high P/E ratios on both a non-risk-adjusted and a risk-adjusted basis.[9] Because a P/E ratio is publicly available information that may be used to generate superior returns, this flies in the face of the more common conclusions on the semistrong form of the efficient market hypothesis. Banz's[10] and Reinganum's[11] research indicates that small firms tend to provide higher returns than larger firms even after considering risk. Perhaps fewer institutional investors in smaller firms make for a less-efficient market and superior potential opportunities.

Additional evidence of this nature continues to accumulate, and in a later section covering special situations and anomalies, we present an extended discussion of some of these items and other possible contradictions to the acceptance of the semistrong version of the efficient market hypothesis. We also comment on measurement problems in that section.

Thus, even if the semistrong form of the efficient market hypothesis appears to be generally valid, exceptions can be noted. Also, it is possible that while most analysts may not be able to add additional insight through fundamental analysis, there are exceptions to every rule. It can be assumed that some analysts have such *extraordinary* insight and capability in analyzing publicly available information that they can perceive what others cannot. Also, if you take a very long-term perspective, the fact that a stock's value is in short-term equilibrium may not discourage you from taking a long-term position or attempting to find long-term value.

---

[8] Shyam Sunder, "Stock Price and Risk Related to Accounting Changes in Inventory Valuation," *Accounting Review*, April 1975, pp. 305–15.

[9] S. Basu, "Investment Performance of Common Stocks in Relation to Their Price-Earnings Ratios: A Test of the Efficient Market Hypothesis," *Journal of Finance*, June 1977, pp. 663–82. Also, S. Basu, "The Information Content of Price-Earnings Ratios," *Financial Management*, Summer 1975, pp. 53–64.

[10] Rolf W. Banz, "The Relationship between Returns and Market Value of Common Stocks," *Journal of Financial Economics*, March 1981, pp. 3–18.

[11] Marc R. Reinganum, "Misspecification of Capital Asset Pricing—Empirical Anomalies Based on Earnings Yield and Market Values," *Journal of Financial Economics*, March 1981, pp. 19–46.

STRONG FORM OF THE EFFICIENT MARKET HYPOTHESIS

The **strong form of the efficient market hypothesis** goes beyond the semistrong form to state that stock prices reflect not only all public information but *all* information. Thus, it is hypothesized that insider information is also immediately impounded into the value of a security. In a sense, we go beyond the concept of a market that is highly efficient to one that is perfect.

The assumption is that no group of market participants or investors has monopolistic access to information. If this is the case, then no group of investors can be expected to show superior risk-adjusted returns under any circumstances. Obviously, the Securities and Exchange Commission doesn't think this is true, because insider trading is illegal and punishable by stiff fines and jail time.

Unlike the weak and semistrong forms of the efficient market hypothesis, major test results are not supportive of the strong form of the hypothesis. For example, specialists on security exchanges have been able to earn superior rates of return on invested capital. The book they keep on unfilled limit orders appears to provide monopolistic access to information. An SEC study actually found that specialists typically sell above their latest purchase 83 percent of the time and buy below their latest sell 81 percent of the time.[12] This implies wisdom that greatly exceeds that available in a perfect capital market environment. Likewise, an institutional investor study, also sponsored by the SEC, indicated that specialists' average return on capital was more than 100 percent.[13] While these returns have decreased somewhat recently in a more competitive environment, specialists still appear to outperform the market.

www.sec.com

Another group that appears to use nonpublic information to garner superior returns is corporate insiders. As previously described, an insider is considered to be a corporate officer, member of the board of directors, or substantial stockholder. The SEC requires that insiders report their transactions to that regulatory body. A few weeks after reporting to the SEC, the information becomes public. Researchers can then go back and determine whether investment decisions made by insiders appeared, on balance, to be wise. Did heavy purchases by insiders precede strong upward price movements, and did sell-offs precede poor market performance? The answer appears to be yes. Research studies indicate insiders consistently achieve higher returns than would be expected in a perfect capital market.[14] Although insiders are not allowed to engage in short-term trades (of six months or less) or illegal transactions to generate trading profits, they are allowed to take longer-term positions, which may prove to be profitable. It has even been demonstrated that investors who follow the direction of inside traders after information on their activity becomes public may enjoy superior returns.[15] (This, of course, represents contrary evidence to the semistrong form of the efficient market hypothesis as well.)

Even though there is evidence on the activity of specialists and insiders that would cause one to reject the strong form of the efficient market hypothesis (or at least not to accept it), the range of participants with access to superior information is not large. For example, tests on the performance of mutual fund managers have consistently indicated they are not able to beat the market averages over the long term.[16]

---

[12] Securities and Exchange Commission, *Report of the Special Study of the Security Markets*, part 2 (Washington, DC: U.S. Government Printing Office).

[13] Securities and Exchange Commission, *Institutional Investor Study Report* (Washington, DC: U.S. Government Printing Office).

[14] For an overview, see Alexandra Peers, "Insiders Reap Big Gains from Big Trades," *The Wall Street Journal*, September 23, 1992, pp. C1, C12.

[15] Michael S. Rozeff and Mir. A. Zaman, "Market Efficiency and Insider Trading: New Evidence," *Journal of Business*, January 1988, pp. 24–25.

[16] Richard A. Ippolito, "On Studies of Mutual Fund Performance," 1962–1991, *Financial Analysts Journal*, January–February 1993, pp. 42–50.

Although mutual fund managers may get the first call when news is breaking, that is not fast enough to generate superior returns.

While the strong form of the efficient market hypothesis suggests more opportunity for superior returns than the weak or semistrong forms, the premium is related to monopolistic access to information rather than other factors.

It should also be pointed out that those who act *illegally* with insider information may initially achieve superior returns from their special access to information, but the price of their actions may be high. For example, Ivan Boesky and Michael Milken, convicted users of illegal insider information in the late 1980s, were forced to give up their gains, pay heavy fines, and serve jail sentences. In their particular cases, they traded on insider information about mergers well before the public was informed. Although they were not officers of the companies or on the boards, they had special fiduciary responsibilities as money managers that they violated.

ABNORMAL RETURNS

In most instances, special or **abnormal returns** refer to gains beyond what the market would normally provide after adjustment for risk. This is also referred to as an **anomaly**. Transactions cost must also be covered to qualify as an anomaly. In the remainder of this chapter, we explore such topics as market movements associated with mergers and acquisitions, the underpricing of new stock issues, the effect of an exchange listing on a stock's valuation, the stock market impact of a firm repurchasing its own shares, and the small-firm and low-P/E effects. Many qualify as anomalies. By identifying and understanding anomalies, the reader may be able to find opportunities for stock market gains. Some of these strategies will relate back directly or indirectly to the efficient markets discussion.

MERGERS AND ACQUISITIONS

Many stocks that were leaders in daily volume and price movement in the last decade represented firms that were merger candidates—that is, companies that were being acquired or anticipated being acquired by other firms. The stocks of these acquisition candidates often increased by 40–60 percent or more over a relatively short period. The list of acquired companies includes such well-known names as Gilette, People Soft, Pixar, Cadbury, and McAfee.

www.duracell.com
www.turner.com
www.quakeroats.com

Premiums for Acquired Company

The primary reason for the upward market movement in the value of the acquisition candidate is the high premium that is offered over current market value in a merger or acquisition. The **merger price premium** represents the difference between the offering price per share and the market price per share for the candidate (before the impact of the offer). For example, a firm that is selling for $25 per share may attract a purchase price of $37.50 per share. Quite naturally, the stock goes up in response to the offer and the anticipated consummation of the merger.

As expected, researchers have consistently found that there are abnormal returns for acquisition candidates.[17] A study has indicated the average premium

[17] Gershon Mandelker, "Risk and Return: The Case of Merging Firms," *Journal of Financial Economics,* December 1974, pp. 303–35; Donald R. Kummer and J. Ronald Hoffmeister, "Valuation Consequences of Cash Tender Offers," *Journal of Finance,* May 1978, pp. 505–6; Peter Dodd, "Merger Proposals, Management Discretion and Stockholder Wealth," *Journal of Financial Economics,* December 1980, pp. 105–38; and Steven Kaplan, "The Effect of Management Buyouts on Operating Performance and Value," *Journal of Financial Economics,* October 1989, pp. 217–54.

TABLE 9-1 **Premiums Offered in Mergers and Acquisitions**

Acquiring Firm	Target Company	Price Bid for Target Firm's Common Stock	Value of Target Firm Three Months before Announcement	Premium Offered (%)
JPMorgan Chase	Bank One	46.25	32.5	42.31
Hewlett Packard	3COM	7.90	4.21	87.65
Xerox	Affiliated Computer Services	63.11	45.03	40.15
Baker Hughes	BJ Services Company	17.44	15.64	11.51
Stanley Works	Black & Decker	57.56	37.9	51.87
On Semiconductor	California Micro Devices	4.70	3.18	47.80
Sanolfi-Aventis	Chatten Inc.	93.50	63.85	46.44
Kraft	Cadbury	13.80	9.5	45.26
EXXON	XTO Energy	51.69	40.47	27.72
Intel	McAfee	48.00	33.02	45.36

These are meger terms and offers and many might not be completed but the premiums demonstrate the point we make.

paid in a recent time period was approximately 40 to 60 percent, and there was an associated upward price movement of a similar magnitude.[18] The premium was based on the difference between the price paid and the value of the acquisition candidate's stock *three months* before announcement of the merger. Some examples of premiums paid during 2009–2010 are presented in Table 9–1.

The only problem from an investment viewpoint is that approximately two-thirds of the price gain related to large premiums occurs before public announcement. It is clear that people close to the situation are trading on information leaks. The highly prestigious investment banking house of Morgan Stanley was embarrassed by charges brought by the U.S. Attorney's Office that two of its former merger and acquisition specialists were conspiring to use privileged information on takeovers to make profits on secret trading accounts.[19]

www.morganstanley.com

Those who attempt to legitimately profit by investing in mergers and acquisitions can follow a number of routes. First, some investors try to identify merger candidates before public announcement to capture maximum profits. This is difficult. While researchers have attempted to identify financial and operating characteristics of acquisition candidates, the information is often contradictory and may even change over time.[20] In prior time periods, acquisition candidates were often firms with sluggish records of performance, whereas many of the recent acquirees are high-quality companies that have unusually good records of performance.

Some alert analysts keep a close eye on securities undergoing unusual volume or pricing patterns (this could be for any number of reasons). Other investors identify industries where companies are being quickly absorbed and attempt to guess which firm will be the next to be acquired. Prime examples of such industries in recent times were banking, telecommunications, pharmaceuticals, and energy.

[18] Henry Oppenheimer and Stanley Block, "An Examination of Premiums and Exchange Ratios Associated with Merger Activity during the 1975–78 Period" (Financial Management Association Meeting, 1980).

[19] "Two Former Morgan Stanley Executives Accused of Plot Involving Takeover Data," *The Wall Street Journal*, February 4, 1981, p. 2.

[20] Robert J. Monroe and Michael A. Simkowitz, "Investment Characteristics of Conglomerate Targets: A Discriminant Analysis," *Southern Journal of Business*, November 1971, pp. 1–15; and Donald J. Stevens, "Financial Characteristics of Merger Firms: A Multivariate Analysis," *Journal of Financial and Quantitative Analysis*, March 1973, pp. 149–58.

TABLE 9-2 Stock Movement of Potential Acquirees in Canceled Mergers

Acquirer-Potential Acquiree	Preannouncement	One Day after Announcement	One Day after Cancellation
Mead Corporation–Occidental Petroleum	20⅜	33¼	23¼
Olin Corp.–Celanese	16	23¾	16¾
Chicago Rivet–MITE	20¾	28⅛	20¾

While trying to guess an acquisition candidate before public announcement can be potentially profitable, it requires that an investor tie up large blocks of capital in betting on an event that may never come to pass. Others prefer to invest at the time of announcement of a merger or acquisition. A gain of the magnitude of 15 percent or more may still be available (over a few months' time period). Perhaps a stock that was $25 before any consideration of merger moves up to $33 on announcement. If the acquisition price is $37.50, there may still be a nice profit to be made. The only danger is that the announced merger may be called off, in which case the stock may sharply retreat in value. Examples of other price drops associated with merger cancellations are shown in Table 9–2.

The wise investor must carefully assess the likelihood of cancellation. Special attention must be given to such factors as the possibility of antitrust action, the attitude of the target company's management toward the merger, the possibility of unhappy stockholders' suits, and the likelihood of poor earnings reports or other negative events. In a reasonably efficient market environment, the potential price gain that exists at announcement may be well correlated with the likelihood of the merger being successfully consummated. That is to say, if it appears the merger is almost certain to go through, the stock may be up to $36.50 at announcement based on an anticipated purchase price of $37.50. If a serious question remains, the stock may only be at $32. When a merger becomes reasonably certain, arbitrageurs come in and attempt to lock in profits by buying the acquisition candidate at a small spread from the purchase price.

One of the most interesting features of the latest merger movement was the heavy incidence of **unfriendly takeovers**, that is, the bidding of one company for another against its will. Such events often lead to the appearance of a third company on the scene, referred to as a **white knight**, whose function is to save the target company by buying it out, thus thwarting the undesired suitor. The new suitor is generally deemed to be friendly to the interests of the target company and may be invited by it to partake in the process. One of the best examples of a white knight goes back to 1984, when Chevron acquired Gulf Oil and saved it from a hostile takeover by Boone Pickens and his Mesa Petroleum. In 2006, Bayer bought Schering to rescue it from the clutches of Merck of Germany. As one might guess, these multiple-suitor bidding wars often lead to unusually attractive offers. A 40 to 60 percent premium may ultimately parlay into an 80 to 100 percent gain or more. For example, the bidding for Gulf Oil sent the stock from 38 to 80.

www.chevron.com
www.ussteel.com

Two of the more notable white knight rescues during the financial crisis of 2008 were not from hostile takeovers of rival bidders but to save the companies from bankruptcy. JP Morgan Chase acquired Bear Stearns with intervention from the Federal Reserve and the U.S. Treasury. Both the Fed and the Treasury thought the bankruptcy of Bear Stearns could cause a collapse of the financial system. Later, PNC Financial Services bought National City Corp., also to save it from bankruptcy, and Bank of America bought Merrill Lynch for the same concerns.

Acquiring Company Performance

What about the acquiring company's stock in the merger and acquisition process? Is this a special situation; that is, does this stock also show abnormal market gains associated with the event? A study by Mandelker indicated that it did not.[21] Long-term economic studies indicate that many of the anticipated results from mergers may be difficult to achieve.[22] There is often an initial feeling of optimism that is not borne out in reality. The **synergy**, or "2 + 2 = 5," effect associated with broadening product lines or eliminating overlapping functions may be offset by the inability of management to mesh divergent philosophies. Sometimes, there is also a fear that too high a price may have been paid.

A good example of the reaction to a merger announcement for the acquiring company was presented in October 2003 when Bank of America announced it was going to acquire Fleet Boston Financial. On the day of the announcement of the merger, Bank of America shares fell by 10 percent from $82 per share to $73.80. Analysts claimed the banking giant was paying too high a price for the Northeast bank holding company (the premium was approximately 40 percent over the then current market value of Fleet). Bank of America tried to explain the merger to investors on the premise that it would give Bank of America even greater power as a retail banker and a foothold in the lucrative Northeast. At least initially, investors weren't convinced. Of course, the shareholders in Fleet Boston Financial were quite pleased as their stock climbed from $31.80 to $39.20 on the day of the announced merger (a gain of approximately 23 percent).

Form of Payment

Another consideration in a merger is the form of payment. Cash offers usually carry a slightly higher premium than stock offers because of the immediate tax consequences to the acquired firm's shareholders. When stock is offered, the tax obligation may be deferred by the acquired company's stockholders until the stock of the acquiring firm is actually sold. This may occur relatively soon or many years in the future.

While stock was the popular medium of payment a decade or two ago, this is no longer the case. Acquiring firms have shown a strong preference for using cash to buy the shares of the merger candidate.[23]

NEW STOCK ISSUES

Another form of a special situation is the initial issuance of stock by a corporation. There is a belief in the investment community that securities may be underpriced when they are issued to the public for the first time. That is to say, when a company **goes public** by selling formerly privately held shares to new investors in an initial public offering, the price may not fully reflect the value of the security.

Why does this so-called underpricing occur, and what is the significance to the investor? The underpricing may be the result of the investment banker's firm commitment to buy the shares when distributing the issue. That is, the investment banker normally agrees to buy the stock from Company A at a set price and then

[21] Mandelker, "Risk and Return," pp. 303–35. Also see Anup Agrawal, Jeffrey F. Jaffe, and Gershon Mandelker, "The Post-Merger Performance of Acquiring Firms," *Journal of Finance,* September 22, 1992, pp. 1605–21.

[22] T. Hogarty, "The Profitability of Corporate Managers," *Journal of Business,* July 1970, pp. 317–27. For a contrary opinion, see Paul M. Healy, Krisha G. Paleps, and Richard S. Ruback, "Does Corporate Performance Improve after Mergers?" *Journal of Financial Economics,* April 1992, pp. 132–65.

[23] For further justification of type of payment, see Kenneth J. Martin, "The Method of Payment in Corporate Acquisitions, Investment Opportunities and Management Ownership," *Journal of Finance,* September 1996, pp. 1227–46.

resells it to the public (along with other investment bankers, dealers, and brokers). The investment banker must be certain the issue will be fully subscribed to at the initial public market price or the banker (and others) will absorb losses or build up unwanted inventory. To protect his position, the investment banker may underprice the issue by 5 to 10 percent to ensure adequate demand.

Studies by Miller and Reilly;[24] Ibbotson, Sindelar, and Ritter;[25] Muscarella and Vetsuypens;[26] and others have indicated positive **excess returns** are related to the issue of the stock. Miller and Reilly, for example, observed positive excess returns of 9.9 percent one week after issue. However, the efficiency of the market comes into play after the stock is actively trading on a regular basis, and any excess returns begin to quickly disappear. Excess returns represent gains above the market averages after adjusting for the relative risk of the investment. The lesson to be learned is that, on average, the best time to buy a new, unseasoned issue is on initial distribution from the underwriting syndicate (investment bankers, dealers, brokers), and the best time to sell is shortly after. These new issues may actually underperform the market over the long term.[27]

The point has been strongly made by recent research by Barry and Jennings.[28] They calculated positive excess returns of 8.69 percent on the first date of trading for new issues but discovered that 90 percent of that gain occurred on the opening transaction.

Participating in the distribution of a new issue is not always as easy as it sounds. A really hot new issue may be initially oversubscribed, and only good customers of a brokerage house may be allocated shares. Such was the case in the feverish atmosphere that surrounded the initial public trading of NexGen, Netscape, Microsoft, Apple Computer, and Genentech. Genentech actually went from $35 to $89 in the first 20 minutes of trading (only to quickly come back down). For the most part, customers with a regular brokerage account and a desire to participate in the new-issues market can find adequate opportunities for investment, though perhaps in less spectacular opportunities than those described above.

www.netscape.com
www.microsoft.com
www.applecomputer.com
www.genentech.com

Performance of Investment Bankers

Research studies indicate that large, prestigious investment banking houses do not generally provide the highest initial returns to investors in the new issues they underwrite.[29] The reason for this is that the upper-tier investment bankers tend to underwrite the issues of the strongest firms coming into the market. Less uncertainty is associated with these strong firms.[30] These firms generally shop around among the many investment bankers interested in their business and eventually negotiate terms that would allow for very little underpricing when they reach the market. (They want most of the benefits to go to the corporation, not to the initial stockholders.)

[24] Robert E. Miller and Frank K. Reilly, "An Examination of Mispricing Returns, and Uncertainty for Initial Public Offerings," *Financial Management,* Winter 1987, pp. 33–38.

[25] Roger G. Ibbotson, J. Sindelar, and Jay R. Ritter, "Initial Public Offerings," *Journal of Applied Corporate Finance,* Fall 1988, pp. 37–45.

[26] Chris Muscarella and Mike Vetsuypens, "A Simple Test of *Barron's* Model of IPO Underpricing," *Journal of Financial Economics,* September 1989, pp. 125–35.

[27] Jay Ritter, "The Long-Term Performance of Initial Public Offerings," *Journal of Finance,* March 1991, pp. 3–27.

[28] Christopher B. Barry and Robert H. Jennings, "The Opening Performance of Initial Offerings of Common Stock," *Financial Management,* Spring 1993, pp. 54–63.

[29] Brian M. Neuberger and Carl T. Hammond, "A Study of Underwriters' Experience with Unseasoned New Issues," *Journal of Financial and Quantitative Analysis,* March 1974, pp. 165–74. Also, see Dennis E. Logue, "On the Pricing of Unseasoned New Issues, 1965–1969," *Journal of Financial and Quantitative Analysis,* January 1973, pp. 91–103; and Brian M. Neuberger and Chris A. La Chapelle, "Unseasoned New Issue Price Performance on Three Tiers: 1976–1980," *Financial Management,* Autumn 1983, pp. 23–28.

[30] Richard Carter and Steven Manaster, "Initial Public Offerings and Underwriter Reputation," *Journal of Finance,* September 1990, pp. 1045–67.

EXCHANGE LISTINGS

A special situation of some interest to investors is an **exchange listing**, in which a firm trading over-the-counter now lists its shares on an exchange (such as the American or New York Stock Exchange). Another version of a listing is for a firm to step up from an American Stock Exchange listing to a New York Stock Exchange listing.

An exchange listing may generate interest in a security (particularly when a company moves from the over-the-counter market to an organized exchange). The issue will now be assigned a specialist who has responsibility for maintaining a continuous and orderly market.[31] An exchange listing may also make the issue more acceptable for margin trading and short selling. Large institutional investors and foreign investors may also consider a listed security more appropriate for inclusion in their portfolios.

Listed firms must meet certain size and performance criteria provided in Table 9–3 (and previously mentioned in Chapter 2 for the NYSE). Although the criteria are not highly restrictive, meeting these standards may still signal a favorable message to investors.

A number of research studies have examined the stock market impact of exchange listings. As might be expected, a strong upward movement is associated with securities that are to be listed, but there is also a strong sell-off after the event has occurred. Research by Van Horne,[32] Fabozzi,[33] and others[34] indicates that the total effect may be neutral. Research by Ying, Lewellen, Schlarbaum, and Lease (YLSL) would tend to indicate an overall gain.[35]

The really significant factor is that regardless of whether a stock has a higher net value a few months after listing as opposed to a few months before listing, there still may be profits to be made. This would be true if the investor simply bought the stock four to six weeks before listing and sold it on listing. Because an application approval for listing is published in the weekly bulletin of the New York Stock Exchange well before the actual date of listing, a profit is often possible. The study by YLSL, cited above, indicates there may be an opportunity for abnormal returns on a risk-adjusted basis in the many weeks between announcement of listing and actual listing (between 4.40 and 16.26 percent over normal market returns, depending on the time period). In this case, YLSL actually reject the semistrong form of the efficient market hypothesis by suggesting there are substantial profits to be made even after announcement of a new listing. The wise investor may wish to sell on the eventual date of listing because sometimes a loss in value may occur at that point.

The reader should also be aware of the potential impact of delisting on a security, that is, the formal removal from a New York Stock Exchange or American Stock Exchange listing, and a resumption of trading over-the-counter. This may occur because the firm has fallen substantially below the requirements of the exchange. As you would expect, this has a large negative effect on the security. Merjos found that 48 of the 50 firms in her study declined between the last day of trading on an

[31] This is not always a superior arrangement to having multiple market makers in the over-the-counter market. It depends on how dedicated the specialist is to maintaining the market. Some banks and smaller industrial firms may choose the competitive dealer system in the over-the-counter market in preference to the assigned specialist. For a truly extensive overview of research on stock listings, see H. Kent Baker and Sue E. Meeks, "Research on Exchange Listings and Delistings: A Review and Synthesis," *Financial Practice and Education*, Spring 1991, pp. 57–71.

[32] James C. Van Horne, "New Listings and Their Price Behavior," *Journal of Finance*, September 1970, pp. 783–94.

[33] Frank J. Fabozzi, "Does Listing on the AMEX Increase the Value of Equity?" *Financial Management*, Spring 1981, pp. 43–50.

[34] Richard W. Furst, "Does Listing Increase the Market Value of Common Stock?" *Journal of Business*, April 1970, pp. 174–80; and Waldemar M. Goulet, "Price Changes, Managerial Accounting and Insider Trading at the Time of Listing," *Financial Management*, Spring 1974, pp. 303–6.

[35] Louis K. W. Ying, Wilbur G. Lewellen, Gary G. Schlarbaum, and Ronald C. Lease, "Stock Exchange Listing and Securities Returns," *Journal of Financial and Quantitative Analysis*, September 1977, pp. 415–32.

www.nyse.com

TABLE 9-3 NYSE Listing Standards

This chart is to be used for an initial evaluation only. For a more complete discussion of the minimum numerical standards applicable to U.S. companies, see Section 102.00 of the Listed Company Manual.

Criteria	Standard
Distribution & Size Criteria	
Must meet all 3 of the following:	
Round-lot Holders[(a)]	400 U.S.
Public Shares[(b)]	1,100,000 outstanding
Market Value of Public Shares[(b,c)]:	
IPOs, Spin-offs, Carve-outs, Affiliates	$40 million
All Other Listings	$100 million
Stock Price Criteria	
All issuers must have a $4 stock price at the time of listing	
Financial Criteria	
Must meet 1 of the following standards:	
Alternative #1—Earnings Test	
Aggregate pre-tax income for the last 3 years[(d)]	$10 million
Minimum in each of the 2 most recent years	$2 million
Third year must be positive	
OR	
Aggregate pre-tax income for the last 3 years[(d)]	$12 million
Minimum in the most recent year	$5 million
Minimum in the next most recent year	$2 million
Alternative #2a—Valuation with Cash Flow	
Global Market Capitalization[(f)]	$500 million
Revenues (most recent 12-month period)	$100 million
Adjusted Cash Flow:	
Aggregate for the last 3 years	$25 million
All 3 years must be positive	
Alternative #2b—Pure Valuation with Revenues	
Global Market Capitalization[(f)]	$750 million
Revenues (most recent fiscal year)	$75 million
REITs	
Stockholders' Equity[(b)]	$60 million

Source: NYSE Euronext. This publication may not contain the most up-to-date information. Please see www.nyse.com/regulation/nyse/1147474807344.html.

exchange and the resumption of trading over-the-counter.[36] The average decline was 17 percent. While the value was not risk adjusted, it is large enough to indicate the clear significance of the event. Other studies have found similar results.[37]

STOCK REPURCHASE

The **repurchase** by a firm of its own shares provides for an interesting special situation. The purchase tends to increase the demand for the shares while decreasing the effective supply. Before we examine the stock market effects of a repurchase, we briefly examine the reasons behind the corporate decision.

[36] Anna Merjos, "Stricken Securities," *Barron's,* March 4, 1963, p. 9.

[37] Gary C. Sanger and James D. Paterson, "An Empirical Analysis of Common Stock Delistings," *Journal of Financial and Quantitative Analysis,* June 1990, pp. 261–72.

the real world of investing

IBM REPURCHASES COMMON STOCK WORTH BILLIONS OF DOLLARS

IBM has bought back over $100 billion of its own common stock since 1995 and over $73 billion since 2003. In May 2007, IBM borrowed $11.5 billion to buy back $12.5 billion of its stock. It used $1 billion of cash and borrowed the rest through an international subsidiary. Borrowing from an international subsidiary allowed IBM to use cash generated overseas. If IBM had repatriated the earnings from overseas to the United States, it would have been subject to income taxes on repatriated earnings, but this maneuver allowed them to use the money and avoid taxes. In February 2008 the board of directors authorized $15 billion dollars for the company's stock repurchase program and in October 2009 added another $5 billion.

There are many reasons why companies will repurchase their own stock. First, they usually have a large free cash flow and no major new capital budgeting projects or acquisitions to make. If they raise the dividend, stockholders expect the dividend to remain stable or rise. By repurchasing common stock they create no expectation that this process will continue indefinitely. In the case of IBM, an investor might expect this repurchase program to continue from year to year, but it would not be possible to predict the dollar amount. In 1994 IBM had 2.350 billion shares outstanding, and by 2009 the company had 1.275 billion shares outstanding. There hasn't been a year since 2004 when IBM has not repurchased common stock. As you can imagine, this has helped increase their earnings per share, because fewer shares inflate earnings per share. It has also allowed them to increase their dividend per share from $.25 in 1994 to $2.15 per share in 2009. Over the last 10 years, earnings per share have grown 9.5 percent and dividends increased 14.5 percent. During this same time revenues have only grown 5.0 percent. One negative consequence of large stock repurchases like IBM's buybacks is that the book value shrinks as equity is taken off the balance sheet. In the case of IBM, the book value per share grew only 5 percent over these last 10 years.

Reasons for Repurchase

In some cases, management believes the stock is undervalued in the market. Prior research studies indicated that repurchased securities generally underperformed the popular market averages before announcement of repurchase.[38] Thus, management or the board of directors may perceive this to be an excellent opportunity because of depressed prices. Others, however, might see the repurchase as a sign that management is not creative or that it lacks investment opportunities for the normal redeployment of capital.[39] Past empirical studies indicated that firms that engage in repurchase transactions often have lower sales and earnings growth and lower return on net worth than other, comparable firms.[40] However, in the bull market of the 1990s, many of the firms repurchasing their own shares were among the strongest and most respected on Wall Street. Examples include Exxon, GE, IBM, Merck, and Monsanto.

Actual Market Effect

From the viewpoint of an anomaly, the key question is, What is the stock market impact of the repurchase? Is there money to be made here or not? Much of the earlier research said no.[41] A number of studies based on data from the 1970s and 1980s took a more positive viewpoint.[42] Recent research, published in 1995, by

[38] Richard Norgaard and Connie Norgaard, "A Critical Evaluation of Share Repurchase," *Financial Management,* Spring 1974, pp. 44–50; and Larry Y. Dann, "Common Stock Repurchases: An Analysis of Returns to Bondholders and Stockholders," *Journal of Financial Economics,* June 1981, pp. 113–38.

[39] Charles D. Ellis and Allen E. Young, *The Repurchase of Common Stock* (New York: The Ronald Press, 1971), p. 61.

[40] Norgaard and Norgaard, "A Critical Evaluation."

[41] A good example is Ellis and Young, *The Repurchase of Common Stock,* p. 156.

[42] Terry E. Dielman, Timothy J. Nantell, and Roger L. Wright, "Price Effects of Stock Repurchasing: A Random Coefficient Regression Approach," *Journal of Financial and Quantitative Analysis,* March 1980, pp. 175–89; Larry Y. Dann, "Common Stock Repurchases: An Analysis of Returns to Bondholders and Stockholders," *Journal of Financial Economics,* June 1981, pp. 113–38; Theo Vermaelen, "Common Stock Repurchases and Market Signaling: An Empirical Study," *Journal of Financial Economics,* June 1981, pp. 139–83; and R. W. Masulis, "Stock Repurchase by Tender Offer: An Analysis of the Causes of Common Stock Price Changes," *Journal of Finance,* May 1980, pp. 305–19.

Ikenberry, Lakonishok, and Vermaelen (ILV) gives only a conditionally positive response.[43]

The researchers found that the immediate reaction to share repurchase announcements was only minimal. For the 1,239 repurchases included in the study, the average gain was only 3.5 percent. One reason for the small increase might be the skepticism with which share repurchases are often viewed. Approximately 90 percent of stock repurchases are announced as future intentions to make open market purchases rather than firm commitments (so-called tender offers). Many analysts are hesitant to accept the premise that there will be a follow-through. A 50 million share repurchase program might be announced, but only 15 million shares might actually be repurchased over time.

Nevertheless, in this latest study, the researchers did find large positive returns over a long period of time following a stock repurchase announcement, even though the initial reaction was muted. Over a four-year time period following the month of announcement, the stocks in the study had an average abnormal return of 12.1 percent (return over and above comparable firms with equal risk).

While there was undoubtedly skepticism about follow-through at time of announcement, the most important factor influencing future market performance was the type of stock involved in the repurchase. For value-oriented stocks with solid fundamentals, the average abnormal return was 45.3 percent over the four-year time horizon.[44] For high-flying "glamour stocks," the returns were neutral to slightly negative (in comparison to similar firms).

The predominant argument for the beneficial effects of the repurchase is that management knows what it is doing when it purchases its *own* shares. In effect, management is acting as an insider for the benefit of the corporation, and we previously observed that insiders tend to be correct in their investment decisions. This factor may provide positive investment results. Of course, these are merely average results over many transactions, and not all tender offers will prove to be beneficial events. The investor must carefully examine the number of shares to be repurchased, the reasons for repurchase, and the future impact on earnings and dividends per share.

THE SMALL-FIRM AND LOW-P/E-RATIO EFFECTS

Two University of Chicago doctoral studies in the early 1980s contended that the true key to superior risk-adjusted rates of return rests with investing in firms with small **market capitalizations**. (Market capitalization refers to shares outstanding times stock price.) In a study of New York Stock Exchange firms, covering from 1936 to 1975, Banz indicates that the lowest quintile (bottom 20 percent) of firms in terms of market capitalization provide the highest returns even after adjusting for risk. Banz suggests, "On average, small NYSE firms have had significantly larger risk-adjusted returns than larger NYSE firms over a 40-year period."[45]

Some criticized Banz for using only NYSE firms in his analysis and for using a time period that included the effects of both a depression and a major war. Small firms had incredibly high returns following the Depression. A similar type study, produced by Reinganum[46] at about the same time, overcame these criticisms. Reinganum examined 2,000 firms that were traded on the New York Stock Exchange or

[43] David Ikenberry, Josef Lakonishok, and Theo Vermaelen, "Market Underreaction to Open Market Share Repurchases," *Journal of Financial Economics,* October 1995, pp. 181–208.

[44] The most important valuation measure used by Ikenberry, Lakonishok, and Vermaelen was book-to-market value, a topic covered in a later section of the chapter.

[45] Rolf W. Banz, "The Relationship between Returns and Market Value of Common Stocks," *Journal of Financial Economics,* March 1981, pp. 3–18.

[46] Marc R. Reinganum, "Misspecification of Capital Asset Pricing—Empirical Anomalies Based on Earnings Yield and Market Values," *Journal of Financial Economics,* March 1981, pp. 19–46. Also, "A Direct Test of Roll's Conjecture on the Firm Size Effect," *Journal of Finance,* March 1982, pp. 27–35; and "Portfolio Strategies Based on Market Capitalization," *Journal of Portfolio Management,* Winter 1983, pp. 29–36.

TABLE 9-4 Synopsis of Results—Reinganum Study

(1) Grouping[a]	(2) Median Market Value (Capitalization, in millions)	(3) Median Share Price	(4) Average Annual Return
MV 1	$ 4.6	$ 5.24	32.77%
MV 2	10.8	9.52	23.51
MV 3	19.3	12.89	22.98
MV 4	30.7	16.19	20.24
MV 5	47.2	19.22	19.08
MV 6	74.2	22.59	18.30
MV 7	119.1	26.44	15.64
MV 8	209.1	30.83	14.24
MV 9	434.6	34.43	13.00
MV 10	1,102.6	44.94	9.47

[a] MV = Market value.

Source: This material is reprinted with permission from Institutional Investor, Inc. from the article by Marc R. Reinganum, "Portfolio Strategies Based on Market Capitalization," *Journal of Portfolio Management,* Winter 1986, pp. 29-36.

the American Stock Exchange between 1963 and 1980. He annually divided the 2,000 firms into 10 groupings based on size, with the smallest category representing less than $5 million in market capitalization and the largest grouping representing a billion dollars or more.

A synopsis of the results from the Reinganum study is presented in Table 9–4. Column 2 indicates the median value of the market capitalization for the firms in each group. Column 3 is the median stock price for firms in each group, while column 4 indicates average annual return associated with that category.

As observed in column 4, the smallest capitalization group (MV 1) outperformed the largest capitalization group (MV 10) by more than 23 percentage points per year. Although not included in the table, in 14 out of the 18 years under study, the MV 1 group showed superior returns to the MV 10 group. In another similar analysis, Reinganum found that $1 invested in the smallest capitalization group would have grown to $46 between 1963 and 1980, while the same dollar invested in the largest capitalization group would have only grown to $4. As did Banz, Reinganum adjusted his returns for risk and continued to show superior risk-adjusted returns.

Such superior return evidence drew criticisms from different quarters. Roll suggested that small-capitalization studies underestimate the risk measure (beta) by failing to account for the infrequent and irregular trading patterns of stocks of smaller firms.[47] Stoll and Whaley maintained that transaction costs associated with dealing in smaller capitalization firms might severely cut into profit potential.[48] They indicated the average buy-sell spread on small-capitalized, low-priced stocks might be four or five times that of large-capitalization firms. Reinganum has maintained that even after accounting for these criticisms, small-capitalization firms continue to demonstrate superior risk-adjusted returns.[49]

Given that there might be advantages to investing in smaller firms, why haven't professional money managers picked up on the strategy? This, in part, is a catch-22. Part of the reason for the inefficiency in this segment of the market that allows for superior returns is the absence of institutional traders. This absence means less information is generated on the smaller firms, and the information that is generated

[47] Richard Roll, "A Possible Explanation of the Small Firm Effect," *Journal of Finance,* September 1981, pp. 879–88.

[48] H. A. Stoll and R. E. Whaley, "Transaction Costs and the Small Firm Effect," *Journal of Financial Economics,* March 1985, pp. 121–43.

[49] Reinganum, "Misspecification of Capital Asset Pricing," pp. 19–46.

TABLE 9-5 P/E Ratios and Performance: The Electronics Industry (1970-1980)

Quintile	Average P/E	Average Quarterly Return (risk-adjusted)	Average Beta
1	7.1	8.53	1.15
2	10.3	4.71	1.12
3	13.4	4.34	1.13
4	17.4	2.53	1.19
5	25.5	1.86	1.29

Source: This material is reprinted with permission from Institutional Investor, Inc. from the article by John W. Peavy III and David A. Goodman, "The Significance of P/Es for Portfolio Returns," *Journal of Portfolio Management,* Winter 1983, pp. 43-47.

is reacted to in a less immediate fashion. Studies suggest an important linkage between the absence of organized information and superior return potential.[50]

Advocates of the small-firm effect argue that it is this phenomenon alone, rather than others, such as the low-P/E-ratio effect, that leads to superior risk-adjusted returns. Peavy and Goodman argued that the low-P/E-ratio effect is also important.[51] In following up on the earlier work of Basu[52] on the importance of P/E ratios, they compensated for other factors that may have resulted in superior returns, such as the small size of the firm, the infrequent trading of stock, and the overall performance of an industry. They did this by using firms that had a market capitalization of at least $100 million, that had an active monthly trading volume of at least 250,000 shares, and that were in the same industry. Thus, none of these factors was allowed to be an intervening variable in the relationship between returns and the level of P/E ratios.

After following these parameters, Peavy and Goodman showed a significant relationship between the firm's P/E ratios and risk-adjusted returns. Firms were broken down into quintiles based on the size of their P/E ratios. Quintile 1 contained firms with the lowest P/E ratios, quintile 2 had the next lowest P/E ratios, and so on up the scale. A portion of their results is presented in Table 9–5.

Note that lower P/E stocks have higher risk-adjusted returns. Although Table 9–5 shows data only for the electronics industry, a similar pattern was found for other industries.

In summarizing this section, some researchers such as Banz and Reinganum argue that small size is the primary variable leading to superior returns, while others argue that it is the low-P/E-ratio effect.

THE BOOK VALUE TO MARKET VALUE EFFECT

Just to make sure that finance professors and their students do not sleep too soundly at night, we have another theory to explain why certain stocks outperform the market. Professors Fama and French maintain that the ratio of book value to market value and size are more important than P/E ratios, leverage, or other variables in explaining stock market performance. Since we've already discussed size,

[50] Avner Arbel and Paul Strebel, "Pay Attention to Neglected Firms," *Journal of Portfolio Management,* Winter 1983, pp. 37–42.

[51] John W. Peavy III and David A. Goodman, "The Significance of P/Es for Portfolio Returns," *Journal of Portfolio Management,* Winter 1983, pp. 43–47.

[52] S. Basu, "Investment Performance of Common Stocks in Relation to Their Price-Earnings Ratios: A Test of the Efficient Market Hypothesis," *Journal of Finance,* June 1977, pp. 663–82.

let's concentrate on book value to market value. The Fama-French study says that the higher the ratio of book value to market value (lower the ratio of market value to book value) the higher the potential return on the stock.[53]

This conclusion is somewhat surprising to students who have been taught that book value, which is based on historical cost rather than current replacement value, is not an important variable. The newer logic is that stocks having a book value that approaches market value are more likely to be undervalued than stocks with book values that are perhaps only 20 percent of market value. The latter figure implies that the stock is trading at five times its book value (or net worth) as shown on the corporate books:

$$\frac{\text{Book value}}{\text{Market value}} \leftrightarrow \frac{\text{Market value}}{\text{Book value}}$$
$$0.20 \leftrightarrow 5\times$$

The high ratio of 5× means the company may be due for a correction as opposed to a stock that is trading at very close to book value.

With this third theory in mind, the investor may wish to keep his or her eye on stocks that meet some or all of the attributes previously discussed, that is, small size, low P/E ratios, and a high book-to-market value ratio.

OTHER STOCK-RELATED ANOMALIES

Although the authors have attempted to highlight the major special situations related to stocks in the preceding pages, there are other opportunities as well. While only brief mention will be made in this section, the student may choose to follow up the footnoted references for additional information.

The January Effect Because stockholders may sell off their losers in late December to establish tax losses, these stocks are often depressed in value in early January and may represent bargains and an opportunity for high returns.[54] In fact, the January effect and the potential for high returns has attracted so much attention that it often is used as a variable to explain other phenomena as well as itself. For example, Keim has found that roughly half the small-firm effect for the year occurs in January.[55] Actually, as more and more investors begin anticipating and playing the January effect, it has moved up in time (everyone wants to be the first one to arrive). Part of the January effect may be viewed in December now.

The Weekend Effect Research evidence indicates that stocks tend to peak in value on Friday and generally decline in value on Monday. Thus, the theory is that the time to buy is on late Monday and the time to sell is on late Friday. While over many decades this observation is valid,[56] generally the price movement is too small to profitably cover transaction costs. However, if you *know* you are going to sell a stock that you have held for a long time, you may prefer to do so later in the week rather than early in the week.

---

[53] Eugene F. Fama and Kenneth R. French, "The Cross Section of Stock Returns," *Journal of Finance,* June 1992, pp. 427–65. The Fama and French study dealt with nonfinancial firms. A similar study with financial firms produced the same type of results. See Brad M. Barber and John D. Lyon, "Firm Size, Book-to-Market Ratio, and Security Returns: A Holdout Sample of Financial Firms," *Journal of Finance,* June 1997, pp. 875–83.

[54] Ben Branch and J. Ryan, "Tax-Loss Trading: An Inefficiency Too Large to Ignore," *Financial Review,* Winter 1980, pp. 20–29.

[55] Donald B. Keim, "Size-Related Anomalies and Stock Return Seasonality," *Journal of Financial Economics,* March 1983, pp. 13–32. Also see Richard Roll, "Vas ist Das? The Turn of the Year Effect and the Return Premium of Small Firms," *Journal of Portfolio Management,* Winter 1983, pp. 18–28.

[56] Frank Cross, "The Behavior of Stock Prices on Fridays and Mondays," *Financial Analysts Journal,* November–December 1973, pp. 67–69; Kenneth R. French, "Stock Returns and the Weekend Effect," *Journal of Financial Economics,* March 1980, pp. 55–69; and Lawrence Harris, "A Transaction Data Study of Weekly and Interdaily Patterns in Stock Returns," *Journal of Financial Economics,* May 1986, pp. 99–117.

the real world of investing

SPECIAL SITUATION: IS BAD NEWS SOMETIMES GOOD NEWS FOR INVESTORS?

Event	Reaction Dates	DJIA % Gain/ Loss During Reaction Dates[a]	DJIA Percentage Gain Days After Reaction Dates 22	63	126
Fall of France	05/09/1940–06/22/1940	(17.1)	(−0.5)	8.4	7.0
Pearl Harbor	12/06/1941–12/10/1941	(6.5)	3.8	(2.9)	(9.6)
Truman upset victory	11/02/1948–11/10/1948	(4.9)	1.6	3.5	1.9
Korean War	06/23/1950–07/13/1950	(12.0)	9.1	15.3	19.2
Eisenhower heart attack	09/23/1955–09/26/1955	(6.5)	0.0	6.6	11.7
Sputnik	10/03/1957–10/22/1957	(9.9)	5.5	6.7	7.2
Cuban missile crisis	08/23/1962–10/23/1962	(9.4)	15.1	21.3	28.7
JFK assassination	11/21/1963–11/22/1963	(2.9)	7.2	12.4	15.1
U.S. bombs Cambodia	04/29/1970–05/26/1970	(14.4)	9.9	20.3	20.7
Kent State shootings	05/04/1970–05/14/1970	(4.2)	0.4	3.8	13.5
Arab oil embargo	10/18/1973–12/05/1973	(17.9)	9.3	10.2	7.2
Nixon resigns	08/09/1974–08/29/1974	(15.5)	(7.9)	5.7	12.5
U.S.S.R. in Afghanistan	12/24/1979–01/03/1980	(2.2)	6.7	4.0	6.8
Hunt silver crisis	02/13/1980–03/27/1980	(15.9)	6.7	16.2	25.8
Falkland Islands war	04/01/1982–05/07/1982	4.3	(8.5)	(9.8)	20.8
U.S. invades Grenada	10/24/1983–11/07/1983	(2.7)	3.9	(2.8)	(3.2)
U.S. bombs Libya	04/15/1986–04/21/1986	2.6	(4.3)	(4.1)	(1.0)
Financial panic '87	10/02/1987–10/19/1987	(34.2)	11.5	11.4	15.0
Invasion of Panama	12/15/1989–12/20/1989	(1.9)	(2.7)	0.3	8.0
Gulf War ultimatum	12/24/1990–01/16/1991	(4.3)	17.0	19.8	18.7
Gorbachev coup	08/16/1991–08/19/1991	(2.4)	4.4	1.6	11.3
ERM U.K. currency crisis	09/14/1992–10/16/1992	(6.0)	0.6	3.2	9.2
World Trade Center bombing	02/26/1993–02/27/1993	(0.5)	2.4	5.1	8.5
Russia, Mexico, Orange County	10/11/1994–12/20/1994	(2.8)	2.7	8.4	20.7
Oklahoma City bombing	04/19/1995–04/20/1995	0.6	3.9	9.7	12.9
Asian stock market crisis	10/07/1997–10/27/1997	(12.4)	6.8	10.5	25.0
Russian LTCM crisis	08/18/1998–10/08/1998	(11.3)	15.1	24.7	33.7
Terrorist Attack— World Trade Center, Pentagon	09/11/2001–09/17/2001	(7.1)	5.7	6.1	10.5

[a] Losses are given in parentheses.

The Value Line Ranking Effect

application example

www.valueline.com

The *Value Line Investment Survey* contains information on approximately 1,700 stocks. Using a valuation model, each company is rated from 1 through 5 for profitable market performance over the next 12 months. One is the highest possible rating, and 5 is the lowest. One hundred stocks are always in category 1. Researchers have generally indicated that category 1 stocks provide superior risk-adjusted returns over the other four categories and the market in general.[57] Of course, frequent trading may rapidly cut into these profits. Figure 9–1 presents the strong performance of the Value Line Group 1 category compared with the other four categories.

[57] Fisher Black, "*Yes,* Virginia, There Is Hope: Test of the Value Line Ranking System," *Financial Analysts Journal,* September–October 1973, pp. 10–14; Clark Holloway, "A Note on Testing an Aggressive Strategy Using Value Line Ranks," *Journal of Finance,* June 1981, pp. 711–19; and Scott E. Stickel, "The Effect of *Value Line Investment Survey* Rank Changes on Common Stock Prices," *Journal of Financial Economics,* March 1985, pp. 121–43.

FIGURE 9-1 Value Line Performance

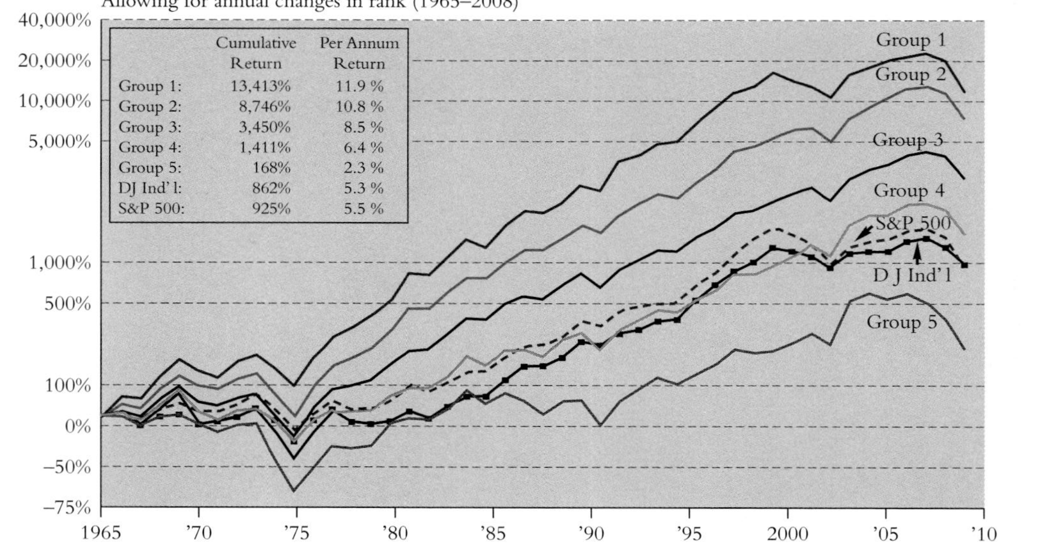

Record of Value Line Rankings for Timeliness (without allowing for changes in rank each week)†

APRIL 16, 1965 TO DECEMBER 31, 2008

Group	'65*	'66	'67	'68	'69	'70	'71	'72	'73	'74	'75	'76	'77	'78	'79	'80	'81	'82	'83	'84	'85	'86	'87
1	33.6%	−3.1%	39.2%	31.2%	−17.7%	−8.9%	26.5%	10.1%	−17.1%	−23.1%	51.6%	35.3%	15.8%	19.8%	25.6%	50.2%	−1.9%	33.7%	25.2%	−8.6%	38.6%	23.5%	−1.2%
2	18.9	−6.0	31.9	26.3	−16.3	−4.0	17.4	7.5	−26.2	−27.8	53.0	36.3	12.7	16.1	30.8	37.4	0.7	29.0	22.2	−0.1	29.5	18.7	0.4
3	8.9	−9.7	30.1	21.4	−20.7	−5.5	12.2	6.2	−27.0	−28.5	52.9	33.8	5.2	9.2	27.6	20.8	2.7	25.5	26.7	−1.6	26.6	11.5	−4.1
4	0.8	−7.2	25.1	25.1	−26.8	−11.7	14.2	3.2	−29.1	−33.6	48.4	36.1	−0.2	2.4	23.1	13.2	−0.9	18.1	35.2	−12.3	24.6	1.5	−9.1
5	−1.2	−12.4	28.4	25.9	−35.7	−13.1	10.5	2.9	−43.1	−36.8	42.1	38.2	−2.8	4.0	39.9	8.4	−4.2	19.9	30.0	−17.1	18.7	−12.1	−17.9
Avg.	10.1	−7.9	29.9	24.6	−22.1	−7.5	14.9	5.5	−27.7	−29.6	51.2	35.1	5.8	9.6	28.0	23.4	0.9	25.0	27.5	−4.7	27.0	10.2	−4.9

Group	'88	'89	'90	'91	'92	'93	'94	'95	'96	'97	'98	'99	'00	'01	'02	'03	'04	'05	'06	'07	'08	'65* to 2008
1	16.0%	28.7%	−6.6%	56.7%	10.1%	18.5%	4.6%	31.3%	27.0%	25.8%	9.3%	23.7%	−11.7%	−7.4%	−15.0%	40.1%	12.2%	11.3	5.7%	5.4%	−45.0%	13,413%
2	19.7	20.3	−8.7	29.8	19.9	13.6	−5.3	27.1	21.4	31.3	8.5	13.9	13.2	4.8	−17.3	37.9	18.8	15.0	15.6	3.9	−40.1	8,746
3	23.2	19.6	−18.6	30.0	17.5	15.3	−1.6	22.8	16.1	24.1	4.8	14.5	13.0	10.2	−18.8	38.6	15.8	7.8	15.2	6.4	−34.2	3,450
4	27.2	12.4	−22.8	34.1	15.6	16.5	−2.9	20.2	14.3	26.6	0.6	13.5	14.0	23.3	−16.2	58.2	16.5	2.4	16.7	1.4	−38.2	1,411
5	20.0	3.3	−33.0	43.8	19.9	20.3	−9.3	15.7	15.8	24.4	−4.0	2.8	11.6	16.4	−14.5	90.1	12.3	−8.7	9.1	−12.0	−50.9	168
Avg.	22.6	17.8	−17.6	33.4	17.3	15.7	−2.6	23.2	17.4	26.1	4.4	14.0	11.4	11.0	−17.5	45.4	16.0	7.3	14.6	3.7	−38.0	3,351
																			Dow Jones Industrials			862%
																			S&P 500			925%

* April through December.

† Arithmetic Averaging.

Source: Value Line Selection & Opinion, January 30, 2009, p. 3719.

The Surprise-Earnings Effect As indicated in the discussion of efficient markets, accounting information tends to be quickly impounded in the value of a stock, and there appears to be little opportunity to garner superior returns from these data. Even if a firm reports a 20 percent increase in earnings, there is likely to be little market reaction to the announcement if the gain was generally anticipated. However, an exception to this rule may relate to truly *unexpected* earnings announcements.[58] If they are very positive, the stock may go up for a number of days after the announcement and thus provide a superior investment opportunity. The opposite would be true of a totally unexpected negative announcement.

The latter factor was particularly evident in the momentum market of the mid- to late 1990s. Stocks that had superior market performance, such as Microsoft, Intel, and Hewlett-Packard, were expected to produce ever-increasing earnings to justify their high valuation. If they did not, the punishment was swift and strong. For example, when Intel announced that its earnings would be below predictions for the second quarter of 1997, its stock dropped 25 points in the first hour of trading.

TRULY SUPERIOR RETURNS OR MISMEASUREMENT?

In our discussions in the previous chapter and in this chapter, we pointed out the possibility that high returns may be the result of a superior strategy in a less than efficient capital market or an anomaly. It also may be the result of mismeasurement, thus showing that you got a superior risk-adjusted return when you did not. You simply misspecified the extent of the risk (beta) component or used the wrong model. If all risk-adjusted superior return studies were the result of misspecification, we could then once again assume the market is perfectly efficient.

The predominant view is that while there is some mismeasurement, many opportunities truly reflect market inefficiencies. There are "special situations" that if properly analyzed provide an opportunity for abnormally high risk-adjusted returns. The most literal and unbending interpretations of efficient markets no longer carry the weight they did two decades ago.[59]

---

[58] Richard Rendleman, Charles Jones, and Henry A. Latane, "Empirical Anomalies Based on Unexpected Earnings and the Importance of Risk Adjustments," *Journal of Financial Economics,* November 1982, pp. 269–87.

[59] Eugene F. Fama, "Efficient Capital Markets: II," *Journal of Finance,* December 1991, pp. 1575–1617.

exploring the web

Web Address	Comments
marketwatch.com/tools/ipo	**Marketwatch IPO Section**
www.redherring.com	**Provides free information on public offerings and links to related sites**
www.thehfa.com	**Web site for the hedge fund association providing information about the industry**
www.hedgefundcenter.com	**Education site on hedge funds**

SUMMARY

The efficient market hypothesis maintains that the market adjusts very rapidly to the supply of new information, and because of this, securities tend to be correctly priced at any given time (or very rapidly approaching this equilibrium value).

The efficient market hypothesis has been stated and tested in three different forms.

1. The weak form states there is no relationship between past and future prices (they are independent over time).
2. The semistrong form suggests all public information is currently impounded in the price of a stock.
3. The strong form suggests *all* information, public or otherwise, is included in the value of a security.

Research tends to support the weak form of the efficient market hypothesis, which causes many researchers to seriously question the overall value of technical analysis. However, many on Wall Street would vigorously debate this position. The semistrong form of the efficient market hypothesis is also reasonably supported by research, and this fact would tend to question the value of fundamental analysis by the individual investor. (It is, however, the collective wisdom of all fundamental analysis that leads to the efficient market hypothesis in the first place.) There are some contradictions to the semistrong form of the efficient market hypothesis, and much research is aimed at supplying additional contradictory data. The strong form of the efficient market hypothesis is not generally accepted.

In this chapter, we also examined various forms of anomalies. Perhaps none has received more attention than the great wave of mergers and acquisitions of the last decade. Because of the premiums paid by the acquiring companies, there is substantial upward potential in the stocks of the acquired firms.

Next, we observe the price patterns of firms going public (selling their stock to the general public for the first time). There appear to be abnormal returns after issue, and then the efficiency of the market comes strongly into play.

Exchange listings may or may not provide higher values for the securities involved; the research is somewhat contradictory in this regard. However, the interesting feature suggested by the Ying, Lewellen, Schlarbaum, and Lease research is that there may be excess returns between the point of announcement and listing (regardless of whether there is a sell-off after listing). This is at variance with the semistrong form of the efficient market hypothesis.

There is also conflicting evidence on the impact of a firm's repurchase of its own shares in the marketplace. Recent research, however, indicates that while there may not be an immediate positive effect, over the longer term the results are positive.

Studies of the small-firm effect indicate there may be superior return potential in investing in smaller capitalization firms. Others suggest it is the low P/E ratios or high book value to market value of many of these firms that leads to superior returns.

Finally, researchers have indicated some special opportunities for profits related to seasonality, unexpected earnings reports, and the Value Line ranking system.

KEY WORDS AND CONCEPTS

abnormal returns 242
anomaly 242
efficient market hypothesis 236
excess returns 246
exchange listing 247
goes public (initial public offering) 245
market capitalizations 250
merger price premium 242
repurchase 248
semistrong form of the efficient market hypothesis 238
strong form of the efficient market hypothesis 241
synergy 245
unfriendly takeovers 244
weak form of the efficient market hypothesis 237
white knights 244

DISCUSSION QUESTIONS

1. Under the efficient market hypothesis, what is the assumption about the processing of new information, and what effect does this have on security pricing?
2. What does the weak form of the efficient market hypothesis suggest? What are the two major ways in which it has been tested?
3. Would low correlation coefficients over time between stock prices tend to prove or disprove the weak form of the efficient market hypothesis?
4. Under the semistrong form of the efficient market hypothesis, is there anything to be gained from a corporate treasurer changing accounting methods to increase earnings per share when there is no associated economic benefit or gain?
5. Why does fundamental analysis tend to make the market efficient?
6. Suggest some studies that would indicate the market is not completely efficient in the semistrong form.
7. What does the strong form of the efficient market hypothesis suggest? Are major test results generally supportive of the strong form?
8. How do specialists, insiders, and mutual fund managers fare in terms of having access to superior information to generate large returns? (Comment on each separately.)
9. Define special or abnormal returns.
10. What is the basis for upward movement in the stock of an acquisition candidate?
11. Do the stocks of acquiring companies tend to show strong upward market movement as a result of the merger process? Comment on the reasoning behind your answer.
12. Why does abnormal return potential sometimes exist in the new-issues market?
13. What are some factors to consider before buying a new issue?
14. What was the major finding of the Ying, Lewellen, Schlarbaum, and Lease study? How does this relate to the semistrong form of the efficient market hypothesis?
15. What are some reasons a firm may repurchase its own stock?
16. What is likely to be the immediate market reaction to the announcement of a share repurchase program? Does this change over the long term?
17. According to researchers such as Banz and Reinganum, what is the general performance of small firms relative to larger firms?
18. What criticisms of the small-firm effect were offered by Roll, and Stoll and Whaley? Were these considered valid by Reinganum?

19. Advocates of the small-firm effect argue that it is this factor *alone* that leads to superior risk-adjusted returns. Does the Peavy and Goodman study support this position?

20. What does Table 9–5 on page 252 indicate about the relationship between a firm's P/E ratio and its average quarterly return?

21. What does the research by Fama and French indicate about the importance of the ratio of book value to market value? If a stock has a book value that is 20 percent of market value, is it thought to possibly be undervalued or overvalued (due for a correction)?

22. What is meant by the statement that "mismeasurement or misspecification of risk could give the false appearance of superior returns"?

WEB EXERCISE

Go to **www.nasdaq.com/reference/IPOs.stm**.
There you will find a table called "Pricings" with a list of recent public offerings. There are four colored symbols to the side of each company with each symbol representing different information about the company. If you scroll across the symbols you will find "Key Data," "Financials," "Filings," and "Experts."

1. Pick a company from the list and click on the "Financials" symbol. Write down or print off the company's basic financial data.

2. Next click on the symbol for "Filings," which can be found in the right hand corner of the "Financials" box. What forms did the company have to file with the SEC?

3. Again slide your cursor over the symbols and click on "Experts." What investment bank was the lead underwriter and what other investment bankers participated in the offering?

4. Next click on the symbol "Key Data." When was the issue priced and at what price did the underwriters sell the stock? What is the ticker symbol (it appears above the company name)?

5. In the bottom left hand corner are four links to information. Click on "View Company Description" and print or write what the company does.

6. Use the "Back" button to take you to the previous screen and click on "View Use of Proceeds." How will the company use the proceeds from the stock offering?

Note: From time to time, companies redesign their Web sites, and occasionally a topic we have listed may have been deleted, updated, or moved into a different location.

chapter ten

BEHAVIORAL FINANCE AND TECHNICAL ANALYSIS

OBJECTIVES

1. Understand how behavioral finance influences investment decisions.
2. Discuss how behavioral finance alters utility theory's assumption of rational behavior.
3. Distinguish between fundamental and technical analysis.
4. Appreciate how technical analysis is related to patterns of stock price movement.
5. Describe the contrary opinion rules and the smart money rules.
6. Discuss the key indicator series and its attempt to track the direction of the market.

OUTLINE

You may wonder how the two areas of behavioral finance and technical analysis are related. This is not discussed in the finance literature, but there is a relationship between what the two schools of thought try to explain.

For years economics and finance have assumed that human beings act in a totally rational fashion and therefore make cold rational decisions about risk-return trade-offs and maximizing utility, but psychologists have found that human beings do not behave as rationally as economists suppose. Models based on rationality are convenient because then the theories reach nice, rational conclusions. But what happens when people don't behave rationally? This is the question that behavioral economics and behavioral finance are trying to answer. You could call behavioral finance the psychology of financial behavior.

Do investors make consistently rational decisions? Can they really predict future cash flows with some degree of accuracy? Do they buy securities at the right time and sell them at the right time? Do they really maximize their utility? Of course, technical analysis also attempts to answer some of these questions, making the assumption that investors behave consistently and will follow the same historical chart patterns, and also that, given a certain chart, they can predict that markets will behave in a predictable way. Technical analysis looks at the behavior of small investors (odd-lot theory) and concludes that they are usually wrong. Technical analysis also looks at the behavior of professional investors (newsletter writers and mutual fund managers) and concludes that investors should do the opposite of a heavily weighted majority opinion.

Although doing the opposite of the current trend may seem like rational behavior, following the crowd may also seem rational. For years fundamental value investors have touted the concept of being a contrarian: Do the opposite of the crowd. Bernard Baruch, in the early part of the 20th century, was noted for saying, "Buy straw hats in winter"—in other words, buy things when they are out of favor. Another saying: "Buy when there is blood in the streets"—buy when the crowd is fearful and markets have plummeted. Are these rational behaviors? If they are, why do investors have such a hard time getting themselves to buy when things are out of favor? Does fear dominate rational behavior? Is going against the crowd overruled by wanting to do what everyone else is doing? Think about tattoos. The first people to get tattooed were going against the crowd, but eventually many others followed them. Now, not getting tattooed is going against the crowd. What is perceived to be rational at one time might not be perceived to be rational at a future time. In the next section we will cover some of the main findings of behavioral finance research.

MARKET BUBBLES

There have been irrational **market bubbles** for centuries. One of the earliest documented bubbles was tulip mania in Holland. Charles Mackay documented the tulip mania bubble in his 1841 book, *Extraordinary Popular Delusions and the Madness of Crowds*. Tulip bulbs at the time soared to prices equal to many times the annual income of a skilled craftsman. Eventually the price of tulip bulbs plummeted and many speculators were ruined. Another well-known economic bubble was the Florida land bubble of the 1920s, which possibly was similar to the 2006–2008 U.S. real estate bubble. In the roaring twenties, people flocked to Miami because it was considered a tropical paradise, and speculators pushed prices up. Credit was easy and prices became inflated, only to collapse in 1925–1926 as hurricanes battered Florida and investors couldn't find buyers for their housing developments. The great stock market crash of 1929 and the depression that followed left whole cities unfinished. Does this sound similar to the financial crisis in 2006–2008, when money was cheap and speculators built houses in Nevada, Florida, Arizona, California, and other places? People continued to bid up prices because it was thought that house prices never decline. This too proved to be fallacious. And let us not forget the tech bubble of the 1990s, when companies that had no earnings, dividends, or cash flow sold at 10 to 30 times sales because it was the only valuation metric that could be used. Companies that sold for hundreds of dollars per share with no earnings eventually went bankrupt. The NASDAQ index, which was dominated by tech companies, peaked above 5,100 in March 2000 and fell to less than 1,200 in July 2002. By October 2010, the NASDAQ composite index was at 2,400, less than half of its previous high 10 years earlier. These are examples of the irrationality of markets.

HEURISTICS

Heuristics are techniques for problem solving that are based on experiential learning; these are often referred to as "rules of thumb." A heuristic often relies on discovery and is used to come to an optimal solution. One general heuristic for solving a problem is to use common sense. Heuristics are nonreflective, intuitive

the real world of investing

THE SUPER BOWL AS A PREDICTOR OF THE STOCK MARKET

Folklore says that the winning Super Bowl team will predict the direction of the stock market for the rest of the year. In 2010 the Super Bowl was played on February 7 between the Indianapolis Colts and the New Orleans Saints. According to the folklore, no matter which of these teams won the Super Bowl, the market should have gone up.

The theory goes that if a team from the old NFL (National Football League) beats a team from the old AFL (American Football League), the market will go up. This indicator has been true 34 out of the last 43 Super Bowls, or 79 percent of the time. That is a pretty high correlation, and so many people think this indicator works even though there is no cause and effect involved. However, the indicator is starting to become difficult to calculate. For example, the Indianapolis Colts used to be the Baltimore Colts, who were an NFL team. New Orleans was also an NFL team, and so the market should have gone up in 2010 no matter who won (New Orleans won, by the way). Or it could be instead that the economy recovered, and therefore the market went up? Which makes more sense?

When the two leagues combined and became the National Football Conference and the American Football Conference, teams were moved from one league to another to create divisional balance and maintain old rivalries. For example, the Cleveland Browns and Pittsburgh Steelers were moved from the old NFL to the new AFC. Now, of course, the Baltimore Ravens are the old Cleveland Browns and Cleveland has a new Browns team. Because new teams, such as the Tampa Bay Buccaneers and the Tennessee Titans, have entered the league, and because of realignment of divisions, it takes some sleuthing to decide which team represents which old league. We are waiting for the day when two brand-new teams play in the Super Bowl and there will be no indicator. What will be the prediction if Cleveland someday wins the Super Bowl?

This isn't the only silly indicator out there. You can find plenty of events that correlate with the stock market. For example, the hemline theory says that as skirts get shorter, the market goes up. The theory is that a higher hemline indicates more willingness to take risk. Be careful about what you believe. Just because something has a high correlation does not guarantee that it makes sense or is a reliable predictor. Unless there is cause and effect, don't take that high correlation at face value. Mark Hulbert of MarketWatch reminds us that David Leinweber, a visiting professor from Caltech's economics department, at one time found that the highest correlation to the S&P 500 index was butter production in Bangladesh.

mechanisms for coping with complexity. Two psychologists, Amos Tversky and Daniel Kahneman, were pioneers in the development of behavioral economics and finance. Their first significant research focused on three heuristics (rules of thumb): representativeness, availability, and anchoring-and-adjustment.

Representativeness

Judgment by **representativeness** occurs when people assess the chances that an event will occur by determining how similar the event is to a stereotype. This can explain why investors may see patterns in random walk data, or fail to appreciate the phenomenon of regression to the mean.

Analysts often extrapolate past earnings trends and tend to undervalue earnings coming out of a recession and overvalue earnings leading into a recession.

Availability

Psychologists know that people have selective memories and that we tend to remember those events that made a big impression on us. Many years after an event, people who experienced the same event may remember it quite differently. **Availability** refers to the fact that we remember more-recent events more intensely than distant events. The more available the event is to our memory, the more likely it will influence our behavior. The more easily we can bring something to mind, the more likely it will influence our decisions. If we see an accident on the highway, we will drive more carefully for a while. Upward or downward movements in the market for extended periods of time may influence our investment decisions.

Anchoring-and-Adjustment

According to the **anchoring-and-adjustment** heuristic, people make estimates from an existing or initial value and then adjust this value to reach the final conclusion. The adjustment is usually not sufficient to reach the actual answer. Werner DeBondt uses the example of the "first-impression syndrome" to illustrate this point: "After meeting someone for the first time (say at a dinner party), we may be slow to adjust our opinion at a later date—even if the context completely changes (say a job interview). In other words, what some television advertisements for cosmetic products tell us is often true: you don't get a second chance to make a first impression."[1]

To summarize these heuristics, it is fair to say that people are influenced by social trends, current fads, and common beliefs. These beliefs may be false, but we may adhere to them because they are our reference points. Just because everyone else is buying tech stocks, this is not necessarily a good reason for you to buy them. Superstitions are thought by most to be false, and yet there are buildings that do not list a "13th" floor (the elevator buttons might read . . . 11, 12, 14A, 14B, 15, . . .). Are we to think there exists no 13th floor in those buildings? One of the authors of this text once checked into a hotel in Hong Kong, and the desk clerk looked very pale when handing over the key. When asked if something was wrong, the clerk explained that the room number, which was 444, meant bad luck or even death. Well, we are still alive and writing.

PROSPECT THEORY[2]

You are probably familiar with the economic concept of utility theory, wherein individuals maximize their utility by reaching their highest indifference curves. These concepts were taught in your introductory economics classes. In investments, we take utility theory and apply it to portfolio selection theory by assuming that investors maximize their return for a given level of risk. If individuals acted rationally, utility theory would work fine. Kahneman and Tversky tested this theory with a series of experiments and found some surprising results. Their model, referred to as **prospect theory**, is an alternative to utility theory and shows results that differ from standard utility theory. In general, Kahneman and Tversky point out that people don't accurately use the probability of expected values when given a choice between certain outcomes and probable outcomes. For example, consider the following choices:

A. A $450 guaranteed amount

B. A 50% probability of $1,000 and a 50% probability of $0; expected value $500

Using standard utility, option B would be the rational choice. Having run many types of experiments similar to the above choices, Kahneman and Tversky found that the dominant choice was the guaranteed amount, rather than the higher expected value. They termed this behavior the **certainty effect**, when investors exhibited risk aversion by choosing sure gains rather than probable gains. Other

[1] Werner DeBondt, presentation at the Center for Behavioral Finance, Institute for Media and Communications Management, University of St. Gallen, Switzerland, February 3, 2005. Copyright © 2005 Werner DeBondt. Used with permission.

[2] Daniel Kahneman and Amos Tversky, *Econometrica* 47, no. 2 (March 1979), pp. 263–291.

experiments found that investors also made risky choices when faced with a sure loss versus a probable loss that creates a gambling effect.

They found that people don't consider all information common to all prospects (choices) and that they make decisions in isolation from this common information. This leads to inconsistent choices when faced with the same alternatives presented in different forms. This led Kahneman and Tversky to create another alternative model that looks at gains and losses rather than the ending wealth position. A rational investor would try to maximize wealth, rather than focus only on gains and losses. Assume an investor starts with a given amount of wealth called the reference point; it appears that people have a stronger reaction to losses, which decrease their wealth, than to an equal gain that would increase their wealth. Thus, the utility curve for gains and losses is not equal. Given a beginning value, investors have a different risk preference for gains than for losses. This is different from the portfolio theory developed by Harry Markowitz, which creates an efficient frontier where investors locate the optimum point, found at the intersection of the efficient frontier with the investor's indifference curves, which maximizes their return for a given level of risk. So, in summary, prospect theory is another indication that investors are not the rational beings we learn about in our economics courses.

Others built on what Kahneman and Tversky started. Richard Thaler endorsed their alternative model and found other behaviors that didn't fit the standard utility theory model. Thaler found that investors underweighted opportunity costs, failed to ignore sunk costs, sometimes refused to make a choice, and suffered regret either for making a bad investment or for a good one that they didn't buy. It seems that the regret felt for taking an action that turned out poorly is more powerful than the regret felt for not taking an action that would have turned out positively. This leads to myopic loss aversion, where the investor is more sensitive to short-term losses than long-term losses.

OVERREACTION

In 1985, Werner DeBondt and Richard Thaler published an article in *The Journal of Finance* titled "Does the Stock Market Overreact?" Some have called this article the beginning of behavioral finance, because it moved the topic from behavioral economics to finance. The authors found that people systematically overreact to unexpected and dramatic news events, which causes inefficiencies in the stock market. Investors overreact to both good and bad news, and past winners become losers and past losers become winners.[3] DeBondt cites a series of empirical tests that support the idea that the overreaction bias influences stock prices. For instance:

> Consider, for example, all companies listed on the New York Stock Exchange since December 1925. On average, the 50 NYSE stocks that did the worst during an initial five-year period later outperform the 50 NYSE stocks that did the best. When one controls for risk, the difference in performance is, on average, about eight percent a year. Contrarian strategies of this type, or similar strategies based on price-earnings ratios, are profitable in many different countries. What is noteworthy about the winner/loser effect is that it was the first asset-pricing anomaly predicted and discovered by behavioral theory.[4]

Overreaction and the winner/loser effect can possibly be explained by our inability to forecast correctly. In business school we learn to run regressions and

---

[3] Werner F. M. DeBondt and Richard H. Thaler, "Does the Stock Market Overreact?" *Journal of Finance* 40, no. 3 (1985), pp. 793–805.

[4] Werner DeBondt, presentation at the Center for Behavioral Finance, Institute for Media and Communications Management, University of St. Gallen, Switzerland, February 3, 2005.

extrapolate the past into the future. With the sustainable growth model we assume that the company will stay in equilibrium and that the ratios for return on equity, asset turnover, and financial leverage will stay constant. We build Excel spreadsheets driven by sales growth and expect the income and balance sheet relationships to remain the same, and more and more analysts rely on management to "give earnings guidance." The winner/loser effect may occur because analysts, traders, and investors simply extrapolate past trends and don't catch changes going on within the company. DeBondt points out that there is some evidence that an arbitrage strategy leads to superior return. Buying stocks from the bottom 20 percent of the most pessimistic analyst forecasts and selling stocks short from the 20 percent with the most optimistic forecasts gives superior risk-adjusted returns that increase with an increased holding period from one to five years.

OTHER BEHAVIORAL ISSUES

Our purpose in presenting the section on behavioral finance is not to cover the complete literature but to introduce you to an alternative concept of investing that gives more focus to the investor's behavior. Many of the behaviors are not explainable, but they are interesting and have an impact on the way people make decisions in almost everything they do in life. Following are some of the other issues behavioral analysts have looked at.

Mental accounting involves **framing**, where investors have a frame of reference (for example, the price of a stock they purchased) that influences their decision to buy, sell, or hold. There is a tendency to divide investment accounts into different piles, such as low-risk safe accounts, high-quality investments, risky investments, speculative investments, play money, and so on. Unfortunately, this type of mental accounting doesn't allow investors to focus on their total wealth but instead involves them more in the gains-and-losses game discovered by Kahneman and Tversky.

Momentum investing strategies seem to work, and Richard Driehaus of Driehaus Capital has been one of the more successful investors using these strategies. Momentum occurs when a stock is moving in one direction in a consistent fashion. As investors see the upward momentum, they pile on and push the price up higher. *Investors Business Daily* is a financial newspaper that publishes momentum numbers and endorses this style of investing. Of course, momentum can have a downward slope as more and more sell. When the momentum stops, this can lead to the winner/loser proposition, where the extrapolation of past trends ends up leading to overvaluation and undervaluation.

Herding is another issue. Herding refers to "follow the leader" mentality: Everybody else is doing this, so I should do it too, because perhaps they know something I don't. In other words, herding brings us back to our opening vignette about the tulip bulbs. The crowd is not always right. Herding is more prevalent with institutional investors than with individual investors. Terrance Odean has published research that indicates investors sell their winners too soon and hold their losers too long. This goes directly against the old Wall Street wisdom of "let your winners run and sell your losers." Odean and Brad Barber are also responsible for our last point, which is that men and women investors have quite different styles. Men suffer from overconfidence and trade 45 percent more than women, thereby underperforming because of transaction costs.

As you read through the technical analysis section, see if you can find any applications of behavioral finance embedded in the theories of technical trading rules. There may be good reasons why being a contrarian investor and going against the crowd seems to be a good investment strategy.

the real world of investing

THE JANUARY BAROMETER

The January barometer says that as January goes, so goes the whole year. If January ends with higher stock prices, then the market will end the year with higher prices. This has been true more often than not, but can there be any reason to believe this predictor really works? The statistical support for this indicator is very weak, and the supposition that there is a cause-and-effect relation is even less reasonable. Mark Hulbert of MarketWatch points out that over the last 113 years, this indicator has been right 72 times, or 64 percent of the time. He also mentions another indicator that says the market will be up from February through December, and this one has also been right 73 out of 113 years, or 65 percent of the time.

He creates two hypothetical portfolios starting with $10,000 each in 1897. The Perennial Bull portfolio buys on the first day of February every year and goes to cash in January. The January Barometer portfolio buys on the first day of February only if the market was up in January. Neither portfolio is credited with interest on cash. The January Barometer is out of the market 41 years and earns no return, while the Perennial Bull is only in cash every January. At the end of 2009 the Perennial Bull portfolio had $979,220 and the January Barometer was worth $496,209. Even if interest were credited to the January Barometer, the portfolio would not have outperformed the Perennial Bull. Be careful what you believe; too many investment advisory services who tout technical analysis take some of these indicators at face value.

Source: Mark Hulbert, "January by the Numbers," *MarketWatch*, January 29, 2010.

TECHNICAL ANALYSIS

In this section, we examine a technical approach to investment timing. In this approach, analysts and market technicians examine prior price and volume data, as well as other market-related indicators, to determine past trends in the belief that they will help forecast future ones. Technical analysts place much more emphasis on charts and graphs of *internal market data* than on such fundamental factors as earnings reports, management capabilities, or new-product development. They believe that even when important fundamental information is uncovered, it may not lead to profitable trading because of timing considerations and market imperfections.

At the outset, be aware there are many disagreements and contradictions in the various areas we examine. As previously implied, advocates of technical analysis do not place much emphasis on fundamental analysis, and vice versa. Even more significant, proponents of the efficient market hypothesis would suggest that neither works.

In light of the various disagreements that exist, we believe it is important that the student be exposed to many schools of thought. For example, we devote this chapter to technical analysis and offer research findings that relate to the value of the technical approach. Our philosophy throughout the chapter is to recognize that there sometimes is a gap between practices utilized by brokerage houses (and on Wall Street) and beliefs held in the academic community, yet the student should be exposed to both.

Technical analysis is based on a number of basic assumptions:

1. Market value is determined solely by the interaction of demand and supply.
2. It is assumed that though there are minor fluctuations in the market, stock prices tend to move in trends that persist for long periods.
3. Reversals of trends are caused by shifts in demand and supply.
4. Shifts in demand and supply can be detected sooner or later in charts.
5. Many chart patterns tend to repeat themselves.

For our purposes, the most significant items to note are the assumptions that stock prices tend to move in trends that persist for long periods, and these trends can be detected in charts. The basic premise is that past trends in market movements can be used to forecast or understand the future. The market technician generally assumes there is a lag between the time he perceives a change in the value of a security and when the investing public ultimately assesses this change.

In developing the tools of technical analysis, we shall divide our discussion between (a) the use of charting and (b) the key indicator series to project future market movements.

THE USE OF CHARTING

Charting is often linked to the development of the Dow theory in the late 1890s by Charles Dow. He was the founder of the Dow Jones Company and editor of *The Wall Street Journal*. Many of his early precepts were further refined by other market technicians, and it is generally believed the Dow theory was successful in signaling the market crash of 1929.

Essential Elements of the Dow Theory

The **Dow theory** maintains that there are three major movements in the market: daily fluctuations, secondary movements, and primary trends. According to the theory, daily fluctuations and secondary movements (covering two weeks to a month) are only important to the extent they reflect on the long-term primary trend in the market. Primary trends may be characterized as either bullish or bearish in nature.

In Figure 10–1, we look at the use of the Dow theory to analyze a market trend. Note that the primary movement in the market is positive despite two secondary movements that are downward. The important facet of the secondary movements is that each low is higher than the previous low and each high is higher than the previous high. This tends to confirm the primary trend, which is bullish.

Under the Dow theory, it is assumed that this pattern will continue for a long period, and the analyst should not be confused by secondary movements. However, the upward pattern must ultimately end. This is indicated by a new pattern in which a recovery fails to exceed the previous high (abortive recovery) and a new low penetrates a previous low as indicated in Figure 10–2. For a true turn in the market to occur, the new pattern of movement in the Dow Jones Industrial Average must also be confirmed by a subsequent movement in the Dow Jones Transportation Average as indicated on the bottom part of Figure 10–2.

A change from a bear to a bull market would require similar patterns of confirmation. While the Dow theory has proved helpful to market technicians, there is

FIGURE 10-1 Presentation of the Dow Theory

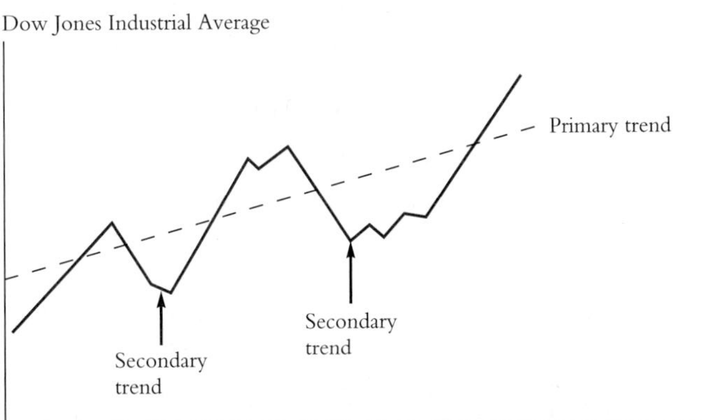

FIGURE 10-2 Market Reversal and Confirmation

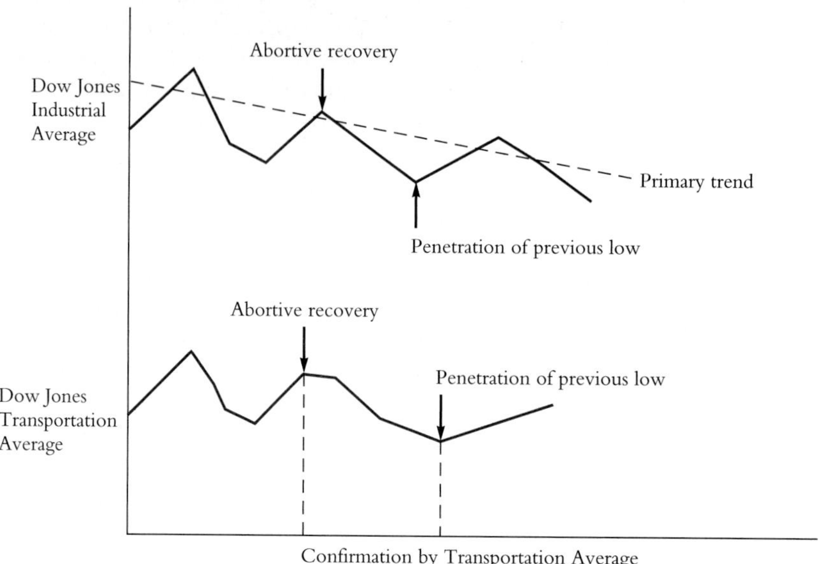

always the problem of false signals. For example, not every abortive recovery is certain to signal the end of a bull market. Furthermore, the investor may have to wait a long time to get full confirmation of a change in a primary trend. By the time the transportation average confirms the pattern in the industrial average, important market movements may have already occurred.

Support and Resistance Levels

Chartists attempt to define trading levels for individual securities (or the market) where there is a likelihood that price movements will be challenged. Thus, in the daily financial press or on television, the statement is often made that the next barrier to the current market move is at 13,000 (or some other level). This assumes the existence of support and resistance levels. As indicated in Figure 10–3, a support

FIGURE 10-3 Support and Resistance

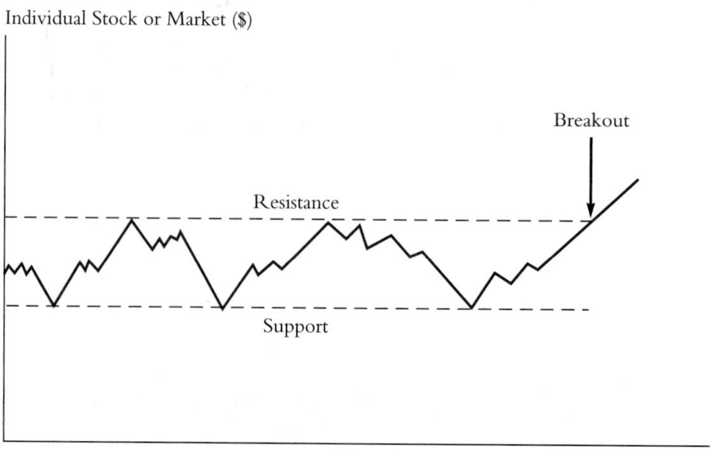

level is associated with the lower end of a trading range and a resistance level with the upper end.

Support may develop each time a stock goes down to a lower level of trading because investors who previously passed up a purchase opportunity may now choose to act. It is a signal that new demand is coming into the market. When a stock reaches the high side of the normal trading range, **resistance** may develop because some investors who bought in on a previous wave of enthusiasm (on an earlier high) may now view this as a chance to get even. Others may simply see this as an opportunity to take a profit.

A breakout above a resistance point (as indicated in Figure 10–3) or below a support level is considered significant. The stock is assumed to be trading in a new range, and higher (lower) trading values may now be expected.

A good example of support and resistance levels can be found in the trading pattern of IBM in the 1990s. After trading in the $150 to $170 range in the early 1990s, the stock hit rock bottom in mid-1993 at $40 per share. Part of the decline was due to a loss in earnings per share (EPS) in 1993 for the first time in decades. However, the stock did find support at $40 per share as investors began to purchase the stock in anticipation of a possible comeback. Lou Gerstner Jr., a highly respected executive, had come on board as chairman and CEO. He immediately began eliminating redundant operations as well as implementing a strategic pattern for future growth. By 1996, the stock was in the $90s range and made a number of attempts to break through a resistance point of 100. After several tries, the stock finally crossed the 100 resistance barrier and then made an almost uninterrupted run up to $200 in mid-1997. The stock then split two for one. By April 2011 it was in the post-split $160 range. IBM will undoubtedly continue to face new support and resistance levels in the future.

Volume

The amount of volume supporting a given market movement is also considered significant. For example, if a stock (or the market in general) makes a new high on heavy trading volume, this is considered to be bullish. Conversely, if the market makes a new high on light volume this may indicate a temporary move that is likely to be reversed.

A new low on light volume is considered somewhat positive because of the lack of investor participation. When a new low is established on the basis of heavy trading volume, this is considered to be very bearish.

In early 2007 the New York Stock Exchange averaged a volume of close to 2.5 billion shares daily. When the volume jumped to 3.5 or 4.0 billion shares, technical analysts took a very strong interest in the trading pattern of the market.

For an individual stock, the same principles also apply. In 2010, Intel had average daily volume of 71 million shares. However, movements on volumes of 90 to 100 million shares or more were considered significant.

Types of Charts

Until now, we have been using typical line charts to indicate market patterns. Technicians also use bar charts and point and figure charts. We shall examine each.

Bar Chart A bar chart shows the high and low price for a stock with a horizontal dash along the line to indicate the closing price. An example is shown in Figure 10–4.

FIGURE 10-4 Bar Chart

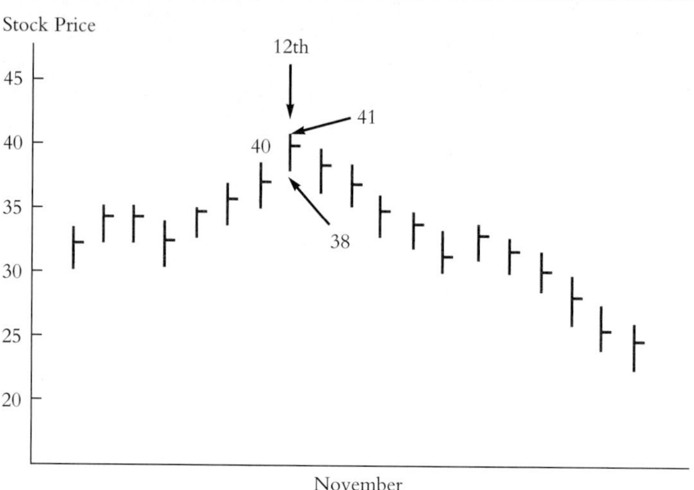

FIGURE 10-5 Bar Chart of Market Average

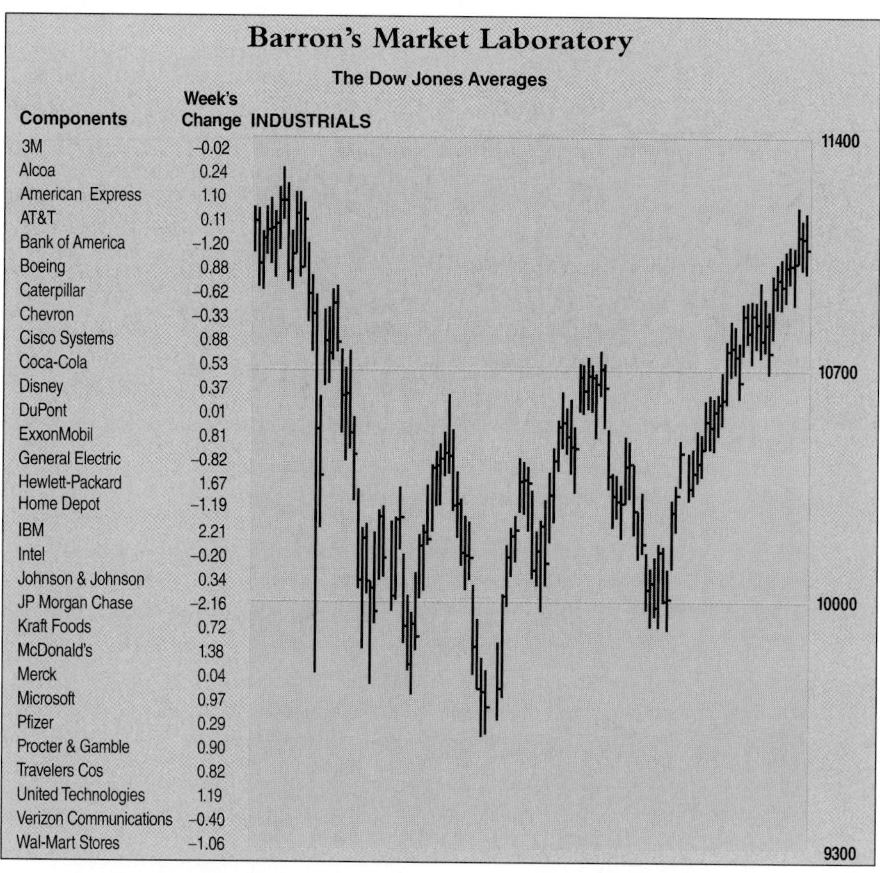

Barron's Market Laboratory

The Dow Jones Averages

Components	Week's Change
3M	-0.02
Alcoa	0.24
American Express	1.10
AT&T	0.11
Bank of America	-1.20
Boeing	0.88
Caterpillar	-0.62
Chevron	-0.33
Cisco Systems	0.88
Coca-Cola	0.53
Disney	0.37
DuPont	0.01
ExxonMobil	0.81
General Electric	-0.82
Hewlett-Packard	1.67
Home Depot	-1.19
IBM	2.21
Intel	-0.20
Johnson & Johnson	0.34
JP Morgan Chase	-2.16
Kraft Foods	0.72
McDonald's	1.38
Merck	0.04
Microsoft	0.97
Pfizer	0.29
Procter & Gamble	0.90
Travelers Cos	0.82
United Technologies	1.19
Verizon Communications	-0.40
Wal-Mart Stores	-1.06

Source: *Barron's*, October 18, 2010, p. M47. Reprinted with permission of *Barron's*, Copyright © 2010 Dow Jones & Company, Inc. All Rights Reserved Worldwide.

We see on November 12 the stock traded between a high of 41 and a low of 38 and closed at 40. Daily information on the Dow Jones Industrial Average is usually presented in the form of a bar chart, as indicated in Figure 10–5.

Trendline, published through a division of Standard & Poor's, provides excellent charting information on a variety of securities traded on the major exchanges

FIGURE 10-6 Chart Representation of Market Bottoms and Tops

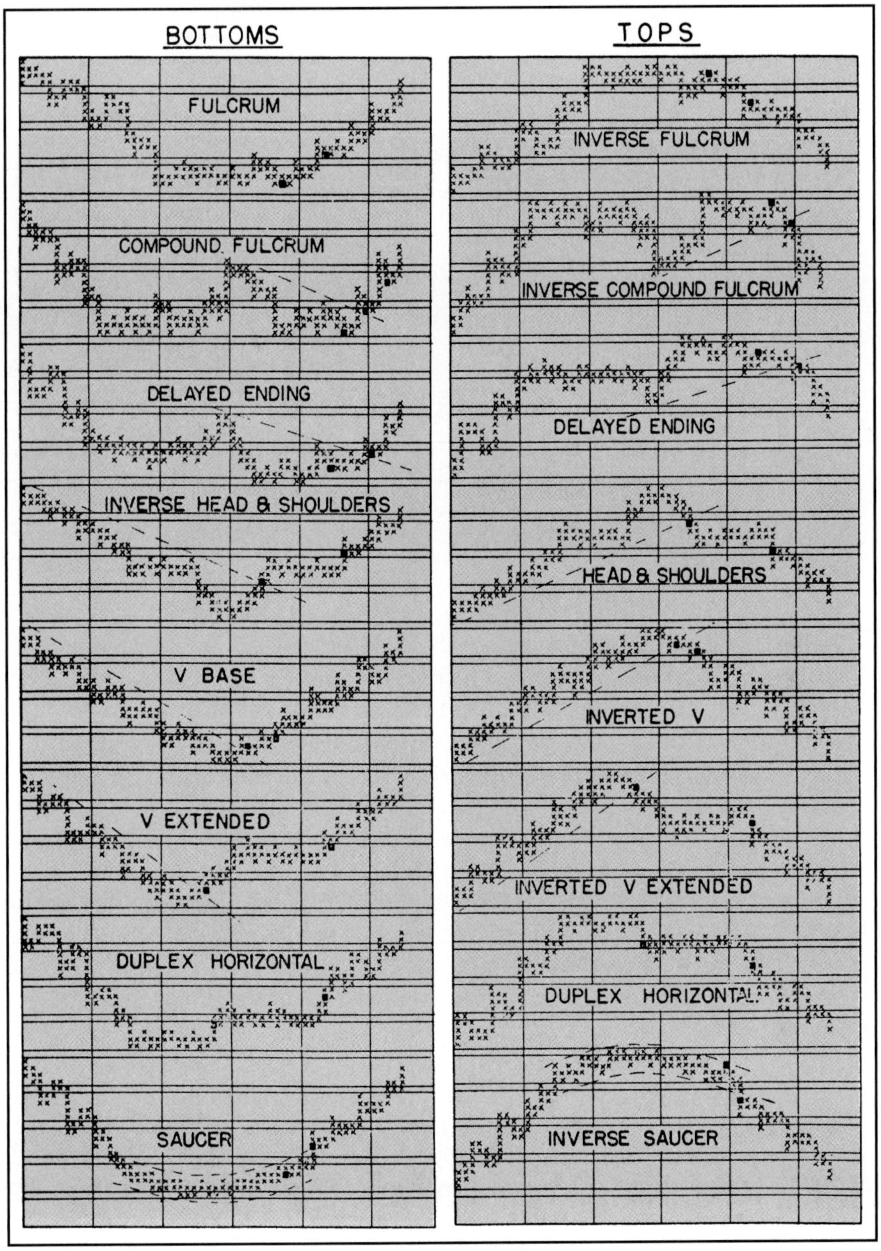

and is available at many libraries and brokerage houses. Market technicians carefully evaluate the charts, looking for what they perceive to be significant patterns of movement. For example, the pattern in Figure 10–4 on the previous page might be interpreted as a head-and-shoulder pattern (note the head in the middle) with a lower penetration of the neckline to the right indicating a sell signal. In Figure 10–6 we show a series of the price-movement patterns presumably indicating market bottoms and tops.

Although it is beyond the scope of this book to go into interpretation of chart formations in great detail, special books on the subject are suggested at the end of our discussion of charting.

Point and Figure Chart A point and figure chart (PFC) emphasizes significant price changes and the reversal of significant price changes. Unlike a line or bar

FIGURE 10-7 Point and Figure Chart

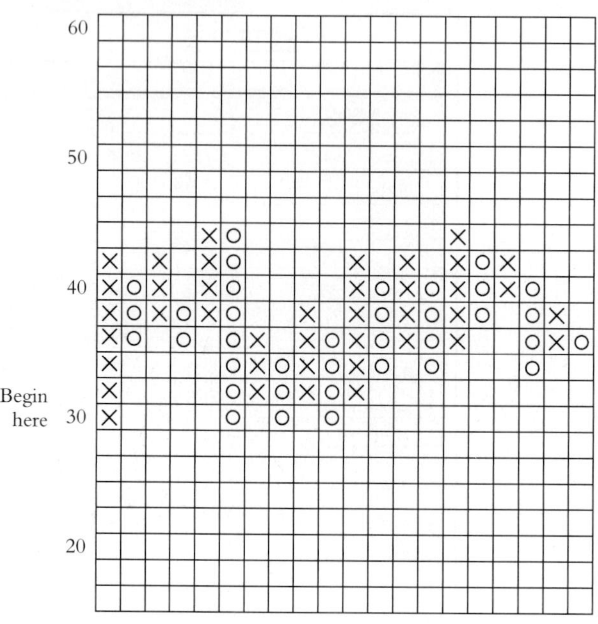

chart, it has no time dimension. An example of a point and figure chart is presented in Figure 10–7.

The assumption is that the stock starts at 30. Only moves of two points or greater are plotted on the graph (some may prefer to use one point). Advances are indicated by Xs, and declines are shown by Os. A reversal from an advance to a decline or vice versa calls for a shift in columns. Thus, the stock initially goes from 30 to 42 and then shifts columns in its subsequent decline to 36 before moving up again in column 3. A similar pattern persists throughout the chart.

Chartists carefully read point and figure charts to observe market patterns (where there is support, resistance, breakouts, congestion, and so on). Students with a strong interest in charting may consult such books as Colby, *The Encyclopedia of Technical Market Indicators,*[5] and DeMark, *The New Science of Technical Analysis.*[6] The problem in reading charts has always been to analyze patterns in such a fashion that they truly predict stock market movements before they unfold. To justify the effort, one must assume there are discernible trends over the long term.

KEY INDICATOR SERIES

In the former television series *Wall Street Week,* host Louis Rukeyser traditionally watched a number of indicators on a weekly basis and compared the bullish and bearish indicators to determine what the next direction of the market might be.

In this section, we examine bullish and bearish technical indicator series. We first look at contrary opinion rules, then smart money rules, and finally, overall market indicators.

Contrary Opinion Rules

The essence of a **contrary opinion rule** is that it is easier to figure out who is wrong than who is right. If you know your neighbor has a terrible sense of direction and you spot him taking a left at the intersection, you automatically take a right. In the stock market there are similar guidelines.

[5] Robert W. Colby, *The Encyclopedia of Technical Market Indicators,* Second Edition (Burr Ridge, IL: McGraw-Hill, 2002).

[6] Thomas R. DeMark, *The New Science of Technical Analysis* (New York: John Wiley & Sons, 1994).

FIGURE 10-8 **Comparing Standard & Poor's 500 Index and the Odd-Lot Index**

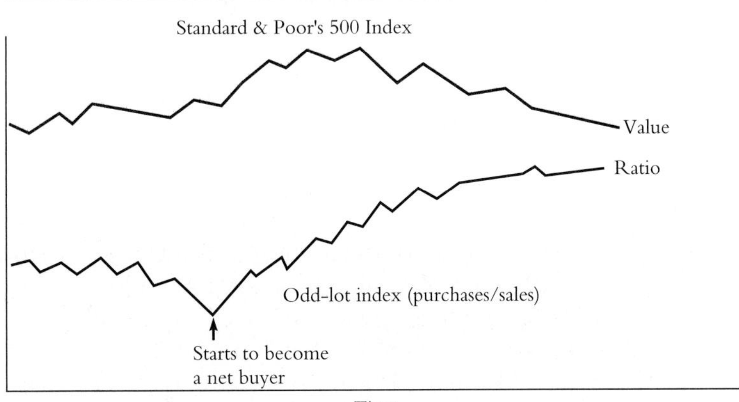

Odd-Lot Theory An odd-lot trade is one of less than 100 shares, and only small investors tend to engage in odd-lot transactions. The odd-lot theory suggests you watch very closely what the small investor is doing and then do the opposite. The weekly edition of *Barron's* breaks down odd-lot trading on a daily basis in its "Market Laboratory—Stocks" section. It is a simple matter to construct a ratio of odd-lot purchases to odd-lot sales. On October 8, 2010, for example, 16,261,100 odd-lot shares were purchased, and 16,910,900 shares were sold, indicating a ratio of 0.962. The ratio has historically fluctuated between 0.50 and 1.45.

www.barrons.com

The odd-lot theory actually suggests that the small trader does all right most of the time but badly misses on key market turns. As indicated in Figure 10–8, the odd-lot trader is on the correct path as the market is going up; that is, selling off part of the portfolio in an up market (the name of the game is to buy low and sell high). This net selling posture is reflected by a declining odd-lot index (purchase-to-sales ratio). However, as the market continues upward, the odd-lot trader suddenly thinks he or she sees an opportunity for a killing in the market and becomes a very strong net buyer. This precedes a fall in the market.

The odd-lot trader is also assumed to be a strong seller right before the bottom of a bear market. Presumably, when the small trader finally gets grandfather's 50 shares of AT&T out of the lockbox and sells them in disgust, it is time for the market to turn upward.

As if to add injury to insult, a corollary to the odd-lot theory says one should be particularly sensitive to what odd-lot traders do on Monday because odd-lotters tend to visit each other over the weekend, confirm each other's opinions or exchange hot tips, and then call their brokers on Monday morning. The assumption is that their chatter over the barbecue pit or in the bowling alley is even more suspect than their own individual opinions.

While the odd-lot theory appeared to have some validity in the 1950s and 1960s, it was not a particularly valuable tool in the last four decades. However, the odd-lotters outguessed many of the professional money managers in selling off before the stock market debacle of the mid-1970s and late 1980s, and they began buying in advance of a recovery. The same was true in the 500-plus-point market decline of October 1997 and the 300-point advance in the fall of 2003.

Short Sales Position A second contrary opinion rule is based on the volume of short sales in the market. As you recall from Chapter 3, a short sale represents the selling of a security you do not own with the anticipation of purchasing the security in the future to cover your short position. Investors would only engage in a short sale transaction if they believed the security would, in fact, be going down in price in the near future so they could buy back the security at a lower price to cover the short sale. When the aggregate number of short sellers is large (that is, they are bearish), this is thought to be a bullish signal.

The contrary opinion stems from two sources: first, short sellers are sometimes emotional and may overreact to the market; second and more important, there now is a built-in demand for stocks that have been sold short by investors who will have to repurchase the shares to cover their short positions.

Daily short sale totals for the New York Stock Exchange are recorded in *The Wall Street Journal*. Also once a month (around the 20th), *The Wall Street Journal* reports on total short sale figures for the two major exchanges as well as securities traded on those exchanges (based on midmonth data). This feature usually contains comments about current trends in the market.

Technical analysts compute a ratio of the total short sales positions on an exchange to average daily exchange volume for the month. The normal ratio is between 2.0 and 3.0. A ratio of 2.5 indicates that the current short sales position is equal to two and a half times the day's average trading volume.

As the short sales ratio (frequently called the short interest ratio) approaches the higher end of the normal trading range, this would be considered bullish (remember this is a contrary opinion trading rule). As is true with many other technical trading rules, its use in predicting future performance has produced mixed results.[7]

Applied to individual stocks, the same type of principles apply. If traders are aggressively short-selling MMM, Cisco Systems, or Microsoft, it may be time to buy.

Investment Advisory Recommendations A further contrary opinion rule states that you should watch the predictions of the investment advisory services and do the opposite. This has been formalized by Investors Intelligence (an investment advisory service itself) into the Index of Bearish Sentiment. When 60 percent or more of the advisory services are bearish, you should expect a market upturn. Conversely, when only 15 percent or fewer are bearish, you should expect a decline.[8]

Figure 10–9 gives a summary of bullish and bearish sentiments from the "Market Laboratory—Economic Indicators" section of *Barron's*. This is published under the heading of "Investor Sentiment Readings." Let's concentrate our attention on the AAII Index (American Association of Individual Investors Index). Since the percentage of bears is much closer to 15 percent than 60 percent, this indicates a possible sell under contrary opinion rules.

Lest one take investment advisory services too lightly, however, observe the market impact of a recommendation by Joseph Granville, publisher of the *Granville Market Letter*. On Tuesday, January 6, 1981, Granville issued a late-evening warning to his subscribers to "sell everything." He helped cause a $40 billion decline in market values the next day. Although subsequent events proved Granville wrong in his prediction of an impending bear market, the fact that one man could trigger such a reaction is an indication of the number of people who are influenced by the suggestions of advisory services. Granville has been followed by many other so-called gurus in the 1980s, 1990s, and 2000s, most of whom have their day in the sun and then eventually fall into disrepute as they fail to call a major turn in the market or begin reversing their positions so often that investors lose confidence. No doubt a new series of such stars will appear in the future.

Put-Call Ratio A final contrary opinion rule applies to the put-call ratio. Puts and calls represent options to sell or buy stock over a specified time period at a given price. A put is an option to sell, and a call is an option to buy. Options have become very popular since they began trading actively on organized exchanges in 1973. As you will see in Chapter 14, there are many sophisticated uses for options

---

[7] Joseph Vu and Paul Caster, "Why All the Interest in Short Interest?" *Financial Analysts Journal*, July–August 1987, pp. 77–79.

[8] John R. Dortman, "The Stock Market Sign Often Points the Wrong Way," *The Wall Street Journal*, January 26, 1989, p. C1.

FIGURE 10-9 Investor Sentiment Readings

INVESTOR SENTIMENT READINGS

High bullish readings in the Consensus stock index or in the Market Vane stock index usually are signs of Market tops; low ones, market bottoms.

	Last Week	2 Weeks Ago	3 Weeks Ago
Consensus Index			
Consensus Bullish Sentiment	58%	56%	63%
Source: Consensus Inc., P.O. Box 520526, Independence, Mo. Historical data available at (800) 383-1441.editor@consensus-inc.com			
AAII Index			
Bullish	47.1%	49.0%	42.5%
Bearish	26.8	27.7	31.6
Neutral	26.1	23.2	25.9
Source: American Association of Individual Investors, 625 N. Michigan Ave., Chicago, Ill. 60611 (312) 280-0170.			
Market Vane			
Bullish Consensus	56%	54%	54%
Source: Market Vane, P.O. Box 90490, Pasadena, CA91109 (626) 395-7436.			
FC Market Sentiment			
Indicator	54.9%	54.5%	55.9%
Source: First Coverage 260 Franklin St., Suite 900 Boston, MA02110-3112 (617) 303-0180. info@firstcoverage.com			

Source: *Barron's,* October 18, 2010, p. M53. Reprinted with permission of *Barron's,* Copyright © 2010 Dow Jones & Company, Inc. All Rights Reserved Worldwide.

to implement portfolio strategies (particularly to protect against losses). However, there is also a great deal of speculation by individual investors in the options market. Because some of this speculation is ill-conceived, ratios based on options may tell you to do the opposite of what option traders are doing.

The ratio of put (sell) options to call (buy) options is normally about 0.60. There are generally fewer traders of put options than call options. However, when the ratio gets up to 0.65 to 0.70 or higher, this indicates increasing pessimism by option traders. Under a contrary opinion rule, this indicates a buy signal (he turned left so you turn right). If the put-call ratio goes down to 0.40, the decreasing pessimism (increasing optimism) of the option trader may indicate that it is time to sell if you are a contrarian. The put-call ratio has a better than average record for calling market turns. Put-call ratio data can be found in the "Market Week—Options" section of *Barron's.*

VIX (The Fear Index) One way investors can measure risk is to look at the volatility of the market. Risk can be measured using an implied volatility index called the **VIX**. The VIX is the Chicago Board Options Exchange Volatility Index, which measures the expected movement in the Standard & Poor's 500 Index. The VIX helps put and call investors determine the premiums that should be attached to options. The higher the VIX, the more risk and volatility expected, and therefore the higher the option premium. The VIX is calculated as an annualized number and is expressed as a percentage. For example, if the VIX is at 25, the expectation is that the market (the Standard and Poor's 500 Index) could move up or down by 25 percent during the next 30 days.

Stock market investors use the VIX to measure the level of risk premiums they should use in determining their required rate of return. The higher the VIX, the

FIGURE 10-10 VIX 1990-2010

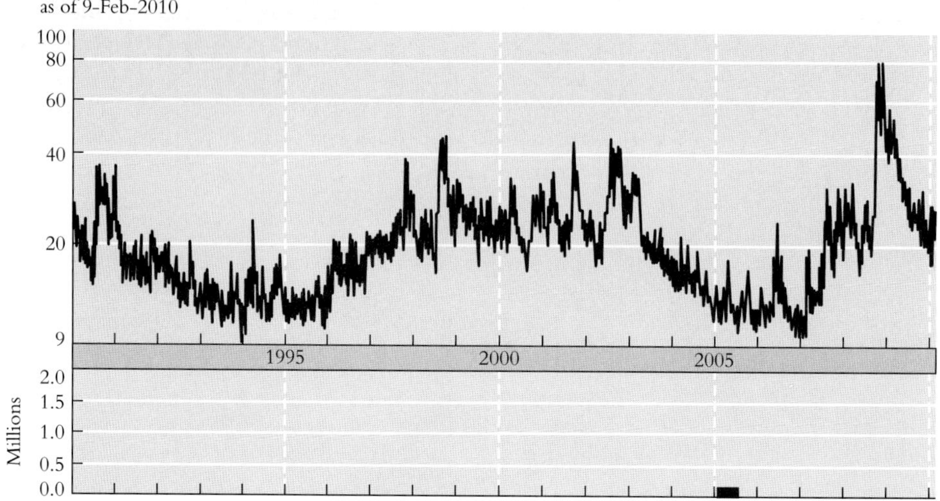

Source: Copyright 2010 Yahoo! Inc. http://finance.yahoo.com/

higher the volatility risk. As the VIX increases, so does the investor's required return. Figure 10–10 shows that the VIX peaked at 80 during the November–December period of 2008 (at the height of the financial crisis) and remained relatively high through 2009. A normal risk range is between 10 and 20 percent.

Smart Money Rules

Market technicians have long attempted to track the pattern of sophisticated traders in the hope that they might provide unusual insight into the future. We briefly observe theories related to bond market traders and stock exchange specialists.

Barron's Confidence Index

The ***Barron's* Confidence Index** is used to observe the trading pattern of investors in the bond market. The theory is based on the premise that bond traders are more sophisticated than stock traders and pick up trends more quickly. The theory suggests that a person who can figure out what bond traders are doing today may be able to determine what stock market investors will be doing in the near future.

application example

Barron's Confidence Index is actually computed by taking the yield on 10 top-grade corporate bonds, dividing by the yield on 40 intermediate-grade bonds,[9] and multiplying by 100:

$$\text{Barron's Confidence Index} = \frac{\text{Yield on 10 top-grade corporate bonds}}{\text{Yield on 40 intermediate-grade bonds}} \times 100 \quad \textbf{(10–1)}$$

The index is published weekly in the "Market Laboratory—Bonds" section of *Barron's.* What does it actually tell us? First, we can assume that the top-grade bonds in the numerator always have a smaller yield than the intermediate-grade bonds in the denominator. The reason is that the higher quality issues can satisfy investors with smaller returns. The

[9] The 40 bonds compose the Dow Jones 40 bond averages.

bond market is very representative of a risk-return trade-off environment in which less risk requires less return and higher risk necessitates a higher return.

With top-grade bonds providing smaller yields than intermediate-grade bonds, the Confidence Index is always less than 100 (percent). The normal trading range is between 80 and 96, and it is within this range that technicians look for signals on the economy. If bond investors are bullish about future economic prosperity, they are rather indifferent between holding top-grade bonds and holding intermediate-grade bonds, and the yield differences between these two categories is relatively small. This would indicate the Confidence Index may be close to 96. An example is presented below in which top-grade bonds are providing 8.4 percent and intermediate-grade bonds are yielding 9.1 percent:

$$\textit{Barron's}\text{ Confidence Index} = \frac{\text{Yield on 10 top-grade corporate bonds}}{\text{Yield on 40 intermediate-grade bonds}} \times 100$$

$$= \frac{8.4\%}{9.1\%} \times 100 = 92(\%)$$

Now let us assume that investors become quite concerned about the outlook for the future health of the economy. If events go poorly, some weaker corporations may not be able to make their interest payments, and thus, bond market investors will have a strong preference for top-quality issues. Some investors continue to invest in intermediate- or lower-quality issues but only at a sufficiently high yield differential to justify the risk. We might assume that the *Barron's* Confidence Index will drop to 83 because of the increasing spread between the two yields in the formula:

$$\textit{Barron's}\text{ Confidence Index} = \frac{\text{Yield on 10 top-grade corporate bonds}}{\text{Yield on 40 intermediate-grade bonds}} \times 100$$

$$= \frac{8.9\%}{10.7\%} \times 100 = 83(\%)$$

The yield on the intermediate-grade bonds is now 1.8 percentage points higher than that on the 10 top-grade bonds, and this is reflected in the lower Confidence Index reading. As confidence in the economy is once again regained, the yield spread differential narrows, and the Confidence Index goes up.

Market technicians assume there are a few months of lead time between what happens to the Confidence Index and what happens to the economy and stock market. As is true with other such indicators, it has a mixed record of predicting future events. One problem is that the Confidence Index is only assumed to consider the impact of investors' attitudes on yields (their demand pattern). We have seen in the 1990s and 2000s that the supply of new bond issues can also influence yields. Thus, a very large bond issue by General Electric or ExxonMobil may drive up high-grade bond yields even though investor attitudes indicate they should be going down.

Short Sales by Specialists Another smart money index is based on the short sales positions of specialists. Recall from Chapter 2 that specialists make markets in various securities listed on the organized exchanges. Because of the uniquely close position of specialists to the action on Wall Street, market technicians ascribe unusual importance to their decisions. One measure of their activity that is frequently monitored is the ratio of specialists' short sales to the total amount of short sales on an exchange.

When we previously mentioned short sales in this chapter, we suggested that a high incidence of short selling might be considered bullish because short sellers often overreact to the market and provide future demand potential to cover their short position. In the case of market specialists, this is not necessarily true. These sophisticated traders keep a book of limit and stop orders on their securities so that they have a close feel for market activity at any given time, and their decisions are considered important.

The normal ratio of specialist short sales to short sales on an exchange is about 45 percent. When the ratio goes up to 50 percent or more, market technicians interpret this as a bearish signal. A ratio under 40 percent is considered bullish.

Overall Market Rules

Our discussion of key indicator series has centered on both contrary opinion rules and smart money rules. We now briefly examine two overall market indicators: the breadth of the market indicator series and the cash position of mutual funds.

Breadth of the Market A breadth of the market indicator attempts to measure what a broad range of securities is doing as opposed to merely examining a market average. The theory is that market averages, such as the Dow Jones Industrial Average of 30 stocks or the Standard & Poor's 500 Stock Average, are weighted toward large firms and may not be representative of the entire market. To get a broader perspective of the market, an analyst may examine all stocks on an exchange.

The technician often compares the advance-declines with the movement of a popular market average to determine whether there is a divergence between the two. Advances and declines usually move in concert with the popular market averages but may move in the opposite direction at a market peak or bottom. One of the possible signals for the end of a bull market is when the Dow Jones Industrial Average is moving up but the number of daily declines consistently exceeds the number of daily advances on the New York Stock Exchange. This indicates that conservative investors are investing in blue-chip stocks but that there is a lack of broad-based confidence in the market.

application example

TABLE 10-1 Comparing Advance-Decline Data and the Dow Jones Industrial Average (DJIA)

	(1)	(2)	(3)	(4)	(5)	(6)
Day	Advances	Declines	Unchanged	Net Advances or Declines	Cumulative Advances or Declines	DJIA
1	1607	1507	201	+100	+100	+33.38
2	1550	1560	188	−10	+90	+20.51
3	1504	1602	194	−98	−8	+13.08
4	1499	1506	295	−7	−15	+35.21
5	1530	1573	208	−43	−58	−12.02
6	1550	1562	186	−12	−70	+50.43
7	1455	1650	200	−155	−225	+30.10
8	1285	1815	212	−530	−755	+21.30

In Table 10–1, we look at an example of divergence between the advance-decline indicators on the New York Stock Exchange and the Dow Jones Industrial Average (DJIA).

In Column 4, we see the daily differences in advances and declines. In Column 5, we look at the cumulative pattern by adding or subtracting each new day's value from the previous total. We then compare the information in Column 4 and Column 5 to the Dow Jones Industrial Average (DJIA) in Column 6. Clearly, the strength in the Dow Jones Industrial Average is not reflected in the advance-decline data, and this may be interpreted as signaling future weakness in the market.

Breadth of the market data can also be used to analyze upturns in the market. When the Dow Jones Industrial Average is going down but advances consistently lead declines, the market may be positioned for a recovery. Some market technicians develop sophisticated weighted averages of the daily advance-declines to go along with the data in Table 10–1. Daily data on the Dow Jones Industrial Average and advancing and declining issues can be found in the "Stock Market Data Bank" section of *The Wall Street Journal*.

While a comparison of advance-decline data to market averages can provide important insights, there is also the danger of false signals. Not every divergence between the two signals a turn in the market, so analysts must be careful in their interpretations. The technical analyst must look at a wide range of variables. With the advent of decimalization of stock prices in 2001, many technicians think this indicator has lost some of its usefulness because now stocks only have to advance or decline a penny to make the list.

Mutual Fund Cash Position Another overall market indicator is the cash position of mutual funds. This measure indicates the buying potential of mutual funds and is generally representative of the purchasing potential of other large institutional investors. The cash position of mutual funds, as a percentage of their total assets, generally varies between 5 and 20 percent.[10]

At the lower end of the boundary, it would appear that mutual funds are fully invested and can provide little in the way of additional purchasing power. As their cash position goes to 15 percent or higher, market technicians assess this as representing significant purchasing power that may help to trigger a market upturn. While the overall premise is valid, there are problems in identifying just what is a significant cash position for mutual funds in a given market cycle. It may change in extreme market environments.

exploring the web

Web Address	Comments
www.bigcharts.com	**Provides data, charts, and technical indicators, free**
http://moneywatch.bnet.com	**Has technical charts and information**
www.quicken.com	**Contains some technical analytical data and charts**
www.stockworm.com	**Has technical charts**
www.stockcharts.com	**Provides free technical charts and education on technical analysis**
www.investopedia.com	**Has primer on technical analysis**
www.stocksites.com	**Contains links to technical analysis sites and related finance sites**

[10] The cash dollars are usually placed in short-term credit instruments as opposed to stocks and bonds.

SUMMARY

Following the discussion of fundamental analysis in Chapters 5 though 8 and the discussion of efficient markets and anomalies in Chapter 9, we turn to behavioral finance and technical analysis in this chapter.

Behavioral finance is the application of psychology to financial decision-making regarding risk-return trade-offs. Behavioral finance examines how investors make decisions, and finds that their decision making is not as rational as economic utility theory would imply. Prospect theory, developed by Kahneman and Tversky, found that investors prefer a sure thing over the probability of a higher return. This is especially true when faced with a 50 percent probability of a positive return and a 50 percent probability of a zero return, even when the expected value is greater than the sure thing. We also find that investors are reluctant to take losses and are more likely to sell their winners and keep their losers.

Investors often overreact to good news and bad news, and this phenomenon reinforces the idea of investing based on contrary opinion rules. When the market sells stocks on bad news to the extent that they become oversold (undervalued), then perhaps it is time to buy. When the market buys stocks on good news and pushes their price to unreasonable levels because of overreaction, then perhaps it is time to sell or sell short.

Technical analysis is based on the study of past price and volume data, as well as associated market trends, to predict future price movements. Technical analysis relies heavily on charting and the use of key market indicators to make forecasts. Technical analysts also observe support and resistance levels in the market as well as data on volume. Line, bar, and point and figure charts are used to determine turns in the market.

Market technicians also follow a number of key indicator series to predict the stock market—contrary opinion indicators, smart money indicators, and general market indicators.

Although there have been traditional arguments about whether fundamental or technical analysis is more important, a great deal of current attention is directed to the efficient market hypothesis and its implications for all types of analysis. This topic will be discussed in the following chapter.

KEY WORDS AND CONCEPTS

DISCUSSION QUESTIONS

1. Discuss market bubbles and offer an opinion on why you think investors have trouble spotting bubbles.
2. Describe the three heuristics that investors use as "rules of thumb."
3. If you "buy straw hats in winter" or buy "when there is blood in the street," what kind of investor are you?
4. How does prospect theory differ from standard economic utility theory?
5. What does the overreaction hypothesis state, and what are its implications for investors?

6. Mental accounting and framing are two behavioral traits investors exhibit. How do these traits influence decision making?
7. How can momentum investing lead to the winner/loser proposition?
8. What does behavioral research indicate about the difference between men and women investors, on average?
9. What is technical analysis?
10. What are the views of technical analysts toward fundamental analysis?
11. Outline the basic assumptions of technical analysis.
12. Under the Dow theory, if a recovery fails to exceed the previous high and a new low penetrates a previous low, what does this tell us about the market?
13. Also under the Dow theory, what other average is used to confirm movements in the Dow Jones Industrial Average?
14. What is meant by a support level for a stock or a market average? When might a support level exist?
15. In examining Figure 10–7 on page 272, if the next price movement is to 34, will a shift to a new column be indicated? (Assume the current price is 36.)
16. What is the logic behind the odd-lot theory? If the odd-lot index starts to move higher in an up market, what does the odd-lot theory indicate the next movement in the market will be?
17. If the Investors Intelligence Service has a bearish sentiment of 70 percent, would you generally want to be a buyer or seller?
18. What is the logic behind *Barron's* Confidence Index?
19. If the advance-decline movement in the market is weak (more declines than advances) while the DJIA is going up, what might this indicate to a technician about the market?
20. Categorize the following as either contrary opinion or smart money indicators (as viewed by technicians):
    a. Short sales by specialists.
    b. Odd-lot positions.
    c. Short sales positions.
    d. *Barron's* Confidence Index.
    e. Investment advisory recommendations.
    f. Put-call ratio.

WEB EXERCISE

Exercise 1

Assume you want to see how much momentum a stock has going forward (a form of technical analysis). Go to **http://finance.yahoo.com**.

1. In the "Get Quotes" box put in the symbol for any stock and press Enter. If you do not have a preference, use pg (Procter & Gamble).
2. Click on "Basic Chart" in the left column. Looking at the entire graph, has the overall momentum generally been up or down? Write a one- to two-sentence answer for this and the following questions.
3. If you were to draw a straight line of best fit through the data, what stock price would you be projecting for the future?
4. Have the peaks generally been associated with high or low volumes? What about the lows?
5. In the left column, click on "Analyst Opinion." Has the "Mean Recommendation" gone up or down over the last week? Is this consistent with the future outlook line you constructed in part 3?

www.mhhe.com/hirtblock10e

6. Scroll down to "Upgrades and Downgrades History." What firm(s) are the most bullish on this stock? What firms are the most bearish?

Exercise 2

1. Log on to BigCharts at **http://bigcharts.marketwatch.com**.
2. Put Johnson & Johnson's ticker symbol (JNJ) in the upper left hand box and click on "Advanced Chart."
3. Click on "compare to" and under "Index" choose S&P 500. Then click on "Draw Chart." You should have a 1 year graph comparing J&J with the S&P 500 index. How has Johnson & Johnson performed compared to the S&P for the last year?
4. Now go to the "Time" dropdown and choose 5 years, then click on "Draw Chart." Repeat this drill for 1 decade and then all data. Can you offer some explanation as to why there is such a disparity between the performance of Johnson & Johnson and the S&P for the various time periods? Assume that you are a student with a 40-year time horizon and then assume you are advising a 70-year-old. Does this information have a different significance to each of these age categories? In what way?
5. Reset the time frame to 1 decade. Now click on "Indicators" and under "Moving Average" choose SMA, then next to it type the number 200. Note you must click on "Draw Chart" every time you change a setting. Is Johnson & Johnson priced below or above its 200-day smoothed moving average? What might the significance of this be? How has Johnson & Johnson performed compared to the S&P 500 during this time?
6. Now choose A/D Line under "Upper Indicators." This is the advance/decline line for the NYSE index. Has J&J advanced and declined in tangent with the A/D line or has it shown a different pattern?
7. Next click on P/E Ratio under "Lower Indicator 1." A separate graph below the price graph will appear. What has been happening to J&J price earnings ratio over this time period?
8. Then choose Rolling EPS under "Lower Indicator 2." A second graph will appear showing the earnings per share over the last decade. What has been happening to EPS over the last 10 years?
9. Finally, under "Lower Indicator 3" choose Money Flow, which measures the flow of money into and out of a particular stock. A third graph will appear showing the money flow. How does the money flow correspond with Johnson & Johnson's price performance?
10. If you find this exercise interesting you can go back and use 1 month, 6 months, 1 year, and any other time period that might be of interest and see how the variables change.
11. For an even more advanced charting program, you can go back to the beginning of the exercise and use interactive charting methods rather than advanced charting methods. The interactive charting might require you to download a Java-based program before you can access the program. With the interactive charting tool, you now have a tool for decision making that includes technical indicators and some fundamental indicators. You can repeat this exercise by changing many of the variables. Some of the technical indicators that are available are not discussed in this chapter; it is not the purpose of this exercise to demonstrate advanced technical analysis but to expose you to the many ways technical analysts construct methods to analyze trends in the market. Since most academics believe in a less than efficient market system, don't expect your professor to believe in the power of all these methods or even to be able to explain them.

Note: From time to time, companies redesign their Web sites, and occasionally a topic we have listed may have been deleted, updated, or moved into a different location.

FIXED-INCOME AND LEVERAGED SECURITIES

PART [four] 4

chapter 11
BOND AND FIXED-INCOME FUNDAMENTALS

chapter 12
PRINCIPLES OF BOND VALUATION AND INVESTMENT

chapter 13
CONVERTIBLE SECURITIES AND WARRANTS

chapter eleven

BOND AND FIXED-INCOME FUNDAMENTALS

OBJECTIVES

1. Explain the fundamental characteristics of a bond issue.
2. Describe the differences among bonds offered by the U.S. government, state and local governments, and corporations.
3. Explain the difference between a private placement and public distribution of a bond.
4. Explain the meaning and impact of bond ratings.
5. Understand how to read bond quotes in the financial press.
6. Describe the characteristics of other forms of fixed-income securities such as preferred stock, money market funds, etc.

OUTLINE

As the reader will observe in various sections of this chapter, bonds actually represent a more substantial portion of new offerings in the capital markets than common stock. Some of the most financially rewarding jobs on Wall Street go to sophisticated analysts and dealers in the bond market. If you are to be a player in this market, you must understand the terms and financial ramifications of bond trading.

In this chapter, we examine the fundamentals of the bond instrument for both corporate and government issuers, with an emphasis on the debt contract and security provisions. We also look at the overall structure of the bond market and the ways in which bonds are rated. The question of bond market efficiency is also considered. While most of the chapter deals with corporate and government bonds, other forms of fixed-income securities also receive attention. Thus, there is a brief discussion of short-term, fixed-income investments (such as certificates of deposit and commercial paper) as well as preferred stock.

In Chapter 12, we shift the emphasis to actually evaluating fixed-income investments and devising strategies that attempt to capture profitable opportunities in the market. In Chapter 13, we look at the interesting concept of convertible securities and warrants. We begin our discussion by considering the key elements that go into a bond contract.

THE BOND CONTRACT

A bond normally represents a long-term contractual obligation of the firm to pay interest to the bondholder as well as the face value of the bond at maturity. The major provisions in a bond agreement are spelled out in the **bond indenture**, a complicated legal document often more than 100 pages long, administered by an independent trustee (usually a commercial bank). We shall examine some important terms and concepts associated with a bond issue.

The **par value** represents the face value of a bond. Most corporate bonds are traded in $1,000 units, while many federal, state, and local issues trade in units of $5,000 or $10,000.

Coupon rate refers to the actual interest rate on the bond, usually payable in semiannual installments. To the extent that interest rates in the market go above or below the coupon rate after the bond is issued, the market price of the bond will change from the par value. A bond initially issued at a rate of 8 percent will sell at a substantial discount from par value when 12 percent is the currently demanded rate of return. We will eventually examine how the investor makes and loses large amounts of money in the bond market with the swings in interest rates. A few corporate bonds are termed **variable-rate notes** or **floating-rate notes**, meaning the coupon rate is fixed for only a short period and then varies with a stipulated short-term rate such as the rate on U.S. Treasury bills. In this instance, the interest payment rather than the price of the bond varies up and down. In recent times, zero-coupon bonds have also been issued at values substantially below maturity value. With **zero-coupon bonds**, the investor receives return in the form of capital appreciation over the life of the bond since no semiannual cash interest payments are received.

The **maturity date** is the date on which final payment is due at the stipulated par value.

Methods of bond repayment can occur under many different arrangements. Some bonds are never paid off, such as selected **perpetual bonds** issued by the Canadian and British governments, and have no maturity dates. A more normal procedure would simply call for a single-sum lump payment at the end of the obligation. Thus, the issuer may make 40 semiannual interest payments over the next 20 years plus one lump-sum payment of the par value of the bond at maturity. There are also other significant means of repayment.

The first is the **serial payment** in which bonds are paid off in installments over the life of the issue. Each serial bond has its own predetermined date of maturity and receives interest only to that point. Although the total bond issue may span more than 20 years, 15 to 20 maturity dates are assigned. Municipal bonds are often issued on this basis. Second, there may be a **sinking-fund provision** in which semiannual or annual contributions are made by a corporation into a fund administered by a trustee for purposes of debt retirement. The trustee takes the proceeds and goes into the market to purchase bonds from willing sellers. If no sellers are available, a lottery system may be used to repurchase the required number of bonds from among outstanding bondholders.

Third, debt may also be retired under a call provision. A **call provision** allows the corporation to call or force in all of the debt issue prior to maturity. The corporation usually pays a 3 to 5 percent premium over par value as part of the call provision arrangement. The ability to call is often *deferred* for the first 5 or 10 years of an issue (it can only occur after this time period).

The opposite side of the coin for a bond investor is a put provision. The **put provision** enables the bondholder to have an option to sell a long-term bond back to the corporation at par value after a relatively short period (such as three to five years). This privilege can be particularly valuable if interest rates have gone up since the initial issuance, and the bond is currently trading at 75 to 80 percent of par. A put bond generally carries a lower interest rate than conventional bonds (perhaps 1 to 2 percent lower) because of this protective put privilege. If one buys a put bond and interest rates go down and bond prices up (perhaps to $1,200), the privilege is unnecessary and is merely ignored.

SECURED AND UNSECURED BONDS

We have discussed some of the important features related to interest payments and retirement of outstanding issues. At least of equal importance is the nature of the security provision for the issue. Bond market participants have a long-standing practice of describing certain issues by the nature of asset claims in liquidation. In actuality, pledged assets are sold and the proceeds distributed to bondholders only infrequently. Typically, the defaulting corporation is reorganized, and existing claims are partially satisfied by issuing new securities to the participating parties. Of course, the stronger and *better secured* the initial claim, the higher the quality of the security to be received in a reorganization.

A number of terms are used to denote **secured debt**, that is, debt backed by collateral. Under a **mortgage** agreement, real property (plant and equipment) is pledged as security for a loan. A mortgage may be senior or junior in nature, with the former requiring satisfaction of claims before payment is given to the latter. Bondholders may also attach an **after-acquired property clause** requiring that any new property be placed under the original mortgage.

A very special form of a mortgage or collateralized debt instrument is the **equipment trust certificate** used by firms in the transportation industry (railroads, airlines, etc.). Proceeds from the sale of the certificate are used to purchase new equipment, and this new equipment serves as collateral for the trust certificate.

Not all bond issues are secured or collateralized by assets. Most federal, state, and local government issues are unsecured. A wide range of corporate issues also are unsecured. There is a set of terminology referring to these unsecured issues. A corporate debt issue that is unsecured is referred to as a **debenture**. Even though a debenture is not secured by a specific pledge of assets, there may be priorities of claims among debenture holders. Thus, there are senior debentures and junior or subordinated debentures.

If liquidation becomes necessary because all other avenues for survival have failed, secured creditors are paid off first out of the disposition of the secured assets. The proceeds from the sale of the balance of the assets are then distributed among unsecured creditors, with those holding a senior ranking being satisfied before those holding a subordinate position (subordinated debenture holders).[1]

Unsecured corporate debt may provide slightly higher yields because of the greater suggested risk. However, this is partially offset by the fact that many unsecured debt issuers have such strong financial statements that security pledges may not be necessary.

Companies with less favorable prospects may issue income bonds. **Income bonds** specify that interest is to be paid only to the extent that it is earned as current income. There is no legally binding requirement to pay interest on a regular basis, and failure to make interest payments cannot trigger bankruptcy proceedings. These issues appear to offer the corporation the unusual advantage of paying interest as a tax-deductible expense (as opposed to dividends) combined with freedom from the

[1] Those secured creditors who are not fully satisfied by the disposition of secured assets may also participate with the unsecured creditors in the remaining assets.

binding contractual obligation of most debt issues. But any initial enthusiasm for these issues is quickly reduced by recognizing that they have very limited appeal to investors. The issuance of income bonds is usually restricted to circumstances where new corporate debt is issued to old bondholders or preferred stockholders to avoid bankruptcy or where a troubled corporation is being reorganized.

THE COMPOSITION OF THE BOND MARKET

Having established some of the basic terminology relating to the bond instrument, we are now in a position to take a more comprehensive look at the bond market. Corporate issues must vie with offerings from the U.S. Treasury, federally sponsored credit agencies, and state and local governments (municipal offerings). The relative importance of the four types of issues is indicated in Figure 11–1.

Over the 40-year period presented in Figure 11–1, the two fastest growing users of funds (borrowers) were the U.S. government and corporations. The former's needs can be attributed to persistent federal deficits that must be financed by increased borrowing.

In the case of corporations, strong growth combined with the need to finance mergers and leveraged buyouts has led to increased borrowing requirements. State and local governments have been active participants with municipal bond issues used to finance local growth and cover local deficits. Please observe the explosive growth in long-term borrowing by all sectors of the economy since 1990.

U.S. Government Securities

U.S. government securities take the form of Treasury bills, Treasury notes, and Treasury bonds (only the latter two are considered in Figure 11–1). The distinction among the three categories relates to the life of the obligation. A fourth category, termed Treasury strips, has other attributes and is also discussed.

Treasury bills (T-bills) have maturities of 91 and 182 days. Treasury bills trade on a discount basis, meaning the yield the investor receives occurs as a result of the difference between the price paid and the maturity value (and no actual interest is paid). A further discussion of this is presented later in the chapter.

Treasury bills trade in minimum units of $1,000, and there is an extremely active secondary, or resale, market for these securities. Thus, an investor buying a Treasury bill from the government with an initial life of approximately six months would have

FIGURE 11-1 Long-Term Funds Raised by Business and Government

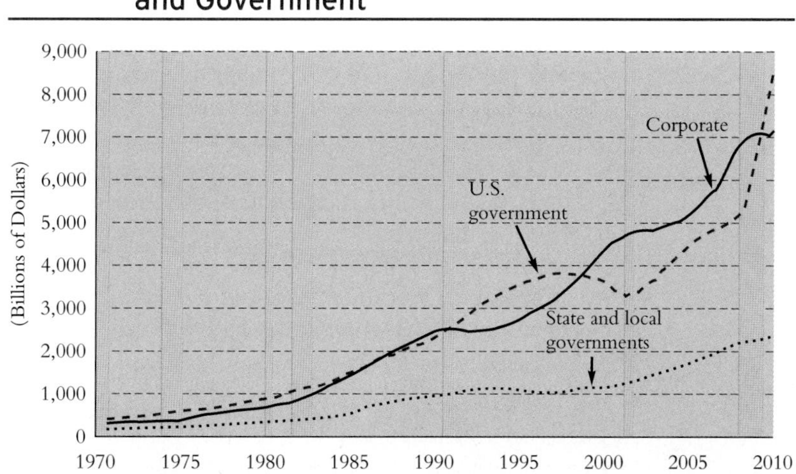

Note: Shaded areas indicate U.S. recessions.

Source: St. Louis Federal Reserve, FRED database, http://research.stlouisfed.org.

no difficulty selling it to another investor after two or three weeks. Because the T-bill now has a shorter time to run, its market value would be a bit closer to par.

A second type of U.S. government security is the **Treasury note**, which is considered to be of intermediate term and generally has a maturity of 1 to 10 years. Finally, **Treasury bonds** are long term in nature and mature in 10 to 30 years. Unlike Treasury bills, Treasury notes and bonds provide direct interest and trade in units of $1,000 and higher. Because there is no risk of default (unless the government stops printing money or the ultimate bomb explodes), U.S. government securities provide lower returns than other forms of credit obligations. Interest on U.S. government issues is fully taxable for IRS purposes but is exempt from state and local taxes.

Treasury securities may also trade in the form of **Treasury strips** (strip-Ts). Treasury strips pay no interest, and all returns to the investor come in the form of increases in the value of the investment (as is true of Treasury bills also). Treasury strips are referred to as zero-coupon securities because of the absence of interest payments.

As an example, 25-year Treasury strips might initially sell for 29.5 percent of par value. You could buy a 25-year, $10,000 Treasury strip for $2,950.[2] All your return would come in the form of an increase in value. Of course, you could sell at the going market price before maturity should you so desire.

Actually the U.S. Treasury does not offer Treasury strips directly. It allows government security dealers to strip off the interest payments and principal payment from regular Treasury notes and bonds and repackage them as Treasury strips. For example, on a 25-year Treasury bond, there would be an annuity of 50 semiannual interest payments and one final principal payment. Each of these 50 payments could be stripped off and sold as a zero-coupon strip.[3] Those who desired short-term Treasury strips would buy into the early payments. The opposite would be true for an investor with a long-term orientation.

The Internal Revenue Service taxes zero-coupon bonds, such as Treasury strips, as if interest were paid annually even though no cash flow is received until maturity. The tax is based on amortizing the built-in gain over the life of the instrument. For tax reasons, zero coupons are usually only appropriate for tax-deferred accounts such as individual retirement accounts, 401(k) plans, or other nontaxable pension funds.

Inflation-Indexed Treasury Securities

In January 1997, the U.S. Treasury began offering 10-year notes that were intended to protect investors against the effects of inflation. The maturities were later expanded to include longer terms to maturity.

Here's how these inflation-indexed Treasury notes work. The investor receives two forms of return as a result of owning the security. The first is annual interest that is paid out semiannually, and the second is an automatic increase in the initial value of principal to account for inflation.

These securities are formally called **Treasury Inflation Protection Securities (TIPS)**. TIPS might pay 3.5 percent in annual interest and, assuming a 3 percent rate of inflation, an additional 3 percent to compensate for inflation. As implied in the preceding paragraph, the 3 percent inflation adjustment is not paid in cash but is added on to the principal value of the bond. Assume the bond had an initial par value of $1,000. At the end of the first year, the principal value would go up to $1,030. Thus, during the first year, the investor would receive $35 (3.5 percent) in cash as interest payments, plus enjoy a $30 increase in principal. On a 10-year indexed Treasury security, this procedure continues for each of the remaining nine years and at maturity, the security is redeemed at the indexed value of the principal by the Treasury. If the

[2] The yield is approximately 5 percent. Zero-coupon securities are also offered by corporations and are discussed more fully in Chapter 18.

[3] Any one payment, such as the first, may be stripped from many hundreds of Treasury bonds at one time to provide a $10,000 Treasury strip.

investor needs to sell before the maturity date, he or she can sell it in the secondary market to other investors at a value approximating the appreciated principal value.[4]

The reader should be aware that the base against which the 3.5 percent annual interest is paid is the inflation-adjusted value of the security. Thus, in the second year, the interest payment would be \$36.05 (3.5% × \$1,030). In each subsequent year, there is a similar adjustment depending on the prior year's rate of inflation.

Assuming inflation remains at 3 percent over the 10-year time period, the inflation-adjusted value of the principal will increase to \$1,344 (10 periods compounded at 3 percent). The investor is effectively getting a return of 6.5 percent in the form of interest and appreciation of principal. Of course, if inflation averages 6 percent over the life of the investment, the investor will get a return of 9.5 percent. The interest payment (real return) will remain at 3.5 percent, but the inflation adjustment will supply the extra return.

Through inflation-indexed Treasury notes, the investor is protected against the effect of inflation. This may be quite a benefit if inflation is high, but the security can provide an inferior return compared with other investments in a low-inflation environment.

Also, the investor should be aware that the annual adjustment in principal is treated as taxable income each year even though no cash is received until redemption at maturity. For this reason, inflation-indexed Treasury securities are more appropriate for tax-deferred or nontaxable accounts.

Federally Sponsored Credit Agency Issues

www.fanniemae.com
www.fhlbanks.com

Securities issued by federal agencies represent obligations of various agencies of the government such as the Federal National Mortgage Association and the Federal Home Loan Bank. Although these issues are authorized by an act of Congress and are used to finance federal projects, they are not direct obligations of the Treasury but rather of the agency itself.

While the issues are essentially free of risk (there is always the implicit standby power of the government behind the issues), they carry a slightly higher yield than U.S. government securities simply because they are not directly issued by the Treasury. Agency issues have been particularly active as a support mechanism for the housing industry. The issues generally trade in denominations of \$5,000 and up and have varying maturities of from 1 to 40 years, with an average life of approximately 15 years. Examples of some agency issues are presented below:

	Minimum Denomination	Life of Issue
Federal Home Loan Bank	\$10,000	12–25 years
Federal Intermediate Credit Banks	5,000	Up to 4 years
Federal Farm Credit Bank	50,000	1–10 years
Export-Import Bank	5,000	Up to 7 years

Interest on agency issues is fully taxable for IRS purposes and is generally taxable for state and local purposes although there are exceptions. (For example, interest on obligations issued by the Federal Farm Credit Bank is subject to state and local taxes, but those of the Federal Home Loan Bank are not.)

www.ginniemae.gov

One agency issue that is of particular interest to the investor because of its unique features is the **GNMA (Ginnie Mae) pass-through certificate**. These certificates represent an undivided interest in a pool of federally insured mortgages.

[4] Other factors can come into play in pricing this security, but they unnecessarily complicate this basic example.

Actually, GNMA, the Government National Mortgage Association, buys a pool of mortgages from various lenders at a discount and then issues securities to the public against these mortgages. Security holders in GNMA certificates receive monthly payments that essentially represent a pass-through of interest and principal payments on the mortgages. These securities come in minimum denominations of \$25,000, are long term, and are fully taxable for federal, state, and local income tax purposes. A major consideration in this investment is that the investor has fully consumed his or her capital at the end of the investment. (Not only has interest been received monthly but also all principal has been returned over the life of the certificate, and therefore, there is no lump-sum payment at maturity.)

Because mortgages that are part of GNMA pass-through certificates are often paid off early as a result of the sale of a home or refinancing at lower interest rates, the true life of a GNMA certificate tends to be much less than the quoted life. For example, a 25-year GNMA certificate may actually be paid off in 12 years. This feature can be a negative consideration because GNMA certificates are particularly likely to be paid off early when interest rates are going down and homeowners are refinancing. The investor in the GNMA certificate is then forced to reinvest the proceeds in a low interest rate environment.

State and Local Government Securities

Debt securities issued by state and local governments are referred to as **municipal bonds**. Examples of issuing agencies include states, cities, school districts, toll roads, or any other type of political subdivision. The most important feature of a municipal bond is the tax-exempt nature of the interest payment. Dating back to the U.S. Supreme Court opinion of 1819 in *McCullough v. Maryland,* it was ruled that the federal government and state and local governments do not possess the power to tax each other. An eventual by-product of the judicial ruling was that income from municipal bonds cannot be taxed by the IRS. Furthermore, income from municipal bonds is also exempt from state and local taxes if bought within the locality in which one resides. Thus, a Californian buying municipal bonds in that state would pay no state income tax on the issue. However, the same Californian would have to pay state or local income taxes if the originating agency were in Texas or New York.

We cannot overemphasize the importance of the federal tax exemption that municipal bonds enjoy. The consequences are twofold. First, individuals in high tax brackets may find highly attractive investment opportunities in municipal bonds.[5] The formula used to equate interest on municipal bonds to other taxable investments is:

application example

$$Y = \frac{i}{(1 - T)} \tag{11–1}$$

where:

Y = Equivalent before-tax yield on a taxable investment
i = Yield on the municipal obligation
T = Marginal tax rate of the investor

If an investor has a marginal tax rate of 35 percent and is evaluating a municipal bond paying 6 percent interest, the equivalent before-tax yield on a taxable investment would be:

$$\frac{5\%}{(1 - 0.35)} = \frac{5\%}{0.65} = 7.69\%$$

[5] It should be noted that any capital gain on a municipal bond is taxable as would be the case with any investment.

TABLE 11-1 Marginal Tax Rates and Return Equivalents

Yield on Municipal	28% Bracket	32% Bracket	35% Bracket	39% Bracket
3%	4.16%	4.41%	4.62%	4.91%
4	5.55	5.88	6.15	6.56
5	6.94	7.35	7.69	8.20
6	8.33	8.88	9.23	9.84
7	9.72	10.29	10.77	11.47
8	11.11	11.76	12.31	13.11
9	12.50	13.23	13.85	14.75

Thus, the investor could choose between a *non*-tax-exempt investment paying 7.69 percent and a tax-exempt municipal bond paying 5 percent and be indifferent between the two. Table 11–1 presents examples of trade-offs between tax-exempt and non-tax-exempt (taxable) investments at various interest rates and marginal tax rates. Clearly, the higher the marginal tax rate, the greater the advantage of tax-exempt municipal bonds.

A second significant feature of municipal bonds is that the yield the issuing agency pays on municipal bonds is lower than the yield on taxable instruments. Of course, a municipal bond paying 5 percent may be quite competitive with taxable instruments paying more. Average differentials are presented in Table 11–2 on the next page. You should notice in Table 11–2 that the yield differences between municipal bonds and corporate bonds is normally 1 to 3 percentage points. Corporate bond yields had an average premium of over 27 percent over the period 1979–2009. A major distinction that is also important to the bond issuer and investor is whether the bond is of a general obligation or revenue nature.

General Obligation versus Revenue Bonds A **general obligation issue** is backed by the full faith, credit, and "taxing power" of the governmental unit. For a **revenue bond**, on the other hand, the repayment of the issue is fully dependent on the revenue-generating capability of a specific project or venture, such as a toll road, bridge, or municipal arena.

Because of the taxing power behind most general obligation (GO) issues, they tend to be of extremely high quality. Approximately three-fourths of all municipal bond issues are of the general obligation variety, and very few failures have occurred in the post–World War II era. Revenue bonds tend to be of more uneven quality, and the economic soundness of the underlying revenue-generating project must be carefully examined (though most projects are quite worthwhile).

Municipal Bond Guarantee A growing factor in the municipal bond market is the third-party guarantee. Whether dealing with a general obligation or revenue bond, a fee may be paid by the originating governmental body to a third-party insurer to guarantee that all interest and principal payments will be made. There are four private insurance firms that guarantee municipal bonds, the largest of which are the Municipal Bond Investors Assurance (MBIA) and the American Municipal Bond Assurance Corporation (AMBAC). Municipal bonds that are guaranteed carry the highest rating possible (AAA) because all the guaranteeing insurance companies are rated AAA. Approximately 30 percent of municipal bond issues are guaranteed. During the financial crisis, both MBIA and AMBAC were in serious trouble, as investors were concerned that they didn't have enough capital to guarantee their municipal bonds. The recession caused severe damage to many municipalities' bond ratings.

A municipal bond that is guaranteed will carry a lower yield and have a better secondary or resale market. This may be important because municipal bonds, in

TABLE 11-2 Comparable Yields on Long-Term Municipals and Taxable Corporates (Yearly Averages)

Year	High-Grade Municipal Bonds Standard & Poors	Corporate Aaa Bonds Moody's	Yield Difference	% Premium
2009	4.64%	5.31%	0.67%	14.44%
2008	4.80	5.63	0.83	17.29
2007	4.42	5.56	1.14	25.79
2006	4.42	5.59	1.17	26.47
2005	4.29	5.24	0.95	22.14
2004	4.63	5.63	1.00	21.60
2003	4.73	5.67	0.94	19.87
2002	5.05	6.49	1.44	28.51
2001	5.19	7.08	1.89	36.42
2000	5.77	7.62	1.85	32.06
1999	5.43	7.04	1.61	29.65
1998	5.12	6.53	1.41	27.54
1997	5.55	7.26	1.71	30.81
1996	5.75	7.37	1.62	28.17
1995	5.95	7.59	1.64	27.56
1994	6.19	7.96	1.77	28.59
1993	5.63	7.22	1.59	28.24
1992	6.41	8.14	1.73	26.99
1991	6.89	8.77	1.88	27.29
1990	7.25	9.32	2.07	28.55
1989	7.24	9.26	2.02	27.90
1988	7.76	9.71	1.95	25.13
1987	7.37	9.38	2.01	27.27
1986	7.38	9.02	1.64	22.22
1985	9.18	11.37	2.19	23.86
1984	10.15	12.71	2.56	25.22
1983	9.47	12.04	2.57	27.14
1982	11.57	13.79	2.22	19.19
1981	11.23	14.17	2.94	26.18
1980	8.51	11.94	3.43	40.31
1979	6.39	9.63	3.24	50.70
			Full Period Average	27.20%
			2000-2009 Average	24.46%
			1990-2009 Average	26.40%

Source: Board of Governors of the Federal Reserve System, Interest Rates and Bond Yields.

general, do not provide as strong a secondary market as U.S. government issues. The market for a given municipal issue is often small and fragmented, and high indirect costs are associated with reselling the issue.

Corporate Securities

Corporate bonds are the dominant source of new financing for U.S. corporations.

Bonds normally supply 80 to 85 percent of firms' external financial needs. Even during the great bull stock market of the 1990s, corporations looked as heavily as ever to the debt markets to provide financing (this was justified by the decreasing interest rates during this period).

TABLE 11-3 Comparative Yields on Single A Bonds

Year	Public Utilities	Industrials	Yield Difference
2009	5.86%	5.82%	0.04%
2007	6.23	6.31	−0.08
2005	5.68	5.77	−0.09
2003	6.28	6.12	0.16
2001	7.82	7.52	0.30
1999	8.24	7.85	0.39
1997	7.15	6.94	0.21
1995	7.17	6.95	0.22
1993	7.34	7.26	0.08
1991	8.73	8.56	0.17
1989	9.42	9.37	0.05
1987	10.98	10.17	0.81
1985	10.75	11.30	−0.55
1983	13.54	13.00	0.54
1981	16.44	15.27	1.17

Source: *Mergent Bond Record* (published by Mergent, Inc. New York, NY). Selected issues.

The corporate market may be divided into a number of subunits, including *industrials, public utilities, rails and transportation,* and *financial issues* (banks, finance companies, etc.). The industrials are a catchall category that includes everything from high-technology companies to discount chain stores. Public utilities represent the largest segment of the market and have issues that run up to 40 years in maturity. Because public utilities are in constant need of funds to meet ever-expanding requirements for power generation, telephone services, and other essential services, they are always in the bond market to raise new funds. The needs associated with rails and transportation as well as financial issues tend to be less than those associated with public utilities or industrials. Table 11–3 shows comparative yields for the two main categories.[6] Normally, public utilities have had slightly higher yields than industrials for the same credit rating.

The higher yields on public utility issues represent a supply-demand phenomenon more than anything else. A constant stream of new issues to the market can only be absorbed by a higher yield pattern. In other cases, the higher required return may also be associated with quality deterioration as measured by profitability and interest coverage. During 1983–84, the default of the Washington State Power Authority on bonds issued to construct power-generating facilities sent waves through the bond market. Again in 1984, when Public Service of Indiana canceled construction of a partially complete nuclear power plant, nuclear utility issues (both stocks and bonds) suffered severe price erosion, and the bond market demanded high-risk premiums on bonds of almost all nuclear utilities. In 2001, the public utility bond market was once again "spooked" by the energy crisis and blackouts in northern California.

Corporate bonds of all types generally trade in units of $1,000, and this is a particularly attractive feature to the smaller investor who does not wish to purchase in units of $5,000 to $10,000 (which is necessary for many Treasury and federally sponsored credit agency issues). Because of higher risk relative to government

[6] Financial and transportation issues are generally not broken out of the published data.

issues, the investor will generally receive higher yields on corporates as well. All income from corporates is taxable for federal, state, and local purposes. Finally, corporate issues have the disadvantage of being subject to calls. When buying a bond during a period of high interest rates, the call provision must be considered a negative feature because the high-yielding bonds may be called in for early retirement as interest rates go down.

BOND MARKET INVESTORS

Having considered the issuer or supply side of the market, we now comment on the investor or demand side. The bond market is dominated by large institutional investors (insurance companies, banks, pension funds, mutual funds) even more than the stock market. Institutional investors account for 80 to 85 percent of the trading in key segments of the bond market. However, the presence of the individual investor is partially felt in the corporate and municipal bond market where the incentives of low denomination ($1,000) corporate bonds or tax-free municipal bonds have some attraction. Furthermore, in the last decade individual investors have made their presence felt in the bond market through buying mutual funds that specialize in bond portfolios.

Institutional investors' preferences for various sectors of the bond market are influenced by their tax status as well as by the nature of their obligations or liabilities to depositors, investors, or clients. For example, banks traditionally have been strong participants in the municipal bond market because of their substantial tax obligations. Their investments tend to be in short- to intermediate-term assets because of the short-term nature of their deposit obligations (the funds supplied to the banks). One problem that banks find in their bond portfolios is that such investments are often preferred over loans to customers when the economy is weak and loan demand is sluggish. Not so coincidentally, this happens to be the time period when interest rates are low. When the economy improves, interest rates go up, and so does loan demand. To meet the loan demand of valued customers, banks liquidate portions of their bond portfolios. The problem with this recurring process is that banks are buying bonds when interest rates are *low* and selling them when interest rates are *high*. This can cause losses in the value of the bank portfolio.

The bond investor must be prepared to deal in a relatively strong primary market (new issues market) and a relatively weak secondary market (resale market). While the secondary market is active for many types of Treasury and agency issues, such is not the case for corporate and municipal issues. Thus, the investor must look well beyond the yield, maturity, and rating to determine if a purchase is acceptable. The question that must be considered is: How close to the going market price can I dispose of the issue if that should be necessary? If a 5 or 10 percent discount is involved, that might be unacceptable. Unlike the stock market, the secondary market in bonds tends to be dominated by over-the-counter transactions (although listed bonds are traded as well).

A significant development in the last decade has been the heavy participation of foreign investors in U.S. bond markets. Foreign investors now bankroll between 10 to 15 percent of the U.S. government's debt. While these investors have helped to finance the U.S. government's deficits, they can be a disruptive factor in the market when they decide to partially withdraw their funds. This happened in the mid-1990s when the declining value of the dollar and fear of inflation in the United States caused many foreign investors to temporarily cash in their investments. Because the U.S. government fears the flight of funds provided by foreign investors, it is sensitive to their needs and desires.

DISTRIBUTION PROCEDURES

In February 1982, the Securities and Exchange Commission began allowing a process called shelf registration under SEC Rule 415. **Shelf registration** permits large companies to file one comprehensive registration statement that outlines the firm's plans for future long-term financing. Then, when market conditions seem appropriate, the firm can issue the securities through an investment banker without further SEC approval. Future issues are said to be sitting on the shelf, waiting for the most advantageous time to appear. An issue may be on the shelf for up to two years.

Approximately half of the new public bond issues are distributed through the shelf registration process. The rest are issued under more traditional procedures in which the bonds are issued shortly after registration by a large syndicate of investment bankers in a highly structured process.

Private Placement

A number of bond offerings are sold to investors as a **private placement**; that is, they are sold privately to investors rather than through the public markets. Private placements are most popular with investors such as insurance companies and pension funds, and they are primarily offered in the corporate sector by industrial firms rather than public utilities. The lender can generally expect to receive a slightly higher yield than on public issues to compensate for the extremely limited or nonexistent secondary market and the generally smaller size of the borrowing firm in a private placement.

BOND RATINGS

Bond investors tend to place much more emphasis on independent analysis of quality than do common stock investors. For this reason, both corporate financial management and institutional portfolio managers keep a close eye on bond rating procedures. The difference between an AA and an A rating may mean the corporation will have to pay ¼ point more interest on the bond issue (perhaps 8½ percent rather than 8¼ percent). On a $100 million, 20-year issue, this represents $250,000 per year (before tax), or a total of $5 million over the life of the bond.

www.moodys.com
www.standardandpoors.com

The two major bond-rating agencies are Moody's Investors Service and Standard & Poor's (a subsidiary of McGraw-Hill, Inc.). They rank thousands of corporate and municipal issues as well as a limited number of private placements, commercial paper, preferred stock issues, and offerings of foreign companies and governments.

U.S. government issues tend to be free of risk and therefore are given no attention by the bond-rating agencies. Moody's, founded in 1909, is the older of the two bond-rating agencies and covers twice as many securities as Standard & Poor's (particularly in the municipal bond area). A smaller firm, Fitch Ratings Inc., acquired Duff & Phelps, another rating agency, in an attempt to diversify and expand its rating coverage.

The bond ratings, generally ranging from an AAA to a D category, are decided on a committee basis at both Moody's and Standard & Poor's. There are no fast and firm quantitative measures that specify the rating a new issue will receive. Nevertheless, measures pertaining to cash flow and earnings generation in relationship to debt obligations are given strong consideration. Of particular interest are coverage ratios that show the number of times interest payments, as well as all annual contractual obligations, are covered by earnings. A coverage of 2 or 3 may contribute to a low rating, while a ratio of 5 to 10 may indicate the possibility of a strong rating. Operating margins, return on invested capital, and returns on total assets are

the real world of investing

THE BOND-RATING GAME: WHO REALLY RUNS THE CORPORATION?

When Shell Canada (**www.shellcanada.com**), an integrated oil company with many U.S. investors, decided to sell its coal business, it called Moody's and Standard & Poor's first. Although its own financial analysis indicated the move was appropriate, it would not have made the decision without the blessings of the two major U.S. bond-rating agencies as well as similar rating agencies in Canada. The sell-off provided a $120 million write-off that could have caused a downgrading of Shell Canada's double-A rating, and the firm was not about to take a chance.

The firm's concern was well justified. Its action was taken in June 1991 (a recession year). During the first six months of 1991, 422 corporations suffered a downgrading in ratings while only 88 had an increase. In the prior decade, the big causes for downgradings were the effects of acquisitions or attempts by corporations to defend themselves against takeovers. In the 2000s, these factors were less important, and the major concern was poor earnings performance.

Three good rules for firms to follow in dealing with bond-rating agencies is never surprise the agencies, tell all, and show good intent. A number of years ago, Manville Corporation (**www.jm.com**) was severely downgraded not for poor performance, but because it took Chapter 11 bankruptcy protection as a way to face asbestos damage litigation. The decision may have been right at the time, but the firm did not have the blessings of the bond-rating agencies.

also evaluated along with debt-to-equity ratios.[7] Financial ratio analysis makes up perhaps 50 percent of the evaluation. Other factors of importance are the nature of the industry in which the firm operates, the relative position of the firm within the industry, the pricing clout the firm has, and the quality of management. Decisions are not made in a sterile, isolated environment. Thus, it is not unusual for corporate management or the mayor to make a presentation to the rating agency, and on-site visitations to plants or cities may occur.

www.financialservicesinc.ubs.com

The overall quality of the work done by the bond-rating agencies may be judged by the agencies' acceptance in the business and academic community. Their work is very well received. Although UBS and some other investment houses have established their own analysts to shadow the activities of the bond-rating agencies and look for imprecisions in their classifications (and thus potential profits), the opportunities are not great. Academic researchers have generally found that accounting and financial data were well considered in the bond ratings and that rational evaluation appeared to exist.[8]

One item lending credibility to the bond-rating process is the frequency with which the two major rating agencies arrive at the same grade for a given issue (this occurs well over 50 percent of the time). When "split ratings" do occur (different ratings by different agencies), they are invariably of a small magnitude. A typical case might be AAA versus AA rather than AAA versus BBB. While one can question whether one agency is looking over the other's shoulder or "copying its homework," this is probably not the case in this skilled industry.

Nevertheless, there is room for criticism. While initial evaluations are quite thorough and rational, the monitoring process may not be wholly satisfactory. Subsequent changes in corporate or municipal government events may not trigger a rating change quickly enough. One sure way a corporation or municipal government will get a reevaluation is for them to come out with a new issue. This tends to generate a review of all existing issues.

---

[7] Similar appropriate measures can be applied to municipal bonds, such as debt per capita or income per capita within a governmental jurisdiction.

[8] James O. Horrigan, "The Determination of Long-Term Credit Standing with Financial Ratios," *Empirical Research in Accounting: Selected Studies,* supplement to *Journal of Accounting Research* 4 (1966), pp. 44–62; Thomas F. Pogue and Robert M. Soldofsky, "What's in a Bond Rating?" *Journal of Financial and Quantitative Analysis,* June 1969, pp. 201–8; and George E. Pinches and Kent A. Mingo, "A Multivariate Analysis of Industrial Bond Ratings," *Journal of Finance,* March 1973, pp. 1–18.

Actual Rating System

Table 11–4 shows an actual listing of the designations used by Moody's and Standard & Poor's. Note that Moody's combines capital letters and small *a*'s, and Standard & Poor's uses all capital letters. Fitch, the smallest rating company, is not listed in Table 11–4 but would have ratings similar to those for S&P and Moody's.

The first four categories are assumed to represent investment-grade quality. Large institutional investors (insurance companies, banks, pension funds) generally confine their activities to these four categories. Moody's also modifies its basic ratings with numerical values for categories Aa through B. The highest in a category is 1, 2 is the midrange, and 3 is the lowest. A rating of Aa2 means the bond is in the midrange of Aa. Standard & Poor's has a similar modification process with pluses and minuses applied. Thus, AA+ would be on the high end of an AA rating, AA would be in the middle, and AA− would be on the low end.

It is also possible for a corporation to have issues outstanding in more than one category. For example, highly secured mortgage bonds of a corporation may be rated AA, while unsecured issues carry an A rating.

The level of interest payment on a bond is inverse to the quality rating. If a bond rated AAA by Standard & Poor's pays 6.5 percent, an A quality bond might pay 7.0 percent; a BB, 8.0 percent; and so on. The spread between these yields changes from time to time and is watched closely by the financial community as a barometer of future movements in the financial markets. A relatively small spread between two rating categories would indicate that investors generally have confidence in the

TABLE 11-4 Description of Bond Ratings

Quality	Moody's	Standard & Poor's	Description
High grade	Aaa	AAA	Bonds that are judged to be of the best quality. They carry the smallest degree of investment risk and are generally referred to as "gilt edge." Interest payments are protected by a large or exceptionally stable margin, and principal is secure.
	Aa	AA	Bonds that are judged to be of high quality by all standards. Together with the first group, they comprise what are generally known as high-grade bonds. They are rated lower than the best bonds because margins of protection may not be as large.
Medium grade	A	A	Bonds that possess many favorable investment attributes and are to be considered as upper-medium-grade obligations. Factors giving security to principal and interest are considered adequate.
	Baa	BBB	Bonds that are considered as medium-grade obligations—they are neither highly protected nor poorly secured.
Speculative	Ba	BB	Bonds that are judged to have speculative elements; their future cannot be considered as well assured. Often the protection of interest and principal payments may be very moderate.
	B	B	Bonds that generally lack characteristics of the desirable investment. Assurance of interest and principal payments or of maintenance of other terms of the contract over any long period may be small.
Default	Caa	CCC	Bonds that are of poor standing. Such issues may be in default, or there may be elements of danger present with respect to principal or interest.
	Ca	CC	Bonds that represent obligations that are speculative to a high degree. Such issues are often in default or have other marked shortcomings.
	C		The lowest-rated class in Moody's designation. These bonds can be regarded as having extremely poor prospects of attaining any real investment standing.
		C	Rating given to income bonds on which interest is not currently being paid.
		D	Issues in default with arrears in interest and/or principal payments.

Sources: *Mergent Bond Record.*

economy. As the yield spread widens between higher and lower rating categories, this may indicate loss of confidence. Investors are demanding increasingly higher yields for lower rated bonds. Their loss of confidence indicates they will demand progressively higher returns for taking risks. This logic was previously covered in Chapter 10 as part of the discussion of the *Barron's* Confidence Index.

JUNK BONDS OR HIGH-YIELD BONDS

Lower quality bonds are sometimes referred to as **junk bonds** or high-yield bonds. Any bond that is not considered to be of investment quality by Wall Street analysts is put in the junk bond category. As previously indicated, investment quality means the bond falls into one of the four top investment-grade categories established by Moody's and Standard & Poor's. This indicates investment-grade bonds extend down to Baa in Moody's and BBB in Standard & Poor's (Table 11–4). A wide range of quality is associated with junk bonds. Some are very close to investment quality (such as the Ba and BB bonds), while others carry ratings in the C and D categories.

Bonds tend to fall into the junk bond category for a number of reasons. First are the so-called fallen angel bonds issued by companies that once had high credit rankings but now face hard times. Second are emerging growth companies or small firms that have not yet established an adequate record to justify an investment-quality rating. Finally, a major part of the junk bond market is made of companies undergoing a restructuring either as a result of a leveraged buyout or as part of fending off an unfriendly takeover offer. In both these cases, equity capital tends to be replaced with debt and a lower rating is assigned.

Many junk bonds behave more like common stock than bonds and rally on good news, actual interest payments, or improving business conditions. Several institutions such as Merrill Lynch and Fidelity Investments manage mutual funds with a junk bond emphasis.

The main appeal of junk bonds historically is that they provided yields 300 to 800 basis points higher than that for AAA corporate bonds or U.S. Treasury securities. Also, until the recession of 1990–91, there were relatively few defaults by junk bond issuers. Thus, the investor got a substantially higher yield with only a small increase in risk.

However, in the 1990–91 recession, junk bond prices tumbled by 20 to 30 percent, while other bond values stayed firm. Examples of junk bond issues that dropped sharply in value included those issued by Rapid-American Corporation, Revco, Campeau Corporation, and Resorts International. Many of these declines were due to poor business conditions. However, the fall of Drexel Burnham Lambert, the leading underwriter of junk bond issues, also contributed to the difficulties in the market. That problem was further compounded when Michael Milken, the guru of junk bond dealers, was sentenced to 10 years in prison for illegal insider trading.

As the economy came out of the recession of 1990–91, junk bonds once again gained in popularity. Many of these issues had their prices battered down so low that they appeared to be bargains. As a result, junk bonds recovered and continued to perform exceptionally well throughout the 1990s—so much so that the spread between the yield on junk bonds and U.S. Treasury securities was half of its historical spread in 1997. While these securities took a hit in 2001 as the economy slowed down, they rallied strongly as the economy improved in 2003 (they were up 25 percent). These securities appear to have a place in the portfolio of investors with a higher than average risk tolerance. This is particularly true for bonds that are in the low- to mid-B rating categories. During 2010, high-yield junk bonds rallied with big gains of 15.6 percent. Between October 2009 and October 2010, yields on triple C (CCC) rated bonds moved from 14.5 percent to 10.8 percent. During this period double A (AA) rated bonds moved from 3.9 percent to 2.7 percent.

BOND QUOTES

application example

Barron's publishes bond values on a weekly basis. Table 11–5 provides an excerpt from the quote sheet for corporate bonds.

TABLE 11-5 **Quotes on Corporate Bonds**

CORPORATE BONDS

For the week ending Friday, October 15, 2010
Forty most active fixed-coupon corporate bonds

COMPANY (TICKER)	COUPON	MATURITY	LAST PRICE	LAST YIELD	**EST SPREAD	UST†	EST $ VOL (000's)
Bank Of America (BAC)	5.625	Jul 01, 2020	103.011	5.224	265	10	819,375
Jpmorgan Chase (JPM)	4.400	Jul 22, 2020	100.175	4.377	181	10	567,756
Jp Morgan Chase (JPM)	4.250	Oct 15, 2020	99.126	4.359	179	10	460,221
Morgan Stanley (MS)	5.500	Jul 24, 2020	103.107	5.091	253	10	442,643
Citigroup (C)	5.375	Aug 09, 2020	102.753	5.015	245	10	438,823
Barclays Bank (BACR)	5.140	Oct 14, 2020	99.305	5.230	268	10	338,421
Manitowoc Co (MTW)	8.500	Nov 01, 2020	101.625	8.218	565	10	298,055
General Electric Capital (GE)	4.375	Sep 16, 2020	99.972	4.378	179	10	281,945
Bank Of America (BAC)	3.700	Sep 01, 2015	100.019	3.695	250	5	274,956
Regency Energy Partners Lp* (RGNC)	6.875	Dec 01, 2018	102.250	6.505	400	10	250,957
Kraft Foods (KFT)	5.375	Feb 10, 2020	111.686	3.867	128	10	236,075
Wells Fargo (WFC)	3.625	Apr 15, 2015	105.346	2.362	118	5	227,962
Jpmorgan Chase (JPM)	6.400	May 15, 2038	110.367	5.653	164	30	212,746
Bank Of America (BAC)	4.500	Apr 01, 2015	103.703	3.591	240	5	212,670
Citigroup (C)	6.000	Dec 13, 2013	110.061	2.646	208	3	208,438
Jpmorgan Chase (JPM)	3.400	Jun 24, 2015	103.584	2.581	139	5	207,025
Raytheon (RTN)	4.875	Oct 15, 2040	97.614	5.030	104	30	195,185
Bp Capital Markets (BPLN)	5.250	Nov 07, 2013	109.262	2.096	154	3	187,787
Citigroup (C)	4.750	May 19, 2015	105.505	3.440	225	5	185,252
Gerdau Trade (GGBRD)	5.750	Jan 30, 2021	103.500	5.305	271	10	175,803
Anadarko Petroleum (APC)	6.375	Sep 15, 2017	110.138	4.639	205	10	174,812
Bp Capital Markets (BPLN)	4.500	Oct 01, 2020	104.461	3.953	139	10	173,563
Transocean (RIG)	6.500	Nov 15, 2020	111.133	5.075	251	10	172,832
General Electric Capital * (GE)	6.875	Jan 10, 2039	113.296	5.901	199	30	166,867
Csn Islands Xii (CSNABZ)	7.000	Dec 23, 2049	98.625	7.104	314	30	166,429
Petroleos Mexicanos (PEMEX)	6.625	Sep 28, 2049	102.850	6.425	242	30	166,213
Block Financial Llc (HRB)	5.125	Oct 30, 2014	95.500	6.410	522	5	166,160
Hess (HES)	5.600	Feb 15, 2041	102.685	5.418	143	30	165,994
General Electric Capital (GE)	3.500	Jun 29, 2015	104.814	2.408	122	5	161,790
Wells Fargo (WFC)	5.750	Feb 01, 2018	112.810	3.724	114	10	158,068
Morgan Stanley (MS)	6.750	Apr 15, 2011	103.041	0.648	n.a.	2	154,113
Jpmorgan Chase (JPM)	5.500	Oct 15, 2040	99.087	5.563	156	30	143,300
Anadarko Petroleum * (APC)	5.950	Sep 15, 2016	108.912	4.228	304	5	140,857
Ubs Ag (Stamford Branch) (UBS)	4.875	Aug 04, 2020	106.882	4.017	145	10	139,930
Merrill Lynch And Co (BAC)	6.400	Aug 28, 2017	108.414	4.937	237	10	139,610
Citigroup (C)	8.500	May 22, 2019	123.049	5.145	258	10	138,376
Wells Fargo (WFC)	5.500	May 01, 2013	109.848	1.518	95	3	137,689
Cemex Finance Llc (CEMEX)	9.500	Dec 14, 2016	101.200	9.235	805	5	133,667
Canadian Imperial Bank Of Commerce (CM)	1.450	Sep 13, 2013	100.778	1.176	61	3	129,960

Volume represents total volume for each issue; price/yield data are for trades of $1 million and greater. * Denotes a security whose last round lot trade did not take place on the last business day prior to publication. ** Estimated spreads, in basis points (100 basis points is one percentage point), over the 2, 5, 10 or 30-year hot run Treasury note/bond. 2-year: 0.375 09/12; 5-year: 1.250 09/15; 10-year: 2.625 08/20; 30-year: 4.375 05/40. †Comparable U.S. Treasury issue.

Source: MarketAxess Corporate BondTicker - www.bondticker.com

Source: *Barron's*, October 18, 2010, p. M52. Reprinted with permission of *Barron's*,

Starting in the first column, the company name is followed by the annual coupon rate and maturity date. For example, the table shows JPMorgan Chase bonds with a coupon rate of 6.40 percent and maturing in 2038. The "Last Price" is 110.367. The quote does not represent actual dollars, but percent of par value because corporate bonds trade in units of $1,000.

The 110.367 represents $1,103.67 ($1,000 × 110.367 percent). The next item of interest in the table is "Last Yield." This represents the true rate of return the bond investor is receiving and is 5.653 percent. More formally, this is referred to as yield to maturity and is covered in chapter 12 "Principles of Bond Valuation and Investment." The other three columns represent the yield spread in basis points over U.S. Treasuries with the next column displaying the appropriate maturity of the U.S. Treasury. The last column is the volume.

If interested in further information on a bond, you could proceed to *Mergent Bond Record* published by Mergent, Inc., or the *Bond Guide,* published by Standard & Poor's. For example, using *Mergent Bond Record,* as shown in Table 11–6, you could determine

TABLE 11-6 Background Data on Bond Issues

CUSIP	ISSUE	MOODY'S® RATING	INTEREST DATES	CURRENT CALL PRICE	CALL DATE	SINK FUND PROV	CURRENT PRICE		YIELD TO MAT.	2006 HIGH	2006 LOW	AMT. OUTST. MIL. $	ISSUED	ISSUED PRICE
61746SBS	Morgan Stanley nt 5.05 01/21/11	Aa3	J&J 21	N.C.	-	No	98.23	bid	5.47	107.60	98.70	2000	10/18/05	99.73
61746SBQ	nt fltg rt 5.08 10/15/15	Aa3	J&J 15	N.C.	-	No	100.48	bid	5.02	102.03	99.05	2400	10/18/05	100.00
617446YT	Morgan Stanley Dean Witter & Co nt fltg rt 4.85 01/18/11	Aa3	J,A,J&O 18	N.C.	-	No	100.18	bid	4.81	—	—	1750	01/10/06	100.00
618270AB	[5] [4] Morris Pubg Group LLC / Fin Co sr sub nt ser b 7 08/01/13	B1	F&A 01	103.50	fr 08/01/08	No	94.50	bid	7.97	100.00	94.13	300	05/12/04	0.00
620076AH	Motorola Inc deb 7.5 05/15/25	Baa2	M&N 15	N.C.	-	No	114.72	bid	6.27	120.36	115.66	400	05/08/95	99.30
620076AK	deb 6.5 09/01/25	Baa2	M&S 01	N.C.	-	No	103.96	bid	6.17	109.30	105.94	400	08/29/95	99.28
620076AP	deb 6.5 11/15/28	Baa2	M&N 15	—	-	No	104.37	bid	6.17	110.56	106.47	445	11/18/98	99.58
620076AC	deb 8.4 08/15/31	Baa2	F&A 15	N.C.	-	No	115.77	bid	7.21	121.93	118.08	3	08/12/91	100.00
620076AM	deb 5.22 10/01/97	Baa2	A&O 01	—	-	No	78.32	bid	6.12	80.95	77.88	300	10/07/97	75.55
620076AF	nt 7.6 01/01/07	Baa2	J&J 01	N.C.	-	No	101.52	bid	5.51	102.93	102.42	117.9	01/02/92	99.84
620076AG	nt 6.5 03/01/08	Baa2	M&S 01	N.C.	-	No	101.14	bid	5.87	103.60	102.29	114.2	03/01/93	99.34
620076AN	nt 5.8 10/15/08	Baa2	A&O 15	N.C.	-	No	100.82	bid	5.45	103.81	100.95	83.8	10/15/98	99.87
620076AR	nt 7.625 11/15/10	Baa2	M&N 15	—	-	No	109.11	bid	5.41	112.99	110.66	527	11/08/00	99.70
620076AX	nt 8 11/01/11	Baa2	M&N 01	—	-	No	112.20	bid	5.48	116.50	113.99	600	12/14/01	0.00
620076AU	sr nt 4.608 11/16/07	Baa2	F,M,A&N 16	N.C.	-	No	98.97	bid	5.27	99.96	99.25	1200	08/11/04	101.78
620076AQ	Motorola, Inc. jr sub def int deb 6.68 03/31/39	Baa3r	—	N.C.	-	No	—	.	—	—	—	20	01/29/99	0.00
620103AE	Motors & Gears Inc sr nt ser d 10.75 11/15/06	Caa3	M&N 15	100.00	NoChange	No	98.50	bid	13.29	95.75	93.00	270	01/16/98	0.00
624581AB	[5] [4] Movie Gallery Inc sr nt 11 05/01/12	Caa3	M&N 01	105.50	fr 05/01/08	No	46.75	bid	26.93	88.00	70.50	325	08/05/05	0.00
55345RAC	MQ Assocs Inc sr disc nt ser b 0 08/15/12	Caa3	F&A 15	109.00	fr 08/15/08	No	27.50	bid	—	63.50	56.00	136	10/14/04	0.00
62475BAA	MSC Med Svcs Co sr secd 2nd priority nt fltg rt rule 144a 12.41 10/15/11	B3	J,A,J&O 15	103.00	fr 10/15/07	No	81.00	bid	17.50	99.00	90.00	150	06/15/05	99.00
55375UAB	[5] [4] MSW Energy Hldgs II LLC / MSW Energy Fin Co II Inc sr secd nt ser b 7.375 09/01/10	Ba3	M&S 01	103.69	fr 09/01/07	No	103.00	bid	6.61	104.00	102.00	225	06/01/04	0.00
55375TAB	[5] [4] MSW Energy Hldgs LLC / MSW Energy Fin Co Inc sr secd nt ser b 8.5 09/01/10	Ba3	M&S 01	104.25	fr 09/01/07	No	106.25	bid	6.88	107.25	105.50	200	11/19/03	0.00
553758AC	[4] MSX Intl Inc sr sub nt 11.375 01/15/08	Ca	J&J 15	100.00	fr 01/15/07	No	65.00	bid	36.20	72.25	66.00	130	07/22/98	0.00
553758AK	[4] MSX Intl Inc / MSX Intl Ltd sr secd nt 11 10/15/07	B3	F&A 01	100.00	fr 08/01/06	No	96.00	bid	13.87	99.50	99.50	75.5	11/21/03	0.00
553768AA	MTR Corp Ltd nt 7.5 11/08/10	Aa3	M&N 08	N.C.	-	No	108.26	bid	5.48	111.79	110.14	600	11/01/00	99.15
628530AE	[5] [4] Mylan Labs Inc sr nt 5.75 08/15/10	Ba1	F&A 15	—	-	No	98.25	bid	6.21	—	—	150	12/16/05	0.00
628530AF	sr nt 6.375 08/15/15	Ba1	F&A 15	103.19	fr 08/15/10	No	100.00	bid	6.38	—	—	350	12/16/05	0.00
635405AQ	National City Corp sr nt 4.9 01/15/15	A1	J&J 15	N.C.	-	No	94.90	bid	5.62	99.15	96.30	400	01/05/05	99.52
635405AR	sr nt fltg rt 5.08688 06/16/10	A1	M,J,S&D 16	N.C.	-	No	99.49	bid	5.22	100.80	99.02	300	06/09/05	99.95
632381AA	National Coal Corp sr secd nt rule 144a 10.5 12/15/10	Caa2	J&D 15	105.25	fr 12/15/08	No	0.00		—	100.00	100.00	55	12/23/05	100.00

Source: *Mergent Bond Record,* April 2010, p. 158.

information about a firm. Let's look at Mylan Labs' 5.75 issue due on August 15, 2010. The code designation in the left margin indicates the industry classification of the firm. Also, the firm has a Moody's bond rating of Bal. The *Mergent Bond Record* further indicates that the bond's interest is payable on F&A (February 15 and August 15) of each year ("Interest Dates" column). The current price of the bond in \$982.50 (\$1,000 × 98.25%).

Quotes on Government Securities

application example

Table 11–7 features quotes on U.S. government securities. Treasury notes and bonds are traded as a percentage of par value, similar to corporate bonds. Historically, price changes in the market have been rather small, and bonds are quoted in $\frac{1}{32}$ of a percentage point. For example, the price for the 4.250 Treasury note due January 2010 is quoted as 105.27 bid and 105.28 asked.[9] These prices translate into $105\frac{27}{32}$ percent and $105\frac{28}{32}$ percent of \$1,000.

The bid price on a \$1,000 note would be 105.84375 percent × \$1,000 or \$1,058.4375:

$$\begin{array}{r} 105.84375\% \text{ (same as } 105\tfrac{27}{32}) \\ \underline{\times \$1{,}000} \\ \$1{,}058.4375 \end{array}$$

The asking price is 105.8750 percent × \$1,000 or \$1058.750:

$$\begin{array}{r} 1{,}058.750\% \text{ (same as } 105\tfrac{28}{32}) \\ \underline{\times \$1{,}000} \\ \$1{,}058.750 \end{array}$$

[9] The bid price is the value at which the bond can be sold, and the asked price is the value at which it can be bought.

which *existing* issues are constantly traded between investors. The bond market is more of a primary market, with the emphasis on new issues. Thus, bond investors are not constantly changing their portfolios with each new action of the corporation. Many institutional investors, such as insurance companies, are not active bond traders in existing issues but, instead, buy and hold bonds to maturity.

THE GLOBAL BOND MARKET

The global bond market is in excess of $50 trillion. The United States makes up approximately 48 percent of the market, with no one else even close. Japan has an 18 percent market position, followed by Germany at 11 percent.

The astute U.S. investor may wish to scout the entire world bond market for investments. In certain years, foreign bonds perform better than U.S. bonds. For example, in 1996, the total return in the U.S. bond market was 1.4 percent, whereas it was 30.4 percent in Italy and 17.8 percent in the United Kingdom (these latter two values represent returns translated to U.S. dollars). Going back further to 1994, there was a negative return of 7.8 percent in the United States, while the return in Germany was 9.1 percent and 8.5 percent in Japan (once again the two latter returns are translated to U.S. dollars). The high foreign returns can be related to more favorable interest rate conditions (declining rates) and/or an increasing value of the currency against the dollar.

Of course, in many years the U.S. bond market is the best-performing market in the world. The U.S. investor must carefully assess world market conditions, but there are potential benefits to international diversification, as explained in Chapter 19.

Dollar-Denominated Bonds

There are key terms associated with the international bond investments. **Dollar-denominated bonds** are bonds in which the payment is in dollars, and these may take the form of **Yankee bonds** or **Eurodollar bonds**. Examples of dollar-denominated Yankee and Eurodollar bonds and foreign-pay bonds are presented in Table 11–8. Yankee bonds are issued by foreign governments, corporations, or major agencies (such as the World Bank) and are traded in the United States and denominated (payable) in U.S. dollars. To the U.S. investor, they appear the same as any other domestically traded bond.

Eurodollar bonds are also denominated in dollars, but they are issued and traded outside the United States. The issuing firm is normally a major U.S. corporation raising money overseas. Even though the term *euro* is used in the title Eurodollar, it could be issued in any country outside the United States.

Foreign-Pay Bonds

Foreign-pay bonds are issued in a foreign country and payable in that country's currency. For example, a Japanese government bond payable in yen would

TABLE 11-8 Global Bonds

Issuer	Type	Maturity	Rating	Currency Denomination
Petro-Canada	Yankee	2021	Baa1	U.S. dollar
Bank America Corp.	Eurodollar	2009	Aa2	U.S. dollar
North American Holdings	Eurodollar	2013	Baa3	U.S. dollar
Nippon Credit Bank	Foreign-pay	2009	Baa3	Yen
Robo Securities (European firm)	Foreign-pay	2008	Aaa	Euro

Source: *Mergent Bond Record,* January 2004. Copyright © 2004 Mergent, Inc. Used with permission.

represent a foreign-pay bond. There is currency exposure to a U.S. investor in a foreign-pay bond in that the yen (or some other currency) may go up or down against the dollar.

OTHER FORMS OF FIXED-INCOME SECURITIES

Our interest so far in this chapter has been on fixed-income securities, primarily in the form of bonds issued by corporations and various sectors of the government. There are other significant forms of debt instruments from which the investor may choose, and they are primarily short term in nature.

Certificates of Deposit (CDs) The **certificates of deposit (CDs)** are provided by commercial banks and savings and loans (or other thrift institutions) and have traditionally been issued in small amounts such as $1,000 or $10,000, or large amounts such as $100,000. The investor provides the funds and receives an interest-bearing certificate in return. The smaller CDs usually have a maturity of anywhere from six months to eight years, and the large $100,000 CDs, 30 to 90 days.

The large CDs are usually sold to corporate investors, money market funds, pension funds, and so on, while the small CDs are sold to individual investors. One main difference between the two CDs, besides the dollar amount, is that there may be a secondary market for the large CDs, which allows these investors to maintain their liquidity without suffering an interest penalty. Investors in the small CDs have no such liquidity. Their only option when needing the money before maturity is to redeem the certificate to the borrowing institution and suffer an interest loss penalty.

Small CDs have been traditionally regulated by the government, with federal regulatory agencies specifying the maximum interest rate that can be paid and the life of the CD. In 1986, all such interest-rate regulations and ceilings were phased out, and the free market now determines returns. Any financial institution is able to offer whatever it desires. Almost all CDs are federally insured for up to $100,000 in the event of the collapse of the financial institution offering the instrument. This feature became particularly important in the late 1980s and early 1990s as a result of the problems in the savings and loan and banking industries.

Commercial Paper Another form of a short-term credit instrument is **commercial paper**, which is issued by large corporations to the public. Commercial paper usually comes in minimum denominations of $25,000 and represents an unsecured promissory note. Commercial paper carries a higher yield than small CDs or government Treasury bills and is in line with the yield on large CDs. The maturity is usually 30, 60, or 90 days (though up to six months is possible).

Bankers' Acceptance This instrument often arises from foreign trade. A **bankers' acceptance** is a draft drawn on a bank for approval for future payment and is subsequently presented to the bank for payment. The investor buys the bankers' acceptance from an exporter (or other third party) at a discount with the intention of presenting it to the bank at face value at a future date. Bankers' acceptances provide yields comparable to commercial paper and large CDs and have an active secondary or resale market.

Money Market Funds **Money market funds** represent a vehicle to buy short-term fixed-income securities through a mutual fund arrangement.[12] An individual with a small amount to invest may pool funds with others to buy higher-yielding large CDs and other similar instruments indirectly through the fund. There is a great deal of flexibility in withdrawing funds through check-writing privileges.

[12] Most brokerage houses also offer money market fund options.

Money Market Accounts **Money market accounts** are similar to money market funds but are offered by financial institutions rather than mutual funds. Financial institutions introduced money market accounts in the 1980s to compete with money market funds. These accounts pay rates generally competitive with money market funds and normally allow up to three withdrawals (checks) a month without penalty. One advantage of a money market account over a money market fund is that it is normally insured by the federal government for up to $100,000. However, because of the high quality of investments of money market funds, this advantage is not particularly important in most cases.

Both money market funds and money market accounts normally have minimum balance requirements of $500 to $1,000. Minimum withdrawal provisions may also exist. Each fund or account must be examined for its rules. In any event, both provide much more flexibility than a certificate of deposit in terms of access to funds with only a slightly lower yield.

PREFERRED STOCK AS AN ALTERNATIVE TO DEBT

Finally, we look at preferred stock as an alternative to debt because some investors may elect to purchase preferred stock to satisfy their fixed-income needs. **Preferred stock** pays a stipulated annual dividend but does not include an ownership interest in the corporation. A $50 par value preferred stock issue paying $3.50 in annual dividends would provide an annual yield of 7.0 percent.

Preferred stock as an investment falls somewhere between bonds and common stock as far as protective provisions for the investor. In the case of debt, the bondholders have a contractual claim against the corporation and may force bankruptcy proceedings if interest payments are not forthcoming. Common stockholders have no such claim but are the ultimate owners of the firm and may receive dividends and other distributions after all prior claims have been satisfied. Preferred stockholders, on the other hand, are entitled to receive a stipulated dividend and must receive the dividend before any payment to common stockholders. However, the payment of preferred stock dividends is not compelling to the corporation as is true in the case of debt. In bad times, preferred stock dividends may be omitted by the corporation.

While preferred stock dividends are not tax deductible to the corporation, as would be true with interest on bonds, they do offer certain investors unique tax advantages. The tax law provides that any corporation that receives preferred or common stock dividends from another corporation must add only 30 percent of such dividends to its taxable income. Thus, if a $5 dividend is received, only 30 percent of the $5, or $1.50, would be taxable to the corporate recipient.[13]

Because of this tax feature, preferred stock may carry a slightly lower yield than corporate bond issues of similar quality as indicated in Table 11–9. During the financial crisis that began in 2007, preferred stock was perceived as much riskier than high-grade bonds, and the yield spread widened so that preferred stock sold at a 2.95 percent premium to bonds.

Features of Preferred Stock

Preferred stock may carry a number of features that are similar to a debt issue. For example, a preferred stock issue may be *convertible* into common stock. Also, preferred stock may be *callable* by the corporation at a stipulated price, generally slightly above par. The call feature of a preferred stock issue may be of particular interest in that preferred stock has no maturity date as such. If the corporation wishes to take preferred stock off the books, it must call in the issue or purchase the shares in the open market at the going market price.

[13] An individual investor does not enjoy the same tax benefit.

TABLE 11-9 Yields on Aa Corporate Bonds and High-Grade Preferred Stock

Year	Moody's Aa Industrial Bonds	Preferred Stock	Yield Spread
2009	5.44%	8.39%	−2.95%
2007	5.83	7.90	−2.07
2005	5.34	6.59	−1.25
2003	5.85	6.32	−0.47
2001	6.86	6.97	−0.11
1999	7.64	7.43	0.21
1997	6.90	6.69	0.21
1995	6.88	7.49	−0.61
1993	7.05	6.97	0.08
1991	8.33	8.09	0.24
1989	8.98	8.96	0.02
1987	9.82	9.76	0.06
1985	10.47	10.65	−0.18
1983	12.39	12.46	−0.07
1981	14.88	14.78	0.10

Sources: Winans International U.S. Preferred Stock Index™—Yield Only. Mergent Bond Record (published by Mergent, Inc. New York, NY). Selected issues.

An important feature of preferred stock is that the dividend payments are usually *cumulative* in nature. That is, if preferred stock dividends are not paid in any one year, they accumulate and must be paid before common stockholders can receive any cash dividends. If preferred stock carries an $8 dividend and dividends are not paid for three years, the full $24 must be paid before any dividends go to common stockholders. This provides a strong incentive for the corporation to meet preferred stock dividend obligations on an annual basis even though preferred stock does not have a fixed, contractual obligation as do bonds. If the corporation gets behind in preferred stock dividends, it may create a situation that is difficult to get out of in the future. Being behind or in arrears on preferred stock dividends can make it almost impossible to sell new common stock because of the preclusion of common stock dividends until the preferred stockholders are satisfied.

exploring the web

Web Address	Comments
www.investinginbonds.com	**Provides bond information and trading**
www.moodys.com	**Provides bond information; some is fee-based**
www.bondsonline.com	**Provides bond information**
www.smartmoney.com	**Provides information on bond yields, bond investing, and related topics**
www.briefing.com	**Provides some bond trading information and general information about bonds**
www.teachmefinance.com	**Education site pertaining to finance and bonds**
www.investorguide.com	**Links to sites provide information on government and corporate bonds**

SUMMARY

Debt continues to play an important role in our economy from both the issuer's and the investor's viewpoints. The primary fund raisers in the bond market are the U.S. Treasury, federally sponsored credit agencies, state and local governments, and corporations.

Bond instruments are evaluated on the basis of many factors, including yield, maturity, method of repayment, security provisions, and tax treatment. The greater the protection and privileges accorded the bondholder, the lower the yield.

A significant feature for a bond issue is the rating received by Moody's Investors Service or Standard & Poor's. The ratings generally range from AAA to D and determine the required yield to sell a security in the marketplace. Although there are no firm and fast rules to determine a rating, strong attention is given to such factors as cash flow and earnings generation in relation to interest and other obligations (coverage ratios) as well as to operating margins and return on invested capital and total assets. Qualitative factors are also considered.

The bond market appears to be reasonably efficient in terms of absorbing new information into the price of existing issues. Some researchers have suggested that the bond market may be slightly less efficient than the stock market in pricing outstanding issues because of the lack of a highly active secondary, or resale, market for certain issues. Insurance companies, pension funds, and bank trust departments are not normally active traders in their bond portfolios.

Short-term investors with a need for fixed income may look to certificates of deposit, commercial paper, bankers' acceptances, money market funds, money market accounts, and the previously discussed government securities as sources of investment. Such factors as maturity, yield, and minimum amount must be considered.

Finally, preferred stock may also be thought of as an alternative form of a fixed-income security. Although dividends on preferred stock do not represent a contractual obligation to the firm as would be true of interest on debt, they must be paid before common stockholders can receive any payment.

KEY WORDS AND CONCEPTS

after-acquired property clause 286
bankers' acceptance 304
bond indenture 285
call provision 285
certificates of deposit (CDs) 304
commercial paper 304
coupon rate 285
debenture 286
dollar-denominated bonds 303
effective yield 302
equipment trust certificate 286
Eurodollar bonds 303
floating-rate notes 285
foreign-pay bonds 303
general obligation issue 291
GNMA (Ginnie Mae) pass-through certificates 289
income bonds 286
junk bonds 298
maturity date 285
money market accounts 305
money market funds 304
mortgage 286
municipal bonds 290
par value 285
perpetual bonds 285
preferred stock 305
private placement 295
put provision 286
revenue bond 291
secured debt 286
serial payment 285
shelf registration 295
sinking-fund provision 285
Treasury bills 287
Treasury bonds 288
Treasury Inflation Protection Securities (TIPS) 288
Treasury note 288
Treasury strips 288
variable-rate notes 285
Yankee bonds 303
zero-coupon bonds 285

DISCUSSION QUESTIONS

1. What are some of the major provisions found in the bond indenture?
2. Does a serial bond normally have only one maturity date? What types of bonds are normally issued on this basis?
3. Explain how a sinking fund works.
4. Why do you think the right to call a bond is often deferred for a time?
5. What is the nature of a mortgage agreement?
6. What is a senior security?
7. Discuss the statement, "A debenture may not be more risky than a secured bond."
8. How do zero-coupon securities, such as Treasury strips, provide returns to investors? How are the returns taxed?
9. What are the two forms of returns associated with inflation-indexed Treasury securities?
10. What is an agency issue? Are they direct obligations of the U.S. Treasury?
11. What tax advantages are associated with municipal bonds?
12. Distinguish between general obligation and revenue bonds.
13. How might an investor reduce the credit risk in buying a municipal bond issue?
14. What is an industrial bond?
15. What is shelf registration?
16. What is meant by the private placement of a bond issue?
17. What is a split bond rating?
18. What is meant by the term *junk bond*? What quality rating does it fail to meet?
19. What does a bond quote of 72¼ represent in dollar terms?
20. Why might the bond market be considered less efficient than the stock market?
21. What is the advantage of a money market fund? How does it differ from a money market account?
22. Why would a corporate investor consider preferred stock over a bond? What is meant by the cumulative feature of preferred stock issues?

PRACTICE PROBLEMS AND SOLUTIONS

Treasury bill

1. Assume a $1,000 Treasury bill is quoted to pay 6 percent interest over a four-month period.
   a. How much interest would the investor receive?
   b. What will be the price of the Treasury bill?
   c. What will be the effective yield?

Treasury Inflation Protection Securities (TIPS)

2. You buy a $1,000 inflation-indexed Treasury security that pays 5.5 percent annual interest. Assume inflation is 4 percent in the first two years you own the security.
   a. What is the inflation-adjusted value of the security after two years?
   b. How much interest will be paid in the third year? The basis for computing interest is the inflation-adjusted value after year two.

Solutions

1. *a.* 6% annual interest ÷ 3 = 2% interest for 4 months
   Note: 6% is divided by 3 above because 4 months represents ⅓ of a year.
   $1,000 × 2% = $20 interest
   b. Price = $1,000 − $20 = $980
   c. $\text{Effective yield} = \frac{\text{Interest}}{\text{Price}} \times 3 = \frac{\$20}{\$980} \times 3 = 2.04\% \times 3 = 6.12\%$

2. *a.*

Par value (beginning of year 1)	$1,000
Inflation adjustment	1.04
Inflation adjustment value (end of year 1)	$1,040
Inflation adjustment (beginning of year 2)	$1,040
Inflation adjustment	1.04
Inflation-adjusted value (end of year 2)	$1,081.60

b. Interest in third year: 5.5% × $1,081.60 = $59.49

PROBLEMS

Municipal bond

1. If an investor is in a 34 percent marginal tax bracket and can purchase a municipal bond paying 7.25 percent, what would the equivalent before-tax return from a nonmunicipal bond have to be to equate the two?

Municipal bond

2. If an investor is in a 30 percent marginal tax bracket and can purchase a straight (nonmunicipal bond) at 8.37 percent and a municipal bond at 6.12 percent, which should he or she choose?

Bond quotes

3. Using the data in Table 11–6 on page 300, indicate the closing *dollar* value of the National City Corp. bonds that pay 4.9 percent interest and mature January 15, 2015. State your answer in terms of dollars based on a $1,000 par value bond.

Interest payments

4. Using the data in Table 11–6 on page 300, indicate the semiannual interest payment dates for the Motorola bonds that mature in 2031. (For the item in question, look under "Interest Dates.") The two dates are six months apart. How much will the semiannual payments be?

Bond quotes

5. Using the data in Table 11–7 on page 301, indicate the asking price for the 6.000 percent government note maturing in August 2009 (09). The asking price is the purchase price for the note. State your answer based on a $1,000 par value.

Treasury bill

6. Assume a $1,000 Treasury bill is quoted to pay 5 percent interest over a six-month period.

a. How much interest would the investor receive?
b. What will be the price of the Treasury bill?
c. What will be the effective yield?

Treasury bill

7. In problem 6, if the Treasury bill had only three months to maturity,

a. How much interest would the investor receive?
b. What would be the price of the Treasury bill?
c. What would be the effective yield?

Treasury strip

8. The price of a Treasury strip note or bond can be found using Appendix C toward the back of the text. It is simply the present value factor from the table times the maturity (par) value of the Treasury strip. Assume you are considering a $10,000 par value Treasury strip that matures in 25 years. The discount rate is 7 percent. What is the price (present value) of the investment?

Treasury strip

9. Review the instructions in problem 8. Now assume as alternative A you are considering a $10,000 par value Treasury strip that matures in 20 years. The discount rate is 6 percent. You also are considering alternative

B, which represents a $10,000 par value Treasury strip that matures in 16 years. The discount rate is 8 percent. Which has the lower price (present value)?

Treasury Inflation Protection Securities (TIPS)

10. You buy a $1,000 inflation-indexed Treasury security that pays 4 percent annual interest. Assume inflation is 5 percent in the first two years you own the security.
    a. What is the inflation-adjusted value of the security after two years?
    b. How much interest will be paid in the third year? The basis for computing interest is the inflation-adjusted value after year two.

Treasury Inflation Protection Securities (TIPS)

11. You buy a 10-year, $1,000 inflation-indexed Treasury security that pays 3 percent annual interest. Assume inflation is 3 percent for the first five years and 6 percent for the last five years. What will be the value of the bond after 10 years? (Use Appendix A to help you in your calculations.) Disregard the 3 percent annual interest.

Comparative after-tax returns

12. A corporation buys $100 par value preferred stock of another corporation. The dividend payment is 7.8 percent of par. The corporation is in a 35 percent tax bracket.
    a. What will be the after-tax return on the dividend payment? Fill in the following table.

Par value	______
Dividend payment (%)	______
Actual dividend	______
Taxable income (30% of dividend)	______
Taxes (35% of taxable income)	______
After-tax return (Actual dividend − Taxes)	______
Percent return = $\frac{\text{After-tax return}}{\text{Par value}}$	______

    b. Assume a second investment in a $1,000 par value corporate bond pays 8.6 percent interest. What will be the after-tax return on the interest payment? Fill in the table below.

Par value	______
Interest payment (percent)	______
Actual interest	______
Taxes (35 percent of interest)	______
After-tax return (Actual interest − Taxes)	______
Percent return = $\frac{\text{After-tax return}}{\text{Par value}}$	______

    c. Should the corporation choose the corporate bond over the preferred stock because it has a higher quoted yield (8.6 percent versus 7.8 percent)?

Comparative after-tax returns

13. Milton Simon owns 200 shares of preferred stock of the Global Travel Corp. The shares were intended to pay $4.75 annually but have not paid a dividend in five years. Because the dividends are cumulative, the company cannot pay

dividends to common stockholders until it eliminates its obligation to preferred stockholders.

a. Can the preferred stockholders force Global Travel Corp. to pay dividends for the last five years with a threat of forcing the firm into bankruptcy?

b. Assume Global Travel Corp. does not have the cash to pay the five years of past preferred stock dividends but will offer new common stock shares to make up for the deficiency. The firm will offer a common stock payout that equals the five-year deficiency, plus provide an additional 20 percent premium in common stock shares to keep the preferred stockholders satisfied. What is the value of the common stock payout for each preferred stock share? Note that the preferred stockholders will still retain ownership of their original shares, only the deficiency in past dividends will be eliminated.

c. Assume Milton Simon receives the proceeds from his 200 shares and reinvests them in either a U.S. government security paying 5.6 percent or a municipal bond paying 4.5 percent. Milton is in a 35 percent tax bracket. How much will he have in cash on an after-tax return basis from each investment? (Disregard a tax on the common stock payout, only consider a potential tax on the returns from his investment.)

CRITICAL THOUGHT CASE (A Classic Example)–FOCUS ON ETHICS

Gail Rosenberg still had her head in the clouds when she joined Salomon Brothers, Inc., in June 2009. While she was proud of her newly awarded MBA from the Wharton School of Business at the University of Pennsylvania, she was even prouder of joining the most prestigious investment banking house on Wall Street, the famous Salomon Brothers. She had received five job offers, but this was the one she wanted. Not only would she train with the best and brightest on Wall Street, but she also would be working for a firm in which 90 employees made more than $1 million a year. How many Fortune 500 companies, law firms, or other employers could claim such a record? She was pleased with her own starting salary of $110,000 a year and could see matters only getting better in the future.

After some general training and apprenticeship-type work, she was assigned to the government bond-trading unit in February 2010. Here she would help in the bidding and distributing of U.S. Treasury bills and notes. Salomon Brothers was the largest participant among investment banking houses in this field, so she knew she would quickly learn the ropes.

Her first major participation would be in the Treasury bill auction for May 2010. Salomon Brothers would bid on behalf of many of its clients and probably have some influence on the ultimate price and yield at which the Treasury bills were sold. As Gail got on her computer to help process orders, she noticed Salomon Brothers submitted bids for clients that did not exist. It was no surprise to Gail that Salomon Brothers captured 85 percent of the bidding and virtually controlled the pricing of the securities.

In a state of shock, Gail went to her immediate supervisor and reported what she had observed on her computer screen. She was told to calm down, that she was no longer in school, and she was witnessing a common practice on "The Street." She was further informed that John Gutfreund, chairman of the board of Salomon Brothers, and President Thomas Strauss implicitly approved of such practices. She felt a little like Oliver North in the Iran-Contra affair cover-up. She

www.mhhe.com/hirtblock10e

had worked very hard to get to this tender point in her career and was now disillusioned.

Question

1. What strategy or advice can you offer to Gail Rosenberg?

WEB EXERCISE

In this exercise, we will examine how the yield on municipal bonds relates to the yield on taxable bonds and also how bond ratings affect the yield that a bond pays. Go to **www.bondsonline.com**.

1. Click on "Today's Market," then on "Composite Bond Yields," and then on "Click for Data." Under the Municipal Bonds table, write down the yield on 20-year, AAA-rated bonds. Divide this value by (1 − 0.35). The value 0.35 is assumed to represent the investor's marginal tax bracket. The answer you get is intended to represent the equivalent before-tax yield on a taxable investment.

   Now compare this value to the yield on the 20-year, AAA-rated corporate bond (which represents the yield on a before-tax basis of a taxable investment). What is the difference between this value and the value you just computed? Of course, they will never be the same because of the inefficiencies in the market and different tax rates for investors.
2. Bond ratings and yields were discussed in the chapter. Click on "US Corporate Bond Spreads" along the left margin. These spreads represent the difference in yields between a given rated bond and a risk-free Treasury bond. We will work with 10-year issues. As an example, a Aaa/AAA industrial bond usually pays 20 to 50 basis points (percentage points) more than a Treasury bond. The AAA industrial is very low risk, but it is still riskier than a Treasury bond issued by the U.S. government.
3. What is the yield spread for a 10-year, A3/A− industrial bond? How many basis points is it greater than a 10-year, Aaa/AAA industrial bond?
4. What is the yield spread on the highest rated junk bond (10-year column)? Look up Ba1/BB+.
5. What is the yield spread of the lowest rated junk bond (10-year column)?
6. Generally speaking, what happens to the yield spread as the maturity period increases from 1 year to 30 years for all different categories of bond ratings?

Note: From time to time, companies redesign their Web sites, and occasionally a topic we have listed may have been deleted, updated, or moved into a different location.

CFA MATERIAL

The following material contains sample questions and solutions from a prior Level I CFA exam. While the terminology is slightly different from that in this text, you can still view the skills that are necessary for the CFA exam.

CFA Exam Question

The investment manager of a corporate pension fund has purchased a U.S. Treasury bill with 180 days to maturity at a price of $9,600 per $10,000 face value. He has computed the discount yield at 8 percent.

a. *Calculate* the bond equivalent yield for the Treasury bill. *Show* calculations. (*3 minutes*)

b. *Briefly state two* reasons why a Treasury bill's bond equivalent yield is always different from the discount yield. (*2 minutes*)

Solution: Morning Section (I–86) (5 points)

a. $\text{BEY} = \frac{(F - P)}{P} \times \frac{365}{N}$

where:

BEY = Bond equivalent yield
F = Face value
P = Price
N = Days to maturity

$$\text{BEY} = \frac{(\$100 - \$96)}{\$96} \times \frac{365}{180} = 8.45\%$$

b. (1) The bond equivalent yield is computed using the actual purchase price of the instrument in the denominator, while the discount yield is calculated using the face value.

(2) The bond equivalent yield is based on a 365-day year, whereas the discount yield is computed using a 360-day year.

chapter twelve 12

PRINCIPLES OF BOND VALUATION AND INVESTMENT

OBJECTIVES

1. Describe how the valuation of a bond is based on present value techniques.
2. Explain the differences among various concepts of yield such as yield to maturity, yield to call, and anticipated realized yield.
3. Describe the techniques for anticipating changes in interest rates.
4. Develop an investment strategy for investing in bonds.
5. Describe how bond swaps may be used to increase after-tax returns.

OUTLINE

The old notion that a bond represents an inhcrently conservative investment can be quickly dispelled. A $1,000, 10 percent coupon rate bond with 25 years to maturity could rise $214.80 or fall $157.60 in response to a 2 percent change in interest rates in the marketplace. Investors enjoyed a total return of 43.79 percent on long-term high-grade corporate bonds in 1982 and 25.37 percent in 1985. However, the same bond investors would have had a negative total return in 13 of the 38 years between 1968 and 2006. Losses were as high as 10 percent.

This type of movement in the market creates opportunities for an investor. As a student of finance, you should not view bonds as a place where you temporarily park funds while waiting to make stock market investments. Investors in the bond markets are often richly rewarded or harshly punished based on their ability to predict interest rates and the future movement of bond prices.

Perhaps the investment banking team of Goldman Sachs is the most aggressive of the high prestige investment houses when it comes to bond trading. For five straight years, it showed large gains in its own proprietary bond trading portfolio. However, in the third quarter of 2003, it failed to hedge its large mortgage bond portfolio and when interest rates went up, its bond portfolio went down. When the poor bond trading performance of this heavy hitter on Wall Street was announced after the third quarter, its stock went down by 5.9 percent in one day.

In this chapter, we examine the valuation process for bonds, the relationship of interest rate changes to the business cycle, and various investment and speculative strategies related to bond maturity, quality, and pricing.

FUNDAMENTALS OF THE BOND VALUATION PROCESS

application example

The price of a bond at any given time represents the present value of future interest payments plus the present value of the par value of the bond at maturity. We say that:

$$V = \sum_{t=1}^{n} \frac{C_t}{(1+i)^t} + \frac{P_n}{(1+i)^n} \quad \textbf{(12–1)}$$

where:

V	=	Market value or price of the bond
n	=	Number of periods
t	=	Each period
C_t	=	Coupon or interest payment for each period, t
P_n	=	Par or maturity value
i	=	Interest rate in the market

We can use logarithms and various mathematical calculations to find the value of a bond or simply use Tables 12–1 and 12–2 to determine the present value of C_t and P_n and add the two. (Expanded versions of these two tables are presented in appendixes at the end of the text.)[1]

Assume a bond pays 10 percent interest or \$100 (C_t) for 20 years (n) and has a par (P_n) or maturity value of \$1,000. The interest rate (i) in the marketplace is assumed to be 12 percent. The present value of the bond, using annual compounding, is shown to be \$850.90 as follows:

Present Value of Coupon Payments (C_t) (from Table 12-1 or Appendix D)	Present Value of Maturity Value (P_n) (from Table 12-2 or Appendix C)
$n = 20$, $i = 12\%$	$n = 20$, $i = 12\%$
\$100 × 7.469 = \$746.90	\$1,000 × 0.104 = \$104.00
Present value of coupon payments	= \$746.90
Present value of maturity value	= 104.00
Value of bond	= \$850.90

[1] Students who have difficulty with the time value of money may wish to review Appendix E.

TABLE 12-1 Present Value of an Annuity of $1 (coupon payments, C_t)

Number of periods (n)	INTEREST RATE (i) 4 Percent	5 Percent	6 Percent	8 Percent	9 Percent	10 Percent	12 Percent
1	0.962	0.952	0.943	0.926	0.917	0.909	0.893
2	1.886	1.859	1.833	1.783	1.759	1.736	1.690
3	2.775	2.723	2.673	2.577	2.531	2.487	2.402
4	3.630	3.546	3.465	3.312	3.240	3.170	3.037
5	4.452	4.329	4.212	3.993	3.890	3.791	3.605
10	8.111	7.722	7.360	6.710	6.418	6.145	5.650
15	11.118	10.380	9.712	8.559	8.061	7.606	6.811
20	13.590	12.462	11.470	9.818	9.129	8.514	7.469
30	17.292	15.372	13.765	11.258	10.274	9.427	8.055
40	19.793	17.160	15.046	11.925	10.757	9.779	8.244

TABLE 12-2 Present Value of a Single Amount of $1 (par or maturity value, P_n)

Number of periods (n)	INTEREST RATE (i) 4 Percent	5 Percent	6 Percent	8 Percent	9 Percent	10 Percent	12 Percent
1	0.962	0.952	0.943	0.926	0.917	0.909	0.893
2	0.925	0.907	0.890	0.857	0.842	0.826	0.797
3	0.889	0.864	0.840	0.794	0.772	0.751	0.712
4	0.855	0.823	0.792	0.735	0.708	0.683	0.636
5	0.822	0.784	0.747	0.681	0.650	0.621	0.567
10	0.676	0.614	0.558	0.463	0.422	0.386	0.322
15	0.555	0.481	0.417	0.315	0.275	0.239	0.183
20	0.456	0.377	0.312	0.215	0.178	0.149	0.104
30	0.308	0.231	0.174	0.099	0.075	0.057	0.033
40	0.208	0.142	0.097	0.046	0.032	0.022	0.011

application example

Because the bond pays 10 percent of the par value when the competitive market rate of interest is 12 percent, investors will pay only $850.90 for the issue. This bond is said to be selling at a discount of $149.10 from the $1,000 par value. The discount is determined by several factors, such as the years to maturity, the spread between the coupon and market rates, and the level of the coupon payment. While the $850.90 price was calculated using annual compounding, coupon payments on most bonds are paid semiannually. To adjust for this, we *divide* the annual coupon payment and required interest rate in the market by two and *multiply* the number of periods by two. Using the same example as before but with the appropriate adjustments for semiannual compounding, we show a slightly lower price of $849.30 as follows:

Present Value of Coupon Payments (C_t) (from Table 12-1 or Appendix D)	Present Value of Maturity Value (P_n) (from Table 12-2 or Appendix C)
$n = 40$, $i = 6\%$	$n = 40$, $i = 6\%$
$50 × 15.046 = $752.30	$1,000 × 0.097 = $97.00
Present value of coupon payments	= $752.30
Present value of maturity value	= 97.00
Value of bond	= $849.30

We see a minor adjustment in price as a result of using the more exacting process. To check our answer, Table 12–3 presents an excerpt from a bond table indicating prices for 10 percent and 12 percent annual coupon rate bonds at various market rates of interest (yields to maturity) and time periods. Although the values are quoted on an annual basis, the assumption is that semiannual discounting, such as that shown in our second example, was utilized. Note that for a bond with a 10 percent coupon rate, a 12 percent market rate (yield to maturity), and 20 years to run, the value in the table is 84.93. This is assumed to represent 84.93 percent of par value. Since the par value of the bond in our example was $1,000, the answer would be $849.30 ($1,000 × 84.93%). This is the answer we got in our second example. A typical modern bond table may be 1,000 pages long and cover time periods up to 30 years and interest rates from ¼ to 30 percent. For professionals working with bonds on a continual basis, financial calculators and computers are quite common and have a quicker response time.

TABLE 12-3 Excerpts from Bond Value Table

	COUPON RATE (10 PERCENT)				COUPON RATE (12 PERCENT)				
Yield to Maturity (percent)	1 Year	5 Years	10 Years	20 Years	1 Year	5 Years	10 Years	20 Years	Yield to Maturity (percent)
8%	101.89%	108.11%	113.50%	119.79%	103.77%	116.22%	127.18%	139.59%	8%
9	100.94	103.96	106.50	109.20	102.81	111.87	119.51	127.60	9
10	100.00	100.00	100.00	100.00	101.86	107.72	112.46	117.16	10
11	99.08	96.23	94.02	91.98	100.92	103.77	105.98	108.02	11
12	98.17	92.64	88.53	**84.93**	100.00	100.00	100.00	100.00	12
13	97.27	89.22	83.47	78.78	99.09	96.41	94.49	92.93	13
14	96.38	85.95	78.81	73.34	98.19	92.98	89.41	86.67	14

RATES OF RETURN

Bonds are evaluated on a number of different types of returns, including current yield, yield to maturity, yield to call, and anticipated realized yield.

Current Yield

The **current yield**, which is shown in *The Wall Street Journal* and many daily newspapers, is the annual interest payment divided by the price of the bond. An example might be a 10 percent coupon rate $1,000 par value bond selling for $950. The current yield would be:

$$\frac{\$100}{\$950} = 10.53\%$$

The 10.53 percent indicates the annual cash rate of return an investor would receive in interest payments on the $950 investment but does not include any adjustments for capital gains or losses as bond prices change in response to new market interest rates. Another problem with current yield is that it does not take into consideration the maturity date of a debt instrument. A bond with 1 year to run and another with 20 years to run would have the same current yield quote if interest payments were $100 and the price were $950. Clearly, the one-year bond would be preferable under this circumstance because the investor would not only get $100 in interest but also a $50 gain in value ($1,000 − $950) within a *one-year* period, as the price goes to its $1,000 maturity value.

Yield to Maturity

Yield to maturity is a measure of return that considers the annual interest received, the difference between the current bond price and its maturity value, and the number of years to maturity. More importantly, **yield to maturity** is the same concept as the internal rate of return or true yield on an investment. That is, it is the interest rate (i) at which you can discount the future coupon payments (C_t) and maturity value (P_n) to arrive at a known current value (V) of the bond. Now, we are assuming that you know the current value (price) of the bond, the coupon payments, the maturity value, and the number of periods to maturity and that you want to know what the true yield to maturity is on the bond.

Restating Formula 12–1 below, the unknown is now assumed to be i, the interest rate in the market. The interest rate in the market is always going to be the same as the yield to maturity (the bond will yield what the market dictates):

$$V = \sum_{t=1}^{n} \frac{C_t}{(1 + \textcircled{i})^t} + \frac{P_n}{(1 + \textcircled{i})^n}$$

Unknown

Let us compute the value of i. We will use annual analysis to facilitate the calculations. First, we do an easy problem to demonstrate the process, and then we extend the analysis to a more involved calculation.

Assume V (market value or price of the bond) is \$850.90, C_t (coupon or interest payment for each period) is \$100, P_n (par or maturity value) is \$1,000, and n (number of periods) is 20. What i will force the future cash inflows to equal \$850.90? Let's use 12 percent, and prove that it works:

Present Value of Coupon Payments (C_t) (from Table 12-1 or Appendix D)	Present Value of Maturity Value (P_n) (from Table 12-2 or Appendix C)
$n = 20$, $i = 12\%$	$n = 20$, $i = 12\%$
\$100 × 7.469 = \$746.90	\$1,000 × 0.104 = \$104.00
Present value of coupon payments	= \$746.90
Present value of maturity value	= 104.00
Value of bond	= \$850.90

An i of 12 percent gave us the \$850.90 we desired because we used the same *12 percent* we employed earlier in the chapter to get \$850.90. (We turned the problem around.) Thus, 12 percent is the yield to maturity.

Let us now go to a situation where we presumably do not know the answer in advance. It should be mentioned at this point that if you have a financial calculator, you may wish to follow the recommended steps for the calculator (such as those shown in Appendix F on page 609 for the Texas Instruments BAII Plus or the Hewlett-Packard 12C) to find yield to maturity. Because the authors cannot assume this is the case, we will introduce you to a trial-and-error method of solution. Please feel free to use the approach that is best for you.

Interpolation We cannot always assume that the value we derive from the interest rates in the tables will allow us to arrive at the exact value for the bond. Using your calculator is an important skill because the interest rates in the tables are expressed in whole numbers while interest rates in the real world are usually not in whole numbers. Therefore you can refer to the calculator example in Appendix F on page 612 for a more accurate way to determine the value of a bond when given the coupon rate, market interest rate, and maturity.

application example

Assume a bond is paying a 7 percent coupon rate (C_t), has 15 periods to maturity (n), is selling for \$839.27 (V), and has a par maturity value (P_n) of \$1,000. What is the value of i? Using a trial-and-error process, we will need to make a first guess at the value of i and try it out. Because the bond is selling for less than par value (\$1,000), we can assume that the interest rate is greater than 7 percent. Why? Anytime a bond is trading at an interest rate (i) greater than the coupon rate, it will sell for less than par value, and that is the case in this example. Of course, if the coupon rate were greater than the interest rate (i), the bond would sell for more than par value. It would be paying more than the market is demanding and would sell at a premium rather than a discount.

Remember that our first trial-and-error calculation in this example must be at an interest rate (i) greater than 7 percent. Let's try 8 percent for the 15 periods to maturity:

Present Value of Coupon Payments (C_t) (from Table 12-1 or Appendix D)	Present Value of Maturity Value (P_n) (from Table 12-2 or Appendix C)
$n = 15, i = 8\%$	$n = 15, i = 8\%$
\$70 × 8.559 = \$599.13	\$1,000 × 0.315 = \$315
Present value of coupon payments	= \$599.13
Present value of maturity value	= 315.00
Value of bond	= \$914.13

The answer of \$914.13 is higher than our desired answer of \$839.27. To bring the answer down, we use a higher interest rate. The next try is at 9 percent:

Present Value of Coupon Payments (C_t) (from Table 12-1 or Appendix D)	Present Value of Maturity Value (P_n) (from Table 12-2 or Appendix C)
$n = 15, i = 9\%$	$n = 15, i = 9\%$
\$70 × 8.061 = \$564.27	\$1,000 × 0.275 = \$275
Present value of coupon payments	= \$564.27
Present value of maturity value	= 275.00
Value of bond	= \$839.27

Obviously, 9 percent is the interest rate that equates the future coupon payments (C_t) *and maturity value* (P_n) to the bond value of \$839.27. Thus, we say that 9 percent is the yield to maturity.

The Formula for Approximate Yield to Maturity Most likely you will never use this approximation formula in the real world. Instead you will look up the bond yield on a Bloomberg terminal or possibly use a calculator. The reason we include the formula for the *approximate yield to maturity* is because it is a very intuitive way of explaining exactly what goes on in the calculation.

If you examine the formula, you will see that the numerator consists of the annual coupon payment in dollars plus an annual increase or decrease in bond value. If the bond is selling at a discount to par value, the bond will increase to par over the life of the bond. Likewise, if it is selling at a premium, it will decrease to par over the life of the bond. Because the increase or decrease is divided by the number of years to maturity, the numerator assumes an equal change in value over the years. So the numerator becomes the average return per year in dollars.

The denominator is essentially the weighted average of the dollars invested over the periods to maturity. Instead of taking a simple average, the denominator uses a

FIGURE 12-1 Relationship between Time to Maturity and Bond Price

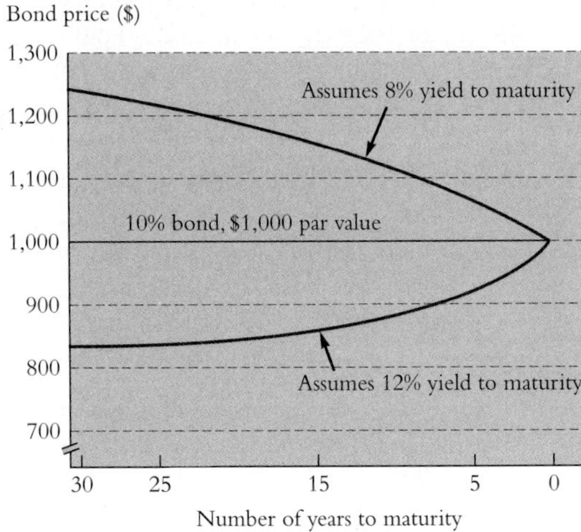

The relationship in the graph is not symmetrical in nature.

weighted average with the market value of the bond weighted at 60 percent and the par value weighted at 40 percent. The weights adjust for the fact that the bond does not approach its par value in a straight line but in a curvilinear fashion. Figure 12–1 shows the price paths that a bond would follow when selling at a premium or a discount. This is what the weighted average in the denominator adjusts for.

So we finally have an approximate yield to maturity as the average annual return in dollars divided by the weighted average on the initial investment. Surprisingly, the formula is fairly accurate, even though it doesn't use the time value of money to calculate the solution.

The formula is:[2]

$$Y' = \frac{C_t + \dfrac{P_n - V}{n}}{(0.6)V + (0.4)P_n} \tag{12–2}$$

Plugging values into the formula on an annual basis, we find:

Y' = Approximate yield to maturity
C_t = Coupon payment = $100
P_n = Par or maturity value = $1,000
V = Market value = $850.90
n = Number of periods = 20

$$Y' = \frac{\$100 + \dfrac{\$1{,}000 - \$850.90}{20}}{(0.6)\$850.90 + (0.4)\$1{,}000}$$

$$= \frac{\$100 + \dfrac{\$149.10}{20}}{\$510.54 + \$400}$$

$$= \frac{\$100 + \$7.45}{\$910.54}$$

$$= \frac{\$107.45}{\$910.54} = 11.80\%$$

[2] This formula is recommended by Gabriel A. Hawawini and Ashok Vora, "Yield Approximations: A Historical Perspective," *Journal of Finance*, March 1982, pp. 145–56. It tends to provide the best approximation.

Actually, the true yield to maturity is 12.00 percent, so the approximate yield to maturity of 11.80 percent is 0.20 percent below the actual yield. In the jargon of bond trading, each 1/100 of 1 percent is referred to as a **basis point**, so the difference is 20 basis points. The approximate yield to maturity method tends to understate exact yield to maturity for issues trading at a discount (in this case, the bond is priced at $850.90). The opposite effect occurs for bonds trading at a premium (above par value).[3]

In the interest of simplicity, we will use approximation formulas in the next two sections related to yield to call and anticipated realized yield, but keep in mind these are only estimates of the exact answers.

Yield to Call

As discussed in the preceding chapter on bond fundamentals, not all fixed-income securities are held to maturity. To the extent a debt instrument may be called in before maturity, a separate calculation is necessary to determine yield to the call date. The answer is termed the **yield to call**. Assume a 20-year bond was initially issued at 11.5 percent interest rate, and after two years, rates have dropped. Let us assume the bond is currently selling for $1,180, and the yield to maturity on the bond is 9.48 percent. However, the investor who purchases the bond for $1,180 may not be able to hold the bond for the remaining 18 years because the issue can be called. Under these circumstances, yield to maturity may not be the appropriate measure of return over the expected holding period.

In the present case, we assume the bond can be called at $1,090 five years after issue. Thus, the investor who buys the bond two years after issue can have his bond called back after three more years at $1,090. To compute yield to call, we determine the approximate interest rate that will equate a $1,180 investment today with $115 (11.5 percent) per year for the next three years plus a payoff or call price value of $1,090 at the end of three years. We can adjust Formula 12–2 (approximate yield to maturity) to Formula 12–3 (approximate yield to call):

$$Y'_c = \frac{C_t + \dfrac{P_c - V}{n_c}}{(0.6)V + (0.4)P_c} \qquad \textbf{(12–3)}$$

On an annual basis, we show:

Y'_c = Approximate yield to call

C_t = Coupon payment = $115

P_c = Call price = $1,090

V = Market value = $1,180

n_c = Number of periods to call = 3

$$\begin{aligned} Y'_c &= \frac{\$115 + \dfrac{\$1{,}090 - \$1{,}180}{3}}{(0.6)\$1{,}180 + (0.4)\$1{,}090} \\ &= \frac{\$115 + \dfrac{-\$90}{3}}{\$708 + \$436} \\ &= \frac{\$115 - \$30}{\$1{,}144} \\ &= \frac{\$85}{\$1{,}144} \\ &= 7.43\% \end{aligned}$$

[3] In all our bond problems, we assume we buy the bond at the beginning of an interest payment period. To the extent there is accrued interest, we would have to modify our calculations slightly.

The yield to call figure of 7.43 percent is 205 basis points less than the yield to maturity figure of 9.48 percent cited above. Clearly, the investor needs to be aware of the differential, which represents the decrease in yield the investor would receive if the bond is called. Generally, any time the market price of a bond is equal to or greater than the call price, the investor should do a separate calculation for yield to call.[4]

In the case where market interest rates are much lower than the coupon, there is always the chance the company will call the bond. Because of this possibility, the call price often serves as an upper price limit, and further reductions in market interest rates will not cause this callable bond to increase in price. In other words, investors' capital gain potentials may be quite limited with bonds subject to a call.

Anticipated Realized Yield

Finally, we have the case where the investor purchases the bond with the intention of holding the bond for a period that is different from either the call date or the maturity date. Under this circumstance, we examine the **anticipated realized yield**. This represents the return over the expected holding period.

Assume an investor buys a 12.5 percent coupon bond for $900. Based on her forecasts of lower interest rates, she anticipates the bond will go to $1,050 in three years. The formula for the approximate realized yield is:

$$Y'_r = \frac{C_t + \dfrac{P_r - V}{n_r}}{(0.6)V + (0.4)P_r} \qquad \textbf{(12–4)}$$

The terms are:

Y'_r = Anticipated realized yield
C_t = Coupon payment = $125
P_r = Realized price = $1,050
V = Market price = $900
n_r = Number of periods to realization = 3

$$\begin{aligned} Y'_r &= \frac{\$125 + \dfrac{\$1{,}050 - \$900}{3}}{(0.6)\$900 + (0.40)\$1{,}050} \\ &= \frac{\$125 + \dfrac{\$150}{3}}{\$540 + \$420} \\ &= \frac{\$175}{\$960} \\ &= 18.23\% \end{aligned}$$

The anticipated return of 18.23 percent would not be unusual in periods of falling interest rates.

Reinvestment Assumption

Throughout our analysis, when we have talked about yield to maturity, yield to call, and anticipated realized yield, we have assumed that the determined rate also represents an appropriate rate for reinvestment of funds. If yield to maturity is 11 or 12 percent, then it is assumed that coupon payments, as they come in, can also be reinvested at that rate. To the extent that this is an unrealistic assumption,

[4] Bond tables may also be used to find the exact value for yield to call. A source is *The Thorndike Encyclopedia of Banking and Financial Tables* (Boston: Warren, Gorham & Lamont, 1981).

the real world of investing

SO YOU WANT A LONG MATURITY—HOW ABOUT 1,000 YEARS?

That's right—bonds of Canadian Pacific Limited have a 1,000-year maturity. By then the cost of a postage stamp should be a few million dollars.

On a more serious note, five major corporations recently offered 50-year bonds, the longest maturities in U.S. history. The following firms participated:

TVA (**www.tva.com**)	$1 billion
Boeing (**www.boeing.com**)	$275 million
Conrail (**www.conrail.com**)	$250 million
Ford Motor (**www.ford.com**)	$200 million

All were issued at about ¼ percent above comparable 30-year issues of the same firm. Because long-term interest rates were considered low at the time for highly rated corporate bonds (approximately 7½ percent), one can clearly see the motivation to the issuing firm.

What about the investor? Half a century is a long time to be tied in to an investment. Look back 50 years ago; we didn't know about computers, space shots to the moon, or artificial heart transplants. What new events will transpire during the next 50 years?

Nevertheless, approximately $2 billion of these 50-year issues were absorbed in the marketplace. Some investors were motivated by the fact that the maturity of the issues matched their liabilities. An example would be insurance companies with long-term policy commitments. Others recognized that the price sensitivity of a 50-year bond is not much greater than a 30-year bond. Although bond price sensitivity increases with maturity, it increases at a greatly decreasing rate with long maturity obligations. For example, an interest rate increase of 2 percent on a 30-year, 8 percent, $1,000 par value bond will cause a price decline to $811.16. On a 50-year bond, the same 2 percent increase will cause a price decline to $802.20—only about a $9 difference. The extra ¼ percent interest on the 50-year bonds apparently justified accepting the slightly greater price sensitivity exposure.

Also keep in mind that if interest rates fall below the initial issue rate any time over the next 50 years, the investor may have the opportunity for capital appreciation. Fifty years is a long opportunity to wait for a depression, a stock market crash, or other type of event that might drive down interest rates.

An added feature was that the issuers were all in the A to AAA category so that the threat of bankruptcy was thought to be relatively small. However, keep in mind that a lot can happen over a 50-year period. By that time, there may not even be conventional airplanes, automobiles, or gasoline, the primary products of many of the issuers.

investors will wish to temper their thinking. For example, if it is anticipated that returns can be reinvested at a higher rate in the future, this increases true yield, and the opposite effect would be present for a decline in interest rates. The reinvestment topic is more fully developed in Chapter 18.

THE MOVEMENT OF INTEREST RATES

In developing our discussion of bond valuation and investments, we observed that lower interest rates bring higher bond prices and profits. A glance back at Table 12–3 on page 317 (right-hand portion) indicates a 12 percent coupon rate, 20-year bond will sell for $1,171.60 if yields to maturity on competitive bonds decline to 10 percent and for $1,276.00 when yields decline to 9 percent. The maturity of the bond is also important, with the impact on price being greater for longer-term obligations.

The investor who wishes to make a substantial profit in the bond market must try to anticipate the turns and directions of interest rates. While much of the literature on efficient markets indicates that this is extremely difficult,[5] Wall Street economists, bank economists, and many others rely on interest-rate forecasts to formulate financial strategies. The fact that short-term and long-term rates do not

[5] Michael J. Prell, "How Well Do the Experts Forecast Interest Rates?" Federal Reserve Bank of Kansas City, *Monthly Review*, September–October 1973, pp. 3–13; Oswald D. Bowlin and John D. Martin, "Extrapolations of Yields over the Short Run: Forecast or Folly?" *Journal of Monetary Economics*, 1975, pp. 275–88; and Richard Roll, *The Behavior of Interest Rates* (New York: Basic Books, 1970).

necessarily move in the same direction or move with the same magnitude makes the task even more formidable. Nevertheless, some historical analysis and knowledge of interest rate patterns over the business cycle are useful in making investment decisions.

Interest rates have long been viewed as a coincident indicator in our economy; that is to say, they are thought to move in concert with industrial production, gross domestic product, and similar measures of general economic health. This is generally true, although in the last five recessions, the change in interest rates has actually lagged behind the decline in industrial production.

While inflationary expectations have the greatest influence on long-term rates, a number of other factors also influence overall interest rates. The demand for funds by individuals, businesses, and the government represents one side of the equation, with the desire for savings and Federal Reserve policy influencing the supply side.

Term Structure of Interest Rates

Of general importance to understanding the level of interest rates is the development of an appreciation for the relationship between the level of interest rates and the maturity of the debt obligation. There is no one single interest rate but, rather, a whole series of interest rates associated with the given maturity of bonds.

The **term structure of interest rates** depicts the relationship between maturity and interest rates. It is sometimes called a yield curve because yields on existing securities having maturities from three months to 30 years are plotted on a graph to develop the curve. To eliminate any business risk consideration, the securities analyzed are usually U.S. Treasury issues. Examples of four different types of term structures are presented in Figure 12–2.

FIGURE 12-2 Term Structure of Interest Rates

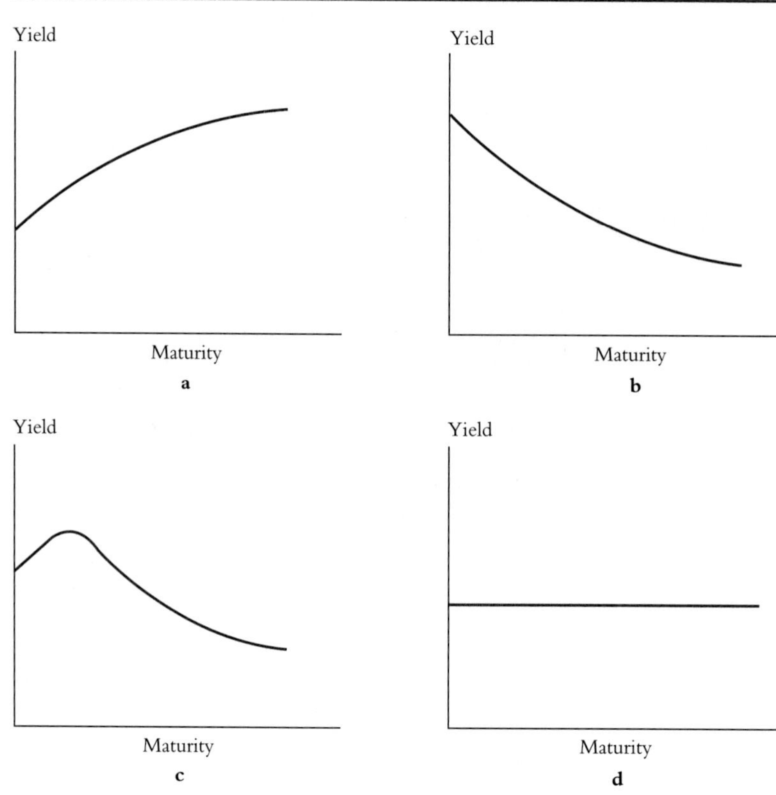

In panel *a,* we see an ascending term structure pattern in which interest rates increase with the lengthening of the maturity dates. When the term structure is in this posture, it is a general signal that interest rates will rise in the future. In panel *b,* we see a descending pattern of interest rates, with this pattern generally predictive of lower interest rates. Panel *c* is a variation of panel *b,* with the hump representing intermediate-term interest rates. This particular configuration is an even stronger indicator that interest rates may be declining in the future. Finally, in panel *d,* we see a flat-term structure indicating investor indifference between debt instrument maturity. This generally indicates that there is no discernible pattern for the future of interest rates. Several theories of interest rates are used to explain the particular shape of the yield curve. We review three of these theories.

Expectations Hypothesis The dominant rationale for the shape of the term structure of interest rates rests on a phenomenon called the **expectations hypothesis**. The hypothesis is that any long-term rate is an average of the expectations of future short-term rates over the applicable time horizon. Thus, if lenders expect short-term rates to be continually increasing, they will demand higher long-term rates. Conversely, if they anticipate short-term rates to be declining, they will accept lower long-term rates. An example may be helpful. Suppose the interest rate on a one-year Treasury security is 6 percent, and that after one year, it is assumed that a new one-year Treasury security may be bought to yield 8 percent. At the end of year 2, it is assumed that a third one-year Treasury security may be bought to yield 10 percent. In other words, the investor can buy (this is sometimes called roll over) three one-year Treasury securities in yearly succession, each with an expected one-year return.

But what about investors who buy one-, two-, or three-year securities today? The yield they will require will be based on expectations about the future. For the one-year security, there is no problem. The 6 percent return will be acceptable. But investors who buy a two-year security now will want the average of the 6 percent they could expect in the first year and the 8 percent expected in the second year, or 7 percent.[6] An investor who buys a three-year security will demand an average of 6, 8, and 10 percent, or an 8 percent return. Higher expected interest rates in the future will mean that longer maturities will carry higher yields than will shorter maturities. The reverse would be true if interest rates were expected to go down.

The expectations hypothesis tends to be reinforced by lender/borrower strategies. If investors (lenders) expect interest rates to increase in the future, they will attempt to lend short-term and avoid long-term obligations so as to diminish losses on long maturity obligations when interest rates go up. Borrowers have exactly the opposite incentive. When interest rates are expected to go up, they will attempt to borrow long term now to lock in the lower rates. Thus, the desire of lenders to lend short term (and avoid long term) and the desire of borrowers to borrow long term (and avoid short term) accentuates the expected pattern of rising interest rates. The opposite motivations are in effect when interest rates are expected to decline.

Liquidity Preference Theory The second theory used to explain the term structure of interest rates is called the **liquidity preference theory**, which states that the shape of the term structure curve tends to be upward sloping more than any other pattern. This reflects a recognition of the fact that long maturity obligations are subject to greater price-change movements when interest rates change. Because

[6] The expectations hypothesis actually uses the geometric mean (compound growth rate) rather than the arithmetic mean (simple average) used in the example. For a short number of years, the two means would be quite similar.

of the increased risk of holding longer-term maturities, investors demand a higher return to hold long-term securities relative to short-term securities. This is called the liquidity preference theory of interest rates. Since short-term securities are more easily turned into cash without the risk of large price changes, investors pay a higher price for short-term securities and thus receive a lower yield.

Market Segmentation Theory The third theory related to the term structure of interest rates is called the **market segmentation theory** and focuses on the demand side of the market. The theory is that there are several large institutional participants in the bond market, each with its own maturity preference. Banks tend to prefer short-term liquid securities to match the nature of their deposits, whereas life insurance companies prefer long-term bonds to match their long-run obligations. The behavior of these two institutions, as well as that of savings and loans, often creates pressure on short-term or long-term rates but very little pressure in the intermediate market of five- to seven-year maturities. This theory helps to focus on the accumulation or liquidation of securities by institutions during the different phases of the business cycle and the resultant impact on the yield curve.

We have now covered all three explanations of the term structure of interest rates. As stated earlier, the expectations hypothesis is probably the most dominant theory, but all three theories have some part in the creation of the term structure of interest rates.

Before concluding our discussion of the term structure of interest rates and proceeding to the development of investment strategies, one final observation is significant. Short-term rates, which are most influenced by Federal Reserve policy in attempting to regulate the money supply and economy, are much more volatile than long-term rates. An examination of Figure 12–3 indicates that *short-term* rates on 3-month marketable certificates of deposit are more volatile than *long-term,* high-grade corporate bond rates even though they move in the same direction over time.

Interest rates in the late 1970s and early 1980s were in the stratosphere of 15 percent for long-term AAA corporate bonds and 18 percent for 3-month CDs. The major impetus for this move was rampant inflation, so as inflation subsided, rates

FIGURE 12-3 Relative Volatility of Short-Term and Long-Term Interest Rates

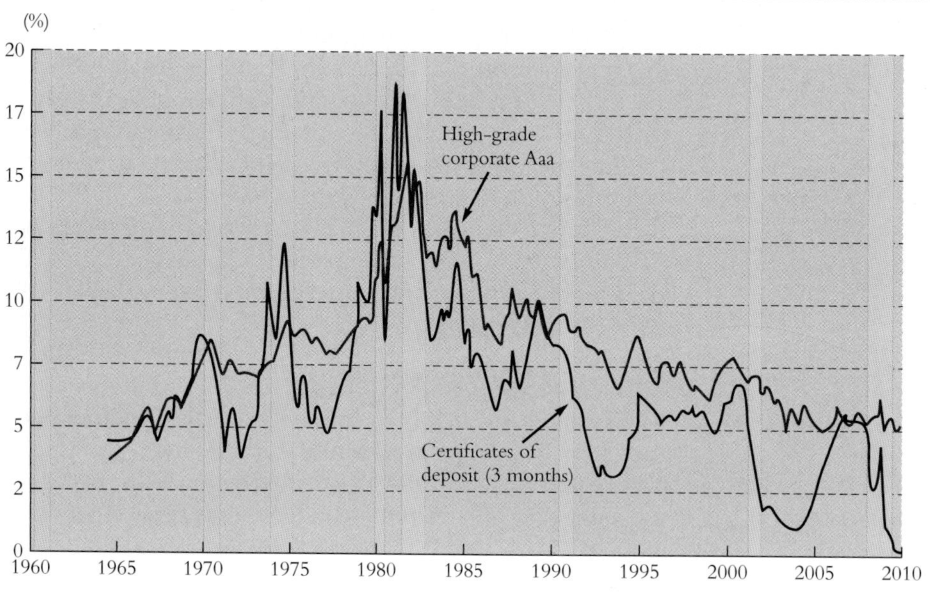

Source: Federal Reserve Bank of St. Louis, FRED Economic Data, Global Financial Database.

came down with a lag. In the period from 2000 to 2010, long-term rates on the highest-quality corporate bonds moved down from over 7.5 percent to a little under 5 percent. However, the short-term rates moved to less than 0.5 percent in 2010. Much of the decline was again due to low to zero inflation and the financial crisis and ensuing recession. The unknown that worries some is whether the government's huge stimulus spending, used to extricate the economy from the recession, may eventually cause inflation to rear its ugly head and push interest rates back up to new highs. Of course, the other set of experts worry about a double-dip recession and deflation, and think that a 3.8 percent yield on 30-year U.S. Treasury bonds is a bargain. In finance and economics, one can always find experts with opposite opinions, and only time will tell who was right.

INVESTMENT STRATEGY: INTEREST RATE CONSIDERATIONS

Thus far in this chapter, we have examined the different valuation procedures for determining the price or yield on a bond and the methods for evaluating the future course of interest rates. We now bring this knowledge together in the form of various investment strategies.

When the bond investor believes interest rates are going to fall, he will take a bullish position in the market by buying long-term bonds and try to maximize the price movement pattern associated with a change in interest rates. The investor can do this by considering the *maturity, coupon rate,* and *quality* of the issue.

Because the impact of an interest rate change is much greater on long-term securities, the investor generally looks for extended maturities. The impact of various changes in yields on bond prices for 12 and 6 percent coupon rate bonds can be examined in Table 12–4. For example, looking at the −2% line for

TABLE 12-4 Change in Market Prices of Bonds for Shifts in Yields to Maturity

12 Percent Coupon Rate

	MATURITY (YEARS)				
Yield Change	1	5	10	20	30
+3%	−2.69%	−10.30%	−15.29%	−18.89%	−19.74%
+2	−1.81	−7.02	−10.59	−13.33	−14.04
+1	−0.91	−3.57	−5.01	−7.08	−7.52
−1	+0.92	+3.77	+5.98	+8.02	+8.72
−2	+1.86	+7.72	+12.46	+17.16	+18.93
−3	+2.81	+11.87	+19.51	+27.60	+30.96

6 Percent Coupon Rate

	MATURITY (YEARS)				
Yield Change	1	5	10	20	30
+3%	−2.75%	−11.67%	−19.25%	−27.39%	−30.82%
+2	−1.85	−7.99	−13.42	−19.64	−22.52
+1	−0.94	−4.10	−7.02	−10.60	−12.41
−1	+0.95	+4.33	+7.72	+12.46	+15.37
−2	+1.92	+8.90	+16.22	+27.18	+34.59
−3	+2.91	+13.74	+25.59	+44.63	+58.80

the 12 percent coupon bond in the upper part of the table, we see a 2 percent drop in competitive yields would cause a 1.86 percent increase in value for a bond with 1 year to maturity but an 18.93 percent increase in value for a bond with 30 years to maturity. For the same 2 percent drop in rates, the 6 percent coupon bond would increase 1.92 percent (1 year to maturity) and 34.59 percent (30 years to maturity). The relationship between these two bonds further shows that the lower 6 percent coupon bond is more price sensitive than the higher 12 percent coupon bond.

We can also observe that the effect of interest rate changes is not symmetrical. Drops in interest rates cause proportionally greater gains than increases in interest rates cause losses, particularly as we lengthen the maturity. An evaluation of the 30-year column in Table 12–4 confirms that both bonds are more price sensitive to a decline in yields than to a rise in yields.[7]

Although we have emphasized the need for long maturities in maximizing price movement, the alert student will recall that short-term interest rates generally move up and down more than long-term interest rates as was indicated in Figure 12–2. What if short-term rates are more volatile—even though long-term rates have a greater price impact—which do we choose then? The answer is fairly direct. The mathematical impact of long maturities on price changes far outweighs the more volatile feature of short-term interest rates. A 1-year, 12 percent debt instrument would need to have an interest rate *change* of almost *9 percent* to have the equivalent impact of a 1 percent change in a 30-year debt obligation.

Bond-Pricing Rules

The relationships we presented in this section can be summarized in a set of bond-pricing rules. Prices of existing bonds have a relationship to maturities, coupons, and market yields for bonds of equal risk. These relationships are evident from an examination of previously presented Table 12–4. If you look at the change in bond prices in Table 12–4, you may be able to describe many of the relationships presented in the following list:

1. Bond prices and interest rates are inversely related.
2. Prices of long-term bonds are more sensitive to a change in yields to maturity than short-term bonds.
3. Bond price sensitivity increases at a decreasing rate as maturity increases.
4. Bond prices are more sensitive to a decline in market yields to maturity than to a rise in market yields to maturity.
5. Prices of low-coupon bonds are more sensitive to a change in yields to maturity than high-coupon bonds.
6. Bond prices are more sensitive when yields to maturity are low than when yields to maturity are high.

Understanding these six bond-pricing relationships is at the heart of creating bond trading and investment strategies. Chapter 18, on duration, provides a more comprehensive analysis of price sensitivity, coupon rates, maturity, market rates, and their combined impact on bond prices.

[7] A sophisticated investor would also consider the concept of *duration*. Duration is defined as the weighted average time to recover interest and principal. For a bond that pays interest (which includes most cases except zero-coupon bonds), duration will be shorter than maturity in that interest payments start almost immediately. Portfolio strategy may call for maximizing duration rather than maturity in order to achieve maximum movement. A complete discussion of this topic is presented in Chapter 18.

Example of Interest-Rate Change

application example

Assume we buy 20-year, $1,000 Aaa bonds at par providing a 12 percent coupon rate. Further assume interest rates on these bonds in the market fall to 10 percent. Based on Table 12–5 below, the new price on the bonds would be $1,171.60 ($1,000 × 117.16).

TABLE 12-5 Sample Bond Table

	COUPON RATE 12 PERCENT		
		Number of Years	
Yield to Maturity	10	20	30
8%	127.18%	139.59%	145.25%
10	112.46	117.16	118.93
12	100.00	100.00	100.00
14	89.41	86.55	85.96

Although we could assume the gain in price from $1,000 to $1,171.60 occurred very quickly, even if the time horizon were one year, the gain is still 17.16 percent. This is only part of the picture. An integral part of many bond–interest rate strategies is the use of margin or borrowed funds. For government securities, it is possible to use margin as low as 5 percent, and on high-quality utility or corporate bonds, the requirement is generally 30 percent. In the preceding case, if we had put down 30 percent cash and borrowed the balance, the rate of return on invested capital would have been 57.2 percent:

$$\frac{\text{Return}}{\text{Investment}} = \frac{\$171.60}{\$300.00} = 57.2\%$$

Although we have to pay interest on the $700 we borrowed, the interest on the bonds (which belongs to the borrower/investor) would have partially or fully covered this expense. Also, if interest rates drop further to 8 percent, our leveraged return could be over 100 percent on our original investment.

Lest the overanxious student sell all his or her worldly possessions to participate in this impressive gain, there are many admonitions. Even though we think interest rates are going down, they may do the opposite. A 2 percent *increase* in interest rates would cause a $133.30 loss or a negative return on a leveraged investment of $300 or a 44.4 percent loss. At the very time it appears that interest rates should be falling due to an anticipated or actual recession, the Federal Reserve may generate the opposite effect by tightening the money supply as an anti-inflation weapon as it did in 1974, 1979, 1981, 1994, and 2001.

Deep Discount versus Par Bonds

Another feature in analyzing a bond is the current pricing of the bond in regard to its par value. Bonds that were previously issued at interest rates significantly lower than current market levels may trade at deep discounts from par. These are referred to as **deep discount bonds**. As an example, the Missouri Pacific 4¾ percent bonds due to mature in 2020 were selling at $699 in January 2007. Their bond rating was Baa2, and the yield to maturity was 7.85 percent.

Deep discount bonds generally trade at a lower yield to maturity than bonds selling at close to par. There are two reasons for this. First, a deep discount bond has

FIGURE 12-4 Yield Spread Differentials on Long-Term Bonds

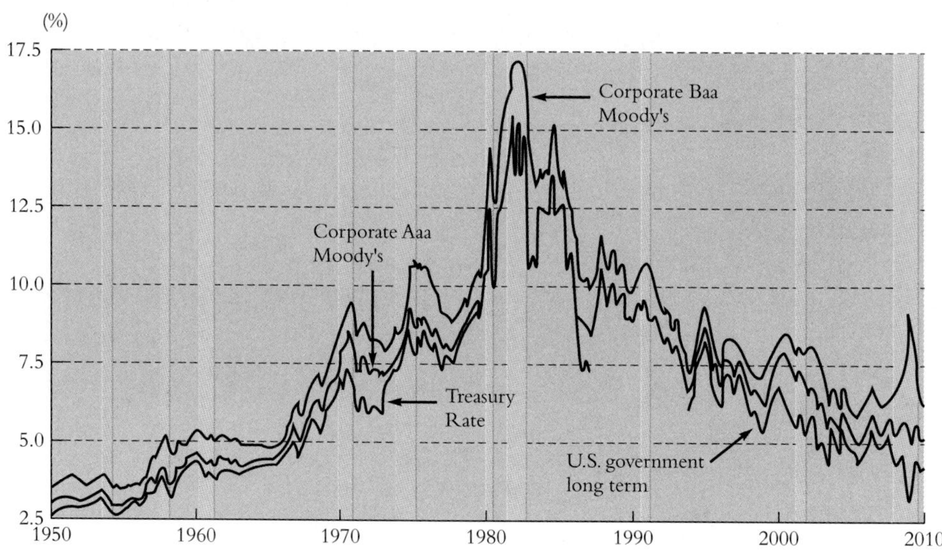

Source: Federal Reserve Bank of St. Louis, FRED Economic Data, http://research.stlouisfed.org.

almost no chance to be called away. Even if prices go up because of falling interest rates, the price is still likely to be below par value. Because of this protection against a call, the investor in deep discount bonds accepts a lower yield. Second, investors in deep discount bonds have the potential for higher percentage price increases (because of the low price base at which the investment is made). Additionally, if the bond is held to maturity, the gain is taxed at the capital gains tax rate. This is not true of zero-coupon bonds that are also sold at a discount from par.

Yield Spread Considerations

As discussed in the previous chapter, different types or grades of bonds provide different yields. For example, the yield on Baa corporate bonds is always above that of corporate Aaa obligations to compensate for risk. Similarly, Aaa corporates pay a higher yield than long-term government obligations. In Figure 12–4, we observe the actual yield spread between Moody's corporate Baa's, Moody's corporate Aaa's, and long-term government securities.

Let's direct our attention to total spread between corporate Baa bonds and government securities (corporate Aaa's fall somewhere in between). Over the long term, the spread appears to be between 75 and 100 basis points.[8] Nevertheless, at certain phases of the business cycle, the yield spread changes. For example, in the early phases of a recession, confidence tends to be at a low ebb, and as a consequence, investors attempt to shift out of lower grade securities into stronger instruments. The impact on the yield spreads can be observed in the recessions of 1969–70, 1973–75, 1981–82, 1990–91, 2000–01, and 2009–10. In all cases, the yield spread between corporate Baa's and government securities went over 150 basis points, only to narrow again during the recovery. Remember that in Chapter 10, about technical analysis, one of the market indicators was the *Barron's* Confidence Index, which measured the ratio of high-grade bonds to medium-grade bonds. The closer the confidence index is to 1.00, the smaller the spread between rates and the more optimistic investors are about the economy. The further the index is below 1.00, the greater the spread in yields and the less the confidence.

[8] The concept of higher yields on Baa bonds should not be confused with that of junk bonds. In the latter case, the yield is substantially higher, but so is the risk of default.

Investors must determine how the yield spread affects their strategy. If they do not need to increase the quality of the portfolio during the low-confidence periods of a recession, they can enjoy unusually high returns on lower-grade instruments relative to higher grades. In the next chapter we examine convertible bonds.

exploring the web

Web Address	Comments
www.smartmoney.com	**Provides some bond information; unique feature is living yield curve**
www.bondsonline.com	**Provides trading, yield curve data**
www.research.stlouis.org	**The Federal Reserve Bank of St. Louis Web site has a wealth of interest rate data**

SUMMARY

The price of a bond is based on the concept of the present value of future interest payments plus the present value of a single-sum payment at maturity. The true return on a bond investment may be measured by yield to maturity, yield to call, or anticipated realized yield. A study of interest rates in the business cycle indicates that while interest rates were at one time a coincident indicator, their movement has tended to lag behind the drop in business activity during recent recessions.

The term structure of interest rates depicts the relationship between maturity and interest rates over a long time horizon. The slope of the curve gives some indication as to future movements, with an ascending pattern generally followed by higher interest rates and a descending pattern associated with a possible decline in the future. While these movements hold true in the long run, it is somewhat difficult to project interest movements in the short run.

An investor who wishes to capture maximum gains from an anticipated interest rate decline should maximize the length of the portfolio while investing in low-coupon, interest-sensitive securities. Deep discount bonds also offer some protection from call provisions.

A complete analysis of a bond portfolio will also include a consideration of the yield spreads between low- and high-quality issues. The spread between long-term U.S. government bonds and corporate Baa's has been as high as 150 basis points or more during certain periods in the 1970s, 1980s, 1990s, and 2000s. This factor can have a strong influence on bond portfolio construction.

KEY WORDS AND CONCEPTS

www.mhhe.com/hirtblock10e

DISCUSSION QUESTIONS

1. Why are bonds not necessarily a conservative investment?
2. How can the market price of a bond be described in terms of present value?
3. Why does a bond price change when interest rates change?
4. Why is current yield not a good indicator of bond returns? (Relate your answer to maturity considerations.)
5. Describe how yield to maturity is the same concept as the internal rate of return (or true yield) on an investment.
6. What is the significance of the yield-to-call calculation?
7. What is the bond reinvestment assumption? Is this necessarily correct?
8. What is the meaning of term structure of interest rates?
9. What does an ascending term structure pattern tend to indicate?
10. Explain the general meaning of the expectations hypothesis as it relates to the term structure of interest rates.
11. Explain the liquidity preference theory as it relates to the term structure of interest rates.
12. How might the market segmentation theory help to explain why short-term rates on government securities increase when bank loan demand becomes high?
13. Under what circumstances would the yield spread on different classes of debt obligations tend to be largest?
14. List the six principles associated with bond-pricing relationships.
15. How do margin requirements affect investor strategy for bonds?
16. Explain the benefits derived from investing in deep discount bonds.
17. What is a bond swap investment strategy? Explain how it might relate to tax planning.

PRACTICE PROBLEMS AND SOLUTIONS

Bond price

1. Given a 9-year bond that sold for $1,000 with an 8 percent coupon rate, what would be the price of the bond if interest rates in the marketplace on similar bonds are now 10 percent? Interest is paid semiannually. Assume a 9-year time period.

Yield to maturity

2. What is the yield to maturity for an 11 percent coupon rate bond priced at $943.50? Assume there are 10 years left to maturity and it is a $1,000 per value bond. Use the trial-and-error approach with annual analysis.

Solutions

1. PV of $40 semiannually for $n = 18$ and $i = 5\%$ (Appendix D)

$40 × 11.690 = $467.60

PV of $1,000 semiannually for $n = 18$ and $i = 5\%$ (Appendix C)

$1,000 × .416 = 416.00

$883.60

2. If the bond is trading below par value, the discoun t rate must be above the coupon rate of 11 percent. Let's try 12 percent.
PV of \$100 annually for $n = 10,\ i = 12\%$
(Table 12–1 or Appendix D)

$$\$110 \times 5.650 = \$621.50$$

PV of \$1,000 annually for $n = 10$ and $i = 12\%$
(Table 12–2 or Appendix C)

$$\$1{,}000 \times .322 = \underline{322.00}$$
$$\$943.50$$

A 12 percent discount rate provides the desired bond value of \$943.50; thus 12 percent is the yield to maturity.

PROBLEMS

Bond price

1. Given a 10-year bond that sold for \$1,000 with a 13 percent coupon rate, what would be the price of the bond if interest rates in the marketplace on similar bonds are now 10 percent? Interest is paid semiannually. Assume a 10-year time period.

Bond price

2. Given a 15-year bond that sold for \$1,000 with a 9 percent coupon rate, what would be the price of the bond if interest rates in the marketplace on similar bonds are now 12 percent? Interest is paid semiannually. Assume a 15-year time period.

Bond price

3. Given the facts in problem 2, what would be the price if interest rates go down to 8 percent? (Once again, do a semiannual analysis.)

Use of bond table

4. Using Table 12–3 on page 317, determine the price of a
   a. 10 percent coupon rate bond, with 20 years to maturity and a 14 percent yield to maturity.
   b. 12 percent coupon rate bond with 10 years to maturity and an 8 percent yield to maturity.

Use of bond table

5. Using Table 12–3 on page 317:
Assume you bought a bond with a 10 percent coupon rate with 20 years to maturity at a yield to maturity of 14 percent. Further assume 10 years later the yield to maturity is 8 percent.
Determine the price of the bond that you initially paid and the bond price with 10 years remaining to maturity. Also, compute the dollar and percentage profit related to the bond over the 10-year holding period.

Current yield

6. What is the current yield of an 8 percent coupon rate bond priced at \$877.60?

Yield to maturity

7. What is the yield to maturity for the data in problem 6? Assume there are 10 years left to maturity. It is a \$1,000 par value bond. Use the trial-and-error approach with annual analysis. [*Hint:* Because the bond is trading for less than par value, you can assume the interest rate (i) for which you are solving is greater than the coupon rate of 8 percent.]

Yield to maturity

8. What is the yield to maturity for a 10 percent coupon rate bond priced at \$1,090.90? Assume there are 20 years left to maturity. It is a \$1,000 par value bond. Use the trial-and-error approach with annual analysis. (*Hint:* Because the bond is trading at a price above par value, first decide whether your initial calculation should be at an interest rate above or below the coupon rate.)

Comparison of yields

9. What is the current yield in problem 8? Why is it slightly higher than the yield to maturity?

www.mhhe.com/hirtblock10e

Current yield and yield to maturity comparison

10. A 15-year, 7 percent coupon rate bond is selling for $839.27.

a. What is the current yield?

b. What is the yield to maturity using the trial-and-error approach with annual calculations?

c. Why is the current yield higher/lower than the yield to maturity?

Approximate yield to maturity

11. What is the approximate yield to maturity of a 14 percent coupon rate, $1,000 par value bond priced at $1,160 if it has 16 years to maturity? Use Formula 12–2 on page 320.

Yield to call

12. *a.* Using the facts given in problem 11, what would be the yield to call if the call can be made in four years at a price of $1,080? Use Formula 12–3 on page 321.

b. Explain why the answer is lower in part *a* than in problem 11.

c. Given a call value of $1,080 in four years, is it likely that the bond price would actually get to $1,160?

Anticipated realized yield

13. *a.* Using the facts given in problem 11, what would be the anticipated realized yield if the forecast is that the bond can be sold in three years for $1,280? Use Formula 12–4 on page 322. Continue to assume the bond has a 14 percent coupon rate ($140) and a current price of $1,160.

b. Now break down the anticipated realized yield between current yield and capital appreciation. (*Hint:* Compute current yield and subtract this from anticipated realized yield to determine capital appreciation.)

Use of bond table

14. An investor places $800,000 in 30-year bonds (12 percent coupon rate), and interest rates decline by 3 percent. Use Table 12–4 on page 327 to determine the current value of the portfolio.

Use of bond table

15. Use Table 12–4 on page 327 to describe the worst possible scenario for a $1,000 bond based on yield change, years to maturity, and coupon rate. What would be the price of the bond?

Expectations hypothesis

16. The following pattern for one-year Treasury bills is expected over the next four years:

Year 1	5%
Year 2	7%
Year 3	10%
Year 4	11%

a. What return would be necessary to induce an investor to buy a two-year security?

b. What return would be necessary to induce an investor to buy a three-year security?

c. What return would be necessary to induce an investor to buy a four-year security?

d. Diagram the term structure of interest rates for years 1 through 4.

Margin purchase

17. *a.* Assume an investor purchases a 10-year, $1,000 bond with a coupon rate of 12 percent. The market rate almost immediately falls to 9 percent. What would be the percentage return on the investment if the buyer borrowed part of the funds with a 25 percent margin requirement? Assume the interest payments on the bond cover the interest expense on the borrowed funds. (You can use Table 12–3 on page 317 in this problem to determine the new value of the bond.)

b. Assume the same bond in part *a* is purchased with 25 percent margin, but market rates go up to 14 percent from 12 percent instead of going down to 9 percent. You can once again use Table 12–3 to determine the price of the bond. What is the percentage loss on the cash investment?

Deep discount bond

18. Assume an investor is trying to choose between purchasing a deep discount bond or a par value bond. The deep discount bond pays 6 percent interest, has 20 years to maturity, and is currently trading at $656.80 with a 10 percent yield to maturity. It is callable at $1,050.

The second bond is selling at its par value of $1,000. It pays 12 percent interest and has 20 years to maturity. Its yield to maturity is also 12 percent. The bond is callable at $1,080.

a. If the yield to maturity on the deep discount bond goes down by 2 percent to 8 percent, what will the new price of the bond be? Do semiannual analysis.

b. If the yield to maturity on the par value bond goes down by 2 percent to 10 percent, what will the new price of the bond be? Do semiannual analysis.

c. Based on the facts in the problem and your answers to parts *a* and *b,* which bond appears to be the better purchase? (Consider the call feature as well as capital appreciation.)

INVESTMENT ADVISOR PROBLEM

Robert Wallace began investing in bonds six months ago through tax-exempt municipal securities. His intent at that point in time was to reduce the tax obligation related to his investment portfolio. However, he began to notice that the price of his bonds changed as interest rates changed, and he even took advantage of this phenomenon by cashing in a couple of his 10-year munis early as interest rates dropped and capital gains were available for the taking.

Because of the bond price–interest rate sensitivity relationship he observed, Robert decided to get more aggressive in his bond investment strategy. He didn't particularly like U.S. government bonds as they pay a lower coupon rate because they have no credit risk. He decided to go for maximum yield on lower-quality corporate bonds while also waiting for interest rates to go down and bond prices to go up. He bought five such 15-year corporate bonds.

In doing a six-months review of Robert Wallace's portfolio, his investment advisor, Brian Gonzalez, said his interest rate strategy was fine, but he was making a fundamental mistake in his type of bond choice based on the "Six Bond-Pricing Rules" found in this chapter. He proceeded to lend him a copy of Hirt and Block's *Fundamentals of Investment Management.*

a. What mistake was Robert Wallace making?

b. Also, from a tax minimization viewpoint, what mistake was Robert Wallace making in the trading of his municipal bonds?

WEB EXERCISE

In this exercise, we will demonstrate how you can get information on the term structure of interest rates and relate yields spreads to the economic outlook. Go to **www.bondsonline.com**.

1. Click on "Today's Market" and then click on "Composite Bond Yields" along the left-hand margin. Select "Click for Data" and write down the yields under "U.S. Treasury Bonds" for three months through 30 years. Plot out the data.
2. Based on the expectations hypothesis, would you expect the future movement in interest rates to be up or down?

www.mhhe.com/hirtblock10e

3. What is the yield on 10-year U.S. Treasuries? What is the yield on 10-year AAA-rated corporate bonds? Compute the differences between the two to get the so-called spread. The normal spread between the two is 30 to 50 basis points, but it expands to 50 to 100 basis points when people become concerned about the economy (they want an increasingly higher yield to take a risk). Based on the number you just computed, what does it appear bond investors are telling us about their outlook for the economy?

Note: From time to time, companies redesign their Web sites, and occasionally a topic we have listed may have been deleted, updated, or moved into a different location.

CFA MATERIAL

The following material contains sample questions and solutions from a prior Level I CFA Exam. While the terminology is slightly different from that in this text, you can still view the skills that are necessary for the CFA exam.

CFA Exam Question

4. *a.* *Briefly explain* why bonds of different maturities have different yields in terms of the (1) expectations, (2) liquidity, and (3) segmentation hypotheses. (*5 minutes*)

b. Briefly describe the implications of each of the three hypotheses when the yield curve is (1) upward sloping, and (2) downward sloping. (*5 minutes*)

Solution: Question 4—Morning Section (I–86) (10 points)

a. (1) The expectations hypothesis maintains that the current long-term rate should equal the average of current and expected future short-term rates. Unless the current and expected future rates are all equal, the averages will be different for different maturities.

(2) The liquidity hypothesis maintains that since longer securities have greater risk, interest rates should increase with maturity as a compensation to investors.

(3) The segmentation hypothesis maintains that individual borrowers are constrained to particular segments of the maturity spectrum. The interest rate for a given maturity will thus depend on the supply and demand for funds in each segment.

b. *Upward sloping yield curve:*

(1) Expectations—short-term interest rates are expected to be higher in the future.

(2) Liquidity—as predicted, longer-term securities have higher return to compensate for risk.

(3) Segmentation—signifies relatively less demand for long-term bonds than short-term bonds.

Downward sloping yield curve:

(1) Expectations—short-term interest rates are expected to be lower in the future.

(2) Liquidity—this is inconsistent with the liquidity hypothesis. When liquidity plus expectations is considered, a decrease in future short-term rates that is larger than the liquidity premium is indicated.

(3) Segmentation—signifies relatively higher demand for long-term bonds than for short-term bonds.

CFA Exam Question

5. You are considering the purchase of a 10 percent, 10-year bond with a par value of $1,000.

a. Using Tables I and II, *compute* the price you should pay for this bond assuming semiannual interest payments and 8 percent yield to maturity. (*2 minutes*)

b. A year from now, you expect that the yield to maturity for this bond will be 6 percent. Using Tables I and II, *compute* the realized compound yield during the year, assuming a reinvestment rate of 5 percent and semiannual interest payments. *Identify* and *comment* on the significance of each of the components of the calculated realized compound yield. (*7 minutes*)

TABLE I Present Value of $1

Periods	3 Percent	4 Percent	5 Percent	6 Percent	7 Percent	8 Percent
4	0.8885	0.8548	0.8227	0.7921	0.7629	0.7350
6	0.8375	0.7903	0.7462	0.7050	0.6663	0.6302
8	0.7874	0.7307	0.6768	0.6274	0.5820	0.5403
10	0.7441	0.6756	0.6139	0.5584	0.5083	0.4632
12	0.7014	0.6246	0.5568	0.4970	0.4440	0.3971
14	0.6611	0.5775	0.5051	0.4423	0.3878	0.3405
16	0.6232	0.5339	0.4581	0.3936	0.3387	0.2919
18	0.5874	0.4936	0.4155	0.3503	0.2959	0.2502
19	0.5703	0.4746	0.3957	0.3305	0.2765	0.2317
20	0.5537	0.4564	0.3769	0.3118	0.2584	0.2145

TABLE II Present Value of $1 Annuity

Periods	3 Percent	4 Percent	5 Percent	6 Percent	7 Percent	8 Percent
4	3.7171	3.6299	3.5460	3.4651	3.3872	3.3121
5	5.4172	5.2421	5.0757	4.9173	4.7665	4.6229
8	7.0197	6.7327	6.4632	6.2098	5.9713	5.7466
10	8.5302	8.1109	7.7217	7.3601	7.0236	6.7101
12	9.9540	9.3851	8.8633	8.3838	7.9427	7.5361
14	11.2961	10.5631	9.8986	9.2950	8.7455	8.2442
16	12.5611	11.6523	10.8378	10.1059	9.4466	8.8514
18	13.7535	12.6593	11.6896	10.8276	10.0591	9.3719
19	14.3238	13.1339	12.0853	11.1581	10.3356	9.6036
20	14.8775	13.5903	12.4622	11.4699	10.5940	9.8181

Solution: Question 5—Morning Section (I–87) (10 points)

a.	$50 × 13.5903 (4% − 20 periods)	=	$ 679.52
	$1,000 × 0.4564	=	456.40
	Value	=	$1,135.92
b.	$50 × 13.7535 (3% − 18 periods)	=	$ 687.68
	$1,000 × 0.5874	=	587.40
	Value of bond 1 year from now	=	$1,275.08

Realized compound yield:
Ending wealth value:

\$1,275.08—ending price of bond
50.00—interest at end of year
50.00—mid-year interest payment
1.25—5% interest on interest for ½ year
\$1,276.33

$$\text{Realized compound yield} = \frac{\$1{,}376.33}{\$1{,}135.92} - 1 = 1.2116 - 1$$

$$= 21.16\%$$

There are three components of the realized compound yield calculated above: price appreciation due to decline in rates from 8 percent to 6 percent, coupon interest, and interest on interest.

The total return in dollars for the year was \$240.41. Of that total return, \$139.16, or about 58 percent, was due to price appreciation; \$100, or about 42 percent, was due to coupon interest; and about 0.5 percent was due to interest on interest.

Because the realized compound yield is calculated over only one year in which rates have fallen, the interest-on-interest component will be very small, and the appreciation component is the largest. Had the coupon been smaller than 10 percent, the appreciation component would have been even larger.

chapter
thirteen

13 CONVERTIBLE SECURITIES AND WARRANTS

OBJECTIVES

1. Understand why investors are attracted to convertible securities and warrants.
2. Explain how convertible securities values are determined.
3. Describe how investors may be forced to convert bonds or preferred stock into common stock.
4. Explain the advantages and disadvantages of convertible securities to the corporate issuer.
5. Describe the accounting requirements associated with convertibles.
6. Explain why warrants represent highly speculative investments.

OUTLINE

Convertible Securities
Conversion Price and Conversion Ratio
- Value of the Convertible Bond
- Bond Price and Premiums
- Comparing the Convertible Bond with a Common Stock Purchase
- Disadvantages of Convertibles
- When to Convert into Common Stock

Advantages and Disadvantages to the Issuing Corporation
Accounting Considerations with Convertibles
Speculating through Warrants
- Valuation of Warrants
- Further Explanation of Intrinsic Value
- Use of Warrants by Corporations
- Impact of Warrants on the Capital Structure

Accounting Considerations with Warrants

An investment in convertible securities or warrants offers the market participant special opportunities to meet investment objectives. For conservative investors, convertible securities can offer regular income and potential downside protection against falling stock prices. Convertibles also offer capital gains opportunities for an investor desiring the appreciation potential of an equity investment. Warrants are more speculative securities than convertibles and also offer the chance for leveraged returns.

These securities have been used as financing alternatives by corporations in periods of high interest rates or tight money. In the 2007–2010 period, when interest rates were very low, companies took advantage of the convertible bond market to sell bonds at coupons in the 1.5 and 2.5 percent range. Stock prices were also low, and so the company got not only the benefit of cheap debt financing but also a high probability that the bond would be converted into common stock at some future date. Also, convertibles have been utilized as a medium of exchange for acquiring other companies' stock in mergers and acquisitions. Convertibles and warrants have advantages to the corporation and to the owner of the security. It is important to realize as we go through this chapter that what is an advantage to the corporation is often a disadvantage to the investor, and vice versa. These securities involve trade-offs between the buyer and the corporation that are considered in the pricing of each security.

CONVERTIBLE SECURITIES

A **convertible security** is a bond or share of preferred stock that can be converted into common stock at the option of the holder. Thus, the owner has a fixed-income security that can be transferred to common stock if and when the performance of the firm indicates such a conversion is desirable.

As an example of a convertible security, we use the Amazon.com 4.75 percent convertible subordinated debenture maturing on February 1, 2009. Amazon.com is a familiar name; the company started its corporate life in 1995 selling books online. It later added CDs and DVDs, video games, and the Kindle book reader, and now, if you go on their Web site **www.amazon.com**, you will find a virtual warehouse of goods to buy, including shoes, computers, software, cell phones, toys, and so on.

Amazon is the biggest online retailer and has had meteoric growth since its beginning. Its sales rose from $15.7 million in 1996 to $1.6 billion in 1999. While the growth rate has not been the same as in the early years, the sales dollars keep climbing. In 2001 Amazon.com made its first operating profit of $35.1 million on sales of $3.12 billion and finally in 2003 made its first after-tax profit of $35.3 million on sales of $5.26 billion. With losses until 2003 and small operating margins, Amazon was not able to generate enough internal funds for expansion and so in 1999, the firm sold the 4.75 percent convertible bonds to raise $1.250 billion. This allowed it to pay off bank debt, buy computers to enhance its infrastructure, and finance the current assets needed in the business.

By the end of 2007, Amazon had posted revenues of $14.8 billion with after-tax income of $476 million, but the convertible bonds were still outstanding. In 2008 Amazon's revenues climbed to $19.1 billion with earnings of $645 million. The stock price reached a high of $97.43 per share in 2008, and Amazon retired the bond. It is a good thing that Amazon's stock reached the price needed to force a conversion, because the convertible notes were due on February 1, 2009. This is a classic case of how to use convertible securities as part of a company's financing strategy. It also shows what benefits will accrue to an investor who wants to benefit from the stock price increase of a growing company, yet receive some income in the process. We will use this Amazon convertible security as our example throughout this section.

In general, the best time for an investor to buy convertible securities is when interest rates are high (bond and preferred prices are depressed) and when stock prices are relatively low. A purchase in this environment increases the probability of a successful investment because rising stock prices and falling interest rates both exert upward pressure on the price of a convertible security. This will become more apparent as we proceed through the discussions in the chapter. Table 13–1 shows the details of the Amazon.com convertible bond with the data taken from the company's annual report and from Standard & Poor's. We will rely on this information as we go through the various calculations required to understand convertible bonds.

CONVERSION PRICE AND CONVERSION RATIO

Table 13–1 shows that the Amazon.com convertible bond is convertible at $78.03 into 12.81558 shares of common stock. The $78.03 is called the **conversion price** and the 12.81558 is called the **conversion ratio**. Normally you will find only one

TABLE 13-1 **Amazon.com 4.75 Percent Convertible Subordinated Notes: Due February 1, 2009**

Convertible at $78.03 into 12.81558 shares subject to adjustment for stock splits and stock dividends.

$23.75 Semiannual interest payable on February 1 and August 1.

Regular calls beginning February 1, 2005 through each of the following years.

Call Price

$1,019.00 February 1, 2005–January 31, 2006

$1,014.25 February 1, 2006–January 31, 2007

$1,009.50 February 1, 2007–January 31, 2008

$1,000.00 After January 31, 2008

of these pieces of information and have to calculate the other. If you find the conversion price stated in the annual report or another financial source, divide the conversion price into the par value of $1,000 to find how many shares you will receive. The conversion ratio is shown in Formula 13–1.

$$\text{Conversion ratio} = \frac{\text{Face value or Par value}}{\text{Conversion price}} \qquad \textbf{(13–1)}$$

If we go through the calculation for the Amazon.com bond, it would be as follows:

$$\frac{\$1{,}000 \text{ (Face value or Par value)}}{\$78.03 \text{ per share (Conversion price)}} = 12.81558 \text{ shares}$$

Value of the Convertible Bond

The Amazon.com convertible bond was originally sold at its par value of $1,000 but the stock was highly speculative and very volatile. Even the common stock price around the day of the convertible bond offering was volatile. On February 1, 1999, Amazon's common stock sold at $57.9375 per share. The next day it fell to $55.125 and on February 3 it rose to $62.875. Clearly Amazon was part of the Internet bubble story of the 1999–2000 period.

application example

A convertible bond has two calculated values, a **pure bond value**, which is the value of the bond if it trades without any conversion features, and a **conversion value**, which is the value of the bond based on the common stock price and the number of shares the bondholder could receive based on the conversion ratio. What would be the conversion value of the Amazon.com bond based on the common stock price on February 1, 1999, the day of the offering, and the two days after? We can find this by multiplying the conversion ratio by the market price per share of the common stock.

Conversion ratio	× Common stock price	= **Conversion value**	(13–2)
12.81558 shares	× $57.9375	= $742.50 February 1, 1999 (IPO date)	
12.81558 shares	× $55.125	= $706.46 February 2, 1999	
12.81558 shares	× $62.875	= $805.78 February 3, 1999	

The amount of $742.50 indicates the value of the underlying shares of common stock each bond represents on the day of the offering, but we can also see how the conversion value changes with the stock price. Two days after the offering the conversion value was up over $60 to $805.78.

How do we calculate the pure bond value? In the case of Amazon.com assume that a similar bond without the conversion privilege carries a yield to maturity of 6 percent. We use the same techniques that we applied in Chapter 12 to value a bond. We would take the semiannual coupon of $23.75, the number of periods to maturity would be 20 six-month periods, and we would use the 3 percent yield, which is one-half of the annual yield to maturity of 6 percent. The pure bond value would be as follows:

$23.75 × 14.877 (*PV* interest factor for an annuity)	=	$353.33
$1,000.00 × .554 (*PV* interest factor for a single amount)	=	$554.00
Pure bond value		$907.33

The pure bond value is considered the **floor value**, or minimum price at which the bond will sell in the market. The conversion value and pure bond value for the Amazon.com convertible bond are graphed in Figure 13–1. You should be aware that it is possible for the pure bond value to change if interest rates change. In other words, the pure bond value will follow the bond pricing rules presented in Chapter 12, and bond prices will be inversely related to interest rates. We could see this relationship if we recalculated the pure bond value at an 8 percent yield to maturity. Following the same method as in the 6 percent example we would find a pure bond value of $778.76 at an 8 percent yield to maturity. This would cause the pure bond value line to move down in Figure 13–1.

In examining Figure 13–1, realize that the investor will always take the higher of the two values between the pure bond value and the conversion value. When the stock price is low and the conversion value is less than the pure bond value, the bond will have a minimum price of at least the pure bond value of $907.33. This makes sense because the bond has a value based on its guaranteed interest payment and par value at maturity. When the conversion value is higher than the pure bond value, the price of the bond will sell at least at the conversion value, because the investor could convert to stock and have the higher market value created by a high stock price.

FIGURE 13-1 Amazon.com Convertible Bond on Day of Issue (February 1, 1999)

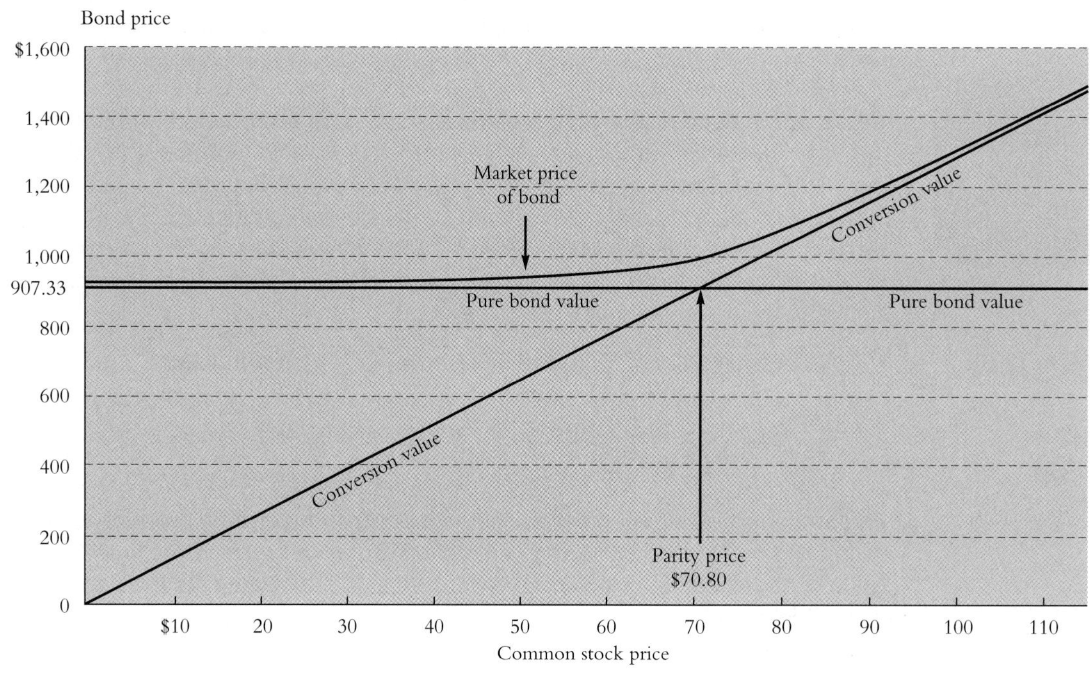

The point where the conversion value and pure bond value are equal is called the **parity price**, and the stock price at that point was \$70.80. To find this parity point we simply divide the \$907.33 pure bond value by the conversion ratio of 12.81558 shares. The important issue here is that when the stock is selling at less than \$70.80, the pure bond value will create a minimum or floor price, and when the common stock is selling at more than \$70.80, the conversion value will be higher than the pure bond value and determine the minimum value an investor would pay.

Bond Price and Premiums

Why is the market price line higher than both the pure bond value and the conversion value? You may wonder why the market price is \$1,000 while the pure bond value is \$907.35 and the conversion value is \$742.50 on the first day of trading. The difference between the market price of \$1,000 and the conversion value of \$742.50 is \$257.50. This \$257.50 is called the **conversion premium** or the amount that investors are willing to pay above and beyond the value of the 12.81558 shares of common stock they would receive upon conversion. In this case the conversion premium is 34.68 percent:

$$\text{Conversion premium} = \frac{\text{Market price of bond} - \text{Conversion value}}{\text{Conversion value}} \qquad \textbf{(13–3)}$$

$$= \frac{\$1{,}000 - 742.50}{\$742.50} = \$257.50/\$742.50 = 34.68\%$$

People are willing to pay a conversion premium for several reasons. In the case of Amazon.com, the premium is slightly higher than the usual 20 to 25 percent paid on new offerings. One reason for the premium is that Amazon.com common stock paid no dividend at all while the bond paid \$47.50 per year. At that rate the investor will recover the \$257.50 premium in a little over five years' time. While the analysis of dividends versus interest is always an important consideration, you also have to realize that a bond is less risky because it has a higher claim on assets and income than common stock, and the income is a legal contractual agreement.

Another reason for the premium is that the bond price will rise as the stock price rises because of the option of converting the bond to 12.81558 shares of stock. If the common stock price rises, the convertible bond investor benefits while an investor in a nonconvertible bond of the same company would not benefit. Also the pure bond value places a floor value under the investment to make the convertible bond less volatile than the underlying common stock. This floor value creates a **downside limit** if the common stock should fall below the parity price. One way to compute this downside protection is to calculate the difference between the market price of the bond and pure bond value as a percentage of the market price. We call this measure the **downside risk**.

$$\text{Downside risk} = \frac{\text{Market price of bond} - \text{Pure bond value}}{\text{Market price of bond}} \qquad \textbf{(13–4)}$$

$$= \frac{\$1{,}000 - 907.33}{\$1{,}000} = \frac{\$92.67}{\$1{,}000} = 9.267\%$$

The Amazon.com downside risk is only 9.267 percent, which means that even if the common stock fell to \$50 per share and had a \$641 conversion value, the bond would have a minimum value of \$907.33. The market price will slowly approach the pure bond value as the common stock price falls and it will slowly approach the conversion value as the common stock price rises. In fact, you should notice that the conversion premium is the largest at the parity price, because this is the price at which the risk-return trade-offs to the investor are the highest. At the parity point, there is no downside risk if the stock price should fall, and if the stock price should rise, the investor will benefit from the increase in conversion value.

The conversion premium is also affected by several other variables. The more volatile the stock price as measured by beta or standard deviation of returns, the higher the conversion premium. In the case of Amazon.com that is true. This higher premium occurs because the potential for capital gains is larger than on less volatile stocks. The longer the term to maturity, the higher the premium—because there is a greater chance that the stock price could rise, making the bond more valuable.

Figure 13–2 presents two graphs of the Amazon.com convertible bond and depicts the conversion premium in Panel (a) and the downside risk in Panel (b).

FIGURE 13-2 Amazon.com Convertible Bond—Conversion Premium and Downside Risk

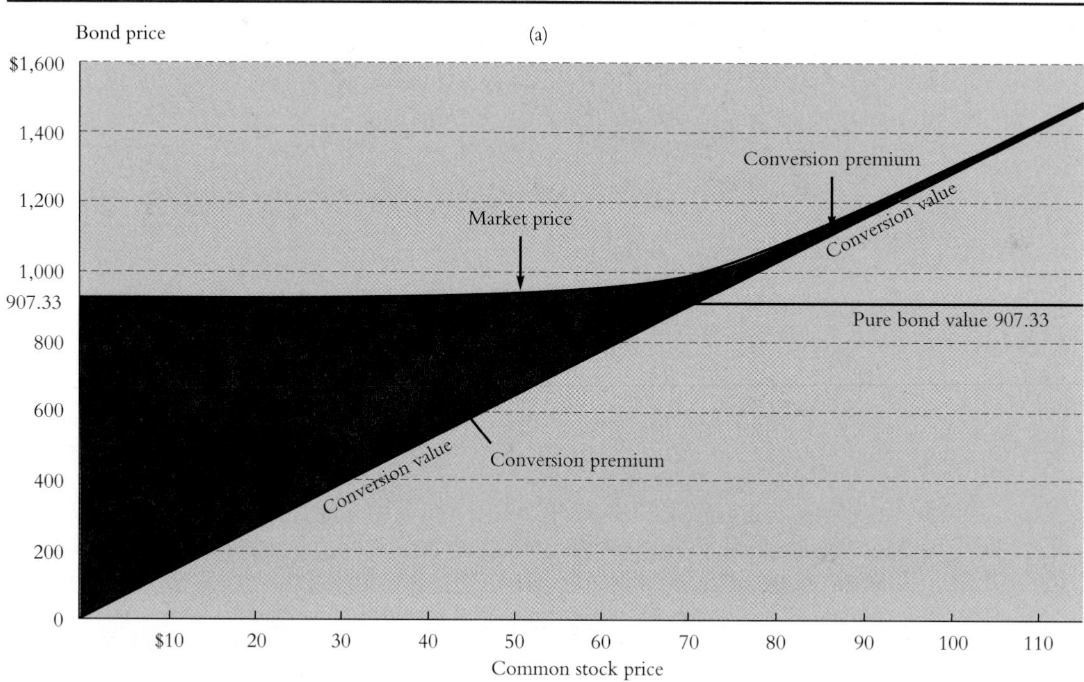

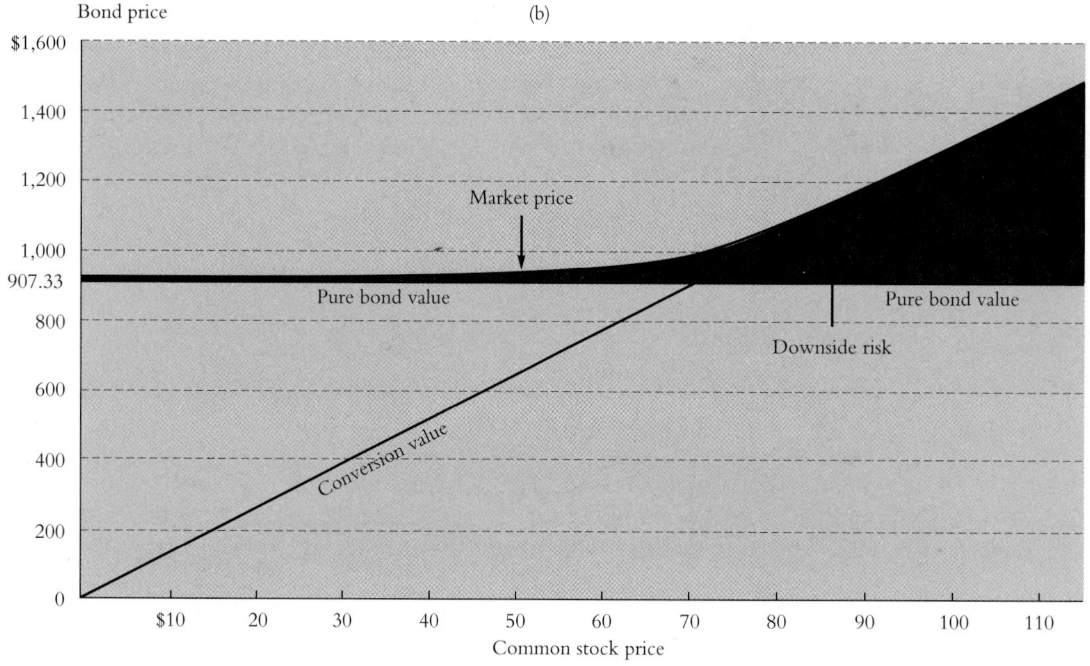

TABLE 13-2 Amazon.com Bond Prices, Stock Prices, Conversion Values, and Conversion Premiums

	BOND PRICE		STOCK PRICE		CONVERSION VALUE		CONVERSION PREMIUM AT HIGH AND LOW STOCK PRICE	
Year	High	Low	High	Low	High	Low	High	Low
2008	$1,001.00	$ 990.00	$ 97.43	$34.68	$1,248.62	$444.44	−19.83%	122.75%
2007	1,015.00	1,009.50	101.09	36.30	1,295.53	465.21	−21.65	117.00
2006	992.50	955.50	48.58	25.76	622.58	330.13	59.42	189.43
2005	1023.40	928.80	50.00	30.60	640.78	392.16	59.71	136.84
2004	1020.70	1000.00	57.82	33.51	741.00	429.45	37.75	132.86
2003	1011.25	733.75	60.41	19.61	774.19	251.31	30.62	191.97
2002	765.00	493.75	25.00	9.03	320.39	115.72	138.77	326.66
2001	545.00	350.00	22.37	5.51	286.68	70.61	90.10	395.65
2000	1,173.75	370.00	91.50	14.88	1,172.63	190.63	0.10	94.09
1999	1,512.50	760.00	113.00	57.38	1,448.16	735.29	4.44	3.36

Note in Panel (a) that as the stock price gets higher, the conversion premium declines. This is because the investor is getting almost no downside protection. This is confirmed by the presence of large downside risk at high stock prices in Panel (b).

Table 13–2 tracks the actual performance of the Amazon.com convertible bond since the offering in 1999 until it was called in 2008. We have presented the high and low prices for the market price of the bond, the common stock price, the conversion value, and the conversion premium that arises from these price fluctuations. Table 13–2 demonstrates the point made in the previous paragraph; in 1999 when the highest Amazon.com stock price was $113, the conversion value was $1,448 and the conversion premium was 4.44 percent. On the other hand, when the stock price hit its low of $5.51 in 2001, the conversion value fell to $70.61 and the conversion premium went up to 395.65 percent.

Another important point is the ability of the company to call the bond for redemption. In most cases the companies who issue convertible bonds are hoping that the stock price rises and thus creates a conversion value that is higher than the par value or call value. If you return to Table 13–1 on page 341, you will find the call prices for 2005 through 2009. For example, if the Amazon.com convertible bond should have a conversion value of $1,100 in the first call period, Amazon could call the bonds and the investors would have a choice between the call price of $1,019 and 12.81558 shares of common stock worth $1,100. The rational bondholders would convert and take the higher value of the shares. This is known as **forced conversion**. There are two advantages to the corporation of forced conversion. First, the company doesn't have to pay off the debt with cash, and second, they most likely will reduce their cash outflows for interest expense. Since the majority of companies selling convertible securities do not pay a dividend on their common stock, the elimination of interest is a cash flow benefit. This may not always be the case—some companies sell convertibles in their growth stages, and by the time the bonds mature or are called, the common dividend can actually be a higher cash outflow on an after-tax basis than the interest savings.

At the beginning of 2008, Amazon had $899 million of debt outstanding, having already repurchased $351 million in previous years when the bond was priced quite a bit below par value. As it turned out, in February 2008 Amazon's board of directors authorized the retirement of the 4.75 percent coupon bonds before the February 1, 2009, maturity date. They called for the bonds' redemption, and over the course of several months during 2008 the bonds were retired. Holders of the bonds ended up converting $605 million of principal into 7.8 million shares of common stock; the other $294 million was paid out in cash. Fortunately Amazon's timing was good—several months after the last redemption (on November 19, 2008), their stock hit $35.75, and the market price was never above the conversion price at any time up to February 1, 2009. If Amazon had waited until maturity to call the bonds, they would have paid off the bonds with $899 million of cash instead of being able to convert a good portion of the bond into common stock. By 2010 Amazon had healthy cash flows and very little long-term debt, the majority of their debt being current liabilities, which reflected the nature of their retail model.

Comparing the Convertible Bond with a Common Stock Purchase

application example

Would you have been better off putting $1,000 into Amazon.com common stock on February 1, 1999, or $1,000 into the convertible bond? The answer depends largely on whether the common stock went up in price, and whether it went up fast enough to outpace the income you may have received from the bond. If the common stock price went down, then the answer is pretty clear, you would be better off owning the convertible bond. On August 12, 2008, Amazon.com stock closed at a price of $87.25. Assume this is the day you tendered your bond under the redemption program. During this time period (1999–2008) Amazon.com paid no dividends on its common stock. Table 13–3 demonstrates the analysis that we used to answer the question we posed in the first sentence of this paragraph.

The trade-off the investor makes in the stock versus the convertible security investment decision is whether to buy stock and receive more shares and a lower cash flow or to buy the convertible bond with fewer shares (because of the premium) but higher cash flow from interest. In this case, the stock price increased and the bond price stayed fairly close to its par value of $1,000 on the day of the initial offering. The investor who bought stock was able to buy 4.44 more shares because no premium was paid. This provided $387.39 in extra stock value on August 12, 2008, or (4.44 shares × $87.25). The convertible bond investor received 19 semiannual interest payments for interest of $451.25. The total advantage to the bondholder was $63.80 (the difference between the numbers in the last column in Table 13–3) and much less risk than owning the common stock. The ending value in the table does not assume reinvested interest payments which would have increased the bondholder's return even more. Both the stock and bond investors would be happy with the return.

TABLE 13-3 Comparing Returns between Purchasing Amazon.com Common Stock or Convertible Bond

	Amount Invested Feb. 1, 1999	Amazon.com Shares Purchased or Controlled	Stock Price Aug. 12, 2008	Ending Stock or Bond Value Aug. 12, 2008	Plus Total Dividends or Interest	Ending Value
Stock	$1,000	17.25625	$87.25	$1,505.61	$ 0.00	$1,505.61
Bond	1,000	12.81558	87.25	1,118.16*	451.25	1,569.41
		4.44			Difference $	63.80

*Quoted bond value. This is not based on conversion.

Table 13–4 on the next page presents a selection of convertible bonds and helps illustrate basic concepts. While an occasional bond such as 3M or Amgen (in the table) carries a Value Line bond rating of B, most bonds are low-end investment grade or high yield junk bonds with ratings of G or less. We have divided up the bonds into four categories: Bonds selling at a discount to par value, bonds selling at close to par value, bonds selling at a premium to par value, and zero-coupon bonds that include all of the three previous categories. Looking at the dividend yields in Column (11), we can see that most of the underlying common stocks pay no or small dividends. Also in Column (13), we see the notation NCB, which means not a callable bond. This may mean that the call date has not yet arrived or that the bond is noncallable throughout its life.

Looking at the bonds by categories, we can make some generalizations that are more often true than false, although we are sure there are exceptions. First when you look at the bonds selling at a discount you can see that the conversion premiums in Column (9) are relatively high compared to the bonds selling at a premium. The bonds selling at a premium are so far past the parity price that the advantages to investors have mostly evaporated and so has the premium. The bonds selling close to par have bond prices that are relatively close to their pure bond values. For the most part, these bond prices are being supported by their pure bond values rather than their conversion values based on the underlying stock price.

Convertible preferred stock selections are presented in Table 13–5 on page 349 and are listed from the lowest to highest conversion premiums. They exhibit the same type of characteristics as convertible bonds, except that most of the preferred stocks were issued at $50 per share and not the $1,000 par of the bonds. Also note the dividend yield of the preferred stock (Column 10) is generally higher as we move down the table from low to high conversion premiums.

Disadvantages of Convertibles

It has been said that everything has a price, and purchasing convertible securities at the wrong price can eliminate one of their main advantages. For example, once convertible bonds begin rising in value, or the pure bond value declines substantially due to higher interest rates, the downside protection becomes meaningless. In the case of Priceline.com in Table 13–4 under "Bonds Selling at a Premium," the market price of the bond is $7,405.90 (Column 4) and the pure bond value is $770 (Column 10). Purchasing any of the five bonds in the premium category would provide almost no downside protection at all because if the stock price declines, the bond price will follow the stock price down.

Another drawback for the purchaser of convertible bonds is that they pay lower yields than "straight" nonconvertible bonds. Therefore, convertible bondholders accept below-market yields in the hope of price appreciation through common stock performance. The interest rate on convertible bonds is generally one-third or more below that for bonds in a similar risk class. For example, while a straight bond might pay 6 percent, a convertible bond for the same company could pay 4 percent or less.

From an institutional investor's standpoint, many convertible securities lack liquidity because of small trading volume or because they are small in dollar size. In general, institutional investors would like to own convertible issues when the size of the total bond issue is $200 million or more.

When to Convert into Common Stock

Convertible securities generally have a call provision, which gives the corporation the option of redeeming the bond at a specified price before maturity. The call price is usually at a premium over par value ($1,000) in the early years of callability,

TABLE 13-4 Selected Convertible Bonds

Convertible Bond Issues	(1) Coupon	(2) Maturity	(3) Value Line's Bond Rating+	(4) Bond Price	(5) Conversion Price	(6) Conversion Ratio	(7) Common Stock Price	(8) Conversion Value	(9) Conversion Premium	(10) Pure Bond Value	(11) Stock Dividend Yield	(12) Bond Current Yield	(13) Call Price
Bonds Selling at a Discount													
Sun Power Corp.	4.500%	2015	G	$ 795.40	22.53	44.385	12.07	535.70	48%	820	nil	5.70%	0
C&D Technologies	5.500	2026	I	401.30	4.84	206.718	0.56	115.80	247	nc	nil	13.70	NCB
Motorola (Liberty Media)	3.500	2031	E	522.20	27.16	36.819	7.64	281.30	86	660	nil	6.70	1000
Nash Finch	1.613	2035	H	478.30	107.39	9.312	39.22	365.20	31	400	1.80%	3.40	NCB
Chesapeake Energy	2.250	2038	E	741.20	85.89	11.643	20.78	241.90	206	730	1.40	3.00	NCB
Hercules Offshore	3.375	2038	I	729.70	50.08	19.969	2.27	45.30	999	800	nil	4.60	NCB
Bonds Selling at Close to Par													
Griffon Corp	4.000%	2023	G	$ 999.30	24.13	41.442	11.97	496.10	101%	860	nil	4.00%	1000
NII Holdings	2.750	2025	G	1,001.70	50.08	19.967	38.37	766.10	31	1000	nil	2.70	1000
Diodes	2.250	2026	G	1,000.20	58.50	17.095	16.02	273.90	265	920	nil	2.20	NCB
Mentor Graphics	6.250	2026	G	1,002.10	17.97	55.654	8.86	493.10	103	930	nil	6.20	0
Tech Data	2.750	2026	E	1,001.00	54.26	18.431	36.75	677.30	48	950	nil	2.70	NCB
GSI Commerce	2.500	2027	G	998.80	30.00	33.333	22.15	738.00	35	780	nil	2.50	NCB
Pier 1 Imports	6.375	2036	H	1,003.80	15.19	65.833	6.36	418.70	140	980	nil	6.40	NCB
Bonds Selling at a Premium													
Priceline.com	0.750%	2013	G	$7,405.90	40.38	24.765	297.19	7359.90	1%	770	0%	0.10%	NCB
TRW Automotive	3.500	2015	H	1,428.40	29.55	33.839	36.83	1246.30	15	730	0	2.50	0
FLIR Systems	3.000	2023	F	2,618.80	11.10	90.122	26.96	2429.70	8	730	nil	1.10	1000
Milennium Chemical	4.000	2023	E	3,641.30	14.08	71.009	47.97	3406.30	7	990	1.90	1.10	NCB
WebMD Corp.	3.125	2025	G	1,464.70	35.03	28.550	51.22	1462.30	0	890	0	2.10	NCB
Informatica	3.000	2026	G	1,549.10	20.00	50.000	30.54	1527.00	1	960	nil	1.90	NCB
Akamai Tech	1.000	2033	G	2,866.90	15.45	64.725	44.22	2862.10	0	970	nil	0.30	NCB
Zero Coupon Bonds													
Costco Wholesale	0%	2017	D	$1,259.30	44.03	22.710	55.31	1256.10	0%	740	1.50%	0%	784.36
CSX Corp.	0	2021	D	1,809.70	28.18	35.492	50.39	1788.40	1	910	1.90	0	906.61
Supervalue	0	2031	D	385.00	103.70	9.643	10.99	10.60	263	380	3.20	0	375.68
3M	0	2032	B	883.80	105.71	9.460	84.01	794.70	11	890	2.50	0	891.49
Amgen Inc	0	2032	B	751.30	112.87	8.860	55.02	487.50	54	700	nil	0	781.29
Anixter	0	2033	F	717.00	66.37	15.067	46.99	708.00	1	430	nil	0	NCB

+Value Line's Bond Ratings go from A to L with A being the highest and L being the lowest rating. The A rating would correspond to a Standard & Poor's AAA rating.

nil = the yield is insignificant or zero

Source: *The Value Line Convertibles Survey*, August 23, 2010. Copyright © 2010 Value Line Publishing, Inc. Used with permission.

TABLE 13-5 **Selected Convertible Preferred Stocks**

Convertible Preferred Issues	(1) Dividend	(2) Call Price	(3) Preferred Stock Price	(4) Common Stock Price	(5) Conversion Ratio (in shares)	(6) Conversion Value	(7) Conversion Premium	(8) Pure Value	(9) Common Dividend Yield	(10) Preferred Dividend Yield
Annaly Mortgage Mgt.	$ 1.500	NC	$ 39.10	$17.39	2.416	$ 42.01	−7%	$ 14.00	15.60%	3.80%
Kansas City Southern	51.250	$1,000.00	1125.00	34.44	33.333	1147.99	−2	483.00	nil	4.60
Reinsurance Group	2.875	50.00	60.43	46.71	1.215	56.75	3	50.00	1	4.80
Vornado Realty Trust A	3.250	50.00	116.00	81.00	1.385	112.19	3	42.00	3.20	2.80
Crown Castle Intl.	3.125	50.00	57.86	38.76	1.356	52.56	10	30.00	nil	5.40
Williams Cos.	2.750	50.00	97.88	19.44	4.591	89.25	10	36.00	2.60	2.80
Ford Capital Trust II	3.250	50.65	46.56	12.15	2.825	34.32	36	27.00	nil	7.00
Affliated Managers	2.550	NC	38.91	68.25	0.333	22.73	71	33.00	nil	6.60
Huntington Bancshares A	85.000	NC	996.01	5.66	83.668	473.56	110	na	0.70	8.50
El Paso	2.375	50.00	36.38	11.61	1.202	13.96	161	23.00	0.30	6.50
Lucent Tech Capital	77.500	1000.00	775.00	2.71	40.331	109.30	609	731.00	nil	10.00

NC = noncallable preferred

nil = the yield is insignificant or zero

Source: *The Value Line Convertibles Survey*, August 23, 2010.

and it generally declines over time to par value. We know that as the price of the common stock goes up, the convertible security will rise along with the stock so the investor has no incentive to convert bonds into stock. However, the corporation may use the call privilege to force conversion before maturity, as Amazon.com did in our opening example. Companies usually force conversion when the conversion value is well above the call price. Investors will take the shares rather than the call price since the shares are worth more. This enables the company to turn debt into equity on its balance sheet and makes new debt issues a better risk for future lenders because of higher interest coverage and a lower debt-to-equity ratio.

Corporations may also encourage voluntary conversion by using a step-up in the conversion price over time. When the bond is issued, the contract may specify the following conversion provisions.

	Conversion Price	Conversion Ratio
First five years	$40	25.0 shares
Next three years	45	22.2 shares
Next two years	50	20.0 shares
Next five years	55	18.2 shares

At the end of each time period, there is a strong inducement to convert rather than accept an adjustment to a higher conversion price and a lower conversion ratio. This is especially true if the bond's conversion value is the dominating influence on the market price of the bond. In the case where the conversion value is below the pure bond value and where the interest income is greater than the dividend income, an investor will most likely not be induced to convert through the step-up feature.

About the only other reason for voluntarily converting in the case stated above is if the dividend income received on the common stock is greater than the interest income on the bond. Even in this case, risk-averse investors may want to hold the bond because interest payments are legally required whereas dividends may be reduced.

ADVANTAGES AND DISADVANTAGES TO THE ISSUING CORPORATION

Having established the fundamental characteristics of the convertible security from the investor's viewpoint, let us now examine the factors a corporate financial officer must consider in weighing the advisability of a convertible offer for the firm.

It has been stated that the interest rate paid on convertible issues is normally lower than that paid on a straight debt instrument. Also, the convertible feature may be the only device for allowing smaller corporations access to the bond market.

Convertible bonds are also attractive to a corporation that believes its stock is undervalued. For example, assume a corporation's $1,000 bonds are convertible into 20 shares of common stock at a conversion price of $50. Also assume the company's common stock has a current price of $45, and new shares of stock might be sold at only $44.[1] Thus, the corporation will effectively receive $6 over current market price, assuming future conversion. Of course, one can also argue that if the firm had delayed the issuance of common stock or convertibles for a year or two, the stock might have gone up from $45 to $60 or $65, and new common stock might have been sold at this lofty price.

[1] There is always a bit of underpricing to ensure the success of a new offering.

To translate this to overall numbers for the firm, if a corporation needs $10 million in funds and offers straight stock now at a new price of $44, it must issue 227,272 shares ($10 million/$44 per share). With convertibles, the number of shares potentially issued is only 200,000 shares ($10 million/$50 per share). Finally, if no stock or convertible bonds are issued now and the stock goes up to a level at which new shares can be offered at a price of $60, only 166,667 will be required ($10 million/$60).

Another matter of concern to the corporation is the accounting treatment accorded to convertibles. In the funny-money days of the 1960s' conglomerate merger movement, corporate management often chose convertible securities over common stock because the convertibles had a nondilutive effect on earnings per share. As indicated in the following section on reporting earnings for convertibles, the rules were changed.

ACCOUNTING CONSIDERATIONS WITH CONVERTIBLES

Before 1969, the full impact of the conversion privilege as it applied to convertible securities, warrants (long-term options to buy stock), and other dilutive securities was not adequately reflected in reported earnings per share. Because all of these securities may generate additional common stock in the future, the potential effect of this **dilution** (the addition of new shares to the capital structure) should be considered. The accounting profession has applied many different measures to earnings per share over the years, most recently replacing the concepts of primary earnings per share and fully diluted earnings per share with **basic earnings per share** and **diluted earnings per share**. In 1997, the Financial Accounting Standards Board issued "Earnings per Share" *Statement of Financial Accounting Standards No. 128* that covered the adjustments that must be made when reporting earnings per share.

If we examine the financial statements of the XYZ Corporation in Table 13–6 we find that the earnings per share reported are not adjusted for convertible securities and are referred to as basic earnings per share.

Diluted earnings per share adjusts for all potential dilution from the issuance of any new shares of common stock arising from convertible bonds, convertible preferred stock, warrants, or any other options outstanding. The comparison of basic and diluted earnings per share give the analyst or investor a measure of the potential effects of these securities.

TABLE 13-6 XYZ Corporation

1. Capital section of balance sheet:	
Common stock (1 million shares at $10 par)	$10,000,000
4.5% convertible debentures (10,000 debentures of $1,000; convertible into 40 shares per bond, or a total of 400,000 shares)	10,000,000
Retained earnings	20,000,000
Net worth	$40,000,000
2. Condensed income statement:	
Earnings before interest and taxes	$ 2,950,000
Interest (4.5% of $10 million of convertibles)	450,000
Earnings before taxes	$ 2,500,000
Taxes (40%)	1,000,000
Earnings after taxes	$ 1,500,000
3. Basic earnings per share:	

$$\frac{\text{Earnings after taxes}}{\text{Shares of common stock}} = \frac{\$1{,}500{,}000}{1{,}000{,}000} = \$1.50$$

We get diluted earnings per share for the XYZ Corporation by assuming that 400,000 new shares will be created from potential conversion, while at the same time, allowing for the reduction in interest payments that would occur as a result of the conversion of the debt to common stock. Since before-tax interest payments on the convertibles are \$450,000, the after-tax interest cost (\$270,000) will be saved and can be added back to income. After-tax interest cost is determined by multiplying interest payments by one minus the tax rate (1 − 0.4) times \$450,000 = \$270,000. Making the appropriate adjustments to the numerator and denominator, we show diluted earnings per share as \$1.26 in Formula 13–5.

$$\begin{aligned}\text{Diluted earnings per share} &= \frac{\text{Adjusted earnings after taxes}}{\text{Shares outstanding} + \text{All convertible securities}}\\ &= \frac{\$1{,}500{,}000 \ \text{(Reported earnings)} + \$270{,}000 \ \text{(Interest savings)}}{1{,}000{,}000 + 400{,}000} \qquad \textbf{(13–5)}\\ &= \frac{\$1{,}770{,}000}{1{,}400{,}000}\\ &= \$1.26\end{aligned}$$

We see a \$0.24 reduction from the basic earnings per share figure of \$1.50 in Table 13–6. The new figure is the value that a security analyst would utilize.

SPECULATING THROUGH WARRANTS

A **warrant** is an option to buy a stated number of shares of stock from the issuing company at a specified price over a given time period. Warrants can trade between investors, but at the expiration of the warrant, the final owner of the warrant will have to decide whether to exercise the option to purchase stock or to let the warrant expire without exercising the option. For example, if a warrant entitles the holder to purchase one share at the exercise price of \$20 per share and the stock is trading at \$30 per share, the investor will give the company \$20 per share and have stock worth \$30 for a \$10 gain. If the stock price is less than \$20 at expiration, then the warrant expires worthless.

The Redback Networks warrants listed in Table 13–7 demonstrate the relationships discussed above. Redback Networks, a casualty of the Internet bubble, emerged from Chapter 11 bankruptcy proceedings on January 2, 2004. The company provides advanced telecommunications networking equipment that enables telephone companies and service providers to give high-speed Internet access to corporate networks. The warrants listed in Table 13–7 were part of Redback's bankruptcy refinancing package. They were given to former investors with the hope that if the company recovers and does well, the stock will rise and the

TABLE 13-7 Redback Networks Warrants in November 2006 and January 2007

		(1)	(2)	(3)	(4)	(5)	(6)	(7)
Company Name	Common Stock Exchange Listing & Warrant Ticker Symbol	Warrant Price	Per Share Stock Price	Per Share Exercise Price	Intrinsic Value [(2) − (3)] × (6)	Speculative Premium [(3) − (2)] × (6) + (1)	Shares per Warrant	Date of Valuation
Redback Networks	OTC, RBAKW	10.85	14.73	5.00	9.73	\$1.12	1.00	November 13, 2006
Redback Networks	OTC, RBAKW	20.02	25.02	5.00	20.02	0.00	1.00	January 1, 2007

Source: *Value Line Convertibles Survey,* November 13, 2006; S&P Stock Reports, August 28, 2010; and Ericsson's 2007 Annual Report.

former stockholders may be able to recover a portion of their losses. On November 13, 2006, the common stock was selling at $14.73 per share (Column 2) and the exercise price for the warrant was $5.00 per share (Column 3). Since the warrant allowed the holder to buy one share of stock for each warrant held, the warrant had a value of $9.73 (Column 4) since you could buy stock for $5.00 and sell it for $14.73. However, because the warrant was actually selling for $10.85 (Column 1) instead of the $9.73 it was worth, it was selling above its true value by $1.12 (Column 5). The warrant had about four years before expiration, and speculators may have been willing to gamble on the potential increase in price of the common stock.

Speculators would have been well rewarded because on December 19, 2006, Ericsson offered to buy Redback for $2.1 billion or $25.02 per share. The sale closed in January 2007. At this price, the warrant would be worth an intrinsic value of $20.02 per warrant ($25.02 − $5). Anyone who bought the warrant on November 13 at $10.85 would have a nice profit of $9.17 per warrant or about an 84 percent return in less than seven weeks. It pays to be lucky as well as smart.

Most warrants allow the holder to buy one share of common stock per warrant on the date of issue, but if the common stock performs well and the stock splits, the warrant gets adjusted to reflect the stock split. For example, if a company with an original ratio of 1 share per warrant had a 2 for 1 stock split, the new ratio would be 2 shares of stock per warrant while a 3 for 2 stock split would give the warrant holder 1.5 shares per warrant.

Warrants are usually issued as a sweetener to a bond offering, and they may enable the firm to issue debt when this would not be feasible otherwise. The warrants allow the bond issue to carry a lower coupon rate and are usually detachable from the bond after the issue date. After being separated from the bond, warrants have their own market price and may trade on a different market from the common stock. After the warrants are exercised, the initial debt with which they were sold remains in existence.

Because a warrant is dependent on the market movement of the underlying common stock and has no "security value" as such, it is highly speculative. If the common stock of the firm is volatile, the value of the warrants may change dramatically.

Valuation of Warrants

Because the value of a warrant is closely tied to the underlying stock price, we can develop a formula for the minimum or intrinsic value of a warrant:

$$I = (M - EP) \times N \quad \textbf{(13–6)}$$

where:

I = The intrinsic or minimum value of the warrant
M = The market value of the common stock
EP = The option or exercise price of the warrant
N = The number of shares each warrant entitles the holder to purchase

Assume that the common stock of the Graham Corporation is $25 per share and that each warrant carries an option to purchase one share at $20 over the next 10 years. The purchase price stipulated in the warrant is the **option** or **exercise price**. Using Formula 13–6, the intrinsic value is $5 or [($25 − 20) × 1]. The **intrinsic value** in this case is equal to the market price of the common stock minus the option price of the warrant times the number of shares each warrant represents. Because the warrant has 10 more years before it expires and is an effective vehicle for speculative trading, it may well trade for over $5. If the warrant were selling for $9, we would say it had an intrinsic value of

$5 and a speculative premium of $4. The **speculative premium** is equal to the price of the warrant, minus the intrinsic value when the warrant entitles the holder to purchase one share. When the number of shares is different than one, the calculation of the speculative premium has to be modified as shown in Formula 13–7.

$$SP = (W - I) \times N \qquad \textbf{(13–7)}$$

where:

SP = The speculative premium
W = The warrant price
I = The intrinsic value of the warrant
N = The number of shares each warrant represents

The speculative premium represents the amount that the stock price must rise by its expiration date for you to break even on the purchase of the warrant. In the example of Graham Corporation, if you pay $9 for the warrant when the intrinsic value is only $5, the stock would have to rise by $4 for you to recover the premium you paid. On the exercise date there is no speculative premium because you have run out of time to speculate.

As long as there is time to expiration left, investors can gamble on a rise in the stock price and be willing to pay a speculative premium. Even if the stock were trading at less than $20 (the exercise price), the warrant might still have some value in the market. Speculators might purchase the warrant with the hope that the common stock price would increase sufficiently to make the warrant valuable. If the common stock were selling for $15 per share, thus giving the warrant a negative intrinsic value, the warrant might still command a value of $1 or $2 in anticipation of increased common stock value.

Further Explanation of Intrinsic Value

The typical relationship between the market price and the intrinsic value of a warrant is depicted in Figure 13–3. We assume the warrant entitles the holder to purchase one new share of common stock at $20.

FIGURE 13-3 Market Price Relationships for a Warrant

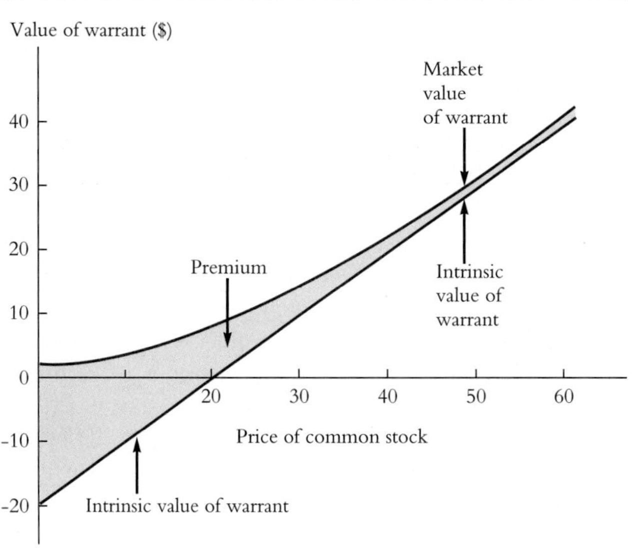

TABLE 13-8 Leverage in Valuing Warrants

(A)	(B)
Stock price = \$25; warrant price = \$5[a] + 10-point movement in stock price	Stock price = \$50; warrant price = \$30 + 10-point movement in stock price.
New warrant price = \$15 (10-point gain)	New warrant price = \$40 (10-point gain)
Percentage gain in warrant $= \frac{\$10}{\$5} \times 100 = 200\%$	Percentage gain in warrant $= \frac{\$10}{\$30} \times 100 = 33\%$

[a] The warrant price would, of course, be greater than \$5 because of a premium. Nevertheless, we use \$5 for ease of computation.

Although the intrinsic value of the warrant is theoretically negative at a common stock price between 0 and \$20, the warrant still carries some value in the market. Also, observe that the difference between the market price of the warrant and its intrinsic value is diminished at the upper ranges of value. Two reasons may be offered for this declining premium.

First, the speculator loses the ability to use leverage to generate high returns as the price of the stock goes up. When the price of the stock is relatively low, say, \$25, and the warrant is in the \$5 to \$10 range, a 10-point movement in the stock could mean a 200 percent gain in the value of the warrant, as indicated in part A of Table 13–8. At the upper levels of stock value, much of this leverage is lost, as indicated in part B of the table. At a stock value of \$50 and a warrant value of approximately \$30, a 10-point movement in the stock would produce only a 33 percent gain in the warrant.

Another reason speculators pay a very low premium at higher stock prices is that there is less downside protection. A warrant selling at \$30 when the stock price is \$50 is more vulnerable to downside movement than is a \$5 to \$10 warrant when the stock is between \$20 and \$30.

Warrant premiums are also influenced by the same factors that affect convertible bond premiums. More volatile common stocks will have greater potential to create short-run profits for warrant speculators, so the higher the price volatility, the greater the premium. Also, the longer the option has before expiration, the higher the premium will be. This "time premium" is worth more the longer the common stock has to reach and surpass the option price of the warrant.

Table 13–9 depicts six warrants divided into in-the-money warrants and out-of-the-money warrants. Many of the relationships just presented are illustrated in this

TABLE 13-9 Selected Warrants as of August 23, 2010

Company Name	Common Stock Exchange Listing & Warrant Ticker Symbol	(1) Warrant Price	(2) Per Share Stock Price	(3) Per Share Exercise Price	(4) Intrinsic Value [(2) − (3)] × (6)	(5) Speculative Premium [(3) − (2)] × (6) + (1)	(6) Speculative Premium as a % of Stock Price (5)/(2)	(7) Shares per Warrant	(8) Due Date
Out of the Money—No Intrinsic Value									
Federal Mogul	OTC, FEMOW	\$0.37	17.59	\$45.82	\$0.00	\$28.60	163%	1.00	12/27/14
New Gold	ASE, NGDAF	1.11	5.56	15.00	0.00	10.55	190	1.00	6/28/17
Owens Corning	NYSE, OCWAW	2.66	25.74	43.00	0.00	19.92	77	1.00	10/31/13
Resolute Energy	ASE, REN/W	1.86	11.18	13.00	0.00	3.68	33	1.00	9/28/14
In the Money—Positive Intrinsic Value									
Funtalk China Holdings	OTC, FTLUF	3.26	8.06	5.00	3.06	0.20	2	1.00	12/13/13
Iridium Communications	OTC, IRDMW	3.36	9.35	7.00	2.35	1.01	11	1.00	2/14/13

Source: *The Value Line Convertibles Survey,* August 23, 2010.

table. For example, the **out-of-the-money warrants** have no intrinsic value because the stock price (Column 2) is less than the exercise price (Column 3). The **in-the-money warrants** will always have an intrinsic value, because the stock price is above the exercise price. Speculative premiums as a percentage of the stock price also demonstrate three things. First, New Gold Warrants expiring in 2017 have a larger speculative premium than those warrants expiring in 2013 and 2014. This demonstrates the influence of time. Second, as the stock price approaches the exercise price, the speculative premiums decline. And third, in-the-money warrants have smaller speculative premiums than out-of-the-money warrants. Table 13–9 also demonstrates the calculations for Formulas 13–6 and 13–7.

Use of Warrants by Corporations

As previously indicated, warrants may allow for the issuance of debt under difficult circumstances. While a straight debt issue may not be acceptable or may be accepted only at extremely high rates, the same security may be well received because detachable warrants are included. Warrants may also be included as an add-on in a merger or acquisition agreement. A firm might offer $20 million in cash plus 10,000 warrants in exchange for all the outstanding shares of the acquisition candidate.

The use of warrants has traditionally been associated with such aggressive, "high-flying" firms as biotechs, airlines, and conglomerates.

As a financing device for creating new common stock, warrants may not be as desirable as convertible securities. A corporation with convertible bonds outstanding may force the conversion of debt to common stock through a call, while no similar device is available to the firm with warrants. The only possible inducement might be a step-up in the option price—whereby the warrant holder must pay a progressively higher option price if he does not exercise by a given date.

Impact of Warrants on the Capital Structure

The capital structure of the firm after the exercise of a warrant also is somewhat different from that created after the conversion of a debenture. In the case of a warrant, the original debt outstanding remains in existence after the detachable warrant is exercised, whereas the conversion of a debenture extinguishes the former debt obligation. If a warrant is exercised, the company sells shares of stock at the exercise price and receives the cash flow from the sale. The exercise of the warrant will increase the number of shares of common stock and provide cash for corporate purposes. The combination of the two will increase assets and lower the debt-to-asset ratio as more equity is provided. The conversion of a convertible security provides no new cash.

As an example, Biodel Inc., a small biotech company with several promising drugs in the pipeline, needed more money to continue its research program. According to Dow Jones Newswires, on August 25, 2010, Biodel entered into an agreement with two institutional investors to sell 2.4 million shares of stock at $3.93 to raise about $9.4 million. The stock had 2.4 million warrants attached that were exercisable at $4.716. Biodel has a promising new diabetes drug under review by the Food and Drug Administration, and if the drug is approved, the stock is expected to move significantly higher. In order to provide the capital required, the investors demanded the warrants as a "sweetener," which is usual for a highly risky investment like this. If the diabetes drug is not approved, Biodel could end up relatively worthless.

ACCOUNTING CONSIDERATIONS WITH WARRANTS

As with convertible securities, the potential dilutive effect of warrants must be considered. In calculating the earnings per share resulting from conversion of warrants, accountants use the treasury stock method. Under this method the accountant must compute the number of new shares that could be created by the exercise of all

the real world of investing

VENTURE CAPITALISTS LOVE CONVERTIBLES AND WARRANTS

Venture capital is normally raised in the early stages of growth for a firm, well before the company has "gone public" (sold its shares in the public market).

Even successful, rapidly developing young companies often have needs for capital that far outstrip their profit-generating capability, their ability to borrow, or the resources of their owners. This is where the venture capitalist comes in. He or she provides funding (seed capital) with the hope that his or her capital will eventually be harvested in the form of a successful public offering of stock at some point in the future.

Venture capitalists are normally overwhelmed with potential proposals for funding. The acceptance rate is lower than 1 out of 100. When the Basses of Fort Worth, the Pritzkers of Chicago, or other venture capitalists see a deal, they always have their eye out for the next Microsoft or Intel. The odds are long, but the potential payout is great. Not only do venture capitalists provide funding, but they also may share their expertise in management, marketing, finance, and so on. Some venture capitalists even specialize in certain areas such as biotechnology or computer software. Often, the financing takes place in sequential stages. This means that additional funding after the original funding will only take place if certain goals are met. These goals may relate to profitability ratios, new product development, market penetration, and so on.

The venture capitalist often provides relatively low-cost debt financing, but with the understanding that the funding carries with it the potential to participate in a major way in any successful public offering of stock in the future. While the venture capitalist may not care about owning a direct equity interest in the company while it is private, he or she wants to participate in ownership when there is a public distribution of shares.

Convertibles and warrants fit very well into these investment parameters. With convertibles the venture capitalist is able to receive interest income and enjoy a relatively high priority of claims among other suppliers of capital. At the time an equity position becomes desirable, he or she can merely convert the debt to common stock.

Another alternative is to provide the venture capitalist with warrants as part of the compensation package for extending debt financing. As incentive, the exercise price on the warrants may be set at one-fifth to one-tenth of the anticipated potential price for a public offering.

When convertibles or warrants are used in early-stage financing, one can think of the interest payments on the related debt as providing singles or doubles to the venture capitalist. What he or she is really hoping for is a grand slam home run in the form of a successful public offering that is fully subscribed to and one in which the stock continues to go up in value after the offering.

warrants, with the provision that the total can be reduced by the assumed use of the cash proceeds to purchase a partially offsetting amount of shares at the market price. Assume that warrants to purchase 10,000 shares at $20 are outstanding and the current price of the stock is $50. We show the following:

1. New shares created	10,000
2. Reduction of shares from cash proceeds (computed below)	4,000
Cash proceeds—10,000 shares at $20 = $200,000	
Current price of stock—$50	
Assumed reduction in shares outstanding from cash proceeds =$200,000/$50 = 4,000	
3. Assumed net increase in shares from exercise of warrants (10,000 − 4,000)	6,000

In computing earnings per share, we will add 6,000 shares to the denominator with no adjustment to the numerator, which will lower earnings per share. If earnings per share had previously been $1 based on $100,000 in earnings and 100,000 shares outstanding, EPS would now be reduced to $0.943:

$$\frac{\text{Earnings}}{\text{Shares}} = \frac{\$100{,}000}{106{,}000} = \$0.943$$

With warrants included in computing diluted earnings per share, their impact on reported earnings is important from both the investor and corporate viewpoints.

exploring the web

Web Address	Comments
http://beginnersinvest.about.com/od/convertiblebonds/Convertible_Bonds.htm	**Provides links to information concerning convertible bond issues**
www.numa.com	**Provides calculator for convertible bonds**
www.marketwatch.com/investing	**Getting Started section contains general information on convertible bonds**
www.bondsonline.com	**Provides information about convertible bonds**

SUMMARY

Convertible securities and warrants offer the investor an opportunity for participating in increased common stock values without owning common stock directly. Convertible securities may be in the form of debt or preferred stock, though most of our examples refer to debt.

Convertible securities provide a guaranteed income stream and a floor value based on required yield on the investment. At the same time, they have an established conversion ratio to common stock (par value/conversion price). The conversion value of an issue is equal to the conversion ratio times the current value of a share of common stock. The conversion value is generally less than the current market price of the convertible issue. Actually, the difference between the market price of the convertible issue and the conversion value is referred to as the conversion premium. The conversion premium is influenced by the volatility of the underlying common stock, the time to maturity, the dividend payment on common stock relative to the interest rate on the convertibles, and other lesser factors. Generally, when the common stock price has risen well above the conversion price (and the convertible is trading well above par), the conversion premium will be quite small, as indicated in Panel (a) of Figure 13–2 on page 344. The small premium is attributed to the fact that the investor no longer enjoys significant downside protection.

A warrant is an option to buy a stated number of shares of stock (usually one) at a specified price over a given time period. Warrants are often issued as a sweetener to a bond issue and may allow the firm to issue debt where it would not normally be feasible. The warrants are generally detachable from the bond issue. Thus, if the warrants are exercised, the bond issue still remains in existence (this is clearly different from a convertible security).

KEY WORDS AND CONCEPTS

DISCUSSION QUESTIONS

1. Why would an investor be interested in convertible securities? (What do they offer to the investor?)

2. What are the disadvantages of investing in convertible securities?

3. When is the best time to buy convertible bonds?

4. How can you determine the conversion ratio from the conversion price?

5. How do you determine the conversion value?

6. What is meant by the pure bond value?

7. For bonds that have conversion premiums in excess of 100 percent, what can you generally infer about the stock price?

8. How does the volatility of a stock influence the conversion premium?

9. How might a step-up in the conversion price force conversion?

10. Why do corporations use convertible bonds?

11. What is meant by the dilutive effect of convertible securities?

12. What is a warrant?

13. For what reasons do firms issue warrants?

14. Please explain why warrants are highly speculative.

15. Why do investors tend to pay a smaller premium for a warrant as the price of the stock goes up?

16. If warrants were initially a detachable part of a bond issue, will the amount of debt be reduced if the warrants are eventually exercised? Contrast this with a convertible security.

17. What type of firm generally issues warrants?

PRACTICE PROBLEMS AND SOLUTIONS

Conversion terms

1. The Noble Corporation has a $1,000 face (par) value bond. Its conversion price is $25. Its stock is selling for $22 per share. The bond is selling for $990.

a. What is the conversion ratio?

b. What is the conversion value?

c. What is the conversion premium (in dollars and percent)?

Pure bond value

2. Balfour, Inc., has a $1,000 par value bond outstanding. The bond pays $60 per share in interest and matures in 20 years. Market rates are eight percent. What is the floor value (pure bond value)? Use semiannual analysis.

Solutions

1. *a.* Conversion ratio = Face value ÷ Conversion price
= $1,000 ÷ 25 = 40

b. Conversion value = Conversion ratio × Common stock
= 40 × $22 = $880

c. Conversion premium ($) = Market price of bond − Conversion value
= $990 − $880
= $110

$$\text{Conversion premium (\%)} = \frac{\text{Market price of bond} - \text{Conversion value}}{\text{Conversion value}}$$

$$= \frac{\$110}{\$880} = 12.50\%$$

2. *PV* of \$30 semiannually for $n = 40$ and $i = 4\%$ (Appendix D)

$$\$30 \times 19.793 = \$593.79$$

PV of \$1,000 for $n = 40$ and $i - 4\%$ (Appendix B)

$$\$1{,}000 \times .208 = \underline{208.00}$$

$$\$801.79$$

PROBLEMS

Conversion terms

1. A convertible bond has a face value of \$1,000, and the conversion price is \$50 per share. The stock is selling at \$42 per share. The bond pays \$60 per year interest and is selling in the market for \$930. It matures in 15 years. Market rates are 10 percent per year.
   a. What is the conversion ratio?
   b. What is the conversion value?
   c. What is the conversion premium (in dollars and percent)?
   d. What is the floor value or pure bond value?

Downside risk

2. Compute the downside risk as a percentage in problem 1. What does this mean?

Downside risk

3. Under what circumstances might the downside risk of a convertible bond increase? Relate your answer to interest rates in the market.

Conversion premium

4. Lowrey Metals Corporation has a \$1,000 convertible bond outstanding that has a market value of \$1,100. It has a coupon rate of 7 percent and matures in 10 years. The conversion price is \$40. The common stock currently is selling for \$37.
   a. What is the conversion premium (in percentage terms)?
   b. At what price does the common stock need to sell for the conversion value to be equal to the current bond price?

Pure bond value

5. In problem 4, market rates of interest for comparable bonds are 10 percent and the pure bond value is \$813.17. What will happen to the pure bond value if market rates of interest go to 12 percent? (You may wish to consult Chapter 12 for computing bond values.)

Downside risk

6. Based on your answer to problem 5, what is the downside risk as a percentage? Use the bond price from problem 4.

Conversion premium and changing stock value

7. Layne Resources, Inc., has a \$1,000 face value convertible bond outstanding that has a market value of \$1,020. It has a coupon rate of 5 percent and matures in 12 years. The conversion price is \$20. The common stock currently is selling for \$16.
   a. What is the conversion premium (in percent)?
   b. At what price does the common stock need to sell for the conversion value to be equal to the current bond price?
   c. Assume the common stock price goes up to \$26 and the conversion premium goes down to \$15. What will be the price of the bond?
   d. What was the percentage gain in the price of the common stock? What was the percentage gain in the price of the bond?
   e. What was the primary reason the conversion premium went down from \$120 to \$15?

Comparative analysis of stock and convertible bonds

8. Assume you bought a convertible bond two years ago for \$900. The bond has a conversion ratio of 32. When the bond was purchased, the stock was selling for \$25 per share. The bond pays \$75 in annual interest. The stock pays no cash dividend. Assume after two years the stock price rises to \$35 and the firm forces investors to convert to common stock by calling the bond (there is no conversion premium at this time).

   Would you have been better off if you had (*a*) bought the stock directly or (*b*) bought the convertible bond and eventually converted it to common stock? Assume you would have invested \$900 in either case. Disregard taxes, commissions, and so forth. (*Hint:* Consider appreciation in value plus any annual income received. See Table 13–3 on page 346 for an example.)

EPS and convertibles

9. Given the following data, compute diluted earnings per share.

Common stock (500,000 shares at $4.00 par value)	$2,000,000
Convertible debentures at 7 percent (6,000 bonds at $1,000 each; convertible into 20 shares per bond)	6,000,000
Retained earnings	8,000,000
Earnings before interest and taxes	3,420,000
Interest	420,000
Earnings before taxes	3,000,000
Earnings after taxes (50%)	$1,500,000

Valuing warrants

10. Assume a firm has warrants outstanding that permit the holder to buy one new share of stock at $25 per share. The market price of the stock is now $34.

a. What is the intrinsic value of the warrant?

b. Why might the warrant sell for $2 in the market even if the stock price is $22?

Valuing warrants

11. Northern Airlines has warrants outstanding that allow the holder to purchase 1.45 shares per warrant at $15 per share (option price). The common stock is currently selling for $19.

a. What is the intrinsic value of the warrant?

b. If the stock sold for $12.50, how large would the negative intrinsic value be?

Comparative analysis of stock and warrants

12. A firm has warrants outstanding that allow the holder to buy one share of stock at $25 per share. Also, assume the stock is selling for $30 per share, and the warrants are now selling for $7 per warrant (this, of course, is above intrinsic value). You can invest $1,000 in the stock or the warrants (for purposes of the computation, round to two places to the right of the decimal point). Assume the stock goes to $40, and the warrants trade at their intrinsic value when the stock goes to $40. Would you have a larger total dollar profit by initially investing in the stock or the warrants?

EPS and warrants

13. Assume a corporation has $400,000 in earnings and 200,000 shares outstanding ($2 in earnings per share). Also assume there are warrants outstanding to purchase 40,000 shares at $25 per share. The stock is currently selling at $40 per share. In considering the effect of the warrants outstanding, what would revised earnings per share be?

INVESTMENT ADVISOR PROBLEM

Chad Smith had decided to invest in convertible bonds because he liked the downside protection that goes with the upside potential. When he bought the 5.85 percent convertible bonds of Morgan Electronics, he was told that the bonds had a floor value of $820.70 with unlimited upside potential. Each bond was convertible into 28 shares of common stock. At the time he purchased the bonds, the firm's common stock was selling for $33 per share, providing a conversion value of $924. His actual purchase price for the bonds was $988.75.

After two months the stock price advanced to $40, the conversion value of the bond went up to $1,120, and the market value of the bond climbed to $1,145.

Chad was quite pleased with his investment when he left for a three-month job assignment in Europe. During that time period he did not track his investments, but when he returned to the United States, he was shocked to find his convertible bond was trading at $740.32.

He immediately called his investment advisor, Gina Gillespie, and asked her what had caused the steep decline in value. Gina was quite astute in making investments and was a Chartered Financial Analyst (CFA). She suggested that two factors must have taken place for this type of decline to happen. What are these two factors?

WEB EXERCISE

Scholastic Corp. is a major publisher of children's books, including the Harry Potter series. To get more information on Scholastic Corp. go to **http://finance.yahoo.com**.

1. On the home page, enter the ticker symbol for Scholastic Corp. (SCHL) in the left-hand search box and click "Get Quotes."
2. Write down the volume traded for the day and the P/E ratio (trailing).
3. Now record the stock price.
4. Scholastic has convertible securities outstanding. Based on the conversion ratio of 26.022, what is the current conversion value of Scholastic Corp.?
5. Assume the convertible bond is presently trading at 90 dollars above the conversion value. What is the conversion premium? You may refer to Formula 13–3 on page 343 to help you with this calculation.

Note: From time to time, companies redesign their Web sites, and occasionally a topic we have listed may have been deleted, updated, or moved into a different location.

CFA MATERIAL

The following material contains a sample question and solution from a prior Level I CFA exam. While the terminology is slightly different from that in this text, you can still view the skills that are necessary for the CFA exam.

CFA Exam Question

6. In examining a company's straight debentures and subordinated convertible debentures, both issued at the same time with the same maturity and at par, you note that the coupon and yield for the subordinated convertible debenture are lower than for the straight debenture. *Discuss* the return potential for the convertible bond in an environment of stable interest rates and rising stock prices that would explain its lower coupon and yield. (*5 minutes*)

Solution: Question 6—Morning Section (5 points)

The reason for the lower coupon and yield is that convertible bonds and preferred stock have the ability to act like common stock on the upside and be valued as a straight bond on the downside. This is demonstrated by the graph in Figure 13–4.

As shown, it has the upside potential of common stock and the downside protection of a bond. Thus, it could have a rate of return approaching common stock with substantially lower risk because it is protected on the downside. Also, the convertible bond has an income advantage relative to common stock until the point at which parity value drives the current yield below the dividend yield.

FIGURE 13-4 Return Distributions—Stocks, Bonds, Convertible Securities

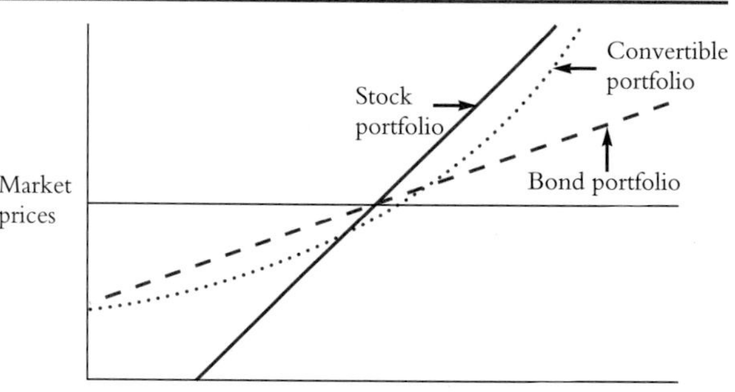

DERIVATIVE PRODUCTS

PART 5 [five]

14

chapter fourteen

PUT AND CALL OPTIONS

OBJECTIVES

1. Understand the basic concept of an option.
2. Distinguish between put and call options.
3. Define strike price, intrinsic value, and speculative premium.
4. Describe speculative and hedging strategies with options.
5. Explain how option contracts are closed out at expiration.
6. Be aware of the tax and commission factors associated with options.

OUTLINE

The word **option** has many different meanings, but most of them include the ability or right to choose a certain alternative. One definition provided by *Webster's* is "the right, acquired for a consideration, to buy or sell something at a fixed price within a specified period of time." This definition is very general and applies to puts, calls, warrants, real estate options, or any other contract entered into between two parties where a choice of action or decision can be put off for a limited time at a cost. The person acquiring the option pays an agreed-upon sum to the person providing the option. For example, someone may want to buy your house for its sale price of $100,000. The buyer does not have the money but will give you $2,000 in cash if you give him the right to buy the house at $100,000 for the next 60 days. If you accept, you have given the buyer an option and have agreed not to sell the house to anyone else for the next 60 days. If the buyer raises $100,000 within the 60-day limit, he may buy the house, giving you the $100,000. Perhaps he gets the $100,000 but also finds another house he likes better for $95,000. He will not buy your house, but you have a $2,000 option premium and must now find someone else to buy your house. By selling the option, you tied up the sale of your house for 60 days, and if the option is not exercised, you have forgone an opportunity to sell the house to someone else.

The most widely known options are puts and calls on common stock. A **put** is an option to sell 100 shares of common stock at a specified price for a given period. **Calls** are the opposite of puts and allow the owner the right to buy 100 shares of common stock from the option seller (writer). Contracts on listed puts and calls have been standardized and can be bought on several different exchanges.

OPTIONS MARKETS

Before the days of options trading on exchanges, puts and calls were traded over-the-counter by the Put and Call Dealers Association. These dealers would buy and sell puts and calls for their own accounts for stocks traded on the New York Stock Exchange and then try to find an investor, hedger, or speculator to take the other side of the option. For example, if you owned 1,000 shares of GE and you wanted to write a call option giving the buyer the right to buy 1,000 shares of GE at $30 per share for six months, the dealer might buy the calls and look for someone who would be willing to buy them from him.

This system had several disadvantages. Dealers had to have contact with the buyers and sellers, and the financial stability of the option writer had to be endorsed (guaranteed) by a brokerage house. The option writer either had to keep the shares on deposit with the brokerage firm or put up a cash margin. Options in the same stock could exist in the market at various strike prices (price at which the option could be exercised) and scattered expiration dates. This meant that when an option buyer wanted to exercise or terminate the contract before expiration, he or she would have to deal directly with the option writer. This does not make for an efficient, liquid market. Unlisted options also reduced the striking price of a call by any dividends paid during the option period, which did not benefit the writer of the call.

Listed Options Exchanges

www.cboe.com

The Chicago Board Options Exchange was established in 1973 as the first exchange for call options. The market response was overwhelming, and within three years, the American, Pacific, and Philadelphia exchanges were also trading call options. By 2010, there were over 3,600 individual equity options traded on the options exchanges. The securities traded have expanded from individual common stocks to include options on stock indexes such as the Nasdaq 100 and the Standard & Poor's 500 Indexes. The ability to buy and sell options on indexes provides a good hedging strategy for portfolio managers, and it allows individual traders to speculate on market movements. The details, of these strategies are covered in Chapter 16, while this chapter concentrates on options for individual common stocks.

Option markets thrive under volatile pricing conditions and uncertainty. The period 2000 through 2010 has provided ample volatility in the markets, and the 2010 average daily trading volume was 14.1 million contracts.

Table 14–1, from the Options Clearing Corporation's Web site (**www.optionsclearing.com**), shows the growth in options trading since 1973. The Options Clearing Corporation is equally owned by its major trading exchanges, which include the American Exchange (AMEX), the Philadelphia Exchange (PHLX), the Pacific Exchange, the Chicago Board Options Exchange (CBOE), and the International Securities Exchange.

TABLE 14-1 Options Data from the Options Clearing Corporation–Statistics

Annual Volume and Open Interest

	VOLUME				AVERAGE DAILY VOLUME		OPEN INTEREST		
Date	Equity	Non-Equity	Futures	OCC Total	Options	Futures	Options	Futures	No. of Equity Issues
2010	3,610,436,931	288,631,739	26,618,135	3,925,686,805	15,578,122	105,628	282,283,772	747,814	3,654
2009	3,366,967,321	245,669,797	12,383,935	3,625,021,053	14,385,004	49,143	256,722,514	728,655	3,529
2008	3,284,761,345	297,811,236	5,173,737	3,587,746,318	14,180,815	20,450	235,799,395	124,710	3,439
2007	2,592,102,961	270,723,257	9,242,341	2,872,068,559	11,405,682	36,822	266,246,756	429,556	3,361
2006	1,844,181,918	183,665,668	8,400,889	2,036,248,475	8,079,074	33,470	218,804,688	1,387,071	3,038
2005	1,369,048,282	135,263,258	5,705,738	1,510,017,278	5,992,132	22,642	181,692,388	1,069,315	2,672
2004	1,083,649,226	98,390,870	2,271,202	1,184,311,298	4,699,648	9,013	149,841,144	164,742	2,534
2003	830,308,227	77,550,428	2,592,193	910,450,848	3,612,900	10,286	121,897,374	197,822	2,227
2002	709,784,014	70,673,329	310,299	780,767,642	3,105,746	8,693	93,122,926	50,952	2,306
2001	722,680,249	58,581,686		781,261,935	3,150,250		81,597,318		2,261
2000	672,871,757	53,856,182		726,727,939	2,883,841		67,635,806		2,364
1999	444,765,224	63,126,259		507,891,483	2,015,442		52,835,522		2,579
1998	329,641,875	76,701,323		406,343,198	1,612,473		32,670,928		2,724
1997	272,998,701	80,824,417		353,823,118	1,398,510		24,853,067		2,400
1996	199,117,729	95,679,973		294,797,702	1,160,621		18,226,729		2,080
1995	174,380,236	112,916,673		287,296,909	1,140,068		14,911,275		1,720
1994	149,932,665	131,449,737		281,382,402	1,116,597		12,292,826		1,512
1993	131,726,101	100,935,994		232,662,095	919,614		11,060,293		1,294
1992	106,484,452	95,511,305		201,995,757	795,259		8,281,401		1,104
1991	104,850,686	93,950,914		198,801,600	785,777		6,415,025		937
1990	111,425,744	98,497,004		209,922,748	829,734		5,543,190		808
1989	141,839,748	85,176,912		227,016,660	900,860		6,835,710		701
1988	114,927,723	81,020,868		195,948,591	774,501		5,998,106		641
1987	164,431,851	140,737,084		305,168,935	1,206,201		6,582,144		590
1986	141,930,945	147,280,190		289,211,135	1,143,127		7,962,816		490
1985	118,555,989	114,354,558		232,910,547	924,248		8,517,379		462
1984	118,925,239	77,512,122		196,437,361	776,432		6,997,632		395
1983	135,658,976	14,397,099		150,056,075	593,107		11,885,189		396
1982	137,264,816	41,389		137,306,205	543,394		9,789,204		375
1981	109,405,782			109,405,782	432,434		9,495,497		354
1980	96,728,546			96,728,546	382,326		5,865,776		241
1979	64,264,863			64,264,863	254,011		4,199,696		220
1978	57,231,018			57,231,018	227,107		3,636,918		217
1977	39,637,328			39,637,328	157,291		3,343,185		222
1976	32,373,925			32,373,925	127,960		2,746,882		202
1975	18,103,018			18,103,018	71,553		1,109,227		44
1974	5,682,907			5,682,907	22,462		380,840		40
1973	1,119,245			1,119,245	6,470		242,825		32

Source: http://www.optionsclearing.com, March 22, 2011.

The International Securities Exchange (ISE) is the "new kid on the block." The ISE traded its first option on May 26, 2000, and since then it has grown to be a significant member of the Options Clearing Corporation, accounting for 18 percent of the trades during October 2010. The International Securities Exchange is an electronic communications network (ECN), providing electronic trading in options. The move to electronic trading in the equity markets, which was covered in Chapter 2, has made its way to the options markets. Before the ISE started, the Chicago Board Options Exchange accounted for 45.5 percent of the trading volume in 2000, but by 2010 its market share had dropped to 27.0 percent. Obviously the ISE has taken a bite out of the CBOE. In addition to clearing options, the Options Clearing Corporation started clearing futures trades in 2002 for an electronic communication network specializing in futures trades so Table 14–1 includes nine years of futures volume.

There are several reasons the listed options markets are so desirable compared with the previous method of over-the-counter trading for options before 1973. The contract period was standardized with three-, six-, and nine-month expiration dates on three calendar cycles:

Cycle 1: January/April/July/October

Cycle 2: February/May/August/November

Cycle 3: March/June/September/December

The use of three cycles spread out the expiration dates for the options so that not all contracts came due on the same day.[1] Each contract expires at 11:59 p.m. Eastern time on the Saturday immediately following the third Friday of the expiration month. For all practical purposes, any closing out of positions must be done on that last Friday while the markets are open.

In an attempt to satisfy demand for longer-term options, **long-term equity anticipation securities (LEAPS)** were added and provided options with up to two years of expiration. LEAPS have generally been limited to blue-chip stocks such as Coca-Cola, Dow Chemical, General Electric, IBM, and others. LEAPS have the same characteristics as the short-term options, but because of their long-term nature, they have higher prices.

Another important feature of option trading is the standardized **exercise price** (strike price). This is the price the contract specifies for a buy or sell. For all stocks over $25 per share, the striking price normally changes by $5 intervals, and for stocks selling under $25 per share, the strike price usually changes by $2.50 a share. As the underlying stocks change prices in the market, options with new striking prices are added. For example, a stock selling at $30 per share when the January option is added will have a striking price of 30, but if the stock gets to 32.50 (halfway to the next striking price), the exchange may add another option (to the class of options) with a 35 strike price or even a 32.50 strike price.

This standardization of expiration dates and strike prices creates more certainty when buying and selling options in a changing market and allows more efficient trading strategies because of better coordination between stock prices, strike prices, and expiration dates. Dividends no longer affect the option contract as they did in the unlisted market. Transactions occur at arm's length between the buyer and seller without any direct matchmaking needed on the part of the broker. The ultimate result of these changes in the option market is a highly liquid, efficient market where speculators, hedgers, and arbitrageurs all operate together.

SINGLE Systems (a hypothetical company) call and put options are presented in Table 14–2 on the next page as an example of different strike prices (15, 17.50, 20, 22.50, 25) and expiration months of December, January, and April. Calls represent options to buy stock, and puts represent options to sell stocks. SINGLE Systems common stock closed at $18.93 (first column) on November 8, but during the last 52 weeks its price had fallen from a high of $57.63 to as low as $11.06. The values within Table 14–2, such as 4.20 and 4.50, reflect the prices of the various options contracts. This information will take on greater meaning as we go through the chapter.

[1] Additional cycles have also been added.

THE OPTIONS CLEARING CORPORATION

Much of the liquidity and ease of operation of the option exchanges is due to the role of the **Options Clearing Corporation**, which functions as the issuer of all options listed on the five exchanges—the CBOE, the AMEX, the Philadelphia Exchange, the International Securities Exchange, and the Pacific Coast Exchange. Investors who want to trade puts and calls need to have an approved account with a member brokerage firm; on opening an account, they receive a prospectus from the Options Clearing Corporation detailing all aspects of option trading.

Options are bought and sold through a member broker the same as other securities. The exchanges allow special orders, such as limit, market, and stop orders, as well as orders used specifically in options trading, such as spread orders and straddle orders. The order process originates with the broker and is transacted on the floor of the exchange. Remember that for every order there must be a buyer and seller (writer) so that the orders can be "matched." Once the orders are matched, they are filed with the Options Clearing Corporation, which then issues the necessary options or closes the position.[2]

Option Premiums

Before investors or speculators can understand various option strategies, they must be able to comprehend what creates option premiums (prices). In Table 14–2, using SINGLE Systems as an example, we can see that the common stock closed at $18.93 per share and that calls and puts are available at a variety of strike prices ranging from $15 to $25. Calls (left-hand side) allow the option holder to buy the stock at the strike price. The January 17.50 calls closed at 2.80 ($280 for one call on 100 shares), while the January 20 call closed at 1.50. The 15 and 17.50 call options are said to be **in-the-money** because the market price of $18.93 is above the **strike** (or purchase) **price** of 15 and 17.50. The 20, 22.50, and 25 calls are **out-of-the-money** because the strike price is above the market price. If SINGLE Systems common were trading at 20, the calls with a strike price of 20 would be **at-the-money** because the stock price and the strike price are equal. In this example, the stock price of $18.93 is 1.07 away from the January 20 put and call. Puts (right-hand side) are the opposite of calls. Because the put allows the holder to sell the stock at the strike price, in-the-money puts would have strike prices greater than $18.93 and out-of-the-money puts would have strike prices less than $18.93.

TABLE 14-2 SINGLE Systems Prices on November 8

Closing Stock Price	Strike Price	CALLS—LAST			PUTS—LAST		
		December	January	April	December	January	April
$18.93	$15.00	$4.20	$4.50	n/a	$0.40	$0.65	n/a
18.93	17.50	2.40	2.80	n/a	1.05	1.40	n/a
18.93	20.00	1.10	1.50	$2.50	2.20	2.60	$3.40
18.93	22.50	0.40	0.70	1.60	3.70	4.20	5.00
18.93	25.00	n/a	0.30	1.10	n/a	6.30	7.10

Note: n/a indicates either that the put or call was not traded on that day or that the option was not offered.

[2] In a transaction, holders and writers of options are not contractually linked but are committed to the Options Clearing Corporation.

Intrinsic Value

application example

In-the-money *call* options have an **intrinsic value** equal to the market price minus the strike price. In the case of the SINGLE Systems January 17.50 call, the intrinsic value is 1.43 as indicated by Formula 14–1:

Intrinsic value (call) = Market price − Strike price **(14–1)**
= 18.93 − $17.50
= 1.43 (SINGLE Systems January 17.50 call)

Options that are out-of-the-money have no positive intrinsic value. If we use Formula 14–1 for the SINGLE Systems January 20 call, we calculate a negative intrinsic value of 1.07. When the market price minus the strike price is negative, the negative value represents the amount the stock price must increase to have the option at-the-money where the strike price and market price are equal. In actual practice, an option cannot have a negative value.

The intrinsic value for the in-the-money put options equals the strike price minus the market price. In the case of the SINGLE Systems January 20 put, the intrinsic value is 1.07 as indicated by the Formula 14–2. Notice that this in-the-money put has a value in the opposite direction from the call:

Intrinsic value (put) = Strike price − Market price **(14–2)**
= $20.00 − $18.93
= $1.07 (SINGLE Systems January 20.00 put)

Because puts allow the owner to sell stock at the strike price, in-the-money put options exist where the strike price is above the market price of the stock. Out-of-the-money puts have market prices for common stock above the strike price.

Speculative Premium (Time Value)[3]

application example

Returning to the SINGLE Systems January 17.50 call, we see in Table 14–2 that the total premium is 2.80, while the previously computed intrinsic value is 1.43. This call option has an additional **speculative premium** of 1.37 due to other factors. The total premium (option price) is a combination of the intrinsic value plus a speculative premium. This relationship is indicated in Formula 14–3 and shown in Figure 14–1 below:

Total premium = Intrinsic value + Speculative premium **(14–3)**
= 1.43 + 1.37
= 2.80

FIGURE 14-1 Components of the Total Premium on a Call Option

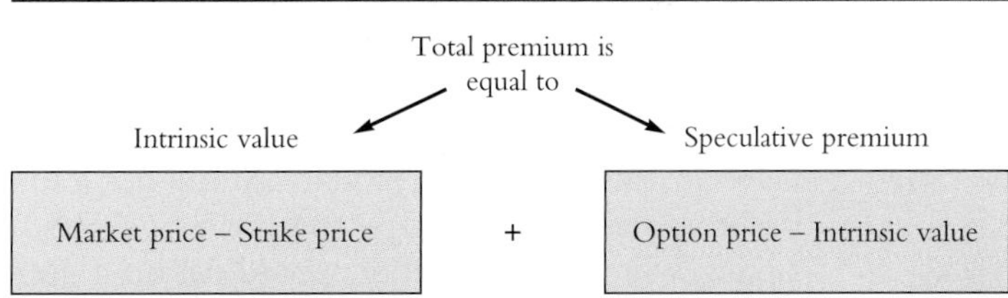

[3] People often refer to the speculative premium as time value because time may be the overriding factor affecting the speculative premium.

TABLE 14-3 Speculative Premiums on November 8 for SINGLE Systems January Options

Market Price on November 8	Strike Price	Total Premium	–	Intrinsic Value	=	Speculative Premium	Speculative Premium as a Percentage of Stock Price
$18.93	$15.00 Jan Call	$4.50		$3.93		$0.57	3.01%
18.93	17.50 Jan Call	2.80		1.43		1.37	7.24
18.93	20.00 Jan Call	1.50		−1.07		2.57	13.58
18.93	22.50 Jan Call	0.70		−3.57		4.27	22.56
18.93	25.00 Jan Call	0.30		−6.07		6.37	33.65

Generally, the higher the volatility of the common stock—as measured by the stock price's standard deviation or by its beta—and the lower the dividend yield, the greater the speculative premium. The longer the exercise period, the higher the speculative premium, especially if market expectations over the duration of the option are positive. Finally, the deeper the option is in-the-money, the smaller the leverage potential and therefore the smaller the speculative premium. Most often, we examine the speculative premium separately to see if it is a reasonable premium to pay for the possible benefits.

The speculative premium can be expressed in dollars or as a percentage of the common stock price. A speculative premium expressed in percent indicates the increase in the stock price needed for the purchaser of a call option to break even on the expiration date. Table 14–3 shows this point.[4] Notice that the SINGLE Systems January 15 call option, which is deep in the money, has the lowest speculative premium, while the 25 call option has the highest. Realize that the 25 call option has a cash value of only 0.30 (the total premium), and the other 6.07 represents the required increase in the stock price for the market price and the strike price to be equal. The 33.65 percent speculative premium for the January 25 call option represents the percentage movement in stock price by the expiration date for a break-even position. At expiration, there will be no speculative premium. The option will reflect only the intrinsic value and possibly even a discount because of commission expenses incurred on exercise.

Speculative Premiums and the Time Factor

Table 14–4 provides a look at premiums for the in-the-money and out-of-the-money call options with varying times to expiration. Since the quotes are as of November, the December options will expire first, then the January options, and finally the April options. The option premiums increase with more time to expiration.

SINGLE Systems' speculative premiums in Table 14–4 demonstrate that percent speculative premiums increase with time across all series of strike prices. The speculative premiums are also lowest with the in-the-money 15 and 17.50 calls because of the low leverage potential and the downside risk if the stock declines. The 25 call option has a high speculative premium, but an option writer (seller) *would not reap much cash inflow*. Generally, out-of-the-money call options have high speculative premiums, but little of the premium may be in the form of cash. As previously indicated in Table 14–3, the January 25 call has a total premium of 0.30. The fact that the cash premium is only $0.30 ($30 on 100 shares) is an important consideration for an option writer. Commissions would eat up a good portion of the cash inflow.

[4] As applied to put options, the speculative premium indicates the decrease in stock price needed for the purchaser of a put option to break even on the expiration date.

TABLE 14-4 Speculative Premiums over Time (SINGLE Systems Call Options, November 8)

Market Price	Strike Price	December Total Premium (Option Price)	Speculative Premium	Premium Percent	January Total Premium (Option Price)	Speculative Premium	Premium Percent	April Total Premium (Option Price)	Speculative Premium	Premium Percent
$18.93	$15.00	$4.20	$0.27	1.43%	$4.50	$0.57	3.01%	n/a	n/a	n/a
18.93	17.50	2.40	0.97	5.12	2.80	1.37	7.24	n/a	n/a	n/a
18.93	20.00	1.10	2.17	11.46	1.50	2.57	13.58	$2.50	$3.57	18.86%
18.93	22.50	0.40	3.97	20.97	0.70	4.27	22.56	1.60	5.17	27.31
18.93	25.00	n/a	n/a	n/a	0.30	6.37	33.65	1.10	7.17	37.88

SINGLE System's 52 Week High = 57.63; low 11.06.

Speculative Premiums, Betas, and Dividend Yields Table 14–5 demonstrates the relationship of betas and dividend yields to the speculative premium. Each of the six options is in-the-money, and the price of their common stock is between .06 percent and 5.51 percent above their strike price, which makes them relatively comparable. While the relationships in this table don't hold for all options, we have structured this example to make two points. Although the betas (second column from the right in Table 14–5) in this example don't decline in rank order, it is clear that the high-beta stocks have the highest speculative premiums. High-beta stocks have a greater probability of participating in a market upturn, and so speculators will pay a higher speculative premium on a call option for the chance to participate in an up market. A beta is usually calculated over a five-year period and is only one measure of risk. Shorter-term volatility measures such as six-month or one-year standard deviations may influence a trader's willingness to pay a high or low speculative premium as well.

Also, stocks with low dividend yield are more likely to have a high speculative premium than high-dividend-yield stocks. In this table the dividend yields and premiums are inversely related. High-dividend-yield stocks are the ones favored by call writers, and therefore, the speculative premiums are lower because there is a larger number of speculators willing to write calls for these stocks.

In the case of Amazon.com, the speculative premium is higher than Apple's because its stock price is closer to the strike price, which gives it better leverage and more "bang for the buck." Disney on the other hand, has a high beta but its dividend reduces its speculative premium compared to the three high-beta stocks that don't pay a dividend. Dividends seem to be the dominant influence on speculative premiums, but this may be misleading because most high-beta stocks are growth stocks with low or no dividends.

TABLE 14-5 Speculative Premiums Related to Betas and Dividend Yields (In-the-Money Call Options)

Company Name	January 2011 Strike Price	October 18 2010 Market Price	Percent Above Strike	Intrinsic Value	Option Premium Asked	Speculative Premium (Time Value) Dollars	Speculative Premium (Time Value) Percent	Beta	Expected Dividend Yield
Apple	$310.00	$318.00	2.58%	$8.00	$26.75	$18.75	5.90%	1.03	0.00%
Amazon.com	160.00	163.56	2.23	3.56	15.00	11.44	6.99	1.12	0.00
e-Bay	25.00	25.72	2.88	0.72	2.14	1.42	5.52	1.08	0.00
Disney	34.00	34.75	2.21	0.75	1.94	1.19	3.42	1.07	1.00
3M	85.00	89.66	5.48	4.66	6.65	1.99	2.22	0.89	2.34
Pfizer Inc.	17.50	17.80	1.71	0.30	0.96	0.66	3.71	0.87	4.00

Source: Merrill Lynch On-Line and E-Trade, October 18, 2010.

Dividends and betas are only two variables that affect speculative premiums. Other factors, such as market conditions or individual company conditions, can also have a strong bearing on speculative premiums. 3M and Pfizer are the high yield dividend stocks but Pfizer's stock price is just over the strike price while 3M is deeper in the money. The stock price in relation to the strike price also has a big influence on the speculative premium which accounts for Pfizer's higher speculative premium. If interest rates are increasing, interest-sensitive stocks may suffer, and the speculative premiums on puts might rise while the speculative premiums on calls decline. As always, future expectations for a company will dominate historical information if that information is now considered irrelevant by the market.

Speculative Premiums per Day Speculative premiums can be deceiving. The novice may attempt to write the options with the highest total premium or speculative premium, while the buyer may think the smallest dollar investment provides the greatest advantage. These notions are not usually true if we look at speculative premiums on a per day basis. For example, the previously discussed SINGLE Systems calls have the following speculative premiums per day. The information is based on a strike price of 20 and expiration months of December, January, and April. Note that the speculative premium is divided by the number of days to expiration to arrive at the speculative premium per day:

Month	Strike Price	Speculative Premium	Days to Expiration	Speculative Premium per Day
December	$20	11.46%	43	0.267%
January	20	13.58	71	0.191
April	20	18.86	162	0.116

An examination of daily premiums suggests that call writers should write short-lived calls on a continuous basis to get a maximum return. In this case, the December calls give the maximum premium per day. On the other hand, call buyers get more time for less premium per day by purchasing the April calls.

Understanding option premiums is important if the investor is to make sense out of option strategies. Various strategies involving calls and puts are covered in the next section. Appendix 14A presents the Black-Scholes option pricing model, a much more sophisticated way of analyzing option prices and their time premiums and speculative premiums. This appendix is primarily designed for those who wish to achieve a more advanced understanding of the theoretical basis for option pricing; it is not essential for the standard reading of the text.

BASIC OPTION STRATEGIES

Option strategies can be very aggressive and risky, or they can be quite conservative and used as a means of reducing risk. Option buyers and writers both attempt to take advantage of the option premiums discussed in the preceding section. In theory, many option strategies can be created, but in practice, the market must be liquid enough to execute these strategies. Although volume on the underlying common stock has continued to increase, much of the option activity has been absorbed by options on the Standard & Poor's 100 and 500 Stock Indexes, where large institutional investors can transact portfolio strategies on the market rather than on individual stocks.

Any reduction of individual option trading reduces the ability to create workable strategies for specific companies. For example, the lack of a liquid market can keep institutional investors from executing hedging strategies involving several hundred thousand shares. Even with these limitations in mind, the average investor can still find many opportunities for option strategies. In this section, we discuss the possible uses of calls and puts to achieve different investment goals. Table 14–6

TABLE 14-6 November Call Option Quotes over Three Months

			SEPTEMBER 28 49 DAYS TO EXPIRATION		OCTOBER 19 28 DAYS TO EXPIRATION		NOVEMBER 2 14 DAYS TO EXPIRATION	
Company Name	**Expiration Month**	**Strike Price**	**Option Price**	**Common Stock Price**	**Option Price**	**Common Stock Price**	**Option Price**	**Common Stock Price**
American Travel	November	$ 30.00	n/a	$33.10	$2.80	$ 31.17	$2.85	$ 32.01
American Travel	November	32.50	n/a	33.10	1.60	31.17	1.35	32.01
American Travel	November	35.00	$ 1.95	33.10	0.75	31.17	0.35	32.01
American Travel	November	40.00	0.55	33.10	0.15	31.17	n/a	32.01
Bow Wing Inc.	November	35.00	2.00	33.50	1.25	33.45	0.95	34.35
SINGLE Systems	November	15.00	0.40	12.18	2.35	16.72	2.50	17.26
SINGLE Systems	November	17.50	0.15	12.18	1.00	16.72	0.90	17.26
SINGLE Systems	November	20.00	n/a	n/a	0.30	16.72	0.25	17.26
Deli USA	November	20.00	2.40	18.53	5.50	24.05	6.00	24.92
Deli USA	November	22.50	1.25	18.53	2.65	24.05	n/a	24.92
Deli USA	November	25.00	1.05	21.55	1.35	24.05	1.05	24.92
Howard & David	November	17.50	2.00	18.08	1.30	18.29	0.50	16.92
Home Delivery	November	40.00	2.10	38.37	2.40	40.41	1.60	40.32
Home Delivery	November	45.00	n/a	n/a	n/a	40.41	0.20	40.32
International Optics	November	100.00	2.40	91.72	5.80	102.65	n/a	109.50
International Optics	November	110.00	1.25	91.72	1.50	102.65	2.45	109.50
Intelligent Systems	November	20.00	2.60	20.39	n/a	24.15	6.50	26.30
Intelligent Systems	November	25.00	0.45	20.39	1.15	24.15	2.05	26.30
Orisis Gaming	November	12.50	1.35	12.58	n/a	14.54	2.05	14.45
Orisis Gaming	November	15.00	0.45	12.58	0.95	14.54	0.45	14.45
World Airways	November	15.00	1.20	15.04	0.30	13.17	0.15	13.48

Note: n/a indicates that the quote was not available because the option did not trade on that date or was not yet listed because the stock price was too far below the strike price.

provides option quotes as of three different dates for our examples. All the options expire in November. We ignored commissions in most examples, but commissions can be a significant hidden cost in some types of option strategies.

Buying Call Options

The Leverage Strategy Leverage is a very common reason for buying call options when the market is expected to rise during the exercise period. The use of calls in this way is similar to warrants discussed in Chapter 13, but calls have shorter lives. The call option is priced much lower than common stock, and the leverage is derived from a small percentage change in the price of the call option. For example, for our hypothetical company, SINGLE Systems, on September 28 its common stock closed at $12.18 per share and the November 15 call option closed at $0.40 (see Table 14–6).

About three weeks later on October 19, the stock closed at $16.72 for a $4.54 gain on the stock or 37.27 percent ($4.54/$12.18). The November 15 call option closed at $2.35 on October 19, for a $1.95 gain of 487.5 percent ($1.95/$0.40). The call option increased by 13.1 times the percentage move in the common stock price over this three-week span. The relationship is indicated below.

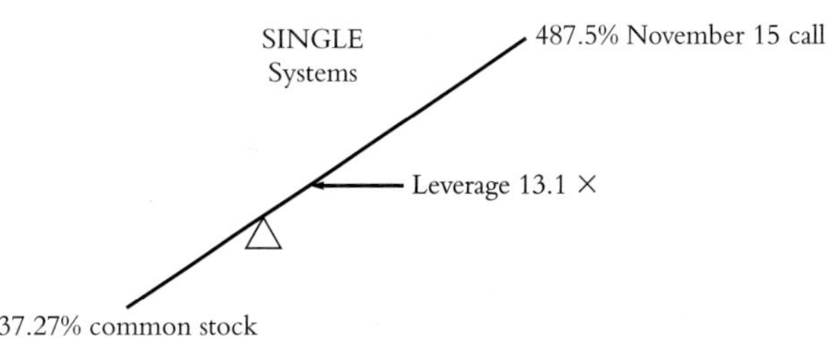

Figure 14–2 depicts the relationship between profit and loss opportunities for the SINGLE Systems November 15 call option, assuming the option is held until the day of expiration (no speculative premium exists at expiration).

As long as the common stock closes under 15, the call buyer loses the whole premium of \$0.40 (100 × \$0.40 = \$40). At a price of \$15.40 the call buyer breaks even because the option is worth an intrinsic value of \$0.40. As the stock increases past \$15.40, the profit starts accumulating. At a price of \$19.40, the profit equals \$400 at expiration. If the option is sold before expiration, a speculative premium may increase the profit potential.

An investor striving for maximum leverage generally buys options that are out-of-the-money or slightly in-the-money. Buying high-priced options for \$10 or \$15 that are well in-the-money limits the potential for leverage. You may have to invest almost as much in the options as you would in the stock.

Playing the leverage game doesn't always work. Let's once again look at Table 14–6. If on September 28 a speculator assumed that Howard & David's stock price would go up and bought the November 17.50 call option for \$2.00, two periods later, on November 2, the Howard & David call option would have been worth \$0.50 per share. A \$1.50 loss occurred in the option price.The decline in Howard & David stock from \$18.08 to \$16.92 was only \$1.16, or a 6.4 percent loss, while at the same time the option lost 75 percent of its value, going from \$2.00 to \$0.50. A loss of \$1.50 per share would equal a \$150 loss on one call option. If the stock price stays below \$17.50 until expiration, the owner of the November 17.50 call can expect to lose the current call premium of \$0.50. It is not hard to lose all your money under these circumstances—leverage works in reverse, too.

Call Options Instead of Stock Many people do not like to risk large amounts of money and view call options as a way of controlling 100 shares of stock without a large dollar commitment. For example, assume you could buy 100 shares of common stock for \$40 per share (\$4,000) or a call option with a strike price of 40 at a cost of \$4 or \$400. You choose to spend the \$400 and invest the \$3,600 difference (\$4,000 − \$400) in short-term money market securities at 4 percent. Assume the call option has six months to expiration. During the six months your common stock falls from \$40 per share to \$30 per share, and your call option is worthless at expiration. During this time your short-term money market securities generated

FIGURE 14-2 SINGLE Systems November 15 Call Option (excludes commissions)

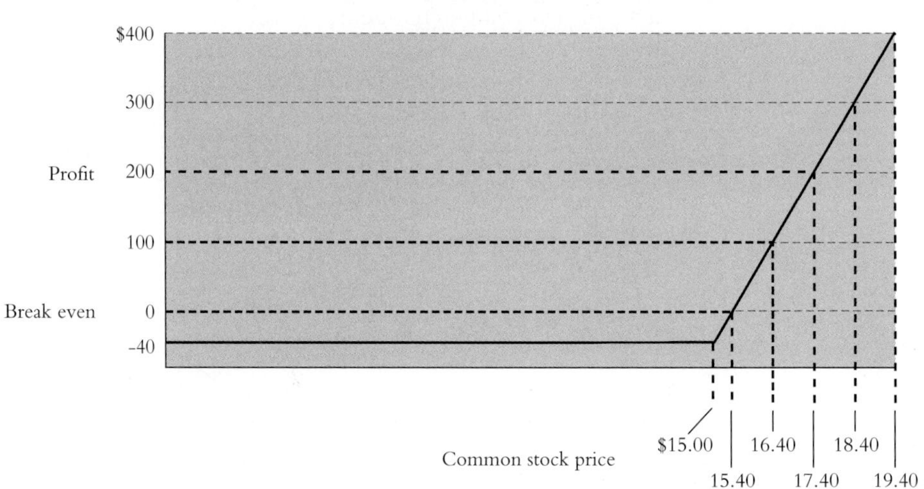

$72 of interest income,[5] which helps offset your $400 loss on your call option. Your total loss on your call investment was $328 ($400 − $72), but if you had bought the common stock, you would have lost $1,000, or $10 per share on 100 shares. When stock prices are falling, this strategy can reduce an investor's losses. This strategy works to the investor's advantage because in the end the loss is less for owning the call option than it would have been for owning 100 shares of stock outright.[6] This will not always be the case.

Had your stock only declined in value by 1¢ to $39.99, you still would have lost $328 on your call option. If you had bought the stock you would have only lost $1.00 (1¢ × 100 shares). One thing to remember is that the purchaser of the call option cannot lose more than the initial purchase price of $400. This will be slightly offset by the $72 of interest earned. Of course, there is the possibility that the stock rises to $50 per share and both the stock purchaser and the option purchaser will show profits. Paying commissions to buy and sell will reduce profits.

Protecting a Short Position Calls are often used to cover a short sale against the risk of rising stock prices. This is called hedging your position. By purchasing a call, the short seller guarantees a loss of no more than a fixed amount while at the same time reducing any potential profit by the total premium paid for the call. Again refer to Table 14–6 on page 373, and assume you sold 100 shares of Intelligent Systems short at $20.39 on September 28, and bought a November 25 call for $0.45 as protection against a rise in the price of the stock. By November 2, the stock rises to $26.30 for a $591 loss on the short position [($26.30 − $20.39) × 100 shares]. This loss has been partially offset by an increase in the November 25 call option price from $0.45 to $2.05, or a $160 gain [($2.05 − $0.45) × 100 shares = $160]. The loss on the short sale has been cut from $591 to $431, or reduced by the $160 profit on the call option.

Reconsider the initial $0.45 call premium. If the stock goes up, the call limits your loss, but if the stock goes down as expected, your profit on the short position may be reduced by the call premium. If Intelligent Systems had declined to $18 and generated a profit of $2.39 ($20.39 − $18) per share, this gain would have been reduced by the loss of $0.45 on the call option. Writing a call to protect a short sale is equivalent to buying an insurance policy that you hope you won't need.

Guaranteed Price Often, an investor thinks a stock will rise over the long term but does not have cash currently available to purchase the stock. The important point for this strategy is that the investor wants to own this stock eventually but does not want to miss out on a good buying opportunity (based on expectations). Perhaps the oil stocks are depressed, or semiconductors have hit bottom. A call option can be utilized. The investor could be anticipating a cash inflow in the future when he or she plans to exercise the call option with a tax refund, a book royalty check, or even the annual bonus.

Please refer back to Table 14–6 on page 373. On September 28, assume an investor buys an Orisis Gaming November 12.50 call option for $1.35. The intrinsic value for the November 12.50 call option is $0.08 because the stock is selling for $12.58 per share. The speculative premium is equal to the option price of $1.35 minus the intrinsic value of $0.08, or $1.27. By November 2, she has received her $1,250 royalty check and exercises the option to buy the stock at $12.50 when the stock is selling at $14.45. For tax purposes the cost or basis of these 100 shares of Orisis is the strike price of $12.50 plus the option premium of $1.35, or a total cost of $13.85 per share. If she had waited until November 2 to buy the stock, she would

[5] The approximate calculation is $3,600 × 4% × 180/360 = $72.

[6] It should be pointed out we are talking about absolute dollar losses. On a percentage basis, the options would be the bigger losers.

have paid an extra $0.60 per share above $13.85, or $14.45. Her strategy locked in a guaranteed price just as it was supposed to. There is always the possibility that the stock price declines to below your strike price; in that case, you buy the stock in the market directly and consider your option premium an insurance policy.

Writing Call Options

Writers of call options take the opposite side of the market from buyers. The writer is similar to a short seller in that he or she expects the stock to decline or stay the same. For short sellers to profit, prices must decline, but because writers of call options receive a premium, they can make a profit if prices stay the same or even rise less than the speculative premium. Option writers can write **covered options**, meaning they own the underlying common stock, or they can write **naked options**, meaning they do not own the underlying stock.

Writing covered call options is often considered a hedged position because if the stock price declines, the writer's loss on the stock is partially offset by the option premium. A potential writer of a covered call must decide if he is willing to sell the underlying stock if it closes above the strike price. If not, the writer must repurchase the call option before the option is exercised by the owner.

Returning to Table 14–6 on page 373 for another set of option quotes, find the Bow Wing November 35 call options on September 28. The market price of the common stock is $33.50 and the writer for a November 35 call option will receive $2.00 per share.

Remember, the writer agrees to sell 100 shares at the 35 strike price as the consideration for the premium. The 35 call option would be a good write if the stock closed at $35 per share or less because the call would not get exercised and the writer would keep the $2.00 premium. If the stock closed at $35 or higher, then the call could get exercised, and the writer would have to buy and deliver 100 shares at $35. More likely, the option writer would buy back the option for its price in the market to avoid having the option exercised. If the ending value of the stock were 40, the option writer could buy back the 35 call for 5. The purchase at $5 would be offset by the initial receipt of the $2 premium and the total loss before commissions would be $3. Figure 14–3 shows this relationship between profit and loss and the common stock price in writing a naked option.

FIGURE 14-3 Bow Wing 35 November Call, Payoff Graph for Writing One Naked Call

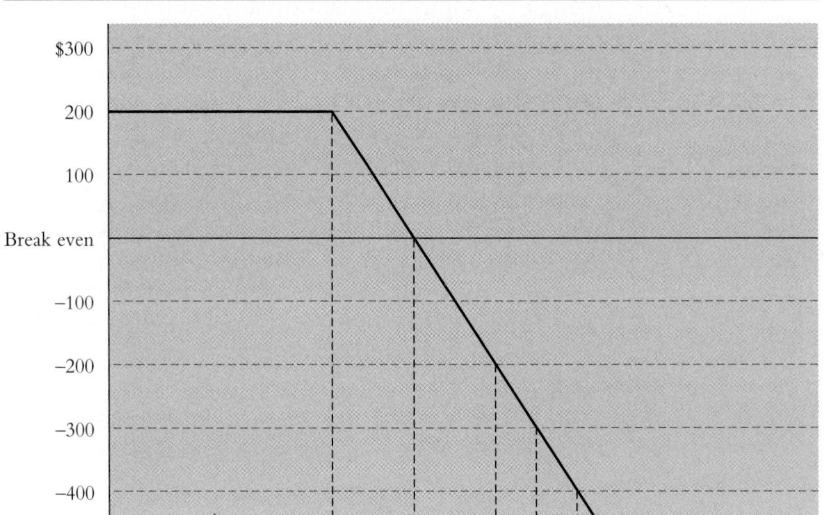

Let's now go to covered call options. Assume an investor bought 100 shares of Bow Wing at \$33.50 on September 28. He also sold a November 35 call option for \$2. If the stock ends up at \$35, he will make a total profit of \$350, a \$150 capital gain on the stock (100 shares × \$1.50) plus the \$200 option premium (100 × \$2). Of course, if the stock really goes up in value, the covered call option writer will wish he had not written the call option. The increased cost to buy back the option will severely cut into the profit on the long position in the stock.

application example

Let's look at what actually happened with Bow Wing. By November 2, Bow Wing stock closed at \$34.35, and at that point, the covered call writer would make money, and a naked call writer would also make money. The covered call writer is assumed to have bought 100 shares at \$33.50 per share at the time he or she wrote the option for \$2.00 on September 28. The naked option writer merely sold the option for \$2.00. It is further assumed the covered option writer would receive a \$17 dividend during the period. Also note that the November 35 option is only worth \$0.95 on November 2. The analysis is presented at the top of the next page:

Bow Wing Example

Covered Writer		Naked Writer	
− Initial investment (100 × 33.50)	−\$3,350.00	− Margin (30% × \$3,350)	−\$1,005.00
+ Option premium (100 × 2.00)	200.00	+ Option premium	200.00
+ Dividend	17.00	(no dividends received)	
+ Ending stock value (100 × 34.35)	3,435.00	+ Ending value margin	1,005.00
Gain	302.00	Gain	200.00
Investment = \$3,350 − \$200.00	\$3,150.00	Investment	\$1,005.00
Percent return on initial investment	9.6%	Return on investment	19.9%

Because the stock price ended at less than the strike price, neither the covered writer nor the naked writer needed to buy back their option as of November 2. They both had profits—with the covered writer ahead of the naked writer by \$102 with \$17 from the dividend and \$85 from the capital gain on the stock, while the naked writer was ahead in percentage terms (19.9 percent versus 9.6 percent) because of a smaller initial investment. The naked writer was required to put up a margin on 30 percent of the value of the stock to ensure the ability to close out the option write if the stock should rise significantly. The capital was returned to the naked call writer when it was no longer needed as collateral. If the stock price had risen, the naked writer was exposed to unlimited risk because he either had to close out the position at a loss or purchase the stock above the strike price and deliver it at a loss. The covered writer had limited risk because he owned the stock and could deliver it or close out the position before it was called.

Another critical decision for a call writer is the choice of months. In the section on option premiums, we examined percentage premiums per day and found that the shortest expiration dates usually provided the highest daily speculative premium. In most cases, the call writer chooses the short-term options and as they expire, writes another short-term option. Annualized returns of 12 to 15 percent are not uncommon for continuously covered writing strategies.

Buying Put Options

The owner (buyer) of a put may sell 100 shares of stock to the put writer at the strike price. The strategy behind a put is similar to selling short or writing a call except losses are limited to the total investment (premium), and no more risk exposure is possible if the stock rises. Buying a put in anticipation of a price decline is one method of speculating on market price changes. The same factors influencing call premiums also apply to put premiums except that expectations for the direction for the market are the opposite.

Let's assume that the New Age Internet Co. was selling at $50 per share in July 2011, already down from its all-time high of $200 per share. You expected it to decline and possibly collapse as many other "new economy" companies had already done. You decided to buy a put rather than sell the stock short because you did not want to take the risk of unlimited loss if the stock should reverse and go back to $200. You found an at-the-money 50 put with an expiration date of April 2012 for an option premium of $7. This was a high premium, but New Age had been a quite volatile stock and often moved $4 or $5 per share in one day.

You bought the put for $700 and hoped that the stock price declined. By April 2012, the company was almost bankrupt and the stock was selling at $5 per share, and at expiration your put option had an intrinsic value of $45 per share. For your $700 investment you received $4,500 when you sold the put for a profit of $3,800 on a $700 investment. That's a good conclusion; but, of course, it doesn't always happen that way.

Puts can also help you offset a potential decline in the price of common stock that you continue to hold for tax purposes. For example, assume you own ABZ Company at a gain and you would like to defer taking a profit until next year. You can protect yourself from a decline in the stock price by buying a put. If the stock falls, the put will make money as the stock loses money. In this case the put becomes an insurance policy against the potential decline in the stock. You can hold the put along with your stock and keep buying new puts if necessary until you are ready to sell your stock.

USING OPTIONS IN COMBINATIONS

Spreads

Now that you have studied puts and calls from both the buyer's and writer's perspectives, we briefly proceed with a discussion of spreads. Most combinations of options are called **spreads** and consist of buying one option (going long) and writing an option (going short) on the same underlying stock. Spreads are for the sophisticated investor and involve many variations on a theme. For an in-depth discussion of spreads, the reader may wish to consult Appendix 14B.

Straddles

A **straddle** is a combination of a put and call on the same stock with the same strike price and expiration date. It is used to play wide fluctuations in stock prices and is usually applied to individual stocks with high betas and a history of large, short-term fluctuations in price. The speculator using a straddle may be unsure of the direction of the price movement but may be able to make a large enough profit on one side of the straddle to cover the cost of both options even if one option expires worthless.

For example, assume a put and a call can be bought for $5 apiece on ABC October 50s when ABC Corporation is selling at 50 with six months to expiration. The total investment is 10 ($1,000). If the stock should rise from 50 to 65 at expiration, the call would provide a profit of 10 (15 value − 5 cost), and the put would be left to expire worthless for a loss of 5. This would provide a net gain of 5, or $500. The same type of example can be drawn if the price goes way down. Some who engage in spreads or straddles might attempt to close out one position before the other. This expands the profit potential but also increases the risk.

OTHER OPTION CONSIDERATIONS

Many factors have not been covered in detail because of their changing nature over time. Tax laws relating to options are constantly changing, and some items, such as capital gains, have been revised several times in the last few years. We do know that the tax laws have a significant impact on spread positions and also on the tax treatment where put options are involved. The recognition of the year in which a gain or loss is declared can still be affected by option strategies in combination with stock positions. The best advice we can give is to check the tax consequences of any option strategy with your accountant or stockbroker.

Commissions vary among brokerage houses and are not easy to pinpoint for option transactions since quantity discounts exist. Because many option positions involve small dollar investment outlays, commissions of $25 to $50 for buying and selling can significantly alter your returns and even create losses. Commissions on acquiring common stock through options are higher than the transaction costs of options, and this is a motivating force in closing out option transactions before expiration. Overall, commissions on options tend to be more significant than commissions on commodities or other highly leveraged investments.

exploring the web

Web Address	Comments
www.cboe.com	**Chicago Board Options Exchange Web site. A good source of education and data.**
www.amex.com	**American Stock Exchange trades options and has a Web site section on options.**

SUMMARY

Put and call options are an exciting area of investment and speculation. We have discussed the past history of over-the-counter options trading and more recent trading of options on the listed options exchanges, such as the CBOE. The markets are more efficient, and the standardized practices of the listed exchanges have made options more usable for many investors and widened the number of option strategies that can be employed.

Option premiums (option prices) are affected by many variables such as time, market expectations, stock price volatility, dividend yields, and in-the-money/out-of-the-money relationships. The total premium consists of an intrinsic value plus a speculative premium that declines to zero by the expiration date. Calls are options to buy 100 shares of stock, while puts are options to sell 100 shares of stock.

www.mhhe.com/hirtblock10e

Understanding the benefits and risks of trading options is complicated. Options can be risky or used to reduce risk. Calls can be bought for leverage, to cover a short position, or as an alternative to investing in the underlying common stock while buying time to purchase the stock (waiting for the financial resources to exercise the call). Calls are written either as a hedge on a long position in the underlying stock or to speculate on a price decline. Puts are bought to hedge a long position against a price decline or as an alternative to selling short. A writer of a put may speculate on a price increase or use the write as a hedge against a short position (if the price goes up, he will come out ahead on the writing of the put to partially offset the loss on the short sale).

Spreads are combinations of buying and writing the same options for an underlying common stock. In general, spreads reduce the risk of loss while limiting the gain. Straddles are a combination of a put and a call option in a stock at the same exercise date and strike price. They are used to profit from stocks showing large, short-term price fluctuations.

Other factors affect option profitability, such as taxes and commissions, and in general, each investor or speculator should check out his or her own situation and factor in the appropriate information with regard to taxes and commissions.

KEY WORDS AND CONCEPTS

DISCUSSION QUESTIONS

1. What exchanges trade stock options?
2. How has the option market been expanded to go beyond individual stocks?
3. What is meant by the exercise or strike price on an option?
4. What factors influence a speculative premium on an option?
5. Why would a high-beta stock often have a greater speculative premium than a low-beta stock?
6. Comment on the statement, "The novice may attempt to write the options with the highest total premium or speculative premium, while the buyer may think the smallest investment provides the greatest leverage."
7. What does the speculative premium as a percentage of stock price indicate for a call option?
8. Comment on how leverage works in purchasing a call option.
9. Assume you wish to control the price movement of 100 shares of stock. You may buy 100 shares of stock directly or purchase a call option on the 100 shares. Which strategy is likely to expose you to the larger potential dollar amount of loss? Which strategy is likely to expose you to the larger potential percent loss on your investment?
10. Explain how options can be used to protect a short position.

11. What are two option strategies to take advantage of an anticipated decline in stock prices? (Relate one to call options and the other to put options.)

12. What is the difference between writing a covered and a naked call option?

13. In general, if the price of the underlying stock is going up, what will happen to the price of a put option? Briefly explain.

14. Why might small commissions of $25 to $50 be important in option trades?

PRACTICE PROBLEMS AND SOLUTIONS

Option trading terms

1. A stock is selling for $42.80 with an option available at a $40 strike price. The 40 call option price is at $6.50.

a. What is the intrinsic value of the 40 call?

b. What is the speculative premium on the 40 call option?

c. What percentage of the common stock price does the speculative premium represent?

Covered call options

2. Ann Smith purchases 100 shares of stock at $52 per share and wishes to hedge her position by writing a 100-share call option on her holdings. The option has a $50 strike price and a premium of $6.50. If the stock is selling at $47 at the time of expiration, what will be the overall dollar gain or loss on this covered option play? (Consider the change in stock value as well as the gain or loss on the option.)

Solutions

1. *a.* Intrinsic value = Market price − Strike price

$2.80 = $42.80 − $40.00

b. Speculative premium = Total premium − Intrinsic value

$3.70 = $6.50 − 2.80

c. $$\frac{\text{Speculative premium}}{\text{Common stock price}} = \frac{\$3.70}{42.80} = 8.64\%$$

2.

− Initial investment (100 shares at $52)	($5,200)
+ Option premium	650
+ Ending value of stock ($47 per share)	4,700
Gain	$ 150

PROBLEMS

Exercise (strike) price

1. A stock has an exercise (strike) price of $40.

a. If the stock price goes to $41.50, is the exchange likely to add a new strike price?

b. If the stock price goes to $42.75 is the exchange likely to add a new strike price?

Option trading prices

2. Look at the option quotes in Table 14–2 on page 368.

a. What is the closing price of the common stock of SINGLE Systems?

b. What is the highest strike price listed?

c. What is the price of a December 20 call option?

d. What is the price of a January 22.50 put option?

Option trading terms

3. Assume a stock is selling for $66.75 with options available at 60, 65, and 70 strike prices. The 65 call option price is at $4.50.

a. What is the intrinsic value of the 65 call?

b. Is the 65 call in the money?

c. What is the speculative premium on the 65 call option?

d. What percentage does the speculative premium represent of common stock price?
e. Are the 60 and 70 call options in the money?

Option trading terms

4. Assume a stock is selling for $48.50 with options available at 40, 50, and 60 strike prices. The 50 call option price is at 2.75.
a. What is the intrinsic value of the 50 call?
b. Is the 50 call in the money?
c. What is the speculative premium on the 50 call option?
d. What percentage of common stock price does the speculative premium represent?
e. Are the 40 and 60 call options in the money?

Option trading terms

5. In the case of Deli USA in Table 14–6 on page 373:
a. What is the intrinsic value of the November 20 call option on October 19?
b. What is the total premium (option price) for the option on that date?
c. What is the speculative premium?

Option trading terms

6. In the case of American Travel in Table 14–6 on page 373:
a. What is the intrinsic value of the November 32.50 call option on November 2?
b. How much is the speculative premium on that date?
c. By what percentage does the stock need to go up by expiration to break even on the call option?

Speculative premium per day

7. Assume on May 1 you are considering a stock with three different expiration dates for the 60 call options. The percentage of the speculative premium for each date is as follows:

May	2.8%
August	6.7
November	10.9

Each contract expires at 11:59 p.m. eastern time on the Saturday immediately following the third Friday of the expiration month. For purposes of this problem, assume the May option has 21 days to run, the August option has 112 days, and the November option has 203 days.
a. Compute the percentage speculative premium per day for each of the three dates.
b. From the viewpoint of a call option purchaser, which expiration date appears most attractive (all else being equal)?
c. From the viewpoint of a call option writer, which expiration date appears most attractive (all else being equal)?

Leverage strategy

8. Assume New Tech, Inc., is trading at $48 and its November call option is $2.20. If the stock ends up at $60 and the option at $11, what is the leverage factor?

Naked call options

9. Assume an investor writes a call option for 100 shares at a strike price of 30 for a premium of 5.75. This is a naked option.
a. What would the gain or loss be if the stock closed at 26?
b. What would the break-even point be in terms of the closing price of the stock?

Covered call options

10. Assume you purchase 100 shares of stock at $44 per share and wish to hedge your position by writing a 100-share call option on your holdings. The option has a 40 strike price and a premium of 8.50. If the stock is selling at 38 at the time of expiration, what will be the overall dollar gain or loss on this covered option play? (Consider the change in stock value as well as the gain or loss on the option.) Note that the stock does not pay a cash dividend.

Covered call options

11. In problem 10, what would be the overall gain or loss if the stock ended up at
    a. $41
    b. $25
    c. $57
    d. $70
    [Disregard the stock being called away in parts *a, c,* and *d.* Assume you will repurchase the options.]

Commission considerations

12. Though commissions are not explicitly considered in problems 9 through 11, might they be significant?

Put options

13. Assume a 40 July put option is purchased for 6.50 on a stock selling at $35 per share. If the stock ends up on expiration at 38.75, what will be the value of the put option?

Protecting a short position with options

14. Assume you sell 100 shares of Bowie Corporation short at $72. You also buy a 70 call option for 5.25 to protect against the stock price going up.
    a. If the stock ends up at $90, what will be your overall gain or loss?
    b. If the stock ends up at $50, what will be your overall gain or loss?
    c. If you have an unprotected short sale position (no call option), what is the most you could lose?

Protecting a short position with options

15. Assume you sell 100 shares of Alston Corporation short at $43. You also buy a 40 call option for $4.80 to protect against the stock price going up.
    a. If the stock ends up at $60, what will be your overall gain or loss?
    b. If the stock ends up at $20, what will be your overall gain or loss?
    c. What is the most you can lose under this short sale–call option plan?
    d. If you have an unprotected short sale position (no call option), what is the most you could lose?
    e. Under the conditions described in part *d,* if you had a limit order to buy the stock and close out the position at $54, what is the most you could lose?

INVESTMENT ADVISOR PROBLEM

Allison Hughes had seen her 1,000 shares in Southern Energy Company go from $24 to $32 per share since she bought them in February 2010. The stock also paid a $1 per share dividend. In mid-December 2010 she faced a dilemma. She strongly believed that Southern Energy would be denied a rate increase by the state of Georgia in January 2011, and that the stock would decline by 10–20 percent in value. Allison had a master's degree in public administration from the University of Georgia and was quite astute in following regulatory actions.

She also knew there could be undesirable tax consequences from selling immediately (December 2010). She called her investment advisor, Hal James, a financial consultant with Merrill Lynch, to get his suggestions.

Hal made it quite clear that there would be undesirable tax consequences from selling in December 2010. Not only would she have to claim the $8 gain on her 1,000 shares on her 2010 tax return, but she would not qualify for preferential tax treatment for long-term capital gains, which requires a one-year holding period and she had only owned the stock since February 2010. Thus, she would be exposed to a maximum short-term capital gains rate of 35 percent instead of a maximum long-term rate of 15 percent.

He suggested that Allison look at two different option strategies that would protect her against a decline in stock value if she continued to hold the shares for up to 12 months.

What might these two different option strategies be?

www.mhhe.com/hirtblock10e

WEB EXERCISE

This exercise will give you an opportunity to view online data on options. Go to **www.cboe.com**.

1. Complete the steps below for the following three stocks, one at a time:
   MSFT (Microsoft)
   CSCO (Cisco)
   IBM (IBM)
2. Put your cursor on "QUOTES & DATA" and click on "Delayed Quotes."
3. Then click on "Enter Symbol" and enter the ticker symbol. Write down the "Last" sale price.
4. Then click on "Options Chain" and scoll down and record the "Strike Price" and the "Last Trade" value.
5. Is each option either in-the-money or out-of-the-money?
6. Compute the intrinsic value and speculative premium for each option.

Note: From time to time, companies redesign their Web sites, and occasionally a topic we have listed may have been deleted, updated, or moved into a different location.

APPENDIX 14A

THE BLACK-SCHOLES OPTION PRICING MODEL*

Theory

In 1973, Fischer Black and Myron Scholes published their derivation of a theoretical option pricing model. They started with three securities: riskless bonds, shares of common stock, and call options. The shares of common stock and call options were combined to form a riskless hedge that, by definition, had to duplicate the return of a discount bond with the same maturity length as the option. Using the riskless-hedge concept as a basis, Black and Scholes then proceeded with their model derivation.

Black and Scholes made the following assumptions:

1. Markets are frictionless. This means there are no taxes or transactions costs; all securities are infinitely divisible; all market participants may borrow and lend at the known and constant riskless rate of interest; there are no penalties for short selling.
2. Stock prices are lognormally distributed, with a constant variance for the underlying returns.
3. The stock neither pays dividends nor makes any other distributions.
4. The option may be exercised only at maturity.

Given the above assumptions and the riskless hedging strategy, Black and Scholes derived a call option pricing model that may be expressed as:

$$c = (S)[N(d_1)] - (X)(e^{-rt})[N(d_2)] \qquad \textbf{(14A–1)}$$

where:

$$d_1 = \frac{\ln(S/X) + [r + (\sigma^2/2)](T)}{(\sigma)(\sqrt{T})} \qquad \textbf{(14A–2)}$$

$$d_2 = d_1 - (\sigma)/(\sqrt{T}) \qquad \textbf{(14A–3)}$$

* This appendix was developed by Professor Carl Luft of DePaul University in consultation with the authors.

The terms are defined as follows:

c	=	Price of the call option
S	=	Prevailing market price of a share of common stock on the date the call option is written
X	=	Call option's striking price (exercise price)
r	=	Annualized prevailing short-term riskless rate of interest
T	=	Length of the option's life expressed in annual terms
σ^2	=	Annualized variance associated with the underlying security's price changes
$N(\cdot)$	=	Cumulative normal density function

At maturity ($T = 0$) the call option must sell for either its intrinsic value or zero, whichever is greater. This boundary condition may be expressed mathematically as:

$$c = \text{Max}(0, S - X) \quad \textbf{(14A–4)}$$

It can be shown that given a put option and a call option, with the same striking price, and one share of the underlying stock, one can form a portfolio that will earn an amount equal to the option's striking price no matter what value the stock takes at expiration. From this relationship, the value of a put option can be determined mathematically as:

$$p = (X)(e^{-rt}) - S + c \quad \textbf{(14A–5)}$$

with the boundary condition,

$$p = \text{Max}(0, X - S) \quad \textbf{(14A–6)}$$

Formula 14A–5 is known as the put-call parity relationship, and Formula 14A–6 shows that at maturity the put must sell for either its intrinsic value or zero.

Inspection of Formulas 14A–1 through 14A–6 reveals that both the call and put option prices are a function of only five variables: S, the underlying stock's market price; X, the striking price; T, the length of the option's life; σ^2, the volatility of the stock price changes; and r, the riskless rate of interest. All of these variables are easily observed or estimated. Previously developed option pricing models relied on variables that were based on individual investor risk preferences or on expected values of the stock price. Since the Black-Scholes model does not rely on such variables, it is superior to prior models.

To understand the behavior of options, it is necessary to examine the relationship of the option price to each of the five inputs. For call options, the price is positively related to the stock's price, the riskless rate of interest, the volatility, and the time to maturity; whereas an inverse relationship exists between the call option price and the striking price. Put options exhibit positive relationships with the striking price and volatility, negative relationships with the underlying stock price and riskless rate, and either a positive or negative relationship with time.

These relationships are easy to grasp if one realizes that options will not be exercised unless they have an intrinsic value. Consider first the price of the underlying stock. As it increases, calls go in the money and gain intrinsic value while puts fall out of the money and lose intrinsic value. If the stock price declines, then the reverse is true. This explains the positive relationship between the call price and the stock price and the inverse relationship between the put price and the stock price. Higher striking prices cause lower intrinsic values for call options but result in greater intrinsic values for put options. In this case, the loss of intrinsic value causes the inverse relationship between the call option and striking price, while the gain in intrinsic value causes the positive relationship between the put price and the striking price. The positive relationship of both put and call prices to the volatility can be explained by the fact that options written on higher volatility stocks have a relatively better chance of being in-the-money at expiration than do options written on lower volatility stocks. The positive relationship of the call price to the risk-free rate reflects the fact that the intrinsic value increases because the present value of the exercise price decreases as the risk-free rate rises. For put options, such rate increases and declining present values of exercise prices cause a loss of intrinsic value and account for the inverse relationship between the put option price and risk-free rate. Finally, the positive relationship of the call price to time is caused by an increasing intrinsic value due to lower present values of the exercise price for longer time periods. A more complex relationship exists for put options.

Intuitively, one might expect a strictly positive relationship between the put option price and time. Such a relationship will occur if the put is at-the-money or out-of-the-money, while a negative relationship can exist for deep in-the-money puts. The reason for this inverse relationship lies embedded in the stock's price behavior. Since stock prices cannot be less than zero, the put option has a maximum value that equals the strike price. Investors who own deep in-the-money put options that are close to their maximum value because of extremely low stock prices are prohibited from exercising these options by assumption 4. Thus, time is working against these investors since they run the risk of losing intrinsic value if the stock price rises before expiration.

After deriving the model, Black and Scholes subjected it to empirical testing. They implemented the riskless-hedging strategy by combining options and stock in proportions dictated by the model and comparing these hedged returns to observed Treasury bill returns. They hypothesized that if the model provided equilibrium, or fair option prices, then the hedged returns should equal the returns generated by the investment in riskless securities. In effect, they attempted to create a synthetic Treasury bill by combining options and stock. If the returns from the option-stock hedge were not equal to the Treasury bill return, it meant the model was unable to provide equilibrium option prices. On the other hand, if there was no significant difference between the hedge and Treasury bill returns, then it could be concluded that the model provided equilibrium prices. The results of the Black-Scholes empirical test showed no significant difference between the option-stock hedged returns and the Treasury bill returns. Thus, Black and Scholes concluded the model did provide equilibrium prices.

The theoretical derivation and empirical justification of an option pricing model by Black and Scholes was an extremely important accomplishment with far-reaching implications. Basically, it meant that model-generated prices could be considered as the equilibrium, or correct, prices. Thus, an investor could use the model to determine whether the market had mispriced an option. Mispriced options spawn arbitrage opportunities. Given such an opportunity, the most obvious way to benefit is to form a riskless hedge by combining options and stock and then maintaining the hedge until the option's market price adjusts to the equilibrium model price. This strategy will provide arbitrage profits since the level of risk that is being assumed equals that of a Treasury bill, but the profits earned when the mispriced option adjusts to the equilibrium, or model price, will exceed the profits earned from investing in a Treasury bill.

Application

The data in Table 14A–1 illustrate the mechanics of the Black-Scholes option pricing model.

Column 1 simply denotes the stock's ticker symbol, while Columns 2 through 7 provide the required inputs for the model. Notice that the option maturity is

TABLE 14A-1 Illustrative Data for Black-Scholes Option Model

(1) Stock Symbol	(2) (*S*) Stock Price	(3) (*X*) Strike Price	(4) (*T*) Days to Maturity Dividend by Days in Year	(5) (*r*) Risk-Free Rate	(6) (σ) Standard Deviation of Returns	(7) (σ^2) Variance of Stock Returns
CFL	33	35	180/365	0.09	0.20	0.0400
GAH	42	40	50/365	0.10	0.23	0.0529

expressed in calendar days and the volatility is given as the standard deviation of returns. The call and put option prices (for both stocks) implied by the data will not be computed.

When the values from Table 14A–1 for CFL stock are used in Formulas 14A–2 and 14A–3, we obtain the following answers for d_1 and d_2.

$$
\begin{aligned}
d_1 &= \frac{\ln(33/35) + [0.09 + (0.04/2)][(0.4932)]}{(0.2)\,(\sqrt{0.4932})} \\
&= \frac{-0.0588 + 0.0543}{0.1405} \\
&= -0.032 \\
d_2 &= -0.032 - 0.1405 \\
&= -0.1725
\end{aligned}
$$

To obtain values for $N(d_1)$ and $N(d_2)$, the Standard Normal Distribution Function Table (Table 14A–2) on the next page must be used. The $N(d_1)$ and $N(d_2)$ values are found by first locating the row and column entries in the table that correspond to the computed d_1 and d_2 values. For CFL stock, the row entry is −0.0, and the column entry is 3. This value of −0.03 approximates the computed d_1 value of −0.032. For d_2, the row entry is −0.1, and the column entry is 7, yielding a value of −0.17, approximating the computed value of −0.1725 for d_2.

Locating the d_1 and d_2 values yield the table entries that define the values of $N(d_1)$ and $N(d_2)$. For CFL stock, the $N(d_1)$ value is 0.4880, while the $N(d_2)$ value is 0.4325. In this example, these values are only approximations, since −0.03 and −0.17 are approximations. If one desires more precise $N(d_1)$ and $N(d_2)$ values, they can be obtained through interpolation. For these examples, the approximations are sufficient.

At this point, all the necessary values for computing the option price have been found. Determining the options' prices via Formulas 14A–1 and 14A–5 is all that remains to be done. Thus, the CFL call option price is:

$$
\begin{aligned}
c &= (33)(0.4880) - (35)[e^{-(0.09)(0.4932)}](0.4325) \\
&= 16.1040 - (35)(0.9566)(0.4325) \\
&= 16.1040 - 14.4805 \\
&= 1.6235
\end{aligned}
$$

and the CFL put option price is:

$$
\begin{aligned}
p &= (35)\,[e^{-(0.09)(0.4932)}] - 33 + 1.6235 \\
&= (35)(0.9566) - 33 + 1.6235 \\
&= 2.1045
\end{aligned}
$$

Since each option controls 100 shares of stock, the theoretical call price is \$162.35, while the put's theoretical price is \$210.45.

www.mhhe.com/hirtblock10e

TABLE 14A-2 Standard Normal Distribution Function

t	0	1	2	3	4	5	6	7	8	9
−3.0	.0013									
−2.9	.0019	.0018	.0017	.0017	.0016	.0016	.0015	.0015	.0014	.0014
−2.8	.0026	.0025	.0024	.0023	.0023	.0022	.0021	.0021	.0020	.0019
−2.7	.0035	.0034	.0033	.0032	.0031	.0030	.0029	.0028	.0027	.0026
−2.6	.0047	.0045	.0044	.0043	.0041	.0040	.0039	.0038	.0037	.0036
−2.5	.0062	.0060	.0059	.0057	.0055	.0054	.0052	.0051	.0049	.0048
−2.4	.0082	.0080	.0078	.0075	.0073	.0071	.0069	.0068	.0066	.0064
−2.3	.0107	.0104	.0102	.0099	.0096	.0094	.0091	.0089	.0087	.0084
−2.2	.0139	.0136	.0132	.0129	.0125	.0122	.0119	.0116	.0113	.0110
−2.1	.0179	.0174	.0170	.0166	.0162	.0158	.0154	.0150	.0146	.0143
−2.0	.0227	.0222	.0217	.0212	.0207	.0202	.0197	.0192	.0188	.0183
−1.9	.0287	.0281	.0274	.0268	.0262	.0256	.0250	.0244	.0239	.0233
−1.8	.0359	.0351	.0344	.0336	.0329	.0322	.0314	.0307	.0300	.0294
−1.7	.0446	.0436	.0427	.0418	.0409	.0401	.0392	.0384	.0375	.0367
−1.6	.0548	.0537	.0526	.0516	.0505	.0495	.0485	.0475	.0465	.0455
−1.5	.0668	.0655	.0643	.0630	.0618	.0606	.0594	.0582	.0571	.0559
−1.4	.0808	.0793	.0778	.0764	.0749	.0735	.0721	.0708	.0694	.0681
−1.3	.0968	.0951	.0934	.0918	.0901	.0885	.0869	.0853	.0838	.0823
−1.2	.1151	.1131	.1112	.1093	.1075	.1056	.1038	.1020	.1003	.0985
−1.1	.1357	.1335	.1314	.1292	.1271	.1251	.1230	.1210	.1190	.1170
−1.0	.1587	.1562	.1539	.1515	.1492	.1469	.1446	.1423	.1401	.1379
−0.9	.1841	.1814	.1788	.1762	.1736	.1711	.1685	.1660	.1635	.1611
−0.8	.2119	.2090	.2061	.2033	.2005	.1977	.1949	.1921	.1894	.1867
−0.7	.2420	.2389	.2358	.2326	.2297	.2266	.2236	.2206	.2177	.2148
−0.6	.2743	.2709	.2676	.2643	.2611	.2578	.2546	.2514	.2483	.2451
−0.5	.3085	.3050	.3015	.2981	.2946	.2912	.2877	.2843	.2810	.2776
−0.4	.3446	.3409	.3372	.3336	.3300	.3264	.3228	.3192	.3156	.3121
−0.3	.3821	.3783	.3745	.3707	.3669	.3632	.3594	.3557	.3520	.3483
−0.2	.4207	.4168	.4129	.4090	.4052	.4013	.3974	.3936	.3897	.3859
−0.1	.4602	.4562	.4522	.4483	.4443	.4404	.4364	.4325	.4286	.4247
−0.0	.5000	.4960	.4920	.4880	.4840	.4801	.4761	.4721	.4681	.4641

(continued)

A second example (using GAH stock) again uses the variables from Table 14A–1 and substitutes them into Formulas 14A–2 and 14A–3 to derive d_1 and d_2 as follows:

$$d_1 = \frac{\ln(42/40) + [0.10 + (0.0529/2)](0.1370)}{(0.23)(\sqrt{0.1370})}$$

$$= \frac{0.0488 + 0.0173}{0.0851}$$

$$= 0.7767$$

$$d_2 = 0.7767 - 0.0851$$

$$= 0.6916$$

The $N(d_1)$ and $N(d_2)$ values from the standard normal distribution table (Table 14A–2) are 0.7823 and 0.7549, respectively. As mentioned in the previous example, greater precision is possible through interpolation.

TABLE 14A-2 Standard Normal Distribution Function (*concluded*)

t	0	1	2	3	4	5	6	7	8	9
0.0	.5000	.5040	.5080	.5120	.5160	.5199	.5239	.5279	.5319	.5359
0.1	.5398	.5438	.5478	.5517	.5557	.5596	.5636	.5675	.5714	.5753
0.2	.5793	.5832	.5871	.5910	.5948	.5987	.6026	.6064	.6103	.6141
0.3	.6179	.6217	.6255	.6293	.6331	.6368	.6406	.6443	.6480	.6517
0.4	.6554	.6591	.6628	.6664	.6700	.6736	.6772	.6808	.6844	.6879
0.5	.6915	.6950	.6985	.7019	.7054	.7088	.7123	.7157	.7190	.7224
0.6	.7257	.7291	.7324	.7357	.7389	.7422	.7454	.7486	.7517	.7549
0.7	.7580	.7611	.7642	.7673	.7704	.7734	.7764	.7794	.7823	.7852
0.8	.7881	.7910	.7939	.7967	.7995	.8023	.8051	.8079	.8106	.8133
0.9	.8159	.8186	.8212	.8238	.8264	.8289	.8315	.8340	.8365	.8189
1.0	.8413	.8438	.8461	.8485	.8508	.8531	.8554	.8577	.8599	.8621
1.1	.8643	.8665	.8686	.8708	.8729	.8749	.8770	.8790	.8810	.8830
1.2	.8849	.8869	.8888	.8907	.8925	.8944	.8962	.8980	.8997	.9015
1.3	.9032	.9049	.9066	.9082	.9099	.9115	.9131	.9147	.9162	.9177
1.4	.9192	.9207	.9222	.9236	.9251	.9265	.9279	.9292	.9306	.9319
1.5	.9332	.9345	.9357	.9370	.9382	.9394	.9406	.9418	.9429	.9441
1.6	.9452	.9463	.9474	.9484	.9495	.9505	.9515	.9525	.9535	.9545
1.7	.9554	.9564	.9573	.9582	.9591	.9599	.9608	.9616	.9625	.9633
1.8	.9641	.9649	.9656	.9664	.9671	.9678	.9686	.9693	.9700	.9706
1.9	.9713	.9719	.9726	.9732	.9738	.9744	.9750	.9756	.9761	.9767
2.0	.9773	.9778	.9783	.9788	.9793	.9798	.9803	.9808	.9812	.9817
2.1	.9821	.9826	.9830	.9834	.9838	.9842	.9846	.9850	.9854	.9857
2.2	.9861	.9864	.9868	.9871	.9875	.9878	.9881	.9884	.9887	.9890
2.3	.9893	.9896	.9898	.9901	.9904	.9906	.9909	.9911	.9913	.9916
2.4	.9918	.9920	.9922	.9925	.9927	.9929	.9931	.9932	.9934	.9936
2.5	.9938	.9940	.9941	.9943	.9945	.9946	.9948	.9949	.9951	.9952
2.6	.9953	.9955	.9956	.9957	.9959	.9960	.9961	.9962	.9963	.9964
2.7	.9965	.9966	.9967	.9968	.9969	.9970	.9971	.9972	.9973	.9974
2.8	.9974	.9975	.9976	.9977	.9977	.9978	.9979	.9979	.9980	.9981
2.9	.9981	.9982	.9982	.9983	.9984	.9984	.9985	.9985	.9986	.9986
3.0	.9987									

Given the above values, the GAH call and put prices are computed as:

$$
\begin{aligned}
c &= (42)(0.7823) - (40)[e^{-(0.10)(0.1370)}](0.7549) \\
&= 32.8566 - (40)(0.9864)(0.7549) \\
&= 32.8566 - 29.7853 \\
&= 3.0713 \\
p &= (40)[e^{-(0.10)(0.1370)}] - 42 + 3.0713 \\
&= (40)(0.9864) - 42 + 3.0713 \\
&= 0.5273
\end{aligned}
$$

These calculations indicate the theoretically correct price (for 100 shares) for the call is $307.13 and that $52.73 is the theoretically correct price for the put.

Suppose the market had priced the GAH call at $262.50. How would you be able to earn arbitrage profits? According to Black and Scholes, you would buy the undervalued calls at $262.50 and sell shares of GAH stock at $42 per share to form a riskless hedge and thus obtain arbitrage profits when equilibrium is established.

However, to implement such a strategy, an investor must know how many shares to combine with each option to form the riskless hedge. This information is provided by $N(d_1)$ and is known as the hedge ratio or delta.

Since each option controls 100 shares of stock, the appropriate arbitrage activity in this example is to sell 0.7823 shares of GAH stock for every option purchased. Practically speaking, one cannot buy and sell fractional shares. Thus, 78 shares should be sold for each option that is purchased. If the market had overpriced the option, then the arbitrageur would sell options and purchase 78 shares for each option sold. In either case, the hedge's risk level will equal that of a Treasury bill, but the hedge's returns will exceed the Treasury bill's return, thus generating arbitrage profits.

APPENDIX 14B

THE USE OF OPTION SPREADS AND STRADDLES

We will look at two primary types of option spreads: vertical spreads and horizontal spreads. Vertical spreads involve buying and writing two contracts at different striking prices with the same month of expiration. Horizontal spreads consist of buying and writing two options with the same strike price but different months, and a diagonal spread is a combination of the vertical and horizontal spreads. Table 14B–1 presents an example of XYZ Corporation demonstrating the options, months, and strike prices involved in each type of spread. There are more complicated spreads than these, such as the butterfly spread, variable spread, and domino spread. We cannot attempt to explain all of these spreads in the space available, so we will concentrate on vertical bull spreads and vertical bear spreads.

Because spreads require the purchase of one option and the sale of another option, a speculator's account will have either a debit or credit balance. If the cost of the long option position is greater than the revenue from the short option position, the speculator has a net cash outflow and a debit in his account. When your spread is put on with a debit, it is said you have "bought the spread." You have "sold the spread" if the receipt from writing the short option position is greater than the cost of buying the long option position and you have a credit balance. For example, the difference between the option prices for a vertical spread on XYZ

TABLE 14B-1 Spreads (Call Options)

VERTICAL SPREAD			OPTION PRICES		
	Market Price	Strike Price	(October)	January	April
XYZ	36⅜	(35)	(4)	6	6½
	36⅜	(40)	(2)	3⅜	4
	36⅜	45	11/16	1½	6
HORIZONTAL SPREAD					
	Market Price	Strike Price	October	(January)	(April)
XYZ	36⅜	(35)	4	(6)	(6½)
	36⅜	40	2	3⅜	4
	36⅜	45	11/16	1½	6
DIAGONAL SPREAD					
	Market Price	Strike Price	(October)	January	(April)
XYZ	36⅜	(35)	(4)	6	6½
	36⅜	(40)	2	3⅜	(4)
	36⅜	45	11/16	1½	6

Corporation in Table 14B–1 with October strike prices of 35 and 40 is $2 ($4 − $2). The $2 difference between these two option prices could be either a debit or credit, depending on whether a bull or bear spread is used. In either case, the profit or loss from a spread position results in the change between the two option prices over time as the price of the underlying stock goes up or down.

Vertical Bull Spread

In a bull spread, the expectation is that the common stock price will rise. The speculator can buy the common stock outright, or if he wants to profit from an expected price increase but reduce his risk of loss, he can enter into a bull spread. Vertical bull spreads limit both the maximum gain and maximum loss available. They are usually debit positions because the spreader buys the higher-priced, in-the-money option and shorts (writes) an inexpensive, out-of-the-money option. Using Table 14B–1 for an XYZ October vertical bull spread, we would buy the October 35 at 4 and sell the October 40 at 2 for a debit of 2 (price spread). This represents a $200 investment. Assume that three weeks later, XYZ stock rises from 36⅜ to 42 with the October 35 selling at 7½ (previously purchased at 4) and the October 40 at 4½ (previously sold at 2). Table 14B–2 shows the result of closing out the spread.

Because the investment was only $200, the total return of $100 provided a 50 percent return. However, returns on spreads can be greatly altered by commissions. If the following spread incurred commissions of $25 in and $25 out, the percentage return could be cut in half to 25 percent.

The maximum profit at expiration is equal to the difference in strike prices ($5 in this case) minus the initial price spread ($2 in this case). For the XYZ vertical bull spread, the maximum profit is $300, and the maximum loss is the original debit of $200. At expiration, all speculative premiums are gone, and each option sells at its intrinsic value. Table 14B–3 shows maximum profit and loss at various closing market prices at expiration. Remember, our initial investment is $200.

TABLE 14B-2 Profit on Vertical Bull Spread

XYZ October 35		XYZ October 40		Price Spread
Bought at	4	Sold at	2	2
Sold at	7½	Bought at	4½	3
Gain	3½	(Loss)	(2½)	1
		Net gain	$100	
		Investment	$200	
		Return	50%	

TABLE 14B-3 XYZ Vertical Bull Spread

XYZ STOCK PRICE AT EXPIRATION 35				XYZ STOCK PRICE AT EXPIRATION 40				XYZ STOCK PRICE AT EXPIRATION 45			
October 35		October 40		October 35		October 40		October 35		October 40	
Bought at	4	Sold at	2	Bought at	4	Sold at	2	Bought at	4	Sold at	2
Expired at[a]	0	Expired at[a]	0	Sold at[a]	5	Expired at[a]	0	Sold at[a]	10	Bought at[a]	5
(Loss)	(4)	Gain	2	Gain	1	Gain	2	Gain	6	Loss	(3)
(Net loss) (2)				Net gain 3				Net gain 3			
($200) = 100 percent loss				$300 = 150 percent gain				$300 = 150 percent gain			

[a] All call options on date of expiration equal their intrinsic value.

FIGURE 14B-1 Profit and Loss Relationships on Spreads and Calls

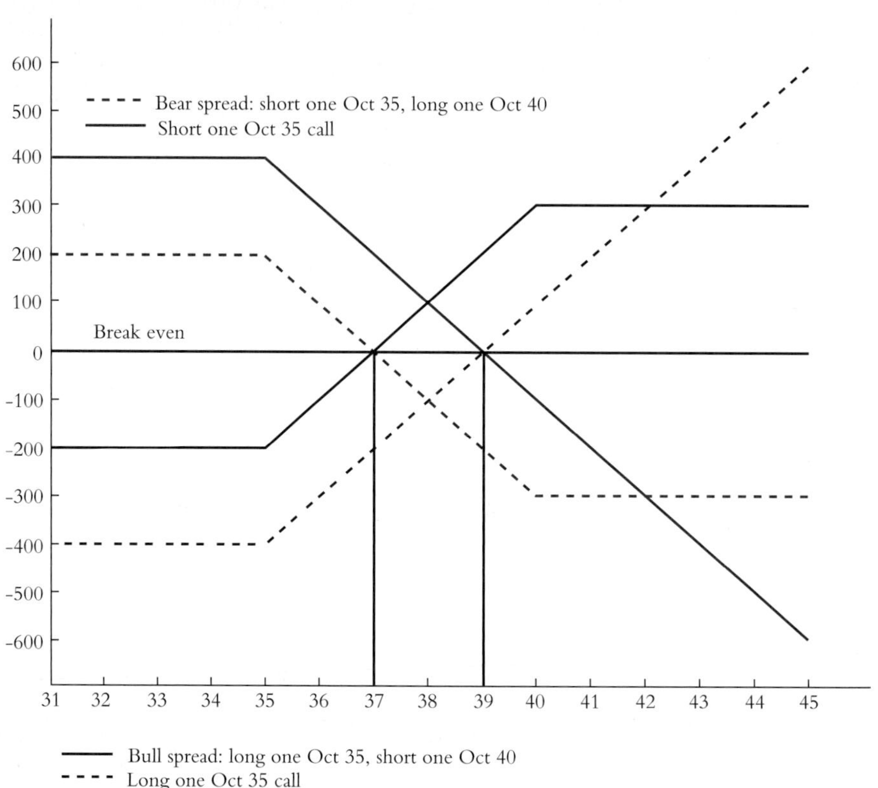

As Table 14B–3 indicates, profit does not increase after the stock moves through the 40 price range. Every dollar of increased profit on the long position is offset by $1 of loss on the short position after the stock passes a price of 40. One of the important but difficult aspects of spreading is forecasting a range of prices rather than just the direction prices will move. If a speculator is bullish, he or she may buy a call instead of spreading. The potential loss is higher with the call but still limited, while the possible gain is unlimited. The relationship between long calls and bull spreads starts in the *bottom* of Figure 14B–1. Note the maximum loss with the bull spread is $200 and $400 with a long call. The break-even point is also $2 less for the bull spread ($37 versus $39). However, the long call has unlimited profit potential, and the bull spread is locked in at $300 at a stock price of $40 or higher. The spread position lowers the break-even point by $2 per share but also limits potential returns—a classic case of risk-return trade-off.

Vertical Bear Spread

The speculator enters a bear spread anticipating a decline in stock prices. Instead of selling short or writing a call with both having unlimited risk, he spreads by selling short the call with the lower strike price (highest premium) and covers the upside risk with the purchase of a call having a higher strike price. This creates a credit balance. In a sense, the bear spread does the opposite of the vertical bull spread as seen in Table 14B–4 in which we show profits and losses from the strategy if XYZ ends up at 35 or at 40. With a bear spread, the price spread of 2 is the

TABLE 14B-4 XYZ Vertical Bear Spread

XYZ STOCK PRICE AT EXPIRATION 35				XYZ STOCK PRICE AT EXPIRATION 40			
October 35		**October 40**		**October 35**		**October 40**	
Sold at	4	Bought at	2	Sold at	4	Bought at	2
Expired at	0	Expired at	0	Bought at	5	Expired at	0
Gain	4	(Loss)	(2)	(Loss)	1	(Loss)	2
		Net gain 2 $200				Net loss (3) $(300)	

maximum gain if the stock closes at 35 or less at expiration, while the maximum loss equals 3, the difference between the exercise prices minus the price spread. The relationship between bear spreads and writing a call option is also demonstrated in Figure 14B–1 (the comparison starts at the *top* of the figure).

chapter fifteen

COMMODITIES AND FINANCIAL FUTURES

OBJECTIVES

1. Explain how commodities and financial futures can be used for speculation or for hedging.
2. Describe the different types of commodities and financial futures contracts that are available.
3. Explain how margin is used in the futures markets to magnify gains (or losses).
4. Explain the difference between the cash and the futures markets.
5. Describe how currency futures and interest rate futures are currently utilized in a business environment.
6. Explain the role of interest rate swaps as an alternative to futures.

OUTLINE

What do pork bellies, soybeans, Japanese yen, and Treasury bills have in common? They are all items on which contracts may be traded in the commodities and financial futures markets. While numerous examples are given in this chapter of the use of futures contracts by people who are in the commodities business (farmers, millers, etc.), keep in mind that commodities and futures contracts can be used by others as well. In early 2007, the euro was appreciating in value against the U.S. dollar. By betting for or against this trend continuing, you could make or lose a lot of money. By May 2010 the euro bottomed out at $1.19 per euro, and by November 4, 2010, it had reached $1.42. Hopefully investors playing these trends in the futures markets guessed right. The same could be said about betting for or against the continued increase in copper prices, which went from $2 per pound in November 2005 to $4 in 2008, down to less than $1.40 in January 2009, only to bounce back up to $4.19 in April of 2011.

A **futures contract** is an agreement that provides for the delivery of a specific amount of a commodity at a designated time in the future at a given price. An example might be a contract to deliver 5,000 bushels of corn next September at $2.40 per bushel. The person who sells the contract does not need to have actual possession of the corn, nor does the purchaser of the contract need to plan on taking possession of the corn. Almost all commodities futures contracts are closed out or reversed before the actual transaction is to occur. Thus, the seller of a futures contract for the delivery of 5,000 bushels of corn may simply later buy back a similar contract for the purchase of 5,000 bushels and close out his position. The initial buyer also reverses his position. More than 99 percent of all contracts are closed out in this fashion rather than through actual delivery. The commodities futures market is similar to the options market in that there is a tremendous volume of activity, but very few actual items ever change hands.

The futures markets were originally set up to allow grain and livestock producers and processors to **hedge** (protect) their positions in a given commodity. For example, a wheat producer might have a five-month lead time between the planting of his crop and the actual harvesting and delivery to the market. While the current price of wheat might be $5.50 a bushel, there is a tremendous risk that the price might change before delivery to the market. The wheat farmer can hedge his position by offering to sell futures contracts for the delivery of wheat. Even though he will probably close out or reverse these futures contracts before the call for actual delivery, he will still have effectively hedged his position. Let's see how this works. If the price of wheat goes down, he will have to sell his crop for less than he anticipated when he planted the wheat, but he will make up the difference on the wheat futures contracts. That is, he will be able to buy back the contracts for less than he sold them for. Of course, if the price of the wheat goes up, the extra profit he makes on the crop will be lost on the futures contracts as he now has to buy back the contracts at a higher price.[1]

A miller who uses wheat as part of his processing faces the opposite dilemma in terms of pricing. The miller is afraid the price of wheat might go up and ultimately cut into his profit margin when he takes actual delivery of his product. He can hedge his position by buying futures contracts in wheat. If the actual price of wheat does go up, the extra cost of producing his product will be offset by the profits he makes on his futures contracts.

The commodities market allows the many parties in need of hedging opportunities to acquire contracts. Although some of this could be accomplished on a private basis (one party in Kansas City calls another party in Chicago on the advice of his banker), this would be virtually impossible to handle on a large-scale basis. Liquid, fluid markets such as those provided by the commodity exchanges are necessary to accomplish this function.

While the hedgers are the backbone and basic reason for the existence of commodity exchanges, they are not the only significant participants. We also have the speculators who take purely long or short positions without any intent to hedge actual ownership. Thus, there is the speculator in wheat or silver who believes that the next major price move can be predicted to such an extent that a substantial profit can be made. Because commodities are purchased on the basis of a small investment in the form of margin (usually running 2 to 10 percent of the value of the contract), there is substantial leverage on the investment, and percentage returns and losses are greatly magnified. The typical commodities trader often suffers many losses with the anticipation of a few very substantial gains. Commodities speculation, as opposed to hedging, represents somewhat of a gamble, and stories have been told of reformed commodities speculators who gave up the chase to spend the rest of their days merely playing the slot machines. Nevertheless, commodity speculators are quite important to the liquidity of the market.

[1] The hedger not only reduces risk of loss but also eliminates additional profit opportunities. This may be appropriate for farmers since they are not in the risk-taking business but rather in agriculture.

the real world of investing

CAN DERIVATIVES BE DANGEROUS?

Derivatives such as futures, options, swaps, caps, floors, and collars keep making headlines. While derivatives are basically neutral instruments, their misuse or overindulgence by investors may not be. Not only are derivatives growing into a multitrillion dollar market, but they are spreading worldwide. Congressional committees and governmental organizations such as the Federal Reserve and U.S. Treasury Department are calling for increased regulation.

Why? The answer may be that many derivatives intended for use in a neutral or defensive way are being utilized in a speculative, highly risky fashion. One can compare the misuse of a derivative with driving an automobile in an irresponsible manner. Although the automobile is basically sound, if it is driven at 95 miles per hour in a rainstorm down a steep hill, it can indeed be a danger to society.

Corporate treasurers at such firms as Procter & Gamble (**www.pg.com**) and Bank One Corporation (**www.bankone.com**) found themselves behind the "eight ball" when they went from using derivatives to protect against interest rate exposure to attempting to generate huge profits from guessing the next move in interest rates. They had unprotected, exposed positions that became very costly when they guessed wrong.

Another example of derivatives causing great harm was the financial crisis of 2007–2009. It is well known by now that the subprime mortgage market made loans to high-risk individuals on the assumption that housing prices would continue to rise. These mortgages were packaged up into marketable mortgage-backed securities (MBSs), which in turn led to complicated collateralized debt obligations (CDOs). These marketable securities were then insured by credit default swaps (CDSs), which were derivative products. When housing prices fell and the collateral behind these mortgage-backed securities evaporated, the insurance provided by the credit default swaps was not sufficient to prevent a market collapse. This story could take up a whole chapter, but the point we make is that derivatives have to be used very carefully in a regulated environment.

Because derivatives can be used in a highly sophisticated fashion, derivatives trading is not easily understood by many corporate auditors. The derivatives trader may take positions that move in five directions on financial markets throughout the world, which the auditor may not have the expertise to follow and analyze. For that reason, it is particularly important that the board of directors and top management of a corporation have clearly stated policies and boundaries on the trading of derivatives. They also must implement adequate monitoring policies to ensure that their directions are being followed.

TYPES OF COMMODITIES AND EXCHANGES

Commodities and financial futures can be broken down into a number of categories based on their essential characteristics. As indicated in Table 15–1, there are five primary categories. In each case, we show representative items that fall under the category.

The first four categories represent traditional commodities, but category five came into prominence in the 1970s and 1980s—with foreign exchange futures originating in 1972, interest rate futures beginning in 1975, and stock index futures in 1982. Because foreign exchange and interest rate financial futures have tremendous implications for financial managers, we will give them special attention later in this chapter. We will defer discussion of stock index futures to Chapter 16 so that they can be given *complete coverage* as a separate topic.

The commodities listed in Table 15–1 trade on various commodity exchanges in the United States and Canada (see Table 15–2). Although the exchanges are well organized and efficient in their operation, a few still run a small percentage of their trades using the open outcry system, complete with various hand signals for bids and asks. In most cases these exchanges, such as the ICE Exchange, have become totally electronic. The Chicago Mercantile Exchange and Chicago Board of Trade conduct over 80 percent of their trades electronically, and over time their open outcry trading floors will fade away.

www.cbot.com

The largest commodity exchange is the Chicago Board of Trade, now part of the CME Group, which reflects a merger between the Chicago Mercantile Exchange and the Chicago Board of Trade. Although some exchanges, such as the Minneapolis

TABLE 15-1 Categories of Commodities and Financial Futures

(1)	(2)	(3)
Grains and oilseeds:	Livestock and meat:	Food and fiber:
Corn	Cattle—feeder	Cocoa
Oats	Cattle—live	Coffee
Soybeans	Hogs—live	Cotton
Wheat	Pork bellies	Orange juice
Barley	Turkeys	Potatoes
Rye	Broilers	Sugar
	Rice	
	Butter	

(4)	(5)
Metals and petroleum:	Financial futures:
Copper	a. Foreign exchange:
Gold	Euro, yen, peso, etc.
Platinum	b. Interest rate futures:
Silver	Treasury bonds
Mercury	Treasury bills
Heating oil no. 2	Municipal bonds
	Eurodollars
	c. Stock index futures:
	S&P 500
	Value Line
	Dow Jones Industrial Average

TABLE 15-2 Major United States and Canadian Commodity Exchanges

Chicago Board of Trade (CBOT) Part of CME group
Chicago Mercantile Exchange (CME) Part of CME group
Also controls International Monetary Market (IMM)
Commodity Exchange (CMX)
ICE Futures Canada (ICE-C)
ICE Futures U.S. (ICE-US)
Kansas City Board of Trade (KC)
Minneapolis Grain Exchange (MPLS)
New York Coffee, Sugar, and Cocoa Exchange (CSCE)
New York Mercantile Exchange (COMEX)
New York Mercantile Exchange (NYMEX)

Grain Exchange, are highly specialized, most exchanges trade in a number of commodities. For example, the Chicago Board of Trade deals in such diverse products as corn, oats, soybeans, wheat, silver, and Treasury Bonds.

www.cftc.gov

The activities of the commodity exchanges are primarily regulated by the Commodity Futures Trading Commission (CFTC), a federal regulatory agency established by Congress in 1975. The CFTC has had a number of jurisdictional disputes with the SEC over the regulation of financial futures.

Types of Commodities Contracts

The commodity contract lists the type of commodity and the denomination in which it is traded (bushels, pounds, troy ounces, metric tons, percentage points,

TABLE 15-3 Size of Commodity Contracts

Contract	Trading Units	Size of Contract Based on Fall 2010 Prices (in dollars)
Corn	5,000 bushels	$ 26,000
Oats	5,000 bushels	17,600
Wheat	5,000 bushels	36,000
Pork bellies	40,000 pounds	43,400
Coffee	37,500 pounds	67,725
Cotton	50,000 pounds	50,650
Sugar	112,000 pounds	28,500
Copper	25,000 pounds	90,300
Gold	100 troy ounces	140,000
Silver	5,000 troy ounces	125,000
Treasury bonds	$100,000	131,750
Treasury bills	$1,000,000	998,200

etc.). The contract will also specify the standardized unit for trade (5,000 bushels, 30,000 pounds, etc.). A further designation will indicate the month in which the contract ends, with most commodities having a whole range of months from which to choose. Typically, contracts run as long as a year into the future, but some interest rate futures contracts extend as far as three years.

Examples of the sizes of futures contracts are presented in Table 15–3. Be aware that there may be many different forms of the same commodity (such as spring wheat or amber/durum wheat).

ACTUAL COMMODITIES CONTRACT

To examine the potential gain or loss in a commodities contract, let's go through a hypothetical investment. Assume we are considering the purchase of a December wheat contract (it is now May 1). The price on the futures contract is $7.20 per bushel. Since wheat trades in units of 5,000 bushels, the total price is $36,000. As we go through our example, we will examine many important features associated with commodity trading—beginning with margin requirements.

Margin Requirements

Commodity trading is based on the use of margin rather than on actual cash dollars. Margin requirements are typically 2 to 10 percent of the value of the contract and may vary over time or even among exchanges for a given commodity. For our example, we will assume a $2,000 margin requirement on the $36,000 wheat contract.[2] That was the specified margin on the Kansas City Board of Trade on August 5, 2010. The $2,000 would represent 5.56 percent of the value of the contract ($36,000).

Margin requirements on commodities contracts are much lower than those on common stock transactions, where 50 percent of the purchase price has been the requirement since 1974. Furthermore, in the commodities market, the margin payment is merely considered to be a good-faith payment against losses. There is no actual borrowing or interest to be paid.[3]

In addition to the initial margin requirements, **margin maintenance requirements** (minimum maintenance standards) run 60 to 100 percent of the value of the initial margin. In the case of the wheat contract, the margin maintenance requirement

[2] The amount of margin required also differs between speculative and hedging activities. For example, $2,500 represents the margin for speculation. The margin for hedging is $2,000 in this case.

[3] It should also be pointed out that a customer may need a minimum account balance of $5,000 or greater to open a commodity account.

might be $1,400 (70% × $2,000). If our initial margin of $2,000 is reduced by $600 due to losses on our contract, we will be required to replace the $600 to cover our margin position. If we do not, our position will be closed out, and we will take our losses.

The margin requirement, relative to size, is even less for financial futures. For example, on a 13-week $1 million Treasury bill contract, the investor must post only an initial margin of $405 in November 2010. Similar requirements exist for other types of financial futures.

Note that the high risk inherent in a commodities contract is not so much a function of volatile price movements as it is the impact of high leverage made possible by the low initial margin requirements. A 5 percent price move may equal or exceed the size of our initial investment in the form of the margin deposit. This is similar to the type of leverage utilized in the options market as described in Chapter 14. However, the action in the commodities market is much quicker. You can be asked to put up additional margin within hours after you establish your initial position.

Market Conditions

Because the price of every commodity moves in response to market conditions, each investor must determine the key market variables that influence the value of his or her contract. In the case of wheat, the investor may be particularly concerned about such factors as weather and crop conditions in the Midwest, the price of corn as a substitute product, the carryover of wheat supply from the previous year, and potential wheat sales to other countries.

Gains and Losses

application example

In the previous example, assume we guessed right in our analysis of the wheat market; we purchased a December futures contract for $7.20 per bushel, and the price goes to $7.60 per bushel (recall that the contract was for 5,000 bushels). With a $0.40 increase per bushel, we have established a dollar gain of $2,000 (5,000 bushels × $0.40 per bushel profit). With an initial margin requirement of $2,000 we have made a percentage profit of 100 percent, as indicated in the following formula:[4]

$$\frac{\text{Dollar gain}}{\text{Amount of margin deposit}} = \frac{\$2{,}000}{\$2{,}000} \times 100 = 100\%$$

If this transaction occurred over one month, the annualized gain would be 1,200 percent (100% × 12 = 1,200%). Note that all of this was accomplished by a $.040 movement in the price of a December wheat contract from $7.20 to $7.60 per bushel.

Actually, we may choose to close out the contract or attempt to let the profits run. We also may use the profits to establish the basis for margin on additional futures contracts. A paper gain of $2,000 is enough to provide the $2,000 margin on a second wheat contract.

We are now in a position to use an inverse pyramid to expand our position. With two contracts outstanding, a mere $0.20 price change will provide $2,000 in profits:

$0.20	Price change
× 10,000	Bushels (two contracts)
$2,000	Profits (can be applied to third contract)

The new $2,000 in profits can be used to purchase a third contract, and now with 15,000 bushels under control, a $0.1333 price change will generate enough profits for a fourth contract. Of course the pyramid scheme cuts both ways. As you leverage your position with more contracts, increasingly smaller price drops can wipe out your position.

[4] This does not include commissions, which are generally less than $100 for a complete transaction (buy and sell).

Inverse pyramiding begins to sound astounding since eventually a 1¢ or ½¢ change in the price of wheat will trigger enough profits for a new contract. Of course, great risks are associated with such a process. It is like building a house with playing cards. If one tumbles, the whole house comes down. The investor can become so highly leveraged that any slight reversal in price can trigger margin calls. While it is often wise to let profits run and perhaps do some amount of pyramiding, prudence must be exercised.

Our primary attention up to this point has been on contracts that are making money. What are the implications if there is an immediate price reversal after we have purchased our December wheat contract? You will recall there was a margin maintenance requirement of $1,400 based on our initial margin of $2,000. In this case, a $600 loss would call for an additional deposit to bring our margin position up to $2,000. How much would the price of wheat have to decline for us to get this margin call to increase our deposit? With a 5,000-bushel contract, we are talking about a mere decline of $0.12 per bushel:

$$\frac{\$600 \text{ loss}}{5{,}000 \text{ bushels}} = \$0.12 \text{ per bushel}$$

This could happen in a matter of minutes or hours after our initial purchase. When we get the margin call, we can either elect to put up the additional $600 and continue with the contract or tell our commodities broker to close out our contract and take our losses. If we put up the $600, our broker could still be on the phone a few minutes later asking for more margin because the price has shown further deterioration. Because investors often buy multiple contracts, such as 10 December wheat contracts, the process can be all the more intense. In the commodities market, the old adage of "cut your losses short and let your profits run" probably has its greatest significance. Even a seasoned commodities trader might determine that he is willing to lose 80 percent of the time and win only 20 percent of the time, but those victories will represent home runs and the losses mere outs.

Price Movement Limitations

Because of the enormous opportunities for gains and losses in the commodities markets, the commodity exchanges do limit maximum daily price movements in a commodity. Some examples are shown in Table 15–4.

These daily trading limits obviously must affect the efficiency of the market somewhat. If market conditions indicate that the price of wheat should decline by

TABLE 15-4 Maximum Daily Price Changes

Commodity	Exchange[a]	Normal Price Range[b]	Maximum Daily Price Change (from previous close)[c]
Corn	CBOT	$3.00–$6.00	$0.30 per bushel
Oats	CBOT	$1.50–$4.00	0.20 per bushel
Wheat	CBOT	$4.50–$8.50	0.60 per bushel
Pork bellies	CBOT	$0.70–$1.20	0.03 per pound
Copper	CMX	$1.50–$4.50	No limit
Silver	CBOT	$10.00–$30.00	No limit
Treasury bills	IMM of CME	85% of par and up	No limit

[a] CBOT (Chicago Board of Trade), CMX (Commodity Exchange), IMM (International Monetary Market), CME (Chicago Mercantile Exchange).

[b] Normal price ranges refer to the calendar year 2009-2010 trading ranges.

[c] These values may change slightly from exchange to exchange and are often temporarily altered in response to rampant speculation.

$0.70 and the daily limit is $0.60, then obviously the price of wheat is not in equilibrium as it opens the following morning. However, the desire to stop market panics tends to override the desire for total market efficiency in the commodity markets. Nevertheless, the potential intraday trading range is still large. Recall, for example, that a $0.40 change in the price of wheat is enough to place tremendous pressure on the investor to repeatedly increase his margin position. On the typical 5,000-bushel contract, this $0.40 price change would represent a daily loss of $2,000.

READING MARKET QUOTES

We turn our attention to interpreting market quotes in the daily newspaper. Table 15–5 shows an excerpt from the September 14, 2010, edition of *The Wall Street Journal* covering ten different types of contracts (this represents about 30 percent of the contracts reported for that day).

In each case, we see a choice of months for which a contract may be purchased. For example, corn, which trades on the Chicago Board of Trade (CBOT), has futures contracts for March, May, July, September, and December. Some commodities offer a contract for virtually every month. To directly examine some of the terms in the table, we produce a part of the corn contract (CBOT) in Table 15–6.

TABLE 15-5 Examples of Price Quotes on Commodity Futures

Agriculture Futures

	OPEN	HIGH	LOW	SETTLE	CHG	OPEN INT
Corn (CBT)-5,000 bu.; cents per bu.						
Sept	463.25	471.75	462.50	**469.25**	5.25	4,407
Dec	477.25	486.50	476.25	**483.50**	5.25	811,763
Ethanol (CBT)-29,000 gal.; $ per gal.						
Oct	2.000	2.010 ▲	1.999	**2.009**	.039	661
Dec	1.889	1.893	1.876	**1.890**	.026	1,834
Oats (CBT)-5,000 bu.; cents per bu.						
Sept	325.00	326.50 ▲	325.00	**322.00**	5.00	13
Dec	324.50	335.00 ▲	323.50	**333.00**	9.00	9,927
Soybeans (CBT)-5,000 bu.; cents per bu.						
Sept	1021.00	1031.00	1018.75	**1025.25**	1.75	967
Nov	1030.75	1041.00	1022.75	**1034.50**	3.50	306,022
Soybean Meal (CBT)-100 tons; $ per ton.						
Sept	296.70	298.30	293.00	**296.80**	-.40	548
Dec	293.70	296.30	291.00	**293.50**	-.20	128,908
Soybean Oil (CBT)-60,000 lbs.; cents per lb.						
Sept	41.35	41.64	41.35	**41.34**	.09	959
Dec	41.86	42.14	41.60	**41.81**	.05	164,603
Rough Rice (CBT)-2,000 cwt.; cents per cwt.						
Sept	1165.00	1169.00	1163.00	**1165.50**	7.50	39
Nov	1176.50	1194.50	1175.00	**1186.50**	7.50	13,015
Wheat (CBT)-5,000 bu.; cents per bu.						
Sept	705.75	722.00	705.75	**713.75**	9.00	2,165
Dec	738.00	754.50	732.75	**745.00**	8.25	267,539
Wheat (KC)-5,000 bu.; cents per bu.						
Sept	759.00	765.50	754.50	**757.50**	10.25	64
Dec	759.00	777.00	755.50	**769.50**	10.25	106,346
Wheat (MPLS)-5,000 bu.; cents per bu.						
Sept	754.75	755.00	749.50	**755.00**	12.25	36
Dec	756.00	773.25	753.50	**767.50**	10.50	28,646

Source: *The Wall Street Journal*, September 14, 2010, p. C8. Reprinted with permission of *The Wall Street Journal*,

TABLE 15-6 Price Quotes for Corn Contracts

	Open	High	Low	Settle	Change	Open Interest
Corn (CBOT)–5,000 bushels; cents per bushel						
Sept	463.25	471.75	462.50	469.25	5.25	4,407
Dec	477.25	486.50	476.25	483.50	5.25	811,763

Source: *The Wall Street Journal*, September 14, 2010, p. C8. Reprinted with permission of *The Wall Street Journal*,

The first line in the table indicates that we are dealing in corn traded on the CBOT. We then note that corn is traded in 5,000-bushel units and quoted in cents per bushel. Quotations in cents per bushel require some mental adjustment. For example, 200 cents per bushel would actually represent $2 per bushel. We generally move the decimal point two places to the left and read the quote in terms of dollars. For example, the September 2010 opening price was $4.6325 per bushel.

Across the top of the table we observe that we are given information on the open, high, low, settle (close), and change from the previous day's close. The last column represents the open interest, or the number of actual contracts presently outstanding for that delivery month.

THE CASH MARKET AND THE FUTURES MARKET

Many commodity futures exchanges provide areas where buyers and sellers can negotiate **cash** (or **spot**) **prices**. The cash price is the actual dollar value paid for the immediate transfer of a commodity. Unlike a futures contract, there must be a transfer of the physical possession of the goods. Prices in the cash market are somewhat dependent on prices in the futures market. Thus, it is said that the futures markets provide an important service as a price discovery mechanism. By cataloging price trends in everything from corn to cattle, the producers, processors, and handlers of more than 50 commodities are able to observe price trends in categories of interest.

THE FUTURES MARKET FOR FINANCIAL INSTRUMENTS

The major event in the commodities markets for the last three decades has been the development of financial futures contracts. With the great volatility in the foreign exchange markets and in interest rates, corporate treasurers, investors, and others have felt a great need to hedge their positions. Financial futures also appeal to speculators because of their low margin requirements and wide swings in value.

Financial futures may be broken down into three major categories: currency futures, interest-rate futures, and stock index futures (the latter is covered in depth in Chapter 16). Trading in currency futures began in May 1972 on the International Monetary Market (part of the Chicago Mercantile Exchange). Interest rate futures started trading on the Chicago Board of Trade in October 1975 with the GNMA certificate. Trading in financial futures, regardless of whether they are currency or interest rate futures, is very similar to trading in traditional commodities such as corn, wheat, copper, or pork bellies. There is a stipulated contract size, month of delivery, margin requirement, and so on. We will first look at currency futures and then shift our attention to interest rate futures.

CURRENCY FUTURES

Futures are available in the currencies listed below:

Euro	Mexican peso
Australian dollar	New Zealand dollar
Brazilian real	Russian ruble
Canadian dollar	Swiss franc
Japanese yen	

The futures market in currencies provides many of the same functions as the older and less formalized market in foreign exchange operated by banks and specialized brokers, who maintain communication networks throughout the world. In either case, one can speculate or hedge. The currency futures market, however, is different in that it provides standardized contracts and a strong secondary market.

application example

Let's examine how the currency futures market works. Assume you wish to purchase a currency futures contract in Mexican pesos. The standardized contract is 500,000 pesos. The value of the contract is quoted in cents per peso. Assume you purchase a December futures contract in May, and the price on the contract is \$0.08860 per peso. The total value of the contract is \$44,300 (500,000 × \$0.08860). The typical margin on a peso contract is \$2,500.

We also assume the peso strengthens relative to the dollar. This might happen because of decreasing U.S. interest rates, declining inflation in Mexico, or any number of other reasons. Under these circumstances, the currency might rise to \$0.09010 (the peso is worth more cents than it was previously). The value of the contract has now risen to \$45,050 (500,000 × \$0.09010). This represents an increase in value of \$750:

\$45,050	Current value
−44,300	Original value
\$750	Gain

With an original margin requirement of \$2,500, this represents a return of 30 percent:

$$\frac{\$750}{\$2{,}500} \times 100 = 30\%$$

On an annualized basis, it could even be higher. Of course, the contract could produce a loss if the peso weakens against the dollar as a result of higher interest rates in the United States or increasing inflation in Mexico. With a normal margin maintenance requirement of \$1,200, a \$300 loss on the contract will call for additional margin.

Corporate treasurers often try to hedge an exposed position in their foreign exchange dealings through the currency futures market. Assume a treasurer closes a deal today to receive payment in two months in Japanese yen. If the yen goes down relative to the dollar, he will have less value than he anticipated. One solution would be to sell a yen futures contract (go short). If the value of the yen goes down, he will make money on his futures contract that will offset the loss on the receipt of the Japanese yen in two months.

Table 15–7 lists the typical size of contracts for four other foreign currencies that trade on the International Monetary Market.

TABLE 15-7 Contracts in Currency Futures

Currency	Trading Units	Size of Contract Based on Fall 2010 Prices
Euro	125,000	\$168,350
Canadian dollar	100,000	97,230
British pound	62,500	98,800
Japanese yen	12,500,000	148,275

INTEREST RATE FUTURES

Since the inception of the interest rate futures contract with GNMA certificates in October 1975, the market has been greatly expanded to include Treasury notes, Treasury bills, municipal bonds, federal funds, and Eurodollars. There is almost unlimited potential for futures contracts on interest-related items.

Interest rate futures trade on a number of major exchanges, including the Chicago Board of Trade, the International Monetary Market of the Chicago Mercantile Exchange, and the New York Futures Exchange. There is strong competition between Chicago and New York City for dominance in this business, with Chicago being not only the historical leader but also the current leader.

Table 15–8 shows examples of quotes on interest rate futures. Direct your attention to the first category, Treasury bonds (CBOT), trading on the Chicago Board of Trade.

The bonds trade in units of $100,000, and the quotes are in percent of par value taken to 32nds of a percentage point. Although it is not shown in these data, the bonds on which the futures are based are assumed to be new, 15-year Treasury instruments paying 5 percent interest. In the first column for the September contract for Treasury bonds, we see an opening price of 131-110. This indicates a value of $131\frac{10}{32}$ percent times stated (par) value. We thus have a contract value of $131,312.50 ($131\frac{10}{32} \times \$100,000$). This represents the opening value. The entire line in Table 15–8 reads as follows:

	Open	High	Low	Settle	Change	Open Interest
Sept	131-100	132-100	130-200	132-030	18	16,301

The **settle price**, or closing price is $132\frac{3}{32}$, which represents a positive change of 18 or $\frac{18}{32}$nds from the close of the previous day. The close for the previous day is not always the same as the open for the current day.[5] Since the value of the

TABLE 15-8 Examples of Price Quotes on Interest Rate Futures

Interest Rate Futures

	OPEN	HIGH	LOW	SETTLE	CHG	OPEN INT
Treasury Bonds (CBT)-$100,000; pts 32nds of 100%						
Sept	131-110	132-100	130-200	**132-030**	18.0	16,301
Dec	130-020	130-300	129-050	**130-220**	18.0	648,985
Treasury Notes (CBT)-$100,000; pts 32nds of 100%						
Sept	124-085	125-010	124-000	**124-300**	16.5	52,923
Dec	123-110	124-010	122-300	**123-290**	16.5	1,651,185
5 Yr. Treasury Notes (CBT)-$100,000; pts 32nds of 100%						
Sept	119-275	120-132	119-267	**120-125**	12.2	25,777
Dec	119-040	119-192	118-297	**119-175**	13.0	879,857
2 Yr. Treasury Notes (CBT)-$200,000; pts 32nds of 100%						
Sept	109-175	109-207	109-175	**109-207**	3.0	7,534
Dec	109-107	109-142	109-095	**109-137**	2.7	681,812
30 Day Federal Funds (CBT)-$5,000,000; 100 - daily avg.						
Sept	99.810	99.818	99.810	**99.815**	.002	50,853
Nov	99.800	99.810	99.800	**99.805**	...	82,628
1 Month Libor (CME)-$3,000,000; pts of 100%						
Sept	...	...	...	**99.7427**	.0002	8,816
Nov	99.7100	99.7200	99.7100	**99.7175**	.0100	11,884
Eurodollar (CME)-$1,000,000; pts of 100%						
Sept	99.7050	99.7100 ▲	99.7050	**99.7078**	.0028	767,307
Dec	99.5550	99.5950	99.5550	**99.5850**	.0300	1,085,462
March'11	99.4450	99.5200	99.4400	**99.5150**	.0600	1,046,183
June	99.3050	99.4200	99.3050	**99.4150**	.0700	863,653

Source: *The Wall Street Journal,* September 14, 2010, p. C8. Reprinted with permission of *The Wall Street Journal,*

[5] A number of overnight events can cause the difference. In this case, we can assume the close for the previous day was $106\frac{13}{32}$.

futures went up, we can assume interest rates decreased. Finally, we see an open interest of 16,301, indicating the number of contracts outstanding for September. Because this September contract was close to expiration, the open interest is small compared to December.

application example

Assume we buy a futures contract for $132\frac{3}{32}$ or \$132,093.75 ($132\frac{3}{32}\% \times \$100{,}000$). The margin requirement on the Chicago Board of Trade is \$3,375 with a \$2,500 margin maintenance requirement. In this case, it may be that we bought the futures contract because we anticipate easier monetary policy by the Federal Reserve, which will trigger a decline in interest rates and an increase in bond prices. If interest rates decline by 0.6 percent (60 basis points), Treasury bond prices will increase by approximately $1\frac{17}{32}$.[6] On a \$100,000 par value futures contract, this would represent a gain of \$1,531.25 as indicated below:

$$\begin{array}{r} \$100{,}000 \\ \underline{\times\ 1\tfrac{17}{32}\%}\ (1.53125\%) \\ \$1{,}531.25 \end{array}$$

With a \$3,375 initial margin, the \$1,531.25 profit represents an attractive return on our original \$3,375 investment of 45.37 percent:

$$\frac{\$1{,}531.25}{\$3{,}375.00} = 45.37\%$$

Note, however, that if interest rates go up by even a small amount, our Treasury bond futures contract value will fall, and there may be a margin call.

As is true of other commodities, when we trade in interest rate futures, we do not take actual title or possession of the commodity unless we fail to reverse our initial position. The contract merely represents a bet or hedge on the direction of future interest rates and bond prices.

Hedging with Interest Rate Futures

Interest rate futures have opened up opportunities for hedging that can only be compared with the development of the agricultural commodities market more than a century ago. Consider the following potential hedges against interest rate risks.

1. A corporate treasurer is awaiting a new debt issue that will occur in 60 days. The underwriters are still putting the final details together. The great fear is that interest rates will rise between now and then. The treasurer could hedge his or her position in the futures market by selling a Treasury bond or other similar security short. If interest rates go up, the price to buy back the interest rate futures will be lower, and a profit will be made on the short position. This will partially or fully offset the higher interest costs on the new debt issue.
2. A corporate treasurer is continually reissuing commercial paper at new interest rates or borrowing under a floating prime agreement at the bank. He or she fears that interest rates will go up and make a big dent in projected profits. By selling (going short) interest rate futures, the corporate treasurer can make enough profit on interest rate futures if interest rates go up to compensate for the higher costs of money.

[6] This is derived from a standard bond table and not explicitly calculated in the example.

3. A mortgage banker has made a forward commitment to provide a loan at a set interest rate one month in the future. If interest rates go up, the resale value of the mortgage in the secondary market will go down. He or she can hedge the position by selling or going short on an interest rate futures contract.
4. A pension fund manager has been receiving a steady return of 6 percent on his short-term portfolio in 90-day Treasury bills. He is afraid interest rates will go down and he will have to adjust to receiving lower returns on the managed funds. His strategy might be to buy (go long on) a Treasury bill futures contract. If interest rates go down, he will make a profit on his futures contract that will partially or fully offset his decline in interest income for one period. Of course, if he is heavily invested in long-term securities and fearful of an interest rate rise, a sell or short position that would provide profits on an interest rate rise would be advisable. This would offset part of the loss in the portfolio value due to increasing interest rates.
5. A commercial banker has most of her loans on a floating prime basis, meaning the rate she charges will change with the cost of funds. However, some of the loans have a fixed rate associated with them. If the cost of funds goes up, the fixed-rate loans will become unprofitable. By selling or going short on interest rate futures, the danger of higher interest rates can be hedged away by the profits she will make on the interest rate futures. Similarly, a banker may make a commitment to pay a set amount of interest on certificates of deposit for the next six months. If interest rates go down, the banker may have to lend the funds at a lower rate than she is currently paying. If she buys a futures contract, then lower interest rates will increase the value of the contract and provide a profit. This will offset the possible negative profitability spread described earlier.

An Actual Example

application example

Assume an industrial corporation has a $10 million, 15-year bond to be issued in 60 days. Long-term rates for such an issue are currently 7.75 percent, and there is concern that interest rates will go up to 8 percent by the time of the issue. The corporate treasurer has figured out that the extra ¼ point would have a present value cost of $213,975 over the life of the issue (on a before-tax basis):

$10,000,000	
× ¼%	
$ 25,000	
× 8.559	Present value factor for 15 years at 8 percent (Appendix D)
$ 213,975	Present value of future costs

To establish a hedge position, he sells 94 Treasury bond futures short. We assume they are currently selling at 107 (107% × $100,000), equaling $107,000 each. The total value of the hedge would be $10,058,000 (94 Treasury bond contracts × $107,000). This is roughly equivalent to the $10 million size of the corporate bond issue. If interest rates go up by ¼ point, the profit on the Treasury bond futures contract (due to falling prices with a short position) will probably offset the present value of the increased cost of the corporate bond issue.

Of course, we do not suggest that both rates (on Treasury bonds and corporate bonds) would move exactly together. However, the general thrust of the example should be apparent. We are actually establishing a **cross-hedging** pattern by using one form of security (Treasury bonds) to hedge another form of security (corporate bonds). This is often necessary. Even when the same security is used, there may be differences in maturity dates so that a perfect hedge is difficult to establish.

Many financial managers prefer **partial hedges** to complete hedges. They are willing to take away part of the risk but not all of it. Others prefer no hedge at all because it locks in their position. While a hedge ensures them against loss, it precludes the possibility of an abnormal gain.

Nevertheless, in a risk-averse financial market environment, most financial managers can gain by hedging their position as described in the many examples in this section. Companies such as Burlington Northern, Eastman Kodak, and McDonald's have established reputations for just such actions. Others have not yet joined the movement because of a lack of appreciation or understanding of the highly innovative financial futures market. Much of this will change with the passage of time.

OPTIONS AS WELL AS FUTURES

www.cboe.com

In late 1982, many exchanges began offering options on financial instruments and commodities. For example, the Chicago Board Options Exchange began listing put and call options on Treasury bonds. Also, the American Stock Exchange started trading options on Treasury bills and Treasury notes, and the Philadelphia Exchange offered foreign currency options. The Chicago Board of Trade, the Chicago Mercantile Exchange, and other exchanges have also added options. The relationship, similarities, and dissimilarities between option contracts and futures contracts are given much greater attention in the following chapter. For now it suffices to say that the futures contract requires an initial margin, which can be parlayed into large profits or immediately wiped out, whereas an option requires the payment of an option premium, which represents the full extent of an option purchaser's liability. In Chapter 16 we also see there are options to purchase futures, which combine the elements of both types of contracts.

INTEREST RATE SWAPS

No chapter relating to hedging interest rate risk would be complete without a discussion of the **interest rate swap**.

The basic premise of interest rate swaps is that one party is able to trade one type of risk exposure to another party, and both parties are able to rebalance their portfolios with less risk. For example, Bank A may be obligated to pay a fixed rate on a $100,000 certificate of deposit (CD) for the next five years. The bank is fearful that rates may go down and that it will be paying more on the CD than it will be receiving on loans. Under these circumstances, Bank A may try to find a "counterparty" who has the opposite type of problem. Perhaps Company B is borrowing money from a finance company at a variable rate and is fearful that rates will go up. Assume it has a $100,000 loan that is also due over the next five years.

Under these circumstances, Bank A will agree to pay Company B a variable rate on a hypothetical $100,000 of principal (referred to as notational principal).[7] In return, Company B will agree to pay Bank A a fixed rate on the same hypothetical principal. Both parties have used this swap agreement to eliminate their risk. Let's see how.

[7] There is no principal actually put up. The $100,000 is merely used to keep score on who owes whom and is referred to as "notational principal."

Because Bank A is paying a variable rate and receiving a fixed rate, if rates go down (its original fear), it will come out ahead on the swap agreement. Let's say rates start out at 8 percent (fixed and variable), but variable rates go down to 5 percent. Bank A will receive a net payment of $3,000 from Company B on the hypothetical principal:

$100,000 Hypothetical Principal	
Bank A pays variable (5%)	$5,000
Company B pays fixed (8%)	8,000
Net payment of B to A	$3,000

The swap agreement has effectively protected Bank A against lower interest rate exposure that it has with the customer who owns the $100,000 CD. It has achieved this through an entirely unrelated interest rate swap agreement with Company B.

At the same time, Company B has protected itself against its original fear that interest rates will go up. For example, if interest rates go from 8 percent to 11 percent, it will make $3,000 on the interest rate swap with Bank A:

$100,000 Hypothetical Principal	
Bank A pays variable (11%)	$11,000
Company B pays fixed (8%)	8,000
Net payment of A to B	$ 3,000

This $3,000 profit will offset the exposure that company B has on its loan with the finance company. It has also achieved its goal through an interest rate swap agreement with Bank A.

We have presented the most basic type of swap agreement (although you may not think so!). The point is that interest rate swap agreements are not, initially, as structured as are futures and options contracts (contract months, strike prices, etc.). The counterparties can start out with a blank piece of paper and put together any kind of deal they desire. Major financial institutions such as Goldman Sachs, JPMorgan Chase, and Credit Suisse often serve as facilitators or dealers in bringing parties together for a transaction.

CREDIT DEFAULT SWAPS

A **credit default swap (CDS)** is a derivatives contract, which is traded in the unregulated over-the-counter market. After the financial crisis exposed the risk of not having a standardized product or a central clearing organization, both the ICE Exchange and the Chicago Mercantile Exchange created standardized products that would be cleared by the exchanges. According to the Chicago Mercantile Exchange, a credit default swap "is a derivatives contract in which a credit protection buyer makes a fixed payment periodically to a credit protection seller in exchange for a specified contingent payout following a default event on the asset(s) underlying the CDS."[8]

[8] *Review of CME Group's Credit Default Swap Margin Model and Financial Safeguards for CDS Clearing,* Risk Management Consulting Services Inc., April 18, 2009, p. 2. http://www.cmegroup.com/company/files/Review_of_CME_Group_CDS_Margin_Model_and_Financial_Safeguards.pdf. Copyright © 2010 CME Group, Inc.

Originally credit default swaps were created to hedge against a debt default. If the holder of a debt obligation is concerned about the default of the underlying security, he could find someone (usually a financial institution) who would guarantee payment in the case of a default. This hedge is similar to credit insurance when the buyer of the CDS actually owns the underlying debt. However, owning the underlying debt isn't a requirement of the over-the-counter derivative contract, so buyers can speculate on the probability of a default without owning the debt security. The price paid by the buyer seeking protection would be similar to an insurance premium paid for automobile insurance. However, for a speculator, it would be more like buying life insurance on someone else hoping they die and collecting the death benefit. The price is referred to as a CDS spread and is paid quarterly at an annualized rate. Credit default swaps are bought for a specified period of time, ranging from 1 to 10 years.

One of the risks of credit default swaps is that the other counterparty will not be able to cover the debt in case of a default. When Lehman Brothers went bankrupt in September 2008, the unregulated and nonstandardized nature of the CDS came home to roost and destroyed many once-profitable firms, like AIG, MBIA, and AMBAC, that had insured many of these derivative products.

Our goal here is to familiarize you with credit default swaps as derivative instruments, but more than likely they deserve to be covered more fully in a risk management or derivatives class.

exploring the web

Web Address	Comments
www.cme.com	**CME Group Inc., a CME/Chicago Board of Trade Company**
www.cbot.com	**CME Group Inc., a CME/Chicago Board of Trade Company**
www.euronext.com	**Euronext**
www.kcbot.com	**Kansas City Board of Trade**
www.mgex.com	**Minneapolis Grain Exchange**

SUMMARY

In this chapter, we broke down the commodities futures market into traditional commodities (such as grains, livestock, and meat) and financial futures primarily in currencies and interest rates.

A commodities futures contract is an agreement that provides for the delivery of a specific amount of a commodity at a designated time in the future. It is not intended that the purchaser of a contract take actual possession of the goods but, rather, that he or she reverse or close out the contract before delivery is due. The same is true for the seller.

Primary participants in the commodities market include both speculators and hedgers. We first examine speculators. A speculator buys a commodities contract (goes long) or sells a commodities contract (goes short) because he believes he can anticipate the direction in which the market is going to move. A hedger buys or sells a commodities futures contract to protect an underlying position he or she might have in the actual commodity.

Many commodity futures exchanges provide areas where buyers and sellers can negotiate cash (spot) prices. The cash price is the actual dollar paid for the immediate delivery of the goods. Near-term futures prices and cash prices tend to approximate each other.

Currency and interest rate futures represent important financial futures. Although these markets only came into existence in the 1970s, they have seen explosive growth. The contract on financial futures is very similar to that on basic, traditional commodities; only the items traded and units of measurement are different.

Currency futures relate to many different currencies and enable financial managers to hedge their position in foreign markets. There is also active participation by speculators.

Interest rate futures cover Treasury bonds, Treasury bills, Treasury notes, certificates of deposit, and similar items.

In the current environment of volatile interest rates, interest rate futures offer an excellent opportunity to hedge dangerous interest rate risks. Possible hedgers include corporate financial officers, pension fund managers, mortgage bankers, and commercial bankers.

KEY WORDS AND CONCEPTS

cash or spot prices 402
credit default swap 408
cross hedge 407
financial futures 402
futures contract 395
hedge 395
interest rate swap 407
margin maintenance requirements 398
partial hedges 407
settle price 404

DISCUSSION QUESTIONS

1. What is a futures contract?
2. Do you have to take delivery or deliver the commodity if you are a party to a futures contract?
3. Explain what hedging is.
4. Why is there substantial leverage in commodity investments?
5. What are the basic categories of items traded on the commodity exchanges?
6. What group has primary regulatory responsibility for the activities of the commodity exchanges?
7. How does the concept of margin on a commodities contract differ from that of margin on a stock purchase?
8. Indicate some factors that might influence the price of wheat in the commodities market.
9. What is meant by a daily trading limit on a commodities contract?
10. How does the cash market differ from the futures market for commodities?
11. What are the three main categories of financial futures? Which two are discussed in this chapter?
12. How does the currency futures market differ from the foreign exchange market?
13. Describe the Treasury bonds that are part of the futures contract that trades on the Chicago Board of Trade (size of units, maturity, assumed initial interest rate).
14. How can using the financial futures markets for interest rates and foreign exchange help financial managers through hedging? Briefly explain, and give one example of each.
15. Explain how interest rate swaps can reduce risks for the counterparties.

PRACTICE PROBLEMS AND SOLUTIONS

Gain on commodities contract

1. Beth Stern purchases a 37,000-pound coffee contract at $1.05 per pound with an initial margin requirement of 7 percent. The price goes up to $1.11 in four months. What are the percentage of profit and the annualized gain?

Hedging

2. Dan Richards anticipates taking 80,000 bushels of soybeans to the market in three months. The current cash price for soybeans is $5.75. He can sell a three-month futures contract for soybeans at $5.78, and he decides to sell eight 5,000-bushel futures contracts at that price. Assume that in three months, when Dan Richards takes the soybeans to market and also closes out the futures contracts (buys them back), the price of soybeans has fallen to $5.63.
   a. What is his total loss in value over the three months on the actual soybeans he produced and took to market?
   b. How much did his hedge in the futures market generate in gains?
   c. What is his overall net loss considering the answer in part *a* and the partial hedge in part *b*?

Solutions

1. .06 gain × 37,000 pounds = $2,220
   Amount of margin = 7% × (37,000 × $1.05)
   = 7% × $38,850
   = $2,719.50

$$\frac{\$2{,}220}{\$2{,}719.50} = 81.63\% \text{ profit}$$

$$81.63\% \times {}^{12}\!/_{4} = 244.89\% \text{ annualized gain}$$

2. *a.* Loss per bushel $5.75 − $5.63 = $12 per bushel

$ .12	Loss per bushel
80,000	Bushels
$ 9,600	Total loss on actual soybeans

   b. Gain per bushel on futures contracts = $5.78 − $5.63 = $.15 per bushel
   Eight contracts equals 40,000 bushels

$ .15	Gain per bushel
40,000	Bushels (8 × 5,000)
$ 6,000	Total gain on futures contract

   c.

Total loss on actual soybeans	$9,600
Total gain on futures contract	6,000
Net loss	$3,600

PROBLEMS

Gain on commodities contract

1. You purchase a 5,000-bushel contract for corn at $1.90 per bushel ($9,500 total). The initial margin requirement is 7 percent. The price goes up to $1.98 in one month. What is your percentage profit and the annualized gain?

Loss on commodities contract

2. An investor purchases a 25,000-pound contract for copper at $2.10 per pound with an initial margin requirement of 6 percent. The price goes down to $2.06 after a year. What are the dollar and percentage losses?

Gain or Loss on commodities contract

3. Sterling Jones purchases a 5,000-troy ounce contract on silver at $13.00 an ounce. At the same time he purchases a 112,000 pound sugar contract at 0.191 cents a pound. If the price of silver goes down to $12.94 at the same

time the price of sugar goes up to 0.196 cents, will Sterling have an overall net gain or loss?

Hedging

4. Farmer Tom Hedges anticipates taking 100,000 bushels of oats to the market in three months. The current cash price for oats is $2.15. He can sell a three-month futures contract for oats at $2.20. He decides to sell 10 5,000-bushel futures contracts at that price. Assume that in three months when Farmer Hedges takes the oats to market and also closes out the futures contracts (buys them back), the price of oats has tumbled to $2.03

a. What is his total loss in value over the three months on the actual oats he produced and took to market?

b. How much did his hedge in the futures market generate in gains?

c. What is the overall net loss considering the answer in part *a* and the partial hedge in part *b*.

Hedging

5. The Health Food Corporation anticipates the need to purchase 80,000 bushels of soybeans in six months to use in their products. The current cash price for soybeans is $5.50 a bushel. A six-month futures contract for soybeans can be purchased at $5.53.

a. Explain why Health Food Corporation might need to purchase futures contracts to hedge their position.

b. To completely hedge their exposure, how many contracts will they need to purchase? Soybeans trade in 5,000-bushel contracts.

c. If the cash price of soybeans ends up at $5.75 per bushel after six months, by how much will the actual cost of 80,000 bushels of soybeans have gone up?

d. After the futures contracts are closed out (sold at $5.75 also), what will be the gain on the futures contracts?

e. Considering the answers to parts *c* and *d,* what is their net position?

Margin maintenance

6. With a 5,000-bushel contract for $25,000, assume the margin requirement is $2,000 and the maintenance margin is 80 percent of the margin requirement. How much would the price per bushel have to fall before additional margin is required?

Generating margin

7. If contracts are written on a 5,000-bushel basis requiring $3,000 of margin and you control 12 contracts, how much would the price per bushel have to change to generate enough profit to purchase an additional contract?

Pyramiding

8. Referring to problem 7, how many contracts would need to be controlled to generate enough profit for a new margin contract if the price changed by only 1¢ per bushel?

Currency futures

9. You purchase a futures contract in euros for $170,000. The trading unit is 125,000 euros.

a. What is the ratio of cents to euros in this contract? (Divide the dollar contract size by the size of the trading unit.)

b. Assume you are required to put up $4,000 in margin and the euro increases by 3¢ (per euro). What will be your return as a percentage of margin?

Treasury bond futures

10. Maxwell Securities buys a $100,000 par value, September 2010 Treasury bond contract at the quoted settle price in Table 15–8 on page 404.

a. What is the dollar value of the contract? Use the settle price in your calculation.

b. There is an initial margin requirement of $3,375 and a margin maintenance requirement of $2,500. If an interest-rate increase causes the bond to go down by 0.8 percent of par value, will Maxwell be called upon to put up more margin?

c. Assume Maxwell's investment is for six months. To have a 100 percent annualized return on the initial $3,375 margin, by what percent of par value must the bond increase?

Hedging by corporate treasurer

11. The treasurer of the Larson Corporation is going to bring an $8 million issue to the market in 120 days. It will be a 25-year issue. The interest rate environment is highly volatile, and even though long-term interest rates are currently 10¼ percent, there is a fear that interest rates will be up to 11 percent by the time the bonds get to the market.

a. If interest rates go up by ¾ point, what is the present value of the extra interest this increase will cost the corporation? Use an 11 percent discount rate, and disregard tax considerations.

b. Assume the corporation is going to short September Treasury bonds as quoted near the top of Table 15–8 on page 404 for the CBOT (Chicago Board of Trade). Based on the settle price, how many contracts must they sell to equal the $8 million exposed position? Round to the nearest whole number of contracts.

c. Based on your answer in part *b,* if Treasury bond prices increase by 2.8 percent of par value in each contract in response to a ½ percent decline in interest rates over the next 45 days, what will be the total loss on the futures contracts?

Hedging by corporate treasurer

12. Should the treasurer of the Larson Corporation feel she has failed in her tasks if the circumstance in part *c* of problem 11 takes place?

CRITICAL THOUGHT CASE–FOCUS ON ETHICS

Milt Samuals joined Garrett Construction Company in 2005 in the budgeting section of the corporate treasurer's office. He worked with a team of two accountants and a senior vice president of finance to provide pro forma budgets and financial statements. Although his undergraduate degree was in finance with an emphasis on investments, he still felt he was acquiring experience with his budgeting work. Nevertheless, he was quite excited when he learned that he was being shifted to a new department in the treasurer's office in which he would share responsibility for managing the excess funds of the corporation as well as participate in the hedging function that the corporation undertook to offset interest rate exposure.

By 2010, he had moved to the top position in the hedging area. Samuals had the major responsibility for hedging against interest rate increases that might take place from the time Garrett Construction Company agreed to undertake a project until the time it was completed. The period often ran from 6 to 12 months. Samuals used financial derivatives such as interest rate futures and swaps to accomplish his purpose. Most often, he employed Treasury bond futures. He would sell (short) them to protect against interest rate increases. If interest rates went up, the market value of the bonds covered under the contract would go down, and he could close out or cover his position at a profit. As he explained it, he would establish the sales price at approximately $100,000, and if interest rates went up, he could buy them back at perhaps $95,000. The $5,000 profit he made on the derivatives would help cover the added interest expense that Garrett Construction Company experienced on its loan at the bank as a result of increasing interest rates. Of course, if interest rates went down, he would lose money on the futures contract, but that would be offset by the lower interest the company would pay. Basically, he was neutralizing the company's position regardless of what happened to interest rates. If the company had a large amount of interest rate exposure, Samuals might engage in 10 or 20 contracts at one time.

Although Samuals was acquiring expertise in his hedging function, he eventually found himself becoming somewhat bored with his normal hedging activities. While he continued to hedge the company's interest rate exposure, he also began speculating on interest rate movements for the company. These contracts had nothing to do with the company's interest rate exposure. For example, if he thought interest rates were going down, he would buy Treasury bond futures contracts. If rates did go down, the value of the bonds covered under the contract would go up, and he would sell (cover) his position at a nice profit. Because only a small amount of margin (cash) was involved, he could really use leverage to establish spectacular gains (though sometimes there were losses).

For the most part, Samuals was doing well, and he could not wait to tell Roger Garrett, the president of the company, about the new activity he had decided to undertake and how well he was doing for the company. He felt certain an added bonus was coming.

Question

1. If you were Roger Garrett, would you be inclined to reward Milt Samuals with an added bonus?

WEB EXERCISE

We will examine the futures contracts for a typical commodity. Go to **www.cbot.com**.

1. Put your cursor on "Agriculture" and click on "Soybeans."
2. Write down the settle prices for the first six contracts listed. Remember to move the decimal point two places to the left to go from dollars to cents.
3. Does the pattern of settle prices appear to be upward or downward with the passage of time? What might this tell you about anticipated future price movements for soybeans?
4. Click on "Learn More" then click on "News." See if you can find a story that validates the pattern shown in exercise 3. If you can, write a one-sentence summary. If not, bypass this question. (Appropriate news stories are not always available.)

Note: From time to time, companies redesign their Web sites, and occasionally a topic we have listed may have been deleted, updated, or moved into a different location.

www.mhhe.com/hirtblock10e

chapter sixteen

STOCK INDEX FUTURES AND OPTIONS

OBJECTIVES

1. Understand the difference between derivatives on stock indexes and individual stocks.
2. Appreciate the role of derivatives in hedging and speculation.
3. Distinguish between futures and options and the consequences of using each.
4. Describe the importance of derivatives in forecasting future stock movements.
5. Explain how to design a hedge based on the volatility of a portfolio.
6. Describe specific examples of stock index hedging.

OUTLINE

Back in Chapter 14, you learned about the use of put and call options to speculate or hedge positions in individual stocks. But for those who have multiple stocks in their portfolio, this can be an expensive and time-consuming process. Wouldn't it be easier for you just to speculate or hedge using a market index such as the Standard & Poor's 500 Stock Index? That way you could take a major position with just one transaction. How did all this get started?

In February 1982, the Kansas City Board of Trade began trading futures on a stock index, the Value Line Index. This event ushered in a new era of futures and options trading related to equities.

A futures contract or option on an index allows the investor to participate in the movement of an entire index rather than an individual security. Currently, futures and options relate to such indexes or averages as the Dow Jones Industrial Average, the Standard & Poor's 500 Stock Index, the Nasdaq 100 Stock Index, and many other market measures.

application example

If an investor purchases a **futures contract on a stock market index**, he puts down the required margin, and gains or losses on the transaction are based on the movement of the index. For example, an investor may purchase a futures contract on the Standard & Poor's 500 Stock Index with $20,000 in margin. The actual contract value is based on the index value times 250. If the S&P 500 Futures Index were at 1,250, the initial contract value would be $312,500 (250 × 1,250). If the index went up or down by eight points, the investor would gain or lose $2,000 (250 × ±8). Because the initial investment is $20,000 in margin, we see a gain or loss of 10 percent ($2,000/$20,000 = 10%). Since this might happen over a one- or two-day period, the annualized return or loss could be quite high.

If the investor is trading in **stock index options** instead of futures, he might choose to participate in the Standard & Poor's 500 Stock Index options. If the S&P 500 Index were again assumed to be at 1,250, an option to purchase the index at a strike price of 1,250 in two months might carry a premium (option price) of $25. The option price is multiplied by 100 to get a total value of the option of $2,500 (100 × $25). If the S&P 500 Index closed out at 1,290 at expiration, the option price will be $40 (1,290 market value −1,250 strike price), and a profit of $1,500 will be achieved over the two months:

$4,000	Final value (100 × $40)
− 2,500	Purchase price (100 × $25)
$1,500	Profit

As we go further into the chapter, you will see there are not only futures and options on stock market indexes but also **options to purchase futures** on stock market indexes. This represents a combination of a futures and option contract.

Stock index futures have grown faster than any new futures trading outlet in history. In their first six months of trading, the average daily volume was 4.5 times as great as the volume on Treasury bond futures during a comparable period of infancy. The same sort of pattern has occurred in index option trading.

THE CONCEPT OF DERIVATIVE PRODUCTS

Trading in stock index futures and options has had a tremendous impact on the financial markets in the United States. Stock index futures and options are sometimes referred to as **derivative products** because they derive their existence from actual market indexes but have no intrinsic characteristics of their own.[1] These derivative products are thought to make market movements more volatile. The primary reason is that enormous amounts of securities can be controlled by relatively small amounts of margin payments or option premiums. Also, these derivative products are often used as part of program trading. **Program trading** means that computer-based trigger points are established in which large volume trades are initiated by institutional investors. Stock index futures and options facilitate program trading because a large volume of securities can be controlled. The presence of program trading, as supported by the use of stock index futures and options, was blamed by many for the 508-point market crash in the Dow Jones Industrial Average on October 19, 1987. It was thought that too many institutional investors were moving in the same direction (to sell) at one time. Increased stock price volatility since the market crash has also been blamed on program trading and the use of stock index futures and options.

Actually, these are somewhat controversial topics. A study by the Chicago Mercantile Exchange suggests program trading and the use of derivative products

[1] Interest rate futures and options are also considered to be derivative products.

has no negative effect on the market's volatility. These trading tools merely help the market reach a new equilibrium level (in terms of value) more quickly.[2]

It is the contention of the authors that stock index futures and options have many useful purposes, which we will cover throughout the chapter. We will also try to point out potential negatives where they exist.

TRADING STOCK INDEX FUTURES

There are major stock index futures contracts on the Dow Jones Industrial Average (Chicago Board of Trade), the Mini Dow Jones Industrial Average[3] (Chicago Board of Trade), the S&P 500 Index (Chicago Mercantile Exchange), the Mini S&P 500 Index (Chicago Mercantile Exchange), the Nasdaq 100[4] (Chicago Mercantile Exchange), the Mini Nasdaq 100 (Chicago Mercantile Exchange), and the Russell 1000 (New York Board of Trade).[5] Examples of these stock index futures contracts are shown in Table 16–1.[6]

You will note in Table 16–1 that the title line for each contract (such as the DJ Industrial Average) indicates the appropriate multiple times the value in the table. For the DJ Industrial Average the multiplier is 10, and for the Mini DJ Industrial Average it is 5 (the intent of the latter is to create a smaller contract based on the

TABLE 16-1 Stock Index Futures (September 14, 2010)

Index Futures

	OPEN	HIGH	LOW	SETTLE	CHG	OPEN INT
DJ Industrial Average (CBT)-$10 x index						
Sept	10515	10560	10515	**10538**	79	9,770
Dec	10405	10498	10405	**10472**	79	519
Mini DJ Industrial Average (CBT)-$5 x index						
Sept	10538	10556	10537	**10538**	79	66,911
Dec	10469	10492	10469	**10472**	79	26,080
S&P 500 Index (CME)-$250 x index						
Sept	1120.00	1123.90	1116.00	**1121.20**	11.40	223,964
Dec	1109.40	1118.80	1108.90	**1116.20**	11.30	136,883
Mini S&P 500 (CME)-$50 x index						
Sept	1112.50	1124.00	1112.00	**1121.25**	11.50	1,863,017
Dec	1110.00	1119.00	1108.00	**1116.25**	11.25	1,367,848
Nasdaq 100 (CME)-$100 x index						
Sept	1908.00	1926.00	1908.00	**1919.25**	27.00	24,026
Dec	1895.75	1923.00	1895.75	**1916.75**	27.00	1,731
Mini Nasdaq 100 (CME)-$20 x index						
Sept	1896.5	1925.3	1896.5	**1919.3**	27.0	299,175
Dec	1895.8	1922.8	1895.3	**1916.8**	27.0	129,297
Mini Russell 2000 (ICE-US)-$100 x index						
Sept	637.70	653.90	637.70	**650.70**	14.70	250,348
Dec	636.00	651.30	636.00	**648.20**	14.70	195,101
Mini Russell 1000 (ICE-US)-$100 x index						
Sept	617.90	617.90	617.90	**617.40**	7.70	18,548
Dec	613.50	615.90 ▲	612.40	**614.80**	7.60	1,979
U.S. Dollar Index (ICE-US)-$1,000 x index						
Sept	82.68	82.68	82.06	**82.09**	-.61	6,402
Dec	83.08	83.08	82.02	**82.19**	-.83	20,918

Source: *The Wall Street Journal*, September 14, 2010, p. C8. Reprinted with permission of *The Wall Street Journal*, Copyright © 2010 Dow Jones & Company, Inc. All Rights Reserved Worldwide.

[2] *Report of the Committee of Inquiry Appointed by the Chicago Mercantile Exchange to Examine the Events Surrounding October 19, 1987* (Chicago: The Chicago Mercantile Exchange, December 17, 1987).

[3] A mini index contract is similar to the normal contract but carries a smaller total value.

[4] The Nasdaq 100 is made up of the 100 largest companies on the Nasdaq.

[5] There are also additional contracts on the Russell 2000 and other indexes.

[6] An alternative way to trade the S&P 500 is through SPDRs, an exchange traded fund; for the Dow Jones Industrial Average it is Diamonds. There are actual shares that trade on the American Stock Exchange and mimic the performance of the index. For example, Diamonds trade at 1/100th the value of the DJIA. If the Dow is at 11,000, a Diamond share of stock will trade for 110. If the DJIA increases to 12,000 over time, the Diamond shares will go up to 120. Diamonds fall under the topic of exchange traded funds, a topic discussed in Chapter 4.

TABLE 16-2 Value of Contracts

	September Settle Price	Multiplier	Contract Value
Dow Jones Industrial Average	10,538.00	10	$105,380
Mini Dow Jones Industrial Average	10,538.00	5	52,690
S&P 500 Index	1,121.20	250	280,300
Mini S&P 500 Index	1,121.20	50	56,060
Nasdaq 100	1,919.25	100	191,925
Mini Nasdaq 100	1,919.25	20	38,385
Mini Russell 2000	650.70	100	65,070
Mini Russell 1000	617.40	100	61,740
U.S. Dollar Index	82.09	1000	82,090

DJ Industrial Average). For the S&P 500 Index, the multiplier is 250, and for the Mini S&P 500, it is 50, and so on. Looking at the September settle price for each of the indexes, we see the value of the contracts in Table 16–2.

If the investor thinks the market is going up, he will purchase a futures contract. If he thinks the market is going down, he will sell a futures contract and hope the market will decline so that the contract can be closed out (repurchased) at a lower value than the sales price. Selling futures contracts can also be used to hedge a large stock portfolio. If the market goes down, what you lose on your portfolio you can recoup in your futures contract.

In the example in Table 16–2, the investor has nine contracts from which to choose. Although not covered here, there are also futures contracts on other indexes.

We shall direct our attention for now to the S&P 500 Index futures contract (although the same basic principles would apply to other contracts).

Part of the material from Table 16–1 that pertains to the S&P 500 Index futures contract is reproduced in Table 16–3 so we can examine a number of key features related to the contract.

Trading Cycle

The trading cycle is made up of the four months of March, June, September, and December. The last day of trading for a contract is the third Thursday of the ending month.

Margin Requirement

As previously mentioned, the basic margin requirement for buying or selling an S&P 500 futures contract on the Chicago Mercantile Exchange was $28,125 in 2010. Based on the September 2010 contract value (found on the third line in Table 16–2), this represents a margin requirement of 10.03 percent ($28,125/$280,300).

There is also a margin maintenance requirement of $22,500. Thus, if the initial margin or equity in the account falls to this level, the investor will be required to supply sufficient cash or securities to bring the account back to $28,125. A drop from $28,125 to $22,500 represents $5,625. Because the contract trades at 250 times the index, a decline of 22.5 points in the S&P contract value would cause a loss of $5,625. The investor would be asked to put up that amount in new funds.

www.cmegroup.com

If the investor can prove he is hedging a long position, the margin requirement will be less. For example, if an investor owns a portfolio of stocks that roughly equals the value of the index futures contract ($280,300 in this case), the initial

the real world of investing

THE S&P IS NOT YOUR FATHER'S INDEX

Just as Buick and Chevrolet claim their latest models are not to be confused with "your father's car," similar claims are made for the Standard & Poor's 500 Index. This is of potential interest because the S&P 500 Index is the most popular venue on which to trade futures contracts.

Thomas McManus, U.S. investment strategist at NatWest Securities, was quoted in *The Wall Street Journal* as saying, "The S&P 500 is higher growth, more global, less cyclical, and more diversified than it has ever been and therefore deserves a higher (price-to-earnings) multiple."* While the last point about higher multiple is subject to debate, the changing characteristics of the Index are not.

The biggest change has been the inclusion of more technology and financial firms, industries that have shown a particularly strong performance during the 1990s. Between 1989 and 2006, the two industries combined have grown from 14 percent of the S&P 500 Index to 36 percent. While much of the growth can be attributed to market value gains that have outstripped the rest of the market, this is not the only explanation. For example, the number of financial firms represented in the S&P 500 has grown from 40 in the late 1980s to 74 in 2006. Furthermore, Microsoft was not added to the S&P 500 Index until 1994, but in mid-2006 represented 2.0 percent of the value of the index.

The changes are not only in technology and finance, but in many other areas as well. One hundred and five changes in the Index have taken place since 1995. There has been a deemphasis on public utilities, energy, steel, and old-style retail establishments and a renewed emphasis on health care, multinationals, and entertainment, as well as technology and finance.

The S&P 500 Index represents a shinier, faster (in terms of growth) model than it was in your father's day The same can also be said of the Dow Jones Industrial Average, which in early 2001 dropped Woolworth, Bethlehem Steel, Texaco, and Westinghouse Electric in favor of more widely traded stocks as represented by Hewlett-Packard, Johnson & Johnson, Citigroup, and Wal-Mart stores.

* Greg Ip, "S&P 500 Is Not Your Father's Index," *The Wall Street Journal*, July 29, 1997, pp. C1, C29. Reprinted with permission of *The Wall Street Journal*,

margin requirement is reduced. Since a hedged position is not as risky as a speculative position, less initial margin is required.[7]

Cash Settlement

In traditional commodity futures markets, the potential for physical delivery exists. One who is trading in wheat could actually decide to deliver the commodity to close out the contract. As discussed in Chapter 15, this happens only a very small percentage of the time, but it is possible. The stock index futures market, on the other hand, is purely a **cash-settlement** market. There is never the implied

TABLE 16-3 S&P Index Futures Contract (CME), 500 Multiplier (September 14, 2010)

	Open	High	Low	Settle	Change
September	1,120.00	1,123.90	1,116.00	1,121.20	11.4
December	1,109.40	1,118.80	1,109.00	1,116.20	11.3
March	—	—	—	—	—
June	—	—	—	—	—

Value of S&P 500 Stock Index (September 14, 2010), 1,121.10.

[7] It should be mentioned that on a hedged position, the margin maintenance requirement is the same as the original margin.

potential for future delivery of the Standard & Poor's 500 Stock Index. An investor simply closes out (or reverses) his position before the settlement date. If he does not, his account is automatically credited with his gains or debited with his losses, and the transaction is completed.[8]

One of the advantages of a cash-settlement arrangement is that it makes it impossible for a "short squeeze" to develop. A short squeeze occurs when an investor attempts to corner a market in a commodity, such as silver, so that it is not possible for those who have short positions to make physical delivery. Clearly, with a cash-settlement position, this can never happen.

Basis

The term **basis** represents the difference between the stock index futures price and the value of the actual underlying index.[9] The basis for the S&P 500 contract for September and December 2010 is shown below:

	September	December
Stock index futures price	1,121.20	1,116.20
Actual underlying index	1,121.10	1,121.10
Basis	0.10	−4.90

In this example, the basis indicates that a premium is being paid over the actual value for September. This is generally thought to be a positive sign. If the index futures price is below the actual underlying index, as it is in December, there is a negative basis.

An excellent discussion of the ability of stock index futures to forecast the actual underlying index is presented in an article by Zeckhauser and Niederhoffer in the *Financial Analysts Journal*.[10] A part of their thesis is that futures contracts move instantaneously to reflect market conditions, whereas the actual underlying index moves more slowly. If the market makes an important move, some of the stocks that are part of the actual underlying index will not yet have reacted. Thus, initial, significant, and potentially predictive information may be found in the futures market quotes.

Also, at times, futures or options markets stay open later or begin trading earlier than the actual underlying stock markets. This can be very beneficial not only in providing lead time information on market movements, but also in giving the trader an opportunity to take a position before the opening or after the closing of the stock market.

Overall Features

Many of the important features related to stock index futures on the various exchanges are presented in Table 16–4. This table can serve as a ready reference guide to trading commodities in various markets.

[8] Actually, the account is adjusted daily to reflect the gains and losses. This is known as marking the customer's position to market.

[9] The same concept can be applied to other types of futures contracts.

[10] Richard Zeckhauser and Victor Niederhoffer, "The Performance of Market Index Futures Contracts," *Financial Analysts Journal*, January–February 1983, pp. 59–65.

TABLE 16-4 Specifications for Stock Index Futures Contracts

Index and Exchange	Index	Contract Size and Value (in dollars)	Contract Months
Dow Jones Industrial Average Chicago Board of Trade (CBOT)	Value of 30 stocks in DJIA	10 × DJIA	March June September December
Mini Dow Jones Industrial Average Chicago Board of Trade (CBOT)	Same as above	5 × DJIA	March June September December
S&P 500 Index Index & Options Market (IOM) of Chicago Mercantile Exchange (CME)	Value of 500 selected stocks on NYSE, AMEX, and Nasdaq, weighted to reflect market value of issues	250 × S&P 500	March June September December
Mini S&P 500 Index Index & Options Market (IOM) of Chicago Mercantile Exchange (CME)	Same as above	50 × S&P 500 Index	March June September December
Mini Russell 2000 Intercontinental Exchange (ICE)	Index for the 2000 smallest stocks in the Russell 3000 index	100 × Russell 2000 Index	March June September December
Mini Russell 1000 Intercontinental Exchange (ICE)	Index for the 1000 largest stocks in the Russell 3000 index	100 × Russell 1000 Index	March June September December
Nasdaq 100 Stock Index Index and Options Market (IOM) of Chicago Mercantile Exchange (CME)	Index for the 100 largest stocks on the Nasdaq, weighted to reflect market value of issues	100 × Nasdaq 100 Stock Index	March June September December
Mini Nasdaq 100 Stock Index Index and Options Market (IOM) of Chicago Mercantile Exchange (CME)	Index for the 100 largest stocks on the Nasdaq, weighted to reflect market value of issues	20 × Nasdaq 100 Stock Index	March June September December
U.S. Dollar Index Intercontinental Exchange (ICE)	Index value for the U.S. Dollar against a basket of six currencies	1000 × U.S. dollar index	March June September December

USE OF STOCK INDEX FUTURES

There are a number of actual and potential users of stock index futures. As is true of most futures contracts, the motivation may be either speculation or the opportunity to hedge.

Speculation

The speculator may use stock index futures in an attempt to profit from major movements in the market. He or she may have developed a conviction about the next move in the market through fundamental or technical analysis. For example, those who utilize fundamental analysis may determine that P/E ratios are relatively low or that earnings performance should be extremely good in the next two quarters, so they wish to bet on the market moving upward. Market technicians might observe that a resistance or support position in the market is being penetrated and that it is time to take a position based on the anticipated consequences of that penetration.

While the market participant could put his or her money in individual stocks, it might be more efficient and less time consuming to simply invest in stock index futures. In buying futures on the S&P 500 Index, the investor is capturing the performance of 500 securities.

Two types of risks are associated with investments: systematic or market-related risks, and unsystematic or firm-related risks. Because many believe only systematic risk is assumed to be rewarded in an efficient capital market environment (unsystematic risk can be diversified away), the investor may wish to be exposed only to systematic risk. Stock index futures represent an efficient approach to only taking systematic, market-related risk.

Another advantage of stock index futures is that there is less manipulative action and insider trading than with individual securities. While it is possible (though not legal) for "informed" insider trading to cause an individual stock to move dramatically in the short term, such activity is not as likely for an entire index. This advantage, however, should not be overstated. Unusual trading activity of stock index futures comes under the scrutiny of federal regulators from time to time.

Stock index futures also offer leverage potential. A $280,300 S&P futures contract can be established for $28,125 in margin and with no interest on the balance.[11] If you were investing $280,300 in actual stocks through margin, you would have to put up a minimum of $140,150 (50 percent) in margin and pay interest on the balance. The margin requirement is still considerably lower than that on an outright stock purchase. Also, the commissions on a stock index futures contract are minuscule in comparison with commissions on securities of comparable value.

application example

Volatility and Profits or Losses Before the market crash of 1987, the average daily move on the S&P 500 Index was approximately 0.50 (one-half point per day). It has been moving up ever since. In the volatile 2007–2010 period, the daily average move has been in the seven-point range, but the range between the high and low has fluctuated between 5 and 20 points. A seven-point upward move in an S&P 500 futures contract (say, from 1260 to 1267) means a daily gain of $1,750 (recall the contract has a multiplier of 250). With a margin requirement of $20,000, that is an 8.75 percent, one-day return on your money:

$ 7	Gain on futures contract
× 250	Multiplier
$ 1,750	Dollar gain
$28,125	Margin
6.22%	Percent gain

This translates into a 2,270.30 percent annualized return (6.22% × 365). By contrast, if the $28,125 were invested in a 5 percent certificate of deposit, only $3.85 in interest would accrue on a daily basis. The difference here, of course, is that the $1,750 average daily movement related to the index may be up or down, whereas the $3.85 is only up.

When a stock index futures contract starts to run against an investor, he or she can bail out and cut losses. If the contract value is going down rapidly, the investor will be continually called on to put up more margin as the margin position is being depleted. That puts tremendous pressure on the investor. He or she must decide

[11] As mentioned in Chapter 15, margin on futures contracts merely represents good-faith money, and there is never any interest on the balance.

whether to put up more margin and hold the position in hopes of a comeback or close out the position and take a loss.

Not all speculation in stock index futures must necessarily be based on the market going up. You can also speculate that the market will go down. You simply sell a contract with the anticipation of repurchasing it at a lower price later. Margin requirements are similar, and gains come from a declining market and losses from an increasing market. If the index goes up rapidly, the investor will be called on to put up more margin.[12]

Hedging

Up to now our discussion of stock index futures has mainly related to speculating (or anticipating the next major move in the market). Perhaps the most important use of stock index futures is for hedging purposes. An investor who has a large diversified portfolio may think the market is about to decline. A portfolio manager who suffers a 20 percent decline in his or her portfolio actually requires a 25 percent gain from the new lower base to break even.

A portfolio manager faced with the belief that a declining market is imminent may be inclined to sell part or all of the portfolio. The question becomes, is this realistic? First, large transaction costs are associated with selling part or all of a portfolio and then repurchasing it later. Second, it may be difficult to liquidate a position in certain securities that are thinly traded. For example, a mutual fund or pension fund that tries to sell 10,000 shares of a small over-the-counter stock may initially find a price quote of $25 but only be able to close out its relatively large position at $23.50. A $15,000 loss would be suffered. Furthermore, the fund might find the same type of problem in reacquiring the stock after the overall market decline is over. This problem could be multiplied by 25 or 50 times, depending on the number of securities in the portfolio. Although larger, more liquid holdings would be easier to trade, significant transactions costs are still involved.

A more easily executed defensive strategy would be to sell one or more stock index futures as a hedge against the portfolio. If the stock market does go down, the loss on the portfolio will be partially or fully offset by the profit on the stock index futures contract(s) because they are bought back at a lower price than the initial sales price.

application example

As an example, assume a corporate pension fund has $20 million in stock holdings. The investment committee for the fund is very bearish in its outlook, fearing that the overall market could go down by 20 percent in the next few months and a $4 million loss would be suffered. The pension fund decides to fully hedge its position.

The fund is going to use S&P 500 Index futures for the hedge. We shall assume the futures can be sold for $1,260, with a settlement date in three months. Before the number of contracts for execution is determined, the portfolio manager must consider the relative volatility of his portfolio. If the portfolio is more volatile than the market, this must be factored into the decision-making process. As discussed in Chapter 1, the beta coefficient indicates how volatile a stock is relative to the market. If a stock has a beta of 1.20, it is 20 percent more volatile than the market. We shall assume the $20 million portfolio discussed above has a weighted average beta of 1.15 (that is, the portfolio is 15 percent more volatile than the market).

To determine the number of contracts necessary to hedge the position, we use the following formula:

$$\frac{\text{\$ Value of portfolio}}{\text{\$ Value of contract}} \times \text{Weighted beta of portfolio} = \text{Number of contracts} \qquad \textbf{(16–1)}$$

[12] The margin maintenance requirements are similar to those on a long position.

In the example under discussion, we would show:

$$\frac{\$20,000,000}{1,260 \times 250} \times 1.15 = \text{Number of contracts}$$

In the first term of the formula, the numerator is the size of the portfolio being hedged. The denominator is the size of each contract and, in the example, is found by multiplying the S&P futures contract value of 1,260 by 250. The first term is then multiplied by the weighted beta value of 1.15. The answer works out as:

$$\frac{\$20,000,000}{\$315,000} \times 1.15 = 63.49 \times 1.15 = 73 \text{ contracts (rounded)}$$

The portfolio can be effectively hedged with 73 contracts.

Assume the market does go down but only by 10 percent instead of the 20 percent originally anticipated. Let's demonstrate that the hedge has worked. Since the portfolio has a beta of 1.15, its decline would be 11.5 percent (10% × 1.15). With a $20 million portfolio, the loss would be $2.3 million. To offset this loss, we will have a gain on 73 contracts. The gain is shown as follows:

1,260.00	S&P Index futures contract (sales price)
−126.00	Decline in price on the futures contract (10% × 1,260.00)
1,134.00	Ending value (purchase price)

The 126.00 point decline on the index futures contract indicates the profit made on each of the contracts.[13] They were sold for $1,260.00 and repurchased for $1,134.00. With 73 contracts, the profit on the stock index futures contracts is $2,299,500.

$31,500	Profit per contract (126.00 × $250)
× 73	Number of contracts
$2,299,500	Total profit

The gain of approximately $2.3 million on the stock index futures contracts offsets the loss of $2.3 million on the portfolio. The small difference between the two values represents the fact that we rounded values. Actually, executing a perfect hedge may be further complicated by a number of other factors such as the lack of an appropriate index to match against the portfolio and the change in basis over time. Also, the portfolio may not move exactly in accordance with the beta. No doubt, many real-world factors can complicate any hedge.

While a stock index futures hedge offers the advantage of protecting against losses, it takes away the upside potential. If the market goes up by 10 percent instead of down, the gain on the portfolio may be wiped out by the loss on the stock index futures contracts. The investor could be forced to buy back the futures contract for 10 percent more than the selling price. Because some portfolio managers are afraid of losing all their upside potential in a hedged position, they may wish to hedge less than 100 percent of their portfolio.

While the hedging procedure just described can be potentially beneficial to portfolio managers, it can be potentially detrimental to the market in general if overused. Actually, protecting a large portfolio against declines is sometimes referred to as **portfolio insurance**. It is potentially a good strategy, but what if many investors initiate their portfolio-insurance strategies at the same time? Perhaps they are worried because there has been an increase in the prime rate or a

[13] Note that the futures contract is assumed to move on a one-to-one basis with the market. The actual relationship may not be this precise.

bad report on inflation. If everyone rushes to sell stock index futures at the same time this will drive down not only stock index futures prices but the stocks in the indexes as well (such as those in the S&P 500 Stock Index). An overall panic can result. The chain reaction is that a whole new round of portfolio-insurance–induced sales is triggered.

Other Uses of Hedging

Hedging with stock index futures has a number of other uses besides attempting to protect the position of a long-term investment portfolio. These include the following.

Underwriter Hedge As described in Chapter 9, the investment banker (underwriter) has a risk exposure from buying stock from the issuing corporation with the intention of reselling it in the public markets. If there is weakness during the distribution period, the potential resale price could fall below the purchase price, and the underwriter's profit would be wiped out. To protect against this market risk, the underwriter could sell stock index futures contracts. If the market goes down, presumably, the loss on the stock will be compensated for by the gain on the stock index futures contract as a result of being able to repurchase it at a lower price. This, of course, is not a perfect hedge. It is possible that the individual stock could go down while the market is going up, and losses on both the stock and stock index futures contract would occur (writing options directly against the stock might be more efficient, but in many cases such options are not available).

Specialist or Dealer Hedge As indicated in Chapter 2, a specialist on an exchange or a dealer in the over-the-counter market buys and sells stocks for his own inventory for temporary holding. He may, at times, assume a larger temporary holding than desired, with all the risks associated with that exposure. Stock index futures can reduce the market (or systematic) risk, although the use of futures cannot reduce the specific risk associated with a security.

Retirement or Estate Hedge As we move into the next two or three decades, large retirement funds will be accumulated from voluntary retirement plans. A retirement plan participant who has accumulated a large sum in an equity fund may feel a need to hedge his or her position in certain time periods in the economy (where liquidation is neither tax advantageous or possible). A futures contract may provide that hedge. Also, a person with responsibility for an estate may be locked into a portfolio during the period of probate (validation of the will process) and wish to hedge his or her position with a stock index futures contract.

Tax Hedge An investor may have accumulated a large return on a diversified portfolio in a given year. To maintain the profitable position but defer the taxable gains until the next year, futures contracts may be employed.

Arbitraging

While stock index futures started out as a major tool for speculating and hedging, they are now also widely used for arbitraging. Basically, an **arbitrage** is set up when a simultaneous trade (a buy and a sell) occurs in two different markets and a profit is locked in. Assume the S&P 500 Stock Index has a value of 1,250 based on the market value of all the stocks in the index. Also, assume the S&P 500 Stock Index futures contract, due to expire in two months, is selling for 1,260. There is a 10-point positive basis between the futures contract and the underlying index. A sophisticated institutional investor may decide to arbitrage based on the difference. He or she will simultaneously sell a futures contract for 1,260 and buy a basket of stocks that matches[14] the S&P 500 Stock Index for $1,250. Because at expiration the futures contract and underlying index will have the same value, a 10-point profit is locked in at the time of arbitraging. For example, if at expiration, the S&P 500 Stock Index has a value of 1,262, a gain of 12 will occur on the purchase, and a loss of 2 will be associated with the sale for a net profit of 10 per contract. If thousands of such contracts are involved, the profits can be substantial, and the potential for losses in a true arbitrage is nonexistent.

As you might assume, index arbitraging is in the exclusive providence of wealthy, sophisticated investors. For this reason, many smaller investors are somewhat resentful of the process and claim it tends to disrupt the normal operations of the marketplace. While there is nothing inherently wrong with arbitraging, it is sometimes a target for criticism by regulators. This is because it involves the process of program trading, discussed earlier in the chapter. However, there are very few arbitrage opportunities that exist and when they do exist, the behavior of the arbitrage traders will drive the prices to equilibrium.

TRADING STOCK INDEX OPTIONS

Stock index options also allow the market participant to speculate or hedge against major market movements, although there is no opportunity for arbitraging. Stock index options are similar in many respects to the standard put and call options on individual stocks discussed in Chapter 14. The purchaser of an option pays an initial premium and then closes out the option at a given price in the future. One essential difference between stock index options and options on individual securities is that, in the former case, there is only a cash settlement of the position, whereas in the latter case (individual securities), you can force the option writer to deliver the securities.

There are stock index options on the Dow Jones Industrial Average, the S&P 500, Nasdaq 100, Russell 2000, and other indexes. They all trade on the Chicago Board Options Exchange. Examples of stock index options for the S&P Index at different strike prices are presented in Table 16–5.

Actual Option Trade in the S&P 500 Index

application example

We will use the data from Table 16–5 for our example. Note in the footnote of Table 16–5 that the S&P 500 Index closed at 1148.67 on September 24, 2010. With this value in mind, we can examine the strike prices and premiums for the various contracts. The premium is multiplied by 100 to determine the total cash value involved. The premium for the October 1,090 strike price is 61.05.

TABLE 16-5 S&P 500 Index Option (September 24, 2010)

Strike Price	CALLS Oct	CALLS Nov	CALLS Dec	PUTS Oct	PUTS Nov	PUTS Dec
1,090	**61.05**	73.96	—	**6.00**	19.00	—
1,095	—	—	—	6.55	—	—
1,100	54.00	65.78	74.00	7.10	21.05	31.00
1,105	49.25	—	—	8.00	—	—

The multiplier times the premium is 100.

Value of the S&P 500 Index = 1,148.67.

[14] Actually, arbitraging has become sufficiently sophisticated through mathematics and computer analysis that all 500 stocks do not actually have to be purchased. Perhaps 10 or 15 key stocks bought in large quantities will be sufficient to adequately represent the S&P 500 Index. Commissions on such transactions tend to be extremely small. Mutual funds and exchange traded funds that replicate the S&P 500 index can also be purchased.

Assume that the investor bought an October 1,090 call option for a price of 61.05 on September 24, 2010, and when the contract expired the S&P 500 Index was 1,160 under an optimistic assumption and 1,020 under a pessimistic assumption. At an index value of 1,160, the option value is 70 (1,160 − 1,090). The ending or expiration price is 70 points higher than the strike price. Also, keep it in mind that the option cost is 61.05. The profit is shown in Table 16–6.

At an ending value of 1,020 (pessimistic assumption), the option is worthless and there is a loss of $6,150, as indicated in Table 16–6. Remember, these are 1,090 call options.

TABLE 16-6 Gains and Losses on Call Option

	1,160 Optimistic Assumption	1,020 Pessimistic Assumption
Final value (100 × 70)	$7,000	$ 0
Purchase price (100 × 61.50)	−6,150	−6,150
Profit or loss	$ 850	−6,150

Let's shift our attention to put options. If an October 1,090 put option (the option to sell at 1,090 rather than to buy at 1,090) had been acquired on September 24, 2010, we can see in Table 16–5 (put column) that the price of the option would be 6.00. Let's assume that when the option expired, the S&P 500 Index was 1,160 under what is now the pessimistic assumption and 1,020 under what is now the optimistic assumption.

At an index value of 1,160, no value is associated with a put option that allows you to sell at 1,160. No one would want to use the option to sell at 1,090 if the index value were 1,160. Because the put option cost 6.00, there is a loss of $600, as indicated in Table 16–7. At a final S&P value of 1,020, the put option to sell at 1,090 has a value of 70. With a cost of 6.00, a profit of 64 occurs, which translates into $6,400. This is also shown in Table 16–7.

TABLE 16-7 Gains and Losses on Put Option

	1,160 Pessimistic Assumption	1,020 Optimistic Assumption
Final value (100 × 70)	$ 0	$7,000
Purchase price (100 × 6)	600	−600
Profit or loss	−600	$6,400

HEDGING WITH STOCK INDEX OPTIONS

The discussion of stock index options thus far has pertained to speculation about market moves. Stock index options can also be used for hedging. Like stock index futures, stock index options can be utilized to protect a portfolio or for special purposes by underwriters, specialists, dealers, tax planners, and others.

At times, options may offer a hedging advantage over futures to investors who are limited by law from purchasing futures contracts. On the other hand, futures generally allow for a more efficient hedge than options. If the market goes down by 20 or 25 percent, chances are good that a completely hedged short futures position (selling futures contracts) will compensate for losses in a portfolio. An option write, used to hedge a portfolio, may be inadequate. Perhaps the option premium income represents 10 percent of the portfolio, but the market goes down by 25 percent. Fifteen percent of the loss will be unprotected. Buying a put option may overcome this problem, but the cash outflow to purchase the put option could involve substantial funds. Clearly, both futures and options have their advantages and disadvantages.

There are also options on industry indexes that can be used for hedging or speculation. For example, the American Stock Exchange has index options on high-tech and pharmaceutical companies, and the Philadelphia Exchange covers gold/silver, oil services, semiconductors, and public utilities. The trading in industry options is basically the same as trading in overall market options.

OPTIONS ON STOCK INDEX FUTURES

We have discussed *stock index futures* and *stock index options,* so a natural extension of our discussion is to consider the third form of stock index trading, *options on stock index futures*. The three forms of index trading are listed below for reference.

1. Stock index futures.
2. Stock index options.
3. Options on stock index futures.

An option on stock index futures (item 3 above) gives the holder the right to purchase the stock index *futures contract* at a specified price over a given period. This is slightly different from the stock index option (item 2) that gives the holder the right to purchase the *underlying index* at a specified price over a given time period.[15]

The primary topic for discussion in this section is represented by the left-hand column in Figure 16–1, an option on a stock index futures contract. The value of an option to purchase a stock index futures contract will depend on the outlook for the futures contract.

Normally, the premiums on the call options increase substantially with the passage of time. This gain in value is not only a function of the extended time period associated with the option but is also due to the fact that the S&P futures contract

FIGURE 16-1 Comparison of Option Contracts

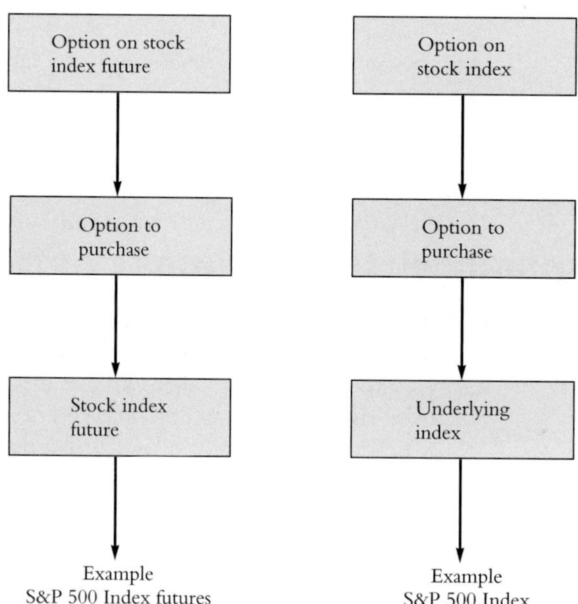

[15] Because of cash-settlement procedures, the actual index will never actually be purchased, and the gain or loss will be settled for cash.

normally has a higher value with the passage of time.[16] Thus, options on stock index futures not only have a time premium (all options do) but may also have an additional premium (or discount) depending on the relationship of the far-term futures market to the near-term futures market.

Options on stock index futures may be settled on a cash basis, or the holder of a call option may exercise the option and force the option writer to produce a specified futures contract. There are also puts for options on stock index futures.

[16] Of course, if the market outlook were highly pessimistic, there would be a decline in the S&P futures contract with the passage of time.

exploring the web

Web Address	Comments
www.cboe.com	**Web site for major options exchange**
www.schaeffersresearch.com	**Offers technical analysis for options**
www.marketwatch.com/investing	**Contains some information and tracking on stock options**
www.888options.com	**Educational site on options**
www.cbot.com	**Web site for the Chicago Board of Trade providing information, quotes, and educational features**
www.pcquote.com	**Provides research and quotes on options and commodities**
www.euronext.com/home_derivatives-2153-EN.html	**Home site for the London International Financial Futures and Options market (Euronext)**
www.cme.com	**Home site for the Chicago Mercantile Exchange containing quotes and information about futures**
www.cftc.gov	**Home site for the future market regulator Commodities Futures Trading Commission**

SUMMARY

For the investor who wishes to trade in stock indexes, there are three basic types of securities: stock index futures, stock index options, and options on stock index futures.

Stock index futures and options offer the potential for speculation as well as for hedging. With stock index futures, the margin is relatively low, which allows for a strong leverage potential. In hedging a portfolio position, the investor should consider the beta of his or her portfolio and adjust the number of contracts accordingly. Basis in the futures market represents the difference between the stock index futures price and the value of the actual underlying index. Basis may present the investor with a potential clue about the future direction of the market. The stock index futures market and the stock index option market trade on a cash-settlement basis. No securities ever change hands as the settlement is always in cash.

Investors in stock index futures may also engage in arbitraging procedures in which a simultaneous trade (a buy and a sell) occurs in the stock index futures contract and in the underlying securities in the index. This allows the investor to

www.mhhe.com/hirtblock10e

lock in a profit. The use of arbitraging, portfolio insurance, and program trading has been blamed by some for the market crash in October 1987 and the subsequent volatility in the market after the crash.

The stock index option contract is generally similar to the option contract on individual securities. The investor has an opportunity to buy puts and calls, and the premium is related to the future prospects for the index.

The third form of stock index contracts, an option on stock index futures, combines the option concept with the futures market. Instead of an option on an actual index, you have an option on a stock index futures contract. The contract may be settled either with cash or with securities.

KEY WORDS AND CONCEPTS

DISCUSSION QUESTIONS

1. Why are stock index futures and options sometimes referred to as derivative products? Why do some investors believe derivative products make the markets more volatile?
2. Why does a hedging position require less initial margin than a speculative position?
3. What is meant by the concept of cash settlement?
4. What does the term *basis* mean in the futures market? If there is a premium and it expands with the passage of time, what is the general implication?
5. Why does a down market put tremendous pressure on a speculator if he or she is the purchaser of a contract in anticipation of a market increase? Relate this answer directly to margin.
6. Why is it unrealistic for a portfolio manager to sell a large portion of his portfolio if he thinks the market is about to decline?
7. How does the beta of a portfolio influence the number of contracts that must be used in the hedging process?
8. What are some complicating factors in attempting to hedge a portfolio?
9. Why might the overuse of portfolio insurance be dangerous to the market?
10. What is an arbitrage position?
11. What is an essential difference between stock index options and options on individual securities in terms of settlement procedures?
12. Under what circumstance might a portfolio manager be more likely to use index option contracts instead of futures contracts to hedge a portfolio? What is the counter argument for futures contracts over index options?
13. Explain the difference between a stock index option and an option on stock index futures.
14. Suggest two reasons an option on a stock index futures contract that has a distant expiration date might have a high premium.

PRACTICE PROBLEMS AND SOLUTIONS

Gains and losses on S&P futures

1. *a.* An investor bought a March S&P 500 Index futures contract in December for 1271.05. After four months the contract value went up to 1292.10. The contract has a multiplier of 250. What is the dollar profit?

b. With an initial margin of $20,000, what is the percent return on margin? On an annualized basis, what is this return?

c. There is a $16,000 margin maintenance requirement. If the contract value went from its original value of 1271.05 down to 1252.81, would there be a call for more margin?

Gains and losses on S&P call and put options

2. Assume the following options are available on the S&P 500 Index. The Index is currently at 1235.

May 1240 call 21
May 1240 put 26

If the Index ends up at 1290 at the expiration date, what will be the gain or loss on the (*a*) call option and (*b*) put option?

Solutions

1. *a.*

Latest value	1292.10
Original value	1271.05
Gain	21.05
Multiplier	$ 250
Total profit	$5,262.50

b. Percent return on initial margin

$$\frac{\$5,262.50}{20,000.00} = 26.31\%$$

$$\text{Annualized return} = 26.31\% \times 12/4 = 78.93\%$$

c.

Latest value	1252.81
Original value	1271.05
Loss	(18.24)
Multiplier	$ 250
Total loss	$ (4,560)

$$\text{Current margin} = \text{Original margin} - \text{Loss}$$
$$\$15,440 = \$20,000 - \$4,560$$

Because the margin is below $16,000, there would be a call for more margin.

2. *a.* May call option

Purchase price	21
Expiration value (1290 − 1240)	50
Gain	29
Total gain ($100 × 29)	$ 2,900

b. May put option

Purchase price	26
Expiration value (no value)	0*
Loss	−26
Total loss ($100 × −26)	−2,600

*The option to sell at 1,240 has no value when the index is at 1,290.

PROBLEMS

Stock index futures

1. Based on the information in Table 16–1 on page 417, what is the total value of an S&P 500 Index futures contract for December 2010? Use the settle price and the appropriate multiplier. Also, if the required margin is $28,125, what percent of the contract value does margin represent?

Gain on S&P futures

2. In problem 1, if the S&P Index futures contract goes up to $1,283.60, what will be the total dollar profit on the contract? What is the percent return on the initial margin? If this price change occurred over four months, what is the annualized return? (Multiply by 12/4.)

Loss on S&P futures and margin

3. Return to problem 1 and assume that margin must be maintained at a minimum level of $22,500. If the S&P Index futures contract goes from its initial value down to $1,051.80, will there be a call for more margin?

Computing settle price

4. Based on the information in Table 16–1 on page 417, assume you buy a Dow Jones (DJ) Industrial Average September contract at the settle price. You hold the contract for six months and enjoy a gain in value of $15,000. What is the settle price after six months?

Computing settle price

5. Based on the information in Table 16–1 on page 417, assume you buy a Nasdaq 100 December contract at the settle price. You hold the contract for one month and suffer a loss of $3,000. What is settle price after one month?

Computing basis

6. Examine Table 16–1 on page 417. Using settle prices, what is the value of the basis for each of the September 2010 and December 2010 DJ Industrial Contracts? Assume the actual DJ is 11,100.

Hedging and betas

7. Northern States Life Insurance Company has a $14 million stock portfolio. The company is very aggressive and the portfolio has a weighted beta of 1.30.
   a. Assume they use S&P 500 Index futures contracts to hedge the portfolio for the next 90 days and the contracts can be sold at 1,290. The contracts have a multiplier of 250. With the appropriate beta adjustment factor, how many contracts should be sold? Round the final answer to the nearest whole number.
   b. If Dow Jones (DJ) Industrial Average contracts selling at 11,150 were used instead, how many contracts should be sold? These contracts have a multiplier of 10. Once again, consider the appropriate beta adjustment factor and round your final answer to the nearest whole number.

Hedging and betas

8. The New Horizon Pension Fund decides to hedge its $40 million stock portfolio on June 1. The portfolio has a beta of 1.10. It will use Nasdaq futures contracts selling at 1,571 to hedge. These contracts have a multiplier of 100.
   a. With the appropriate beta adjustment factor and rounding the final answer to the nearest whole number, how many contracts should be sold?
   b. Assuming that by September 1 the market has gone down by 20 percent and the stock portfolio moves in accordance with its beta, what will be the total dollar decline in the portfolio?
   c. Assume the Nasdaq Index futures contracts decline by 20 percent from 1,571. What will be the total dollar gain on the futures contracts? In the process, compare the sale price of 1,571 with the current value, multiply by 100, and then multiply this value by the number of contracts. How does the total dollar gain on the futures contracts compare with the portfolio loss in part *b*?
   d. Now assume that because of changing basis, the stock index futures contract does not move parallel to the market. Although the market goes down by 20 percent, the stock index futures decline by only 15 percent. What will be the gain on the futures contracts? How does this compare with the loss in portfolio value in part *b*?

S&P 500 call options

9. The following problem relates to data in Table 16–5 on page 426. Assume you purchase a November 1100 (strike price) S&P 500 call option. Compute your total dollar profit or loss if the index has the following values at expiration:

a. 1150
b. 1190
c. 1230

S&P 500 call options

10. Using data from Table 16–5 on page 426, assume you purchase a December 1100 (strike price) S&P 500 put option. Compute your total dollar profit or loss if the index has the following values at expiration:

a. 1260
b. 1210
c. 1100

Hedging with the S&P 500 options

11. The Topps Company has a $1 million funded pension plan for its employees. The portfolio beta is equal to 1.12. Assume the company sells (writes) 60 October 1100 (strike price) call option contracts on the S&P 500 Index as shown in Table 16–5 on page 426. Each contract trades in units of 100. At the time the options were written, the index had a value of 1,148.67.

a. What are the proceeds from the sale of the call options?
b. Assume the market goes down by 14 percent. Considering the portfolio beta, what will be the total dollar decline in the portfolio?
c. Assume the S&P 500 Index shown at the bottom of Table 16–5 also goes down by 14 percent at expiration. What will be the value of the index at that time?
d. Based on your answer to part *c,* what will be your profit or loss on the option writes?
e. Considering your answers to parts *b* and *d,* what is your net gain or loss?

Using puts to hedge

12. Assume that in problem 11 the firm had purchased 80 October 1100 put option contracts on the S&P 500 Index listed in Table 16–5 on page 426, instead of selling the call options. If the S&P 500 Index goes down by 14 percent (see 11*c*) at expiration,

a. What will be your profit on the puts? Comparing that to your loss on the stock portfolio in problem 11*b,* what is your net overall gain or loss?
b. Compare the protection afforded by the call-writing hedge in problem 11 with the protection afforded by the put purchase in this problem.
c. Suggest any modifications to the call writing or put purchase strategy that would allow you to increase your protection even more. A general statement is all that is required.

Using calls and puts to hedge

13. Garner Money Management, Inc., is in charge of a $50 million portfolio. Its beta is equal to the market. To hedge its position, it sells (writes) 200 December 1100 call option contracts on the S&P 500 Stock Index as shown in Table 16–5 on page 426. It also buys 300 December 1100 put option contracts on the same index shown in Table 16–5. Instead of going down, the market goes up by 10 percent (as does the portfolio), and the S&P 500 Stock Index ends at 1,263.00.

Consider the change in the portfolio value and the gains or losses on the call and put options. Each option contract trades in units of 100. What is the overall net gain or loss of Garner Money Management as a result of the changes in the market?

INVESTMENT ADVISOR PROBLEM

Katie Winstead had just completed a course in investments and was ready to start investing. She had inherited $4,000 from her grandfather and wanted to put the money to work. Because the market had recently declined by 10 percent and the time period was early January, she thought a market recovery might be in order.

She had learned in her investments class about the importance of diversification so she was hesitant to buy just one or two stocks. She decided instead to buy a stock index futures contract. She knew she could get maximum "bang for her bucks" through the low margin requirement on a stock index futures contract.

She initially looked at the Dow Jones Industrial Average futures contract, which had a contract value of $105,380 and a margin requirement of $7,500. She knew the margin requirement normally ran 6 to 7 percent of the size of the contract so she was not surprised with the $7,500 requirement. However, since she had only $4,000 in funds, this contract was out of her reach. She also had a preference for technology stocks as opposed to the diversified stocks that were part of the Dow Jones Industrial Average. She decided to call her family's investment advisor, Sharon Lewis, to see what she might suggest.

Sharon directed her to Table 16–2 on page 418 in the Hirt and Block text and reminded her that the margin requirement was normally 6 to 7 percent of the value of the contract.

a. Given the amount of Katie's funds and her other preferences, which contract might be best for her?

b. How else might she get maximum "bang for the bucks" in investing in stock index plays?

BROADENING THE INVESTMENT PERSPECTIVE

PART [six] 6

17 chapter seventeen

A BASIC LOOK AT PORTFOLIO MANAGEMENT AND CAPITAL MARKET THEORY

OBJECTIVES

1. Understand the basic statistical techniques for measuring risk and return.
2. Explain how the portfolio effect works to reduce the risk of an individual security.
3. Discuss the concept of an efficient portfolio.
4. Explain the importance of the capital asset pricing model.
5. Understand the concept of the beta coefficient.
6. Discuss the required return on an individual stock and how it relates to its beta.

OUTLINE

Assume it's 8:00 on Sunday evening, and you are watching a sporting event on ESPN. Commercials come on and, along with the latest shiny BMW and Lexus models, there is an ad about mutual funds.

www.fidelity.com

We could take any mutual fund as an example, but in this particular case, we will use the Fidelity Blue Chip Growth Fund. The title of the fund is laden with upscale words. Fidelity is the best-known mutual fund company in the world (with scores of other funds besides this one). The term blue chip implies high quality and growth and indicates that the fund invests in companies that have strong possibilities to enhance their value. The ad for this fund indicated its value had gone up 21.64 percent over the last 12 months.

However, the real issue is how much risk or volatility the investor was exposed to in achieving this high return. There are two dimensions to any investment: risk and return, and this typical ad is only covering one: return. If the fund had to take an inordinately high amount of risk to achieve this result, it is certainly a less commendable performance. The truth is the fund did have a high degree of risk exposure, with 25.1 percent of its assets invested in technology stocks.

In this chapter, we develop a more complete understanding of how the investor perceives risk and demands compensation for it. We eventually build toward a theory of portfolio management that incorporates these concepts. While the use of mathematical terms is an essential ingredient to a basic understanding of portfolio theory, more involved or complicated concepts are treated in appendixes at the end of the chapter.

As indicated in Chapter 1, risk is generally associated with uncertainty about future outcomes. The greater the dispersion of possible outcomes, the greater the risk. We also observed in Chapter 1 that most investors tend to be risk-averse; that is, all things being equal, investors prefer less risk to more risk and will increase their risk-taking position only if a premium for risk is involved. Each investor has a different attitude toward risk. The inducement necessary to cause a given investor to withdraw funds from a money market account to drill an oil well may be quite different from yours. For some, only a very small premium for risk is necessary, while others may not wish to participate unless there are exceptionally high rewards. We begin the chapter with a formal development of risk measures.

FORMAL MEASUREMENT OF RISK

Having defined risk as uncertainty about future outcomes, how do we actually measure risk? The first task is to design a probability distribution of anticipated future outcomes. This is no small task. The possible outcomes and associated probabilities are likely to be based on economic projections, past experience, subjective judgments, and many other variables. For the most part, we are forcing ourselves to write down what already exists in our head. Having established the probability distribution, we then determine the expected value and the dispersion around that expected value. The greater the dispersion, the greater the risk.

Expected Value

application example

To determine the **expected value**, we multiply each possible outcome by its probability of occurrence. Assume we are considering two investment proposals where *K* represents a possible outcome and *P* represents the probability of that outcome based on the state of the economy. If we were dealing with stocks, *K* would represent the price appreciation potential plus the dividend yield (total return). Table 17–1 presents the data for two investments, *i* and *j*.

TABLE 17-1 Return and Probabilities for Investments *i* and *j*

Investment *i*			Investment *j*	
Return K_i	P_i (Probability of K_i Occurring)	Possible State of the Economy	Return K_j	P_j (Probability of K_j Occurring)
5%	0.20	Recession	20%	0.20
7	0.30	Slow growth	8	0.30
13	0.30	Moderate growth	8	0.30
15	0.20	Strong economy	6	0.20

We will say that $\overline{K}_i$ (the expected value of investment i) equals ΣK_iP_i. In this case, the answer would be 10.0 percent, as shown under Formula 17–1:

$$\overline{K}_i = \Sigma K_i P_i \quad \textbf{(17–1)}$$

K_i	P_i	K_iP_i
5%	0.20	1.0%
7	0.30	2.1
13	0.30	3.9
15	0.20	3.0
		10.0% = ΣK_iP_i

Standard Deviation

application example

The commonly used measure of dispersion is the **standard deviation**, which is a measure of the spread of the outcomes around the expected value. The formula for the standard deviation is:

$$\sigma_i = \sqrt{\Sigma(K_i - \overline{K}_i)^2 P_i} \quad \textbf{(17–2)}$$

Let's determine the standard deviation for investment i around the expected value ($\overline{K}_i$) of 10 percent.

K_i	$\overline{K}_i$	P_i	$(K_i - \overline{K}_i)$	$(K_i - \overline{K}_i)^2$	$(K_i - \overline{K}_i)^2P_i$
5%	10%	0.20	−5%	25%	5.0%
7	10	0.30	−3	9	2.7
13	10	0.30	+3	9	2.7
15	10	0.20	+5	25	5.0
					15.4% = $\Sigma(K_i - \overline{K}_i)^2P_i$

$$\sigma_i = \sqrt{\Sigma(K_i - \overline{K}_i)^2 P_i} = \sqrt{15.4\%} = 3.9\%$$

The standard deviation of investment i is 3.9 percent (rounded). To have some feel for the relative risk characteristics of this investment, we compare it with the second proposal, investment j.

We assume investment j is a countercyclical investment. It does well during a recession and poorly in a strong economy. Perhaps it represents a firm in the housing industry that is most profitable when the economy is sluggish and interest rates are low. Under these circumstances, people will avail themselves of low-cost financing to purchase a new home, and the stock of the firm will do well. In a booming economy, interest rates will advance rapidly, and the financing of housing will become expensive. Thus, we have a countercyclical investment. The outcomes and probabilities of outcomes for investment j are as follows:

The expected value for investment j is:

$$\overline{K}_j = \Sigma K_j P_j$$

K_j	P_j	K_jP_j
20%	0.20	4.0%
8	0.30	2.4
8	0.30	2.4
6	0.20	1.2
		$\overline{K}_j$ = 10.0%

The standard deviation for investment j is:

$$\sigma_j = \sqrt{\Sigma(K_j - \overline{K}_j)^2 P_j}$$

K_j	$\overline{K}_j$	P_j	$(K_j - \overline{K}_j)$	$(K_j - \overline{K}_j)^2$	$(K_j - \overline{K}_j)^2 P_j$
20%	10%	0.20	+10%	100%	20.0%
8	10	0.30	−2	4	1.2
8	10	0.30	−2	4	1.2
6	10	0.20	−4	16	3.2
					25.6% = $\Sigma(K_j - \overline{K}_j)^2 P_j$

$$\sigma_j = \sqrt{\Sigma(K_j - \overline{K}_j)^2 P_j} = \sqrt{25.6\%} = 5.1\% \text{ (rounded)}$$

We now see we have two investments, each with an expected value of 10 percent but with varying performances in different types of economies and different standard deviations ($\sigma_i = 3.9$ percent versus $\sigma_j = 5.1$ percent).[1]

PORTFOLIO EFFECT

application example

An investor who is holding only investment i may wish to consider bringing investment j into the portfolio. If the stocks are weighted evenly, the new portfolio's expected value will be 10 percent. We define K_p as the expected value of the portfolio:

$$K_p = X_i\overline{K}_i + X_j\overline{K}_j \quad \textbf{(17–3)}$$

The X values represent the weights assigned by the investor to each component in the portfolio and are 50 percent for both investments in this example. The $\overline{K}_i$ and $\overline{K}_j$ values were previously determined to be 10 percent. Thus we have:

$$K_p = 0.5(10\%) + 0.5(10\%) = 5\% + 5\% = 10\%$$

[1] Actually, rather than use the standard deviation, we can also use its squared value, termed the *variance,* to describe risk. That is, we may use σ^2 (the standard deviation squared) to describe the risk in an individual secuity.

What about the standard deviation for the combined portfolio (σ_p)? If a weighted average were taken of the two investments, the new standard deviation would be 4.5 percent:

$$X_i\sigma_i + X_j\sigma_j$$
$$0.5(3.9\%) + 0.5(5.1\%) = 1.95\% + 2.55\% = 4.5\%$$

The interesting element is that the investor in investment *i* would appear to be losing from the combined investment. His expected value remains at 10 percent, but his standard deviation has increased from 3.9 to 4.5 percent. Given that he is risk-averse, he appears to be getting more risk rather than less risk by expanding his portfolio.

There is one fallacy in the analysis. *The standard deviation of a portfolio is not based on the simple weighted average of the individual standard deviations (as the expected value is).* Rather, it considers significant interaction between the investments. If one investment does well during a given economic condition while the other does poorly and vice versa, there may be significant risk reduction from combining the two, and the standard deviation for the portfolio may be less than the standard deviation for either investment (this is the reason we do not simply take the weighted average of the two).

Note in Figure 17–1 the risk-reduction potential from combining the two investments under study. Investment *i* alone may produce outcomes anywhere from 5 to 15 percent, and investment *j*, from 6 to 20 percent. By combining the two, we narrow the range for investment (*i, j*) from 7.5 to 12.5 percent. Thus, we have reduced the risk while keeping the expected valuc constant at 10 percent. We now examine the appropriate standard deviation formula for the two investments.

Standard Deviation for a Two-Asset Portfolio

The standard deviation for a two-asset portfolio is presented in Formula 17–4:[2]

$$\sigma_p = \sqrt{X_i^2\sigma_i^2 + X_j^2\sigma_j^2 + 2X_iX_jr_{ij}\sigma_i\sigma_j} \quad \textbf{(17–4)}$$

FIGURE 17–1 Investment Outcomes under Different Conditions

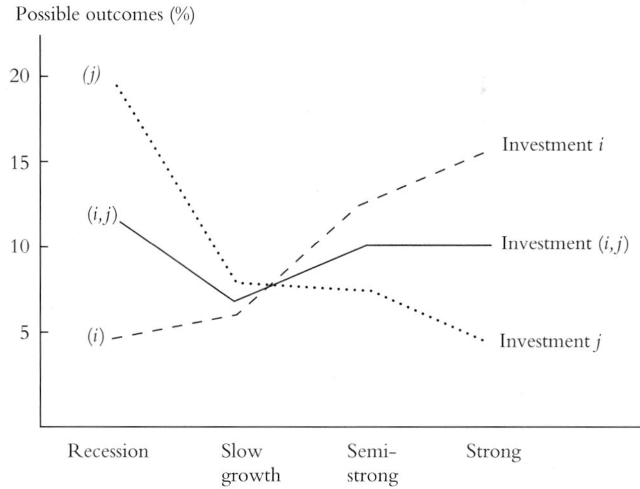

[2] For a multiple asset portfolio, the expression is written as:

$$\sigma_p = \sqrt{\sum_{i=1}^{N} X_i^2\sigma_i^2 + 2\sum_{i=1}^{N-1}\sum_{j=1+1}^{N} X_iX_jr_{ij}\sigma_i\sigma_j}$$

N is the number of securities in the portfolio.

FIGURE 17–2 Correlation Analysis

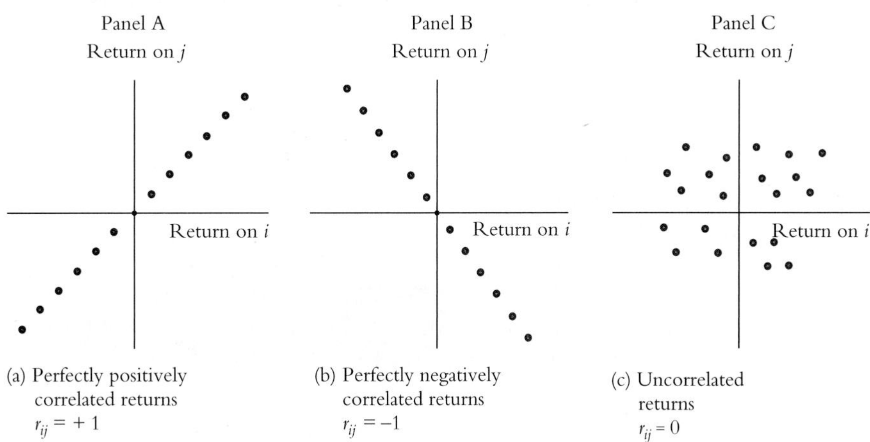

(a) Perfectly positively correlated returns $r_{ij} = +1$

(b) Perfectly negatively correlated returns $r_{ij} = -1$

(c) Uncorrelated returns $r_{ij} = 0$

The only new term in the expression is r_{ij}, the **correlation coefficient** or measurement of joint movement between the two variables. The value for r_{ij} can be from -1 to $+1$, although for most variables, the correlation coefficient falls somewhere in between these two values. Figure 17–2 demonstrates the concept of correlation. In Panel A, assets *i* and *j* are perfectly correlated, with r_{ij} equal to $+1$. As *i* increases in value, so does *j* in exact proportion to *i*. In Panel B, assets *i* and *j* exhibit a perfect negative correlation, with r_{ij} equal to -1. As *i* increases, *j* decreases in exact proportion to *i*. Panel C demonstrates assets *i* and *j* having no correlation at all, with r_{ij} equal to 0.

application example

The actual computation of the correlation coefficient for investments *i* and *j* is covered in Appendix 17A. It is not necessary to go through Appendix 17A before proceeding with our discussion, though some readers may wish to do so. As indicated in Appendix 17A, the correlation coefficient (r_{ij}) between our investment *i* and investment *j* is -0.70. This indicates the two investments show a high degree of negative correlation. Plugging this value into Formula 17–4, along with other previously determined values, the standard deviation (σ_p) for the two-asset portfolio can be computed:[3]

$$\sigma_p = \sqrt{X_i^2\sigma_i^2 + X_j^2\sigma_j^2 + 2X_iX_jr_{ij}\sigma_i\sigma_j}$$

where:

$$\begin{aligned}
X_i &= 0.5, \sigma_i = 3.9 \\
X_j &= 0.5, \sigma_j = 5.1 \\
r_{ij} &= -0.70 \\
\sigma_p &= \sqrt{(0.5)^2(3.9)^2 + (0.5)^2(5.1)^2 + 2(0.5)(0.5)(-0.7)(3.9)(5.1)} \\
&= \sqrt{(0.25)(15.4) + (0.25)(25.6) + 2(0.35)(-0.7)(19.9)} \\
&= \sqrt{3.85 + 6.4 + (0.5)(-13.93)} \\
&= \sqrt{3.85 + 6.4 - 6.97} \\
&= \sqrt{3.28} = 1.8\%
\end{aligned}$$

[3] Note that the squared values, such as $(3.9)^2 = 15.4$, are the reverse of earlier computations. Previously, we found the square root of 15.4 to be 3.9 (see computation under Formula 17–2). The use of rounding introduces slight discrepancies where we square numbers for which we previously found the square root.

The standard deviation of the portfolio of 1.8 percent is less than the standard deviation of either investment i (3.9 percent) or j (5.1 percent). Any time two investments have a correlation coefficient (r_{ij}) less than +1 (perfect positive correlation), some risk reduction will be possible by combining the assets in a portfolio. In the real world, most items are positively correlated; the extent that we can still get risk reduction from positively correlated items gives extra meaning to portfolio management. Note the impact of various assumed correlation coefficients for the two investments previously described in terms of individual standard deviations:[4]

Correlation Coefficient (r_{ij})	Portfolio Standard Deviation (σ_p)
+1.0	4.5
+0.5	3.9
0.0	3.2
−0.5	2.3
−0.7	1.8
−1.0	0.0

The conclusion to be drawn from our portfolio analysis discussion is that the most significant risk factor associated with an individual investment may not be its own standard deviation but how it affects the standard deviation of a portfolio through correlation. As we shall later observe in this chapter, there is not considered to be a risk premium for the total risk or standard deviation of an individual security, but only for that risk component that cannot be eliminated by various portfolio diversification techniques.

DEVELOPING AN EFFICIENT PORTFOLIO

We have seen how the combination of two investments has allowed us to maintain our return of 10 percent but reduce the portfolio standard deviation to 1.8 percent. We also saw in the preceding table that different coefficient correlations produce many different possibilities for portfolio standard deviations. A shrewd portfolio manager may wish to consider a large number of portfolios, each with a different expected value and standard deviation, based on the expected values and standard deviations of the individual securities and, more importantly, on the correlations between the individual securities. Though we have been discussing a two-asset portfolio case, our example may be expanded to cover 5-, 10-, or even 100-asset portfolios.[5] The major tenets of portfolio theory that we are currently examining were developed by Professor Harry Markowitz in the 1950s, and so we refer to them as the Markowitz portfolio theory. In 1990 Markowitz won the Nobel Prize in economics for this work.

Assume we have identified the following risk-return possibilities for eight different portfolios (there may also be many more, but we will restrict ourselves to this set at the top of the next page for now):

---

[4] Each is assumed to represent 50 percent of the portfolio.

[5] The incremental benefit from reduction of the portfolio standard deviation through adding securities appears to diminish fairly sharply with a portfolio of 10 securities and is quite small with a portfolio as large as 20. A portfolio of 14 to 16 securities is generally thought to be of sufficient size to enjoy the majority of desirable portfolio effects. See W. H. Wagner and S. C. Lau, "The Effect of Diversification on Risk," *Financial Analysts Journal,* November–December 1971, pp. 48–53.

Portfolio	K_p	σ_p
A	10%	1.8%
B	10	2.1
C	12	3.0
D	13	4.2
E	13	5.0
F	14	5.0
G	14	5.8
H	15	7.2

In diagramming our various risk-return points in the table above, we show the values in Figure 17–3.

Although we have only diagrammed eight possibilities, we see an efficient set of portfolios would lie along the ACFH line in Figure 17–3. This line is efficient because the portfolios on this line dominate all other attainable portfolios. This line is called the **efficient frontier** because the portfolios on the efficient frontier provide the best risk-return trade-off. That is, along this efficient frontier we can receive a maximum return for a given level of risk or a minimum risk for a given level of return. Portfolios do not exist above the efficient frontier, and portfolios below this line do not offer acceptable alternatives to points along the line. As an example of *maximum return* for a given level of risk, consider point F. Along the efficient frontier, we are receiving a 14 percent return for a 5 percent risk level, whereas directly below point F, portfolio E provides a 13 percent return for the same 5 percent standard deviation.

To also demonstrate that we are getting *minimum* risk for a given return level, we can examine point A in which we receive a 10 percent return for a 1.8 percent

FIGURE 17–3 Diagram of Risk-Return Trade-Offs

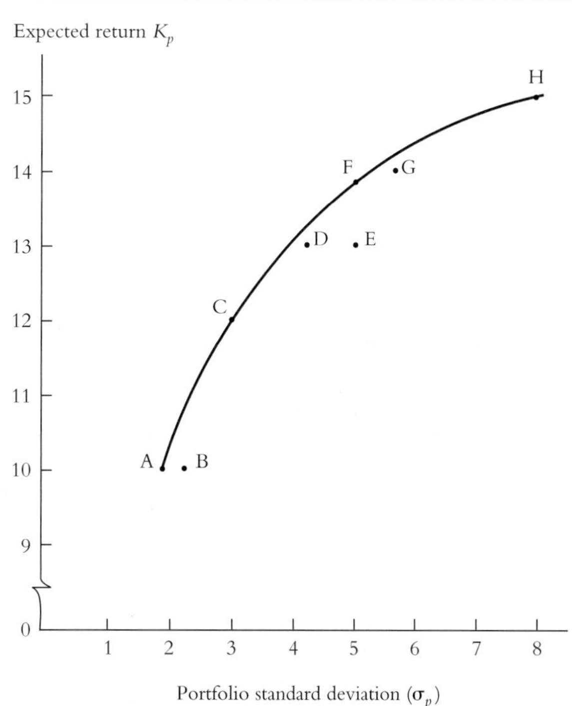

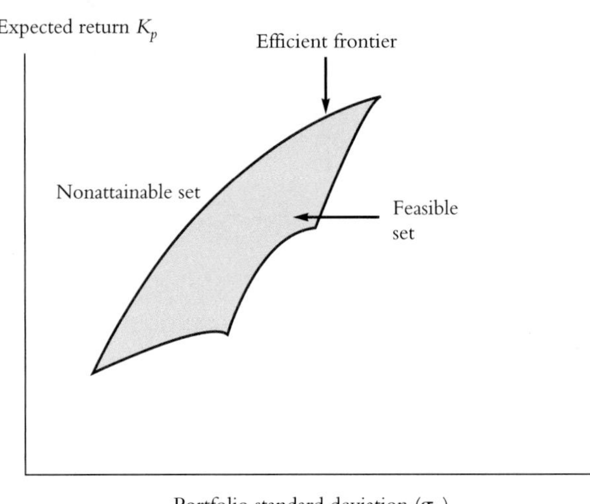

risk level, whereas to the right of point A, we get the same 10 percent return from B, but a less desirable 2.1 percent risk level. One portfolio can consist of various proportions of two assets or two portfolios. For example, we can connect the points between A and C by generating portfolios that combine different percentages of portfolio A and portfolio C and so on between portfolios C and F and portfolios F and H. Although we have shown but eight points (portfolios), a fully developed efficient frontier may be based on a virtually unlimited number of observations as is presented in Figure 17–4.

In Figure 17–4, we once again view the efficient frontier in relationship to the feasible set and note that certain risk-return possibilities are not attainable (and should be disregarded). At this point in the analysis, we can stipulate that the various points along the efficient frontier are all considered potentially optimal and a given investor should choose the most appropriate single point based on individual risk-return trade-off desires. We would say that a low-risk-oriented investor might prefer point A in Figure 17–3, whereas a more-risk-oriented investor would prefer point F or H. At each of these points, the investor is getting the best risk-return trade-off for his or her own particular risk-taking propensity.

Risk-Return Indifference Curves

To actually pair an investor with an appropriate point along the efficient frontier, we look at his or her indifference curve as illustrated in Figure 17–5.

The **indifference curves** show the investor's trade-off between risk and return. The steeper the slope of the curve, the more risk-averse the investor is. For example, in the case of Investor B (I_B in Figure 17–5), the indifference curve has a steeper slope than for Investor A (I_A). This means Investor B will require more incremental return (more of a risk premium) for each additional unit of risk. Note that to take risks, Investor B requires approximately twice as much incremental return as Investor A between points X and Y. However, Investor A is still somewhat risk-averse and perhaps represents a typical investor in the capital markets.

Once the shape of an investor's indifference curve is determined, a second objective can be established—to attain the highest curve possible. For example, Investor A, initially shown in Figure 17–5, would have a whole set of similarly shaped indifference curves as presented in Figure 17–6.

FIGURE 17–5 Risk-Return Indifference Curves

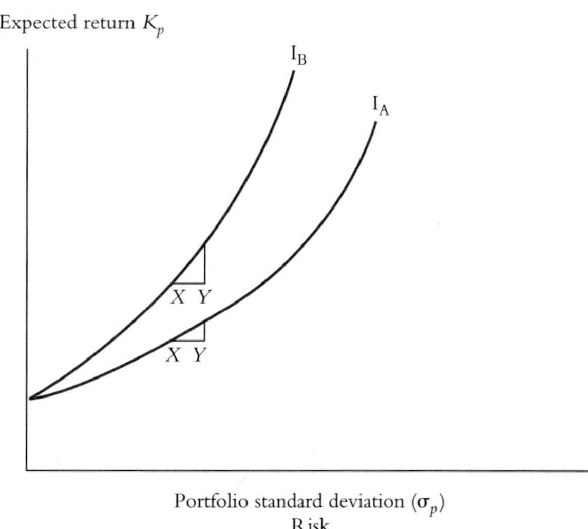

FIGURE 17–6 Indifference Curves for Investor A

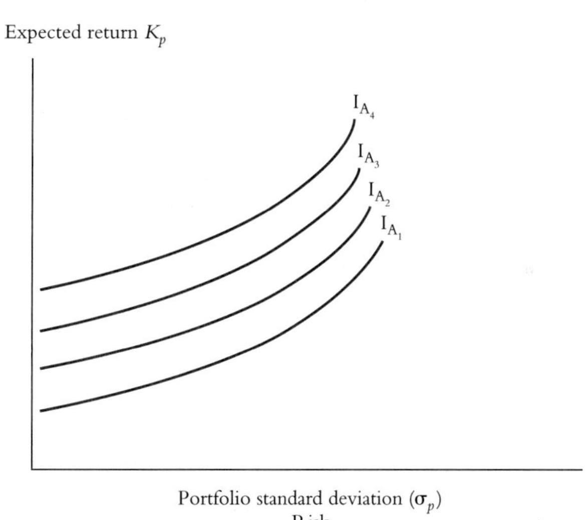

While he is indifferent to any point along a given curve (such as I_{A4}), he is not indifferent to achieving the highest curve possible (I_{A4} is clearly superior to I_{A1}). I_{A4} provides more return at all given risk levels. The only limitation to achieving the highest possible indifference curve is the feasible set of investments available.

Optimum Portfolio

The investor must theoretically match his own risk-return indifference curve with the best investments available in the market as represented by points on the efficient frontier. We see in Figure 17–7 that Investor A will achieve the highest possible indifference curve at point C along the efficient frontier.

This is the point of tangency between his own indifference curve (I_{A3}) and the efficient frontier. Both curves have the same slope or risk-return characteristics at this point. While a point along indifference curve (I_{A4}) might provide a higher level

FIGURE 17–7 Combining the Efficient Frontier and Indifference Curves

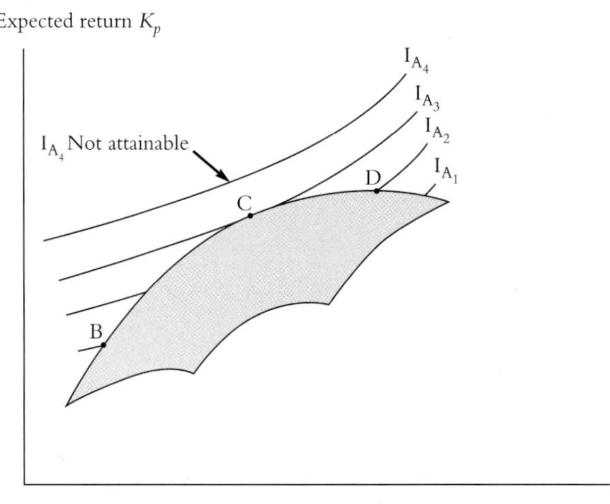

of utility, it is not attainable. Also, any other point along the efficient frontier would cross a lower level indifference curve and be inferior to point C. For example, points B and D cross I_{A2}, providing less return for a given level of risk than I_{A3}. Investors must relate the shape of their *own* risk-return indifference curves to the efficient frontier to determine that point of tangency providing maximum benefits.

CAPITAL ASSET PRICING MODEL

The development of the efficient frontier in the previous section gives insight into optimum portfolio mixes in an appropriate risk-return context. Nevertheless, the development of multiple portfolios is a rather difficult and tedious task. Professors Sharpe, Lintner, and others have allowed us to take the philosophy of efficient portfolios into a more generalized and meaningful context through the **capital asset pricing model**. Under this model, we examine the theoretical underpinnings through which assets are valued based on their risk characteristics.

The capital asset pricing model (CAPM) takes off where the efficient frontier concluded through the introduction of a new investment outlet, the risk-free asset (R_F). A risk-free asset has no risk of default and a standard deviation of 0 ($\sigma_{RF} = 0$) and is the lowest assumed safe return that can be earned. A U.S. Treasury bill or Treasury bond is often considered representative of a risk-free asset. Under the capital asset pricing model, we introduce the notion of combining the risk-free asset and the efficient frontier with the development of the R_FMZ line as indicated in Figure 17–8.

The R_FMZ line opens up the possibility of a whole new set of superior investment opportunities. That is, by combining some portion of the risk-free asset as represented by (R_F) with M (a point along the efficient frontier), we create new investment opportunities that will allow us to reach higher indifference curves than would be possible simply along the efficient frontier. The only point along the efficient frontier that now has significance is point M, where the straight line from R_F is tangent to the old efficient frontier. Let us further examine the R_FMZ line.

We can reach points along the R_FMZ line in a number of different ways. To be at point R_F, we would simply buy a risk-free asset. To be at a point between R_F and M, we would buy a combination of R_F and the M portfolio along the efficient

FIGURE 17–8 Basic Diagram of the Capital Market Line

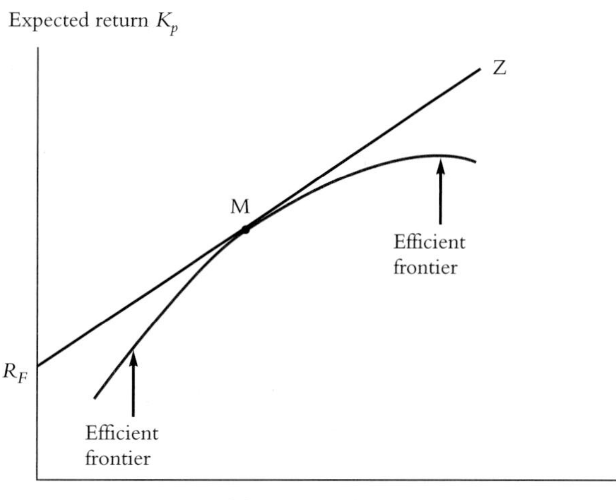

FIGURE 17–9 The Capital Market Line and Indifference Curves

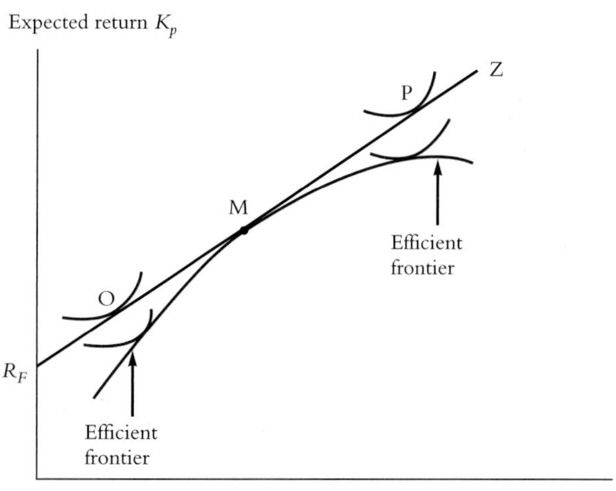

frontier. To be at a point between M and Z, we buy M with our available funds and then borrow additional funds to further increase our purchase of the M portfolio (an example of this would be to be at point P in Figure 17–9). To the extent that M is higher than R_F and we can borrow at a rate equal to R_F or slightly higher, we can get larger returns with a combination of buying M and borrowing additional funds to buy M.

We also note that point M is considered the optimum "market basket" of investments available (although you may wish to combine this market basket with risk-free assets or borrowing). If you took all the possible investments that investors could acquire and determined the optimum basket of investments, you would come up with point M (because it is along the efficient frontier and tangent to the R_F line). Point M can be measured by the total return on the Standard & Poor's 500 Stock Average, the Dow Jones Industrial Average, the New York Stock Exchange

Index, or similar measures. If point M or the market were not represented by the optimum risk-return portfolio for all investments at a point in time, then it is assumed there would be an instantaneous change, and the market measure (point M) would once again be in equilibrium (be optimal).

Capital Market Line

application example

The previously discussed R_FMZ line is called the **capital market line (CML)** and is once again presented in Figure 17–10.

The formula for the capital market line in Figure 17–10 may be written as:

$$K_P = R_F + \left(\frac{K_M - R_F}{\sigma_M - 0}\right)\sigma_P$$

We indicate that the expected return on any portfolio (K_P) is equal to the risk-free rate of return (R_F) plus the slope of the line times a value along the horizontal axis (σ_P), indicating the amount of risk undertaken. We can relate the formula for the capital market line to the basic equation for a straight line as follows:

$$\text{Straight line } Y = a + bX$$

$$\text{Capital market line } K_P = R_F + \left(\frac{K_M - R_F}{\sigma_M}\right)\sigma_P \qquad \textbf{(17–5)}$$

In using the capital market line, we start with a minimum rate of return of R_F and then say any additional return is a reward for risk. The reward for risk or risk premium is equal to the market rate of return (K_M) minus the risk-free rate (R_F) divided by the market standard deviation (σ_M). If the market rate of return (K_M) is 12 percent and the risk-free rate of return (R_F) is 6 percent, with a market standard deviation (σ_M) of 20 percent, there is a risk premium of 0.3:

$$\frac{K_M - R_F}{\sigma_M} = \frac{12\% - 6\%}{20\%} = \frac{6\%}{20\%} = 0.3$$

FIGURE 17–10 Illustration of the Capital Market Line

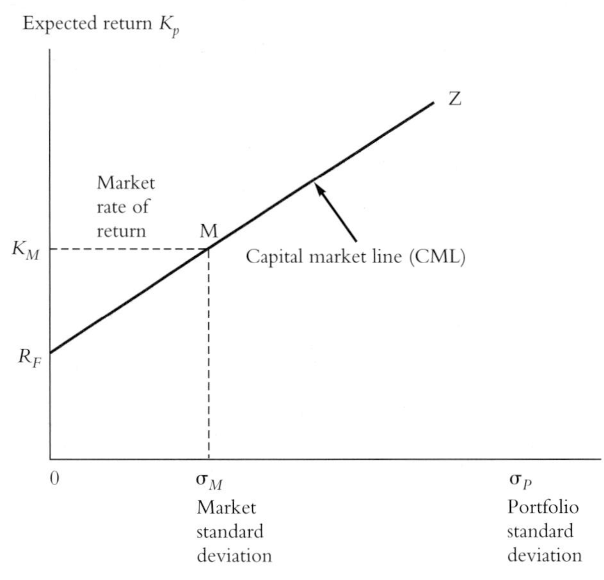

Then, if the standard deviation of our portfolio (σ_P) is 22 percent, we can expect a return of 12.6 percent along the CML computed as follows:

$$K_P = R_F + \left(\frac{K_M - R_F}{\sigma_M}\right)\sigma_P$$

$$K_P = 6\% + \left(\frac{12\% - 6\%}{20\%}\right)22\%$$

$$= 6\% + (0.3)22\%$$

$$= 6\% + 6.6\% = 12.6\%$$

The essence of the capital market line is that the way to get larger returns is to take increasingly higher risks. Thus, the only way to climb up the K_P *return* line in Figure 17–10 is to extend yourself out on the σ_P *risk* line. Portfolio managers who claim highly superior returns may have taken larger than normal risks and thus may not really be superior performers on a risk-adjusted basis. We shall see in the following chapter that the best way to measure a portfolio manager is to evaluate his returns relative to the risks taken. Average to slightly above average returns based on low risk may be superior to high returns based on high risk. One does not easily exceed market-dictated constraints for risk and return.

RETURN ON AN INDIVIDUAL SECURITY

We have been examining return expectations for a portfolio; we now turn our attention to an individual security. Once again the return potential is closely tied to risk. However, when dealing with an individual security, the premium return for risk is not related to *all* the risk in the investment as measured by the standard deviation (σ). The reason for this is that the standard deviation includes two types of risk, but only one is accorded a premium return under the capital asset pricing model.

We now begin an analytical process that allows us to get at the two forms of risk in an individual security. The first form of risk is measured by the beta coefficient. While some of the concepts discussed below were briefly covered in Chapter 1, a much more comprehensive discussion is provided in this chapter.

Beta Coefficient

In analyzing the performance of an individual security, it is first important to measure its relationship to the market through the **beta coefficient**. Let us lay the groundwork for understanding beta. In the case of a potential investment, stock *i,* we can observe its relationship to the market by tracing its total return performance relative to the market total return over the last five years.[6]

Year	Stock *i* Return (K)	Market Return (K_M)
1	4.8%	6.5%
2	14.5	11.8
3	19.1	14.9
4	3.7	1.1
5	15.6	12.0

We see that stock *i* moves somewhat with the market. Plotting the values in Figure 17–11, we observe a line that is upward sloping at slightly above a 45-degree angle.

[6] Although monthly calculations are often used, we can satisfy the same basic learning objectives with annual data, and the analysis is easier to follow.

FIGURE 17–11 Relationship of Individual Stock to the Market

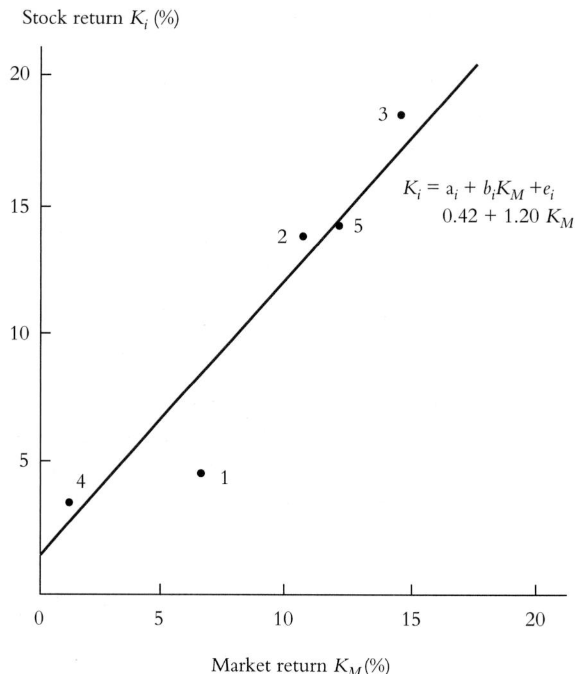

A straight line of best fit has been drawn through the various points representing the following formula:

$$K_i = a_i + b_iK_M + e_i \quad \textbf{(17–6)}$$

K_i represents the anticipated stock return based on Formula 17–6 where: a_i (alpha) is the point at which the line crosses the vertical axis; b_i (beta) is the slope of the line; K_M is the independent variable of market return; and e_i is the random error term. The $a_i + b_iK_M$ portion of the formula describes a straight line, and e_i represents deviations or random, nonrecurring movements away from the straight line. In the present example, the formula for the straight line is $K_i = 0.42 + 1.20\ K_M$ (indicating a beta or line slope of 1.2). These values can be approximated by drawing a line of best fit as indicated in Figure 17–11 or through the use of least squares regression analysis presented in Appendix 17B. Basically, the equation tells us how volatile our stock is relative to the market through the beta coefficient. In the present case, if the market moves up or down by a given percentage, our stock is assumed to move 1.2 times that amount.

Because beta measures the correlation of a stock's total return to a market index, the beta of the market when regressed on itself will always be 1.0. With a beta of 1.2, our stock is considered to be 20 percent more volatile than the market and therefore riskier. A stock with average volatility would have a beta of 1.0, the same beta as the market. A stock having a beta of less than 1.0 would have less risk than the market.

Systematic and Unsystematic Risk

Previously, we mentioned the two major types of risk associated with a stock. One is the market movement or beta (b_i) risk. If the market moves up or down, a stock is assumed to change in value. This type of risk is referred to as **systematic risk**. The second type of risk is represented by the error term (e_i) and indicates changes in value not associated with market movement. It may represent the temporary influence of a competitor's new product, changes in raw material prices, or unusual economic and government influences on a given firm. These changes are peculiar to an individual security or industry at a given point and are not directly correlated with the market. This second type of risk is referred to as **unsystematic risk**.

Because unsystematic risk is associated with an individual company or industry, it may be diversified away in a large portfolio and is not a risk inherent in investing in common stocks. Thus, by picking stocks that are less than perfectly correlated, unsystematic risk may be eliminated. For example, the inherent risks of investing in cyclical semiconductor stocks may be diversified away by investing in countercyclical housing stocks. Researchers have indicated that all but 15 percent of unsystematic risk may be eliminated with a carefully selected portfolio of 10 stocks, and all but 11 percent, with the portfolio of 20 stocks.[7]

The systematic risk (beta) cannot be diversified away even in a large portfolio. Therefore, the market compensates an investor with a higher expected return when that investor buys securities with a high beta, or with a lower expected return than the market when the investor buys securities with a beta less than the market. Using this method of risk adjustment, the capital asset pricing model creates a linear risk-return trade-off using the market as the reference point for risk and return.

Because unsystematic risk can be diversified away, systematic risk (b_i) is the only relevant risk under the capital asset pricing model. Thus, even though we can describe total risk as:

$$\text{Total risk} = \text{Systematic risk} + \text{Unsystematic risk}$$

in a diversified portfolio, unsystematic risk approaches 0.

Security Market Line

We actually express the trade-off between risk and return for an *individual stock* through the **security market line (SML)** in Figure 17–12. Whereas in Figure 17–11, we graphed the relationship that allowed us to compute the beta (b_i) for a security, in Figure 17–12 we now take that beta and show what the anticipated or required return in the marketplace is for a stock with that characteristic. The security market line (SML) shows the risk-return trade-off for an individual stock in Figure 17–12, just as the capital market line (CML) accomplished that same objective for a portfolio in Figure 17–10 on page 448.

FIGURE 17–12 Illustration of the Security Market Line

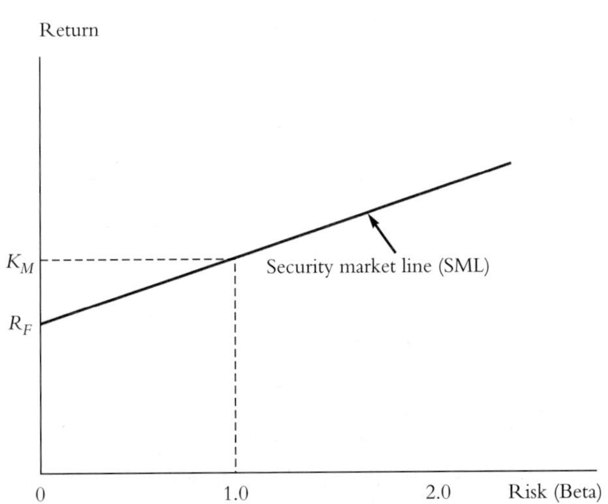

[7] Wagner and Lau, "The Effect of Diversification on Risk."

Once again, we stress that the return is not plotted against the total risk (σ) for the individual stock but only that part of the risk that cannot be diversified away, commonly referred to as the systematic or beta risk. The actual formula for the security market line (SML) is:

$$K_i = R_F + b_i(K_M - R_F) \qquad \textbf{(17–7)}$$

application example

The mathematical derivation of the formula is presented in Appendix 17C. As we did with the capital market line for portfolio returns, with the security market line we start out with a basic rate of return for a risk-free asset (R_F) and add a premium for risk. In this case, the premium is equal to the beta on the stock times the difference between the market rate of return (K_M) and the risk-free rate of return (R_F). If R_F = 6 percent, K_M = 12 percent, and the stock has a beta (b_i) of 1, the anticipated rate of return, using Formula 17–7, would be the same as that in the market, or 12 percent.

$$K_i = 6\% + 1(12\% - 6\%) = 6\% + 6\% = 12\%$$

Because the stock has the same degree of risk as the market in general, this would appear to be logical. If the stock has a beta of 1.5, the added systematic risk would call for a return of 15 percent, whereas a beta of 0.5 would indicate the return should be 9 percent. The calculations are indicated below:

Beta = 1.5

$$K_i = 6\% + 1.5(12\% - 6\%) = 6\% + 1.5(6\%) = 6\% + 9\% = 15\%$$

Beta = 0.5

$$K_i = 6\% + 0.5(12\% - 6\%) = 6\% + 0.5(6\%) = 6\% + 3\% = 9\%$$

Because the beta factor is deemed to be important in analyzing potential risk and return, much emphasis is placed on knowing the beta for a given security. Bloomberg, Value Line, Standard & Poor's, and various brokerage houses and investment services publish information on beta for a large number of securities. A representative list is presented in the table below:

Corporation	Beta (November 12, 2010)
Bank America (**www.bankofamerica.com**)	1.75
American Express (**www.americanexpress.com**)	1.47
DuPont (**www.dupont.com**)	1.11
Disney (**www.disney.com**)	1.07
Southwest Airlines (**www.southwest.com**)	0.97
Coca Cola (**www.coca-cola.com**)	0.71
Abbott Labs (**www.abbottlabs.com**)	0.68
Southern Company (**www.southerncompany.com**)	0.68

However, there is a good chance that you will find a wide range of beta calculations for some companies. First, it depends on what index beta is calculated against. A beta compared to the Standard & Poor's 500 will be different from a beta calculated against the return on the Value Line Index or the Wilshire 5000 index. Second, betas will differ based on the time period used for the regression of the return on the stock to the return on the market. The standard practice is to use the stock's return compared to the return on the Standard & Poor's 500 Index for a regression over the last 60 months. Third, because beta is used as an expected value, the raw beta may

the real world of investing

STUDENTS AS PORTFOLIO MANAGERS—THE NUMBER OF PROGRAMS CONTINUES TO GROW

It started at TCU and the University of Wisconsin more than 40 years ago. Now students manage part of the university endowment in more than 200 colleges and universities worldwide. This is no simulation.

The largest such program is at Ohio State University, where the students are enrolled in courses that allow them to manage more than $10 million of the permanent endowment of the university. Other schools such as UCLA, Indiana University, the University of Southern California, Southern Methodist University, Notre Dame, Gannon College, Virginia Military Institute, DePaul University, and Texas Christian University have similar programs. Professor Edward C. Lawrence of the University of Missouri–St. Louis tracks all the programs across the country as to size, value, and source of funding. Some schools operate with as little as a few thousand dollars, while the typical program size is $150,000 to $200,000.

The authors are most familiar with the student-managed fund at Texas Christian University, where they have both served as faculty advisors. The students manage $1.5 million in stocks and bonds and have power to make their own investment decisions. The faculty advisors do not even have veto power (don't ask if they sweat a lot!). The students receive six hours of academic credit for their work and do intensive work to analyze securities and balance the portfolio. The students also have their own committees operating in such areas as economics and accounting.

As would be true of other professional money managers, they provide annual reports, in which they compare their performance with their own goals as well as with the popular market averages. DePaul University has added a new wrinkle by creating a second student managed fund that specializes only in international securities. This fund started in 2010 with $100,000 and focuses on four world regions outside of the U.S. and Canada.

not be a good indicator of what an investor should expect in the future. For this reason some financial institutions will adjust beta for a tendency to regress to the mean of one. That means that high betas will be adjusted down toward 1 and low beta stocks will be adjusted up toward 1. The adjustments may not all be equal. Betas are meant to be used in judging the risk of a portfolio, because portfolio betas are quite stable, whereas betas of individual stocks can change significantly over time.

ASSUMPTIONS OF THE CAPITAL ASSET PRICING MODEL

Having evaluated some of the implications of the CAPM, it is important that students be aware of some of the assumptions that go into the model.

1. All investors can borrow or lend an unlimited amount of funds at a given risk-free rate.
2. All investors have the same one-period time horizon.
3. All investors wish to maximize their expected utility over this time horizon and evaluate investments on the basis of means and standard deviations of portfolio returns.
4. All investors have the same expectations—that is, all investors estimate identical probability distributions for rates of return.
5. All assets are perfectly divisible—it is possible to buy fractional shares of any asset or portfolio.
6. There are no taxes or transactions costs.
7. The market is efficient and in equilibrium or quickly adjusting to equilibrium.

Listing these assumptions indicates some of the necessary conditions to create the CAPM. While at first they may appear to be severely limiting, they are similar to those often used in the standard economic theory of the firm and in other basic financial models.

The primary usefulness in examining this model or similar risk-return trade-off models is to provide some reasonable basis for relating return opportunity with

FIGURE 17–13 Test of the Security Market Line

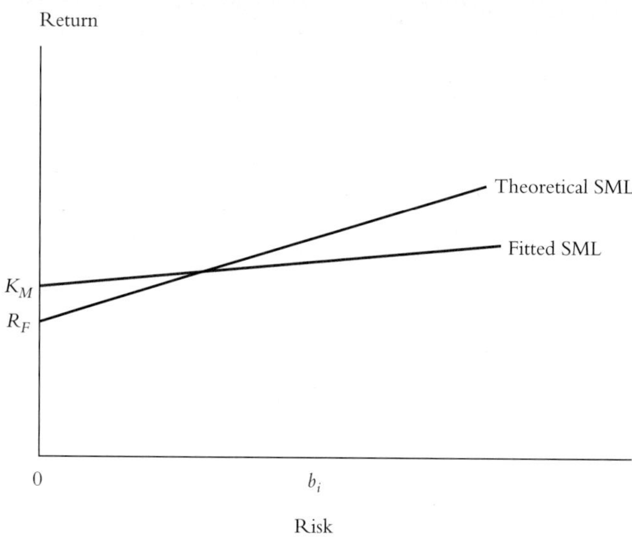

risk on the investment. Portfolio managers find risk-return models helpful in explaining their performance or the performance of their competitors to clients. A competitor's portfolio that has unusually high returns may have been developed primarily on the basis of high-risk assets. To the extent that this can be explained on the basis of capital market theory, the competitor's performance may look less like superior money management and more like a product of high risk taking. As we shall see in Chapter 22, many of the techniques for assessing portfolio performance on Wall Street are explicitly or implicitly related to the risk-return concepts discussed in this chapter.

Although empirical tests have somewhat supported the capital asset pricing model, a number of testing problems remain. To develop the SML in which stock returns (vertical axis) can be measured against beta (horizontal axis), an appropriate line must be drawn. Researchers have some disagreement about R_F. (Is it represented by short-term or long-term Treasury rates?) There is also debate about what is the approximate K_M, or market rate of return. Some suggest the market proxy variable will greatly influence the beta and that difficulties in dealing with this problem can bring the whole process under attack.[8]

When empirical data are compared with theoretical return expectations, there is some discrepancy in that the theoretical SML may have a greater slope than the actual line fitted on the basis of real-world data as shown in Figure 17–13.[9]

There may also be a possible problem in that betas for individual securities are not necessarily stable over time (rather than remaining relatively constant at 1.3 or perhaps 0.7, they tend to approach 1 over time). Thus, a beta based on past risk may not always reflect current risk.[10] Because the beta for a portfolio may be more stable than an individual stock's beta, portfolio betas are also used as a systematic

[8] Richard Roll, "A Critique of the Asset Pricing Theory's Test," *Journal of Financial Economics,* March 1977, pp. 129–76. Also, "Ambiguity When Performance Is Measured by the Securities Market Line," *Journal of Finance,* September 1978, pp. 1051–69.

[9] Franco Modigliani and Gerald A. Pogue, "An Introduction to Risk and Returns," *Financial Analysts Journal,* March–April 1974, pp. 68–86, and May–June 1974, pp. 69–86.

[10] Robert A. Levy, "On the Short-Term Stationary of Beta Coefficients," *Financial Analysts Journal,* November–December 1971, pp. 55–62. Also, Marshall E. Blume, "Betas and Their Regression Tendencies," *Journal of Finance,* June 1975, pp. 785–95.

risk variable. A portfolio beta is simply the weighted average of the betas of the individual stocks. We can say:

$$b_P(\text{portfolio beta}) = \sum_{i=1}^{n} x_i b_i \qquad \textbf{(17–8)}$$

and

$$K_P = R_F + b_P(K_M - R_F) \qquad \textbf{(17–9)}$$

By examining portfolio betas rather than individual stock betas, we overcome part of the criticism leveled at the instability of betas in the capital asset pricing model. Many of the other criticisms have also evoked new research that may provide different approaches or possible solutions to past deficiencies in the model. One such approach is the arbitrage pricing theory described in Appendix 17D.

SUMMARY

The investor is basically risk-averse and therefore will demand a premium for incremental risk. In an efficient market context, the ability to achieve high returns may be more directly related to absorption of additional risk than superior ability in selecting stocks (this remains a debatable point that proponents of fundamental and technical analysis would argue).

Risk for an individual stock is measured in terms of the standard deviation (σ_i) around a given expected value ($\overline{K}_i$). The larger the standard deviation, the greater the risk. For a portfolio of stocks, the expected value (K_P) is the weighted average of the individual returns; but this is not true for the portfolio standard deviation (σ_P). The portfolio standard deviation is also influenced by the interaction between the stocks. To the extent the correlation coefficient (r_{ij}) is less than +1, there will be some reduction from the weighted average of the standard deviation of the individual stocks that we are combining. A negative correlation coefficient will provide substantial reduction in the portfolio standard deviation.

The CAPM supersedes some of the findings of classic portfolio theory with the introduction of the risk-free asset as represented by (R_F) into the analysis. The assumption is that an individual can choose an investment combining the return on the risk-free asset with the market rate of return, and this will provide superior returns to the efficient frontier at all points except M, where they are equal.

The capital asset pricing model also calls for an evaluation of individual assets (rather than portfolios). The security market line in Figure 17–12 on page 451 shows the same type of risk-return trade-off for individual securities as the capital market line does for portfolios. Investors in individual assets are only assumed to be rewarded for systematic, market-related risk, known as the beta (b_i) risk. All other risk is assumed to be susceptible to diversification.

A number of assumptions associated with the capital asset pricing model are subject to close review and challenge. However, it still remains the most widely used approach to risk management.

KEY WORDS AND CONCEPTS

DISCUSSION QUESTIONS

1. Define risk.
2. What is an expected value?
3. What is the most commonly used measure of dispersion?
4. In a two-asset portfolio, is the portfolio standard deviation a weighted average of the two individual stocks' standard deviation? Explain.
5. What does the correlation coefficient (r_{ij}) measure? What are the two most extreme values it can take, and what do they indicate? In the real world, are more variables positively or negatively correlated?
6. What are the two characteristics of points along the efficient frontier? Do portfolios exist above the efficient frontier?
7. What does the steepness of the slope of the risk-return indifference curve indicate?
8. Describe the optimum portfolio for an investor in terms of indifference curves and the efficient frontier.
9. What new investment variable or outlet allowed market researchers to go from the Markowitz portfolio theory (including the efficient frontier) to the capital asset pricing model?
10. In examining the *capital market line* as part of the capital asset pricing model, to increase portfolio return (K_P) what other variable must you increase?
11. In terms of the capital asset pricing model:
    a. Indicate the two types of risks associated with an individual security.
    b. Which of these two is the beta risk?
    c. What risk is assumed not to be compensated for in the marketplace under the capital asset pricing model? Why?
12. What can be assumed in terms of volatility for a stock that has a beta of 1.2?
13. What does the security market line indicate? In general terms, how is it different from the capital market line?
14. In regard to the capital asset pricing model, comment on disagreements or debates related to R_F (the risk-free rate) and K_M (market rate of return).
15. Are betas of individual stocks necessarily stable (constant) over time?

PRACTICE PROBLEMS AND SOLUTIONS

Expected value and standard deviation

1. An investment has the following range of outcomes and probabilities.

Outcomes	Probability of Outcomes
10%	0.30
15	0.40
20	0.30

Calculate the expected value and the standard deviation (round to two places after the decimal point where necessary).

Capital market line and security market line

2. *a.* Using the formula for the capital market line (Formula 17–5 on page 448), if the risk-free rate (R_F) is 5 percent, the market rate of return (K_M) is 11 percent, the market standard deviation (σ_M) is 10 percent, and the standard deviation of the portfolio (σ_P) is 14 percent, compute the anticipated return (K_P).
   b. Using the formula for the security market line (Formula 17–7 on page 452), if the risk-free rate (R_F) is 7 percent, the beta (b_i) is 1.50, and the market rate of return (K_M) is 13 percent, compute the anticipated rate of return (K_i).

Solutions

1. Expected Value $\overline{K}_i = \Sigma K_i P_i$

K_i	P_i	K_iP_i
10%	0.30	3.0%
15	0.40	6.0
20	0.30	6.0
		15.0% = $\Sigma K_iP_i = \overline{K}_i$

Standard deviation = $\sigma_i = \sqrt{\Sigma(K_i - \overline{K}_i)^2 P_i}$

K_i	$\overline{K}_i$	P_i	$(K_i - \overline{K}_i)$	$(K_i - \overline{K}_i)^2$	$(K_i - \overline{K}_i)^2 P_i$
10%	15%	.30	−5%	25%	7.5%
15	15	.40	0	0	0
20	15	.30	5	25	7.5
					15.0% = $\Sigma(K_i - \overline{K}_i)^2 P_i$

$$\sigma_i = \sqrt{\Sigma(K_i - \overline{K}_i)^2 P_i} = \sqrt{15\%} = 3.87\%$$

2. *a.*
$$K_p = R_f + \left(\frac{K_M - R_f}{\sigma_M}\right)\sigma_p$$
$$= 5\% + \left(\frac{11\% - 5\%}{10\%}\right) 14\%$$
$$= 5\% + \left(\frac{6\%}{10\%}\right) 14\%$$
$$= 5\% + .6(14\%)$$
$$= 5\% + 8.4\%$$
$$= 13.4\%$$

b.
$$K_i = R_F + b_i(K_M - R_F)$$
$$= 7\% + 1.50(13\% - 7\%)$$
$$= 7\% = +1.50(6\%)$$
$$= 7\% + 9\% = 16\%$$

PROBLEMS

Expected value

1. The Infidelity Mutual Fund projects three possible outcomes for next year: weak performance (−5 percent), good performance (10 percent), and outstanding performance (30 percent). The good performance has a 50 percent chance of happening and is twice as likely as the other two outcomes. What is the expected value?

Expected value and standard deviation

2. An investment has the following range of outcomes and probabilities:

Outcomes	Probability of Outcomes
6%	0.20
9	0.60
12	0.20

Calculate the expected value and the standard deviation (round to two places after the decimal point where necessary).

Portfolio expected value and standard deviation

3. Given another investment with an expected value of 12 percent and a standard deviation of 2.2 percent that is countercyclical to the investment in problem 2, what is the expected value of the portfolio and its standard deviation if both are combined into a portfolio with 40 percent invested in the first investment and 60 percent in the second? Assume the correlation coefficient (r_{ij}) is -0.40.

Portfolio standard deviation

4. What would be the portfolio standard deviation if the two investments in problem 3 had a correlation coefficient (r_{ij}) of $+0.40$?

Portfolio standard deviation

5. If the two investments above were perfectly positively correlated ($r_{ij} = +1$), what would be the portfolio standard deviation?

Efficient frontier

6. Assume the following risk-return possibilities for 10 different portfolios. Plot the points in a manner similar to Figure 17–3, on page 443, and indicate the approximate shape of the efficient frontier.

Portfolio	K_P	σ_P
1	9.0%	1.5%
2	9.0	2.0
3	10.0	3.0
4	10.0	4.0
5	12.0	4.0
6	11.5	5.0
7	13.5	5.5
8	13.0	6.0
9	15.0	7.0
10	14.5	7.8

Efficient frontier

7. Referring to problem 6, if a new portfolio, no. 11, has a K_P value of 13.8 percent and a standard deviation (σ_P) of 7.1 percent, will it qualify for the efficient frontier?

Capital market line

8. Using the formula for the capital market line (Formula 17–5 on page 448), if the risk-free rate (R_F) is 8 percent, the market rate of return (M_K) is 12 percent, the market standard deviation (σ_M) is 10 percent, and the standard deviation of the portfolio (σ_P) is 12 percent, compute the anticipated return (K_P).

Capital market line

9. Recompute the answer to problem 8 based on a portfolio standard of 16 percent. In terms of capital market theory, explain why K_P has increased.

Security market line

10. Using the formula for the security market line (Formula 17–7 on page 446), if the risk-free rate (R_F) is 7 percent, the beta (b_i) is 1.25, and the market rate of return (K_M) is 11.8 percent, compute the anticipated rate of return (K_i).

Beta consideration

11. If another security had a lower beta than indicated in problem 10, would K_i be lower or higher? What is the logic behind your answer in terms of risk?

Plotting best fit to data

12. Assume the following values for a stock's return and the market return.

Year	Stock *i* Return (K)	Market Return (K_M)
1	14.9%	10.3%
2	3.8	2.2
3	9.0	10.5
4	18.2	12.8
5	6.0	3.4

Plot the data and draw a line of best fit similar to that in Figure 17–11 on page 450. No equation is necessary.

Least squares regression analysis

13. Using the formulas in Appendix 17B, compute a least squares regression equation for problem 12. (Round beta and alpha to two places after the decimal point.)

Rate of return

14. Use the beta (b_i) from problem 13, and plug it into the formula for the security market line (Formula 17–7 on page 452). Assume the risk-free rate (R_F) is 7 percent and the market rate of return (K_M) is 12.6 percent. What is the value of the anticipated rate of return (K_i)?

15. Assume you own a portfolio of 10 stocks. The table below lists the dollars invested and the beta for each stock. Compute the portfolio beta and comment on the effect of the high risk and low risk stocks on the portfolio beta.

	Invested	Beta
A.	$10,000	1.00
B.	6,000	1.50
C.	12,000	0.80
D.	8,000	1.40
E.	10,000	1.10
F.	15,000	1.05
G.	5,000	1.85
H.	8,000	1.60
I.	12,000	0.75
J.	14,000	0.90

WEB EXERCISE

In this web exercise, we will show how to determine the required rate of return for a stock using the capital asset pricing model.

1. The formula for the capital asset pricing model is:

$$K_i = R_F + b_i(K_M - R_F) \qquad \textbf{(17–7)}$$

K_i is the required rate of return that we are solving for; R_F is the risk-free rate, and we shall assume it is 4.6 percent; b_i is the systematic risk of a stock that we will estimate; $(K_M - R_F)$ is the equity risk premium or the amount the market is assumed to earn over the risk-free rate in the long term. We will use 6.4 percent in this example.

2. Now we are in a position to estimate the beta for a company and compute K_i, the required rate of return.

While Value Line, Bloomberg, and other financial services provide estimates of beta, they are often very different. In this exercise, we are going to have you eyeball a value for beta. Go to **finance.yahoo.com**.

3. Enter Oracle (ORCL) in the search box on the left and click "Get Quotes."

4. Along the left margin, click on "Basic Chart."

5. Then on the "Range" line, click on "2y."

6. Then on the "Compare" line, select S&P 500 and click "Compare."

7. Eyeball the relative volatility of ORCL to the Standard & Poor Index (GSPC) and estimate a beta (such as 1.1 or 1.3) based on the relative volatility of the stock versus the index.

8. Use this beta and the previously presented information on R_F and $(K_M - R_F)$ to compute K_i.

9. Follow this procedure for:
   a. McDonald's (MCD)
   b. Bank of America (BAC)
   c. Coca-Cola (KO)
10. What conclusion can you draw between the relationship of beta (b_i), a risk measure, and the required rate of return (K_i)?

Note: From time to time, companies redesign their Web sites, and occasionally a topic we have listed may have been deleted, updated, or moved into a different location.

APPENDIX 17A

THE CORRELATION COEFFICIENT

There are a number of formulas for the correlation coefficient. We shall use the statement:

$$r_{ij} = \frac{\text{cov}_{ij}}{\sigma_i \sigma_j} \qquad \textbf{(17A–1)}$$

Here, cov_{ij} (covariance) is an *absolute* measure of the extent to which two sets of variables move together over time. Once we have determined this value, we simply divide by $\sigma_i\sigma_j$ to get a relative measure of correlation (r_{ij}).

The formula for the covariance is:

$$\text{cov}_{ij} = \Sigma(K_i - \overline{K}_i)(K_j - \overline{K}_j)P \qquad \textbf{(17A–2)}$$

We take our K and P values from investment i and investment j in this chapter on page 437 to compute the following:

K_i	$\overline{K}_i$	$(K_i - \overline{K}_i)$	K_j	$\overline{K}_j$	$(K_j - \overline{K}_j)$	$(K_i - \overline{K}_i)(K_j - \overline{K}_j)$	P	$(K_i - \overline{K}_i)(K_j - \overline{K}_j)P$
5%	10%	−5%	20%	10%	+10%	−50%	0.20	−10.0%
7	10	−3	8	10	−2	+6	0.30	+1.8
13	10	+3	8	10	−2	−6	0.30	−1.8
15	10	+5	6	10	−4	−20	0.20	−4.0
								−14.0%

$$\text{cov}_{ij} = \Sigma(K_i - \overline{K}_i)(K_j - \overline{K}_j)P = -14.0\%$$

Using the values in the chapter for σ_i equal to 3.9 and σ_j equal to 5.1, we determine:

$$r_{ij} = \frac{\text{cov}_{ij}}{\sigma_i \sigma_j} = \frac{-14.0}{(3.9)(5.1)} = \frac{-14.0}{19.9} = -0.70$$

APPENDIX 17B

LEAST SQUARES REGRESSION ANALYSIS

We will show how least squares regression analysis can be used to develop a linear equation to explain the relationship between the return on a stock and return in the market.

We will develop the terms in the expression:

$$K_i = a_i + b_i K_M + e_i$$

(e_i is the random error term and will not be quantified in our analysis.)

Using the data from the chapter on page 449,

Year	K_i	K_M
1	4.8%	6.5%
2	14.5	11.8
3	19.1	14.9
4	3.7	1.1
5	15.6	12.0

the mathematical equation to solve for b_i is:

$$b_i = \frac{N\Sigma K_i K_M - \Sigma K_i \Sigma K_M}{N\Sigma K_M^2 - (\Sigma K_M)^2} \quad \textbf{(17B–1)}$$

For a_i, we use the following formula (which is dependent on a prior determination of b_i):

$$a_i = \frac{\Sigma K_i - b_i \Sigma K_M}{N} \quad \textbf{(17B–2)}$$

We compute four columns of data and plug the values into our formulas.

K_i	K_M	$K_i K_M$	K_M^2
4.8	6.5	31.20	42.25
14.5	11.8	171.10	139.24
19.1	14.9	284.59	222.01
3.7	1.1	4.07	1.21
15.6	12.0	187.20	144.00
$\Sigma K_i = 57.7$	$\Sigma K_M = 46.3$	$\Sigma K_i K_M = 678.16$	$\Sigma K_M^2 = 548.71$

Also N (number of observations) = 5.

$$\begin{aligned} b_i &= \frac{N\Sigma K_i K_M - \Sigma K_i \Sigma K_M}{N\Sigma K_M^2 - (\Sigma K_M)^2} \\ &= \frac{5(678.16) - 57.7(46.3)}{5(548.71) - (46.3)^2} \\ &= \frac{3390.80 - 2671.51}{2743.55 - 2143.69} = \frac{719.29}{599.86} = 1.20 \end{aligned}$$

Using our beta value, we now compute alpha:

$$\begin{aligned} a_i &= \frac{\Sigma K_i - b_i \Sigma K_M}{N} \\ &= \frac{57.7 - 1.2(46.3)}{5} \\ &= \frac{57.7 - 55.6}{5} = \frac{2.1}{5} = 0.42 \end{aligned}$$

In summary:

$$\begin{aligned} K_i &= a_i + b_i K_M \\ &= 0.42 + 1.20\ K_M \end{aligned}$$

APPENDIX 17C

DERIVATION OF THE SECURITY MARKET LINE (SML)

First, we graph the SML based on covariance (Figure 17C–1).[1]

Along the vertical axis we show return, and along the horizontal axis, covariance of return with the market.[2] We can describe our equation for the SML in terms of the slope of the line.

$$K_i = R_F + \frac{(K_M - R_F)}{(\sigma_M^2 - 0)} \text{cov}_{iM} \qquad \textbf{(17C–1)}$$

We then rearrange our terms:

$$K_i = R_F + \left(\frac{\text{cov}_{iM}}{\sigma_M^2}\right)(K_M - R_F) \qquad \textbf{(17C–2)}$$

The systematic risk of an individual asset is measured by its covariance with the market (cov_{iM}). We can convert this to a relative measure by dividing through by the market variance (σ_M^2). The *relative* systematic movement of an individual asset with the market is referred to as the beta regression coefficient. Thus, we show in Formula 17C–3:

$$b_i = \frac{\text{cov}_{iM}}{\sigma_M^2} \qquad \textbf{(17C–3)}$$

Substituting beta into Formula 17C–2, we show:

$$K_i = R_F + b_i(K_M - R_F) \qquad \textbf{(17C–4)}$$

FIGURE 17C–1 Derivation of the SML

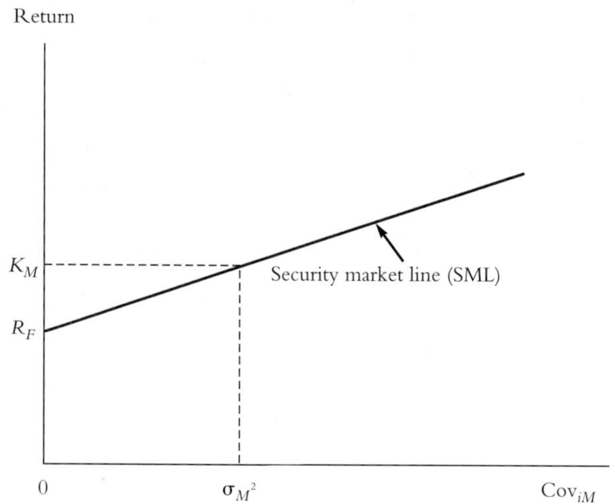

[1] The concept of covariance is described in Appendix 17A.

[2] Actually, σ_M^2 represents the covariance of the market with the market (a bit redundant). The cov_{MM} equals σ_M^2. The covariance of a variable with itself is equal to the variance.

APPENDIX 17D

ARBITRAGE PRICING THEORY

An alternative theory to the capital asset pricing model for explaining stock prices and stock returns is the arbitrage pricing theory (APT). This is a fairly sophisticated theory and will be of interest to those who wish to learn more about asset pricing.

Arbitrage pricing theory assumes a linear return generating model that makes the return on an investment a function of more than one factor. The capital asset pricing model also uses a linear return generating model but assumes that returns are a function of a stock's sensitivity to the equity risk premium. APT acknowledges that a stock's return may be a function of many factors. The arbitrage pricing model is a more generalized model than the CAPM and less restrictive in its assumptions; it does not assume equilibrium markets or make assumptions about investor preferences. However, the concept of arbitrage behavior will drive markets to equilibrium as investors try to make risk-free profits.

Arbitrage behavior assumes one good should always have the same price. If two different prices are found for gold in London and New York, an arbitrageur could sell short the high-priced gold and buy the low-priced gold. This behavior would drive the price of high-priced gold down and the price of low-priced gold up until the price of gold was the same. Theoretically, by selling short, the investor can use the proceeds from the short sale to buy long, and therefore, the transaction can be made without any investment. This makes the transaction a no-cost riskless transaction. Arbitrage relies on the behavior of market participants to take advantage of prices in disequilibrium, and through this arbitrage mechanism, prices will move into equilibrium.

The arbitrage pricing model describes the expected return on a stock as a function of several factors. While there is no universal agreement on what factors have the greatest impact on stock returns, Chen[1] and Roll and Ross[2] suggest there are a few major factors. These are changes in expectations about:

1. Interest rate risk.
2. Business-cycle risk.
3. Inflation.
4. The risk of changing risk premiums.

The return-generating process using the APT model appears in Formula 17D–1. We have listed four factors here, but there could be as few as one factor or many other factors. Three or four factors probably capture the most significant return sensitivities.

$$K_{i,t} = a_i + b_{i,1} F_{1,t} + b_{i,2} F_{2,t} + b_{i,3} F_{3,t} + b_{i,4} F_{4,t} + e_{i,t} \qquad \textbf{(17D–1)}$$

where:

$K_{i,t}$ = Return on stock i at time t
a_i = Expected return on stock i
$b_{i,j}$ = Sensitivity of stock i to factor j
$F_{j,t}$ = Value of factor j at time t
$e_{i,t}$ = Random term unique to stock i at time t

[1] Nai-fu Chen, "Some Empirical Tests of the Theory of Arbitrage Pricing," *Journal of Finance,* December 1983, pp. 1393–1414.

[2] Richard Roll and Stephen A. Ross, "An Empirical Investigation of the Arbitrage Pricing Theory," *Journal of Finance,* December 1980, pp. 1073–1103.

If a_i is the expected return on the stock, then the effect of the factors is expected to be zero (0). In other words, the market has already incorporated expectations about these factors into the stock's price. What will affect the actual return on stock i are any surprises in these factors that were not anticipated. For example, if factor 1 is changing real GDP and if real GDP goes up more than expected, stocks that are sensitive to changes in real GDP will go up, while those stocks that are not sensitive to the business cycle will be unaffected. Conversely, if inflation is factor 2 and if it increases more than expected, stocks that are subject to inflationary pressures will decline in price, while those that are not sensitive to changes in inflation will not be affected. The sensitivity to these various factors shows up in the b_i for each factor.

The random term e_i represents the unexpected portion of the return on security i, which is not explained by the factors. It captures unexpected events unique to firm i. For example, a new product announcement, a merger, or a takeover will affect firm i only. These unexpected events were not impounded into the stock's expected return, a_i.

The b_i's (factor sensitivities) reflect the sensitivity of the factor on the stock's return. Like the capital asset pricing model, the factor sensitivity for a portfolio is the sum of the weighted beta for each factor based on the percentage of market value that each stock contributes to the portfolio.

Let us take two stocks, x and y. Two factors affect the returns of both stocks, and the random variable e_i is eliminated because we assume that in a diversified portfolio, e_i approaches zero (0):

$$K_x = 12\% + 3F_{1,t} - 2F_{2,t}$$
$$K_y = 15\% + 1F_{1,t} - 6F_{2,t}$$

Each factor will have an impact on portfolio risk in proportion to the amount invested in each stock and the sensitivity of each factor on the stock's return. For example, if factor 1 represents the impact of changing real GDP (the business cycle risk), an unexpected increase in real GDP would increase the return on stock x by 3 percent. The same 1 percent unexpected change in GDP would increase the return on stock y by 1 percent. These effects show up in the factor sensitivities (b_i) of 3 for K_x and 1 for K_y.

If the second factor represents inflation, we can see that a 1 percent unexpected increase in inflation will cause a reduction in return of 2 percent for stock x and 6 percent for stock y. When we combine stocks x and y into a portfolio weighted 40 percent stock x and 60 percent stock y, we end up with portfolio risk dependent on the percentage of each stock in the portfolio and each stock's sensitivity to factors affecting risk. We multiply both sides of the return equations by the portfolio weights:

$$\begin{aligned}(0.4)K_x &= (0.40) \times 12\% + (0.40) \times (3)F_{1,t} - (0.40) \times (2)F_{2,t} \\ &= 4.8\% \qquad\qquad + 1.2F_{1,t} \qquad\qquad -0.8F_{2,t}\end{aligned}$$

Forty percent of stock x will contribute 4.8 percent expected return to the portfolio and will have a factor sensitivity of 1.2 to the business-cycle risk and a negative factor sensitivity of 0.8 to the inflation risk:

$$\begin{aligned}(0.6)K_y &= (0.60) \times 15\% + (0.60) \times (1)F_{1,t} - (0.60) \times (6)F_{2,t} \\ &= 9.0\% \qquad\qquad + 0.6F_{1,t} \qquad\qquad -3.6F_{2,t}\end{aligned}$$

Sixty percent of stock y will contribute 9.0 percent expected return to the portfolio and will have a factor sensitivity of 0.6 to the business-cycle risk and a negative factor sensitivity of 3.6 to the inflation risk. When we combine the two stocks into a portfolio, we end up with a portfolio having an expected return of 13.8 percent and having a sensitivity to factor 1 (business-cycle risk) of 1.8 and a negative sensitivity to factor 2 (inflation risk) of 4.4:

$$\begin{aligned}\text{Portfolio return } K_P &= (4.8\% + 9\%) + (1.2 + 0.6) - (0.8 + 3.6) \\ &= 13.8\% \qquad + 1.8F_{1,t} \qquad -4.4F_{2,t}\end{aligned}$$

We have structured a portfolio that will be moderately sensitive to any unexpected events having to do with changes in real GDP and highly susceptible to unexpected changes in inflation.

It is important to understand that the sign in front of the factor sensitivity indicates whether the unexpected event is directly related to returns or inversely related to returns. For example, we assume unexpected increases in inflation reduce stock returns while unexpected decreases in inflation increase stock returns. Thus, we have a minus sign before the second factor.

Application to Portfolio Management

From the portfolio manager's point of view, the arbitrage pricing theory can help measure the sensitivity of a portfolio to various macro factors that could potentially affect the actual return on one stock or a portfolio. This model allows investment managers to structure portfolios that are either highly sensitive or insensitive to certain kinds of risk exposures. If a manager were concerned about a recession and this information were not yet factored into stock prices, he or she could create a portfolio that insulated the returns on the portfolio from unpleasant surprises. On the other hand, if the market had factored in expectations for a recession and the manager expected good business-cycle news, he or she could buy stocks sensitive to business-cycle news.

Problems

Arbitrage Pricing Theory

17D–1. Under arbitrage pricing theory, assume two stocks have the following equations.

$$\begin{aligned}K_x &= 14\% + 2F_{1,t} - 3F_{2,t} \\ K_y &= 10\% + 1F_{1,t} - 4F_{2,t}\end{aligned}$$

The first factor relates to unexpected increases in real GDP, and the second factor relates to unexpected increases in interest rates.

If a portfolio consists of 60 percent of stock *x* and 40 percent of stock *y*, what will be the equation for portfolio return (K_P)?

17D–2. Assume the following two stocks are available for purchase. (There is only one risk factor.)

$$\begin{aligned}K_a &= 20\% + 4F \\ K_b &= 12\% + 3F\end{aligned}$$

We will sell stock *b* and replace three-fourths of its value with stock *a* and one-fourth of its value with a risk-free asset yielding 6 percent.

a. What is the new weighted average for the risk factor?
b. What is the new weighted average return?
c. Has the investor benefited from a risk-return perspective?

18

chapter eighteen

DURATION AND BOND PORTFOLIO MANAGEMENT

OBJECTIVES

1. Understand that duration is a better measure of the life of a bond than maturity.
2. Be able to use present value techniques to compute duration.
3. Explain the effect that duration has on bond price sensitivity to interest rates changes.
4. Explain how the reinvestment rate for inflows may materially affect the final value of an investment.
5. Describe the uses of duration in the management of bond portfolios.
6. Explain the use of bond ladders and their rationale in portfolio management.

OUTLINE

REVIEW OF BASIC BOND VALUATION CONCEPTS

In Chapter 12, we discussed the principles of bond valuation. The value of a bond was established in Formula 12–1 on page 315 as follows:

$$V = \sum_{t=1}^{n} \frac{C_t}{(1 = i)^t} + \frac{P_n}{(1 + i)^n}$$

where:

V = Market value or price of the bond
n = Number of periods
t = Each period
C_t = Coupon or interest payment for each period, t
P_n = Par or maturity value
i = Interest rate in the market

Based on this equation, as interest rates in the market rise, the price of the bond will decline because the present value of the cash flows is worth less at a higher discount rate. The opposite is true if interest rates decline. We also demonstrated in Table 12–4 on page 327 that bonds with long-term maturities were generally more sensitive to changes in interest rates than were short-term bonds. Reproduction of part of Table 12–4 below shows that a 30-year bond exhibits larger price changes in response to a change in yield than do shorter-term obligations. For example, a 2 percent drop in interest rates would cause a 1.86 percent increase in value for a bond with one year to maturity, but an 18.93 percent price change for a bond with 30 years to maturity. Given the relationship between the life of a bond and the price sensitivity just described, it is particularly important that we have an appropriate definition of the life or term of a bond.

(Reproduction of Table 12-4) Change in Market Prices of Bonds for Shifts in Yields to Maturity (12 percent coupon rate)

Yield Change	MATURITY (YEARS)				
	1	5	10	20	30
+3%	−2.69%	−10.30%	−15.29%	−18.89%	−19.74%
+2	−1.81	−7.02	−10.59	−13.33	−14.04
+1	−0.91	−3.57	−5.01	−7.08	−7.52
−1	+0.92	+3.77	+5.98	+8.02	+8.72
−2	+1.86	+7.72	+12.46	+17.16	+18.93
−3	+2.81	+11.87	+19.51	+27.60	+30.96

The first inclination is to say that the term of a bond is an easily determined matter. One merely needs to look up the maturity date on a Bloomberg terminal, and the matter is settled. However, the notion of effective life of a bond is more complicated than this. The situation is somewhat analogous to the quoted coupon rate on the bond not really conveying the true yield to maturity on the obligation. Similarly, the maturity date on a bond may not convey all important information about the life of a bond.

In studying the true characteristics about the life of a bond, not only must the final date and amount of the maturity payment be considered but also the pattern of coupon payments that occurs in the interim. If you were to receive $1,000 after 20 years and no interest payments during the term of the obligation, clearly the effective life is 20 years. But suppose in addition to the $1,000, you were also to receive $100 per year for the next 20 years. Part of the payment is coming early and part of the payment is coming late, and the weighted average term of the payout is certainly less than 20 years. The higher the coupon payments relative to the maturity payment, the shorter the weighted average life of the payout. The **weighted average life** refers to the time period over which the coupon payments and maturity payment on a bond are recovered. In the next section, we shall go through the simple mathematics of computing the weighted average life of the payout; for now it is enough to know that such a concept exists.

The important consideration is that *bond price sensitivity* can be more appropriately related to *weighted average life* than to just the maturity date. While many bond analysts simply relate price sensitivity to maturity (and we did that also in Chapter 12), there is a more sophisticated approach related to weighted average life.

Before we move on to calculate weighted average life, there is an investment decision we wish you to consider. Assume you have to decide whether to invest in an 8 percent coupon rate bond with a 20-year maturity or a 12 percent coupon rate bond with a 25-year maturity. Which bond will have the larger increase in price if interest rates decline? You may choose the 25-year, 12 percent coupon rate bond because it has the longer maturity, but don't answer too quickly on this. Let's consider weighted average life and then come back to this question of price sensitivity.

DURATION

The concept of weighted average life of a bond falls under the general topic of duration. We shall first of all do a simple example of weighted average life and then more formally look at duration. Assume we have a five-year bond that provides $80 per year for the next five years plus $1,000 at the end of five years. For ease of calculation, we are using annual coupon payments in our analysis. Semiannual analysis would change the answer only slightly. An approach to computing weighted average life is presented in Table 18–1.

TABLE 18-1 Simple Weighted Average Life

(1) Year, t	(2) Cash Flow	(3) Annual Cash Flow (2) ÷ by Total Cash Flow	(4) Year × Weight (1) × (3)
1	$ 80	0.0571	0.0571
2	80	0.0571	0.1142
3	80	0.0571	0.1713
4	80	0.0571	0.2284
5	80	0.0571	0.2855
5	1,000	0.7145	3.5725
Total cash flow →	$1,400	1.0000	4.4290

First, we see that the weighted average life of the bond, based on the annual cash flows, is 4.4290 years. Let's see how this is calculated. In column (1) is the year in which each cash flow falls, and in column (2) is the size of the cash flow for each year plus the total cash flow. Column (3) calls for dividing the annual cash flow in column (2) by the total cash flow at the bottom of column (2) to determine what percentage of the total it represents. For example, the annual cash flow of $80 on the first line of column (2) represents 0.0571 of the total cash flow of $1,400.

($80 ÷ $1,400 = 0.0571.) The same basic procedure is followed for all subsequent years. In column (4), each year is multiplied by the weights (percentages) developed in column (3). For example, year 1 is multiplied by 0.0571 to arrive at 0.0571 in column (4). Year 2 is multiplied by 0.0571 to arrive at 0.1142 in column (4). This procedure is followed for each year and each weight. The final answer is 4.4290 for the weighted average life of the bond.

If you can understand the approach presented in Table 18–1, you should have no difficulty following a more formal and appropriate definition of weighted average life called duration. **Duration** represents the weighted average life of a bond where the weights are based on the *present value* of the individual cash flows relative to the *present value* of the total cash flows. An example of duration is presented in Table 18–2. Present value calculations are based on the market rate of interest (yield to maturity) for the bond, which in this case, we shall assume to be 12 percent.

application example

The only difference between Tables 18–1 and 18–2 is that in Table 18–2, the cash flows are present valued before the weights are determined. Thus, the cash flows (2) are multiplied by the present value factors at 12 percent (3) to arrive at the present value of cash flows (4). The total present value of cash flows at the bottom of column (4) is also the same as the price of the bond. In column (5), weights for each year are determined by dividing the present value of each annual cash flow (4) by the total present value of cash flows [bottom of column (4)]. For example, in year 1, the present value of the cash flow is $71.44, and this is divided by the total present value of cash flows of $855.40 to arrive at 0.0835 in column (5). Similarly, the weight in year 2, as shown in column (5), is determined by dividing $63.76 by $855.40 to arrive at 0.0745. In column (6), each year is multiplied by the weights developed in column (5). For example, year 1 is multiplied by 0.0835 to arrive at 0.0835 in column (6). Year 2 is multiplied by 0.0745 to arrive at 0.1490. This procedure is followed for each year, and the values are then summed.

The final answer for duration (the weighted average life based on present value) is 4.2498. This 4.2498 duration is referred to as **Macaulay duration**, named after Frederick Macaulay, who developed this concept more than 100 years ago. Duration, once determined, is the most representative value for effective bond life and the measure against which bond price sensitivity should be evaluated.

TABLE 18-2 Duration Concept of Weighted Average Life

(1) Year, *t*	(2) Cash Flow (*CF*)	(3) *PV* Factor at 12 Percent	(4) *PV* of Cash Flow (*CF*)	(5) *PV* of Annual Cash Flow (4) ÷ by Total *PV* of Cash Flows	(6) Year × Weight (1) × (5)
1	$ 80	0.893	$ 71.44	0.0835	0.0835
2	80	0.797	63.76	0.0745	0.1490
3	80	0.712	56.96	0.0666	0.1998
4	80	0.636	50.88	0.0595	0.2380
5	80	0.567	45.36	0.0530	0.2650
5	$1,000	0.567	567.00	0.6629	3.3145
		Total *PV* of → cash flows (*V*)	$855.40	1.0000	4.2498 ↑ Duration

the real world of investing

INTERNATIONAL BOND MANAGERS—CHANGING INTEREST RATES AND BOND PRICES

International bond managers have their hands full managing interest rate risk around the globe. In addition to changing interest rates, these managers also have to pay attention to currency fluctuations, local economies, and government intervention into the money markets. During the last decade (2000–2010), interest rates in the world's largest economies all declined. In fact, interest rates have been in a secular decline since 1982. At the beginning of 2000, 10-year U.S. Treasury bonds were yielding slightly more than 6 percent. Between 2002 and 2007 the rates on 10-year Treasury bonds traded in a narrow range of 4 percent, plus or minus about 75 basis points. The collapse of the housing bubble in the United States and in Europe, and the financial crisis that followed, caused rates on 10-year Treasury bonds to fall below 3 percent. The recessions of 2001 and 2007–2009 forced central banks to keep monetary policy easy with low interest rates in an effort to stimulate the economy. Similar patterns were present for the British gilts and other European countries.

At the end of 2010, money managers were faced with the difficulty of not knowing when this low interest rate environment would end or, once it did end, what the new equilibrium rates established in the markets would be. Given that a 1 percent increase in interest rates can cause a high duration bond to lose significant value, bond managers had to guess right.

It is difficult to forecast changes in interest rates, and most bankers admit that any forecast of interest rates more than three months into the future is hazardous. There are always unexpected changes in inflation, GDP, central bank policy, and so on.

All these factors can impact world bond prices and create price fluctuations. Given the sophistication of these international bond managers, let's give them the benefit of the doubt and assume they can actually forecast changing interest rates over the next three months. Let's also assume they can make money by shorting bonds whose prices will fall as interest rates rise and buying long those bonds whose prices will rise as interest rates fall.

How do bond managers know whether an increase in rates by ¼ percent on a 1.8 percent Japanese bond will change the price more or less than a ½ percent increase on a 5.5 percent German bond? They will most likely have to use the concept of *duration* to calculate which bond is most price sensitive to a change in interest rates. The fact that all international bonds will not have the same maturity may appear to complicate the decision, but duration measures bond price sensitivity and considers the current market interest rate, the maturity of the bond, and the bond's coupon rate. This is just what the international trader needs to make decisions in this fast-moving world of international interest rate movements.

The formula for duration can be formally stated as follows:

$$\text{Macaulay duration (D)} = \underbrace{\frac{CF\ PV}{V}}_{\text{Weight}}\underbrace{(1)}_{\text{Year}} + \underbrace{\frac{CF\ PV}{V}}_{\text{Weight}}\underbrace{(2)}_{\text{Year}} + \underbrace{\frac{CF\ PV}{V}}_{\text{Weight}}\underbrace{(3)}_{\text{Year}} + \ldots + \underbrace{\frac{CFPV}{V}}_{\text{Weight}}\underbrace{(n)}_{\text{Year}} \quad \textbf{(18–1)}$$

where:

CF = Yearly cash flow for each time Period

PV = Present value factor for each time period (from Appendix C at the end of the book)

V = Total present value or market price of the bond

n = Number of periods to maturity[1]

[1] Using the symbols from Formula 12–1, duration can also be stated as:

$$\text{Duration} = \sum_{t=1}^{n} \frac{C_t \frac{1}{(1+i)^t}}{V}(t) + \frac{P_n \frac{1}{(1+i)^n}}{V}(n)$$

If semiannual analysis is used throughout the calculation, the answer should be divided by two to convert the figure to annual terms.

TABLE 18-3 Duration for 8 Percent Coupon Rate Bonds with Maturities of 1, 5, and 10 Years Discounted at 12 Percent

(1) Year, *t*	(2) Cash Flow (*CF*)	(3) *PV* Factor at 12 Percent	(4) *PV* of Cash Flow (*CF*)	(5) *PV* of Annual Cash Flow (4) ÷ by Total *PV* of Cash Flows	(6) Year × Weight (1) × (5)
1-YEAR BOND					
1	$ 80	0.893	$ 71.44	0.0741	0.0741
1	1,000	0.893	893.00	0.9259	0.9259
			Total *PV* of cash flows → $964.44	1.0000	1.0000 ↑ Duration
5-Year Bond					
1	$ 80	0.893	$ 71.44	0.0835	0.0835
2	80	0.797	63.76	0.0745	0.1490
3	80	0.712	56.96	0.0666	0.1998
4	80	0.636	50.88	0.0595	0.2380
5	80	0.567	45.36	0.0530	0.2650
5	1,000	0.567	567.00	0.6629	3.3145
			Total *PV* of cash flows → $855.40	1.0000	4.2498 ↑ Duration
10-Year Bond					
1	$ 80	0.893	$ 71.44	0.0923	0.0923
2	80	0.797	63.76	0.0824	0.1648
3	80	0.712	56.96	0.0736	0.2208
4	80	0.636	50.88	0.0657	0.2628
5	80	0.567	45.36	0.0586	0.2930
6	80	0.507	40.56	0.0524	0.3144
7	80	0.452	36.16	0.0467	0.3269
8	80	0.404	32.32	0.0418	0.3344
9	80	0.361	28.88	0.0373	0.3357
10	80	0.322	25.76	0.0330	0.3330
10	$1,000	0.322	322.00	0.4160	4.1600
			Total *PV* of cash flows → $774.08	1.0000	6.8381 ↑ Duration

In Table 18–3, we observe durations for an 8 percent coupon rate bond with maturities of 1, 5, and 10 years. The discount rate is 12 percent. The procedure used to compute duration in Table 18–3 is the same as that employed in Table 18–2. Although many calculations are involved, you should primarily direct your attention to the last value presented in column (6) for each of the three bonds. This value represents the duration of the issue.

We see in Table 18–3 that the duration for a 1-year bond is 1.0. Since all cash flows are paid at the end of year 1, duration equals the maturity.[2] As maturity increases (to 5 and 10 years), duration increases but less than the maturity of the bond. With a 5-year bond, duration is 4.2498, and with a 10-year bond, duration is 6.8381. Duration is increasing at a decreasing rate because the principal repayment

[2] If semiannual analysis were used, the duration would be slightly less than the maturity in the first year.

in the last year becomes a smaller percentage of the total present value of cash flow, and the annual coupon payments become more important.[3]

DURATION AND PRICE SENSITIVITY

Once duration is computed, its most important use is in determining the price sensitivity of a bond. In Table 18–4, we consider the maturity, duration, and percentage price change for an 8 percent coupon rate bond based on a 2 percent decrease and on a 2 percent increase in interest rates. The *market* rate of interest for computing duration in Table 18–4 is 8 percent. Duration is related not only to maturity but also to coupon rate and market rate of interest. For example, in Table 18–3, the coupon rate of interest was 8 percent, and the market rate of interest was 12 percent. In the calculations in Table 18–4, the coupon rate is 8 percent, and the initial market rate of interest is assumed to be 8 percent. Because of the different market rates of interest in Tables 18–3 and 18–4, the duration for a given maturity (such as 5 or 10 years) will be different. The point just discussed will be further clarified later in the chapter, so even if you do not fully understand it, you should read on.

We see in Table 18–4 that the longer the maturity or duration, the greater the impact of a 2 percent change in interest rates on price. However, we shall also observe how much more closely the percentage change in price parallels the change in duration as compared with maturity. For example, between 25 and 50 years, duration increases very slowly [column (2)], and the same can be said for the increase in the percentage impact that a 2 percent decline in interest rates has on price [column (3)]. This is true despite the fact that the maturity period has increased by 100 percent, from 25 to 50 years.

TABLE 18-4 Duration and Price Sensitivity (8 percent coupon rate bond)

(1) Maturity	(2) Duration	(3) Impact of a 2% Decline in Interest Rates on Price	(4) Impact of a 2% Increase in Interest Rates on Price
1	1.0000	+1.89%	−1.81%
5	4.3121	+8.42	−7.58
10	**7.2470**	+14.72	−12.29
20	10.6038	+22.93	−17.03
25	11.5290	+25.57	−18.50
30	12.1585	+27.53	−18.85
40	12.8787	+30.09	−19.55
50	13.2123	+31.15	−19.83

application example

As a rough measure of price sensitivity, one can multiply duration times the change in interest rates to determine the percentage change in the value of a bond.

$$\text{Percentage change in the value of a bond approximately equals} \rightarrow \text{Duration} \times \text{Change in interest rates} \quad \textbf{(18–2)}$$

The sign in the final answer is reversed because interest rate changes and bond prices move in opposite directions. For example, if a bond has a duration of 7.2470 years,

[3] A sinking-fund provision can also have an effect on duration, causing the weighted average life of the bond to be shorter.

and interest rates go down by 2 percent, a rough measure of bond value appreciation is +14.494 percent (7.2470 × 2). Columns (2) and (3) in Table 18–4, across from 10 years maturity, indicate this is a good approximation. That is, when duration was 7.2470, a 2 percent drop in interest rates actually produced a 14.72 percent increase in bond prices (not too many basis points away from our formula value of +14.494 percent).[4] The approximation gets progressively less accurate as the term of the bond is extended. It is also a less valid measure for interest rate increases (and the associated price decline). Even with these qualifications, one can observe a more useful relationship between price changes and duration than between price changes and maturity.

It is for this reason that the analyst must have a reasonable feel for the factors that influence duration. The length of the bond affects duration, but as previously mentioned, it is not the only variable. Duration is also influenced by market rate of interest and the coupon rate on the bond. It is theoretically possible for these two factors to outweigh maturity in determining duration. That is to say, it is possible that a bond with a shorter maturity than another bond may actually have a longer duration and be more price sensitive to interest rate changes.

Duration and Market Rates

Market rates of interest (yield to maturity) and duration are inversely related. The higher the market rate of interest, the lower the duration. This is because of the present-value effect that is part of duration. Higher market rates of interest mean lower present values. For example, in Table 18–2 on page 469, if the market rate of interest in column (3) had been 16 percent instead of 12 percent, the final answer for duration would have been 4.1859. The new value is computed in Table 18–5. Clearly, it is less than the 4.2498 duration value in Table 18–2.

To expand our analysis, in Table 18–6 on the next page we see the duration values for an 8 percent coupon rate bond at different market rates of interest. As market rates of interest increase, duration decreases. This can be easily seen in the 20-year row

TABLE 18-5 **Duration of an 8 Percent Coupon Rate Bond with a 16 Percent Market Rate of Interest**

(1) Year, *t*	(2) Cash Flow (*CF*)	(3) *PV* Factor at 16 Percent	(4) *PV* of Cash Flow (*CF*)	(5) *PV* of Annual Cash Flow (4) ÷ by Total *PV* of Cash Flows	(6) Year × Weight (1) × (5)
1	$ 80	0.862	$ 68.96	0.0935	0.0935
2	80	0.743	59.44	0.0806	0.1612
3	80	0.641	51.28	0.0695	0.2085
4	80	0.552	44.16	0.0598	0.2392
5	80	0.476	38.08	0.0516	0.2580
5	$1,000	0.476	476.00	0.6451	3.2255
		Total *PV* of cash flows →	$737.92	1.0000	4.1859 ↑ Duration

[4] The approximation can be slightly improved by using modified duration instead of actual duration. Modified duration is explained later in this chapter, as is convexity. This is not required reading to understand the material in the chapter, but it may prove interesting to the more advanced student.

TABLE 18-6 Duration Values at Varying Market Rates of Interest (based on 8 percent coupon rate bond)

	MARKET RATES OF INTEREST				
Maturity (Years)	4 Percent	6 Percent	8 Percent	10 Percent	12 Percent
1	1.0000	1.0000	1.0000	1.0000	1.0000
5	4.3717	4.3423	4.3121	4.2814	4.2498
10	7.6372	7.4450	7.2470	7.0439	6.8381
20	12.3995	11.4950	10.6038	9.7460	8.9390
25	14.2265	12.8425	11.5290	10.3229	9.2475
30	15.7935	13.8893	12.1585	10.6472	9.3662
40	18.3274	15.3498	12.8787	10.9176	9.3972
50	20.2481	16.2494	13.2123	10.9896	9.3716

(reading across). At a 4 percent market rate of interest, duration for the 8 percent coupon rate bond is 12.3995. At 8 percent, it is 10.6038, and at 12 percent, 8.9390.

Also note in Table 18–6 that an equal change in market rates of interest will have a bigger impact on duration when rates move down than when they move up. For example, in the 50-year row, a 4 percentage point decrease in market rates of interest (say, from 8 percent to 4 percent) causes duration to increase by 7.0358 years, from 13.2123 to 20.2481 years. A similar increase from 8 percent to 12 percent would cause duration to decrease by only 3.8407 years, from 13.2123 to 9.3716 years.

Duration and Coupon Rates

In the previous section, we learned that duration is inversely related to the market rate of interest. We now look at the relationship between duration and the coupon rate on a bond. As the coupon rate rises, duration decreases. Why? The answer is that high coupon rate bonds tend to produce higher annual cash flows before maturity and thus tend to weight duration toward the earlier to middle years. On the other hand, low coupon rate bonds produce less annual cash flows before maturity and have less influence on duration. Duration is weighted more heavily toward the final payment at maturity, and duration tends to be somewhat closer to the actual maturity on the bond. At the extreme, a zero-coupon bond has the same maturity and duration.

The relationship between duration and coupon rates can be seen in Table 18–7. Here three different coupon rate bonds are presented. Each bond is assumed to have a maturity of 25 years. The best way to read the table is to pick a market rate of interest in the first column and then read across the table to determine the

TABLE 18-7 Duration and Coupon Rates (25-year bonds)

	COUPON RATES		
Market Rate of Interest	4 Percent	8 Percent	12 Percent
4%	16.2470	14.2265	13.3278
6	14.7455	12.8425	12.0407
8	13.2459	11.5290	10.8396
10	11.8112	10.3229	9.7501
12	10.4912	9.2475	8.7844

FIGURE 18-1 The Effect of Coupon Rates on Duration

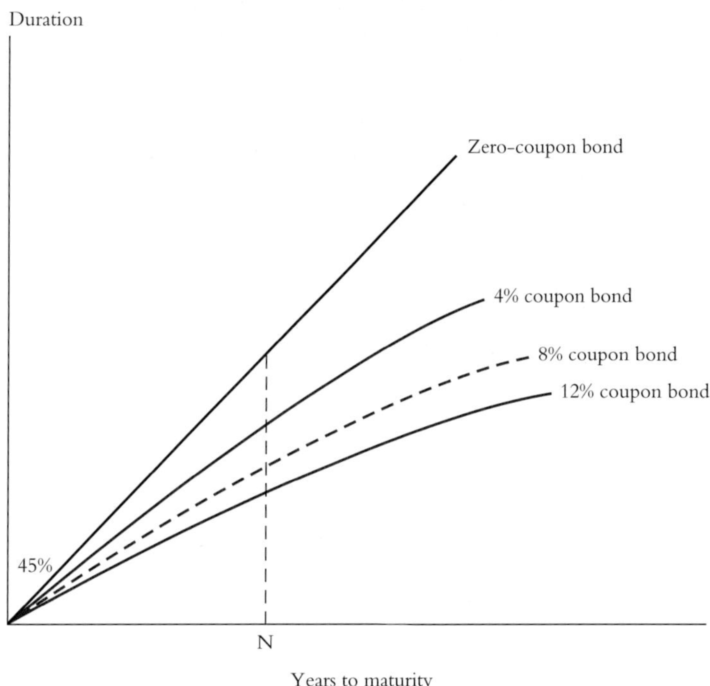

duration at various coupon rates. For example, at an 8 percent market rate of interest, duration is 13.2459 at a 4 percent coupon rate, 11.5290 at an 8 percent coupon rate, and 10.8396 at a 12 percent coupon rate. Clearly, the higher the coupon rate, the lower the duration (and vice versa).

The impact of coupon rates on duration is also demonstrated in Figure 18–1 above. Note that with a zero-coupon bond, the line is at a 45-degree angle; that is, duration and years to maturity are always the same value. There is only one payment, and it is at maturity.

You can also observe in Figure 18–1 that progressively higher coupon rates lead to a lower duration. As an example, go to point N on the horizontal axis and observe duration for 4 percent, 8 percent, and 12 percent interest. Clearly the higher the coupon rate, the lower the duration value.

Because the higher the duration, the greater the price sensitivity, it follows that an investor desiring maximum price movements will look toward lower coupon rate bonds. As previously demonstrated, low coupon rate and high duration go together, and high duration leads to maximum price sensitivity. The relationship of low coupon rates to price sensitivity was briefly discussed in Chapter 12 under investment strategy. We now see that the unnamed explanatory variable at that point was duration.

BRINGING TOGETHER THE INFLUENCES ON DURATION

The three factors that determine the value of duration are the maturity of the bond, the market rate of interest, and the coupon rate. Duration is positively correlated with maturity but moves in the opposite direction of market rates of interest and coupon rates; that is, the higher the market rate of interest or the coupon rate, the lower the duration. Earlier in this chapter, you were asked to consider whether you should invest in an 8 percent coupon rate, 20-year bond or a 12 percent coupon rate, 25-year bond. Since we were assuming interest rates were going to go down, you were looking for maximum price volatility. Had you not studied duration, you probably would have selected the bond with the longer maturity. This would generally be a valid assumption as indicated in Chapter 12. However, the primary emphasis to the sophisticated bond investor when assessing price volatility, or sensitivity, is duration.

Note that the bond with the longer maturity (25 years versus 20 years) also has a higher coupon rate (12 percent versus 8 percent). The first factor (longer maturity) would indicate higher duration, but the second factor (higher coupon rate) would indicate a lower duration. What is the net effect? The answer can be found in earlier tables in this chapter. Let's assume that the *market rate* of interest is 12 percent for both bonds. Table 18–6 on page 474 presented information on 8 percent coupon rate bonds for varying maturities and market rates of interest. To determine the duration on the 8 percent coupon rate, 20-year bond, assuming a 12 percent market rate of interest, we read across the 20-year row to the last column in the table and see the answer is 8.9390. (Note that all bonds in Table 18–6 have an 8 percent coupon rate, so we must identify the value associated with 20 years and a 12 percent market rate of interest.)

To determine the duration for the 12 percent coupon rate, 25-year bond with a 12 percent market rate of interest, we must go to Table 18–7 on page 474. Note that all bonds in this table have a 25-year maturity, so read down to a market rate of interest of 12 percent and across to a coupon rate of 12 percent. The value for duration on this bond is 8.7844.

Based on this analysis, the answer to the question posed earlier in the chapter is that the bond with the shorter maturity (8 percent coupon rate for 20 years) has a higher duration than the bond with the greater maturity (12 percent for 25 years) and thus is the most price sensitive.[5]

Bond	Duration
8%, 20 years	8.9390 ← greater price sensitivity
12%, 25 years	8.7844

In actuality, if interest rates went down by 2 percent, the 8 percent, 20-year bond would go up by 18.5 percent, while the 12 percent, 25-year bond would increase by only 17.9 percent.

DURATION AND ZERO-COUPON BONDS

Characteristics of zero-coupon bonds were briefly described in Chapter 11. As previously mentioned, Figure 18–1 on the previous page depicts the duration of zero-coupon bonds as a 45-degree line relative to years to maturity. This graphically indicates that the duration of a zero-coupon bond equals the number of years it has to maturity. For all bonds of equal risk and maturity, the zero-coupon bond has the greatest duration and therefore the greatest price sensitivity. This price risk is one that is often lost in the image of safety that zero-coupons have when backed by U.S. government securities.

[5] As previously indicated, if we vary the market rate of interest, we can also influence the outcome to our question.

TABLE 18-8 Duration of Zero-Coupon versus 6 Percent Coupon Bonds (market rate of interest is 4 percent)

(1) Years to Maturity	(2) Duration of Zero-Coupon Bond	(3) Duration of 6 Percent Coupon Bond	(4) Relative Duration of Zero-Coupon to 6 Percent Coupon Bonds (2) ÷ (3)
10	10	7.86	1.2723
20	20	12.87	1.5540
30	30	16.34	1.8360
40	40	18.82	2.1254

A classic headline in *The Wall Street Journal* on June 1, 1984, appeared as follows: "Zero-Coupon Bonds' Price Swings Jolt Investors Looking for Security."[6] It was reported that between March 31, 1983, and March 31, 1984, Salomon Brothers' 30-year zero coupon CATs (Certificates of Accrual on Treasury Securities) declined 25 percent in price, while returns on conventional 30-year government bonds declined only a few percentage points. The article cited one client buying $100,000 of zero-coupons, thinking they were similar to short-term Treasury bill investments, only to find out four weeks later that his zero-coupon bonds had declined in value by $25,000.

To put the volatility of a zero-coupon bond into better perspective, we compare the duration of a zero-coupon bond to that of a 6 percent coupon bond for several maturities in Table 18–8. Note that the market rate of 4 percent with a low coupon bond creates a fairly high duration.

The far right column in Table 18–8 indicates the ratio of duration between zero-coupon and 8 percent coupon rate bonds. As stressed throughout the chapter, duration represents a measure of price sensitivity. Thus, for a 10-year maturity period, a zero-coupon bond is almost 1½ times as price sensitive as a 6 percent coupon rate bond (the ratio in the last column is 1.2723). For a 20-year maturity period, it is over 1.5 times more price sensitive, and for 40 years the price sensitivity ratio is over two times greater (2.1254). This might explain why zero-coupons were much more sensitive to rising interest rates during 1983–84 as described in the story in *The Wall Street Journal*. Of course, tremendous profits can be made in zero-coupon bonds when there is a sharp drop in interest rates as in early 1985 and again in 1997, early 2003, and 2008, with the Federal Reserve maintaining low rates until 2011.

THE USES OF DURATION

Duration is primarily used as a measure to judge bond price sensitivity to interest rate changes. Because duration includes information on several variables (maturity, coupon rate, and market rate of interest), it captures more information than any one of them. It therefore allows more accurate decisions for complex bond strategies. One such strategy involves the timing of investment inflows to provide a needed cash outlay at a known future date. Perhaps $1 million is needed after five years. Everything is tailored to this five-year time horizon. If interest rates go up, there will be a decline in the value of the portfolio but a higher reinvestment rate opportunity for inflows. Similarly, if interest rates go down, there will be capital appreciation for the portfolio but a lower reinvestment rate opportunity. By tying all the investment decisions to a duration period, the portfolio manager can take

[6] Randall Smith, "Zero-Coupon Bonds' Price Swings Jolt Investors Looking for Security," *The Wall Street Journal*, June 1, 1984, p. 19.

advantage of these counter forces to ensure a necessary outcome. This strategy is called **immunization** and is used by insurance companies, pension funds, and other institutional money managers to protect their portfolios against swings in interest rates. For a more comprehensive discussion of immunization strategies, an article by Fisher and Weil is an appropriate source.[7] For an excellent criticism of duration and immunization strategy, see Yawitz and Marshall.[8] One of the problems with duration analysis is that it often assumes a parallel shift in yield curves. Although long-duration bonds are clearly more price sensitive than shorter-duration bonds, there is no assurance that long- and short-term interest rates will move by equal amounts.

BOND REINVESTMENT ASSUMPTIONS AND TERMINAL WEALTH ANALYSIS

Reinvestment Assumptions

As indicated in the previous section, one concern an investor may have when purchasing bonds is that the interest income will not be reinvested to earn the same return the coupon payment represents. This may not be a problem for an individual consuming the interest payments, but it could be a serious concern for individuals building a retirement portfolio or a pension fund manager accumulating funds for future payout to retirees. The crucial issue is the amount of money accumulated at the time the retirement fund will be used to cover living expenses. One major determinant of the ending value of a retirement fund is the rate of return on coupon payments as they are reinvested.

Since the middle 1970s, interest rates have generally been more volatile than during previous periods. This has caused more emphasis on the management of fixed-income securities, not only in the selection of maturity but also in the switching from short- to long-term securities. These volatile rates have caused more emphasis on concepts such as duration to measure bond price sensitivity and on total return as a measure of bond management success. Given that interest rates change daily and by large amounts over a year, what impact would a lower or higher **reinvestment assumption** have on the outcome of your retirement nest egg?

First, let us look at Table 18–9. The material covers the compound sum of \$1 and assumes all interest is reinvested at the stated rate in order to find the ending value of \$1 invested to maturity. For our current analysis, we are assuming annual interest (though the answer changes only slightly if we use semiannual interest).

The table values are given in \$1 amounts, so for a \$1,000 bond we would just move the decimal three places to the right. A \$1,000 bond having a 12 percent coupon

TABLE 18-9 Compound Sum of \$1.00 = $(1 + i)^n \times \$1$

Period	7 Percent	8 Percent	9 Percent	10 Percent	11 Percent	12 Percent
10	\$ 1.967	\$ 2.159	\$ 2.367	\$ 2.594	\$ 2.839	\$ 3.106
20	3.870	4.661	5.604	6.727	8.062	9.646
30	7.612	10.063	13.268	17.449	22.892	29.960
40	14.974	21.725	31.409	45.259	65.001	93.051

[7] Lawrence Fisher and Roman L. Weil, "Coping with Risk of Interest Rate Fluctuations: Returns to Bondholders from Naive and Optimal Strategies," *Journal of Business,* October 1971, pp. 408–31.

[8] Jess B. Yawitz and William J. Marshall, "The Shortcomings of Duration as a Risk Measure for Bonds," *Journal of Financial Research,* Summer 1981, pp. 91–101.

rate with interest being reinvested at 12 percent would compound to $93,051 over 40 years, while a 7 percent coupon bond reinvested at 7 percent would compound to only $14,974 over a similar period. A difference of 5 points in the rates creates a total difference of $78,077. This is quite a large difference. Notice that the longer the compounding period, the larger the amount. From further inspection of Table 18–9, other comparisons can be made between years and total ending values.

The importance of the reinvestment assumption can also be viewed from the perspective of its contribution to total wealth. For example, an investor owning a 40-year bond with a 12 percent coupon rate and an assumed reinvestment rate of 12 percent will have an accumulated value of $93,051. In terms of payout, $4,800 (40 × $120) comes directly from 40 years of 12 percent interest payments, $1,000 comes from principal, and the balance of $87,251 comes from interest that is earned on the annual interest payments. In this case, interest on interest represents 93.8 percent of the overall return ($87,251/$93,051). This $87,251 assumes that the interest payments are reinvested at the 12 percent coupon rate over the life of the bond. This is seldom the case in the real world and so terminal wealth calculations provide a more accurate answer to our rate of return over the life of the bond.

Terminal Wealth Analysis

application example

Now, we will assume a reinvestment assumption different from the coupon rate. Take the two extreme values from Table 18–9 on page 478 of 12 percent and 7 percent. Assume you buy a bond having a 12 percent coupon rate, but the interest can only be reinvested at 7 percent. To find the ending value of this investment, we will need to use a **terminal wealth table.**

Table 18–10 on the next page is called a terminal wealth table because it generates the ending value of the investment at the end of each year, assuming the bond has a *maturity* date corresponding to that year. Let's use 10 years as an example in examining Table 18–10. If the bond matures in 10 years, the $1,000 principal in column (2) will be recovered. Also the investor will receive $120 in annual interest (12 percent of $1,000) in year 10 as indicated in column (3). In column (4), the accumulated interest up to the *beginning* of year 10 is shown. The reinvestment rate on this previously accumulated interest is a mere 7 percent as indicated in column (5). The interest on the previously accumulated interest is $100.62 (0.07 × $1,437.38). Finally, the total interest for year 10 is shown in column (7). This consists of the coupon interest of $120 and the interest on interest of $100.62 and totals to $220.62. The total ending value of the portfolio is shown in column (8). The ending value consists of the recovered principal of $1,000 plus the accumulated interest of $1,437.38 up to the beginning of year 10 plus the total interest paid in year 10 of $220.62. The ending wealth value (portfolio sum) thus shown in column (8) is $2,658.00. The value is summarized below:

Recovered principal	$1,000.00	Column (2)
Accumulated interest (beginning of year 10)	1,437.38	Column (4)
Total annual interest (during year 10)	220.62	Column (7)
Ending wealth value (portfolio sum)	$2,658.00	Column (8)

A $1,000 investment that grows to $2,658.00 after 10 years is the equivalent of a $1 investment that grows to 2.65800 as indicated in column (9). The annual percentage return for a $1 investment that grows to 2.65800 after 10 years is 10.26 percent as indicated in column (10).

TABLE 18-10 Terminal Wealth Table (12 percent coupon with 7 percent reinvestment rate on interest)

(1) Years to Maturity	(2) Principal	(3) Annual Coupon Interest	(4) Accumulated Interest[a]	(5) Reinvestment Rate on Interest	(6) Interest on Interest	(7) Total Annual Interest	(8) Portfolio Sum	(9) Compound Sum Factor	(10) Annual Percentage Return
0.0	$1,000.00								
1.0	1,000.00	$120.00	$ 0.00			$ 120.00	$ 1,120.00	1.12000	12.00%
2.0	1,000.00	120.00	120.00	0.07	$ 8.40	128.40	1,248.40	1.24840	11.73
3.0	1,000.00	120.00	248.40	0.07	17.39	137.39	1,385.79	1.38579	11.48
4.0	1,000.00	120.00	385.79	0.07	27.01	147.01	1,532.80	1.53280	11.26
5.0	1,000.00	120.00	532.80	0.07	37.30	157.30	1,690.10	1.69010	11.06
6.0	1,000.00	120.00	690.10	0.07	48.31	168.31	1,858.41	1.85841	10.86
7.0	1,000.00	120.00	858.41	0.07	60.90	180.09	2,038.50	2.03850	10.71
8.0	1,000.00	120.00	1,038.50	0.07	72.70	192.70	2,231.20	2.23120	10.55
9.0	1,000.00	120.00	1,231.20	0.07	86.18	206.18	2,437.38	2.43738	10.40
10.0	1,000.00	120.00	1,437.38	0.07	100.62	220.62	2,658.00	2.65800	10.26
11.0	1,000.00	120.00	1,658.00	0.07	116.06	236.06	2,894.06	2.89406	10.14
12.0	1,000.00	120.00	1,894.06	0.07	132.58	252.58	3,146.64	3.14664	10.02
13.0	1,000.00	120.00	2,146.64	0.07	150.26	270.26	3,416.90	3.41690	9.91
14.0	1,000.00	120.00	2,416.90	0.07	169.18	289.18	3,706.08	3.70608	9.80
15.0	1,000.00	120.00	2,706.08	0.07	189.43	309.43	4,015.51	4.01551	9.71
16.0	1,000.00	120.00	3,015.51	0.07	211.09	331.09	4,346.60	4.34660	9.61
17.0	1,000.00	120.00	3,346.60	0.07	234.26	354.26	4,700.86	4.70086	9.54
18.0	1,000.00	120.00	3,700.86	0.07	259.06	379.06	5,079.92	5.07992	9.44
19.0	1,000.00	120.00	4,079.92	0.07	285.59	405.59	5,485.51	5.48551	9.37
20.0	1,000.00	120.00	4,485.51	0.07	313.99	433.99	5,919.50	5.91950	9.29
21.0	1,000.00	120.00	4,919.50	0.07	344.37	464.37	6,383.87	6.38387	9.22
22.0	1,000.00	120.00	5,383.87	0.07	376.87	496.87	6,880.74	6.88074	9.16
23.0	1,000.00	120.00	5,880.74	0.07	411.65	531.65	7,412.39	7.41239	9.09
24.0	1,000.00	120.00	6,412.39	0.07	448.87	568.87	7,981.26	7.98126	9.04
25.0	1,000.00	120.00	6,981.26	0.07	488.69	608.69	8,589.95	8.58995	8.98
26.0	1,000.00	120.00	7,589.95	0.07	531.30	651.30	9,241.25	9.24125	8.92
27.0	1,000.00	120.00	8,241.25	0.07	576.89	696.89	9,938.14	9.93814	8.87
28.0	1,000.00	120.00	8,938.14	0.07	625.67	745.67	10,683.81	10.68381	8.82
29.0	1,000.00	120.00	9,683.81	0.07	677.87	797.87	11,481.68	11.48168	8.78
30.0	1,000.00	120.00	10,481.68	0.07	733.72	853.72	12,335.40	12.33540	8.73
31.0	1,000.00	120.00	11,335.40	0.07	793.48	913.48	13,248.88	13.24888	8.69
32.0	1,000.00	120.00	12,248.88	0.07	857.42	977.42	14,226.30	14.22630	8.65
33.0	1,000.00	120.00	13,226.30	0.07	925.84	1,045.84	15,272.14	15.27214	8.61
34.0	1,000.00	120.00	14,272.14	0.07	999.05	1,119.05	16,391.19	16.39119	8.57
35.0	1,000.00	120.00	15,391.19	0.07	1,077.38	1,197.38	17,588.57	17.58857	8.53
36.0	1,000.00	120.00	16,588.57	0.07	1,161.20	1,281.20	18,869.77	18.86977	8.50
37.0	1,000.00	120.00	17,869.77	0.07	1,250.88	1,370.88	20,240.65	20.24065	8.46
38.0	1,000.00	120.00	19,240.65	0.07	1,346.85	1,466.85	21,707.50	21.70750	8.43
39.0	1,000.00	120.00	20,707.50	0.07	1,449.53	1,569.53	23,277.03	23.27703	8.40
40.0	1,000.00	120.00	22,277.03	0.07	1,559.39	1,679.39	24,956.42	24.95642	8.37

[a] At beginning of year.

A similar analysis can be done for all other maturity periods running from 1 to 40 years. One thing to notice from Table 18–10 is that the longer the maturity period of the bond, the greater the effect the low 7 percent reinvestment rate has on the bond. For 5 years, the annual percentage return [column (10)] is 11.06 percent; for 15 years, 9.71 percent; and for 40 years, 8.37 percent.

What is the actual difference between the ending value for a 40-year, 12 percent coupon rate bond assuming a *12 percent* reinvestment rate and the 40-year, *7 percent* reinvestment rate just presented in Table 18–10? Earlier in this section, Table 18–9 demonstrated that a 12 percent coupon rate bond with an assumed 12 percent reinvestment rate for 40 years would grow to $93,051. In Table 18–10, we see that a 12 percent coupon rate bond with a 7 percent reinvestment rate will grow to only $24,956.42 after 40 years. It should be evident that it is not only the coupon rate that matters but the reinvestment rate as well.

If the bond were not held to maturity in our analysis, then we would have to rely on the realized rate of return analysis developed in Chapter 12. The realized rate of return approach would assume that the bond is not held to maturity and that it is sold at either a gain or a loss. In the case of the bond analyzed in the terminal wealth table (Table 18–10), we know that since interest rates are assumed to decline, any sale of the bond before maturity should result in a capital gain. How large that capital gain would be will be dependent on its duration. Terminal wealth analysis is a way of analyzing the reinvestment assumption when bonds are held to maturity, while the realized yield approach assumes bonds are actively traded to take advantage of interest rate swings.

Zero-Coupon Bonds and Terminal Wealth

One of the benefits of zero-coupon bonds is that they lock in a compound rate of return (or reinvestment rate) for the life of the bond *if held to maturity*. There are no coupon payments during the life of the bond to be reinvested, so the originally quoted rate holds throughout if held to maturity. If a $1,000 par value, 15-year zero-coupon bond is quoted at a price of $183 to yield 12 percent, you truly have locked in a 12 percent reinvestment rate. Some would say you have not only locked in 12 percent but have thrown away the key. In any event, zero-coupon bonds allow you to predetermine your reinvestment rate.

Of course, if a zero-coupon bond is sold before maturity, there could be large swings in the sales price of the bond because of its high duration characteristics. Under this circumstance, the locked-in reinvestment concept for the zero-coupon bond loses much of its meaning. It is valid only when the zero-coupon bond is held to maturity.

MODIFIED DURATION AND CONVEXITY

Modified Duration

If we want to more accurately measure bond price sensitivity resulting from the impact of a change in interest rates, we can use the term **modified duration**, which is Macaulay duration divided by (1 plus the yield to maturity denoted as i). Macaulay duration is simply the duration value computed in the main body of the chapter:

$$\text{Modified duration } (D^*) = \text{Macaulay duration } (D)/(1 + i) \qquad \textbf{(18–3)}$$

For example, let's take the 10-year bond in Table 18–4 on page 472 of the chapter with a duration of 7.2470. To get modified duration we use 7.2470 ÷ (1 + 0.08), where 0.08 represents the 8 percent yield to maturity. The modified duration for this 10-year bond equals 6.712. The basic reason for calculating a modified duration is that it is more accurate than Macaulay duration in measuring the change in the price of the bond for a given change in the interest rate:

$$\text{Percentage change in the value of a bond approximately equals} \rightarrow \text{Modified duration} \times \text{Change in interest rate} \quad \textbf{(18–4)}$$

This equation is similar to Formula 18–2 on page 472 except that modified duration is used instead of normal or Macaulay duration. For example, if interest rates in the market move from 8 to 10 percent on the 10-year bond described in Table 18–4 of the chapter, this equation would predict that the price of the bond would decrease by 12.42 percent. This is derived as follows using Formula 18–3:

Percentage change in the value of a bond approximately equals:

$$6.712 \times 2\%$$

$$6.712 \times 2 = 13.42\%$$

The sign in the final answer changes because interest rate changes and bond prices move in opposite directions. The true answer is a modified duration of −13.42. When this negative number is multiplied by a negative change in yield to maturity, the product is a positive change in the bond price. Conversely, when −13.42 is multiplied by an increase in yield to maturity, the change in bond price will be negative. We can write this equation as

$$\Delta P = \Delta Y \times D^* \quad \textbf{(18–5)}$$

where:

ΔY = change in yield to maturity

D^* = modified duration expressed as a negative number

ΔP = percentage change in the bond price

As was true of Macaulay duration, modified duration becomes less accurate as the maturity of the bond is increased or the change in yield to maturity becomes large. The reason for the loss of accuracy in predicting the change in the bond's price comes from the issue of **convexity** presented on the next page.

If we look at Figure 18–2, we can see the yield to maturity and modified duration for a series of U.S. Treasury securities. If we start with the top of the list, we see

FIGURE 18-2 U.S. Treasury Yield Curve

The curve shows the yield to maturity of current bills, notes, and bonds; all data as of 3 p.m. ET.

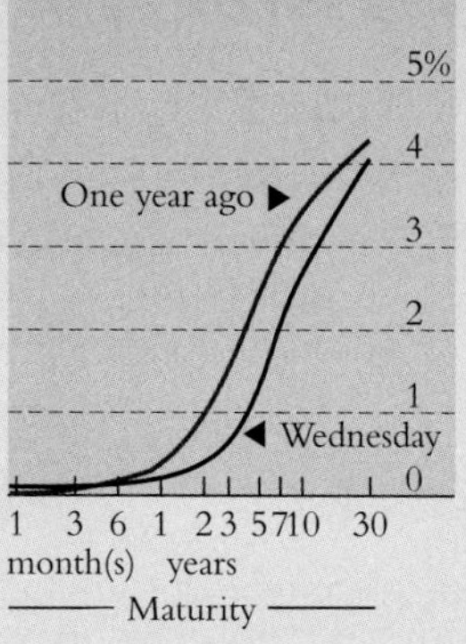

Ryan Index	Yield to Maturity	Modified Duration	TOTAL RETURN Month to-Date	Quarter to-Date	Year to-Date	12-Month
30-year Treasury	4.043%	17.25	−5.68%	−5.68%	14.08%	8.78%
10-year Treasury	2.716	8.54	−1.49	−1.49	12.89	10.15
7 year Treasury	2.028	6.45	−0.60	−0.60	12.78	11.49
Five-year Treasury	1.328	4.83	−0.03	−0.03	9.60	9.13
Ryan Index	1.859	7.00	−1.28	−1.28	9.52	7.96
3 year Treasury	0.622	2.94	0.13	0.13	5.13	5.14
Two-year Treasury	0.414	1.99	0.06	0.06	2.40	2.47
1 Year Treasury	0.223	0.98	0.06	0.06	0.80	0.90
Six-month Treasury	0.183	0.50	0.02	0.02	0.23	0.27
Ryan Cash Index-a	0.173	0.45	0.03	0.03	0.32	0.38
Three-month bill	0.142	0.25	0.02	0.02	0.16	0.21
One-month bill	0.142	0.08	0.01	0.01	0.10	0.11

a-Performance of a cash investment

Sources: *The Wall Street Journal Asia,* October 29-31, 2010, p. 28. Ryan ALM. Reprinted with permission of *The Wall Street Journal,*

a 30-year bond with a modified duration of 17.25 and a 10-year bond with a modified duration of 8.54. At the other end of the spectrum, the 3-year Treasury has a modified duration of 0.622 and the 1-year Treasury has a modified duration of 0.223. It is clear that if interest rates go up over the long term, bonds have a lot more to lose than short-term Treasuries. For example, if we assume that rates rise 50 basis points (0.5 percent), the 30-year bond will lose 8.62 percent of its value (−17.25 × 0.5) whereas the 3-year Treasury will lose 0.31 percent of its value (0.622 × 0.5).

We can also see the performance of the bonds in the last four columns from the current month of October 2010, the quarter, the year-to-date, and the last 12 months. Looking at the year-to-date figures, we can tell that rates have come down over that time period, and that the 30-year bond has given the highest return. If interest rates reverse and go up, the opposite will happen.

Convexity

The approximation formula used with the modified duration generates a linear relationship in bond price changes when in fact actual bond price changes are not linear. We can see from Table 18–4 on page 472 that a 2 percent change in interest rates does not create equal percentage changes in bond prices for both increases and decreases in interest rates [columns (3) and (4)]. Table 18–4 demonstrates that a decrease in interest rates for a 10-year maturity bond causes a bigger increase in the bond price (14.72 percent) than the change in price caused by a 2 percent increase in rates (−12.29 percent).

Using Figure 18–3 to explain convexity, we start at point B where the bond price (V) and approximation price begin in equilibrium at the market interest rate i. An increase in interest rates $+i$, estimates that the price of the bond using modified duration estimates will fall to $-V_{D^*}$ while the actual price only falls to $-V$. The difference between the estimated price and the actual price is due to the convexity of bond prices. For a decrease in interest rates $-i$, the modified duration estimates a price of $+V_{D^*}$ while the actual price is really $+V$. Looking at the differences between the estimates and reality, it can be observed that with a decline in interest rates, modified duration underestimates the bond price and that with an increase in interest rates, modified duration overestimates the bond price.

Convexity is only one of the issues that the analyst must understand in measuring the impact of bond price changes caused by interest rate fluctuations. While

FIGURE 18-3 Convexity

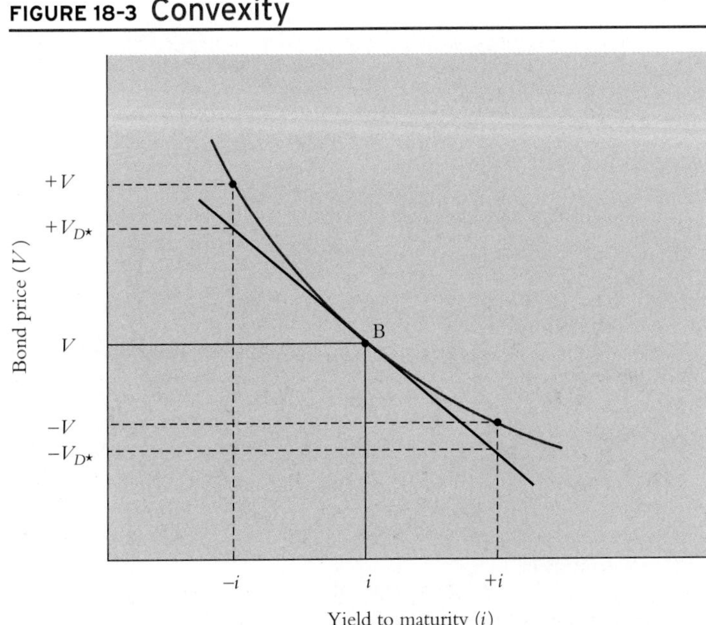

convexity makes duration a less than perfect measure for predicting bond price changes, it does not negate its value to the analyst in predicting bond price changes in individual bonds or bond portfolios.

BOND PORTFOLIO STRATEGIES WITH CHANGING INTEREST RATES

It should be clear by now that rising interest rates cause bond prices to fall and falling interest rates cause bond prices to rise. As a summary, we should also understand that long-term bonds with low or zero coupons are much more price sensitive to a change in rates than short-term bonds with high coupons. These relationships are all captured by modified duration and reinforced by Figure 18–2 on page 482.

So what should your strategy be when rates are expected to rise or fall? When rates are expected to rise, long-term bonds will lose more value than short-term bonds. The trap that many individual investors fall into is chasing the highest yield, ignoring this interest-rate risk. The interest-rate risk occurs when rates rise and you have locked yourself into long-term securities that will lose significant value. Although it is true that the U.S. Treasury securities listed in Figure 18–2 are risk free (free of the default risk), they are not immune to interest-rate risk. Fixed income securities like corporate bonds and U.S. Treasury bonds should be bought with a careful eye to changing interest-rate expectations. Chasing the highest yield is not a good idea when rates are expected to rise, but locking in a high yield to maturity when rates are expected to fall is a good idea.

Figure 18–4 from the St. Louis Federal Reserve Bank depicts the long-term interest-rate trend in 10-year and 3-month Treasury securities. It is clear that U.S.

FIGURE 18-4 10-Year and 3-Month Treasury Securities

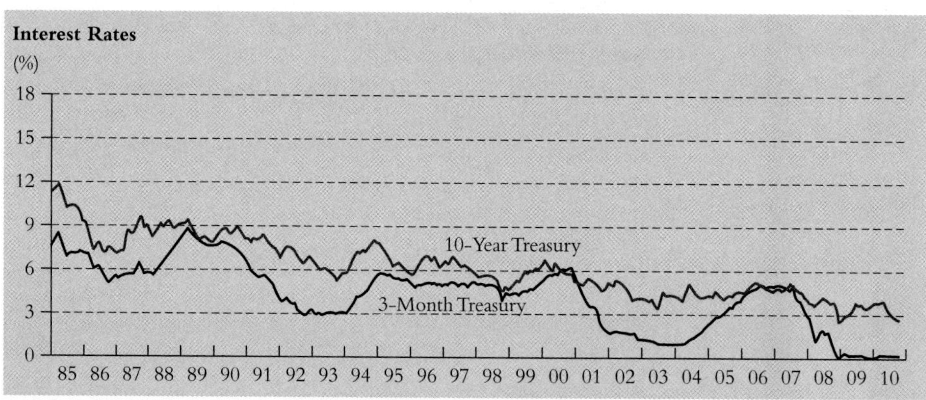

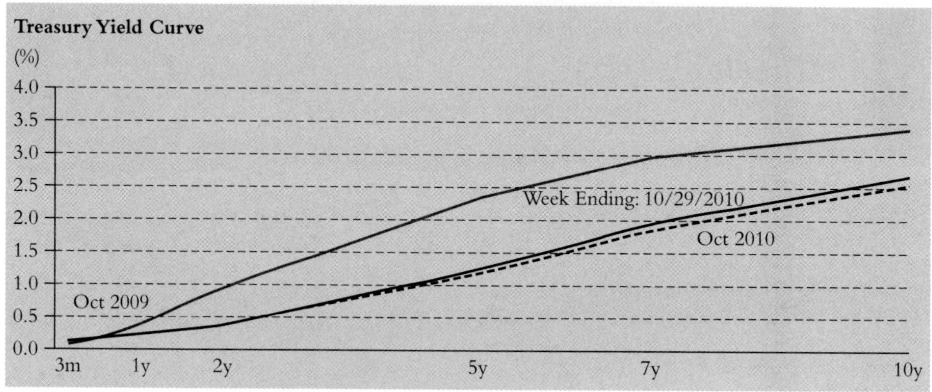

Source: Material reprinted from the Federal Reserve Bank of St. Louis, November 1, 2010.

interest rates have been in a secular decline since the early 1980s. There are a few upside short-lived moves, but the rates are currently the lowest since the Great Depression of the 1930s. The second part of the graph shows the yield curve in October 2009 and 2010, and we can observe that over this time it has moved down about 1 percent at the long end of the maturities and about 0.5 percent at the 2-year maturity. This explains the rates of returns for the Treasury Securities depicted in Figure 18–2 on page 482. It is fairly clear that rates don't have much lower to go and have a much higher probability of moving up than down. How should we structure a bond portfolio to maximize our long-term returns?

BOND LADDERS

A very common way of investing in bonds is to take an averaging approach rather than an all-or-nothing approach. Clearly, if we expect rates to go up, we want to stay with short maturities. If we are right and rates go up, we will be able to reinvest at higher and higher rates as market yields rise. Once we think rates have peaked, we might then create a portfolio with long maturities to lock in those high rates. This sounds easy on paper, but in practice correct forecasting is difficult. This is why bond traders pay attention to Federal Reserve Board policy and especially understand the material presented in Chapter 5 on the economy.

Let's see how a **bond ladder** would work with rates that are expected to rise. The bond ladder presented in Table 18–11 assumes semiannual compounding and investments spaced out in six-month maturities. The table assumes that the five-year market rates rise by 50 basis points each six months and that when the investor's 6-month security matures, she can reinvest the proceeds at a higher rate than she had previously been receiving. At the end of six months her old five-year security now has four and one-half years left to maturity, and she is still locked in to the other nine bonds. After six months she can reinvest in a new five-year bond to yield 3.5 percent. This investment brings her annualized yield up to 2.05 percent from 1.75 percent. After another six months, another bond matures, and she can now roll it over into a 4.0 percent five-year bond and increase her annualized yield to 2.38 percent.

Notice also that the income generated from the portfolio rises from $875 to $1,187.50 over the course of one year. An important consideration is whether you will be spending the income or reinvesting the income. Table 18–11 assumes that the income is not reinvested. If the investor is able to reinvest the interest, the portfolio will grow over time. In this example an investor reinvesting income would reinvest both the principal and the accumulated interest into the 5-year maturity. For example in the period 0 plus 6 months the 5-year treasury would now be $10,875 in principal and in the period 0 plus 1 year, the next 5-year treasury would be $11,025.

As market rates continue to rise, this strategy will gradually bring your portfolio yield up to a higher level without your portfolio suffering a large loss in value. When you estimate that rates have peaked or reached a plateau, when that six-month bond matures you can take the proceeds and invest in a 10-year or 30-year bond that will lock in a high rate of return. In fact, to avoid the reinvestment risk (reinvesting at a lower rate), you might want to buy zero-coupon bonds to lock in a high yield without worrying about what rate you will receive when you reinvest the proceeds from a coupon bond.

Bond ladders can be built in monthly intervals, quarterly intervals, and annual intervals, or for any time period that makes the investor comfortable. The need for cash flow should be considered when deciding on the intervals. Using zero-coupon bonds to build long-term ladders is also a strategy that investors can use to have the cash available for a desired purpose. However, zero-coupon bond ladders are much better constructed when interest rates are expected to fall, because you don't want to lock in a low reinvestment rate when rates are expected to rise. You can build a 5-year, 7-year, or 10-year ladder, or even longer. However, you

TABLE 18-11 Bond Ladder with Rising Rates

Time Period 0
Yield Available Today for the Following Maturities

Maturities	Yields to Maturity	Investment	Interest Earned	
6 months	0.50%	$ 10,000	$ 25.00	
1 year	0.75	10,000	37.50	
1.5 years	1.00	10,000	50.00	
2 Years	1.25	10,000	62.50	
2.5 years	1.50	10,000	75.00	
3 years	2.00	10,000	100.00	
3.5 years	2.25	10,000	112.50	
4 years	2.50	10,000	125.00	
4.5 years	2.75	10,000	137.50	
5 years	3.00	10,000	150.00	
		$100,000	$875.00	**Income for 6 months**
			1.75%	**Annualized Yield**

Time Period 0 + 6 Months
Yields Available Six Months from Today
As your 6-month bond comes due, you roll it into a new five-year bond at 3.5%

Maturities	Yields to Maturity	Investment	Interest Earned	
6 months	0.75%	$ 10,000	$ 37.50	
1 year	1.00	10,000	50.00	
1.5 years	1.25	10,000	62.50	
2 Years	1.50	10,000	75.00	
2.5 years	2.00	10,000	100.00	
3 years	2.25	10,000	112.50	
3.5 years	2.50	10,000	125.00	
4 years	2.75	10,000	137.50	
4.5 years	3.00	10,000	150.00	
5 years	3.50	10,000	175.00	
		$100,000	$1,025.00	**Income for 6 months**
			2.05%	**Annualized Yield**

You have increased your annualized yield by 30 basis points or 0.30% from 1.75% to 2.05%

Time Period 0 + 1 Year
Yields Available One Year from Today
Another six-month bond comes due, and you roll it into a new five-year bond at 4.0%

Maturities	Yields to Maturity	Investment	Interest Earned	
6 months	1.00%	$ 10,000	$ 50.00	
1 year	1.25	10,000	62.50	
1.5 years	1.50	10,000	75.00	
2 Years	2.00	10,000	100.00	
2.5 years	2.25	10,000	112.50	
3 years	2.50	10,000	125.00	
3.5 years	2.75	10,000	137.50	
4 years	3.00	10,000	150.00	
4.5 years	3.50	10,000	175.00	
5 years	4.00	10,000	200.00	
		$100,000	$1,187.50	**Income for 6 months**
			2.38%	**Annualized Yield**

You have increased your annualized yield by 33 basis points, or 0.33%, from 2.05% to 2.38%

want a short-term ladder when rates are expected to rise and a long-term ladder when rates are expected to fall.

BOND SWAPS

The term **bond swap** refers to selling out of a given bond position and immediately buying into another one with similar attributes in an attempt to improve overall portfolio return or performance.

Often there are bonds that appear to be comparable in every respect with the exception of one characteristic. For example, *newly issued bonds* that are the equivalent in every sense to outstanding issues generally trade at a slightly higher yield.

Swaps may also be utilized for tax-adjustment purposes and are very popular at the end of the year. Assume you own a single-A-rated AT&T bond that you bought five months ago, and you are currently sitting on a 20 percent capital loss because of rising interest rates. You bought a high-duration bond when you thought rates were on their way down and you guessed wrong. You can sell the bond and claim the loss (up to $3,000) against other income or to offset capital gains on other securities. Net losses greater than $3,000 can be carried forward to future periods. This loss will save you income equal to the loss times your marginal income tax rate. You can take the proceeds from the sale and reinvest in a bond of equal risk, and you will have increased your total cash returns because of tax benefits. Financial institutions will take advantage of tax swaps and are not limited to the $3,000 taxable loss limit as are individual investors.

Another common swap is the **pure pickup yield swap**, in which a bond owner thinks she can increase the yield to maturity by selling a bond and buying a different bond of equal risk. The key to this swap is that the bond price of one or both bonds has to be in disequilibrium. This assumes that the market is less than totally efficient. By selling the bond that is overpriced and purchasing the bond that is underpriced, the investor is increasing the yield on the investment. If by chance the true quality and risk of the two bonds are different, the bond trader may have swapped for nothing, or may even end up losing on the trade. Institutional bond traders often will forecast an increase or decrease in a bond's rating. If the bond rating is expected to rise because of better corporate financial performance, the yield would go down and the price would go up. The trader might buy the bond in advance of an expected rating increase with proceeds from the sale of a bond that is expected to have a stable rating or a decline in its rating. Other types of swaps exist for arbitrages associated with interest-payment dates, call transactions, conversion privileges, or any quickly changing factor in the market.

SUMMARY

In Chapter 18, we have taken the concepts developed in Chapter 12 and expanded on the principles of bond price volatility and total return. We developed the concept of duration so that the student has a basic understanding of its meaning and some of its applications. In general, we have shown that duration is the number of years, on a present-value basis, that it takes to recover an initial investment in a bond. More specifically, each year is weighted by the present value of the cash flow as a proportion of the present value of the bond and then summed. The higher the duration, the more sensitive the bond price is to a change in interest rates. Duration as one number captures the three variables—maturity, coupon rate, and market rate of interest—to indicate the price sensitivities of bonds with unequal characteristics. Generally, bond duration increases with the increase in number of years to maturity. Duration also increases as coupon rates decline to zero, and finally, duration declines as market interest rates increase.

Zero-coupon bonds are highlighted as the most price sensitive of bonds to a change in market interest rates, and comparisons are made between zero-coupon bonds and coupon bonds. Duration's primary use is in explaining price volatility, but it also has applications in the insurance industry and other areas of investments where interest rate risk can be reduced by matching duration with predictable cash outflows in a process called immunization.

An important concept has to do with the reinvestment of interest at rates other than the coupon rate. The method used to explain the effect on the total return is terminal wealth analysis, which assumes that the investment is held to maturity and that all proceeds over the life of the bond are reinvested at the reinvestment rate. In general, the longer the maturity, the more total annualized return approaches the reinvestment rate. If the reinvestment rate is significantly different from the coupon rate, the annualized return can differ greatly from the coupon rate in as little as five years.

Modified duration was presented along with the concept of convexity. This concept creates a more accurate estimate of a bond's price sensitivity with changing interest rates. This was followed by portfolio strategies using bond ladders and swaps as ways to manage bond portfolios.

KEY WORDS AND CONCEPTS

bond ladder 485
bond swaps 485
convexity 482
duration 469
immunization 478
Macaulay duration 469
modified duration 481
pure pickup yield swap 487
reinvestment assumption 478
terminal wealth table 479
weighted average life 468

DISCUSSION QUESTIONS

1. Why is the weighted average life of a bond less than the maturity date?
2. Define duration.
3. How can duration be used to determine a rough measure of the percentage change in the price of a bond as a result of interest rate changes?
4. Comment on the statement, "It is possible that a bond with a shorter maturity than another bond may actually have a longer duration and be more price sensitive to interest rate changes." Explain why a bond with a shorter maturity than another bond could have a longer duration.
5. As market rates of interest become higher, what impact does this have on duration?
6. What happens to duration as the coupon rate on a bond issue declines from 12 percent to 0 percent with the maturity date remaining constant?
7. Why are the maturity date and duration the same for a zero-coupon bond?
8. Should an investor who thinks interest rates are going down seek low or high coupon rate bonds? Relate your answer to duration and price sensitivity.
9. Why are zero-coupon bonds the most price sensitive of any type of bond issue?
10. Why is the reinvestment rate assumption critical to bond portfolio management?
11. What is a terminal wealth table? How is terminal wealth analysis different from the realized yield approach in Chapter 12?
12. Why is it said that zero-coupon bonds lock in the reinvestment rate?
13. Is the locked-in reinvestment assumption valid for zero-coupon bonds if they are sold before maturity? Explain.
14. How would you construct a bond ladder if you thought interest rates would rise? What if you thought rates would fall?

PRACTICE PROBLEMS AND SOLUTIONS

Duration

1. Compute the duration for the data in this problem. Use an approach similar to that in Table 18–2 on page 469. A discount rate of 10 percent should be applied.

Year	Cash Flow
1	70
2	70
3	70
3	$1,000

Reinvestment

2. You have invested $1,000 in a 10 percent coupon bond that matures in three years. You are investing the interest income in a fund earning 6 percent. At the end of three years, what will be your portfolio sum? Follow the procedure in Table 18–10 (first eight columns).

Solutions

1.

(1) Year, *t*	(2) Cash Flow (*CF*)	(3) *PV* Factor at 10%	(4) *PV* of Cash Flow (*CF*)	(5) *PV* of Annual Cash Flow (4) ÷ Total *PV* of Cash Flows	(6) Year × Weight (1 × 5)
1	70	.909	$ 63.63	.0688	.0688
2	70	.826	57.82	.0625	.1250
3	70	.751	52.57	.0568	.1704
3	1,000	.751	751.00	.8119	2.4357
		Total *PV* of Cash Flows →	$925.02	1.0000	2.7999 ↑ Duration

2.

(1) Years to Maturity	(2) Principal	(3) Annual Coupon Interest	(4) Accumulated Interest (beginning of year)	(5) Reinvestment Rate on Interest	(6) Interest on Interest	(7) Total Annual Interest	(8) Portfolio Sum
0.0	$1,000	—	—	—	—	—	—
1.0	1,000	$100	0	—	—	100.00	$1,100.00
2.0	1,000	100	100.00	0.06	$ 6.00	106.00	1,206.00
3.0	1,000	100	206.00	0.06	12.36	112.36	**$1,318.36**

PROBLEMS

Weighted average life

1. Compute the simple weighted average life for the following data. Use an approach similar to that in Table 18–1 on page 468.

Year	Cash Flow
1	$ 105
2	105
3	105
4	105
5	105
5	$1,000

Duration

2. Compute the duration for the data in problem 1. Use an approach similar to that in Table 18–2 on page 469. A discount rate of 13 percent should be applied.

Price sensitivity

3. As part of your answer to problem 2, you computed the price of the bond [column (4)]. This is the same as the PV of cash flows in column (4).
   a. Recompute the price of a bond based on an 11 percent discount rate (market rate of interest).
   b. What is the percentage change in the price of the bond as interest rates decline by 2 percent from 13 percent to 11 percent?
   c. Approximate this same value by multiplying the duration computed in problem 2 times the change in interest rates (2 percent). The answer in part *c* should come reasonably close to the answer in part *b*. However, they will not be exactly the same.

Comparative duration

4. *a.* Compute the duration for the following data. Use a discount rate of 13 percent.

Year	Cash Flow
1	$ 50
2	50
3	50
4	50
5	50
5	$1,000

   b. Explain why the answer to part *a* is higher than the answer to problem 2.
   c. If in part a the discount rate were 10 percent instead of 13 percent, would duration be longer or shorter? You do not need to actually compute a value; merely indicate an answer based on the discussion material in the text.

Comparative duration

5. You are considering the purchase of two $1,000 bonds. Your expectation is that interest rates will drop, and you want to buy the bond that provides the maximum capital gains potential. The first bond has a coupon rate of 6 percent with four years to maturity, while the second has a coupon rate of 14 percent and comes due six years from now. The market rate of interest (discount rate) is 8 percent. Which bond has the best price movement potential? Use duration to answer the question.

Comparative duration

6. Ted Bear thinks that recent Federal Reserve policy is going to push interest rates up. He is considering keeping only one of the three bonds in his portfolio. He knows that bond A has a duration of 5.3128, bond B has a duration of 3.2056, and bond C has the following characteristics:

Par Value	$1,000
Life	4 years
Coupon rate	5 percent
Discount rate	10 percent

Which one of the three bonds should he keep?

Comparative duration

7. Assume you desire maximum duration to take advantage of anticipated interest rate declines. Answer the following questions based on information taken from Tables 18–6 and 18–7 on page 474.

a. Would you prefer an 8 percent coupon rate bond with a 20-year maturity or a 12 percent coupon rate bond with a 25-year maturity? The market rate of interest is 8 percent.

b. Would you prefer an 8 percent coupon rate bond with a 20-year maturity or a 4 percent coupon rate bond with a 25-year maturity? The market rate of interest is 12 percent.

c. Would you prefer an 8 percent coupon rate bond with a 20-year maturity or a 12 percent coupon rate bond with a 25-year maturity? The market rate of interest is 12 percent.

Zero-coupon bond and duration

8. A 30-year, $1,000 par value zero-coupon bond provides a yield of 11 percent.

a. Compute the current price of the zero-coupon bond. (*Hint:* Simply take the present value of the ending $1,000 payment.)

b. What is the duration of the bond?

c. Does the bond have a longer or shorter duration than a 50-year, 8 percent coupon rate bond, where the duration on the latter bond is based on a 12 percent market rate of interest (consult Table 18–6)?

d. Assume you were going to put the zero-coupon bond(s) from part *a* in a nontaxable individual retirement account. If you wish to have $30,000 after 30 years, how much would you need to invest today?

e. If a $1,000 par value zero-coupon rate bond had a 40-year maturity and provided a yield of 13 percent, what would be the current price of the zero-coupon bond?

Return on zero-coupon bond

9. Assume you buy a 20-year, $1,000 par value zero-coupon bond that provides a 10 percent yield. Almost immediately after you buy the bond, yields go down to 8 percent.

a. What will be your gain on the investment?

b. What will be your percentage gain?

Yield on zero-coupon bond

10. You buy a zero-coupon bond for $200 and 15 years later sell it for $728.40. What rate of return did you earn?

Reinvestment assumption

11. You have invested $1,000 in a 13 percent coupon bond that matures in five years. This bond is held in your individual retirement account, and you are not concerned about tax consequences. You are investing the interest income in a money market fund earning 8 percent. At the end of five years, what will be your portfolio sum? Follow the procedure in Table 18–10 on page 480 (first eight columns).

Annual return with reinvestment assumption

12. In problem 11, what is the annual percentage return? An approximation will be sufficient.

Modified duration and price changes

13. Use Figure 18–3 and the modified duration for the securities given to answer the following questions.

a. Compute the expected change in price for the 30-year Treasury if interest rates go up by 75 basis points. Assuming the bond is selling for $1,000, what would the dollar change be?

b. Compute the expected change in price for the 30-year Treasury if interest rates go down by 20 basis points.

c. Compute the expected change in price for the 10-year Treasury if interest rates go up 0.75 percent.

d. If you think rates will rise, which bond would you rather own?

Bond ladder calculations

14. You expect interest rates to rise on five-year bonds by 1 percent per year over the next three years from their artificially low rate of 2 percent. Currently you can buy the following securities at the yields listed below. You invest $10,000 into each bond and spend the income from the portfolio. Refer to Table 18–11 for the structure of this problem.

1-year bond 0.50%
2-year bond 1.00%
3-year bond 1.50%
4-year bond 1.75%
5-year bond 2.00%

a. Build a five-year bond ladder with the above data and compute the annual rate of return.
b. At the end of the first year, reinvest the $10,000 that matures into a new five-year bond yielding 2.50% and compute the return on the portfolio.
c. At the end of the second year, reinvest the $10,000 that matures into a new five-year bond yielding 3.00% and compute the return on the portfolio.
d. Finally, at the end of the third year, rates have peaked and you reinvest the $10,000 that matures into another five-year bond yielding 4.00%. Compute the yield on your portfolio.
e. How much did the return on the last portfolio differ from the return on the new portfolio?

WEB EXERCISE

To maximize your understanding of duration, it is helpful to calculate the duration on an actual bond issue. Go to **www.investinginbonds.com**.

1. Put your cursor on "BOND MARKET & PRICES" and click on "Corporate Market At-A-Glance."
2. Click on "Most Active Bonds During the Last Trading Day."
3. Scroll down until you see a bond with a coupon rate over 5 percent, a maturity rate of less than six years in the future, a high price of at least 70, and a yield of at least 5 percent.
4. You are going to use the techniques in Table 18–2 to calculate the duration of the bond. You will need a calculator for ease of computation. Examining Table 18–2 of the chapter:
a. Set up column (1). Even if the bond you have selected does not end in exactly a given number of years, round to the nearest year.
b. Set up column (2). Use the coupon rate on the screen and multiply it times $1,000 to get cash flow. Also, assume a $1,000 cash flow in the final year.
c. To get the discount rate in column (3), round the yield value on the screen to the nearest whole number.
d. Compute the present value of the cash flows for each year, and sum them as is shown in column (4).
e. To get the values in column (5), divide each value in column (4) by the sum of column (4).
f. Multiply the year number in column (1) by the values in column (5) to get the values in column (6). When you total the values, you have completed the process of computing duration.
5. How does the duration of the bond compare to the bond's rounded value for maturity? What percentage of maturity does it represent?
6. If interest rates go down by 2 percent, how much will this bond price increase? Use Formula 18–2 and remember to change the sign to positive in your answer.

Note: From time to time, companies redesign their Web sites, and occasionally a topic we have listed may have been deleted, updated, or moved into a different location.

CFA MATERIAL

The following material contains sample questions and solutions from a prior Level I CFA exam. While the terminology is slightly different from that in this text, you can still view the skills that are necessary for the CFA exam.

CFA Exam Question

Question 7 is composed of two parts, for a total of 10 minutes.

7. You are asked to consider the following bond for possible inclusion in your company's fixed-income portfolio:

Issuer	Coupon	Yield to Maturity	Maturity	Duration
Wiser Company	8%	8%	10 Years	7.25 years

a. I. Explain why the Wiser bond's duration is less than its maturity.
II. Explain whether a bond's duration or its maturity is a better measure of the bond's sensitivity to changes in interest rates. (*4 minutes*)

b. Briefly explain the impact on the duration of the Wiser Company bond under *each* of the following conditions:
I. The coupon is 4 percent rather than 8 percent.
II. The yield to maturity is 4 percent rather than 8 percent.
III. The maturity is 7 years rather than 10 years. (*6 minutes*)

Solution: Question 7—Morning Section (10 points)

a. I. The Wiser bond's duration is less than its maturity because some of the bond's cash flow payments (i.e., the coupons) occur before maturity. Since duration measures the weighted average time until cash flow payment, its duration is less than its maturity. Bond duration is defined as

$$D = \frac{\sum_{t=1}^{N} PVCF_t \times t}{\sum_{t=1}^{N} PVCF_t}$$

II. For coupon bonds, duration is a better measure of the bond's sensitivity to changes in interest rates. Using the bond's maturity is deficient as a benchmark because it measures only when the final cash flow is paid and ignores all of the interim flows. Duration is a better measure because it measures the weighted average time until cash flow and thus is a more representative measure of the bond's overall cash flow sensitivity to interest rate changes. Duration takes into account coupon (inverse relationship) and yield to maturity (inverse relationship) as well as time to maturity.

b. I. Duration will increase. As the coupon decreases, a proportionately higher weight is given to the redemption payment, and therefore, the duration increases.
II. Duration will increase. As rates decline, all of the cash flows increase in value, but the longest ones increase at the greatest rate. Therefore, the redemption payment has much greater effect, causing the duration to increase.
III. Duration will decrease. The elapsing of time is accompanied by the reduction of total coupon payments and the shortening of time until the redemption payment. Therefore, because the redemption payment comes sooner, the duration decreases.

chapter nineteen

INTERNATIONAL SECURITIES MARKETS

OBJECTIVES

1. Describe the diversification benefits of international investments.
2. Explain the difference between market performance in developed countries versus that in emerging countries.
3. Describe the return potential in foreign markets versus that in the United States.
4. Explain the effect of currency fluctuations on rates of return.
5. Understand the various methods of participating in foreign investments.
6. Describe the risks and obstacles associated with foreign investments.

OUTLINE

In Chapters 1 and 17, we discussed the advantage of diversification in terms of risk reduction. To reduce risk exposure, the investor may desire a broad spectrum of securities from which to choose. An investor who lives in California would hardly be expected to limit all his investments to that geographic boundary. The same might be said for an investor living in the United States or Germany or Japan. The advantages of crossing international boundaries may be substantial in terms of diversification benefits.

Companies operating in different countries will be affected differently by international events such as crop failures, energy prices, wars, tariffs, trade between countries, and the value of local currencies relative to other currencies, especially the U.S. dollar. Furthermore, despite the up and down markets in the United States, there is almost certain to be a bull market somewhere in the world for the investor who likes to keep his chips on the table at all times.

Of course, there are some disadvantages to investing in international securities. The main drawback would appear to be the more complicated nature of the investment. Currently, one cannot simply pick up the phone and ask a broker to buy 100 shares of any stock listed on a foreign exchange. Some foreign markets have very low liquidity or require citizenship for ownership, or U.S. brokers may be restricted from dealing in these securities.

The primary focus of this chapter is international equities, although investments may certainly include fixed-income securities and real assets. We shall examine the composition of world equity markets, the diversification and return benefits to a portfolio that can be derived from foreign investments, the obstacles that are present, and finally, the methods of participating in foreign investments directly and indirectly.

THE WORLD EQUITY MARKET

The world equity markets grew rapidly from 1992 to 2009 but experienced a few bumps along the way, such as the Asian currency crisis of 1997–1998, the collapse of the Internet bubble in the United States in 2000–2002, and the bursting of the U.S. real estate bubble in 2007–2009. Throughout this time, developed markets haven't made much headway. In 1996 the developed world had capital markets valued at almost $18 trillion, and three years later in 1999 they were valued at $33 trillion. Three years later (2002) the markets had declined to $21 trillion, only to recover to $36.5 trillion in 2005. The interesting thing is that by the end of 2009 these developed markets were valued at $34.9 trillion, not much more than the $33 trillion they were worth in 1999.

Table 19–1 shows the changes in the values of developed countries between 2005 and 2009. We can see that countries like Australia, Canada, Hong Kong, France, Spain, and Germany have increased their percentages of the total, largely at the expense of the United States and Japan. Figure 19–1 shows that the three regions of developed

TABLE 19-1 Market Capitalization of Developed Countries (in millions of U.S. dollars)

Country	Year-End 2005	Percent of Total	Year-End 2009	Percent of Total	% Change, 2005-2009
Australia	$ 804,074	2.20%	$ 1,258,456	3.61%	56.5%
Austria	126,324	0.35	53,578	0.15	−57.6
Belgium	327,065	0.90	261,429	0.75	−20.1
Bermuda	2,125	0.01	1,360	0.00	−36.0
Canada	1,480,891	4.05	1,680,958	4.82	13.5
Cyprus	6,583	0.02	4,993	0.01	−24.2
Denmark	178,038	0.49	186,852	0.54	5.0
Finland	209,504	0.57	91,021	0.26	−56.6
France	1,710,029	4.68	1,972,040	5.65	15.3
Germany	1,221,250	3.34	1,297,568	3.72	6.2
Greece	145,013	0.40	54,717	0.16	−62.3
Hong Kong	1,006,228	2.75	2,291,578	6.56	127.7
Iceland	27,799	0.08	1,128	0.00	−95.9
Ireland	114,134	0.31	29,883	0.09	−73.8
Italy	798,167	2.18	317,317	0.91	−60.2
Japan	4,736,513	12.96	3,377,892	9.68	−28.7
Luxembourg	51,254	0.14	105,559	0.30	106.0
Netherlands	727,515	1.99	542,533	1.55	−25.4
New Zealand	40,620	0.11	67,061	0.19	65.1
Norway	190,952	0.52	227,233	0.65	19.0
Portugal	66,981	0.18	98,650	0.28	47.3
Singapore	208,300	0.57	310,766	0.89	49.2
Spain	960,024	2.63	1,297,227	3.72	35.1
Sweden	403,948	1.11	432,296	1.24	7.0
Switzerland	938,624	2.57	1,070,694	3.07	14.1
U.K.	3,058,182	8.37	2,796,444	8.01	−8.6
U.S.	16,997,982	46.52	15,077,286	43.19	−11.3
Developed World	**$36,538,119**	**100%**	**$34,906,519**	**100%**	**−4.5%**

Source: *Global Stock Markets Factbook 2010*, Standard & Poor's, p. 29.

FIGURE 19–1 Developed Markets by Geographical Areas

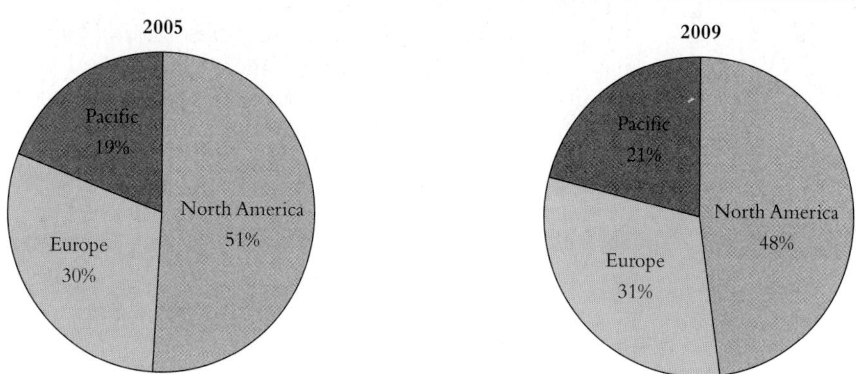

Source: *Global Stock Markets Factbook 2010,* Standard & Poor's Corp. 2010, p. 25.

countries have not changed much, but North America has lost 3 percent while the Pacific has picked up 2 percent and Europe 1 percent. Asia has benefited from the growth of China, and Europe has benefited from the integration and growth of the European Union. Australia and Canada have both benefited from the increased prices of raw materials such as copper, oil, bauxite, and other minerals. These two natural-resource-rich economies have not suffered as much as Europe and the United States, which were still recovering from the financial crisis as 2010 came to an end. All in all, the developed markets lost 4.5 percent of their market values over 2005–2009. Fortunately, 2010 brought rising stock markets to most of the world economies.

What is most surprising is the dramatic rise of the emerging-market countries, as shown in Table 19–2. While the developed world markets were shrinking, the emerging markets were growing by 93.5 percent during this same time period, led by China's amazing growth story. In 2005 these emerging markets had a market value of $7.1 trillion, which was about 19.5 percent of the developed market's capitalization. By 2009 these emerging markets were valued at $13.8 trillion, which totaled 39.5 percent of the developed markets' $34.9 trillion market cap.

Some of this 20 percent relative increase can be credited to China's growth from $780 billion in 2005 to $5 trillion in 2009, or a 541 percent increase in value. Of the ten largest emerging markets, India and Brazil grew by over 100 percent and Russia by 57 percent. Although countries like Tunisia (217%), Kazakhstan (448%), Indonesia (117%), Serbia (118%), and Colombia (189%) grew very rapidly, they were small markets to begin with and didn't influence the overall total all that much. However, if they keep growing at the same rate for another four years, they will become significant markets.

China however, increased by over $4.3 trillion dollars and was the major reason for the large increase in value. There are several reasons for China's emergence as the second largest stock market capitalization in the world. First, the country has had annual GDP growth of close to 10 percent per year for the last decade. This vaulted it into second place for the world's largest economy, ahead of Japan and behind the United States. More importantly, China has become a mixed economy, with a one-party system embracing its own form of capitalism. Many state-owned companies were privatized and became public companies listed on the Shanghai and Shenzhen stock exchanges. Additionally, many Chinese companies are now listed and traded on the New York Stock Exchange and the NASDAQ market. With this we have to also include Hong Kong's stock market, which grew from $1 trillion to $2.3 trillion during the same time period. Hong Kong is a special administrative region of China, and many Chinese companies with global interests are listed on the Hong Kong Stock Exchange. A significant benefit for Hong Kong is that it still operates under a British style legal system.

You might wonder why China, the second largest economy in the world, is still considered an emerging market. There are several reasons. One of the major

TABLE 19-2 Market Capitalization of Emerging Markets Greater than 2 Billion in Capitalization (in millions of U.S. dollars)

Country	Year-End 2005	% of Total	Year-End 2009	% of Total	% Change 2005-2009
Argentina	$ 61,478	0.86%	$ 48,942	0.35%	−20.39%
Bahrain	17,364	0.24	16,933	0.12	−2.48
Bangladesh	3,035	0.04	7,068	0.05	132.88
Bolivia	2,200	0.03	2,792	0.02	26.91
Brazil	474,647	6.65	1,167,335	8.45	145.94
Bulgaria	5,086	0.07	7,103	0.05	39.66
Chile	136,446	1.91	209,475	1.52	53.52
China	780,763	10.94	5,007,646	36.27	541.38
Colombia	46,016	0.64	133,301	0.97	189.68
Cote d'Ivorie	2,327	0.03	6,141	0.04	163.90
Croatia	12,918	0.18	25,637	0.19	98.46
Czech Republic	38,345	0.54	52,688	0.38	37.41
Ecuador	3,214	0.05	4,248	0.03	32.17
Egypt	79,672	1.12	89,953	0.65	12.90
El Salvador	3,623	0.05	4,432	0.03	22.33
Estonia	3,495	0.05	2,654	0.02	−24.06
Ghana	1,661	0.02	2,508	0.02	50.99
Hungary	32,576	0.46	28,288	0.20	−13.16
India	553,074	7.75	1,179,235	8.54	113.21
Indonesia	81,428	1.14	178,191	1.29	118.83
Iran	38,724	0.54	63,299	0.46	63.46
Israel	120,114	1.68	182,095	1.32	51.60
Jamaica	13,028	0.18	6,201	0.04	−52.40
Jordan	37,639	0.53	31,865	0.23	−15.34
Kazakhstan	10,521	0.15	57,655	0.42	448.00
Kenya	6,384	0.09	10,756	0.08	68.48
Korea	718,180	10.06	836,462	6.06	16.47
Kuwait	130,080	1.82	95,938	0.69	−26.25
Lebanon	4,929	0.07	12,893	0.09	161.57
Lithuania	8,183	0.11	4,477	0.03	−45.29
Malaysia	181,236	2.54	255,952	1.85	41.23
Mauritius	2,617	0.04	4,740	0.03	81.12
Mexico	239,128	3.35	340,565	2.47	42.42
Morocco	27,220	0.38	62,910	0.46	131.12
Nigeria	19,356	0.27	33,325	0.24	72.17
Oman	15,269	0.21	17,302	0.13	13.31
Pakistan	45,937	0.64	33,239	0.24	−27.64
Panama	5,074	0.07	8,048	0.06	58.61
Peru	35,995	0.50	69,753	0.51	93.79
Philippines	40,153	0.56	80,132	0.58	99.57
Poland	93,873	1.32	135,277	0.98	44.11
Qatar	87,316	1.22	87,856	0.64	0.62
Romania	20,588	0.29	30,325	0.22	47.29
Russia	548,579	7.69	861,424	6.24	57.03
Saudi Arabia	646,104	9.05	318,765	2.31	−50.66
Serbia	5,409	0.08	11,522	0.08	113.02
Slovak Republic	4,393	0.06	4,672	0.03	6.35
Slovenia	7,899	0.11	11,772	0.09	49.03

(continued)

TABLE 19-2 Market Capitalization of Emerging Markets Greater than 2 Billion in Capitalization (in millions of U.S. dollars) *(concluded)*

Country	Year-End 2005	% of Total	Year-End 2009	% of Total	% Change 2005-2009
South Africa	565,408	7.92	704,822	5.10	24.66
Sri Lanka	5,720	0.08	8,133	0.06	42.19
Taiwan	485,617	6.81	695,865	5.04	43.30
Thailand	124,864	1.75	138,189	1.00	10.67
Trinidad and Tobago	16,972	0.24	11,145	0.08	−34.33
Tunisia	2,876	0.04	9,120	0.07	217.11
Turkey	161,537	2.26	225,735	1.63	39.74
Ukraine	24,976	0.35	16,790	0.12	−32.78
United Arab Emirates	225,568	3.16	109,620	0.79	−51.40
Vietnam	461	0.01	21,199	0.15	4498.48
West Bank and Gaza	4,461	0.06	4,461	0.03	0.00
Others under $2 Billion	64,207	0.90	17,689	0.13	−72.45
Emerging Markets	**$7,135,963**	**100%**	**$13,806,558**	**100%**	**93.48%**

economic variables separating emerging from developed countries is per capita income. This is why a small country like Luxembourg is considered developed and countries like India, China, and Russia are considered emerging. China also does not have a free-floating currency that can be exchanged in international financial markets. This will come in time, but even when it happens the per capita income of 1.4 billion people will not merit developed nation status.

In Table 19–2 the emerging-market countries with the 10 biggest market capitalizations are highlighted. These 10 countries (Brazil, China, India, Korea, Malaysia, Mexico, Russia, Saudi Arabia, South Africa, and Taiwan) make up 82 percent of the total capitalization of the emerging markets. Only those countries with market capitalizations greater than $2 billion made it into the table. There are many more small countries with stock markets that didn't get listed. They account for 0.13 percent of the total and $17 billion of value.

One way to keep emerging markets in perspective is to compare their size with some well-known U.S. companies. Table 19–3 lists the 20 largest U.S. companies by market capitalization as of September 20, 2010. The comparison isn't perfect, because the country capitalizations end December 31, 2009, and Table 19–3 lists as of September 2009. However, the comparison still makes the proper point. These 20 companies have a total market value of $3.4 trillion, which would put them in third place in the world, ranking slightly ahead of Japan. Exxon, Apple, Microsoft, Berkshire Hathaway, and Wal-Mart, the top five, account for $1.189 trillion in market capitalization. Only China in the emerging-market list would be above them.

The small size of many emerging markets explains the low liquidity of these markets and also explains why small capital flows in and out of these markets can create wide swings in securities prices. If you examine the list, you will see that most of these countries do not have capital markets as big as Exxon Mobil. If we put Exxon Mobil into Table 19–2, it would rank 10th, behind Malaysia and ahead of all the rest. When investors suddenly decide they want to own stocks in emerging-market economies, money managers of mutual funds specializing in these countries have a difficult time placing all the money flows without driving prices up dramatically. That is why most mutual funds specializing in single countries are closed-end funds. If you remember from Chapter 4, closed-end funds have a fixed number of shares. This protects the fund from having larges inflows and outflows of new capital chasing hot-country markets. Open-end funds could not protect themselves as well from these flows, and would eventually have to close to new investors because they would not have any place to put the new money as these markets become overvalued.

TABLE 19-3 **20 Largest U.S. Companies by Market Capitalization (in billions of $)**

Exxon Mobil	XOM	$ 312.28
Apple	AAPL	256.28
Microsoft	MSFT	220.38
Berkshire Hathaway	BRKA	206.18
Wal-Mart Stores	WMT	194.58
General Electric	GE	175.48
Procter & Gamble	PG	173.90
Johnson & Johnson	JNJ	170.30
AT&T	T	168.10
IBM	IBM	165.90
Google	GOOG	161.50
JPMorgan Chase	JPM	161.30
Chevron	CHV	159.70
Oracle	ORCL	138.40
Pfizer	PFE	137.90
Wells Fargo	WFC	136.50
Bank of America	BAC	135.60
Coca-Cola	KO	133.60
Cisco Systems	CSCO	123.80
Merck & Co.	MRK	111.70
		$3,443.38

Note: Prices as of September 20, 2010.

Investors often equate emerging markets to high growth, and there is some truth to this when taken in a portfolio context. Between 1992 and 2009 the developed markets increased in market capitalization from $9.9 trillion to $34.9 trillion, a 252 percent increase, or an annualized rate of 5.6 percent. During this same time period the emerging markets increased from $882 billion to $13.8 trillion, a 14,653 percent increase, or an annualized rate of 17.1 percent. In some countries the growth has increased during the last five years. For example, China's market capitalization grew 551 percent from 2005 to 2009, or at an annual rate of close to 54 percent, much higher than its GDP growth rate. This rapid growth is due to many formerly state-owned companies becoming public companies. Other countries like Venezuela fell out of the ranking completely.

A geographical breakdown of the emerging markets is depicted in Figure 19–2. The relationships among the emerging countries have changed dramatically over this time period. The Middle East and Africa have gone from 31 percent of the emerging markets to 15 percent, a 50 percent decrease. South Asia and Latin America have remained relatively the same, at 13 percent and 15 percent, respectively. Eastern and Central Europe went from 11 percent to 9 percent. The big winner, again because of China, was East Asia, which moved from 29 percent to 48 percent of the total emerging markets. The interesting thing about Figure 19–2 is that every region except the Middle East and Africa increased in market size by significant amounts. China's growth simply overwhelmed the other fast-growing regions.

As emerging markets have grown, there are more opportunities to own equity positions in these markets. It is useful to look at the different market structures and institutional characteristics of these and other markets.

Markets are structured quite differently. For example, continuous auction markets are the standard in developed countries such as the United States, Japan, United Kingdom, Germany, Canada, Hong Kong, and others. In many smaller emerging markets, there is not enough continuous buying and selling of securities to create the liquid markets necessary for continuous auction markets; instead, exchanges may

FIGURE 19-2 Regional Weights of Emerging Markets

	2005		2009	
Mideast and Africa	31%	$2,200,854	15%	$ 2,082,237
South Asia	14	996,426	13	1,797,106
East Asia	29	2,038,315	48	6,684,874
Eastern and Central Europe	11	809,970	9	1,196,279
Latin America	15	1,042,548	15	2,031,702
		$7,088,113		$13,792,198

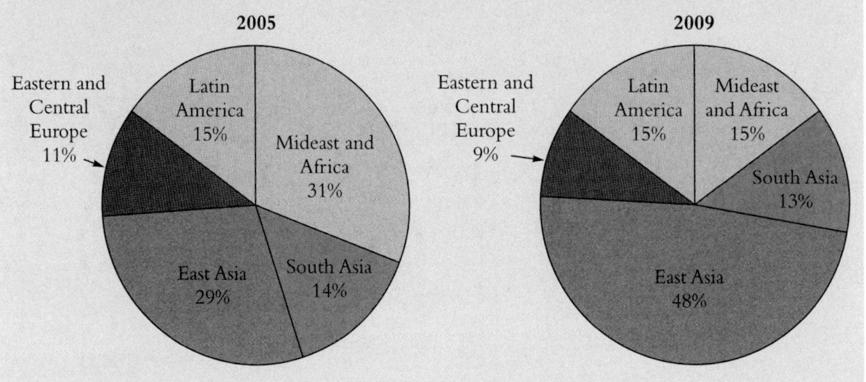

trade shares once or twice per day. Some markets have specialists, automated trading, and computer-directed trading, while others do not. Even in the developed markets, most exchanges do not allow trading in options and futures on the stock exchanges. While most exchanges do not have limits on price movements, some exchanges limit prices within a band of 5 or 10 percent on a daily basis. Transaction taxes can be significant on foreign exchanges, ranging from 0 percent in Mexico to 2.4 percent in the Netherlands. Taxes at very high levels can reduce trading, liquidity, and potential returns. Many exchanges use some form of margin, which allows investors to purchase securities with a percentage of borrowed money, and some do not allow this practice at all. In some countries such as Korea, foreign investors may not be allowed to buy shares of companies at all. The moral is, do not assume that foreign markets function like those in the United States. Emerging markets usually have higher transactions costs, less liquidity, and are generally less efficient. Institutional practices around the world can have significant impacts on your rates of return.

DIVERSIFICATION BENEFITS

One of the benefits of foreign investing is that not all foreign markets move in the same direction across time, so a diversified portfolio consisting of stocks from many countries will have less volatility than a purely domestic portfolio of stocks and could even have a higher rate of return. This benefit has not always been perfect, and in the 1987 market crash, 19 of 23 markets declined more than 20 percent. This is unusual given the low degree of correlation between the historical returns of different countries. An article by Richard Roll[1] pointed out that the most significant factor relating to the size of the market decline in each country was the beta of that market to the world market index.

In Table 19–4, we see the stock market movements for a number of key countries over 30 years. Each year there is a wide range of performance numbers among these eight countries; the highest and lowest yearly returns are highlighted.

[1] Richard Roll, "The International Crash of 1987," *Financial Analysts Journal,* September–October 1988, pp. 19–35.

TABLE 19-4 The Best- and Worst-Performing Equity Markets, 1976-2009 (in U.S. dollars)

	Germany	Switzerland	United Kingdom	Australia	Hong Kong	Japan	Canada	United States
1976	6.6	10.5	*(12.70)*	(10.2)	**40.7**	25.6	9.7	23.8
1977	25.8	28.7	**58.0**	11.9	*(11.20)*	15.9	(2.1)	(7.2)
1978	26.9	21.9	14.6	21.8	18.5	**53.3**	20.4	*6.5*
1979	(2.2)	12.1	22.1	43.6	**83.5**	*(11.9)*	51.8	18.5
1980	*(9.1)*	(7.3)	41.1	55.3	**72.7**	30.3	22.6	32.4
1981	(8.2)	(9.5)	(10.6)	*(23.9)*	(15.8)	**15.8**	(10.7)	(4.9)
1982	12.3	3.4	9.2	(22.6)	*(44.5)*	(0.5)	2.4	**21.5**
1983	25.9	19.3	17.2	**56.0**	*(3.0)*	24.9	33.4	22.2
1984	(3.8)	(11.1)	5.4	*(12.6)*	**46.8**	17.1	(7.6)	6.2
1985	**139.2**	107.4	52.8	20.9	51.6	43.4	15.9	31.6
1986	37.2	34.3	27.1	43.8	56.0	**99.7**	*10.7*	18.2
1987	*(23.4)*	(8.8)	36.5	10.3	(4.1)	**43.2**	14.6	5.2
1988	23.1	*7.1*	*7.1*	**38.0**	28.0	35.5	18.0	16.5
1989	**48.8**	27.1	23.1	10.8	8.3	*1.8*	25.2	31.4
1990	(10.8)	(7.8)	**6.0**	(21.0)	3.7	*(36.4)*	(15.3)	(5.6)
1991	8.7	13.6	12.0	n.a.	**43.4**	*6.5*	8.7	30.3
1992	(13.2)	13.3	(6.2)	(16.2)	**28.3**	*(23.1)*	(15.7)	2.8
1993	33.7	47.5	*3.2*	36.3	**107.7**	25.3	17.0	9.0
1994	3.3	2.4	(4.7)	2.9	*(31.0)*	**20.7**	(4.9)	(0.9)
1995	14.8	**42.4**	17.2	8.3	18.2	*0.0*	16.1	34.7
1996	18.6	3.1	28.2	23.1	**38.8**	*(17.0)*	27.7	23.5
1997	21.9	**44.1**	21.5	(5.2)	*(19.5)*	*(28.4)*	9.4	31.1
1998	23.0	**23.2**	16.9	5.0	*(10.8)*	*6.9*	(8.5)	23.0
1999	18.7	*(5.0)*	17.5	22.7	63.7	**67.4**	35.2	20.7
2000	(9.9)	**11.2**	(10.9)	(5.3)	(10.3)	*(29.3)*	5.4	(4.8)
2001	(21.6)	(22.5)	(14.0)	**3.3**	(16.8)	*(28.5)*	(16.8)	(11.2)
2002	*(29.9)*	(10.9)	(14.2)	**1.6**	(16.3)	(8.7)	(10.8)	(21.4)
2003	**65.2**	36.3	34.2	53.8	45.3	38.6	56.7	*31.9*
2004	16.9	15.9	21.3	**34.4**	23.2	16.9	24.7	*12.5*
2005	11.4	17.0	9.1	16.6	11.6	28.0	**28.6**	*6.6*
2006	34.1	29.2	24.1	**36.3**	29.1	*(0.2)*	14.8	14.47
2007	28.6	5.1	1.7	18.5	**29.9**	*(5.8)*	28.6	2.68
2008	(47.4)	(32.3)	(52.0)	(41.0)	**14.3**	(27.7)	*(54.2)*	(41.16)
2009	17.1	24.1	51.0	64.4	**72.4**	*4.9*	67.7	28.45

n.a.: not sufficient information.

Bold color numbers represent lowest returns and bold black numbers represent highest returns.

Before 1996 data sources were Templeton International; Morgan Stanley Capital International Perspective, Geneva. Located in *Barron's* January issues.

Note: From 1996 through 2009, S&P/Citigroup BMI World Total Return Indices were used. These are broad market indices.

There are several issues worth noting. No country continually outperforms the others on an annual basis. Hong Kong has the highest returns 11 out of 34 years and Japan had the lowest returns 13 out of 34 years. Canada has had the highest return once and the lowest return twice.

Table 19–4 further shows that the developed markets in 2000, 2001, and 2002 were mostly in negative territory except for Switzerland, Australia, and Canada. In 2003 through 2005 all eight countries had gains, with the United States in last place each year. When markets move in the same direction, you sometimes hear that international markets don't provide any risk reduction. Occasionally markets move together because of some global economic force. In 1989 and 1997 during the October collapses of the U.S. markets and right after the September 11, 2001, attacks on New York's World Trade Center and the Pentagon in Washington, D.C., markets around the world reacted together as they fell in sympathy with the U.S.

markets. In 2008, when the subprime mortgage market collapsed, note that seven of these markets suffered losses between −27.7 percent (Japan) and −54.2 percent (Canada). Only Hong Kong had a positive return, of 14.7 percent. In 2009 all markets rebounded, some with significant gains. International events that cause markets to move in unison have caused many market analysts to surmise that markets are more connected than they used to be for several reasons:

1. We have a global economy where international companies do business across borders. This phenomenon will cause economies across these geographical regions to become more intertwined and less diverse.
2. We have a European Monetary Union using the euro as the single currency. With the European Central Bank harmonizing monetary policy across the region, these European markets are more economically intertwined.

Although all these stories make sense, we should recognize that over the long run, the world economies and their markets do not move directly with the U.S. economy on a consistent basis.

Let us look at a U.S. investor based on the data in Table 19–4 on the previous page. In 1976, a 23.8 percent return could be earned in the United States, while a 12.7 percent loss occurred in the United Kingdom. In 1977, this situation was reversed with a 7.2 percent loss in the United States and a 58 percent return in the United Kingdom. If an investor had held equal positions in both countries, returns would have been less volatile (risky), and a U.S. investor would have had a greater total return. Diversification reduces portfolio volatility and at the same time offers opportunities for higher returns than a single country portfolio.

One way to consider **diversification benefits** is to measure the extent of correlation of stock movements. The **correlation coefficient** measures the movement of one series of data over time to another series of data, in this case stock market returns. The correlation coefficient can be between −1 and +1. A coefficient of +1 indicates a perfect positive relationship as the two variables move together up and down. A coefficient of −1 indicates a perfect negative relationship as the two variables move opposite of each other. A zero coefficient describes a series that has no relationship. Any time you can diversify into assets that have a correlation coefficient of less than +1, you reduce the amount of risk assumed. Such a measure is presented in Table 19–5, in which stock movements for a number of developed countries are compared with those of the United States.

Five sets of correlation coefficients are presented: one long-term set from 1960 to 1980, and four short-term sets: from June 1981 through September 1987, from July 1991 through July 1996, from December 2000 through December 2005, and from December 2005 to December 2009. The countries are listed from the highest correlation to the lowest, based on 1960 to 1980 data. By comparing the five sets of correlations, we can see there is not a great amount of stability among the time periods, with some countries such as Italy going from 12th to 11th place to 4th place and back to 13th place in the latest period. Canada, because of its close ties with the U.S. economy, is highly correlated with the U.S. markets.

The best risk-reduction benefits can be found by combining U.S. securities with those from countries having low correlations. Countries with high correlations provide the least benefit from diversification.

The fourth period presented does show some interesting changes from all the previous periods. First, the correlations are higher for almost all countries. Second, the average correlation coefficient is 0.77 versus 0.27 for the previous period. We could find some causal effects. Many of these countries are now in the European Monetary Union with a common currency. Their economies have begun to work together with a European Central Bank to coordinate monetary policy, and it is possible that these countries have become more highly correlated among themselves.

TABLE 19-5 Correlations of Foreign Stock Movements with U.S. Stock Movements

Country	Correlation 1960–1980	Rank	Correlation 6/81 to 9/87	Rank	Correlation 7/91 to 7/96	Rank	Correlation 12/00 to 12/05	Rank	Correlation 12/05 to 12/09	Rank
United States	1.00		1.00		1.00		1.00		1.00	
Netherlands	0.73	(1)	0.47	(4)	0.32	(5)	0.86	(5)	0.98	(4)
Canada	0.71	(2)	0.72	(1)	0.70	(1)	0.80	(7)	0.96	(8)
Australia	0.70	(3)	0.33	(7)	0.17	(9)	0.72	(9)	0.99	(1)
United Kingdom	0.62	(4)	0.51	(2)	0.32	(6)	0.82	(6)	0.99	(1)
Switzerland	0.45	(5)	0.50	(3)	0.18	(8)	0.72	(10)	0.96	(8)
Sweden	0.40	(6)	0.28	(9)	0.29	(7)	0.90	(2)	0.98	(4)
Belgium	0.39	(7)	0.25	(10)	0.34	(3)	0.73	(11)	0.97	(6)
Denmark	0.24	(8)	0.35	(6)	0.08	(12)	0.66	(12)	0.99	(1)
Japan	0.22	(9)	0.33	(8)	0.08	(12)	0.36	(13)	**0.69**	(11)
Hong Kong	n.a.		0.25	(10)	0.16	(10)	0.97	(1)	**0.67**	(12)
France	0.21	(10)	0.39	(5)	0.36	(2)	0.87	(4)	0.97	(6)
Germany	0.21	(11)	0.21	(13)	0.14	(11)	0.89	(3)	0.87	(10)
Italy	0.21	(12)	0.22	(12)	0.33	(4)	0.77	(8)	**0.45**	(13)
Average Correlation	**0.42**		**0.37**		**0.27**		**0.77**		**0.88**	

Sources: Roger G. Ibbotson, Richard C. Carr, and Anthony W. Robinson, "International Equity and Bond Returns," *Financial Analysts Journal,* July-August 1982, pg. 71; Richard Roll, "The International Crash of 1987," *Financial Analysts Journal,* September-October 1988, pg. 20-21; JPMorgan Correlation Calculator, www.jpmorgan.com; *Global Stock Markets Factbook 2006,* Standard & Poor's, 2006, p. 68; and *Global Stock Markets Factbook 2010,* Standard & Poor's, 2010. p. 25.

It is also possible that the United States has been the engine of growth for a lagging Europe and Japan and that as the U.S. economy slowed down, it affected the rest of the world. However, we should be forewarned that just as correlations can rise, they can also fall in the next period. The moral of this story is that you can still reap strong diversification benefits even with 77 percent correlations. Perhaps you can't achieve them as easily as with correlations of 38 and 27 percent, but nevertheless, they are still good reasons to include foreign stocks in your portfolio.

The fifth period in Table 19–5 covers some very difficult economic years in the world economies. In 2005 the markets had barely recovered from the bursting Internet bubble. By the end of 2007 it was apparent that the U.S. housing bubble was creating problems for U.S. banks, and by 2008 the financial crisis was in full bloom in the United States and Europe. Housing prices fell and continued to fall through 2010. Many banks were saved through government intervention while others were left to fail. In the United States, over 400 banks failed in 2009. This crisis happened in England, Ireland, the United States, Spain, and other countries. Many felt the world was on the brink of another 1930s-era Great Depression, and stock prices fell.

As we mentioned previously in Table 19–4, seven out of the eight developed countries experienced significant stock price declines. So it is no wonder when we look at Table 19–5 that 9 of the 13 countries had correlations with the United States of between 0.96 and 0.99. Japan and Hong Kong had correlations of 0.69 and 0.67, respectively, and Italy was the lowest with a correlation of 0.45. These correlations were significantly higher than in the other four periods, and so the question that faces us is whether this is a permanent transformation of the markets or whether the markets will revert back to the mean with lower correlations possible in the future. Only time will tell. One thing is clear: the emerging markets will have lower correlations with the developed markets than the developed markets will have between themselves.

Table 19–6 lists the world stock market performance in local currencies of 88 countries. The developed countries are highlighted in color, the emerging markets are not.

TABLE 19-6 World Stock Market Performance, 2009 (Ranked by % Change in Price Indices in Local Currency)

Rank	Market	% Change in Price Index	Rank	Market	% Change in Price Index
1	Russia	133.8	45	Macedonia	31.0
2	Iceland	131.4	46	Australia	30.9
3	Argentina	103.6	47	Canada	30.7
4	Israel	103.0	48	Czech Republic	30.2
5	Peru	101.0	49	Spain	29.8
6	Turkey	96.6	50	South Africa	28.6
7	Kazakhstan	95.7	51	Saudi Arabia	27.5
8	Ukraine	90.1	52	Ireland	27.0
9	Indonesia	87.0	53	United States	23.5
10	Brazil	82.7	54	Greece	22.9
11	Sri Lanka	82.4	55	France	22.3
12	China	80.0	56	United Kingdom	22.1
13	India	79.4	57	Italy	20.7
14	Taiwan	78.3	58	Bulgaria	19.1
15	Hungary	73.4	59	New Zealand	18.9
16	Norway	70.4	60	Germany	18.5
17	Singapore	64.5	61	Switzerland	18.3
18	Thailand	63.2	62	Oman	17.0
19	Romania	61.7	63	Croatia	16.4
20	Pakistan	59.4	64	United Arab Emirates	14.8
21	Vietnam	56.8	65	Iran	14.0
22	Philippines	54.0	66	Panama	13.3
23	Colombia	53.5	67	Slovenia	10.4
24	Hong Kong	52.0	68	Bangladesh	10.3
25	Korea	49.7	69	St. Kitts & Nevis	9.0
26	Tunisia	48.4	70	Japan	5.6
27	Estonia	47.2	71	Jamaica	4.0
28	Chile	46.9	72	Botswana	2.9
29	Poland	46.9	73	Latvia	2.8
30	Lithuania	46.0	74	Qatar	1.1
31	Malaysia	45.2	75	Namibia	−2.0
32	Cyprus	45.0	76	Guyana	−3.0
33	Sweden	44.0	77	Morocco	−6.2
34	Mexico	43.5	78	Kenya	−7.8
35	Austria	42.5	79	Jordan	−8.2
36	Mauritius	40.4	80	Trinidad & Tobago	−9.2
37	Luxembourg	39.8	81	Kuwait	−10.0
38	Egypt	38.4	82	Ecuador	−16.2
39	Netherlands	36.3	83	Bahrain	−19.2
40	Finland	34.1	84	Nepal	−24.0
41	Portugal	33.5	85	Slovak Republic	−25.7
42	Lebanon	32.9	86	Côte d'Ivoire	−25.9
43	Denmark	32.1	87	Nigeria	−33.8
44	Belgium	31.6	88	Ghana	−46.6

Notes: Returns are based on survey responses and data provided by the local market.

Source: *Global Stock Markets Factbook 2010,* Standard & Poor's, p. 22.

Out of the top 32 countries, only 4 of them (Iceland, Norway, Singapore, and Hong Kong) were developed countries. Singapore and Hong Kong both have strong economic ties to China's economy. Down the list, from number 52 to 61, you will find many of the world's major economies with Japan in last place at number 70. Although their returns are not low, they pale in comparison to the emerging-market returns above them. There are no correlation coefficients with this table, but we can expect that there would be many instances of low correlations for this one-year period if we ran regressions for 52 weeks. Table 19–6 simply reinforces the idea that there are many markets where an investor can diversify and get better returns than their local market. Of course, these returns are in local currencies, and as we discuss later in the chapter, currency exchange rates can make some of these returns quite different in U.S. dollars.

RETURN POTENTIAL IN INTERNATIONAL MARKETS

Actually, risk reduction through effective international diversification is only part of the story. Not only does the investor have less risk exposure, but there is also the potential for higher returns in many foreign markets. Why? A number of countries have had long-term growth rates superior to those of the United States in terms of real GDP. These would include Norway, Singapore, and China. Second, many countries have become highly competitive in traditional U.S. products such as automobiles, steel, and consumer electronics. Third, many nations (Germany, Japan, France, Canada) enjoy higher individual savings rates than the United States, and this leads to capital formation and potential investment opportunity. This is not to imply that the United States does not have the strongest and best regulated securities markets in the world. It clearly does. However, it is a more mature market than many others, and there may be abundant opportunities for high returns in a number of foreign markets.

One current investment thesis is to invest in the **BRICs**. This stands for the markets of Brazil, Russia, India, and China. The reasoning is that these are large economies with young populations. They will grow faster than the United States and they will provide some risk reduction through correlation coefficients less than one and they will provide higher returns. The data on their returns are shown in Table 19–7.

All of the markets outperformed the U.S. market with correlation coefficients that would reduce the volatility of a U.S. portfolio. While an investor could have made a fortune in Russia, it is not as easy as you might think for a large portfolio manager to get a big enough piece of the action to improve his/her returns. As you can see from the market capitalization column, the United States is much larger than the other markets, although China is now one-third the size of the U.S. markets. These countries could have investment restrictions on outside investors and ownership limits on just how much of a company a foreign investor could own. Nevertheless, the individual investor can diversify his or her portfolio by buying mutual funds or exchange-traded funds on these countries' indexes. Then there is always the question of trust. Would you trust the Russian market with your money and if so, how much of it? How much risk is there in these markets? Are you a long-term investor or a short-term investor? If you are a short-term investor, these markets have higher standard deviations of returns than the U.S. markets and you could lose a lot of money in a short period of time.

Some Market Differences between Countries

Markets around the world differ in many ways. Some of the differences are cultural, such as the willingness to take risk and expectations for returns. Others are related to accounting issues and government regulation of markets. We can summarize some of these differences by looking at a few basic investment ratios, such as price to earnings, dividend yield, and price to book value.

The problem with comparing price–earnings ratios across countries is that the earnings might not be computed using the same accounting standards. What may be a low P/E in some countries might be a high P/E in other countries with more liberal accounting standards. There is a strong movement among the developed countries to harmonize their accounting standards, but this movement has been going on for over a decade, and agreement hasn't been reached on one standard to fit all countries.

Dividends are another area where wide differences appear. In some countries, such as the United Kingdom, investors expect dividends to be paid, and British companies generally have higher payout ratios and dividend yields than their U.S.

TABLE 19-7 The BRICs vs. the U.S. Markets

	Brazil	Russia	India	China	U.S. S&P 500
1996	63.80%	0.00%	−7.90%	65.20%	22.96%
1997	44.80	231.50	12.40	30.20	33.36
1998	−33.50	0.00	−8.70	−4.00	28.58
1999	151.90	190.10	97.80	19.20	21.04
2000	−10.70	6.90	−24.20	51.70	−9.10
2001	−11.00	94.00	−23.30	−17.40	−11.89
2002	−17.00	47.60	10.30	−20.70	−22.10
2003	97.30	48.00	98.10	10.30	28.68
2004	17.80	15.00	17.90	−15.40	10.88
2005	27.70	101.70	36.30	−8.30	4.91
2006	49.82	92.71	48.06	210.76	15.79
2007	92.71	42.17	122.15	156.61	5.49
2008	−56.99	−73.57	−64.52	−55.13	−37.00
2009	98.06	116.88	82.69	79.25	26.46
Annual Rate of Return	**23.47**	**43.61**	**16.15**	**20.38**	**6.19**

Returns of the BRICs from Beginning of 1996 to End of 2009

	Annualized Returns 1996-2009	Standard Deviation of Returns	Ending Value of $1 Invested in 1996	Market Capitalization in Millions 2009
Brazil	23.47%	57.55%	$ 19.13	$ 1,167,335
Russia	43.61	77.30	158.69	861,424
India	16.15	53.00	8.14	1,179,235
China	20.38	70.51	13.42	5,007,646
United States	6.19	20.58	2.32	15,077,286

Correlations with the U.S. Broad Market Index

	Correlation Coefficient with S&P 500 1996-2009	Correlation Coefficient with S&P 500 2000-2005	Correlation Coefficient with S&P 500 2005-2009
Brazil	0.64	0.94	0.90
Russia	0.35	−0.07	0.95
India	0.53	0.83	0.82
China	0.51	0.11	0.66
United States	1.00	1.00	1.00

counterparts in the same industry. For example, at the time of this writing Royal Dutch Shell had a dividend yield of 5.13 percent, while Exxon Mobil had a dividend yield of 2.50 percent and Chevron a dividend yield of 3.40 percent.

Book value is the basis of value in many countries, and, again because of accounting differences, book value may vary widely between countries. Those countries that allow aggressive expensing of capital purchases will have lower book values than those countries that have conservative depreciation practices.

CURRENCY FLUCTUATIONS AND RATES OF RETURN

To track the performance of selected world markets, the most comprehensive quotations come from MSCI. Their Web site provides daily quotes on international equity indexes and bond indexes. Some are available only to customers and subscribers, but many are available to the public. Table 19–8 shows the returns of

TABLE 19-8 Developed Markets MSCI Data in Local Currencies and U.S. Dollars

MSCI Index	USD 1 Yr	Local Currency 1 Yr	USD 3 Yr	Local Currency 3 Yr	USD 5 Yr	Local Currency 5 Yr	USD 10 Yr	Local Currency 10 Yr
Austria	**−9.740%**	**−1.080%**	−23.560%	−21.560%	−8.780%	−11.360%	**7.690%**	**2.820%**
Belgium	−2.110	7.270	−19.940	−17.850	−7.550	−10.170	−0.770	−5.260
Denmark	18.980	30.650	−3.880	−1.360	9.520	6.410	9.250	4.310
Finland	0.160	9.770	−21.880	−19.830	−1.270	−4.070	−5.650	−9.910
France	−7.330	1.560	−12.680	−10.390	0.120	−2.730	0.450	−4.090
Germany	2.710	12.560	−11.420	−9.100	4.430	1.470	1.930	−2.670
Greece	−51.930	−47.320	−37.580	−35.950	−15.910	−18.290	−5.640	−9.890
Ireland	−20.490	−12.860	−39.410	−37.820	−22.480	−24.680	−10.540	−14.590
Italy	−18.560	−10.740	−20.680	−18.610	−7.120	−9.750	−2.970	−7.360
Netherlands	−2.750	6.570	−11.950	−9.650	1.690	−1.190	−0.750	−5.240
Norway	−1.960	5.120	−13.980	−11.270	3.020	0.860	8.610	3.900
Portugal	−13.310	−5.000	−18.740	−16.620	0.980	−1.880	1.290	−3.290
Spain	−24.290	−17.030	−15.990	−13.790	2.090	−0.810	4.700	−0.030
Sweden	12.350	12.890	−3.900	−1.020	6.630	3.090	3.910	0.010
Switzerland	5.420	2.370	−4.650	−8.480	3.530	−2.260	4.330	−1.670
United Kingdom	**0.540**	**6.060**	**−11.290**	**−3.560**	**−0.940**	**0.610**	**−0.060**	**−1.170**
Europe	−2.870	3.200	−12.210	−9.000	0.340	−1.520	0.770	−2.800
Emu	−8.740	0.010	−15.230	−13.010	−0.290	−3.120	0.070	−4.460
Europe ex Emu	3.020	6.280	−9.130	−4.770	0.980	0.180	1.500	−1.100
Europe ex Uk	−4.500	1.780	−12.660	−11.490	1.040	−2.420	1.270	−3.520
Nordic Countries	8.920	14.050	−10.050	−7.920	4.820	1.440	2.260	−2.160
Australia	**3.320**	**−2.670**	**−6.890**	**−9.940**	**6.330**	**0.310**	**10.420**	**3.600**
Hong Kong	**19.360**	**19.440**	**−2.730**	**−2.840**	**9.250**	**9.250**	**5.240**	**5.180**
Japan	7.500	−0.100	−8.710	−17.020	−3.630	−10.260	−1.850	−4.460
New Zealand	0.440	−3.480	−14.160	−14.810	−6.320	−8.490	5.520	−1.210
Singapore	20.810	13.390	0.180	−3.420	12.950	7.090	7.310	4.170
Pacific	7.820	0.780	−7.330	−14.140	−0.280	−6.450	0.860	−2.260
Pacific ex Japan	8.360	3.320	−5.230	−7.640	7.500	2.820	8.360	3.470
Canada	10.220	6.200	−3.650	−2.210	6.960	3.770	7.770	3.290
Usa	6.540	6.540	−6.600	−6.600	−0.860	−0.860	−1.490	−1.490
North America	6.870	6.510	−6.350	−6.260	−0.300	−0.530	−0.980	−1.210
Eafe	0.430	1.930	−10.710	−10.990	0.140	−3.330	0.800	−2.800
Far East	9.420	2.410	−7.690	−15.210	−1.940	−8.050	−0.890	−3.340
Israel	1.130	−1.740	1.230	−0.910	6.180	1.560	2.880	1.550
The World Index	3.850	4.360	−8.420	−8.560	−0.110	−1.920	−0.240	−1.950
Easea Index (Eafe ex Japan)	−1.370	3.050	−11.250	−8.830	1.290	−1.010	1.590	−2.190
Kokusai Index (World ex Jp)	3.470	5.000	−8.390	−7.410	0.310	−0.820	−0.030	−1.590
Singapore Free	20.810	13.390	0.180	−3.420	12.950	7.090	7.310	4.170

November 17, 2010, for MSCI Large and Midcap Country Indexes (unweighted).

MSCI Indexes for developed countries for a 1-, 3-, 5-, and 10-year period both in local currencies and in U.S. dollars. The data are consolidated from several tables on the MSCI Web site and also include indexes for regions, such as the Pacific, North America, Europe, and the Far East, and a **World Index** that is a weighted index of the developed markets. There are a few other indexes that take out a major economic power, such as the United Kingdom, so we see "(Europe ex U.K.)."

There are several things to take away from this table. First, the investor needs to know what he or she wants to measure. Individual investors are less motivated to compare their performance to a benchmark, but professional investors have no choice but to make this comparison. If you are a mutual fund manager in charge of a regional portfolio for Europe, you need a benchmark to see if you outperformed. These MSCI indexes provide just that for many managers and are possibly the most widely used indexes for professional portfolio managers.

Another factor that is important to both individual investors and professional investors is the time period used to measure performance. Behavioral finance research shows that individual investors often chase last year's mutual fund winners, and professional managers are glad to outperform their benchmark because they know it will attract new money. Unfortunately, last year's winners are often next year's losers. Investors should look for consistency of performance. Can the manager outperform year after year? We can't ignore the long-term return comparisons. One of the major factors that will influence a manager's returns beside security selection is the movement of currency exchange rates. Table 19–8 makes that point very well.

First, let us take a look at Hong Kong. Because the Hong Kong dollar is pegged to the U.S. dollar, there is very little variation in the return expressed in local currency or U.S. currency. The Hong Kong dollar is pegged at about 7.75–7.80 to 1 U.S. dollar, with some minor fluctuations in that range. Now let's look at the United Kingdom, where local returns are priced in British pounds. In the 3-year return column, the return in pounds was −3.56 percent, whereas the return when translated into U.S. dollars was −11.29 percent. During this time the pound fell against the dollar, and when the return was translated from pounds to dollars, there were fewer dollars available, lowering the return by 7.73 percent. On the other hand, if we take Australia for the 1- and 10-year returns, we can see that in both periods the Australian dollar rose against the U.S. dollar, and so when the currency was translated into U.S. dollars, the returns were enhanced by the exchange rate.

We now explicitly consider the effect of **currency fluctuations** (changes in currency values) as well as rates of return in different countries. For example, assume an investment in Switzerland produces a 10 percent return. But suppose at the same time the Swiss franc declines in value by 5 percent against the U.S. dollar. The Swiss franc profits are thus worth less in dollars. In the present case, the gain on the investment would be shown as follows:

110%	(Investment with 10% profit)
	(Adjusted value of Swiss franc relative to U.S. dollar)
× 0.95	(1.00 − 0.05 decline in currency)
104.5%	Percent of original investment

The actual return in U.S. dollars would be 4.5 instead of 10 percent. Of course, if the Swiss franc appreciated by 5 percent against the dollar, the Swiss franc profits converted to dollars would be worth considerably more than 10 percent. The values are indicated below:

110%	(Investment with 10% profit)
	(Adjusted value of Swiss franc relative to U.S. dollar)
× 1.05	(1.00 + 0.05 increase in currency)
115.5%	Percent of original investment

TABLE 19-9 J.P. Morgan Overseas Government Bond Index

	LOCAL CURRENCY			Foreign Currency vs. U.S. Dollar	U.S. DOLLAR		
Country	Index	Wkly % Chg	YTD % Chg		Index	Wkly % Chg	YTD % Chg
Australia	728.43	−0.28	5.27	**10.92%**	1006.43	−1.93	16.77
Belgium	489.64	−0.71	5.34	**−4.73**	546.99	−4.58	0.36
Canada	616.19	−0.93	6.59	**4.33**	796.99	−1.18	11.21
Denmark	588.47	−0.20	11.41	**−4.88**	655.07	−4.08	5.97
France	541.28	−0.26	**8.18**	**−4.72**	599.77	−4.16	**3.07**
Germany	405.98	−0.11	8.64	**−4.72**	445.14	−4.01	3.51
Italy	765.55	−1.75	1.76	**−4.73**	626.52	−5.58	−3.05
Japan	246.80	−0.51	2.59	**12.87**	362.21	−2.76	15.79
Netherlands	436.70	−0.22	8.50	**−4.73**	478.08	−4.12	3.37
Spain	653.11	−1.70	−0.99	**−4.73**	575.71	−5.54	−5.67
Sweden	652.88	−0.02	5.81	**4.60**	552.89	−4.57	10.68
U.K.	623.07	−1.40	7.66	**0.03**	533.62	−2.18	7.69
U.S.	495.72	−0.75	8.56	**0.00**	495.72	−0.75	8.56
Non-U.S.	409.98	−0.58	4.47	**3.51**	455.90	−3.45	8.14
Global	436.97	−0.72	5.72	**2.29**	492.06	−2.62	8.14

YTD–Year to date. Yields-Semi-annual. Dec. 31, 1987 = 100

Source: J.P. Morgan Government Bond Index, *Barron's,* November 15, 2010, p. MW52. Reprinted with permission of *Barron's,*

The 10 percent gain in the Swiss franc investment has produced a 15.5 percent gain in U.S. dollars. A U.S. investor in foreign securities must consider not only the potential trend of security prices but also the trend of foreign currencies against the dollar.

This point will become more apparent as we look at Table 19–9, which depicts rates of return on the JP Morgan Overseas Government Bond Index for 12 developed countries from January 1, 2010, through November 12, 2010. During this period, the U.S. dollar was mixed against the rest of the world. This can be seen by comparing the return in local currency against the return in U.S. dollars (YTD change column). In every case of the European Union countries, the return in U.S. dollars is lower than the returns in local currencies.

Let's examine the currency effects in France year-to-date (YTD). In this instance, the return in the local currency was 8.18 percent (third column) while the return in U.S. dollars was 3.07 percent (seventh column). The change in the dollar versus the euro caused a positive return in local currency to have a negative effect on the U.S. currency. The return was reduced from 8.18 percent in euros to 3.07 percent in dollars. If you were French this would not have a negative effect on your return, but if you were an international investor translating returns to U.S. dollars, the negative impact would definitely reduce your returns. We would compute the returns as follows:

108.18%	(Investment with 8.18% profit)
	(Adjusted value of the French euro to the U.S. dollar)
× 0.9528	(1.000 − .0472 decline in currency)
1.0307%	Percent of original investment

The ending value of 1.0307 indicates a gain of approximately 3.07 percent from the initial value of 100 percent.[2] If we were merely to subtract the foreign currency loss of 4.72 percent from the 8.18 percent profit, the answer would be

[2] Due to rounding and other statistical adjustments, not all values adjusted to U.S. dollars come out as precisely as this.

a loss of 3.46 percent, but this is not the correct procedure. The gain of 8.18 percent was on an initial base of 100 percent, but the foreign currency loss of 4.72 percent was on an ending value of 108.18 percent. The resulting loss in U.S. dollar terms is the 4.72 percent, which leaves investors with 103.07 percent of their original investment.

You can see that several countries had their currency fall against the dollar by 4.72–4.73 percent (middle column). These countries are all in the Monetary Union and have their currencies pegged to the euro. Those countries that are not in the Monetary Union, such as Australia, Canada, Japan, Sweden, and the United Kingdom all had different percentage devaluations against the U.S. dollar.

Those who track the performance in foreign markets usually make adjustments so that the reported returns are in U.S. dollars that have already been adjusted for **foreign currency effects**. For example, most of the returns in prior tables of this chapter have already been adjusted for the foreign currency effect.

One might justifiably ask, how important is the foreign currency effect in relation to the overall return performance in the foreign currency? Do events in foreign exchange markets tend to overpower actual returns achieved in specific investments in foreign countries? Normally, the foreign currency effect is only about 10 to 20 percent as significant as the actual return performance in the foreign currency.[3] However, when the dollar is rising or falling rapidly over a short period, the impact can be much greater. For example, the returns to U.S. investors in Japanese securities between 1985 and 1988 were increased by 50 percent from the gain in the yen against the dollar.

In a well-diversified international portfolio, the changes in foreign currency values in one part of the world normally tend to cancel changes in other parts of the world. Also, those who do not wish to have foreign currency exposure of any sort may use forward exchange contracts, futures market contracts, or put options on foreign currency to hedge away the risk. Finally, there are those who believe in parity theories that suggest one should get additional compensation in local returns to make up for potential losses in foreign currency values. This latter point is a purely theoretical matter that provides little comfort in the short run.

The authors would suggest that those considering international investments be sensitive to the foreign currency effect but not be overly discouraged by it. The superior return potentials from foreign investments previously shown in this chapter, are computed *after* considering the foreign exchange effect on U.S. dollar returns. While foreign currency swings have been *wider* in recent times, they are still not a major deterrent to an internationally diversified portfolio.

OTHER OBSTACLES TO INTERNATIONAL INVESTMENTS

Other problems are peculiar to international investments. Let us consider some of them.

Political Risks

Many firms operate in foreign political climates that are more volatile than that of the United States. There is the danger of nationalization of foreign firms or the restriction of capital flows to investors. There also may be the danger of a violent overthrow of the political party in power. Furthermore, many countries have been unable to meet their foreign debt obligations, and this has important political implications.

The informed investor must have some feel for the political/economic climate of the foreign country in which he or she invests. Of course, problems sometimes create opportunities. Local investors may overreact to political changes occurring

[3] Bertrand Jacquillat and Bruno Solnik, "Multinationals Are Poor Tools for Diversification," *Journal of Portfolio Management,* Winter 1978, pp. 8–12.

in their environment. Because all their eggs are in one basket, they may engage in an oversell in regard to political changes. A less impassioned outside investor may identify an opportunity for profit.

Nevertheless, political risk represents a potential deterrent to foreign investment. The best solution for the investor is to be sufficiently diversified around the world so that a political or economic development in one foreign country does not have a major impact on his or her portfolio (this can be accomplished through a mutual fund or through other means discussed later in the chapter).

Tax Problems

Many major foreign countries may impose a 15 to 30 percent withholding tax against the dividends or interest paid to nonresident holders of equity or debt securities. However, it is often possible for *tax-exempt* U.S. investors to secure an exemption or rebate on part or all of the withholding tax. Also, taxable U.S. investors can normally claim a U.S. tax credit for taxes paid in foreign countries. The problem is more likely to be one of inconvenience and paper shuffling rather than loss of funds.

Lack of Market Efficiency

U.S. capital markets tend to be the most liquid and efficient in the world. Therefore, an investor who is accustomed to trading on the New York Stock Exchange may have some difficulties adjusting to foreign markets. A larger spread between the bid (sell) and asked (buy) price in foreign countries is likely. Also, an investor may have more difficulty executing a large transaction (the seller may have to absorb a larger discount in executing the trade). Furthermore, as a general rule, commission rates are higher in foreign markets than in the United States.

Administrative Problems

There can also be administrative problems in dealing in foreign markets in terms of adjusting to the various local systems. For example, in the Hong Kong, Swiss, and Mexican stock markets, you must settle your account one day after the transaction; in London, there is a two-week settlement procedure; and in France, there are different settlement dates for cash and forward markets. The different administrative procedures of foreign countries simply add up to an extra dimension of difficulty in executing trades. (As implied throughout this section, there are ways to avoid most of these difficulties by going through mutual funds and other investment outlets.)

Information Difficulties

The U.S. securities markets are the best in the world at providing investment information. The Securities and Exchange Commission, with its rigorous requirements for full disclosure, is the toughest national regulator of investment information. Also, the United States has the Financial Accounting Standards Board (FASB) continually providing pronouncements on generally accepted accounting principles for financial reporting. Publicly traded companies are required to provide stockholders with fully audited annual reports. In the United States, we are further spoiled by the excellent evaluative reports and ratings generated by Moody's, Standard & Poor's, Value Line, and other firms. We also have extensive economic data provided by governmental sources such as the Department of Commerce and the Federal Reserve System.

Many international firms, trading in less sophisticated foreign markets, simply do not provide the same quantity or quality of data. This would be particularly true of firms trading in some of the smaller foreign markets. Even when the information is available, there may be language problems for the analyst who does not speak German, French, Portuguese, and so on.

Also, the analyst must be prepared to analyze the firm in light of the standards that are generally accepted in the foreign market in which the company operates. For example, Japanese companies often have much higher debt ratios than U.S. firms. A debt-to-equity ratio of three times is not unusual in Japan, whereas in the United States, the standard is closer to 1:1. The analyst may be inclined to "mark down" the Japanese firm for high debt unless he or she realizes the different features at play in the Japanese economy. For example, in Japan there are normally very close relationships between the lending bank and the borrower, with the lender perhaps having an equity position in the borrower and with interlocking boards between the two. This diminishes the likelihood of the lender calling in the loan in difficult economic periods. Also, the Japanese make extensive use of reserve accounts that tend to give the appearance of a smaller asset or equity base than actually exists. This pattern of understatement is further aided by a strict adherence to historical cost valuation. When appropriate adjustments are made for these effects on financial reporting, a Japanese debt-to-equity ratio of 3:1 may not be a matter of any greater concern than a U.S. debt-to-equity ratio of 1:1.

Corporate Governance

Another issue that deals with information flows to investors is the idea of **corporate governance**. Corporate governance has to do with the management of the company and the transparency of the transactions within the company. Are outside investors treated fairly? Are the financial statements audited and shared with minority stockholders? This becomes very important in emerging economies because many companies have evolved as family businesses, and the family runs the company as they always have even though it may be publicly traded. In other words, is the company run for the benefit of the shareholders or the benefit of the family or majority owners? The issue of corporate governance is also related to the rules and regulations of the stock exchange and the government regulatory authority similar to our Securities and Exchange Commission.

METHODS OF PARTICIPATING IN FOREIGN INVESTMENTS

The avenues to international investment include investing in firms in their own foreign markets, purchasing the shares of foreign firms trading in the United States, investing in mutual funds and closed-end funds with a global orientation, buying the shares of multinational corporations, and entrusting funds to private money managers who specialize in international equities. We shall examine each of these alternatives.

Direct Investments

The most obvious but least likely alternative would be to directly purchase the shares of a firm in its own foreign market through a foreign broker or an overseas branch of a U.S. broker. The investor might consider such firms as Toshiba or Fanuc on the Tokyo Stock Exchange, Consolidated Rutile on the Sydney Stock Exchange, or Hoechst on the Frankfurt Stock Exchange. This approach is hampered by all the difficulties and administrative problems associated with international investments. There could be information-gathering problems, tax problems, stock-delivery problems, capital-transfer problems, and communication difficulties in executing orders. Only the most sophisticated money manager would probably follow this approach (although this may change somewhat in the future as foreign markets become better coordinated).

A more likely route to direct investment would be to purchase the shares of foreign firms that actually trade in U.S. securities markets. Hundreds of foreign firms actively trade their securities in the United States on the New York Stock Exchange.

www.nortel.com

Firms such as Royal Bank of Canada (RY), Inc., and Canada Pacific Railway (CP) (both Canadian firms) trade their stocks *directly* on the New York Stock Exchange. Most of the other foreign firms trade their shares in the United States through **American depository receipts (ADRs)**. The ADRs represent the ownership interest in a foreign company's common stock. If you go to the New York Stock Exchange Web site **www.nyse.com**, you will be able to access the entire list of foreign companies traded on the NYSE. There are also American Depository Receipts listed on the Nasdaq, with one of the most widely traded being L.M. Ericcson of Sweden.

www.syngenta.com

www.british-airways.com

An American depository receipt is created when the shares of a foreign company are purchased and put in trust in a foreign branch of a New York bank. The bank receives and can issue depository receipts to the American shareholders of the foreign firm. These ADRs allow foreign shares to be traded in the United States. Because many countries have securities priced higher or lower than the traditionally priced U.S. securities, each ADR may have a claim on more or less than one share of the foreign stock. For example, Switzerland is known for very high-priced shares, and each ADR of the pharmaceutical firm Syngenta is exchangeable for one-fifth of a share of the common stock. While in the United Kingdom (England), share prices are low and 1 ADR in British Airways, for example, is exchangeable into 10 shares of British Air.

www.sony.com

www.honda.com

When you call your broker and ask to purchase Sony Corporation or Honda Motor Company, Ltd. (which are represented by ADRs), you will notice virtually no difference between this transaction and buying shares of General Motors or Eastman Kodak. You will receive your dividends in dollars and get your reports about the company in English. Generally, you will pay your normal commission rates.

Indirect Investments

The forms of indirect investments in the international securities include (*a*) purchasing shares of multinational corporations, (*b*) purchasing mutual funds or closed-end investment funds specializing in worldwide investments, (*c*) investing in exchange traded funds, and (*d*) engaging the services of a private firm specializing in foreign investment portfolio management.

www.exxon.com

Purchasing Shares of Multinational Corporations

Multinational corporations, that is, firms with operations in a number of countries, represent an opportunity for international diversification. For example, the major oil companies have investments and operations throughout the world. The same can be said for large banking firms and mainframe computer manufacturers. When one buys ExxonMobil, to some extent one is buying exposure to the world economy. Many U.S. firms such as IBM, General Electric, Coca-Cola, Citigroup, Chevron, Hewlett-Packard, Procter and Gamble, and others have more than 50 percent of their sales from foreign countries and a large amount of profits that are generated in foreign currencies. The foreign income exposes the earnings per share to currency fluctuations, but earnings may also benefit from a higher growth rate in foreign countries than in the United States.

Although buying shares in a U.S. multinational firm is an easy route to take to experience worldwide economic effects, some researchers maintain that multinationals do not provide the major *investment* benefits that are desired. Jacquillat and

the real world of investing

THE GROWTH OF AMERICAN DEPOSITORY RECEIPTS

After years of going unnoticed, the benefits that American depository receipts (ADRs) offer American investors are now better understood. To avoid investor difficulties in collecting dividends, receipts are created that provided proof of ownership of the shares held abroad. This makes it less expensive and less troublesome for shareholders to collect dividends on their own.

Many companies from around the world are scrambling to get their stocks traded on American exchanges. This move to Wall Street allows foreign companies to expand their capital while filling the growing demand for ADRs by American investors. Although ADRs are considered to be more liquid, less expensive, and easier to trade than buying foreign companies' stock directly on that country's exchange, there are some drawbacks.

ADRs are treated like domestic stock on the American front and are traded in dollars, but they are still traded in their local currencies on their home markets. The gains or losses an investor can receive from changes in the currency exchange rate can also be offset by capital gains or losses on the investment itself. For those with short time horizons, this can be a serious problem, but for those with long-run interests, many experts argue that the dollar will usually even itself out, and high returns will win out.

There is still a lack of communication between companies and their shareholders abroad. It is difficult for individual investors to keep daily tabs on a foreign company without the aid of a broker.

Even though the SEC requires companies trading ADRs on American exchanges to use the U.S. standard of accounting, many "pink-sheet" ADRs not traded on an exchange are free from such restrictions. Pink sheets are price quotes for smaller or thinly traded over-the-counter companies. These companies are trying, however, to improve their accounting methods to catch the interests of foreign investors.

Politics can also be a disadvantage in ADRs. If a country is going through political turmoil, such unrest can send the stock price soaring or cause it to crash. The hefty taxes the foreign government takes out of the dividends can also be burdensome. To be reimbursed for the amount deducted, a U.S. investor has to request a credit by the Internal Revenue Service.

A final warning is to beware of management. History shows that in emerging economies, inexperienced companies often have tried to expand their business into markets in which they have little knowledge.

Solnik found that multinationals provide very little risk reduction over and above purely domestic firms (perhaps only 10 percent).[4] The prices of multinational shares tend to move very closely with their own country's financial markets despite their worldwide investments. Thus, U.S. multinationals may not do well in a U.S. bear market even if they have investments in strong markets in other countries. This leaves us to turn to mutual funds and closed-end investment companies as potential international investments.

Mutual Funds and Closed-End Investment Companies As described in Chapter 4, mutual funds offer the investor an opportunity for diversification as well as professional management. Nowhere is the mutual fund concept more important than in the area of international investments. Those who organize the funds usually have extensive experience in investing overseas and are prepared to deal with the administrative problems. This, of course, does not necessarily lead to superior returns, but the likelihood for inexperienced blunders is reduced.

One may also invest in closed-end investment companies specializing in international equity investments. As described in Chapter 4, a closed-end investment company has a fixed supply of shares outstanding and trades on a national exchange or over-the-counter, much as an individual company does. It may trade at a premium or discount from its net asset value. An example of an international closed-end fund is the Japan Fund.

Closed-end funds are popular international investment vehicles because they have a fixed number of shares outstanding and they don't accept new money. This is beneficial for investors in emerging markets because these markets are small and

[4] Ibid.

illiquid and cannot absorb large amounts of new cash. Investors often chase rising markets, and in the case of open-end funds, a large flow of cash into emerging markets mutual funds might actually be enough to overly influence the market. That is why you generally find open-end funds in the large developed markets and closed-end funds in the emerging markets.

Exchange-Traded Funds This type of fund was covered in Chapter 4 along with mutual funds, so this section is just a short focus on their use for international investing. Investors can use **exchange-traded funds (ETFs)** to buy a portfolio of international securities. Almost all ETFs are some type of index fund, which buys a basket of securities representing an underlying country index, such as the FTSE in London, the DAX in Germany, or the Hang Seng Index in Hong Kong. The ETF can track a broad stock index, a bond index, or an industry or sector index. There are now hundreds of these funds; for a representative sample you can go to the Barclays iShare Web site at **http://us.ishares.com/product_info/fund/index.htm**. Mutual fund companies are also getting into the act, and so you can also find ETFs on the Vanguard or Fidelity Web sites. Table 19–10 shows a list of exchange-traded funds and their correlation coefficients with the U.S. S&P 500 (GSPC) for the two years of 2009–2010. There are also cross correlations between the countries, and looking at Chile we find low correlations to the others countries in the list. The ticker symbols are in the second column, in case you want to do further research on any of the funds.

The two year correlations are lower than the five year correlations presented in Table 19–5 for 2005–2009. This demonstrates the instability of the correlations. In all cases except Chile, the correlations between the U.S. and the countries in the list range between .75 and .89. Remember that combining any asset with a correlation coefficient of less than 1.00 will reduce the risk (volatility) of the portfolio. Of course, the lower the correlation coefficient, the better the risk reduction. If you can add assets with higher returns than the U.S. market then you have a win-win situation.

TABLE 19-10 Country Correlation Matrix

The following table shows return correlations between various countries (as represented by exchange traded funds) over the past two years.

		^GSPC	EZA	EWQ	EWG	EWC	EWD	EWU	EWA	EWJ	EWY	EWT	EWZ	ECH	EWW	EIS
United states	^GSPC															
South Africa	EZA	**0.86**														
France	EWQ	**0.89**	0.84													
Germany	EWG	**0.89**	0.84	0.96												
Canada	EWC	**0.86**	0.83	0.83	0.84											
Sweden	EWD	**0.86**	0.80	0.91	0.91	0.81										
United Kingdom	EWU	**0.88**	0.82	0.91	0.89	0.83	0.86									
Australia	EWA	**0.88**	0.85	0.88	0.86	0.84	0.82	0.86								
Japan	EWJ	**0.81**	0.72	0.80	0.80	0.71	0.76	0.77	0.77							
South Korea	EWY	**0.81**	0.77	0.76	0.77	0.75	0.74	0.75	0.81	0.73						
Taiwan	EWT	**0.75**	0.75	0.74	0.73	0.70	0.71	0.72	0.79	0.69	0.84					
Brazil	EWZ	**0.87**	0.85	0.83	0.82	0.86	0.80	0.83	0.84	0.73	0.79	0.76				
Chile	**ECH**	**0.65**	**0.59**	**0.64**	**0.64**	**0.64**	**0.64**	**0.66**	**0.64**	**0.55**	**0.57**	**0.51**	**0.66**			
Mexico	EWW	**0.87**	0.81	0.83	0.82	0.83	0.79	0.82	0.81	0.71	0.76	0.72	0.86	0.64		
Israel	EIS	**0.78**	0.71	0.77	0.75	0.71	0.75	0.72	0.76	0.65	0.67	0.67	0.73	0.58	0.71	
Turkey	TUR	**0.84**	0.81	0.80	0.79	0.75	0.77	0.79	0.80	0.70	0.76	0.72	0.80	0.57	0.79	0.70

Source: www.assetcorrelation.com. Used with permission.

SUMMARY

Investments in international securities allow the investor to diversify a portfolio beyond the normal alternatives. Because different foreign markets are influenced by varying and often contradictory factors, effective risk reduction can be provided. An example might be a sharp and unexpected increase in energy prices. The negative impact on oil importers will likely be offset by the positive impact on oil exporters.

Investments in selected foreign equity markets may also provide excellent return opportunities. A number of countries have had superior real GDP growth performance in comparison with the United States. They may also have greater savings rates and higher capital formation. Furthermore, a number of countries are becoming more competitive in traditional U.S. products such as automobiles, steel, and consumer electronics. Emerging countries may offer even greater return and risk-reduction benefits than investments in better established markets. However, many of the problems of international investments can surface in these less developed countries.

In assessing the risk reduction potential of adding international securities to a portfolio, the investor has to consider the correlation between the countries and the assets.

The impact of currency fluctuations on returns is an added dimension to international investments. Not only must the investor determine whether the security will provide a positive return, but he or she must also evaluate the possibility of the return being enhanced or diminished by changes in currency relationships with the U.S. dollar.

International investing can also present political risks, tax problems, administrative issues, liquidity problems, and corporate governance obstacles. To offset these problems investors may want to consider indirect investments such as mutual funds and exchange-traded funds rather than direct investments.

KEY WORDS AND CONCEPTS

American depository receipts (ADRs) 513
BRICs 505
corporate governance 512
correlation coefficient 502
currency fluctuations 508
diversification benefits 502
exchange-traded funds (ETFs) 515
foreign currency effects 510
multinational corporations 513
World Index 508

DISCUSSION QUESTIONS

1. Does an investor who achieves international diversification through foreign investments necessarily have to accept lower returns?
2. Why does Canada represent a relatively poor outlet for achieving risk reduction for U.S. investors? (Merely use your own judgment in answering this question.)
3. In discussing return potential in foreign markets, indicate why a number of foreign countries may have higher return possibilities than the United States.
4. According to researcher Bruno Solnik, how much larger would a pure U.S. portfolio have to be in relation to a well-diversified international portfolio to achieve the same risk-reduction benefits?
5. Explain how currency fluctuations affect the return on foreign investments.

6. Suggest two types of strategies to reduce or neutralize the impact of currency fluctuations on portfolio returns.
7. Suggest how foreign political risk may create a potential investment opportunity.
8. Are foreign markets likely to be more or less efficient than U.S. markets? What effect does this have on bid-ask spreads and the ability to absorb large transactions?
9. Explain why high debt ratios in Japan may not be as great a problem as one might first assume.
10. What are some of the key problems in investing directly in foreign securities?
11. Explain the concept of an ADR.
12. Why did Jacquillat and Solnik indicate that multinational firms may provide very little risk-reduction benefits in comparison with domestic firms?
13. Why might mutual funds be particularly beneficial in the international area?

PRACTICE PROBLEMS AND SOLUTIONS

Foreign currency effects

1. Assume you invest in the French equity market and have a 15 percent return (quoted in euros).
   a. If during this period the euro appreciated by 12 percent against the dollar, what would be your actual return translated into U.S. dollars?
   b. If the euro declined by 8 percent against the dollar, what would be your actual return translated into dollars?
   c. Recompute the answer based on a 30 percent decline in the euro against the dollar.

Solutions

1. *a.*

115%	(15% Profit)
× 1.12	(adjusted value of the euro relative to the U.S. dollar)
128.8%	Percent of original investment
28.8%	Actual gain translated into U.S. dollars

b.

115%	(15% Profit)
× 0.92	(adjusted value of the euro relative to the U.S. dollar)
105.8%	Percent of original investment
5.8%	Actual gain translated into U.S. dollars

c.

115%	(15% Profit)
× 0.70	(adjusted value of the euro relative to the U.S. dollar)
80.5%	Percent of original investment
19.5%	Actual loss translated into U.S. dollars

PROBLEMS

Foreign currency effects

1. Assume you invest in the British equity market and have a 10 percent decline (quoted in British pounds).
   a. If during this period the pound appreciated by 10 percent against the dollar, what would be your actual return translated into U.S. dollars?
   b. If during this period the pound appreciated by 20 percent against the dollar, what would your actual return be translated into U.S. dollars?
   c. Recompute the answer based on a 20 percent decline in the pound against the U.S. dollar.

www.mhhe.com/hirtblock10e

Foreign currency effects

2. Assume you invest in the German equity market and have a 20 percent return (quoted in euros).
   a. If during this period the euro appreciated by 10 percent against the dollar, what would be your actual return translated into U.S. dollars?
   b. If the euro declined by 15 percent against the dollar, what would your actual return be translated into U.S. dollars?
   c. Recompute the answer based on a 25 percent decline in the euro against the dollar.

Foreign currency effects

3. Assume you invest in the Japanese equity market and have a 25 percent return (quoted in yen). However, during the course of your investment, the yen declines versus the dollar. By what percentage could the yen decline relative to the dollar before all your gain is eliminated?

WEB EXERCISE

Assume you want to see how a foreign currency has performed against the dollar over a recent period of time and the implications for investments in companies that trade in that currency. Go to **www.x-rates.com**.

1. Click on "Currency Calculator" under the menu along the left-hand margin.
2. You will then see "Convert" American dollar and "Into" American dollar in the middle of the page. Go to the first box (Convert American Dollar) and follow the arrow down until you get to the Danish krone. Then click on "Calculate."
3. At the top of the same page you will see in a box the relationship between the Danish krone and the U.S. dollar. Write down this value. To better understand the meaning of the value you have just written down, if it is .178 USD, that means a Danish krone is only worth 17.8 percent of the dollar. Said another way, $1.00 is worth 5.62 Danish krones ($1 \div .178$). If you were to purchase an item in Denmark that cost 11.24 Danish krones, that would cost $2.00 ($2 \times 5.62 = 11.24$).
4. Now click the highlighted statement in the box at the bottom that says "Two currencies." You will see a graphic presentation of the krone versus the dollar over the last few months. Below the graph you will also see the lowest and highest value of the Danish krone versus the U.S. dollar.
5. Assume you bought a stock quoted in Danish krones at the lowest value of the krone to the dollar and sold it at the highest value of the krone to the dollar.* What would be the percentage gain if the stock price did not move? The only change in value would be the gain in the Danish krone to the dollar. Divide the highest value by the lowest value to get your answer.
6. Assume the same factors as before in regard to the krone versus dollar performance, but that the stock also went up by 20 percent. What would be your overall gain? (Multiply 1 plus the percentage gain computed in question number five times 1.20 and subtract 1.)
7. Once again assume the same factors as before in terms of the gain in the krone versus the dollar, but assume the stock went down by 20 percent. What would be your overall loss? (Multiply 1 plus the percentage gain computed in question five times .80 and subtract 1.)

* The assumption in this analysis is that the highest exchange rate follows the lowest exchange rate. While this is not always necessarily the case, the assumption is made to facilitate the analysis.

Note: From time to time, companies redesign their Web sites, and occasionally a topic we have listed may have been deleted, updated, or moved into a different location.

CFA MATERIAL

The following material contains a sample question and solution from a prior Level I CFA exam. While the terminology is slightly different from that in this text, you can still view the skills that are necessary for the CFA Exam.

CFA Exam Question

2. Unique risks are associated with international investing. Briefly describe *four* such risks. (*5 minutes*)

Solution: Question 2—Morning Section (5 points)

Four primary risks are:

1. *Currency fluctuations.* If the value of the investors' domestic currency strengthens after the purchase of foreign securities, the value of the investment declines.
2. *Availability of information.* Quality information about foreign companies may be less readily available to analysts than information about domestic companies. This results because of varying requirements for corporate disclosure, less exhaustive analysis conducted by the foreign financial community, and the use of accounting conventions that differ from those in the country of the investor.
3. *Liquidity.* Foreign equity issues may tend to be smaller (or larger) than those in the investor's country making the accumulation of substantial positions more (or less) difficult.
4. *Sovereign risks.* These risks include the potential for disruptive political, sociological, or psychological developments. Examples of political risk are the possibility of nationalization of local companies, expropriation of assets owned by foreign investors, punitive taxation, and restrictions on the withdrawal of capital.

Other unique risks that might be addressed include the following:

5. High transaction costs, including taxes.
6. Administrative cost/settlement problems.
7. Difficulty in assessing manager skill and high fee structure.

www.mhhe.com/hirtblock10e

chapter twenty

INVESTMENTS IN REAL ASSETS

OBJECTIVES

1. Understand the advantages and disadvantages of real assets.
2. Explain the portfolio significance of the correlations between real estate and other assets.
3. Explain the characteristics of investing in real estate.
4. Discuss the various forms of financing for real estate investments.
5. Explain the traditional appeal of precious metals as a form of investments.
6. Understand the factors that influence the value of collectibles.

OUTLINE

In this chapter, we turn our attention to **real assets**; that is, tangible assets that may be seen, felt, held, or collected. Examples of such assets are real estate, gold, silver, diamonds, coins, stamps, and antiques. This is no small area from which to consider investments. For example, the total market value of all real estate holdings in the United States in the early 2000s was in excess of $10 trillion.

As further evidence of value, in the current decade, a Van Gogh painting sold for $40 million, a 132-carat diamond earring set sold for $6.6 million, and a Honus Wagner baseball card sold for more than $2.3 million.

As was pointed out in Chapter 1, in inflationary environments, real assets have at times outperformed financial assets (such as stocks and bonds). With this in mind, the reader is advised to become familiar with these investment outlets—not only to take advantage of the investment opportunities but also to be well aware of the pitfalls. A money manager who is challenged by clients to include real assets in a portfolio (such as real estate or precious metals) must be conversant not only with the opportunities but also with the drawbacks.

ADVANTAGES AND DISADVANTAGES OF REAL ASSETS

As previously mentioned, real assets may offer an opportunity as an inflation hedge because inflation means higher replacement costs for real estate, precious metals, and other physical items. Real assets also serve as an investment hedge against the unknown and feared. When people become concerned about world events, gold and other precious metals may be perceived as the last safe haven for investments.

Real assets also may serve as an effective vehicle for portfolio diversification. Because financial and real assets at times move in opposite directions, some efficient diversification may occur. A study by Robichek, Cohn, and Pringle in the *Journal of Business* actually indicates that movements among various types of real and monetary assets are less positively correlated than are those for monetary assets alone.[1] The general findings indicate that enlarging the universe of investment alternatives would benefit the overall portfolio construction in terms of risk-return alternatives.

A final advantage of an investment in real assets is the psychic pleasure that may be provided. One can easily relate to a beautiful painting in the living room, a mint gold coin in a bank lockbox, or an attractive real estate development.

There are many disadvantages to consider as well. Perhaps the largest drawback is the absence of large, liquid, and relatively efficient markets. Whereas stocks or bonds can generally be sold in a few minutes at a value close to the latest quoted trade, such is not likely to be the case for real estate, diamonds, art, and other forms of real assets. It may take many months to get the desired price for a real asset, and even then, there is an air of uncertainty about the impending transaction until it is consummated.

Furthermore, there is the problem of dealer spread or middleman commission. Whereas in the trading of stocks and bonds where spreads or commissions are very small (usually 1 or 2 percent), dealer spreads for real assets can be as large as 20 to 25 percent or more. This is particularly true for small items that do not have great value. On more valuable items, such as rare paintings, valuable jewels, or mint gold coins, the dealer spread tends to be smaller (perhaps 5 to 10 percent) but still more than that on securities.

The investor in real assets generally receives no current income (with the possible exception of real estate) and may incur storage and insurance costs. Furthermore, there may be the problem of high unit cost for investments. You cannot easily acquire multiple art masterpieces.

A final drawback or caveat in real assets is the hysteria or overreaction that tends to come into the marketplace from time to time. Gold, silver, diamonds, and coins may be temporarily bid out of all proportion to previously anticipated value. This happened in the late 1980s. The last buyer, who arrives too late, may end up owning a very unprofitable investment. The trick is to get into the recurring cycle early enough to take advantage of the capital gains opportunities that occur for real assets. Also, you should buy items of high enough quality so that you can ride out the setbacks if your timing is incorrect.

In the remainder of this chapter, we will examine real estate, gold, silver, diamonds, and other collectibles as investment outlets. Because real estate lends itself more directly to analytical techniques familiar to students of finance, it will receive a proportionately larger share of our attention.

[1] Alexander A. Robichek, Richard A. Cohn, and John J. Pringle, "Return on Alternative Media and Implications for Portfolio Construction," *Journal of Business*, July 1972, pp. 427–43.

REAL ESTATE AS AN INVESTMENT

Approximately 65 percent of the households in the United States own real estate as a home or investment. Also, many firms in the brokerage and investment community have also moved into real estate. As an example, Merrill Lynch has acquired real estate affiliates to broker property, conduct mortgage banking activities, and package real estate syndications. Pension fund managers are also increasing the real estate component in their portfolios, going from virtually no representation two decades ago to almost 10 percent at present.

Some insight into changing real estate values may be gained from Figure 20–1. We see the gain for a dollar invested in real estate in 1971 as compared with fixed-income investments and small common stock. REITs have returned more than large company stocks, long-term government bonds, and U.S. treasury bills. And they have done this with the collapse of the real estate bubble in 2007–2009. Only small company stocks have outperformed REITs.

Real estate investments may include your own home, duplexes and apartment buildings, office buildings, shopping centers, industrial buildings, hotels and motels, as well as undeveloped land. The investor may participate as an individual, as part of a limited partnership real estate syndicate, or through a real estate investment

FIGURE 20-1 Wealth Indices of Investments in Equity REITs and Basic Series Index (Year-End 1971 = $1.00)

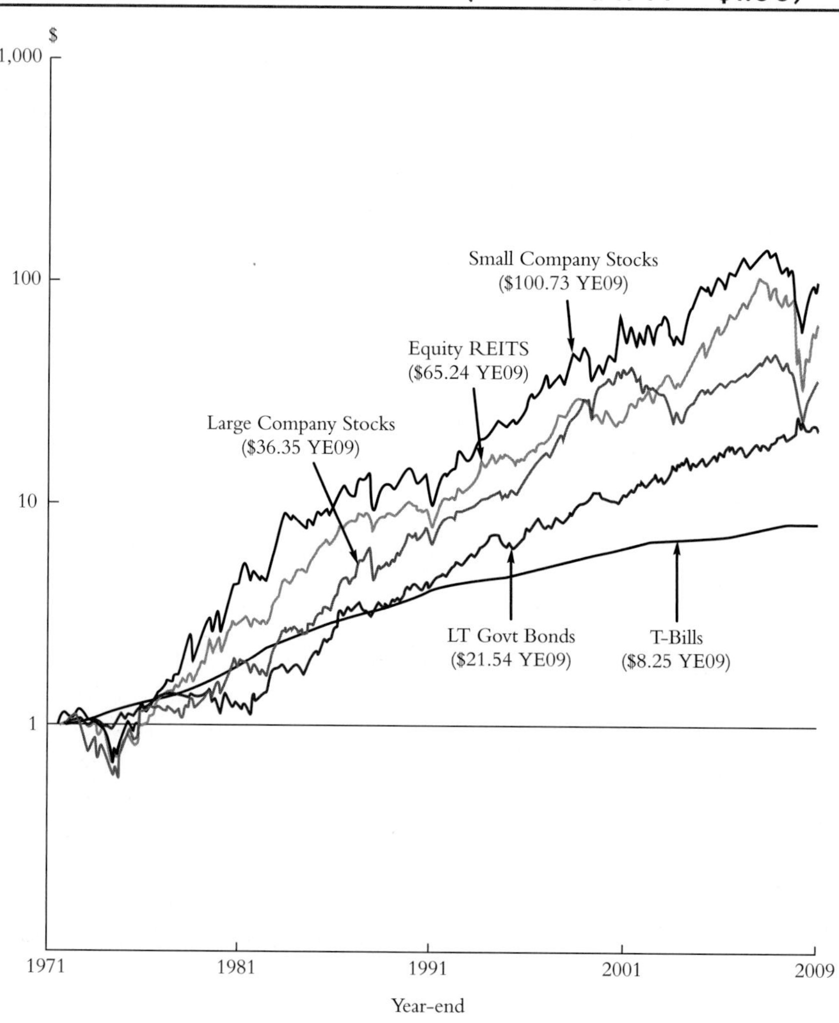

Data from 1971–2009.

trust (REIT). The real estate index represented in Figure 20–1 is the NAREIT Equity Index, which represents all tax-qualified real estate investment trusts on the major U.S. exchanges.

Throughout the rest of the section, we will discuss real estate values in the recent past and relate it to the future outlook. We will also evaluate a typical real estate investment, consider new methods of real estate financing, and examine limited partner syndicates and real estate investment trusts.

REAL ESTATE RETURNS AND CORRELATIONS

The mid-1980s started out as a bad time for real estate with the passage of the Tax Reform Act of 1986. As part of this legislation, the life over which a real estate investor could write off depreciation for tax purposes was extended from 19 years to 27.5 years for residential rental property and to 39 years for commercial property. This meant that an investor had to wait longer to take full advantage of tax deductions related to real estate. Also, real estate investors not actively involved in the management of property were severely restricted in writing off paper losses from real estate against other forms of income.

The effect of tax reform was to make real estate a less attractive investment. Because of the loss of many traditional tax benefits for real estate, some existing properties had less value, and new construction proceeded at a slower pace.

The initial negative impact of tax reform on real estate was also associated with declining economic conditions in various sections of the country during the late 1980s and early 1990s. First, the Southwest (and Texas in particular) was hit with a 70 percent plunge in oil prices in 1986. This meant office buildings, shopping centers, and homes built on an assumption of increasing energy prices to stimulate economic growth went begging for buyers. It was not unusual for a home that was purchased in Dallas, Oklahoma City, or Denver for $300,000 in 1986 to be sold at 50 to 60 percent of that amount five years later. Even as the Southwestern economy began to slowly recover in the early 1990s, real estate–related problems moved into the Northeast, with Massachusetts being hit particularly hard. The next area to suffer was the supposedly immune West Coast in the mid-1990s. Few thought it possible that the ever-growing state of California would see the real estate bubble burst in such dynamic areas as Los Angeles and the San Francisco Bay area.

Over the long term, however, real estate may still have been a good investment. Why? With fewer new properties being developed as a result of tax reform and economic conditions, the glut in office space and apartments in certain sections of the country began to disappear. Furthermore, with fewer new properties brought to the market, rents were going up on existing properties. The eventual effect of higher rents is higher valuation. Evidence of "smart" money starting to flow into real estate markets could be seen in the Dallas–Fort Worth area, in Atlanta, and California markets. Historically, low interest rates have also contributed to the positive pattern. However, the real estate market was starting to heat up at mid-decade, and some analysts became concerned that once again a cooling-off period would take place.

And cool off it did. The real estate bubble burst in 2007, and real estate prices continued to decline throughout 2010. The hardest hit areas were the fast-growth markets of California, Nevada, Arizona, and Florida, where residential housing prices plummeted as much as 50 percent or more. The collapse in real estate prices punctured the idea that prices would only go higher. Because of this myth, many speculators bought properties expecting to flip them and make a fast buck. Some homeowners borrowed against the increased equity in their homes, and when prices fell, their mortgage balance was more than the value of the house. Others had borrowed with little collateral, thanks to the easy credit policies of banks and mortgage brokers. The collapse of the real estate bubble caused a huge problem for the banks and mortgage lenders, as borrowers either couldn't pay their mortgage or simply walked away and left the lenders holding the bag.

The result was the second worst recession since the Great Depression. The recession lasted 18 months, and unemployment peaked at 10 percent, adding pain to the mortgage mess. Foreclosures reached into the millions as lenders repossessed homes for which the borrowers had stopped paying their loans. As history in the preceding paragraphs shows, real estate has had some bumpy rides. This can also be seen in Figure 20–1. However, if we are to be serious investors, we need to consider the long-term portfolio implications of holding real estate. The Ibbotson SBBI 2010 Yearbook states that real estate has had a low correlation with common stocks and bonds over time, and when added to a stock and bond portfolio could increase the return and at the same time lower the standard deviation. The correlation trends can be seen in Figure 20–2. It is possible that the rising correlation in the past few years is simply a reflection that correlations of all assets have a tendency to increase in a crisis. Because REITs are traded in the stock market, they are also affected by market sentiment, and the financial crisis created fear and risk aversion for all risky asset classes.

Figure 20–3 also indicates that real estate has had somewhat volatile returns over time, but that the income stream is fairly stable even when prices are falling. This gives real estate a cash flow advantage for portfolios seeking income. Because REITs must pay out 90 percent of their income, this figure is a pretty clear indication of the stability of real estate returns.

Investors often become fearful when markets collapse, but a contrarian looks at a market collapse as a buying opportunity. Of course, timing the purchase is quite important, but Figure 20–3 shows that after the collapse in 2007–2008, real estate bounced back in 2009. And although the graph doesn't include 2010, REITs continued their recovery during that year.

FIGURE 20-2 Rolling 60-Month Correlations of Equity REITs

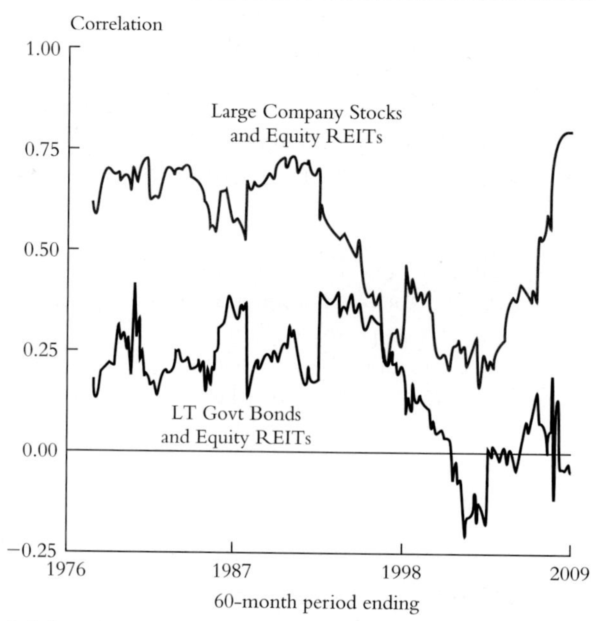

Data from January 1972–December 1976 to January 2005–December 2009.

Source:

FIGURE 20-3 Annual Returns on Equity REITs

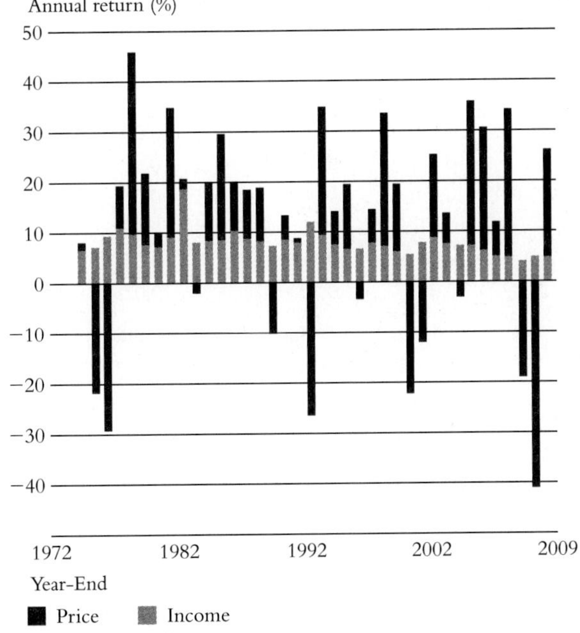

Data from 1972–2009.

In order to take a longer look at real estate returns, we turn to Table 20–1, which includes return data from 1972 to 2009. Notice that real estate has the second highest return compared to other asset classes. Only small common stocks outperform and have a higher standard deviation. Notice that long-term corporate bonds and government bonds have almost the same geometric mean return, with intermediate-term government bonds not too far behind.

Perhaps more important are the long-term correlations found in Table 20–2, which depicts cross correlations and serial correlations between these asset classes. The most important column is the first one, labeled Equity REITs. This column shows that REITs are most highly correlated to small stocks (0.79) and next to large stocks (0.59). We know from Chapter 17 on portfolio theory that whenever we can add an asset to a portfolio with a correlation of less than 1, we can reduce the risk of that portfolio and perhaps increase the portfolio return. In this case, because

TABLE 20-1 Summary Statistics of Annual Returns (%)

	Geometric Mean	Arithmetic Mean	Standard Deviation
Equity REITs	11.6	13.4	19.0
Large Company Stocks	9.9	11.6	18.6
Small Company Stocks	12.9	15.4	23.6
Long-Term Corporate Bonds	8.5	8.9	10.4
Long-Term Government Bonds	8.4	9.1	12.2
Intermediate-Term Government Bonds	7.8	8.0	6.7
Treasury Bills	5.7	5.8	3.1
Inflation	4.5	4.5	3.2

Data from 1972 to 2009.

TABLE 20-2 Serial and Cross-Correlations of Annual Returns

	Equity REITs	Large Company Stocks	Small Company Stocks	LT-Corp. Bonds	LT-Gov't Bonds	IT-Gov't Bonds	T-Bills	Inflation
Equity REITs	1.00							
Large Company Stocks	0.57	1.00						
Small Company Stocks	0.79	0.72	1.00					
Long-Term Corporate Bonds	0.23	0.30	0.16	1.00				
Long-Term Government Bonds	0.00	0.08	−0.07	0.90	1.00			
IT Government Bonds	0.01	0.10	−0.03	0.88	0.92	1.00		
Treasury Bills	0.02	0.10	0.05	0.05	0.09	0.33	1.00	
Inflation	−0.03	−0.10	0.07	−0.40	−0.35	−0.18	0.64	1.00
Serial Correlation	0.13	0.00	0.02	−0.06	−0.30	−0.04	0.82	0.73

Data from 1972 to 2009.

Source:

REITs have the second highest return, we can be sure that real estate's addition to the portfolio will raise the portfolio return.

Although REITs are correlated at a low level to corporate bonds (0.23), they have almost no correlation to government bonds and bills. This is extremely important, because adding an asset with zero correlation to a bond portfolio will have a significant impact on reducing the risk (standard deviation) of the portfolio. Even adding real estate to a blended portfolio of stocks and bonds will have the same impact, because none of the correlations are close to 1. Focusing on the other columns in Table 20–2, we see that large and small common stocks have very low correlations to bonds of all types. Now we move on to the valuation of real estate, so you will have a better idea of what this asset class is worth if you want to add it to your portfolio.

VALUATION OF REAL ESTATE

There are three primary approaches to determining the value of real estate.

The Cost Approach

The first is the **cost approach**. What better place to start than the cost to replace an asset at current prices? This is fairly easy to determine for relatively new property, where the components that went into the structure are easily identified and priced out. For older buildings, the challenge is somewhat greater because the building materials may no longer be in existence or may be currently prohibited (for example, asbestos). Some would assume a building is at least worth its replacement cost, but that it not always the case. A warehouse or apartment complex that is poorly located may be worth far less than the replacement cost. Also, when a certain part of the country is suffering from an economic setback, there may be no desire to replace the asset. Nevertheless, the cost basis serves as a useful estimate of value when used in conjunction with the other two approaches.

Comparative Sales Value

Many in the real estate industry look to the selling price of comparable real estate to determine value. If you are going to put a four-bedroom, three-bathroom house, with 2,500 square feet on the market, what better way to establish value than to look for recent sales prices for comparable property in the neighborhood? This approach is called the **comparative sales value**.

Of course, true comparables are difficult to find. While nearby property may appear to be similar, there can be differences in floor plans, landscape, traffic exposure, and so forth. Nevertheless, if a number of comparables can be identified, the differences may be averaged out or a grid established in which a base price is assigned and then modified for each different element.

Although the comparative sales approach is only a helpful guideline, it does have one indisputable value. *Actual sales* did take place at the recorded price.

The Income Approach

For income-producing property, the **income approach** may be applied. The basic question to be answered is this: "What is the potential annual operating income and at what level should it be valued (capitalized)?"

In its simplest form, this formula may be applied:

$$\frac{\text{Annual net operating income}}{\text{Capitalization rate (Cap rate)}} = \text{Value} \qquad \textbf{(20–1)}$$

The numerator is determined by an analysis of annual rentals, followed by a subtraction of expenses such as property taxes, insurance, etc. The numbers to be applied are future realistic numbers rather than current or historical values. Perhaps the current gross rentals are $35,000 per year but could easily be raised to $40,000 with a minimum of effort. It is this latter number that should be used. The same is true for expenses. If prior tax returns indicate that maintenance and upkeep expenses are too low to maintain the quality of the property, upward adjustments must be made.

The second component in Formula 20–1 is the denominator, the capitalization rate. That is, the rate of return required by investors in similar-type investments. It is normally determined by examining the rate of return on recent transactions. It may be further modified by additional consideration of risk, changes in interest rates, etc.

Assume a property had a projected annual net operating income of $17,500 and a market capitalization rate of 10 percent. The value based on this approach would be $175,000:

$$\frac{\$17{,}500}{0.10} = \$175{,}000$$

While the approach is potentially helpful, it suffers somewhat from oversimplicity. For example, only one number is used for annual net operating income for the foreseeable future when it is quite likely to change over time. Also, different analysts may have difficulty in determining what the capitalization rate should be. At a cap rate of 9 percent, the property is worth $194,444, and at a cap rate of 11 percent, it is only worth $159,091.

Combination of the Three Approaches

In most cases, a final value will be determined by a combination of the three approaches—each imparts significant information, but each also has its shortfalls. While a one-third weighting of the value determined under each approach is appealing, in most cases (particularly those involving litigation), a different weighting approach is likely to be used. Perhaps comparable sales values will receive a 50 percent weighting, the income approach 35 percent, and the cost approach 15 percent.

For those who wish to study a much more comprehensive approach to real estate investment decisions, please see Appendix 20A.

Types of Mortgages

The most frequently used type of mortgage is the fixed-payment mortgage. Based on this arrangement, a constant monthly amount is paid over the life of the loan based on the amount borrowed, the number of years for repayment, and the interest rate. In actuality, a whole set of mortgage arrangements is available as alternatives to the fixed-payment mortgage (particularly for home mortgages). The borrower must now be prepared to consider such alternative lending arrangements as the **adjustable rate mortgage**, the **graduated payment mortgage**, and the **shared appreciation mortgage**.

Adjustable Rate Mortgage (ARM) Under this mortgage arrangement, the interest rate is adjusted regularly. If interest rates go up, borrowers may either increase their normal payments or extend the maturity date of the loan at the same fixed-payment level to fully compensate the lender. Similar downside adjustments can also be made if interest rates fall. Generally, adjustable rate mortgages are initially made at rates 1 to 2 percent below fixed-interest-rate mortgages because the lender enjoys the flexibility of changing interest rates and is willing to share the benefits with the borrower. Adjustable rate mortgages currently account for more than half of the residential mortgage market. Although adjustable rate mortgages usually have an upper boundary (such as 12 or 15 percent or a 6 percent lifetime adjustment over the original borrowing rate), there is a real possibility of default for many borrowers if interest rates reach high levels.

Graduated Payment Mortgage (GPM) Under this type of financial arrangement, the payments start out on a relatively low basis and increase over the life of the loan. This type of mortgage may be well suited to the young borrower who has an increasing repayment capability over the life of the loan. An example would be a 30-year, $60,000 loan at 9 percent that would normally require monthly payments of $583.99 under a standard fixed-payment mortgage. With a graduated payment mortgage, monthly payments might start out as $350 or $400 and eventually progress to more than $700. The GPM plan has been referred to by a few of its critics as the "gyp 'em" plan, in that early payments may not be large enough to cover interest, and therefore, later payments must cover not only the amortization of the loan but also interest on the accumulated, unpaid, early interest. This is not an altogether fair criticism but merely an interpretation of what the graduated payment stream represents.

Shared Appreciation Mortgage (SAM) Perhaps the newest and most innovative of the mortgage payment plans is the shared appreciation mortgage. This provides the lender with a hedge against inflation because he directly participates in any increase in value associated with the property being mortgaged. The lender may enjoy as much as 30 to 40 percent of the appreciation in value over a specified time period, such as 10 years. The lender may take his return from the selling of the property or from the refinancing of the appreciated property value with a new lender. In return for this appreciation-potential privilege, the lender may advance funds at well below current market rates (perhaps at three-fourths of current rates). The shared appreciation mortgage is not yet legal in all states.

Other Forms of Mortgages Somewhat similar to the shared appreciation mortgage is the concept of equity participation that is popular in commercial real estate. Under an **equity participation** arrangement, the lender not only provides the borrowed capital but part of the equity or ownership funds as well. A major insurance company or savings and loan thus may acquire an equity interest of 10 to 25 percent (or more). This financing arrangement becomes popular each time inflation rears its head. Some lenders are simply unwilling to commit capital for long periods without a participation feature.

Borrowers may also look toward a *second mortgage* for financing. Here, a second lender provides additional financing beyond the first mortgage in return for a secondary claim or lien. The second mortgage is generally for a shorter period of time than the initial mortgage. Primary suppliers of second mortgages in recent times have been sellers of property. Often, to consummate a sale, it is necessary for the seller to supplement the financing provided by a financial institution. Sellers providing second mortgages generally advance the funds at rates below the first mortgage rate to facilitate the sale, whereas other second mortgage lenders (non-sellers) will ask for a few percentage points above the first mortgage rate to compensate for the extra risk of being in a secondary claim position.

In some cases, sellers may actually provide all the financing to the buyer. Usually the terms of the mortgage are for 20 to 30 years, but the seller has the right to call in the loan after three to five years if so desired. The assumption is that the buyer may have an easier time finding his own financing at that point in time. This may or may not be true.

FORMS OF REAL ESTATE OWNERSHIP

Ownership of real estate may take many forms. The investor may participate as an individual, in a regular partnership, through a real estate syndicate (generally a limited partnership), or through a real estate investment trust (REIT).

Individual or Regular Partnership

Investing as an individual or with two or three others in a regular partnership offers the simplest way of getting into real estate from a legal viewpoint. The investors pretty much control their own destinies and can take advantage of personal knowledge of local markets and changing conditions to enhance their returns.

As is true with most smaller and less complicated business arrangements, there is a well-defined center of responsibility that often leads to quick, corrective action. However, there may be a related problem of inability to pool adequate capital to engage in large-scale investments as well as the absence of expertise to develop a wide range of investments. Furthermore, there is unlimited liability to the investor(s).

Syndicate or Limited Partnership

To expand the potential for investor participation, a syndicate or limited partnership has traditionally been formed. The **limited partnership** works as follows: A general partner forms the limited partnership and has unlimited liability for the partnership liabilities. The general partner then sells participation units to the limited partners whose liability is limited to the extent of their initial investment (such as $5,000 or $10,000). Limited liability is particularly important in real estate because mortgage debt obligations may exceed the net worth of the participants. The general partner is normally responsible for managing the property, while the limited partners are merely investors.

Although the restricted liability feature of the limited partnership remains attractive, the Tax Reform Act of 1986 generally restricted the use of limited partnerships as tax shelters. Historically, real estate limited partnerships generated large paper losses through accelerated depreciation (though not cash losses), and these paper losses were used to shelter other forms of income (such as a doctor's salary) from taxation. Under the Tax Reform Act of 1986, a taxpayer is no longer allowed to freely use passive losses to offset other sources of income such as salary or portfolio income. Such losses can only be used to offset income from other passive investments.

Real estate limited partnerships still exist but more for limited liability than for tax reasons. The successful partnerships stress strong cash flow generation and capital appreciation potential. In the advanced example in the Appendix to this chapter, a limited partnership was not involved, and the investor actively participated in managing the property. Some small tax write-offs were allowed, but the success of the project was much more dependent on cash flow and potential capital appreciation.

If you decide to invest in a limited partnership, you should follow certain guidelines. You must be particularly sensitive to the front-end fees and commissions the general partner might charge. These can vary anywhere from 5 to 10 percent to as large as 20 to 25 percent. The investor must also be sensitive to any double-dealing the general partner might be doing. An example would be selling property between different partnerships the general partner has formed and taking a commission each time. The inflated paper profits may prove quite deceptive and costly to the uninformed limited partner.

In assessing a general partner and his associated real estate deal, the investor should look at a number of items. First, he should review the prior record of performance of the general partner. Is this the 1st or 10th deal that the general partner has put together? The investor will also wish to be sensitive to any lawsuits against the general partner that might exist. The investor might also wish to ascertain whether he or she is investing in a **blind pool** arrangement where funds are provided to the general partner to ultimately select properties for investment or if specific projects have already been identified and analyzed.

Finally, the investor may have to decide whether to invest in a limited partnership/syndication that is either *public* or *private* in nature. A public offering generally involves much larger total amounts and has gone through the complex and rigorous process of SEC registration. Of course, SEC registration only attempts to ensure that full disclosure has occurred—it does not judge the prudence of the venture. A private offering of a limited partnership syndication is usually local in scope and restricted to a maximum of 35 investors.

Secondary (resale) markets for both public and private limited partnerships exist, but the dealer spreads and commissions tend to be very high. The spreads on desirable property are 10 to 15 percent; on less desirable property, 20 to 30 percent or more. Really bad property may approach total illiquidity. As you might anticipate, a public limited partnership has much more resale potential than a private one.

Real Estate Investment Trust

Another form of real estate investment is the **real estate investment trust (REIT)**. REITs are similar to mutual funds or investment companies and trade on organized exchanges or over-the-counter. They pool investor funds, along with borrowed funds, and invest them directly in real estate or use them to make construction or mortgage loans to investors.

The advantage to the investor of a REIT is that he or she can participate in the real estate market for as little as $10 to $20 per share. Furthermore, this is the most liquid type of real estate investment because of the large secondary market for the shares.

REITs were initiated under the Real Estate Investment Trust Act of 1960. Like other investment companies, they enjoy the privilege of single taxation of income (only the stockholder pays and not the trust). To qualify for the tax privilege of a REIT, a firm must receive at least 75 percent of its income from real estate (i.e., rents and interest on mortgage loans) and distribute at least 95 percent of its income as cash dividends.

REITs may take any of three different forms or combinations thereof. **Equity trusts** buy, operate, and sell real estate as an investment; **mortgage trusts** make long-term loans to real estate investors; and **hybrid trusts** engage in the activities of both equity and mortgage trusts. REITs are generally formed and advised by affiliates of commercial banks, insurance companies, mortgage bankers, and other financial institutions. Representative issues include Bank America Realty, and Connecticut General Mortgage.

www.cigna.com

www.reitnet.com

There are more than 400 REITs from which the investor may choose.[2] In Figure 20–4 on the next page, a *Value Line* data sheet is presented for Weingarten Realty, a typical industry participant. Many other REITs are also presented in *Value Line*.

[2] Further information on REITs may be acquired from the National Association of Real Estate Investment Trusts, 1101 17th St., N.W., Washington, DC 20036.

FIGURE 20-4 Data Sheet for REIT

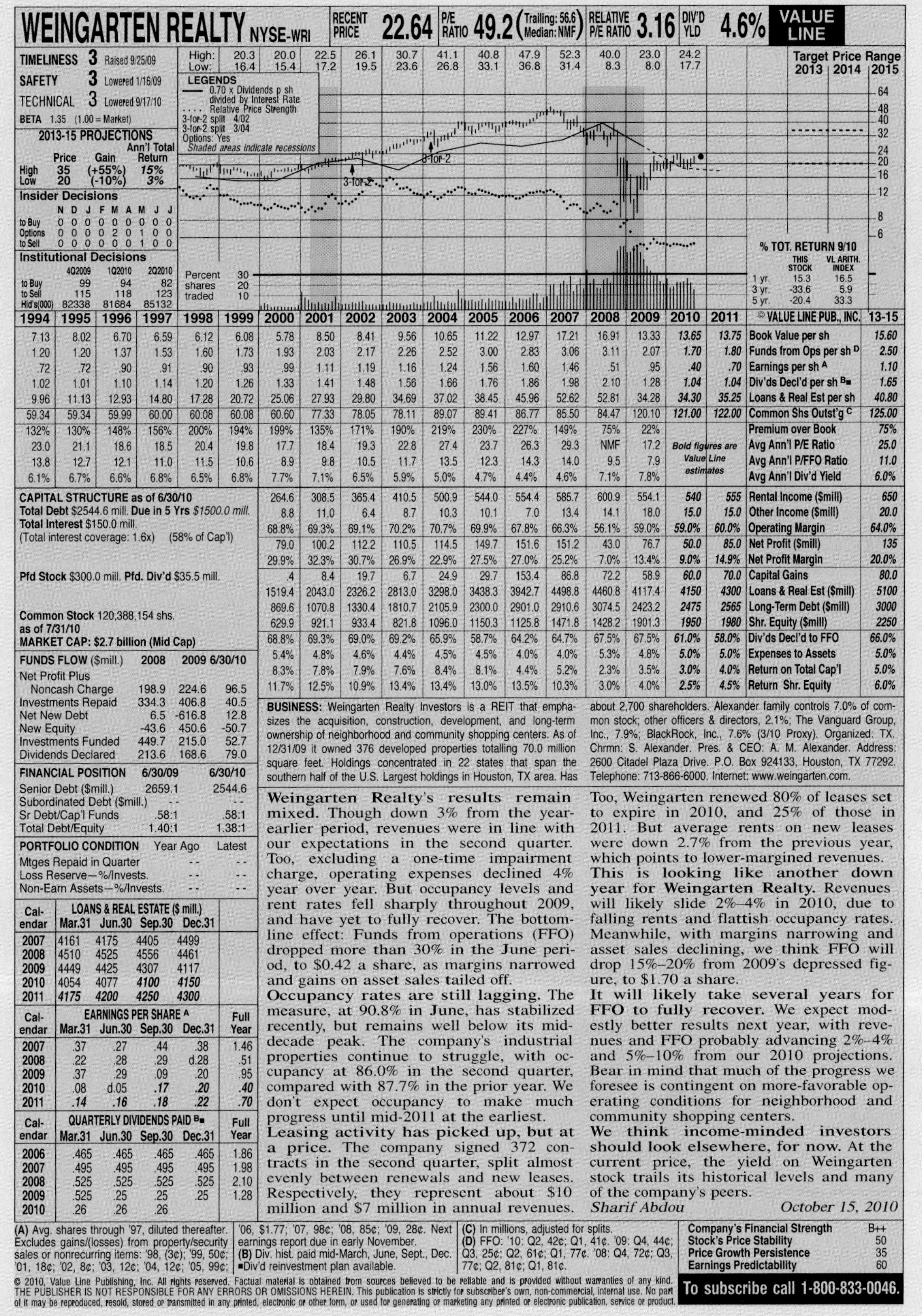

WEINGARTEN REALTY NYSE-WRI

RECENT PRICE 22.64 | P/E RATIO 49.2 (Trailing: 56.6 Median: NMF) | RELATIVE P/E RATIO 3.16 | DIV'D YLD 4.6% | VALUE LINE

TIMELINESS 3 Raised 9/25/09
SAFETY 3 Lowered 1/16/09
TECHNICAL 3 Lowered 9/17/10
BETA 1.35 (1.00 = Market)

	1999	2000	2001	2002	2003	2004	2005	2006	2007	2008	2009	2010
High:	20.3	20.0	22.5	26.1	30.7	41.1	40.8	47.9	52.3	40.0	23.0	24.2
Low:	16.4	15.4	17.2	19.5	23.6	26.8	33.1	36.8	31.4	8.3	8.0	17.7

Target Price Range 2013 | 2014 | 2015

2013-15 PROJECTIONS

	Price	Gain	Ann'l Total Return
High	35	(+55%)	15%
Low	20	(-10%)	3%

Insider Decisions

	N	D	J	F	M	A	M	J	J
to Buy	0	0	0	0	0	0	0	0	0
Options	0	0	0	0	2	0	1	0	0
to Sell	0	0	0	0	0	0	1	0	0

Institutional Decisions

	4Q2009	1Q2010	2Q2010
to Buy	99	94	82
to Sell	115	118	123
Hld's(000)	82338	81684	85132

% TOT. RETURN 9/10

	THIS STOCK	VL ARITH. INDEX
1 yr.	15.3	16.5
3 yr.	-33.6	5.9
5 yr.	-20.4	33.3

© VALUE LINE PUB., INC.	1994	1995	1996	1997	1998	1999	2000	2001	2002	2003	2004	2005	2006	2007	2008	2009	2010	2011	13-15
Book Value per sh	7.13	8.02	6.70	6.59	6.12	6.08	5.78	8.50	8.41	9.56	10.65	11.22	12.97	17.21	16.91	13.33	*13.65*	*13.75*	*15.60*
Funds from Ops per sh [D]	1.20	1.20	1.37	1.53	1.60	1.73	1.93	2.03	2.17	2.26	2.52	3.00	2.83	3.06	3.11	2.07	*1.70*	*1.80*	*2.50*
Earnings per sh [A]	.72	.72	.90	.91	.90	.93	.99	1.11	1.19	1.16	1.24	1.56	1.60	1.46	.51	.95	*.40*	*.70*	*1.10*
Div'ds Decl'd per sh [B]■	1.02	1.01	1.10	1.14	1.20	1.26	1.33	1.41	1.48	1.56	1.66	1.76	1.86	1.98	2.10	1.28	*1.04*	*1.04*	*1.65*
Loans & Real Est per sh	9.96	11.13	12.93	14.80	17.28	20.72	25.06	27.93	29.80	34.69	37.02	38.45	45.96	52.62	52.81	34.28	*34.30*	*35.25*	*40.80*
Common Shs Outst'g [C]	59.34	59.34	59.99	60.00	60.08	60.08	60.60	77.33	78.05	78.11	89.07	89.41	86.77	85.50	84.47	120.10	*121.00*	*122.00*	*125.00*
Premium over Book	132%	130%	148%	156%	200%	194%	199%	135%	171%	190%	219%	230%	227%	149%	75%	22%			*75%*
Avg Ann'l P/E Ratio	23.0	21.1	18.6	18.5	20.4	19.8	17.7	18.4	19.3	22.8	27.4	23.7	26.3	29.3	NMF	17.2	*Bold figures are Value Line estimates*		*25.0*
Avg Ann'l P/FFO Ratio	13.8	12.7	12.1	11.0	11.5	10.6	8.9	9.8	10.5	11.7	13.5	12.3	14.3	14.0	9.5	7.9			*11.0*
Avg Ann'l Div'd Yield	6.1%	6.7%	6.6%	6.8%	6.5%	6.8%	7.7%	7.1%	6.5%	5.9%	5.0%	4.7%	4.4%	4.6%	7.1%	7.8%			*6.0%*
Rental Income ($mill)							264.6	308.5	365.4	410.5	500.9	544.0	554.4	585.7	600.9	554.1	*540*	*555*	*650*
Other Income ($mill)							8.8	11.0	6.4	8.7	10.3	10.1	7.0	13.4	14.1	18.0	*15.0*	*15.0*	*20.0*
Operating Margin							68.8%	69.3%	69.1%	70.2%	70.7%	69.9%	67.8%	66.3%	56.1%	59.0%	*59.0%*	*60.0%*	*64.0%*
Net Profit ($mill)							79.0	100.2	112.2	110.5	114.5	149.7	151.6	151.2	43.0	76.7	*50.0*	*85.0*	*135*
Net Profit Margin							29.9%	32.3%	30.7%	26.9%	22.9%	27.5%	27.0%	25.2%	7.0%	13.4%	*9.0%*	*14.9%*	*20.0%*
Capital Gains							.4	8.4	19.7	6.7	24.9	29.7	153.4	86.8	72.2	58.9	*60.0*	*70.0*	*80.0*
Loans & Real Est ($mill)							1519.4	2043.0	2326.2	2813.0	3298.0	3438.3	3942.7	4498.8	4460.8	4117.4	*4150*	*4300*	*5100*
Long-Term Debt ($mill)							869.6	1070.8	1330.4	1810.7	2105.9	2300.0	2901.0	2910.6	3074.5	2423.2	*2475*	*2565*	*3000*
Shr. Equity ($mill)							629.9	921.1	933.4	821.8	1096.0	1150.3	1125.8	1471.8	1428.2	1901.3	*1950*	*1980*	*2250*
Div'ds Decl'd to FFO							68.8%	69.3%	69.0%	69.2%	65.9%	58.7%	64.2%	64.7%	67.5%	67.5%	*61.0%*	*58.0%*	*66.0%*
Expenses to Assets							5.4%	4.8%	4.6%	4.4%	4.5%	4.5%	4.0%	4.0%	5.3%	4.8%	*5.0%*	*5.0%*	*5.0%*
Return on Total Cap'l							8.3%	7.8%	7.9%	7.6%	8.4%	8.1%	4.4%	5.2%	2.3%	3.5%	*3.0%*	*4.0%*	*5.0%*
Return Shr. Equity							11.7%	12.5%	10.9%	13.4%	13.4%	13.0%	13.5%	10.3%	3.0%	4.0%	*2.5%*	*4.5%*	*6.0%*

CAPITAL STRUCTURE as of 6/30/10
Total Debt $2544.6 mill. **Due in 5 Yrs** *$1500.0 mill.*
Total Interest $150.0 mill.
(Total interest coverage: 1.6x) (58% of Cap'l)

Pfd Stock $300.0 mill. **Pfd. Div'd** $35.5 mill.

Common Stock 120,388,154 shs.
as of 7/31/10
MARKET CAP: $2.7 billion (Mid Cap)

FUNDS FLOW ($mill.)	2008	2009	6/30/10
Net Profit Plus Noncash Charge	198.9	224.6	96.5
Investments Repaid	334.3	406.8	40.5
Net New Debt	6.5	-616.8	12.8
New Equity	-43.6	450.6	-50.7
Investments Funded	449.7	215.0	52.7
Dividends Declared	213.6	168.6	79.0

FINANCIAL POSITION	6/30/09	6/30/10
Senior Debt ($mill.)	2659.1	2544.6
Subordinated Debt ($mill.)	- -	- -
Sr Debt/Cap'l Funds	.58:1	.58:1
Total Debt/Equity	1.40:1	1.38:1

PORTFOLIO CONDITION	Year Ago	Latest
Mtges Repaid in Quarter	- -	- -
Loss Reserve—%/Invests.	- -	- -
Non-Earn Assets—%/Invests.	- -	- -

Cal-endar	LOANS & REAL ESTATE ($ mill.) Mar.31	Jun.30	Sep.30	Dec.31
2007	4161	4175	4405	4499
2008	4510	4525	4556	4461
2009	4449	4425	4307	4117
2010	4054	4077	*4100*	*4150*
2011	*4175*	*4200*	*4250*	*4300*

Cal-endar	EARNINGS PER SHARE [A] Mar.31	Jun.30	Sep.30	Dec.31	Full Year
2007	.37	.27	.44	.38	1.46
2008	.22	.28	.29	d.28	.51
2009	.37	.29	.09	.20	.95
2010	.08	d.05	*.17*	*.20*	*.40*
2011	*.14*	*.16*	*.18*	*.22*	*.70*

Cal-endar	QUARTERLY DIVIDENDS PAID [B]■ Mar.31	Jun.30	Sep.30	Dec.31	Full Year
2006	.465	.465	.465	.465	1.86
2007	.495	.495	.495	.495	1.98
2008	.525	.525	.525	.525	2.10
2009	.525	.25	.25	.25	1.28
2010	.26	.26	.26		

BUSINESS: Weingarten Realty Investors is a REIT that emphasizes the acquisition, construction, development, and long-term ownership of neighborhood and community shopping centers. As of 12/31/09 it owned 376 developed properties totalling 70.0 million square feet. Holdings concentrated in 22 states that span the southern half of the U.S. Largest holdings in Houston, TX area. Has about 2,700 shareholders. Alexander family controls 7.0% of common stock; other officers & directors, 2.1%; The Vanguard Group, Inc., 7.9%; BlackRock, Inc., 7.6% (3/10 Proxy). Organized: TX. Chrmn: S. Alexander. Pres. & CEO: A. M. Alexander. Address: 2600 Citadel Plaza Drive. P.O. Box 924133, Houston, TX 77292. Telephone: 713-866-6000. Internet: www.weingarten.com.

Weingarten Realty's results remain mixed. Though down 3% from the year-earlier period, revenues were in line with our expectations in the second quarter. Too, excluding a one-time impairment charge, operating expenses declined 4% year over year. But occupancy levels and rent rates fell sharply throughout 2009, and have yet to fully recover. The bottom-line effect: Funds from operations (FFO) dropped more than 30% in the June period, to $0.42 a share, as margins narrowed and gains on asset sales tailed off.

Occupancy rates are still lagging. The measure, at 90.8% in June, has stabilized recently, but remains well below its mid-decade peak. The company's industrial properties continue to struggle, with occupancy at 86.0% in the second quarter, compared with 87.7% in the prior year. We don't expect occupancy to make much progress until mid-2011 at the earliest.

Leasing activity has picked up, but at a price. The company signed 372 contracts in the second quarter, split almost evenly between renewals and new leases. Respectively, they represent about $10 million and $7 million in annual revenues. Too, Weingarten renewed 80% of leases set to expire in 2010, and 25% of those in 2011. But average rents on new leases were down 2.7% from the previous year, which points to lower-margined revenues.

This is looking like another down year for Weingarten Realty. Revenues will likely slide 2%–4% in 2010, due to falling rents and flattish occupancy rates. Meanwhile, with margins narrowing and asset sales declining, we think FFO will drop 15%–20% from 2009's depressed figure, to $1.70 a share.

It will likely take several years for FFO to fully recover. We expect modestly better results next year, with revenues and FFO probably advancing 2%–4% and 5%–10% from our 2010 projections. Bear in mind that much of the progress we foresee is contingent on more-favorable operating conditions for neighborhood and community shopping centers.

We think income-minded investors should look elsewhere, for now. At the current price, the yield on Weingarten stock trails its historical levels and many of the company's peers.

Sharif Abdou *October 15, 2010*

(A) Avg. shares through '97, diluted thereafter. Excludes gains/(losses) from property/security sales or nonrecurring items: '98, (3¢); '99, 50¢; '01, 18¢; '02, 8¢; '03, 12¢; '04, 12¢; '05, 99¢; '06, $1.77; '07, 98¢; '08, 85¢; '09, 28¢. Next earnings report due in early November.
(B) Div. hist. paid mid-March, June, Sept., Dec. ■Div'd reinvestment plan available.
(C) In millions, adjusted for splits.
(D) FFO: '10: Q2, 42¢; Q1, 41¢. '09: Q4, 44¢; Q3, 25¢; Q2, 61¢; Q1, 77¢. '08: Q4, 72¢; Q3, 77¢; Q2, 81¢; Q1, 81¢.

Company's Financial Strength	B++
Stock's Price Stability	50
Price Growth Persistence	35
Earnings Predictability	60

Source: Copyright © 2010 by Value Line Publishing, Inc. Reprinted by permission.

GOLD AND SILVER

We now examine a number of other forms of real asset investments. Precious metals represent the most volatile of the investment alternatives. Historically, gold and silver have tended to move up in troubled times and show a decline in value during stable, predictable periods.[3] Observe the movement in the price of gold between 1975 and 2010 in Figure 20–5.

Gold

Major factors that tend to drive up gold prices are fear of war, political instability, and inflation (these were particularly evident in Figure 20–5 after 1979 with the takeover of U.S. embassies in Iran and double-digit inflation). Conversely, moderation in worldwide tensions and lower inflation cause a decline in gold prices.

www.kiplinger.com

Gold may be owned in many different forms, and a survey by *Kiplinger's Personal Finance Magazine* indicated that 35 percent of the U.S. population with incomes of more than $50,000 per year owned gold (directly or indirectly) or other forms of precious metals. Let's examine the different forms of gold ownership.

Gold Bullion Gold bullion includes gold bars or wafers. The investor may own anywhere from 1 troy ounce to 10,000 troy ounces (valued at approximately $13.5 million in 2010). Smaller bars generally trade at a 6 to 8 percent premium over pure gold bullion value, with larger bars trading at a 1 to 2 percent premium. Gold bullion may provide storage problems, and unless the gold bars remain in the custody of the bank or dealer who initially sells them, they must be reexamined before being sold.

FIGURE 20-5 Movement in Gold Prices, 1975–2010

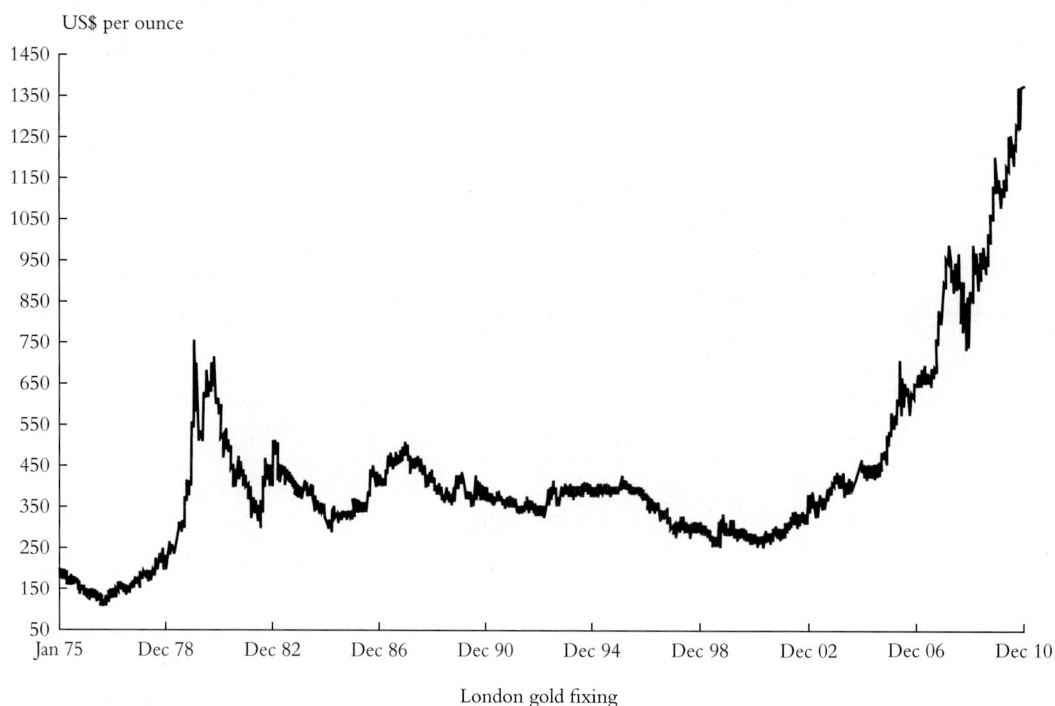

Source: © www.kitco.com, November 15, 2010.

[3] As previously pointed out, this pattern was not evident in the 1990s but is still thought to carry long-term validity.

Gold Coins Many of the storing and assaying costs associated with gold bullion can be avoided by investing directly in gold coins. There are three basic outlets for investing in gold coins. First, there are *gold bullion coins,* such as the South African Krugerrand, the Mexican 50 peso, and the Canadian Maple Leaf. These coins trade at a small premium of 2 to 3 percent over pure bullion value and afford the investor an excellent outlet for taking a position in the market. A second form is represented by *common date gold coins* that are no longer minted, such as the U.S. double eagle, the British sovereign, or the French Napoleon. These coins may trade at as much as 50 to 100 times their pure gold bullion value because of their value as collectibles. Finally, there are gold coins that are *old* and *rare* and that may trade at a numismatic value into the thousands or hundreds of thousands of dollars.

Gold Stocks In addition to gold bullion and gold coins, the investor may take a position in gold by simply buying common stocks of firms that have heavy gold-mining positions. Examples of such companies listed on U.S. exchanges include Newmont Mining (U.S.-based), Placer Dome Inc. (Canada-based), and ASA Limited (U.S.-based). Because these securities often move in the opposite direction of the stock market as a whole, they may provide excellent portfolio diversification.

www.placerdome.com

www.barrick.com

Gold Futures Contracts Finally, the gold investor may consider trading in futures contracts. Gold futures are traded on five different U.S. exchanges and on many foreign exchanges.[4]

Exchange-Traded Gold Fund (GLD) State Street Global Advisors launched an ETF that invested in gold in November of 2004. By April 2011 the ETF had approximately $52 billion of assets of which 100 percent were invested in gold. The exchange-traded fund pays out zero income so the investor is only buying the ability to cash in on gold's price appreciation or to lose out on it's declining price. The fund's price is set at 10 percent of an ounce of gold.

Silver

Silver has many of the same investment characteristics as gold in terms of being a hedge against inflation and a potential safe haven for investment during troubled times. Silver moved from $5 a troy ounce in 1976 to more than $50 an ounce in early 1980 and then back to $12 an ounce in 2006, only to hit $29 an ounce in 2010.

More so than gold, silver has heavy industrial and commercial applications. Areas of utilization include photography, electronic and electrical manufacturing, electroplating, dentistry, and silverware and jewelry. It is estimated that industrial uses of silver exceed annual production by 150 million ounces per year. Furthermore, the supply of silver does not necessarily increase with price because silver is a by-product of copper, lead, zinc, and gold. Because of the undersupply factor, many consider silver to be appropriate for long-term holding.

Investment in silver can also take many different forms. Some may choose to buy *silver bullion* in the form of silver bars. Because the price of silver generally is 1/25 to 1/75 the price of gold and larger bulk is involved for an equivalent dollar size investment, the storage and carrying costs can be quite high. Second, *silver coins* may be bought in large bags or as rare coins for their numismatic value. Keep in mind that dimes, quarters, and half-dollars minted during and before 1965 were 90 percent pure silver. As a third outlet, the investor may wish to consider *silver futures contracts.* Finally, the investor may purchase *stocks* of firms that have interests in silver mining, such as Hecla Mining or Echo Bay Mines.

www.hecla-mining.com

[4] There are also options on gold futures on the Comex.

the real world of investing

BASEBALL CARDS AS COLLECTIBLES

Although we most often associate baseball cards with the 10-year-old child who coaxes $2.00 from his parents to buy a pack of cards in the drugstore, there is actually a half-billion dollar a year industry out there. There are 100,000 serious baseball card collectors and millions of child arbitragers doing business on a daily basis.

Other forms of sports memorabilia have value as well. A baseball clearly autographed by Babe Ruth is worth about $8,000. An authentic Lou Gehrig game-worn uniform carries a $310,000 price tag. A truly enterprising collector went so far as to pay $500 for the dental records of Eddie Cicotte, a long-deceased pitcher for the infamous Chicago Black Sox of 1919.

In 2007, a 1910 Honus Wagner tobacco baseball card sold for more than $2.3 million. The previous high for the Wagner card was $1.1 million in 2001. In 1985, it had changed hands at $110,000. Why all the upside momentum? Wagner did not approve of smoking, and when his card appeared in a tobacco-related set around 1910, he forced the American Tobacco Company to pull all but 100 off the market. Now, only 40 Wagner cards are thought to exist, and the law of supply and demand has clearly set in.

Also, other forms of baseball memorabilia (besides cards) have done extremely well in the last few years. It all started with the Sotheby's (**www.sothebys.com**) auction of the Barry Halper memorabilia collection in 2000. Mr. Halper, a multimillionaire and minority owner of the New York Yankees, had the largest memorabilia collection of items such as autographed baseballs (going back to the 1920s), players' uniforms, and Ty Cobb and Babe Ruth signed documents in existence. The auction brought in two and three times the anticipated value of cherished items and started a renewed interest in memorabilia. As evidence, Mastro Fine Sports (**www.mastronet.com**) of Burr Ridge, Illinois, conducts memorabilia auctions over the Internet four or five times a year and normally grosses $10 to $12 million per auction. A 1927 Yankees autographed baseball, which was worth $5,000 a few years ago, recently went for $70,000. An autographed copy of the 1948 *Babe Ruth Story* purchased by one of the authors for $1,100 in 1999 went for $4,000 in May 2001. The ill-fated Cubs' Bartman "fan-interference ball" sold for $106,600 in December 2003. Finally, the sale of a Lou Gehrig uniform topped $350,000 in 2006.

PRECIOUS GEMS

Precious gems include diamonds, rubies, sapphires, and emeralds. Diamonds and other precious gems have appeal to investors because of their small size, easy concealment, and great durability. They are particularly popular in Europe because of a long-standing distrust of paper currencies as a store of value.

The distribution of diamonds is under virtual monopolistic control by De Beers Consolidated Mines of South Africa, Ltd. It controls the distribution of approximately 80 percent of the world's supply and has a stated policy of maintaining price control. Diamonds have generally enjoyed a steady, somewhat spectacular movement in price. For example, the price of a "D" color, one-carat, flawless, polished diamond increased more than tenfold between 1974 and 1980.

Of course, not all diamonds have done so well. Furthermore, there have been substantial breaks in the market, such as in 1974 and 1980–82 when diamond prices declined by one-fourth and more. Even with large increases in value, the diamond investor does not automatically come out ahead. Dealer markups may be anywhere from 10 to 100 percent so three to five years of steady gain may be necessary to show a substantial profit.

In no area of investment is product and market knowledge more important. Either you must be an expert yourself or know that you are dealing with an "honest" expert. Diamonds are judged on the basis of the four *c*'s (color, clarity, carat weight, and cut), and the assessment of any stone should be certified by a member of the

Gemological Institute of America. As is true of most valuable items, the investor is well advised to purchase the highest quality possible. You are considerably better off using the same amount of money to buy a higher quality, smaller carat diamond than a lesser quality, high-carat diamond.

OTHER COLLECTIBLES

A listing of other collectibles for investment might include art, antiques, stamps, Chinese ceramics, rare books, and other items that appeal to various sectors of our society. Each offers psychic pleasure to the investor as well as the opportunity for profit.

Anyone investing in a collectible should have some understanding of current market conditions and of the factors that determine the inherent worth of the item. Otherwise, you may be buying someone else's undesirable holding at a premium price. It is important not to get swept away in a buying euphoria. The best time to buy art, antiques, or stamps is when the bloom is off the market and dealers are overburdened with inventory, not when there is a weekly story in *The Wall Street Journal* or *BusinessWeek* about overnight fortunes being made. There seems to be a pattern or cycle in the collectibles market the same as in other markets (arts, antiques, and stamps actually do move together).

As is true of other markets, the wise investor in the collectibles market must be sensitive to dealer spreads. A price guide that indicates a doubling in value every two or three years may be meaningless if the person with whom you are dealing sells for $100 and buys back for $50. The wise investor/collector can best maintain profits by dealing with other collectors or investors and eliminating the dealer or middleman from the transaction where possible.

www.money.com

www.coinworld.com

www.linns.com

Such periodicals as *Money* magazine and *Collector/Investor* provide excellent articles on the collectibles market. Specialized periodicals, such as *American Arts and Antiques, Coin World, Linn's Stamp News, The Sports Collectors Digest,* and *Antique Monthly,* also are helpful. The interested reader can find books on almost any type of collectible in a public library or large bookstore.

exploring the web

Web Address	Comments
www.realtor.com	**Has property search function, mortgage evaluation function**
moneycentral.msn.com	**Has property valuation function along with mortgage financing calculator**
www.quicken.com	**Provides mortgage financing information and payment calculator**
www.nareit.com	**Web site for the industry trade group and provides information and data on REITs**
www.hsh.com	**Contains database of current residential mortgage rates**
www.realestate.com	**Provides information on property listings and mortgage financing and reports on property values and analysis**
www.gmacrealestate.com	**Provides property search, valuation calculation, and mortgage information**
www.housevalues.com	**Will estimate residential property values and provide report for homes in cities in its database**

SUMMARY

Investments in real assets must be considered in a total portfolio concept. They offer a measure of inflation protection, an opportunity for efficient diversification, and psychic pleasure to the investor.

A disadvantage is the absence of a large, liquid market such as that provided by the securities markets. There also may be a large dealer or middleman spread, and the investor may have to forgo current income.

The hysteria that grips these markets from time to time not only creates substantial opportunities for profit but also dictates that the investor must be particularly cautious about market timing. It can be quite expensive to be the last buyer in a gold or silver boom.

Valuing real estate requires many of the analytical techniques that are utilized in valuing stocks and bonds. The basic methods are the cost approach, comparable sales value, and the income approach. Often a weighted combination of the three is used to appraise real estate. A more sophisticated approach to valuing real estate is to do an in-depth cash flow/present value analysis as demonstrated in the appendix to the chapter.

Gold and silver represent two highly volatile forms of real assets in which price movements often run counter to events in the economy and the world. Bad news is good news (and vice versa) for precious-metal investors. Gold and silver may generally be purchased in bullion or bulk form, as coins, in the commodities futures market, or indirectly through securities of firms specializing in gold or silver mining.

Precious gems and other collectibles, such as art, antiques, stamps, Chinese ceramics, and rare books, have caught the attention of investors in various time periods. Although there are many warning signs at times, the wise and patient investor can do well over the long run. The investor should understand the factors that determine value before taking a serious investment position.

KEY WORDS AND CONCEPTS

adjustable rate mortgage 528
blind pool 530
comparative sales value 526
cost approach 526
equity participation 528
equity trusts 530
graduated payment mortgage 528
hybrid trusts 530
income approach 527
limited partnership 529
mortgage trusts 530
real assets 520
real estate investment trust (REIT) 530
shared appreciation mortgage 528
straight-line depreciation 539

DISCUSSION QUESTIONS

1. Why might real assets offer an opportunity as an inflation hedge?
2. Explain why real assets might add to effective portfolio diversification.
3. What are some disadvantages of investing in real estate?
4. What two factors have hurt real estate in recent times? Why might the future outlook be more positive?
5. What are the three primary approaches to real estate valuation? Should they be combined?
6. What is an adjustable rate mortgage?
7. For what type of borrower is the graduated payment mortgage best suited?

8. Explain a shared appreciation mortgage.
9. What is meant by a seller loan with a call privilege?
10. How is liability handled in a limited partnership?
11. What are REITs? What are the three types of REITs?
12. What are some factors that drive up the price of gold? What are factors that drive it down?
13. What are three different ways to invest in gold coins?
14. Suggest some commercial and industrial uses of silver. What forms can silver investments take?
15. Explain how the dealer spread can affect the rate of return on a collectible item.

INVESTMENT ADVISOR PROBLEM

Lance O'Brien thought he had finally hit the right investment for the $35,000 he had saved over the last 10 years while working as a store manager at a Zale's jewelry store in Tulsa, Oklahoma. It was a duplex near the downtown area of the city.

The property carried a price tag of $148,000 and produced net operating income of $13,000 per year. It was Lance's plan to put down his full $35,000 and borrow the balance. He felt the property would provide a steady income for his family (wife and two children).

Before he closed the deal, he decided to talk over the purchase with his father-in-law, Justin Maxwell, who worked as an investment advisor at a financial planning firm. Justin brought up the following questions:

a. Is the real estate likely to provide adequate liquidity?
b. All things being equal, is the duplex likely to provide a good hedge against inflation?
c. Does the duplex provide adequate diversification? If Lance wanted greater liquidity and diversification, what other form of real estate investment might he consider?
d. If the operating income from the duplex is capitalized (valued) at 8.5 percent, is he getting a good investment in terms of value?

How would Lance answer these questions?

WEB EXERCISE

Although the chapter covers many types of real assets, we will concentrate on real estate. The assumption is that you are interested in what property may be available in a given area. Go to **www.coldwellbanker.com**.

1. On the home page, under "Properties," do the following.
2. Put in your home city and state. Also select a maximum price such as $250,000, and click "Search."
3. Move down until you see a price that you or your parents can afford.
4. Write down the price, the number of bedrooms, the number of baths, and the square feet.
5. Does the property appear attractive to you?

Note: From time to time, companies redesign their Web sites, and occasionally a topic we have listed may have been deleted, updated, or moved into a different location.

APPENDIX 20A

A COMPREHENSIVE ANALYSIS FOR REAL ESTATE INVESTMENT DECISIONS

In any valuation of an asset, the ultimate worth is based on the present value of future cash flows. This not only applies to stocks, bonds, oil wells, and new business ventures, but to real estate as well.

To determine cash flow variables, we will follow these six steps:

1. Determine the purchase price, the size of the mortgage, and the annual mortgage payment.
2. Compute the net operating income for each year of the anticipated holding period.
3. Translate this to annual cash flow during the holding period.
4. Project the selling price of the property after the holding period.
5. Discount the annual cash flows and the anticipated selling price after the holding period back to the present to determine the present value of the future benefits.
6. Compare the upfront cash commitment to the present value of future benefits to determine if the property provides a positive net present value.

We will now discuss each of these steps.

1. Determine the Purchase Price and Financing Assume the Baily apartment complex (six units) can be purchased for $180,000. Discussion with a mortgage banker (lender) indicates a loan for 80 percent of the value would be available at 12 percent for 20 years. Thus, the loan would be for $144,000:

$$\$180{,}000 \times 80\% = \$144{,}000$$

The balance of the purchase price would be put up in cash ($36,000):

$$\$180{,}000 - \$144{,}000 = \$36{,}000$$

Next, we look up the annual mortgage payment. Examining Table 20A–1 below, we see on the first line that the annual mortgage payment for 20 years at 12 percent is $19,280.

2. Determine the Net Operating Income for Each Year We will assume the buyer intends to hold the property for four years and then sell it. Thus, we determine the value each year in Table 20A–2. The values are assumed to slightly increase with the passage of time. Next we translate net operating income into cash flow.

3. Determine Annual Cash Flow Up until now we have only computed income from operations. The real issue is how much cash flow is being generated. Other

TABLE 20A-1 Annual Mortgage Payment for a 20-Year Loan (principal amount equals $144,000)

	8%	10%	12%	14%	16%
Annual mortgage payment	$ 14,667	$ 16,913	($ 19,280)	$ 21,742	$ 24,287
First-year interest expense	11,520	14,400	17,280	20,160	23,040
Total interest over the life of the loan	149,340	194,260	241,600	290,840	341,700

TABLE 20A-2 Annual Net Operating Income

	Year 1	Year 2	Year 3	Year 4
Gross annual rental				
(6 units × $450 × 12 months in first year)	$32,400	$34,100	$36,400	$38,100
Less 5% vacancy rate	1,620	1,705	1,820	1,905
Net rental income	$30,780	$32,395	$34,580	$36,195
Less operating expenses				
Property taxes	$ 5,000	$ 5,100	$ 5,200	$ 5,300
Maintenance	1,500	1,550	1,650	1,710
Utilities	1,960	2,072	2,205	2,310
Insurance	2,200	2,240	2,290	2,340
Total operating expenses	$10,660	$10,962	$11,345	$11,660
Net operating income	$20,120	$21,433	$23,235	$24,535

TABLE 20A-3 Taxable Income or Loss

	Year 1	Year 2	Year 3	Year 4
Net operating income	$20,120	$21,433	$23,235	$24,535
Less				
Depreciation	5,096	5,096	5,096	5,096
Interest expense	17,280	17,040	16,767	16,405
Taxable income (loss)	$ (2,256)	$ (703)	$ 1,372	$ 3,034

nonoperating factors that must be considered are interest expense, depreciation, taxable income or losses (and related taxes or tax shield benefits), and repayment of the mortgage.

In Table 20A–3, we subtract depreciation and interest expense from net operating income to determine taxable income or loss for each year. But before we look at the bottom line in Table 20A–3, let's briefly discuss depreciation and interest expense. **Straight-line depreciation** is based on a straight-line deduction of the value of the depreciable asset over a period for 27.5 years. This time period applies to rental residential property and is mandated under the Tax Reform Act of 1986.

You may recall the purchase price of the property was $180,000. We assume $40,000 of the purchase price represents land (which cannot be depreciated), so the amount of depreciable assets is $140,000. Assuming 27.5-year straight-line depreciation, 3.64 percent (1 ÷ 27.5 years) can be deducted each year. Based on $140,000 in depreciable assets, the annual write-off is $5,096 per year (line 3 in Table 20A–3). Depreciation is a particularly valuable deduction because it reduces taxable income but does not represent an actual cash payment.

The deduction for interest expense is also important and changes from year to year as the loan balance becomes smaller. The interest expense is merely given in this case (line 4 of Table 20A–3), but it can be easily computed through interest amortization tables. As an example, in the first year the beginning loan balance is $144,000, and with 12 percent interest, interest owed in the first year is $17,280.

We now look to the bottom line of Table 20A–3. The main observation is that there are taxable losses in the first two years and taxable income in the last two years. The losses in the first two years may potentially be used to offset income from other sources. To the extent the investor is actively involved with

TABLE 20A-4 Tax Shield Benefits or Taxes Owed

	Year 1	Year 2	Year 3	Year 4
Taxable income (or loss)	$(2,256)	$(703)	$1,372	$3,034
Tax rate	30%	30%	30%	30%
Tax shield benefits or taxes owed	$ 677	$ 211	$ (412)	$ (910)

TABLE 20A-5 Annual Cash Flow

	Year 1	Year 2	Year 3	Year 4
Net operating income	$20,120	$21,433	$23,235	$24,535
Tax shield benefit or taxes owed	677	211	(412)	(910)
Annual mortgage payment	(19,280)	(19,280)	(19,280)	(19,280)
Cash flow	$ 1,517	$ 2,364	$ 3,543	$ 4,345

the property (it is not a passive investment under the terms of the Tax Reform Act of 1986), he or she will be able to use the losses as a tax shield (shelter) for other income.

Assuming the investor is in a 30 percent tax bracket, the taxable losses in Years 1 and 2 translate into the tax shield benefits shown in Table 20A–4. Of course, the taxable income in Years 3 and 4 will require that taxes be paid.

We are now in a position to achieve our goal in step 3: determine annual cash flow. We have three forms of cash flow coming in. The first is net operating income (Table 20A–2), and the second is annual tax shield benefits or taxes owed (Table 20A–4). The third annual cash flow is the annual mortgage payment.[1] We can turn back to the circled item in Table 20A–1 to easily determine this value. It will apply to each of the four years of the holding period.

The three sources of cash flow are brought together in Table 20A–5 to determine the total annual value of cash flow.

We now move on to step 4. That is, after determining the annual cash flows during the four-year holding period, it is time to look at the potential sales price for the property after the holding period.

4. Project the Sales Price The investor initially paid $180,000 for the property, and we assume it increases in value by 6 percent per year over the four-year holding period. Using Appendix A for four periods at 6 percent, the compound sum factor is 1.262. This translates into a sales value of $227,160:

$180,000	Purchase price
× 1.262	Compound sum factor
$227,160	Value after 4 years

The investor, who is now the seller, will likely have to pay a real estate commission and other fees, which we will assume total 7 percent. The amount is $15,901 (7% × $227,160). This leaves the investor with a value of $211,259:

$227,160	Sales price
− 15,901	Commission and fees
$211,259	Net proceeds

[1] The interest component of the annual mortgage payment was deducted in computing taxable income or loss, but it was not subtracted out as a cash item. Therefore, it is appropriately included as part of the annual mortgage payment to determine cash flow.

To the extent the net proceeds exceed the book value of the property, a capital gains tax will also have to be paid. The book value of the property is equal to the initial purchase price minus depreciation to date. The purchase price was $180,000, and four years of depreciation at $5,096 per year have been taken (third line of Table 20A–3 on page 539). Thus the book value is:

$ 180,000	Purchase price
− 20,384	4 years of depreciation (4 × $5,096)
$159,616[2]	Book value

The difference between the net proceeds from the sale and the book value is $51,643:

$211,259	Net proceeds
− 159,616	Book value
$ 51,643	Capital gain

The profit is categorized as a capital gain and it is subject to a maximum tax rate of 15 percent.[3] You will recall the investor paid a 30 percent tax on normal operating income, but investments held for over a year normally qualify for preferential capital gains treatment.

The capital gains tax in this case would be $7,746 (15% × $51,643). This would leave the investor with funds from the sale of $203,513:

$211,259	Net proceeds
− 7,746	Capital gains tax
$203,513	Funds from the sale

From this sum, the investor must pay off the mortgage balance that exists after four years as he or she closes out the ownership position. The mortgage banker informs us this is equal to $134,432.[4]

The cash flows from the sale minus the mortgage balance leave the investor with net cash flow from the sale of $69,081:

$203,513	Funds from the sale
− 134,432	Payoff of mortgage
$ 69,081	Net cash flow (from sale)

5. Determine the Present Value of All Benefits Because we have computed the annual cash flows from the four years of operations as well as the net cash flow from selling the property, we are now in a position to determine the present value of the benefits. We assume the investor in this particular example has a required return of 12 percent on real estate investments, and we use that as the discount rate in Table 20A–6. The present value of the future cash flows is $52,461.

---

[2] This value is the same as taking depreciable assets of $140,000 minus depreciation to date of $20,384 and adding back $40,000 in original land value:

$140,000	Depreciable assets
− 20,384	Depreciation to date
$119,616	
+ 40,000	Land
$159,616	Book value

[3] The recaptured depreciated amount could be taxed at 30 percent; however, we will disregard this complication.

[4] This value is computed by subtracting the repayment of principal each year from the initial mortgage.

TABLE 20A-6 Present Value of the Cash Flows

Year	Cash Flow (Table 20A-5)	Present Value Factor (12%)	Present Value
1	$ 1,517	0.893	$ 1,355
2	2,364	0.797	1,884
3	3,543	0.712	2,523
4	$73,426[a]	0.636	$46,699
		Total present value of cash flows	$52,461

[a] Fourth-year annual cash flow of $4,345 plus net cash flow from the sale of $69,081.

6. Compare the Upfront Cash Payment to the Benefits The upfront cash investment was $36,000, and the present value of all future cash flows is $52,461. This indicates a net present value for the investment of $16,461:

$52,461	Present value of future cash flows
− 36,000	Upfront cash investment
$16,461	Net present value

Clearly, the project earns well in excess of the required return on the investment of 12 percent and is an acceptable investment. The actual yield or interest rate of return is slightly in excess of 22 percent. But keep in mind that real estate may be a very illiquid investment, and almost all the return is based on a 6 percent annual increase in value. The annual operating gains are almost negligible. Nevertheless, this does appear to be an attractive investment.

PRACTICE PROBLEMS AND SOLUTIONS

1. An investor is considering purchasing a fourplex for $190,000. A loan for 20 years at 80 percent of the purchase price is available at 12 percent. Determine the size of the loan and the amount that he will have to put up in cash.
2. The investor intends to hold the property for three years and then sell it. He is going to compute net operating income for the first year and then assume that this amount will grow by 6 percent over the next two years.

   Given the information below, compute the net operating income for the first year (following the procedure in Table 20A–2 on page 539). Then assume that the amount will grow by 6 percent per year to determine net operating income in the second and third years.

Gross annual rental (4 units at $450 per month), 5% vacancy rate	
Property taxes	$2,800
Maintenance	900
Utilities	800
Insurance	1,250

Solutions

1.

$190,000	
80%	
$152,000	Size of loan
$190,000	Purchase price
152,000	Loan
$ 38,000	Cash investment

2.

First Year – Net Operating Income	
Gross annual rental	$21,600
(4 units × 450 × 12 months in the first year)	
Less 5% vacancy rate	1,080
Net rental income	$20,520

Less operating expenses:	
Property taxes	$2,800
Maintenance	900
Utilities	800
Insurance	1,250
Total operating expenses	$ 5,750
Net operating income	$14,770

	Year 1	Year 2	Year 3
Net operating income (6% increase after 1st year)	$14,770	$15,656	$16,595

PROBLEMS

Real estate Investment analysis

1. An investor is considering purchasing an apartment complex for $240,000. A loan for 20 years at 75 percent of the purchase price is available at 10 percent.
   a. Determine the size of the loan and the amount that will have to be put up in cash. Assume the annual mortgage payment is $21,142.
   b. The investor intends to hold the property for three years and then sell it. He is going to compute net operating income for the first year and then assume that amount will grow by 5 percent over the next two years.

   Given the information below, compute net operating income for the first year (following the procedure in Table 20A–2 on page 539). Then assume that amount will grow by 5 percent per year to determine net operating income in the second and third years.

First Year Data	
Gross annual rental (8 units at $500 per month), 6% vacancy rate:	
Property taxes	$6,600
Maintenance	1,900
Utilities	2,360
Insurance	2,600

   c. Determine depreciation for each of the first three years. The building has a value of $190,000 (the remaining $50,000 is land value). Assume straight-line depreciation with a 27.5 year write-off.
   d. Assume interest expense for the first three years is as follows:

Year 1	$18,000
Year 2	17,686
Year 3	17,340

Based on the information you computed in parts *b* and *c* and the data given in part *d,* compute taxable income (use a procedure similar to Table 20A–3 on page 539).

e. Determine taxes owed for each of the three years. Use a procedure similar to the last two columns of Table 20A–4 on page 540. Assume a tax rate of 35 percent.

f. Using net operating income from part *b,* taxes owed from part *d,* and annual mortgage payments for each of the three years of $21,142, compute cash flow for each of the three years. Use a procedure similar to that in Table 20A–5 on page 540.

g. Assume the property increases in value by 8 percent per year over the next three years. Use Appendix A to determine how much the initial value of $240,000 will grow to after three years.

h. Deduct from the sales value computed in part *g,* 6 percent in commissions and fees to arrive at net proceeds.

i. Assume the property has a book value of $219,252. Subtract this value from net proceeds computed in part *h*. The difference represents capital gains.

j. Multiply the capital gains times 15 percent to get the capital gains tax.

k. Subtract the capital gains tax (part *j*) from the net proceeds (part *h*) to get funds from the sale.

l. You must pay off (subtract) the remaining mortgage of $169,600 from the funds from the sale (part *k*) to arrive at net cash flow from the sale.

m. Determine the present value of all the benefits at a discount rate of 9 percent from Appendix C. Set this up in a similar fashion to Table 20A–6 on page 542. The cash flow in Years 1 and 2 can be found in part *f.* The cash flow for Year 3 is the sum of Year 3 from part *f* plus the value in part *m.*

n. Subtract the upfront cash investment of $60,000 ($240,000 purchase price minus $180,000 initial mortgage) from the total percent value of cash flows (part *m*) to determine the net present value. Should the property be purchased based on the net present value?

chapter twenty-one

ALTERNATIVE INVESTMENTS: PRIVATE EQUITY AND HEDGE FUNDS

OBJECTIVES

1. Explain the different types of private equity/venture capital funds available for investing.
2. Explain how alternative investments can help diversify a portfolio and enhance the risk/return trade-off.
3. Understand the private equity process, from fundraising through the distribution of profits, including the time horizon for the entire process to be complete.
4. Describe the relationship between general partners and limited partners, and discuss how the two share returns.
5. Understand the different hedge fund strategies and how they generate returns and lower risk.

OUTLINE

CORE SATELLITE PORTFOLIOS

One method professional managers use to manage pension funds, endowment funds, foundations, and other large portfolios that have a long-term focus with a required payout is the **core satellite portfolio approach**. The reason we mention large portfolios is because some of these alternative investments require large amounts of money to enter the game. Figure 21–1 is a basic picture of how a manager might think of investing in alternative investments after he has established a basic domestic stock and bond portfolio.

Why do alternatives make sense for institutional investors? First, most of these asset classes (hedge funds, private equity, real estate, international, and natural resources) are not highly correlated with common stock portfolios or bonds, and perhaps not even highly correlated among themselves. So a basic reason is to

FIGURE 21–1 Core-Satellite Portfolio Structure

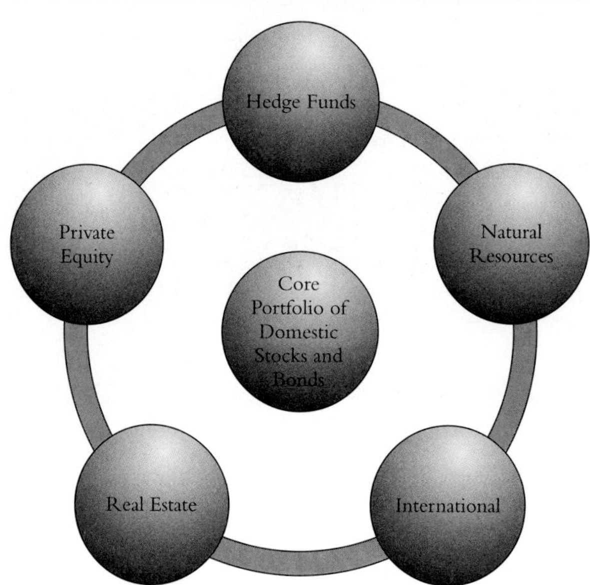

reduce the standard deviation of the portfolio while perhaps increasing the rate of return at the same time. We have already covered real estate and international stock markets, and in both cases demonstrated how these two asset classes can reduce correlation and increase returns. Several of the other asset classes in Figure 21–1 do the same thing.

Natural resources include many categories, such as minerals like gold, silver, platinum, copper, lead, and tin. It can also include petroleum, timber, farmland, and commodities such as grains, sugar, coffee, and other agricultural products. Not all of these will be direct investments, but they could be bought through hedge funds, private equity funds, and real estate investment trusts.

PRIVATE EQUITY

The term **private equity** refers to all equity investments in nonpublic companies. The most common categories are venture capital, leveraged buyouts, and mezzanine debt, and sometimes a category called "special situations" is included. For example, special situations might include infrastructure investing, an area that has gained in popularity. Besides the traditional venture capital firms that specialize in making these types of investments, many corporations have set up venture capital divisions to invest in companies that might have technologies or products that could be compatible with their products. Venture capital investments by companies such as Intel, Microsoft, Google, and Apple may eventually lead to an acquisition or partnership with the venture firm or technology that can be licensed and used in their products.

Venture Capital

Venture capital firms raise money for investment into a variety of companies at various stages of their development. Venture capital firms can be sorted in terms of corporate development: early-stage, middle-stage (sometimes referred to as expansion stage), and late-stage investing. Venture capital firms generally specialize in one of these areas rather than cover the whole spectrum. Before a venture capital firm gets involved with an investment in a startup company, the company must have a track record and will most likely have investors who helped finance the company's initial stage of development.

When an individual gets an idea for a new product or company, he or she often asks friends and relatives for help in financing the startup company. These investors are usually called **angel investors** because they have faith in the person starting the company and are willing to risk their capital to help get it started. Sometimes this capital is called **seed capital**, because it helps plant the seed that could turn into a large, productive company. If this seed capital gets the company off the ground, then the owners have a chance to get early-stage capital from a venture capital firm. For example, in Google's case Andy Bechtolsheim, co-founder of Sun Microsystems, provided the first $100,000 of funding to Google in August 1998.[1]

Early-Stage Venture Capital **Early-stage venture capital** is highly risky, and the failure rate for venture capital investors is quite high. These types of investors generally expect to fail often and succeed rarely, but the key is to invest in many companies and hope that you hit a home run (to use a baseball analogy) in more than one of the investments. Google would be an example of more than just a home run; perhaps a game-winning, grand slam walk-off home run would be more like it. There are many venture capital firms, but the center of venture capital for technology-based companies is Silicon Valley in California. For example, it was Kleiner Perkins Caufield & Byers (KPCB) and Sequoia Capital that provided the initial venture capital for Google on June 7, 1999. These two venture capital firms were major competitors, as are most early-stage venture capital companies. The two together provided Google with $25 million.[2] See the Real World of Investing box for other companies that KPCB has funded and developed.

One of the benefits the private equity firm brings to a startup private company is experience, which most entrepreneurs don't have. Early-stage companies are often in the process of preparing their marketing, manufacturing, and sales plans. A private equity company has marketing and finance specialists in their firm and partners who know the industry and can give advice. They have developed a cadre of experts over the years and can match the venture capital startup with experts who can help develop a better business model and strategy. For a company looking for venture capital, it is not just about finding money, but also about finding a private equity firm that can help grow the business.

Private Equity Funds for Middle- and Late-Stage Companies

Once a private company is well organized and growing, it may need more capital, and so there are private equity funds that invest in middle-stage (expansion stage) and late-stage developed companies. **Middle-stage or expansion companies** are four or five years away from an initial public offering and are growing their market. In this stage they are getting their production ramped up to meet market demand and have established a market niche. They may not need late-stage capital if they can generate enough profit to continue their growth. **Late-stage companies** are producing and shipping goods and are often two or three years away from an initial public offering. Late-stage financing helps increase the financial resources and dresses up the balance sheet for the public offering. It often allows an expansion of business through larger inventory and an increased sales staff. However, when a company is successful, it is the early-stage investors that make the biggest profits in the end. The angel investors' ownership position can become so diluted by the venture capital infusions that they often don't participate in the grand slam home run like the early-stage investors.

Buyout Funds **Buyout funds** purchase existing public companies or a division of a public company that needs to be restructured. Often these companies are in

[1] Kopytoff, Verne, and Dan Fost. "For early Googlers, key word is $$$," San Francisco Chronicle, April 29, 2004. Sourced from Wikipedia November 22, 2010.

[2] ibid

the real world of investing

KLEINER PERKINS CAUFIELD & BYERS, VENTURE CAPITAL AT ITS BEST

Kleiner Perkins Caufield & Byers (KPCB) is committed to helping entrepreneurs build enduring market-changing institutions, defining new business sectors or expanding existing ones. Since 1972 their partners have supported hundreds of entrepreneurs in building more than 600 companies, including such household names as Amazon, Sun, Genentech, Intuit, VeriSign, and Google. These are well-known names, and ones that got their start with some help from KPCB. As stated on the KPCB Web site:

> We work tirelessly on behalf of entrepreneurs and share the benefits of our experience to develop new enterprises. Our Relationship Capital creates an informal, far-reaching network to assist entrepreneurs as they learn from one another and build the great businesses of tomorrow . . . We're constantly on the lookout for ideas with the promise to invent new business categories or radically alter existing ones. Our passion is for new technologies and new applications of technology that will drive high-impact change.

Examples of KPCB's focus areas include green technology, information technology, and life sciences. In the area of green technology, it focuses on scientific breakthroughs in biology and material technology that might reduce our dependence on fossil fuels and reduce atmospheric CO_2 levels. KPCB feels that this area of investment could be the hot spot of the 21st century. It has partnered with Al Gore and his Generation Investment Management in the hopes that his connections and expertise will help KPCB find viable firms in this area. Here are two examples of private companies in this area that KPCB has invested in:

Fisker Automotive
Fisker Automotive is a green American premium sports car company with a mission to create a range of beautiful, environmentally friendly cars that make environmental sense without compromise.

GreatPoint Energy
Commercializing a proprietary catalytic process for converting coal (and other carbon-based feedstocks) into clean-burning, pipeline-quality natural gas.

KPCB has been a leader since their founding in 1972. Over the years it has funded and helped to develop some of the world's major technology companies, such as Sun, EA, Xilinx, Symantec, Intuit, Juniper, Netscape, VeriSign, Amazon, ISS, and Google. KPCB invests across

financial trouble or do not have enough capital to compete efficiently. Some might be called turnaround companies because they are heading in the wrong direction. Many of these companies have bad management or lack of management depth across key areas. These funds are often referred to as leveraged buyout funds (LBOs) because they use a minimum amount of equity and a large amount of debt to acquire the company, with the hopes of using free cash flow from operations to pay off the debt. After many years, the debt is paid off, the company is restructured, and an initial public offering is made to exit the company and get a return on the investments. Not all leveraged buyouts work out, and some end up in bankruptcy, overburdened with debt they can't pay off.

One very well-known buyout fund is Kohlberg Kravis and Roberts (KKR), which has had great success taking companies private through leveraged buyouts. One of the most famous deals was the Duracell Company. Kraft Foods acquired Duracell through the acquisition of Dart Industries. After a while it became clear to the management of Duracell that Kraft wasn't giving this division the attention they needed to grow their business. Duracell's management thought that Kraft didn't understand the battery market or the advertising necessary to grow the brand. Management made an offer to buy the division from Kraft with the help of KKR, and in 1988 KKR invested $1.9 billion in a management leveraged buyout. We call this a management leveraged buyout because management of Duracell stayed intact and held 30 percent of the equity in the company after the buyout. Duracell now had the capital they needed to expand advertising and research. As in most leverage buyouts, the firm streamlined operations by selling off some assets to pay down debt and additionally downsized the number of employees.

All in all the plan worked very well, and in a record amount of time. KKR took the company public in 1989, raising about $450 million but retaining 61 percent of the company. In 1995, KKR had a secondary offering of more shares that brought

a broad area of technology, including consumer, enterprise, semiconductors, security, and communications. As the KPCB website explains:

> We are a selective hands-on firm. We invest in what we believe to be the category-defining companies. With every investment, we aim to make a difference and to build enduring, significant institutions. We invest primarily in early stage ventures often incubating new companies around proven entrepreneurs and good ideas.

On October 21, 2010, KPCB raised a $250 million private equity fund to invest in social networking entrepreneurs.

Another area of KPCB focus is the life sciences industry:

> We were the first venture capital firm to form a dedicated Life Sciences Group practice. We have partnered with scientists and entrepreneurs to build over 100 companies and their breakthrough products in medical devices, drugs, vaccines, personalized medicine, diagnostics, and healthcare IT and services. We have worked shoulder to shoulder with the teams in our companies to pioneer recombinant DNA, monoclonal antibodies, molecular diagnostics, implantable therapeutic devices, combinatorial chemistry, non-viral vaccines, laser treatments, and protein drug discovery. Our family of companies includes Genentech, Hybritech, GenProbe, Align, Millennium Pharmaceuticals, eHealthinsurance, WebMD, Genomic Health, Idec Pharmaceuticals, and many others using innovation (or innovative technologies) to help solve important unmet medical needs. KPCB has built a powerful and large network of scientists, executives, policy experts, and business development activities so that we can help young companies translate their dreams from "bench to bedside" faster and more effectively. We have founded and co-led several important conferences, such as the annual "Laguna Biotech CEO Meeting at Laguna Niguel," now in its 22nd year. We are actively looking for new and exciting opportunities.

One example of KPCB's private equity investments in this area is Pacific Biosciences:

> **Pacific Biosciences**
> Commercializing a disruptive 3rd-Generation DNA sequencing system based on Single Molecule Real Time (SMRT) detection technology.

Source: Kleiner Perkins Caufield & Byers: website: http://www.kpcb.com/portfolio/, accessed November 22, 2010.

their ownership position down to 29 percent, and in 1996 Gillette bought all of Duracell for over $7 billion. As you can imagine, KKR made a very nice profit on this deal, as did the original management team. So if you ever wondered why some Gillette razors now come equipped with batteries, you have the answer. Gillette thought that Duracell would be a great fit because Gillette was already selling its products in thousands of consumer stores worldwide and could use their distribution system for Duracell batteries. In 2005, Procter & Gamble bought Gillette for $51 billion in one of the biggest consumer product mergers of all time.

Raising Capital for a Private Equity Fund

Private equity funds raise capital from private investors who must meet standards of wealth and income to be an approved investor and must sign a disclosure stating that they are qualified investors. For example, to be a **qualified investor** an individual may need to have income of $250,000 for the past three years and $1 million in assets, not including a home. In other words, the investor needs at least $1 million of financial assets. Most qualified investors have much more than $1 million in financial assets, and some of the largest investors in private equity are public and private pension funds. As you can imagine, the economic situation in 2008–2010 has reduced investors' appetite for risk. Table 21–1 shows the number of funds that successfully raised capital during the years 2005 through the third quarter of 2010.

In Table 21–1, 2007 was the peak year, with 252 funds raising capital. By 2009 there were only 151 funds that raised capital for venture capital investments. Additionally, the number of new and follow-on funds started to decline in 2009 and 2010. A **follow-on fund** is defined as an existing fund that is raising another fund. This fund could be one in a series of funds developed by the same venture capital company.

TABLE 21-1 Venture Capital Funds: New vs. Follow-On Funds

Years	New Funds	Follow-On Funds	Total
2005	54	191	245
2006	67	176	243
2007	77	175	252
2008	63	166	229
2009	42	109	151
2010	35	89	124

Source: Thomson Reuters and National Venture Capital Association, www.thomsonreuters.com.

Funds that have been successful and in existence for 20 or 30 years could be starting their eighth or ninth fund, or even more. New funds are often started by experienced individuals at a private equity fund, who decide to leave and develop their own private equity fund. Table 21–1 also shows the number of new and follow-on funds, and again the peak is in 2007, after which the trend is down.

One interesting thing about raising a new fund or a follow-on fund is the commitment the investor makes when she is accepted as a qualified investor. Suppose an individual investor agrees to invest \$1 million, or a pension fund agrees to invest \$25 million, in a new \$500 million venture capital fund. The fund expects to invest this \$500 million into private companies, but it will not have identified the future investments that it will make with these funds. Because of this, the fund does not expect all of the money an investor agrees to invest to be deposited at the beginning of the fund. Once the fund raises the \$500 million in commitments, it will close the fund and begin accepting proposals from companies seeking funding, and it will also begin looking for places to invest its funds. When the fund finds a potential investment, it will make a capital call on its investors, and they will be obligated to make a payment into the fund to cover their share of the investment. Sometimes it will take up to four or five years for a fund to be fully invested, and an investor might have capital returned from successful investments before she has put in all the capital she has committed.

Table 21–2 presents the amount of capital raised by venture capital firms from 1995 through the third quarter of 2010, by stage of development. Notice that 1999

TABLE 21-2 Private Equity by Stage of Development

Year	Seed	Early Stage	Expansion or Middle Stage	Late Stage	Total	Number of Deals
1995	\$1,140,354,900	\$ 1,674,250,000	\$ 3,410,434,000	\$ 1,118,199,800	\$ 7,343,238,700	1,863
1996	1,223,235,800	2,496,181,800	5,265,986,100	1,549,197,400	10,534,601,100	2,601
1997	1,281,483,100	3,345,858,700	7,255,481,400	2,196,206,900	14,079,030,100	3,201
1998	1,641,533,200	4,999,919,700	9,754,737,400	3,208,238,200	19,604,428,500	3,694
1999	**3,474,361,100**	**10,764,387,300**	**28,699,996,900**	**8,492,631,300**	**51,431,376,600**	**5,555**
2000	**2,963,221,500**	**23,710,056,700**	**57,376,141,200**	**16,004,232,900**	**100,053,652,300**	**7,979**
2001	713,673,300	8,116,263,400	21,682,518,800	7,699,761,400	38,212,216,900	4,546
2002	314,262,400	3,690,849,800	11,770,670,400	5,091,943,500	20,867,726,100	3,158
2003	335,087,600	3,480,769,500	9,441,997,300	5,649,531,200	18,907,385,600	2,991
2004	462,989,600	3,843,210,800	9,080,413,800	8,411,098,500	21,797,712,700	3,146
2005	917,781,900	3,841,796,800	8,342,733,800	9,499,584,000	22,601,896,500	3,194
2006	1,243,334,400	4,203,229,300	11,010,855,700	9,606,611,900	26,064,031,300	3,748
2007	1,499,801,400	5,717,302,600	10,861,533,200	11,955,863,300	30,034,500,500	4,029
2008	1,717,927,500	5,267,831,300	10,347,162,800	10,727,484,900	28,060,406,500	4,014
2009	1,728,423,000	4,654,190,700	5,718,834,400	6,148,939,400	18,250,387,500	2,916
2010 3Q	1,511,057,100	4,003,281,700	6,202,269,200	4,972,685,100	16,689,293,100	2,497

Source: PricewaterhouseCoopers/National Venture Capital Association Money Tree™ Report. Data: Thomson Reuters.

and 2000 were the peak years, with $51 billion and $100 billion in capital raised. These were the Internet bubble years, when any stock that had anything to do with Internet technology or computers sold at extremely high price–earnings multiples or high price to sales per share multiples if the company had no earnings.

More often than not these companies had no earnings, but the venture capitalists were afraid to miss out on potential opportunities to make a killing. Many companies that started out in this period became well-known and profitable companies, such as Amazon, eBay, and Google, and made fantastic returns for their investors. Hundreds of others went out of business without ever generating a profit. The year 1999 saw 5,555 deals funded, and 7,979 deals were funded in 2000. The deals in the year 2000 were more than the total of the deals for 1995, 1996, and 1997 combined. Looking back, one can see the evidence of a bubble much more clearly now than during the period. The $100 billion raised in 2000 was more than the total raised during the next four years, when the bubble burst. The stock market started down in 2000 and suffered three years of losses in a row during 2000–2002.

Private equity funds specialize in certain industries. For example, one fund may raise capital for investing in biotechnology and another might specialize in social networking Web site development or Internet-related companies. Others might specialize in energy or infrastructure projects. Table 21–3 gives a view of investments by industry over the period 2003–2010. You can see from the table that software has been a hot area for all periods and accounts for almost 19 percent of the funds invested over this eight-year period. Biotechnology runs a close second place with over 16 percent invested, and is followed by medical devices and equipment with a little over 10 percent of funds raised. Industrial and energy are next, with semiconductors and telecommunications close behind. The rest of the industries hold small percentages with little variation over time. Table 21–3 gives a good list of the categories of venture capital and private equity investments, and it shows that the money primarily goes to industries with the most innovation and growth opportunities. However, it also demonstrates that there are basic industries such as business services, health care services, financial services, and consumer products that also take a small share of the pie.

TABLE 21-3 Amount Invested by Industry (in millions)

	2003	2004	2005	2006	2007	2008	2009	2010	Total	Percent
Biotechnology	$ 3,563	$ 4,155	$ 3,685	$ 4,364	$ 5,164	$ 4,457	$ 3,626	$ 3,149	$ 32,163	**16.87%**
Business Products & Services	649	397	341	547	639	482	242	331	3,629	1.90
Computers and Peripherals	400	614	545	525	527	441	336	329	3,717	1.95
Consumer Products & Services	159	268	307	358	393	374	372	354	2,587	1.36
Electronics/Instrumentation	185	361	405	709	548	613	313	340	3,474	1.82
Financial Services	398	509	879	445	575	494	372	465	4,137	2.17
Healthcare Services	211	365	402	363	279	181	108	196	2,106	1.10
Industrial/Energy	674	785	825	1,837	2,877	4,415	2,339	2,440	16,192	**8.49**
IT Services	655	726	1,001	1,360	1,788	1,872	1,106	1,175	9,682	5.08
Media and Entertainment	824	888	1,128	1,718	1,990	1,715	1,205	885	10,353	5.43
Medical Devices & Equipment	1,545	1,827	2,226	2,811	3,740	3,462	2,564	1,902	20,077	**10.53**
Networking and Equipment	1,702	1,536	1,474	1,198	1,546	756	752	474	9,439	4.95
Other	1,030	900	57	4	1	0	9	27	2,029	1.06
Retailing/Distributions	6,436	185	208	188	359	266	186	133	7,961	4.17
Semiconductors	1,782	2,062	1,997	2,152	2,234	1,649	864	895	13,635	7.15
Software	4,428	5,286	4,801	4,878	5,373	5,212	3,273	2,903	36,154	**18.96**
Telecommunications	1,666	1,834	2,320	2,608	2,000	1,671	583	689	13,372	7.01
Grand Total	**$26,308**	**22,697**	**22,602**	**26,064**	**30,035**	**28,060**	**18,250**	**16,689**	**190,706**	**100.00**

Source: PricewaterhouseCoopers/National Venture Capital Association Money Tree™ Report. Data: Thomson Reuters.

TABLE 21-4 Corporate Venture Capital Group Investment Analysis, 1995 through Q3 2010

Corporate Venture Capital Group Investment Analysis 1995 through Q3 2010

Year	Count of All Venture Capital Deals	Number of Deals with CVC Involvement	Calculated Percentage of Deals with CVC Involvement	$M Average Amount of All VC Deals	$M Average Amount of CVC Participation	Total VC Investment $M	Total CVC Investment $M	Calculated Percentage of Dollars Coming from CVCs
1995	1,864	141	7.6%	$ 3.94	$3.29	7,343.24	463.78	6.3%
1996	2,601	219	8.4	4.05	3.67	10,534.05	803.07	7.6
1997	3,201	329	10.3	4.39	2.82	14,067.43	926.16	6.6
1998	3,694	500	13.5	5.31	3.36	19,598.99	1,680.06	8.6
1999	5,555	1,209	21.8	9.25	6.30	51,377.81	7,611.76	14.8
2000	7,979	1,972	24.7	12.54	7.75	100,021.64	15,276.74	15.3
2001	4,546	965	21.2	8.39	4.83	38,140.62	4,657.66	12.2
2002	3,158	552	17.5	6.60	3.52	20,852.47	1,941.42	9.3
2003	2,991	438	14.6	6.32	2.95	18,904.86	1,293.16	6.8
2004	3,146	515	16.4	6.93	2.90	21,787.47	1,493.98	6.9
2005	3,194	510	16.0	7.07	2.88	22,594.65	1,466.42	6.5
2006	3,750	625	16.7	6.96	3.27	26,111.13	2,042.64	7.8
2007	4,029	726	18.0	7.44	3.33	29,976.55	2,416.41	8.1
2008	4,013	752	18.7	6.99	2.85	28,067.19	2,144.51	7.6
2009	2,917	368	12.6	6.26	3.72	18,254.08	1,367.32	7.5
9M10	2,498	321	12.9	6.70	4.49	16,737.79	1,440.96	8.6

Source: PricewaterhouseCoopers/National Venture Capital Association MoneyTree™ Report, Data: Thomson Reuters.

Corporate Venture Capital Funds

As mentioned earlier in this chapter, one area that is often under the radar is investments by large public companies into small private companies. For example, in 2009 over 30 percent of the investments made in biotechnology were made by corporate venture capital funds. These funds could be part of a large pharmaceutical company looking for biotech companies that may be developing new drugs but need capital for the phase I, II, and III trials required by the Federal Drug Administration. In the software area, 14 percent of the investments were made by corporate funds. These could be funds operated by a technology company such as Microsoft, Oracle, EMC, or Adobe, or other software-oriented companies looking for ways to improve their software offerings. A third area is the industrial/energy area. In 2009 this area accounted for almost 12 percent of corporate private equity investment, but in the third quarter it amounted to 26.7 percent of the total. The rapid increase in this area is due to the rise of energy initiatives for wind, solar, and other non-carbon-related green-energy technologies.[3]

Table 21–4 shows corporate venture capital activity from 1995 through the third quarter of 2010. The table presents the total venture capital deals and the number of deals with corporate venture capital involvement and their percentage of participation. It also shows that corporations were no smarter than the rest of the market, as their activity also peaked in 1999 and 2000 at the height of the Internet bubble. The table also presents the average dollars involved per deal and the average size of the corporate deals. Since 2002, corporate venture capital funds participated on average in about 16 percent of the deals but accounted for only about 8 percent of the dollars invested.

[3] Source: PricewaterhouseCoopers/National Venture Capital Association Money Tree™ Report. Data: Thomson Reuters.

One advantage a corporate investor has is the ability to lend industry expertise to the company, and we can assume that the corporate venture capital funds invest in related areas where they do have the expertise. Another advantage is the ability to help market and test a product, and to eventually share in the revenue stream. This has turned out to be true in the pharmaceutical industry with new drug development. If the drug passes phase III trials and gets approved by the Federal Drug Administration, a large pharmaceutical company has the sales force and marketing muscle to sell the new approved drug through its distribution channels. This usually results in shared revenue and often results in the acquisition of the smaller biotech company.

Exiting Venture Capital Deals

One question that concerns investors is when they will get their money back. This is also a concern of the fund managers, because there are two major ways to recover your investment. The company can become a publicly owned company through an initial public offering, as was the case for Duracell, or the fund can find a merger partner who will buy the company. The timing of initial public offerings is dependent on the tone of the overall market. During the market downturn of 2000–2002 and again in 2008–2010, IPOs were difficult to achieve, and many venture capital funds held their companies off the market. If you were an investor in a fund, you were forced to wait for the market to recover in order to get fair value out of the company. Table 21–5 presents a view of mergers and acquisitions and

TABLE 21-5 Venture-Backed Liquidity Events by Year/Quarter 2004-2010

Quarter Year	Total M&A Deals	M&A Deals with Disclosed Values	*Total Disclosed M&A Value (in mil. $)	Average M&A Deal Size (in mil. $)	**Number of IPOs	Total Offer Amount (in mil. $)	Average IPO Offer Amt (in mil. $)
2004	**349**	**188**	**$16,043.8**	**$85.3**	**94**	**$10,481.6**	**$111.5**
2005	**350**	**163**	**17,324.7**	**106.3**	**57**	**4,482.4**	**78.6**
2006	**377**	**164**	**19,034.8**	**116.1**	**57**	**5,117.1**	**89.8**
2007–1	88	31	4,640.3	149.7	18	2,190.6	**121.7**
2007–2	90	37	3,912.1	105.7	25	4,146.8	**165.9**
2007–3	108	55	11,261.7	204.8	12	945.2	**78.8**
2007–4	93	45	9,645.8	214.4	31	3,043.8	**98.2**
2007	**379**	**168**	**29,460.0**	**175.4**	**86**	**10,326.3**	**120.1**
2008–1	109	42	4,983.2	118.6	5	282.7	**56.5**
2008–2	87	27	3,321.2	123.0	0	0.0	**0.0**
2008–3	89	32	3,080.2	96.3	1	187.5	**187.5**
2008–4	66	18	2,390.9	132.8	0	0.0	**0.0**
2008	**351**	**119**	**13,775.4**	**115.8**	**6**	**470.2**	**78.4**
2009–1	65	15	666.0	44.4	0	0.0	**0.0**
2009–2	65	13	2,570.1	197.7	5	720.7	**144.1**
2009–3	69	23	1,392.4	60.5	3	572.1	**190.7**
2009–4	74	41	8,924.3	217.7	4	349.3	**87.3**
2009	**273**	**92**	**13,552.7**	**147.3**	**12**	**1,642.1**	**136.8**
2010–1	121	31	5,586.6	180.2	9	936.2	**104.0**
2010–2	97	22	2,932.2	133.3	17	1,274.9	**75.0**
2010–3	104	27	3,843.0	142.3	14	1,249.1	**89.2**
2010	**322**	**80**	**12361.8**	**154.5**	**40**	**3,460.2**	**86.5**

* Only accounts for deals with disclosed values.

** Includes all companies with at least one U.S. VC Investor that trades on U.S. exchanges, regardless of domicile.

Source: Thomson Reuters & National Venture Capital Association.

initial public offerings between 2004 and 2010 for venture capital funds. These are called liquidity events because of the way the fund monetizes its investment and gets cash out the deal.

Several observations can be made from Table 21–5. First, initial public offerings suffered more of a decline than mergers and acquisitions. The average size of the IPO market stayed within the normal range throughout this seven-year period, but the number of offerings was very sensitive to the stock market. If we compare 2004–2007 IPO data, we see that IPOs averaged about 74 per year during the four-year period, with 94 being the high in 2004 and 57 being the low in 2005 and 2006. With only six IPOs in 2008 and twelve in 2009, venture capital funds were not able to exit their investments using an initial public offering during these two years. In the first three quarters of 2010, IPO activity picked up as the stock market recovered. Forty IPOs took place during this period, with more to come in the fourth quarter. Mergers and acquisitions were more stable over this seven-year period, although 2008 and 2009 showed some drop-off from the high of 2007. During times when a firm cannot exit a private equity investment, it can use free cash flow to pay investors special dividends. This would occur after the capital structure is normalized for the industry and there is enough cash flow available for reinvestment into the company. This behavior would depend on whether the industry is a growth industry or more mature.

Returns on Venture Capital Investments

Another major issue for investors is what kinds of annualized returns they will receive from private equity investments. One of the reasons individuals, pension funds, and endowment funds invest in private equity funds is the expectation of receiving higher returns than from the stock market. Have investors really been rewarded with higher returns? There are several issues that affect the return an investor will receive. The first issue is the fee charged by the private equity fund. The normal practice is to take 20 percent of the profits for the **general partners** (the fund managers) and 80 percent of the profits for the **limited partners** (the investors). The 20 percent profit for the fund managers is referred to as **carried interest**. Most funds will have some **hurdle rate** that the limited partners will get before the general partners take their cut off the top. The hurdle rate usually is clustered around 8 and 10 percent but can be higher or lower. It is also sometimes referred to as the preferred rate.

A more important issue than fees is the type of fund and its history of success. Follow-on funds of successful private equity firms with a track record of ranking in the top quartile of returns generally exhibit higher returns than those funds in the bottom 75 percent. In other words, if you can get your money invested in the funds with a top track record, you stand to make better returns. Funds in the top quartile earn more than twice as much as the median return, and funds in the bottom quartile earn less than 2 percent on average.[4] The problem becomes getting into the right fund, because everyone wants into the follow-on funds where the previous funds have exhibited top quartile performance. Often these funds are closed to new investors and open only to those investors who participated in previous funds. This creates a problem for new investors trying to invest in private equity.

Venture capital returns are judged by **vintage year**—the year the fund made its first investment. Because a fund might make investments over a five-year period and not exit all investments in the fund for as many as five or more years, it is difficult to judge rates of return on a short-term basis. A fund may have exited some investments and still have a portfolio of other investments that it is grooming for an IPO, merger, or acquisition.

[4] Hirt, Geoffrey, Thomas Galuhn and Paul Rice, "Private Equity Fund of Funds," *The Handbook of Alternative Investments*, John Wiley & Sons, Inc., New York, pp. 141–159.

TABLE 21-6 U.S. Venture Capital Index Returns

US Venture Capital Index Returns for the Periods Ending 6/30/2010, 3/31/2010 and 6/31/2009

For the Period Ending	Qtr.	1 Year	3 Years	5 Years	10 Years	15 Years	20 Years
June 30, 2010	0.4	6.4	−2.7	4.3	−4.2	38.1	24.3
March 31, 2010	0.7	6.5	−0.7	4.9	−3.7	38.2	24.0
June 30, 2009	0.2	−17.1	1.3	5.7	14.3	36.3	22.7
Other Indices at June 30, 2010							
DJIA	−9.6	18.9	−7.4	1.7	1.7	7.5	8.9
NASDAQ Composite	−12.0	14.9	−6.8	0.5	−6.1	5.6	7.9
S&P 500	−11.4	14.4	−9.8	−0.8	−1.6	6.2	7.7

Note: Because the U.S. Venture Capital index is capital weighted, the largest vintage years mainly drive the index performance.

Sources: Cambridge Associates LLC. Dow Jones & Company, Inc., Standard and Poor's, and Thomson Datastream.

Table 21–6 gives the returns for all venture capital investments compared to stock market equity indexes for the Dow Jones Industrial Average, the NASDAQ Composite, and the Standard & Poor's 500 Index. Venture capital returns for 3-, 5-, 10-, and 20-year periods exceed those of the stock market. As you might remember from previous tables, raising venture capital funds is a lumpy process, and not all years have the same amount of capital raised. For that reason the returns on venture capital are heavily influenced by the amount of capital raised in any vintage year. Years with large amounts of investments, such as 1999 and 2000, have a great weight on 10-year returns. Perhaps Table 21–7 gets this point across in a different way. The table is based on a $1 investment. The first column reflects the vintage year. The second column reflects the amount of capital that was returned to the investors, while the third column shows the value of the companies still left in the funds. This value could be higher or lower depending on the exit price received for the company.

The last column combines columns 2 and 3. As you go down through the years, you can see that the distributions get smaller and the residual value gets larger. For example, vintage years 2005–2010 have most of the value in the residual column, and as the stock market rises, this residual value will most likely rise with it. Eventually the fund will start to exit their investments and distribute capital. We can see that the 1995 vintage year was the best year, with every dollar invested getting $6.14 back in capital distributions and a small $.05 left in residual value. This is reflected in Table 21–6 in the 15-year return column with an annual rate of 38.1 percent. We won't really know if the vintage years of 2000 and later will be good or bad until after most of the capital is returned to the investors.

Correlations of Private Equity with Other Assets

Besides higher expected returns, private equity has low correlations with other assets. A look at Table 21–8 shows that a combination of buyout and venture capital shown in the All Private Equity column has lower correlations than just venture capital, which is riskier and generally invested in smaller companies. Short-term U.S. T-bills and the Lehman Brothers Aggregate Government Bond Index have negative correlations with all three columns, and it is clear that an investor who wants to balance off the risk of a bond portfolio would find good

TABLE 21-7 Vintage Year Multiples per $1 Invested

Vintage Year Multiples Analysis Pooled Mean Net to Limited Partners As of June 30, 2010

Vintage Year	Distribution to Paid in Capital (DPI)	Residual Value to Paid in Capital (RVPI)	Total Value to Paid in Capital (TVPI)
1981–1994	3.23	0.01	3.24
1995	6.14	0.05	6.19
1996	4.93	0.09	5.02
1997	2.98	0.07	3.05
1998	1.30	0.15	1.46
1999	0.67	0.24	0.91
2000	0.50	0.41	0.91
2001	0.45	0.57	1.02
2002	0.43	0.54	0.97
2003	0.38	0.73	1.11
2004	0.21	0.89	1.10
2005	0.12	0.87	0.99
2006	0.05	0.91	0.97
2007	0.03	0.95	0.98
2008	0.02	1.00	1.02
2009	0.00	1.01	1.01
Overall	**1.09**	**0.44**	**1.53**

Source: Cambridge Associates.

TABLE 21-8 Correlations of All Private Equity with Other Assets

	All Private Equity	Buyouts	Venture Capital
90 Day T-Bills	−0.16	−0.19	−0.14
LB Aggregate Bond	−0.15	−0.14	−0.04
ML High Yield Bond	0.17	0.04	0.09
NAREIT Equity	0.18	0.07	0.19
MSCI EAFE	0.25	0.11	0.38
Russell 1000 Value	0.35	0.13	0.40
Russell 2000 Value	0.38	0.13	0.42
S&P 500	0.40	0.13	0.50
Russell 1000 Growth	0.40	0.15	0.55
Russell 2000 Growth	0.48	0.18	0.70

risk reduction by combining bonds with private equity. The category with the highest correlations is the Russell 2000 small cap growth index. The Russell 2000 is 70 percent correlated to Venture Capital, but only 18 percent correlated to Buyouts.[5] The story of private equity and venture capital is higher returns and lower correlations, both of which are good reasons to have them in a diversified portfolio. Now we move on to hedge funds as another alternative investment strategy in addition to private equity.

[5] Hirt, Geoffrey, Thomas Galuhn and Paul Rice, "Private Equity Fund of Funds," *The Handbook of Alternative Investments,* John Wiley & Sons, Inc., New York, 2002, pp. 141–159.

HEDGE FUNDS

Hedge funds have been around for a while. They really came into vogue in the 1990s and have become much maligned in the financial crisis of 2007–2010. **Hedge funds** are private limited partnerships that are unregulated by the Securities and Exchange Commission. Actually, the name is somewhat misleading, because hedge funds do not restrict their activities to hedging or reducing risk. Rather, the term is a generic name for funds that engage in a wide range of activities in an attempt to generate superior returns. They normally are neither bullish nor bearish, but engage in buying, short selling, and transacting puts and calls at the same time in an attempt to gain an edge in return while also reducing the volatility of their portfolio. They tend to be highly leveraged. Hedge fund managers charge management fees of 1 to 2 percent, but more importantly, like private equity funds they are compensated with 20 percent of the profits. Also like private equity funds, hedge funds may have to achieve a hurdle rate for the limited partners before they can take their 20 percent share of the profits. Hedge funds have the same requirements for qualified investors as private equity funds do, and for the most part the same types of investors: wealthy individuals, pension funds, endowment funds, and foundations.

Hedge Fund Strategies

There are too many different styles of hedge funds to cover all of them in this chapter, but we will try to give an overview of some key strategies so you can get a feel for how they operate. Hedge funds are very secretive and do their best to hide their trades. In a sense, hedge funds are paranoid that other hedge funds will copy their strategies or bet against their strategies, and in the process ruin opportunities for returns. If you remember the concept of dark pools from Chapter 2, you can imagine why hedge funds like using dark pools for trading. Hedge funds will also spread out their buys and sells through many brokerage houses so that no one broker can figure out their strategies.

Alfred Jones created the first hedge fund in 1949. Its major characteristic was that it hedged against a falling market. Jones used both short sales and leverage to create a conservative portfolio. He thought that in a bull market strong stocks would outperform weaker stocks, and that in a down market the strong stocks would go down less than the weak stocks. His strategy was to first identify the strong and weak stocks, and for this Jones used traditional stock selection strategies. He would buy the strong stocks, short the weak stocks, and use leverage to enhance his returns. He did this so well that over time his methods were copied. By 1968 there were 200 hedge funds. Some of them became quite famous, such as George Soros Quantum Fund and Michael Steinhardt's, Steinhardt's Partners.[6]

Long/Short Equity Funds Most **long/short equity funds** involve a strategy similar to that devised by Alfred Jones. The traditional fund might be one-third short and two-thirds long, and with the use of leverage, 133 percent invested. The more the long-term bias, the greater will be the long-term percentage of the portfolio versus the short percentage. This type of fund is not market neutral and would have a net long bias. They generally try to construct a portfolio that will have a higher beta in rising markets and a lower beta in falling markets. The manager has the ability to shift between growth and value and to use options and futures as hedges. The fund could specialize in a specific industry such as health care broadly defined, technology, financials, consumers stocks, and so forth. Long/short equity funds are the most popular types of funds and make up the largest segment of the hedge fund universe.

[6] Tremont Advisers and TASS Investment Research LTD. "Hedge Funds," *The Handbook of Alternative Investments*, John Wiley & Sons Inc. New York, 2002, pp. 14–15.

Market Neutral or No-Bias Funds Hedge funds that are neither long nor short in their strategy are either **market neutral funds** or **no-bias funds**. They intend to make their profits by making good stock selections and having a balance between long and short positions. A 50–50 percent breakdown would be a perfect balance, but a no-bias hedge fund index will allow as much as a 20 percent long or 20 percent short position for limited amounts of time. A common strategy in this type of fund would be to pair two stocks in the same industry. You would buy the one that you think is the most undervalued and sell short the one that you think is the most overvalued. The manager would do this across many industries with the overall goal of making a profit on the spread between the two price changes. In rising markets the long position should rise more than the short position, and in down markets the short position should fall more than the long position. The difference between the two price changes is the profit for each paired trade.

Short Bias Funds The **short bias fund** always has a negative bias and can be 100 percent short or a blend of short and long. The typical short bias fund might hold $100 to $120 of short positions and $0 to $40 of long positions for each $100 of capital. The key is that the net exposure has to be short. A short bias fund does not necessarily have to believe that the market will fall—only that the stocks in the short portfolio will fall. The Internet bubble and the collapse of the financial markets and the falling stock markets made short sellers some money. Unfortunately there were fewer short sellers taking advantage of these markets because many of them folded up shop in the bull market of the 1990s. Short sellers borrow stock from a counterparty and sell it in the market. They are required to keep a cash balance to repurchase the stock. They are also required to keep a margin balance above the sale price to guarantee that they can buy back the stock if it goes against them on the upside. Individual investors would have to start with a 50 percent margin and perhaps keep a maintenance margin of 30 percent. Short funds may have different requirements with their brokers that allow lower maintenance margins. Short sellers may use puts and calls in their strategies and sell forward contracts on stock index futures to help implement or hedge their strategy.

Event-Driven Funds Any change in the value of a company due to an event can create an opportunity to profit. **Event-driven funds benefit** from many types of events that can cause a change in value, but because the change in value is uncertain, event funds have to consider the probability of the event creating value. Some examples of events could be proxy battles, corporate restructurings, spin-offs, litigation outcomes, leveraged buyouts, share buybacks, leveraged recapitalizations, mergers and acquisitions, and bankruptcy announcements. Event-driven strategies are the second most popular strategies behind long/short equity.[7] Both distressed funds and merger arbitrage funds are event-driven strategies. Distressed companies are in some form of reorganization due to bankruptcy proceedings, whereas mergers create new companies and a change in ownerships and value.

Distressed Funds **Distressed funds** can invest in any type of distressed security, including common stock, preferred stock, or debt. Companies with distressed securities are usually in bankruptcy, or close to bankruptcy, and in need of legal action. The fund manager thinks there will be some value after the bankruptcy and after creditors have been paid, and that the market is not valuing the security accurately. The security in question is usually debt, because in bankruptcy proceedings common stockholders are almost always wiped out. It could be that the company will be restructured under Chapter 11 bankruptcy law and will regain some value as

[7] Tremont Advisers and TASS Investment Research LTD. "Hedge Funds," *The Handbook of Alternative Investments*, John Wiley & Sons Inc. New York, 2002, p. 20.

debt holders are willing to exchange some debt for equity or forgive a significant amount of debt, hoping to get back more of their money with an ongoing firm than with a dead firm. Some fund managers get actively involved in the restructuring process; others take a passive approach with a diversified portfolio of distressed securities. It is also possible that the fund could provide equity capital in the restructuring process and become an equity holder of the reorganized company.

Merger Arbitrage Funds **Merger arbitrage funds** make their money betting on the completion or failure of the merger. When a merger is announced, there is usually a premium offered by the acquiring company for the target company's common stock. Once a company is "in play," other bidders might enter and bid up the price of the target company. A merger arbitrage fund might play the odds and buy the target company expecting a higher offer or a bidding war. That happened in 2010 when Dell and Hewlett Packard entered a bidding war for 3PAR Company. According to 3PAR's Web site, 3PAR is "the leading global provider of utility storage, a category of highly virtualized and dynamically tiered storage arrays built for public and private cloud computing." Dell started the bidding for 3PAR with an offer of $1.15 billion net of 3PAR's cash on August 16, 2010. Seven days later, Hewlett Packard entered the bidding with an offer of $1.5 billion. Dell countered with a raised bid of $1.6 billion. One day later Dell raised its bid to $27 per share and Hewlett Packard raised its offer to $30 per share, or more than $2 billion. Dell made one final offer of $32 per share, with HP topping that at $33 per share, or $2.4 billion. If a merger arbitrage manager had gotten into 3PAR when the bidding started, they could have made a large profit. The final price of $2.4 billion was $1.25 billion higher than Dell's original offer, or a little over 108 percent higher.

A more common merger arbitrage play would be an ongoing merger, where there is some probability that the merger might not go through because of antitrust or other regulatory issues. Table 21–9 presents an example of a merger offer made by Southwest Airlines for Airtran Holdings Inc., another discount carrier. The data are from the Dow Jones Newswires, November 26, 2010.

In the case of Southwest Airlines, there is currently a premium of $0.32 over the $7.43 share price of Airtran, or a 4.31 percent premium. When the expected closing date of the merger is estimated, the premium is annualized at 24.18 percent. A merger arbitrage manager could play this two ways. The fund manager could buy Airtran long, expecting the merger to be completed, and at the same time sell Southwest short

TABLE 21-9 Merger Arbitrage Opportunities

AirTran Holdings Inc. (AAI), Southwest Airlines Co. (LUV)
Premium offered: $0.32, or 4.31%
Acquirer: LUV
Target: AAI
Offer per share: 0.293 shares and $3.75 per share
Value of offer per share: $7.75
Value of outstanding common equity securities: $1,049,505,000
Acquirer share price: $13.63
Target share price: $7.43
Expected closing: By First Half 2011 1/30/2011
Annualized gain: 24.18%

Note: Under the terms of the agreement, AAI holders will receive $3.75 in cash and 0.321 LUV share for each share as long as the total value of the deal is between $7.25 and $7.75 a share. If LUV's stock jumps above $12.50, the stock portion of the deal will be lowered so the overall consideration of the merger equals $7.75 a share. Likewise, AAI holders will receive more LUV shares if the stock falls below $10 to maintain the $7.25 a share price tag.

Source: Dow Jones Newswires November 26, 2010.

in an amount that equals the 0.293 shares of Airtran and the $3.75 per share that would come with the completion of the merger. When the merger is complete, the Southwest shares that were exchanged for the Airtran stock and the cash received would be used to cover the short sale. If the merger doesn't go through because of antitrust issues, then Airtran stock would fall back to its pre-merger price of $4.50 and the merger arbitrage manager would lose money. To cover this possibility, the fund manager could buy some Airtran puts. Of course, the premium paid for the puts would reduce the profit potential, but the purchase would reduce the negative effect if the merger fails. If all things go according to plan, the fund would pocket the 24 percent annualized return found in Table 21–9.

If the merger arbitrage fund manager expects the merger to fail because of antitrust competition issues, he could short Airtran stock, hoping that it would fall back to its premerger price of $4.50. The risk of this position is that the merger might go through, in which case the manager would lose the $0.32 per share premium. The negative effects are not so bad compared to the possible returns if the merger fails.

Convertible Arbitrage Convertible securities were covered in Chapter 13, and understanding the basics presented in that chapter will help you understand convertible arbitrage strategy. **Convertible arbitrage** is centered on convertible preferred stock and convertible bonds. The strategy can be U.S. oriented or globally focused. The common strategy is to buy the convertible security for the income and sell the common stock short. Common stocks of companies issuing convertibles usually have very low or nonexistent dividends, and so owning the convertible security generates income, and shorting the common stock creates a cash account that earns interest. Additionally, if the common stock pays a dividend, the short position is obligated to pay that dividend, which would reduce the cash flow.

Remember from Chapter 13 that a convertible bond has two sources of value. It has a floor value equal to the pure bond value, and it has a conversion value equal to the conversion ratio times the common stock price. One strategy would be for a convertible arbitrage fund to sell the common stock short when the conversion value is less than the pure bond value and buy the bond. If the stock price declines, the fund will make money on the short sale and not lose any money on the long bond position. If the stock price moves up dramatically and the conversion value is far enough above the pure bond value to trigger a call, the fund will take the shares from the conversion of the bond to stock and use the shares to cover its short position. What this means is that the fund manager has to keep the proper hedge ratio between the common stock shares and the convertible bond.

Other Types of Hedge Funds There are many other types of hedge funds, such as currencies, commodities, global macro, fixed-income arbitrage, managed futures, and multistrategy funds. In general these funds will make bets on market moves. For example, a currency fund could short the U.S. dollar and buy the euro long because they thought the U.S. dollar would decline and the euro would rise. A commodity fund could buy wheat long and sell soybeans short, expecting wheat to rise and soybeans to either fall, stay even, or rise less than wheat. In the case of commodity hedges, the manager has to pay attention to the different-size contracts and their dollar value. Then the manager has to choose a hedge ratio between the two commodities that establishes either a perfect hedge, a long hedge, or a short hedge. A long hedge would mean the two contracts are tilted toward a long position in the commodity that is expected to rise. A short hedge would be the opposite.

Hedge Fund Performance

Table 21–10 shows the short-term and long-term performance of a selection of hedge fund indexes as tracked by the Credit Suisse Dow Jones Hedge Fund Indexes. The indexes are all expressed in U.S. dollars, and the returns are for the year-to-date

TABLE 21-10 Credit Suisse Dow Jones Hedge Fund Indexes

Index/Sub Strategies	Currency	YTD Return	1 Year Return	Avg Annl*	Std Dev*	Sharpe*
Dow Jones Credit Suisse Hedge Fund Index	USD	8.02%	11.27%	9.34%	7.72%	0.77
Convertible Arbitrage	USD	9.64	12.98	7.87	7.12	0.63
Dedicated Short Bias	USD	−15.64	−21.66	−3.36	17.07	−0.40
Emerging Markets	USD	10.10	13.81	8.23	15.29	0.32
Equity Market Neutral	USD	−0.03	−0.83	5.19	10.66	0.17
Event Driven	USD	8.22	13.08	10.23	6.09	1.12
Distressed	USD	6.98	11.93	11.06	6.64	1.15
Multi-Strategy	USD	9.10	13.94	9.84	6.50	0.99
Risk Arbitrage	USD	3.50	4.96	7.19	4.18	0.90
Fixed Income Arbitrage	USD	11.00	13.75	5.23	5.96	0.31
Global Macro	USD	11.10	13.37	12.46	10.07	0.90
Long/Short Equity	USD	5.18	9.01	10.10	10.00	0.67
Managed Futures	USD	11.00	10.67	6.63	11.75	0.27
Multi-Strategy	USD	7.14	9.44	8.18	5.47	0.87

* Average Annual Index data begins January 1994. Monthly Standard Deviation annualized. Sharpe ratio calculated using the rolling 90-day T-bill rate.

Source: http://www.hedgeindex.com/hedgeindex/en/default.aspx?cy=USD. The Dow Jones Credit Suisse Hedge Fund Index(es)[SM] are calculated, distributed and marketed by Dow Jones Indexes, the marketing name and a licensed trademark of CME Group Index Services LLC ("CME Indexes"), and have been licensed for use. "Dow Jones Indexes" and "Dow Jones Credit Suisse Hedge Fund Indexes[SM]" are service marks of Dow Jones Trademark Holdings, LLC or Credit Suisse AG, as the case may be. All content of the Dow Jones Credit Suisse Hedge Fund Indexes are proprietary to CME Indexes and Credit Suisse Index Co., Inc.

return (YTD) from January 1, 2010, to October 31, 2010, and the one-year return from October 2009 to October 2010. The average annual return is based on the period January 1994 to October 2010. The standard deviation of the various indexes is given as well as the Sharpe ratio, which is a measure of risk and return. The higher the Sharpe ratio, the better the return for the given amount of risk. The Sharpe ratio is more fully explained in Chapter 22.

The long-term annual returns are probably more significant than the short-term returns, because they reflect many different time periods and consolidate many types of funds over this 16-year period. Notice that the dedicated short bias funds have negative returns across all the time periods. Given that the markets have a long-term upward trend, it isn't surprising that the long-term performance of short sellers has been negative. The dedicated short bias also has the largest standard deviation, but as we would suspect, these funds did great in the down markets of 2000–2002 and for periods between 2008 and 2010. The key to the short bias funds is to be invested at the right time. The event-driven strategies and the fixed-income arbitrage have very small standard deviations and good returns when compared to the Standard & Poor's 500 index. The Ibbotson SBBI Classic 2010 Yearbook has an annual rate of return for large stocks from 1994 to 2009 at 7.6 percent. The long-term standard deviation for large stocks from 1926 to 2009 was 20.5 percent. The standard deviation for this same time period for long-term government bonds was 9.8 percent and for intermediate government bonds was 5.7 percent. Even though the time periods are not exactly the same, they do give a reference point to the standard deviations in Table 21–10. So in most cases the risk/return trade-off with hedge funds turns out to be positive.

Hedge Fund Correlations

The Credit Suisse Dow Jones Hedge Fund Index was formerly the Credit Suisse Tremont Index and the data in Table 21–11 compares the aggregate hedge fund index found on the first line in Table 21–10 to the asset classes found in Table 21–11.

TABLE 21-11 Historical Correlations of Hedge Funds Relative to Other Asset Classes, January 1994–February 2011

	Credit Suisse Dow Jones Hedge Fund Index	Mesirow Multi-Strategy Hedge Fund Index	S&P 500	Lehman Aggregate Bond	MSCI EAFE	MSCI Emerging Market	GS Commodity Index	Dow Jones Real Estate Index
Credit Suisse Dow Jones Hedge Fund Index	1.00	0.71	0.56	0.16	0.61	0.60	0.35	0.35
Mesirow Multi-Strategy Composite	0.71	1.00	0.42	(0.01)	0.53	0.53	0.34	0.30
S&P 500	0.56	0.42	1.00	0.07	0.84	0.72	0.22	0.58
Lehman Aggregate Bond	0.16	(0.01)	0.07	1.00	(0.07)	(0.04)	0.03	0.14
MSCI EAFE	0.61	0.53	0.84	(0.07)	1.00	0.78	0.24	0.52
MSCI Emerging Market	0.60	0.53	0.72	(0.04)	0.78	1.00	0.31	0.46
Goldman Sachs Commodity Index	0.35	0.34	0.22	0.03	0.24	0.31	1.00	0.18
Dow Jones Real Estate Index	0.35	0.30	0.58	0.14	0.52	0.46	0.18	1.00

Source: Mesirow Financial, Chicago, Illinois.

This table of cross correlations is from Mesirow Financial's Advanced Strategy Group that manages $14 billion in a fund of hedge funds. In other words, it groups hedge funds managed by others into hedge fund portfolios to reach a risk-return tradeoff on the efficient frontier that we discussed in chapter 17. Each client may choose a different risk return tradeoff on the efficient frontier and Mesirow Financial could structure an individual portfolio to meet the client's objectives. The correlations in the table run from 1994 through February of 2011.

It is clear from examining the table that hedge funds are not highly correlated to other asset classes. As would be expected, the highest correlation of 71 percent is with Mesirow Financial's Multi-Strategy Composite fund. This is a Mesirow internal index that combines their many fund strategies into one portfolio. The Credit Suisse Hedge Fund Index is correlated with the S&P 500 Index at 0.56, the MSCI EAFE at 0.61 and the MSCI Emerging market index at 0.60. This would indicate that the Credit Suisse Dow Jones Hedge Fund Index is about 60 percent correlated with common stocks. When compared to the Dow Jones real estate index and the Goldman Sachs commodity index the correlation falls to 0.35 for both asset classes. The lowest correlation is with the Lehman Aggregate Bond Index at 0.16. In fact, if you look down the 5th column, the Lehman Aggregate Bond Index has the lowest correlation with all the other asset classes. Looking at some other correlations, we find that the Goldman Sachs Commodity Index has only a 14 percent correlation with the Dow Jones Real Estate Index and that commodities have low correlations to the other asset classes in this table.

While these long-term correlations don't measure what is happening in the current market over the short term, they do give a reasonable view of a continuous investment strategy in the hedge fund asset class.

According to Altegris Investments (**www.altegris.com**), hedge fund correlations with the Standard & Poor's 500 Index for the period November 2005 to October 2010 have increased over the long-term trend. Hedge funds overall were 0.80 correlated with the S&P 500 Index over this time period. However, some other hedge fund strategies maintained relatively low correlations. These hedge fund strategies had the following correlations over this time period: market neutral (0.38), convertible arbitrage (0.66), event-driven (0.80), and currency (0.50). In all cases, correlations of less that 1.00 can help reduce the volatility of a portfolio and its risk. For an update on these correlations, log on to the Altegris Web site.

SUMMARY

Institutional investors use the core satellite portfolio approach to diversify their portfolios with alternative investments. In previous chapters we presented real estate and real assets, international investments, and commodities. In this chapter we present private equity and hedge funds as other ways to diversify a portfolio.

The term *private equity* refers to any kind of equity investment in nonpublic companies. It is a broad term that includes angel capital, many forms of venture capital, and leveraged buyouts. Venture capital essentially is divided into four types of investments, depending upon the company's stage of development. Angel investors are the first to provide money to a private company. These are usually friends and family members and occasionally wealthy investors who like the company's ideas. These angel investors help get the company off the ground and started. Sometimes venture capital firms will provide seed capital, which is also money to help get a firm started. After startup, a company that needs more capital might turn to a venture capital fund that specializes in early-stage investing. Sometimes private companies need middle-stage venture capital to expand the business, and some venture capital companies specialize in late-stage venture capital, which usually occurs two to three years before the company is ready for an initial public offering. Leverage is used in various ways in buyout funds; an example is the case of Duracell and Gillette. Publicly traded corporations also use internal venture capital funds.

Both private equity and hedge funds provide diversification opportunities for investors who have portfolios consisting of stocks and bonds. In both cases the correlation coefficients are less than 1, and in many cases they are quite low or even negative to some asset classes. Correlations of less than 1 help reduce the risk in a portfolio, and if the returns are higher than a traditional stock/bond portfolio, then the risk/return trade-off is positive. An investor may be able to increase his return and at the same time decrease his risk by using private equity and hedge funds in his portfolio mix. Data were presented on both returns and correlations for these two asset classes.

Hedge funds like private equity funds are partnerships that are not regulated by the Securities Exchange Commission. These partnerships include the general partners, who manage the fund, and the investors who are limited partners with limited liability. Hedge funds do their best to conduct their trading in a way that does not disclose their strategy. They are very protective of their trades and often use dark pools and many brokers to disguise their trading strategies. Only qualified investors can invest in hedge funds and private equity. These investors must meet wealth and income standards before they can invest and must be considered sophisticated investors, given the risks that both private equity and hedge funds encompass.

In this chapter we covered the basic hedge fund styles but not the exotic ones. The most common type of hedge fund is the long/short equity fund. These funds have a long bias but use short sales (20 to 40 percent) to balance the portfolio and decrease volatility. There are also market neutral funds, or no-bias and short bias funds. We discuss event-driven funds such as distressed funds and merger arbitrage funds. These funds are driven by an event that changes the structure and value of the company. The event could be bankruptcy, a merger or acquisition, a spin-off, a restructuring of some type, or even a significant stock repurchase or recapitalization. Finally, drawing on your knowledge of convertible bonds from Chapter 13, we presented convertible arbitrage strategies.

KEY WORDS AND CONCEPTS

angel investors 547

buyout funds 547

carried interest 554

convertible arbitrage funds 560

core satellite portfolio approach 545

distressed funds 558

early-stage venture capital 547
event-driven funds 558
follow-on fund 549
general partners 554
hedge funds 557
hurdle rate 554
late-stage companies 547
limited partners 554
long/short equity funds 557
market neutral or no-bias funds 558
merger arbitrage funds 559
middle-stage or expansion companies 547
private equity 546
seed capital 547
short bias funds 558
venture capital firms 546
vintage year 554

DISCUSSION QUESTIONS

1. Why would an investor want to diversify a portfolio with alternative investments?
2. What is private equity, and what does it include?
3. Explain why an angel investor can be important to a company just starting out.
4. Describe the risk and return for early-stage venture capital funds.
5. What other benefits besides dollars do private equity funds bring to an early-stage company?
6. Compare and contrast middle-stage and late-stage venture capital funds.
7. Describe the strategy behind buyout funds.
8. Define a "qualified investor."
9. What is a follow-on fund?
10. How is the private equity market related to the stock market?
11. When an investor in a limited partnership commits $1 million, how does the private equity fund collect the money?
12. Why do public corporations have venture capital funds, and what impact do they have in the venture capital arena?
13. What is the life of a venture capital fund, and how long might it take for an investor to get his or her investment back?
14. In order to turn an investment into a tangible return, a venture capital fund must have an exit strategy. What exit strategies exist, and how are they affected by the stock market?
15. Describe how the returns of a venture capital fund are distributed between the general partners and the limited partners (investors).
16. Why is the vintage year important in analyzing venture capital returns?
17. How are private equity returns correlated with 90-day T-bills and the Lehman Brothers Aggregate Bond Index? What implications does this have in constructing a portfolio?
18. Describe the legal structure of a hedge fund.
19. Why do hedge funds like dark pools?
20. What would be the normal strategy for a long/short equity hedge fund?
21. How does a market neutral hedge fund expect to make profits?
22. Describe the two types of event-driven hedge funds presented in this chapter.
23. For a typical merger arbitrage play with an ongoing merger, how does the hedge fund manager make a profit if he or she expects the merger to be completed?
24. Explain how a convertible arbitrage fund works.
25. Explain the concept of a core-satellite portfolio and why it is commonly used by large pension funds. Include a discussion of how private equity and hedge funds fit into this type of portfolio.

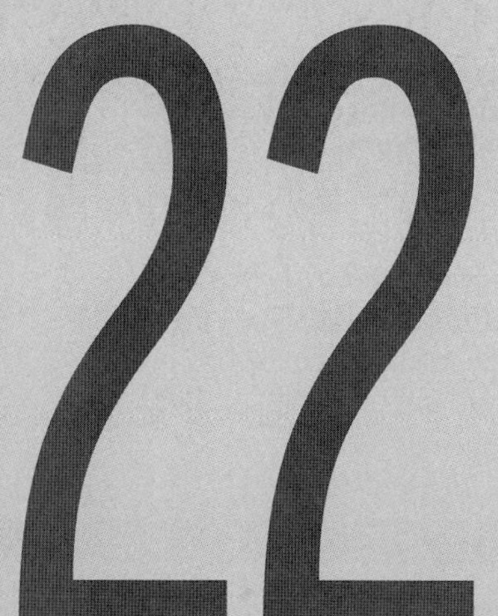

chapter twenty-two

MEASURING RISKS AND RETURNS OF PORTFOLIO MANAGERS

OBJECTIVES

1. Appreciate the importance of historical trends.
2. Explain how return is measured against risk for portfolio managers.
3. Discuss the adequacy of performance for professional money managers.
4. Describe the success of portfolio managers in diversifying their portfolios.
5. Explain the process of asset allocation.
6. Show how results can be measured against benchmarks.

OUTLINE

In the bull market days of the last decade, many portfolio managers have turned in performances that were superior to the market averages. These high returns were often achieved by taking larger than normal risks through investing in aggressive growth companies or concentrating in a limited number of high-tech companies. These portfolio managers or their representatives often proclaimed their superior ability in managing money and extrapolated past returns into the future to indicate the potential returns to the investor. A typical statement might be: "The Rapid Growth Fund has earned 20 percent per year over the past 10 years. The investor who places funds with us has the possible opportunity to see the funds grow from a $100 investment today to $619.20 in 10 years at this historical growth rate of 20 percent." There is very little attempt to relate rate of return directly to risk exposure or to provide warnings about the likelihood of repeating past performance.

This is important to you because bull markets often lull investors into looking for the highest stock returns while paying little heed to the relative risk of individual stock portfolios. The crash of 1987 drove home the concept of risk and return. If an investor had been invested in bonds rather than stock on October 19, 1987, he or she would have seen the value of bonds rise as the Federal Reserve pushed interest rates down by pumping liquidity into the market. Money market securities would have been another safe haven, but investors in common stocks lost out during the crash on a worldwide basis.

In this chapter, we examine historical trends and studies of risk-return performance for professional money managers. We evaluate the setting of objectives, the achievement of efficient diversification, and the measurement of return related to risk. In some of this discussion, we relate back to the capital asset pricing model developed in Chapter 17.

LEARNING FROM HISTORICAL TRENDS

Historical trends can provide important insights. Observe the comparative performance of seven different asset classes over 83 years in Figure 22–1. (This figure was previously shown in another context in Chapter 1.) Note that small company stocks[1] have both the highest return (11.9 percent)[2] and the largest risk (a standard deviation of 32.8 percent). The standard deviation is 2.75 times the return. While

FIGURE 22-1 Basic Summary Statistics of Annual Total Returns from 1926 to 2009

Series	Geometric Mean	Arithmetic Mean	Standard Deviation	Distribution
Large company stocks	9.8%	11.8%	20.5%	
Small company stocks*	11.9	16.6	32.8	
Long-term corporate bonds	5.9	6.2	8.3	
Long-term government bonds	5.4	5.8	9.6	
Intermediate-term government bonds	5.3	5.5	5.7	
U.S. Treasury bills	3.7	3.7	3.1	
Inflation	3.0	3.1	4.2	

-90% 0% 90%

Source: *Ibbotson SBBI 2010 Classic Yearbook,* p. 28, Copyright © 2011 Morningstar. All rights reserved. Used with permission.

[1] Small company stocks are those that are in the lowest 20 percent of the New York Stock Exchange market capitalizations.

[2] The geometric mean is the true annual compound rate of return that has been earned, whereas the arithmetic mean is simply an average of the annual returns. It is the former that is most meaningful in this context.

FIGURE 22-2 Wealth Indices of Investments in U.S. Capital Markets Index, 1925–2009 (year-end 1925 = $1.00)*

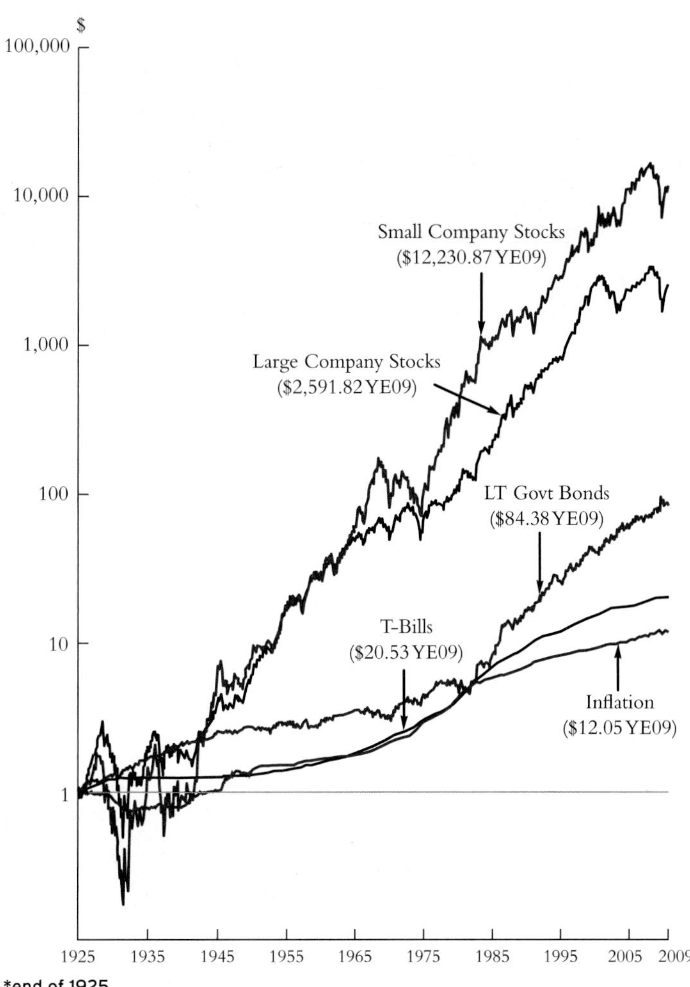

*end of 1925

Source: *Ibbotson SBBI 2010 Classic Yearbook*, p. 25, Copyright © 2011 Morningstar. All rights reserved. Used with permission.

much of this risk can be diversified away in a well-designed portfolio, we cannot automatically assume the investor is taking such action.

Second in return performance are large company stocks[3] with an annual return of 9.8 percent and a standard deviation of 20.5 percent. The ratio of the standard deviation to the return is 2.09 times. There is both a sacrifice in return and a reduction of risk compared to small company stocks. Corporate and government bonds appear to play in another ballpark with a return approximately one-half that of stocks and also considerably less risk.

Let's concentrate on stocks for now. The compound rate of return can have an enormous impact on value. In examining stock returns between the end of 1925 and 2009, Figure 22–2 indicates that $1 invested in large company stocks would have grown to $2,591.82 during this time period.[4] For those of you who had

[3] Large company stocks are those in the S&P 500 Stock Index.

[4] Note the capital appreciation part of the return is relatively small, emphasizing the importance of dividends to total returns.

great-grandfathers who invested $10,000 back in 1925, your current wealth would be $25,918,200.

If you are not satisfied with your current wealth, examine Figure 22–2. As you can see over a comparable time period, one dollar invested in small company stocks would have grown to $12,230.87, and your grandfather's $10,000 would have grown to $122,308,700. Over the long run, bonds and T-bills don't come close to generating as much wealth.

Holding Period

Since you have read in this text that stocks are riskier than other investments, the question becomes, How dangerous are such investments? The answer is, It depends. If you are a short-term trader, the risk is high and losses of 50 to 75 percent are possible.

But the beauty is, if you have a long-term perspective, mistakes can be overcome. Nowhere is that more apparent than in the first column of Table 22–1 at the top of the next page. At the top left of the table you see "Annual Returns." Let's go to the riskiest class, small company stocks on the second line below annual returns. The worst year between 1926 and the present was 1937 with a loss of 58.01 percent (shown as minimum value return in the third and fourth columns). The best year was 1933 with a gain of 142.57 percent (shown as maximum value return in the first and second columns). The difference between the best and worst is 200.58 percent (plus 142.57 percent to minus 58.01 percent). That's a large variance.

However, notice the "20-Year Rolling Period Returns" for small company stocks on the second line of this section. These are returns for any and all 20-year periods between 1926 and 2009. For small company stocks, the very best 20-year period (maximum value return) was 1942–1961 with an annual return of 21.13 percent. That's good news, but even better news is that the *worst* 20-year holding period (minimum value return) was 1929–1948 with a *positive* annual return of 5.74 percent. (Don't forget that period includes the market crash of 1929 and the aforementioned loss of 58.01 percent in 1937.) Thus over the long term, stocks are a relatively safe investment. You may also wish to examine other types of assets over other time periods (such as large company stocks over 10-year rolling periods).

All this information indicates a potentially bright future for individual investors with an appropriate time horizon, but what about professional money managers such as mutual funds, bank trust departments, and so on? Unfortunately, they are not accorded the luxury of a long-term time horizon. Their performance is not only measured annually, but quarterly as well. There is a large body of material related to measuring the performance of professional money managers and a discussion of some of that material follows.

STATED OBJECTIVES AND RISK

A first question to be posed to a professional money manager is: Have you followed the basic objectives that were established? These objectives might call for maximum capital gains, a combination of growth plus income, or simply income (with many variations in between). The objectives should be set with an eye toward the capabilities of the money managers and the financial needs of the investors. The best way to measure adherence to these objectives is to evaluate the risk exposure the fund manager has accepted. Anyone who aspires to maximize capital gains must, by nature, absorb more risk. An income-oriented fund should have a minimum risk exposure.

TABLE 22-1 Maximum and Minimum Values of Returns for 1-, 5-, 10-, and 20-Year Holding Periods (compound annual rates of return in percent)

1926-2009

Annual Returns	Maximum Value Return and Year(s)		Minimum Value Return and Year(s)		Times Positive (Out of 84 years)	Times Highest Returning Asset
Large company stocks	53.99	1933	−43.34	1931	60	16
Small company stocks	142.87	1933	−58.01	1937	58	37
Long-term corporate bonds	42.56	1982	−8.09	1969	67	6
Long-term government bonds	40.36	1982	−14.90	2009	62	10
Intermediate-term gov't bonds	29.10	1982	−5.14	1994	75	3
U.S. Treasury bills	14.71	1981	−0.02	1938	81	6
Inflation	18.16	1946	−10.30	1932	74	6
5-Year Rolling Period Returns	**Maximum Value Return and Year(s)**		**Minimum Value Return and Year(s)**		**(Out of 80 overlapping 5-year periods)**	**Times Highest Returning Asset**
Large company stocks	28.56	1995–99	−12.47	1932	69	23
Small company stocks	45.90	1941–45	−27.54	1932	69	43
Long-term corporate bonds	22.51	1982–86	−2.22	1969	77	7
Long-term government bonds	21.62	1982–86	−2.14	1969	74	4
Intermediate-term gov't bonds	16.98	1982–86	0.96	1959	80	2
U.S. Treasury bills	11.12	1979–83	0.07	1942	80	0
Inflation	10.06	1977–81	−5.42	1932	73	1
10-Year Rolling Period Returns	**Maximum Value Return and Year(s)**		**Minimum Value Return and Year(s)**		**(Out of 75 overlapping 10-year periods)**	**Times Highest Returning Asset**
Large company stocks	20.06	1949–58	−1.38	2008	71	20
Small company stocks	30.38	1975–84	−5.70	1938	73	43
Long-term corporate bonds	16.32	1982–91	0.98	1956	75	6
Long-term government bonds	15.56	1982–91	−0.07	1959	74	2
Intermediate-term gov't bonds	13.13	1982–91	1.25	1956	75	2
U.S. Treasury bills	9.17	1978–87	0.15	1942	75	1
Inflation	8.67	1973–82	−2.57	1935	69	1
20-Year Rolling Period Returns	**Maximum Value Return and Year(s)**		**Minimum Value Return and Year(s)**		**(Out of 65 overlapping 20-year periods)**	**Times Highest Returning Asset**
Large company stocks	17.88	1980–99	3.11	1948	65	9
Small company stocks	21.13	1942–61	5.74	1948	65	55
Long-term corporate bonds	12.13	1982–01	1.34	1969	65	0
Long-term government bonds	12.09	1982–01	0.69	1969	65	1
Intermediate-term gov't bonds	9.97	1981–00	1.58	1959	65	0
U.S. Treasury bills	7.72	1972–91	0.42	1950	65	0
Inflation	6.36	1966–85	0.07	1945	65	0

Source: *Ibbotson SBBI 2010 Classic Yearbook*, p. 32, Copyright © 2011 Morningstar. All rights reserved. Used with permission.

A classic study by John McDonald published in the *Journal of Financial and Quantitative Analysis* indicates that mutual fund managers generally follow the objectives they initially set. As indicated in Figure 22–3, he measured the betas and standard deviations for 123 mutual funds and compared these with the funds' stated objectives. In Panel (a), we see the fund's beta dimension along the horizontal axis and the fund's stated objective along the vertical axis. Inside the

FIGURE 22-3 Risk and Fund Objectives for 123 Mutual Funds

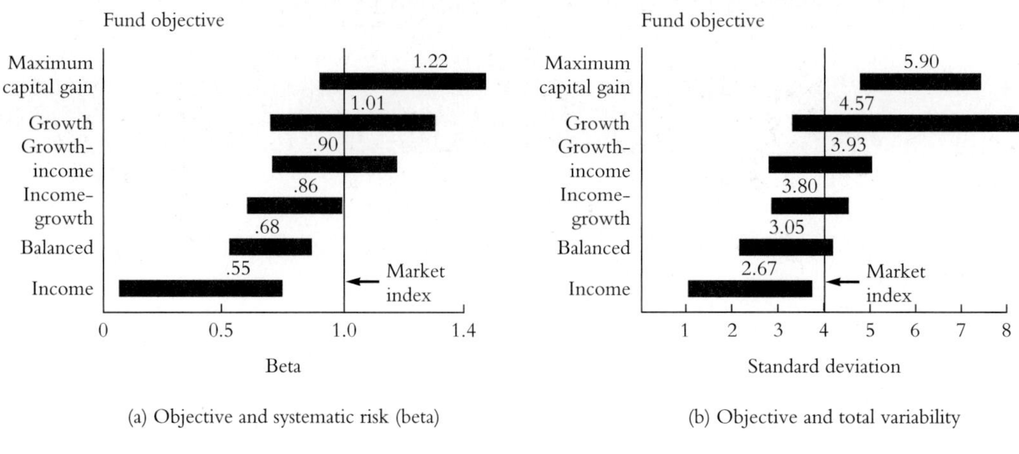

(a) Objective and systematic risk (beta)

(b) Objective and total variability

• Mean

Source: John G. McDonald, "Objectives and Performance of Mutual Funds, 1960–1969" *Journal of Financial and Quantitative Analysis,* Vol. 9, June 1974, p. 316. Copyright © 1974 School of Business Administration, University of Washington. Reprinted with the permission of Cambridge University Press. Used with permission.

panel, we see the association between the two. For example, funds with an objective of maximum capital gains had an average beta of 1.22, those with a growth objective had an average beta of 1.01, and so on all the way down to an average beta of 0.55 for income-oriented funds. In Panel (b) of Figure 22–3, a similar approach was used to compare the fund's objective with the portfolio standard deviation.

In both cases of using betas and portfolio standard deviations, we see that the risk absorption was carefully tailored to the fund's stated objectives. Funds with aggressive capital gains and growth objectives had high betas and portfolio standard deviations, while the opposite was true of balanced and income-oriented funds. Other studies have continually reaffirmed the position established in this seminal study by McDonald.

Adherence to objectives as measured by risk exposure is important in evaluating a fund manager because risk is one of the variables a money manager can directly control. While short-run return performance can be greatly influenced by unpredictable changes in the economy, the fund manager has almost total control in setting the risk level. He can be held accountable for doing what was specified or promised in regard to risk. Most lawsuits brought against money managers are not for inferior profit performance but for failure to adhere to stated risk objectives. Although it may be appropriate to shift the risk level in anticipation of changing market conditions (lower the beta at a perceived peak in the market), long-run adherence to risk objectives is advisable.

MEASUREMENT OF RETURN IN RELATION TO RISK

In examining the performance of fund managers, the return measure commonly used is excess returns. Though the term **excess returns** has many definitions, the one most commonly used is total return on a portfolio (capital appreciation plus dividends) minus the risk-free rate:

$$\text{Excess returns} = \text{Total portfolio return} - \text{Risk-free rate}$$

Thus, excess returns represent returns over and above what could be earned on a riskless asset. The rate on U.S. government Treasury bills is often used to represent the risk-free rate of return in the financial markets (though other definitions are possible). Thus, a fund that earns 12 percent when the Treasury bill rate is 6 percent has excess returns of 6 percent.

Once computed, excess returns are then compared with risk. We look at three different approaches to comparing excess returns to risk: the **Sharpe approach**, the **Treynor approach**, and the **Jensen approach**.

Sharpe Approach

application example

In the Sharpe approach,[5] the excess returns on a portfolio are compared with the portfolio standard deviation:

$$\text{Sharpe measure} = \frac{\text{Total portfolio return} - \text{Risk-free rate}}{\text{Portfolio standard deviation}} \qquad \textbf{(22–1)}$$

The portfolio manager is thus able to view excess returns per unit of risk. If a portfolio has a return of 10 percent, the risk-free rate is 6 percent, and the portfolio standard deviation is 18 percent, the Sharpe measure is 0.22:

$$\text{Sharpe measure} = \frac{10\% - 6\%}{18\%} = \frac{4\%}{18\%} = 0.22$$

This measure can be compared with other portfolios or with the market in general to assess performance. If the market return per unit of risk is greater than 0.22, then the portfolio manager has turned in an inferior performance. Assume there is a 9 percent total market return, a 6 percent risk-free rate, and a market standard deviation of 12 percent. Then the Sharpe measure for the overall market is:

$$\frac{9\% - 6\%}{12\%} = \frac{3\%}{12\%} = 0.25$$

The portfolio measure of 0.22 is less than the market measure of 0.25 and represents an inferior performance. Of course, a portfolio measure above 0.25 would have represented a superior performance.

Treynor Approach

application example

The formula for the second approach for comparing excess returns with risk (developed by Treynor[6]) is:

$$\text{Treynor measure} = \frac{\text{Total portfolio return} - \text{Risk-free rate}}{\text{Portfolio beta}} \qquad \textbf{(22–2)}$$

The only difference between the Sharpe and Treynor approaches is in the denominator. While Sharpe uses the portfolio standard deviation—Formula 22–1, Treynor uses the portfolio beta—Formula 22–2. Thus, one can say that Sharpe uses total risk, while Treynor uses

[5] William F. Sharpe, "Mutual Fund Performance," *Journal of Business*, January 1966, pp. 119–38.

[6] Jack L. Treynor, "How to Rate Management of Investment Funds," *Harvard Business Review*, January–February 1965, pp. 63–74.

only the systematic risk, or beta. Implicit in the Treynor approach is the assumption that portfolio managers can diversify away unsystematic risk, and only systematic risk remains.

If a portfolio has a total return of 10 percent, the risk-free rate is 6 percent, and the portfolio beta is 0.9, the Treynor measure would be:

$$\frac{10\% - 6\%}{0.9} = \frac{4\%}{0.9} = \frac{0.04}{0.9} = 0.044$$

This measure can be compared with other portfolios or with the market in general to determine whether there is a superior performance in terms of return per unit of risk. Assume the total market return is 9 percent, the risk-free rate is 6 percent, and the market beta (by definition) is 1; then the Treynor measure as applied to the market is 0.03:

$$\frac{9\% - 6\%}{1.0} = \frac{3\%}{1.0} = \frac{0.03}{1.0} = 0.030$$

This would imply the portfolio has turned in a superior return to the market (0.044 versus 0.030). Not only is the portfolio return higher than the market return (10 percent versus 9 percent), but the beta is less (0.9 versus 1.0). Clearly, there is more return per unit of risk.

Jensen Approach

application example

In the third approach, Jensen emphasizes using certain aspects of the capital asset pricing model to evaluate portfolio managers.[7] He compares their actual excess returns (Total portfolio return − Risk-free rate) with what should be required in the market, based on their portfolio beta.

The required rate of excess returns in the market for a given beta is shown in Figure 22–4 on page 573 as the **market line**. If the beta is 0, the investor should expect to earn no more than the risk-free rate of return because there is no systematic risk. If the portfolio manager earns only the risk-free rate of return, the excess returns will be 0. Thus, with a beta of 0, the expected excess returns on the market line are 0. With a portfolio beta of 1, the portfolio has a systematic risk equal to market, and the expected portfolio excess returns should be equal to market excess returns. If the market return (K_M) is 9 percent and the risk-free rate (R_F) is 6 percent, the market excess returns are 3 percent. A portfolio with a beta of 1 should expect to earn the market rate of excess returns ($K_M - R_F$), equal to 3 percent. Other excess returns expectations are shown for betas ranging from 0 to 1.5. For example, a portfolio with a beta of 1.5 should provide excess returns of 4.5.

Adequacy of Performance

Using the Jensen approach, the adequacy of a portfolio manager's performance can be judged against the market line. Did he or she fall above or below the line? While it would appear that portfolio manager Y in Figure 22–4 at the top of the next page had inferior returns in comparison with portfolio manager Z (approximately 2.1 percent versus 3.9 percent), this notion is quickly dispelled when one considers risk. Actually, portfolio manager Y performed above risk-return expectations as indicated by the

[7] Michael C. Jensen, "The Performance of Mutual Funds in the Period 1945–1964," *Journal of Finance,* May 1968, pp. 389–416.

FIGURE 22-4 Risk-Adjusted Portfolio Returns

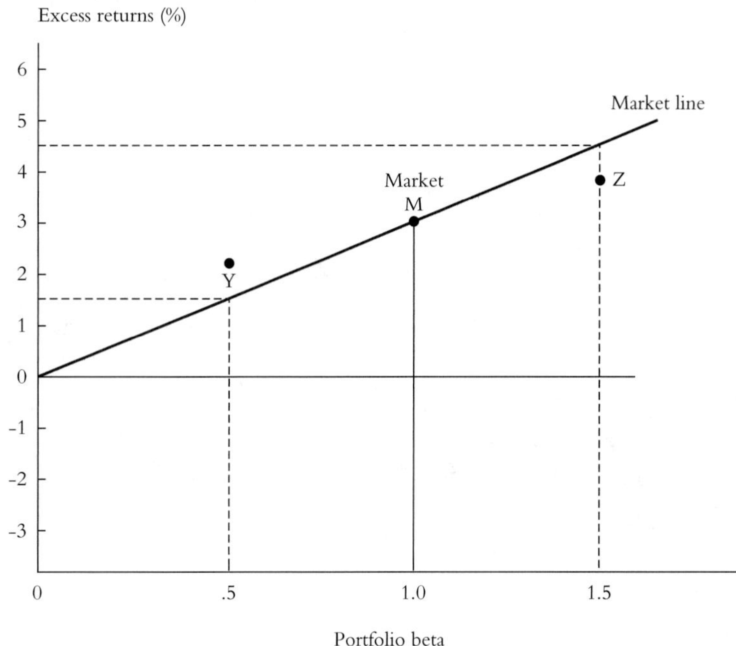

market line, while portfolio manager Z was below his risk-adjusted expected level. The vertical difference from a fund's performance point to the market line can be viewed as a measure of performance. This value, termed **alpha** or **average differential return**, indicates the difference between the return on the fund and a point on the market line that corresponds to a beta equal to the fund. In the case of fund Z, the beta of 1.5 indicated an excess return of 4.5 percent along the market line, and the actual excess return was only 3.9 percent. We thus have a negative alpha of 0.6 percent (3.9% − 4.5%). Clearly, a positive alpha indicates a superior performance, while a negative alpha leads to the opposite conclusion.

A key question for portfolio managers in general is: Can they consistently perform at positive alpha levels? That is, can they generate returns better than those available along the market line, which are theoretically available to anyone? The results of the classic study conducted by John McDonald on 123 mutual funds are presented in Figure 22–5.

The upward-sloping line is the market line, or anticipated level of performance based on risk. The small dots represent performance of the funds. About as many funds underperformed (negative alpha below the line) as overperformed (positive alpha above the line). Although a few high-beta funds had an unusually strong performance on a risk-adjusted basis, there is no consistent pattern of superior performance.

Around this same time period (the 1960s), the studies by Sharpe and Jensen[8] actually showed that mutual funds underperformed common stock indexes. Since then, there has been a raging debate about the adequacy of performance of mutual funds. In an excellent 1993 article in the *Financial Analysts Journal,* Richard Ippolito analyzed 21 major studies relating to mutual fund performance over the last four decades.[9] In examining the Ippolito material, we are left with the impression that mutual fund

[8] Sharpe, "Mutual Fund Performance"; Jensen, "The Performance of Mutual Funds in the Period 1945–1964."

[9] Richard A. Ippolito, "On Studies of Mutual Fund Performance, 1962–1991," *Financial Analysts Journal,* January–February 1993, pp. 42–50.

FIGURE 22-5 Empirical Study of Risk-Adjusted Portfolio Returns—Systematic Risk and Return

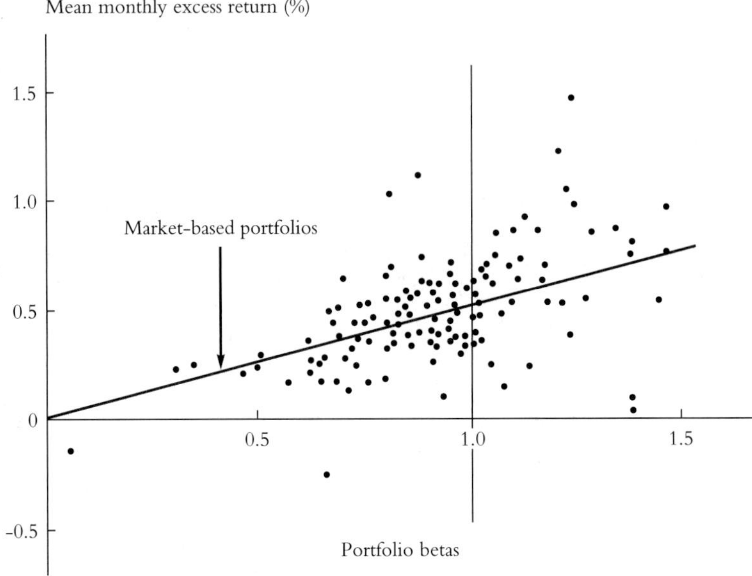

Source: John G. McDonald, "Objectives and Performance of Mutual Funds, 1960–1969" *Journal of Financial and Quantitative Analysis,* Vol. 9, June 1974, p. 316. Copyright © 1974 School of Business Administration, University of Washington. Reprinted with the permission of Cambridge University Press. Used with permission.

managers are not inferior performers; however, we would be hard pressed to say that investing in mutual funds will provide returns that are higher than those reported in the popular common stock market indexes such as the Standard & Poor's 500 Index or New York Stock Exchange Index (after adjustment for the fund's risk).

What the Ippolito article suggests is that mutual funds are efficient gatherers of information and that, on average, they use the information well in their investment activities. However, there are costs associated with acquiring this information, and wise use of the information covers the cost of its acquisition.

www.russell.com

Another study was done by Thomas Goodwin, in which he breaks down excess returns (in this case relative to the standard deviation) for various types of investment styles as shown in Figure 22–6 on the next page. The study is of 212 actively managed funds from 1986 to 1995 and uses the Frank Russell database. Risk-adjusted excess returns are shown on the x-axis and the percentage of time they occur is shown on the y-axis. The important factor to note is that the plusses and minuses are pretty close to evening out. There is no statistically significant positive or negative excess returns for any of the six management styles.

Thus, we are left with the conclusion that after all factors are considered and after four decades of debate, mutual funds are neither superior nor inferior to the overall market in terms of risk-adjusted returns.[10] Studies of other types of money managers besides mutual funds, such as pension funds and endowment funds, have reached similar conclusions.[11] Perhaps, it is not surprising that more investors are shifting their assets to **index funds**, in which fund managers merely attempt to produce the same results as those that could be attained from investing in a market index, such as the Standard & Poor's 500 Stock Index.

[10] For further confirmation of this point, see Mark M. Carhart, "On Persistence of Mutual Fund Performance," *Journal of Finance,* March, 1997, pp. 57–82. Carhart says successful funds cannot replicate good performance over the long term, but bad-performing funds may persist in their poor performance.

[11] Stephen A. Berkowitz, Louis D. Finney, and Dennis E. Logue, *The Investment Performance of Corporate Pension Plans,* New York: Quorum Books, 1988.

FIGURE 22-6 Excess Returns: Based on Six Different Management Styles (1986–1995)

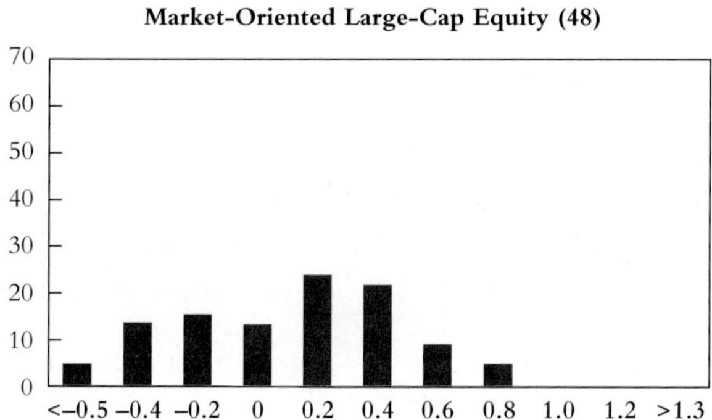

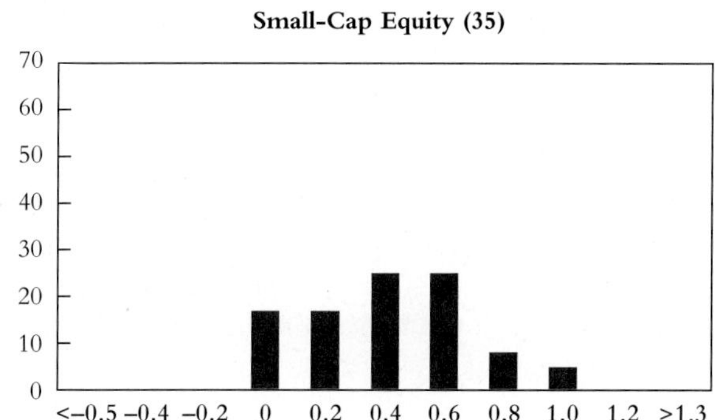

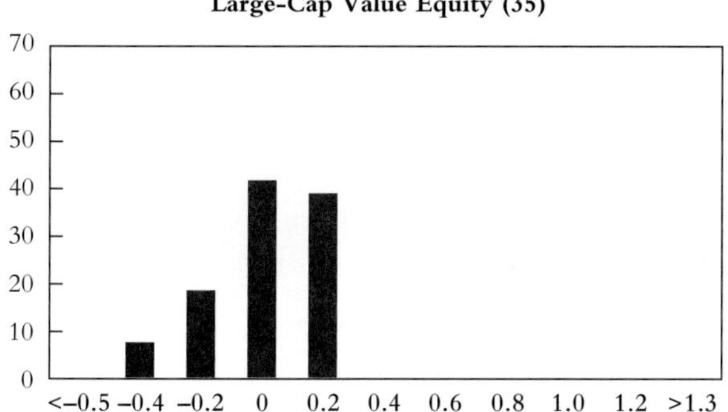

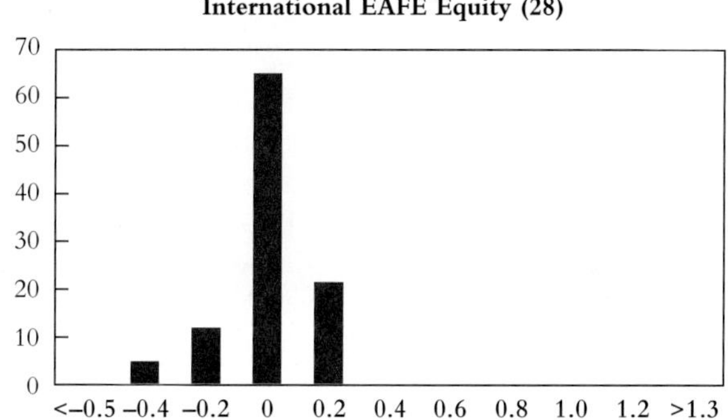

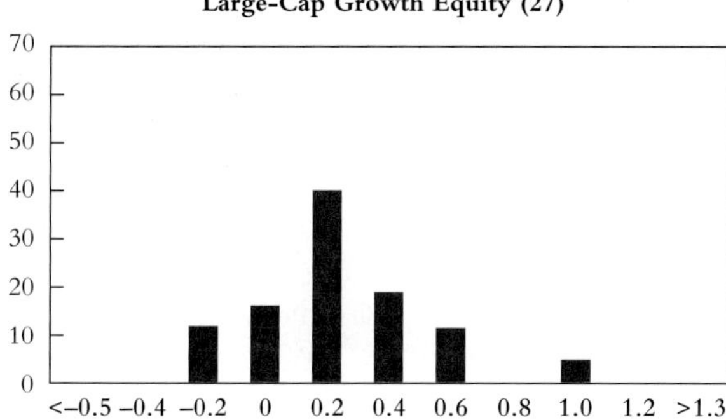

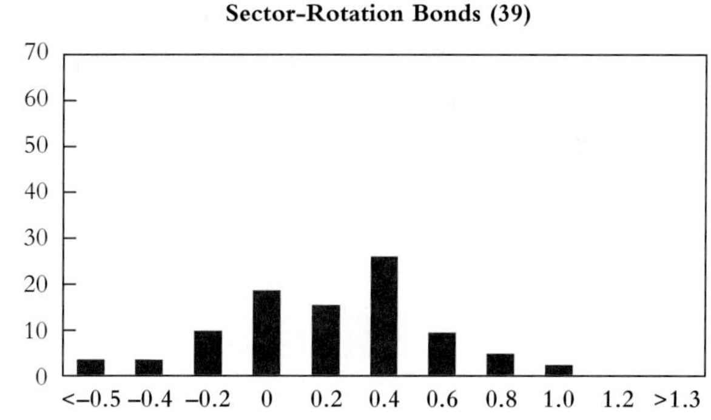

Note: Midpoints of ranges. Information ratios are on the *x*-axes; relative frequencies, in percentages, are on the *y*-axes. The number after the management style is the number of funds in that category.

Source: Thomas H. Goodwin, "The Information Ratio," from *Financial Analysts Journal,* July/Aug 1998:41.

DIVERSIFICATION

An important service a money manager can provide is effective diversification of asset holdings. Once we at least partially accept the fact that superior performance on a risk-adjusted basis is a difficult achievement, we begin to look hard at other attributes money managers may possess. For example, we can ask: Are mutual fund managers effective diversifiers of their holdings?

As previously discussed in Chapter 17 and in this chapter, there are two measures of risk: systematic and unsystematic. Systematic risk is measured by the portfolio's

the real world of investing

IF YOU CAN'T BEAT THEM, JOIN THEM: THE GROWTH OF INDEX FUNDS

An index fund is one that attempts to replicate the performance of a popular market average such as the Standard & Poor's 500 Index (**www.standardandpoors.com**). The largest index fund is the Vanguard Index 500 (**www.vanguard.com**) (based on the S&P 500), which has tripled in size over the last decade.

Why all the growth? As pointed out in the chapter, it is somewhat difficult for mutual funds and other professional money managers to consistently beat the market averages. Between 1981 and 2009, the Standard & Poor's 500 Index went up at a 10.6 percent compound annual growth rate. A mutual fund, such as the Vanguard Index 500, that passively tracks that average is going to represent stiff competition for actively managed funds and has outperformed them 80 percent of the time.

A passively managed stock fund invests in a portfolio that matches the S&P 500 Index on a daily basis. Thus if IBM's percent of the Index goes up on a given day as a result of a large price gain, and Procter & Gamble's percentage goes down, IBM will be purchased and Procter & Gamble sold to match the percentage composition of the index at the end of the day.

The management fee and expenses for a passively managed fund are approximately 0.20 percent. This is quite low because of the absence of salaries for security analysts, portfolio managers, and so on. For actively managed funds, which do incur the above costs, the typical management fee is 0.75 to 1.25 percent.

Index funds have also spread to other areas such as Fidelity's (**www.fidelity.com**) funds that track the Wilshire 5000 Equity Index (**www.wilshire.com**), and the Morgan Stanley Capital Markets International Index (**www.morganstanley.com**).

While actively managed funds have experienced difficulty in beating the performance of index funds, many optimistic investors consider it almost un-American to accept the "average performance" of index funds. Thus, the hope for finding that one great fund will always continue. Ninety percent of mutual funds are still actively managed.

(or individual stock's) beta. Under the capital asset pricing model, higher betas are rewarded with relatively high returns, and vice versa. As the market goes up 10 percent, our portfolio might go up 12 percent (beta of 1.2), and a similar phenomenon may occur on the downside. Unsystematic risk is random or nonmarket related and may be generally diversified away by the astute portfolio manager. Under the capital asset pricing model, there is no market reward for unsystematic risk since it can be eliminated through diversification.

The question for a portfolio manager then becomes: How effective have you been in diversifying away the nonrewarded, unsystematic risk? Put another way, to what extent can a fund's movements be described as market related rather than random in nature? If we plot a fund's excess returns over an extended period against market excess returns, we can determine the joint movement between the two as indicated in Figure 22–7 on the next page. In panel (a) we plot the fund's basic points. In panel (b) we draw a regression line through these points. Of importance to the present discussion is the extent to which our line fits the data. If the points of observation fall very close to the line, the independent variable (excess market returns) is largely responsible for describing the dependent variable (excess returns for fund X).

The degree of association between the independent and dependent variables is measured by **R^2 (coefficient of determination)**.[12] R^2 may take on a value anywhere between 0 and 1. A high degree of correlation between the independent and dependent variables will produce an R^2 of 0.7 or better. In panel (b) of Figure 22–7 it is assumed to be 0.90.

[12] R^2 also represents the correlation coefficient squared. Thus, we can square Formula 17A–1 in Chapter 17. Another statement is:

$$R^2 = \frac{1''' \Sigma(y''' y_c)^2/n}{\Sigma(y''' \bar{y})^2/n}$$

where y_c represents points along the regression line, and y is the average value of the independent variable.

FIGURE 22-7 Relationship of Fund's Excess Returns to Market Excess Returns

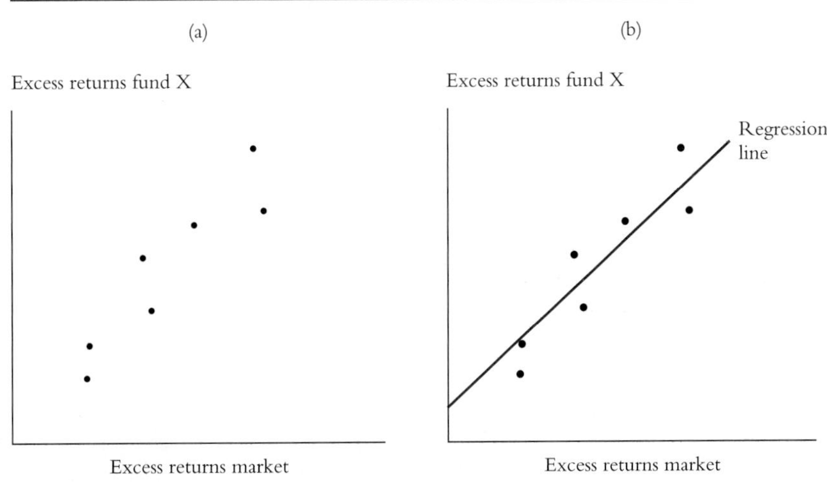

FIGURE 22-8 Example of Lower Correlation

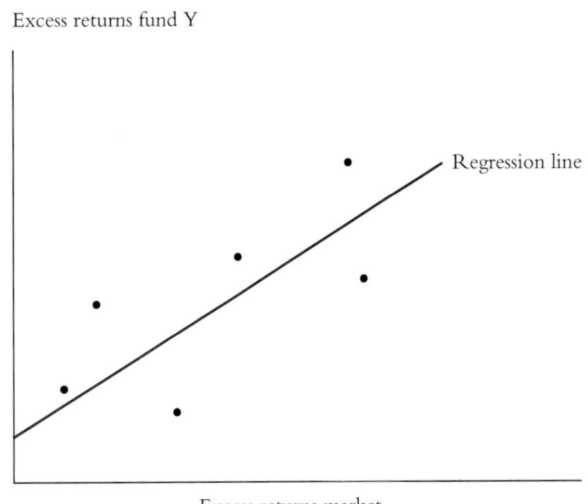

In Figure 22–8, the points do not fall consistently close to the regression line, and the R^2 value is assumed to be only 0.55. In this instance, we say the independent variable (excess market returns) was not the only major variable in explaining changes in the dependent variable (excess returns for fund Y).

The points in Figure 22–8 imply that the portfolio manager for fund Y may not have been particularly effective in his diversification efforts. Many other factors besides market returns appear to be affecting the portfolio returns of fund Y, and these could have been diversified away rather than allowed to influence returns. In this instance, we say there is a high degree of unsystematic, or non-market-related, risk. Because unsystematic risk is presumed to go unrewarded in the marketplace under the capital asset pricing model, there is evidence of inefficient portfolio diversification.

FIGURE 22-9 Quarterly Returns Attributable to Market Fluctuations: 100 Mutual Funds

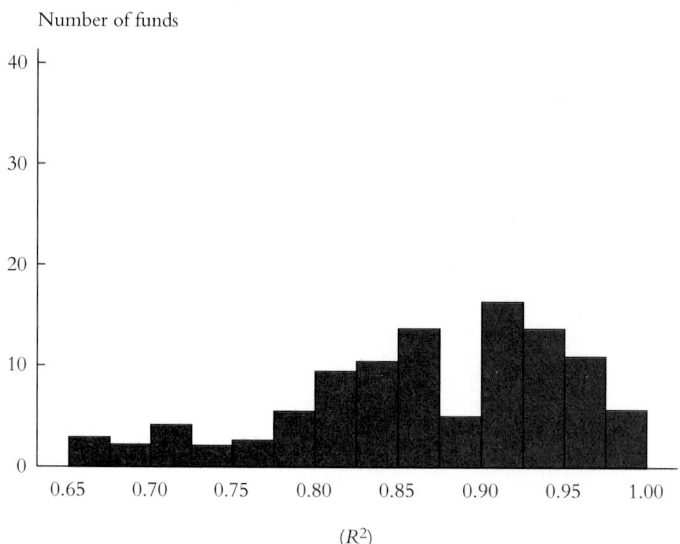

Source: Pierce, Fenner & Smith, *Investment Performance Analysis, Comparative Survey,* 1974.

What do empirical data tell us about the effectiveness of portfolio managers in achieving diversification? How have they stacked up in terms of R^2 values for their portfolios? As indicated in Figure 22–9, their record is generally good.

The Merrill Lynch study of 100 mutual funds in Figure 22–9 shows an average R^2 value of approximately 0.90 with very few funds falling below 0.70. The actual range is between 0.66 and 0.98. Studies by McDonald, Jensen, and Gentry have led to similar conclusions.

Although many mutual funds invest in 80 to 100 securities to achieve effective diversification, this is often more than is necessary. A high degree of diversification can be achieved with between 10 and 20 efficiently selected stocks.

OTHER ASSETS AS WELL AS STOCKS

This chapter has dealt primarily with the ability to measure risk and return as it relates to portfolios of common stock. Most professionally managed funds have portfolios that are also diversified across asset classes. Brinson, Hood, and Beebower (BHB) examined 91 large corporate pension plans and found that the average plan included investments in stocks, bonds, T-bills, and real estate.[13] The combined asset mix makes performance evaluation more complex than the Sharpe, Treynor, and Jensen measures discussed earlier in the chapter, which can be applied only to the stock portion of the portfolio.

BHB suggest that performance of portfolios diversified across asset classes be compared with a portfolio that consists of the pension plan's normal percentage distribution between asset classes. BHB use the Standard & Poor's 500 Index, the Shearson Lehman Government/Corporate Bond Index, and 30-day Treasury bills as the measurement indicator for each of these asset classes. For an investment manager to generate superior performance, he or she would have to outperform a passively managed portfolio maintaining the plan's mix of asset classes.

[13] Gary P. Brinson, Randolph Hood, and Gilbert L. Beebower, "Determinants of Portfolio Performance," *Financial Analysts Journal,* July–August 1986, pp. 39–44.

TABLE 22-2 Summary Statistics of Annual Returns (%), 1926-2009

Portfolio (Always Rebalance)	Geometric Mean	Arithmetic Mean	Standard Deviation
100% large company stocks	9.8	11.8	20.5
90% stocks/10% bonds	9.6	11.2	18.5
70% stocks/30% bonds	8.9	10.0	14.7
50% stocks/50% bonds	8.1	8.7	11.4
30% stocks/70% bonds	7.2	7.5	9.3
10% stocks/90% bonds	6.0	6.4	8.9
100% long-term gov't. bonds	5.4	5.8	9.6

Source: *Ibbotson SBBI Classic Yearbook,* 2010, Morningstar Inc., p. 34. Based on copyright works by Ibbotson and Sinquefield.

Ignoring real estate and focusing on stocks, bonds, and T-bills, BHB found that, in general, the actual mean average total return on managed portfolios over the period was 9.01 percent versus 10.11 percent for the benchmark portfolio. In other words, active management cost the pension plans 1.10 percent per year. Of course, over other time periods the managed portfolios could reflect superior results. Stressed throughout the BHB analysis is also the fact that determining the appropriate asset allocation mix (stocks versus bonds versus T-bills) is much more important than simply picking winning or losing stocks. Asset managers lose their jobs not so much because they picked stock A over stock B, but because they had a poorly allocated portfolio under a given market condition.

Table 22–2 shows the benefits of diversification from the risk-return trade-off between large stocks and bonds. The data are from the *Ibbotson Classic 2010 Yearbook,* based on the period 1926 to 2009. The table shows what happens to returns and standard deviations, given a mix of stocks and bonds that are rebalanced every year to maintain their original percentages at the beginning of the year. At the extremes lie the 100 percent stock and bond portfolios. Focus on the first three lines. As we move to a 90 percent stock and 10 percent bond portfolio, the returns drop slightly, and the standard deviation drops 2 percent. As we go to the 70 percent stock and 30 percent bond portfolio, we see that the returns have dropped 0.9 percent from the 100 percent bond portfolio, and the standard deviation has dropped 5.8 percent. This is a risk-return tradeoff that many investors would welcome. If the portfolios are not rebalanced, the large stock portion becomes an increasingly larger percentage of the portfolio, because stocks outperform bonds. Without rebalancing, the diversification benefits decline as the portfolio standard deviation approaches the standard deviation of large stocks.

A SPECIFIC EXAMPLE–ASSET ALLOCATION

Suppose a portfolio manager is charged with the responsibility of overseeing the performance of a $100 million portfolio. At the end of each quarter, she must report her performance to the plan sponsor, which we shall assume is a pension fund committee for a large corporation.

After intensive analysis of the economy using many of the approaches presented in Chapter 5, she decides to allocate her funds in the manner shown in column (1) of Table 22–3. The designation of funds into various categories of assets is called **asset allocation**. The second column represents her returns from each category during the course of the year. The third column shows the percentage invested (Column 1) times the returns (Column 2) and, in effect, represents her weighted return for each category and her total return for the year.

TABLE 22-3 Comparison of Managed and Benchmark Portfolios

	MANAGED PORTFOLIO			BENCHMARK PORTFOLIO		
	(1) Asset Allocation	(2) Returns	(3) Weighted Returns	(4) Asset Allocation	(5) Returns	(6) Weighted Returns
Asset Class						
Equities:						
Domestic large capitalization	30%	9%	2.70%	30%	10%	3.00%
Domestic small capitalization	20	15	3.00	15	13	1.95
International	20	18	3.60	10	14	1.40
Total equities	70%		9.30%	55%		6.35%
Fixed income:						
Domestic bonds	11%	8%	0.88%	15%	9%	1.35%
Foreign bonds	8	10	0.80	10	12	1.20
Total fixed income	19%		1.68%	25%		2.55%
Real estate	7	10%	0.70	15	11%	1.65
Cash equivalents	4	4	0.16	5	4	0.20
Total portfolio	100%		11.84%	100%		10.75%

On the right side of the table, we see a representative benchmark portfolio that is the standard for measuring her performance. In Column 4, we observe the asset allocation; in Column 5, the return for each category; and in Column 6, the weighted returns for the benchmark portfolio.

For ease of presentation, we shall assume the risk associated with her portfolio is the same as that for the benchmark portfolio. Later we will consider the implications of different risk exposure.

In observing Table 22–3, note the overall results in Column 3 for the portfolio manager and those in Column 6 for the benchmark portfolio. The portfolio manager outperformed the benchmark portfolio by 1.09 percent; that is, her total return was 11.84 percent, while the benchmark portfolio had a 10.75 percent return.

The question is, How was this superior result achieved? In this particular case, she held a larger equity position (70 percent) than the benchmark portfolio (55 percent), which turned out to be fortunate because the stock market was moving up throughout the year (all categories of equities had strong positive returns).

We can further break down the performance of equities based on the three major categories of stock. Actually, for domestic, large capitalization stocks (those with $9 billion or more in market value), she slightly underperformed the market (9 percent versus 10 percent). An appropriate market measure for the benchmark portfolio of large capitalization stocks would be the Standard & Poor's 500 Index.[14] Notice that her performance on small capitalization stocks was 2 percent higher than the market portfolio (15 percent versus 13 percent). An appropriate market measure for the benchmark portfolio of small capitalization stocks would be the Russell 2000 Index.

Finally, she achieved a high rate of return on international equities, exceeding the benchmark return by a full 4 percent (18 percent versus 14 percent). The appropriate benchmark portfolio measure might be the Dow Jones World Index. We might even decide to break down our international equity investments and the benchmark comparisons by different areas of the world such as Mexico, Europe, Asia/Pacific, and so on. Further comparisons can be made among investments in established markets and emerging markets. The effect that the changing value of the dollar had on returns could also be considered.

[14] We could also add another category of MidCap stocks, but we have omitted it to shorten the presentation.

the real world of investing

MY SECTOR UNDERPERFORMED, BUT I STILL WANT A RAISE

An important part of managing the stock component of a portfolio is the allocation of funds to the various sectors of the economy. A sector is a major grouping of companies in an area such as energy, technology, and so on. Obviously, a sector analyst wants his or her sector to perform well relative to a benchmark, such as the Standard and Poor's 500 Technology Index, but in the event he or she falls short in performance, the next best thing is to be underweighted (have a smaller percentage participation of the sector in your portfolio than that represented in the S&P 500 Index). Similarly, one might have cause for concern if he or she overperforms but is underweighted. All this comes back to the desire of portfolio managers to beat the overall S&P 500 Index. To understand these points, please observe the accompanying table.

The sectors listed are those used by Standard and Poor's (S&P) to break down the equity market into 10 different components. Column (1) shows your firm's asset allocation among the sectors. Column (2) indicates the S&P 500 weightings for the sectors at a given point in time, and Column (3) shows the difference in weights.

Next, the portfolio return is shown for each sector over a three-month holding period (Column 4), and in Column (5), the values are shown for the equivalent S&P 500 sectors. Then, in Column (6), the portfolio sector performance is shown relative to the comparable S&P sector. Column (7) is the all-important measure in which the difference in weights (Column 3) is multiplied by the sector over- or underperformance (Column 6). Thus, Column (7) indicates whether a positive or negative overall contribution is being made by each sector of the total equity return.

The math in Column (7) is a little tricky. When you multiply a percentage by a percentage, the answer tends to be very small. Look at industrials as an example (fourth line from the bottom). The value in Column (3) is 3.2 percent and the value in Column (6) is 5 percent. When the two percentages are multiplied by each other, the answer is 0.16 percent ($0.032 \times 0.05 = 0.0016$).

Overall, the portfolio outperformed the S&P by 1.39 percent as shown at the bottom of Column (7). The largest positive contribution was energy (0.63 percent).

Assume you are in charge of information technology (third line from the top). You had the misfortune of underperforming by 3.2 percent (Column 6), but because you were underweighted by 9.8 percent (Column 3), you actually delivered a positive impact of 0.31 percent. A negative times a negative equals a positive. The question is: Do you ask for the raise?

Sector Return Analysis

Sector	(1) Portfolio Weighting	(2) S&P Weighting	(3) Difference in Weighting	(4) Portfolio Return	(5) S&P Return	(6) Sector Over- or Under-performance	(7) = (3) × (6) Sector Allocation Contribution
Telecommunications services	6.0%	5.6%	0.4%	2.0%	−3.0%	5.0%	0.02%
Utilities	3.1	3.9	−0.8	−2.0	4.0	−6.0	0.05
Information technology	8.0	17.8	−9.8	4.0	7.2	−3.2	0.31
Materials	3.3	2.8	0.5	5.0	4.2	0.8	0.01
Financials	15.6	17.6	−2.0	8.1	9.2	−1.1	0.02
Consumer discretionary	14.6	13.1	1.5	9.0	12.1	−3.1	−0.05
Industrials	14.7	11.5	3.2	9.0	4.0	5.0	0.16
Energy	14.3	7.0	7.3	18.0	9.4	8.6	0.63
Health care	17.0	13.3	3.7	14.9	10.7	4.2	0.16
Consumer staples	3.4	7.4	−4.0	6.8	8.8	−2.0	0.08
							1.39%

In moving to fixed-income securities, our portfolio manager underperformed the benchmark portfolio, both domestically (8 percent versus 9 percent) and internationally (10 percent versus 12 percent). The same slight underperformance can be found in real estate (10 percent versus 11 percent). However, with only 19 percent of assets allocated to fixed income and 7 percent to real estate in the managed portfolio, this underperformance is not a problem.

In summary, our portfolio manager had a strong performance because of an equity position (70 percent) that was much higher than the benchmark portfolio (55 percent); that is, she benefited from superior asset allocation. She also gained from superior stock selection in the small capitalization and international equity areas; these factors more than overcame the slightly inferior performance in other categories.

Earlier in the chapter, we talked about risk considerations in measuring performance. Although we will not make a formal evaluation of risk in this case, certain factors are worthy of note. To the extent that the managed portfolio is riskier than the benchmark portfolio, the superior return would have to be partially discounted. Of course, if it is less risky than the market, the superior performance becomes even more meaningful.

While the higher equity component in the managed portfolio might imply greater risk, the large degree of international diversification could easily compensate for this factor. International securities may offset shocks in the U.S. market, and vice versa. Also, the managed portfolio appears to be more liquid than the benchmark portfolio, with real estate representing 7 percent of the holdings versus 15 percent for the benchmark portfolio. This is true in spite of a slightly lower cash position in the managed portfolio.

One last factor is worthy of note in discussing the performance of the portfolio manager. The results presented in Table 22–3 on page 580 represent annual data. As mentioned earlier, the portfolio manager will not only need to present annual information for evaluation but normally reports quarterly to the investor as well. Because there is always strong pressure for performance, short-term swings in the market can test a portfolio manager's convictions. For example, when the stock market is going down, a portfolio manager with a large equity position (perhaps 70 percent or greater) may be under pressure to lighten up on stocks because of negative returns. However, down markets are normally the best time to buy, not to sell. This principle may be severely tested when a portfolio manager has to report a quarterly loss but, at the same time, suggests that unusually good buying opportunities now exist. While the stock market generally provides superior returns in comparison with other investments over the long term, such may not be the case over a short period of time. Well-informed portfolio managers, and those for whom they work, generally use a three- to five-year time horizon to determine whether performance is acceptable. However, in the world of money management, one or two bad quarters can sometimes mean the loss of an account.

exploring the web

Web Address	Comments
www.morningstar.com	**Provides analysis of mutual fund portfolios and modern portfolio theory statistics for mutual funds tracked by Morningstar and for personal portfolios; some analysis is fee-based**
www.financialengines.com	**Provides portfolio analysis and information on personal financial planning**
www.stockworm.com	**Site will track and evaluate portfolios**
finance.yahoo.com	**Provides analysis of mutual funds using Morningstar data**

SUMMARY

The ability of portfolio managers to meet various goals and objectives is considered in this chapter. Many portfolio managers appear to demonstrate superior performances during market boom years. However, when this performance is adjusted for risk, any perceived superiority may quickly vanish.

Some concepts related to the capital asset pricing model may be used to evaluate the performance of money managers. Portfolio beta values are shown along the horizontal axis, while the market line indicates expected returns. Portfolio managers that are able to operate above the line (positive alphas) are thought to be superior managers, while the opposite would be true of those falling below the line. Research indicates that, on average, portfolio managers do not beat the popular averages or random portfolios on a risk-adjusted basis.

Nevertheless, mutual funds (or other managed portfolios) do have some desirable attributes. As indicated by a Merrill Lynch study (and others as well), mutual funds tend to be very efficient diversifiers. Their average correlation with the market (R^2) tends to be approximately 90 percent, indicating only 10 percent unsystematic, or nonrewarded, risk. In general, mutual fund managers also do a good job of constructing portfolios that are consistent with their initially stated objectives (that is, maximum capital gains, growth, income, etc.).

In a specific evaluation of a professional money manager, one may wish to judge how assets were allocated between stocks, bonds, real estate, cash equivalents, and so forth, and whether this was effective over a given time period. Furthermore, the performance within each asset classification can be compared with a benchmark portfolio's return. All of this analysis enables one to determine the overall adequacy of performance and how it was produced.

KEY WORDS AND CONCEPTS

alpha (average differential return) 573
asset allocation 579
average differential return 573
excess returns 570
index funds 574
institutional investors 588
Jensen approach 571
market line 572
R^2 (coefficient of determination) 576
Sharpe approach 571
Treynor approach 571

DISCUSSION QUESTIONS

1. What is a risk-adjusted return?
2. In evaluating a mutual fund manager, what would be the first point to analyze?
3. How can risk exposure be measured?
4. How are excess returns defined?
5. What is the Sharpe approach to measuring portfolio risk? If a portfolio has a higher Sharpe measure than the market in general under the Sharpe approach, what is the implication?
6. How does the Treynor approach differ from the Sharpe approach? Which of the two measures assumes unsystematic risk will be diversified away?
7. Under the Jensen approach, how is the market line related to the beta?
8. Explain alpha as a measure of performance.
9. What conclusions can be drawn from the empirical studies of portfolio (fund) managers' performances? Are they superior?

www.mhhe.com/hirtblock10e

10. If investment companies do not offer returns that are, on average, any better than the market in general, why would someone invest in them?

11. What does a high R^2 (correlation) between a fund's excess returns and the market's excess returns indicate about the fund manager's ability to effectively diversify?

12. According to the Brinson, Hood, and Beebower (BHB) study, are asset allocation decisions (stocks versus bonds, etc.) more or less important than individual stock selection decisions?

PRACTICE PROBLEMS AND SOLUTIONS

Sharpe approach to measuring performance

1. A firm that evaluates portfolios uses the Sharpe approach to measuring performance. How would it rank the following three portfolios?

	Portfolio Return	Risk-Free Rate	Portfolio Standard Deviation
Tinker Investment Co.	12%	5%	15%
Evers Group	9	5	22
Lawson Money Managers	13	5	16

Treynor approach to measuring performance

2. Now assume the money managers are evaluated using the Treynor approach. The portfolio betas are as follows:

	Portfolio Beta
Tinker Investment Co.	0.95
Evers Group	1.10
Lawson Money Managers	1.40

Rank the three money managers.

Solutions

1. $$\text{Sharpe Measure} = \frac{\text{Total portfolio return} - \text{Risk-free rate}}{\text{Portfolio standard deviation}}$$

$$\text{Tinker} = \frac{12\% - 5\%}{15\%} = \frac{7\%}{15\%} = .467$$

$$\text{Evers} = \frac{9\% - 5\%}{22\%} = \frac{4\%}{22\%} = .182$$

$$\text{Lawson} = \frac{13\% - 5\%}{16\%} = \frac{8\%}{16\%} = .500$$

Ranking	
Lawson	.500
Tinker	.467
Evers	.182

2. $\text{Treynor Measure} = \dfrac{\text{Total portfolio return} - \text{Risk-free rate}}{\text{Portfolio beta}}$

$$\text{Tinker} = \frac{12\% - 5\%}{.95} = \frac{7\%}{.95} = .074$$

$$\text{Evers} = \frac{9\% - 5\%}{1.10} = \frac{4\%}{1.10} = .036$$

$$\text{Lawson} = \frac{13\% - 5\%}{1.40} = \frac{8\%}{1.40} = .057$$

Ranking	
Tinker	.074
Lawson	.057
Evers	.036

PROBLEMS

Sharpe approach to measuring performance

1. A firm that evaluates portfolios uses the Sharpe approach to measuring performance. How would it rank the following three portfolios? (Round to three places to the right of the decimal point.)

	Portfolio Return	Risk-Free Rate	Portfolio Standard Deviation
Grange Money Managers	10.0%	7%	14%
Harmon Group	10.2	7	18
Luckman Investment Company	14.0	7	22

Treynor approach to measuring performance

2. Assume a second firm that evaluates portfolios uses the Treynor approach to measuring performance. The firm is also evaluating the three portfolios in problem 1. The portfolio betas are as follows:

	Portfolio Beta
Grange Money Managers	1.18
Harmon Group	0.90
Luckman Investment Company	1.25

a. Using the Treynor approach, how would the second firm rank the three portfolios? (Round to three places to the right of the decimal point.)
b. Explain why any differences have taken place in the rankings between problems 1 and 2*a*.
c. If the Treynor approach is utilized and the market return is 10 percent (with a risk-free rate of 7 percent), which of the portfolios outperformed the market? The market beta is always 1.

Jensen approach to measuring performance

3. Assume the Jensen approach to portfolio valuation is being used.
a. Draw a market line similar to that in Figure 22–4 on page 573. That is, show 0 excess returns at a 0 portfolio beta and 3 percent excess returns at a portfolio beta of 1. Now graph the three portolios.
b. Which portfolio(s) over- or underperformed the market?

Asset allocation and returns

4. A portfolio manager has the following asset allocation and returns on his portfolio. Fill in the values in Column (3). Use Table 22–2 on page 579 as a guideline on how to proceed.

	(1) Portfolio Manager Asset Allocation	(2) Portfolio Manager Returns	(3) Portfolio Manager Weighted Returns
Asset Class			
Equities:			
Domestic large capitalization	25%	10%	
Domestic small capitalization	20	13	
International	5	20	
Total equities	50%		
Fixed income:			
Domestic bonds	20%	7%	
Foreign bonds	7	8	
Total fixed income	27%		
Real estate	3	10%	
Cash equivalents	20	5	
Total portfolio	100%		

The benchmark portfolio with which he is being compared is shown below:

	(1) Benchmark Portfolio Asset Allocation	(2) Benchmark Portfolio Returns	(3) Benchmark Portfolio Weighted Returns
Asset Class			
Equities:			
Domestic large capitalization	30%	9%	2.70%
Domestic small capitalization	25	12	3.00
International	17	18	3.06
Total equities	72%		8.76%
Fixed income:			
Domestic bonds	13%	6%	0.78%
Foreign bonds	6	7	0.42
Total fixed income	19%		1.20%
Real estate	3	9%	0.27
Cash equivalents	6	4	0.24
Total portfolio	100%		10.47%

a. Explain why the portfolio manager under- or overperformed the benchmark portfolio.

b. If cash equivalents had been reduced by the portfolio manager to 15 percent and had been invested in international equities at his indicated rate of return, would the portfolio manager have under- or overperformed the benchmark portfolio?

5. *a.* Fill the blanks in the table below for a quarterly comparison of sectors with the S&P 500 Index (see the box on page 581).

Sector	(1) Portfolio Weighting	(2) S&P Weighting	(3) Differences in Weighting	(4) Portfolio Return	(5) S&P Return	(6) Sector Over- or Under-performance	(7) Sector Allocation Contributions
Telecommunications services	2.7%	5.8%	______	2.0%	3.3%	______	______
Utilities	8.1	3.7	______	3.2	1.8	______	______
Information technology	15.5	18.2	______	5.9	2.6	______	______
Materials	5.2	2.5	______	3.8	1.8	______	______
Financials	12.1	18.1	______	5.0	2.0	______	______
Consumer discretionary	10.8	13.3	______	1.8	3.0	______	______
Industrials	15.2	12.1	______	4.1	5.0	______	______
Energy	9.1	7.8	______	4.3	9.0	______	______
Health care	17.1	11.9	______	10.6	4.8	______	______
Consumer staples	4.2	6.6	______	1.2	12.5	______	______

b. Did the portfolio manger under- or overperform the S&P 500?
c. Which sector made the largest positive contribution?
d. Which sector made the largest negative contribution?

INVESTMENT ADVISOR PROBLEM

Lauren McGill had just graduated from California State University at Fullerton (Cal State–Fullerton) and accepted a job with Bank of America as a credit analyst for $45,000 a year. Her long-term career plan was to become a senior loan officer in the energy sector or a bank president. Since she was only 22, she had at least four decades to reach her goal.

In her first year of work, she decided to put $3,000 in an IRA (Individual Retirement Account). She was not sure whether the money should go into stocks, bonds, or CDs. She told her 50-year-old uncle of her plans for an IRA, and he had this warning for her. "Be careful with the stock market. It can go up one minute and down the next. I made $10,000 in the market last year and lost $12,000 this year when the Federal Reserve started raising interest rates."

Lauren respected her uncle's knowledge about the import–export business, in which he had 30 years of experience, but did not deem him to be an expert in financial planning.

She decided to check out his logic as it applied to her IRA with Susan Wolinsky, an investment advisor in the trust department of Bank of America.

a. What advice do you think Susan should give Lauren in regard to the short-term volatility of the stock market as it applies to her IRA?
b. Referring back to "Retirement and Estate Planning Considerations" in Chapter 1, what tax advantage will an IRA allow Lauren?
c. If Lauren puts away $3,000 a year for the next 40 years and the funds grow at 11 percent, how much will she have accumulated at that time?

WEB EXERCISE

1. For the following five stocks, you will write in their 1-year return following their beta.

   Home Depot (HD)
   American International Group (AIG)
   Harley Davidson (HDI)
   Consolidated Edison (ED)
   CISCO Systems (CSCO)

2. To get the 1-year return go to **www.bloomberg.com**. The 1-year return can be found by typing the ticker symbol into the "Search Quotes and News" box in the upper right-hand corner of the screen and then hitting "Enter." The 1-year return will show up at the end of the summary table.
3. Fill in the table below:

Company	Beta	1-Year Return
Home Depot (HD)	1.30	
American International Group (AIG)	0.95	
Harley Davidson (HDI)	1.10	
Consolidated Edison (ED)	0.65	
CISCO Systems (CSCO)	1.45	

4. Have the riskier companies provided higher returns as they are supposed to? Do not be surprised by your answer one way or the other.

Note: From time to time, companies redesign their Web sites, and occasionally a topic we have listed may have been deleted, updated, or moved into a different location.

APPENDIX 22A

THE MAKEUP OF INSTITUTIONAL INVESTORS

Having discussed measurement and portfolio management techniques for institutional investors, we will now take a more specific look at the participants. **Institutional investors**, as opposed to individual investors, represent organizations that are responsible for bringing together large pools of capital for reinvestment. Our coverage will center on investment companies (including mutual funds), pension funds, life insurance companies, bank trust departments, and endowments and foundations.

Investment Companies (including Mutual Funds)

Investment companies take the proceeds of individual investors and reinvest them in other securities according to their specific objectives. Income and capital gains are generally distributed to stockholders and are subject to single taxation under Subchapter M of the Internal Revenue Code. Investment companies were discussed at some length in Chapter 4.

TABLE 22A-1 Percentage of Institutional Market Held by Institutional Investors

	Percent
1. Private noninsured pension funds	28.3%
2. Open-end investment companies	16.1
3. Other investment companies	1.9
4. Life insurance companies	5.0
5. Property-liability insurance companies	4.7
6. Personal trust funds	26.4
7. Common trust funds	1.6
8. Mutual savings banks	0.9
9. State and local retirement funds	4.8
10. Foundations	7.5
11. Educational endowments	2.8
	100%

Source: Compiled from a review of annual reports from the Securities and Exchange Commission and the New York Stock Exchange.

Other Institutional Investors

Other institutional investors (along with investment companies) and their extent of market participation are presented in Table 22A–1. Total institutional holdings are more than $10 trillion. We will briefly comment on pension funds, insurance companies, bank trust departments, and foundations and endowments.

Pension Funds Pension funds represent an important and growing sector of the institutional market and may be private or public. Private funds represent well over half of the pension fund market. The benefits that accrue under private pension funds may be insured or uninsured, with the latter arrangement occurring most frequently. Public pension funds are run for the benefit of federal, state, or local employees.

Insurance Companies Insurance companies may be categorized as either "life" or "property and casualty." Life insurance companies must earn a minimum rate of return assumed in calculating insurance premiums, and public policy emphasizes safety of assets. Part of life insurance company assets are in privately placed debt or mortgages, with the balance in bonds and stocks. Property and casualty insurance companies enjoy more lenient regulation of their activities and generally have a larger percentage of their assets in bonds and stocks.

Bank Trust Departments The emphasis in bank trust departments is on managing other people's funds for a fee. Banks may administer individual trusts or commingled (combined) funds in a common trust fund. Often a bank will establish more than one common trust fund to serve varying needs and objectives. The overall performance of bank trust departments has been mixed, with the usual number of leaders and laggards. Bank trust management is highly concentrated with a relatively small number of trust departments holding the majority of funds. Out of approximately 3,000 bank trust departments, the top 10 hold one-third of all assets, and the largest 60 hold two-thirds.

Foundations and Endowments Foundations represent nonprofit organizations set up to accomplish social, educational, or charitable purposes. They are often established through the donation of a large block of stock in which the donor was one of the corporate founders. Examples include the Ford, Carnegie, and Rockefeller foundations. Endowments, on the other hand, represent permanent capital funds that are donated to universities, churches, or civic organizations. The management of endowment funds is often quite difficult because of the pressure for current income to maintain operations (perhaps the university library) while at the same time there is a demand for capital appreciation. Measurement of performance for foundations and endowments is moving more to a total-return basis (annual income plus capital appreciation) rather than the traditional interest-earned or dividend-received basis.

appendices

appendix **A**
COMPOUND SUM OF $1

appendix **B**
COMPOUND SUM OF AN ANNUITY OF $1

appendix **C**
PRESENT VALUE OF $1

appendix **D**
PRESENT VALUE OF AN ANNUITY OF $1

appendix **E**
TIME VALUE OF MONEY AND INVESTMENT APPLICATIONS

appendix **F**
USING CALCULATORS FOR FINANCIAL ANALYSIS

APPENDIX A Compound Sum of $1 $S = PV(1 + i)^n$

	PERCENT										
Period	1%	2%	3%	4%	5%	6%	7%	8%	9%	10%	11%
1	1.010	1.020	1.030	1.040	1.050	1.060	1.070	1.080	1.090	1.100	1.110
2	1.020	1.040	1.061	1.082	1.103	1.124	1.145	1.166	1.188	1.210	1.232
3	1.030	1.061	1.093	1.125	1.158	1.191	1.225	1.260	1.295	1.331	1.368
4	1.041	1.082	1.126	1.170	1.216	1.262	1.311	1.360	1.412	1.464	1.518
5	1.051	1.104	1.159	1.217	1.276	1.338	1.403	1.469	1.539	1.611	1.685
6	1.062	1.126	1.194	1.265	1.340	1.419	1.501	1.587	1.677	1.772	1.870
7	1.072	1.149	1.230	1.316	1.407	1.504	1.606	1.714	1.828	1.949	2.076
8	1.083	1.172	1.267	1.369	1.477	1.594	1.718	1.851	1.993	2.144	2.305
9	1.094	1.195	1.305	1.423	1.551	1.689	1.838	1.999	2.172	2.358	2.558
10	1.105	1.219	1.344	1.480	1.629	1.791	1.967	2.159	2.367	2.594	2.839
11	1.116	1.243	1.384	1.539	1.710	1.898	2.105	2.332	2.580	2.853	3.152
12	1.127	1.268	1.426	1.601	1.796	2.012	2.252	2.518	2.813	3.138	3.498
13	1.138	1.294	1.469	1.665	1.886	2.133	2.410	2.720	3.066	3.452	3.883
14	1.149	1.319	1.513	1.732	1.980	2.261	2.579	2.937	3.342	3.797	4.310
15	1.161	1.346	1.558	1.801	2.079	2.397	2.759	3.172	3.642	4.177	4.785
16	1.173	1.373	1.605	1.873	2.183	2.540	2.952	3.426	3.970	4.595	5.311
17	1.184	1.400	1.653	1.948	2.292	2.693	3.159	3.700	4.328	5.054	5.895
18	1.196	1.428	1.702	2.206	2.407	2.854	3.380	3.996	4.717	5.560	6.544
19	1.208	1.457	1.754	2.107	2.527	3.026	3.617	4.316	5.142	6.116	7.263
20	1.220	1.486	1.806	2.191	2.653	3.207	3.870	4.661	5.604	6.727	8.062
25	1.282	1.641	2.094	2.666	3.386	4.292	5.427	6.848	8.623	10.835	13.585
30	1.348	1.811	2.427	3.243	4.322	5.743	7.612	10.063	13.268	17.449	22.892
40	1.489	2.208	3.262	4.801	7.040	10.286	14.974	21.725	31.409	42.259	65.001
50	1.645	2.692	4.384	7.107	11.467	18.420	29.457	46.902	74.358	117.39	184.57

APPENDIX A Compound Sum of $1 *(concluded)*

	PERCENT										
Period	12%	13%	14%	15%	16%	17%	18%	19%	20%	25%	30%
1 . . .	1.120	1.130	1.140	1.150	1.160	1.170	1.180	1.190	1.200	1.250	1.300
2 . . .	1.254	1.277	1.300	1.323	1.346	1.369	1.392	1.416	1.440	1.563	1.690
3 . . .	1.405	1.443	1.482	1.521	1.561	1.602	1.643	1.685	1.728	1.953	2.197
4 . . .	1.574	1.630	1.689	1.749	1.811	1.874	1.939	2.005	2.074	2.441	2.856
5 . . .	1.762	1.842	1.925	2.011	2.100	2.192	2.288	2.386	2.488	3.052	3.713
6 . . .	1.974	2.082	2.195	2.313	2.436	2.565	2.700	2.840	2.986	3.815	4.827
7 . . .	2.211	2.353	2.502	2.660	2.826	3.001	3.185	3.379	3.583	4.768	6.276
8 . . .	2.476	2.658	2.853	3.059	3.278	3.511	3.759	4.021	4.300	5.960	8.157
9 . . .	2.773	3.004	3.252	3.518	3.803	4.108	4.435	4.785	5.160	7.451	10.604
10 . . .	3.106	3.395	3.707	4.046	4.411	4.807	5.234	5.696	6.192	9.313	13.786
11 . . .	3.479	3.836	4.226	4.652	5.117	5.624	6.176	6.777	7.430	11.642	17.922
12 . . .	3.896	4.335	4.818	5.350	5.936	6.580	7.288	8.064	8.916	14.552	23.298
13 . . .	4.363	4.898	5.492	6.153	6.886	7.699	8.599	9.596	10.699	18.190	30.288
14 . . .	4.887	5.535	6.261	7.076	7.988	9.007	10.147	11.420	12.839	22.737	39.374
15 . . .	5.474	6.254	7.138	8.137	9.266	10.539	11.974	13.590	15.407	28.422	51.186
16 . . .	6.130	7.067	8.137	9.358	10.748	12.330	14.129	16.172	18.488	35.527	66.542
17 . . .	6.866	7.986	9.276	10.761	12.468	14.426	16.672	19.244	22.186	44.409	86.504
18 . . .	7.690	9.024	10.575	12.375	14.463	16.879	19.673	22.091	26.623	55.511	112.46
19 . . .	8.613	10.197	12.056	14.232	16.777	19.748	23.214	27.252	31.948	69.389	146.19
20 . . .	9.646	11.523	13.743	16.367	19.461	23.106	27.393	32.429	38.338	86.736	190.05
25 . . .	17.000	21.231	26.462	32.919	40.874	50.658	62.699	77.388	95.396	264.70	705.64
30 . . .	29.960	39.116	50.950	66.212	85.850	111.07	143.37	184.68	237.38	807.79	2,620.0
40 . . .	93.051	132.78	188.88	267.86	378.72	533.87	750.38	1,051.7	1,469.8	7,523.2	36,119.
50 . . .	289.00	450.74	700.23	1,083.7	1,670.7	2,566.2	3,927.4	5,988.9	9,100.4	70,065.	497,929.

APPENDIX B Compound Sum of an Annuity of $1 $S_A = A\left[\frac{(1+i)^n - 1}{i}\right]$

Period	PERCENT										
	1%	2%	3%	4%	5%	6%	7%	8%	9%	10%	11%
1 . . .	1.000	1.000	1.000	1.000	1.000	1.000	1.000	1.000	1.000	1.000	1.000
2 . . .	2.010	2.020	2.030	2.040	2.050	2.060	2.070	2.080	2.090	2.100	2.110
3 . . .	3.030	3.060	3.091	3.122	3.153	3.184	3.215	3.246	3.278	3.310	3.342
4 . . .	4.060	4.122	4.184	4.246	4.310	4.375	4.440	4.506	4.573	4.641	4.710
5 . . .	5.101	5.204	5.309	5.416	5.526	5.637	5.751	5.867	5.985	6.105	6.228
6 . . .	6.152	6.308	6.468	6.633	6.802	6.975	7.153	7.336	7.523	7.716	7.913
7 . . .	7.214	7.434	7.662	7.898	8.142	8.394	8.654	8.923	9.200	9.487	9.783
8 . . .	8.286	8.583	8.892	9.214	9.549	9.897	10.260	10.637	11.028	11.436	11.859
9 . . .	9.369	9.755	10.159	10.583	11.027	11.491	11.978	12.488	13.021	13.579	14.164
10 . . .	10.462	10.950	11.464	12.006	12.578	13.181	13.816	14.487	15.193	15.937	16.722
11 . . .	11.567	12.169	12.808	13.486	14.207	14.972	15.784	16.645	17.560	18.531	19.561
12 . . .	12.683	13.412	14.192	15.026	15.917	16.870	17.888	18.977	20.141	21.384	22.713
13 . . .	13.809	14.680	15.618	16.627	17.713	18.882	20.141	21.495	22.953	24.523	26.212
14 . . .	14.947	15.974	17.086	18.292	19.599	21.015	22.550	24.215	26.019	27.975	30.095
15 . . .	16.097	17.293	18.599	20.024	21.579	23.276	25.129	27.152	29.361	31.772	34.405
16 . . .	17.258	18.639	20.157	21.825	23.657	25.673	27.888	30.324	33.003	35.950	39.190
17 . . .	18.430	20.012	21.762	23.698	25.840	20.213	30.840	33.750	36.974	40.545	44.501
18 . . .	19.615	21.412	23.414	25.645	28.132	30.906	33.999	37.450	41.301	45.599	50.396
19 . . .	20.811	22.841	25.117	27.671	30.539	33.760	37.379	41.446	46.018	51.159	56.939
20 . . .	22.019	24.297	26.870	29.778	33.066	36.786	40.995	45.762	51.160	57.275	64.203
25 . . .	28.243	32.030	36.459	41.646	47.727	54.865	63.249	73.106	84.701	98.347	114.41
30 . . .	34.785	40.588	47.575	56.085	66.439	79.058	94.461	113.28	136.31	164.49	199.02
40 . . .	48.886	60.402	75.401	95.026	120.80	154.76	199.64	259.06	337.89	442.59	581.83
50 . . .	64.463	84.579	112.80	152.67	209.35	290.34	406.53	573.77	815.08	1,163.9	1,668.8

APPENDIX B Compound Sum of an Annuity of $1 *(concluded)*

	PERCENT										
Period	12%	13%	14%	15%	16%	17%	18%	19%	20%	25%	30%
1 . . .	1.000	1.000	1.000	1.000	1.000	1.000	1.000	1.000	1.000	1.000	1.000
2 . . .	2.120	2.130	2.140	2.150	2.160	2.170	2.180	2.190	2.200	2.250	2.300
3 . . .	3.374	3.407	3.440	3.473	3.506	3.539	3.572	3.606	3.640	3.813	3.990
4 . . .	4.779	4.850	4.921	4.993	5.066	5.141	5.215	5.291	5.368	5.766	6.187
5 . . .	6.353	6.480	6.610	6.742	6.877	7.014	7.154	7.297	7.442	8.207	9.043
6 . . .	8.115	8.323	8.536	9.754	8.977	9.207	9.442	9.683	9.930	11.259	12.756
7 . . .	10.089	10.405	10.730	11.067	11.414	11.772	12.142	12.523	12.916	15.073	17.583
8 . . .	12.300	12.757	13.233	13.727	14.240	14.773	15.327	15.902	16.499	19.842	23.858
9 . . .	14.776	15.416	16.085	16.786	17.519	18.285	19.086	19.923	20.799	25.802	32.015
10 . . .	17.549	18.420	19.337	20.304	21.321	22.393	23.521	24.701	25.959	33.253	42.619
11 . . .	20.655	21.814	23.045	24.349	25.733	27.200	28.755	30.404	32.150	42.566	56.405
12 . . .	24.133	25.650	27.271	29.002	30.850	32.824	34.931	37.180	39.581	54.208	74.327
13 . . .	28.029	29.985	32.089	34.352	36.786	39.404	42.219	45.244	48.497	68.760	97.625
14 . . .	32.393	34.883	37.581	40.505	43.672	47.103	50.818	54.841	59.196	86.949	127.91
15 . . .	37.280	40.417	43.842	47.580	51.660	56.110	60.965	66.261	72.035	109.69	167.29
16 . . .	42.753	46.672	50.980	55.717	60.925	66.649	72.939	79.850	87.442	138.11	218.47
17 . . .	48.884	53.739	59.118	65.075	71.673	78.979	87.068	96.022	105.93	173.64	285.01
18 . . .	55.750	61.725	68.394	75.836	84.141	93.406	103.74	115.27	128.12	218.05	371.52
19 . . .	63.440	70.749	78.969	88.212	98.603	110.29	123.41	138.17	154.74	273.56	483.97
20 . . .	72.052	80.947	91.025	102.44	115.38	130.03	146.63	165.42	186.69	342.95	630.17
25 . . .	133.33	155.62	181.87	212.79	249.21	292.11	342.60	402.04	471.98	1,054.8	2,348.80
30 . . .	241.33	293.20	356.79	434.75	530.31	647.44	790.95	966.7	1,181.9	3,227.2	8,730.0
40 . . .	767.09	1,013.7	1,342.0	1,779.1	2,360.8	3,134.5	4,163.21	5,529.8	7,343.9	30,089.	120,393.
50 . . .	2,400.0	3,459.5	4,994.5	7,217.7	10,436.	15,090.	21,813.	31,515.	45,497.	280,256.	1,659,731.

APPENDIX C Present Value of $1 $PV = S\left[\frac{1}{(1+i)^n}\right]$

Period	PERCENT											
	1%	2%	3%	4%	5%	6%	7%	8%	9%	10%	11%	12%
1	0.990	0.980	0.971	0.962	0.952	0.943	0.935	0.926	0.917	0.909	0.901	0.893
2	0.980	0.961	0.943	0.925	0.907	0.890	0.873	0.857	0.842	0.826	0.812	0.797
3	0.971	0.942	0.915	0.889	0.864	0.840	0.816	0.794	0.772	0.751	0.731	0.712
4	0.961	0.924	0.885	0.855	0.823	0.792	0.763	0.735	0.708	0.683	0.659	0.636
5	0.951	0.906	0.863	0.822	0.784	0.747	0.713	0.681	0.650	0.621	0.593	0.567
6	0.942	0.888	0.837	0.790	0.746	0.705	0.666	0.630	0.596	0.564	0.535	0.507
7	0.933	0.871	0.813	0.760	0.711	0.665	0.623	0.583	0.547	0.513	0.482	0.452
8	0.923	0.853	0.789	0.731	0.677	0.627	0.582	0.540	0.502	0.467	0.434	0.404
9	0.914	0.837	0.766	0.703	0.645	0.592	0.544	0.500	0.460	0.424	0.391	0.361
10	0.905	0.820	0.744	0.676	0.614	0.558	0.508	0.463	0.422	0.386	0.352	0.322
11	0.896	0.804	0.722	0.650	0.585	0.527	0.475	0.429	0.388	0.350	0.317	0.287
12	0.887	0.788	0.701	0.625	0.557	0.497	0.444	0.397	0.356	0.319	0.286	0.257
13	0.879	0.773	0.681	0.601	0.530	0.469	0.415	0.368	0.326	0.290	0.258	0.229
14	0.870	0.758	0.661	0.577	0.505	0.442	0.388	0.340	0.299	0.263	0.232	0.205
15	0.861	0.743	0.642	0.555	0.481	0.417	0.362	0.315	0.275	0.239	0.209	0.183
16	0.853	0.728	0.623	0.534	0.458	0.394	0.339	0.292	0.252	0.218	0.188	0.163
17	0.844	0.714	0.605	0.513	0.436	0.371	0.317	0.270	0.231	0.198	0.170	0.146
18	0.836	0.700	0.587	0.494	0.416	0.350	0.296	0.250	0.212	0.180	0.153	0.130
19	0.828	0.686	0.570	0.475	0.396	0.331	0.277	0.232	0.194	0.164	0.138	0.116
20	0.820	0.673	0.554	0.456	0.377	0.312	0.258	0.215	0.178	0.149	0.124	0.104
25	0.780	0.610	0.478	0.375	0.295	0.233	0.184	0.146	0.116	0.092	0.074	0.059
30	0.742	0.552	0.412	0.308	0.231	0.174	0.131	0.099	0.075	0.057	0.044	0.033
40	0.672	0.453	0.307	0.208	0.142	0.097	0.067	0.046	0.032	0.022	0.015	0.011
50	0.608	0.372	0.228	0.141	0.087	0.054	0.034	0.021	0.013	0.009	0.005	0.003

APPENDIX C Present Value of $1 *(concluded)*

	PERCENT												
Period	**13%**	**14%**	**15%**	**16%**	**17%**	**18%**	**19%**	**20%**	**25%**	**30%**	**35%**	**40%**	**50%**
1	0.885	0.877	0.870	0.862	0.855	0.847	0.840	0.833	0.800	0.769	0.741	0.714	0.667
2	0.783	0.769	0.756	0.743	0.731	0.718	0.706	0.694	0.640	0.592	0.549	0.510	0.444
3	0.693	0.675	0.658	0.641	0.624	0.609	0.593	0.579	0.512	0.455	0.406	0.364	0.296
4	0.613	0.592	0.572	0.552	0.534	0.515	0.499	0.482	0.410	0.350	0.301	0.260	0.198
5	0.543	0.519	0.497	0.476	0.456	0.437	0.419	0.402	0.320	0.269	0.223	0.186	0.132
6	0.480	0.456	0.432	0.410	0.390	0.370	0.352	0.335	0.262	0.207	0.165	0.133	0.088
7	0.425	0.400	0.376	0.354	0.333	0.314	0.296	0.279	0.210	0.159	0.122	0.095	0.059
8	0.376	0.351	0.327	0.305	0.285	0.266	0.249	0.233	0.168	0.123	0.091	0.068	0.039
9	0.333	0.300	0.284	0.263	0.243	0.225	0.209	0.194	0.134	0.094	0.067	0.048	0.026
10	0.295	0.270	0.247	0.227	0.208	0.191	0.176	0.162	0.107	0.073	0.050	0.035	0.017
11	0.261	0.237	0.215	0.195	0.178	0.162	0.148	0.135	0.086	0.056	0.037	0.025	0.012
12	0.231	0.208	0.187	0.168	0.152	0.137	0.124	0.112	0.069	0.043	0.027	0.018	0.008
13	0.204	0.182	0.163	0.145	0.130	0.116	0.104	0.093	0.055	0.033	0.020	0.013	0.005
14	0.181	0.160	0.141	0.125	0.111	0.099	0.088	0.078	0.044	0.025	0.015	0.009	0.003
15	0.160	0.140	0.123	0.108	0.095	0.084	0.074	0.065	0.035	0.020	0.011	0.006	0.002
16	0.141	0.123	0.107	0.093	0.081	0.071	0.062	0.054	0.028	0.015	0.008	0.005	0.002
17	0.125	0.108	0.093	0.080	0.069	0.060	0.052	0.045	0.023	0.012	0.006	0.003	0.001
18	0.111	0.095	0.081	0.069	0.059	0.051	0.044	0.038	0.018	0.009	0.005	0.002	0.001
19	0.098	0.083	0.070	0.060	0.051	0.043	0.037	0.031	0.014	0.007	0.003	0.002	0
20	0.087	0.073	0.061	0.051	0.043	0.037	0.031	0.026	0.012	0.005	0.002	0.001	0
25	0.047	0.038	0.030	0.024	0.020	0.016	0.013	0.010	0.004	0.001	0.001	0	0
30	0.026	0.020	0.015	0.012	0.009	0.007	0.005	0.004	0.001	0	0	0	0
40	0.008	0.005	0.004	0.003	0.002	0.001	0.001	0.001	0	0	0	0	0
50	0.002	0.001	0.001	0.001	0	0	0	0	0	0	0	0	0

APPENDIX D Present Value of an Annuity of $1 $PV_A = A\left[\frac{1 - \frac{1}{(1+i)^n}}{i}\right]$

Period	PERCENT 1%	2%	3%	4%	5%	6%	7%	8%	9%	10%	11%	12%
1	0.990	0.980	0.971	0.962	0.952	0.943	0.935	0.926	0.917	0.909	0.901	0.893
2	1.970	1.942	1.913	1.886	1.859	1.833	1.808	1.783	1.759	1.736	1.713	1.690
3	2.941	2.884	2.829	2.775	2.723	2.673	2.624	2.577	2.531	2.487	2.444	2.402
4	3.902	3.808	3.717	3.630	3.546	3.465	3.387	3.312	3.240	3.170	3.102	3.037
5	4.853	4.715	4.580	4.452	4.329	4.212	4.100	3.993	3.890	3.791	3.696	3.605
6	5.795	5.601	5.417	5.242	5.076	4.917	4.767	4.623	4.486	4.355	4.231	4.111
7	6.728	6.472	6.230	6.002	5.786	5.582	5.389	5.206	5.033	4.868	4.712	4.564
8	7.652	7.325	7.020	6.733	6.463	6.210	5.971	5.747	5.535	5.335	5.146	4.968
9	8.566	8.162	7.786	7.435	7.108	6.802	6.515	6.247	5.995	5.759	5.537	5.328
10	9.471	8.983	8.530	8.111	7.722	7.360	7.024	6.710	6.418	6.145	5.889	5.650
11	10.368	9.787	9.253	8.760	8.306	7.887	7.499	7.139	6.805	6.495	6.207	5.938
12	11.255	10.575	9.954	9.385	8.863	8.384	7.943	7.536	7.161	6.814	6.492	6.194
13	12.134	11.348	10.635	9.986	9.394	8.853	8.358	7.904	7.487	7.103	6.750	6.424
14	13.004	12.106	11.296	10.563	9.899	9.295	8.745	8.244	7.786	7.367	6.982	6.628
15	13.865	12.849	11.939	11.118	10.380	9.712	9.108	8.559	8.061	7.606	7.191	6.811
16	14.718	13.578	12.561	11.652	10.838	10.106	9.447	8.851	8.313	7.824	7.379	6.974
17	15.562	14.292	13.166	12.166	11.274	10.477	9.763	9.122	8.544	8.022	7.549	7.102
18	16.398	14.992	13.754	12.659	11.690	10.828	10.059	9.372	8.756	8.201	7.702	7.250
19	17.226	15.678	14.324	13.134	12.085	11.158	10.336	9.604	8.950	8.365	7.839	7.366
20	18.046	16.351	14.877	13.590	12.462	11.470	10.594	9.818	9.129	8.514	7.963	7.469
25	22.023	19.523	17.413	15.622	14.094	12.783	11.654	10.675	9.823	9.077	8.422	7.843
30	25.808	22.396	19.600	17.292	15.372	13.765	12.409	11.258	10.274	9.427	8.694	8.055
40	32.835	27.355	23.115	19.793	17.160	15.046	13.332	11.925	10.757	9.779	8.951	8.244
50	39.196	31.424	25.730	21.482	18.256	15.762	13.801	12.233	10.962	9.915	9.042	8.304

APPENDIX D Present Value of an Annuity of $1 *(concluded)*

Period	13%	14%	15%	16%	17%	18%	19%	20%	25%	30%	35%	40%	50%
	PERCENT												
1	0.885	0.877	0.870	0.862	0.855	0.847	0.840	0.833	0.800	0.769	0.741	0.714	0.667
2	1.668	1.647	1.626	1.605	1.585	1.566	1.547	1.528	1.440	1.361	1.289	1.224	1.111
3	2.361	2.322	2.283	2.246	2.210	2.174	2.140	2.106	1.952	1.816	1.696	1.589	1.407
4	2.974	2.914	2.855	2.798	2.743	2.690	2.639	2.589	2.362	2.166	1.997	1.849	1.605
5	3.517	3.433	3.352	3.274	3.199	3.127	3.058	2.991	2.689	2.436	2.220	2.035	1.737
6	3.998	3.889	3.784	3.685	3.589	3.498	3.410	3.326	2.951	2.643	2.385	2.168	1.824
7	4.423	4.288	4.160	4.039	3.922	3.812	3.706	3.605	3.161	2.802	2.508	2.263	1.883
8	4.799	4.639	4.487	4.344	4.207	4.078	3.954	3.837	3.329	2.925	2.598	2.331	1.922
9	5.132	4.946	4.772	4.607	4.451	4.303	4.163	4.031	3.463	3.019	2.665	2.379	1.948
10	5.426	5.216	5.019	4.833	4.659	4.494	4.339	4.192	3.571	3.092	2.715	2.414	1.965
11	5.687	5.453	5.234	5.029	4.836	4.656	4.486	4.327	3.656	3.147	2.752	2.438	1.977
12	5.918	5.660	5.421	5.197	4.988	4.793	4.611	4.439	3.725	3.190	2.779	2.456	1.985
13	6.122	5.842	5.583	5.342	5.118	4.910	4.715	4.533	3.780	3.223	2.799	2.469	1.990
14	6.302	6.002	5.724	5.468	5.229	5.008	4.802	4.611	3.824	3.249	2.814	2.478	1.993
15	6.462	6.142	5.847	5.575	5.324	5.092	4.876	4.675	3.859	3.268	2.825	2.484	1.995
16	6.604	6.265	5.954	5.668	5.405	5.162	4.938	4.730	3.887	3.283	2.834	2.489	1.997
17	6.729	6.373	6.047	5.749	5.475	5.222	4.988	4.775	3.910	3.295	2.840	2.492	1.998
18	6.840	6.467	6.128	5.818	5.534	5.273	5.003	4.812	3.928	3.304	2.844	2.494	1.999
19	6.938	6.550	6.198	5.877	5.584	5.316	5.070	4.843	3.942	3.311	2.848	2.496	1.999
20	7.025	6.623	6.259	5.929	5.628	5.353	5.101	4.870	3.954	3.316	2.850	2.497	1.999
25	7.330	6.873	6.464	6.097	5.766	5.467	5.195	4.948	3.985	3.329	2.856	2.499	2.000
30	7.496	7.003	6.566	6.177	5.829	5.517	5.235	4.979	3.995	3.332	2.857	2.500	2.000
40	7.634	7.105	6.642	6.233	5.871	5.548	5.258	4.997	3.999	3.333	2.857	2.500	2.000
50	7.675	7.133	6.661	6.246	5.880	5.554	5.262	4.999	4.000	3.333	2.857	2.500	2.000

appendix E

TIME VALUE OF MONEY AND INVESTMENT APPLICATIONS

OVERVIEW

Many applications for the time value of money exist. Applications use either the compound sum (sometimes referred to as *future value*) or the present value. Additionally some cash flows are annuities. An **annuity** represents cash flows that are equally spaced in time and are constant dollar amounts. Car payments, mortgage payments, and bond interest payments are examples of annuities. Annuities can either be present value annuities or compound sum annuities. In the next section, we present the concept of compound sum and develop common applications related to investments.

COMPOUND SUM

Compound Sum: Single Amount

In determining the **compound sum,** we measure the future value of an amount that is allowed to grow at a given rate over a period of time. Assume an investor buys an asset worth $1,000. This asset (gold, diamonds, art, real estate, etc.) is expected to increase in value by 10 percent per year, and the investor wants to know what it will be worth after the fourth year. At the end of the first year, the investor will have $1,000 × (1 + 0.10), or $1,100. By the end of year two, the $1,100 will have grown by another 10 percent to $1,210 ($1,100 × 1.10). The four-year pattern is indicated below:

1st year: $1,000 × 1.10 = $1,100
2nd year: $1,100 × 1.10 = $1,210
3rd year: $1,210 × 1.10 = $1,331
4th year: $1,331 × 1.10 = $1,464

After the fourth year, the investor has accumulated $1,464. Because compounding problems often cover a long time, a generalized formula is necessary to describe the compounding process. We shall let:

S = Compound sum
P = Principal or present value
i = Interest rate, growth rate, or rate of return
n = Number of periods compounded

The simple formula is:

$$S = P(1 + i)^n \qquad \textbf{(E–1)}$$

In the preceding example, the beginning amount, P, was equal to $1,000; the growth rate, i, equaled 10 percent; and the number of periods, n, equaled 4, so we get:

$$S = \$1{,}000(1.10)^4, \text{ or } \$1{,}000 \times 1.464 = \$1{,}464$$

The term $(0.10)^4$ is found to equal 1.464 by multiplying 1.10 four times itself. This mathematical calculation is called an exponential, where you take (1.10) to the fourth power. On your calculator, you would have an exponential key y^x where y represents (1.10) and x represents 4. For students with calculators, we have prepared Appendix F for both Hewlett-Packard and Texas Instruments calculators.

For those not proficient with calculators or who have calculators without financial functions, Table E–1 is a shortened version of the compound sum table found in Appendix A. It can be used easily. The table tells us the amount $1 would grow to if it were invested for any number of periods at a given rate of return. Using this table for our previous example, we find an interest factor for the compound sum in the row where $n = 4$ and the column where $i = 10$ percent. The factor is 1.464, the same as previously calculated. We multiply this factor times any beginning amount to determine the compound sum.

When using compound sum tables to calculate the compound sum, we shorten our formula from $S = P(1 + i)^n$ to:

$$S = P \times S_{IF} \qquad \textbf{(E–2)}$$

where S_{IF} equals the interest factor for the compound sum found in Table E–1 or Appendix A. Using a new example, assume $5,000 is invested for 20 years at 6 percent. Using Table E–1, the interest factor for the compound sum would be 3.207, and the total value would be:

$$\begin{aligned} S &= P \times S_{IF} \qquad (n = 20, i = 6\%) \\ &= \$5{,}000 \times 3.207 \\ &= \$16{,}035 \end{aligned}$$

Example—Compound Sum, Single Amount

Problem: Mike Donegan receives a bonus from his employer of $3,200. He will invest the money at a 12 percent rate of return for the next eight years. How much will he have after eight years?

TABLE E-1 Compound Sum of $1 ($S_{IF}$)

Periods	1%	2%	3%	4%	6%	8%	10%
1	1.010	1.020	1.030	1.040	1.060	1.080	1.100
2	1.020	1.040	1.061	1.082	1.124	1.166	1.210
3	1.030	1.061	1.093	1.125	1.191	1.260	1.331
4	1.041	1.082	1.126	1.170	1.262	1.360	1.464
5	1.051	1.104	1.159	1.217	1.338	1.469	1.611
10	1.105	1.219	1.344	1.480	1.791	2.159	2.594
20	1.220	1.486	1.806	2.191	3.207	4.661	6.727
30	1.348	1.811	2.427	3.243	5.743	10.063	13.268

Solution: Compound sum, single amount:

$$S = P \times S_{IF} \quad (n = 8, i = 12\%) \quad \text{Appendix A}$$
$$= \$3{,}200 \times 2.476 = \$7{,}923.20$$

Compound Sum: Annuity

Our previous example was a one-time single investment. Let us examine a **compound sum of an annuity** where constant payments are made at equally spaced periods and grow to a future value. The normal assumption for a compound sum of an annuity is that the payments are made at the end of each period, so the last payment does not compound or earn a rate of return.

Figure E–1 demonstrates the timing and compounding process when $1,000 per year is contributed to a fund for four consecutive years. The $1,000 for each period is multiplied by the compound sum factors for the appropriate periods of compounding. The first $1,000 comes in at the end of the first period and has three periods to compound; the second $1,000 at the end of the second period, with two periods to compound; the third payment has one period to compound; and the last payment is multiplied by a factor of 1.00 showing no compounding at all.

Because compounding the individual values is tedious, compound sum of annuity tables can be used. These tables simply add up the interest factors from the compound sum tables for a single amount. Table E–2 is a shortened version of Appendix B, the compound sum of an annuity table showing the compound sum factors for a specified period and rate of return. Notice that all the way across the table, the factor in period one is 1.00. This reflects the fact that the last payment does not compound.

One example of the compound sum of an annuity applies to the individual retirement account (IRA) and Keogh retirement plans. The IRA allows workers to invest $3,000 per year in a tax-free account and the Keogh allows a maximum of $40,000 per year to be invested in a retirement account for self-employed individuals.[1] Assume Dr. Piotrowski shelters $40,000 per year from age 35 to 65. If she

FIGURE E-1 Compounding Process for Annuity

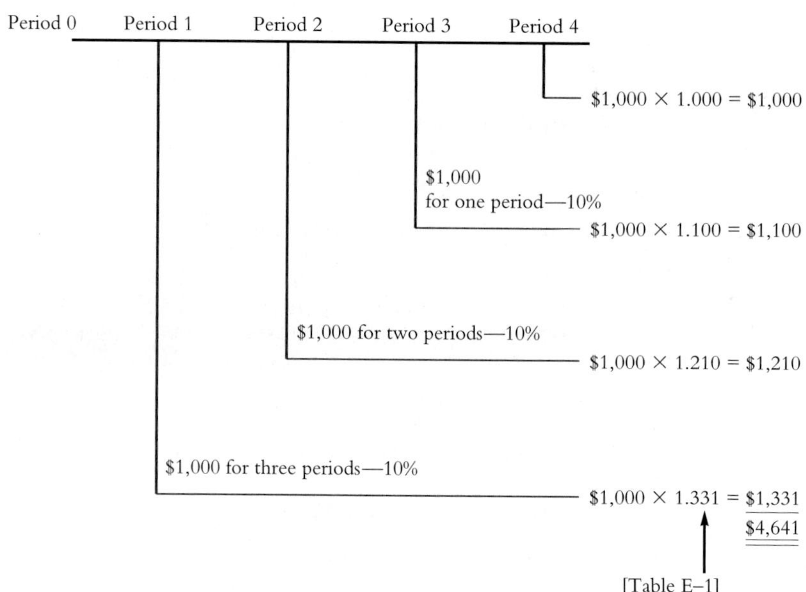

[1] The annual allowable deductibles are scheduled to increase between 2001 and 2011.

TABLE E-2 Compound Sum of an Annuity of \$1 (SA_{IF})

Periods	1%	2%	3%	4%	6%	8%	10%
1	1.000	1.000	1.000	1.000	1.000	1.000	1.000
2	2.010	2.020	2.030	2.040	2.060	2.080	2.100
3	3.030	3.060	3.091	3.122	3.184	3.246	3.310
4	4.060	4.122	4.184	4.246	4.375	4.506	4.641
5	5.101	5.204	5.309	5.416	5.637	5.867	6.105
10	10.462	10.950	11.464	12.006	13.181	14.487	15.937
20	22.019	24.297	26.870	29.778	36.786	45.762	57.275
30	34.785	40.588	47.575	56.085	79.058	113.280	164.490

makes 30 payments of \$40,000 and earns a rate of return of 8 percent, her Keogh account at retirement would be more than \$4 million.

$$\begin{aligned} S &= R \times SA_{IF} \qquad (n = 30, i = 8\% \text{ return}) \\ &= \$40{,}000 \times 113.280 \\ &= \$4{,}531{,}200 \end{aligned} \tag{E–3}$$

While this seems like a lot of money in today's world, we need to measure what it will buy 30 years from now after inflation is considered. One way to examine this is to calculate what the \$40,000 payments would have to be if they only kept up with inflation. Let's assume inflation of 3 percent over the next 30 years and recalculate the sum of the annuity:

$$\begin{aligned} S &= R \times SA_{IF} \qquad (n = 30, i = 3\% \text{ inflation}) \\ &= \$40{,}000 \times 47.575 \\ &= \$1{,}903{,}000 \end{aligned}$$

To maintain the purchasing power of each \$40,000 contribution, Dr. Piotrowski needs to accumulate \$1,903,000 at the estimated 3 percent rate of inflation. Since her rate of return of 8 percent is 5 percentage points higher than the inflation rate, she is adding additional purchasing power to her portfolio.

Example—Compound Sum, Annuity

Problem: Sonny Outlook invests \$2,000 in an IRA at the end of each year for the next 40 years. With an anticipated rate of return of 11 percent, how much will the funds grow to after 40 years?

Solution: Compound sum, annuity:

$$\begin{aligned} S &= R \times SA_{IF} \qquad (n = 40, i = 11\%) \qquad \text{Appendix B} \\ &= \$3{,}000 \times 581.83 = \$1{,}745{,}490 \end{aligned}$$

PRESENT VALUE CONCEPT

Present Value: Single Amount

The **present value** is the exact opposite of the compound sum. A future value is discounted to the present. For example, earlier we determined the compound sum of \$1,000 for four periods at 10 percent was \$1,464. We could reverse the process to state that \$1,464 received four years from today is worth only \$1,000 today if one

FIGURE E-2 Relationship of Present Value and Compound Sum

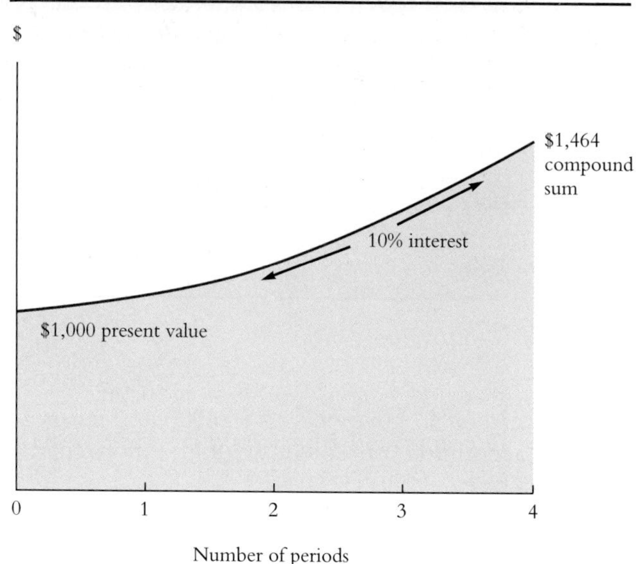

can earn a 10 percent return on money during the four years. This $1,000 value is called its present value. The relationship is depicted in Figure E–2.

The formula for present value is derived from the original formula for the compound sum. As the following two formulas demonstrate, the present value is simply the inverse of the compound sum.

$$S = P(1 + i)^n \text{ Compound sum}$$
$$P = S \times 1/(1 + i)^n \text{ Present value} \qquad \textbf{(E–4)}$$

The present value can be determined by solving for a mathematical solution to the above formula, or by using Table E–3, the Present Value of $1. When we use Table E–3, the present value interest factor $1/(1 + i)^n$ is found in the table and represented by PV_{IF}. We substitute it into the formula above:

$$P = S \times PV_{IF} \qquad \textbf{(E–5)}$$

Let's demonstrate that the present value of $1,464, based on our assumptions, is worth $1,000 today:

$$P = S \times PV_{IF} \quad (n = 4, i = 10\%) \quad \text{Table E–3 or Appendix C}$$
$$= \$1{,}464 \times 0.683$$
$$= \$1{,}000$$

TABLE E-3 Present Value of $1 ($PV_{IF}$)

Periods	1%	2%	3%	4%	6%	8%	10%
1	0.990	0.980	0.971	0.962	0.943	0.926	0.909
2	0.980	0.961	0.943	0.925	0.890	0.857	0.826
3	0.971	0.942	0.915	0.889	0.840	0.794	0.751
4	0.961	0.924	0.888	0.855	0.792	0.735	0.683
5	0.951	0.906	0.863	0.822	0.747	0.681	0.621
10	0.905	0.820	0.744	0.676	0.558	0.463	0.386
20	0.820	0.673	0.554	0.456	0.312	0.215	0.149
30	0.742	0.552	0.412	0.308	0.174	0.099	0.057

Present value becomes very important in determining the value of investments. Assume you think a certain piece of land will be worth \$500,000 10 years from now. If you can earn a 10 percent rate of return on investments of similar risk, what would you be willing to pay for this land?

$$\begin{aligned} P &= S \times PV_{IF} \qquad (n = 10, i = 10\%) \\ &= \$500{,}000 \times 0.386 \\ &= \$193{,}000 \end{aligned}$$

This land's present value to you today would be \$193,000. What would you have 10 years from today if you invested \$193,000 at a 10 percent return? For this answer, we go to the compound sum factor from Table E–1 on page 601:

$$\begin{aligned} S &= P \times S_{IF} \qquad (n = 10, i = 10\%) \\ &= \$193{,}000 \times 2.594 \\ &= \$500{,}642 \end{aligned}$$

The compound sum would be \$500,642. The two answers do not equal \$500,000 because of the mathematical rounding used to construct tables with three decimal points. If we carry out the interest factors to four places, 0.386 becomes 0.3855 and 2.594 becomes 2.5937 and the two answers will be quite similar.

Near the end of the compound sum of an annuity section, we showed that Dr. Piotrowski could accumulate \$4,531,200 by the time she retired in 30 years. What would be the present value of this future sum if we brought it back to the present at the rate of inflation of 3 percent?

$$\begin{aligned} P &= S \times PV_{IF} \qquad (n = 30, i = 3\%) \\ &= \$4{,}531{,}200 \times 0.412 \\ &= \$1{,}866{,}854 \end{aligned}$$

The amount she will have accumulated will be worth \$1,866,854 in today's dollars. If the rate of inflation averaged 6 percent over this time, the amount would fall to \$788,429 (\$4,531,200 × 0.174). Notice how sensitive the present value is to a 3 percentage point change in the inflation rate. Another concern is being able to forecast inflation correctly. These examples are simply meant to heighten your awareness that money has a time value and financial decisions require this to be considered.

Example—Present Value, Single Amount

Problem: Barbara Samuels received a trust fund at birth that will be paid out to her at age 18. If the fund will accumulate to \$400,000 by then and the discount rate is 9 percent, what is the present value of her future accumulation?

Solution: Present value, single amount:

$$\begin{aligned} P &= S \times PV_{IF} \qquad (n = 18, i = 9\%) \qquad \text{Appendix C} \\ &= \$400{,}000 \times 0.212 = \$84{,}800 \end{aligned}$$

Present Value: Annuity

To find the **present value of an annuity,** we are simply finding the present value of an equal cash flow for several periods instead of one single cash payment. The analysis is the same as taking the present value of several cash flows and adding them. Since we are dealing with an annuity (equal dollar amounts), we can save time by creating tables that add up the interest factors for the present value of single amounts and make present value annuity factors. We do this in Table E–4, a shortened version of Appendix D. Before using Table E–4, let's compute the present

TABLE E-4 Present Value of an Annuity of $1 ($PVA_{IF}$)

Periods	1%	2%	3%	4%	6%	8%	10%
1	0.990	0.980	0.971	0.962	0.943	0.926	0.909
2	1.970	1.942	1.913	1.886	1.833	1.783	1.736
3	2.941	2.884	2.829	2.775	2.673	2.577	2.487
4	3.902	3.808	3.717	3.630	3.465	3.312	3.170
5	4.853	4.713	4.580	4.452	4.212	3.993	3.791
8	7.652	7.325	7.020	6.773	6.210	5.747	5.335
10	9.471	8.983	8.530	8.111	7.360	6.710	6.145
20	18.046	16.351	14.877	13.590	11.470	9.818	8.514
30	25.808	22.396	19.600	17.292	13.765	11.258	9.427

value of $1,000 to be received each year for five years at 6 percent. We could use the present value of five single amounts and Table E–3 on page 604.

Period	Receipt	*IF* @ 6%	
1	$1,000 ×	0.943 =	$ 943
2	$1,000 ×	0.890 =	$ 890
3	$1,000 ×	0.840 =	$ 840
4	$1,000 ×	0.792 =	$ 792
5	$1,000 ×	0.747 =	$ 747
		4.212	$4,212 Present value

Another way to get the same value is to use Table E–4. The present value annuity factor under 6 percent and 5 periods is equal to 4.212, or the same value we got from adding the individual present value factors for a single amount. We can simply calculate the answer as follows:

where:

A = The present value of an annuity
R = The annuity amount
PVA_{IF} = The interest factor from Table E–4

$$A = R \times PVA_{IF} \qquad (n = 5, i = 6\%) \qquad \textbf{(E–6)}$$
$$= \$1{,}000 \times 4.212$$
$$= \$4{,}212$$

Present value of annuities applies to many financial products such as mortgages, car payments, and retirement benefits. Some financial products such as bonds are a combination of an annuity and a single payment. Interest payments from bonds are annuities, and the principal repayment at maturity is a single payment. Both cash flows determine the present value of a bond.

Example—Present Value, Annuity

Problem: Ross "The Hoss" Sullivan has just renewed his contract with the Chicago Bears for an annual payment of $3 million per year for the next eight years. The newspapers report the deal is worth $24 million. If the discount rate is 14 percent, what is the true present value of the contract?

Solution: Present value, annuity:

$$A = R \times PVA_{IF} \quad (n = 8, i = 14\%) \quad \text{Appendix D}$$
$$= \$3{,}000{,}000 \times 4.639 = \$13{,}917{,}000$$

Present Value: Uneven Cash Flow

Many investments are a series of uneven cash flows. For example, buying common stock generally implies an uneven cash flow from future dividends and the sale price. We hope to buy common stock in companies that are growing and have increasing dividends. Assume you purchased Caravan Motors common stock. You expect to hold the stock for five years and then sell it at $60. You also expect to receive dividends of $1.60, $2.00, $2.00, $2.50, and $3.00 during those five years.

What would you be willing to pay for the common stock if your required return on a stock of this risk is 14 percent. Let's set up a present value analysis for an uneven cash flow using Appendix C, the present value of a single amount. Since this is not an annuity, each cash flow must be evaluated separately. For simplicity, we assume all cash flows come at the end of the year. Also, the cash flow in the fifth year combines the $3.00 dividend and expected $60 sale price.

Year	Cash Flow	PV_{IF} 14%	Present Value
1	$ 1.60	0.877	$ 1.40
2	2.00	0.769	1.54
3	2.00	0.675	1.35
4	2.50	0.592	1.48
5	63.00	0.519	32.70
Present value of Caravan Motors under these assumptions:			$38.47

If you were satisfied that your assumptions were reasonably accurate, you would be willing to buy Caravan at any price equal to or less than $38.47. This price will provide you with a 14 percent return if all your forecasts come true.

Example—Present Value, Uneven Cash Flow

Problem: Joann Zinke buys stock in Collins Publishing Company. She will receive dividends of $2.00, $2.40, $2.88, and $3.12 for the next four years. She assumes she can sell the stock for $50 after the last dividend payment (at the end of four years). If the discount rate is 12 percent, what is the present value of the future cash flows? (Round all values to two places to the right of the decimal point.) The present value of future cash flows is assumed to equal the value of the stock.

Solution: Present value, uneven cash flow:

Year	Cash Flow	PV_{IF} 12%	Present Value
1	$ 2.00	0.893	$ 1.79
2	2.40	0.797	1.91
3	2.88	0.712	2.05
4	53.12	0.636	33.78
			$39.53

The present value of the cash flows is $39.53.

Example—Present Value, Uneven Cash Flow

Problem: Sherman Lollar wins a malpractice suit against his accounting professor, and the judgment provides him with $3,000 a year for the next 40 years, plus a single lump-sum payment of $10,000 after 50 years. With a discount rate of 10 percent, what is the present value of his future benefits?

Solution: Present value, annuity plus a single amount:

Annuity

$$\begin{aligned} A &= R \times PVA_{IF} \qquad (n = 40, i = 10\%) \qquad \text{Appendix D} \\ &= \$3{,}000 \times 9.779 = \$29{,}337 \end{aligned}$$

Single amount

$$\begin{aligned} P &= S \times PV_{IF} \qquad (n = 50, i = 10\%) \qquad \text{Appendix C} \\ &= \$10{,}000 \times 0.009 = \$90 \end{aligned}$$

Total present value = $29,337 + $90 = $29,427

appendix F

USING CALCULATORS FOR FINANCIAL ANALYSIS

This appendix is designed to help you use either an algebraic calculator (Texas Instruments BAII Plus Business Analyst) or the Hewlett-Packard 12C Financial Calculator. We realize that most calculators come with comprehensive instructions, and this appendix is only meant to provide basic instructions for commonly used financial calculations.

There are always two things to do before starting your calculations as indicated in the first table: Clear the calculator, and set the decimal point. If you do not want to lose data stored in memory, do not perform steps 2 and 3 in the first box below.

Each step is listed vertically as a number followed by a decimal point. After each step you will find either a number or a calculator function denoted by a box [ ]. Entering the number on your calculator is one step and entering the function is another. Notice that the HP 12C is color coded. When two boxes are found one after another, you may have an [f] or a [g] in the first box. An [f] is orange coded and refers to the orange functions above the keys. After typing the [f] function, you will automatically look for an orange-coded key to punch. For example, after [f] in the first Hewlett-Packard box (right-hand panel), you will punch in the orange-color-coded [REG]. If the [f] function is not followed by another box, you merely type in [f] and the value indicated.

	Texas Instruments BAII Plus	Hewlett-Packard 12C
First clear the calculator.	1. [CE/C] [CE/C] Clears Screen	1. [CLX] Clears Screen
	2. [2nd] [CLR WORK] Clears the regular memory registers	2. [f]
	3. [2nd] [CLR TVM] Clears the time value of money memory register	3. [REG] Clears Memory
	4. [CF] [2nd] [CLR WORK] Clears cash flow register	
Set the decimal point	1. [2nd] [FORMAT] 4 [ENTER]	1. [f] 2. 4 (# of decimals)
Set the number of periods per year.	1. [2nd] [P/Y] 1. [ENTER]	

The [g] is coded blue and refers to the functions on the bottom of the function keys. After the [g] function key, you will automatically look for blue-coded keys. This first occurs on page 609 of this appendix. The TI BAII Plus is also color coded. The gold [2nd] key, located near the top left corner of the calculator, refers to the gold functions above the keys. Upon pressing the [2nd] key, the word "2nd" appears in the top left corner, indicating the gold function keys are active.

Familiarize yourself with the keyboard before you start. In the more complicated calculations, keystrokes will be combined into one step.

In the first four calculations on this page and on page 611 we simply instruct you how to get the interest factors for Appendices A, B, C, and D. We have chosen to use examples as our method of instruction.

	Texas Instruments BAII Plus	Hewlett-Packard 12C
A. Appendix A Compound Sum of $1	To Find Interest Factor	To Find Interest Factor
	1. 1	1. 1
$i = 9\%$ or 0.09; $n = 5$ years		
	2. +	2. [enter]
$S_{IF} = (1 + i)^n$		
	3. 0.09 (interest rate)	3. 0.09 (interest rate)
Sum = Present Value × S_{IF}		
	4. [=]	4. [+]
$S = P \times S_{IF}$		
	5. [y^x]	5. 5 (# of periods)
Check the answer against the number in Appendix A. Numbers in the appendix are rounded. Try different rates and years.	6. 5 (# of periods)	6. [y^x] answer 1.5386
	7. = answer 1.538624	
B. Appendix B Compound Sum of an Annuity of $1	To Find Interest Factor	To Find Interest Factor
	Repeat steps 1 through 7 in part A of this section. Continue with step 8.	Repeat steps 1 through 6 in part A of this section. Continue with step 7.
$i = 9\%$ or 0.09; $n = 5$ years		
$SA_{IF} = \frac{(1 + i)^n - 1}{i}$	8. [−]	7. 1
Sum = Receipt × SA_{IF}	9. 1	8. [−]
$S = R \times SA_{IF}$		9. 0.09
Check your answer with Appendix B. Repeat example using different numbers and check your results with the number in Appendix B. Numbers in appendix are rounded.	10. [÷]	10. [÷] answer 5.9847
	11. 0.09	
	12. [=] answer 5.9847106	

	Texas Instruments BAII Plus	Hewlett-Packard 12C
C. Appendix C Present Value of $1	To Find Interest Factor	To Find Interest Factor
	Repeat steps 1 through 7 in part A of this section. Continue with step 8.	Repeat steps 1 through 6 in part A of this section. Continue with step 7.
i = 9% or 0.09; n = 5 years		
$PV_{IF} = (1 + i)^n$		
	8. [1/x] answer 0.6499314	7. [1/x] answer 0.6499
Present Value = Sum × PV_{IF}		
$P = S \times PV_{IF}$		
Check the answer against the number in Appendix C. Numbers in the appendix are rounded.		
D. Appendix D Present Value of an Annuity of $1	To Find Interest Factor	To Find Interest Factor
i = 9% or 0.09; n = 5 years	Repeat steps 1 through 8 in parts A and C. Continue with step 9.	Repeat steps 1 through 7 in parts A and C. Continue with step 8.
$PV_{IF} = \frac{1 - [(1/(1+i)^n]}{i}$	9. [−]	8. 1
Present Value = Annuity × PVA_{IF}	10. 1	9. [−]
	11. [=]	10. [CHS]
$A = R \times PVA_{IF}$		
	12. [+/−]	11. 0.09
Check your answer with Appendix D. Repeat example using different numbers and check your results with the number in Appendix D. Numbers in appendix are rounded.	13. [÷]	12. [÷] answer 3.8897
	14. 0.09	
	15. [=] answer 3.8896513	

On the following pages, you can determine bond valuation, yield to maturity, net present value of an annuity, net present value of an uneven cash flow, internal rate of return for an annuity, and internal rate of return for an uneven cash flow.

BOND VALUATION USING BOTH THE TI BAII PLUS AND THE HP 12C

Solve for V = Price of the bond, given:

C_t = \$80 annual coupon payments or 8 percent coupon (\$40 semiannually)
P_n = \$1,000 principal (par value)
n = 10 years to maturity (20 periods semiannually)
i = 9.0 percent rate in the market (4.5 percent semiannually)

You may choose to refer to Chapter 12 for a complete discussion of bond valuation.

	Texas Instruments BAII Plus	Hewlett-Packard 12C
Bond Valuation	Clear TVM memory [2nd] [CLR TVM]	Clear Memory [f] [REG]
All steps begin with number 1. Numbers following each step are keystrokes followed by a box [ ]. Each box represents a keystroke and indicates which calculator function is performed.	Set decimal to 2 places	Set decimal to 3 places
	[2nd] [FORMAT]	[f] 3
	2 [ENTER]	
	[2nd] [STO]	1. 9.0 (yield to maturity)
	1. 40 (semiannual coupon)	2. [i]
The Texas Instruments calculator requires that data be adjusted for semiannual compounding.	2. [PMT]	3. 8.0 (coupon in percent)
	3. 4.5 (yield to maturity) semiannual basis	4. [PMT]
The Hewlett-Packard 12C internally assumes that semiannual compounding is used and requires annual data to be entered. The HP 12C is more detailed in that it requires the actual day, month, and year. If you want an answer for a problem that requires a given number of years (e.g., 10 years), simply start on a date of your choice and end on the same date 10 years later, as in the example.	4. [I/Y]	5. 1.092011 (today's date month-day-year)*
	5. 1000 principal	6. [enter]
	6. [FV]	7. 1.092021 (maturity date month-day-year)*
	7. 20 (semiannual periods to maturity)	8. [f]
	8. [N]	9. [Price] Answer 93.496
	9. [CPT]	
	10. [PV] answer 934.96	Answer is given as % of par value and equals \$934.96. If Error message occurs, clear memory and start over.
	Answer is given in dollars, rather than % of par value.	*See instructions in the third paragraph of the first column.

YIELD TO MATURITY ON BOTH THE TI BAII PLUS AND HP 12C

Solve for Y = Yield to maturity, given:

V = \$895.50 price of bond
C_t = \$80 annual coupon payments or 8 percent coupon (\$40 semiannually)
P_n = \$1,000 principal (par value)
n = 10 years to maturity (20 periods semiannually)

You may choose to refer to Chapter 12 for a complete discussion of yield to maturity.

	Texas Instruments BAII Plus	Hewlett-Packard 12C
Yield to Maturity	Clear TVM memory	Clear Memory [f] [REG]
All steps are numbered. All numbers following each step are keystrokes followed by a box [ ]. Each box represents a keystroke and indicates which calculator function is performed.	[2nd] [CLR TVM]	
	Set decimal to 2 places	Set decimal [f] 2
	1. 20 (semiannual periods)	1. 89.55 (bond price as a percent of par)
The payment for a bond is normally an outflow of cash, while the receipt of the periodic interest payments and the repayment of the bond is an inflow of cash. The TI BAII Plus requires that inflows be entered as a positive number while outflows as a negative number. Before entering the current value of the bond, be sure to change the sign to negative.	2. [N]	2. [PV]
	3. 1000 (par value)	3. 8.0 (coupon in %)
	4. [FV]	4. [PMT]
	5. 40 (semiannual coupon)	5. 1.092011 (today's date)*
	6. [PMT]	6. [enter]
The Texas Instruments BAII Plus does not internally compute to a semiannual rate, so that data must be adjusted to reflect semiannual payments and periods. The answer received in step 11 is a semiannual rate, which must be multiplied by 2 to reflect an annual yield.	7. 895.50 (bond price)	7. 1.092021 (maturity date)*
	8. [+/−]	8. [f]
	9. [PV]	9. [YTM] answer 9.65%
The Hewlett-Packard 12C internally assumes that semiannual payments are made and, therefore, the answer in step 9 is the annual yield to maturity based on semiannual coupons. If you want an answer on the HP for a given number of years (e.g., 10 years), simply start on a date of your choice and end on the same date 10 years later, as in the example.	10. [CPT]	In case you receive an Error message, you have probably made a keystroke error. Clear the memory
	11. [I/Y] answer 4.83%	[f] [REG]
	12. [×]	and start over.
	13. 2	
	14. [=] answer 9.65% (annual rate)	*See instructions in the third paragraph of the first column.

NET PRESENT VALUE OF AN ANNUITY ON BOTH THE TI BAII PLUS AND THE HP 12C

Solve for A = Present value of annuity, given:

n = 10 years (number of years cash flow will continue)
PMT = \$5,000 per year (amount of the annuity)
i = 12 percent (cost of capital K_a)
Cost = \$20,000

	Texas Instruments BAII Plus	Hewlett-Packard 12C
Net Present Value of an Annuity	Clear TVM memory [2nd] [CLR TVM]	[f] [REG] clears memory
All steps are numbered and some steps include keystrokes. All numbers following each step are keystrokes followed by a box [ ]. Each box represents a keystroke and indicates which calculator function is performed on that number.	Set decimal to 2 places	Set decimal to 2 places [f] 2
	1. 10 (years of cash flow)	1. 20000 (cash outflow)
	2. [N]	2. [CHS] changes sign
The calculation for the present value of an annuity on the TI BAII plus requires that the project cost be subtracted from the present value of the cash inflows.	3. 5000 (annual payments)	3. [g]
	4. [PMT]	4. [CFo]
	5. 12 (cost of capital)	5. 5000 (annual payments)
	6. [I/Y]	6. [g] [CFj]
The HP 12C could solve the problem exactly with the same keystrokes as the TI. However, since the HP uses a similar method to solve uneven cash flows, we elected to use the method that requires more keystrokes but which includes a negative cash outflow for the cost of the capital budgeting project.	7. [CPT]	7. 10 [g] [N_j] (years)
	8. [PV]	8. 12 [i] (cost of capital)
	9. [+/−]	9. [f] [NPV]
	10. [−]	answer \$8,251.12
	11. 20,000	If an Error message appears, start over by clearing the memory with [f] [REG]
To conserve space, several keystrokes have been put into one step.	12. [=] answer \$8,251.12	

NET PRESENT VALUE OF AN UNEVEN CASH FLOW ON BOTH THE TI BAII PLUS AND HP 12C

Solve for *NPV* = Net present value, given:

n = 5 years (number of years cash flow will continue)
PMT = \$5,000 (yr. 1); 6,000 (yr. 2); 7,000 (yr. 3); 8,000 (yr. 4); 9,000 (yr. 5)
i = 12 percent (cost of capital K_a)
Cost = \$25,000

Net Present Value of an Uneven Cash Flow

All steps are numbered and some steps include several keystrokes. All numbers following each step are keystrokes followed by a box [ ]. Each box represents a keystroke and indicates which calculator function is performed on that number.

Because we are dealing with uneven cash flows, the TI BAII requires that each number must be entered. These numbers are entered into the cash flow register of the calculator. The CFo symbol stands for the cash flow in period 0. Each additional cash flow will be represented by C and the period. For example, C01 is for period 1, C02 is for period 2, etc.

The HP 12C requires each cash flow to be entered in order. The [CFo] key represents the cash flow in time period 0. The [CFj] key automatically counts the year of the cash flow in the order entered and so no years need to be entered. Finally, the cost of capital of 12% is entered and the [f] key and [NPV] key are used to complete the problem.

Texas Instruments BAII Plus

Clear cash flow register
[CF] [2nd] [CLR WORK]

Set decimal to 2 places

[2nd] [FORMAT] 2 [ENTER]

1. [CF]
2. 25000 (cash outflow)
3. [+/−] changes sign
4. [ENTER]
5. [↓] C01 appears
6. 5000 [ENTER]
7. [↓] [↓] C02 appears
8. 6000 [ENTER]
9. [↓] [↓] C03 appears
10. 7000 [ENTER]
11. [↓] [↓] C04 appears
12. 8000 [ENTER]
13. [↓] [↓] C05 appears
14. 9000 [ENTER]
15. [NPV] I appears
16. 12 [ENTER]
17. [↓]
18. [CPT] answer −\$579.10

Negative Net Present Value

Hewlett-Packard 12C

[f] [REG] clears memory

Set decimal to 2 places

[f] 2

1. 25000 (cash outflow)
2. [CHS] changes sign
3. [g] [CFo]
4. 5000 [g] [CFj]
5. 6000 [g] [CFj]
6. 7000 [g] [CFj]
7. 8000 [g] [CFj]
8. 9000 [g] [CFj]
9. 12 [i]
10. [f] [NPV]

answer −\$579.10
Negative Net Present Value

If you receive an Error message, you have probably made a keystroke error. Clear memory with [f] [REG]

and start over with step 1.

INTERNAL RATE OF RETURN FOR AN ANNUITY ON BOTH THE TI BAII PLUS AND HP 12C

Solve for *IRR* = Internal rate of return, given:

n = 10 years (number of years cash flow will continue)
PMT = $10,000 per year (amount of the annuity)
Cost = $50,000 (this is the present value of the annuity)

	Texas Instruments BAII Plus	Hewlett-Packard 12C
Internal Rate of Return of an Annuity	Clear memory [TVM] [2nd] [CLR TVM]	[f] [REG] clears memory
All steps are numbered and some steps include several keystrokes. All numbers following each step are keystrokes followed by a box [ ]. Each box represents a keystroke and indicates which calculator function is performed on that number.	1. 10 (years of cash flow)	1. 50,000 (cash outflow)
	2. [N]	2. [CHS] changes sign
	3. 10,000 (annual payments)	3. [g]
	4. [PMT]	4. [CFo]
	5. 50,000 (present value)	5. 10,000 (annual payments)
The calculation for the internal rate of return on an annuity using the TI BAII Plus requires relatively few keystrokes.	6 [+/−]	6. [g] [Cfj]
	7. [PV]	7. 10 [g] [Nj] (years)
The HP 12C requires more keystrokes than the TI BAII Plus, because it needs to use the function keys [f] and [g] to enter data into the internal programs. Both calculators require that the cash outflow be expressed as a negative.	8. [CPT]	8. [f] [IRR]
	9. [I/Y]	answer is 15.10%
	answer is 15.10%	If an Error message appears, start over by clearing the memory with [f] [REG]
To conserve space, several keystrokes have been put into one step.	At an internal rate of return of 15.10%, the present value of the $50,000 outflow is equal to the present value of $10,000 cash inflows over the next 10 years.	

INTERNAL RATE OF RETURN WITH AN UNEVEN CASH FLOW ON BOTH THE TI BAII PLUS AND HP 12C

Solve for *IRR* = Internal rate of return (return which causes present value of outflows to equal present value of the inflows), given:

n	=	5 years (number of years cash flow will continue)
PMT	=	\$5,000 (yr. 1); 6,000 (yr. 2); 7,000 (yr. 3); 8,000 (yr. 4); 9,000 (yr. 5)
Cost	=	\$25,000

	Texas Instruments BAII Plus	Hewlett-Packard 12C
Internal Rate of an Uneven Cash Flow	Clear cash flow register [CF] [2nd] [CLR WORK]	[f] [REG] clears memory
All steps are numbered and some steps include several keystrokes. All numbers following each step are keystrokes followed by a box [ ]. Each box represents a keystroke and indicates which calculator function is performed on that number.	Set decimal to 2 places	
	1. [CF]	1. 25000 (cash outflow)
	2. 25000 (cash outflow)	2. [CHS] changes sign
	3. [+/−] changes sign	3. [g] [CFo]
Because we are dealing with uneven cash flows, the TI BAII Plus requires each number must be entered. These numbers are entered into the cash flow register of the calculator. The CFo symbol stands for the cash flow in period 0. Each additional cash flow will be represented by C and the period. For example, C01 is for period 1, C02 is for period 2, etc.	4. [ENTER]	4. 5000 [g] [CFj]
	5. [↓] C01 appears	5. 6000 [g] [CFj]
	6. 5000 [ENTER]	6. 7000 [g] [CFj]
	7. [↓] [↓] C02 appears	7. 8000 [g] [CFj]
	8. 6000 [ENTER]	8. 9000 [g] [CFj]
	9. [↓] [↓] C03 appears	9. [f] [IRR]
	10. 7000 [ENTER]	answer 11.15%
	11. [↓] [↓] C04 appears	If you receive an Error message, you have probably made a keystroke error. Clear memory with [f] [REG]
The HP 12C requires each cash flow to be entered in order. The [CFo] key represents the cash flow in time period 0. The [CFj] key automatically counts the year of the cash flow in the order entered and so no years need to be entered. To find the internal rate of return, use the [f] [IRR] keys and complete the problem.	12. 8000 [ENTER]	
	13. [↓] [↓] C05 appears	and start over with step 1.
	14. 9000 [ENTER]	
	15. [IRR]	
	16. [CPT] answer 11.15%	

glossary

A

abnormal return Gains beyond what the market would normally provide after adjustment for risk.

adjustable rate mortgage A mortgage in which the interest rate is adjusted regularly to current market conditions. It is sometimes referred to as a variable rate mortgage.

advances Increases in the prices of various stocks as measured between two points in time. Significant advances in a large number of stocks indicate a particular degree of market strength. Also see declines.

after-acquired property clause The stipulation in a mortgage bond indenture requiring all real property subsequently obtained by the issuing firm to serve as additional bond security.

aftermarket performance The price experience of new issues in the market.

algorithmic trading Algorithimic trading is the use of mathematical models that automatically execute trades when defined market or individual stock conditions exist.

alpha The value representing the difference between the return on a portfolio and a return on the market line that corresponds to a beta equal to the portfolio. A portfolio manager who performs at positive alpha levels would generate returns better than those available along the market line.

American depository receipts (ADRs) These securities represent the ownership interest in a foreign company's common stock. The process is as follows: The shares of the foreign company are purchased and put in trust in a foreign branch of a New York bank. The bank, in turn, receives and can issue depository receipts to the American shareholders of the foreign firm. These ADRs (depository receipts) allow foreign shares to be traded in the United States much like any other security. Through ADRs, one can purchase the stock of Sony Corporation, Honda Motor Co., Ltd., and hundreds of other foreign corporations.

anchoring-and-adjustment Making judgments from an existing value and then adjusting this value to reach the final conclusion.

angel investors Investors who are often friends and relatives who provide financing (seed capital) for a startup company.

annuities Cash flows that are equally spaced in time and are constant dollar amounts.

anomalies Deviations from the basic proposition that the market is efficient.

anticipated rate of inflation The expected rate of inflation that is included in the risk-free rate of return.

anticipated realized yield The return received on a bond held for a period other than that ending on the call date or the maturity date. In computing the anticipated realized yield, the investor considers both coupon payments and expected capital gains.

arbitrage An arbitrage is instituted when a simultaneous trade (a buy and a sale) occurs in two different markets and a profit is locked in.

arbitrage pricing theory A theory for explaining stock prices and stock returns. While the capital asset pricing model bases return solely on one form of systematic risk (market risk), arbitrage pricing theory can utilize several sources of risk (GDP, unemployment, etc.). Under this theory, it is assumed the investor will not be allowed to earn a return greater than that dictated by the various sensitivity factors affecting returns. To the extent that he does, arbitrageurs will eliminate the extra returns by selling the security and buying other comparable securities—thus the term "arbitrage pricing theory." Unlike the capital asset pricing model, there is no necessity to define K_M (the market rate of return).

asset allocation The designation of assets in various categories for investment purposes. The typical allocation is between stocks, bonds, and cash equivalents.

asset-utilization ratios Ratios that indicate the number of times per year that assets are turned over. They show the activity in the various asset accounts.

at-the-money An option on a stock that has a market value equal to the strike price.

automatic reinvestment plan A plan offered by a mutual fund in which the fund automatically reinvests all distributions to a shareholder account.

availability Availability refers to the fact that more-recent events have more influence on our decisions than distant events.

average differential return The alpha value that indicates the difference between the return on a portfolio or fund and a return on the market line that corresponds to a beta equal to the portfolio or fund.

B

back-end load An exit fee for selling a mutual fund.

balance sheet A financial statement that indicates, at a given point, what the firm owns and how these assets are financed in the form of liabilities and ownership interest.

balanced funds Mutual funds that combine investments in common stock, bonds, and preferred stock. Many balanced funds also invest in convertible securities as well. They try to provide income plus some capital appreciation.

banker's acceptance A short-term debt instrument usually issued in conjunction with a foreign trade transaction. The acceptance is a draft that is drawn on a bank for approval for future payment and is subsequently presented to the payer.

***Barron's* Confidence Index** An indicator utilized by technical analysts who follow smart money rules.

Movements in the index measure the expectations of bond investors whom some technical analysts see as astute enough to foresee economic trends before the stock market has time to react.

basic earnings per share Earnings per share unadjusted for dilution.

basis The difference between the futures price and the value of the underlying item. Thus, on a stock index futures contract, basis represents the difference between the stock index futures price and the value of the underlying index. The basis may be either positive or negative, with the former indicating optimism and the latter signifying pessimism.

basis point One basis point is equal to 0.01 percent. It is used as a unit to measure changes in interest rates.

BATS Exchange BATS Exchange was formed in 2005 as an electronic communication network and has become one of the largest exchanges in the world and includes BATS Europe.

behavioral finance An offshoot of cognitive psychology which suggests that people are not consistent in how they view equivalent events if they are presented in different contexts. This behavior can lead to irrational investment decisions.

best efforts The issuing firm, rather than the investment banker, assumes the risk for a distribution. The investment banker merely agrees to provide his best effort to sell the securities.

beta A measurement of the volatility of a security with the market in general. A greater beta coefficient than 1 indicates systematic risk greater than the market, while a beta of less than 1 indicates systematic risk less than the market.

beta coefficient *See* beta.

beta-related hedge A stock index futures hedge in which the relative volatility of the portfolio to the market is considered in determining the number of contracts necessary to offset a given dollar level of exposure. If a portfolio has a beta greater than 1, then extra contracts may be necessary to compensate for high volatility.

beta stability The amount of consistency in beta values over time. Instability means prior beta values may not be reflective of future beta values.

Black-Scholes option pricing model A formal model used to determine the theoretical value of an option. Such factors as the riskless interest rate, the length of the option, and the volatility of the underlying security are considered. For a more complete discussion, see Appendix 14A.

blind pool A form of limited partnership for real estate investments in which funds are provided to the general partner to select properties for investment.

bond indenture A lengthy, complicated legal document that spells out the borrowing firm's responsibilities to the individual lenders in a bond issue.

bond ladder A bond ladder is a portfolio of bonds bought with maturities that are equally spaced over a defined time period. For example the ladder could have a five-year life with 10 bonds coming due at 6-month intervals.

bond mutual funds Mutual funds that specialize in bond investments and interest income.

bond price sensitivity The sensitivity of a change in bond prices to a change in interest rates. Bond price sensitivity is influenced by the duration of the bond in that the longer the duration of a bond, the greater the price sensitivity. A less sophisticated but acceptable approach is to tie price sensitivity to the maturity of the bond rather than the duration.

bond swaps The selling of a given bond position and immediately buying into another one with similar attributes in an attempt to improve overall portfolio return or performance.

bottom-up approach A method for choosing stocks that starts with picking individual companies and then looking at the industry and economy to see if there is any reason an investment in the company should not be made.

breadth of market indicators Overall market rules used by technical analysts in comparing broad market activity with trading activity in a few stocks. By comparing all advances and declines in NYSE-listed stocks, for example, with the Dow Jones Industrial Average, analysts attempt to judge when the market has changed directions.

BRICs The BRICs represent the investment portfolio of Brazil, Russia, India, and China the four largest emerging markets.

bull spread An option strategy utilized when the expectation is that the stock price will rise. The opposite strategy is a bear spread.

business cycle Swings in economic activity encompassing expansionary and recessionary periods and, on average, occurring over four-year periods.

buying the spread A term indicating the cost from writing the call is more than the revenue of the short position. The opposite results in "selling the spread."

buyout fund Buyout funds usually purchase existing public companies or a division of a public company and take it private with the intention to sell it in the public market for a profit after it has been restructured and is more profitable.

C

call option An option to buy 100 shares of common stock at a specified price for a given period.

call provision A mechanism for repaying funds advanced through a bond issue. A provision of the bond indenture allows the issuer to retire bonds before maturity by paying holders a premium above principal.

calls *See* call option.

capital appreciation A growth in the value of a stock or other investments as opposed to income from dividends or interest.

Capital Asset Pricing Model A model that relates the return on an asset to the risk-free rate of a U.S. government treasury security adjusted for the risk of the asset and the risk of the market. The model reflects that the higher the risk the higher the required rate of return.

capital asset pricing model A model by which assets are valued based on their risk characteristics. The required return for an asset is related to its beta.

capital gain or loss Occurs when a stock held for investment purposes is sold at a gain or loss.

capital market line (CML) The graphic representation of the relationship of risks and returns with various portfolios of assets. The line is part of the capital asset pricing model.

carried interest The share of the profits allocated to the general partners is called the carried interest and is often 20 percent of the profits even though they may only have a 2 percent investment in the fund.

cash or spot price The dollar value paid for the immediate transfer of a commodity.

cash settlement Closing out a futures or options contract for cash rather than calling for actual delivery of the underlying item specified in the contract—for example, pork bellies and T-bills. The stock index futures markets and stock index options markets are *purely* cash-settlement markets. There is never even the implied potential for future delivery of the S&P 500 Stock Index or other indexes.

CBOE Chicago Board Options Exchange, the first and largest exchange for options.

certainty effect When given a choice between a guaranteed outcome and a probable outcome investors often choose the certain outcome rather than a higher probable outcome. This indicates risk aversion.

certificates of deposit Savings certificates that entitle the holder to the receipt of interest. These instruments are issued by commercial banks and savings and loans (or other thrift institutions).

certified financial planner (CFP) A financial planner who has been appropriately certified by the College for Financial Planning in Denver. He or she must demonstrate skills in risk management, tax planning, retirement and estate planning, and other similar areas.

chartered financial analyst (CFA) A security analyst or portfolio manager who has been appropriately certified through experience requirements and testing by the CFA Institute in Charlottesville, Virginia.

charting Use by technical analysts of charts and graphs to plot past stock price movements that are used to predict future prices.

circuit breakers Circuit breakers shut down the market for a period of time (usually 30 minutes) if there is a dramatic drop in stock prices.

closed-end fund A closed-end investment fund has a fixed number of shares, and purchasers and sellers of shares must deal directly with each other rather than with the fund. Closed-end funds trade on an exchange or over-the-counter.

coincident indicators Economic indicators that change direction at roughly the same time as the general economy.

combined earnings and dividend model A model combining earnings per share and an earnings multiplier with a finite dividend model. Value is derived from both the present value of dividends and the present value of the future price of the stock based on the earnings multiplier (P/E).

commercial paper A short-term credit instrument issued by large business corporations to the public. Commercial paper usually comes in minimum denominations of $25,000 and represents an unsecured promissory note.

commission broker An individual who represents a stock brokerage firm on the floor of an exchange and who executes sales and purchases stocks for the firm's clients across the nation.

commodities Such tangible items as livestock, farm produce, and precious metals. Users and producers of commodities hedge against future price fluctuations by transferring risks to speculators through futures contracts.

commodity futures A contract to buy or sell a commodity in the future at a given price.

comparable sales approach An approach to appraising real estate in which value is determined by the sales price for similar property.

compound sum The future value of an amount that is allowed to grow at a given interest rate over a period of time.

compound sum of an annuity Constant payments are made at equally spaced time periods and grow to a future value.

constant-dollar method Adjusting for inflation in the financial statements by using the consumer price index.

constant-growth model A dividend valuation model that assumes a constant growth rate for dividends.

construction and development trust A type of REIT that makes short-term loans to developers during their construction period.

Consumer Price Index An index used to measure the changes in the general price level.

contrary opinion rules Guidelines, based on such factors as the odd-lot or the short sales position, used by technical analysts who predict stock market activity on the assumption that such groups as small traders or short sellers are often wrong. *Also see* smart money rules.

conversion premium The amount, expressed as a dollar value or as a percentage, by which the price of the convertible security exceeds the current market value of the common stock into which it may be converted.

conversion price The face value of a convertible security divided by the conversion ratio gives the price of the underlying common stock at which the security is convertible. An investor would usually not convert the security into common stock unless the market price was greater than the conversion price.

conversion ratio The number of shares of common stock an investor receives when exchanging convertible bonds or shares of convertible preferred stock for shares of common stock.

conversion value The value of the underlying common stock represented by convertible bonds or convertible preferred stock. This dollar value is obtained by multiplying the conversion ratio by the per share market price of the common stock.

convertible arbitrage funds Convertible arbitrage funds is centered on convertible bonds and preferred stock. The common strategy is to buy the convertible bond for its income stream and short the common stock. If the convertible security increases in value and gets called for redemption the arb will take the shares received from conversion and cover the short position. This means that the hedge ratio has to be correct so that the shares received by conversion equal the shares sold short.

convertible security A corporate bond or a share of preferred stock that, at the option of the holder, can be converted into shares of common stock of the issuing corporation. Sometimes convertible securities can be exchanged for other assets or securities held by the issuing company.

convexity Convexity describes the nonlinear relationship of a bond's value to its maturity.

core-satellite portfolio A core-satellite portfolio structure used alternative assets to increase the return and reduce the risk of a core portfolio of stocks and bonds.

corporate governance The accuracy and transparency of financial statements and operations of the company by management. Good corporate governance includes fair treatment of shareholders.

corporate venture capital funds Generally a large corporation that invests in small companies that need financial capital.

correlation coefficient The measurement of joint movement between two variables.

cost approach An approach to appraising real estate (or other assets) in which value is determined by the cost to replace the asset at current prices.

coupon rate The stated, fixed rate of interest paid on a bond.

covered options The process of writing (selling) options on stock that is already owned.

covered writer A writer of an option who owns the stock on which the option is written. If the stock is not owned, the writer is deemed naked.

credit default swaps A credit default swap (CDS) is a derivative contract in which a credit protection buyer makes a fixed payment periodically to a credit protection seller in exchange for a specified contingent payout following a dafault event on the asset(s) underlying the CDS.

creditor claims Claims represented by debt instruments offered by financial institutions, industrial corporations, or the government.

cross hedge A hedging position in which one form of security is used to hedge another form of security (often because differences in maturity dates or quality characteristics make a perfect hedge difficult to establish).

crossover point In the industry life cycle curve or company life cycle curve, the point where the industry or company moves from the growth phase (accelerating growth) to the expansion stage (decelerating growth). This crossover point is very important because the price-earning ratio will adjust downward once the market realizes the growth rate has slowed down.

currency fluctuations Changes in the relative value of one currency to another. For example, the French franc may advance or decline in relation to the dollar. To the extent a foreign currency appreciates relative to the dollar, returns on foreign investments will increase in terms of dollars. The opposite would be true for declining foreign currencies.

currency futures Futures contracts for speculation or hedging in different nations' currencies.

current-cost method Adjusting for inflation in the financial statements by revaluing assets at their current cost.

current ratio Current assets divided by current liabilities.

current yield The annual dollar amount of interest paid on a bond divided by the price at which the bond is currently trading in the market.

cyclical indicators Factors that economists can observe to measure the progress of economic cycles. Leading indicators move in a particular direction in advance of the movement of general business conditions, while lagging indicators change direction after general conditions, and coincident indicators move in unison with the economy.

cyclical industry An industry such as automobiles, whose financial health is closely tied to the condition of the general economy. Such industries tend to make the type of products whose purchase can be postponed until the economy improves.

D

dark pools Dark pools are electonic networks used by institutional investors to cross trades annonymously. They are called dark pools because no one can see who is at either end of the trade.

database A form of organized, stored data. It is usually fed into the computer for additional analysis.

debenture An unsecured corporate bond.

debt-utilization ratios Ratios that indicate how the firm is financed between debt (lenders) and equity (owners) and the firm's ability for meeting cash payments due on fixed obligations, such as interest, lease payments, licensing fees, or sinking-fund charges.

declines Decreases in the prices of various stocks as measured between two points in time. Significant declines in a large number of stocks indicate a particular degree of market weakness. *Also see* advances.

deep discount bond A bond that has a coupon rate far below rates currently available on investments and that consequently can be traded only at a significant discount from par value. It may offer an opportunity for capital appreciation.

deficit (government) The government spends more than it receives.

defined benefit plan A defined benefit plan specifies the amount of the retirement benefit based on income and years of service.

defined contribution plan A defined contribution plan transfers the risk of money management from employers to employees with the ending balance in the account. The retirement benefit is based on the employee's investment choices and performance over the life of the accumulation period.

derivative products Securities that derive their existence from other items. Stock index futures and options are sometimes thought of as derivatives because they derive their existence from actual market indexes but have no intrinsic characteristics of their own.

diagonal spread A combination of a vertical and horizontal spread.

diluted earnings per share EPS adjusted for all potential dilution from the issuance of any new shares of common stock arising from convertible bonds, convertible preferred stock, warrants, or any other options outstanding.

dilution The reduction in earnings per share that occurs when earnings remain unchanged yet the number of shares outstanding increases, as in the conversion of convertible bonds or preferred stock into common stock.

direct equity claim Representation of ownership interests through common stock or other instruments to purchase common stock, such as warrants and options.

discount rate The interest rate at which future cash flows are discounted to a present value.

dispersion The distribution of values or outcomes around an expected value.

distressed funds Distressed funds invest in any type of security that is on the verge of bankruptcy or in bankruptcy or where legal actions may have created an undervalued asset in the eye of the hedge fund manager.

diversification Lack of concentration in any similar security, industry, or country. A portfolio composed of many different securities is diversified.

diversification benefits Risk reduction through a diversification of investments. Investments that are negatively correlated or that have low positive correlation provide the best diversification benefits. Such benefits may be particularly evident in an internationally diversified portfolio.

dividend payout ratio Annual dividends per share divided by annual earnings per share.

dividend valuation model Any one of a number of stock valuation models based on the premise that the value of stock lies in the present value of its future dividend stream.

dividend yield Annual dividends per share divided by market price.

dollar-cost averaging The investor buys a fixed dollar's worth of a given security at regular intervals regardless of the security's price or the current market outlook. This provides a certain degree of discipline and also means more shares will be purchased at low prices rather than high prices since the amount of the regular investment is fixed and only the number of shares purchased varies.

dollar-denominated bonds Foreign bonds that are denominated (payable) in U.S. dollars.

Dow Jones Equity Market Index An index that includes 700 stocks in 82 industry groups. Unlike the Dow Jones Industrial Average, it includes stocks from the New York Stock Exchange, the American Stock Exchange, and the Nasdaq National Market System and is much more broadly based.

Dow Jones Industrial Average An index of stock market activity based on the price movements of 30 large corporations. The average is price-weighted, which means each stock is effectively weighted by the magnitude of its price.

Dow Jones World Industry Groups A table in *The Wall Street Journal* that shows the leading and lagging industries for a given day around the world. Specific price change information on more than 100 industries is also provided.

Dow Jones World Index An international stock index that covers 25 countries in three major sectors of the world. It shows this information individually and collectively.

Dow theory The theory, developed by Charles Dow in the late 1890s and still in use today, that the analysis of long-term (primary) stock market trends can yield accurate predictions for future price movements.

downside limit The lowest value a convertible bond should fall to based on its pure bond value (and an assumption that interest rates stay constant).

downside protection The protection that a convertible bond investor enjoys during a period of falling stock prices. While the underlying common stock and the convertible bond may both fall in value, the bond will fall only to a particular level because it has a fundamental, or pure, bond value based on its assured income stream.

downside risk The possibility that an asset, such as a security, may fall in value as a result of fundamental factors or external market forces. The limit of the downside risk for a convertible bond can be computed as the difference between the bond's market price and its pure bond value divided by the market price.

Du Pont analysis A system of analyzing return on assets through examining the profit margin and asset turnover. Also, the value of return on equity is analyzed through evaluating return on assets and the debt/total assets ratio.

duration The weighted average life of a bond. The weights are based on the present values of the individual cash flows relative to the present value of the total cash flows. Duration is a better measure than maturity when assessing the price sensitivity of bonds; that is, the impact of interest rate changes on bond prices can be more directly correlated to duration than to maturity.

E

early-stage venture capital Financial capital that is invested in companies that are just getting started that are only one or two years old.

earnings per share The earnings available to holders of common stock divided by the number of common stock shares outstanding.

earnings valuation model Any one of a number of stock valuation models based on the premise that a stock's value is some appropriate multiple of earnings per share.

EBITDA Earnings before interest, taxes, depreciation, and amortization. It emphasizes operating income rather than the normally reported earnings after taxes.

Economic Growth and Tax Reconciliation Act of 2001 A tax act passed by the Bush administration that lowers marginal tax rates, phases out the estate tax, and provides a number of other tax benefits. It is scheduled to be rescinded in 2011 unless it is renewed.

effective diversification The diversification of a portfolio to remove unsystematic risk.

effective yield Securities sold at a discount from par value like U.S. treasury bills have a yield that is higher than the yield quoted on the par value because the interest payment is received on an investment of less than par value. The effective yield is sometimes referred to as the true yield or the actual yield.

efficient frontier A set of investment portfolios in which the investor receives maximum return for a given level of risk or a minimum risk for a given level of return.

efficient hedge A hedge in which one side of the transaction effectively covers the exposed side in terms of movement.

efficient market The capacity of the market to react to new information, to avoid rapid price fluctuations, and to engage in increased or reduced trading volume without realizing significant price changes. In an efficient market environment, securities are assumed to be correctly priced at any point in time.

efficient market hypothesis (EMH) The concept that there are many participants in the securities markets who are profit maximizing and alert to information so that there is almost instant adjustment to new information. The weak form of this hypothesis suggests there is no relationship between past and future prices. The semistrong form maintains that all forms of public information are already reflected in the price of a security, so fundamental analysis cannot determine under- or overvaluation. The strong form suggests that all information, insider as well as public, is impounded in the value of a security.

efficient portfolio A portfolio that combines assets so as to minimize the risk for a given level of return.

Electronic Book The database system that covers all stocks listed on the New York Stock Exchange and keeps track of limit orders and market orders for the specialist.

electronic communication networks (ECNs) These are electronic trading systems that automatically match buy and sell orders at specified prices. ECNs are also known as alternative trading systems (ATSs) and have been given Security Exchange Commission approval to be more fully integrated into the national market system by choosing to either act as a broker-dealer or as an exchange.

emerging countries Foreign countries that have not fully developed their economic systems and productive capacity. Examples might include Chile, Jordan, Korea, Thailand, and Zimbabwe. A number of these emerging countries may represent good risk-reduction potential for U.S. investors because the factors that influence their economic welfare may be quite different from critical factors in the United States. Investments in these countries, at times, may also provide high returns.

Employment Act of 1946 This act set up the four economic goals that dictated monetary policy for the Federal Reserve Board.

equal-weighted index Each stock, regardless of total market value or price, is weighted equally. It is as if there were $100 invested in every stock in the index. The Value Line Index is a prime example of an equal-weighted index.

equipment trust certificate A secured debt instrument used by firms in the transportation industry that provides for bond proceeds to purchase new equipment, which in turn is collateral for the bond issue.

equity participation The lender also participates in an ownership interest in the property.

equity risk premium (ERP) The extra return investors require for investing in common stock rather than in risk-free U.S. government securities. The extra return is a function of the historical returns of stocks versus U.S. government securities.

equity trust A type of REIT that buys, operates, and sells real estate as an investment as opposed to mortgage trusts.

Eurodollar bonds Bonds that are denominated (payable) in dollars but that are issued and traded outside the United States.

event-driven funds Event-driven funds take investment positions in many types of events such as mergers and acquisitions, bankruptcy announcements, corporate restructurings, proxy battles, spin-offs, and more. Any event that causes the price of an asset not to be fairly priced will attract event-driven hedge funds.

excess returns Returns in excess of the risk-free rate or in excess of a market measure such as the S&P 500 Stock Index.

exchange listing A firm lists its shares on an exchange (such as the American or New York Stock Exchange).

exchange privilege A feature offered by a mutual fund sponsor in which a shareholder is able to move money between various funds under the management of the sponsor at a very minimal processing charge and without a commission.

exchange-traded funds (ETFs) The American Stock Exchange created exchange-traded funds that are similar to index mutual funds. Their structure is different than mutual funds but they allow an investor to buy an index such as the Standard and Poor's 500 on the AMEX just the same as buying common stock.

exercise price (warrant) The price at which the stock can be bought using the warrant.

expectations hypothesis The hypothesis that explains the term structure of interest rates, stating that a long-term interest rate is the average of expected short-term interest rates over the applicable time period. If, for example, long-term rates are higher than short-term rates, then according to the expectations hypothesis, investors must expect that short-term rates will be increasing in coming periods.

expected value The sum of possible outcomes times their probability of occurrence.

extraordinary gains and losses Gains or losses from the sale of corporate fixed assets, lawsuits, or similar events that would not be expected to occur often, if ever again.

F

Fed The Federal Reserve serves as the central banking authority for the United States. The Fed enacts monetary policy, and it plays a major role in regulating commercial banking operations and controlling the money supply.

federal deficit A situation in which the federal government spends more money than it receives through taxes and other revenue sources.

federal surplus A situation in which taxes and other government revenues provide more money than is needed to cover government expenditures.

FIFO A method of inventory valuation in which it is assumed that inventory purchased first is sold first (first-in, first-out).

financial asset A financial claim on an asset (rather than physical possession of a tangible asset) usually documented by a legal instrument, such as a stock certificate.

financial futures A contract to trade futures on interest rates, foreign exchange, and stock indexes.

financial hedging Reducing exposure to financial risks such as changes in interest rates, currency value, or stock price. Hedging may entirely or partially eliminate negative effects of a market movement.

financial risk Financial risk occurs when a firm uses too much financial leverage (high debt to asset ratio) and risks bankruptcy.

financial-service companies Firms that provide a broad range of financial services to diversify their consumer base. Services may include brokerage activities, insurance, banking, and so forth.

fiscal policy Government spending and taxing practices designed to promote or inhibit various economic activities.

flash crash On May 6, 2010, the market fell 1,000 points in a matter of minutes. This event became known as the flash crash.

floating-rate notes The coupon rate on the note or bond is fixed for only a short time and then varies with a stipulated short-term rate such as the rate on U.S. Treasury bills.

floor broker An independent stockbroker who is a member of a stock exchange and who executes trades, for a fee, for commission brokers experiencing excessive volumes of trading.

floor value A value that an income-producing security will not fall below because of the fundamental value attributable to its assured income stream.

flow-of-funds analysis Analysis of the pattern of financial payments between business, government, and households.

follow-on fund A follow-on fund is defined as an existing fund that is raising another fund.

forced conversion When the company calls the convertible security knowing that the owners will take the stock and thus convert the debt to equity.

foreign currency effects To the extent a foreign currency appreciates relative to the dollar, returns on foreign investments will increase in terms of dollars. The opposite would be true for declining foreign currencies.

foreign funds Mutual funds that specialize in foreign markets and foreign securities.

foreign-pay bonds Bonds issued in a foreign country and payable in that country's currency. For example, a Japanese government bond payable in yen would represent a foreign-pay bond.

foreign political risks The risks associated with investing in firms operating in foreign countries. There is the danger of nationalization of foreign firms or the blockage of capital flows to investors. There also may be the danger of violent overthrow of the political party in power, with all the associated implications. Punitive legislation against foreign firms or investors is another political risk.

forward price-earnings ratio The market price of a stock divided by the earnings per share expected over the next 12 months.

fourth market The direct trading between large institutional investors in blocks of listed stocks.

framing Framing is related to mental accounting. Investors keep a frame of reference such as the purchase price of a stock, and this influences their decision to buy, sell, or hold.

free cash flow After-tax earnings plus depreciation (and amortization) less necessary capital expenditures and anticipated dividend payments. Free cash flow emphasizes the amount of funds available to redeploy in the business or to be used for acquisitions.

fundamental analysis The valuation of stocks based on fundamental factors, such as company earnings, growth prospects, and so forth.

funded pension plan Current income is charged with pension liabilities in advance of the actual payment, and funds are set aside.

futures contract An agreement that provides for sale or purchase of a specific amount of a commodity at a designated time in the future at a given price.

futures contract on a stock market index A futures contract based on a market index, such as the Standard & Poor's 500 Stock Index or the NYSE Composite Index.

G

general obligation issue A municipal bond backed by the full faith, credit, and "taxing power" of the issuing unit rather than the revenue from a given project.

general partners General partners are the fund managers who invest their own money and money from the limited partners. They oversee the investments in the fund and get compensated for their efforts with a share of the profits.

The Global Dow This is a stock index of 150 worldwide corporations. It only includes blue-chip stocks and is created by the Dow Jones Company, the publisher of the Wall Street Journal.

GNMA (Ginnie Mae) pass-through certificates Fixed-income securities that represent an undivided interest in a pool of federally insured mortgages. GNMA, the Government National Mortgage Association, buys a pool of securities from various lenders at a discount and then issues securities to the public against these mortgages.

going public Selling privately held shares to new investors in the over-the-counter market for the first time.

government securities Bonds issued by federal, state, or local governmental units or government agencies. Whereas corporate securities' returns are paid through company earnings, government securities are repaid through taxes or the revenues from projects financed by the bonds.

graduated payment mortgage A type of mortgage in which payments start out on a relatively low basis and increase over the life of the loan.

greed index A contrary opinion index that measures how "greedy" investors are. Greed is thought to be synonymous with bullish sentiment, or optimism. Under the assumptions of the greed index, the more greedy or optimistic investors are, the more likely the market is to fall and vice versa.

gross domestic product (GDP) A measure of output from U.S. factories and related consumption in the United States. It does not include products made by U.S. companies in foreign markets.

growth company A company that exhibits rising returns on assets each year and sales that are growing at an increasing rate (growth phase of the life-cycle curve). Growth companies may not be as well known as growth stocks.

growth funds Mutual funds with the primary objective of capital appreciation.

growth stock The stock of a firm generally growing faster than the economy or market norm.

growth with income funds Mutual funds that combine a strategy of capital appreciation with income generation.

H

hedge funds Hedge funds are private limited partnerships that are unregulated by the Securities and Exchange Commission. These funds are only open to qualified investors and can invest in almost any type of asset. They are managed by a general partner who normally takes 20 percent of the profits from the fund. They normally are neither bullish nor bearish, but engage in buying, short selling, transacting in puts and calls, etc. attempting to earn superior returns.

hedging A process for lessening or eliminating risk by taking a position in the market opposite to your original position. For example, someone who owns wheat can sell a futures contract to protect against future price declines.

herding Herding refers to a follow-the-leader mentality where investors all do the same thing as the majority.

heuristic A technique for problem solving based on experiential learning. Heuristics are nonreflective, intuititive mechanisms for coping with complexities.

hidden assets Assets that are not readily apparent to investors in a traditional sense, but add substantial value to the firm.

high-frequency trading Computerized trades in thousandths of one second generated by mathematical equations.

horizontal spread Buying and writing two options with the same strike price but maturing in different months.

house brokers Brokers who got their name because they represent NYSE member firms such as Merrill Lynch or Smith Barney, which used to be known as investment houses. House brokers either trade for clients of the investment house or for the firm's direct account.

hurdle rate This is the rate of return that must be achieved for the limited partners before the general partners can take their share of the profits.

hybrid trust A form of REIT that engages in the activities of both equity trusts and mortgage trusts.

I

Ibbotson study A study examining comparative returns on stocks and fixed-income securities from the mid-1920s to the present.

immunization Immunizing or protecting a bond portfolio against the effects of changing interest rates on the ending value of the portfolio. The process is usually tied to a time horizon. In the process, if interest rates go up, there will be a decline in the value of the portfolio, but a higher reinvestment rate opportunity for inflows. Conversely, if interest rates go down, there will be capital appreciation for the portfolio, but a lower reinvestment rate opportunity. By tying all the investment decisions to a specified duration period, the portfolio manager can take advantage of these counter forces to ensure a necessary outcome.

income approach An approach to appraising real estate by dividing annual net operating income by an appropriate capitalization rate, which is based on the required return by investors on similar-type property.

income bond A corporate debt instrument on which interest is paid only if funds are available from current income.

income statement A financial statement that shows the profitability of a firm over a given period.

income-statement method A method of forecasting earnings per share based on a projected income statement.

independent brokers Individuals on the NYSE that are employees of small "boutique firms." These independent brokers can provide execution services to member firms or nonmember firms as well as for house brokers who need extra help.

index fund A fund investing in a portfolio of corporate stocks, the composition of which is determined by the Standard & Poor's 500 Index or some other index.

indifference curves These curves show the investor's trade-off between risk and return. The steeper the slope of the curve, the more risk-averse the investor is.

indirect equity claim An indirect claim on common stock such as that achieved by placing funds in investment companies.

individual retirement account (IRA) An IRA allows a qualifying taxpayer to deduct $3,000 from taxable income and invest the funds at a bank, savings and loan, brokerage house, mutual fund, or other financial institution. The funds are normally placed in interest-bearing instruments, or perhaps in other securities, such as common stock. The income on the funds is allowed to grow tax-free until withdrawn at retirement. The annual allowable deduction is scheduled to increase to $5,000 over the decade.

industry factors The unique attributes that must be considered in analyzing a given industry or group of industries. Examples include industry structure, supply/demand of labor and materials, and government regulation.

industry life cycles Cycles that are created because of economic growth, competition, availability of resources, and the resultant market saturation of the particular goods and services offered. The stages are development, growth, expansion, maturity, and decline.

inflation A general increase in the prices of goods and services.

inflation-adjusted accounting Restating financial statements to show the effect of inflation on the balance sheet and income statement. This is supplemental to the normal presentation based on historical data.

inflationary expectations A value representing future expectations about the rate of inflation. This value, combined with the real rate of return, provides the risk-free required return for the investor.

initial public offering (IPO) The process of bringing private companies to the public market for the first time.

insider trading Trading by those who had special access to unpublished information. If the information is used to illegally make a profit, there may be large fines and possible jail sentences.

institutional investor A type of investor (as opposed to individual investors) representing organizations responsible for bringing together large pools of capital for investment. Institutional investors include investment companies, pension funds, life insurance companies, bank trust departments, and endowments and foundations.

in-the-money A term that indicates when the market price of a stock is above the striking price of the call option. When the strike price is above the market price, the call option is out of the money.

in-the-money warrants Warrants that have market prices higher than their exercise prices and have positive intrinsic values.

Intercontinental Exchange (ICE) The Intercontinental Exchange was founded in 2000 and trades futures contracts in the U.S. and Europe.

interest rate futures Futures contracts involving Treasury bills, Treasury bonds, Treasury notes, commercial paper, certificates of deposit, and GNMA certificates.

interest rate swaps The trading of interest rate exposure between two or more parties so that each participant may be able to rebalance his portfolio with less risk. Fixed-rate exposure and variable-rate exposure are normally exchanged.

international tax problems Many foreign countries impose a 7.5 to 15 percent withholding tax against the dividends or interest paid to nonresident holders of equity or debt securities. However, it is often possible for tax-exempt U.S. investors to secure an exemption or rebate on part or all of the withholding tax. Also, taxable U.S. investors can normally claim a U.S. tax credit for taxes paid in foreign countries. The problem is more likely to be one of inconvenience and paper shuffling rather than loss of funds.

internationally oriented funds Mutual funds and closed-end investment companies that invest in worldwide securities. Some funds specialize in Asian holdings, others in South African, and so on.

intrinsic value Value of a warrant or option equal to market price minus the strike (exercise) price.

inverse pyramiding A process of leveraging to control commodities contracts in which the profits from one contract are used to purchase another contract on margin, and profits on this contract are applied to a third, and so on.

investment The commitment of current funds in anticipation of the receipt of an increased return of funds at some point.

Investment Advisor Act of 1940 This act was set up to protect the public from unethical investment advisers. Any adviser with more than 15 public investment clients must register with the SEC and file semiannual reports.

investment banker One who is primarily involved in the distribution of securities from the issuing corporation to the public. An investment banker also advises corporate clients on their financial strategy and may help to arrange mergers and acquisitions.

investment banking The underwriting and distribution of a new security issue in the primary market. The investment banker advises the issuing concern on price and other terms and normally guarantees sale while overseeing distribution of the securities through the selling brokerage houses.

investment companies A type of financial institution that takes proceeds of individual investors and reinvests them in securities according to their specific objectives. A popular type of investment company is the mutual fund.

J

Jensen measure of portfolio performance Jensen compares excess returns (total portfolio returns minus the risk-free rate) to what should be required in the market based on the portfolio beta. For example, if the portfolio beta is 1, the portfolio has a systematic risk equal to the market, and the expected portfolio excess returns should be equal to market excess returns (the market rate of return minus the risk-free rate). The question then becomes: Did the portfolio manager do better or worse than expected? The portfolio manager's excess returns can be compared to the market line of expected excess returns for any beta level.

junk bonds (high-yield bonds) High-risk, low-grade bonds rated below BBB. They often perform like common stock and may provide interesting investment opportunities.

K

K_e The term representing required rate of return based on the capital asset pricing model. It is the discount rate applied to future dividends and price.

key indicators Various market observations used by technical analysts to predict the direction of future market trends. Examples include the contrary opinion and smart money rules.

L

lagging indicators Economic indicators that usually change direction after business conditions have turned around.

late-stage companies Late-stage companies are producing and shipping goods that are often two or three years away from an initial public offering.

leading indicators Economic indicators that change direction in advance of general business conditions.

least squares trend analysis A statistical methodology to make projections.

least squares trendline A trendline that minimizes the squared distance of the individual values from the line.

leveraged buyouts The management of the company or some other investor group borrows the needed cash to repurchase all the shares of an existing company. The balance sheet of the company serves as the collateral base to make the borrowing possible. After the leveraged buyout, the company may be taken private for a time in which unprofitable assets are sold and debt reduced. The intent is then to bring the company to the public market once again (or resell it to another company) at a large profit over the initial purchase price.

LIFO A method of inventory valuation in which it is assumed inventory purchased last is sold first (last-in, first-out).

limit order A condition placed on a transaction executed through a stockbroker to assure that securities will be sold only if a specified minimum price is received or purchased only if the price to be paid is no more than a given maximum.

limited partners Limited partners provide the majority of the financial capital and have a liability limited to their investment. They share in the profits from the fund's investment.

limited partnership A business arrangement in which there is the limited liability protection of a corporation with the tax provisions of a regular partnership. All profits or losses are directly assigned to the partners. The general partner has unlimited liability.

Lipper Mutual Fund Investment Performance Averages Lipper publishes indexes for growth funds, growth-with-income funds, and balanced funds. Lipper also shows year-to-date and weekly performance for many other categories of funds.

liquidity The capacity of an investment to be retired for cash in a short period with a minimum capital loss.

liquidity preference theory A theory related to the term structure of interest rates. The theory states the term structure tends to be upward sloping more than any other pattern. This reflects a recognition of the fact that long maturity obligations are subject to greater price change movements than short maturity obligations when interest rates change. Because of increased risk of holding longer-term maturities, investors demand a higher return to hold such securities. Thus, they have a preference for short-term liquid obligations.

liquidity ratios Ratios that demonstrate the firm's ability to pay off short-term obligations as they come due.

load fund A mutual fund that charges a commission.

long position A market transaction in which an investor purchases securities with the expectation of holding the securities for cash income or for resale at a higher price in the future. *Also see* short position.

long/short equity funds The traditinal long/short equity fund is one-third short and two-thirds long and uses leverage to be 133 percent invested.

long-term anticipation securities (LEAPS) Longer-term options with expiration dates of up to two years.

Lorie and Fisher study A University of Chicago study indicating comparative returns on financial assets over half a decade. It is similar to the Ibbotson and Sinquefield study in many respects.

low-load fund The commission or load is only 2 to 3 percent instead of the normal 7.25 percent.

M

Macaulay duration The standard definition of duration of a bond, which is based on the weighted average life as represented by the present value of cash inflows.

manager risk Professional money managers may be good, bad, or neutral. The risk is that your funds are managed by a poor money manager or that the fund manager cannot consistently outperform the market.

margin account A trading account maintained with a brokerage firm on which the investor may borrow a percentage of the funds for the purchase of securities.

The broker lends the funds at interest slightly above the prime rate.

margin maintenance requirement The amount of money that must be "deposited" to hold a margin position if losses reduce the initial margin that was put up.

margin requirements The amount of money that must be "deposited" to purchase a commodity contract or shares of stock on margin.

market A mechanism for facilitating the exchange of assets through buyer-seller communication. The communication, and not a central negotiating location, is the requisite condition for a market to exist, though some transactions (for example, trades at the various stock exchanges) do involve a direct meeting of buyers and sellers or their agents.

market bubbles A market bubble occurs when prices are grossly overrvalued due to speculation.

market capitalization The total market value of the firm. It is computed by multiplying shares outstanding times stock price.

market line On a graph, excess returns are shown on the vertical axis, the portfolio beta is shown on the horizontal axis, and the market line describes the relationship between the two.

market neutral funds Market neutral funds have no bias toward a long or short position and try to make their profits by good stock selections using 50 percent long and 50 percent short.

market rate of interest The coupon rate of interest paid on bonds currently issued. Of course, a previously issued bond that is currently traded may be sold at a discount or a premium so that the buyer in effect receives the market rate even if the coupon rate on this older bond is substantially higher or lower than market rates. The market rate is also known as the yield to maturity.

market segmentation theory A theory related to the term structure of interest rates that focuses on the demand side of the market. There are several large institutional participants in the bond market, each with its own maturity preferences. Banks tend to prefer short-term liquid securities to match the nature of their deposits, whereas life insurance companies prefer long-term bonds to match their long-run obligations. The behavior of these two institutions and of savings and loans often creates pressure on short-term or long-term rates but very little on the intermediate market of five- to seven-year maturities. This theory helps to focus on the accumulation or liquidation of securities by institutions during the different phases of the business cycle and the resultant impact on the yield curve.

maturity date The date at which outstanding principal must be repaid to bondholders.

mental accounting Mental accounting occurs when investors divide investments into different types of accounts and lose sight maximizing total wealth.

merger arbitrage funds Merger arbitrage funds make their money betting on the completion or failure of an announced merger. A merger arbitrageur can take either side of the bet by assuming the merger will be completed or that it will fail. In general the arb would buy the security that is expected to rise and short the security that is expected to decline.

merger price premium The difference between the offering price per share and the market price per share of the merger candidate (before the impact of the offer).

middle-stage companies Middle-stage or expansion companies are four or five years away from an initial offering and are growing their market.

modified duration Macaulay duration divided by one plus yield to maturity. It provides a better measure of bond price sensitivity to interest rate changes than does Macaulay duration.

momentum investing Momentum investing is an investing style that buys stocks that are performing consistently well compared to the market in general. On a relative basis momentum stocks rise faster than the market, and momentum investors like to find these kinds of stocks.

monetarist An economic analyst who believes monetary policy tools, and not fiscal policy, can best provide a stable environment of sustained economic growth.

monetary policy Direct control of interest rates or the money supply undertaken by the Federal Reserve to achieve economic objectives. Used in some cases to augment or offset the use of fiscal policy.

money market account Accounts offered by financial institutions to compete with money market funds. The minimum deposit is $500 to $1,000, with a maximum of three checks drawn per month.

money market fund A type of mutual fund that invests in short-term government securities, commercial paper, and repurchase agreements. Most offer checkwriting privileges.

money supply The level of funds available at a given time for conducting transactions in our economy. The Federal Reserve can influence the money supply through its monetary policy tools. There are many different definitions of the money supply. For example, M1 is currency in circulation plus private checking deposits, including those in interest-bearing NOW accounts. M2 adds in savings accounts and money market mutual funds, and so on.

monopolies Dominance of an industry by one company. Monopolies are not common in the United States due to antitrust laws, but they do exist by government permission in the area of public utilities.

mortgage A lien against real property.

mortgage trust A form of REIT in which long-term loans are made to real estate investors.

multinational corporations Firms that have operations in a number of countries. Multinationals are frequently found in such industries as oil, mainframe computers, and banking.

municipal bonds Tax-exempt debt securities issued by state and local governments (including special political subdivisions).

mutual fund A pooling of funds by investors for reinvestment. The funds are administered by professional managers. Technically, only an open-end (see definition) investment fund is considered to be a mutual fund.

mutual fund cash position An overall market rule that asserts that by examining the level of uncommitted funds held by large institutional investors, analysts can measure the potential demand for stocks and thereby anticipate market movements.

N

naked options The process of writing (selling) options on a stock that is not currently owned. It is highly speculative.

Nasdaq indexes Index measures for components of the over-the-counter market. The OTC indexes are value-weighted.

Nasdaq Stock Market Nasdaq was formerly referred to as the National Association of Securities Dealers Automated Quotation system. This is where all over-the-counter stocks trade through electronic medium. Eventually the over-the-counter market became known as the Nasdaq Stock Market.

net asset value The net asset value (NAV) represents the current value of an investment fund. It is computed by taking the total value of the securities, subtracting out the liabilities, and dividing by the shares outstanding.

net debtor-creditor hypothesis Since inflation makes each dollar worth less, it is often argued that a person or firm that is a net debtor gains from inflation because payments of interest and return of principal are made with continually less valuable dollars. Conversely, a net creditor loses real capital because the loans are repaid in less valuable dollars.

net working capital Current assets minus current liabilities.

New York Stock Exchange The NYSE is the largest stock exchange in the world based on value of stocks traded. It owns the American Stock Exchange and merged with Euronext, a large European exchange.

New York Stock Exchange Index A market value-weighted measure of stock market changes for all stocks listed on the NYSE.

no-bias funds No-bias funds are the same as market neutral funds. *See* market neutral funds.

no-load mutual fund A mutual fund on which no sales commission must be paid. The fund's shares are sold, not through brokers, but rather through the mail or other direct channels.

nominal GNP Gross national product expressed in current, noninflation-adjusted dollars.

nominal return A return that has not been adjusted for inflation.

nonconstant growth model Dividend valuation model that does not assume a constant growth rate for dividends.

O

odd-lot theory The contrary opinion rule stating that small traders (who generally buy or sell odd lots) often misjudge market trends, selling just before upturns and buying before downturns. The theory has not been useful in predicting trends observed in recent years.

oligopolies Industries that have few competitors. Oligopolies are quite common in large, mature U.S. industries such as automobiles, steel, oil, airlines, and aluminum. The competition between companies in an oligopoly can be intense, and profitability can suffer as a result of price wars and battles over market share. Increasingly, oligopolistic industries are facing international competition, which has altered their competitive strategies.

online broker A brokerage firm that executes transactions on its Internet Web site at a minimum cost to the customer.

open-end fund An open-end investment fund stands ready at all times to sell or redeem shares from stockholders. There is no limit to the number of shares. Technically, a mutual fund is considered to be an open-end investment fund. *Also see* closed-end fund.

open-market operations The Federal Reserve's action of buying or selling government securities to expand or contract the amount of money in the economy.

operating margin Operating income divided by sales.

operating risk Operating risk focuses on the volatility of operating earnings. Given the cyclical nature of the economy and the stability of the industry, this risk can be measured by the standard deviation of operating earnings.

option The right acquired for a consideration to buy or sell something at a fixed price within a specified period.

option premium The intrinsic value plus a speculative premium.

option price The specified price at which the holder of a warrant may buy the shares to which the warrant entitles purchase.

Options Clearing Corporation Issues all options listed on the exchanges that trade in options.

options on industry indexes An option index contract tailored to a given industry. Thus, one who wishes to speculate on a given industry's performance or hedge against holdings in that industry can use industry index options (subindexes).

options to purchase stock index futures An option to purchase a stock index futures contract at a specified price over a given time. This security combines the options concept with the futures concept.

organized exchanges Institutions, such as the New York Stock Exchange, the American Stock Exchange, or any of the smaller regional exchanges, that provide a central location for the buying and selling of securities.

out-of-the-money The strike price is above the market price of a stock on a call option or below the market price of a stock on a put option.

out-of-the-money warrants Warrants that have market prices less than their exercise price and have no intrinsic value.

overall market rules Guidelines, such as breadth of market indicators or mutual fund cash positions, used by technical analysts who predict stock market activity based on past activity.

overreaction Investors have a tendancy to overreact to information. As a result they buy winners and sell losers assuming the past will repeat itself.

over-the-counter bulletin board market (OTC. BB) Mechanism that provides quotes on unlisted firms. The firms represented, however, file regulatory reports to the SEC (unlike those listed on pink sheets).

over-the-counter market Not a specific location but rather a communications network through which trades of bonds, nonlisted stocks, and other securities take place. Trading activity is overseen by the National Association of Securities Dealers (NASD).

P

par bonds Bonds that are selling at their par or maturity values rather than at premium or discounted prices. Par value on a corporate bond is generally $1,000.

par value (bond) The face value of a bond, generally $1,000 for corporate issues, with higher denominations for many government issues.

parity price The price to compensate for inflation exposure.

partial hedge A hedge position in which only part of the risk is eliminated or lessened.

peak The point in an economic cycle at which expansion ends and a recession begins.

perpetual bond A bond with no maturity date.

personal savings/personal disposable income The rate at which people are saving their disposable income. This has implications for the generation of funds to modernize plant and equipment and increase productivity.

pink sheets Sheets that provide quotes on companies not listed on an exchange or on the over-the-the-counter bulletin board market. The companies do not file reports with the SEC.

Porter's Five Competitive Forces Porter divides the competitive structure of an industry into (1) threat of entry by new competitors, (2) threat of substitute goods, (3) bargaining power of buyers, (4) bargaining power of suppliers, and (5) rivalry among existing competitors.

portfolio The term applied to a collection of securities or investments.

portfolio effect The effect obtained when assets are combined into a portfolio. The interaction of the assets can provide risk reduction such that the portfolio standard deviation may be less than the standard deviation of any one asset in it.

portfolio insurance Protecting a large portfolio against a decline. A common strategy is to sell stock index futures contracts in anticipation of a decline.

portfolio manager One responsible for managing large pools of funds. Portfolio managers may be employed by insurance companies, mutual funds, bank trust departments, pension funds, and other institutional investors.

preferred stock A hybrid security that generally provides fixed returns. Preferred stockholders are paid returns after bondholder claims are satisfied but before any returns are paid to common stockholders. Though preferred stock returns are fixed in amount, they are classified as dividends (not interest) and are not tax deductible to the issuing firm.

present value The exact opposite of the compound sum. A future value is discounted to the present.

present value of an annuity The present value of an equal cash flow for several periods is determined.

price-earnings ratio The multiplier applied to earnings per share to determine current value. The P/E ratio is influenced by the earnings and sales growth of the firm, the risk or volatility of its performance, the debt-equity structure, and other factors.

price ratios Ratios that relate the internal performance of the firm to the external judgment of the marketplace in terms of value.

price-weighted average Each stock in the average is weighted by its price. The higher the price, the greater the relative weighting. The Dow Jones Industrial Average represents a price-weighted average.

primary market A market in which an investor purchases an asset (via an investment banker) from the issuer of that asset. The purchase of newly issued shares of corporate stock is an example of primary market activity. Subsequent transfers of the particular asset occur in the secondary market.

private equity Equity ownership of companies that are privately owned and not traded on public stock markets.

private placement The company sells its securities to private investors such as insurance companies, pension funds, and so on rather than through the public markets. Investment bankers may also aid in a private placement on a fee basis. Most private placements involve debt rather than common stock.

profitability ratios Ratios that allow the analyst to measure the ability of the firm to earn an adequate return on sales, total assets, and invested capital.

program trading Computer-based trigger points are established in which large volume trades are indicated. The technique is used by institutional investors.

prospect theory Prospect theory is an alternative theory to utility theory and states that people don't accurately use the probablility of expected values when given a choice between certain outcomes and probable outcomes.

prospectus A document that must accompany a new issue of securities. It contains the same information appearing in the registration statement, such as a list of directors and officers, financial reports certified by a CPA, the underwriters, the purpose and use for the funds, and other reasonable information that investors need to know.

public placement Public distribution of securities through the financial markets.

pure bond value The fundamental value of a bond that represents a floor price below which the bond's value should not fall. The pure bond value is computed as the present value of all future interest payments added to the present value of the bond principal.

pure competition Companies in pure competition do not have a differentiated product, and they compete intensely.

pure pickup yield swap A bond swap where a bond owner thinks he or she can increase the yield to maturity by selling a bond and buying a different bond of equal risk. This implies market disequilibrium.

put An option to sell 100 shares of common stock at a specified price for a given period.

put provision This provision enables a bond investor to have an option to sell a long-term bond back to the corporation at par value after a relatively short period (such as three to five years). This privilege can be particularly valuable if interest rates have gone up and bond prices have gone down.

Q

qualified investor A qualified investor is someone who has significant financial wealth to be considered sophisticated and able to take risk. A common standard is someone who has, at the minimum, income of $250,000 for the past three years and $1 million in assets not including a home.

quick ratio Current assets minus inventory (i.e., cash, marketable securities, and accounts receivables) divided by current liabilities.

R

R^2—the coefficient of determination It measures the degree of association between the independent variable(s) and the dependent variable. It may take on a value anywhere between 0 and 1.

real asset A tangible piece of property that may be seen, felt, held, or collected, such as real estate, gold, diamonds, and so on.

real estate investment trust (REIT) An organization similar to a mutual fund where investors pool funds that are invested in real estate or used to make construction or mortgage loans.

real GDP Gross domestic product expressed in dollars that have been adjusted for inflation.

real rate of return The return that investors require for allowing others to use their money for a given period. This is the value that investors demand for passing up immediate consumption and allowing others to use their savings until the funds are returned. Because the term *real* is employed, this means it is a value determined *before* inflation is added.

reinvestment assumption with bonds The assumed rate of reinvestment for inflows from a bond investment. It is normally assumed that inflows can be reinvested at the yield to maturity of the bond. This, however, may not be valid. Interest rates may go up or down as inflows from coupon payments come in and need to be reinvested. A more valid approach is to assign appropriate reinvestment rates to inflows and then determine how much the total investment will be worth at the end of a given period. This process is known as terminal wealth analysis.

reported income versus adjusted earnings Reported income is generally based on historical cost accounting, whereas adjusted earnings have been modified for inflation (on inventory and plant and equipment).

representativeness Representativeness occurs when people make a judgment by assessing the chance that the event will occur based on a similar event or streotype.

repurchase A purchase by a firm of its own shares in the marketplace.

required rate of return The total return required on an investment. For common stock, it is composed of the risk-free rate plus an equity risk premium. Once determined, it becomes the discount rate applied to future cash flows.

reserve requirements Percentages of bank deposit balances stipulated by the Federal Reserve as unavailable for lending. By increasing or reducing reserve requirements, the Fed can contract or expand the money supply.

resistance *See* resistance level.

resistance level The technical analyst's view that as long as a given long-term trend continues, prices of a particular stock or of the market as a whole will not rise above the upper end of the normal trading range (the resistance level) because at that point, investors sell in an attempt to get even or take a profit.

retention ratio The percentage of earnings retained in the firm for investment purposes.

return on equity Net income divided by stockholder's equity.

revenue bond A municipal bond supported by the revenue from a specific project, such as a toll road, bridge, or municipal coliseum.

risk Uncertainty concerning the outcome of an investment or other situation. It is often defined as variability of returns from an investment. The greater the range of possible outcomes, the greater the risk.

risk-adjusted return The amount of return after adjustment for the level of risk incurred to achieve the return.

risk-free rate The required rate of return before risk is explicitly considered. It is composed of the real rate of return plus a rate equivalent to inflationary expectations. It is referred to as R_F.

risk premium A premium assumed to be paid to an investor for the risk inherent in an investment. It is added to the risk-free rate to get the overall required return on an investment.

rotational investing An investment strategy that refers to the practice of moving in and out of various industries over the business cycle. As the business cycle moves from a trough to a peak, different industries benefit from the economic changes that accompany the business cycle.

Roth IRA Works in the opposite fashion from a traditional IRA. You do not get a deduction for an initial contribution up to $3,000, but the money is allowed to accumulate tax free, and there is no tax at the time of withdrawal if certain conditions are met.

Russell 1000 Index The index includes the 1,000 largest firms out of the Russell 3000 Index. It is value-weighted.

Russell 2000 Index The index includes the 2,000 smallest firms out of the Russell 3000 Index. It is value-weighted.

Russell 3000 Index The index is composed of the 3,000 largest U.S. stocks as measured by market capitalization. It is value-weighted.

S

secondary market A market in which an investor purchases an asset from another investor rather than the issuing corporation. The activity of secondary markets sets prices and provides liquidity. *Also see* primary market.

sector funds Mutual funds that specialize in a given segment of the economy such as energy, medical technology, computer technology, and so forth. While they may offer the potential for high returns, they are clearly less diversified and more risky than a typical mutual fund.

secured bond A bond that is collateralized by the pledging of assets.

secured debt Debt that is backed by collateral.

Securities Act of 1933 Enacted by Congress to curtail abuses by securities issuers, the law requires full disclosure of pertinent investment information and provides for penalties to officers of firms that do not comply.

Securities Acts Amendments of 1975 Enacted to increase competition in the securities markets, this legislation prohibits fixed commissions on public offerings of securities and directs the Securities and Exchange Commission to develop a single, nationwide securities market.

Securities and Exchange Commission (SEC) The federal government agency created in 1934 to enforce securities laws. Issuers of securities must register detailed reports with the SEC, and the SEC polices such activities as insider trading, investor conspiracies, and the functionings of the securities exchanges.

Securities Exchange Act of 1934 Created the Securities and Exchange Commission to regulate the securities markets. The act further empowers the Board of Governors of the Federal Reserve System to control margin requirements.

Securities Investor Protection Corporation (SIPC) Created under the Securities Investor Protection Act of 1970, this agency oversees the liquidation of insolvent brokerage firms and provides insurance on investors' trading accounts.

security analyst One who studies various industries and companies and provides research reports and valuation studies.

security market line (SML) The graphic representation of risk (as measured by beta) and return for an individual security.

seed capital Seed capital is financial capital used to help start up a company and is usually provided by angel investors.

semistrong form of efficient market hypothesis The hypothesis states that all public information is already impounded into the value of a security, so fundamental analysis cannot determine under- or overvaluation.

serial payment A mechanism for repaying funds advanced through a bond issue. Regular payments systematically retire individual bonds with increasing maturities until, after many years, the entire series has been repaid.

settle price The term for the closing price on futures contracts.

shared appreciation mortgage A type of mortgage in which the lender participates in any increase in value associated with the property being mortgaged.

Sharpe measure of portfolio performance Total portfolio return minus the risk-free rate divided by the portfolio standard deviation. It allows the portfolio manager to view excess returns in relation to total risk. Comparisons between various portfolios can be made based on this relative risk measure.

shelf registration Large companies file one comprehensive registration statement that outlines the firm's plans for future long-term financing. Then, when market conditions seem appropriate, the firm can issue the securities through an investment banker without further SEC approval. Future issues are said to be sitting on the shelf, waiting for the most advantageous time to appear. An issue may sit on the shelf for up to two years.

short-bias funds The short-bias fund always has a negative bias and can be 100 percent short or a blend of short and long, but always with a higher percentage of short positions than long positions.

short position (short sale) A market transaction in which an investor sells borrowed securities in anticipation of a price decline. The investor's expectation is that the securities can be repurchased (to replace the borrowed shares) at a lower price in the future. *Also see* long position.

short sales position theory The contrary opinion rule stating that large volumes of short sales can signal an impending market upturn because short sales must be covered and thereby create their own demand. *Also,* the average short seller is often thought to be wrong.

sinking-fund provision A mechanism for repaying funds advanced through a bond issue. The issuer makes periodic payments to the trustee, who retires part of the issue by purchasing the bonds in the open market.

small-firm effect A market theory that suggests small firms produce superior returns compared to larger firms on both an absolute and risk-adjusted basis.

smart money rules Guidelines, such as Barron's Confidence Index, used by technical analysts who predict stock market activity based on the assumption that sophisticated investors will correctly predict market trends and that their lead should be followed. *Also see* contrary opinion rules.

sold directly The least-used method for distributing securities by a public corporation. The securities are sold directly to the public by the corporation without the assistance of an investment banker.

specialist or dealer hedge A specialist on an exchange or dealer in the over-the-counter market buys and sells stocks for his own inventory for temporary holding (as a part of his market-making function). At times, he may assume a larger temporary holding than desired with all the risks associated with that exposure. Stock index futures or options can reduce the market, or systematic, risk, although they cannot reduce the specific risk associated with a security.

specialty funds Mutual funds that have special purposes that do not neatly fit into another category. Examples include the Phoenix Fund, the Calvert Social Investment Fund, and the United States Gold Shares.

speculative premium The difference between an option or warrant's price and its intrinsic value. That an investor would pay something in excess of the intrinsic value indicates a speculative desire to hold the security in anticipation of future increases in the price of the underlying stock.

spot market The term applied to the cash price for immediate transfer of a commodity as opposed to the futures market where no physical transfer occurs immediately.

spreads A combination of options that consists of buying one option (going long) and writing an option (going short) on the same stock.

Standard & Poor's 100 Index An index composed of 100 blue-chip stocks on which the Chicago Board Options Exchange currently has individual option contracts.

Standard & Poor's 400 Industrial Index An index that measures price movements in the stocks of 400 large industrial corporations listed primarily on the New York Stock Exchange.

Standard & Poor's 400 MidCap Index An index composed of 400 middle-size firms that have total market values between $1.2 billion and $9 billion.

Standard & Poor's 500 Stock Index An index of 500 major U.S. corporations. In 2004 there were 373 industrial firms, 15 transportation firms, 47 utilities, and 65 financial firms. This index is value-weighted.

Standard & Poor's 600 SmallCap Index An index of the smallest capital stocks covered by Standard & Poor's. The stocks normally have a market capitalization of less than $1 billion (there is some overlap with the Standard & Poor's MidCap Index in terms of size).

Standard & Poor's 1500 Stock Index An index that combines the S&P 500, the S&P 400 MidCap, and the S&P SmallCap 600.

Standard & Poor's International Oil Index A value-weighted index of oil firms. Options on the index have been traded on the Chicago Board Options Exchange.

standard deviation A measure of dispersion that considers the spread of outcomes around the expected value.

statement of cash flows Formally established by the Financial Accounting Standards Board in 1987, the purpose of the statement of cash flows is to emphasize the critical nature of cash flows to the operations of the firm. The statement translates accrual-based net income into actual cash dollars.

stock dividend A dividend paid by issuing more stock, which results in retained earnings being capitalized.

stock index futures A futures contract on a specific stock index, such as the Standard & Poor's 500 Stock Index or the NYSE Composite Index.

stock index options An option contract to purchase (call) or sell (put) a stock index. Popular contracts include the S&P 100 Index, the Dow Jones Industrial Average, and others. The purchaser of a stock index option pays an initial premium and then closes out the option at a given price in the future.

stock pickers Investors who follow the bottom-up approach to selecting stocks. They pick an individual stock and then merely check it out against the industry and economy.

stock split The result of a firm dividing its shares into more shares with a corresponding decrease in par value.

stop order A mechanism for locking in gains or limiting losses on securities transactions. The investor is not assured of paying or receiving a particular price but rather agrees to accept the price prevailing when the broker is able to execute the order after prices have reached some predetermined figure.

straddle A combination of a put and call on the same stock with the same strike price and expiration date.

straight-line depreciation A method of depreciation in which the project cost is divided by the project life to calculate each year's depreciation amount.

strike price The price that the contract specifies at which a security covered by an option may be bought or sold. It is the same as the exercise price.

strong form of the efficient market hypothesis A hypothesis that says all information, insider as well as public, is reflected in the price of a security.

Super Dot The computer system that allows New York Stock Exchange members to electronically transmit all market and limit orders directly to the specialist at the trading post or member trading booth.

support *See* support level.

support level Technical analyst's view that as long as a given long-term trend continues, prices of a particular stock or of the market as a whole will not fall below the lower end of a normal trading range (the support level) because at that point, low prices stimulate demand.

surpluses (government) Government revenues exceed expenditures.

sustainable growth model A model that looks at how much growth a firm can generate by maintaining the same financial relationships as the year before. The interaction between return on equity and the retention of equity for reinvestment is considered.

syndicate A group of investment bankers that jointly shares the underwriting risk and distribution responsibilities in a large offering of new securities. Each participant is responsible for a predetermined sales volume. One or a few firms serve as the managing underwriters.

synergy A more-than-proportionate increase in performance from the combination of two or more parts.

systematic risk Risk inherent in an investment related to movements in the market that cannot be diversified away.

systematic withdrawal plan A plan offered by a mutual fund in which the investor receives regular monthly or quarterly payments from investment in the fund.

T

TALF TALF stands for Term Asset Backed Securities Loan Facility. This facility allowed the Federal Reserve to buy up to $1 trillion of asset-backed securities.

target date funds A target date fund (sometimes called a life-cycle fund) manages your portfolio asset mix based on your age and the date of your expected retirement.

TARP TARP stands for the Troubled Asset Relief Program. It provided financial support to the banking system during the financial crisis of 2007–2010. This program allowed the U.S. Treasury to purchase or insure up to $700 billion of troubled assests that were primarily subprime mortgages or securities collateralized by mortgages.

tax hedge An investor may have accumulated a large return on a diversified portfolio in a given year. To maintain the profitable position but defer the taxable gains until the next year, stock index futures or options contracts may be employed. For individual securities, individual stock options may be used when available.

tax risk Tax risk arises when investors in tax free retirement accounts retire in higher marginal income tax brackets than they had while working and sheltering retirement income. Usually the tax free compounding will overcome some of this risk. But there is the risk that you will pay higher taxes in retirement than you did while working.

Taxpayer Relief Act of 1997 Legislation that changed the holding period and tax rates applied to capital gains and losses. It also covered other items such as new forms of IRAs, estate taxes, etc.

tax swaps Selling of one bond position and buying into a similar one to take advantage of a tax situation. For example, one might sell a bond that has a short-term capital loss to take the deduction and replace it with a similar bond.

technical analysis An analysis of price and volume data as well as other related market indicators to determine past trends that are believed to be predictable into the future. Charts and graphs are often utilized.

term structure of interest rates This depicts the relationship between maturity and interest rates for up to 30 years.

terminal wealth table A table that indicates the ending or terminal wealth from a bond investment based on the reinvestment of the inflows at a specified rate (which may be different from the coupon rate). The initial investment can then be compared with the terminal wealth (compound interest plus principal) and an overall rate of return computed.

third market The trading between dealers and institutional investors, through the over-the-counter market, of NYSE-listed stocks. The third market accounts for an extremely small share of total trading activity.

Tokyo Nikkei 225 Average The most widely watched country index outside the United States. It covers 225 large Japanese companies.

top-down approach A method for choosing stocks that goes from the macroeconomic viewpoint to the individual company.

trailing price-earnings ratio The market price of a stock divided by the earnings per share for the last 12 months.

trading range The high and low spread of prices that a stock normally sells within.

Treasury bill A short-term U.S. government obligation. A Treasury bill is purchased at a discount and is readily marketable.

Treasury bond A long-term U.S. government bond.

Treasury Inflation Protection Securities (TIPS) The investor receives two forms of return as a result of owning the security. The first is annual interest that is paid out semiannually, and the second is an automatic increase in the initial value of principal to account for inflation.

Treasury note An intermediate-term (1 to 10 years) U.S. government bond.

Treasury stock Stock issued but not outstanding by virtue of being held (after it is repurchased) by the firm.

Treasury strips These government securities pay no interest and all returns to the investor come in the form of increases in the value of the investment. The bond is stripped of interest payments and traded based on the present value of the principal at maturity.

trend analysis Comparable analysis of performance over time.

Treynor measure of portfolio performance Total portfolio return minus the risk-free rate divided by the portfolio beta. Unlike the Sharpe measure, which uses the portfolio standard deviation in the denominator, the risk measure here is the beta, or systematic risk. It enables the portfolio manager to view excess return in relation to nondiversifiable risk. The assumption is that all other types of risk have been diversified away. Once computed, the Treynor measure allows for comparisons between different portfolios.

trough The point in an economic cycle at which recession ends and expansion begins.

U

underpricing In selling formerly privately held shares to new investors in the over-the-counter market, the price might not fully reflect the value of the issue. Underpricing is used to attempt to ensure the success of the initial distribution.

underwriter hedge A hedge, based on stock index futures or options contracts, used to offset the risk exposure associated with the underwriting of new securities by an investment banker. If the market goes down, presumably the loss on the stock being underwritten will be compensated for by the gain on the stock index futures or options contract as a result of being able to repurchase it at a lower price. This, of course, is not a perfect hedge. The stock could go down while the market is going up, and losses on both the stock and stock index contract would occur (writing options directly against the stock may be more efficient, but in many cases such options are not available).

underwriting Refers to the guarantee the investment banking firm gives the selling firm to purchase its securities at a fixed price, thereby eliminating the risk of not selling the whole issue of securities.

unfriendly takeover A merger or acquisition in which the firm acquired does not wish to be acquired.

unfunded pension plan Payments to retirees are made out of current income and not out of prior funding.

unit investment trusts (UITs) These are formed by investment companies with the intention of acquiring a portfolio of fixed income to be passively managed over a fixed period. The trust is then terminated.

unseasoned issue An issue that has not been formerly traded in the public markets.

unsystematic risk Risk of an investment that is random in nature. It is not related to general market movements. It may represent the temporary influence of a competitor's new product, changes in raw material prices, or unusual economic or government influences on a firm. It may generally be diversified away.

V

valuation The process of attributing a value to a security based on expectations of the future performance of the issuing concern, the relevant industry, and the economy as a whole.

valuation model A representation of the components that provide the value of an investment, such as a dividend valuation model used to determine the value of common stock.

Value Line Average The index represents 1,700 companies from the New York and American Stock Exchanges and the over-the-counter market. Many individual investors use the Value Line Index because it more closely corresponds to the variety of stocks the average investor may have in his or her portfolio. It is an equal-weighted index, which means each of the 1,700 stocks, regardless of market price or total market value, is weighted equally.

value-weighted index Each company in the index is weighted by its own total market value as a percentage of the total market value for all firms in the index. Most major indexes such as the S&P 500, S&P 400, and NYSE Index, are value-weighted. With value-weighted indexes, large firms tend to be weighted more heavily than smaller firms.

variability The possible different outcomes of an event. As an example, an investment with many different levels of return would have great variability.

variable-rate mortgage A mortgage in which the interest rate is adjusted regularly.

variable-rate notes *See* floating-rate notes.

venture capital Financial capital that is invested in private companies to help them grow.

vertical spread Buying and writing two contracts at different striking prices with the same month of expiration.

vesting A legal term meaning pension benefits or rights cannot be taken away.

vintage year Vintage year is the year that the fund made its first investment.

VIX The VIX is sometimes called the "fear index" because it measures the volatility of the market. It is calculated as an annualized number and is expressed as a percentage. For example, a VIX of 25 indicates that the S&P 500 could move up or down by 25 percent during the next 30 days. The higher the VIX, the higher the volatility risk.

W

warrant A right or option to buy a stated number of shares of stock at a specified price over a given period. It is usually of longer duration than a call option.

warrant breakeven The price movement in the underlying stock necessary for the warrant purchaser to break even, that is, recover the initial purchase price of the warrant.

weak form of efficient market hypothesis A hypothesis suggesting there is no relationship between past and future prices of securities.

weighted average life The weighted average time period over which the coupon payments and maturity payment on a bond are recovered.

white knight A firm that "rescues" another firm from an unfriendly takeover by a third firm.

Wiesenberger Financial Services An advisory service that provides important information on mutual funds.

Wilshire 5000 Equity Index A stock market measure comprising 5,000 equity securities. It includes all New York Stock Exchange and American Stock Exchange issues and the most active over-the-counter issues. The index represents the total dollar value of all 5,000 stocks. By measuring total dollar value, it is, in effect, a value-weighted measure.

World Index A value-weighted index of market performance in 19 major countries as compiled by Capital International, S.A., of Geneva, Switzerland.

Y

Yankee bonds Bond issued by foreign governments, foreign corporations, or major agencies that are traded in the United States and denominated (payable) in U.S. dollars.

yield curve A curve that shows interest rates at a specific point for all securities having equal risk but different maturity dates. Usually, government securities are used to construct such curves. The yield curve is also referred to as the term structure of interest rates.

yield spread The difference between the yields received on two different types of bonds, or bonds with different ratings. It is important to investment strategy because during periods of economic uncertainty, spreads increase because investors demand larger premiums on risky issues to compensate for the greater chance of default.

yield to call The interest yield that will be realized on a callable bond if it is held from a given purchase date until the date when it can be called by the issuer. The yield to call reflects the fact that lower overall returns may be realized if the issuer avoids some later payments by retiring the bonds early.

yield to maturity The internal rate of return or true yield on a bond. It is the interest rate (i) at which you can discount the future coupon payments (C_t) and maturity value (P_n) to arrive at the current value of a bond (v). It is synonymous with market rate of interest.

Ying, Lewellen, Schlarbaum, and Lease study A research study that indicates there may be an opportunity for abnormal returns on a risk-adjusted basis in the many weeks between announcement of the listing and actual listing of a security.

Z

zero-coupon bonds Bonds designed to pay no interest, in which the return to the investor is in the form of capital appreciation over the life of the issue.

Index

D

E

F

G

H

I

N

O

P

T

U